Twomey on Partnership

Second Edition

To my parents
Michael and Anne Twomey

Twomey on Partnership

Second Edition

by

MICHAEL TWOMEY

B.C.L, LL.M., Ph.D., Solicitor
Judge of the High Court

Editor

MAEDHBH CLANCY

LL.B (Ling. Franc), Solicitor
Of Counsel, Arthur Cox

Bloomsbury Professional

DUBLIN · LONDON · EDINBURGH · NEW DELHI · NEW YORK · SYDNEY

BLOOMSBURY PROFESSIONAL

Bloomsbury Publishing Plc

The Fitzwilliam Business Centre, 26 Upper Pembroke Street, Dublin 2, Ireland
41–43 Boltro Road, Haywards Heath, RH16 1BJ, UK

**BLOOMSBURY and the Diana logo are trademarks of
Bloomsbury Publishing Plc**

British Library Cataloguing-in-Publication Data
A catalogue record for this book is available from the British Library.

ISBN: HB: 978 152650 485 2
       epub: 978 152650 487 6
       epdf: 978 152650 486 9

Typeset by Marlex Editorial Services Ltd, Dublin, Ireland
Printed and bound by CPI Group (UK) Ltd, Croydon, CR0 4YY

To find out more about our authors and books visit www.bloomsburyprofessional.com
Here you will find extracts, author information, details of forthcoming events
and the option to sign up for our newsletters

Foreword to the First Edition

It is with very great pleasure and unlimited confidence that I both welcome and enthusiastically recommend this book on Partnership law.

For this welcome and recommendation there are many compelling reasons. First and foremost it fills a massive gap in the present, if relatively recently constructed, cornucopia of legal textbooks directly aimed at the study and practice of Irish law. That gap is the law of partnership. It is, indeed, surprising that, as far as I can discover, no book has been published in Ireland, within this lawyer's favourite period of the memory of man, on this subject which is of such general importance in our legal system and of particular importance to lawyers as the vehicle in which a very high proportion indeed of one branch of our legal profession, namely the solicitors, is driven.

The author of this book, Michael Twomey, has not only a very distinguished academic record but has also had experience of practice as a solicitor. From this background it is not surprising, though it is of tremendous value, that he has written a book which is a dual textbook in the sense that it is an excellent academic guide to the study of the law of partnership and at the same time a wholly accessible, clear and analytical book for the use of both legal practitioners and judges.

Consideration of the table of contents alone indicates the extremely careful and logical structure which has been imposed on potentially diffuse subject matter, and consideration of the contents of the book immediately shows that this clear, analytical and logical approach has been carried over as well into the text and the manner of its presentation. The conclusions reached by the author are supported throughout by reference either to the statutes applicable, to the decisions interpreting them or to decisions applying the relevant common law principles.

The excellence of the structure of the book is best demonstrated by a mere recital of the sectional headings which are: The Nature of Partnership; Relations between Partners and Third Parties; Relations between Partners *Inter Se*; Dissolution of Partnerships; and last, but by no means least, a highly informative section on the special problems of Limited Partnerships.

Without the slightest hint of chauvinism the author has, in support of the conclusions stated by him in this book, quoted to a remarkable extent the decisions of the Irish courts both in the 19th and 20th centuries. The existence of such a large body of Irish decisions on partnership law, I would readily confess, was unknown to me and I suspect that it may come as a surprise to a great number of lawyers. The industry which must have been involved in finding and analysing this body of case law was great and the result of it makes a major contribution to our legal publications.

The book contains in addition to statements of the law and conclusions drawn from them a limited, but most persuasively stated, number of suggestions as to how our statute law might be amended and extended so as to make the laws of partnership a more appropriate and flexible legal mechanism.

Accordingly, I not only repeat my very enthusiastic recommendation of this book to academic and practising lawyers and to the judiciary, but would also, notwithstanding the doctrine of the separation of powers, extend that recommendation to legislators as well.

Thomas A Finlay
Chief Justice of the Supreme Court (1985–1994)

Preface to the First Edition

The partnership structure is one of the most popular forms of business in Ireland. It is the most common business arrangement for professionals such as accountants, solicitors, doctors, dentists, vets, architects, engineers etc, many of whom will be restricted from practising through companies. In addition, partnership is the default form of business organisation, so that any time two or more people carry on any form of business together (from farming to playing in a rock-band) without incorporating, they will be in partnership. Combined with this is the fact that the partnership structure has become the business and investment vehicle of choice for those who seek out its tax, accountancy and disclosure advantages over limited liability companies. Furthermore, in recent times, limited partnerships and investment limited partnerships have gained in popularity because of their uses as venture capital vehicles and in collective investment funds.

Against this backdrop, it is surprising that the state of partnership law in this country has received such scant attention to date. This is in stark contrast to the position in our neighbouring jurisdictions of Scotland, England and Wales, where legal practitioners have had the benefit of a number of treatises on the law of partnership for well over a century. Despite the existence of hundreds of Irish cases in the area, the dearth of Irish research on partnership law has often led to only the English legal position being pleaded before the Irish courts. This has resulted in the Irish courts sometimes accepting without argument statements in English textbooks as representing the legal position in Ireland.

The need for an analysis of the law of partnership is particularly great at present, in light of the calls for multi-disciplinary partnerships between the professions, the proposed introduction of limited liability partnerships in the United Kingdom and the possibility of incorporation for professional practices.

The usefulness of a textbook on partnership law was recognised by the Irish courts as long ago as 1864 in the *Bagnalstown and Wexford Railway Company* case, where Berwick J expressly relied on the first edition of Lord Lindley's book on partnership law. In the same case, Blackburne LJ noted that it was "a subject of regret that there is a difference between the state of law in England and in Ireland". The intervening period has seen further divergence in the law of partnership, hastened by Ireland's independence from the United Kingdom. Yet, if they were alive today, Berwick J and Blackburne LJ might be surprised to learn that there was still no text on this important area of law in Ireland or Northern Ireland. The author's aim is to fill this regrettable gap in the Irish legal textbook landscape. This task has been approached by examining the decisions of the Irish courts and partnership legislation from the 18th century up to the present day. Only once it is definitively known what the state of partnership law is in Ireland, may one critically examine it. This examination forms a secondary aim of the book and for which purpose the position in other jurisdictions was examined, notably, in England and Wales, Scotland, America, Australia, New Zealand, Canada and South Africa. In this way, it is hoped to assist in the development of partnership law in this jurisdiction generally and also to contribute to the debates on the incorporation of professional practices, the formation of multi-disciplinary practices and the provision of limited liability professional partnerships. Whilst all reasonable care has been taken to state the law as of 31 May 2000, no liability can be accepted for any errors or omissions. The author would however welcome all comments or suggested improvements to the text.

Michael Twomey
Dublin
www.partnershiplaw.ie

31 May 2000

Acknowledgment to the First Edition

A work on partnership law of necessity traverses several distinct areas of law ranging from such areas as agency, contract, equity, torts and property to issues of practice and procedure. In undertaking the present task, I was lucky enough to be able to fall back on the assistance of leading practitioners, academics and judges in these and other fields. This work has benefited enormously from their input. Each one gave very generously of their time from the early stages where they advised on and encouraged the undertaking of this project to the later stages where they painstakingly reviewed and contributed to chapters of the text. I wish to acknowledge their enormous contribution to this work for which I am most grateful.

Thanks are due to the former Supreme Court Chief Justice, Mr Justice Tom Finlay, for reviewing the work *in toto,* for his very helpful comments thereon and his very kind foreword; I am particularly grateful to Professor Victor Brudney who welcomed me to Harvard Law School as a Visiting Researcher. The majority of this book was researched there during my time as a Visiting Researcher in partnership law and I am indebted to Professor Brudney and other members of Harvard Law School for their advice and encouragement of this project. I am also grateful to Judge Bryan McMahon for his comments on tort-related issues; Professor John Wylie, University of Cardiff and A&L Goodbody, Professor David Gwynn Morgan, University College Cork and Dr Hilary Delany, Trinity College Dublin, for their contribution to the property and equity sections of the text; Tom Courtney, solicitor, for his assistance with several chapters relating to company law matters; Paul Gallagher SC for his review of the section on litigation between partners; Professor Robert Clark and Blanaid Clark of University College Dublin for their comments on the chapters on contractual aspects of partnerships; Nigel Martin, partner, A&L Goodbody for his contribution to the section on partnership agreements; Michael Dickson, partner, A&L Goodbody and Des Peelo, accountant, for their suggestions regarding financial and accounting aspects of partnerships; Benedict Ó Floinn BL for his comments on practice and procedural aspects of litigation by and against partnerships; the former Official Assignee in Bankruptcy, Gerard Rubotham BL for his comments on the bankruptcy of partners; Martina Kelly from the Securities and Exchanges Supervision department of the Central Bank for her comments on investment limited partnerships; Professor Brian Carroll, University College Cork and Professor Dick Webb, Auckland University, New Zealand for their comments on the section on the dissolution of partnerships. In addition, I would like to thank the staff of Butterworths Ireland including Gerry McCallion, Toni Ryder, Madeleine Roche, Ciara Fitzpatrick, and also Marian Sullivan who typeset the work in a very professional manner, John Bergin who produced a detailed index and in particular my editor Louise Leavy who was always most professional and of considerable assistance during all the stages of this project.

Because of the similarity between the law of partnership on both sides of the border, this book considers Northern Ireland case law from both before and after 1922. In this regard, I was lucky enough to receive comments on the book from Lord Justice Anthony Campbell of the Northern Ireland Court of Appeal, former Lord Justice John

MacDermott and Lisa Glennon of Queen's University Belfast. For their comments on other chapters of the text and their encouragement in relation to this work, I am grateful to Dr John Breslin of University College Dublin, Professor Mary Condon of Osgoode Hall Law School in Toronto and Professor William Binchy of Trinity College Dublin. I also owe a debt of gratitude to Stephen Hamilton, Marcus Beresford and the partners in A&L Goodbody for establishing the Rodney Overend Educational Trust which assisted in the research costs of this work. I had the privilege of working with Rodney and his father, Brian, during my time in A&L Goodbody. I was also lucky enough to get to know Rodney on a personal level because of our shared interest in any form of sporting activity. It was therefore a particular honour for me to be the first recipient of the scholarship established in his honour.

On a personal level, this book would never have been published without the support and encouragement at different times of Mary Keane and my parents. Finally, my biggest debt of gratitude is due to Anne to whom I will always be grateful for her support and encouragement from the inception of this project to its completion.

Preface to the Second Edition

I was delighted to be given the opportunity to edit the second edition of this work, which has been of such value to practitioners and academics alike since it was first published in 2000.

The partnership structure continues to be an essential part of the Irish business landscape, and this edition has been updated to examine relevant Irish case-law since the first edition was published. Notable decisions of the courts of the United Kingdom are also considered, as the Partnership Act 1890 continues to apply there also.

While the seminal partnership statutes, the Partnership Act 1890 and the Limited Partnerships Act 1907, have not been the subject of recent amendment in Ireland (albeit that, in the United Kingdom, some changes have been made to the 1907 Act, and more are expected), the new Legal Services Regulation Act 2015 will introduce significant reforms for the legal profession in Ireland. When its provisions are commenced in full, and detailed framework regulations are made by the Legal Services Regulatory Authority, the 2015 Act will allow practising barristers to enter into partnership with one another, and with practising solicitors. These new forms of partnership will be known as 'legal partnerships'. It will also be possible for practising lawyers (both solicitors and barristers) to enter into partnership with non-lawyers. That form of partnership will be known as a 'multi-disciplinary practice'. In a significant development for the Irish legal profession, both partnerships of solicitors, and legal partnerships, will be able to apply for authorisation as a 'limited liability partnership', with the partners in such a partnership then benefitting from limited liability. Each of these new partnership models will continue, for the most part, to be subject to the 1890 Act. At the time of writing, the framework regulations for both legal partnerships and limited liability partnerships are expected in early 2019, albeit that the position regarding the introduction of multi-disciplinary practices is considerably less certain. The 2015 Act, and the new business models that it provides for, are considered in detail in the new Chapter 30 of this second edition.

It is worth noting that while the Irish investment limited partnership, introduced by the Investment Limited Partnerships Act 1994, has proven less popular than anticipated in Ireland (with only seven such partnerships currently authorised by the Central Bank of Ireland at the time of writing), reforms in this area are expected shortly. In July 2017, the Minister for Finance and Public Expenditure and Reform announced that approval had been given for a Bill to be drafted to amend the 1994 Act to further enhance Ireland's status as a fund domicile. That Bill (currently known as the Investment Limited Partnership and Irish Collective Asset-management Vehicle (Amendment) Bill) is expected to be published in the first half of 2019.

I was very fortunate to receive considerable support when editing this work. Particular thanks are due to the Hon. Mr Justice Michael Twomey for entrusting me with the role of editor, and for his guidance; Maureen O'Neill of MON Legal Consulting for her contribution to the chapter on anti-competitive provisions; my colleagues, Dr Thomas B Courtney and William Johnston, for their encouragement; the team at

Bloomsbury Professional, in particular Sandra Mulvey for her assistance; and my husband Jeremy and daughter Sophia for their support.

While every effort has been taken to state the law as of 1 December 2018, no liability is accepted for any errors or omissions.

Maedhbh Clancy
Dublin

22 December 2018

Contents

Chapter 3   Characteristics of a Partnership

Chapter 6   Types of Partners

Chapter 7   Partner by Holding Out

Chapter 8   Types of Partnerships

Chapter 9   Illegal Partnerships

Part B Relations between Partners and Third Parties

Chapter 10   Liability of a Partner for the Acts of his Co-Partners

Chapter 11 Nature and Duration of Liability

Chapter 12 Litigation by and against Partners

Part C Relations between Partners Inter Se

Chapter 13 Management Rights of Partners

Chapter 14   Financial Rights of Partners

Chapter 15   Fiduciary Duties of Partners

Chapter 16   Partnership Property

Chapter 17   Partnership Capital

Chapter 18   The Goodwill of a Partnership

Chapter 19   Shares in a Partnership

Chapter 20   Litigation between Partners

Chapter 21   The Terms of the Partnership Agreement

Chapter 22   Anti-Competitive Provisions

Part D Dissolution of Partnerships

Chapter 23   Causes of Dissolution

Chapter 24   Death of a Partner

Chapter 25   Dissolution by the Court

Chapter 26   Post-Dissolution and Winding Up of a Partnership

Chapter 27 Bankruptcy

Part E Limited Partnerships

Chapter 28   Limited Partnerships

Chapter 29   Investment Limited Partnerships

Chapter 30   LLPs, Legal Partnerships and Multi-disciplinary Practices

Contents

Table of Cases

D

H

I

J

K

M

N

O

P

X

Y

Table of Legislation

Bunreacht na hÉireann

United Kingdom

European Legislation

International Treaties and Conventions

Statutory Instruments

Other Jurisdictions

PART A
NATURE OF A PARTNERSHIP

Chapter 1

Introduction

[1.01] Before embarking on a detailed analysis of the law of partnership as it exists today, it is helpful to first consider partnerships from a historical perspective and to deal in general terms with the sources of modern partnership law. Accordingly, it is proposed to begin with the following areas:

    I.   Historical Background; and

    II.   Sources of Partnership Law.

I.   HISTORICAL BACKGROUND

[1.02] Partnership is a form of business structure which is as old as any form of human co-operative activity and, accordingly, the law of partnership has a long history which can be traced back to the *societas* of Roman times. The *societas* was a contract whereby two or more persons agreed to combine property or labour in a common stock for the sake of sharing the gain. The Eastern Roman Emperor Justinian (AD 527–565) instructed his lawyers to codify the law which applied to the *societas*, which they did by publishing the *Institutes*.[1] However, the law of partnership only really began to take off in the middle of the eighteenth century, when Lord Mansfield became Chief Justice. During this time, he began creating a common law for commercial matters which was based largely on the customs of merchants. An important part of this commercial law was the law of partnership.[2] One of the earliest reported Irish cases from this period is *Hayden v Carroll* which was heard in 1777.[3] This case was heard by Lord Chancellor Clare, Lord Yelverton and Lord Carleton and involved the formation of a banking partnership in Waterford between one Henry Hayden and Bartholomew Rivers. It remains important to this day in the context of the distribution of a partner's estate on his bankruptcy.[4]

[1.03] By the middle of the nineteenth century, partnerships were used for all types of business enterprises in Ireland, ranging from the building of railway lines from Enfield to Edenderry[5] to the Beamish and Crawford brewing partnership in Cork.[6] Indeed, until

---

[1]   Book III, Title XXV of the *Institutes* (AD 533) details an account of the *societas*.

[2]   One of Lord Mansfield's most noteworthy partnership cases is that of *Fox v Hanbury* (1776) 2 Cowp 445 which deals with the relative rights to partnership property of partners and their separate creditors. This decision was approved by Johnston J in *Provincial Bank of Ireland v Tallon* [1938] IR 361.

[3]   *Hayden v Carroll* (1796) 3 Ridg PC 545.

[4]   See para **[27.99]**. See also *Vincett v Hackett* (1829) 2 Ir Law Rec 258, which concerned a banking partnership in Nenagh, Co Tipperary.

[5]   The subject of litigation in *Bagnell v Edwards* (1875) 10 Ir Eq 215.

[6]   The subject of litigation in *Beamish v Beamish* (1869) 4 Ir Eq R 120.

the advent of the joint stock company with the passing of the Joint Stock Companies Acts 1844 and 1856, partnerships were, for all intents and purposes, the only vehicle in which two or more persons could pool their expertise and finances to pursue a common business goal. In fact, up to the end of the nineteenth century and, in particular, prior to the popularisation of the family company by *Salomon's* case[7] in 1897, partnerships continued to be the predominant vehicle for the carrying on of business. It follows that this period was one in which there was a rich vein of partnership litigation resulting in the development of a considerable number of common law and equitable principles by the courts. By the end of the nineteenth century, it was decided to partially codify these principles into one partnership statute, the Partnership Act 1890 (referred to throughout this work as the 1890 Act), and this Act forms the basis of modern partnership law. It should be noted that the wealth of pre-1890 caselaw which gave rise to the 1890 Act remains applicable today unless it is inconsistent with the express provisions of that Act.[8]

Relationship between Partnership Law and Company Law

[1.04] Before considering the details of Irish partnership law, it is appropriate to consider the historical links between partnerships and the main form of business enterprise today, the limited liability company.[9] The strong link which exists today between partnerships and companies can be attributed, in part, to the fact that modern company law has its roots in partnership law. The change by business enterprises from using partnerships to using companies was an evolving process throughout the nineteenth century and early twentieth century. During this time, large partnerships were known as deed of settlement companies, as their constitutions were contained in deeds of settlement whereby certain persons became trustees of the partnership property.[10] This practice of using trustees developed in large partnerships as a means of circumventing the rule that all persons interested in litigation should be joined as parties.[11] By creating a trust, the trustee of the partnership was allowed to sue and be sued on behalf of the partnership. Where the trust was created by deed, it became known as a deed of settlement. These deed of settlement partnerships became known as

---

7 *Salomon v Salomon* [1897] AC 22.
8 Partnership Act 1890, s 46. To quote Sir Frederick Pollock, the draftsman of the 1890 Act, that Act has to be 'read and applied in light of the decisions which have built up the existing rules': Pollock, *A Digest of the Law of Partnership* (11th edn, 1920) at p ix.
9 See generally Lannon, *Company Law the Background* (1997); Courtney, *The Law of Companies* (4th edn, 2016) at para [1.051] et seq; Hutchinson, *Keane on Company Law* (5th edn, 2016) at para [2.02] et seq.
10 See generally Morse, *Palmer's Company Law* at para 1.103; DuBois, *The English Business Company after the Bubble Act, 1720-1800* (1938) at p 215 et seq; Holdsworth, *A History of English Law* (1932) Vol VIII, Ch IV at para 4; Formoy, *The Historical Foundations of Modern Company Law* (1923).
11 *Lloyd v Loaring* (1802) 6 Ves Jun 773.

companies, but, as noted by James LJ in *Smith v Anderson*,[12] a deed of settlement company was:

> 'a partnership which is constantly changing, a partnership today consisting of certain members, and tomorrow consisting of some only of these members along with others who have come in so that there will be a constant shifting of the partnership.'[13]

[1.05] Gradually, modern company law developed from these deed of settlement companies by legislative enactment and judicial decision, both of which drew from partnership principles.[14] As noted by Ronan LJ in *Coolmoyne and Fethard Co-operative Creamery v Bulfin*:[15]

> 'It has been often said that companies are of the nature of partnerships ... since the members of a company under the [Companies Act 1862] are partners in a special sort of partnership modified and governed by statutory provisions'.[16]

[1.06] These special types of partnerships, or in the words of Bruce LJ 'these extended partnerships called joint-stock companies',[17] developed into what is now the modern limited liability company. It is for this reason that many of today's company law provisions can trace their roots back to partnership law, eg the right of a director to inspect the books of account of his company under s 284(1) of the Companies Act 2014 is the direct descendant of the right of a partner to inspect the firm's books of account under s 24(9) of the 1890 Act. Similarly, the right of a court to wind up a company on just and equitable grounds under s 569(1)(e) of the 2014 Act is clearly a descendant of the right of the court to wind up a partnership on just and equitable grounds under s 35(f) of the 1890 Act. The relationship also works in reverse, so for example certain partnerships are deemed to be unregistered companies under Part 22 of the 2014 Act and thus may be wound up under that Act.[18]

---

12 *Smith v Anderson* (1880) 15 Ch D 247.

13 *Smith v Anderson* (1880) 15 Ch D 247 at 273–274.

14 This reliance on partnership law by early company lawyers is also evident in the first company law textbooks, see, for example, Lord Lindley's leading work on the law of partnership in England, which in 1860 was entitled a *Treatise on the Law of Partnership, including its Application to Companies*. This work is now to be found as a work on partnership law only: see l'Anson Banks, *Lindley & Banks on Partnership* (20th edn, 2017).

15 *Coolmoyne and Fethard Co-operative Creamery v Bulfin* [1917] 2 IR 107.

16 *Coolmoyne and Fethard Co-operative Creamery v Bulfin* [1917] 2 IR 107 at 131, quoting in part from the judgment of Buckley LJ in *Newton v Birmingham Small Arms Co* [1906] 2 Ch 378 at 386. However note that s 1(2) of the 1890 Act now provides that the relationship between members of a company is not a partnership. In this way, it is the provisions of the Companies Act 2014 which apply to companies rather than the terms of the 1890 Act. See para **[2.29]**. Nonetheless, the close relationship between companies and partnerships continues on another level as evidenced by the application of partnership law principles to those companies which are in form companies, but in substance partnerships and therefore called quasi-partnerships, see para **[8.67]** et seq.

17 *Keene's Executors* 3 De GM & G 272 at 279.

18 See further para **[27.06]**.

[1.07] The common ground which exists between partnership law and company law is also responsible for the growth of the company law doctrine which applies partnership principles to those companies which resemble partnerships and are known as quasi-partnerships.[19] Indeed, it is suggested elsewhere in this work that this cross-fertilisation should also operate in the reverse direction.[20]

Popularity of Partnerships

[1.08] Despite the all-pervasive nature of the limited liability company, the partnership structure remains a popular vehicle for doing business.[21] This can be attributed to a number of factors.

[1.09] First, partnership is the residual form of business association which arises when two or more people go into business together. Thus, if the participants do not adopt a particular form for their enterprise, the most common being the limited liability company, they will invariably end up being in partnership. This is because it is very easy to form a partnership, as, in most cases, it does not require any written agreement, but simply an oral understanding that the participants will carry on business in common with a view to profit. For example the members of a rock band will, in the absence of contrary agreement, be a partnership and, if they do not agree on the specific terms of the partnership as between themselves, the default rules set out in s 24(1) of the 1890 Act regarding the sharing of profits will apply to them.[22] It follows that one of the reasons that partnerships remain popular is that they are the default form of business association.

[1.10] Second, certain professions are restricted directly or indirectly from practising through the medium of a registered company. In some cases, this is because in such professional practices, the relation of the firm to its clients or patients is considered to be of such a nature as to require personal responsibility. Therefore, where two or more

---

[19] See generally para **[8.67]** et seq.

[20] See the reference to a quasi-company, para **[8.105]** et seq.

[21] Since partnerships, unlike companies, are not required to be registered, it is not possible to determine the precise number of partnerships operating in Ireland. One indication of the popularity of partnerships is the fact that thousands of partnerships have registered business names under the Registration of Business Names Act 1963. It should be borne in mind that this Act only applies to partnerships which carry on business under a name other than the names of all the partners and that the terms of this Act are not enforced to a great degree by the Companies Registration Office. See further para **[3.70]**.

[22] See for example *Joyce v Morrisey* [1999] EMLR 233 concerning the band *The Smiths*. At the time that the preliminary issues were tried, the members of the band agreed that they had been in partnership, however the question arose as to whether the profits were to be shared equally between them, or whether they were to be shared in proportion to the contributions actually made to the band by each member. As no agreement had been reached between the band members rebutting the presumption at s 24 of the 1890 Act that all partners are to share equally in the profits of the partnership's business, the profits made by the band were to be shared equally between them.

dentists,[23] veterinary surgeons[24] or doctors[25] wish to carry on business together, they will invariably do so in partnership.

[1.11] While at the time of writing, two or more solicitors remain restricted from practising through the medium of a registered company and that is expected to remain the position for the foreseeable future,[26] the Legal Services Regulation Act 2015 has introduced the possibility of limited liability for both firms of solicitors currently constituted as ordinary partnerships, and "legal partnerships" (partnerships in which at least one partner is a practising barrister and the other partners are practising solicitors, practising barristers, or a combination of both). It makes provision for such firms of solicitors and legal partnerships to benefit from limited liability by applying for authorisation as limited liability partnerships (LLPs). At the time of writing the relevant provisions of the 2015 Act are not yet operative, consultations by the newly-established Legal Services Regulatory Authority are continuing, and the regulations on the operation and management of LLPs, which the Legal Services Regulatory Authority is mandated to make, have not yet been made.[27]

[1.12] Regarding accountants who wish to carry on business together, those who wished to be appointed as auditors were previously restricted from incorporating by s 187(2)(g) of the Companies Act 1990 (which provided that a body corporate could not be appointed as a company's auditor). That restriction was removed in 2010[28] to allow for

---

23 Dentists Act 1985, s 52(1).

24 Veterinary Practice Act 2005, s 54(2). See McVeigh, 'Partnership Agreements', Veterinary Ireland Journal (July 2017) Volume 7 Number 7, at pp 346–347. Note that in its 2008 Report on Competition in Professional Services (veterinary practitioners) the Competition Authority (now the Competition and Consumer Protection Commission) recommended that the Veterinary Practice Act 2005 be amended to allow for incorporated veterinary practices having regard to the perceived benefits of incorporation, including improved access to capital and business skills. At p 57 of its Report, the Competition Authority in particular noted that: 'There is no evidence from any profession or any other economic sector to suggest that incorporation leads to a diminution in quality of service. In fact, the requirement for collective accountability that is implicit in a firm of highly qualified professionals acts as a guarantee of professional behaviour' (although it is difficult to see how the professional behaviour of highly qualified practitioners would differ depending on whether they operate in partnership or by way of an incorporated body).

25 See the Medical Council's *Guide to Professional Conduct and Ethics for Registered Medical Practitioners* (8th edn, 2016) at para 54.1 and s 43 of the Medical Practitioners Act 2007. See also the Pharmacy Act 2007, s 63(1) which provides that it is professional misconduct for a registered pharmacist to have an interest in a medical practice.

26 By virtue of the Solicitors Act 1954, s 64(1), which provides that a body corporate or a director, officer or servant a body corporate, shall not do any act that could imply that the body corporate is qualified, or recognised by law as qualified, to act as a solicitor. While s 70 of the Solicitors (Amendment) Act 1994 gives the Law Society of Ireland (with the agreement of the Minister for Justice and Equality, following consultation with the Minister for Business, Enterprise and Innovation) the power to make regulations which provide for the incorporation of solicitors' practices, no such regulations have, at the time of writing, been made.

27 See further paras **[30.14]** and **[30.15]**.

28 By reg 6(b) of the European Communities (Statutory Audits) (Directive 2006/43/EC) Regulations 2010.

statutory auditors to be formed as bodies corporate and still be able to be appointed as a company's auditor. The Statutory Audits Regulations,[29] at the time of writing soon to be revoked when the relevant commencement order is made under the Companies (Statutory Audits) Act 2018, and their replacement, Part 27 of the Companies Act 2014 do not restrict a body corporate from acting as a statutory auditor but this has not resulted in all statutory audit firms being constituted as bodies corporate – the Companies Act 2014 still expressly contemplates the possibility of a partnership being appointed as statutory auditor.[30]

[1.13] Third, partnerships offer a number of advantages over limited liability companies as a vehicle for business. Although partners in ordinary partnerships[31] suffer from unlimited liability:[32]

– they are tax-transparent,[33] so that only the partners are taxed while in a company, the company and the shareholders are taxed;

– they are tax-efficient, since the partners are subject to lesser social insurance contributions than the combined rate payable by employers and employees;[34]

– they are not required to file accounts;[35]

– partners may withdraw their capital contributions without any restrictions;[36]

– the partnership structure permits the concentration of the ownership and management of an enterprise in the same hands (ie the partners), while under company law, there is a requirement that the ownership of the enterprise be in

---

[29] European Union (Statutory Audits) (Directive 2006/43/EC, as amended by Directive 2014/56/EU, and Regulation (EU) No 537/2014) Regulations 2016 (SI 312/2016).

[30] Companies Act 2014, s 380(4) which provides that '[the] appointment of a firm (not being a body corporate) by its firm name to be the statutory auditors of a company' shall be deemed to be an appointment of those who are partners in that firm during the term of its appointment and who are also themselves qualified to be statutory auditors.

[31] But not limited partners in limited partnerships, limited partners in investment limited partnerships or members of LLPs, see para **[28.01]** et seq, para **[29.01]** et seq and para **[30.37]** et seq, respectively.

[32] But note that a limited liability company may be a partner and in this way the partner's liability is effectively limited. Indeed it is arguable that in many cases this advantage of limited liability that companies have over partnerships is illusory since directors and shareholders in limited liability companies will often have to give personal guarantees to third party creditors and banks.

[33] See generally in relation to the tax transparency of limited partnerships, para **[28.13]**.

[34] See the Social Welfare (Consolidation) Act 2005, s 13 and s 21.

[35] Save in special circumstances, see European Communities (Accounts) Regulations 1993 (SI 396/1993). This statutory instrument was introduced to implement Council Directive 90/605/EEC. See generally para **[14.66]**. But note that under s 358 of the Companies Act 2014, a company (known as a 'small company') also does not have to have its accounts audited provided that it meets two of three 'qualifying conditions' (a turnover not exceeding €12 million, a balance sheet total not exceeding €6 million and an average employee number of 50 or less) in its first financial year, and in certain other financial years.

[36] Cf the position of companies under ss 84–87 of the Companies Act 2014. See generally Courtney, *The Law of Companies* (4th edn, 2016) at para [10.002] et seq; Hutchinson, *Keane on Company Law* (5th edn, 2016) at para [15.04].

the hands of the shareholders, while its management must be vested in the directors.[37]

Indeed, even where the founders of a business decide to incorporate, partnership law will still apply to any co-operative business venture between that company and another company or companies since the law of partnership applies to partnerships between legal persons such as companies as it does to partnerships between natural persons.[38]

[1.14] Fourth, legislation has been enacted which enables partners to have limited liability in certain circumstances under the Limited Partnerships Act 1907 Act. These partnerships have proved relatively popular with tax-based financiers and venture capitalists, since they combine the advantage of limited liability and tax transparency with the easy withdrawal of capital; however, the 1907 Act has remained largely unchanged in Ireland since its introduction and there is a growing sense that modernisation of that Act is needed. Limited reforms have been made to limited partnership law in England in both 2009 and 2017,[39] and the manner in which limited partnerships are currently used in Scotland is under review.[40]

[1.15] Fifth, the partnership was given further scope as an investment vehicle by the enactment of the Investment Limited Partnerships Act 1994 which allows it to be used as vehicle for collective investments (other than UCITS).[41] An investment limited partnership is subject to a specific Central Bank of Ireland authorisation and supervision regime as an alternative investment fund.[42] Despite initial expectations, it has not proven popular, with only seven investment limited partnerships being subject to existing authorisations from the Central Bank at 31 May 2018. However, the 1994 Act will shortly be revised[43] to take account of the perceived limitations on its usefulness which have been viewed by the funds industry as having a negative effect on the attractiveness of the Irish investment limited partnership both domestically and to international private equity funds.[44]

---

[37] However, it should be noted that the directors and shareholders can be the same people.

[38] Unless of course, the companies use a special purpose joint venture company, see para **[2.29]**.

[39] See further para **[28.11]**.

[40] See further paras **[1.43]** and **[28.11]**.

[41] See generally in relation to investment limited partnerships, para **[29.01]** et seq.

[42] Within the meaning of the European Union (Alternative Investment Fund Managers) Regulations 2013 which transposed Directive 2011/61/EU of the European Parliament and of the Council of 8 June 2011 on Alternative Investment Fund Managers (the AIFMD) into Irish law.

[43] In July 2017, the Minister for Finance and Public Expenditure and Reform announced approval of the drafting of the Investment Limited Partnerships (Amendment) Bill. In its Government Legislation Programme Autumn 2018, the Government confirmed that the Heads of Bill for what is now referred to as the 'Investment Limited Partnership and Irish Collective Asset-management Vehicle (Amendment) Bill' had been drafted, and that the draft Bill itself is a priority for publication. See further paras **[1.44]** and **[29.05]**. The British parliament introduced a new form of limited partnership, the private fund limited partnership, in April 2017 with a view to further enhancing Britain's status as a fund domicile. This was done by way of an amendment to the Limited Partnerships Act 1907 as it applies in the United Kingdom. See further para **[28.11]**.

[44] See further paras **[1.44]** and **[29.05]**.

[1.16] Finally, as mentioned above, the Legal Services Regulation Act 2015 makes provision for the formation of legal partnerships of barristers, legal partnerships of barristers and solicitors, LLPs (which will either be firms of solicitors, or legal partnerships) and multi-disciplinary practices (partnerships providing both legal services and non-legal services). While, at the time of writing, consultations by the newly-formed Legal Services Regulatory Authority are ongoing and it is not yet possible to form one of these new structures in Ireland, the Authority indicated in the minutes of its April 2018 meeting that it is working towards implementing the framework for legal partnerships in the third quarter of 2018. In its April 2018 First Strategic Plan 2018–2020, it also signalled its intention to introduce the enabling framework for LLPs in the fourth quarter of 2018. The position regarding multi-disciplinary practices is, at the time of writing, less certain.[45]

II.   SOURCES OF PARTNERSHIP LAW

[1.17] The law of partnership is a combination of statutory provisions (the main one being the 1890 Act) and the common law, both of which will now be considered.

Partnership Legislation

[1.18] In contrast to the twentieth century which saw the enactment of just two partnership Acts,[46] and the twenty-first century which has so far seen the enactment of just one relevant Act,[47] the active state of the law of partnership in Ireland in the eighteenth and nineteenth centuries is evidenced by the number of partnership statutes which were enacted during that time. All, but the 1890 Act itself, have been repealed, although some only as recently as 1962 by the Statute Law Revision (Pre-Union Irish Statutes) Act of that year. Before dealing with the 1890 Act, it is proposed to refer to these other partnership statutes.

Repealed partnership statutes

[1.19] The first partnership statute enacted in Ireland was in 1741 and was entitled an Act for the better Regulation of Partnerships to encourage Trade and Manufacture in Ireland,[48] which was amended in 1771.[49] These Acts provided for persons to be entitled to enter into a contract of partnership and in particular to empower the majority of partners to sell the share of a partner who fails to make his capital contribution.[50] These

---

45   See, further, para **[30.71]**.

46   The Limited Partnerships Act in 1907 and the Investment Limited Partnerships Act in 1994.

47   The Legal Services Regulation Act in 2015, albeit that initial steps have been taken to draft an Act to amend the Investment Limited Partnerships Act 1994. See further paras **[1.44]** and **[29.05]**.

48   15 Geo 2, c 7.

49   An Act for amending an Act for better regulation of partnerships to encourage the trade and manufacture in Ireland (11 & 12 Geo 3, c 25).

50   Both of these seventeenth century statutes on partnership remained part of Irish law until their repeal in 1962 by the Statute Law Revision (Pre-Union Irish Statutes) Act 1962. The wholesale repeal of the pre-Union statutes was criticised, obiter, by Kenny J in *Browne v Fahy* (5 October 1975) HC.

two Acts were designed to facilitate 'the establishing of fisheries, opening and working of mines, and the carrying on and improving the linen manufacture'.[51] Banking was a particularly popular object of eighteenth century partnerships and, in subsequent years, the control of banking partnerships became a concern because of the number of banks which collapsed or defrauded customers during this time. The nineteenth century is marked by the considerable number of cases concerning failed banking partnerships.[52] Until the enactment of the Liability of Members of Banking and other Joint Stock Companies Act 1879, banks were not entitled to limited liability and banking business was invariably carried on through the medium of a partnership. Therefore prior to that time, a number of statutes were enacted (the Irish Banking Acts 1755–1825)[53] which provided for the regulation of banking co-partnerships[54] in Ireland.

[1.20] The next major legislative step in partnership law came in 1865 with the passing of Bovill's Act (An Act to amend the Law of Partnership).[55] Since the eighteenth century, the courts had accepted that a person who shared in the profits of a business was liable as a partner for the losses of that business.[56] However, it was considered unjust that a person who was merely lending money to a firm at a rate of return fluctuating with and payable out of the profits of the firm should be treated as a partner. This view culminated with the seminal decision in *Cox v Hickman*[57] where it was held

---

[51] Section I of 15 Geo 2, c 7.

[52] See the summary of these banking failures in Limerick, Cork, Waterford, Newry, Clonmel, etc, outlined in *Nichols v Murray* (1828) 2 Ir Law Rec (os) 181 and the cases cited in fn **53** many of which related to one particularly notorious bank, namely the Tipperary Joint Stock Bank. See also Breslin, *Banking Law in the Republic of Ireland* (1st edn, 1998) at pp 12 et seq.

[53] Ie An Act for promoting Public Credit of 1755 (29 Geo 2, c 16), An Act to establish the Bank of Ireland of 1821 (1 & 2 G 4, c 72), An Act to make Members of Copartnerships liable and to enable such Copartnerships to sue and be sued of 1824 (5 Geo 4, c 73) and An Act for the better Regulation of Copartnerships of certain Bankers of 1825 (6 G 4, c 42). The Act of 1824 was the subject of litigation in a number of cases, see, for example, *Thompson v Kelly* (1843) 6 Ir LR 32 (concerning the Belfast Banking Company) and *Keily v Whitaker* (1838) Ir LR 28 (concerning the Southern Bank of Ireland). See also *Re Ginger* (1856) 5 Ir Ch R 174; *Reid v Mitchell* (1842) 4 Ir LR 322; *May v Hodges* (1843) 5 Ir LR 584; *Wright v Murphy* (1841) 4 Ir LR 258; *Thompson v Kelly* (1843) 6 Ir LR 32; *Howard v Love* (1847) 10 Ir LR 505; *Murray v Comyn* (1859) 11 Ir CLR 239; *Thomson v Birnie* (1840) 2 Ir LR 234; *McDowell v Bergin* (1861) 12 Ir CLR 391; *Durand v Potter* (1841) 1 Ir Leg Rep 224; *McDowell v Doyle* (1857) 7 Ir CLR 598; *Dudgeon v O'Connell* (1849) 12 Ir Eq R 566; *Grimshaw v Bowden* (1847) 11 Ir LR 399; *Nichols v Murray* (1828) 2 Ir Law Rec (os) 181; *Kiely v Whitaker* 1 Ir LR 28; *Taylor v Hughes* (1844) 7 Ir Eq R 529; *Sugrue v Hibernian Bank* (1828) 2 IR LR 285; *Ex p Kennedy* (1856) Ir Jur 278; *Ex p Stirling* (1858) 6 Ir Ch R 180; *Carroll v Kennedy* (1856) 2 Ir Jur 15; *Davies v Kennedy* (1869) 3 Ir Eq R 668 aff'd *sub nom Copland v Davies* (1872) LR 5 HL 358; *Acheson v Hodges* (1841) 3 Ir Eq R 516; *O'Flaherty v McDowell* (1857) 10 ER 1248 overruling *Fawcett v Hodges* (1841) 3 Ir Eq R 232. See generally Breslin, *Banking Law in the Republic of Ireland* (1st edn, 1998) at pp 12 et seq.

[54] The term 'co-partnership' was commonly used at that time but it has the same meaning as the term 'partnership'.

[55] 28 & 29 Vict, c 86.

[56] See *Grace v Smith* (1775) 2 Wm Blacks 998 and *Waugh v Carver* (1793) 2 H Blacks 235.

[57] *Cox v Hickman* (1860) 8 HL Cas 268.

that the sharing of the profits of a business was not determinative of partnership, but rather that this was simply prima facie evidence of partnership which could be rebutted.[58] Bovill's Act expanded on this principle by removing any presumption of partnership or liability as a partner in four situations in which a person receives a share of the profits of a business, ie where the receipt of profits is consideration for the sale of the goodwill of a business, is in repayment of a loan, is remuneration for services, or is an annuity to the widow or family of a deceased partner. The terms of Bovill's Act remain applicable to this day because, while the Act itself was repealed by the passing of the 1890 Act, its terms were incorporated, with slight modification, into ss 2(3) and 3 of the 1890 Act. It follows that cases decided under Bovill's Act between 1865 and 1890 remain relevant in interpreting those sections of the 1890 Act.

The first limited partnership statute

[1.21] An interesting first for the Irish parliament was the introduction of the first limited partnership statute in the common law world, when it enacted the Anonymous Partnerships Act 1781[59] and amended it in 1786.[60] This Act granted limited liability to certain partners, called anonymous partners, provided they took no part in the management of the partnership, while the active partners were liable for the partnership debts. It was adopted in New South Wales, New Zealand, South Australia and Victoria.[61] However, while limited partnerships continued in all of the aforesaid jurisdictions, the Anonymous Partnerships Act of 1781 was repealed in Ireland in 1862[62] and the limited partnership was not re-introduced until the enactment of the Limited Partnerships Act in 1907.

[1.22] The Anonymous Partnerships Act 1781 is also significant since it was the first legislative expression of one of the cornerstones of partnership law, ie that a person who takes part in a business is liable for the firm's losses, since it would be 'unjust that any man who takes a share of the profits should not also answer for the losses of the firm to

---

58   This principle is now contained in s 2(3) of the 1890 Act.

59   21 & 22 Geo 3, c 46: its full title is an Act to promote Trade and Manufacture, by regulating and encouraging partnerships. This Anonymous Partnership Act was the subject of litigation in *Lindsay and Company v Loughead* (1847) 10 Ir LR 26. There, Pigot CB held that proceedings which were issued by the plaintiff as 'Samuel Lindsay and Company' did not mention the Anonymous Partnership Act, which Statute entitled the original partner or surviving partner to sue on behalf of the firm. On this basis, the Court held that the proceedings were defective as not showing any title in the plaintiffs to sue.

60   26 G 3, c 34, its full title is an Act for more effectually promoting Partnerships in Trade, by amending the Laws respecting the same.

61   New South Wales: Anonymous Partnerships Act 1853 (17 Vic, c 9); Queensland: Mercantile Act 1867, ss 53– 68; South Australia: Anonymous Partnerships Act 1853 (17 Vic, c 20); Victoria: Anonymous Partnerships Act 1853 (17 Vic, c 5); New Zealand: Special Partnership Act 1858. See generally Fletcher, *Higgins and Fletcher on The Law of Partnership in Australia and New Zealand* (8th edn, 2001); Fletcher, *The Law of Partnership in Australia* (9th edn, 2007)

62   Companies Act 1862, s 205 and 3rd Sch (25 & 26 Vict c 89).

its creditors'.[63] This principle was reflected in the provisions of the Anonymous Partnerships Act which established the personal liability of a partner for the acts of the firm.

Partnership Act 1890

[1.23] The only eighteenth or nineteenth century partnership statute which is still in force is the 1890 Act. This seminal piece of legislation was drafted by Sir Frederick Pollock in 1879, but was not enacted until 1890, by which time it had undergone substantial amendment. This Act was drafted with the aim of reducing the mass of pre-1890 caselaw into a series of principles of partnership law. In this respect it was partially successful, and to this day, in analysing any partnership issue, recourse should first be made to the principles contained in the 1890 Act. In Ireland, it has not been the subject of any substantive amendment or modernisation since its enactment, and no changes are expected in the short term as, at the time of writing, the key focus areas are the reform of the investment limited partnership framework, and the development of legal partnerships and LLPs as business models for the Irish legal community. In the UK, while both the Law Commission and the Scottish Law Commission commented in 2003 that:

> 'Although the 1890 Act has been regarded as a reasonably successful example of codification of a branch of the common law, and has operated almost without amendment for over a hundred years, it contains a number of conceptual flaws ...'.[64]

there has also been little in the way of change to the framework of the 1890 Act, with any recent legislative changes in the UK focusing instead on the areas of limited partnerships[65] and LLPs.[66]

[1.24] Although enacted prior to the establishment of Saorstát Éireann, there can be no doubt that the 1890 Act was carried over into the laws of Ireland in 1922. Any doubts which might have existed about this issue were quickly dispelled in the 1923 case of

---

63   McKenna, 'On Partnerships with Limited Liability' (1854) Journal of Dublin Statistical Society 1 at 17. Another rationale for making a person who receives a share of the profits liable for the acts of the firm was to prevent 'an infraction of the usury laws', which prohibited the charging of exorbitant interest on loans by the receipt of a share of the profits in return for the loan. These laws were repealed by the Usury Law Repeals Act 1854.

64   At para 1.16 of The Law Commission and The Scottish Law Commission *Partnership Law: A Joint Consultation Paper* (Consultation Paper No 159; Discussion Paper No 111). Despite various issues being identified as part of that consultation, most notably a recommendation that separate legal personality be introduced for partnerships generally, the reforms proposed by both Commissions relating to ordinary partnerships (ie those subject only to the 1890 Act) did not progress. Minor reforms in the area of limited partnerships were introduced however, as to which see para **[28.11]**. For further information on the reforms proposed in 2003, see Berry, 'The Partnership Bill 2003: unnecessary tinkering or much-needed reform?' (2005) Journal of Business Law, 70–90; Henning, 'Partnership law review: the joint consultation papers and the Limited Liability Partnership Act in brief historical and comparative perspective' (2004) Company Lawyer, 25(6), 163–170; Deards, 'The Partnership Bill: under starter's orders' (2004) Company Lawyer, 25(2), 41–48).

65   See further para **[28.11]**.

66   See further paras **[1.38]** and **[30.38]**.

Murphy v Power,[67] in which the Irish Court of Appeal[68] accepted the application of the 1890 Act in Saorstát Éireann.

[1.25] The 1890 Act is divided into the following five parts and this format is followed in this text, save that the fifth part of this work deals with limited partnerships, investment limited partnerships, LLPs and other key aspects of the Legal Services Regulation Act 2015:

> Part I   Nature of partnership;
>
> Part II   Relations of partners to persons dealing with them;
>
> Part III Relations of partners to one another;
>
> Part IV Dissolution of partnership and its consequences;
>
> Part V   Supplemental.

Limited partnership legislation

[1.26] As has been noted, the 1890 Act forms the basis of partnership law in Ireland. However, in addition to the 1890 Act, there are two other partnership statutes which are in operation today namely the Limited Partnerships Act 1907 and the Investment Limited Partnerships Act 1994, and one partnership-related statute where key provisions are not yet operative, namely the Legal Services Regulation Act 2015 (and more particularly Part 8 (*Legal Partnerships, Direct Professional Access, Multi-disciplinary Practices and Limited Liability Partnerships*) thereof). The 1907 Act provides for the formation of a partnership, in which at least one partner has limited liability, known as the limited partner, and one has unlimited liability, known as the general partner. The 1994 Act also provides for the creation of a partnership, in which at least one partner is a limited partner and one is a general partner. These investment limited partnerships are subject to a specific Central Bank authorisation and supervision regime as alternative investment funds within the meaning of the European Union (Alternative Investment Fund Managers) Regulations 2013, and are very specialised partnerships since they are also collective investment undertakings. The 2015 Act provides for the setting up of legal partnerships (ie partnerships of barristers, and partnerships of solicitors and barristers),[69] LLPs (a model that will be available to both firms of solicitors and legal partnerships) and multi-disciplinary practices (partnerships which will provide both legal and non-legal services, at least one partner in which must be a practising solicitor or a practising barrister). Limited partnerships, investment limited partnerships, LLPs

---

67   *Murphy v Power* [1923] 1 IR 68.

68   The court comprised Molony CJ, Ronan and O'Connor LJJ.

69   A partnership of solicitors is not a 'legal partnership' for the purposes of the Legal Services Regulation Act 2015. As practising solicitors were already capable of entering into partnership with one another before the 2015 Act was introduced, the 2015 Act does not regulate ordinary partnerships of solicitors generally, but does provide that a partnership of solicitors may apply to be authorised as an LLP (Legal Services Regulation Act 2015, Part 8).

and other business models contemplated by the 2015 Act are considered separately in Part E of this work.

Common Law

[1.27] In addition to the partnership legislation regard must also be had to the partnership law as established by the courts.

Status of pre-1890 and post-1890 caselaw

[1.28] As much of the partnership caselaw predates the 1890 Act, it is important to bear in mind that the 1890 Act does not replace this common law. The 1890 Act describes itself as an Act to 'declare' and amend the law of partnership, a fact recognised by O'Hanlon J in the High Court case of *MacCarthaigh v Daly*.[70] The 1890 Act is not, nor was it intended to be, a complete codification of the pre-1890 caselaw. By its express terms, the 1890 Act provides that the pre-existing caselaw continues in force except in so far as inconsistent with the 1890 Act. Section 46 provides that:

> The rules of equity and of common law applicable to partnership shall continue in force except so far as they are inconsistent with the express provisions of this Act.

This approach may be supported in principle since the principles in the 1890 Act are simply summaries of the large body of caselaw which existed at that time and to understand the principles, recourse must be had to those cases. The draftsman of the 1890 Act, Sir Frederick Pollock, made this clear, when he stated in the preface to his *Digest of the Law of Partnership*, that:

> 'Unless the Law has been purposely altered, which in a codifying Act is a rare exception, the decisions are still the material from which the rule of law has been generalised.'[71]

[1.29] In the 1923 case of *Murphy v Power*,[72] the new courts of Saorstát Éireann got an early opportunity to consider the status of pre-1890 partnership law cases. Ronan LJ expressly relied on cases decided prior to the passing of the 1890 Act, observing that:

> 'The law of partnership at present is partly regulated – and I say this advisedly – by the Partnership Act 1890 ... It will be observed that the Partnership Act does not purport to abrogate the case law on the subject; but, on the contrary, declares that "the rules of equity and common law applicable to partnership shall continue in force except so far as they are inconsistent with the express provisions of this Act" (sect 46). The Act therefore has to be read and applied in the light of the decisions which have built up the existing rules.'[73]

---

[70] *MacCarthaigh v Daly* [1985] IR 73, where he stated (at 119) that 'the Partnership Act 1890 ... was largely declaratory of the common law'.

[71] Gower, *Pollock on the Law of Partnership* (15th edn, 1952) at pp (xiii)–(xiv).

[72] *Murphy v Power* [1923] 1 IR 68.

[73] *Murphy v Power* [1923] 1 IR 68 at 74, quoting in part from Sir Frederick Pollock's preface to his *Digest on the Law of Partnership* (7th edn).

However, the express terms of s 46 of the 1890 Act must not be ignored, so that where a provision of the 1890 Act is clear, any pre-1890 caselaw must be read subject to those provisions and in the event of a conflict, those provisions will take precedence over the earlier caselaw.

[1.30] A second reason to have recourse to pre-1890 caselaw is that there are many important areas of partnership law which have been dealt with by the courts, but which were not addressed by the 1890 Act, such as the status of partnership goodwill and the administration of partnership assets in the event of a partner's insolvency.

Status of pre-1922 decisions of the courts of the United Kingdom

[1.31] This work treats as binding on the Irish courts, the pre-1922 decisions of the courts of the United Kingdom and of Ireland on the grounds that they became part of Irish law on the establishment of Saorstát Éireann, save to the extent that they are inconsistent with the Irish Constitution.[74] This is, of course, subject to the pre-1890 decisions of the courts of the United Kingdom and of Ireland not being inconsistent with the terms of the 1890 Act.[75]

Post-1922 decisions of the courts of the United Kingdom

[1.32] Post-1922 decisions of the courts of the United Kingdom on partnership law matters, although clearly not binding on the Irish courts, are regarded as persuasive authority.[76] Insofar as these decisions consider the terms of the 1890 Act, they will be regarded as strongly persuasive, since the 1890 Act applies in Northern Ireland, England and Wales[77] and Scotland[78] in almost the exact same format as it does in Ireland.[79] A similar approach is taken to decisions of the courts of former colonies of the United

---

[74] See the judgment of McCarthy J in *Irish Shell Ltd v Elm Motors Ltd* [1984] ILRM 595. See also *Vone Securities Ltd v Cooke* [1975] IR 59; *McKinley v Minister for Defence* [1992] 2 IR 333. However, a different view has been expressed by Walsh J (with whom O'Higgins CJ agreed) in *Gaffney v Gaffney* [1975] IR 133 where he felt that statute law only, and not caselaw, was carried forward into Irish law in 1922.

[75] Partnership Act 1890, s 46.

[76] See for example the judgments of Costello J in *M McM v J McC* [1994] 1 IR 293 at 303 and of McCarthy J in *Irish Shell Ltd v Elm Motors Ltd* [1984] ILRM 595 and, more recently, the judgment of Kearns P in *Nevin & Anor v Nevin* [2013] IEHC 80 in which he stated that the decisions of the English courts are of persuasive authority post-1922, and that the decisions of the superior courts in the United Kingdom 'can be highly persuasive…'.

[77] See generally l'Anson Banks, *Lindley & Banks on Partnership* (20th edn, 2017). See also Blackett-Ord and Haren, *Partnership Law* (5th edn, 2015); Prime & Scanlan, *The Law of Partnership* (1995).

[78] See generally Brough, *Miller on Partnership* (2nd edn, 1994).

[79] There have been some minor amendments made to the 1890 Act in these jurisdictions, but the only significant difference between the application of the Act in Ireland and these different jurisdictions is evident from the Act itself, ie s 4(2) which provides that in Scotland, a firm is a legal person distinct from its members.

Kingdom,[80] such as America,[81] New Zealand,[82] Canada[83] and Australia[84] which have implemented the 1890 Act in whole or in part into their law.[85]

Application of Equitable Principles

[1.33] Since the passing of the Supreme Court of Judicature Act (Ireland) 1877, the administration of law and equity has been merged and it is important to bear in mind that the law of partnership is today subject to the application of equitable principles. This point is particularly important for partnerships, since a relationship of trust is the basis for every partnership and therefore the partnership relationship will be subject to additional duties which attach to such positions under the law of equity. In the High Court case of *Williams v Harris*,[86] McWilliam J adopted the following approach to partnership issues, in the context of the winding up of partnerships, but which is of general application to all partnership matters:[87]

> 'in winding up a partnership the procedure belongs to an equitable jurisdiction which, though theoretically concurrent, is practically exclusive. It depends on the principles which Courts of Equity apply to persons who are in possession of property under

---

[80]   One jurisdiction which never adopted a Partnership Act is South Africa, see generally Joubert, *The Law of South Africa*, Vol 19 (Partnership) (1997); Henning, 'The universal partnership proper: recognising the concept of a partnership extending beyond the commercial sphere' (Comp Law 2013, 34(8), 231–233). See also Henning and Snyman, 'Revision of the law of partnership in the United States of America: A commendable precedent' (1997) 114 SALJ 684.

[81]   See generally Hurt, Smith, Bromberg and Ribstein, *Bromberg & Ribstein on Partnership* (2nd edn) and Hurt, Smith, Bromberg and Ribstein, *Bromberg & Ribstein on Limited Liability Partnerships, the Revised Uniform Partnership Act, and the Uniform Limited Partnership Act* (2018 edn).

[82]   See generally Webb and Molloy, *Principles of the Law of Partnership* (6th edn, 1996). See also Fletcher, *Higgins and Fletcher on The Law of Partnership in Australia and New Zealand* (8th edn, 2001).

[83]   See generally Manzer, *A Practical Guide to Canadian Partnership Law* (1996) (updated annually).

[84]   See generally Fletcher, *The Law of Partnership in Australia* (9th edn, 2007).

[85]   See for example the American Uniform Partnership Act 1997 (Last Amended 2013), the New South Wales Partnership Act 1892, the Queensland Partnership Act 1891, the South Australian Partnership Act 1891, the Tasmanian Partnership Act 1891, the Victoria Partnership Act 1958, the Western Australian Partnership Act 1895 and the New Zealand Partnership Act 1908. See also the Ontario Partnerships Act, RSO 1990, c P.5; the British Columbia Partnership Act, RSBC 1996, c 348; the Alberta Partnership Act, RSA 2000, c P-3; the Manitoba Partnership Act, CCSM c P30; the Saskatchewan Partnership Act, RSS 1978, c P-3; the New Brunswick Partnership Act, RSNB 1973, C P-4; the Newfoundland and Labrador Partnership Act, RSNL 1990, c P-3; the Nova Scotia Partnership Act, RSNS 1989, c 334; the Prince Edward Island Partnership Act, RSPEI 1988, c P-1; the Yukon Partnership and Business Names Act, RSY 2002, C 166; and the Northwest Territories Partnership Act, RSNWT 1988, c P-1.

[86]   *Williams v Harris* (15 January 1980) HC.

[87]   He was quoting from Viscount Haldane in *Hugh Stevenson v Aktiengesellschaft* [1918] AC 240.

circumstances in which they are treated as standing in a fiduciary relationship. It is more than and different from the procedure which applies when the rights of parties arise merely out of the rules of the common law which apply to contracts.'[88]

It is important therefore to bear in mind that the rules of equity will have a particular application to the resolution of partnership law issues.

Position in Northern Ireland

[1.34] While ostensibly this work deals with the law of partnership in Ireland, of necessity, it will also refer to the legal position in Northern Ireland. This is because the 1890 Act and the Limited Partnerships Act 1907 apply in both jurisdictions. It follows that the reliance herein on decisions of those Commonwealth jurisdictions in which the 1890 Act or an adaptation thereof still exists, will be of equal relevance in Northern Ireland. In addition, much of the Irish caselaw on partnership matters pre-dates 1922 and is therefore equally applicable in Northern Ireland. For these reasons, there is arguably no other branch of law which is so similar north and south of the border and it is suggested that decisions of the Northern Irish courts since 1922 should therefore be treated as being of a strongly persuasive nature in this jurisdiction and vice-versa.

Descriptive Terms used in Partnership Law

[1.35] The terms 'general partnership' and 'general partner' have at times been used by partnership legislation, legal commentators and the courts to describe a partnership and partners which are governed by the 1890 Act.[89] However, it is contended that the use of the term 'general' leads immediately to confusion between a partnership governed by the 1890 Act and one governed by the Limited Partnerships Act 1907 or the Investment Limited Partnerships Act 1994 where the term is used to distinguish between a partner with unlimited liability ('a general partner') and a partner with limited liability ('a limited partner'). In order to avoid confusion with a general partner in a limited partnership or in an investment limited partnership, it is suggested that a partnership which is governed by the 1890 Act should be referred to as an ordinary partnership and a partner therein as an ordinary partner. This terminology is used throughout this work. Indeed it is suggested that consideration should be given to adopting such a change in the 1890 Act.

[1.36] Another important nomenclature issue regarding partnerships which is the cause of considerable confusion is the use of the term 'dissolution' of a partnership. As is noted in detail elsewhere in this text, the word 'dissolution' may refer to a technical dissolution of a partnership (in which there is simply a change of membership) or to a general dissolution of a partnership (in which there is a winding up of the firm). The term dissolution when used in the 1890 Act usually, but not always, refers to a general

---

[88]   *Williams v Harris* (15 January 1980) HC at pp 7–8 of the transcript.

[89]   See for example s 5 of the Limited Partnerships Act 1907. See also l'Anson Banks, *Lindley & Banks on Partnership* (20th edn, 2017) at para 5-68.

dissolution[90] and throughout this work every effort is made to clarify whether one is dealing with a general dissolution or a technical dissolution.

The Future

Limited liability partnerships

[1.37] Limited liability partnerships (LLPs) have existed in the United States since 1991 and have proved popular with professional partnerships as a means of restricting partners' liability.[91] They differ from limited partnerships under the Limited Partnerships Act 1907 since all the partners are granted a limit on their personal liability for the firm's obligations, yet they are not required to forgo a say in the management of the firm in return for this protection.

[1.38] As a result of high profile negligence cases against professional partnerships in the United Kingdom,[92] pressure was brought to bear by large accountancy partnerships on the British parliament to introduce limited liability for partners in ordinary partnerships. The result was the Limited Liability Partnerships Act 2000, which introduced LLPs to England and Wales, and to Scotland.[93] LLPs formed under that Act are bodies corporate with separate legal personality,[94] have unlimited corporate capacity[95] and are not partnerships for the purposes of the 1890 Act.[96] Instead, they are formed in a manner similar to companies, by way of an incorporation document which

---

90   See for example ss 38, 39 and 40 of the 1890 Act which clearly refer to a general dissolution. On the other hand see s 31(2) of the 1890 Act which refers firstly to a general dissolution, then a technical dissolution ('In case of a dissolution of the partnership, whether as respects all the partners or as respects the assigning partner') and s 42(1) which clearly refers to a technical dissolution.

91   They were first introduced in Texas and are now to be found throughout the United States. They permit ordinary partnerships, by making a filing or registration, to obtain a form of limited liability. The LLP was first introduced in Texas as a reaction to litigation against law and accountancy partnerships for their part in advising on the establishment of loan and savings associations which failed in large numbers. The suits alleged joint and several liability against partners, many of whom had nothing to do with the failed associations. To protect the innocent partners in professional partnerships (such as lawyers, accountants, doctors, architects and engineers) against vicarious liability claims in the future, it was proposed that partners in a registered LLP would not be liable for liabilities arising from negligence committed by another partner. This proposal went on to form the basis of the first LLP statute. At the time of writing, in all but nine US states, there is a full corporate-type liability shield, while in the remaining states, the partners remain vicariously liable for ordinary contract-type debts. In all other respects, these partnerships are subject to the law of ordinary partnerships. See generally Hurt, Smith, Bromberg and Ribstein, *Bromberg & Ribstein on Limited Liability Partnerships, the Revised Uniform Partnership Act, and the Uniform Limited Partnership Act* (2018 edn).

92   Such as *ADT Ltd v BDO Binder Hamlyn* [1996] BCC 808, in which an award of Stg£65m was made on foot of a finding of negligent misrepresentation.

93   See l'Anson Banks, *Lindley & Banks on Partnership* (20th edn, 2017) at para 2-39 et seq.

94   Limited Liability Partnerships Act 2000, s 1(2).

95   Limited Liability Partnerships Act 2000, s 1(3).

96   Limited Liability Partnerships Act 2000, s 1(5).

must be registered with Companies House (following which the LLP will receive a 'certificate of incorporation').[97] The members of the LLP may be individuals or corporates, and it must have at least two 'designated members' who will have a greater level of responsibility than the other members. LLPs formed under that Act tend to put in place a 'limited liability partnership agreement' to regulate their internal governance. Its members are the agents of the LLP and not agents of each other, and the LLP is tax transparent with each member paying tax on its share of the profits. Provision has been made for a clawback of certain drawings by the partners if the LLP becomes insolvent within two years of such drawings, subject to certain conditions being met.[98] LLPs were then introduced in Northern Ireland from November 2004 under the Limited Liability Partnerships Act (Northern Ireland) 2002.[99]

[1.39] The Legal Services Regulation Act 2015 introduced a framework for LLPs in Ireland. Once the relevant provisions of that Act become operative, a firm of solicitors or a legal partnership (a partnership between barristers, or between solicitors and barristers) will be able to apply for authorisation to operate as an LLP under s 125 of that Act. Unlike the position under English law, an LLP in Ireland will not have separate legal personality. As such, while the English law LLP is more akin to a body corporate, an Irish law LLP will remain more aligned with the law of ordinary partnership. This absence of separate legal personality also means that the relatively recent body of LLP-related English caselaw will be of less persuasive authority in Ireland than caselaw relating to the 1890 Act or to the Limited Partnerships Act 1907.[100]

[1.40] A partner in an Irish LLP will not (as a result of being a partner in the LLP) be personally liable for the debts, obligations or liabilities of the LLP, of himself *qua* partner or of another partner in the LLP, or of any employee, agent or representative of the LLP. The possibility of limited liability is expected to prove attractive to the majority of partnerships of solicitors, in particular as it will enable the risks to which partners are exposed to be reduced, and as it may reduce the cost of professional indemnity insurance. The LLP framework is considered further elsewhere in this work.[101]

Limited partnership reform?

[1.41] While in Ireland, there have been no substantive proposals to re-examine the law in relation to limited partnerships, some limited changes have been introduced by the

---

97   According to the 'Official Statistics: Incorporated companies in the UK: July to September 2018' (and excluding LLPs in liquidation or otherwise in the course of being removed from the Companies House LLP Register of Members), there were 50,342 LLPs on that register at the end of June 2018 (46,820 were incorporated in England and Wales, 2,889 were incorporated in Scotland, and 633 were incorporated in Northern Ireland).
98   Limited Liability Partnerships Regulations 2001, Sch 3 (which amended the Insolvency Act 1986).
99   C 12 (NI). This Act was repealed by s 1286(2) of the Companies Act 2006 (the repeal took full effect from 1 October 2009) with s 1286(1)(a) of the Companies Act 2006 extending the laws in effect in Great Britain at that time in relation to LLPs (including the Limited Liability Partnerships Act 2000) to Northern Ireland.
100 See further Keane, 'LLP service' Law Society Gazette, November 2017 at p 44.
101 See para **[30.37]** et seq.

British parliament to the limited partnership framework applicable in England and Wales, Scotland and Northern Ireland. The British parliament signalled in 2006 that it would introduce the reforms to the limited partnership framework proposed by the Law Commission and Scottish Law Commission in their 2003 report[102] on their 2001 consultation on the reform of limited partnership law.[103] A formal consultation was then carried out by the Department of Business, Energy and Industrial Strategy in 2008,[104] proposing the repeal of the Limited Partnerships Act 1907, the inclusion of provisions dealing with limited partnerships in the 1890 Act, and changes to the provisions relating to the establishment, registration and de-registration of limited partnerships, the liability of limited partners to third parties, and the rights and obligations of general partners and limited partners. However, based on the responses received to that consultation, only the changes regarding the registration of limited partnerships were progressed, and these became law in 2009 by way of the Legislative Reform (Limited Partnerships) Order 2009.

[1.42] In April 2017, the British parliament introduced a variation on its limited partnership regime, aimed at collective investment schemes, with a view to making the United Kingdom more attractive to the global funds industry.[105] The new regime allows a limited partnership to elect to be treated as a private fund limited partnership if it meets certain conditions – it must have a written partnership agreement in place, and it must be a collective investment scheme. A private fund limited partnership will benefit from a 'white list' of certain actions that will not be considered as management activity[106] and the provisions of the limited partnership regime regarding capital contributions and more general administrative matters have also been amended insofar as a limited partnership successfully elects to be treated as a private fund limited partnership.[107]

[1.43] Following reports that limited partnerships registered in Scotland were being used as vehicles for criminal activity (such as money laundering, organised crime and tax evasion), and in light of the comparatively significant increase in the number of limited partnerships being registered in Scotland when compared with England, Wales and

---

[102] The Law Commission and the Scottish Law Commission *Partnership Law: Report on a Reference under Section 3(1)(e) of the Law Commissions Act 1965* (Law Co No 283) (Scot Law Com No 192).

[103] *Limited Partnerships Act 1907, Joint Consultation Paper* (The Law Commission Consultation Paper No 161; The Scottish Law Commission Discussion Paper No 118)

[104] *Reform of Limited Partnership Law: Legislative Reform Order to repeal and replace the Limited Partnerships Act 1907 – A consultation document – August 2008.*

[105] The Legislative Reform (Private Fund Limited Partnerships) Order 2017 which amends the Limited Partnerships Act 1907 as it applies in the United Kingdom by including specific provisions dealing with the regime for private fund limited partnerships.

[106] What constitutes management activity has long been a source of concern for limited partners, as a limited partner can lose its limited liability status if it becomes involved in the management of the limited partnership. See further para **[28.79]** et seq.

[107] See further, 'Private Fund Limited Partnerships – The Advent of Certainty?' Legal Ease with Lexis® PSL, Butterworths Journal of International Banking and Financial Law, July/August 2017, 454.

Northern Ireland,[108] the Department for Business, Energy and Industrial Skills published a '*Review of Limited Partnership Law: call for evidence*' in January 2017, which closed in March 2017. In that call for evidence, views and evidence were sought as to why registrations of limited partnerships in Scotland had increased, the economic uses of limited partnerships, the characteristics of limited partnerships that might enable criminal activity, and other related matters. Following that call for evidence, the Department published a consultation (*Limited Partnerships: Reform of Limited Partnership Law*) on 30 April 2018,[109] outlining that while evidence provided in response to its January 2017 call for evidence had shown an ongoing need for limited partnerships as business entities, evidence had also been provided of suspected criminal activity involving limited partnerships registered in Scotland. As such, the consultation sought views on how the law in relation to limited partnerships could be reformed to reduce the risk of misuse. In particular, consideration is being given to requiring that a UK limited partnership file an annual statement confirming that its principal place of business remains in the UK and providing evidence that the address in question is truly its principal place of business (and not merely an address for service of notices and proceedings). Alternatively, consideration is being given to allowing a UK limited partnership to have its principal place of business in another jurisdiction, while requiring it to have an additional service address in its country of registration (ie England and Wales, Scotland, or Northern Ireland). The consultation is also seeking views on whether UK limited partnerships should be required to prepare accounts and reports similar to those required of a private company, and whether the Registrar of Companies should be given the power to strike-off limited partnerships.

Changes to investment limited partnership framework

[1.44] The investment limited partnership framework has proven considerably less popular than originally expected in Ireland. At the time of writing, there are only seven investment limited partnerships with authorisations from the Central Bank of Ireland.[110] As mentioned above,[111] an investment limited partnership is subject to a specific authorisation and supervision regime by the Central Bank as an alternative investment fund, but the Irish funds industry has long viewed the current investment limited partnership framework as having considerable limitations which lessen its attractiveness both domestically and to international private equity firms. In July 2017, the Minister for Finance and Public Expenditure and Reform announced that approval had been given for a Bill to be drafted to amend the Investment Limited Partnerships Act 1994.

---

108 The Department of Business, Energy and Industrial Strategy: *Review of Limited Partnership Law: call for evidence* (January 2017) noted, at p 18, that between March 2011 and March 2016, there had been a 236% increase in the number of limited partnerships registered in Scotland, whereas the number of limited partnerships registered in England and Wales, and in Northern Ireland, during the same period increased by only 26%.

109 This consultation closed on 23 July 2018. At the time of writing, the Department for Business, Energy and Industrial Skills has not confirmed what reforms may be introduced in light of responses received to the consultation.

110 Central Bank of Ireland Register of Authorised Investment Limited Partnerships (30 September 2018).

111 See para **[1.15]** above.

The purpose of the Bill is to align the investment limited partnership framework with the framework introduced by the Alternative Investment Fund Managers Directive,[112] and to further enhance Ireland's status as a fund domicile. At the time of writing, that Bill is known as the Investment Limited Partnership and Irish Collective Asset-management Vehicle (Amendment) Bill 2017, but only draft Heads of Bill have been prepared.[113]

---

[112] Directive 2011/61/EU of the European Parliament and of the Council of 8 June 2011 on Alternative Investment Fund Managers, transposed into Irish law by the European Union (Alternative Investment Fund Managers) Regulations 2013 (SI 257/2013).

[113] In its Government Legislation Programme for Spring/Summer 2018, the Government confirmed that the Heads of Bill had been prepared, and that it was in the process of determining whether the draft should be referred to the relevant Oireachtas Committee for pre-legislative scrutiny.

Chapter 2

The Definition and Existence of a Partnership

INTRODUCTION

[2.01] '[T]he difficulty whether a man is a partner or not has been of frequent occurrence, and ... there are few questions of law on which there has been a greater diversity of judicial opinion.'

Per Gibson J in *Cullimore v Savage South Africa*.[1]

Despite these rather ominous words from Gibson J, this chapter will attempt to clarify the approach to determining whether a partnership exists in a particular case.

[2.02] The question of whether a partnership exists is governed by ss 1(1) and 2 of the 1890 Act. Section 1(1) contains the definition of a partnership and each of its six components must be satisfied for a partnership to exist. Section 2 of the 1890 Act sets out eight rules which assist in determining whether a partnership exists in a particular case. Undoubtedly, if an enterprise satisfies the definition of partnership in s 1(1), then it is not necessary to consider the application of the rules in s 2 of the Act. These rules will, however, be of assistance in cases of doubt.

[2.03] This chapter follows the approach taken by ss 1(1) and 2 of the 1890 Act by considering the existence of a partnership under the following headings:

    I.   The Definition of a Partnership; and
    II.   The Rules for the Existence of a Partnership.

A consideration of both the definition of a partnership and the rules for assisting in this determination is important for a clear understanding of the nature of the partnership relationship. It will be of particular importance to those who draft agreements which are designed to fall on either side of the partnership line.

Overview

[2.04] In considering the definition of partnership, namely that the parties be carrying on business in common with a view to profit, it will be seen that this definition may be divided into six separate requirements. While each of these six prerequisites must be satisfied, it is clear that the requirement which allows for the greatest variety of interpretation on the part of the courts is that the parties be carrying on business 'in common'. It is this requirement which goes to the very root of the partnership relationship and much of this chapter is taken up with determining whether the alleged partners are acting in common, or, to put it another way, whether their relationship is sufficiently proximate for them to be partners with the attendant legal consequences.

---

[1]   *Cullimore v Savage South Africa* [1903] 2 IR 589 at 605. See generally Northam and Smith, 'Unincorporated association or partnership?' (1996) 1 Commercial Lawyer 6.

While the question of whether parties are acting in common is an objective test, the courts are undoubtedly influenced both by the general consequences of such a finding and the specific consequences of the case before them and it is useful to briefly consider both.

[2.05] The general consequences of a finding of partnership which are considered in detail in subsequent chapters, include such important issues as the fact that partners are, as a matter of partnership law, held to be each others' agents for the purposes of the partnership business,[2] they are held to owe each other a fiduciary duty in their partnership dealings,[3] they must account to each other for the use of the partnership name, property or business connection,[4] they share profits and losses equally,[5] and as a group the partners have see-through status[6] for tax purposes.[7]

[2.06] On the other hand, the specific consequences of a finding of partnership in a particular case depend on the circumstances in which the claim of partnership is being made in that case. The most common situations in which a claim arises are either: (i) where A is being sued by a third party or by B, on the grounds that he is B's partner and therefore jointly liable for the damage caused by B to that third party or for the losses incurred by the firm; or (ii) where A seeks to establish that a partnership exists between himself and B in order to substantiate A's claim for a share of the profits of their joint enterprise.[8] The specific consequences of a finding of partnership in either case are quite different, since in one case, a finding of partnership will result in A sharing in the benefits of the enterprise, while in the other case, a finding of partnership will result in A being liable to an unlimited degree for the partnership losses.[9]

[2.07] Although the question of whether persons are carrying on business 'in common' is the same in all cases, it is clear that both the general and specific consequences of such a finding weigh heavily on the mind of the court in applying the test in a particular case.[10] It is perhaps not surprising, therefore, that the courts do not take a formalistic

---

2   Paragraph **[10.01]** et seq.
3   Paragraph **[15.01]** et seq.
4   Paragraph **[15.27]**.
5   Paragraph **[14.04]** et seq.
6   Paragraph **[1.13]**.
7   It may also be observed that some of these consequences will be relevant in determining the existence of a partnership. For example parties who act as each others' agents are more likely to be found to be partners than if they had not so acted, see para [2.71].
8   Another situation, although less common than the other two, is where B is bankrupt and his creditors seek to gain priority of their debts over those debts owed by B to A, on the grounds that A was B's partner. See generally regarding the deferral of a partner's debt on the bankruptcy of his partner, para **[27.124]** et seq.
9   In such a case, one party will be denying a partnership relationship exists and under the Rules of the Superior Courts, Ord 21, r 7, a person who denies the alleged constitution of any partnership is required to deny it specifically in his defence.
10   See for example the analysis below of the High Court decisions in *O'Kelly v Darragh* [1988] ILRM 309, *DPP v McLoughlin* [1986] IR 355, and *Griffin v Minister for Social, Community and Family Affairs and Deasy v Minister for Social, Community and Family Affairs* (2 October 2001) HC at para **[2.116]** et seq. Contrast also the different results obtained in *Pilsworth v Mosse* (1863) 14 Ir Ch R 163 and in *Barklie v Scott* (1827) 1 Hud and Bro 83, which are considered at para **[2.20]** et seq.

approach to determining whether the parties are acting 'in common',[11] and it will be seen that a finding of partnership results from an analysis of a combination of factors, such as whether the parties were co-owners of the business, whether they managed and controlled that business together, whether they shared profits from that business[12] and whether they conducted themselves as mutual agents for the purposes of the partnership business.

[2.08] For this reason, it is true to say that in each case in which the question of whether a partnership exists is determined, all the relevant factors require to be weighed up to determine the true nature of the relationship, with due regard being paid to the consequences of such a finding.[13] The analysis that follows seeks to assist in determining the importance to be attached to the facts of a particular case.

I. THE DEFINITION OF A PARTNERSHIP

[2.09] Partnership is defined in s 1(1) of the 1890 Act as: 'the relation which subsists between persons carrying on a business in common with a view of profit.'[14] This definition may be divided into six requirements, each of which must be satisfied for a partnership to exist, and they will be considered in turn:

1. relation;
2. which subsists between persons;

---

[11]   Of note are the comments of the Scottish Court of Session (Inner House) in *Worbey v Campbell* [2017] CSIH 49 – even if parties are found to have entered into a working relationship with a view to profit, it does not automatically follow that this is being done 'in common' (otherwise almost every business relationship would be a partnership and that '… would be a consequence of failing to give proper regard to the important words in the definition of partnership, "carrying on a business *in common*"'). See further para **[2.68]**.

[12]   Although it is important to note that the sharing of profits is not a prerequisite to the existence of a partnership – see *M Young Legal Associates v Zahid* [2006] 1 WLR 2562 (CA) and *Hodson v Hodson* [2009] EWHC 430 (Ch).

[13]   As was done by Costello J in *DPP v McLoughlin* [1986] IR 355. In that case, the fact that the members of the crew were not liable for the losses of a fishing venture was outweighed by the fact that the profits of the venture were divided amongst the crew in a manner to be determined amongst the crew and by custom, so as to support a finding of partnership, see further para **[2.116]**. In *Griffin v Minister for Social, Community and Family Affairs and Deasy v Minister for Social, Community and Family Affairs* (2 October 2001) HC, both cases concerning share fishermen, Carroll J was critical of the approach taken by the Appeals Officer who had not used the decision in *DPP v McLoughlin* as the starting point when considering whether the share fishermen were in partnership, or were in an employer-employee relationship. See generally l'Anson Banks, 'Partners in Law' (1996) Commercial Law 25; Walthall, 'What do you mean "we", Kemo Sabe?' Partnership law and client responsibilities of office sharing lawyers: *Hartwick v Hartley*' (1998) 28 Cumberland LR 601; Veron, 'Taxation of Income of Family Partnerships' (1945) 59 Harv LR 209 at 222 et seq.

[14]   In *M Young Legal Associates v Zahid* [2006] 1 WLR 2562 (CA), Wilson LJ (in dismissing an appeal against the judgment of HHJ Howarth, sitting as a judge of the High Court, Chancery Division, Manchester District Registry, on 26 August 2005) cited with approval the statement of HHJ Howarth in which he noted that the question of whether a relationship between two people carrying on business in common with a view of profit existed was a '… simple test, factually not necessarily simple at all. (contd.../)

3. carrying on;
4. a business;
5. in common;
6. with a view of profit.

Since the most nebulous of these requirements is that the parties are acting in common, much of this section and the rules for the existence of a partnership will be concerned with this issue. For this reason, this factor will be considered last, the other factors being almost procedural pre-requisites, in the sense that they will be satisfied quite easily in most cases. First, however, it should be noted that the onus of proving the existence of a partnership is on the person alleging it.[15]

1. 'Relation'

Partnership is based in contract

[2.10] By virtue of s 1(1) of the 1890 Act, a partnership must consist of a subsisting relationship between two or more parties. This relationship is consensual and is based in contract. The fact that the 'relation' referred to in s 1(1) is based in contract is not stated in s 1(1) but it is clear from other sections of the 1890 Act. Thus, s 35(b) of the 1890 Act talks of a dissolution being granted by the court where one partner is permanently incapable of performing his part of the partnership 'contract', s 41 refers to the rescission of a partnership 'contract' in certain circumstances and s 19 allows the partners to vary the mutual rights and duties of their 'agreement'.[16] Jessel MR has described partnership as:

> 'a contract of some kind undoubtedly – a contract, like all contracts, involving the mutual consent of the parties; a contract for the purpose of carrying on a commercial business – that is a business bringing profit in some shape or another between the partners.'[17]

---

14 (\...contd) I accept also that whatever label the parties chose to describe themselves by on their own notepaper is not determinative. You look at the reality, you do not look at the form or the window dressing.' Wilson LJ went on to note that a conclusion as to whether or not a partnership exists must be taken by reference to all of the features of the agreement between the parties, and not just (in that case) the apparent absence of a direct link between the fixed amount paid to a partner, and the firm's profits. See also *Samarkand Film Partnership No 3 v Revenue and Customs Commissioners* [2011] UKFTT 610 (TC) where it was noted that the component parts of this definition must still be met if and when the composition of the partnership changes ie when a new partner is admitted.

15 Per Campbell J in *Hanna v Barnes* (26 June 1992) HC NI at p 4 of the transcript.

16 This fact is also implicit in the margin note to s 19 of the 1890 Act which refers to variation by consent of the 'terms of partnership'.

17 *Polley v Driver* (1876) 5 Ch D 458 at 471. Although '...while partnership is a consensual arrangement based on agreement, it is more than a simple contract' (per Lord Millett in *Hurst v Bryk* [2002] 1 AC 185). While there need not be a written contract between the parties (see para **[2.11]**), there must be a binding agreement between them – see the comments of Newey J in *Achom v Lalic* [2014] EWHC 1888 (Ch) where he quoted from the judgment of Morgan J in *McPhail v Bourne* [2008] EWHC 1235 (Ch).

Similarly in *DPP v McLoughlin*,[18] Costello J put the matter thus:

> 'in determining the existence of a partnership ... regard must be paid to the true contract
> and intention of the parties as appearing from the whole facts of the case.'[19]

No requirement that contract be in writing

[2.11] Although the partnership relationship is contractual, there is no requirement that this contract be in writing and in many cases the 'relation' is based on an oral contract.[20] For example in *Crowley v O'Sullivan (No 2)*,[21] the parties had drawn up heads of agreement which had not been signed for their purchase of a shop in Bantry and its operation by them as partners. However, the defendant refused to sign the deed of partnership when it was prepared. In the High Court, Palles CB (Andrews and Johnson JJ concurring) held that an oral partnership agreement had been concluded between the parties and damages were awarded against the defendant for his refusal to comply with the agreement. In *AIB PLC v Higgins & ors*,[22] four individuals formed a partnership for the purposes of purchasing and developing lands at Duleek, Co Meath. No written partnership agreement was entered into between them, but they did not dispute the existence of the partnership. Kelly J noted that:

> '[there] was no deed or written instrument governing the partnership but that did not make
> it any less a partnership within the meaning of the statutory definition.'

[2.12] However, for both registered farm partnerships and registered succession farm partnerships, the partnership agreement must be in writing.[23] Investment limited partnerships are also required to have a written partnership agreement in place.[24] Legal partnerships and multi-disciplinary practices, which will be capable of establishment under the Legal Services Regulation Act 2015 once the remaining provisions of that Act are commenced, will also be required to have written partnership agreements in place.[25]

---

18   *DPP v McLoughlin* [1986] IR 355.
19   *DPP v McLoughlin* [1986] IR 355 at 360. Later on p 360, Costello J refers to the 'contractual relationship' which existed between the partners, although there was no formal written contract between them.
20   See for example *DPP v McLoughlin* [1986] IR 355. See also *Marsella v J&P Construction Limited* [2004] IEHC 369 in which Peart J noted (albeit when finding that the plaintiff and a third party joined by the defendant to the proceedings were not partners), that no partnership agreement 'either verbal or written' had been entered into between them. However, where the parties draft a partnership agreement but leave it unsigned, if evidence is not presented regarding its date and authorship should a dispute arise in respect of provisions of that draft which have not been acted upon by the parties, a court is unlikely to base its conclusions on that draft – see *Condon v Allied Irish Bank plc & ors* [2018] IEHC 92 per Ní Raifeartaigh J at para 45 of the judgment.
21   *Crowley v O'Sullivan (No 2)* [1900] 2 IR 478.
22   *AIB PLC v Higgins & ors* [2010] IEHC 219.
23   SI 273/2017. See further para **[8.111]**.
24   Investment Limited Partnerships Act 1994, s 3.
25   See the definitions of 'legal partnership' and 'multi-disciplinary practice' in s 2(1) of the 2015 Act. See, further, paras **[30.27]** and **[30.73]**.

Agreement containing blanks may be binding

[2.13] Where the partnership contract is in writing, it may be held to be enforceable even where it is executed containing a number of spaces which were unintentionally left blank, provided that the whole agreement (as distinct from a clause) is not thereby rendered illusory or meaningless. This is clear from *Heslin v Fay (1)*.[26] In that case, the partnership agreement provided for Heslin to contribute £2,000 to the capital of the firm, while the other three partners, who had already been partners together, were to jointly contribute £8,000, consisting partly of the partnership assets of their pre-existing partnership.[27] However, the agreement was executed by the partners without filling in the blanks which referred to the value to be put on the pre-existing partnership assets and the amount of cash to be contributed by the other three partners. After a number of years of trading, the partners ended up in court. The capital had been contributed by the partners substantially in line with the partnership agreement and not surprisingly, Sullivan LC (Fitzgibbon and Barry LJJ concurring) accepted the validity of the partnership between them, notwithstanding the presence of these blanks.

Partnership relationship is consensual

[2.14] It has been noted that the partnership relationship is based in contract. It follows that one may not become a partner without agreeing to do so. As noted by McWilliam J in *Williams v Harris*:[28]

> 'To have any partnership there must, of necessity, be an agreement, be it implied, by parol, in writing under hand or, as here, by deed.'[29]

Thus, one may not become a partner against one's will and in this sense the partnership relationship may be described as being consensual.[30] In *Hunter v Stoney*,[31] a mother

---

[26] *Heslin v Fay (1)* (1884) 15 LR Ir 431.

[27] *Heslin v Fay (1)* (1884) 15 LR Ir 431 at 434. The agreement stated: 'The said £8,000 worth of capital to be contributed by the said Patrick McCabe Fay, Patrick J Kehoe and William F Moloney, shall be composed of (1) £ ___, being the costs and expenses of obtaining the houses Nos. 68 and 69, North King-street, Dublin, and in fitting, painting and repairing the warehouses and buildings erected thereon. Secondly of £ ___, being the cost price of stock-in-trade, machinery, implements and plant, brought into the premises by the said Patrick McCabe Fay, Patrick J Kehoe and William F Moloney. And thirdly, of £ ___, cash contributed by the said Patrick McCabe Fay, Patrick J Kehoe and William F Moloney; and that the share of the said Christopher Heslin shall be £2,000, and shall be contributed in cash.'

[28] *Williams v Harris* (15 January 1980) HC rev'd on appeal [1980] ILRM 237 on other grounds.

[29] At p 12 of the transcript.

[30] In *Friends First Finance Ltd v Lavelle & anor* [2013] IEHC 201, the unquestioning acceptance by Friends First of a 'Proposal for a High Net Worth Client' in the name of a (non-existent) partnership in connection with a loan application by Peter Lavelle, and the opening by Friends First of a client profile on their systems in the name of that partnership, listing the personal details of Mr Lavelle and his spouse, without any questions being raised as to the form of the partnership, the existence of a partnership deed or the intentions of the partnership, was sharply criticised by Charleton J as an 'abrogation of responsibility' and, in part, led to Mrs Lavelle successfully establishing a *non est factum* defence. Also of interest is the decision in *McPhail v Bourne* [2008] EWHC 1235 (Ch), a dispute between members of the band *Busted* regarding the ownership of various songs. (contd.../)

signed a partnership agreement for a partnership called The Saint Patrick's Assurance Company of Ireland in her son's name, unknown to her son. As soon as he became aware, he disclaimed this interest and when the son was subsequently sued as a partner in the firm, MacMahon MR dismissed the action on the grounds that he was not a partner.[32]

Where the parties do not agree to be 'partners' per se

[2.15] It is important to note that when one talks of consenting to being a partner, it is not necessary that the person agree to become a partner as such or use the term 'partner' in his discussions or in the agreement. Indeed, the person may believe that he is not a partner, as he may believe that he is an employee or independent consultant. Nonetheless, such a person will be a partner if he consents to carry on business in common with others with a view to profit, the requirement that he consent to being a partner thereby being satisfied.[33] *Greenham v Gray*[34] involved an agreement between the plaintiff and the defendant to carry on the trade of cotton-spinning in Drogheda in the defendant's mill. In the agreement, the parties were not described as partners. The word partner was not used nor was its use insisted upon by the plaintiff, because he was afraid to use that term in case it might bring the point to issue and cause the whole agreement to fall apart. Greene B observed:

> 'True it is, that the word "partner" is not mentioned; but if the Court see from the contract that the intention is to create partnership, it is not necessary to have the word mentioned.'[35]

[2.16] Of course, in certain circumstances, the fact that the parties have not discussed the possibility of their being partners will be a factor in a court's decision as to the existence of a partnership, especially where a disaffected employee is seeking a share of the profits of the enterprise on this basis.[36]

---

[30] (\...contd) At the time that the four members of the band had started recording songs together and dealing with those with whom they would later enter into a management agreement, all but one of them was aged 17. In holding that no partnership (express or implied) had been entered into, Morgan J in particular commented that the '... lack of definition in relation to the activities which were the subject of the contract and the alleged partnership and, indeed, the complete lack of appreciation that anything the boys were doing required them to address those questions suggest to me that there was no intention to create a contractual relationship at all.' See, further, Sellars, 'Band formation – ownership of songs and partnership' (Ent LR 2008, 19(8), 185–187).

[31] *Hunter v Stoney* (1831) Glasc 23.

[32] See also *Greville v Venables* [2007] EWCA Civ 878 in which Lloyd LJ observed that if parties have expressly addressed the question of what their business relationship should be, but have not agreed on a final position because one party has not agreed to the other party's partnership proposal, an inference of partnership would contradict what had been expressly discussed between the parties.

[33] Unless, of course, he does so as a member of a company: Partnership Act 1890, s 1(2) and para **[2.29]**.

[34] *Greenham v Gray* (1855) 4 Ir CLR 501.

[35] *Greenham v Gray* (1855) 4 Ir CLR 501 at 509.

[36] See for example *O'Kelly v Darragh* [1988] ILRM 309 which is considered at para **[2.118]**.

[2.17] The converse of Greene B's proposition is also applicable. Therefore, simply because the parties to an agreement use the term 'partner' or 'partnership' is not conclusive evidence that they are partners. If they do not satisfy all of the six requirements of partnership, they will not be partners. Further, if a party holds himself out as being a partner, this also will not be conclusive evidence as to the existence of a partnership if there is evidence that the terms of any future partnership agreement are still being negotiated.[37] Equally, simply because parties may, on occasion, describe themselves as partners when promoting a business opportunity, this does not mean that they are in partnership if no other evidence of a partnership between them exists.[38]

[2.18] Equally, simply because parties to an arrangement are described by legislation as a form of partnership (see the definition of 'hotel partnership' in s 409 of the Taxes Consolidation Act 1997)[39] this will not automatically render their relationship one of partnership unless the six requirements of partnership are met.

Where parties are described as something else

[2.19] Where the parties to an agreement have described themselves as consultants, employers/employees or expressly disavowed the existence of a partnership by using a 'no partnership clause',[40] this will not prevent a partnership coming into existence, provided that the parties satisfy the definition of partnership. If the parties carry on business together in common for profit, it is irrelevant that they may intend or wish not to become partners. In the words of Lord Halsbury:

> 'If a partnership in fact exists, a community of interest in the adventure being carried on in fact, no concealment of name, no verbal equivalent for the ordinary phrases of profit or loss, no indirect expedient for enforcing control over the adventure will prevent the substance and reality of the transaction being adjudged to be partnership ... and no phrasing of it by dextrous draftsmen ... will avail to avert the legal consequence of the contract.'[41]

On this principle, a partnership was held to exist in the Drogheda cotton-spinning case of *Greenham v Gray*,[42] although the plaintiff intended to create a partnership while the

---

37 *McAleenan v AIG (Europe) Limited* [2010] IEHC 128, in which the plaintiff had held herself out, in her application to the Law Society of Ireland for the renewal of her solicitor's practicing certificate, as a partner in the firm in which she was an employee. See para **[7.37]**.

38 *Younes v Chrysanthou* [2016] EWHC 3269 (QB) (judgment of His Honour Judge Waksman QC sitting as a judge of the High Court).

39 Which defines a 'hotel partnership' as including '... any syndicate, group or pool of persons, *whether or not a partnership,* through or by means of which a hotel investment is made' [emphasis added].

40 A typical 'no partnership clause' in a joint venture agreement reads: 'This Agreement will not be deemed to create a partnership between the parties hereto'. See generally Webb, 'Joint venture or partnership?' (1997) New Zealand LJ 159. See generally regarding special purpose joint venture companies, Mercer and Shilling, 'Articles of Association for partnership companies' (1995) 9 Corporate Briefing 4; Sheikh, 'Company law: articles of association' (1995) 6 International Company and Commercial LR 152. Regarding co-ownership and the use of 'no partnership' clauses, see para **[2.89]** et seq and para **[3.22]** et seq.

41 *Adam v Newbigging* (1888) 13 App Cas 308 at 315.

42 *Greenham v Gray* (1855) 4 Ir CLR 501.

defendant did not. So, in determining whether a partnership exists, it will be relevant how the parties describe themselves[43] and whether they intend to be partners as such, yet what is crucial is whether they actually carry on business in common with a view to profit.

The intention of the parties

[2.20] The significance of the state of mind of the parties to an alleged partnership arrangement is illustrated by *Pilsworth v Mosse*.[44] There, the defendant wished not to be a partner in Pilsworth's milling business in Ballyconra, Clornanty and Ballyragget in Co Kilkenny because of a restriction on Mosse, in his partnership agreement with Lyster, from entering any other partnerships. For this reason, Mosse paid capital to Pilsworth in the name of his two sons but the business was carried on only in Pilsworth's name. The agreement between Pilsworth and Mosse provided for Mosse's two sons to be named in the partnership books as the owners of capital in the partnership and entitled them to a share of the profits of the firm. The agreement also provided that in the event of the sons dying, Mosse was entitled to replace them with his other sons, which duly occurred. During the course of the business, Mosse sought money from Pilsworth to purchase property. Pilsworth obliged by paying Mosse out of one of the son's accounts with the firm. On the death of all of the sons and the father, a dispute arose between their respective estates as to the entitlement to the partnership property. Smith MR observed that the sons had never intended to be partners[45] but were simply named in the partnership books so as to avoid a claim that Mosse was in breach of his agreement with Lyster. Accordingly, it was held that the two sons were not partners of Pilsworth but that the partnership was with Mosse, and, therefore, his estate was entitled to the partnership property.

[2.21] That case may be contrasted with the conclusion reached in a similar case, that of *Barklie v Scott*.[46] There, the defendant was a father who set up a partnership business in Sligo for his son by contributing £1,000 on his behalf to the firm. In this case, the father was not prevented from entering a partnership himself. Rather his decision to contribute the £1,000 in capital was clearly a gift for his young son. This fact, combined with the fact that the allegation of partnership was made by a third party seeking to make the defendant liable for the firm's debts, may explain why a different decision was reached in this case. The agreement in this case provided that accounts would be furnished to the

---

43 In *Simpson v Torpey & ors* [2011] IEHC 342, the defendants became involved in property development in Romania, but the legal structure of their development business was unclear. In one letter, the sender was listed as 'RI Investment Group' with an address in Romania. While the letter was signed by one of the defendants using the title 'partner', that defendant gave evidence that this title was used to avoid a potential issue with the translation of the term 'director" from English to Romanian, and Clarke J noted that there was no suggestion that a partnership had been formally put in place between the defendants.

44 *Pilsworth v Mosse* (1863) 14 Ir Ch R 163.

45 *Pilsworth v Mosse* (1863) 14 Ir Ch R 163 at 170, where Smith MR states: 'I think that the affidavit of [one of the sons] is quite consistent with the truth, when he swears, substantially that for years after the death of [Mosse], such a thing as a partnership in favour of [the other son] and himself was never in contemplation of the parties.'

46 *Barklie v Scott* (1827) 1 Hud and Bro 83.

father and that the firm would be directed by the father's advice. The plaintiff, a customer of the firm, sought to make the father liable for the debts of the firm. The father was held not to be a partner in the firm, his advice to the firm being viewed as that of an experienced person to a young man starting off, rather than that of a person carrying on business in common as partner. Jebb J supported his decision on the basis that:

    (i)   the son alone was entitled to a return of the capital;

    (ii)   the father was not entitled to a share of the profits;

    (iii) the plaintiff had previously expressed the view that the father was not a partner;

    (iv) the other partners in the firm never dealt with the father as a partner; and

    (v)   the father was never held out to the world as a partner.

Vague assurances as to partnership unlikely to be sufficient

[2.22] In *Kelly v Byrne trading as Thomas Byrne & Company Solicitors*,[47] a partnership agreement was entered into in 2001 between the plaintiff and the defendant. While it listed three properties (in respect of which no investment transactions were subsequently entered into by the parties) it did not refer to the property that formed the subject of the proceedings. While the plaintiff alleged that there was an understanding between him and the defendant that the plaintiff would be a partner in all of the defendant's property projects, Clarke J found no written evidence of that understanding, and found no provisions in the 2001 partnership agreement that dealt with the property in question. While Clarke J noted that the defendant was likely to have given 'various vague assurances' to the plaintiff that the plaintiff would be involved in other projects, he held that any such assurances did not come 'close to providing a basis for establishing the clear legal relations necessary to determine that a partnership existed'.

The parties' written intentions

[2.23] Notwithstanding the existence of a document (provided to the plaintiff as lender) which described an arrangement as 'a partnership between the two companies', Finlay Geoghegan J found that no partnership existed in *Allied Irish Banks Plc v Galvin Developments (Killarney) Limited & ors*.[48] In reaching that decision, she took into account that the parties seemed to have proceeded on the basis that each would be liable for 50% of the liabilities arising from a property development (ie a co-ownership structure) as distinct from a partnership where each party would have been liable for the entire debt. She also took account of the fact that the co-ownership agreement expressly excluded the application of both the 1890 Act and the Limited Partnerships Act 1907.[49]

---

[47] *Kelly v Byrne trading as Thomas Byrne & Company Solicitors* [2011] IEHC 174.

[48] *Allied Irish Banks Plc v Galvin Developments (Killarney) Limited & ors* [2011] IEHC 314.

[49] Interestingly, the co-ownership agreement, even though it expressly provided that 'the Co-Ownership shall be regulated solely by this Agreement to the exclusion of the Partnership Act 1890 and the Limited Partnership Act 1907 (as amended)', also included a clause providing for particular terms to apply if 'the relationship of the parties the subject of this Agreement is determined to be a partnership'. However, Finlay Geoghegan J noted that, having regard to the co-ownership agreement as a whole, this clause was included as a precaution and did not indicate an intention to create a partnership. Regarding co-ownerships and the use of 'no partnership' clauses, see para **[2.89]** et seq and para **[3.22]** et seq.

The parties' current intentions do not mean that a partnership has always existed

[2.24] In *Bergin v Walsh*,[50] two individuals planned, in 2007, to set up a company in Monaco to acquire and lease certain property in Portlaoise. That decision came towards the end of the business relationship between them. However, Hogan J held that while the fact that the two individuals, Mr Bergin and Mr Walsh, had decided to explore a joint venture together was unsurprising, given that they had worked together for a number of years, this did not of itself mean that one could work backwards from that proposal to decide that a partnership (or a quasi-partnership) had always existed between them. Mr Bergin had operated as a business advisor to Mr Walsh, and received commission payments in respect of previous developments, but there was no evidence that he had been entitled to share in the profits of any of those previous developments.

Ulterior motives of partners

[2.25] In considering the intentions of the parties to an alleged partnership agreement, the motives of the parties may be relevant. Thus, in *Greenham v Gray*[51] the desire of the plaintiff not to upset the negotiations by introducing the term 'partner' was important. This was also the case in *Hanna v Barnes*[52] in which Campbell J held that Barnes studiously avoided using the term 'partner' when it transpired that the enterprise he had embarked upon with Hanna was more successful than he had anticipated and thus that it was too good to share with Hanna. Similarly, in *Pilsworth v Mosse*,[53] the motive of the father was important, ie he wished to be involved in a concern, but not as a partner, in order to comply with the restriction on him from being a party to another partnership agreement. In all cases, these motives were undoubtedly a factor in the classification of the parties as partners.

[2.26] On the other hand, where the only reason a person wishes to form a partnership is for ulterior motives, eg tax avoidance, this will not prevent a partnership coming into existence, unless of course the effect of those motives is to render the partnership illegal.[54] This is clear from *O'Dwyer, Inspector of Taxes v Cafolla & Co*[55] which concerned a chain of fast-food restaurants in O'Connell Street and Capel Street in Dublin. Mr Cafolla, who had run the restaurants as a sole trader, decided to form a partnership with his sons. One of the intentions behind this move seems to have been his desire to benefit from the tax free allowances of his children, and in this way reduce the overall tax bill of the business.[56] The partnership was accepted as being valid and in the Supreme Court, Murnaghan J noted that:

---

50 *Bergin v Walsh* [2015] IEHC 594.
51 *Greenham v Gray* (1855) 4 Ir CLR 501. See further, para **[2.77]**.
52 *Hanna v Barnes* (26 June 1992) HC NI. See further para **[2.75]**.
53 *Pilsworth v Mosse* (1863) 14 Ir Ch R 163. See further, para **[2.20]**.
54 As to the illegality of certain partnerships, see para **[9.01]** et seq.
55 *O'Dwyer, Inspector of Taxes v Cafolla & Co* [1949] IR 210.
56 Note, however, the anti-avoidance provisions of tax legislation which now exist concerning the admission of children into partnerships, see Taxes Consolidation Act 1997, s 798. See also Maguire, *Irish Income Tax 2017* (2017) at para [15.409].

'It is now, I think, settled that it is not material whether Joseph Cafolla entered into the partnership deed with the intention of evading[57] income tax liability. So long as the arrangement entered into by him is a genuine and real transaction, it must have its due legal effect in respect of liability for income tax.'[58]

2. 'which subsists between persons'

[2.27] For a partnership to exist, the contractual relationship referred to in s 1(1) of the 1890 Act must subsist between 'persons'.

Number of parties required to constitute a partnership

[2.28] It is perhaps self-evident, though deserving of specific mention, that the use of the plural form indicates that before a partnership can exist there must be at least two 'persons'. Accordingly, the term 'sole partner' is a contradiction in terms and such a person is most likely to be a sole trader. Yet under Ord 14, r 11 of the Rules of the Superior Courts, an individual, who carries on business under a name other than his own, may be sued in that name 'as if it were a firm name'. This order also provides for the procedural rules which apply to partnerships in such a case. However, it must be remembered that these are simply rules of procedure and do not alter the basic fact that one person may not be a partner with himself, whether he trades under a separate name or not.

Relationships between persons which cannot be partnerships

[2.29] Certain relationships between persons, which might otherwise satisfy the criteria for partnerships, are excluded from constituting partnerships by s 1(2) of the 1890 Act. Section 1(2) provides:

> But the relation between members of any company or association which is—
>
> (a) Registered as a company under the Companies Act 1862, or any other Act of Parliament for the time being in force and relating to the registration of joint stock companies; or
>
> (b) Formed or incorporated by or in pursuance of any other Act of Parliament or letters patent or Royal Charter; or
>
> (c) A company engaged in working mines within and subject to the jurisdiction of the Stannaries:
>
> is not a partnership within the meaning of this Act.

---

[57] By 'evading' income tax, Murnaghan J undoubtedly means 'avoiding' income tax in modern parlance. Murnaghan J was in the minority in the Supreme Court in relation to permitting the use of the childrens' tax-free allowances, but there was no disagreement on the validity of the partnership. As a result of this case, s 448 of the Income Tax Act 1967 (now substantially contained in s 798 of the Taxes Consolidation Act 1997) was enacted to provide that if a trade is carried on by a person in partnership with one or more of his children (or one or more of the children of his civil partner), having previously been carried on by that person on his own, all of the income of the partnership will be treated as the income of that person for so long as the child is under the age of 18 years or unmarried.

[58] *O'Dwyer, Inspector of Taxes v Cafolla & Co* [1949] IR 210 at 233.

Section 1(2)(a) has been adapted to apply to Acts of the Oireachtas and therefore the relation between members of a company formed under the Companies Act 2014 or its predecessor, the Companies Act 1963,[59] will not constitute a partnership.[60]

Promoters of a company prior to incorporation

[2.30] What about the position of the promoters of a company who intend to become members of the company after its formation? May those persons be partners prior to the incorporation of the company? While the promoters of a company, prior to its formation, may share the aim of carrying on business with a view to profit, their immediate object is the formation of a company and, assuming that this is their only business association, they are unlikely to be in partnership.[61] This issue was considered in *Forester v Bell*,[62] where an action to recover money was brought against a member of a proposed company to be called The Irish West Coast Railway Company. The plaintiff had entered into a contract with one member of the provisional committee of this company prior to its formation. However, he took an action to enforce the contract against another member of the committee, on the grounds that all of the members of the committee were liable to him on the contract. He alleged that all of the promoters were in partnership prior to the formation of the company. His claim was rejected, Blackburne CJ holding that:

> '[t]he members of this provisional committee were not partners, nor had any of them a right to bind the others; so that the defendant cannot be visited with liability by any analogy to the case of partners.'[63]

---

[59]   The Companies Act 2014 is an Act relating to the registration of joint stock companies: see Hutchinson, *Keane on Company Law* (5th edn, 2016) at para [2.05], which refers to 'the name joint stock company, still sometimes used to describe the limited liability company of today' and Courtney, *The Law of Companies* (4th edn, 2016) at para [1.075] in which he notes that '[the] first piece of legislation to carry the principles embodied in the Joint Stock Companies Act 1856 through to our modern companies' legislation was also the first in a long line of "Companies Acts"; namely the Companies Act 1862'. An argument by the plaintiff in *Madden v Anglo Irish Bank Corporation plc & anor* [2004] IESC 108 that private companies established for the purposes of a joint venture should be distinguished at law from public companies and treated instead as partnerships was quickly dismissed by Denham J.

[60]   As this section was drafted prior to Irish independence, it is not immediately clear whether this section applies to members of a company formed under the Companies Act 2014 or its predecessor, the Companies Act 1963. However, s 5(4) of the Adaptation of Enactments Act 1922 provides that the term 'Act of Parliament' as used in British Statutes (defined by s 20 of the Adaptation of Enactments Act 1922 as meaning an 'Act of the Parliament of the late United Kingdom of Great Britain and Ireland which was on the 6th day of December, 1922, in force in the area now comprised in Saorstát Éireann') shall mean either an Act of the British Parliament or an Act of the Oireachtas, as the case may require.

[61]   See *Wood v Argyll* (1844) 6 Man & G 928; *Hutton v Thompson* (1846) 3 HLC 161; *Reynell v Lewis* (1846) 15 M & W 517. See also the decision of the English Court of Appeal in *Keith Spicer Ltd v Mansell* [1970] 1 All ER 462. See generally Breeze, 'The liability of the associates in a defective corporation' (1906) 16 Yale LJ 1.

[62]   *Forester v Bell* (1847) 10 Ir LR 555.

[63]   *Forester v Bell* (1847) 10 Ir LR 555 at 557–558.

[2.31] In *Horgan v Murray*,[64] Mr Horgan, Mr Milton and Mr Murray were the sole shareholders in Murray Consultants Limited, a well-known public relations company. They were also three of the directors of the company but Horgan alleged that while there were other directors, all business decisions were taken only with the agreement and consensus of the three, who held regular 'partners' meetings' between themselves. When Milton and Murray sought to replace Horgan with Murray as the managing director of the company and to fundamentally change the way in which the company was run, Horgan sought a number of declarations, including one that he was in partnership with Milton and Murray in Murray Consultants Limited. Horgan claimed that Milton and Murray had breached the partnership agreement which existed independently of, and prior to, the formation of Murray Consultants Limited. However, noting that there was no written agreement regarding any partnership between Horgan, Murray and Milton that existed separately from the relationship between them as co-shareholders in Murray Consultants Limited, counsel for Milton and Murray argued that all individuals who come together to form a company make some form of prior agreement between themselves to form that company, but such prior agreement is not necessarily a partnership agreement. Finding in favour of Milton and Murray, O'Sullivan J concluded that:

'I am unable to agree with [counsel for Mr Horgan] that any basis has been pleaded or established whereby a Court could infer a partnership relationship between the parties to these proceedings which is separate and anterior to their relationship as common shareholding members of [Murray Consultants Limited] ...

I cannot agree that there is any indication on the pleadings that clear evidence will be advanced to show that obligations or rights apart from or additional to those arising under the companies code were contemplated or agreed between the parties. On the contrary, [counsel for Mr Horgan] has accepted in argument that the relationship between the parties under what he submits is an independently subsisting partnership relationship are precisely the same as those which exist between them as fellow shareholding members of the company ...'[65]

[2.32] However, a different conclusion may be reached when the participants are not being sued as alleged partners but where some or all of the participants themselves wish to be treated as partners. This was the case in *De Pol v Cunningham*,[66] in which the Northern Ireland Court of Appeal considered the business arrangement between De Pol and Kennedy. De Pol had been in a flooring partnership with two others. Kennedy agreed that he would provide De Pol with the finance to enable him buy out his partners and transfer the partnership business to a company to be formed by De Pol and Kennedy.

---

[64]   *Horgan v Murray* [1999] IEHC 65.

[65]   O'Sullivan J relied, in part, on the High Court judgment of Murphy J in *Crindle Investments v Wymes* [1998] 4 IR 567 at 576, where it was held that: 'the undertaking was conceived and consciously promoted in the form of a company incorporated under the Companies Act, 1963, and it was the requirements of that legislation which governed the relationship between the parties.' See also *Bradshaw v Murphy & Ors* [2014] IEHC 146 (an application for an interlocutory injunction) in which the plaintiff unsuccessfully alleged that he had entered into a partnership agreement with the defendant to form a company. While it was undisputed that the company had been formed, Finlay Geoghegan J was not satisfied that the parties had *personally* agreed to carry on business with a view to profit.

[66]   *De Pol v Cunningham* (1974) 49 TC 445.

The Inspector of Taxes alleged that capital gains tax was due by De Pol on the transfer of the partnership business to the company, since he was the sole beneficial owner of the partnership business after the purchase from his former partners and immediately prior to its transfer to the company. However, the Court of Appeal (Lowry CJ and Jones LJ, Curran LJ dissenting) held that when De Pol purchased the partnership business using money provided by Kennedy, he was not the sole beneficial owner thereof but that there was a 'community of assets' between De Pol and Kennedy giving rise to a partnership between them which lasted for a month and a half until the company was incorporated and the partnership business transferred thereto.

Relationship between members of other statutory associations

[2.33] It has been noted that the reference in s 1(2) to 'Acts of Parliament' must be interpreted as referring to Acts of the Oireachtas.[67] Therefore, s 1(2)(b) of the 1890 Act is to be interpreted as providing that a partnership is not constituted by the relation between members of companies or associations formed or incorporated under other Acts of the Oireachtas. It follows, for example, that the relationship which exists between the members of associations such as Ervia (formerly Bórd Gáis),[68] building societies,[69] industrial and provident societies[70] and friendly societies[71] does not constitute a partnership. This does not, of course, mean that persons who happen to be members of a company or a statutory association may not form partnerships inter se, but simply that their relationship *qua* members of that association is not a partnership.

Applicability of s 1(2)(c) of the 1890 Act in Ireland

[2.34] Section 1(2)(c) of the 1890 Act excludes from constituting a partnership the relation between members of a company engaged in working mines within and subject to the jurisdiction of the Stannaries, which is in Devon and Cornwall. It remains to be observed that for this reason, this subsection is of little relevance to Ireland and, indeed, the Stannaries jurisdiction no longer exists in England by virtue of s 28 of the Companies Consolidation (Consequential Provisions) Act 1985.[72]

Can a company be a partner?

[2.35] It is clear that intra-company relationships are prevented by the terms of s 1(2)(a) of the 1890 Act from constituting partnerships. It is, however, not apparent from the wording of s 1 whether the term 'persons' in the definition of a partnership is restricted to natural persons or whether non-natural persons such as companies may form a partnership so as to allow inter-company relationships to constitute partnerships.

---

67 Paragraph **[2.29]**.
68 Established under the Gas Acts 1976–2009.
69 Formed under the Building Societies Act 1989–2006. At the date of writing, there are no building societies in existence in Ireland.
70 Registered under the Industrial and Provident Societies Acts 1893–2014.
71 Registered under the Friendly Societies Acts 1896–2014, although because of their objects these societies are likely to fail to satisfy the fifth leg of the definition of partnership, see para **[2.62]**.
72 c 9 of 1985.

Section 19 of the Interpretation Act 1889[73] clarified this point by providing that where the word 'persons' was used in an Act passed after the commencement of the 1889 Act,[74] it was deemed to include 'any body of persons corporate or unincorporate', unless the contrary intention appeared. Section 18 of the Interpretation Act 2005[75] now provides that, when the term 'person' is used in inter alia an Act of the Oireachtas or in a statute which was in force in Saorstát Éireann immediately before the date of the coming into operation of the 1937 Constitution and which continued in force by virtue of Article 50 of the 1937 Constitution, it shall include 'a body corporate … and an unincorporated body of persons'. Accordingly, the relationship between companies or the relationship between a company and individuals may constitute a partnership under Irish law.[76] One of the first acknowledgements of this fact was in the Supreme Court case of *Re Debtor Summons*[77] where Fitzgibbon J, in considering the procedural rules[78] which allow a partnership to be sued in its firm name, observed they did not relate to a company 'except possibly in so far as such a company may lawfully act as or be a partner with one or more natural persons'.[79] Where a company is a partner, partnership

---

[73] 52 & 53 Vict, c 63. Like the 1890 Act, this Act was carried over into the laws of Saorstát Éireann by Article 73 of the 1922 Constitution. It was later repealed by s 3(1)(a) of the Interpretation Act 2005.

[74] The Interpretation Act 1889 commenced on 1 January 1890 and the 1890 Act was passed on 14 August 1890.

[75] The Interpretation Act 2005, s 18 is the equivalent provision of the Interpretation Act 1889, s 19. Section 18 of the Interpretation Act 2005 applies not only to Acts of the Oireachtas, but also to statutes which were in force in Saorstát Éireann immediately before the date of the coming into operation of the 1937 Constitution and which continued in force by virtue of Article 50 of the 1937 Constitution. The carrying over of the 1890 Act into the laws of Ireland by the 1922 Constitution is considered at para **[1.24]** and the 1890 Act then continued in force by virtue of Article 50 of the 1937 Constitution.

[76] See for example *MacCarthaigh v Daly* [1985] IR 73 where the High Court accepted the decision of the Revenue Appeal Commissioner that a partnership existed between a limited company and seven individuals. See also the reference by Carroll J in *The State v Dublin County Council* [1985] IR 1 at 7 to the House of Lords decision in *Harold Holdsworth and Co v Caddies* [1955] 1 WLR 352, wherein it was held that a group of companies was the same as a partnership in which all three companies were partners.

[77] *Re Debtor Summons* [1929] IR 139.

[78] At that time, these Rules were contained in Ord 48A of the Rules of the Supreme Court (Ireland) 1905, but they are now contained in Ord 14, r 1 of the Rules of the Superior Courts (SI 15/1986, as amended).

[79] *Re Debtor Summons* [1929] IR 139 at 148. See also *Williams v Harris* [1980] ILRM 237, where the Supreme Court accepted that a partnership existed between a company and three individuals. The fact that a company may be a partner for the purposes of s 1(1) of the 1890 Act has also been recognised by subsequent legislation, eg s 3 of the Registration of Business Names Act 1963 which requires the partners in a firm who are carrying on business under a name other than the surname or 'corporate name' of the partners to register that name as a business name. Regulation 6 of the European Communities (Accounts) Regulations 1993 applies to, inter alia, partnerships whose members are companies with limited liability. See also the explicit reference to a 'partner company which is a limited partner' in s 1013(2)(b) of the Taxes Consolidation Act 1997 in relation to limited partnerships formed under the Limited Partnerships Act 1907.

law will apply to it as it does to a natural person. However, as is noted elsewhere in this work, partnership law does not generally contemplate corporate partners and therefore one is often left with a situation where the precise application to companies of provisions (which were drafted for natural persons) is left up in the air.[80]

Can a firm be a partner?

[2.36] It is possible for there to be a partnership between two or more partnerships. Indeed, this was recognised prior to the 1890 Act under the terms of Bovill's Act of 1865[81] which defined the term 'person' as including a 'Partnership Firm'.[82] The possibility of there being a partnership between two firms was first recognised by the Irish courts in *McCalmont v Chaine*.[83] In that case, the Irish based consignee, Chaine, was being sued by McCalmont, a partner in a London based firm which carried on business with a Mexican based firm. McCalmont's partner in the London firm was Inglis, and the two of them were also partners in the Mexican firm with Graves. Inglis died and McCalmont took an action against Chaine for money owed in relation to the consignment of goods by Chaine on behalf of the London firm to the Mexican firm. Chaine claimed that, as the London firm and the Mexican firm shared in the profits of the sale of the goods consigned, they were in partnership. He claimed that the action should be struck out as the partners in the Mexican firm should have been joined as co-plaintiffs. Although the London firm had furnished accounts in its own name for a number of years, it was held that there was sufficient evidence of the existence of a partnership between the two firms for the matter to be left to the jury.

[2.37] It remains to be observed that a partnership between firms is known as a group partnership (with each member of each firm being a member of the group partnership) and this subject is considered in detail elsewhere in this work.[84]

3. 'carrying on'

[2.38] The third requirement for a partnership to exist is that the parties to the relationship be 'carrying on' business, in the sense that the business has actually commenced. This raises a number of issues in relation to agreements for a future partnership, retrospective partnerships and in relation to partnership agreements which are not performed.

---

[80] See for example the concept that a partnership is dissolved on the death or bankruptcy of a partner in s 33(1) of the 1890 Act and para **[23.32]**.

[81] An Act to amend the Law of Partnership (28 & 29 Vict, c 86). This Act was repealed by s 48 of the 1890 Act.

[82] Bovill's Act 1865, s 6.

[83] *McCalmont v Chaine* (1835) 3 Ir Law Rec (ns) 215. See also the High Court case of *X v Mulvey* [1947] IR 121 where Maguire J held that a partnership was a 'person' under s 12(1) of the Finance Act 1929. See further the English Court of Appeal case of *Nixon v Wood* (1987) 284 Estates Gazette 1055.

[84] Paragraph **[8.49]**.

An agreement to enter partnership is not 'carrying on' of business

[2.39] Because of the requirement that the parties be carrying on business, it follows that a partnership will not be deemed to exist if the parties have simply agreed to become partners. In *Macken v Revenue Commissioners*,[85] an oral agreement to enter partnership was reached between a father and his two children in September 1953. This oral agreement dealt with such matters as the proportions in which profits, losses, assets and liabilities were to be shared and the trading name of the firm. However in the High Court, Teevan J held that a partnership did not come into existence until April 1954 since the parties only commenced carrying on business at that time.

[2.40] In *Khan v Miah*,[86] the English House of Lords overturned a majority decision of the Court of Appeal as to when a partnership actually commenced. In that case a dispute arose between a group of people who had decided to open an Indian restaurant. Mr L Miah and Mr Ahad made a proposal to Mr M Khan for the opening of the restaurant. Mr L Miah was to be the manager, and Mr Ahad and Mr M Khan were to be the chefs. Mr K Miah was brought in for his commercial expertise. The participants then fell out with one another before the restaurant was opened. However, prior to that falling out, the parties had arranged for Mr K Miah to take a lease of the premises, and subsequently the freehold interest was acquired in Mr K Miah's name. He had also entered into a contract for the design and refurbishment of the premises as a restaurant. A joint account had been opened by Mr K Miah and Mr M Khan. Mr M Khan had provided nearly all of the monies in this account, other than some monies provided by his brother, Mr S Khan. Furniture and equipment was also purchased and a contract for the restaurant's laundry was entered into. Once the dispute arose, Mr M Khan's solicitor sent a letter to the defendants, which had the effect of terminating the business arrangement. The action came to court when Mr M Khan and Mr S Khan sought a declaration that the partnership had been dissolved and a declaration that the premises was held in trust for all the partners. The case initially came before the Court of Appeal, which held by a 2:1 majority that no partnership existed in this case on the grounds that, per Thorpe LJ, the partners could not be said '... to be carrying on the business prior to the date upon which the restaurant opened for the consumption of meals on the premises'. The majority decision of the Court of Appeal was, however, reversed by the House of Lords. The House of Lords accused the Court of Appeal of nominalism in its determination of whether the parties were carrying on business in common for the purposes of the definition of partnership. Lord Millett pointed out that there '... was no rule of law that the parties to a joint venture do not become partners until actual trading commences ...' and noted that '[the] question is not whether the restaurant had commenced trading, but whether the parties had done enough to be found to have commenced the joint enterprise in which they had agreed to engage ...'. He held that for the purposes of the definition of partnership in s 1(1) of the 1890 Act, '... the work of finding, acquiring and fitting out a shop or restaurant begins long before the premises are open for business and the first customers walk through the door. Such work is taken with a view to profit, and may be

---

85   *Macken v Revenue Commissioners* [1962] IR 302.
86   *Khan v Miah* [2001] All ER 20.

undertaken as well by partners as by a sole trader.' As Buxton LJ had pointed out in his dissenting judgment in the Court of Appeal, if it were otherwise, '... every separate transaction entered into before the opening of the restaurant for trade [would have to be] separately litigated in respect of its effect between the parties: be that agency, trust or whatever other legal analysis has to be applied to explain the particular transaction ... It is surely to prevent the implications for the parties of every single piece of business entered into by persons acting jointly in commercial matters having to be separately litigated between them that the law of partnership was conceived.'

[2.41] The test propounded by Lord Millett will necessitate a case-by-case approach being taken to the assessment of preparatory work and whether sufficient steps have been taken to indicate the carrying on of a business beyond simple agreeing to enter into partnership.[87]

[2.42] A conditional agreement for partnership does not constitute the carrying on of business and the parties thereto will not be partners. *Milliken v Milliken*[88] concerned a partnership agreement to run a bookshop at 115 Grafton Street in Dublin between Mrs Milliken, Mr Grant and Mr Bolton. The agreement also contained a provision for the admission of a future partner, Mrs Milliken's son, who was to replace his mother in the firm. Mr Milliken was a party to the agreement and the agreement provided for him to provide services to the firm in return for a salary. The agreement stated that at the expiration of the third year of the partnership, he was to become entitled to his mother's share in the partnership, if his conduct was to the 'reasonable satisfaction' of Mr Grant and Mr Bolton. Before the end of the third year, Mr Milliken was prevented from providing services to the firm by Mr Grant and Mr Bolton, who desired to dissolve the firm. Mr Milliken took an action for the specific performance of the agreement entitling him to become a partner and sought an injunction preventing the dissolution of the firm, on the grounds that as he had a right to become a partner at the end of three years, the firm could not be dissolved without his consent. Blackburne MR held that the use of the words 'reasonable satisfaction' indicated that it was completely within Mr Grant's and Mr Bolton's discretion as to whether to admit Mr Milliken to the firm:

> 'There is, perhaps, no subject on which a man might more reasonably reserve to himself the unlimited right of judging and acting for himself, than in a contract for a future partnership with a young and inexperienced man.'[89]

---

[87] The decisions of the Court of Session (Outer House) and, on appeal, the Court of Session (Inner House) in Scotland in *Worbey v Campbell* ([2016] CSOH 148 and [2017] CSIH 49 respectively) concerning a possible business arrangement to develop and market apps considered the House of Lords judgment in *Khan v Miah* [2001] All ER 20 but as there was no definitive agreement (express or implied) as to the obligations of the parties, or as to how any losses would be shared, the arrangements between the parties in *Worbey v Campbell* (while similar to those in *Khan v Miah*) differed sufficiently for no partnership to be found to exist. A future business arrangement had certainly been contemplated, but no 'concluded contract', written or oral, was found to exist. See further in relation to *Worbey v Campbell*, 'Mobile dating applications and partnership law: *Worbey v Campbell*' Edin LR 2018, 22(2), 274–282.

[88] *Milliken v Milliken* (1845) 8 Ir Eq R 16.

[89] *Milliken v Milliken* (1845) 8 Ir Eq R 16 at 31.

On this basis, he rejected any question of Mr Milliken being in partnership with the defendants and so refused an injunction to prevent the dissolution of the firm.

Option to become a partner

[2.43] An option to become a partner does not constitute the holder of the option a partner, since that person will not, before the exercise of the option, be carrying on business in common with the granter of the option. This is evident from the case of *Re Hall*,[90] where Mallinson entered negotiations with Hall with a view to forming a partnership with Hall in Dublin. To this end, Mallinson managed Hall's business for a year and Hall agreed that at the end of the year Mallinson would have an option to become a partner in the business. Brady LC held that neither the negotiations nor the option were sufficient to constitute Mr Mallinson a partner in Mr Hall's business.[91]

One-sided financial contribution or partnership?

[2.44] In the English High Court case of *Nadeem v Rafiq*[92] (a dispute between two cousins as to when and if a partnership between them had arisen), Nadeem had made a significant financial contribution to a plumbing and heating business at the outset, but Rafiq argued that he was not to be admitted as a partner in the business until he had completed certain training. Nelson J commented that for Nadeem to have put money into the business on such a one-sided basis was improbable, and held that Nadeem had been a partner in the business from the time that the contribution was made. In *Chahal v Mahal*,[93] Mr Chahal had advanced £30,000 on an interest-free and unsecured basis to the defendants in connection with the operation of a caravan site. The defendants claimed that this was a loan, whereas Mr Chahal successfully claimed that a partnership existed between them. The court considered it implausible, on the facts of the case, that Mr Chahal had the financial resources available to him to enable him to simply make a long-term interest-free loan to the defendants, and this influenced the court's decision that there was a partnership between them.[94]

---

[90] *Re Hall* (1864) Ir Ch R 287.

[91] Reliance was placed by Brady LC on *Rawlinson v Clarke* (1846) 15 M & W 292. Of note also is the case of *Gulliver v Brady & ors p/a Matheson Ormsby Prentice* [2003] IESC 68. A memorandum of understanding had been entered into between the parties to the effect that, subject to the fulfilment of certain conditions, Mr Gulliver would be admitted as a full equity partner in the defendant partnership. One of those conditions was that at least 75% of the equity partners would not vote against his admission as a partner. However, a resolution was passed that precluded his admission as a partner, with Mr Gulliver then claiming that he had been made a partner, and had acted as a full equity partner, before that resolution had been passed. The dispute was referred to arbitration, and then settled, with Mr Gulliver leaving the firm.

[92] *Nadeem v Rafiq* [2007] EWHC 2959 (Ch).

[93] *Chahal v Mahal* [2004] EWHC 2589.

[94] That finding was not challenged on appeal. A loan from a sibling to a family partnership was not however found to be a partnership contribution, but was instead regarded as a loan (both in the accounts of the partnership, and by the High Court of England and Wales, in *Mehra v Shah* (1 August 2003) EWHC (the High Court's finding that no partnership existed was upheld on appeal, [2004] EWCA Civ 632).

Can there be a retrospective partnership?

[2.45] A written partnership agreement may legitimately provide that the partnership actually commenced at an earlier date than the date of execution of the agreement, provided that this was actually the case. Thus in *Best v McKay*,[95] a partnership commenced on 16 August 1938. The partnership agreement, which was not signed until February 1939, provided that the agreement commenced on 16 August 1938 and this clause was upheld as valid by Andrews LCJ in the Northern Ireland Court of Appeal (Babbington and Murphy LJJ, concurring). In similar circumstances, in *O'Dwyer, Inspector of Taxes v Cafolla & Co*,[96] the partnership agreement provided that the partnership was deemed to have commenced almost a year prior to the date of execution of the agreement. The decision of the Special Commissioner of the Revenue that the partnership agreement was valid was accepted by the High Court and Supreme Court.

[2.46] However, if the partnership did not actually commence on the earlier date, such a clause will be of no effect. Thus in *Macken v Revenue Commissioners*,[97] the partnership agreement, which was executed in April 1954, contained a provision to the effect that 'the partnership shall be deemed to have commenced on the 1 January 1954'.[98] In the High Court, Teevan J held that this clause was of no effect since the partnership did not commence on 1 January 1954 as the parties were not in fact carrying on business together as of that date.[99]

Where partnership agreement is not performed

[2.47] Another consequence of the requirement that the parties be 'carrying on' business is that a partnership agreement which is not performed will not constitute the parties thereto partners. The case of *Reilly v Walsh*[100] involved two brothers who were builders but who had not entered into partnership. They then agreed with Archdeacon Barton to lease land in Suffolk Street in Dublin and build some houses upon it. However, one brother had a disagreement with Archdeacon Barton and refused to comply with the terms of their agreement and indeed he made every effort to thwart the venture by discouraging third parties from lending to his brother. Despite this, the other brother acquired the land and completed the buildings. It was held that while the original intention was that a partnership be formed between the brothers in relation to the venture, this was never carried into effect and no partnership came into existence since by his actions the errant brother ensured that they never carried on business in common. Richards B (Jackson and Moore JJ concurring) held that the failure of the errant brother to act as a partner, namely his failure to show a duty of good faith to his brother and the fact that, unlike his brother, he never made any contributions to the venture, supported a finding of no partnership.

---

[95] *Best v McKay* (1940) 74 ILTR 125.
[96] *O'Dwyer, Inspector of Taxes v Cafolla & Co* [1949] IR 210.
[97] *Macken v Revenue Commissioners* [1962] IR 302.
[98] *Macken v Revenue Commissioners* [1962] IR 302 at 308.
[99] Teevan J relied on *Waddington v O'Callaghan* (1931) 16 TC 187.
[100] *Reilly v Walsh* (1848) 11 Ir Eq R 22.

All partners need not be actively carrying on the business

[2.48] The requirement in s 1(1) that the partners be 'carrying on' the business does not require all of the partners to be active in the day-to-day operations of the business. This is because a partner may take no active role in the running of the partnership business, yet the business may be transacted on his behalf and if so, he will be a partner, known as a dormant partner. Thus, in a two-partner firm, where one of the partners is a dormant partner, the active partner will appear to be carrying on business on his own account. While the dormant partner will not be taking any active part in the management of the firm's business, he will still be regarded as carrying on business in common with the active partner, since the active partner will be carrying on business on behalf of the dormant partner.[101] Thus in *Y v O'Sullivan*,[102] a business was run after the death of the owner by his executor alone. However, the profits of the business were divided amongst the four residuary legatees, of which the executor was one, and in the High Court Maguire J observed that:

> '[i]t was not open to doubt that, since the death of the deceased, a partnership business has been carried on, by the executor for the benefit of the partners.'[103]

4. 'a business'

[2.49] To constitute a partnership, s 1(1) of the 1890 Act requires the parties to be carrying on a 'business' together.[104] Section 45 of the 1890 Act defines the term 'business' in a non-exclusive manner as 'including every trade, occupation, or profession', thus ensuring that the greatest number of commercial activities fall within the terms of the 1890 Act. In the words of Lord Diplock, 'the word "business" is an etymological chameleon; it suits its meaning to the context in which it is found'.[105]

---

[101] *Cox v Hickman* (1860) 8 HLC 268. As a partner, the dormant partner will be bound by the acts of the active partner which are within the ordinary course of business of the firm, see further para **[6.05]** and para **[10.17]**.

[102] *Y v O'Sullivan* [1949] IR 264.

[103] *Y v O'Sullivan* [1949] IR 264 at 273. See generally regarding dormant partners, para **[6.04]** et seq.

[104] Note the comment of Nugee J in *Dutia v Geldof* [2016] EWHC 547 (Ch) that a partnership under the 1890 Act requires an agreement that the intended partners will carry on business themselves, not that they will have an economic interest in a business to be carried on by someone else. In that case, the parties carried out some preparatory work together, with the ultimate intention of carrying on business by way of a limited liability partnership (which, in the UK, has separate legal personality). Nugee J distinguished the fact pattern in this case to that of *Khan v Miah – Khan v Miah* [2001] All ER 20 involved the question of whether a partnership had commenced; *Dutia v Geldof* instead involved the question of whether the parties' preparatory work was referable to a business they would carry on between themselves, or to the business that the LLP would carry on (no partnership was found to exist in this case).

[105] *Town Investments Ltd v Department of the Environment* [1977] 1 All ER 813 at 819. And it is possible for a business to have different component parts; see *In Re Dent Co* (Ch D) [2017] 3 WLR 198 in which the partnership was involved in two businesses: a farming business which produced 10% of its revenue, and a haulage business which produced 90% of its revenue.

[2.50] Not only is it true to say that the term suits its context, it may also be said that the term suits the commercial environment of the time, and for this reason, care should be taken in considering the impact of precedents from a different era.[106] For example in *French v Styring*,[107] an agreement between two people who owned a racehorse, whereby they agreed to share the horse's winnings and expenses equally, was held not to be a partnership on the basis that the ownership of a horse was not a 'business'. In more recent times, one has witnessed the formation (and occasional flotation) of companies with the sole aim of owning horses and dividing the profits therefrom.[108] Therefore, it is suggested that this decision would not be followed in today's climate, where horse-owning syndicates can literally be big 'business'.[109]

[2.51] Indeed, there would seem to be a reluctance on the part of the courts to remove enterprises from the ambit of the 1890 Act on the technical grounds that the enterprise does not constitute a business. In *O'Kelly v Darragh*,[110] the parties were involved in a psychoendocrine research centre in St James's Hospital in Dublin which provided testing and analysis services to drug companies. When the plaintiff sought a share of the surplus funds in the centre's bank account, the defendant alleged that it was a research fund to accomplish objectives, rather than a business. This argument was rejected by Carroll J, who noted that the centre's operations had been very profitable and that its operations had since been taken over by a company formed by the defendant which had gone public.

Is running a farm a 'business'?

[2.52] In *Murtagh v Costello*,[111] a firm of flour merchants was formed in Athlone to carry on the business of milling and other trading. Certain lands were purchased with partnership money and were used for farming purposes. On the death of one of the partners, a dispute arose as to whether the lands were partnership property or not. It was claimed that they did not constitute partnership property, since they were used for farming and not for trading, on the basis that a farmer is not a trader. Chatterton VC held that the lands were partnership property and noted that:

> 'It was contended that the farming could not be included as part of the trading of the partnership, as a farmer is not in one sense a trader; but there may be a partnership in farming as in any other business.'[112]

---

[106] See for example the judgment of Staughton LJ in *United Bank of Kuwait Ltd v Hammoud* [1988] 1 WLR 1051 at 1063F.

[107] *French v Styring* (1857) 3 Jur NS 670.

[108] Eg Classic Thoroughbreds plc.

[109] The Companies Act 2014, s 1435(c)(iii) explicitly recognises thoroughbred horse breeding as a partnership business and provides that partnerships formed for the purpose of carrying on or promoting the business of thoroughbred horse breeding are exempted from the prohibition in s 1435 on the formation of partnerships with more than 20 members.

[110] *O'Kelly v Darragh* [1988] ILRM 309.

[111] *Murtagh v Costello* (1881) 7 LR Ir 428.

[112] *Murtagh v Costello* (1881) 7 LR Ir 428 at 437.

In the High Court case of *Williams v Harris*,[113] the business of farming and breeding of livestock between a husband, his wife, the defendant and the defendant's company was accepted by McWilliam J as constituting a partnership.

What about a family farm or a family business?

[2.53] Since the running of a farm per se has been held to constitute a 'business', it is necessary to consider the High Court decision in *Walsh v Walsh*[114] that a farm which was operated by a family was not a 'business'. However, it is contended that this decision should not be followed[115] today in view of the attempt by Gavin Duffy J to find what appear to be non-existent differences between Irish and English conditions in order to justify a different application of legal principles. The case involved the relationship between the wife of a deceased farmer and her five children who remained at home to work the family farm in Maolais, Co Mayo in the 1940s. The family members worked the farm for a number of years and pooled the proceeds of their labour to meet the family's outgoings. After the death of a number of the family members, a dispute arose as to the ownership of funds which resulted from the profits of the family farm. Before considering the decision, of significance are the views of Gavin Duffy J on Irish country life at that time:

> 'In applying English law to the facts, one has to begin by recognising the outlook of the persons immediately concerned. One of the persistent characteristics of Irish country life, perhaps, indeed, of peasant life elsewhere, is the prevalence of family feeling, the intense feeling of the family for the family: whatever may be the outlook in the towns, that essentially Christian society of our countryside treats the family in actual practice as the basic unit of social order; that approach to the problem of life was indigenous, natural, traditional, among the unspoilt sections of our people long before the Constitution proclaimed it, though a very human avarice, understandable among men and women who earn their money hard, may at times be a competing factor.'[116]

This attitude does perhaps explain his conclusion regarding the family firm in that case that:

> 'the essence of the combination was the fact that these persons were one family, who were working together for the sake of the family and because they were one family; the purpose of gain was an incidental ... and they were not, so far as the home farm was concerned, carrying on a "business" at all.'[117]

[2.54] Over a half of a century later, Gavan Duffy J's view of family farms is no longer accurate and it is suggested that modern Irish farming, whether by family members or not, is as much a 'business' as the operation by family members of any other commercial activity.[118] It is beyond doubt that a partnership can exist between family

---

113 *Williams v Harris* (15 January 1980) HC and on appeal [1980] ILRM 237. See also *Hawkins v Rogers* [1951] IR 48 (partnership in the owning and running of racehorses).

114 *Walsh v Walsh* [1942] IR 403.

115 Note, however, that part of the case dealing with the timber operations is not tainted in the same way, see further para **[2.72]**.

116 *Walsh v Walsh* [1942] IR 403 at 408.

117 *Walsh v Walsh* [1942] IR 403 at 410.

118 See for example the partnership between a father and his sons in a family fast-food business in *O'Dwyer, Inspector of Taxes v Cafolla & Co* [1949] IR 210.

members and, indeed, much of our partnership litigation is between family members.[119] For this reason, it is apprehended that *Walsh v Walsh*[120] will not be followed today.[121] Rather, it is suggested that the approach of O'Connor MR in the earlier case of *Re Christie*[122] should be followed. In that case it was accepted[123] by O'Connor MR that two brothers who owned and worked the family farm in County Antrim and supported themselves out of the profits were partners in the farming stock and profits.[124]

Mere ownership of property is not a business

[2.55] While the running of a farm may constitute a 'business', it is noted in more detail hereunder[125] that the mere ownership of land or other property is not a 'business' for the purposes of s 1(1) of the 1890 Act.[126] Thus in *Re Littles*,[127] in which the parties carried on a salmon fishery business on the River Bann, it was noted obiter that they would not have been partners if they were not trading as a consequence of owning the land. Brady LC observed that 'the mere occupation of the fishery would not be trading'.[128] In *Hitchins v Hitchins and Anor*,[129] the Supreme Court of New South Wales reiterated that the mere holding of an investment did not constitute the carrying on of business. The

---

119 See for example *Meagher v Meagher* [1961] IR 96. See also the comments of Master Bowles in *Khan v Khan* [2015] EWHC 2625 (Ch) (in the context of an unsuccessful allegation by a son that he was a partner in, rather than an employee of, his father's business) that he could 'readily envisage circumstances whereby someone in the position of [the son] comes to work in a family business, takes a role in the business and is paid, other than on a salaried, or wage paid basis, from the business. In those circumstances, it seems to me that the court might very well find an implied agreement that that person, together with the other family members in the business, were carrying on business in common with a view to profit, for purposes of section 1 of the Partnership Act, and, thus, that that person would be entitled to a share in the partnership business.' Interestingly, Master Bowles also indicated that cultural norms could be a factor for consideration in determining a person's expectations in joining a family business (albeit, in this case, they did not fall to be considered in detail as the court viewed the son as being aware of his status as an employee, and not as partner).
120 *Walsh v Walsh* [1942] IR 403.
121 See also the position in Australia where a family farming enterprise was held to be a partnership in *Harvey v Harvey* (1970) 120 CLR 529.
122 *Re Christie* [1917] 1 IR 17. This case was unsucessfully pleaded in *Walsh v Walsh* [1942] IR 403.
123 This was accepted, rather than decided, by O'Connor MR as it does not appear to have been contested by the parties in that case.
124 See also *Moore v Moore* (27 February 1998) HC NI in which it was held that a partnership in a family farm existed between two brothers and their mother.
125 Paragraph **[2.89]**.
126 See, however, the interesting New Zealand case of *Dickie v Torbay Pharmacy* [1995] 3 NZLR 429, where a group of doctors and an accountant decided to acquire some land for property development purposes. The High Court of New Zealand referred expressly to this arrangement as a co-venture, but clearly treated it as a partnership by applying partnership principles thereto and in particular holding that the accountant owed the doctors a fiduciary duty.
127 *Re Littles* (1843) 6 Ir Eq R 197 and on appeal (1847) 10 Ir Eq R 275.
128 *Re Littles* (1847) 10 Ir Eq R 275 at 283.
129 *Hitchins v Hitchins and Anor* (1998) NSW Lexis 2382, (1998) 47 NSWLR 35.

case involved the plaintiff and her two brothers who were members of a hotel partnership with a number of other individuals. The hotel property and business was jointly owned by all the partners and the joint share of the three Hitchins siblings in the hotel partnership was 18%. This share of the profits of the hotel partnership was paid to the three Hitchins jointly. A dispute arose amongst the three of them regarding the treatment of these co-owned profits. The plaintiff alleged that the hotel profits should have been divided equally between the three since the relationship between the siblings in these co-owned profits itself constituted a separate partnership between the three of them.[130] In the Supreme Court of New South Wales, Bryson J held that the activity of the three, namely investing in a share in the hotel partnership and receiving drawings from it, did not constitute the carrying on of a 'business in common'.[131] Instead he categorised this activity as simply an investment, since there were no 'elements of engaging in trade and a flow of transactions which could be thought of as carrying on a business'.[132] He held that while the three Hitchins were clearly partners in the hotel partnership, they were not partners in a separate partnership of which the business was the joint ownership of a share in the hotel partnership.[133]

Partnerships between spouses and civil partners

[2.56] Like partnerships between family members,[134] there is no reason why a partnership cannot exist between a husband and a wife, or between civil partners.[135] Indeed, it is somewhat surprising that in family law cases, more use has not been made of the terms of the 1890 Act to support claims by one spouse or partner for a share of

---

130 She therefore relied on the default right of partners to an equal share of the profits under s 24(1) of the 1890 Act.

131 He also relied on the rules in s 2 of the 1890 Act regarding co-ownership of property and the sharing of gross returns not of itself constituting partnership, see para **[2.89]** et seq.

132 *Hitchins v Hitchins and Anor* (1998) NSW Lexis 2382 at 2390.

133 Although there was no partnership between the three siblings, Bryson J was able to find for the plaintiff on the grounds that the relationship between the three was fiduciary. He supported this conclusion on the grounds, inter alia, that they were in a close family relationship and that they were common members of the hotel partnership. On this basis, he relied on the equitable principle that 'equality is equity' to hold that the hotel profits should be distributed evenly between the three siblings and he therefore ordered that an account of the distribution of the hotel partnership profits should be taken.

134 See further in relation to such partnerships, para **[2.53]**.

135 In *Williams v Harris* (15 January 1980) HC NI and on appeal [1980] ILRM 237, the partnership was not solely between a husband and wife but also involved the defendant and the defendant's company. See also *Logan v Logan* (2 February 1990) HC NI; cf *McFarlane v McFarlane* [1972] NI 59 and *Northern Bank v McNeill* (14 February 1986) HC NI; *Butler v Butler* (1885) QBD 374. Partnerships between spouses have been recognised in other jurisdictions, see the American case of *Marcrum v Smith* (1921) 206 Ala 456, 91 So 259, 20 ALR 1303, the Australian case of *The Queen v Ross-Jones, ex p Beaumont* (1979) 141 CLR 504 and the New Zealand case of *Cawte v Cawte* (1990) 6 FRNZ 495. See also the English family law case of *Bothe v Amos* [1975] 2 All ER 321. Note that in *Re Gilligan* (1996) The Irish Times, 28 November, the Criminal Assets Bureau claimed in the High Court that the wife of a suspected criminal was a partner of his in 'his conduct of criminal enterprises', but this claim seems to overlook the fact that the resulting partnership would be illegal and therefore immediately dissolved under s 34 of the 1890 Act, see para **[9.27]**. (contd.../)

half of the profits and property of business ventures run with their spouse or partner.[136] A successful claim of partnership would appear to be likely in such situations since the community of interest between a husband and wife, or between civil partners, as a result of the relationship between them will often be such as to lead to the conclusion that any business which is being carried on by them is being carried on by them 'in common' so as to satisfy the definition of partnership.[137] However, it is important to note that it is the way that the spouses and civil partners conduct their business matters which is crucial and not the way they conduct their social activities. This is exemplified by the Ontario case of *Palter v Zeller*.[138] There, the plaintiff was suing a lawyer for the lawyer's misuse of his funds. He also joined the defendant, the lawyer's wife, as he claimed that she, who was also a lawyer and had worked in her husband's law firm, was his partner under the Ontario equivalent of s 1 of the 1890 Act.[139] The plaintiff's claim was rejected as he produced no objective evidence of partnership other than the fact that he knew the couple socially and 'that they were partners in everything they did, including their practice of law'.[140] In the Ontario Court of Justice, Wilkins J observed:

> 'The mere fact that lawyers may be married and behave in an equal social and marital partnership, in my view, has no relationship or impact upon the manner in which they conduct their affairs as contemplated by the Partnership Acts.'[141]

[2.57] However, it is probably not correct to say that the marital relationship or civil partnership will always have no impact on the alleged existence of a partnership between spouses or civil partners. So, if the same allegation of partnership were to be made by one spouse or civil partner, rather than by a third party, it seems likely that the court would pay more heed to the social relationship between the spouses or civil partners and the impact that had upon their business relationship.

Can a single venture constitute 'a business'?

[2.58] It is clear that the requirement in s 1(1), that the parties be carrying on 'business', will be satisfied even where the parties do not carry on trading on a continuous basis, but rather have only come together for a single venture. This is implicit in the terms of s 32 of the 1890 Act, which deals with the dissolution of a partnership entered into for 'a

---

135   (\...contd) See generally Murrie and Magrin, 'Family partnerships and divorce' (1997) NLJ 176. As regards the tax implications and possible pit-falls of partnerships between spouses, see Grattan, '"With all my profits I thee endow": The tax risks of business marriages' (1995) 46 NILQ 72. As regards non-married co-habitants, see Sholar, 'Partnership: implied partnership between nonmarried cohabitants' (1992) 22 Memphis State University LR 391. Note also the tax implications where a person takes a spouse into partnership: Palmer, 'Challenge to husband and wife partnerships' (1994) 15 Tolley's Practical Tax 158.

136   Partnership Act 1890, s 24(1). For a case in which the husband and wife entered marriage and a partnership see the English Court of Appeal case of *White v White* [1998] TLR 422 and in particular see the court's criticisms of the lawyers' failure to appreciate the wife's entitlement under partnership law when the marriage broke-down and the partnership dissolved.

137   See further in relation to the requirement that the parties be acting 'in common', para **[2.68]**.

138   *Palter v Zeller* (1997) 30 OR (3d) 796.

139   The Ontario Partnerships Act, RSO 1990, c P5, s 2.

140   *Palter v Zeller* (1997) 30 OR (3d) 796 at 799, from the plaintiff's statement of claim.

141   *Palter v Zeller* (1997) 30 OR (3d) 796 at 802.

single adventure or undertaking'.[142] Thus, the Australian High Court has held that a one-off venture to promote and finance an Australian tour by the well-known artists Elton John and Cilla Black was a partnership.[143]

[2.59] A more surprising case is that of *Robinson v Anderson*[144] where two solicitors, who were practising in different firms, were jointly retained to conduct litigation on behalf of the same client. The two solicitors agreed to do this and they agreed to share the profit arising from the case between them. A dispute arose as to the division of the profits. Even though this was a once-off arrangement between the solicitors, the court held that they were partners for the purposes of the conduct of that case and thus they were subject to the default rule under partnership law that partners share profits equally, in the absence of contrary agreement.[145] It is contended that if the issue before the court was one solicitor's liability for the acts of the other, a different conclusion might have been reached. Thus, it is suggested that the case should not be taken as authority for the proposition that any time two or more professionals advise the one client that the professionals will be deemed to be in partnership together. Clearly, where two professionals, eg an accountant and a lawyer, give a third party accountancy advice and legal advice respectively, they would not be regarded as carrying on business in common, as required by the definition of partnership.[146] Even where two lawyers (or two accountants) are jointly advising a client in relation to the same subject matter, it is suggested that more than this joint advice would be required for the two professionals to be regarded as partners. Rather, they must have a sufficient degree of proximity so as to be regarded as carrying on 'business in common'.[147]

A series of separate ventures

[2.60] Where an enterprise consists of a series of separate ventures, then the participants will not be in a continuous partnership but a partnership will be formed between them each time there is a new venture. This was the case in *Minister for Social Welfare v Griffiths*.[148] There, the enterprise involved a sharing of the catch between two fishermen every time they went out to sea together. One of the men owned the fishing vessel and it was alleged by the Minister that he was the other fisherman's employer and therefore owed the Revenue Commissioners social insurance payments. In the High Court, Blayney J rejected the Minister's claim and noted that each voyage was a separate venture, with a new partnership being formed for each venture.

---

142   Partnership Act 1890, s 32(b).
143   *Canny Gabriel Castle Jackson Advertising Pty Ltd v Volume Sales (Finance) Pty Ltd* (1974) 131 CLR 321.
144   *Robinson v Anderson* (1855) 20 Beav 98 and 7 De GM & G 239 (appeal). See generally, Walthall, 'What do you mean "we", Kemo Sabe? Partnership law and client responsibilities of office sharing lawyers' (1998) 28 Cumberland LR 601.
145   Partnership Act 1890, s 24(1).
146   Partnership Act 1890, s 1(1).
147   This issue is considered in detail, at para **[2.68]**.
148   *Minister for Social Welfare v Griffiths* [1992] ILRM 667.

Can a criminal activity be a business?

[2.61] While a criminal activity might technically constitute a 'business' for the purposes of s 1(1), the resulting partnership will be an illegal partnership and will therefore be immediately dissolved under the terms of s 34 of the 1890 Act.[149]

5. 'with a view of profit'

[2.62] The fifth requirement for the existence of a partnership is that the relationship between the parties be one which is with a view to profit. The motivation that a profit result from the venture (even if a loss actually results) is at the heart of the partnership relationship. In the words of Lord Lindley:

> 'An agreement that something shall be attempted with a view to gain, and that the gain shall be shared by the parties to the agreement, is the grand characteristic of every partnership, and is the leading feature of nearly every definition of the term.'[150]

The importance of the profit element is clear from other provisions of the 1890 Act. Thus, under s 2(3) of the 1890 Act, the sharing of profits is prima facie evidence of partnership between persons who share in the profits of a business,[151] while s 35(e) of the 1890 Act provides that a partner may apply to court for the dissolution of the partnership, where the business of the partnership can only be carried on at a loss.[152]

Definition of 'profit'

[2.63] The term 'profit' as used in the 1890 Act is not defined. In the Supreme Court case of *Meagher v Meagher*,[153] Kingsmill Moore J[154] adopted the following classic definition of the term 'profit':[155]

> 'If the total assets of the business at the two dates be compared, the increase which they shew at the later date as compared with the earlier date (due allowance ... being made for any capital introduced into or taken out of the business in the meanwhile) represents in strictness the profits of the business during the period in question.'[156]

On this basis, Kingsmill Moore J held that an increase in the capital value of partnership assets, by keeping them unsold, was a profit. That case concerned a firm of builders who bought houses, renovated them and sold them at a profit. The value of the houses had increased between the date of death of one of the partners in the firm and the date of realisation of the assets, as a result of a general increase in property prices. Kingsmill Moore J concluded that:

---

149 See generally in relation to illegal partnerships, para **[9.01]** et seq. Note that in *Re Gilligan* (1996) Irish Times, 28 November, the Criminal Assets Bureau claimed in the High Court that the wife of a suspected criminal was a partner of his in 'his conduct of criminal enterprises'.
150 *Mollwo, March & Co v Court of Wards* (1872) LR 4 PC 419.
151 See further para **[2.95]**.
152 See generally in relation to s 35(e), para **[25.51]**.
153 *Meagher v Meagher* [1961] IR 96.
154 Ó Dálaigh and Maguire JJ concurring.
155 Per Fletcher Moulton LJ in *Re Spanish Prospecting Co Ltd* [1911] 1 Ch 92 at 99.
156 *Meagher v Meagher* [1961] IR 96 at 111.

'It appears to me, therefore, that any increase in value of the assets of the business between the date of the dissolution and the date of realisation, which is attributable to the use[157] of the assets ... is properly to be regarded as profits.'[158]

[2.64] The High Court considered the meaning of 'profit' further in *Irish Life and Permanent PLC & Companies Acts*[159] by reference to the definition adopted by Kingsmill Moore J in *Meagher v Meagher*, with Clarke J stating that:

'As is clear from the authorities to which I have referred,[160] the general meaning of the word profit is that a company, partnership or the like has had an improvement in its assets, not explicable by a change in the amount of capital invested.'

Does a view to profit include a view to gain?

[2.65] While Lord Lindley's description of an 'agreement with a view to gain' as being the grand characteristic of partnership is accurate in most cases, care should be taken to use the term 'profit' rather than 'gain'. This is because the Supreme Court has made a distinction between these two terms. In *Deane v Voluntary Health Insurance Board*,[161] the question arose as to whether the Voluntary Health Insurance Board (VHI) was an undertaking which was 'engaged for gain' so as to fall within the terms of the Competition Act 1991. The VHI collected only such revenue as was necessary to cover its costs, the surplus going to the State's Central Fund. In the High Court, Costello J had held that the term 'for gain' was equivalent to the term 'for profit' and on this basis he held that the VHI was not engaged for gain. However, in the Supreme Court, Finlay CJ (Hederman and Egan JJ concurring) reversed this decision on the grounds that the two terms were not synonymous, but that there is an area of gain (ie non-pecuniary gain) which does not equate to profit.[162] It follows that associations, such as the VHI, which have as their aim the achievement of non-pecuniary gain, will be engaged for gain, but will not be partnerships, since they will not satisfy the fifth element of the definition of partnership.

Where there is no 'view to a profit'

[2.66] The situation where a partnership does not have a view to profit was considered in *MacCarthaigh v Daly*.[163] This was a case stated to the High Court by the Revenue Appeal Commissioner. It concerned a Cork solicitor who had entered into a purported

---

157 Per Kingsmill Moore J: 'In my opinion the increase in value of an asset due to a change in prices during the period of its retention can properly be regarded as a profit derived from *its use*.' ([1961] IR 96 at 110.)

158 *Meagher v Meagher* [1961] IR 96.

159 *Irish Life and Permanent PLC & Companies Acts* [2009] IEHC 567.

160 *Meagher v Meagher* [1961] IR 96, together with *Buckley on the Companies Acts* (14th edn, 1981) and the judgments in *Re Spanish Prospecting Company* [1911] CH 92, *Drown v Gaumont-British Picture Corporation* [1937] Ch 402, *McClelland v Hyde* [1942] NI 1, *Rushden Heel Company Limited v Keane* [1946] 2 All ER 141 and *Wilson v Dunnes Stores (Cork) Limited* (22 January 1976) HC.

161 *Deane v Voluntary Health Insurance Board* [1992] 2 IR 319.

162 Finlay CJ relied on the decision of Jessel MR in *Re Arthur Average Association for British, Foreign and Colonial Ships* (1875) LR 10 Ch App 542.

163 *MacCarthaigh v Daly* [1985] IR 73.

limited partnership[164] with six other limited partners and a general partner. Agreements for the leasing of equipment by the partnership to the Metropole Hotel were completely uneconomical and had the effect of producing a substantial loss for the partnership. Mr Daly wished to use his share of the losses of the partnership to reduce his individual income tax as a solicitor. O'Hanlon J stated that:

> 'I would have some reservations, however, in coming to a conclusion that the arrangement entered into between them should properly be regarded as a partnership at all, since the Partnership Act, 1890, which was largely declaratory of the common law, commenced by defining partnership in s 1 of the Act as "the relation which subsists between persons carrying on a business in common with a view of profit" ... It was fairly conceded in the course of the hearing before the Appeal Commissioner that an important reason behind the scheme was to achieve a tax benefit for the participants.'[165]

For procedural reasons,[166] O'Hanlon J was constrained from overturning the finding of fact by the Appeal Commissioner that a partnership had come into existence. Nonetheless, it seems clear from his judgment that if he was not so constrained, he would have had held that the arrangement did not constitute a partnership because of the absence of the 'view of profit'.

[2.67] This case should therefore operate as a warning to persons who are involved in business ventures which use partnerships for their tax benefits. Where the sole purpose of the partnership is to create a loss, the association will not be a partnership. In some cases this will defeat the purpose of the business venture, ie to benefit from the 'see-through' tax status of a partnership.[167]

6. 'in common'

[2.68] The sixth and final requirement of the definition of partnership is that the parties be acting in common. The other five requirements of the definition of partnership may be regarded as procedural prerequisites which in most cases will be easily established. Thus, an employer and an employee will usually satisfy the five other requirements of the definition of partnership since they will be involved in a relationship between two or more persons carrying on business with a view to profit. They will not however satisfy the requirement that they be carrying on business in common.[168] This requirement goes to the very heart of the question of whether a partnership exists and most cases of doubt

---

[164] In fact, this is one of the rare reported cases dealing with a failure to properly register a limited partnership under the Limited Partnerships Act 1907. Under s 5 of that Act this failure results in the limited partnership being deemed to be a general partnership. See further para **[28.63]**.

[165] *MacCarthaigh v Daly* [1985] IR 73 at 79.

[166] As the appeal to the High Court was from a decision of the Appeal Commissioner by way of case stated, O'Hanlon J relied on the case of *Mara (Inspector of Taxes) v Hummingbird Ltd* [1982] ILRM 421, to hold that the findings on primary facts (that the relationship was a partnership) should not be set aside unless there was no evidence whatever to support them.

[167] As to the tax status of limited partnerships, see para **[28.13]** et seq.

[168] In *Davis v Sean Walshe and Plynth Limited t/a Dew Wholesale* [2003] ELR 1 (14 May 2002) HC, Murphy J noted that the '... issue of partnership or quasi-partnership does not seem to arise in the context of employment by a company'. (contd.../)

about the existence of a partnership revolve around this issue.[169] The importance of the words 'in common' was neatly summarised by the Scottish Court of Session (Inner House) in 2017,[170] when Lord Glennie stated that:

> '... even if the Lord Ordinary had found as a fact that the parties had entered into a business relationship with a view to profit, it would not follow as a matter of law that they were carrying on such business "in common" and therefore in partnership. Were that to be the case, the words "in common" would add nothing. Almost every relationship between parties pursuant to which they carried on business with a view to profit would be classified as a partnership, unless excluded by the terms of section 1 (2) of the 1890 Act. Every joint venture would be a partnership. A company and its employees would be in partnership. The several parties to a construction contract would be in partnership with each other. Parties would find themselves to have been in partnership simply because they were working together in anticipation of concluding a contract. This is not the law – but it would be a consequence of failing to give proper regard to the important words in the definition of partnership, "carrying on a business *in common*".'

[2.69] This issue may be seen as determining whether the parties have a sufficiently proximate relationship to be said to be partners, with the attendant rights and/or liabilities.[171] This is a difficult question of fact which can only be answered by examining all of the circumstances of the case. Accordingly, the purpose of this part of the chapter and the analysis of the rules in s 2 for ascertaining the existence of a partnership which follows,[172] is to isolate the factors which have been considered by the courts in determining this issue.

[2.70] In general terms, parties will be acting in common when they have a community of interest[173] in the business in question or, in other words, are co-owners of the business (as distinct from any property used by the business).[174] A strong indicator of this co-ownership is the fact that they share profits of the business or that they jointly control or

---

168 (\...contd) See, also, the judgment of Master Bowles in *Khan v Khan* [2015] EWHC 2625 (Ch): 'As a matter of trite law, one cannot both be a partner in a business and an employee of the business.' In that case, a son had worked for his father's business and was paid as an employee.

169 For example see *Macken v Revenue Commissioners*, considered at para **[2.80]**, *O'Kelly v Darragh*, para **[2.118]** and *Greenham v Gray*, considered at para **[2.77]**.

170 In *Worbey v Campbell* [2017] CSIH 49.

171 As to this liability, see generally para **[10.01]** et seq.

172 Paragraph **[2.88]** et seq.

173 In *Adam v Newbigging* (1888) 13 AC 308 at 315, Lord Halsbury noted the requirement of a community of interest for a partnership to exist.

174 Note that the definition of partnership in s 102(11) of the American Uniform Partnership Act (1997) (Last Amended 2013) is 'an association of two or more persons to carry on as co-owners a business for profit'. The distinction between co-owning a business and co-owning property used by a business is highlighted by the Northern Ireland Court of Appeal case of *Sinclair v Murray* [1980] NI 26 which concerned a mutual association of taxi drivers. Lowry LCJ seems to have assumed that the association did not constitute a partnership since although the taxis were owned by the association, each taxi-driver drove the taxi not on the business of the association but each was engaged on his own business for his own profit.

manage the business.[175] When parties have this community of interest in the business, the business will be carried on by or on behalf of all the parties and they will all act as each other's agents for the purpose of that business.[176] Accordingly, the question of whether the parties are acting in common is often considered by asking the fundamental question of whether the business is being conducted so as to constitute the relationship of principal and agent between the persons taking the profits and those actually carrying on the business.[177] For this reason, partnership law has been judicially described as that branch of the law of agency which deals with persons working together for an enterprise of which they all are a part.[178] Therefore, it is this factor which will be first considered in determining whether parties are acting in common. However, it is important to bear in mind that the courts do not take a formalistic approach to determining whether the parties are acting in common. More often than not, a finding of partnership will result from a combination of factors[179] and a weighing up by the courts of their relative importance.[180]

Are the parties each other's agent?

[2.71] The importance of whether the alleged partners are agents and principals for each other is clear from *Shaw v Galt*.[181] There, the High Court considered the test to be used in determining whether a partnership exists and O'Brien J (Fitzgerald and Hayes JJ concurring) highlighted the importance of the presence of an agency relationship by referring to the seminal partnership law case of *Cox v Hickman*:[182]

---

[175]   The control of the business by a party will be a strong factor in favour of a finding of partnership, since the rationale for imposing liability on a person as a partner, is that he can control the enterprise and therefore should be made liable for its actions. From an economic perspective, he controls the prices and costs of the enterprise and is best positioned to distribute the risk of loss: see generally Douglas, 'Vicarious Liability and the Administration of Risk' (1929) 38 Yale LJ 584. The importance of the role of an alleged partner in the management of the partnership business in determining his liability is evidenced by the fact that in limited partnerships and investment limited partnerships, the limited partners are granted limited liability in return for their not taking part in the management of the firm. See s 6(1) of the Limited Partnerships Act 1907 and s 6(1) of the Investment Limited Partnerships Act 1994.

[176]   See the interesting Australian case of *Duke Group Ltd (in liq) v Pilmer* [1999] SASC 97 concerning an alleged partnership between the members of an association of accounting firms throughout Australia. It was held that no partnership actually existed in that case.

[177]   Per Blackburn J in *Bullen v Sharp* (1865) LR 1 CP 86 at 111.

[178]   See the judgment of O'Brien J in *Shaw v Galt* (1863) 16 Ir CLR 357 at 374, considered at para **[2.71]**.

[179]   Such as whether the parties are co-owners of the business, whether they manage and control that business together, whether they share profits from that business, whether they share losses of the business and whether they are mutual agents for the purposes of the partnership business.

[180]   See for example the weighing up by Costello J of the different factors in *DPP v McLoughlin* [1986] IR 355, para **[2.116]**.

[181]   *Shaw v Galt* (1863) 16 Ir CLR 357.

[182]   *Cox v Hickman* (1860) 8 HL Cas 268.

'By referring to the judgments of Lord Carnworth (page 304), and of Lord Wensleydale (pages 312 and 313), it will be seen that in their opinion the law of partnership was to be regarded as a branch of the law of principal and agent; and the liability of one partner for the acts of another was in truth the liability of a principal for the acts of his agent ... in page 306, Lord Cranworth ... says:- "... the real ground of the liability is, that the trade has been carried on by persons acting on his behalf." ... The principle to be collected from them appears to be, that a partnership, even as to third parties, is not constituted by the mere fact of two or more persons participating or being interested in the net profits of a business; but that the existence of such partnership implies also the existence of such a relation between those persons as that "each of them is a principal and each an agent for the others" and that each of them is also entitled as partner to an account from the others.'[183]

[2.72] A similar approach was taken by Gavan Duffy J in *Walsh v Walsh*.[184] It has been noted that Gavan Duffy J's peculiar vision of Irish family farming influenced his decision that the running of a family farm was not a partnership business. However, the same concerns did not cloud his judgment regarding timber operations which were carried on by some only of the family and quite separate from the family farm. Accordingly, this aspect of his decision remains of relevance. He noted that while the timber operations were capable of constituting a partnership:

'But, if I call this a partnership, I must face the fact that, as I believe, Pat, the master, would not have tolerated any attempt by a brother, without express consent, to pledge his credit or otherwise act as agent of the group.'[185]

Since this agency was not present, he held that the timber operations did not in fact constitute a partnership. This, therefore, is an example of a case where the consequences of a partnership (ie each partner is his co-partner's mutual agent) were found not to exist and on this basis, it was concluded that there could be no partnership. This is not always the approach which is taken by the courts since they will often find that there is a sufficient community of interest between the parties for them to be partners and the consequence of this finding is that they are mutual agents.[186]

[2.73] However, whichever approach is taken by the courts, the alleged partners must be capable of being each other's agents.[187] Therefore, where it is not possible for the participants in a venture to be in a principal/agent relationship, they will not be partners as they will not be capable of carrying on business 'in common'. So, for example, in *Smith v Anderson*[188] it was held that it was not possible to have a partnership between total strangers, since they did not know each other and therefore could not have agreed to be each other's agent for the purposes of the business.

---

183 *Shaw v Galt* (1863) 16 Ir CLR 357 at 375.
184 *Walsh v Walsh* [1942] IR 403.
185 *Walsh v Walsh* [1942] IR 403 at 411.
186 The mutual agency of partners is considered in detail at para **[10.07]**.
187 But clearly the fact that one person is another's agent is not per se sufficient for there to be the necessary community of interest for a partnership to exist. See for example *Re Shanahans Stamp Auctions Ltd* [1962] IR 386 in which Budd J held that the relationship between an investor in stamps and the company which bought those stamps on his behalf, although a principal/agent relationship, was not a partnership.
188 *Smith v Anderson* (1880) 15 Ch D 247.

[2.74] Similarly, where there is an agency relationship between A and B, but not between B and A, the agency is not mutual and there will be no partnership. Thus in *Re Boyle*,[189] a solicitor in Dublin, Boyle snr, employed his son, Boyle jnr, as a solicitor in his office. The father gave Boyle jnr permission to carry on, for his own benefit, any business given to him personally and to have the free use of his office and staff for such purposes. After the outbreak of the Second World War, Boyle jnr joined the British Army and Boyle snr agreed to act on Boyle jnr's behalf, as his agent, and to transact any business given to him without fee or reward of any kind. The names of the father and son both appeared on the notepaper of the firm, though there was nothing on the notepaper which indicated a partnership. On one occasion during the son's absence, Boyle snr applied for his son's licence not as his agent but as his partner, although before and after this application, Boyle snr applied as agent. While Boyle snr was agent for his son, it was clear that his son was not his agent. Since the agency of the father was being done for the exclusive benefit of the son, there was not a business in common and in these circumstances, the High Court accepted that no partnership existed between them.[190]

Other factors in determining whether a 'business in common'

[2.75] It is now proposed to examine some of the other factors which have been used by the courts in determining whether there is sufficient community of interest for the parties to be held to be carrying on business 'in common'.[191]

[2.76] The case of *Re Hall*[192] involved a business which satisfied the other five requirements of the definition of partnership, but not the requirement that the parties be carrying on business in common. It involved an alleged partnership between Hall and Mallinson in a wholesale woollen business at 9 William Street in Dublin. It was agreed that Mallinson was to manage the business for a year, with a view to seeing whether he wished to become a partner, in which case he would be entitled to a share of the profits. This option was never exercised by Mallinson. On the bankruptcy of Hall, his creditors sought to have moneys owed by Hall to Mallinson subordinated to their debts, on the basis that Mallinson had been in partnership with Hall.[193] However, Brady LC held that no partnership existed on the grounds, inter alia, that:

---

189 *Re Boyle* [1947] IR 61.

190 Similarly, in *Sim v Sim* (1861) 11 Ir Ch R 310, Sim snr had stated in his letter to Sim jnr that he would act 'merely as agent for you' and Smith MR held that no partnership existed, see para **[2.85]**.

191 In *Hanna v Barnes* (26 June 1992) HC NI, Campbell J held that the relationship between the parties was consistent with partnership rather than employer/employee. The factors supporting this conclusion were the contribution by Hanna of his redundancy money to the business, the use by Barnes of the term 'partner' to describe Hanna (albeit on one occasion) and Barnes's leaving three signed cheques with Hanna one of which was used by Hanna for his personal use (thus indicating that Hanna considered himself a partner).

192 *Re Hall* (1864) Ir Ch R 287.

193 This principle whereby a bankrupt partner's debt to his co-partner is subordinated to the debts of the bankrupt partner which are owed to third parties, is considered in detail at para **[27.124]** et seq.

    (i)   Mallinson simply was managing Hall's business for a year;

    (ii)   he did not, in his own name, deal with any customer of the business 'as he would have done if he had been a partner';[194]

    (iii) the name of the firm had not been changed; and

    (iv) he did not sign any bills, letters or other formal documents on behalf of the enterprise.[195]

[2.77] A contrasting case is that of *Greenham v Gray*,[196] in which the parties were held to be carrying on business in common. This case involved an agreement between the plaintiff and the defendant to carry on the trade of cotton-spinning in a mill in Drogheda. The agreement provided that the defendant was to provide the mill in which the enterprise was to be run, while the plaintiff was to have the entire control and management of the business and that he was not to engage in any other trade. The plaintiff claimed a share of the profits in the enterprise on the grounds that he was a partner, while the defendant alleged that the relationship was one of employer/employee. Greene B[197] held that the following factors were inconsistent with the relationship of master and servant. Instead he held that the parties were partners as 'all the clauses taken together prove that it was the intention of the parties to carry on trade together':[198]

    (i)   the plaintiff was to have the entire control and management of the business;

    (ii)   accounts were to be tendered to both the plaintiff and the defendant;

    (iii) the plaintiff was to be paid a salary and one fifth of the profits;

    (iv) the plaintiff was in no way subordinate to the defendant; and

    (v)   each was to have a say in the possible extension of the business.

Contribution of capital is not required for partnership

[2.78] *Greenham v Gray*[199] also highlights that a person may be a partner in a concern, without having to contribute capital, since a partnership was held to exist where Gray contributed all of the capital to the firm in the shape of a mill in Drogheda, while Greenham agreed simply to devote his skill and effort to running the mill. In *Griffin v Minister for Social, Community and Family Affairs* and *Deasy v Minister for Social, Community and Family Affairs*,[200] Carroll J criticised the decision of the Appeals Officer who had concluded that a share fisherman was not an investor in an enterprise because he had not invested capital in it, noting that '… [it] is a mistake of law to conclude that there cannot be a joint enterprise/partnership unless there is a capital investment'. Mr

194 *Re Hall* (1864) Ir Ch R 287 at 301.

195 See also para **[21.89]** where it is contended that if one partner was allowed to prevent the other partner from knowing the true state of affairs of the business, they would not be 'carrying on a business in common' in the true sense of that expression. On this basis, it is contended that the obligation of a partner to render true accounts to his co-partners under s 28 of the 1890 Act is irrevocable.

196 *Greenham v Gray* (1855) 4 Ir CLR 501.

197 Pennefather and Richards BB, concurring.

198 *Greenham v Gray* (1855) 4 Ir CLR 501 at 509.

199 *Greenham v Gray* (1855) 4 Ir CLR 501.

200 *Griffin v Minister for Social, Community and Family Affairs and Deasy v Minister for Social, Community and Family Affairs* (2 October 2001) HC.

Coakley had provided labour, oilskins and knives to the enterprise, which the Appeals Officer had concluded were not an investment. Carroll J disagreed, finding that the Appeals Officer was mistaken in his conclusion that the provision of labour is insufficient to sustain a relationship of joint enterprise or partnership, citing the examples of firms of solicitors and firms of accountants, where some partners may contribute premises, and others may contribute labour. The English courts have also recently reiterated that a capital contribution is not required for a partnership to exist. In *M Young Legal Associates Ltd v Zahid*,[201] while Wilson LJ acknowledged that the fact that a person did not contribute capital to the firm pointed to the absence of partnership, a partnership was found to exist having regard to all of the features of the agreement entered into between the parties. Equally, the contribution of capital by a party to an enterprise is not conclusive evidence of partnership.[202]

One partner with complete control of business?

[2.79] The interesting case of *O'Dwyer, Inspector of Taxes v Cafolla & Co*[203] considered a partnership in which one partner had effective control over all the operations of the business. The partnership resulted from the decision of Mr Cafolla to convert his business from that of a sole trader to a partnership with his sons. It appears that one of the primary reasons for this change was for the business to benefit from the tax-free allowances of each of his sons. However, under the terms of the partnership agreement, Mr Cafolla had almost complete control of the business, since he retained ownership of the premises in which the business was being carried on, he retained ownership of all capital, assets and the goodwill, and was the only signatory on the bank account. He had the right at any time to deal in any way with the assets of the partnership by way of loan, mortgage or compromise. He alone was entitled to employ and dismiss staff and enter contracts on behalf of the firm. The other partners were entitled to draw on the partnership account at any time, but only by cheque drawn by Mr Cafolla and for amounts approved by him. In addition, he had the right at any time to bring the partnership to an end and instead to resume carrying on the business for his sole benefit. The Revenue Commissioners claimed unsuccessfully that in these circumstances, the income of the partnership should be deemed to be the income of Mr Cafolla. As regards the question of the existence of the partnership, it was held by the Special Commissioner of the Revenue, and not subsequently challenged in the High Court or the Supreme Court, that a partnership existed in this case. Indeed in the High Court, Maguire J indicated that there was abundant evidence for such a finding.[204] However, it is seriously doubted whether this case should be followed. While the partnership agreement described each of the sons as partners, it is doubted that there was sufficient evidence of a community of interest in the business, in the sense of control over its operation, for

---

[201] *M Young Legal Associates Ltd v Zahid* [2006] 1 WLR 2562 (CA).

[202] See for example *Pilsworth v Mosse* (1863) 14 Ir Ch R 163, in which capital was contributed by a father on behalf of his son and his son was credited in the partnership books with that capital, but the partnership was held to be with the father. See further para **[2.20]**.

[203] *O'Dwyer, Inspector of Taxes v Cafolla & Co* [1949] IR 210.

[204] *O'Dwyer, Inspector of Taxes v Cafolla & Co* [1949] IR 210 at 222. Although the decision of Maguire J was overturned on appeal by the Supreme Court, the Supreme Court did not disagree with his conclusions regarding the existence of a partnership.

there to have been a partnership. In addition, the mutual agency which should exist between partners was absent, since only Mr Cafolla was entitled to enter contracts on behalf of the firm. For this reason, it is suggested that this decision should not be followed insofar as it treats such a partnership as valid.

Existing business becoming a business in common

[2.80] The issue of whether a partnership exists may sometimes arise in the context of a sole trader's business which is expanded by the admission of third parties, who up to that time had been employees of the sole trader. In such a situation, one must look for perceptible differences in both the inner operations and the outward appearance of the firm to support a finding that the business is now being carried on in common. *Macken v Revenue Commissioners*[205] concerned an oral agreement between Mr Macken, his daughter and his son, whereby Mr Macken agreed to admit his daughter and son as partners into his painting business which, up to then, he had operated as a sole trader. The question for the High Court was whether after the date of the oral agreement the business continued to be carried on as a sole trader or whether the parties were carrying on the business 'in common'. The Revenue Commissioners claimed that no partnership existed at the date of the oral agreement, but that the transfer of the father's business to his children took place on the date of execution of the partnership agreement, a number of months later, and estate duty was to be assessed on this basis. The profits of the business were in fact shared between the three parties for the period between the oral agreement and the written agreement, and the Revenue Commissioners, in assessing income tax, treated the three parties as partners. Nonetheless, Teevan J held that the oral agreement was simply an agreement to enter partnership at a future date and that the partnership did not commence at that time. The parties were not carrying on business in common since there had been no perceptible change in the manner in which the business was carried on after the oral agreement. In addition, the parties had not reached agreement at that time on one of the vital terms of the agreement, namely a determination of which assets were to be brought into the partnership. The other factors considered by Teevan J in determining whether a partnership existed can be framed as questions which may provide assistance[206] in determining whether a business is being carried on in common after a pre-existing business purportedly admits a partner:

---

[205] *Macken v Revenue Commissioners* [1962] IR 302.

[206] This list is neither an exhaustive list of factors nor, in the case of affirmative responses, conclusive evidence that the parties are in partnership. For example in *O'Kelly v Darragh* [1988] ILRM 309, the plaintiff was a co-signatory on the bank account, he supervised the business and received a share of the profits but he was held not to be a partner. In that case, other relevant factors in determining that there was no partnership were the fact that the plaintiff was not involved in the negotiations and agreements for the business of the firm or in getting funds or contract work, see para **[2.118]**. The recent decision of the First Tier Tribunal Tax Chamber in *Ashton v Revenue and Customs Commissioners* [2016] UKFTT 727 (TC) is also of interest when considering whether parties are carrying on a business 'in common' where certain evidence points towards this being the case, and other evidence points towards the 'in common' requirement not being met. In that case, Mr Ashton was an employee of a martial arts instruction business, which had expanded to admit certain employees as partners. Mr Ashton appealed against a decision of HM Revenue and Customs to treat him as self-employed (ie as a partner) rather than as an employee. (contd.../)

(i)   Has the business name of the firm been changed?[207]

(ii)   Are the bank accounts in the names of the purported partners?[208]

(iii) Have notices been issued to those parties who had been contracting with the pre-existing business to advise them of the change in structure?

(iv)   Has a transfer of debts from the pre-existing business to the new business taken place?

(v)   If the pre-existing business was a partnership, has a registration in the Register of Business Names[209] been effected?

(vi)   How was the relationship between the parties treated by the Revenue Commissioners for tax purposes?[210]

---

[206] (\...contd) While the Tribunal found that Mr Ashton had been an employee, but had later completed tax returns on the basis that he was a partner, it also found that he had not signed a partnership agreement, had never received partnership accounts, was not involved in partnership meetings, was paid a bonus based on turnover rather than profits, met his own business expenses and while he was a signatory on the partnership account, had no control over its operation. As such, Mr Ashton was found not to be 'carrying on business in common' with the partners in the firm.

[207] The absence of this factor was relied upon in determining that no partnership existed in *Re Hall* (1864) Ir Ch R 287, see para **[2.76]**.

[208] See also *MacCarthaigh v Daly* [1985] IR 73 in which O'Hanlon J supported his finding that a partnership existed between seven individuals and a company on the grounds that (a) a bank account was opened in the name of the firm, (b) those who adopted the firm name held themselves out as partners to the Revenue Commissioners for VAT purposes and (c) those who adopted the firm name held themselves out as partners to their bank. O'Hanlon J had however reservations about whether the partnership satisfied the fifth requirement of the definition of partnership, see para **[2.66]**. See also the English cases of *Jackson v White and Midland Bank* [1967] 2 Lloyd's Rep 68 (joint bank account was not even prima facie evidence of the existence of a partnership) and *Waddington v O'Callaghan* (1931) 16 TC 187; cf *Dungate v Lee* [1967] 1 All ER 241 where a partnership was found to exist between the parties although the bank account was opened in the defendant's name only. See also the Scottish case of *Saywell v Pope* [1979] STC 824 (absence of a joint bank account may be evidence against the existence of a partnership) and *Northern Bank Ltd v McNeill* (14 February 1986) HC NI. In the latter case, a wife was claiming that the family property was partnership property so as to defeat the claim of the plaintiff bank which wished to rely on it as security for her husband's debts. In addition to relying on the absence of a joint bank account, Murray J found that there was no partnership by relying on the fact that the wife did not consider joining in on a mortgage of the property for the benefit of the business, she was not listed as a partner in the accounts and the husband gave a charge over the property without even consulting with her.

[209] Under the Registration of Business Names Act 1963, s 1, a partnership which is carrying on business under a name other than the names of all the partners must register that name within one month of the adoption of that name. See generally in relation to the application of this Act to partnerships, para **[3.70]** et seq.

[210] This criterion was also used in *MacCarthaigh v Daly* [1985] IR 73, but cf *Moore v Moore* (27 February 1998) HC NI in which Master Ellison noted that there was a partnership between the parties as regards a dairy farm but not as regards a pig breeding business or a barley growing business which were run by the partners individually, although the parties were treated as partners for accountancy and tax purposes in relation to all three businesses.

Where person's name is part of firm name

[2.81] One of the stronger indications of the fact that a person is a partner is the use of the alleged partner's name in the name of the enterprise. However, this will not of course be conclusive evidence of partnership. In *Martin v Sherry*,[211] a client of a solicitor, who was based in Armagh, alleged that the solicitor (Joshua E Peel) was not entitled to his costs as he was a member of a firm (Joshua E Peel & Son) in which one partner (his son, John Peel) had failed to take out his practising certificate for a 10-month period during which the costs were incurred.[212] The Taxing Officer upheld the claim on the grounds that when the costs were earned, the son was a partner. In the Irish Court of Appeal[213] this decision was overturned and it was held that the use of the business name, Joshua E Peel & Son, did not make the son a partner in the firm. Holmes LJ stated:

> 'I have formed the opinion that his son is in no sense of the word a partner in the business ... It is true that the business was carried on in the name of Peel & Son; but this gave the young man no interest in the earnings of the office.'[214]

The other factors which were relevant to the holding that the son was not a partner were that:

  (i)   no deed of partnership was executed;

  (ii) the son did not receive a division of the profits;

 (iii) the son was given no share in the business; and

 (iv) the business continued to be the sole property of the father.

The same principle would apply to a case where the son's name had actually been used, rather than the term '& Son', so that, while this would be stronger evidence of partnership, it would also not be conclusive.

[2.82] Finally, it goes without saying that the absence of some of the foregoing factors which have been held by the courts to be indicators of partnership will not be fatal to the success of a particular case. To illustrate this point, one might consider one such common indicator of partnership, ie the existence of joint bank account in the firm name. This will often be a significant factor in determining the existence of a partnership. Yet in *Re Ferrar, ex p Ulster Banking Company*[215] no bank account was opened by Simms and Ferrar in the name of Simms and Ferrar. Rather, Simms and Ferrar owned and ran their business, namely the publication of a newspaper called the *Belfast Mercury* under the style of 'Simms and Ferrar' and each had a separate account with the bank. It was nonetheless accepted by Macan J that there was a partnership between them.

---

[211] *Martin v Sherry* [1905] 2 IR 62.

[212] Under s 48 of the Solicitor Act Ireland 1898 (61 & 62 Vict, c 17), each member of the firm had to hold a valid practising certificate for costs to be recoverable.

[213] Ashbourne LC and Holmes LJ.

[214] *Martin v Sherry* [1905] 2 IR 62 at 68–69.

[215] *Re Ferrar, ex p Ulster Banking Company* (1859) 9 Ir Ch R 11.

II.　RULES FOR DETERMINING THE EXISTENCE OF A PARTNERSHIP

[2.83] Where the six requirements of the definition of partnership in s 1(1) are clearly satisfied, a partnership will exist and no reference need be made to the rules for determining the existence of a partnership in s 2 of the 1890 Act. However, where one or more of these requirements is not clearly satisfied, most usually the requirement that the parties are acting 'in common', the eight rules listed in s 2 will be of assistance. In addition to these eight rules there is what may be termed the main rule for determining the existence of a partnership, which will be considered first.

Main Rule in Determining the Existence of a Partnership

[2.84] In considering the rules for determining the existence of a partnership in s 2 of 1890 Act, one should bear in mind that these rules are simply aimed at assisting the courts in the application of what has been termed the 'main rule' for determining the existence of a partnership. This rule, although arguably self-evident, was adopted by Costello J in *DPP v McLoughlin*[216] in the following terms:

> 'the main rule to be observed in determining the existence of a partnership, a rule which has been recognised ever since the case of *Cox v Hickman* (1860) 8 HLC 268, is that regard must be paid to the true contract and intention of the parties as appearing from the whole facts of the case.'[217]

It follows that in considering the presence or absence of such factors as the mutual agency of the parties, community of interest, control of the business, sharing of profits, sharing of losses, etc, these factors will not be conclusive in determining whether a partnership exists. Rather, each case must be decided on its own facts and in light of the surrounding circumstances and intentions of the parties.

Admissibility of evidence of partnership

[2.85] In general terms, there would appear to be no restriction on the evidence which a person can produce in support of his claim of partnership. However in *Sim v Sim*,[218] the only evidence produced by the plaintiff as to the existence of a corn-milling partnership in Colooney, Co Sligo with the defendant, were books of an account of the transactions in respect of which the partnership was alleged to exist and drawn up by the plaintiff in his own handwriting. Smith MR held that where a partnership was established, the books of account of the plaintiff would be admissible in evidence as to the terms of the partnership. However, they were not admissible as evidence of the existence of the partnership, where the plaintiff alleged a partnership, while the defendant denied its existence. It is doubted whether this approach is of general application and it is thought that the better approach would be to admit such accounts as evidence of the purported

---

[216] *DPP v McLoughlin* [1986] IR 355.

[217] *DPP v McLoughlin* [1986] IR 355 at 360, quoting from Scammel and l'Anson Banks, *Lindley & Banks on Partnership* (14th edn, 1979) at p 70. See also the statement of Carroll J in *O'Kelly v Darragh* [1988] ILRM 309 at 317: 'The terms of the arrangement between the parties must fairly be considered as a whole.'

[218] *Sim v Sim* (1861) 11 Ir Ch R 310. Note that in that case, the partnership is described as a limited partnership, by which was meant a partnership of limited duration and not a limited partnership, which was first created by the Limited Partnerships Act 1907.

partnership, but to treat them with caution if they are prepared by one party only as clearly they would not constitute sufficient evidence on their own, to establish the existence of a partnership.

Role of conduct of partners in interpreting agreement

[2.86] The terms of any written agreement will, of course, play an important role in determining whether the parties to that agreement are in fact partners. However, the terms thereof will not be conclusive and the court will take into account the actual conduct of the enterprise by the partners to determine if there is a genuine partnership. In *Barklie v Scott*,[219] Jebb J adopted the following statement in relation to the interpretation of written 'partnership' agreements:

'The law, as I apprehend, is, that the transactions of partners are always to be looked at, in order that you may determine between them, *even against the written articles*, what clauses in those articles will bind them, provided those transactions afford higher probability amounting almost to demonstration.'[220]

Thus, although the written agreement in that case provided that the firm was to be governed and directed by the defendant and that accounts were to be furnished to him, the fact that, inter alia, the partners in the firm did not treat him as a partner vitiated a finding of partnership.[221]

Stranger to bankruptcy proceedings cannot be declared a partner

[2.87] It is also to be noted that a bankruptcy court does not have the power to declare a person a bankrupt by making a declaratory order of partnership against a stranger to the bankruptcy proceedings, albeit a partner of the bankrupt. *Re Harris*[222] concerned the bankruptcy of Ms Harris who carried on a garage business in Lower Castlereagh, Co Down. At the bankruptcy hearing it transpired that Mr Rand carried on business with Ms Harris and the bankruptcy judge made an order that Mr Rand, at the time of the adjudication of Ms Harris, was her partner, and that therefore he also should be adjudged a bankrupt. Mr Rand appealed to the Northern Ireland Court of Appeal which noted that he had not committed any act of bankruptcy. Andrews LCJ (Best and Babington LJJ, concurring) held that the bankruptcy court had no jurisdiction[223] to make a declaratory order of partnership against Mr Rand, who was a stranger to those proceedings.[224]

---

[219] *Barklie v Scott* (1827) 1 Hud and Bro 83.

[220] *Barklie v Scott* (1827) 1 Hud and Bro 83 at 96, where Jebb J quotes from Lord Eldon in *Geddes v Wallace* (1820) 2 Bli 270.

[221] The other factors are listed at para **[2.21]**.

[222] *Re Harris* [1939] NI 1.

[223] Under the Bankruptcy (Ireland) Amendment Act 1872, s 66 (general powers of court). This section was repealed in Ireland by the Bankruptcy Act 1988, s 6, but similar powers are now contained in the Bankruptcy Act 1988, ss 135–138.

[224] Andrews LCJ relied on the judgment of Lord Selborne in *Ellis v Silber* (1872) LR 8 Ch AC 83 at 86. Note however that a bankruptcy court is entitled to declare that the debts owed to a person by the bankrupt are deferred to those of other creditors on the grounds that this person is a partner. See for example the cases of *Re Borthwick* (1875) ILTR 155 and *Re Hall* (1864) Ir Ch R 287 and see generally para **[27.124]**.

Rules in 1890 Act for Determining the Existence of a Partnership

[2.88] The rules set out in s 2 of the 1890 Act are aimed at assisting the courts in determining whether the parties are carrying on business 'in common' and thus in determining the existence of a partnership. The section does this by setting out certain situations which have the appearance of partnership (ie the co-ownership of property or the sharing of profits of a business) but which are not sufficient by themselves to satisfy the requirement that the parties be carrying on business in common. Each of the subsections of s 2 will be examined in turn but it is helpful to first set out this section in full:

> In determining whether a partnership does or does not exist, regard shall be had to the following rules:
>
> (1)   Joint tenancy, tenancy in common, joint property, common property, or part ownership does not of itself create a partnership as to anything so held or owned, whether the tenants or owners do or do not share any profits made by the use thereof.
>
> (2)   The sharing of gross returns does not of itself create a partnership, whether the persons sharing such returns have or have not a joint or common right or interest in any property from which or from the use of which the returns are derived.
>
> (3)   The receipt by a person of a share of the profits of a business is *prima facie* evidence that he is a partner in the business, but the receipt of such a share, or of a payment contingent on or varying with the profits of a business, does not of itself make him a partner in the business; and in particular -
>
>   (a)   The receipt by a person of a debt or other liquidated amount by instalments or otherwise out of the accruing profits of a business does not of itself make him a partner in the business or liable as such:
>
>   (b)   A contract for the remuneration of a servant or agent of a person engaged in business by a share in the profits of the business does not of itself make the servant or agent a partner in the business or liable as such:
>
>   (c)   A person being the widow or child of a deceased partner, and receiving by way of annuity a portion of the profits made in the business in which the deceased person was a partner, is not by reason only of such receipt a partner in the business or liable as such:
>
>   (d)   The advance of money by way of a loan to a person engaged or about to engage in any business on a contract with that person that the lender shall receive a rate of interest varying with the profits, or shall receive a share of the profits arising from carrying on the business, does not of itself make the lender a partner with the person or persons carrying on the business or liable as such. Provided that the contract is in writing, and signed by or on behalf of all the parties thereto:
>
>   (e)   A person receiving by way of annuity or otherwise a portion of the profits of a business in consideration of the sale by him of the goodwill of the business is not by reason only of such receipt a partner in the business or liable a such.

(i) Section 2(1) – co-ownership does not of itself create a partnership

[2.89] Section 2(1) of the 1890 Act establishes that co-ownership does not of itself create a partnership between the co-owners *as to property so owned*, even where the co-owners share the profits derived from the use of the property which is co-owned. This section highlights the essential distinction between co-ownership of property which is used in a partnership business (which is not a necessary requirement for a partnership to exist between the parties) and co-ownership of the partnership business which is an important indicator that the parties are carrying on business in common.[225] It is, however, important to note that s 2(1) does not mean that co-owners of a property cannot be in partnership with one another. Even if parties to a property investment describe themselves as a 'co-ownership', they will constitute a partnership if they meet the six separate requirements of the definition of 'partnership' in s 1(1) of the 1890 Act.[226]

[2.90] In *Re Christie*,[227] two brothers, who were co-owners of a farm in Co Antrim, were held not to be partners as to the farm so held. They were, however, held to be partners as to the farming stock and the profits derived from the property. In *Delande v Delahunty*,[228] three individuals, including Delande and Delahunty, were part owners of a ship. On an unprofitable voyage of the ship, Delande made disbursements in his capacity as the ship's manager which were not authorised by Delahunty. Delande sought to recover part of these disbursements from Delahunty on the basis that there existed a partnership between them in the ship and Delahunty was jointly liable for the disbursements. Brady LC held that Delahunty, though a part-owner of the ship, was not a partner of Delande and accordingly was not liable for the disbursements.[229]

---

[225] The distinction between a co-ownership and a partnership was briefly referred to by Finlay Geoghegan J in *Allied Irish Banks plc v Galvin Developments (Killarney) Limited & ors* [2011] IEHC 314 where she noted that the parties had agreed to proceed with their plans for property development using a co-ownership structure in which each party would acquire a 50% interest and would be liable for 50% of the liabilities, rather than using a partnership structure in which 'each side of the joint venture would have been liable for the entire debts of the partnership'.

[226] See further para **[2.09]**.

[227] *Re Christie* [1917] 1 IR 17. See also *Walsh v Walsh* [1942] IR 403 at 411, in which Gavan Duffy J held that, in relation to a dispute between family members regarding the profits of the family farm, 'the true relationship, as a matter of law, was that of co-owners of the common undertaking, and that this co-ownership constituted no partnership.' See further para **[2.53]**.

[228] *Delande v Delahunty* (1857) 5 Ir Jur (ns) 162.

[229] He relied expressly on *Green v Briggs* (1848) 6 Hare 395. A reference to the possibility of there being co-owners of property, who are not partners, was also made in the dissenting judgment of McCarthy J in the Supreme Court case of *Revenue Commissioners v O'Reilly & McGilligan* [1984] ILRM 406. In that case, McCarthy J argued that the term 'body of persons' (in legislation exempting such bodies of persons from income tax) meant any number more than one. In support of his interpretation, he gave the example of co-owners, who were not partners. He observed that if the term 'body of persons' did not include two persons, then it would be possible that 'two persons jointly engaged in the ownership of securities paying interest not deductible at source would enjoy an immunity from tax if they can contrive not to constitute a partnership' ([1984] ILRM 406 at 411–412). (contd.../)

Co-ownership is not required for partnership

[2.91] Section s 2(1) of the 1890 Act states that co-ownership of property alone does not create a partnership as regards that property. Equally, it should be obvious that co-ownership is not a necessary ingredient for partnership.[230] Thus in *Greenham v Gray*[231] a partnership was held to exist between Mr Gray who owned the mill and the plaintiff who had no ownership rights in the mill, but who managed the mill.[232]

(ii) Section 2(2) – sharing gross returns does not create partnership

[2.92] Section 2(2) of the 1890 Act states that the sharing of gross returns does not of itself constitute a partnership between the parties thereto. Gross returns are different from profits, since the profits (or net profits) of a business are the gross returns less the amount of any advances made in that business. For this reason a reference to profits in the 1890 Act is generally to be taken as meaning the net profits. The classic example of a person who shares gross returns is a sales person who is paid a commission for the number of sales made by him, regardless of whether the owner's business makes an overall profit or not. Unlike the receipt of profits, which, as will be seen hereafter, is prima facie evidence of partnership,[233] the receipt of gross returns does not give rise to such a presumption. Rather, s 2(2) provides that the sharing of gross returns does not *of*

---

229 (\...contd) Decisions of courts in other common law jurisdictions where partnership legislation is based on the 1890 Act also merit consideration when considering whether co-owners are, or are not, partners. For example in the Canadian case of *Volzke Construction Limited v Westlock Foods* (1986) 4 WWR 688, the Alberta Court of Appeal held that a partnership existed between Volzke Construction and Westlock Foods (who owned 80% and 20% (respectively) of a shopping centre). Factors which led the Alberta Court of Appeal to its decision were that Volzke Construction and Westlock Foods shared profits jointly, co-owned the property, had a bank account in joint names and had jointly financed the project. The New Zealand courts reached a similar decision in *National Insurance Co of New Zealand v Bray* [1934] NZLR 67. In that case, a syndicate was formed for the purpose of investing in property, with the property being held by a Mr Wheatley on behalf of the syndicate. The plaintiff took an action against Mr Wheatley as a partner in the syndicate for moneys owed by Mr Wheatley to the plaintiff under a contract relating to the property. The court held that the syndicate members were partners, and the plaintiff's action succeeded.

230 The same applies for the other rules in s 2 of the 1890 Act, ie that their corollory does not apply. Note, however, that it is submitted at para **[2.101]** that the corollary of the *presumption* in s 2(3) applies so that the absence of a sharing of profits raises a rebuttable presumption of no partnership.

231 *Greenham v Gray* (1855) 4 Ir CLR 501.

232 See also the English case of *Walker West Developments v FJ Emmet* (1978) 252 EG 1171, in which an arrangement between a builder (who had purchased the land in question) and a developer (to whom the builder contracted to sell that land) that various houses be built by the builder, and sold by the developer, with the profits shared between them, was found to be a partnership. A similar finding had previously been made in *Fenston v Johnstone (Inspector of Taxes)* (1940) 23 TC 29. In that case, a partnership was found to exist between Mr Fenston and Mr Shaw (who had purchased land sourced by Mr Fenston, when Mr Fenston was unable to raise enough money to fund the purchase himself). Mr Shaw and Mr Fenston had agreed that profits and losses arising from the venture would be shared equally.

233 Partnership Act 1890, s 2(3).

itself create a partnership, whether the parties are co-owners of the property which produces the returns or not. The logic for making a person, who shares profits, prima facie a partner, but not a person who shares gross returns, is that a person who shares in the net profits of a business will have an incentive to keep expenses to a minimum and will invariably have a greater degree of control over the running of that business. As such, he is likely to have the requisite community of interest or control to be a partner, unlike a person who is merely concerned about the gross returns of the business.

[2.93] *Lyon v Knowles*[234] is an example of a case in which there was a sharing of gross returns and no partnership between the parties. In that case, Knowles, the owner of a theatre leased the theatre to Dillon, the producer of a play. The owner was to be paid for the letting by a division between the parties of the amount paid by the public to see the plays. Dillon provided the company of actors, selected the plays to be performed and managed the performance. Knowles paid for the printing and advertising, lighting and the doorkeeper. It was held that this sharing of the gross returns did not create a partnership between the owner and the producer. It should be noted that unlike the case of a sharing of net profits, this arrangement might have resulted in Knowles making a profit out of the venture, while Dillon might make a loss or *vice-versa*, in light of their differing expenses, thus vitiating a finding of partnership.

Franchise agreements

[2.94] It remains to be observed that franchisers will often fall into the category of persons who share the gross returns of a business. Under franchise agreements, the franchiser will usually receive a royalty or fee out of the gross returns of the franchisee's business.[235] It is most unusual for franchisers to share in the net profits of a franchisee's business and it is apprehended that these arrangements will rarely have a sufficient degree of proximity between the franchiser and franchisee for them to be carrying on business in common so as to constitute a partnership.

(iii) Section 2(3) – sharing profits is prima facie evidence of partnership

[2.95] Section 2(3) of the 1890 Act provides that the receipt of a share of the profits of a business is prima facie evidence of partnership, but that the receipt alone of such profits does not of itself make the recipient a partner. Although the sharing of profits is an important factor in establishing partnership, the reason why the sharing of profits is not conclusive evidence of partnership is because, as has been noted, the theoretical basis for partnership does not rest in the sharing of profits but rather in the fact that partners carry on business in common.[236] Thus, persons may well share profits of a business venture, but if they do not genuinely carry on business in common then there will be no

---

234   *Lyon v Knowles* (1863) 3 B & Sm 556. See also *Cox v Coulson* [1916] 2 KB 177.

235   See generally in relation to franchise agreements, Ussher and O'Connor (eds), *Doing Business in Ireland* (1998) by Dunn at para 11.02 et seq.

236   Thus in *Bullen v Sharp* (1865) LR 1 CP 86 at 111, Blackburn J stated that: '[t]he true question is... whether the trade is carried on behalf of the person sought to be charged as a partner, the participation in profits being a most important element in determining that question, but not being itself decisive, the test being ... whether it is such a participation in profits as to constitute the relation of principal and agent between the person taking the profits and those actually carrying on the business.' (contd.../)

partnership, eg where the profits are received by them as an employee or consultant, but not as a partner.

Definition of 'profit'

[2.96] It is noted elsewhere that the Supreme Court has defined the term 'profit' as the increase in the value of the total assets of the business, allowance being made for any capital introduced or taken out.[237]

'prima facie evidence'

[2.97] Section 2(3) is curiously drafted. On the one hand it states that the receipt of a share of the profits of a firm is prima facie evidence of partnership. The section then goes on to state that the receipt of a share of profits does not *of itself* make the recipient a partner. This section does not mean that a person is presumed to be a partner where he receives a share of the profits of a business, if no contrary evidence is forthcoming.[238] Invariably, however, the matter will not stop there, as there will be circumstances explaining the decision to share the profits, which will require careful consideration. Rather this section must be taken to mean that the receipt of a share of the profits of a business is simply strong evidence in support of a claim of partnership, but it is not in itself sufficient.[239] This conclusion may be supported in principle, since what makes people partners is not their sharing of a financial interest in a venture, but their joint control, mutual agency and community of interest, and people will commonly share the profits of an enterprise without having these other characteristics. This interpretation of s 2(3) is supported by the statement of Carroll J in *O'Kelly v Darragh*:[240]

> 'However the receipt of a share of the profits is only *prima facie* evidence; and the receipt
> of a share or payment contingent or varying with the profits does not of itself make
> someone a partner in a business (s 2(3) Partnership Act 1890). The terms of the
> arrangement between the parties must fairly be considered as a whole.'[241]

---

[236] (\...contd) See also *M Young Legal Associates v Zahid* [2006] 1 WLR 2562 (CA) and *Hodson v Hodson* [2009] EWHC 430 (Ch), each of which endorsed the view that the sharing of profits is not a prerequisite to the existence of a partnership – the 'view of profit' is essential, but the sharing of profit is not.

[237] Paragraph **[2.63]**.

[238] Since the key to partnership is not the sharing of profits, but the existence of a 'business in common' between the participants, see para **[2.68]**.

[239] Compare the working of s 202(c)(3) of the American Uniform Partnership Act (1997) (Last Amended 2013) which creates a rebuttable presumption of partnership by providing that '[a] person who receives a share of the profits of a business is presumed to be a partner in the business, unless the profits were received in payment: (A) of a debt by installments or otherwise; (B) for services as an independent contractor or of wages or other compensation to an employee; (C) of rent; (D) of an annuity or other retirement or health benefit to a deceased or retired partner or a beneficiary, representative, or designee of a deceased or retired partner; (E) of interest or other charge on a loan, even if the amount of payment varies with the profits of the business, including a direct or indirect present or future ownership of the collateral, or rights to income, proceeds, or increase in value derived from the collateral; or (F) for the sale of the goodwill of a business or other property by installments or otherwise.'

[240] *O'Kelly v Darragh* [1988] ILRM 309.

[241] *O'Kelly v Darragh* [1988] ILRM 309 at 317.

[2.98] In that case, Dr O'Kelly and Dr Darragh shared the profits of an endocrine research business in St James's Hospital in Dublin. At times, the plaintiff received up to 50% of the profits of the business. Nonetheless, the High Court held that this fact was not sufficient evidence of the existence of a partnership and that the share of the profits was received by Dr O'Kelly in his capacity as an employee of the defendant.[242]

[2.99] The English case of *Pratt v Stick*[243] involved the sharing of profits on the sale of a medical practice. One doctor sold his practice to another, but agreed to reside in the house, from which he had practised for three months after the sale in order to introduce patients to the new doctor. It was agreed that he would be entitled to half of the profits and liable for half of the expenses of the practice during this period. Nonetheless, the court held that there was no partnership between the doctors, but that this was an agreement relating to the outright sale of the practice.[244]

[2.100] By way of contrast, in *Re Curry*,[245] the sharing of the profits of a business between Curry and Lever was assumed[246] to constitute a partnership between them. There the two parties had agreed that Mr Lever would write a novel, while Mr Curry would pay all the expenses of writing and publishing the novel. It was agreed that Curry would keep the profit on the first 11,000 sales and they would divide amongst themselves the net profits of the sales in excess of 11,000 copies.[247]

Where no sharing of profits

[2.101] Because of the importance[248] of the sharing of profits to the existence of partnership, it might be argued that where there is no sharing of the profits, it would be reasonable to presume that the parties are not partners. However, this should be no more than a presumption. This is because, while the sharing of profits is a very common

---

242 See further in relation to this aspect of the decision, para **[2.118]**.

243 *Pratt v Stick* (1932) 17 TC 459.

244 See also the judgment of Costello J in *DPP v McLoughlin* [1986] IR 355 at 360, where he quoted s 2(3) of the 1890 Act and added '[b]ut the existence of a profit-sharing term is not by any means conclusive'. The prima facie nature of the sharing of profits is also implicit in the judgment of Teevan J in *Macken v Revenue Commissioners* [1962] IR 302, who noted that the sharing of profits by the parties in that case was 'not of conclusive importance'. See para **[2.80]**.

245 *Re Curry* (1848) 12 Ir Eq R 382.

246 Indeed Macan C stated: 'Now, though I, disclaim all intention of deciding that such a participation in profits would establish a partnership, more especially in a case so peculiarly circumstanced ... yet I shall assume, for the purposes of my judgment, that Mr Lever was, in the strongest sense of the term, a partner' (*Re Curry* (1848) 12 Ir Eq R 382 at 384).

247 See also *Y v O'Sullivan* [1949] IR 264, in which the sharing of the profits of a business amongst residuary legatees was held to constitute a partnership.

248 See for example the statement of Lord Lindley in *Mollwo, March & Co v Court of Wards* (1872) LR 4 PC 419 that: '[a]n agreement that something shall be attempted with a view to gain, and that the gain shall be shared by the parties to the agreement, is the grand characteristic of every partnership, and is the leading feature of nearly every definition of the term.' See also *Martin v Sherry* [1905] 2 IR 62, where the absence of a sharing of the profits was crucial to the decision of the Irish Court of Appeal that there was no partnership, considered at para **[2.81]**.

incident of partnership, it is not a prerequisite of the definition of partnership which simply requires the parties to be carrying on business in common with a *view to profit*. In *M Young Legal Associates Ltd v Zahid*,[249] Wilson LJ referenced the decision in *Walker v Hirsch*[250] when stating that, when one says that participation in profits and losses is not determinative as to the existence of a partnership, this does not mean that such participation is even necessary, and agreed that the fact that a person is paid a specific sum of money for the work he does for a firm does not preclude him from being a partner in that firm. He noted that the wording 'Partnership is the relationship which subsists between persons carrying on a business in common with a view to profit' at s 1(1) of the 1890 Act is sufficiently wide so as to render a person, who receives a fixed payment, a partner, provided that a business is being carried on with a view to profit and, importantly, that the person is carrying on that business in common with another or others. Indeed, Hughes LJ in the same case held that the wording of s 1(1) of the 1890 Act removed any doubt on the question of whether profit sharing was a necessary ingredient of partnership, noting that while the making of profit is an aim of a partnership, the 1890 Act 'studiously abstain[ed] from reference to any necessity that it be shared'. Wilson LJ also reiterated the importance of looking at all of the features of the agreement between the parties when making a determination as to the existence of a partnership, rather than focusing on the apparent absence of a direct link between the fixed amount paid to the party asserting that he is not a partner, and the profits of the partnership.[251]

[2.102] While the carrying on of business with a 'view of profit' is an essential ingredient in a partnership, neither the sharing of profits nor the deriving of a benefit is a prerequisite to the existence of a partnership. In *Hodson v Hodson*,[252] the sixth defendant, Ms Rowlands, denied that she was a partner in a partnership (notwithstanding that she had signed a deed of partnership). She asserted that while she was entitled to 1% of the partnership's profits, this was a nominal amount that she had not received. However, she did acknowledge that she had, to a limited extent, benefitted from her association with the firm by receiving the benefit of the professional indemnity insurance policy taken out by it, and by being able to use the firm's client account for handling client monies. She had also been involved in the management of the firm for a period of time through her supervision of another partner. In his judgment, Arnold J held that Ms Rowlands was a partner at the relevant times and also observed however (in addition to endorsing the decision of Wilson LJ in *M Young Legal Associates Ltd v Zahid*[253] that the sharing of profits is not a prerequisite to the existence of a partnership) that: 'it is not a pre-requisite of partnership that a putative partner should derive benefit from the partnership...[more] importantly, it is again not a pre-requisite for a

---

[249] *M Young Legal Associates Ltd v Zahid* [2006] EWCA Civ 613.

[250] *Walker v Hirsch* (1884) 27 Ch D 460.

[251] In America, there is a rebuttable presumption that profit-sharing leads to a person being a partner in a business (s 202(c)(3) of the Uniform Partnership Act (1997) (Last Amended 2013)). Under the previous Uniform Partnership Act (1914), profit-sharing was instead prima facie evidence of a partnership.

[252] *Hodson v Hodson* [2009] EWHC 430 (Ch).

[253] *M Young Legal Associates Ltd v Zahid* [2006] EWCA Civ 613.

relationship of partnership to exist that one of the partners should also be involved in the management of the partnership.'

Sharing of profits and losses

[2.103] An agreement to share profits is prima facie evidence of partnership, since it is indicative of parties carrying on business in common. However, since the very basis of a business in common is one in which the risks and the rewards are shared, it follows that an agreement to share both profits and losses is an even stronger indication of partnership than an agreement to share profits alone.[254] Equally, however, it is to be noted that the sharing of profits and losses is not conclusive evidence of partnership.[255]

Where the parties share profits but not losses

[2.104] While the existence of a sharing of profits and losses is a strong indicator of a partnership,[256] parties may simply agree to share the profits only of a venture, with one of the parties being liable for any loss. In *Brophy v Holmes*,[257] it was held that no partnership existed between Brophy and Captain Holmes where they agreed to split the profits of a shipping venture to be undertaken by Captain Holmes. This was because Hart LC held that it was inconsistent with the existence of a partnership for Captain Holmes to be solely liable for any loss which resulted from the venture. However, this case cannot be regarded as supporting a principle that the absence of a sharing of losses means that there is no partnership. While it will be easier to prove that the parties are carrying on business in common where there is a sharing of both profits and losses,[258] it is certainly the case that a partnership may exist even where the parties do not share losses. *DPP v McLoughlin*[259] concerned fishing ventures between the skipper/owner of a fishing trawler and his five crew members. The skipper and the crew participated in regular fishing expeditions and the remuneration was agreed by them after the end of each voyage and was based solely on the value of the catch. The crew members were not required to contribute to any loss that may have been sustained on a voyage. In the High Court, Costello J noted that under s 2(3) of the 1890 Act, the sharing of profits was prima facie evidence of partnership and although the losses of the business were not

---

[254] Note that once a partnership is held to exist, the losses are assumed to be shared in the same proportion as the profits: *Re Albion Life Assurance Society* (1880) 16 Ch D 83 and see para **[14.26]**.

[255] *Walker v Hirsch* (1884) 27 Ch D 460, in which Baggallay LJ held that where there is an agreement under which the parties agree to share profits and bear losses in particular proportions, this would be prima facie evidence of an intention to conduct the business as a partnership, but that much will also depend on the general terms of that agreement.

[256] And the absence of a sharing of losses is strong evidence that the parties did not intend to form a partnership: see the American case of *Mill Factors' Corp v Margolies* (1924) 210 AD 739.

[257] *Brophy v Holmes* (1828) 1 Ir Law Rec 495.

[258] *Re Borthwick* (1875) ILTR 155, see para **[2.112]** and *O'Kelly v Darragh* [1986] IR 355, see para **[2.118]** are examples of cases where the absence of any sharing in the losses was a significant factor in the courts' decisions to hold that there was no partnership.

[259] *DPP v McLoughlin* [1986] IR 355. See also Cousins, 'Social Welfare – Persons Engaged in Share Fishing: Employees or Self-employed?' (1994) DULJ 207.

shared, he held that the relationship between the skipper and the crew was a partnership.[260]

Occasional 'coming together' to work as a team and share net profits does not equate to partnership where no sharing of losses or liabilities

[2.105] In *Marsella v J&P Construction Limited*,[261] Peart J considered the relationship between the plaintiff, Mr Marsella, and a third party, Mr O'Grady. Both were plasterers who worked together as a team. There was no partnership agreement between them, but they shared the profits of each job between them, net of overheads and other deductions. When Mr Marsella issued proceedings against the defendant company following a fall from a scaffolding platform, the defendant joined Mr O'Grady on the basis that he had employed Mr Marsella to work on the platform with him, and had assisted in the erection of that platform. In considering the nature of the relationship between Mr Marsella and Mr O'Grady, Peart J noted that it 'defied any strict legal categorisation', but that each was treated by the Revenue Commissioners as a registered subcontractor, and that their working relationship did not involve the assumption by either of them of '... the liability for each other's debts and obligations in the way normally understood in a partnership, and ... [their relationship also contained] a certain informal fluidity'. Peart J found that they were each self-employed persons who came together on occasion to work as a team, without forming a relationship of employer–employee or partnership.

Sharing profits of part of business only

[2.106] Section 2(3) of the 1890 Act simply refers to the sharing of the profits of 'a business' as being prima facie evidence of partnership. The question of whether the

---

[260] The reasons for his finding of partnership are outlined para **[2.116]**. In contrast, *Donnelly and Byrne v Hanlon* (1893) 27 ILTR 73 is an example of a share fishing case in which the crew was not liable to meet any losses from the voyages and this fact was used by the High Court to support a finding that the crew members were not partners with the master of the boat but rather his employees. This case was not considered in *DPP v McLoughlin* above. In this case, the master of the boat was also a part-owner of the boat and he deducted the costs of the expedition from the gross returns and kept half of the resulting profits for himself, the balance being shared equally amongst the crew. These contrasting cases illustrate the very fine line which can sometimes exist between a partnership relationship and an employer/employee relationship. The different conclusions can perhaps be explained by the different consequences of a finding of partnership. In *DPP v McLoughlin* above, a finding of partnership meant that the defendant was not guilty of the criminal offence of failing to make employee returns. In contrast in *Donnelly and Byrne v Hanlon*, a finding of partnership would have operated as a defence to the plaintiffs' civil action for their wages in the Petty Sessions Court which did not have jurisdiction to deal with an action between partners. See also *English Insurance Co v National Benefit Assurance Co (Official Receiver)* [1929] AC 114 where the House of Lords held that no partnership existed between two insurance companies who were parties to a re-insurance contract. The relationship was characterised as one where the plaintiff insurance company was carrying on the business of insurance as principal and the defendant insurance company was receiving a proportion of the premiums paid to the plaintiff insurance company less commission in consideration for the defendant's agreement to indemnify the plaintiff against a proportion of the losses suffered by it.

[261] *Marsella v J&P Construction Limited* [2004] IEHC 369.

sharing of the profits of part of a business only is sufficient to constitute partnership was raised, but not decided, in *Re Borthwick.*[262] However, it is contended that since s 2(3) is simply prima facie evidence of partnership, there is no reason in principle why a person, who shares in the profits of part only of a business, eg because of his specialised skills in that area, may not, in appropriate circumstances, be regarded as carrying on the whole business in common with the other participants or be a partner as to the relevant part of the business only.[263]

Does the sharing of profits imply a sharing also of losses?

[2.107] Once a partnership is held to exist, the 1890 Act provides that, in the absence of a contrary agreement between the partners, the losses of the firm are to be shared amongst the partners in the same proportion as the profits. A separate question is whether two parties, who share the profits of a business, which may or may not be a partnership, must be assumed to share the losses in the same proportion. In both *Greenham v Gray*[264] and in *Grantham v Redmond*[265] it was held that the sharing of profits implies a sharing of losses. However, it is clear from the more recent High Court case of *O'Kelly v Darragh*[266] that this is no longer a principle of Irish law and indeed is not a principle of law in most other jurisdictions.[267] In that case, the parties shared the profits of the business equally but had never discussed who would be liable for any losses, if the business was unprofitable. O'Hanlon J concluded that the plaintiff was not liable for the losses of the venture and for this and other reasons, he was not in partnership with the defendant.[268]

---

[262] *Re Borthwick* (1875) ILTR 155 at 155 where Harrison J noted that: '[w]ithout deciding whether the fact that Kirkpatrick was to get a share in the profits of part of the business only would, of itself, be sufficient to show that he was not a partner, I am clearly of opinion that, on the evidence before me, there was not such a relation between Kirkpatrick and the bankrupt as amounted to a partnership.'

[263] Support for this view is provided by *Moore v Moore* (27 February 1998) HC NI in which it was held that the parties were partners as to the dairy part of a family farm, but not as regards the pig-farming or barley and potato growing.

[264] *Greenham v Gray* (1855) 4 Ir CLR 501. There, Greene B (Richards and Pennefather BB, concurring) held that: '[t]here is no express provision in this contract as to loss, but there is no necessity for a stipulation about loss, if there be one about profits, for the one includes the other ... In the absence of such a stipulation, I am of the opinion that Mr. Greenham is liable for them by the right which the contract gives him to the profits.' ((1855) 4 Ir CLR 501 at 509–10.)

[265] *Grantham v Redmond* (1859) 8 Ir Ch R 449. There Napier LC held that: '[h]owever the net profits turn out, is it not plain that the person who has a right to a share of them must be subject to the liabilities of trade? It may be inconvenient, but there exists this clear principle of law, that the person who is entitled to a share of the profits is subject to liability.' ((1859) 8 Ir Ch R 449 at 453.)

[266] *O'Kelly v Darragh* [1988] ILRM 309.

[267] See for example the decision of *Sowman v David Samuel Trust Ltd (In liquidation)* [1978] 1 WLR 22.

[268] As to these other reasons, see para **[2.118]**.

The remaining subsections

[2.108] The five additional rules referred to in sub-ss (a) to (e) of s 2(3) of the 1890 Act are in fact simply illustrations of the general rule at the start of s 2(3), ie that the receipt of a share of the profits of a business is only prima facie evidence of partnership. These five additional rules are framed as negative statements that the receipt by a person of the profits of a business in the circumstances stated does not of itself make him a partner.

'Liable as such'

[2.109] In each of the five sub-ss (a) to (e) of s 2(3), a person who shares in the profits of a firm is stated not to be a partner or 'liable as such'. This wording can be explained by reference to the common law prior to the enactment of the 1890 Act. In fact these subsections are substantially the same as their predecessors, ss 1–5 of Bovill's Act of 1865.[269] The eighteenth century case of *Grace v Smith*[270] had established the principle that the recipient of a share of the profits of a business was liable for its debts and obligations, just as if he were a full partner. This principle became known as the doctrine of partners as to third persons. This doctrine was overruled in the seminal case of *Cox v Hickman*[271] and the use first in Bovill's Act and then in the 1890 Act of the words 'liable as such' simply reiterates the position at common law, that not only is a person not a partner in these situations, but he is also not liable as a partner.

[2.110] Each of these subsections will now be considered.

(iv) Section 2(3)(a) – payment of debt out of profits of business

[2.111] Section 2(3)(a) of the 1890 Act provides that the receipt of a debt out of the profits of a business does not of itself make the recipient a partner in that business.[272] In *O'Kelly v Darragh*,[273] which is considered below,[274] Carroll J relied on this subsection to observe that the plaintiff's share of the profits in the defendant's endocrine research business was not conclusive evidence of him being a partner, since 'the receipt of a share or payment contingent or varying with the profits does not of itself make someone a partner in a business'.[275]

[2.112] Similarly, *Re Borthwick*[276] may be seen as an example of the principle in s 2(3)(a). Kirkpatrick advanced £800 to Borthwick, a general merchant in Belfast. This

---

[269] An Act to amend the Law of Partnership of 1865 (28 & 29 Vict, c 86). See generally in relation to ss 1–5 of that Act, Anon, 'Loan to trader for share in profits' (1886) 20 ILT&SJ 507.

[270] *Grace v Smith* (1775) 2 Wm Bl 998, which was relied upon in *Waugh v Carver* (1793) 2 H Bl 235.

[271] *Cox v Hickman* (1860) 8 HLC 268. For a detailed analysis of the state of the law prior to *Cox v Hickman* see Scammell and l'Anson Banks, *Lindley & Banks on Partnership* (15th edn, 1984) at p 99 et seq.

[272] See also Anon, 'Loan to trader for share in profits' (1886) 20 ILT&SJ 507.

[273] *O'Kelly v Darragh* [1988] ILRM 309.

[274] Paragraph **[2.118]**.

[275] *O'Kelly v Darragh* [1988] ILRM 309 at 315.

[276] *Re Borthwick* (1875) ILTR 155. Although this case is primarily an example of one within the terms of s 2(3)(b) of the 1890 Act, see para **[2.113]**.

sum was to be used to purchase Irish flax for the business. It was agreed that Kirkpatrick was to be paid interest on this loan as well as half the profits derived from the sale of the flax. On the bankruptcy of Borthwick, it was alleged by his assignees in bankruptcy that Kirkpatrick, as a partner of Borthwick, should have his debt deferred to the other creditors of Borthwick.[277] Harrison J held that Kirkpatrick, although the recipient of a debt out of the profits of Borthwick's business, was not his partner.[278]

(v) Section 2(3)(b) – remuneration of employee out of profits of business

[2.113] Section 2(3)(b) of the 1890 Act provides that the remuneration of an employee by a share in the profits of the business does not of itself make the employee a partner in the business. In *Shaw v Galt*[279] the defendant sought to recover the amount of four bills of exchange which were drawn on the firm of J & W Wallace. As both J Wallace and W Wallace were discharged bankrupts, the plaintiff took an action against Galt, who he alleged was a partner in the firm. The question of whether Galt was a partner in the firm rested on the terms of agreement between J and W Wallace on the one hand and Galt on the other hand. This agreement provided for Galt to undertake services for J and W 'under the superintendence and direction' of J and W Wallace for a period of three years 'in consideration of salary and others'. The agreement also provided that J and W 'as co-partners, and as individuals, and their company firm' agreed to pay Galt a salary of £500 and also that he should be entitled to a sum equivalent to one third part of the net profits of the business, to be ascertained from accounts to be prepared by J and W Wallace. Before ascertaining the profits, both J and W Wallace were to be paid £500 each. In the High Court, O'Brien J[280] distinguished the case of *Greenham v Gray*[281] in which Mr Greenham was held to be a partner. There, Greenham was also paid a fixed sum and a share of the profits in return for his services, namely the managing of a mill. However unlike Galt, in *Greenham v Grey* the accounts of the business were to be tendered to Greenham and he had absolute control over and management of the business. In contrast, Galt's position was that of a servant operating under the direction of J and W Wallace. Accordingly, it was held that he received the share of the profits not 'as profits' but as remuneration in his capacity as an employee of the firm.[282]

[2.114] In the context of persons receiving a share of the profits as employees the reverse situation sometimes arises, ie where a partner (usually a managing partner) receives a payment, confusingly referred to as a 'salary', in addition to his share of the profits. It should be noted that this payment will not alter his status as a partner. As observed by Greene B in *Greenham v Gray*,[283] 'nothing is more common than a

---

[277] See generally in relation to the deferral of a partner's debts on the bankruptcy of his co-partner, para **[27.124]** et seq.

[278] He was held to be his employee, see further para **[2.123]**.

[279] *Shaw v Galt* (1863) 16 Ir CLR 357.

[280] Hayes and Fitzgerald JJ, concurring.

[281] *Greenham v Gray* (1855) 4 Ir CLR 501, see para **[2.77]**.

[282] See also the decision in *Re Borthwick* (1875) ILTR 155 where Kirkpatrick advanced £800 to Borthwick and was to be paid interest on that advance and a share of the profits in lieu of extra salary. He was held to be an employee and not a partner.

[283] *Greenham v Gray* (1855) 4 Ir CLR 501.

managing partner, and nothing unusual in an arrangement that he should receive something additional for his management'.[284]

Employee or partner?

[2.115] The question of whether the relationship between parties who carry on business together is that of partnership or of employer–employee will usually be determined in the context of s 2(3)(b) of the 1890 Act, since the alleged partner will often receive a share of the profits of the business. The rights and obligations of that person will vary considerably depending on whether he is an employee or a partner, so for example he will have the protection of employment legislation if he is an employee but not if he is a partner, while he will have a statutory right under the 1890 Act to a share in the profits of the enterprise if he is a partner but not if he is an employee. The difficulty of drawing a clear line between a partner and employee is illustrated by the different conclusions reached in *DPP v McLoughlin*[285] and *O'Kelly v Darragh.*[286]

[2.116] *DPP v McLoughlin*[287] examined the legal relationship between the skipper/owner of a fishing trawler and his five crew members. The skipper and the crew participated in regular fishing expeditions, although each weekly voyage was a separate venture and no crew member had a contract which entitled him to take part in a subsequent voyage. The crew members were not required to contribute to any loss that might be sustained on a voyage. However, they were not paid wages, but became entitled to a share in the net profits of the fishing expedition. If there was no profit on the catch, the crew received no money, but the skipper sometimes dispersed 'subs' to crew members in particular financial difficulties and these subs were treated in the nature of advances against future shares of the profits. The skipper exercised a large measure of control over the manner in which each member of the crew performed his work, though such control arose as much from the nature of the work as from the contractual relationship which existed. Costello J observed that the receipt of a share of the profits was prima facie evidence of partnership[288] and he held that the relationship between the skipper and the crew was not that of employer/employee but that of partnership. Of importance was the fact that each weekly voyage was a separate venture and no crew member had a contract which entitled him to take part in a subsequent voyage and he was not paid wages but a share of the profits. Of particular significance in Costello J's view was the fact that the skipper did not himself determine the rate of remuneration. This was determined partly by custom and partly by agreement between the crew themselves in consultation with the skipper.[289]

---

284 *Greenham v Gray* (1855) 4 Ir CLR 501 at 509. See further in relation to such payments to managing partners, para **[13.10]** et seq.
285 *DPP v McLoughlin* [1986] IR 355.
286 *O'Kelly v Darragh* [1988] ILRM 309.
287 *DPP v McLoughlin* [1986] IR 355.
288 Partnership Act 1890, s 2(3).
289 Costello J relied in part on the Scottish case of *Parker v Walker & Ors* [1961] SLT 252 and the Canadian case of *Mark Fishing Co v United Fishermen and Allied Workers Union* 24 DLR (3rd ed) 585. Note also the case of *Galvin v Minister for Industry and Commerce* [1932] IR 216 in which the decision of the National Insurance Commissioners that the owner of a fishing boat was an employer of the crew was overturned by the High Court. (contd.../)

[2.117] In *Griffin v Minister for Social, Community and Family Affairs* and *Deasy v Minister for Social, Community and Family Affairs*,[290] Carroll J also examined the legal relationship in respect of two different groups of share fishermen. Carroll J found that the Chief Appeals Officer whose decisions were being appealed to the High Court had erred in not using the decision in *DPP v McLoughlin* as his starting point when assessing whether an employer–employee relationship existed, or whether the relationship was one of joint enterprise or partnership, noting that the legal position is that, where a case involves share fishermen and a similar fact-pattern to that in *DPP v McLoughlin*, the share fishermen are 'legally partners on a joint venture with their respective boat owners' and not employees. In *Griffin*, the expenses of each fishing trip were deducted from the gross profits, with the net profit being divided into thirteen shares (six for the boat to cover loan repayments, fishing gear, repairs and insurances, two for the skipper, and one each for the five crew members). Losses were carried forward to the next trip and the boat was at sea for up to 40 weeks per year. For those weeks when the boat was not at sea, the crew were not paid, and did not receive sick pay, holiday pay or pension contributions. The skipper supplied the boat and if he was unavailable for a trip, selected his replacement. Rather than setting out which factors were indicative of a relationship of joint enterprise or partnership, Carroll J instead focused on which aspects of the decision of the Chief Appeals Officer led to his erroneous decision that the relationship was of employer and employee[291] as follows:

 - he erred in not using the decision of Costello J in *DPP v McLaughlin* as his starting point;
 - he was mistaken in concluding that there could not be a joint enterprise or partnership without a capital investment;
 - he was mistaken in concluding that the provision of labour to a joint enterprise or partnership is insufficient to form a basis for a relationship of joint enterprise or partnership;

289 (\...contd) That case concerned the owner of a boat who gave it to a third party to use for salmon fishing expeditions off the coast of Wexford. In return, the owner got 25% of the profits of the fishing while the third party divided the 75% between himself and the crew. The owner had no role in this arrangement and did not even know the identity of the crew. However, the more difficult question of whether the relationship between the third party and the crew was that of partnership or employment was expressly not considered by Johnston J. Another share-fishing case is that of *Donnelly and Byrne v Hanlon* (1893) 27 ILTR 73, see para [2.104].

290 *Griffin v Minister for Social, Community and Family Affairs and Deasy v Minister for Social, Community and Family Affairs* (2 October 2001) HC. These cases, together with *DPP v McLoughlin*, above, led to the publication of clarification by the Revenue Commissioners of the tax implications of these judgments for share fishermen and women, and boat owners and skippers, now contained at Pt 4, Ch 1 of the Revenue Commissioners *Tax and Duty Manual for Income Tax, Capital Gains Tax and Corporation Tax*.

291 Carroll J also criticised the reliance placed by the Chief Appeals Officer on the US decision in *US v Silk* 331 US 704 which indicates that workers who need to work 'as a matter of economic reality' should be regarded as employees, as this approach is different to the approach taken in Ireland, which requires the existence of an employer–employee relationship.

- regarding losses, it was not material that the loss suffered by one of the share fishermen did not equate to the loss suffered by the boat's owner if the boat could not sail;

- it was not material that a loss suffered by a share fisherman was not a loss of a capital investment;

- he was mistaken in concluding that an agreement to set off losses against the next trip was not a commercial risk; and

- he was mistaken in his view that there must be 'an equal coming together of partners' – in share fishermen cases, the risk to the owner of the boat (damage to his boat) is different to the risk to each of the share fishermen (risk of not being paid if there are no net profits).

[2.118] A contrasting case is *O'Kelly v Darragh*.[292] This involved two doctors who were involved in a pscyhoendocrine centre in St James's Hospital in Dublin which provided testing and analysis services to drug companies. The plaintiff supervised the day-to-day running of the business, whilst the defendant played no active part in the business. The plaintiff and the defendant divided the profits of the business equally between them. When the plaintiff was dismissed by the defendant due to his continued absence from the business, he brought an action for a share of the profits on the basis that he had been a partner. Carroll J noted that the sharing of profits was prima facie evidence of partnership, but that this did not of itself make the relationship a partnership. While the plaintiff was a co-signatory on the bank account for the business, he was not involved in or responsible for getting funds for the continued operation of the business, nor in going out to get contract work for the business. In addition, there had never been a discussion of a partnership between the plaintiff and defendant and there had never been a discussion of whether the plaintiff would have any personal liability if the contract work did not make a profit. On this basis, Carroll J held that, although the plaintiff was entitled to a share of the profits of the business, he was entitled to them, not as a partner, but as an employee.

[2.119] It would be difficult in either of these cases to predict with confidence on which side of the line the court would come down. In close cases such as these, it is apprehended that the circumstances and reason for the claim of partnership will be crucial in determining the outcome. Thus in *DPP v McLoughlin*,[293] the High Court held that the defendant was a partner, rather than an employer of his crew, in order to dismiss criminal proceedings, which were brought against him for failing to file employer returns to the Revenue Commissioners. While in *O'Kelly v Darragh*,[294] the High Court held that the defendant was an employer, rather than a partner, of the plaintiff, in order to dismiss the plaintiff's claim for a share of the profits of the venture after his dismissal due to long periods of absence from the business. A notable recent case in which the High Court considered whether a relationship was that of partnership, or of employer and employee, was that of *McAleenan v AIG*,[295] in which the plaintiff was employed by Michael Lynn & Co, Solicitors in November 2004. The terms and conditions of her

---

[292] *O'Kelly v Darragh* [1988] ILRM 309.
[293] *DPP v McLoughlin* [1986] IR 355.
[294] *O'Kelly v Darragh* [1988] ILRM 309.
[295] *McAleenan v AIG* [2010] IEHC 128.

employment included a provision whereby the possibility of partnership would be discussed once she had been employed by the firm for three years. In 2007, the plaintiff became aware of irregularities in the manner in which Michael Lynn, the principal of the firm, conducted his dealings with various lenders. She contacted the Law Society of Ireland, and resigned. It transpired that Mr Lynn had given multiple undertakings to several lenders in respect of the same properties, and that the charges that were the subject of those undertakings had not been registered in favour of those lenders. Mr Lynn was found guilty of misconduct and struck from the roll of solicitors. AIG sought to avoid the professional indemnity insurance policy that the firm held with it. Ms McAleenan claimed that she was an employee of the firm and entitled to be indemnified under the policy, while AIG claimed that Ms McAleenan had held herself out as a partner in the firm at all material times, and sought to avoid the policy on the basis of material non-disclosure, misrepresentation or untrue statements. In considering whether Ms McAleenan was a partner, or had held herself out as such,[296] Finlay Geoghegan J considered s 1(1) of the 1890 Act and its application to the facts of this particular case. It was common case that Ms McAleenan had joined the firm as an employee, and not as a partner. As to whether she had become a partner between joining the firm in 2004 and resigning in 2007, various facts indicated that she had not: she had remained subject to PAYE, there were meetings regarding a proposed partnership agreement but the Court was satisfied that no agreement had been reached as to the terms on which a partnership would come into existence between Mr Lynn and Ms McAleenan or how profits would be shared between them (indeed, she was given a partnership agreement in July 2007 which she refused to sign), when the business name of the firm was changed, it was registered to Mr Lynn and not to a partnership, Ms McAleenan was given a P45 when she resigned, and the firm's bank account had remained in the sole name of Mr Lynn. However, there were some other factors that contradicted the absence of a partnership:

–   in 2005, Ms McAleenan had indicated to the Law Society of Ireland that she was a partner in the firm – she explained to the Court that she believed herself to be a 'named partner' and that she understood this to mean that she remained an employee, but was 'named' as a partner to clients pending formally entering into partnership with Mr Lynn;

–   Ms McAleenan had ticked 'partner in a solicitor's practice' on her application for a practising certificate in both 2006 and 2007, albeit she struck out the section concerning accounts that was to be completed by partners, and instead completed the section that required completion by employees;

–   in the proposal form for the professional indemnity insurance policy with AIG, the number of partners in the firm was listed as two (although the word 'partner' appeared directly after Mr Lynn's name, but not Ms McAleenan's); and

–   Ms McAleenan's name was included on the firm's notepaper in 2007 – Ms McAleenan indicated to the Court that she had agreed to this as she understood that negotiations regarding her becoming a partner in the firm were close to complete.

---

[296]   As to holding out, see para **[7.01]** et seq.

Finlay Geoghegan J noted the complexities surrounding the concept of 'salaried partner',[297] and the distinction between 'true partners' and a person who holds himself out as, or is held out by the true partners to be, a partner in a partnership.[298] She was satisfied that there was no partnership between Mr Lynn and Ms McAleenan, and that any partnership between them remained under negotiation, citing with approval the observation of Megarry J in *Stekel v Ellice*[299] that '… the question whether or not there is a partnership depends on what the true relationship is, and not on any mere label attached to that relationship'. Finlay Geoghegan J further held that the misrepresentation by Ms McAleenan in the proposal form provided to AIG that she was a partner in the firm was material and made recklessly, thereby entitling AIG to avoid the professional indemnity insurance policy against Ms McAleenan.

[2.120] In *M Young Legal Associates Ltd v Zahid*,[300] Wilson LJ emphasised the importance of examining all of the features of the agreement between the parties when determining if a partnership exists, or whether the relationship is one of employer and employee.[301] He also emphasised the importance of establishing whether the actions of those who are in partnership with one another are expressed to bind the party who claims that he is an employee, and not a partner. If the acts of those partners bind that party then, by virtue of s 5 of the 1890 Act, this (as a 'necessary incident of partnership') would not be consistent with that party being an employee. In *Cobbetts LLP v Hodge*,[302] Mr Hodge was offered the role of an 'employed partner' in the partnership and the relevant partnership deed distinguished between that role and the roles of 'equity partner' and 'junior partner' (a 'junior partner' being a partner with a fixed share of the profits). The definition of 'partners' in the partnership deed expressly excluded 'employed partners', and the partnership deed also provided that an employed partner could not share in the net profits, attend partners' meetings, get involved in the management of the partnership, sign cheques on behalf of the partnership or receive any sum in excess of the remuneration specified in his employment contract. Counsel for the partnership argued that while the terms of the partnership deed might not be determinative, there was nothing in the surrounding circumstances that would alter the position as set out in that deed.[303] Floyd J held that Mr Hodge was in fact an employee, and not a partner.

---

297 As to which, see para **[6.18]** et seq.

298 As to which, see s 14(1) of the 1890 Act and para **[7.10]** et seq.

299 *Stekel v Ellice* [1973] 1 WLR 191.

300 *M Young Legal Associates Ltd v Zahid* [2006] EWCA Civ 613.

301 Wilson LJ viewed that examination as preferable to focusing only on the apparent absence of a link between the profits of the partnership, and the fixed amount paid to the party who claimed that he was not a partner.

302 *Cobbetts LLP v Hodge* [2009] EWHC 786 (Ch).

303 Counsel for Mr Hodge had claimed that there were various factors which indicated that he was a partner rather than an employee, including that he was taxed on a self-employed basis rather than as an employee, had attended partners' meetings and had been represented by the partnership as being a partner on a mortgage application. Those factors were not found to alter the position as set out in the partnership deed, which was clearly worded.

(vi) Section 2(3)(c) – annuity paid to widow or child of deceased partner

[2.121] Section 2(3)(c) of the 1890 Act provides that the payment of an annuity out of the profits of a partnership business to a widow or a child of a deceased partner does not of itself make the recipient a partner. In former times, it was common for the widow or child of a partner to be entitled to an annuity from the partnership on the death of that partner. Now, it is more usual for such an eventuality to be covered by insurance. Thus, partnership agreements commonly require each partner to take out personal life insurance for the benefit of his/her dependants, thereby eliminating any moral obligation, that might otherwise be felt by the continuing partners, to provide for the dependants of their deceased partner.

(vii) Section 2(3)(d) – interest on loan paid to lender out of profits

[2.122] Section 2(3)(d) of the 1890 Act provides that where a loan is made to a person engaged, or about to engage in any business, and the repayment of interest on the loan to that person varies with the profits of the business *or* the lender receives a share of the profits of the business, that does not of itself make the lender a partner in the business or liable as such.[304] However, this is subject to the proviso that the contract is in writing and signed by all the parties thereto. The rule in sub-s (d) is the only one of the five rules in s 2(3) which contains a proviso. Thus, where the loan agreement is not in writing, sub-s (d) will not apply. However, because of the similarity between sub-s (d) and sub-s (a), an oral agreement which thereby falls outside the terms of sub-s (d) may constitute the receipt by a person of a debt out of the profits of a business and so fall within the terms of sub-s (a).[305]

[2.123] *Re Borthwick*[306] is an example of such a case, since the agreement therein was not reduced to writing. In that case, Kirkpatrick advanced £800 to Borthwick for the purpose of Borthwick's general merchant business in Belfast which was to be used to purchase Irish flax for the business. As noted earlier, under the terms of their oral agreement, Kirkpatrick was to receive repayments of interest and principal at a rate of half of the profits derived from the sale of the flax, yet Harrison J held that he was not a partner.[307]

Allegations of partnership between lenders and borrowers

[2.124] The volume of litigation between lenders and borrowers escalated significantly as borrowers increasingly encountered repayment difficulties following the onset of the financial crisis in Ireland in 2008. In many of these cases, borrowers alleged a

---

[304] But he may still be a partner, for example, if he is exercising such control over the business so as to be carrying on business in common with the borrower, see Anon, 'Direct Loan Financing' (1972) 85 Harv LR 1409 at 1425 et seq.

[305] See further in relation to s 2(3)(a) of the 1890 Act, para **[2.111]**. For further historical context, see Henning, 'The origins of the distinction between loan and partnership enshrined in Partnership Act 1890' (2001) Comp Law 22(3), 75–79.

[306] *Re Borthwick* (1875) ILTR 155. Since Kirkpatrick was an employee of Borthwick, this case is also an example of a case which falls within the terms of s 2(3)(b) of the 1890 Act, see para **[2.111]** et seq.

[307] He was held to be an employee, see para **[2.112]**.

partnership relationship with their lenders, although these arguments tended not to find favour.

[2.125] In *Zurich Bank v McConnon*[308] the bank sought summary judgment against Mr McConnon in respect of amounts advanced by the bank to finance the development of a shopping centre in Castleblayney, Co Monaghan. A standstill agreement was entered into, in November 2009, under which the bank agreed to grant a three-month forbearance period to Mr McConnon to enable him to provide the bank with, among other items, a revised business plan. The standstill agreement provided that the forbearance period would enable Mr McConnon and his advisors to prepare both a business plan and feasibility study, and enable the bank to develop revised repayment schedules and loan agreements in respect of Mr McConnon's debt. A report was furnished by Mr McConnon, but rejected by the bank. In dismissing an argument by Mr McConnon that the bank was estopped from taking enforcement action against him in respect of his debt because the bank had not put in place the repayment schedules, thereby not meeting its obligations under the standstill agreement, Birmingham J noted that this argument:

> 'fundamentally [misunderstood] the nature of the relationship between the bank and the defendant. The relationship was not that of partners with a common interest, sharing a risk, rather, the relationship was that of lender and borrower.'

[2.126] Separately, Mr McConnon alleged that the parties had intended to develop the shopping centre (implying a relationship of joint enterprise rather than one of creditor and debtor); however Birmingham J noted that this again indicated a misunderstanding

---

[308] *Zurich Bank v McConnon* [2011] IEHC 75. Birmingham J's comments regarding the bank–borrower relationship not being one of partners with a common interest were cited with approval by Charleton J in *National Asset Loan Management Ltd v Barden* [2013] IEHC 32 in dismissing an argument by the borrower that a development loan provided to him by Allied Irish Banks plc (which was stated to be repayable on demand, with specific amounts to be applied in reduction of the debt on the sale of units in the development, and with the balance of the loan to be repaid at the end of its term) was in fact only repayable by him on a phased basis as and when a buyer was found for each unit in the development. Charleton J noted that if such an argument were accepted, it would '... turn the relationship of lender and borrower into a radically different form of business than that which any reasonable person would contemplate as being encapsulated in the facility letter'. Note also the decision of Barrett J in *KBC Bank Ireland PLC v Osborne* [2015] IEHC 795: in unsuccessfully seeking to defend the bank's application for summary judgment in respect of loans made to him, the defendant borrower alleged that he was in partnership with the bank, largely on the basis that he had kept the bank updated with details of his developments. Barrett J held that this was indicative of nothing more than a prudent borrower seeking to avoid any misunderstandings should repayment difficulties arise, with the borrower's reward being any forbearance provided to him by the bank, and not a relationship of partners. In *ACC Loan Management Ltd v Dolan & Ors* [2016] IEHC 69, Baker J held that neither the 'degree of flexibility' that had entered into the repayment arrangements between the bank and the borrower, nor the commissioning by the bank of its own valuation report, meant that the bank became the defendant's partner, or was engaged in a joint venture with him, and noted that such claims by a small developer '... [ignored] the fact that the Bank was entitled to and did offer indulgence to its customer from time to time, and did so for very sound commercial reasons and in the hope of achieving maximum return on a default loan in the context of a profound property price collapse'.

of the relationship between lenders and borrowers; the bank lent money in the expectation that it would be repaid, and that it would make a profit.[309] Any suggestion that the parties had agreed to enter into a risk-sharing partnership was found by Birmingham J to be 'unstateable'.

Profit-sharing between lenders and borrowers

[2.127] While allegations by borrowers of a partnership-type relationship with their lenders generally find little favour in the courts in the absence of tangible supporting evidence,[310] the question of whether profit-sharing arrangements between lenders and borrowers are indicative of the existence of a partnership relationship has been considered in greater detail, with somewhat different views being expressed. The 1890 Act (at s 2(3)(d)) provides that:

> The advance of money by way of a loan to a person engaged or about to engage in any business on a contract with that person that the lender shall receive a rate of interest varying with the profits, or shall receive a share of the profits arising from carrying on the business, does not of itself make the lender a partner with the person or persons carrying on the business or liable as such. Provided that the contract is in writing, and signed by or on behalf of all the parties thereto.[311]

[2.128] The recent decisions of the Irish courts on the question of whether a profit-sharing arrangement implies a partnership between a lender and a borrower have not specifically referred to the above section of the 1890 Act.

[2.129] The obiter comments of Charleton J in *Irish Bank Resolution Corporation Limited v Cambourne Investments Inc & ors*[312] are of particular note. Part of that litigation involved a loan from Anglo Irish Bank to Cambourne Investments to finance the purchase of certain units in the Parnell Centre in Dublin. Those loans were guaranteed by Peter Curistan (the ultimate beneficial owner of Cambourne Investments via a family trust). A condition of those loans was that Anglo Irish Bank would receive a 25% share of any profits made on the sale of units in the Parnell Centre. The loan agreements between Anglo Irish Bank and Cambourne Investments failed in this case as conditions precedent regarding both a valuation and a loan-to-value ratio which were for

---

[309] In this case, there did not appear to have been a profit-share arrangement built in to the agreements between Zurich Bank and Mr McConnon, so Birmingham J's reference to 'profit' most likely refers to the interest payable on the loan.

[310] For example *KBC Bank Ireland PLC v Osborne* [2015] IEHC 795 where the borrower simply kept his lending bank up to date in relation to his property developments, *ACC Loan Management Ltd v Dolan & Ors* [2016] IEHC 69 where the bank had granted some forbearance to the borrower and commissioned its own valuation report, and *Allied Irish Banks PLC v Likely* [2016] IEHC 579 in which the defendant offered no evidence whatsoever to support her assertions as to the existence of a partnership or agency between the bank and Goodbody Stockbrokers.

[311] Note the comments of Lord Lindley, set out in l'Anson Banks, *Lindley & Banks on Partnership* (20th edn, 2017) at para 5-03, to the effect that the rules set out in s 2 of the 1890 Act are subject to the principle that 'regard must be paid to the true contract and intention of the parties as appearing from the whole facts of the case ...'

[312] *Irish Bank Resolution Corporation Limited v Cambourne Investments Inc & ors* [2012] IEHC 262.

the benefit of both parties were not met.[313] As a result, the enforceability or otherwise of the profit-share clause in the loan agreement did not need to be considered. However, in obiter comments on banking practices generally,[314] Charleton J criticised the profit-sharing arrangement as potentially exposing the bank to a risk of being seen as a partner to the transaction:

> 'One of the puzzling aspects of the Dublin transaction was that Anglo was to obtain a 25% profit share had the Parnell Centre loan resulted in an enhancement of its capital value on eventual sale. Anglo heedlessly adopted an inappropriate risk. Banks are traditionally remunerated on the basis of coldly assessing risk and setting an appropriate interest rate. Profit sharing draws banks directly into property speculation. That is not prudent. In addition, such profit sharing with a borrower by a bank gives rise to the real possibility that a bank will be seen by those on the other side of a transaction as a partner to the business in hand. That is a serious risk but the court does not have to rule on the applicable legal principles due to the failure of the main contract under the facility letters.'

[2.130] In *Vesta Mortgage Investments Limited v Devine*,[315] Vesta applied for summary judgment in respect of the borrower's debt to EBS which Vesta had acquired from EBS in November 2012. The borrower unsuccessfully alleged that a partnership existed between him and EBS in connection with the purchase of a German property. McGovern J held that the relationship was one of lender and borrower, with no evidence of partnership provided by the borrower. While McGovern J quoted Cotton LJ in *Badeley v Consolidated Bank*[316] who held that[317] where a clause in an agreement provides for profit participation, '... it is wrong to say that this is *prima facie* evidence of a partnership ...' as the agreement must be examined as a whole to assess whether it relates to '... a partnership ... a joint business carried on behalf of the two ...' or whether it relates to a relationship of debtor and creditor involving '... a loan secured by giving a certain interest in the profits', McGovern J went on to hold that the agreements in this case were clearly between a lender and a borrower, with no profit-sharing provisions or any other indicators of a partnership.[318] Notably, Lindley LJ in *Badeley v*

---

313   While the loan agreements were not upheld, summary judgment was granted in favour of Anglo Irish Bank for the amount claimed on the basis that 'Once lent, money is repayable' (*Irish Bank Resolution Corporation Limited v Cambourne Investments Inc & ors* [2012] IEHC 262, para 51 of the judgment).

314   *Irish Bank Resolution Corporation Limited v Cambourne Investments Inc & ors* [2012] IEHC 262, at paras 63–70 of the judgment.

315   *Vesta Mortgage Investments Limited v Devine* [2014] IEHC 109.

316   *Badeley v Consolidated Bank* [1888] 38 Ch D 238.

317   *Badeley v Consolidated Bank* [1888] 38 Ch D 238 at 250.

318   McGovern J noted (at para 15 of his judgment in *Vesta Mortgage Investments Limited v Devine* [2014] IEHC 109) that even if a partnership had been established between the defendant and EBS in this case, that would not have given the defendant a defence to the claim for repayment of his debt. Similarly, in *AIB PLC v Flanagan* [2015] IEHC 632, Hedigan J commented that even if the borrower's allegation that one of the bank's employees with whom he dealt was in fact a partner in the borrower's property ventures was true (and Hedigan J did not make a finding as to whether such a partnership had, in fact, existed), that would not release the borrower from his obligation to repay to the bank the sums that he had borrowed from it in his sole name, and that he had covenanted to repay himself.

Consolidated Bank underscored the importance of assessing the relationship between the parties in its entirety before inferring the existence of a partnership:[319]

> 'It is no longer right to infer either partnership or agency from the mere fact that one person shares the profits of another. It may be, and probably it is true, that if all that is known is that one person carries on a business and shares the profits of that business with another, *prima facie* those two are partners, or *prima facie* the person carrying on the business is carrying it on as the agent of the person with whom he shares his profits. That may be true, and I think it is true even now; but when you have a great deal more to consider it appears to me to be a fallacy to say that you are to proceed upon the idea that sharing profits *prima facie* creates a partnership or an agency, and that *prima facie* presumption has to be rebutted by something else.'

[2.131] While reference was not made to the decision in *Badeley v Consolidated Bank*,[320] the most significant recent Irish decision on whether a profit-sharing arrangement between a bank and a borrower could turn a creditor–debtor relationship into one of partnership is that of Kennedy J in *Roche and Anor v Investec Bank plc Ltd & Anor*.[321] Mr Roche, a property developer, claimed that he had been in partnership with the bank and Mr O'Riordan, one of the bank's lending managers who had also entered into consultancy with entities connected with the plaintiffs. A number of the loan facilities in respect of which evidence was presented during the hearing made provision for payment of exit fees, profit-share and/or arrangement fees for the benefit of the bank. Evidence was given by a banking expert on the bank's behalf, and the bank's chief executive officer, that such fees were usual at that time in commercial loan agreements (the arrangements were entered into between 2004 and 2006), and were agreed to in consideration of the risk being assumed by the bank. One particular loan agreement made provision for the bank to receive an arrangement fee of €20,000 and a profit share of 23.5%. The bank argued that it became involved in financing these developments when the underlying arrangements were already well-advanced, and there had been considerable repayment risk for the bank. Kennedy J was satisfied that the relationship remained one of lender and borrower, and '... not one of partners with a common or a shared interest' with the bank looking to ensure that it was repaid and using a fee structure that was by no means unique at that time.[322]

[2.132] In light of these decisions, it is expected that the courts would look to the relationship between the parties as a whole (as contemplated by *Badeley v Consolidated Bank*[323]) and to market practice at the time that the arrangements are entered into (as Kennedy J did in *Roche and Anor v Investec Bank plc Ltd & Anor*[324]) when determining

---

319   *Badeley v Consolidated Bank* [1888] 38 Ch D 238 at 258.

320   *Badeley v Consolidated Bank* [1888] 38 Ch D 238.

321   *Roche and Anor v Investec Bank plc Ltd & Anor* [2015] IEHC 367.

322   Kennedy J cited with approval the decision of Birmingham J in *Zurich Bank v McConnon* [2011] IEHC 75. She also noted the evidence provided by the banking expert that it was standard practice to include provisions in loan facility letters whereby the borrower agreed to pay all costs, including legal and valuation costs, irrespective of whether the transaction proceeded.

323   *Badeley v Consolidated Bank* [1888] 38 Ch D 238.

324   *Roche and Anor v Investec Bank plc Ltd & Anor* [2015] IEHC 356.

whether a profit-share provision for the benefit of a lender is indicative of a creditor-debtor relationship, or of a partnership.

(viii) Section 2(3)(e) – vendor of goodwill who takes a share of the profits

[2.133] Section 2(3)(e) of the 1890 Act provides that a vendor of the goodwill of a business, who receives as part of the consideration, a share of the profits in the business is not *by reason only* of such receipt, a partner or liable as such. In *Hawksley v Outram*,[325] the vendors of a partnership dyeing business were to receive a share of the profits of the business from the purchasers if the debts owing by the business did not exceed the estimate of those debts made by the vendors at the time of the purchase. When specific performance of the agreement was sought, it was alleged that there was a partnership. However, it was held that the vendors were not in partnership with the new owners, as the share of the profits which they received was simply a way of ascertaining the purchase price.

---

[325] *Hawksley v Outram* [1892] 3 Ch 359.

Chapter 3

Characteristics of a Partnership

INTRODUCTION

[3.01] In this chapter, the characteristics of the partnership relationship will be considered both in general and in certain specific situations. This will be done under the following headings:

    I.   The Nature of Partnership in General;
    II.   Partners and Partnerships in Specific Situations;
    III. Status of the Firm Name;
    IV. Registration of Business Names Act 1963; and
    V.   Guarantees involving Partnerships.

Overview

[3.02] Perhaps the most important characteristic of a partnership is the fact that it is not a separate legal entity, rather it is an aggregate of its members.[1] Indeed many of the other characteristics of a partnership which are discussed in this chapter can be traced back to the aggregate nature of the firm, eg, that a firm cannot employ a partner, that a partner cannot be the firm's debtor or creditor, that a partner cannot sue his own firm, etc. Most significantly, it is the aggregate nature of a partnership which renders its tax position so advantageous by comparison with that of a separate legal entity such as a registered company. Thus, since a partnership is not a separate legal entity, the law (and accordingly taxation legislation) looks to (and taxes) the members of the firm, rather than the firm itself. In contrast, a registered company is subject to corporation tax on its profits *and* the members of that company are subject to income tax on any dividend received by them from the company.

[3.03] The fact that a partnership is not a separate legal entity but an aggregate of its members explains in part the confusion surrounding the use by partnerships of firm names. Thus, even though a partnership is not a separate legal entity, it is allowed to trade under a separate name from the names of the partners, in much the same way as a registered company. However, a contract signed in the firm name is with the members of the partnership at the time of the contract. Yet it is sometimes wrongly thought that when a contract is signed by a partnership in the firm name the contract is with a separate legal entity called that firm name. To assist third parties who deal with partnerships which use these firm names, the Registration of Business Names Act 1963 entitles them to discover from a perusal of the register of business names the identity of each of the partners in that partnership. Since third parties who deal with a firm do not have a legal

---

[1]   See generally Jorna, *'The legal nature of partnerships'* (1994) 21 Transactions for the Luyt Centre for Business Law 23.

relationship with the firm per se (as it is not a separate legal entity) but with the partners in the firm, the 1963 Act allows these third parties to identify those with whom they have a legal relationship. However, this right is only as good as the compliance by partnerships with the terms of the 1963 Act and it will be noted hereunder that this is an area which would benefit from considerably stricter enforcement.

I.   THE NATURE OF PARTNERSHIPS IN GENERAL

Not a Separate Legal Entity

[3.04] One of the crucial features of a partnership and one which clearly distinguishes it from a company is that a partnership is not a separate legal entity.[2] Rather it is simply an aggregate of the partners who make up the firm. In the Supreme Court case of *Re A Debtor Summons*,[3] Fitzgibbon J adopted the following description of a partnership:

> '... a firm as such has no existence; partners carry on business both as principals and as agents for each other within the scope of the partnership business; the firm-name is a mere expression, not a legal entity.'[4]

It is noteworthy that in Scotland a partnership is a separate legal entity since it is defined by the 1890 Act as 'a legal person distinct from the partners of whom it is composed'.[5] Accordingly, Scottish decisions on the nature of a partnership do not have the same persuasive authority in this jurisdiction as other decisions of the Scottish courts.[6]

---

[2]   And a legal entity that holds partnership property in trust for a partnership will be treated as a separate legal entity from that partnership: *Bayworld Investments v McMahon & ors (Practising under the Style and Title of McMahon O'Brien & Downes Solicitors)* [2004] IESC 39.

[3]   *Re A Debtor Summons* [1929] IR 139.

[4]   Quoting from Farwell LJ in *Sadler v Whiteman* [1910] 1 KB 868 at 889. See also *Ex p Gliddon* (1884) 13 QBD 43; *Hoare v Oriental Bank Corporation* (1877) 2 App Cas 589; *Ex p Corbett* (1880) 14 ChD 122; *R v Holden* [1912] 1 KB 483. In *Mount Kennett Investment Company & anor v O'Meara & ors* [2012] IEHC 167, Clarke J reiterated the absence of separate legal personality in the context of a firm of solicitors, noting that: '[a] firm of solicitors which is a partnership does not have a separate legal personality to its equity partners. It is not a corporate entity.' See also the observation of Clarke J in *Dunne & Ors v Mahon & Anor* [2014] IESC 24 at para 5.3 of the judgment, that '... the courts have a type of jurisdiction over unincorporated bodies which gives a form of quasi-recognition to the existence of those bodies even though they do not enjoy separate legal personality.' (His comments were made in the context of both clubs and partnerships).

[5]   Partnership Act 1890, s 4(2). See for example the Scottish case of *Jardine-Paterson v Fraser* (1974) SLT 93 and generally Brough, *Miller on Partnership* (2nd edn, 1994) at p 145 et seq. The report published by the English Law Commission and the Scottish Law Commission entitled 'Partnership Law' in 2003 (ref Cm 6015) recommended (at recommendation 20.12 thereof) that a 'partnership should have legal personality separate from the partners but should not be a body corporate'; however, this proposal (along with the majority of other proposals contained in that report) did not progress further.

[6]   This sentence was quoted with approval by Keane J in *Bloxham v Companies Acts* [2017] IEHC 664 at para 96 of his judgment. Most jurisdictions either provide that a partnership is an aggregate of its partners, or a separate legal entity. (contd.../)

A partner is not a debtor or creditor of his firm

[3.05] Since a firm is not a separate legal entity but is simply an aggregate of its members, a partner in a firm cannot be a debtor or creditor of the firm as it is not possible for a person to owe money to himself. This principle underlies the High Court decision in *Foley v Toomey*.[7] There, the plaintiff was a creditor of Philip Toomey and he obtained a judgment and execution order against him. However, Philip Toomey had no goods to answer the judgment. At that time Philip Toomey was in partnership with Denis Toomey and Philip Toomey was due his share of profits from this partnership. For this reason, the plaintiff sought to satisfy his debt by seeking a garnishee order against Denis Toomey, in respect of the debt which was due by the firm to Philip Toomey. This application suffered from the misconception that a firm and a partner may be in creditor/debtor relationship. For this reason, Murnaghan J rejected the application for the garnishee order; instead he amended the application by treating it as a summons for a charging order against a partner's share under s 23 of the 1890 Act.[8]

A firm cannot employ its partners

[3.06] Since a partnership is not a separate legal entity, a partner in a firm cannot be an employee of his firm, since to do so would allow a person to be both an employer and an employee in respect of himself, as was noted by the High Court in *Minister for Social Welfare v Griffiths*.[9]

A firm is sometimes treated as a separate legal entity in commercial life

[3.07] Although a partnership is not a separate legal entity as a matter of law, it is common for the firm to be treated as distinct from the individual partners comprising the firm in commercial life. This follows from the fact that firms do things which are commonly associated with separate legal entities such as adopting names which are unconnected with the partners, having bank accounts and contracts in that name and having partners come and go without any outward change to that firm. As long ago as 1847, this was recognised by the Irish courts, when in *Kerrison v Reddington*[10] Brady LC observed:

---

6   (\...contd) The approach taken by the tax authorities in the State of Delaware is interesting however, insofar as a limited liability company (a body corporate) can elect to be treated as either a body corporate or a partnership for tax purposes. See, further, Montagu, 'Anson and entity classification revisited in light of Brexit: can an LLC constitute a "body corporate"?' (British Tax Review, 2016, 4, 466-489).

7   *Foley v Toomey* (1953) 87 ILTR 141.

8   The order granted by Murnaghan J refers to 'Patrick' Toomey, but this must be taken to be a typing error and to mean Philip Toomey. See generally in relation to charging orders under s 23 of the 1890 Act, para **[19.39]** et seq. A similar case is that of *Belfast Telegraph Newspapers v Blunder Northern Ireland* (13 September 1995), CA in which the plaintiff sought a garnishee order against a bank which had a joint account in the name of the judgment debtor and his partner. Carswell LJ held that the debt could not be attached since it was not due to the judgment debtor alone, but to him jointly with his partner.

9   *Minister for Social Welfare v Griffiths* [1992] ILRM 667, which case is noted hereunder, at para **[3.30]**.

10   *Kerrison v Reddington* (1847) 11 Ir Eq R 451.

'Firms may continue for years after the original parties have ceased to be concerned in them, as very often occurs in England. The old partners retire and new ones come, but still the business is conducted as that of the same firm and often in the same name, and it is the constant course to transfer the debts from the old to the new partners'[11]

[3.08] Allowing this commercial view of partnerships to prevail is convenient while things are running smoothly in the firm's relations with outsiders and amongst the partners. However, once difficulties in either of these relationships arise, it is necessary to rely on the precise legal relationship between the partners. In the words of Lord Lindley, the 'liabilities of the firm are regarded as the liabilities of the partners only in case they cannot be met by the firm and discharged out of its assets'.[12]

Partnership is sometimes treated as if it was a separate legal entity at law

[3.09] Not only is a partnership sometimes treated as a separate legal entity in commercial life but there are also some exceptional cases where, for convenience, the law treats a firm *as if it was* a separate legal entity.[13] This happens under the 1890 Act itself and in the treatment of partnerships under other legislation and by the courts. Under the 1890 Act, some characteristics of a firm are such that it appears to treat it as if it was a separate legal entity. For example property is owned by a partnership,[14] partners are stated to be agents of the 'firm' rather than of their co-partners[15] and it is the firm, rather than the partners, which must indemnify a partner for his business expenses.[16]

[3.10] Under other legislation, the partnership is also treated as if it were an entity. Until 2007, under taxation legislation it was possible to raise an income tax assessment in the name of the precedent partner of a firm in respect of unexhausted profits of the

---

11   *Kerrison v Reddington* (1847) 11 Ir Eq R 451 at 453–454.

12   l'Anson Banks, *Lindley & Banks on Partnership* (20th edn, 2017) at para 3-02.

13   Nowhere was this tension between the legal treatment of the firm as an aggregate and the commercial treatment of it as an entity more marked than in the United States in the early twentieth century. At that time, the seminal partnership legislation, the Uniform Partnership Act (1914), was being drafted. Initially, this Act was drafted by James Ames, Dean of Harvard Law School, a proponent of the theory of the partnership as an entity. However, due to his death, the completion of the Act was done by William Lewis, Dean of the University of Pennsylvania Law School, who was a proponent of the aggregate theory of partnerships. Accordingly, the final draft of the Uniform Partnership Act (1914) adopted the aggregate theory (and was adopted in all US states with the exception of one (Louisiana)). However, in 1986, a subcommittee of the American Bar Association recommended that the entity theory be incorporated into any revision of the Uniform Partnership Act (1914) and that Act has now been replaced by the Uniform Partnership Act 1997 (Last Amended 2013) which has been adopted in approximately three-quarters of US states. The Uniform Partnership Act 1997 (Last Amended 2013) has moved from the aggregate theory back to the entity theory. At s 201(a), it expressly states that 'A partnership is an entity distinct from its partners'. In some areas however, elements of the aggregate theory are retained, including in respect of the joint and several liability of partners, and the concept of a partnership at will.

14   Partnership Act 1890, s 19.

15   Partnership Act 1890, s 5 and s 15.

16   Partnership Act 1890, s 24(2).

partnership trade for a year of assessment.[17] While that is no longer the case, the precedent partner of a firm is required to file returns of the firm's sources of income,[18] and of the firm's chargeable gains[19] and is also deemed to be the 'chargeable person' for self-assessment purposes.[20]

[3.11] An income tax assessment in the firm name had been the subject of the Supreme Court case of *O'Dwyer, Inspector of Taxes v Cafolla & Co*,[21] where O'Byrne J noted:

> 'where a trade or profession is carried on by two or more persons jointly, the tax in respect thereof shall be computed and stated jointly and in one sum ... and a joint assessment shall be made in the partnership name ... This is, in effect, an assessment on the several partners carrying on the trade and is, admittedly enforceable against each and every partner.'[22]

[3.12] A second example of a situation where a firm is treated as if it were a separate legal entity is under Part 22 of the Companies Act 2014. Under Chapter 3 of Part 22 of that Act, a partnership may be wound up as an unregistered company.[23]

[3.13] A final example of a situation where a firm is treated as if it was a separate legal entity is under the Rules of the Superior Courts.[24] Under Ord 14 of these rules, it is possible to bring an action by or against partners in the firm name, rather than in the name of all the partners.[25] As noted by Farwell J: 'the firm-name is a mere expression, not a legal entity, although for convenience under RSC, Ord [14],[26] it may be used for the sake of suing & being sued.'[27]

---

[17] Until 2007, this provision was in the Taxes Consolidation Act 1997, s 1008(4). It was then deleted by the Finance Act 2007, s 30 and replaced by s 1008(2)(a)(ii) of the 1997 Act (inserted by s 30 of the 2007 Act) which provides for an apportionment of those unexhausted profits either in ratios pre-agreed between the partners or, if no such ratios are agreed, in the general ratio already used to attribute profits to each partner's several trade or, if no such ratio exists, equally between them. Separately, note the High Court case of *X v Mulvey* [1947] IR 121 in which Maguire J held that a partnership was a 'person' under the Finance Act 1929, s 12(2).

[18] Taxes Consolidation Act 1997, s 880(2).

[19] Taxes Consolidation Act 1997, s 880(5).

[20] Taxes Consolidation Act 1997, s 959M.

[21] *O'Dwyer, Inspector of Taxes v Cafolla & Co* [1949] IR 210.

[22] *O'Dwyer, Inspector of Taxes v Cafolla & Co* [1949] IR 210 at 237–238. O'Byrne J is referring here to rule 10 of the rules applicable to Cases I and II of Schedule D of the Income Tax Act 1918 now contained in Schedule D of the Taxes Consolidation Act 1997 (as set out in s 18 of that Act).

[23] See generally in relation to the winding up of partnerships as unregistered companies, para **[27.06]** et seq.

[24] SI 15/1986 (as amended) and see generally Ó Floinn, *Practice and Procedure in the Superior Courts* (2nd edn, 2008) at p 147 et seq.

[25] See for example *Magner v Johnstone* [1926] IR 472 where proceedings were brought against a firm in the firm name pursuant to Ord 48A of the Rules of the Supreme Court 1905 (now RSC, Ord 14, r 1).

[26] Farwell J refers to the predecessor of RSC, Ord 14, r 1, namely Ord 48A of the Rules of the Supreme Court 1905.

[27] *Sadler v Whiteman* [1910] 1 KB 868 at 889.

[3.14] As is clear from Farwell J's judgment, the treatment of a partnership *as if it was* an entity, whether by the courts or by the legislature, is simply that. It does not alter the nature of a partnership as an aggregate of the persons comprising the firm. Rather this treatment of a firm as if it were an entity is allowed merely, as noted by Black J, 'for obvious convenience'.[28] One must remember that the law does not deviate from its view of a partnership as an aggregate and it continues to look to the persons comprising the firm.[29]

Partnership Distinguished from a Company

[3.15] In view of the popularity of companies, and, in particular, limited liability companies[30] as a form of business vehicle in Ireland, it is useful to examine the differences between this form of business vehicle and its alternative, the partnership.

Limited liability company

[3.16] Perhaps the most important difference between a limited liability company and a partnership is the fact that the members of a partnership will generally have unlimited liability,[31] while members of a limited liability company are allowed to limit their liability to a fixed amount of money.[32] In many cases, this factor alone will be of such importance as to ensure that a limited liability company, rather than a partnership, is chosen as the appropriate vehicle for a business enterprise.[33] Nonetheless, as noted hereunder, the partnership is not without its advantages, and in certain cases these advantages will outweigh the disadvantage of having unlimited liability. This is particularly so where the partners may be in a position to effectively limit their liability by virtue of their being corporate partners rather than individual partners or by having insurance.

Division of management and ownership in a company

[3.17] Another important difference between partnerships and companies concerns the respective manner in which they are managed and owned. In a partnership, the ownership and management of the firm are generally vested in the same individuals, namely the partners.[34] In contrast, in a company there is a *de jure* (if not always de facto)

---

28 *O'Dwyer, Inspector of Taxes v Cafolla* [1949] IR 210 at 242.
29 For a criticism of the aggregate theory, see Crane, 'The Uniform Partnership Act – A criticism' (1915) 28 Harv LR 762 and for a criticism of the entity theory, see Lewis, 'A Reply to Mr Crane's Criticism' (1916) 29 Harv LR 158. See also Roisin, 'The Entity-Aggregate Dispute: Conceptualism and Functionalism in Partnership Law' (1989) 42 Arkansas LR 395.
30 See generally in relation to limited liability companies, Hutchinson, *Keane on Company Law* (5th edn, 2016); Courtney, *The Law of Companies* (4th edn, 2016); Forde and Kennedy, *Company Law* (5th edn, 2017); Ussher, *Company Law in Ireland* (1986); Morse, *Palmer's Company Law*.
31 Unless it is a limited partnership under the Limited Partnerships Act 1907 (as to which see generally para [28.01] et seq) or an investment limited partnership under the Investment Limited Partnerships Act 1994 (as to which see generally para [29.01] et seq).
32 The amount, if any, unpaid on their shares (Companies Act 2014, s 655).
33 Yet, in some cases it may be argued that this limit on liability is illusory. See para [1.13] ff.
34 Partnership Act 1890, s 24(8) and see generally regarding the management rights of the partners, para [13.01] et seq.

separation between the ownership of the company, which is vested in the shareholders, and the management of the company which is vested in the directors. The principles of company law reflect this separation of powers by providing, inter alia, for the directors to report and be responsible to the shareholders for their management of the company.[35] It should, however, be noted that in some companies this separation of powers will be more apparent than real, since all the shareholders may also be the sole directors of the company. These companies will, therefore, more closely approximate to the partnership model of management than the company model. This fact is reflected in the willingness of the courts to term these companies quasi-partnerships, and by so doing, apply partnership law principles to them.[36]

Double taxation of company's profits

[3.18] It has been seen that unlike a company, a partnership is not a separate legal entity.[37] It is for this reason that partnerships are sometimes viewed as more tax efficient structures than companies. As a separate legal entity, a company pays corporation tax on its profits and, in addition, the members of the company are taxed on any dividends which they receive from the company. For this reason, the profits of an enterprise which is operated as a company may be said to be subject to a form of double taxation. However, if that same enterprise is operated as a partnership, the profits generated by the partnership would not be taxed, since a partnership is not a separate legal entity. Instead, only the profits which are received by the members of the partnership are taxed.

Company required to file financial statements

[3.19] There is no requirement under partnership law that accounts be publicly filed by a partnership and this is another important advantage of partnerships over companies (both limited and unlimited), since limited liability companies are in general required to file their financial statements as, in certain cases, are unlimited companies.[38] However, there is one exception to the general rule that partnerships are not required to file accounts: this is where all the partners in a firm are in fact limited liability companies.

---

[35] This reporting is done by means of the annual general meeting of the company: Companies Act 2014, s 186, and by the fact that the directors may be removed by the shareholders: Companies Act 2014, s 146.

[36] See generally in relation to quasi-partnerships, para **[8.67]** et seq.

[37] See para **[3.04]**.

[38] Companies Act 2014, s 343. See also s 358 of the Companies Act 2014 under which a 'small company' (ie a company which does not exceed two of the following three thresholds, in general for at least two consecutive years: a turnover not exceeding €12 million, a balance sheet total not exceeding €6 million and an average employee number not exceeding 50) also benefits from an audit exemption. In a more recent development, the Companies (Accounting) Act 2017 extended (with effect from 9 June 2017) the requirement to file financial statements to unlimited liability companies that are directly or indirectly owned or controlled by limited liability companies. This change was to address concerns that corporate structures were being set up to circumvent the requirement to file financial statements by interposing a limited liability company (often based outside the EEA) between the unlimited company and its ultimate beneficial owners with the intention of shielding those owners from unlimited liability and making it more difficult to identify those owners.

In such a situation, there is an obligation to file accounts under reg 6 of the European Communities (Accounts) Regulations 1993.[39]

Partnership Distinguished from an EEIG

[3.20] The European Economic Interest Grouping or EEIG was introduced into Irish law by the European Communities (European Economic Interest Groupings) Regulations 1989.[40] An EEIG consists of two or more individuals, companies or firms, who carry on their principal activity or have their central administration in different Member States, but who combine together to develop their own respective economic activities. An EEIG cannot be a partnership, since the members of an EEIG retain their own respective economic activities. Thus, they will not have a 'business in common' and will therefore not satisfy the definition of partnership in s 1(1) of the 1890 Act. The fact that an Irish-registered EEIG may not be a partnership is also clear from the terms of the implementing legislation in Ireland. Article 7 of the 1989 Regulations provides that an EEIG is incorporated on the registration of the contract for the formation of the EEIG and from the date of registration the grouping is a body corporate.[41] Indeed, in view of the absence of a joint business between the members of the EEIG, it is doubtful that an EEIG which is registered in another Member State would be regarded by the Irish courts as a partnership.

Partnership Distinguished from a Club

[3.21] It is noted elsewhere in this work that one of the requirements for a partnership to exist is that the parties have as their aim the making of a profit.[42] In general, clubs do not aim to be profit-making and therefore will not constitute partnerships. Another important difference between clubs and partnerships is that members of a club, unlike members of a partnership, are not by virtue of their membership liable for the acts of their fellow members.[43] In addition, a club is formed on the understanding that its members are not liable to pay any money beyond the subscription required by its rules,[44] while members of a partnership are always subject to unlimited liability for the

---

[39]   SI 396/1993.

[40]   SI 191/1989 which implements Council Regulation (EC) No 2137/85 on the European Economic Interest Grouping.

[41]   Note, however, that for tax purposes, an EEIG is treated as if it was a partnership: Taxes Consolidation Act 1997, s 1014(3).

[42]   Partnership Act 1890, s 1(1) and see generally para [2.62] et seq.

[43]   *Flemyng v Hector* (1836) 2 M & W 172; *Todd v Emly* (1841) 8 M & W 505; *The St James' Club* (1852) 2 De GM & G 383; *Caldicott v Griffiths* (1853) 8 Ex 898. They may be vicariously liable in an appropriate case for a fellow member's act: see *Murphy v Roche et al* (15 May 1987) HC. See also McMahon and Binchy, *Law of Torts* (4th edn, 2013) at para [39.11].

[44]   See for example *Wise v Perpetual Trustee Co* [1903] AC 139. However in *Minnitt v Lord Talbot* (1876) 1 LR Ir 143 and (1881) 7 LR Ir 407, the members of a club were required to advance further sums. The plaintiffs in that case were the members of the committee of the Irish Farmer's Agricultural Club who had advanced money to improve the premises of the club at 42 O'Connell Street, Dublin. (contd.../)

obligations of the firm.[45] The distinction between a club and a partnership was neatly summarised by Hogan J in *Re: Roadstone Group Sports Club: Dunne & ors v Mahon & anor*[46] in which he quoted the observation of Johnston J in *Feeney v McManus*[47] who observed as follows:

> 'A club is the most anomalous group of human beings that is known to the law. It is union of persons for social intercourse or for the promotion of certain pursuits, which are closely allied to social intercourse, and the members usually regulate their conduct in accordance with bye-laws or regulations to which they subscribe. A club has no existence apart from its members… a trading partnership, regulated by the [Partnership Act 1890] has a position and an existence which is superior to those of a club.'

Partnership Distinguished from a Co-Ownership

[3.22] The arrangements between groups of individual investors participating in transactions such as the development of hotels, nursing homes, student accommodation and private hospitals to avail of certain tax benefits have tended to be structured as co-ownerships, rather than partnerships, as that was seen as preferable from a tax perspective. While the majority of these tax benefits have been phased-out, the question of whether an arrangement between various investors in fact constitutes a co-ownership or a partnership remains relevant.[48]

[3.23] Co-ownership agreements often include specific provisions designed to reduce the risk of those agreements, and the relationship between the persons listed as co-owners, being re-characterised as partnership agreements and partners respectively. Such provisions can include:

- an agreement by each co-owner to share in the liabilities of the co-ownership in proportion to his investment in that co-ownership (eg payments made on foot of indemnities);[49]

---

44 (\…contd) They were held to be entitled to a lien on the property of the club which had been acquired with their money. However, when it transpired that on the sale of such property it would not cover all the advances made by the committee members, Sullivan MR ordered that all members of the committee and the members of the club who assented to or subsequently ratified the advance, were liable to indemnify the plaintiffs.

45 See generally regarding the nature of the liability of a partner for the obligations of the firm, para **[11.01]** et seq.

46 *Re: Roadstone Group Sports Club: Dunne & ors v Mahon & anor* [2012] IEHC 214.

47 *Feeney v McManus* [1937] IR 23 at 31–32. See also *Dunne & ors v Mahon & anor* [2014] IESC 24 at paras 5.1–5.3 of the judgment.

48 See, further, l'Anson Banks, *Lindley & Banks on Partnership* (20th edn, 2017) para 5-07 et seq (in particular para 5-08 which summarises the key differences between a co-ownership and a partnership).

49 See for example *Allied Irish Banks plc v Galvin Developments (Killarney) Limited & ors* [2011] IEHC 314 where Finlay Geoghegan J noted that the parties had agreed to proceed with their plans for property development using a co-ownership structure in which each party would acquire a 50% interest and would be liable for 50% of the liabilities, rather than using a partnership structure in which 'each side of the joint venture would have been liable for the entire debts of the partnership'.

- an agreement that the co-owners will share in the gross, rather than the net, profits of the co-ownership;[50]
- a statement that the co-owners are not agents of one another and the act of one will not bind the others, save in accordance with the express provisions of the co-ownership agreement; and
- a specific 'no partnership' clause.[51]

[3.24] As previously mentioned,[52] s 2(1) of the 1890 Act establishes that co-ownership does not of itself create a partnership between the co-owners as to property so owned, even where the co-owners share the profits derived from the use of the property which is co-owned. However, this section seems to have been unduly relied upon in several property investments in recent years. It is important to note that s 2(1) does not say that co-owners of property cannot be partners. It simply says that co-ownership of a property alone does not mean that a partnership exists. This means that those who are not in business together, and are not making joint investments, but instead happen to own property together (perhaps as a result of an inheritance) are not treated, simply as a result of that co-ownership, as partners. Something more than mere co-ownership is required for co-owners of property to satisfy the definition of partnership, and one therefore must fall back on the definition of partnership to see if a partnership exists between co-owners since the real question is whether the parties satisfy the definition of partnership. The definition of partnership in s 1(1) of the 1890 Act is very wide-ranging,[53] since it simply requires two or more people to be carrying on business in common with a view to profit, and this business may be investing in property. In view of the very wide-ranging nature of the definition of partnership in s 1(1) of the 1890 Act, it is difficult to argue, where a group of investors pool their resources to invest in property with a view to making a profit, that they are not in fact carrying on a business so as to be in partnership.

[3.25] Decisions of courts in other common law jurisdictions where the 1890 Act applies, or where partnership legislation is based on the 1890 Act, merit consideration. For example in the Canadian case of *Volzke Construction Limited v Westlock Foods*,[54] the Alberta Court of Appeal held that a partnership existed between Volzke Construction and Westlock Foods (who owned 80% and 20% (respectively) of a shopping centre).

---

50   See generally para **[2.92]** as to s 2(2) of the 1890 Act and why the sharing of gross returns is not of itself an indicator of partnership.

51   See *Fenston v Johnstone (Inspector of Taxes)* [1940] 23 TC 29 in which a partnership was found to exist between Mr Fenston and Mr Shaw (who had purchased land sourced by Mr Fenston, when Mr Fenston was unable to raise enough money to fund the purchase himself). Mr Shaw and Mr Fenston had agreed that profits and losses arising from the venture would be shared equally. The agreement entered into between them expressly provided that '[this] arrangement herein set out shall not constitute any partnership between us'. Wrottesley J in the High Court of England and Wales observed that the use of such wording '…cannot change the character of what is in essence a partnership, at any rate as regards third parties, and in the case before me there is nothing but this one phrase to disturb the presumption arising from the other provisions in the agreement that this is a partnership.'

52   See para **[2.89]**.

53   See para **[2.09]** et seq.

54   *Volzke Construction Limited v Westlock Foods* (1986) 4 WWR 688.

Factors which led the Alberta Court of Appeal to its decision were that Volzke Construction and Westlock Foods shared profits jointly, co-owned the property, had a bank account in joint names and had jointly financed the project. The New Zealand courts reached a similar decision in *National Insurance Co of New Zealand v Bray*.[55] In that case, a syndicate was formed for the purpose of investing in property, with the property being held by a Mr Wheatley on behalf of the syndicate. The plaintiff took an action against Mr Wheatley as a partner in the syndicate for moneys owed by Mr Wheatley to the plaintiff under a contract relating to the property. The court held that the syndicate members were partners, and the plaintiff's action succeeded. In the English case of *Walker West Developments v FJ Emmet*,[56] an arrangement was entered into between a builder (who had purchased the land in question) and a developer (to whom the builder contracted to sell that land) that various houses would be built by the builder, and would then be sold by the developer, with the profits shared between them. That arrangement was found to be a partnership. A similar finding had previously been made in *Fenston v Johnstone (Inspector of Taxes)*.[57] In that case, a partnership was found to exist between Mr Fenston and Mr Shaw (who had purchased land sourced by Mr Fenston, when Mr Fenston was unable to raise enough money to fund the purchase himself). Mr Shaw and Mr Fenston had agreed that profits and losses arising from the venture would be shared equally.

[3.26] It is important to note that where a co-ownership is, in fact, a partnership, certain key terms of the 1890 Act will be implied into the agreement between the parties, most notably:

- the right of a partner to dissolve the partnership under s 26(1);
- the obligation on a partner, under s 30, not to carry on any business of the same nature as, and competing with, the partnership, without the consent of his fellow partners;
- s 33(1), which provides that the partnership will dissolve on the death of a partner; and
- ss 5 to 13, which deal with the liability of a partner for the acts of his co-partners.

While a partnership agreement will often disapply ss 26(1), 30 and 33(1), a co-ownership agreement which has not been drafted on the basis that the co-owners are, in fact, partners, will not have done so, and these provisions will apply by default. While ss 5 to 13 cannot be disapplied to a partnership, a partnership will often address the potential liabilities of its partners by including indemnities in its partnership agreement.

[3.27] The statutory prohibition in s 1435(1) of the Companies Act 2014 on the formation of a partnership with more than 20 members would also apply to a co-ownership that is, in fact, a partnership. If such a co-ownership has more than 20 members, it will be illegal.[58]

---

55   *National Insurance Co of New Zealand v Bray* [1934] NZLR 67.
56   *Walker West Developments v FJ Emmet* (1978) 252 EG 1171.
57   *Fenston v Johnstone (Inspector of Taxes)* (1940) 23 TC 29.
58   See, further, para **[9.17]**.

The Governing Law of a Partnership

[3.28] The principles which determine which law governs a partnership agreement are similar to those for any other contract.[59] For a detailed consideration of the governing law of contracts, reference should be made to the standard works in this area.[60] In general terms, the following points may be made:

(i) where the partners have chosen a governing law, that law in general determines their obligations under the agreement, although the choice may be avoided on public policy grounds, eg where it is an attempt to avoid a mandatory rule of the country with which the agreement is most closely connected;

(ii) where, as often happens in partnership agreements, the partners omit to choose a governing law, the intentions of the partners may be inferred by the other terms of the contract, eg where the partners in a particular profession have chosen an arbitrator who is to be picked by the president of the profession's governing body;[61]

---

59 Note, however, that Regulation (EC) No 593/2008 of the European Parliament and of the Council of 17 June 2008 on the law applicable to contractual obligations (the 'Rome I Regulation') will not apply to partnership agreements as it does to other contracts, since two of the exclusions from the scope of Rome I Regulation are of clear application to partnerships: art 2(f) excludes 'questions governed by the law of companies and other bodies, corporate or unincorporated, such as the creation by registration or otherwise, legal capacity, internal organisation or winding-up of companies and other bodies, corporate or unincorporated, and the personal liability of officers and members as such for the obligations of the company or body' and it also excludes (at art 2(g)) 'the question whether an agent is able to bind a principal, or an organ to bind a company or body corporate or unincorporated, in relation to a third party'. However, in general terms, the rules contained in the Rome I Regulation broadly map the common law rules outlined above. See in relation to the American position, Cooper, 'Transactions with Foreign Partnerships: two disasters to avoid' (1995) 58 Texas BJ 1102. As regards the separate question of the jurisdiction of the courts in a trans-national partnership, reference should be made to the Recast Brussels Regulation (Regulation (EU) No 1215/2012 of the European Parliament and of the Council of 12 December 2012 on jurisdiction and the recognition and enforcement of judgments in civil and commercial matters (recast)) and the Lugano Convention (the Convention on jurisdiction and the recognition and enforcement of judgments in civil and commercial matters done at Lugano on 13 October 2007) and the standard works on this area, ie Binchy, *Irish Conflicts of Law* (1988) at p 123 et seq. Note that under art 4 of the Recast Brussels Regulation, the general rule of jurisdiction is that persons domiciled in a Member State are (whatever their nationality) to be sued in courts of that Member State. Article 22 of the Lugano Convention provides the courts of the contracting state in which an association of natural or legal persons has its seat shall have exclusive jurisdiction (regardless of domicile) in proceedings relating to the validity of its constitution, its nullity or dissolution, or the validity of the decisions of its organs. Under the Ninth Schedule to the Jurisdiction of Courts and Enforcement of Judgments (European Communities) Act 1998 an association has its seat in the State if it was incorporated or formed under the law of the State, or if its central management and control is exercised in the State.

60 Binchy, *Irish Conflicts of Law* (1988) at p 517 et seq; *Dicey, Morris & Collins on the Conflict of Laws* (15th edn, 2012), Ch 10 et seq.

61 See for example *Tzortis v Monrak Line A/B* [1968] 1 WLR 406.

(iii)   where it is not possible to decipher the partners' intentions, the governing law of the partnership agreement is the law which has the closest and most real connection with the contract and transaction.[62]

II.   PARTNERS AND PARTNERSHIPS IN SPECIFIC SITUATIONS

[3.29] In this section, it is proposed to consider the nature of the partnership relationship in a number of specific situations.[63]

A Partner is not an 'Employee' under Employment Legislation

[3.30] The principle that a partner may not be his co-partner's employee should be self-evident from the fact that a partnership is not a separate legal entity[64] and from the definition of a partner as someone who carries on business 'in common' with another.[65] However, it has been argued in the Irish courts that a partner should be treated as an employee for the purposes of employers' social insurance contributions. This occurred in the High Court case of *The Minister for Social Welfare v Griffiths*.[66] This case involved a partnership between two fishermen, Mr Pepper and Mr Griffiths, who worked together on Mr Griffiths' fishing vessel. As part of his case, the Minister conceded that Mr Pepper was a partner of the defendant, but he nonetheless claimed employer contributions from the defendant under the terms of the social welfare legislation. Blayney J had no hesitation in holding that as Mr Pepper was a partner of the defendant's, he could not be the defendant's employee and therefore he held that the defendant could not be liable for employee contributions under the social welfare legislation.

[3.31] However, the courts have taken a more liberal approach to similar statutory interpretations in order to prevent unintended discrimination against partnerships. This was the case in the House of Lords decision in *Kelly v Northern Ireland Housing Executive*.[67] It concerned the invitation by the defendant for applications from firms of solicitors for appointment to a panel which defended public liability claims against the defendant. The plaintiff alleged religious discrimination under the Fair Employment (Northern Ireland) Act 1970 when her firm was unsuccessful. The plaintiff's claim was rejected at first instance on the grounds that the defendant was not an employer since employment was defined by the 1970 Act as including a contract 'personally to execute any work' and the partnership could not personally execute work. The House of Lords allowed the appeal on the basis that a partnership is not a separate legal entity and therefore an activity taken on by a firm would be done 'personally' since any contract would be with all the partners.

---

[62]   See *Cripps Warburg v Cologne Investment* [1980] IR 321 at 333.
[63]   These situations are, of course, not exhaustive. See for example the case comment on *Keeble v Combined Lease Finance Plc* (1996) 19 Construction Law Today 8, CA, regarding the issue of whether a partnership is a debtor under hire-purchase legislation.
[64]   See para **[3.04]**.
[65]   See generally regarding the requirement that partners carry on business in common, para **[2.68]** et seq. See also the judgment of Costello J in *DPP v McLoughlin* [1986] IR 355.
[66]   *The Minister for Social Welfare v Griffiths* [1992] ILRM 667.
[67]   *Kelly v Northern Ireland Housing Executive* [1998] 3 WLR 735.

A Partnership is Generally a 'Person'

[3.32] The question of whether a partnership is a person for the purposes of legislation which refers to a 'person' or 'persons', is deserving of consideration. In general, this matter will be covered by s 18(c) of the Interpretation Act 2005 which provides that unless the context otherwise requires, the term 'person' in an Act of the Oireachtas, in a statute which was in force in Saorstát Éireann immediately before the date of the coming into operation of the 1937 Constitution and which continued in force by virtue of Article 50 of the 1937 Constitution, or in a statutory instrument, is deemed to include an unincorporated body of persons, and therefore includes a partnership.[68] In *Bovale Developments & Companies Acts: Director of Corporate Enforcement v Bailey & anor,*[69] Denham J (with whom Macken and Finnegan JJ concurred) held that PwC (a partnership) was an unincorporated body and therefore a 'person' for the purposes of s 18(c) of the Interpretation Act 2005. The directors of Bovale Developments Limited claimed that as the work done by PwC (which had been retained by the Office of the Director of Corporate Enforcement to examine and report on the books of the company) was done by a team within PwC, this meant that the work had not been done by a 'person', ie by PwC (on the basis that a 'team' could not be a 'person' within the meaning of s 18(c) of the Interpretation Act 2005). Denham J did not share this view, holding that the fact that some members of the team were not partners in the PwC partnership did not invalidate the fact that PwC was responsible for the work.

[3.33] The question of whether a partnership is a 'person' under the Judgment Mortgage (Ireland) Act 1850[70] was considered in *Magner v Johnstone,*[71] without reference to the Interpretation Act 1937 (the predecessor to the Interpretation Act 2005) or its predecessor,[72] since neither applied to this Act. There, a judgment was purportedly registered as a judgment mortgage against a firm's property in Rathkeale, Co Limerick, under the terms of the Judgment Mortgage (Ireland) Act 1850. Section 6 of that Act allows for the registration of a judgment mortgage against a 'person' against whom a judgment has been registered. The partners in the firm argued that the judgment mortgage should not have been registered, as a firm is not a 'person' for the purposes of s 6 of the Judgment Mortgage (Ireland) Act 1850. In the High Court, Meredith J rejected

---

[68] See *Revenue Commissioners v O'Reilly & McGilligan* [1984] ILRM 406 in which it is implicit that an unincorporated body of persons includes a partnership, but see the discussion as to whether a partnership of two members constitutes a body of persons at para **[3.47]**. See also the European Court of Justice case of *Staatssecretaris van Financien v Heerma* (C-23/98) 27 January 2000 which held that the letting of property by a partner to a partnership of which he is a member is an independent activity within the meaning of art 4(1) of the Sixth VAT Directive (Directive 77/388/EEC) so as to give rise to a charge to VAT, since the partner acts in his own name, on his own behalf and under his own responsibility, even if he is at the same time manager of the lessee partnership.

[69] *Bovale Developments & Companies Acts: Director of Corporate Enforcement v Bailey & anor* [2011] IESC 24.

[70] 13 & 14 Vict, c 29. That Act was repealed by s 8(3) and Sch 2 to the Land and Conveyancing Law Reform Act 2009. The law relating to judgment mortgages is now set out in Part 11 (ss 115 to 119) of the Land and Conveyancing Law Reform Act 2009.

[71] *Magner v Johnstone* [1926] IR 472.

[72] The Interpretation Act 1889 (52 & 53 Vict, c 63).

this contention and he held that a firm was a 'person' for the purposes of the Judgment Mortgage (Ireland) Act 1850.

A Partnership may be a 'Consumer'

[3.34] While, traditionally, laws concerning the protection of consumers (most notably, the Consumer Credit Act 1995) have focussed on the protection of individuals acting for personal purposes (ie not for the purposes of a trade, business or profession in which they are engaged),[73] partnerships are included in the definition of 'consumer' in the Central Bank of Ireland's Consumer Protection Code 2012, and partnerships with an annual turnover of €3,000,000 or less in the previous financial year are included in the definition of 'consumer' in the Financial Services and Pensions Ombudsman Act 2017 thereby bringing such partnerships within the definition of 'complainant' in s 2 of that Act, and enabling them to file complaints with the Financial Services and Pensions Ombudsman in respect of financial services providers or pension providers.

[3.35] While at first glance, bringing a partnership within the scope of certain consumer protection legislation may seem inconsistent with the scope of the term 'consumer' in other legislation (such as the Consumer Credit Act 1995, which defines a 'consumer' as a natural person acting outside of his trade, business or profession), most partnerships are small in size, involving a small number of private individuals. Until SI 164/2014, all partnerships came within the definition of 'consumer' for the purposes of making complaints to the then Financial Services Ombudsman. The annual turnover test was introduced by SI 164/2014 from 7 April 2014 onwards. While SI 164/2014 was repealed by the Financial Services and Pensions Ombudsman Act 2017 with effect from 1 January 2018, the €3,000,000 annual turnover threshold was carried over into the new Act. The position until April 2014 was perhaps best summarised by reference to the judgment of MacMenamin J in *Hooper Dolan Financial Ltd v Financial Services Ombudsman & Ors*[74] in which he stated[75] that:

> 'Partnerships … come within the definition of "consumer" for the purposes of the Act of 1942. Some partnerships may be quite sizeable businesses. These are the exception rather than the rule. This fact does not create inconsistency with the principles and policies of the legislation. In the vast majority of cases, partnerships are constituted of private individuals with personal liability. As such, to afford them the status of "consumers", in my view, is not inconsistent with the traditional concept of consumer. Unlike incorporated companies, partnerships are not obliged to file their accounts in any public office or register, and

---

[73] In *Harrington & Anor v Gulland Property Finance Ltd & Anor (No 2)* [2018] IEHC 445, Baker J (at para 152 of the judgment) noted that the borrowers, two brothers, were partners in a business together and, as such, were outside the scope of the definition of 'consumer' in both the Consumer Credit Act 1995 and the European Communities (Unfair Terms in Consumer Contracts) Regulations 1995 (SI 27/1995). See also *AIB plc v Higgins & Ors* [2010] IEHC 219. In that case, Kelly J held that the Consumer Credit Act 1995 had no application to the four individual defendants who had borrowed as a partnership from AIB with a view to investing in property and developing it for profit.

[74] *Hooper Dolan Financial Ltd v Financial Services Ombudsman & Ors* [2011] IEHC 296.

[75] *Hooper Dolan Financial Ltd v Financial Services Ombudsman & Ors* [2011] IEHC 296 at para 97 of the judgment.

accordingly, it would be impractical, and perhaps impossible, to apply a "turnover test" to partnerships without compelling a disclosure of financial information that runs entirely counter to policies to do with the nature and regulation of partnerships ...'

The definition of 'consumer' in the Consumer Protection Code continues to encompass all partnerships, without any turnover test.

Partners and Firms are 'Undertakings' under the Competition Acts

[3.36] Both partners[76] and partnerships[77] are undertakings for the purposes of the Competition Act 2002 and this issue is considered in detail elsewhere in this work.[78]

A Partnership cannot be a Bank

[3.37] At the time of writing, a partnership cannot be granted a banking licence. Since the introduction of the Single Supervisory Mechanism in 2014,[79] under which the European Central Bank is the central banking supervisor in respect of banks within the euro area, a licence to operate as a bank in Ireland can no longer be granted directly by the Central Bank of Ireland. Instead, the Central Bank must make a proposal to the European Central Bank that the European Central Bank grant a banking licence to an applicant provided that the applicant meets certain conditions. One of those conditions is that the applicant must be a body corporate with both its registered office and its head office located in the State (ie it cannot be a natural person or an unincorporated body such as a partnership).[80]

A Partnership can provide other Regulated Financial Services

[3.38] While a partnership cannot be licensed as a bank, under the Central Bank Act 1997 it can be licensed as a bureau de change business, a money transmission business, a home reversion firm, a retail credit firm, a debt management firm or a credit servicing

---

76   *Doyle/Moffit* Competition Authority, Dec No 333, 10 June 1994, Notif CA/1133/92.
77   *Scully Tyrell/Edberg* Competition Authority, Dec No 12, 29 January 1993, Notif CA/57/92.
78   Paragraph **[22.09]**.
79   Under Council Regulation (EU) No 1024/2013 of 15 October 2013 conferring specific tasks on the European Central Bank concerning policies relating to the prudential supervision of credit institutions and see also the European Union (Single Supervisory Mechanism) Regulations 2014 (SI 495/2014). The Single Supervisory Mechanism comprises the European Central Bank and the national competent authorities of the participating EU Member States (including the Central Bank of Ireland as the national competent authority of Ireland). Under the Single Supervisory Mechanism, banks are categorised as 'significant' or 'less significant'. Those categorised as 'significant' are directly supervised by the European Central Bank. The relevant national competent authorities, such as the Central Bank of Ireland, continue to supervise those banks categorised as 'less significant'. In all cases, however, the European Central Bank is the decision-maker with respect to applications for banking licences.
80   Central Bank Act 1971, ss 9 and 9F.

firm.[81] It can also be authorised as an electronic money institution,[82] a payment institution,[83] a credit intermediary[84] or a mortgage credit intermediary.[85]

A Partnership can be authorised as a Trust or Company Service Provider

[3.39] Under the Criminal Justice (Money Laundering and Terrorist Financing) Act 2010, a partnership can also be authorised by the Minister for Justice and Equality to operate as a 'trust or company services provider' providing services for bodies corporate, partnerships and trusts.[86] Unless otherwise specified in the authorisation, any reference to the holder of such an authorisation is a reference to each partner in the partnership.[87]

Partnerships as UCITS or Alternative Investment Funds

[3.40] The question of whether a partnership is subject to the terms of the Unit Trusts Act 1990, the UCITS Regulations[88] or the AIFMD Regulations[89] is considered later in this work in the context of limited partnerships and investment limited partnerships.[90] However, the same principles will apply to the question of whether a limited partnership

---

81 In each case, by the Central Bank under the Central Bank Act 1997. See s 36A(1)(f) of the Central Bank Act 1997 which deals with the revocation of authorisations by the Central Bank, including in circumstances where '… the holder of the authorisation is a partnership …'. An 'authorisation' is in turn defined at s 28(1) as an authorisation to carry on a 'regulated business' (also defined at s 28(1) as '… a bureau de change business, a money transmission business, a home reversion firm, a retail credit firm, a debt management firm or a credit servicing firm').

82 See the European Communities (Electronic Money) Regulations 2011 (SI 183/2011) which (as regards the circumstances in which the Central Bank may withdraw an authorisation), expressly contemplates the holding of such an authorisation by a partnership at reg 27(1)(b)(ii) where it states '… if the holder of the authorisation is a partnership …'.

83 See the European Communities (Payment Services) Regulations 2009 (SI 383/2009) which (as regards the circumstances in which the Central Bank may withdraw an authorisation), expressly contemplates the holding of such an authorisation by a partnership at reg 34(1)(b)(ii) where it states '… if the holder of the authorisation is a partnership …'.

84 See reg 6(1) of the European Communities (Consumer Credit Agreements) Regulations 2010 (SI 281/2010) which defines a credit intermediary as being '… a person (including a firm, within the meaning of the Partnership Act 1890 …' and also s 144(6) of the Consumer Credit Act 1995 which contemplates a partnership carrying on the business of a credit intermediary.

85 See reg 4(1) of the European Union (Consumer Mortgage Credit Agreements) Regulations 216 (SI 142/2016) which defines a mortgage credit intermediary as being '… a person (including a firm, within the meaning of the Partnership Act 1890 …'.

86 This can include acting or arranging for a person to act as a partner in a partnership (Criminal Justice (Money Laundering and Terrorist Financing) Act 2010, s 24(1)).

87 Criminal Justice (Money Laundering and Terrorist Financing) Act 2010, s 86(1).

88 European Communities (Undertakings for Collective Investment in Transferable Securities) Regulations 2011 (SI 352/2011).

89 European Union (Alternative Investment Fund Managers) Regulations 2013.

90 See para **[28.19]**.

or an ordinary partnership falls within the terms of this legislation and, accordingly, reference should be made to that section.

Partnership under the Markets in Financial Instruments Regulations 2017

[3.41] The European Union (Markets in Financial Instruments) Regulations 2017,[91] anticipate that a partnership can be both an authorised investment firm and a market operator of a regulated market.[92] A partnership can be authorised by the Central Bank to operate as an investment firm[93] provided that it meets certain conditions. To require authorisation as an investment firm under the 2017 Regulations, the regular business of the partnership must be '… the provision of one or more investment services to third parties or the performance of one or more investment activities on a professional basis or both …'. If the investment services are not provided by the partnership to third parties, or if the investment activities are not performed by the partnership on a professional basis, the requirement for authorisation as an investment firm under the 2017 Regulations will not apply. If a regulated market (the Main Securities Market of the Irish Stock Exchange is an example of a regulated market) is to be operated by a partnership, that partnership will also require authorisation under the 2017 Regulations as a market operator of that regulated market.

[3.42] Regarding whether, if a person is providing investment services to a third party in respect of interests in a partnership, authorisation under the European Union (Markets in Financial Instruments) Regulations 2017 is required, the position differs slightly from that under the Investment Intermediaries Act 1995. Under the 2017 Regulations, 'transferable securities' are defined as including securities equivalent to shares in partnerships if negotiable on the capital market.[94] As such, it seems that the provision of an investment service to third parties on a professional basis in connection with interest in a partnership could lead to a requirement for authorisation.

Partnership under the Investment Intermediaries Act 1995

[3.43] In general terms, the Investment Intermediaries Act 1995 provides that a person may not give investment advice or be involved in investment business services without authorisation from the Central Bank. It should be noted that, as a result of the introduction of the Markets in Financial Instruments regime in Ireland[95] most investment firms are now authorised under that legislation and only a limited number of investment firms are permitted to be authorised under the 1995 Act. The key issue for partnerships regarding the 1995 Act is whether a partnership could be caught by the terms of that Act if it is carrying on investment business services on its own account. By the express terms

---

91 SI 375/2017 which transposes Directive 2014/65/EU into Irish law.
92 Regulation 148 of the European Union (Markets in Financial Instruments) Regulations 2017 (which deal with the winding up of such an investment firm or market operator by the Court and, at reg 148(10), provide for the Central Bank to have the benefit of s 35 of the 1890 Act when applying for a decree of dissolution).
93 European Union (Markets in Financial Instruments) Regulations 2017, reg 9(1)(a)(iv).
94 European Union (Markets in Financial Instruments) Regulations 2017, reg 3(1).
95 See para **[3.41]**.

of the Act, if the investment business services (or the investment advice) are *not* being provided to a third party on a professional basis the Act will not apply.[96] If this is the case, then the partnership will not fall within the terms of the 1995 Act and, therefore, will not require to be authorised thereunder.

[3.44] As to whether an interest in an ordinary partnership or a limited partnership is an 'investment instrument' under the Investment Intermediaries Act 1995 such that any advice given in relation to such interests would constitute investment advice and require to be given by an 'authorised' investment business firm, it is contended that such an interest does not fall within the definition of investment instrument in s 2(1) of the 1995 Act. While the most likely category it would fall within is that of 'transferable securities', the term 'transferable securities' is clearly intended to be restricted to securities issued by companies or governments.[97] Support for this view is also to be found in Recital 9 of the Investment Services Directive,[98] upon which the 1995 Act is based, since that refers to transferable securities as those classes of securities which are normally dealt in on the capital market, such as government securities, shares in companies, etc. This view is also supported by the fact that a specific inclusion in the definition of 'investment instruments' is made for interests in investment limited partnerships but not for either limited or ordinary partnerships.[99]

Partner Cannot Sue his own Firm

[3.45] As a consequence of the aggregate theory of partnership prevailing, ie that there is no entity only individuals, a partner cannot, as a general rule, sue his firm for a partnership obligation, since this would involve that partner in suing himself. This general rule has been recognised by the High Court in *Hawkins v Rogers*[100] and is considered in detail elsewhere in this work.[101] The rationale for this principle is that, as a partner is jointly liable with his co-partners for the firm's obligations,[102] if he were allowed to sue his firm this is akin to suing himself.[103] Similarly, a partner can, as a general rule, only sue his co-partner for a partnership obligation as part of a partnership action in which there is an account of all partnership dealings between them.[104]

---

96   Investment Intermediaries Act 1995, s 2(1) (definition of 'investment business firm').
97   See part (a) of the definition of 'investment instruments' in the Investment Intermediaries Act 1995, s 2(1).
98   Directive 93/22/EEC.
99   See part (c) of the definition of 'investment instruments' in the Investment Intermediaries Act 1995, s 2(1).
100 *Hawkins v Rogers* [1951] IR 48.
101 Paragraph **[20.07]**.
102 See further regarding a partner's liability for the obligations of his partners, para **[10.01]** et seq.
103 Although there are exceptional cases in which a partner can sue his firm for a partnership obligation, see para **[20.08]**.
104 As to such partnership actions, see generally para **[20.11]**.

The Creation of a Partnership is not a Settlement of Partnership Profits

[3.46] For tax purposes, a settlement is defined widely as any disposition or transfer of any right to money or property.[105] The Supreme Court has held that the creation of a partnership cannot constitute a settlement of partnership profits by one of the partners. This is because at the time of the creation of the partnership, there are no partnership profits to settle as these only come into existence as a result of the creation of the partnership. In *O'Dwyer, Inspector of Taxes v Cafolla*[106] Mr Cafolla converted his successful fast-food business in Dublin into a partnership with a number of his sons. However, after the creation of this partnership, the Revenue Commissioners refused to grant the firm[107] the benefit of the son's tax-free allowances. Instead the Revenue Commissioners sought to have the income of the partnership treated as the income of Mr Cafolla on the basis that the partnership agreement was a 'settlement'[108] by Mr Cafolla, through the medium of a partnership, of income on his children. Section 2(1) of the Finance Act 1937 provided that, where under the terms of a settlement money is paid to the minor child of a settlor, that income is deemed to be the income of the settlor in the first year of the settlement. On this basis, the Revenue Commissioners claimed that all the 'partnership' income should be treated as Mr Cafolla's income for the purposes of income tax. In the Supreme Court, O'Byrne J noted that until the partnership was created, there were no partnership profits to be settled and that the partnership deed at one and the same time created the partnership and provided for the distribution of the profits. He stated that in law:

> 'all the partners are equal and Joseph Cafolla cannot be regarded as settlor any more than any of the other partners. If after the partnership had been created, Joseph Cafolla had proceeded to settle, for the benefit of his children, his own share of the partnership profits or assets, this would have been a settlement within the meaning of the section.'[109]

Thus, while the settling of partnership profits after the creation of the partnership may be a settlement, it is clear that the creation of the partnership itself cannot be a settlement.

Is a Partnership with two Members a 'Body of Persons'?

[3.47] The question of whether a partnership of two members would constitute a 'body of persons' is open to doubt in light of the decision in *Revenue Commissioners v*

---

[105] Taxes Consolidation Act 1997, s 10(1). At the time of the decision in *O'Dwyer, Inspector of Taxes v Cafolla* [1949] IR 210, this definition was contained in s 2 of the Finance Act 1937. As regards the position in Northern Ireland, see s 620(1) of the Income Tax (Trading and Other Income) Act 2005. See generally Grattan, 'With all my profits I thee endow: The tax risks of business marriages' (1995) 46 NILQ 72.

[106] *O'Dwyer, Inspector of Taxes v Cafolla* [1949] IR 210.

[107] The reference is to the firm and not to the individual partners, as a joint assessment was made against the firm, see para **[3.11]**.

[108] A settlement was defined in s 2(2) of the Finance Act 1937 as including 'any disposition, trust, covenant, agreement, or arrangement, and any transfer of money or other property or of any right to any money or other property'.

[109] *O'Dwyer, Inspector of Taxes v Cafolla* [1949] IR 210 at 241–242.

O'Reilly & McGilligan.[110] In that case, the Supreme Court considered the meaning of the term 'body of persons' in s 349 of the Income Tax Act 1967, as that Act exempted certain bodies of persons from income tax. 'Body of persons' was defined in that Act as 'any body politic, corporate, or collegiate, and any company, fraternity, fellowship and society of persons, whether corporate or not corporate'.

[3.48] The case itself involved an attempt by two professionals to benefit from a tax exemption designed for clubs and associations which promoted athletic sport.[111] The two defendants, a solicitor and an accountant, formed a club which promoted skiing and sailing for the defendants, their families and friends. However, the Supreme Court refused to allow them to benefit from this tax exemption on the grounds that their club, which effectively consisted of just the two defendants, did not have the degree of plurality required by the term 'body of persons'. Although the case concerned a club, Henchy J stated obiter that a partnership of two persons would not be a body of persons for the purposes of s 349 of the Income Tax Act 1967. However, this decision must be treated with caution, since it appears to have been made less on principle and more on Henchy J's reluctance to grant the income tax exemption to the two professionals who 'with an engaging spirit of impudent challenge ... choose to call their club by the very number of the relevant section'.[112]

[3.49] Particularly persuasive is the dissenting judgment of McCarthy J who argued that a body of persons means any number more than one. He cogently argued that if it does not include two persons, where does one draw the line, three, four, ten? He also observed that if a body of persons does not include two persons, then under other income tax charging provisions which use the term 'body of persons', it would be possible that:

> 'two persons jointly engaged in the ownership of securities paying interest not deductible at source would enjoy an immunity from tax if they can contrive not to constitute a partnership.'[113]

[3.50] On this basis, it is apprehended that a partnership of two or more persons would indeed constitute a 'body of persons' and that the majority judgment of the Supreme Court and in particular the dicta of Henchy J would not be followed. The question of whether a partnership of two or more persons is a 'body of persons' remains of limited practical relevance since the only legislation of note to use this expression is the modern equivalent of s 349 of the Income Tax Act 1967.[114]

---

110 *Revenue Commissioners v O'Reilly & McGilligan* [1984] ILRM 406.
111 Income Tax Act 1967, s 349.
112 *Revenue Commissioners v O'Reilly & McGilligan* [1984] ILRM 406.
113 *Revenue Commissioners v O'Reilly & McGilligan* [1984] ILRM 406 at 411–412.
114 Taxes Consolidation Act 1997, s 235. See also the European Court of Justice decision in *Gregg v Customs and Excise Commissioners* [1999] All ER 775 in which it was held that a Northern Ireland nursing home partnership fell with the terms 'establishment' and 'organisation' so as to to be exempt from registration for VAT under Article 13(1)(b) and (g) of the Sixth VAT Directive (Directive 77/388/EEC). These terms were held to include natural persons as well as legal persons so as to apply to partnerships.

Status of a Legacy to a Firm

[3.51] A testator may decide to leave a legacy to a partnership, rather than to individual partners. In such a case, it has been established that the legacy is payable to those persons who were partners in the firm at the date of execution of the will.[115] In *Kerrison v Reddington*,[116] Thomas Reddington of Rye Hill, Co Galway, left a sum of money, not to a firm, but to the representatives of the firm of Messrs Alday and Kerrison. That partnership had originally consisted of two partners, but a number of years before the will was executed Alday died and all the assets of the firm became vested in Kerrison, the surviving partner. Accordingly, Brady LC held that the personal representatives of Kerrison should be entitled to the legacy.

Sole Trader Becoming a Partner

[3.52] Where a sole trader wishes to expand his business, he may choose to do so by constituting himself a partnership with one or more third parties. Where this occurs, the sole trader's former business and the new business of the partnership may be identical, but as a matter of law they will generally be treated as distinct.[117] In *Y v O'Sullivan*[118] the sole trader, who carried on a grocery business in Co Kerry died and under the terms of his will he left the business to a number of legatees. The testator's son, who was his sole personal representative, began to run the business after the date of death on the basis of a partnership for the benefit of himself and the residuary legatees. It was claimed by the Revenue Commissioners that under the income tax legislation of the time,[119] the business carried on by the son was the 'same business' as that carried on by the deceased. In the High Court, Maguire J held that these were not the same businesses and therefore any payments in respect of bad debts which were received by the son in his capacity as personal representative of the deceased, as debts due to the estate of the deceased, were not to be included in the trading accounts of the partnership business.

Where sole trader retains control of subsequent partnership business

[3.53] The sole trader's business and that of the resulting partnership will be treated as distinct, even where the sole trader retains considerable powers over what was originally his business alone. In such a case, provided that the consideration for the partnership is adequate, even if not sufficient,[120] the new business will be treated as bona fide as a

---

[115] *Stubbs v Sargon* (1838) 3 My & Cr 507.

[116] *Kerrison v Reddington* (1847) 11 Ir Eq R 451.

[117] In this context, note that the rights of employees in relation to any contract with a partnership for the transfer of its business will be protected by the European Communities (Protection of Employees on Transfer of Undertakings) Regulations 2003 (SI 131/2003). See *Allen & Son v Coventry* [1997] IRLR 399; *Jeetle v Elster* [1985] IRLR 227. See generally Regan and Murphy, *Employment Law* (2nd edn, 2017) at ch 23; Redmond, *Dismissal Law in Ireland* (2nd edn, 2007) at ch 18.

[118] *Y v O'Sullivan* [1949] IR 264.

[119] Income Tax Act 1918 (as amended).

[120] See further in relation to the adequacy and sufficiency of consideration, Clark, *Contract Law in Ireland* (8th edn, 2016) at para 2-09 et seq; McDermott and McDermott, *Contract Law* (2nd edn, 2017) at para [3.12] et seq.

matter of partnership law. This is clear from *O'Dwyer, Inspector of Taxes v Cafolla &
Co.*[121] There, Joseph Cafolla converted his sole trader's business in Dublin into a
partnership with his sons. Under the terms of the partnership agreement, Mr Cafolla
reserved to himself very extensive and far-reaching powers over the direction and
control of the firm. In particular, he had the power to put an end to the partnership at any
time, to reclaim the premises, the stock and the goodwill and to resume the carrying-on
of the business as a sole trader. Nonetheless, it was held by the Special Commissioner of
the Revenue, and it was not subsequently challenged in the High Court or the Supreme
Court, that a partnership existed in this case.[122] Indeed in the High Court, Maguire J
indicated that there was abundant evidence for such a finding.[123] It was argued that Mr
Cafolla was entitled at any time to obtain the beneficial enjoyment of the income of the
firm and therefore the income of the firm should be deemed to be Mr Cafolla's sole
income under s 20(1) of the Finance Act 1922.[124] However, the Supreme Court held, by a
3–2 majority, that the income of the firm arose from the carrying-on of the firm's
business under the terms of the partnership agreement and under this agreement the
sons undertook to devote their whole time to the business of the firm. Thus, although
under the terms of the partnership agreement, Mr Cafolla was able to resume the
restaurant business as a sole trader at any time, by doing so he would not be receiving
the income of 'the firm' (but the income of a new business to be run by him without his
sons). Thus, the firm's income was not something of which he could have beneficial
enjoyment at any time for the purposes of s 20(1) of the Finance Act 1922 and therefore
it was incorrect to deem it to be his income for income tax purposes. In this way, the
Supreme Court maintained the strict distinction between the sole trader's business and
that of the subsequent partnership.

In tenancy cases, sole trader and firm deemed to be one

[3.54] Although in the *Cafolla* case[125] and in *Y v O'Sullivan*,[126] a sole trader's business
was treated as distinct from the subsequent partnership business, the courts have not
taken a consistent approach to this question. It will be seen that where the courts have
desired to achieve an equitable result, particularly in the context of an application for the
renewal of a tenancy, they have treated a partnership and a former sole trader's business

---

121 *O'Dwyer, Inspector of Taxes v Cafolla & Co* [1949] IR 210.
122 However, see para **[2.79]**, where, as a separate issue, it is doubted whether this aspect of the
     decision should be followed.
123 Although the decision of Maguire J was overturned on appeal by the Supreme Court, the
     Supreme Court did not disagree with his conclusions regarding the existence of a partnership.
124 The relevant provision was s 20(1) of the Finance Act 1922 which provided that:

     Any income – of which any person is able, or has, at any time since the 5th day of
     April, nineteen hundred and twenty-two, been able, without the consent of any other
     person by means of the exercise of any power of appointment, power of revocation or
     otherwise howsoever by virtue of or in consequence of a disposition made directly or
     indirectly by himself, to obtain for himself the beneficial enjoyment [shall] be deemed
     for the purposes of the enactments relating to income tax ... to be the income of the per-
     son who is or was able to obtain the beneficial enjoyment thereof ... and not ... the
     income of any other person.
125 *O'Dwyer, Inspector of Taxes v Cafolla & Co* [1949] IR 210.
126 *Y v O'Sullivan* [1949] IR 264.

as one.[127] One such case is that of *Gaffney v Duffy*,[128] which concerned Gaffney, who carried on a bicycle shop business as a sole trader from the respondent's property in Capel Street in Dublin under the terms of a lease. After a number of years in occupation of the premises, Gaffney acquired two partners for his business and he became a dormant partner in the resulting partnership. When Gaffney sought a renewal of his tenancy, an issue arose as to whether Gaffney was to be regarded as continuing to be in occupation of the premises for the term of the lease, even though the business had changed from that of a sole trader to that of a partnership.[129] In the Circuit Court, Judge Shannon held that after he acquired the partners, Gaffney was still the occupier of the premises and was therefore entitled to a new tenancy under the landlord and tenant legislation.[130] Thus in this case, the sole trader of a business was treated as one and the same as the partnership which he formed to take over that business.

Partner Becoming a Sole Trader

[3.55] The contrary position to that of a sole trader becoming a partner is also worthy of consideration.[131] *O'Neill v Whelan*[132] deals with the issue of a partner becoming a sole trader. The case involved an application by a tenant for a new tenancy. The respondent leased a premises in Little Green Street in Dublin to a partnership of potato dealers which consisted of Whelan and Mrs O'Neill. The partnership subsequently dissolved and Mrs O'Neill acquired the business and was granted a lease of the premises in her own name. Subsequently, Mrs O'Neill sought a new tenancy of the premises under the landlord and tenant legislation.[133] In the Circuit Court, Connolly J held that the term a 'tenant for the time being' in s 19(1) of the Landlord and Tenant Act 1931 included the time the partnership was in occupation of the premises as well as the time the sole trader, who was the successor in title to the partnership, was in occupation of the premises. On this basis, Mrs O'Neill had the requisite three-year period as a tenant in the premises and was entitled to a new tenancy.[134] Although s 19(1) of the Landlord and Tenant Act 1931 has since been repealed, the principles underlying these cases are still of relevance to the

---

127 See *O'Neill v Whelan* (1951) 85 ILTR 111, considered at para **[3.55]**.
128 *Gaffney v Duffy* (1953) 87 ILTR 92.
129 Under s 24 of the Landlord and Tenant Act 1931.
130 See Wylie, *Landlord and Tenant Law* (3rd edn, 2014) at para [30.15].
131 Here also, the rights of employees, in relation to any contract with a partnership for the transfer of its business, will be protected by the European Communities (Protection of Employees on Transfer of Undertakings) Regulations 2003 (SI 131/2003). See *Allen & Son v Coventry* [1997] IRLR 399; *Jeetle v Elster* [1985] IRLR 227. See generally Regan and Murphy, *Employment Law* (2nd edn, 2017) at ch 23; Redmond, *Dismissal Law in Ireland* (2nd edn, 2007) at ch 18.
132 *O'Neill v Whelan* (1951) 85 ILTR 111.
133 Ie the Landlord and Tenant Act 1931.
134 Also in this case, the landlord contended that the letting made to the partnership was a letting 'made for or dependant on the continuance of the tenant in any office, employment or appointment' such that when the partnership dissolved the premises were no longer a tenement within s 2 of the Landlord and Tenant Act 1931 and thus O'Neill was not entitled to a new tenancy. However, this contention was rejected by Connolly J who held that the letting to a partnership does not come within the description of a letting 'made for or dependant on the continuance of the tenant in any office, employment or appointment'.

new legislation.[135] Thus, the overriding concern for the courts in these cases, as is evident from *Gaffney v Duffy*[136] and *O'Neill v Whelan*,[137] is to ensure that an equitable result is obtained if the de facto tenant is in possession of the premises for the required period, even if part of this period is as a partner in a firm which occupies the premises.[138]

III. STATUS OF FIRM NAME

[3.56] As has been noted, a partnership is not a separate legal entity, but is an aggregate of its members.[139] It follows that the name used by the firm is no more than a convenient way to describe the partners.[140] Section 4(1) of the 1890 Act provides that:

> Persons who have entered into partnership with one another are for the purposes of this Act called collectively a firm, and the name under which their business is carried on is called the firm-name.

As a result of this section, the term 'firm' usually connotes a partnership, but it is commonly used by the courts and legislation to include other types of business enterprises.[141]

[3.57] Since a firm name is the collective name for the partners in the firm, any time there is a change in the membership of the firm, the firm name takes on a new meaning. Accordingly, where a partnership is referred to by its firm name, this is deemed to be a reference to the members of the firm at the time the name is used. Evidence will be

---

135   Landlord and Tenant (Amendment) Act 1980, s 13(1)(a), as to which see Wylie, *Landlord and Tenant Law* (3rd edn, 2014) at para [30.13] et seq.

136   *Gaffney v Duffy* (1953) 87 ILTR 92.

137   *O'Neill v Whelan* (1951) 85 ILTR 111.

138   A similar result occurred in the Northern Ireland case of *Cairns v Prudential Assurance* [1956] NI 123, a case decided under the Business Tenancies (Temporary Provisions) Act (Northern Ireland) 1952.

139   Paragraph **[3.04]**.

140   See *Re Land Credit Co of Ireland – Weikersheim's Case* (1873) 8 Ch App 831; *Meyer & Co v Faber (No 2)* [1923] 2 Ch 421; *Sadler v Whiteman* [1901] 1 KB 868 at 889 (affirmed in the House of Lords, albeit that other aspects of the first instance judgment were not affirmed [1910] AC 674); *R v Holden* [1912] 1KB 483.

141   For example in s 2(1) of the Investment Intermediaries Act 1995, the term 'investment business firm' is defined as a 'person' and thus includes an individual as well as a body corporate and an unincorporated body of persons by virtue of s 18(c) of the Interpretation Act 2005. See also, for example, the English High Court case of *Nationwide Building Society v Lewis* [1997] 3 All ER 498, in which a sole practitioner's business was referred to by the court as a firm. The comments of Finlay Geoghegan J in *McAleenan v AIG* [2010] IEHC 128 regarding the commonplace use of the term 'firm' to describe different business entities are worth noting. She noted that the term is not only used to describe a partnership, but can also be used to describe a limited company and a practice carried on by a sole practitioner who employs others. The use of the term 'firm' is not determinative of the existence of a partnership, and Finlay Geoghegan J commented that the names of certain firms may imply that they are partnerships (in that case, the name of the firm was 'Michael Lynn & Co., Solicitors' which could have implied that more than one person was involved in the firm and that the firm was a partnership, whereas in fact the firm had a sole principal who in turn employed a number of solicitors and other staff).

admissible to show who is in fact a member of the firm at the relevant time. In *Latouche v Whaley*,[142] under the terms of a deed between the defendant and the banking firm of 'David Latouche and Company', the defendant assigned a judgment to the firm. When one partner in the firm, John Latouche, sought to enforce the deed, the defendant objected on the basis that John Latouche was not named as a party to the deed. The Irish Court of Exchequer held that the use of the firm's name was sufficient designation of all the partners in the firm at the time of the execution and that evidence was admissible to accurately ascertain them. This issue is now governed by the Rules of the Superior Courts,[143] which allow a partnership to sue or be sued in its firm name, in which case the partners suing or being sued are the partners who were members of that firm at the time of the accrual of the cause of action.[144]

[3.58] It is clear that where a conveyance is made to a firm, it will pass the property to the persons who were at the date of the conveyance partners in the firm.[145] For this reason, it is common for large evolving firms to convey property into the names of a number of partners as trustees for the partners from time to time in the firm. In *Gorrie v Woodley*,[146] there was a contract of guarantee by the defendant in favour of a firm called R Meiklejohn & Son of Carrigtwohill, Co Cork. The three partners in that firm took an action, in their own names only, to enforce the guarantee. The defendant argued that the guarantee was not enforceable by the three individuals since the guarantee did not contain their names and thus it did not constitute a sufficient memorandum of the guarantee to satisfy the requirements of the Statute of Frauds (Ireland) 1695. In the High Court, O'Brien J held that the firm name was sufficient to refer to the partners in that partnership and that the statement of claim of the defendants need simply state that the three plaintiffs are the persons described in the guarantee as 'R Meiklejohn & Son'.

Judgment and Judgment Mortgage may be Obtained in Firm Name

[3.59] It has been noted previously that in the High Court case of *Magner v Johnstone*,[147] Meredith J held that a judgment mortgage could be registered in the same name as that in which a judgment could be obtained.[148] Therefore, just as one can obtain a judgment against a firm in a firm name,[149] it is also possible to register a judgment mortgage against a firm name.

---

142 *Latouche v Whaley* (1832) Hayes & Jones 43. See also *Pentland v Gibson* (1833) Alc & Nap 310, see para **[12.16]**.
143 RSC Ord 14, r 1 (SI 15/1986 as amended).
144 See generally in relation to actions by or against firms in the firm name, para **[12.11]** et seq.
145 *Wray v Wray* [1905] 2 Ch 349.
146 *Gorrie v Woodley* (1864) 17 Ir CLR 221.
147 *Magner v Johnstone* [1926] IR 472.
148 Paragraph **[3.33]**.
149 At that time, a judgment could be obtained against a firm in a firm-name, since under Ord 48A of the Rules of the Supreme Court 1905, a firm could be sued in its firm name. Today, Ord 48A has been replaced by Ord 14, r 1 of the Rules of the Superior Courts, as to which, see generally para **[12.11]**.

Effect on Firm Name of a Change in Partners

[3.60] When the constitution of a partnership changes by the addition or departure of a partner, the firm name takes on a new meaning and henceforth it is the manner by which the partnership, as newly constituted, is described.[150] It is of course a separate question as to what the effect of a change of partners may have on a firm's legal position *vis-à-vis* third parties, as distinct from the effect on the firm name. For this reason, care will always have to be taken to identify who was or was not a partner on the date of a transaction or on the date a liability was incurred between a third party and the partnership. This issue will be considered next.

Contracts with the firm before a change in partners

[3.61] Usually, a contract which is entered into with a partnership will be a contract with the firm, as from time to time constituted, in the sense that any change in the firm will not bring the contract to an end. In such a case, the admission or departure of a partner will not terminate the contract.[151]

[3.62] In some instances, however, contracts made with partnerships may be of a personal nature and made solely with the specific partners, who were members of the partnership at the date of execution of the contract for so long as they alone would be partners in the firm. In such cases, the contract may cease to apply in the event of there being any change in the firm, although this will not affect the liability of the partners incurred up to that point. Thus in *Grantham v Redmond*,[152] a contract was entered into by Redmond with the four partners of a firm called the Liverpool and Wexford Steam Navigation Company for the docking of the partners' ship or a replacement thereof in Redmond's wharf in Wexford Harbour. Significantly, under the terms of the contract, the four partners undertook *personally* not to injure Redmond's business interests and Redmond was to receive a share of the profits of the use of the ship on the Liverpool–Wexford line. Subsequently, one of the four partners retired and six other partners joined the firm and the newly constituted firm sought the specific performance of this contract in relation to another ship owned by these nine partners. Napier LC held that it was clear from the terms of the contract that the identity of the original four partners was important to Redmond and therefore he refused to enforce the agreement.[153]

---

150 In *Latouche v Whaley* (1832) Hayes & Jones 43, a deed of assignment had been executed by the defendant in favour of a banking partnership in Castle Street in Dublin called 'David Latouche and Company'. David and John Latouche had originally been partners in that firm, but David Latouche had died. Accordingly, the Irish Court of Exchequer allowed John Latouche to sue on the deed.

151 It is of course a separate question as to the liability of the former partner and the liability of the new partner on the contract and this issue is discussed para **[11.25]** et seq.

152 *Grantham v Redmond* (1859) 8 Ir Ch R 449. See also *Tasker v Shepherd* (1861) 123 RR 697, in which two partners appointed an agent for four and half years. Before the end of that term one of the partners died and it was held that the surviving partner was not obliged to continue to employ the agent since the contract of agency was made by reference to the partnership which existed at the time of the contract.

153 *Grantham v Redmond* (1859) 8 Ir Ch R 449 at 454, Napier LC stated: (contd.../)

[3.63] It will, of course, be a matter of construction of the terms of the transaction to determine if a partnership contract is solely with the partners at the date of execution such that it is to terminate in the event of changes in the firm. It is thought that the contract must be of a somewhat personal nature for this interpretation to be taken and that in large firms with regular changes in the membership, it will be a difficult matter to show that a contract has such a character.

Effect on Partnership of a Change in Firm Name

[3.64] Since a firm name is a mere expression used for convenience to describe the partners,[154] it follows that the legal status of a partnership is not affected by a change in the firm name. Rather, the change in the firm name simply represents a change in the label or title by which the partners are collectively known.

Possible to have more than one firm name

[3.65] Section 4(1) of the 1890 Act does not restrict a partnership to using just one firm name and it has long been accepted that a firm may operate with more than one firm name. Thus in *Dickson v McMaster & Co*,[155] a Belfast linen partnership operated under the names Dickson, McMaster & Co and Dunbar, McMaster & Co. The use of two or more firm names will of course necessitate the registration of each name as a separate business name of the partnership under the Registration of Business Names Act 1963 and this matter is considered in detail below.[156]

Use of '& Company' in the Firm Name

[3.66] It is common for partnerships to include in their firm name the expression '& Company' or a variation thereof. The use of this expression does not indicate, nor can it be interpreted by third parties as indicating, that the business is that of a registered company. The practice of partnerships using this expression can be traced back to the Anonymous Partnerships Act of 1781.[157] Section 2 of this Act provided, inter alia, for firms to carry on business 'in whole name and names whilst living and continuing in credit, with the addition of "and company".' Although this Act has since been repealed, it is clear that partnerships are still entitled to use the expression '& Company' as part of

---

[153]   (\...contd) 'However, I find that Mr Redmond is to participate in the profits, that gives a most substantial reason for saying that the relations must not be altered by the admission of a person on whose conduct or commercial character the profits might depend. Then too, when I find that the four owners pledge themselves personally, as part of the agreement, it is hard to say how that could be carried out against other owners of another vessel.' In this regard the contract in this case resembled a guarantee with the partnership which is subject to special rules, see para **[3.94]** et seq.

[154]   As to this proposition, see para **[3.56]**.

[155]   *Dickson v McMaster & Co* (1866) 11 Ir Jur 202.

[156]   Paragraph **[3.78]**.

[157]   An Act to promote Trade and Manufacture, by regulating and encouraging Partnerships in Ireland (21 & 22 Geo 3, c 46). This Act was repealed by the Companies Act 1862, s 205, 3rd Sch (25 & 26 Vict c 89).

their firm name.[158] It should, however, be noted that partnerships which use this term or a variation thereof are required to register that name as a business name under the Registration of Business Names Act 1963.[159]

Firm Name as a Passing Off

[3.67] The law of passing off is relevant to the firm name which is used by a partnership. A firm commits the tort of passing off if it adopts a name similar to that of another firm, such that it is passing itself off as being that other firm or passing off its goods or services as being those of that firm.[160] In this context, it is to be noted that a firm name may be registered as a trade mark or a service mark under the Trade Marks Act 1996.[161]

Entitlement of Partners to use Firm Name after Dissolution

[3.68] An issue which should be addressed in every partnership agreement is the entitlement of the partners to use the firm name after a dissolution of the firm, whether a technical or a general dissolution.[162] This is because, in the absence of any contrary agreement, each of the partners is entitled to use the firm name after a dissolution of the firm.[163] As noted by Chatterton VC in *Wilson v Williams*:[164]

> 'On a dissolution any of the partners may, unless expressly prohibited by contract from doing so, carry on the same business as before, and use the old name of the firm, and solicit the customers to deal with them.'[165]

[3.69] One reason why a former partner may not want the firm's name used by his partners is because of the risk that he may be held out to be a partner, particularly if the firm name includes his name. This concern does not arise in the case of a deceased partner, since s 14(2) of the 1890 Act provides that the continued use of a firm name or of the deceased partner's name as part thereof, shall not make his estate liable for partnership debts contracted after his death.

IV. REGISTRATION OF BUSINESS NAMES ACT 1963

[3.70] In this section of this chapter, it is proposed to deal with the application of the Registration of Business Names Act 1963[166] to partnerships. This Act is designed to

---

[158] See for example *Maughan v Sharpe* 17 CB (ns) 443; *Wray v Wray* [1905] 2 Ch 349. In *Barr v Barr* (29 July 1992) HC, the partnership used the name 'The North Western Tea Company'.

[159] Registration of Business Names Act 1963, s 3(1)(a). See generally in relation to such registration, para **[3.70]** et seq.

[160] For the requirements of a passing off action see McMahon and Binchy, *Law of Torts* (4th edn, 2013) at para [31.01] et seq.

[161] See generally in relation to such registrations, Clarke, Smyth and Hall, *Intellectual Property Law in Ireland* (4th edn, 2016) at para [34.01] et seq.

[162] As to the difference between a general and a technical dissolution, see para [23.07].

[163] This question of whether a partner is entitled to use a firm name after the dissolution of the firm is considered in detail at para **[18.18]**.

[164] *Wilson v Williams* (1892) 29 LR Ir 176.

[165] *Wilson v Williams* (1892) 29 LR Ir 176 at 181–182.

[166] The filing fees relevant to that Act are contained in the Business Names Regulations 2016 (SI 339/2016).

provide transparency for third parties who deal with all business enterprises, including partnerships. It does this by allowing third parties to establish from a public register (the Register of Business Names) the identity of the partners in a firm who trade under a name different from the names of the partners. Such partnerships are required to comply with two main obligations. First, the firm must register its business name with the registrar (the Registrar of Companies acts as registrar under the 1963 Act)[167] under s 4 of the 1963 Act and second it must publish the names and nationalities (if not Irish) of its partners on its stationery under s 18 of the 1963 Act.

Act applies to a 'person to be registered'

[3.71] The Registration of Business Names Act 1963 applies its terms to a 'person to be registered' under the 1963 Act, and s 3 provides that a partnership is a 'person to be registered' if it comes within the scope of s 3(1)(a) or s 3(1)(c). Section 3(1)(a) provides that a person to be registered includes:

> every firm having a place of business in the State[168] and carrying on business under a business name which does not consist of the true surnames of all partners who are individuals and the corporate names of all partners which are bodies corporate without any addition other than the true Christian names of individual partners or initials of such Christian names.

[3.72] A partnership will not fall under s 3(1)(a) of the Registration of Business Names Act 1963 where the addition to the names of the partners merely indicates that the firm's business is being carried on in succession to a former owner of the business,[169] by the use of the plural form of a surname if two or more of the partners have the same surname[170] or where the firm's business is being carried on by an assignee or trustee in bankruptcy, a trustee of the estate of an arranging debtor, or a receiver or manager appointed by any court.[171] However, in any other situation where the existing partners operate under a name which does not consist solely of their names (eg the use of a former partner's name), the firm will have to comply with the terms of the 1963 Act. It is also the case that the use by two partners (A and B) of the business name AB '& Company' or AB 'and Co' would require registration, since this term is an addition to their names. However, where a body corporate uses a recognised abbreviation for the term 'Company' (eg 'Co') in its business name, s 3(4) of the 1963 Act provides that registration of the business name is not, for this reason alone, required. It is strange that the same exemption was not extended to partnerships, especially since they have been using the term 'Company' for almost a century before the advent of the registered

---

[167] Registration of Business Names Act 1963, s 15(1).

[168] It is interesting to note that in *O'Donnell & anor v Bank of Ireland* [2015] IESC 14, the fact that the appellants had registered their business partnership (Vico Capital) under the Registration of Business Names Act 1963 was one of the factors which indicated to Laffoy J that the centre of main interests of each appellant was located in Ireland for the purposes of the EU Insolvency Regulation (then Council Regulation (EC) No 1346/2000).

[169] Registration of Business Names Act 1963, s 3(2).

[170] Registration of Business Names Act 1963, s 3(3).

[171] Registration of Business Names Act 1963, s 3(5).

company.[172] It is suggested that the failure of the draftsman to extend this exemption to partnerships resulted from a failure to appreciate the use of this term by partnerships and it is contended that the s 3(4) exemption should be extended to partnerships to eliminate the requirement to register a business name solely be virtue of the use of this term.

Every partnership that changes its name is 'a person to be registered'

[3.73] The main application of the Registration of Business Names Act 1963 is to provide transparency to third parties dealing with partnerships, by requiring those partnerships which operate under a name other than the names of all the partners to disclose the names of all the partners in the Register of Business Names. However, in some cases the 1963 Act even applies to partnerships which trade under a name which *does* consist of the names of all the partners. This is because s 3(1)(c) of the 1963 Act defines a person to be registered as including the following:

> every individual or firm having a place of business in the State, who, or a member of which, has either before or after the passing of this Act changed his name, except in the case of a woman in consequence of marriage.

Since this section applies to every firm which changes its name, it follows that a firm of partners (A, B and C), which trades under the firm name (A, B & C) will be subject to the requirements of the 1963 Act where, on the departure of C, the partners change the firm name to A & B, even though the new firm is trading under a name containing only the names of the partners. Clearly this result goes against the spirit of the 1963 Act and there should have been a carve-out for such a situation.

Obligations under the Registration of Business Names Act

[3.74] As a person to be registered under the Registration of Business Names Act 1963, a partnership has two basic obligations:

   (i)   it must register its business name under s 4 of the 1963 Act; and

   (ii)   it must publish the true names of the partners (and their nationalities, if not Irish) on the stationery of the firm under s 18 of the 1963 Act.

Each of these obligations will now be considered.

(i) Registration of Business Name

[3.75] Section 4(1) of the Registration of Business Names Act 1963 requires the firm to register its business name with the registrar. Registration is effected by furnishing (online, or by post or delivery) to the registrar a statement in writing in the prescribed form[173] containing the following particulars in relation to the partnership:[174]

   (i)   its business name, including, in the case of the proprietor of a newspaper, the title of the newspaper;

   (ii)   the general nature of its business;

---

[172] See the Anonymous Partnerships Act of 1781, s 2, discussed at para **[3.66]**. The limited liability company was not introduced until the Limited Liability Act 1855, which was replaced by the Joint Stock Companies Act 1856.
[173] This form is known as a Form RBN1A.
[174] Registration of Business Names Act 1963, s 4(1)(a)–(d), (g).

   (iii)   the principal place of its business;

   (iv)   the present Christian name and surname, any former Christian name or surname, the nationality, if not Irish, the usual residence, and the other business occupation (if any) of each of the individuals who are partners, and the corporate name and registered or principal office in the State of every body corporate which is a partner; and

   (v)   the date of adoption of the business name by the firm.

[3.76] The Form RBN1A[175] must be signed by all the partners (and in the case of corporate partners, by the director or secretary of the corporate partner).[176] It may also be signed by just one individual partner (or a director or secretary of a corporate partner) if that execution is verified by a statutory declaration of the signatory.[177] The form must be filed[178] with the Business Names Section of the Companies Registration Office within one month of the adoption of the business name.[179]

Issue of certificate of business name on registration

[3.77] Upon the filing of the registration statement, the registrar is required to send a certificate of registration of business name to the partnership.[180] The partnership is required to exhibit the certificate in a prominent place at the firm's principal place of business, failing which, each partner is liable on summary conviction to a class C fine.[181]

No monopoly in a registered business name

[3.78] It is important to bear in mind that the registration of a business name by a firm does not give that firm a monopoly in the use of that name. It is possible for another partnership to register the same business name, even if the second partnership carries on the same business as the first registered firm. In such a case, the first registered firm will not have any remedy under the law relating to business names, although it may have other remedies under the law of passing off[182] or for breach of intellectual property rights, if it had registered its business name as a trade mark or as a service mark.[183] Similarly, there is no reason why a firm cannot have more than one registered business

---

[175]   This form is available on the Companies Registration Office's website: www.cro.ie and the most recent version was prescribed by the Business Names Regulations 2016 (SI 339/2016).

[176]   Registration of Business Names Act 1963, s 5(1)(c)(i).

[177]   Registration of Business Names Act 1963, s 5(1)(c)(ii).

[178]   The filing fee is €40 where a paper filing is made, and €20 when an electronic filing is made (Business Names Regulations 2016 (SI 339/2016), reg 5).

[179]   Registration of Business Names Act 1963, s 6(1).

[180]   Registration of Business Names Act 1963, s 8(1). While s 8(1) provides that the certificate will be sent by post or delivered, it is now sent by email to the email address supplied on the Form RBN1A.

[181]   The original fine of £100 set out in the Registration of Business Names Act 1963, s 8(2) was converted to its euro equivalent by virtue of Council Regulations (EC) No 1103/97, (EC) No 974/98 and (EC) No 2866/98 and the Economic and Monetary Union Act 1998, s 6 and then replaced, by virtue of the Fines Act 2010, s 6, with a class C fine (at the time of writing, a class C fine is a fine not exceeding €2,500).

[182]   As to which, see para **[3.67]**.

[183]   As to which, see para **[3.67]**.

name and this, for example, is common amongst accountancy partnerships which have different business names for their audit, tax and consultancy areas of work.

[3.79] The Minister for Business, Enterprise and Innovation may refuse to permit the registration of any business name by a partnership, if, in the Minister's opinion, the name is undesirable.[184]

Change in details registered under s 4

[3.80] The details filed with the registrar as part of the registration process may change, such as where the identity of the partners changes because of the admission or retirement of a partner or where the address of the partnership changes.[185] In such an event, these changes must be notified to the registrar by the filing of a Form RBN2A[186] within one month of the change.[187] In addition, under s 12(1) of the Registration of Business Names Act 1963, a firm which ceases to carry on business under its registered business name is required to notify the registrar by filing a Form RBN3[188] within three months.

Filing of Form RBN2A to notify Registrar of departure of a partner

[3.81] Pursuant to s 7 of the Registration of Business Names Act 1963, the Form RBN2A must be signed by one or all of the partners in the firm.[189] It follows that where the change being notified is the departure of a partner after he has left the firm, the form must be signed by the continuing partners only. For this reason, it is a good practice to have a provision in partnership agreements which requires the continuing partners to sign and file the Form RBN2A in order to ensure that the former partner's name is removed from the Register of Business Names. However, even in the absence of such a provision, the former partner will be able to rely on s 37 of the 1890 Act, which entitles him to 'require the other partner or partners to concur ... in all necessary or proper acts' for the public notification of his retirement. Thus, in *Larkin v Groeger and Eaton*,[190] the continuing partner in an accountancy partnership was ordered[191] to sign the necessary

---

[184]   Registration of Business Names Act 1963, s 14(1).

[185]   Registration of Business Names Act 1963, s 7.

[186]   This form is available on the Companies Registration Office's website: www.cro.ie and the most recent version was prescribed by the Business Names Regulations 2016 (SI 339/2016). The filing fee is €15 where a paper filing is made. An RBN2A can be filed electronically (free of charge) for a change in a partnership's address but not, at the time of writing, for other changes.

[187]   Registration of Business Names Act 1963, s 7.

[188]   This form is available on the Companies Registration Office's website: www.cro.ie and the most recent version was prescribed by the Business Names Regulations 2016 (SI 339/2016). There is no filing fee and either a paper filing or an electronic filing can be made.

[189]   This is because s 7 of the Registration of Business Names Act 1963 provides that the statement to be filed should be signed in the like manner as the statement required on registration. Thus the Form RBN2A may be signed by one partner only, if this execution is verified by a statutory declaration of the signatory.

[190]   *Larkin v Groeger and Eaton* (26 April 1988) HC.

[191]   The order was in fact made by an arbitrator, John Gore Grimes, solicitor, which award was approved by Barrington J in the High Court.

business name form to notify the registrar that the retiring partners were no longer partners in the firm.

Is a change in register of business names constructive notice to third parties?

[3.82] It has been noted that on the departure of a partner, a partnership which has a registered business name must notify this change to the registrar by filing a Form RBN2A. In addition, a firm which does not have to register its business name, because its business name consists of the surname of all the partners, will have to register its business name on the departure of a partner. This is because the firm of A, B & C, after the departure of C, will do one of two things, either of which will result in it being subject to registration. First, it may decide to leave the name unaltered, in which case A and B will be persons to be registered, since they will be using a business name which has an 'addition' to their surnames, namely C's name, and thus they will fall within the terms of s 3(1)(a) of the Registration of Business Names Act 1963. Second, the firm may decide to change its name to A & B, in which case it will fall within the terms of s 3(1)(c) of the 1963 Act as a firm changing its name.[192] It follows that in every case in which a partner leaves a partnership and the partnership continues in business, it will be necessary for the registrar to be notified of the change, either by way of an amendment to an existing business name or by way of the first registration of a business name under the names of the continuing partners.

[3.83] Accordingly, one of the ways in which third parties may be on notice of the departure of a partner[193] from a firm is through an inspection of the firm's business name in the Register of Business Names. Under s 16 of the Registration of Business Names Act 1963, any person may inspect the documents kept by the registrar and obtain a certified or an ordinary copy of such documents upon the payment of a nominal fee.[194] The question may be asked as to whether the filing by a firm of a Form RBN2A in relation to the departure of a partner constitutes constructive notice to third parties of his retirement? In the related area of the advertisement of a partner's retirement in *Iris Oifigiúil*, s 36(2) of the 1890 Act expressly provides that all persons, who had no previous dealings with the firm, are deemed to be on notice of the partner's retirement once it is advertised in *Iris Oifigiúil*. In contrast, the 1963 Act is silent as to whether third persons (whether they had previous dealings with the firm or not) will be deemed to be on notice of the removal of a partner's name from the Register of Business Names. In the absence of any express provision along the lines of s 36(2) of the 1890 Act, it is apprehended that such a filing would not be deemed to be notice to existing or new customers of the firm of the departure of a partner. Support for this view can be found in the Scottish decision of *Welsh v Knarston*[195] in which a former partner was being sued

---

[192] See para **[3.73]**.

[193] Or indeed the commencement of liability for a partner by holding out, where a person is held out to be a partner in the register of business names. See generally regarding partners by holding out, para **[7.01]** et seq.

[194] The inspection fee is €3.50 for any document kept by the registrar in paper form or electronically. A certified copy of a document kept by the registrar or of the certificate of registration costs €12 and an ordinary copy of any other document kept by the registrar costs €2.50: Business Names Regulations 2016 (SI 339/2016).

[195] *Welsh v Knarston* [1972] SLT 96.

for the negligence of his firm. He claimed that he was not liable therefor on the grounds that the plaintiff was on notice of his departure from the firm. The Scottish register of business names for the firm name did not contain his name (since he had never been listed therein as a partner in the first place). However, the defendant claimed that the letterhead of the firm, which was sent to the plaintiff after the defendant's departure, no longer contained his name and that the defendant should be deemed to be on notice of his departure by virtue of this fact. This claim was rejected by the Scottish court, Lord Stott observing that:

> 'In any event the omission of his name from the letter head seems to me to fall short of what would be required to give notice to the pursuers that he had ceased his association with the firm and that he was no longer to be taken as concerning himself with the pursuer's business.'[196]

Penalties

[3.84] Every partner is liable on summary conviction to a class C fine where his firm makes default without reasonable excuse in furnishing a statement of particulars of a business name or a change in particulars of the business name or fails to notify the registrar that the firm has ceased to carry on business under that name.[197] Where a person furnishes a statement which is false in any material particular to the knowledge of the person making the statement, that person shall be liable to a term of imprisonment not exceeding six months and/or to a class C fine.[198]

(ii) Publication of true names and nationalities of partners

[3.85] The second obligation on partnerships which are 'persons to be registered' under the Registration of Business Names Act 1963 is contained in s 18(1)(b). This states that:

> A person required by this Act to be registered shall, in all business letters, circulars and catalogues on or in which the business name appears and which are sent by that person to any person, state in legible characters ...
>
> (b)   in the case of a firm, the present Christian names, or the initials thereof, and present surnames, any former Christian names and surnames and the nationality, if not Irish, of all the partners in the firm or, in the case of a body corporate being a partner, the corporate name.

[3.86] Where default is made in complying with s 18 of the Registration of Business Names Act 1963, every partner is liable on summary conviction to a class E fine.[199] One

---

196   *Welsh v Knarston* [1972] SLT 96 at 98.
197   The original fines of £100 set out in the Registration of Business Names Act 1963, ss 10 and 12 were converted to their euro equivalents by virtue of Council Regulations (EC) No 1103/97, (EC) No 974/98 and (EC) No 2866/98 and the Economic and Monetary Union Act 1998, s 6 and then replaced, by virtue of the Fines Act 2010, s 6, with class C fines (a class C fine is a fine not exceeding €2,500).
198   Registration of Business Names Act 1963, s 11.
199   The original fine of £25 set out in the Registration of Business Names Act 1963, s 18(2) was converted to its euro equivalent by virtue of Council Regulations (EC) No 1103/97, (EC) No 974/98 and (EC) No 2866/98 and the Economic and Monetary Union Act 1998, s 6 and then replaced, by virtue of the Fines Act 2010, s 6, with a class E fine (a class E fine is a fine not exceeding €500).

obvious omission from s 18 of the 1963 Act is the fact that it makes no provision for the names of partners to be stated in modern methods of communication such as electronic mail (and it also does not refer to the use of faxes). Therefore these forms of communication do not appear to be subject to the requirements in s 18 of the 1963 Act.[200]

[3.87] It has been noted that in *Welsh v Knarston*[201] it was held that the removal of a partner's name from the firm's letterhead was not regarded as notice of a partner's departure from the firm.[202]

Solicitors' partnerships

[3.88] It remains to be noted that all partnerships of solicitors are subject to the obligation that the partners' names be listed on the notepaper of the firm, even where the partnership would not be a 'person to be registered' under the Registration of Business Names Act 1963. This is because the Solicitors (Practice, Conduct and Discipline) Regulations 1996[203] require all solicitors' firms to have the partners' names on the notepaper, regardless of whether the firm uses a business name which consists only of the names of the partners.

Importance of Complying with Registration of Business Names Act

[3.89] Although sometimes seen as unnecessary red-tape, registering a business name or updating the registration details of a registered business name is of importance for third parties dealing with a partnership, since it is the means by which third parties know who is behind a particular business name. Nonetheless, there have been few recorded instances of penalties being imposed on partnerships for a breach of the Registration of Business Names Act 1963 and this is undoubtedly due to the lack of any direct enforcement of its provisions by the Minister for Business, Enterprise and Innovation.[204] It is certainly not due to a high level of compliance with the 1963 Act, as anecdotal evidence would suggest that the 1963 Act is more honoured in the breach than the observance. Indeed, it may be argued that this law has fallen into disrepute in much the same way as the law requiring companies to file financial statements had done, prior to the institution of proceedings against directors and companies which led to the striking off of thousands of companies from the register of companies.[205] Undoubtedly a similar effort is required to render the register of business names an up-to-date and practical guide for third parties doing business with partnerships. In this regard it would be preferable if the Registrar of Companies was given the same powers in relation to

---

[200] It is also to be noted that there is no obligation to remove a former partner's name from the firm's stationery, in contrast to the requirement to remove a former partner's name from the Register of Business Names: Registration of Business Names Act 1963, s 7.

[201] *Welsh v Knarston* [1972] SLT 96.

[202] See para [3.83].

[203] SI 178/1996.

[204] Under s 20(1) of the Registration of Business Names Act 1963, the Minister for Business, Enterprise and Innovation is empowered to bring summary proceedings under that Act.

[205] According to the Companies Registration Office, 5,420 companies were involuntarily struck off the register in 2017 (a significant decrease on the figure of 8,302 in 2016 due to a higher compliance rate by companies in respect of filing annual returns).

compliance with the 1963 Act as that Registrar has in relation to the Companies Act 2014.[206]

[3.90] However some hope of continued compliance by partnerships with the terms of the Registration of Business Names Act 1963 is provided by the other consequences of non-compliance. As is noted hereunder, the registration or failure to register under the Act may prove significant as secondary evidence of the date of departure of a partner from a firm, the date of dissolution of the firm or even the existence of a partnership in the first place. Yet more could be done to ensure compliance with the 1963 Act and it is interesting to note that in England, partnerships are further encouraged to comply with Part 41 the Companies Act 2006[207] by the fact that the failure of a partnership to comply with its disclosure obligations under that Act could, if it entered into a contract at a time when it was in breach and then looks to enforce that contract, result in those proceedings being dismissed if the defendant can show that, as a result of the breach, he was unable to pursue a claim against the partnership under the contract or suffered a financial loss as a result thereof.[208]

Register as evidence of departure of partner or dissolution of firm

[3.91] As noted earlier,[209] the filing of certain statements with the registrar is not thought to constitute notice to third parties of the information filed. Nonetheless, under the Registration of Business Names Act 1963, a partnership must notify the registrar of the departure of a partner from the firm[210] or the dissolution of the firm.[211] In the case of a subsequent dispute as to the date of departure of a partner or the dissolution of a firm, it is clear that such actions will provide secondary evidence of the relevant date. In addition, the filing of the necessary forms (and indeed amending the firm's stationery) has the advantage of reducing the likelihood of a former partner being held liable as an 'apparent member' of the firm for debts incurred in the name of the partnership whether under s 36(1) of the 1890 Act[212] or on the basis of continued holding out by the partner(s) under s 14(1) of the 1890 Act.[213]

Register as evidence of the existence of a partnership

[3.92] On the registration of a business name, s 4 of the Registration of Business Names Act 1963 requires the names of the partners in the firm to be stated. Clearly, therefore,

---

[206] Ie under s 343(5) of the Companies Act 2014.

[207] Which replaced the Registration of Business Names Act 1985 with effect from 1 October 2009.

[208] See further, l'Anson Banks, *Lindley & Banks on Partnership* (20th edn, 2017) at para 3.34 et seq; Blackett-Ord and Haren, *Partnership Law* (5th edn, 2015) at para 8.63 et seq. In Nova Scotia, a partnership cannot commence an action unless it is registered under the Partnerships and Business Names Registration Act 1989: *Fischback & Moore of Canada Ltd v Gulf Oil Canada Ltd* (1971) 3 DLR (3d) 606.

[209] See para **[3.82]**.

[210] Registration of Business Names Act 1963, s 7, and see further para **[3.80]**.

[211] Registration of Business Names Act 1963, s 12(1), and see further para **[3.80]**.

[212] See generally regarding the liability of a former partner under s 36(1) of the 1890 Act, para **[11.25]** et seq.

[213] See generally in relation to partnership by holding out, para **[7.01]** et seq.

this registration may be used as supporting evidence of the fact that a partnership existed and that a specific person was or was not a member of the partnership. This was the case in *Macken v Revenue Commissioners*.[214] There, the High Court was faced with a claim by a brother and sister that, prior to their father's death, they had been introduced as partners to their father's painting business. Up to the time of their alleged admission, their father, Patrick Macken, had carried on the business as a sole trader under the name Patrick Macken & Son. After the alleged partnership was created, the business continued to be carried on under this name. Teevan J noted that if, as they alleged, the children were partners in the business, they should have registered the business name 'Patrick Macken & Son' under the Registration of Business Names Act[215] as they would have been carrying on business under a name which was not the name of all three partners. In holding that no partnership had existed between the father and his children, Teevan J relied, inter alia, on this omission by them to register their names in the register of business names as partners.

Register as evidence of the identity of the precedent partner

[3.93] The precedent partner in a firm is the partner who is responsible for making the return of income and chargeable gains of the firm to the Revenue Commissioners.[216] Under s 1007 of the Taxes Consolidation Act 1997, the precedent partner is the partner (resident in the State) who is first named in the partnership agreement (if there is one), is named singly or with precedence over the other partners in the name of the firm or is the precedent acting partner, if the person named with precedence is not an acting partner. In this regard, it has been noted that as part of its compliance with the Registration of Business Names Act 1963, a firm which is subject to that Act is required to list all the partners in the firm's stationery.[217] Therefore, compliance with this obligation under the 1963 Act may impact upon the identity of the firm's precedent partner, since it seems likely that in determining which partner is given precedence, a court will place reliance on the order in which the partners are listed on the firm's notepaper.

V. GUARANTEES INVOLVING PARTNERSHIPS

[3.94] The issue of guarantees and partnerships is deserving of separate treatment in view of the possibility that a continuing guarantee involving a partnership may be revoked under s 18 of the 1890 Act. This is a very important section of the 1890 Act and one that should be borne in mind by anyone who is involved with the giving of guarantees to a partnership or the guaranteeing of the obligations of a partnership. Section 18 re-enacts, with minor modification, the terms of s 4 of the Mercantile Law Amendment Act 1856.[218] It states:

> A continuing guaranty or cautionary obligation given either to a firm or to a third person in respect of the transactions of a firm is, in the absence of agreement to the contrary,

---

[214] *Macken v Revenue Commissioners* [1962] IR 302.
[215] The registration of business names was then governed by the Registration of Business Names Act 1916.
[216] See generally in relation to the precedent partner, para **[6.37]**.
[217] See para **[3.85]**.
[218] 19 & 20 Vict c 97. Section 4 of that Act was repealed by the 1890 Act, s 48.

revoked as to future transactions by any change in the constitution of the firm to which, or of the firm in respect of the transactions of which, the guaranty or obligation was given.

[3.95] Thus, a continuing guarantee is revoked by any change in the constitution of a firm to which the guarantee is given, or by any change in the constitution of a firm, whose liabilities are being guaranteed. The rationale for this rule is founded in the principle of the law of sureties that, where a contract of surety is varied without the consent of the surety, he should be released from his obligations thereunder. This is because a change in the persons guaranteed or to whom the guarantee is given is a variation of the contract and an alteration of the risk and as a result, it operates as a discharge of the guarantee. As noted by Napier LC in *Grantham v Redmond*:[219]

> 'this is the principle of all the cases where a man has become a surety to the banking firm. To change the firm would alter the relation of the parties; and when another person gets a share of the profits, there is a new element introduced, which does change the firm.'[220]

[3.96] This rule of the law of guarantee is based on the principle that a contract of continuing guarantee is subject to the construction *strictissimi juris*.[221] Therefore, such a contract is discharged as to future transactions by a change in the membership of the partnership, which is the creditor or the debtor.

[3.97] Thus a guarantee to a firm of A, B & C of the repayment of money which is from time to time lent by the firm to a third party is, in the absence of contrary agreement, revoked as to future loans when C is replaced by D.[222]

'any change in the constitution of the firm'

[3.98] By its express terms, s 18 revokes continuing guarantees to, or in respect of, a partnership in the event of there being any change in the constitution of the firm, unless there is an agreement to the contrary. Thus, s 18 ensures that a partnership guarantee is automatically revoked by the departure of a partner,[223] the death of a partner,[224] the admission of a new partner[225] or the dissolution of the firm.[226]

'revoked as to future transactions'

[3.99] It is important to bear in mind that the guarantee is not revoked ab initio, but only, in the words of s 18, as to future transactions. Accordingly, transactions which took

---

219 *Grantham v Redmond* (1859) 8 Ir Ch R 449, although the point was obiter as the case did not concern guarantees.

220 *Grantham v Redmond* (1859) 8 Ir Ch R 449 at 454. Napier LC relied on the authority of *Pemberton v Oaks* (1827) 4 Russ 154 and *Chapman v Beckington* (1842) 3 Gale & Dav 33.

221 The strictest letter of the law.

222 *Pemberton v Oaks* (1827) 4 Russ 154.

223 *Myers v Edge* (1797) 7 TR 254; *Dry v Davy* (1839) 8 LJQB 209.

224 *Backhouse v Hall* (1865) 12 ER 1283; *Chapman v Beckington* (1842) 3 Gale & Dav 33; *Weston v Barton* (1812) 4 Taunt 673.

225 *Wright v Russel* (1774) 3 Wils 530.

226 See for example the case of *Phelan v Johnson* (1843) 7 Ir LR 527 where Phelan had given a guarantee to a three man partnership in respect of the liabilities of one Smith to the firm. At a preliminary hearing regarding the service of proceedings, it was argued, but not decided by Brady CB, that the guarantee was discharged by the dissolution of the partnership.

place prior to the change in the constitution of the firm will remain subject to the terms of the guarantee.

'agreement to the contrary'

[3.100] Since s 18 is subject to agreement to the contrary, it is common for banks and other lending institutions to have an express provision in their guarantees that the terms of the guarantee will continue notwithstanding any change in the firm.[227] For example in *Re Pim*,[228] the guarantee obtained by a bank from one of the partners in respect of the firm's borrowings provided that it was 'to be a continuing obligation and binding on him notwithstanding any change in any one or more partners'.[229] In addition to express agreements to the contrary, a contrary agreement may arise by implication from the nature of the guarantee, the conduct of the parties or other surrounding circumstances.[230]

Status of a Solicitor's Lien

[3.101] A solicitor's lien is a lien which a solicitor has over papers, deeds and other documents which he has in his possession but which belong to his clients. The lien arises by operation of law and is as security for fees due to the solicitor by the client. The interaction of this doctrine and s 18 of the 1890 Act is deserving of consideration. In *Ring & Ring v Giles J Kennedy & Co*[231] the defendant held title deeds belonging to the plaintiff as security for professional legal fees due to the defendant from the plaintiff and from a number of companies controlled by the plaintiff. Laffoy J held that a solicitor's lien only extended to costs incurred by the client against whom it is claimed. She relied on *Turner v Deane*[232] in which it was held that an attorney who held title deeds belonging to a partnership had no lien in respect of fees due to the attorney by a member of that partnership on his private account.

---

227 See generally regarding such guarantees Breslin, *Banking Law* (3rd edn, 2013) at para 14-50 et seq; Donnelly, *The Law of Credit and Security* (2nd edn, 2015) at para 18-95 et seq. See also Andrews and Millett, *Law of Guarantees* (7th edn, 2015) at para 4-102 where the importance of clarity of drafting is emphasised. The sensible approach is to include a separate provision in the guarantee that provides that (whether it is given by or in favour of a partnership) it will continue notwithstanding any change to the consittution of that partnership.

228 *Re Pim* (1881) 7 LR Ir 458.

229 *Re Pim* (1881) 7 LR Ir 458 at 460.

230 It might be thought that it should be easier to establish an implicit agreement to the contrary, where the change occurs in a firm to whom the guarantee is given (debtor), than in a firm being guaranteed (creditor). However, it is contended that an implicit agreement to the contrary will be difficult to establish in either case since the risk to the guarantor will be altered by both changes, and an express agreement to the contrary is preferable. Where the change occurs in a creditor firm the change may clearly impact upon the guarantor's exposure since for example, the new partner may decide to increase the loans to the third party. Similarly, where the change occurs in the debtor firm, the change may impact upon the exposure of the guarantor, since the new partner may press for increased loans from the guaranteed third party.

231 *Ring & Ring v Giles J Kennedy & Co* (18 July 1997) HC.

232 *Turner v Deane* [1849] 6 Dow & L 669.

[3.102] As the lien is a form of security for the payment of the solicitor's costs, the question arose in *Pelly v Wathen*[233] as to whether s 18 of the 1890 Act applies to a solicitor's lien, so as to revoke the lien in the event of there being any change in the constitution of the firm of solicitors. However, it was held that a solicitor's lien is not revoked by a change in the constitution of the solicitors' firm.

---

[233] *Pelly v Wathen* (1849) 7 Hare 351.

Chapter 4

Capacity to be a Partner

INTRODUCTION

[4.01] In considering whether a valid partnership exists, regard must be had to the capacity of the parties to enter that arrangement. Since the partnership relationship is based in contract,[1] the rules regarding contractual capacity will apply to a person who proposes to enter into a partnership contract as they do to any contract.[2] In this chapter, consideration will be given to the application of these rules to the partnership contract. Capacity to contract is being considered hereunder in the broad sense of the term; while some of the rules hereunder relate to the personal qualities of the proposed partners (eg the ability to exercise decision-making capacity), others relate to the fact that, with some exceptions, partnerships of more than a certain number of partners are prohibited by statute. These issues will be considered under the following headings:

    I.   Minors;

    II.   Companies;

   III. Persons who require assistance in exercising their decision-making capacity, or who lack the capacity to make partnership-related decisions;

   IV. Bankrupts, Arranging Debtors and Insolvent Debtors;

    V.   Convicts;

   VI. Non-Resident Foreign Nationals;

  VII. Personal Representatives;

 VIII. Partnerships between Spouses and Partnerships between Civil Partners;

   IX. Restricted or Disqualified Directors;

    X.   Size of Partnerships.

Overview

[4.02] A partnership agreement, whether written or oral, like any other type of contract, is subject to the rules governing the capacity of persons to enter a contract. So, for example, when a minor enters a contract of partnership, it is voidable at his instance. Likewise, a company must have the requisite power in its objects clause to enter a

---

[1]   See para **[2.10]**.

[2]   See generally regarding the rules on contractual capacity, Clark, *Contract Law in Ireland* (8th edn, 2016) at para 16-01 et seq; McDermott and McDermott, *Contract Law* (2nd edn, 2017) at para [18.01] et seq; Friel, *The Law of Contract* (2nd edn, 2000) at p 60 et seq. See also *Chitty on Contracts* (32nd edn, 2015) at para [9.001] et seq; Peel, *Trietel – The Law of Contract* (14th edn, 2015) at para [12.001] et seq.

partnership contract[3] and nationals of countries with which Ireland is at war may not enter into a partnership contract governed by Irish law. In this sense, it is understandable that no special provision was made in the 1890 Act regarding the capacity of parties to enter a partnership contract, as distinct from any other type of contract.

[4.03] However, in one respect the 1890 Act is deceptively simple regarding the capacity to enter a partnership contract. This is because it fails to make any reference to fact that the number of partners in a firm is, in many cases, limited to 20 and more importantly that a breach of this limit results in the partnership being illegal and automatically dissolved.[4] Rather the prohibition on partnerships of 20 or more persons is hidden in an obscure section of the Companies Act 2014.[5] Since the 1890 Act is an attempt at the codification of partnership law, it would be preferable if a provision which goes to the very validity of the partnership relationship was contained in that Act. However, a better solution still would be to repeal this prohibition on large partnerships. As is noted hereunder, it was introduced to reduce the task of third parties who, in previous times, had to make each partner a party to an action against a firm. However this rationale is no longer relevant since it is now possible to sue partnerships without joining each of the partners to the action, and several categories of partnership are now exempt from this size restriction.

I.   MINORS

Minor Partner not Liable for Partnership Obligations

[4.04] A minor is someone under 18, unless he or she is married.[6] The general principles which govern the capacity of minors to enter contracts apply also to contracts of partnership. Thus, a minor may be a partner[7] but where a minor enters a partnership, the firm itself will be bound by the actions of the minor, yet, the minor will not during his minority incur liability to his co-partners or to third parties for the debts of the firm or

---

[3]   With the exception of a 'private company limited by shares' (as defined in s 2(1) of the Companies Act 2014) which has (under s 38 of that Act) 'full and unlimited capacity to carry on and undertake any business or activity, do any act or enter into any transaction' and has 'full rights, powers and privileges' for the purposes of doing so.

[4]   The number of partners in a banking partnership is limited to 10 (although at the time of writing it is not possible for a partnership to be authorised as a bank – see paras **[3.37]** and **[9.20]**) and the number of partners in registered farm partnerships and registered succession farm partnerships is also limited to 10 – see para **[8.109]** et seq). While a breach of the limit on the number of partners in a banking partnership would also result in such a partnership being illegal and automatically dissolved, it is submitted that the effect of a partnership that wishes to register as a farm partnership having more than 10 members is that it cannot register as a farm partnership and avail of the benefits that arise from such registration, but a partnership will continue to exist between the parties. A partnership can only be registered as a succession farm partnership if already registered as a registered farm partnership.

[5]   Companies Act 2014, s 1435(1).

[6]   The Age of Majority Act 1985, s 2(1) defines a minor as someone who has not yet reached the age of 18 or is not married (marriage under the age of 18 is void unless an exemption has been granted under Family Law Act 1995, s 33(1)).

[7]   See for example the case of *Re A and M* [1926] 1 Ch 274.

the acts of his co-partners.[8] In addition, the contract is voidable at the instance of the minor partner either during his minority or within a reasonable time after he attains majority. In the House of Lords case of *Lovell and Christmas v Beauchamp*,[9] Lord Herschell noted that:

> 'I think that it is clear that there is nothing to prevent an infant trading, or becoming a partner with a trader, and that until his contract of partnership be disaffirmed he is a member of the trading firm.'[10]

[4.05] Thus, it might be said that the 'incapacity' of a minor is in fact more of a privilege than a disability, since the minor has a one-sided power of avoidance. The case of *Shannon v Bradstreet*[11] concerned a lease of land in Portmahon, Co Dublin by Sir Samuel Bradstreet, then a judge of the High Court. The issue of whether this lease was binding on Sir Samuel's minor son was considered by Redesdale LC who observed that:

> 'it is the peculiar privilege of infants for their protection, that though they are not bound, yet those who enter into contracts with them shall be bound,[12] if it be prejudicial to the infant to rescind the contract.'[13]

[4.06] In the context of partnership contracts, this means that it may be particularly hazardous for a person to enter partnership with a minor, since the adult will be solely liable to the creditors, but with no right of indemnity against the minor. It is however the case that the minor's share of the partnership property is liable for the partnership debts.[14] Thus, while a minor partner is not personally liable for the obligations of the partnership, he is bound to the extent of his capital contribution or any partnership profits due to him.[15]

[4.07] The fact that a minor partner is not liable for the obligations of the firm was an important factor in the decision which was reached in *Cuffe v Murtagh*.[16] That case concerned a milling partnership in Dublin and Athlone. The partnership agreement entitled a partner to nominate a person to succeed him on his death. Under the terms of

---

8   *Lovell and Christmas v Beauchamp* [1894] AC 607. See generally, Anon, 'The Position of an Infant Partner' (1938) 4 Ir Jur 20.
9   *Lovell and Christmas v Beauchamp* [1894] AC 607.
10 *Lovell and Christmas v Beauchamp* [1894] AC 607 at 611.
11 *Shannon v Bradstreet* (1803) 1 Sch & Lef 52.
12 In this context and in the context of the statement of Lord Herschell set out at para **[4.04]**, the obiter statement of Blackburne MR in *Milliken v Milliken* (1845) 8 Ir Eq R 16 at 27 must be taken as incorrect insofar as it seems to suggest that an infant partner could not take an action for the specific performance of the partnership agreement against his adult co-partners: 'there can be no question that if he were still an infant this objection would be fatal to the bill; but he attained his age in October 1884.' Despite this statement, it seems quite clear that a minor partner can enforce a partnership agreement against his co-partners during the course of his minority. This conclusion is consistent with the principle that a partnership agreement with a minor partner is voidable, ie binding on the other parties thereto, but subject to repudiation by the minor: see Beatson, *Anson's Law of Contract* (30th edn, 2017) at p 257; Peel, *Trietel The Law of Contract* (14th edn, 2015) at paras 12-020 and 12-023 et seq.
13 *Shannon v Bradstreet* (1803) 1 Sch & Lef 52 at 54.
14 *Lovell and Christmas v Beauchamp* [1894] AC 607.
15 *Lovell and Christmas v Beauchamp* [1894] AC 607.
16 *Cuffe v Murtagh* (1881) 7 LR Ir 411.

the partnership agreement, the nominee was to be subject to the *same terms and conditions* as the deceased partner. One partner died before his nominated successor reached the age of majority and the question arose as to whether a minor partner could be subject to the *same terms and conditions* as adult partners. Chatterton VC noted that the minor was:

> 'incapable of subjecting himself, by deed or otherwise, to the debts and liabilities of the firm: for though an infant may be a partner, he is not personally responsible for partnership debts.'[17]

On this basis, it was held that the nominee could not be subject to the same terms and conditions as the other partners and therefore could not become a partner until he reached the age of majority. Until this time, it was held that his 'rights of admission remained, therefore, contingent'.[18]

Right of Minor Partner to Repudiate Partnership Agreement

[4.08] In addition to the fact that a minor partner is not liable as a partner during his minority, the second important aspect of partnership agreements with minors is the fact that minor partners may repudiate the contract during their minority or within a reasonable time thereafter.[19] Where the agreement is repudiated, the other partners must apply the partnership property, including the minor's share, to pay off the firm's debts and liabilities.[20] The minor partner will only be entitled to recover any property or money which he has paid to the firm, if he can restore the other partners to the same position as they were in prior to the agreement.[21]

Minor Partner may affirm Agreement on Reaching Majority

[4.09] Rather than repudiating the agreement, the minor partner may decide to affirm the agreement after he reaches the age of majority. Indeed, if the minor partner complies with the terms of the agreement after reaching the age of majority, he will be held to have affirmed the partnership agreement. In *Milliken v Milliken*,[22] a partnership agreement provided for the admission of a minor to a book selling partnership in Grafton Street in place of his mother. Although the minor was clearly not a partner at the time of the execution of this agreement, the partnership agreement was signed by him. After he had attained his majority, the minor took an action for the specific performance of the agreement. His mother's partners claimed that, as he was a minor at the time of the execution of the agreement, this disallowed his claim. Blackburne MR rejected this defence on the grounds that the minor had affirmed the contract:

---

[17] *Cuffe v Murtagh* (1881) 7 LR Ir 411 at 425.
[18] *Cuffe v Murtagh* (1881) 7 LR Ir 411 at 425. See further in relation to a contingent partner, para **[6.17]**.
[19] *Newry and Enniskillen Railway v Coombe* (1849) 18 LJ Ex 325; *Dublin and Wicklow Railway v Black* (1852) 22 LJ Ex 94.
[20] *Burgess v Merrill* (1812) 4 Taunt 468.
[21] *Valentini v Canali* (1889) 61 LT 731; *Ex p Taylor* (1856) 8 De GM & G 254; *Holmes v Blogg* (1818) 2 Moore 553.
[22] *Milliken v Milliken* (1845) 8 Ir Eq R 16.

'there can be no question that if he were still an infant this objection would be fatal to the bill;[23] but he attained his age in October 1884, since which time he has acted on this contract, by performing the services which the agreement specifies, by serving notice of his intention to adopt and abide by it; and by his present bill, which binds him to carry it into execution. I think the authorities[24] warrant me in holding that the plaintiff is as much bound as if he were adult when he signed this agreement.'[25]

[4.10] It is also important to note that where a minor affirms a partnership agreement after attaining his majority, he may not be liable for the firm's obligations which were incurred while he was a minor partner. This is because of the terms of s 2 of the Infants Relief Act 1874 which states:

No action shall be brought whereby to charge any person upon any promise made after full age to pay any debt contracted during infancy, or upon any ratification made after full age of any promise or any contract made during infancy, whether there shall or shall not be any new consideration for such promise or ratification after full age.[26]

[4.11] However the scope of s 2 of the Infants Relief Act 1874 is restricted by virtue of the fact that a person who retains a share in a partnership cannot do so without its incidental obligations.[27] Thus the doctrine of holding out will impose liability upon an adult partner who has recently attained his majority. This is illustrated by *Goode v Harrison*,[28] where the minor was known to be a partner in the firm. On coming of age, he did not give notice of his repudiation of the partnership and he was held as a consequence to be bound to the firm's creditors.

[4.12] If a minor wishes to repudiate a partnership agreement on his coming of age, this should be done clearly and promptly. Otherwise, there is the possibility of his being assumed to have affirmed the partnership contract. Thus, if he continues to share in the profits of the firm he will be held liable for a share of the losses in the firm.[29] Another risk for a minor partner who is equivocal, is that he may be held to be liable to third parties after he reaches the age of majority, on the basis that he allowed himself to be held out as a partner under s 14(1) of the 1890 Act,[30] as exemplified by *Goode v Harrison*.[31]

---

23 As mentioned in fn **12** above, this part of Blackburne MR's obiter statement must be taken to be incorrect.
24 He relies on the authority of *Boys v Ayerst* (1822) 6 Mad 316; *Martin v Mitchell* (1820) 2 Ja & W 427; *Ashfield v Ashfield* (1675) Sir W Jones 157; *Baylis v Dineley* (1815) 3 M & S 477; *Clayton v Ashdown* (1714) 9 Vin Ab 393; *Shannon v Bradstreet* (1803) 1 Sch & Lef 52; *Goode v Harrison* (1821) 5 Bar & Ald 147.
25 *Milliken v Milliken* (1845) 8 Ir Eq R 16 at 27.
26 See for example *Belfast Banking Co v Doherty* (1879) 4 LR Ir 124.
27 *Cork and Bandon Railway Co v Cazenove* (1847) 10 QB 935 per Coleridge and Erle JJ.
28 *Goode v Harrison* (1821) 5 Bar & Ald 147.
29 *Cork and Bandon Railway v Cazenove* (1847) 10 QB 935.
30 See further para **[7.01]** et seq.
31 *Goode v Harrison* (1821) 5 Bar & Ald 147.

No Liability for Holding out by a Minor Partner

[4.13] Just as a minor partner is not liable to third parties for the obligations of the firm of which he is a member, he is also not liable to third parties as a partner by holding out while he remains a minor.[32] Yet, as has been noted, once he reaches majority, he may be subject to such an action.[33]

[4.14] A minor is however liable for his own torts and therefore he may be subject to an action for negligent misstatement or fraudulent misrepresentation during his minority.[34] In *Griffiths v Delaney*,[35] the plaintiff sued a minor partner as a member of a firm but no allegation was made that the minor was guilty of misrepresentation. The action was dismissed and costs were awarded by the High Court to the minor partner. O'Byrne J indicated obiter that he would not have awarded such costs if the minor partner had misrepresented his age. It would seem to follow from this case that the mere membership of a firm by a minor is not a representation by him that he is of full age.[36]

Minor Partner ought not to be Joined as a Defendant

[4.15] *Griffiths v Delaney*[37] also illustrates the principle that, since a minor partner is not liable for the obligations of a firm, in an action against a firm, a minor partner ought not to be joined as a defendant. That case involved an action against the defendant firm for a sum of money owed to the plaintiff for goods[38] supplied to the firm. One of the partners in the firm was a minor. O'Byrne J held that as the 'plaintiff has sued a person against whom he is not entitled to obtain judgment',[39] he should pay the minor partner's costs. Therefore, it may be concluded that if an action is taken against a partnership in the firm name, it should be against 'the firm of Y & Co, other than X, a minor' and that if a judgment is obtained against a firm which has a minor partner the judgment should be 'against the defendant firm, other than X, a minor'.

II.   COMPANIES

[4.16] It has been noted earlier in this work that a company is a 'person' for the purposes of s 1(1) of the 1890 Act and therefore may be a member of a partnership.[40] The

---

32   *Price v Hewitt* (1853) 8 Ex 146; *Green v Greenbank* [1816] 2 Marsh 485; *Glossop v Colman* (1815) 18 RR 741; *Johnson v Pye* (1665) 1 Sid 258.

33   See *Goode v Harrison* (1821) 5 Bar & Ald 147, discussed at para **[4.11]**.

34   See generally in relation to negligent misstatement and fraudulent misrepresentation, McMahon and Binchy, *Law of Torts* (4th edn, 2013) at paras [10.07], [10.71] et seq and [35.01] et seq.

35   *Griffiths v Delaney* (1938) Ir Jur Rep 1. This case is discussed at Anon, 'The Position of an Infant Partner' (1938) 4 Ir Jur 20.

36   See also *Re King, ex p Unity Joint Stock Mutual Banking Association* (1858) 3 De G & J 63.

37   *Griffiths v Delaney* (1938) Ir Jur Rep 1.

38   The goods were not necessaries, which form an exception to the general rule regarding enforcing contracts against minors, see Clark, *Contract Law in Ireland* (8th edn, 2016) at paras 16-06 – 16:09; McDermott and McDermott, *Contract Law* (2nd edn, 2017) at para [18.03] et seq; Friel, *The Law of Contract* (2nd edn, 2000) at p 72.

39   *Griffiths v Delaney* (1938) Ir Jur Rep 1 at 2.

40   See para **[2.35]**. See para **[8.63]** regarding the use of corporate partners to facilitate large partnerships where the 20 partner limit applies.

question of whether a particular company has the capacity to enter a partnership will be determined by an examination of the memorandum of association of that company.[41] Modern memoranda of association for companies tend to either expressly or impliedly permit such activity. That it may be a relatively easy task to find such an authority in the memorandum of association of a company is apparent from the case of *Newstead v Frost*.[42] This case involved an alleged partnership between a company and the well-known British broadcaster, David Frost. Mr Frost had formed a company with a view to reducing his tax liability and he entered into partnership with this company. In its memorandum of association, the company had the power to undertake 'all kinds of financial ... or other operations'. It was held by the House of Lords that this power was sufficient to authorise the company to enter into a partnership.

[4.17] Since the provisions of the 1890 Act were clearly drafted for partnerships between individuals, it is prudent for any partnership with a company or companies to amend or clarify the application of these principles to the corporate partners (in particular, as regards insolvency). This issue is considered in detail elsewhere in this work.[43]

III. PERSONS WHO REQUIRE ASSISTANCE IN EXERCISING THEIR DECISION-MAKING CAPACITY, OR WHO LACK THE CAPACITY TO MAKE PARTNERSHIP-RELATED DECISIONS[44]

[4.18] A person who lacks the capacity to decide whether or not to enter a partnership may validly enter a partnership, provided his partners act bona fide and are unaware of his incapacity.[45] It follows that where a person enters a partnership and subsequently becomes mentally incapacitated, this does not per se dissolve the partnership. In *Re*

---

41 Such an examination will not be necessary for a 'private company limited by shares' (as defined in s 2(1) of the Companies Act 2014) which has (under s 38 of that Act) full and unlimited corporate capacity. The constitution of such a private company limited by shares no longer contains an objects clause (s 19 of the 2014 Act and Sch 1 to that Act).

42 *Newstead v Frost* [1980] 1 All ER 363.

43 See para **[21.23]**.

44 With the signing of the Assisted Decision-Making Capacity Act 2015 into Irish law (albeit that, at the date of writing, many of its provisions remain to be commenced), Ireland's laws regarding individuals who may have difficulty exercising their decision-making capacity have been overhauled in line with the UN Convention on the Rights of Persons with Disabilities. An individual will be assumed to have legal capacity, and various steps will need to be followed to support his ability to make decisions before he can be regarded as lacking capacity to make decisions. Much of the archaic terminology used in previous legislation, such as the Lunacy Regulation (Ireland) Act 1871, will no longer be used, and the new framework will no longer enable an individual's capacity to make decisions to be removed permanently.

45 *Imperial Loan Co v Stone* [1892] 1 QB 599; *Hassard v Smith* (1872) 6 Ir Eq R 429 (lease of land by mentally incapacitated person). See also the New Zealand case of *O'Connor v Hart* [1985] 1 NZLR 159 and before the Privy Council as *Hart v O'Connor* [1985] AC 1000. See generally Clark, *Contract Law in Ireland* (8th edn, 2016) at paras 16.46–16-51; McDermott and McDermott, *Contract Law* (2nd edn, 2017) at para [18.45] et seq; Friel, *The Law of Contract* (2nd edn, 2000) at p 68. (contd.../)

Ferrar, ex p Ulster Banking Co,[46] Ulster Bank sought to prove upon the joint estate of a partnership between Simms and Ferrar. During the course of the partnership, Simms had become of unsound mind, yet Macan J did not regard this fact as sufficient to dissolve the partnership.[47] Instead, he held that when this occurred, Ferrar became the 'sole active partner'. Thus, it may be concluded that, rather than dissolving the partnership, a partner's lack of capacity to make decisions in relation to a partnership in which he is a partner could render him a dormant partner and may not even render him as such if a 'decision-making assistant', a 'co-decision maker' or a 'decision-making representative' is appointed in respect of that partner under the terms of the Assisted Decision-Making Capacity Act 2015 (further detail is set out in the following paragraph).[48]

[4.19] The Assisted Decision-Making Capacity Act 2015 which will, when its key operative provisions are commenced, repeal the existing Lunacy Regulation (Ireland) Act 1871, contemplates a possible recovery of capacity. Once its provisions are fully operative, it will be possible for a partner who has been rendered a dormant partner due to a lack of capacity to revert to being an active partner if his lack of capacity proves temporary, or he may remain as an active partner if supported in his decision-making by a person appointed to assist him under the 2015 Act. The 2015 Act will allow a person who is concerned that his capacity may be called into question to appoint a person as his 'decision-making assistant'[49] or 'co-decision maker'.[50] If appointed by a partner, such a decision-making assistant or co-decision maker will be able to assist that partner in making decisions regarding his 'property and affairs', which will include the carrying out of any contract entered into by him (eg a partnership agreement) and will also expressly include the making of decisions regarding the dissolution of a partnership in which he is a partner.[51] In limited circumstances, it will also be possible for a court order to be granted to appoint a 'decision-making representative' who can perform a similar role.[52] It is of course open to the other partners to apply to court under s 35(a) of the 1890 Act for an order to dissolve the partnership on the grounds that their co-partner is 'of permanently unsound mind'; however, it remains to be seen whether such orders (having regard to the absolute nature of the term 'permanently unsound mind') will be granted in the future having regard to the more case-by-case approach to the assessment of decision-making capacity that underpins the 2015 Act.[53]

---

45 (\...contd) However, it should be noted that the courts may rely on equitable principles to find that the partnership agreement is an unconscionable bargain and, as such, may be set aside, see generally Clark, *Contract Law in Ireland* (8th edn, 2016) at paras 13-32–13-43; McDermott and McDermott, *Contract Law* (2nd edn, 2017) at para [18.25].

46 *Re Ferrar, ex p Ulster Banking Co* (1859) 9 Ir Ch R 11.

47 Macan J notes that '[d]uring a considerable time, while Simms was totally incapable, and when Ferrar had the power to bind the partnership assets, as sole active partner ...' Re *Ferrar, ex p Ulster Banking Co* (1859) 9 Ir Ch R 11 at 15.

48 See further para **[6.04]** in relation to dormant partners.

49 Assisted Decision-Making Capacity Act 2015, s 10.

50 Assisted Decision-Making Capacity Act 2015, s 17.

51 See the definition of 'property and affairs' at s 2(1) of the Assisted Decision-Making Capacity Act 2015.

52 Assisted Decision-Making Capacity Act 2015, s 38.

53 See further para **[25.24]**.

IV. BANKRUPTS, ARRANGING DEBTORS AND INSOLVENT DEBTORS

[4.20] The only reference to bankruptcy in the 1890 Act is in s 33(1) which provides that a partnership is dissolved on the bankruptcy of a partner, unless the partners have agreed otherwise. There is no express prohibition in the 1890 Act on a bankrupt becoming a partner in a firm and it is implicit in s 33(1) that a bankrupt may enter a partnership. However, the wide-ranging restrictions on a bankrupt and on an arranging debtor[54] in s 129 of the Bankruptcy Act 1988 will, in most cases, be as effective as a prohibition on their entering partnership. This section states:

A bankrupt or an arranging debtor who –

(a) either alone or jointly with any other person obtains credit[55] to the extent of €650 or upwards from any person without informing that person that he is a bankrupt or an arranging debtor, or

(b) engages in any trade or business under a name other than that under which he was adjudicated bankrupt or granted protection without disclosing to all persons with whom he enters into any business transactions the name under which he was so adjudicated or granted protection,

shall be guilty of an offence.

[4.21] In view of this provision, it is likely to be impractical for a bankrupt to enter into a partnership. First, under the second leg of this section, if the firm is not trading under the bankrupt's name, every person dealing with the firm would have to be notified of the name under which he was adjudicated bankrupt or granted protection. Second, as is noted elsewhere in this work, partners are mutual agents so that a bankrupt who enters a partnership will be the agent of his co-partners and his co-partners will be his agent.[56] Thus, any obtaining of credit by the firm or by the 'innocent' partners, who fails to notify the third party of the existence of the bankrupt partner, would be attributable to the bankrupt and he would be in breach of the first leg of the section and thereby guilty of a criminal offence.[57]

[4.22] There is no reference in the 1890 Act to the non-judicial debt settlement mechanisms[58] that can be availed of by insolvent individuals[59] under the Personal Insolvency Acts 2012–2015. Those Acts contain wide-ranging restrictions on what a debtor in respect of whom such an arrangement is in place may do. These include, in the

---

54   An arranging debtor is defined by s 3 of the Bankruptcy Act 1988 as a debtor who has been granted an order for protection under Part IV of that Act. However, with effect from 3 December 2013, a debtor can no longer present a petition for court protection from bankruptcy proceedings with a view to entering into an arrangement with his creditors. See further para [27.165].

55   Though if he obtains credit only for his partner or another third party, he would not contravene this section: *R v Godwin* (1980) 71 Cr App R 97, decided under s 155(a) of the Bankruptcy Act 1914.

56   Partnership Act 1890, s 5 and see generally para [10.82] et seq.

57   Bankruptcy Act 1988, s 132.

58   Being debt relief notices, debt settlement arrangements and personal insolvency arrangements.

59   An individual debtor is 'insolvent' for the purposes of the Personal Insolvency Act 2012 if he is unable to pay his debts in full as they fall due (Personal Insolvency Act 2012, s 2(1)).

case of a personal insolvency arrangement or a debt settlement arrangement, a debtor obtaining credit (either alone or with any other person) of more than €650 without disclosing to his potential creditor that he is the subject of such an arrangement,[60] or transferring, leasing, granting security over or otherwise disposing of his property above a prescribed value other than in accordance with the terms of the relevant arrangement.[61] More limited restrictions apply to debtors in respect of whom a debt relief notice is in place – notably the restriction on obtaining credit of more than €650 applies.[62] In practice, these restrictions will make it difficult for debtors in respect of whom a personal insolvency arrangement or a debt settlement arrangement is in place to enter into partnership. Given the low net disposable income thresholds and asset values applicable to debtors who qualify for debt relief notices,[63] it is also very unlikely that such a debtor would be in a position to enter into a partnership during the three-year supervision period during which the debt relief notice will remain in force. Further, as noted above, partners are mutual agents so that a debtor who is the subject of a personal insolvency arrangement, a debt settlement arrangement or a debt relief notice who enters a partnership will be the agent of his co-partners and his co-partners will be his agent.[64] As mentioned above, any obtaining of credit by the firm or by an 'innocent' partner who fails to notify the creditor of the existence of the debtor who is subject to a personal insolvency arrangement, a debt settlement arrangement or a debt relief notice, would be attributable to that debtor and he will be guilty of a criminal offence.[65]

V. CONVICTS

[4.23] Previously, under s 8 of the Forfeiture Act 1870, a convict was incapable of making any contract[66] and was therefore prohibited from entering a partnership agreement. However, the Forfeiture Act 1870 was repealed by the Criminal Law Act 1997 with the result that this general restriction on a convict entering into a partnership agreement was removed.

VI. NON-RESIDENT FOREIGN NATIONALS

[4.24] A distinction needs to be drawn between the capacity of a non-resident foreign national to enter an Irish law partnership contract and the capacity of a resident of a country with which the State is at war, or in respect of which a sanctions regime is in place, to enter an Irish law partnership contract. Non-resident foreign nationals have full contractual capacity to enter a partnership under Irish law.[67] However, nationals of

---

60 Personal Insolvency Act 2012, ss 81(4) (in respect of a debt settlement arrangement) and 118(4) (in respect of a personal insolvency arrangement).
61 Personal Insolvency Act 2012, ss 81(5) (in respect of a debt settlement arrangement) and 118(5) (in respect of a personal insolvency arrangement).
62 Personal Insolvency Act 2012, s 36(7).
63 Under s 26(2) of the Personal Insolvency Act 2012, such a debtor must have net disposable income of €60 or less per month, and assets worth €400 or less.
64 Partnership Act 1890, s 5 and see generally para **[10.82]** et seq.
65 Personal Insolvency Act, s 130.
66 See *O'Connor v Coleman* (1947) 81 ILTR 42.
67 *Pedlar v Johnstone* [1920] 2 IR 450. See also *Porter v Freudenberg* [1915] 1 KB 857; *Wells v Williams* (1697) 1 Salk 46.

countries with which the State is at war may not enter into a partnership agreement under Irish law.[68] Where a non-resident foreign national is a partner and his country of nationality is later at war with Ireland, the partnership is thereby dissolved[69] and the partnership is not reconstituted when that war ends. A foreign national from a country with which Ireland is at war may not sue in the Irish courts during the war[70] but he may be sued in the Irish courts and in such a case he may defend the action. An exception to the foregoing principle appears to be that foreign national who is lawfully residing in the State may enter a partnership contract and sue thereon even if his country of nationality is at war with Ireland.[71] For so long as Ireland retains its neutral status, the latter question of capacity is unlikely to arise. However, a number of European sanctions regulations are directly effective in Ireland and certain of these prohibit the entry into of business arrangements with natural or legal persons, entities, or bodies representing them.[72]

VII. PERSONAL REPRESENTATIVES

[4.25] *Y v O'Sullivan*[73] is authority for the principle that a personal representative has the capacity to be a partner. There, Maguire J noted that it was not 'open to doubt that, since the death of the deceased, a partnership business has been carried on, by the executor for the benefit of the [beneficiaries]'.[74] This issue is considered in detail elsewhere in this work.[75]

VIII. PARTNERSHIPS BETWEEN SPOUSES AND PARTNERSHIPS BETWEEN CIVIL PARTNERS

[4.26] There is no prohibition on spouses [76] or civil partners[77] entering into partnerships. Indeed, in many business relationships between spouses, or between civil partners, it should be an easy matter to prove that they are partners. This is because they should

---

68 *R v Kupfer* [1915] 2 KB 321 at 338. See also *Hugh Stevenson v Aktiengesellschaft für Cartonnagen Industrie* [1918] AC 240. As regards enemy companies see *Kuenigl v Donnersmarck* [1955] 1 QB 515.

69 *Hugh Stevenson v Aktiengescellschaft für Cartonnagen Industrie* [1918] AC 240.

70 *Pedlar v Johnstone* [1920] 2 IR 450. See generally Binchy, *Irish Conflicts of Law* (1988) at pp 171 et seq.

71 See *Volkl v Rotunda Hospital* [1915] 1 KB 857, a case which concerned the right of an alien enemy to sue the defendant for negligence.

72 See for example Council Regulation (EU) 2017/1509 of 30 August 2017 concerning restrictive measures against the Democratic People's Republic of Korea.

73 *Y v O'Sullivan* [1949] IR 264.

74 *Y v O'Sullivan* [1949] IR 264 at 273.

75 See para **[24.28]** et seq.

76 *Butler v Butler* (1885) QBD 374. This is also the position in Australia: *Jones v Jones* [1968] NSWR 206 and *R v Jones* (1979) 141 CLR 504. See also *Bothe v Amos* [1975] 2 All ER 321, which was relied on by Barrington J in *Larkin v Groeger and Eaton* (26 April 1988) HC, though as authority for the repudiation of a partnership by conduct. In *Bothe v Amos*, above, the wife was held to have repudiated the partnership by leaving the marriage.

77 As defined in the Civil Partnership and Certain Rights and Obligations of Cohabitants Act 2010, s 3.

have the requisite degree of community of interest to satisfy the requirement in the
definition of partnership that the business be carried on 'in common'.[78] For this reason,
it is perhaps surprising that the issue is not more commonly pleaded in disputes between
spouses or civil partners, particularly as the default rights of a partner under the 1890
Act might be useful in such a dispute, eg the right to an equal share of the profits[79] and
to have the partnership assets sold on a dissolution to pay off the firm's liabilities with
the surplus being divided between the partners.[80] For example the family law case of *CC
v SC*[81] involved a situation in which the husband used money which was held in a joint
account with his wife to fund an investment and property venture for the benefit of his
wife and their young children. It is suggested that this relationship could have been
categorised as a partnership, with the wife being a dormant partner. Instead, the court
chose to protect the wife's position by the use of the concept of resulting trusts between
the spouses.

[4.27] It is, of course, a separate question as to whether the activity which is being
carried on by the spouses or civil partners is a business in the first place so as to satisfy
the definition of partnership.[82] In this regard, the running of a home would clearly not be
regarded as a business, but, for example, it is apprehended that the running of a family
farm by spouses or civil partners would be regarded as a 'business' so as to be the
subject of a partnership.[83]

IX. RESTRICTED OR DISQUALIFIED DIRECTORS

[4.28] While an individual who is the subject of a restriction order,[84] a restriction
undertaking,[85] a disqualification order[86] or a disqualification undertaking[87] under the
Companies Act 2014 will be restricted or disqualified from being appointed or from
acting in various capacities in respect of a company or (in the case of a disqualification
order or a disqualification undertaking), a friendly society or an industrial and provident
society, such an order or undertaking will not restrict his ability to enter into a
partnership.[88]

---

[78] See generally para [2.68].
[79] Unless this right is excluded by the parties, Partnership Act 1890, s 24(1).
[80] Partnership Act 1890, s 39 and see generally para [26.27].
[81] *CC v SC* (July 1982) HC.
[82] See para [2.56] et seq.
[83] See *Re Christie* [1917] 1 IR 17. Cf *Walsh v Walsh* [1942] IR 403, see further para [2.53].
[84] Companies Act 2014, Pt 14, Ch 3.
[85] Companies Act 2014, Pt 14, Ch 5.
[86] Companies Act 2014, Pt 14, Ch 4.
[87] Companies Act 2014, Pt 14, Ch 5.
[88] This was expressly acknowledged by Keane J in *Fitzpatrick v Connaughton & anor* [2016]
IEHC 533 where he noted (at para 45) that a declaration of restriction (then under s 150 of the
Companies Act 1990, now under Part 14, Chapter 3 of the Companies Act 2014) does not
prevent a person from entering into a business partnership.

X. SIZE OF PARTNERSHIPS

Restriction in Companies Act 2014

[4.29] Prior to the popularisation of the company as a business vehicle in the late nineteenth century,[89] large partnerships became known as 'deed of settlement companies,' as their constitutions were contained in deeds of settlement and thereunder one or more of the partners became trustees of the partnership property.[90] These large partnerships were viewed as 'a public mischief to be repressed'[91] because creditors had to join each partner in any action against the firm. This task was rendered difficult since these associations had large and constantly fluctuating membership.[92] For this reason, the Joint Stock Companies Act 1844[93] provided for the first time a limit on the number of partners in a firm, namely 25. Subsequently, with the passing of s 4 of the Joint Stock Companies Act of 1856,[94] this figure was reduced to 20. This section was replaced by s 4 of the Companies Act of 1862 which provided that partnerships of more than 20 members were unlawful (other than for the business of banking, where the limit was ten),[95] unless registered as a company or formed under some other statute. Although it is now possible to sue a partnership in the name of the firm,[96] the prohibition on partnerships with more than 20 partners remains, subject to a growing number of exceptions. The present day successor to the general prohibition on more than 20 partners is s 1435(1) of the Companies Act 2014 which reads:

> No company, association or partnership[97] consisting of more than 20 persons shall be formed for the purposes of carrying on any business (other than the business of banking), that has for its object the acquisition of gain by the company, association or partnership, or by the individual members thereof, unless:
>
> (a) it is registered as a company under this Act;

---

[89] See para **[1.03]**.

[90] See generally Morse, *Palmer's Company Law* at para 1.103; DuBois, *The English Business Company after the Bubble Act, 1720-1800*, at pp 215 et seq; Holdsworth, *A History of English Law* (1932) Vol VIII, Ch IV, para 4; Formoy, *The Historical Foundations of Modern Company Law* (1923).

[91] Per James LJ in *Smith v Anderson* (1880) 15 ChD 247 at 273.

[92] In *Smith v Anderson* (1880) 15 ChD 247 at 273, James LJ noted that they were 'large fluctuating bodies, so that persons dealing with them did not know with whom they were contracting, and so might be put to great difficulty and expense'.

[93] 7 & 8 Vict, c 110.

[94] 19 & 20 Vict c 47.

[95] This limitation regarding banking partnerships is now contained in s 1436 of the Companies Act 2014.

[96] Rules of the Superior Courts, Ord 14, r 1, see further para **[12.11]**.

[97] Note that s 1435 of the Companies Act 2014 does not apply to investment limited partnerships by virtue of each of s 1435(4) of the 2014 Act (which provides that s 1435 does not apply to an investment limited partnership within the meaning of the Investment Limited Partnerships Act 1994), and s 4(4) of the 1994 Act (which dis-applies s 376 of the Companies Act 1963, the predecessor to s 1435, to investment limited partnerships).

    (b)   it is formed in pursuance of some other statute;[98] or

    (c)   it is a partnership formed for the purpose of—

        (i)   carrying on practice as accountants in a case where each partner is a statutory auditor;

        (ii)   carrying on practice as solicitors in a case where each partner is a solicitor;

        (iii)   carrying on or promoting the business of thoroughbred horse breeding, being a partnership to which, subject to *subsection (5)*, the Limited Partnerships Act 1907 relates;[99] or

        (iv)   the provision of investment and loan finance and ancillary facilities and services to persons engaged in industrial or commercial activities, being a partnership—

            (I)   that consists of not more than 50 persons; and

            (II)   to which, subject to *subsection (5)*, the Limited Partnerships Act 1907 relates.

[4.30] The first point that could be made about this provision is that, to assist prospective partners and their advisers, any restriction on the number of partners could usefully be contained in the 1890 Act which was intended to be a codification of the law of partnership. As matters stand, the 1890 Act contains no indication that there is any restriction on the number of partners in a firm.

[4.31] If a partnership exceeds 20 members, it will be illegal and immediately dissolved.[100] There is however a facility for the Minister for Business, Enterprise and Innovation[101] to make an order under s 1435(2) of the Companies Act 2014 declaring that the provisions of s 1435(1) of the 2014 Act shall not apply to the formation of a specific partnership or type of partnership. The equivalent power under s 13 of the Companies (Amendment) Act 1982 was exercised twice,[102] to exempt both limited partnerships formed for the purposes of carrying on or promoting the business of thoroughbred horse-breeding, and limited partnerships consisting of 50 partners or less formed for the purposes of, and whose main business consists of, the provision of investment and loan finance and ancillary activities and services to persons engaged in

---

[98]   For example limited partnerships (formed under the Limited Partnerships Act 1907, although they are separately governed by size restrictions in s 4(2) of the 1907 Act) and investment limited partnerships (formed under the Investment Limited Partnerships Act 1994). Section 1435(4) also confirms that the restrictions in s 1435(1) do not apply to investment limited partnerships.

[99]   Section 1435(5) provides that s 4(2) of the Limited Partnerships Act 1907 (which inter alia provides that a limited partnership will not consist of more than 20 persons) does not apply to limited partnerships formed for the purpose of carrying on or promoting the business of thoroughbred horse breeding. So this type of partnership is not subject to an upper limit on the number of its partners.

[100]   See para **[9.19]** et seq.

[101]   Jobs, Enterprise and Innovation (Alteration of Name of Department and Title of Minister) Order 2017 (SI 364/2017).

[102]   Companies (Amendment) Act 1982 (Section 13(2)) Order 1988 (SI 54/1988) and Companies (Amendment) Act 1982 (Section 13(2)) Order 2004 (SI 506/2004).

industrial or commercial activities, from s 376 of the Companies Act 1963 – those exemptions have now been expressly incorporated into s 1435(1) of the 2014 Act.

Avoidance of Prohibition on Large Partnerships

[4.32] In order to circumvent this prohibition on partnerships with more than 20 partners, it is possible to use corporate partners,[103] sub-partnerships[104] and parallel partnerships.[105] For example the persons who would otherwise be members of the partnership, were it not for the prohibition, could form a company which itself would be a single member of the partnership. In this way more than 20 people may be interested in the partnership, albeit that the shareholders in the corporate partner will be interested in an indirect fashion. The same principle applies to the use of sub-partnerships and parallel partnerships. However, since these are not separate legal entities, there is the risk that all the members of the sub-partnership and the main partnership (or all the members of the two parallel partnerships) may be regarded as being in partnership together, in which case the maximum number of partners will still be exceeded.

Exemption for Large Accountancy and Law Firms

[4.33] In the late 1970s and 1980s it became apparent that accountancy firms (and to a lesser extent solicitors' firms) had grown to such an extent that the prohibition on more than 20 partners was a potential restriction on their expansion. Attempts were made to overcome the prohibition in s 376 of the Companies Act 1963 (the predecessor to s 1435(1) of the Companies Act 2014) by using parallel partnerships, although it is doubted whether, if tested, these schemes would have been successful in avoiding the prohibition in s 376.[106] However, before they could be tested, s 13(1)(a) of the Companies (Amendment) Act 1982 was enacted which exempted solicitors' and accountancy firms from the prohibition in s 376. Those exemptions are now contained in s 1435 of the 2014 Act, but are restricted to firms in which all the partners are solicitors or in which all the partners are statutory auditors.[107] There is a further exemption at s 1435(1)(b) from the 20 partner limit for partnerships formed under another statute. As legal partnerships of practising barristers, and legal partnerships of practising solicitors and practising barristers (and therefore limited liability partnerships to the extent that they are first established as legal partnerships) together with multi-disciplinary practices will, when these business models become available to the legal community in Ireland under the Legal Services Regulation Act 2015, be formed under that 2015 Act, the exemption at s 1435(1)(b) should also extend to them. Whether any further specific exemptions are added to s 1435 to take account of these new structures remains to be seen and the regulations setting out the finer details of the operating framework for such partnerships have not, at the time of writing, been made.[108]

---

103 See generally, para [8.63].
104 See para [8.45].
105 See para [8.55].
106 See para [8.58] et seq.
107 A statutory auditor is defined in s 2 of the Companies Act 2014 by reference to the new Part 27 of that Act.
108 See further Chapter 30.

Exclusion of banking partnerships

[4.34] By its express terms, s 1435(1) of the Companies Act 2014 does not apply to banking partnerships. These are governed by s 1436 of the 2014 Act which restricts the number of partners in a banking partnership to ten. This provision is of limited practical significance since, at the time of writing, a banking licence cannot be granted to a partnership.[109]

Repeal of section 1435(1)

[4.35] The question remains as to whether s 1435(1) of the Companies Act 2014 serves any useful purpose today. It has been noted that this section has its origins in an attempt to ease the task of creditors who wished to sue partnerships and other unincorporated associations. To sue a partnership, it was necessary at that time to sue each member of the partnership or association and by restricting the membership of such partnerships and associations to 20, this task was rendered practical. However, it is now possible to sue partnerships in the firm name.[110] For this reason, it is submitted that s 1435(1) no longer serves any useful purpose and should be dis-applied in full to ordinary and limited partnerships[111] as has already been done in respect of investment limited partnerships.[112] The 20 partner limit was, insofar as it remained, removed in Great Britain in 2002 under the Regulatory Reform (Reform of 20 Member Limit in Partnerships etc) Order 2002 (SI 2002/3203) and later in Northern Ireland by The Partnerships etc (Removal of Twenty Member Limit) (Northern Ireland) Order 2003.[113]

Registered Farm Partnerships and Succession Farm Partnerships

[4.36] Under s 667C of the Taxes Consolidation Act 1997, a farm partnership that wishes to be registered on the Register of Farm Partnerships maintained by the Minister for Agriculture, Food and the Marine can have no more than 10 partners. To be entered on the Register of Succession Farm Partnerships under s 667D of the 1997 Act, a partnership must already be a registered farm partnership, meaning that a partnership that wishes to be registered as a succession farm partnership can also have no more than 10 partners.[114]

---

[109] See paras [3.37] and [9.20].

[110] See para [12.11].

[111] The same argument supports the repeal of s 1436 of the Companies Act 2014 regarding banking partnerships in light of the current requirement that an Irish bank be a 'body corporate'. See fn **109** above.

[112] Investment Limited Partnerships Act 1994, ss 4(4) and 1435(4).

[113] The limit was removed in respect of both ordinary partnerships and limited partnerships.

[114] See further para [8.109] et seq in relation to registered farm partnerships and registered succession farm partnerships.

Chapter 5

Evidentiary Requirements of Partnership

INTRODUCTION

[5.01] Subject to some limited exceptions, there is no requirement for a partnership to be created by deed or written agreement since it has been noted that it may be created by oral agreement between the parties.[1] However, in certain cases, an oral agreement presents problems of proof and this and the other evidentiary requirements of the partnership agreement are considered in this chapter. Once the agreement has been concluded, it may be varied by express or implicit agreement of the parties and in this chapter reference will also be made to the variation of the terms of partnership agreements. This area will be considered under the following headings:

    I.   Application of Statute of Frauds;

    II.   Consideration; and

    III. Variation of Partnership Agreements.

Overview

[5.02] A partnership agreement, like any other type of contract, is subject to the general rules governing the evidentiary requirements of contracts. So, for example, to be enforceable a partnership agreement must be supported by consideration and if it relates to land it must be in writing or there must be a memorandum in writing thereof as required by the Statute of Frauds (Ireland) 1695.[2] In this sense, it is clear that no special provision was required to be made in the 1890 Act regarding the evidentiary requirements of partnership contracts. One issue which is addressed by the 1890 Act is the important right of the partners to vary the terms of their partnership agreement by their conduct. Thus, the conduct of the partners may be used as evidence of the partners' implicit agreement to vary the original terms of their partnership agreement, even where those original terms are in writing. Therefore from a practical perspective, particular care should be taken by partners who are acting contrary to their express rights as this conduct may be deemed to vary these rights.

---

[1]   Paragraph **[2.11]**. See para **[2.12]** for the limited cases in which a written partnership agreement is required.

[2]   7 Will 3, c 12.

I.   APPLICATION OF THE STATUTE OF FRAUDS

[5.03] The Statute of Frauds (Ireland) 1695 applies to a partnership agreement as it does to any other contract.[3] Under s 4 of the Statute:

> ... no action shall be brought ... whereby to charge the defendant upon any special promise to answer for the debt, default or miscarriage of another person, or to charge any person upon any agreement made upon consideration of marriage, or upon any contract or (sic) sale of lands, tenements or hereditaments, or any interest in or concerning them; or upon any agreement that is not to be performed within the space of one year from the making thereof, unless the agreement upon which such action shall be brought, or some memorandum or note thereof, shall be in writing, and signed by the party to be charged therewith, or some other person thereunto by him lawfully authorised.

Therefore if:

1. a partnership agreement is not to be performed within a year; or

2. a partnership agreement involves the sale of an interest in land; or

3. a partnership is giving or the recipient of a guarantee,

then s 4 will apply thereto and it will not be enforceable, unless there exists a written memorandum of the agreement. Each of these situations will now be examined.

1. 'Agreement not to be performed within the space of one year'

[5.04] A partnership agreement is subject to the terms of s 4 of the Statute of Frauds,[4] if:

(a) it is entered into for more than one year; or

(b) the partnership is not to commence for more than one year from the signing of the partnership agreement; or

(c) it is entered into for more than a year, with a power to determine sooner.

Any of these agreements must be in writing under s 4 of the Statute of Frauds, failing which they are unenforceable. It is important to note that a partnership agreement which is silent as regards its duration, as many partnerships are, is not an agreement to be performed outside the space of a year and therefore will fall outside the terms of the Statute of Frauds.[5]

---

[3] See generally Clark, *Contract Law in Ireland* (8th edn, 2016) at para 4.01 et seq; McDermott and McDermott, *Contract Law* (2nd edn, 2017) at para [5.06] et seq; Friel, *The Law of Contract* (2nd edn, 2000) at p 149 et seq. In England and Wales, the Statute of Frauds 1677 still applies to contracts of guarantee, but has been replaced in respect of contracts for the sale or other disposition of land by s 2(1) of the Law of Property (Miscellaneous Provisions) Act 1989. See also *Anson's Law of Contract* (30th edn, 2016) at p 82 et seq; *Chitty on Contracts* (32nd edn, 2015) at para 5.010 et seq; Treitel, *The Law of Contract* (14th edn, 2015) at para 5-013 et seq.

[4] *Hanau v Ehrlich* [1912] AC 39.

[5] See for example the American cases of *Jacobs v Thomas* (1991) 600 A 2d 1378; *Schaefer v Bork* (1987) 413 NW 2d 873; *Kist v Coughlin* (1943) 50 NE 2d 939; *Stitt v Rat Portgage Lumber Co* (1906) 98 Minn 52.

2. Partnerships involving land

[5.05] Section 4 of the Statute of Frauds also applies to any contract concerning an interest in land. The section will therefore be of relevance where an oral partnership agreement provides for the partnership property to include land or where a partnership is formed exclusively for dealing in land. However, once a partnership is proven to exist, it has been held that the land which is necessary for the carrying on of a trade attaches to the partnership as a necessary incident of the trade.[6] For this reason, once the partnership is proved to exist, parol evidence may be adduced to show that its property consists of land and no reliance may be placed on s 4 of the Statute of Frauds to defeat such a claim.[7] This exception to the Statute of Frauds may be explained by the nature of partnership property. The share of a partner in a partnership is in fact simply his proportion of the partnership property after that property has been turned into money and applied to pay off the partnership debts.[8] This follows from the terms of s 44 of the 1890 Act which provides that partnership property is to be used, on the dissolution of the firm, to pay off the firm's liabilities, advances and capital contributions and the surplus is to be divided amongst the partners.[9] No distinction is made between real property and personal property for this purpose. For this reason, it is said that real property which forms part of the partnership property is subject to the doctrine of conversion and is thereby said to be converted into personal estate. It follows that a contract to enter a partnership for the purpose of acquiring land or where land is a necessary part of the partnership, is not a contract relating to land in the true sense, but primarily a contract relating to personalty.[10] The application of the doctrine of conversion to partnership property (whether real or personal property) is expressly recognised by the 1890 Act, which in s 22 provides that all partnership property is considered to be personalty as

---

[6] See the judgment of the Lord Chancellor in *Forster v Hale* (1800) 5 Ves Jun 308 at 309 that: 'If by facts and circumstances it is established as a fact, that these persons were partners in the colliery, in which land was necessary to carry on the trade, the lease goes as an incident.'

[7] *Gray v Smith* (1889) 43 Ch D 208; *Forster v Hale* (1800) 5 Ves Jr 308; *Dale v Hamilton* (1846) 5 Hare 369; *Re De Nicols* [1900] 2 Ch 410. All these cases concerned s 4 of the Statute of Frauds 1677 which has now been largely repealed in England and Wales, save as regards guarantees. As regards land, see now s 2(1) of the Law of Property (Miscellaneous Provisions) Act 1989, the current equivalent of s 4 of the Statute of Frauds (Ireland) 1695. See also the Scottish case of *Munro v Stein* (1961) SC 362 and the decision of the English Court of Appeal in *Steadman v Steadman* [1974] QB 161.

[8] See generally in relation to the meaning of a partnership share, para **[19.08]**.

[9] See also s 20(1) of the 1890 Act which requires partnership property to be used for the purposes of the partnership.

[10] Similarly, it may be said that an agreement to become partners is not a contract for a transfer of an interest in land, since title to the property is not affected by the agreement. Any real property which is acquired with partnership funds is partnership property and the Statute of Frauds does not prevent partnership ownership. Rather, such a situation involves a resulting trust which is outside the Statute. This is also the position in America where the Statute of Frauds is ubiquitous: *Unit v Kentucky Fried Chicken Corp* (1973) 304 A 2d 320; *Anderson v Property Development* (1977) 555 F 2d 648; *Goben v Barry* (1984) 676 P 2d 90; *Johnson v Johnson* (1985) 490 NYS 2d 344.

between the partners and is therefore subject to the doctrine of conversion.[11] Thus, a contract to enter into partnership which is to acquire land or where land is necessary for the operation of the partnership business is a contract relating to personalty and thus outside the ambit of the Statute of Frauds. For this reason, in *Johnson v Murray*,[12] the British Columbia Supreme Court found that a partnership agreement for the acquisition of land did not comply with the Statute of Frauds, yet the court held that a partner's claim was not barred by the statute.

[5.06] However, where it can be shown that the parties to the agreement are not partners or where the very existence of the partnership cannot be proved, the Statute of Frauds will provide a good defence to a claim that the parties are bound by a contract involving land.[13] Similarly, the Statute of Frauds will provide a good defence if the contract is between the firm and a third party. This explains the dicta of Blayney J in *Guardian Builders Ltd v Seelcon Ltd.*[14] In that case he noted obiter that where a purchaser buys an interest in a partnership which owns land, such that the purchase is in substance a purchase of an interest in land, that contract must comply with the Statute of Frauds.[15] In both cases, the land in question is not partnership property and therefore is not personalty under s 22 of the 1890 Act.[16]

3. Guarantees and partnerships

[5.07] A guarantee, but not an indemnity,[17] is also within the terms of s 4 of the Statute of Frauds, since that section requires there to be a written memorandum of any promise to answer for the debt, default or miscarriage of another person. Thus, where a guarantee is given by a partnership or to a partnership, in order to ensure that it is enforceable, it should be in writing. *Gorrie v Woodley*[18] involved a valid partnership between the members of a firm called Meiklejohn & Son. The three partners in the firm took an action in their own names only to enforce a guarantee given by the defendant to the firm. The defendant disputed the enforceability of the guarantee on the grounds that the guarantee did not contain their names and thus there was not a sufficient memorandum in writing to satisfy the Statute of Frauds. In the High Court, O'Brien J held that the Statute of Frauds had been satisfied since it was sufficient for the statement of claim of the defendants to state that the three plaintiffs were the persons described in the guarantee as 'R Meiklejohn & Son'.

---

[11] See further in relation to this doctrine, para **[16.70]**.
[12] *Johnson v Murray* (1951) 2 WWR (NS) 447.
[13] *Caddick v Skidmore* (1857) 3 Jur NS 1184; *Isaacs v Evans* [1899] WN 261, both of which concern s 4 of the Statute of Frauds 1677.
[14] *Guardian Builders Ltd v Seelcon Ltd* (18 August 1988) HC.
[15] Blayney J relied on the authority of *Boyce v Green* (1826) Batty 608. See p 8 of the transcript.
[16] See for example the Australian case of *Caporn v Dixon* (1904) 6 WALR 71.
[17] See *Barnett v Hyndman* (1840) 3 Ir LR 109 and see generally Clark, *Contract Law in Ireland* (8th edn, 2016) at para 4-06.
[18] *Gorrie v Woodley* (1864) 17 Ir CLR 221.

Part Performance of a Partnership Agreement

[5.08] In order to ensure that the Statute of Frauds was not used as an instrument of fraud, courts allowed the enforcement of contracts which did not comply with the Statute where there had been a part performance of their terms. Initially, it was thought that this equitable doctrine of part performance only applied to cases concerning land.[19] The extension of the doctrine to all agreements governed by the Statute can be supported in principle since clearly it is equally as important to prevent fraud in the case of a partnership guarantee as it is in the case of a partnership involving land. Any doubts about the application of the doctrine of part performance to other contracts and in particular contracts for more than a year was dispelled by the High Court in *Crowley v O'Sullivan (No 2)*.[20] The doctrine of part performance allows an oral agreement which does not satisfy s 4 of the Statute of Frauds to be enforced if it has been part performed, ie where the actions of the person seeking to deny the contract are referable to the alleged contract and consistent with its existence.[21] That case involved an oral partnership agreement between the plaintiff and defendant whereby Crowley agreed to abstain from bidding for some premises in Bantry, Co Cork and O'Sullivan agreed to purchase the premises for the benefit of a partnership, to be entered into between them for at least three years. The premises were duly purchased by O'Sullivan and the parties entered into partnership. After several months, a dispute developed between them and Crowley instituted proceedings to enforce the terms of their oral partnership agreement. He was met with the defence that the agreement did not comply with the Statute of Frauds. In response, Crowley alleged that the performance of the partnership agreement by the parties for a period of seven months constituted part performance so as to satisfy the Statute of Frauds. Although the case itself clearly concerned lands, Palles CB[22] chose not to limit his judgment to contracts in relation to land. He held that the doctrine of part performance also applied to a contract for partnership for more than a year, thus taking the partnership in that case outside the Statute of Frauds.[23]

[5.09] In general terms therefore, where a partnership business has commenced under the terms of an oral partnership agreement, it is apprehended that a partner to that agreement may rely on the doctrine of part performance to take the agreement outside the Statute of Frauds.

---

[19] *Britain v Rossiter* (1879) 11 QBD 123 which was not followed by the High Court in *Crowley v O'Sullivan (No 2)* [1900] 2 IR 478.

[20] *Crowley v O'Sullivan (No 2)* [1900] 2 IR 478.

[21] See generally, Clark, *Contract Law in Ireland* (8th edn, 2016) at para 4-51; McDermott and McDermott, *Contract Law* (2nd edn, 2017) at para [5.120] et seq; Friel, *The Law of Contract* (2nd edn, 2000) at pp 305–306; Trietel, *The Law of Contract* (14th edn, 2015) at para 2-053; *Anson's Law of Contract* (30th edn, 2016) at p 475 et seq.

[22] Andrews and Johnson JJ, concurring.

[23] He relied on *Maddison v Alderson* (1883) 8 AC 467.

II. CONSIDERATION

[5.10] Like all contracts, in order to be enforceable, a contract of partnership must be supported by consideration or be executed as a deed.[24] The consideration provided by the partners need not be adequate, in the sense of being of equal value, but must simply be sufficient, in the sense of being 'something of value in the eyes of the law'.[25] The fact that a contract of partnership is enforceable, even where for example there is a substantial disparity in the size of capital contributions of the partners, is illustrated by *O'Dwyer, Inspector of Taxes v Cafolla & Co*.[26] There, Joseph Cafolla owned Cafolla restaurants, a chain of successful fast-food restaurants in Capel Street and O'Connell Street in Dublin. By converting his sole trader's business into a partnership with his children, he was able to benefit from his children's tax-free allowances in order to reduce the overall tax paid in respect of the business. Under the terms of the partnership agreement, Mr Cafolla contributed all of the business assets and goodwill to the partnership, while his children contributed no capital, but simply undertook to devote their full time to the business. Nonetheless, it was held by the Special Commissioner of the Revenue, and it was not subsequently challenged in the High Court or the Supreme Court, that a valid partnership existed in this case and Maguire J indicated that there was abundant evidence for such a finding.[27]

[5.11] Like any other contract, the consideration for a partnership agreement is legally sufficient where it is simply the undertaking by one party to be bound by the terms of the contract or to be a partner in the case of a partnership agreement. The case of *Drimmie v Davies*[28] involved a dentistry partnership between a father and a son at 27

---

[24] See generally regarding the requirement for consideration, Clark, *Contract Law in Ireland* (8th edn, 2016) at para 2-01 et seq; McDermott and McDermott, *Contract Law* (2nd edn, 2017) at para [3.01] et seq; Friel, *The Law of Contract* (2nd edn, 2000) at p 87 et seq; Trietel, *The Law of Contract* (14th edn, 2015) at para 3-001 et seq; *Anson's Law of Contract* (30th edn, 2016) at p 96 et seq. The Land and Conveyancing Law Reform Act 2009, s 64, reformed the law regarding the execution of deeds. An individual no longer needs to use a seal to make a document a deed (s 64(1)(a)) (although the use by an individual of a seal in such cases will not affect the validity of the deed – the seal will simply be a superfluous addition). To be a deed after 1 December 2009, where an instrument is executed by an individual, it must be described as such (by using the term 'deed' or similar) or it must be otherwise clear on the face of the instrument that the individual intends to execute it as a deed, and it must be signed by the individual in the presence of a witness. See, further, Wylie, *The Land and Conveyancing Law Reform Act 2009: Annotations and Commentary* (2nd edn, 2017) at p 109. Regarding the execution of deeds by companies, see Courtney, *The Law of Companies* (4th edn, 2016) at para [7.061].

[25] *Thomas v Thomas* (1842) 2 QB 581 and Clark, *Contract Law in Ireland* (8th edn, 2016) at para 2-09 et seq; McDermott and McDermott, *Contract Law* (2nd edn, 2017) at para [3.12] et seq; Friel, *The Law of Contract* (2nd edn, 2000) at p 95 et seq; Trietel, *The Law of Contract* (14th edn, 2015) at para 3-013; *Anson's Law of Contract* (30th edn, 2016) at p 104 et seq.

[26] *O'Dwyer, Inspector of Taxes v Cafolla & Co* [1949] IR 210.

[27] Although the decision of Maguire J regarding the tax treatment of the partnership was overturned on appeal by the Supreme Court, the Supreme Court did not disagree with his conclusions regarding the existence of a partnership.

[28] *Drimmie v Davies* [1899] IR 176. See also the High Court case of *Re Clarke* (1906) 40 ILTR 117. (contd.../)

Westmoreland Street in Dublin, whereby the son agreed to pay an annuity to his siblings after his father's death. However, on the death of his father, he refused to honour this term of the partnership agreement. When the children and the personal representatives of the deceased partner sought to enforce this covenant, the son claimed that there was no consideration for this undertaking. As the agreement was under seal, the following comments of Chatterton VC were obiter:

> 'As for the defence that there was no consideration to the defendant for such a covenant, it is unfounded in fact, for he was admitted as a partner, which was a valuable consideration, if any were necessary, and it was one of the terms and conditions stated in the agreement upon which he and his father became partners.'[29]

[5.12] These sentiments were echoed by Fitzgibbon LJ when the son's defence was also rejected by the Irish Court of Appeal:

> '[B]eing under seal it did not require valuable consideration to support it, but even if it did, there was, in my opinion, valuable consideration for it in the fact that the defendant got a share in the business during his father's life, and the right of succession to it on his father's death. *Facio ut facias*[30] is just as good consideration as *do ut des*;[31] the deed of partnership contained covenants binding both father and son, and it was a contract for valuable consideration on both sides.'[32]

[5.13] Finally, reference should be made to the case of *Brophy v Holmes*.[33] It was authority for the principle that a person who did not agree to share the losses of an enterprise could not be a partner on the grounds of insufficiency of consideration. There, Brophy and Holmes entered into an arrangement whereby the profits of the business would be shared equally, but Holmes was to be liable for all the losses. Hart LC was of the opinion that the agreement was void for want of consideration on the basis that both should share the losses equally. It is clear that this case no longer represents the law.[34] There can be no good reason why one or more partners in a firm should not be entitled to be indemnified from loss by the other partners, if this is agreed under the terms of the partnership agreement. It is submitted that the contrary position is too much of a restriction on the freedom of partners to negotiate the terms of their partnership agreement.

---

28   (\...contd) This concerned the question of whether a transaction, whereby a father took his sons into partnership, was a transaction for value, so as to be subject to estate duty. At 119–120, Palles CB (Johnson and Kenny JJ, concurring) noted, obiter that: 'Of course, if arguing the question whether there was consideration sufficient to support a contract, I would point to the extension of the period of the partnership, during which time the sons were bound to give their whole time to the business.'

29   *Drimmie v Davies* [1899] IR 176 at 181.

30   I do in order that you may do.

31   I give that you may give.

32   *Drimmie v Davies* [1899] IR 176 at 186, per Fitzgibbon LJ. Neither Holmes nor Walker LJJ adverted to the consideration issue to find that the personal representative and the children could sue the son.

33   *Brophy v Holmes* (1828) 1 Ir Law Rec 495.

34   See for example *DPP v McLoughlin* [1986] IR 355, where a partnership was held to exist even though the partners did not share the losses, considered at para **[2.104]**.

III.   VARIATION OF PARTNERSHIP AGREEMENTS

[5.14] Whether a partnership agreement is created by deed, by written agreement or orally, the terms of that agreement may be varied in writing, orally or by the conduct of the partners, subject of course to there being sufficient consideration for the variation.[35] The principle that the terms of a written partnership agreement could be varied by the conduct of the parties was recognised by the Irish courts as early as 1827 in the case of *Barklie v Scott.*[36] That case concerned the question of whether the defendant was a partner in the Sligo firm of John Scott, Patrickson & Co in which he invested a sum of money on behalf of his son. The evidence in support of a finding that the defendant was not a partner consisted, inter alia, of a conversation by one of the true partners in the firm to a third party to the effect that the defendant was not a partner. On this basis, the defendant was held not to be a partner, despite the existence of a letter whereby the true partners were to account to the defendant for the profit or loss of the enterprise and to be governed by his advice relating to the business. Jebb J adopted the following principle in relation to the variation of written partnership agreements:[37]

> 'The law, as I apprehend, is, that the transactions of partners are always to be looked at, in order that you may determine between them, even against the written articles, what clauses in those articles will bind them, provided those transactions afford higher probability amounting almost to demonstration.'[38]

[5.15] The variation by the partners of the terms of a partnership agreement, whether written or oral, is now recognised by s 19 of the 1890 Act. As is clear from *Barklie v Scott*[39] above and the wording of s 19 hereunder, the terms of a partnership agreement may be varied by conduct:[40]

> The mutual rights and duties of partners, whether ascertained by agreement or defined by the Act, may be varied by the consent of all the partners, and such consent may be either express or inferred from a course of dealing.[41]

---

35   See generally Clark, *Contract Law in Ireland* (8th edn, 2016) at para 18-32 et seq; McDermott and McDermott, *Contract Law* (2nd edn, 2017) at para [22.64] et seq; Friel, *The Law of Contract* (2nd edn, 2000) at p 119 et seq; Trietel, *The Law of Contract* (14th edn, 2015) at para 3-062; *Anson's Law of Contract* (30th edn, 2016) at p 488 et seq; *Chitty on Contracts* (32nd edn, 2015) at para 4-080 et seq.

36   *Barklie v Scott* (1827) 1 Hud & Bro 83.

37   Quoting from Lord Eldon in *Geddes v Wallace* (1820) 2 Bli 270 at 297–298.

38   *Barklie v Scott* (1827) 1 Hud & Bro 83 at 96.

39   *Barklie v Scott* (1827) 1 Hud & Bro 83.

40   See also *Taylor v Hughes* (1844) 7 Ir Eq R 529 where Sugden LC held that *Const v Harris* (1824) T & R 496 was authority for this principle and he quoted Eldon LJ's statement that: '[a]rticles which have been agreed on to regulate a partnership cannot be altered without the consent of all the partners; but if alterations are made by some of the partners and acquiesced in by all, the Court will hold that to be an adoption of new terms.' On this basis, Sugden LC held that the purchase of one partner's interest in the firm, though allegedly contrary to the express terms of the partnership deed, was valid since it had been done with the consent of all the partners.

41   See also *O'Crowley v O'Sullivan (No 2)* [1900] 2 IR 478.

[5.16] In *Williams v Harris*,[42] the variation of a partnership deed by conduct was accepted by the Supreme Court. The deed provided for six months' notice in writing to be given by a partner retiring from the firm, but no notice was given by the retiring partners in that case. Kenny J noted that:

> 'On 30 July 1976, the plaintiffs gave notice that they retired from the partnership and, although clause 2 of the partnership deed provided for six months notice in writing, all the parties treated 30 July 1976 as the date upon which the partners retired from the partnership.'[43]

On this basis, the Supreme Court accepted that the retirement was effective as of 30 July 1976.

[5.17] There was also a variation by conduct of the partnership agreement in *Larkin v Groeger and Eaton*.[44] That case involved a written partnership agreement between a number of accountants. Within a few months of the commencement of their partnership, difficulties arose between them and these disputes were submitted to arbitration. The arbitrator held that the conduct of the parties, in ignoring their respective obligations under the partnership agreement, had resulted in that agreement ceasing to operate between them 20 months after it was signed. The arbitrator's award was upheld by Barrington J on appeal.

Variation does not Affect Validity of Original Agreement

[5.18] It is perhaps self-evident that a subsequent variation of a partnership agreement does not affect the validity of the terms of the original agreement.[45] Thus in *Crowley v O'Sullivan (No 2)*,[46] there was a variation of the original partnership agreement between the parties by their agreeing to the substitution of the defendant's son for the defendant. Palles CB rejected the claim that this variation affected the validity of the original partnership agreement. He expressly relied on *England v Curling*[47] and observed that the judgment in that case:

> 'goes on to say that partners make constant variations in the terms of their partnership agreement, which may be evidenced not only by writing but by their conduct. In giving judgment Lord Langdale says:- "With respect to a partnership agreement, it is to be observed that all parties being competent to act as they please, they may put an end to or vary it at any moment; a partnership agreement is therefore open to variation from day to day, and *the terms* of such variations may not only be evidenced by writing, but also *by the conduct of the parties* in relation to the agreement and to their mode of conducting their

---

42   *Williams v Harris* [1980] ILRM 237.
43   *Williams v Harris* [1980] ILRM 237 at 240.
44   *Larkin v Groeger and Eaton* (26 April 1988) HC.
45   And also that the variation should not be with a view to terminating the partnership – Arnold J in the Court of Appeal in *Hodson v Hodson* [2009] EWHC 430 (Ch) noted that it was 'difficult to conceive' of a 'variation' to a partnership agreement which in fact caused the termination of the arrangements between the parties.
46   *Crowley v O'Sullivan (No 2)* [1900] 2 IR 478.
47   *England v Curling* (1844) 8 Beav 129 in which the court ordered the execution of a formal partnership agreement between persons who had been partners for 12 years under initialled heads of agreement.

business; when, therefore, there is a variation and alteration of the terms of the partnership, it does not follow that there was not a binding agreement at first.'"[48]

Terms of Partnership Agreement Varied by Partnership Accounts

[5.19] A common manner in which a financial term in a partnership agreement may be varied is by the inclusion of contrary terms in the firm's books or accounts. This is because if a provision is made in the partnership accounts on a regular basis, this will constitute strong evidence of an agreement between the partners regarding this term. Thus in *Hutcheson v Smith*,[49] an attempt was made by one partner in a distillery partnership in Armagh to establish a right to be compensated for his expenses in entertaining clients of the firm.[50] Brady CB rejected this claim noting that:

'If there had been a settlement of account, containing this item, in the first year of the partnership, that would be a fair ground for saying that there was an agreement between the partners to that effect: but such was not the case.'[51]

[5.20] However, where the partner receiving the accounts is not likely to understand the significance of the provision in the accounts, then they will not operate as a variation of the partnership agreement. In the English Court of Appeal case of *Joyce v Morrissey*,[52] a dispute arose between the four members of the rock band 'The Smiths' regarding their sharing of profits. The lead singer (Morrissey) and the lead guitarist (Johnny Marr) were the prime movers behind the band and alleged that they were entitled to 40% of the profits each with 10% each going to the drummer and bass guitarist. They relied in part on the fact that the group's accountants, Ossie Kilkenny & Co, had sent accounts to the drummer showing this split of 40/40/10/10. Waller LJ noted that the default partnership agreement in s 24(1) of the 1890 Act applied at the start of the partnership, namely equal profit-sharing. He held that a variation of this equality of profit-sharing could not be achieved by sending partnership accounts to one's partner and assuming that his silence constituted acceptance of the new terms, particularly where the partner might not be expected to understand the accounts without some explanation.

Consent of all the Partners Required

[5.21] By the express terms of s 19 of the 1890 Act, a variation will only be effective if it is consented to (whether expressly or impliedly) by each of the partners in the firm. It follows that from an evidentiary perspective, it may be more difficult to establish a variation of a partnership agreement in a firm with numerous partners or in a firm containing dormant partners, than in a firm with two or three partners. Of course, on the other hand, in larger professional firms, it is often the case that a more formal approach is taken to partners' conduct by way of documenting decisions by means of minutes of partners' meetings, having handbooks or manuals for partners' conduct, etc. In such

---

[48] *Crowley v O'Sullivan (No 2)* [1900] 2 IR 478 at 487.
[49] *Hutcheson v Smith* (1842) 5 Ir Eq R 117.
[50] The case was heard prior to the passing of the Partnership Act 1890, s 24(2) of which contains the right of a partner to be indemnified for the liabilities incurred in the ordinary conduct of the firm's business. See generally para **[14.40]**.
[51] *Hutcheson v Smith* (1842) 5 Ir Eq R 117 at 123.
[52] *Joyce v Morrissey* [1999] EMLR 233.

cases, proof of a variation of the partnership agreement by the conduct of the partners may be established by having recourse to this documentation.

Care when Partner is Acting Contrary to Terms of Agreement

[5.22] Since a partnership agreement may be varied by a course of dealing between the partners, it follows that care should be taken by any partners who act contrary to, or do not exercise any of their rights under, the partnership agreement. This is because such partners may be surprised to learn that their actions, if consented to by all the partners, may be deemed to constitute a variation of their partnership agreement by implication. For this reason, it would be prudent for a partner who is conducting himself contrary to his express rights under the partnership agreement, to confirm in writing with his co-partners that such actions are not to be construed as a variation of the terms of the partnership agreement. This issue could also arise in the context of the right of partners under the partnership agreement to expel a partner where those partners fail to exercise this right in the face of the misconduct of one partner. If the misconduct has been tolerated by the partners over a long period of time, it could be argued that this conduct by the partners amounts to a variation of the expulsion clause so that the partner may not be expelled for continuing this 'tolerated' misconduct. For this reason, partnership agreements may attempt to circumvent this issue by including a 'No Variation' clause.[53]

[5.23] This issue is illustrated by the case of *Heslin v Fay (1)*.[54] There, the partnership deed for a grocery business provided that the partnership business was to be operated by the firm at North King Street in Dublin and it was to be run independently from a business which was run by some of the partners only in Thomas Street in Dublin. In practice, both firms operated as one business and Heslin, who was a partner in the North King Street firm only, complained of this practice. However, Heslin had acquiesced in this practice by allowing it to continue and this lack of action by him was held to have led to a variation of the partnership deed. Sullivan LC dismissed Heslin's ground of complaint, noting that he 'undid the deed by his own act, and acquiesced in its being disregarded for ten years and he cannot now complain'.[55]

Are New Partners Subject to Previously Agreed Variation?

[5.24] Where a partner joins a firm whose partnership agreement has been varied by the conduct of the partners, an issue may arise as to whether the new partner is bound by the terms of the original agreement or the agreement as varied. It is apprehended that as a matter of contract, an incoming partner will not be bound by the varied terms, unless the variation has been expressly brought to his attention. In many cases, of course, the variation will not be brought to his attention, since it will have taken place by conduct.

[5.25] However, this will not be the case if the new partner is a derivative partner. A derivative partner is a partner who becomes a partner by taking over the outgoing

---

53   An example of such a clause is as follows: 'This Agreement may not be released, discharged supplemented, amended, varied or modified in any manner except by an instrument in writing signed by each of the Partners.' Although, it is to be noted that this clause may itself obviously be varied under s 19 of the 1890 Act.

54   *Heslin v Fay (1)* (1884) 15 LR Ir 431.

55   *Heslin v Fay (1)* (1884) 15 LR Ir 431 at 445.

partner's share *in specie*. In such a case, the incoming partner will be bound by any variation of the terms of the partnership agreement which was consented to by the outgoing partner.[56] To be effective, the transfer of a partnership share *in specie* to an incoming partner requires the consent of all the partners in the firm, since they must consent to the admission of a new partner.[57] Although, not that common in ordinary partnerships, both the Limited Partnerships Act 1907[58] and the Investment Limited Partnerships Act 1994[59] contemplate a limited partner's share being acquired by a third party in this fashion.

[5.26] The more common way in which a partner transfers his interest in an ordinary partnership to a third party is by way of assignment of his share. In such a case, the assignee does not thereby become a partner[60] and therefore no issue arises regarding the assignee being bound by the terms of the varied partnership agreement.

---

[56]   *Const v Harris* (1824) T & R 496.
[57]   A person may not be admitted as a partner, without the consent of all the existing partners, in the absence of contrary agreement between the partners: Partnership Act 1890, s 24(7). See further para **[13.22]**.
[58]   Limited Partnerships Act 1907, s 6(5)(b), see generally para **[28.119]**.
[59]   Investment Limited Partnerships Act 1994, s 18(2), see generally para **[29.126]** et seq.
[60]   Partnership Act 1890, s 31 and see generally para **[19.12]**.

Chapter 6

Types of Partners

INTRODUCTION

[6.01]

> 'Now, there are many kinds of partnership, as everyone knows. There may be a partner only in name, or a partner without having his name in the firm; there may be a sleeping partner, or a partner who is only a clerk.'

Per Ashbourne LC in *Martin v Sherry*.[1]

Throughout this text, reference is made to the term 'partner'. By this is meant a member of an ordinary partnership or 'an ordinary partner',[2] ie a person who carries on business in common with one or more others with a view to profit.[3] As noted by Ashbourne LC, there are a number of different types of partner and this chapter is concerned with these categories and the extent, if any, to which their treatment differs from that of an ordinary partner. Each of the following types of partners will be considered in turn:

    I.   Dormant Partner;

    II.   Salaried Partner;

    III. Fixed Share Partner;

    IV. General Partner and Limited Partner;

    V.   Quasi-Partner;

    VI. Partner by Holding Out;

    VII. Senior and Junior Partners; and

    VIII. Precedent Partner.

Overview

[6.02] In considering the different categories of partners, it will become apparent that in some cases little significance attaches to the application of these labels to partners. So, for example, a dormant partner, precedent partner, senior partner and junior partner will in general have the same rights and duties as an ordinary partner and be subject to the same provisions of the 1890 Act. However, having said that, although a dormant partner is subject to the same liabilities as an ordinary partner, the application of the provisions of the 1890 Act to a dormant partner will produce different results from when the same provisions are applied to an ordinary partner. This difference arises not by virtue of a person's classification as a dormant partner, but because of the characteristics of the partner in question and in particular because dormant partners are usually not known to

---

[1]   *Martin v Sherry* [1905] 2 IR 62 at 66–67.

[2]   As regards the meaning of the term 'ordinary partner', see para **[1.35]**.

[3]   See the definition of partnership in s 1(1) of the 1890 Act, considered at para **[2.09]** et seq.

be partners by third parties, while ordinary partners are. It is for this reason, for example, that a dormant partner may escape liability to a third party for debts incurred after he left the firm, while an ordinary partner may not.[4]

[6.03] In contrast, brief reference will also be made in this chapter to the very different rights and liabilities which attach to partners depending on their classification. Thus, whether a partner is a limited partner or a general partner will determine whether he had limited or unlimited liability for the obligations of the firm.

I.   DORMANT PARTNER

[6.04] While there is no technical definition of a dormant partner, this category of partner may be described as a partner who is not involved in the day-to-day operations of the firm and as a result is not generally known to be a partner.[5] The fact that one or more third parties know that a person is a dormant partner does not of itself prevent that person from being a dormant partner.[6] This looseness regarding the classification of a person as a dormant partner can be explained by the fact that a dormant partner is treated the same as an ordinary partner and therefore not much turns on the fact that someone is classified as a dormant partner. Yet as is noted below, the application of those rights and liabilities to a dormant partner will, in some cases, produce different results by virtue of the characteristic of dormant partners, ie that they are not generally known to be partners and do not take an active part in the business of the firm.[7]

Dormant Partner Treated as an Ordinary Partner

[6.05] A dormant partner has the same rights and obligations as an ordinary partner. For example a dormant partner is bound by the acts of his partners,[8] he is entitled to an equal

---

4   Under s 36(1) of the 1890 Act, see para **[6.14]**.

5   For an example of a dormant partner, see *O'Dwyer, Inspector of Taxes v Cafolla & Co* [1949] IR 210, where an illiterate 80-year-old grandmother, who never took any part in the business, was held to be a dormant partner. See also *Barklie v Scott* (1827) 1 Hud & Bro 83 and *Re McManus* (1858) 7 Ir Ch R 82. For a description of a dormant partner, see the US cases of *Schwaegler Co Inc v Marchesotti* (1948) 199 P 2d 331; *Warner v Modan* (1960) 164 NE 2d 904; *Dygert v Hansen* (1948) 199 P 2d 596. In the United States, s 35(2) of the Uniform Partnership Act (1914) defined a dormant partner as one who is neither known to a third party nor sufficiently active in partnership affairs that his or her presence in the firm formed a basis of the partnership's credit reputation however, this was removed when the Uniform Partnership Act (1997) was put in place, as it was viewed as inconsistent with the general agency rules set out in s 301 of the Uniform Partnership Act (1997) (Last Amended 2013). The terms 'dormant partner' and 'sleeping partner' are often used interchangeably in commentary and in caselaw, but mean the same thing. In *Hodson v Hodson* [2009] EWHC 430 (Ch), Arnold J noted that it is not a prerequisite to the existence of a partnership that a particular partner should be involved in the management of the partnership, stating that it '… is well-established that a sleeping partner can be a partner'. Equally, in *Chahal v Mahal* [2004] EWHC 2859 (Ch) (heard before Hazel Williamson QC sitting as a Deputy Judge of the High Court), the Court noted that that the 'sleeping partner' concept is well-recognised as a matter of English law.

6   *Re Ferrar, ex p Ulster Banking Co* (1859) 9 Ir Ch R 11, see para **[6.11]**.

7   See further paras **[6.08]–[6.15]**.

8   See generally para **[10.01]** et seq.

share of the profits of the firm,[9] he is equally liable to third parties for the losses of the firm,[10] etc. The fact that a dormant partner is in no better or worse a position than an ordinary partner was noted by Hanna J in the High Court case of *Leech v Stokes and Ors*.[11] This case concerned an action by a dormant partner (Mr Leech) in a firm of solicitors against the firm's accountants. He alleged negligence by the accountants in the preparation of the law firm's accounts. The firm of accountants, the precursor of the Irish partnership of KPMG,[12] had been engaged by the active partner in the firm (Mr Fetherstonhaugh) to prepare the accounts. The accountants failed to discover the embezzlement of money by a law clerk in the firm. After Mr Fetherstonhaugh's death, Mr Leech initiated an action against the accountants and Hanna J[13] observed:

> 'As to the legal position, it is clear that anything that Mr Fetherstonhaugh, the acting partner, knew or did, binds the plaintiff, the sleeping partner, who is presumed to have full knowledge of the partnership affairs and methods of business. Mr Leech, therefore can be in no better position than Mr Fetherstonhaugh, and must be taken to stand in his shoes and the case must be tried upon that basis.'[14]

[6.06] The treatment of dormant partners as having the same rights and duties as ordinary partners is also illustrated by *Gaffney v Duffy*.[15] This case concerned a sole trader who carried on a bicycle sales and repair business from the respondent's property in Capel Street in Dublin. He admitted two partners to his business and he became a dormant partner in the resulting partnership. His application for a new tenancy was disputed on the grounds that he was not in continuous occupation of the premises, since he had initially occupied it as a sole trader and then as a dormant partner. Up to that time, the courts had treated *ordinary* partners who became sole traders as being in continuous occupation of a premises despite their change in status, for the purposes of the landlord and tenant legislation.[16] In the Circuit Court, Judge Shannon applied the corollary of this principle to dormant partners.[17] Accordingly, the applicant was treated as still being the occupier of the premises after he became a dormant partner, thus entitling him to a new tenancy under the landlord and tenant legislation.[18]

Different Results in Some Cases

[6.07] It has been noted that the same legal principles apply to dormant partners as apply to ordinary partners. However, the fact that, unlike ordinary partners, dormant partners do not take an active part in the partnership business and are not generally known to be partners means that the application of the same legal principles will often produce different results. The situations in which this is the case will now be considered.[19]

---

[9]   Unless there is a contrary provision in the partnership agreement: Partnership Act 1890, s 24(1).
[10] See generally para **[11.07]** et seq.
[11] *Leech v Stokes and Ors* [1937] IR 787.
[12] Ie Stokes Brothers & Pim.
[13] Hanna J's decision was affirmed by the Supreme Court on appeal, [1937] IR 817.
[14] *Leech v Stokes and Ors* [1937] IR 787 at 792.
[15] *Gaffney v Duffy* (1953) 87 ILTR 92.
[16] *O'Neill v Whelan* (1951) 85 ILTR 111 and see generally para **[3.54]**.
[17] Albeit in reverse.
[18] At that time, the Landlord and Tenant Act 1931.

(i) Dormant partner does not 'habitually act in the partnership business'

[6.08] Section 16 of the 1890 Act provides that notice to a partner who habitually acts in the partnership business of any matter relating to the partnership affairs is deemed to be notice to the firm.[20] By definition, a dormant partner does not habitually act in the partnership business and therefore notice to a dormant partner will not operate as notice to the firm.

(ii) Exclusion of dormant partner's right to manage firm

[6.09] Section 24(5) of the 1890 Act entitles every partner to take part in the management of the firm's business. However, this right is, by its very terms, subject to 'any agreement express or implied between the partners'. As a dormant partner takes no part in the management of the firm, this right will often be either expressly or impliedly excluded by the partners. It will often be the case, however, that the right is not excluded but is simply not exercised by the dormant partner and such a dormant partner will continue to retain the right to take part in the firm's management.

(iii) No right to dissolution on insanity of a dormant partner

[6.10] Section 35(a) of the 1890 Act provides that the court may dissolve a partnership where a partner is of permanently unsound mind. Dissolution on this ground is likely to be extremely rare once the Assisted Decision-Making Capacity Act 2015 comes into full effect.[21] Pending that Act coming into full effect, any application for a partnership to be dissolved under s 35(a) would need to be justified by a mentally incapacitated partner being unable to undertake his obligations under the partnership contract. However, where the partner in question is a dormant partner, who will have no active involvement in the business in the first place, this basis for a dissolution order will not exist. On this basis, it seems that s 35(a) of the 1890 Act will (for so long as it remains a viable ground for seeking dissolution of a partnership), in general, have no application to dormant partners.[22]

(iv) Mentally incapacitated ordinary partner may become a dormant partner

[6.11] While the mental incapacity of an ordinary partner is grounds for an application to court for the dissolution of a partnership (albeit that such an application is unlikely to succeed once the Assisted Decision-Making Capacity Act 2015 comes into full effect),[23]

---

19   The concept of reputed ownership, which has since been repealed (see para **[27.93]**), was held to apply more readily to a dormant partner, than an ordinary partner, since the dormant partner did not have any apparent interest in the property of the bankrupt: *Re Curry* (1848) Ir Eq R 382 at 387.

20   Except in the case of a fraud on the firm committed by or with the consent of that partner: Partnership Act 1890, s 16. See generally in relation to this section, para **[10.126]**.

21   See further para **[4.19]**.

22   See for example the Scottish case of *Eadie v McBean's Curator Bonis* (1885) 12 R 660 and para **[25.27]**.

23   See generally in relation to applications for court dissolutions of partnerships on the grounds of the mental incapacity of a partner, para **[25.22]** et seq.

such a condition does not per se dissolve the firm.[24] If the unaffected partners decide not to apply for a court dissolution, the mentally incapacitated partner will continue as a member of the firm. However, it seems that such an incapacitated partner will thereby become a dormant partner.[25] This is because he will continue to be a partner in the firm but for obvious reasons, will not take any part in the management of the firm. Implicit support for this view is to be found in the decision of Macan J in *Re Ferrar, ex p Ulster Banking Co*.[26] This case involved a two-man partnership called Simms and Ferrar, which owned a newspaper called *The Belfast Mercury*. During the course of the partnership, Simms became of unsound mind. However, Macan J did not hold that this event dissolved the partnership, but rather he recognised the continuance of the partnership after this event and described Ferrar as the sole active partner.[27] Thus, Simms must be viewed as having become a dormant partner in the firm, by virtue of his supervening mental incapacity.

(v) Departure of a dormant partner

[6.12] The fifth situation in which the application of legal principles to a dormant partner will produce different results from their application to an ordinary partner concerns the liability of a partner on his departure from his firm. It is here that the difference between the results is most marked.

[6.13] The principle in question is contained in s 36(1) and 36(3) of the 1890 Act, ie that a partner who leaves a firm is liable for the obligations of the firm incurred to third parties after his retirement, if those third parties dealt with the firm, while he was a partner, and are unaware of his retirement.[28] The rationale for this rule is that such third parties can claim to have relied on the continued membership of this partner in the firm, as they were not notified of his departure. However, in the case of a dormant partner, this rationale is not present, since the dormant partner will not have been known by third parties to be a partner in the firm in the first place. It follows that s 36(1) and 36(3) of the 1890 Act will apply very differently to dormant partners than to ordinary partners.

Application of s 36(1) to dormant partners

[6.14] Section 36(1) of the 1890 Act provides that:

> Where a person deals with a firm after a change in its constitution he is entitled to treat all apparent members of the firm as still being members of the firm until he has notice of the change.

By definition, a dormant partner is unlikely to be an 'apparent member' of a firm. Therefore, when the dormant partner leaves the firm, a third party (who is unaware that he was a partner) will not be able to hold him liable for obligations incurred after his

---

24 See para **[4.18]**.
25 For so long as he remains incapacitated – the Assisted Decision-Making Capacity Act 2015 contemplates a potential return to capacity, see para **[4.19]**.
26 *Re Ferrar, ex p Ulster Banking Co* (1859) 9 Ir Ch R 11.
27 *Re Ferrar, ex p Ulster Banking Co* (1859) 9 Ir Ch R 11 at 15, where he states: '[d]uring a considerable time, while Simms was totally incapable, and when Ferrar had the power to bind the partnership assets, as sole active partner.'
28 See generally para **[11.49]**.

retirement. Of course, if the dormant partner happened to be known by a particular third party to be a partner in the firm, he will, regarding that third party, be an apparent member of the firm and thus subject to s 36(1). It follows that a dormant partner should give notice of his departure from the firm to any third parties who deal with the firm and who are aware that he is a partner.

Application of s 36(3) to dormant partners

[6.15] In its application to dormant partners, s 36(3) of the 1890 Act is the corollary of s 36(1). It provides that a partner who, 'not having been known to the person dealing with the firm to be a partner', retires from the firm, is not liable for partnership debts contracted thereafter.[29] However, a dormant partner, who happens to be known by a third party to be a partner, will not be able to rely on s 36(3) and he should give notice of his retirement to such third parties so as to benefit from s 36(1).

Impact of Registration of Business Names Act 1963

[6.16] The impact of the Registration of Business Names Act 1963 on partnerships has been considered elsewhere in this text.[30] Since a dormant partner is treated in all respects as an ordinary partner he is subject to the terms of the 1963 Act. Therefore, if a firm's business name does not include the surname of a dormant partner, that name must be registered as a business name and the dormant partner's name must be filed in the register of business names as one of the partners in the firm.[31] Similarly, the dormant partner's name must be listed on the stationery of the firm.[32] In this way, it is to be noted that the publicity requirements of the 1963 Act reduce the likelihood of a person retaining his anonymity as a dormant partner.[33]

'Contingent Partner' is not a Dormant Partner

[6.17] The difference between a dormant partner and a 'contingent partner' was considered in *Cuffe v Murtagh*.[34] The case concerned a partnership between a number of flour millers who carried on business in Dublin and Athlone. The partnership agreement entitled a partner to nominate another person to succeed to his share in the firm. If the nominee was a minor, the nomination was to be 'valid though made during the minority of any such nominee, but not to take effect until he should have attained the age of twenty-one'.[35] One partner died before his nominated successor reached 21. The question arose as to whether the nominee was entitled to the share of the deceased

---

29   See generally para **[11.58]**.
30   Paragraph **[3.70]** et seq.
31   Registration of Business Names Act 1963, s 4(1).
32   Registration of Business Names Act 1963, s 18.
33   However, if a third party is unaware of the presence of a dormant partner's name on the stationery, then the partner will remain a dormant partner. Note that in the case of solicitors' partnerships, every solicitors' firm is now required to have the names of all partners on the headed notepaper of the firm, thus reducing the chances of a partner retaining his anonymity: Solicitors (Practice, Conduct and Discipline) Regulations 1996 (SI 178/1996). See further para **[6.21]** et seq.
34   *Cuffe v Murtagh* (1881) 7 LR Ir 411.
35   *Cuffe v Murtagh* (1881) 7 LR Ir 411 at 414.

partner in the interval between the death of the partner and his 21st birthday. In particular, the case considered whether the nominee could be regarded as a dormant partner during this period of time, since if this was the case he would have been entitled to the share of the firm. It was held that he was not a dormant partner, but was a 'contingent partner' since, in the words of Chatterton VC, his 'rights of admission remained ... contingent'[36] on his becoming 21. The Vice-Chancellor supported his decision that the nominee was not a dormant partner by the fact, inter alia,[37] that the partnership was one in which active duties were to be performed by *all* the partners and the fact that there were no existing dormant partners in the firm.

II.   SALARIED PARTNER

[6.18] The term 'salaried partner' is a contradiction in terms since a salaried partner is not a partner but is invariably an employee of a firm[38] who is held out as a being a partner. In commercial terms, salaried partners are commonly found in professional partnerships as middle ranking professionals who are on the rung of the professional ladder somewhere between ordinary partners and salaried employees. They may be on the way up the promotion stakes in a firm or indeed in some cases, they may be former partners who are employed by the firm as 'consultants' before full retirement. Since a salaried partner is held out to be a partner, reference should also be made to the chapter on partners by holding out.[39]

Use of Term 'Salaried Partner' or 'Salary' is not Conclusive

[6.19] Just as the use of the term 'partner' is not conclusive in determining whether a person is an ordinary partner,[40] the use of the term 'salaried partner' is not conclusive in determining whether a person is a salaried partner. The circumstances of each case must be carefully analysed since, for example, the purported salaried partner may be an ordinary partner, whose pre-determined share of the profits of the firm[41] or whose monthly drawings (in advance of the end of year share-out of the profits) is incorrectly described as his 'salary'.[42] To determine whether a person is an ordinary partner or a salaried partner, it is necessary to carefully consider his rights and obligations in order to

---

36   *Cuffe v Murtagh* (1881) 7 LR Ir 411 at 425.

37   In addition, Chatterton VC relied on the fact that the nomination was 'not to take effect' under the terms of the partnership agreement and that the partnership agreement provided that the nominee should be subject to the same terms and conditions as the deceased partner. However, the latter was impossible while the nominee was a minor, since a minor is incapable of subjecting himself to the debts and liabilities of the firm (see para [4.04]).

38   See for example *Casson Beckman & Partners v Papi* [1991] BCLC 299, where the salaried partner was an employee. See generally Strattan 'Salaried Partnerships: some caveats' (1993) 137 Sol Jo 1164. See also the reference by Clarke J to 'fixed income' partners in *Mount Kennett Investment Company & anor v O'Meara & ors* [2012] IEHC 167 where he was referring to salaried partners and noted that any extra income remaining once the costs of running a partnership (including the payment of salaries to salaried partners) is shared between the equity (ie ordinary) partners only.

39   Paragraph [7.01] et seq.

40   See para [2.15].

41   See for example *Watson v Haggitt* [1928] AC 127. An ordinary partner may be entitled to a share of the profits of the firm up to a fixed amount which might be incorrectly termed his salary.

determine whether he satisfies the definition of partnership in s 1(1) of the 1890 Act.[43] As noted by Megarry J in *Stekel v Ellice*:[44]

> 'It seems to me impossible to say that as a matter of law a salaried partner is or is not necessarily a partner in the true sense. He may or may not be a partner, depending on the facts. What must be done, I think, is to look at the substance of the relationship between the parties; and there is ample authority for saying that the question whether or not there is a partnership depends on what the true relationship is, and not on any mere label attached to that relationship.'[45]

[6.20] The above statement of Megarry J in *Stekel v Ellice* was cited with approval by Finlay Geoghegan J in *McAleenan v AIG*,[46] in which she noted the vagueness of the term 'salaried partner', that the term may include both a true partner and a person who is not a true partner, and the importance of looking at the true relationship in each case. This was of particular importance in *McAleenan v AIG* where the court was examining whether the plaintiff had entered into partnership with Michael Lynn, a solicitor who was subsequently struck off the roll of solicitors, rather than whether the plaintiff had joined a partnership that was already in existence.

[6.21] *Stekel v Ellice* was also applied in *M Young Legal Associates v Zahid*[47] in which Wilson LJ was asked to consider whether a person could be a partner in a firm if he was not entitled to share in the profits, but rather it was agreed that he be paid a specific sum, irrespective of the firm's profits, for the work done by him for the firm. Wilson LJ held that s 1(1) of the 1890 Act required that a partnership have the intention of making a profit, but not that it be shared, and the fact that a person was paid a fixed sum without an apparent direct link to the profits of the firm would not of itself preclude that person from being a partner in that firm.

[6.22] Wilson LJ endorsed the views expressed by Mark Blackett-Ord (who himself appeared for the appellant in this particular case) in the 2nd edition of his book on partnership law.[48] In that work, Mr Blackett-Ord cautioned against the use of the term 'salaried partner', commenting that it did not have a universally accepted meaning, could lead to confusion, and could be used to either describe someone who is, in fact, an employee (but is described as a partner to increase his profile), or to describe someone who is, in fact, a partner, who receives a salary rather than a share in the partnership's profits.

---

[42] Or indeed, it may be the 'rent' which is payable by the firm for the use of that partner's premises.

[43] See generally para **[2.01]** et seq.

[44] *Stekel v Ellice* [1973] 1 All ER 465.

[45] *Stekel v Ellice* [1973] 1 All ER 465 at 473.

[46] *McAleenan v AIG* [2010] IEHC 128. Finlay Geoghegan J also endorsed the views expressed at para 5-65 of the 17th edition of *Lindley & Banks on Partnership* (now I'Anson Banks, *Lindley & Banks on Partnership* (20th edn, 2017) at para 5-54 et seq).

[47] *M Young Legal Associates v Zahid* [2006] 1 WLR 2562.

[48] Now in its fifth edition: Blackett-Ord and Haren, *Partnership Law* (5th edn, 2015) in which the author emphasised that the question of whether or not such a person is a true partner will depend on the nature of his agreement with the firm in question.

[6.23] Like the use of the term 'salaried partner', the use of the term 'salary' is not conclusive evidence that the recipient is an employee, since the provision of a salary may, in some cases, simply be a machinery for the division of profits. When one is dealing with the question of whether a person is a salaried or an ordinary partner, an important factor will be whether his 'salary' is payable irrespective of whether the firm has profits. Thus, a person who receives a guaranteed salary from a firm (regardless of the level of profits of the firm) will be most likely a salaried partner, while a person who receives a fixed sum (albeit referred to as a 'salary') which is payable only out of the profits, if any, of the firm, is more likely to be a true partner.[49] In the latter case, if the firm makes a loss, the payment will abate as is illustrated by *Marsh v Stacey*.[50] There, a partnership agreement provided for a 'fixed salary of £1,200 as a first charge on the profits' of the firm to be paid to a junior partner. For two years the profits of the firm were below £1,200. Accordingly, the English Court of Appeal held that the junior partner's 'salary' did not have to be paid by the firm to him as there were insufficient profits.

More Difficult to be a Salaried Partner in a Law Firm

[6.24] In most instances, a salaried partner will be an employee of the firm who is held out to third parties to be a partner in the firm. In most cases the primary manner in which a salaried partner in a firm is held out to be a partner is by his being listed as a partner on the firm's notepaper. In the context of solicitors' partnerships, it is to be observed that the Solicitors (Practice, Conduct and Discipline) Regulations 1996[51] provide that this option is no longer available. For this reason, it is more difficult for law firms to have salaried partners. Paragraph 6(ii) of the Regulations provides that:

> If the names of assistant solicitors are listed on the notepaper, a differentiation shall be made between their names and the names of the partners.

[6.25] Since salaried partners are, as a matter of law, assistant solicitors, this section requires law firms to make a distinction between true partners and salaried partners.[52] Accordingly, law firms are not entitled to give the impression on their notepaper that salaried partners are in fact true partners in the firm.[53] In view of the popularity of salaried partnerships in law firms and the commercial importance thereof, it may be that in using the term 'partner', the drafters of the regulations did not have regard to the fact that it excluded salaried partners from being held out as partners. There would certainly appear to be no good reason why law firms should be restricted from having salaried

---

49 Obviously, this is but one factor to be used in determining this issue. Examples of other factors are whether he receives an indemnity for the losses of the firm from the other partners, whether he is entitled to a share in the goodwill, an interest in the capital and stock of the firm etc. See further in relation to the question of whether a person is a partner, para [2.01] et seq.

50 *Marsh v Stacey* (1963) 107 SJ 512.

51 SI 178/1996. The Regulations came into force on 1 October 1996: para 1(ii).

52 Previously, the only obligation was under s 18 of the Registration of Business Names Act 1963 which provided that it was sufficient for the partners' names to be listed on the notepaper, there being no necessity to differentiate between partners and employees.

53 A breach of these Regulations would constitute an act of misconduct by a solicitor under s 3 of the Solicitors (Amendment) Act 1960 and thus subject him to an inquiry by the Disciplinary Tribunal of the Law Society, with a possible censure by the High Court.

partners, while other professional firms are not so restricted. For this reason, it is suggested that this anomaly should be rectified.

Salaried Partners Have the Worst of Both Worlds

[6.26] In some ways, the salaried partner may be regarded as having the worst of both worlds. This is because as regards the internal control of the firm a salaried partner does not have the rights of a partner. For example he has no right to such matters as a share in the profits or a say in the management of the firm. Yet as regards third parties, he is liable 'as a partner' under s 14(1) of the 1890 Act. This is because a salaried partner invariably allows himself to be held out to be a partner and is liable to third parties who rely on this fact.[54] For this reason, it is common for the true partners in a firm to indemnify the salaried partner in respect of this and other potential liabilities. For the same reason, it is also in the salaried partner's interest to ensure that the firm maintains adequate professional indemnity insurance. In addition, it is to be noted that the partnership itself will be bound by the acts of the salaried partner, since the other partners will invariably have given him apparent authority to bind the firm by their holding him out as their partner.[55]

[6.27] The salaried partner has received little consideration to date in the Irish courts, which is partly due to the fact that only in recent years has it become popular in professional firms as a way to assuage the ambitions of the growing number of prospective partners. In England there has been some judicial consideration of the position of a salaried partner[56] and in *Stekel v Ellice*,[57] Megarry J gave a useful *resumé* of the position of the salaried partner:

> 'Certain aspects of a salaried partnership are not disputed. The term "salaried partner" is not a term of art, and to some extent it may be said to be a contradiction in terms. However, it is a convenient expression which is widely used to denote a person who is held out to the world as being a partner, with his name appearing as a partner on the notepaper of the firm and so on. At the same time, he receives a salary as remuneration, rather than a share of the profits, though he may, in addition to his salary, receive some bonus or other sum of money dependent upon the profits. *Quoad* the outside world it often will matter little whether a man is a full partner or a salaried partner; for a salaried partner is held out as being a partner, and the partners will be liable for his acts accordingly. But within the partnership it may be important to know whether a salaried partner is truly to be classified as a mere employee, or as a partner.'[58]

[6.28] In *M Young Legal Associates Ltd v Zahid*[59] Wilson LJ noted that he saw:

> '... no logic behind a situation in which

---

54 It is important therefore, when considering salaried partners to also consider them to be partners by holding out and thus liable 'as a partner' under s 14(1) of the 1890 Act. See generally para **[7.01]** et seq.
55 See further in relation to the authority of a partner by holding out to bind the firm, para **[7.45]**.
56 See also *Wood v Priestley* [2016] EWHC 2986 (Ch); *Bates van Winkelhof v Clyde & Co LLP* [2014] 1 WLR 2047 (SC).
57 *Stekel v Ellice* [1973] 1 All ER 465.
58 *Stekel v Ellice* [1973] 1 All ER 465 at 472.
59 *M Young Legal Associates Ltd v Zahid* [2006] EWCA Civ 613.

    (a)   an agreement that a person should receive a share of profits, however nominal that share might be, could make him a partner and indeed was *prima facie* evidence thereof (section 2(3) [of the Partnership Act 1890]); and

    (b)   an agreement that a person should receive a share of profits limited to payments in a fixed sum could make him a partner (*In Re Hill* [2934] 1 Ch 623); but

    (c)   an agreement that a person should receive payments in a fixed sum, irrespective of profits, precluded his being a partner.'

Presumption of reliance by third party on holding out of a salaried partner

[6.29] The requirements to be satisfied for a salaried partner to be held liable as a partner by holding out are considered in detail elsewhere in this text.[60] One of these requirements is that for liability to arise under s 14(1) of the 1890 Act, there must be a reliance by the third party on the representation that the salaried partner was a true partner. For present purposes, it suffices to note that in relation to this requirement salaried partners may be treated more strictly than other partners by holding out. This is because there may be a presumption of reliance in certain cases involving salaried partners. The possibility of such a presumption was raised in *Nationwide Building Society v Lewis*.[61] There, the English Court of Appeal noted that as a general rule, to establish liability under s 14(1) of the 1890 Act, there must be direct evidence provided by the third party of his reliance on the holding out.[62] However, the court left open the question of whether, in some circumstances, it may be appropriate to presume such a reliance. In particular, Slade LJ suggested that a person, who deals *exclusively* with a salaried partner, might be entitled to a presumption that he relied on the representation that he was a partner and thus would be relieved from the burden of proving any reliance on the representation that he was a partner. In the event of such a presumption, the burden of proof would switch to the salaried partner who would then have to show that there was no actual reliance by the third party on the representation that he was a partner.

III. FIXED SHARE PARTNER

[6.30] While the concept of fixed share partners (a variation on the salaried partner) may develop further in Ireland following the introduction of limited liability partnerships, it has gained prominence in the United Kingdom. While, as mentioned above, a salaried partner invariably receives a salary without the right to a share in the profits or a say in how the partnership in question is managed, a fixed share partner tends to receive a fixed share of the profits (ie fixed in monetary amount, rather than as a percentage), rather than a salary (which is subject to employer's pay-related social insurance), may be required to make a small contribution to capital, and may have a say in the management of the partnership (albeit generally a limited entitlement to vote).[63]

---

60   Paragraph **[7.06]** et seq.

61   *Nationwide Building Society v Lewis* [1998] 3 All ER 143.

62   For a discussion of this general rule, see para **[7.30]**.

63   But Clarke J's reference to 'fixed income' partners in *Mount Kennett Investment Company & anor v O'Meara & ors* [2012] IEHC 167 would appear to be a reference to salaried, rather than fixed share, partners.

[6.31] In *Tiffin v Lester Aldridge LLP*,[64] Mr Tiffin had been a salaried partner in a partnership which later converted to a limited liability partnership, to which he was admitted as a fixed share partner, following which he was paid monthly drawings rather than a salary, was required to contribute £5,000 to the partnership, became a signatory on the firm's bank accounts, and received a small number of profit share points which entitled him to vote (salaried partners in the partnership had no profit share points or voting rights whatsoever, while true partners had up to 100 profit share points). When his membership of the partnership was terminated, Mr Tiffin took an unfair dismissal claim, arguing that he was an employee. An employment tribunal found that he was a partner, rather than an employee, notwithstanding Mr Tiffin's claim that he did not carry on 'business in common' with the partnership, that his 'view of profit' was extremely small and that there were a number of factors which were consistent with him being an employee rather than a partner. In dismissing the subsequent appeal to the Employment Appeals Tribunal, Silber J observed that the concept of a fixed share partner was relatively new and quoted from *Lindley & Banks on Partnership* in which it was noted that the concept of fixed share partner developed in view of the risk that a salaried partner could be held to be an employee. Indicators of a fixed share partnership are an entitlement to a small share of profits and losses (over and above the fixed profit share), an obligation to make a small capital contribution, and a right to participate to some extent in the management of the firm.[65] While Mr Tiffin claimed that he was not carrying on the business of the firm in common with the partners as he was only entitled to participate in part of the management structure, Silber J, in the Employment Appeals Tribunal's judgment, held that there is no minimum management requirement with which a partner must comply, noting that in many large professional partnerships, true partners do not necessarily each participate in every management decision. Regarding Mr Tiffin's claim that his 'view of profit' was negligible having regard to the relatively small number of profit share points that he held, Silber J again held that there was no requirement that a person's profit share meet a minimum threshold before that person can be treated as a partner.[66]

IV. GENERAL PARTNER AND LIMITED PARTNER

[6.32] Two other categories of partners are general partners and limited partners. Every partner in a limited partnership and in an investment limited partnership must be either a general partner or a limited partner. A general partner is like an ordinary partner since he is liable to an unlimited degree for the debts of the firm, while a limited partner is a partner whose liability for the obligations of the firm is limited to the amount of capital

---

[64] *Tiffin v Lester Aldridge LLP* [2011] IRLR 105 (affirmed on appeal, [2013] EWCA Civ 35).

[65] Note that the paragraph from l'Anson Banks, *Lindley & Banks on Partnership* quoted by Silber J in this case (now para 5-62 of l'Anson Banks, *Lindley & Banks on Partnership* (20th edn, 2017)) states the view of the current editor of that work to be that none of those factors is truly determinative of partnership, consistent with the views expressed by Wilson LJ in *M Young Legal Associates v Zahid* [2006] EWCA (Civ) 613.

[66] On this point, Silber J cited with approval the decision of Wilson LJ in *M Young Legal Associates v Zahid* [2006] EWCA (Civ) 613 in which he held that neither the absence of a right to share in profits nor the absence of a requirement to make a capital contribution is decisive when assessing the existence or otherwise of a partnership.

he has contributed to the partnership. It is not possible to have a limited partner in an ordinary partnership, since in an ordinary partnership every partner's liability is unlimited.[67] It is not proposed to examine the nature of a general partner or a limited partner in this chapter, as they are considered in detail in the context of limited partnerships[68] and investment limited partnerships.[69]

V. QUASI-PARTNER

[6.33] Like the term 'salaried partner', the term 'quasi-partner' is a contradiction in terms, since a quasi-partner is not a partner. Rather, a quasi-partner may be described as a member of a legal entity, usually a company, which although in legal form a company, is in substance a partnership. Since quasi-partnerships are in substance partnerships, the principles of partnership law have been applied by the courts to them and to the quasi-partners. The nature of quasi-partnerships and quasi-partners is considered in detail elsewhere in this work.[70]

VI. PARTNER BY HOLDING OUT

[6.34] A partner by holding out is also a contradiction in terms, since he is not a partner but a person who allows himself to be held out as a partner. As a consequence, he is liable as if he were a partner to third parties who have relied on the representation that he is a partner.[71] This category of partner is considered in detail elsewhere in this text.[72]

VII. SENIOR AND JUNIOR PARTNERS

[6.35] In professional partnerships, one commonly encounters the term 'junior partner' and 'senior partner' to describe the relative status or seniority of partners in a firm. As a matter of general partnership law, these terms have no particular meaning and the rights and obligations of a junior partner will be the same as those of a senior partner. Thus in *Morans v Armstrong*,[73] a partner in a firm claimed that a composition with creditors was not binding on the firm, since it was approved only by a junior partner. This claim was rejected by the Irish Court of Exchequer, where Brady CB observed:

> 'The junior partner binds the others as much as any other partner, or as all the partners together. The world cannot know his department in the establishment, it is enough that he was partner at all.'[74]

[6.36] However, while there is no distinction between senior and junior partners as a matter of general partnership law, the terms of the partnership agreement will often distinguish between their respective rights. Thus, the rights of a junior partner may be restricted *vis-à-vis* the senior partners, regarding such matters as a share of the profits,

---

67   Partnership Act 1890, ss 10 and 12; see generally para **[11.04]**.
68   Paragraph **[28.01]** et seq.
69   Paragraph **[29.01]** et seq.
70   See para **[8.67]** et seq.
71   Liability is imposed under s 14(1) of the 1890 Act.
72   Paragraph **[7.01]** et seq.
73   *Morans v Armstrong* (1840) Arm M & O 25.
74   *Morans v Armstrong* (1840) Arm M & O 25 at 25.

number of votes at partners' meetings and authority to bind the firm, or he may be restricted from doing certain acts without the consent of the senior partner(s).

VIII. PRECEDENT PARTNER

[6.37] The term 'precedent partner' is defined in s 1007 of the Taxes Consolidation Act 1997, which, among other matters, governs the taxation of partners. While tax is assessed on the partners separately and not on the firm,[75] the Revenue Commissioners require a return of income regarding the partnership trade. Under the 1997 Act,[76] one partner in a firm, termed the precedent partner, is required to file (on receipt of a notice from the Inspector of Taxes) a return of the partnership's sources of income, the amount of that income, and such other information, accounts and statements as may be required of him in respect of the relevant year of assessment.[77] The precedent partner must also, when required by notice to do so, file a written statement of the profits or gains arising from each chargeable source in respect of such period as may be specified in the notice.[78] While the 1997 Act provides that such information must be furnished by the precedent partner on request, the precedent partner is also deemed to be the chargeable person for self-assessment purposes and must therefore file the partnership return in respect of each year of assessment irrespective of whether a request is received.[79] He is also responsible for keeping the records required to enable true returns of income tax and chargeable gains to be made in respect of any trade, business or activity carried on by the partnership,[80] and is the person to whom the Revenue Commissioners give notice of their determinations regarding the tax affairs of the partnership.[81] The precedent partner is defined in s 1007(1) of the 1997 Act as follows:

> 'precedent partner', in relation to a partnership, means the partner who, being resident in the State—
>
> (a)   is first named in the partnership agreement,
>
> (b)   if there is no agreement, is named singly or with precedence over the other partners in the usual name of the firm, or
>
> (c)   is the precedent acting partner, if the person named with precedence is not an acting partner,

---

75   Taxes Consolidation Act 1997, s 1008(1).

76   Taxes Consolidation Act 1997, s 880(2), s 951(2) and see also ss 880 and 1008(4).

77   Taxes Consolidation Act 1997 s 880(2). Under s 913(7), details of any chargeable capital gains realised in the relevant year by the partnership and details of chargeable assets acquired by the partnership during that same year must also be included in that partnership return, together with any claim for a joint allowance in respect of the partnership trade (Taxes Consolidation Act 1997, s 1010(9)(a)).

78   Taxes Consolidation Act 1997, s 880(5).

79   Taxes Consolidation Act 1997, s 959M. Partnership returns must, since June 2011, be filed electronically with the Revenue Commissioners.

80   Taxes Consolidation Act 1997, s 886.

81   Taxes Consolidation Act 1997, s 1008(3), s 1010(6) and s 1012(1).

and any reference to precedent partner, shall, in a case in which no partner is resident in the State, be construed as a reference to the agent, manager or factor of the firm resident in the State.[82]

[6.38] It would seem to be implicit in the wording of paragraph (c) of this definition that the partners may nominate a partner to be the precedent partner, in which case this 'precedent acting partner' will be the precedent partner. If there is no partner resident in the State, the Inspector of Taxes may serve a notice on any agent, manager of factor of the partnership resident in the State requiring him to make the partnership return.[83]

---

[82] For a more detailed account of the taxation of partnerships, reference should be made to Maguire, *Irish Income Tax: 2018* (2018) at para 4.501 et seq.

[83] Taxes Consolidation Act 1997, s 1007(1).

Chapter 7

Partner by Holding Out

INTRODUCTION

[7.01] Like the expression 'salaried partner',[1] the expression 'partner by holding out' is a contradiction in terms, since it is used to describe someone who is not in fact a partner.[2] Rather this expression denotes a person who because of his action or inaction is held to be liable to certain third parties as if he were a partner.[3]

[7.02] This area will be considered under the following headings:

    I.   Liability as a Partner by Holding Out;

    II.   Liability under s 14(1);

    III. Consequences of a Finding of Holding Out; and

    IV. Specific Instances of Holding Out.

Overview

[7.03] The doctrine of holding out is set out primarily in s 14(1) of the 1890 Act and also in s 36(1). This doctrine may be seen as an instance of the wider doctrine of estoppel by representation[4] whereby a person who, by his conduct, causes another[5] to alter his

---

1   See generally in relation to salaried partners, para **[6.18]** et seq.

2   For a historical perspective of the doctrine of holding out in Ireland, see Anon, 'The Doctrine of "Holding Out"' (1942) 76 ILT & SJ 225.

3   This paragraph was quoted by Finlay Geoghegan J in *McAleenan v AIG* [2010] IEHC 128 in which she noted, at para 36 of her judgment, that: '[the] law of partnership distinguishes between true partners and apparent partners in the following sense. By true partners is meant persons who are in fact and in law partners to each other in a partnership as defined by s 1 of the Act of 1890. They have, as between themselves, all the rights and liabilities of partners, and similarly in relation to third parties. By an apparent partner, is meant a person who is not a true partner in the sense of being a partner in a partnership with others, but is held out, either by the true partners of the partnership, or by himself, to be a partner in the partnership. By so holding himself out, or being held out, he may become liable to third parties as a partner whilst not being a true partner, either by reason of s 14(1) of the Act of 1890, or by application of the doctrine of estoppel by representation.'

4   *Re Fraser ex p Central Bank of London* [1892] 2 QB 633. See also the judgment of Megaw LJ in *Hudgell Yeates & Co v Watson* [1978] 2 All ER 363 at 374 and the judgment of Gibson LJ in *Nationwide Building Society v Lewis* [1998] 3 All ER 143 at 147. See generally Wilken and Villiers, *The Law of Waiver, Variation and Estoppel* (3rd edn, 2012); Keane, *Equity and the Law of Trusts in Ireland* (3rd edn, 2017) at para [27.03] et seq; Biehler, *Equity and the Law of Trusts in Ireland* (6th edn, 2016) at p 826 et seq. However, as noted at para **[7.05]**, this comparison is not wholly accurate.

5   There must obviously be a third party involved for the estoppel to arise: *Walsh v Butler* (21 January 1997) HC. (contd.../)

position in reliance on a certain state of affairs which the representor knows to be false, is estopped from claiming afterwards that such a state of facts did not exist.[6] Thus, third parties who deal with a partnership in the belief that the firm has a large number of partners might not do so if they knew that there were in fact only two partners and the other 'partners' were in fact employees. The rationale for the doctrine of partner by holding out is clear, ie it seeks to prevent a fraud being suffered by third parties dealing with the firm on the basis of a misrepresentation.[7]

[7.04] Section 14(1) is concerned primarily with the liability of a person who never was a partner to third parties who are led to believe that he is a partner. This chapter also considers briefly the liability of a former partner to persons who dealt with his firm after he ceased to be a partner but who were unaware of his departure. This issue is dealt with by s 36(1) of the 1890 Act.[8] Liability under s 36(1) is also founded in estoppel by representation and is clearly subject to the same rationale. Thus, a former partner who dealt with third parties is estopped from denying that he is a partner, if those third parties were not notified or were not otherwise aware of his departure from the firm. The justice of this principle is clear. There is of course nothing to prevent a claim against a former partner being brought under s 14(1), though as will be seen, the requirements under s 36(1) are easier to satisfy than under s 14(1).

[7.05] Since liability under both s 14(1) and under s 36(1) is founded in the doctrine of estoppel by representation, it follows that even where the strict terms of these sections are not complied with, reliance may be placed on the general principles of estoppel.[9] In

---

5   (\...contd) That case involved an action for personal injuries by the plaintiff against a rugby club. An issue arose as to whether the plaintiff was a member of the club. Morris J rejected the claim that the plaintiff was estopped from denying that he was a member of the club, since the mere act of holding oneself out as a member of the club, *without adverse consequences to a third party*, could not give rise to a situation where he would be estopped from denying that he was a member.

6   *Carr v L &N W Rail Co* (1875) 10 CP 307.

7   While the doctrine of holding out applies for the protection of third parties, it is not relevant when determining whether a partnership exists between possible partners: see *Heffernan & Anor v Murray & Anor* [2015] IEHC 196 where Binchy J noted (at para 61) that '… it is clear from the wording of s 14(1) and from the authorities that this section is for the protection of third parties and not partners themselves'. See also *Greville v Venables* [2007] EWCA Civ 878.

8   This section is considered in more detail in para **[11.85]**.

9   Note, however, the general view of an estoppel as a rule of evidence rather than a rule of substantive law. For this reason it has been stated that it may not give rise to a cause of action (para **[7.05]**), although clearly the doctrine of holding out under s 14(1) does operate as a rule of substantive law. However, this difference between a rule of evidence and a rule of substantive law is, it is suggested, more imaginary than real, since it is the facts set up and not the estoppel which are the source of the substantive legal obligation under the doctrine of estoppel. Thus, once the constituent elements of the estoppel are established, the court does not permit them to be contradicted by the defendant. Then, the legal relationship of the parties is determined according to the facts as represented and not according to the true state of affairs. In this way, estoppel by representation may give rise indirectly to a cause of action where it operates to set up a state of facts which themselves vest a cause of action in the representee. See generally Wilken and Villiers, *The Law of Waiver, Variation and Estoppel* (3rd edn, 2012).

either case, therefore, the essential nature of a finding of liability will be that a third party acted on the faith of a representation that the defendant was a partner and in order to protect such third parties, the law prevents the defendant from denying the truth of those facts. However, the comparison with estoppel by representation is not wholly accurate. It is, of course, true to say that the doctrine of holding out does resemble an estoppel, since it acts like an evidentiary device by benefiting third parties who have relied thereon, without creating a relationship between the true partners and the person represented to be a partner. However, the doctrine of estoppel is generally regarded[10] as not constituting a cause of action and therefore it may normally be invoked only as a shield, rather than as a sword.[11] In contrast, the doctrine of holding out in s 14(1) clearly establishes a cause of action since it expressly provides for the person held out as a partner to be liable as if he were a partner.

I. LIABILITY AS A PARTNER BY HOLDING OUT

[7.06] The position of a partner by holding out is dealt with primarily in s 14(1) of the 1890 Act, but also in s 36(1) of that Act. Section 14(1) of the 1890 Act defines a partner by holding out and establishes his liability. This section states:

> Every one who by words spoken or written or by conduct represents himself, or who knowingly suffers himself to be represented, as a partner in a particular firm, is liable as a partner to any one who has on the faith of any such representation given credit to the firm, whether the representation has or has not been made or communicated to the person so giving credit by or with the knowledge of the apparent partner making the representation or suffering it to be made.

Thus, in broad terms, a person who represents himself or allows himself to be represented as a partner is liable as if he were a partner to anyone who relied on this representation. The liability of a partner by holding out is also dealt with in s 36(1) of the 1890 Act, but only in relation to partners by holding out who were formerly partners in the firm. Section 36(1) states:

> Where a person deals with a firm after a change in its constitution he is entitled to treat all apparent members of the old firm as still being members of the firm until he has notice of the change.

This section applies what may be termed an 'automatic holding out' to a former partner in relation to persons who had dealings with the firm while he was a partner (for convenience, referred to as 'existing customers'), unless those customers are on notice of his departure.

---

10   See for example the statement of O'Hanlon J in *Association of General Practitioners Ltd v Minister for Health* [1995] 2 ILRM 481 at 492 that 'the doctrine of equitable or promissory estoppel cannot create any new cause of action where none existed before'. However, cf the decision of Costello J in *Re JR* [1993] ILRM 657, where he appears to hold that the estoppel in that case could give rise to a cause of action.

11   See the comments of Denning LJ in *Combe v Combe* [1951] 2 KB 215 at 219. See generally Feltham, Hochberg and Leech, *Spencer Bower on The Law Relating to Estoppel by Representation* (4th edn, 2004).

Difference between s 36(1) and s 14(1)

[7.07] Section 36(1) of the 1890 Act is considered in more detail elsewhere in this work[12] and the remainder of this chapter is concerned primarily with liability under s 14(1). However, it is useful at this juncture to note the differences between the two types of holding out in ss 36(1) and 14(1).

[7.08] The first important difference is the much more limited scope of s 36(1) compared to that of s 14(1). Section 14(1) of the 1890 Act applies the principle of holding out to 'every one' and thus includes persons who were never partners in a firm as well as former partners. In contrast, s 36(1) only provides for a holding out in relation to a partner who departs from his firm as is clear from the use of the expression 'still being members of the firm'.[13] The two sections therefore may be relied upon in a case of an alleged holding out against a former partner. The second difference between the two sections is that s 36(1) is more restrictive than s 14(1) in the sense that it only provides for liability by holding out between on the one hand former partners and on the other hand persons who are existing, as distinct from new, customers of the firm. This is not the case with s 14(1), which is equally applicable to all third parties who deal with the firm. A third and important practical difference between these two sections is that a third party is required to prove that he relied on the representation under s 14(1), while under s 36(1), he need not show such reliance, but need only show that he dealt with the firm while the defendant was a partner and that he was not aware that he was no longer a partner when the liability in question was incurred. Finally, a fourth difference between the sections is that under s 36(1), the knowledge of the former partner that he was being held out as still being a partner is irrelevant to his liability. In this sense, s 36(1) may be said to impose automatic liability by holding out on the former partner, unless the existing customers are aware of his departure. In contrast, for liability to ensue under s 14(1), the partner by holding out must have knowledge of the acts which constitute the holding out.[14]

[7.09] The difference in approach of s 14(1) and s 36(1) is justified on the basis of the two different situations with which the sections deal; s 14(1) deals generally with persons who were never partners but held out to third parties to be such, and s 36(1) deals with a former partner's relationship with his former customers or clients. Thus, the fact that a third party is not required to prove any reliance under s 36(1), but is under s 14(1), may be justified on the basis that a reliance by a third party on a person being a partner can be assumed in the case of a person who was a partner (and has retired), but it must be established in the case of a person who was never a partner, but who it is alleged held himself out as such. Similarly, the requirement that a person alleged to be liable under s 14(1) must have knowledge of the facts constituting the holding out should not apply to a former partner, since he must be taken to know that he is likely to be still held out as a partner in his former firm, unless he takes steps to prevent it. In this regard, the difference between the two sections is arguably more apparent than real and the

---

12 See para **[11.85]** et seq.

13 The terms 'depart' and 'departure' are used in the sense of no longer being a member of a firm, regardless of whether this occurs by virtue of a dissolution, expulsion, retirement or otherwise.

14 See para **[7.14]**.

automatic holding out under s 36(1) can be justified by the differing circumstances of a former partner from a person who never was a partner.

II.   LIABILITY UNDER S 14(1)

[7.10] The remainder of this chapter will consider the liability of a person as a partner by holding out under s 14(1) of the 1890 Act, although some reference will be made to liability under s 36(1).[15] However, since both s 14(1) and s 36(1) are examples of the doctrine of estoppel by representation, many of the principles which follow will also be applicable to a holding out under s 36(1).

[7.11] The three requirements which have to be satisfied for a person to be liable as a partner by holding out under s 14(1) will first be considered. These are that there must be:

1.   a holding out;
2.   a reliance by the third party thereon; and
3.   the giving of credit by the third party to the firm.

Each of these requirements will be examined in turn.

1. There Must be a Holding Out

[7.12] As is clear from the express terms of s 14(1) of the 1890 Act, the holding out must constitute a representation that the person is a partner. Section 14(1) provides that it need not be in any particular form and it may be 'by words spoken or written or by conduct'. It is also clear from the wording of s 14(1) that inaction on the part of the person held out is sufficient to constitute a holding out since the section provides that liability may arise where a person 'knowingly suffers' himself to be represented as a partner. Typically, liability will arise under this 'knowingly suffering' heading where the person is aware of a representation by another (whether by a 'real' partner or a third party) of him as a partner and he lets this reference go uncontradicted.[16] A case where the holding out was not allowed go uncontradicted is that of *Re Scott Brothers*[17] which concerned three brothers who were in a partnership which sold seeds in Belfast. The firm went bankrupt and soon afterwards two of the three brothers set up a new firm and advertised in the Belfast papers the fact that the *same* firm would again receive orders for seeds. The third brother, who had gone to England, wrote two letters to one of the brothers protesting against the advertisement and refusing to have anything to do with the matter and stating that he would not consent to having his name used in this way. The issue came to court as the third brother had been served with proceedings by a third party for payment of the new partnership's obligations. In these circumstances Green B set aside the service of the proceedings.

---

[15]   In particular, see para **[7.52]** et seq.
[16]   For example see *Martyn v Gray*, para **[7.22]**.
[17]   *Re Scott Brothers* (1852) 19 LTOS 149. See also *Hunter v Stoney* (1831) Glasc 23, para **[7.15]**.

[7.13] In *Heffernan & Anor v Murray & anor*,[18] the plaintiffs, who had entered into a contract for sale with the first to twelfth defendants (who, together with the second plaintiff, comprised a partnership known as the Ballykisteen Development Partnership) claimed that the thirteenth defendant, Mr Simpson, had held himself out to the plaintiffs as being a partner in the partnership, that the plaintiffs had relied on that holding out when entering into the contract for sale, and that Mr Simpson was therefore liable to them under s 14(1) of the 1890 Act as a partner in respect of that contract for sale. In the High Court, Binchy J noted that while Mr Simpson's name had appeared in various pieces of correspondence leading up to the execution of the contract for sale, his name was removed from the final version of the contract for sale, this change was initialled by the solicitors acting for the plaintiffs and, in light of that, the plaintiff's claim could not succeed on that basis. Citing s 14(1) of the 1890 Act, the plaintiffs continued to claim that Mr Simpson had held himself out as a partner in the partnership in various ways, including by his attendance at partnership meetings, his coordination of various arrangements connected with the partnership's development business, and his negotiation of various matters on behalf of the partnership with the plaintiffs. Binchy J noted that Mr Simpson was heavily involved in the partnership's business, on occasion appeared to have assumed some personal obligations to the plaintiffs and on occasion conducted himself in a manner that would indicate that he might have considered himself to be a partner. However, Binchy J held that simply because Mr Simpson may have considered himself to be a partner at various times, it did not automatically follow that he was a partner. Notably, Ulster Bank, as lender to the partnership, did not treat him as one of the partners, and the partnership agreement clearly listed the partners, and the apportionment of benefits and liabilities as between them, without any reference to Mr Simpson. There did not seem to be any basis on which Mr Simpson could claim an entitlement to a portion of the partnership's profits. As such, the plaintiffs could not prove that Mr Simpson had held himself out as a partner, in particular as he had deliberately taken steps to ensure that he was not a party to the contract for sale by making sure that his name was crossed out.

Making or knowingly suffering the representation

[7.14] Before a person will be held liable as a partner by holding out under s 14(1) of the 1890 Act, there must be a representation that he is a partner in the first place.[19] In the Ontario Court of Justice case of *Palter v Zeller*,[20] the plaintiff took an action against a husband and wife who worked together in the husband's law firm. The plaintiff alleged that the wife was held out as a partner in her husband's law firm. The plaintiff's claim was rejected as he produced no objective evidence likely to suggest to a client of the practice that the husband and wife were holding themselves out as partners. It was not

---

[18] *Heffernan & Anor v Murray & anor* [2015] IEHC 196.
[19] The English Court of Appeal case of *Bass Brewers Ltd v Appleby* [1997] CLY 1423 involved a holding out between accountants. It involved one accountant, a sole practitioner, who entered into a group management agreement with an accountancy partnership whereby the firm allowed the sole practitioner to use the firm's name. When the sole practitioner failed to account for a client's money, the firm was held liable under s 14(1) of the 1890 Act for holding itself out as his partner.
[20] *Palter v Zeller* (1997) 30 OR (3d) 796.

sufficient that the plaintiff knew the couple socially and that he formed the impression 'that they were partners in everything they did, including their practice of law',[21] since the plaintiff's belief that the defendant was holding herself out as a partner was held by Wilkins J to be ill-founded.

[7.15] The representation must be made by the alleged partner by holding out or he must have knowingly suffered such a representation. The requirement that the representation be made by the person himself does not require further comment. As regards the representation being knowingly suffered by the apparent partner, this requires a knowledge on the part of the apparent partner that he is being held out as a partner – if there is no knowledge of the acts which constitute the representation, there can be no liability ascribed to him under s 14(1). In *Re Scott Brothers*,[22] the third brother could not be said to have knowingly suffered the holding out by the other two partners, since he objected vigorously to it and therefore could not be regarded as being liable under s 14(1).[23] In *Hunter v Stoney*,[24] a mother signed a partnership agreement for the Saint Patrick's Assurance Company of Ireland in her son's name. The son was unaware of this fact and therefore he could not be said to have knowingly suffered the representation. As soon as he became aware of it, he disclaimed this interest. Accordingly, when the son was sued as a partner, MacMahon MR held that the action should be dismissed. In *Elite Business Systems UK Ltd v Price*,[25] a father opened a bank account for his son to facilitate his son setting up a business by himself. When subsequently entering into an agreement with Elite Business Systems, the son described himself in one section of the agreement as a sole trader, and in another section indicated that he was in partnership with his father. Lord Phillips MR observed that the father could not reasonably have foreseen that third parties would form a view that he was in partnership with his son simply because he opened a bank account for him. Further, mere carelessness on the part of a person which falls short of knowledge of the representation will be insufficient. This is clear from the English case of *Tower Cabinet Co Ltd v Ingram*.[26] In that case, a partner retired from his firm and due to carelessness on his part omitted to destroy the headed notepaper of the firm which contained his name.[27] It was held that this carelessness did not constitute him knowingly suffering himself to be held out as a partner, as he did not know that the notepaper was used by the firm after his retirement. Clearly, if he had known this fact, he would have been held to have knowingly suffered a holding out.

[7.16] An issue under s 14(1) which has not yet been considered by the courts is the position of a creditor of a firm who receives a share of the profits from the partnership

---

21   *Palter v Zeller* (1997) 30 OR (3d) 796 at 799, from the plaintiff's statement of claim.
22   Paragraph **[7.12]**.
23   Note, however, that *if* the third party was an existing customer of the firm, as distinct from a new customer, liability might be established under s 36(1). This is because the letters were addressed only to the other partners and this would not put the third party on notice of his departure as required to escape liability under s 36(1). See further para **[11.85]**.
24   *Hunter v Stoney* (1831) Glasc 23.
25   *Elite Business Systems UK Ltd v Price* [2005] EWCA Civ 920.
26   *Tower Cabinet Co Ltd v Ingram* [1949] 2 KB 397.
27   Note that the exemption in s 14(2) of the 1890 Act only applies in relation to the use of a firm name after the death of a partner. See further para **[7.50]**.

in payment of a debt. Such a person is not by virtue of his receipt of a share of the profits a partner,[28] but the question arises as to whether he could be liable as a partner by holding out on the basis that the sharing of profits constitutes a holding out by him that he is a partner. The creditor in such a case will invariably be knowingly suffering the actions which constitute the representation, namely the sharing of profits. However, the representation that he is a partner is indirect and differs considerably from a direct representation, such as a person's name appearing on the letterhead as a partner. Accordingly, it might be argued that a creditor should not be liable on the basis of such an indirect holding out, even where the representation is done knowingly. A case for liability might be stronger where the creditor makes an indirect representation of holding out, but is shown to have been aware of the consequences of his being held out as a partner.

How far must a person go to prevent unwanted holding out?

[7.17] It would be a dangerous course of action for someone, who knows that he is being represented by a third party as a partner, to do nothing to prevent such representations. Prudence suggests that such a person should take immediate action to have the representation withdrawn or to inform the public that he is not a partner. If he remains silent, in the knowledge of the representation, he will be regarded as having knowingly suffered the holding out.[29] If the attempts to have the representations stopped are unsuccessful, it may even be necessary to seek an injunction against the third party. This was necessary in the case of *Walter v Ashton*,[30] where an injunction was granted to The Times newspaper to prevent the defendant from advertising the sale of bicycles as 'Times cycles'. The court held that there was a reasonable probability of The Times being exposed to litigation as a partner by holding out. Similarly in *Taylor v Hughes*,[31] the plaintiff left a firm called The Agricultural and Commercial Bank of Ireland. Soon after, he was re-listed as a partner by his former partners. There, Sugden LC granted an injunction to the plaintiff to prevent the firm from placing his name on a list of partners.

A reasonable time in which to prevent representations?

[7.18] Between the time that the apparent partner discovers that representations are being made about him and the time he prevents those representations, it is likely that a number of representations will have been made to third parties. During this period, the apparent partner will know that representations have, or are being made, and the question arises as to whether he is liable under s 14(1) for representations which he is attempting to stop.

[7.19] Although not contemplated by the terms of s 14(1), it is contended that the apparent partner will be given a reasonable period of time from the date of his discovering the representations in order to prevent those representations. Accordingly, he may not be held to have 'knowingly suffered' any representations which are made during this period of time. To find otherwise is without justification in principle. This is

---

28 See the Partnership Act 1890, s 2(3) and see generally para **[2.95]**.
29 See the Scottish case of *J & C Gardner v Anderson and Anor* (1862) 24 D 315.
30 *Walter v Ashton* [1902] 2 Ch 282.
31 *Taylor v Hughes* (1844) 7 Ir Eq R 529.

because, as has been noted,[32] the doctrine of holding out is based on the equitable principle that a person, who by his conduct allows another to believe him to be a partner, is estopped from denying that fact. In the situation under discussion, the apparent partner who attempts to stop representations being made has not done anything 'inequitable' which would to justify his being estopped from denying that he is a partner. On the contrary, he has taken all reasonable efforts to prevent such representations being made.

State of mind of person being held out as partner

[7.20] It is clear that for liability under s 14(1) to arise, there is no requirement on the part of the apparent partner that he intend to hold himself out as a partner.[33] However, he must intend to do those actions which constitute the representation that he is a partner, or be aware of the fact that they are being done.

Representation that person intends to become a partner

[7.21] In the same way as a person who agrees to become a partner at a future date is not a partner,[34] so too a person who holds himself out as willing to become a partner is not liable under s 14(1) of the 1890 Act. Before liability as a partner by holding out will attach, there must be a representation to the effect that the person is a partner, and not simply that he will be a partner.[35]

Apparent partner's name need not be mentioned

[7.22] In order to constitute a sufficient holding out of a person as a partner, there is no requirement for that person's name to be mentioned. This is clear from *Martyn v Gray*,[36] in which a person supplied goods to a mine on the faith of a representation by the captain of the mine. In referring to the defendant, the captain of the mine stated that a capitalist from London, whose name he was not authorised to give, had a large interest in the mine and intended to work it vigorously. The defendant allowed this reference to

---

32 See para **[7.03]**.
33 See for example *Tower Cabinet Co Ltd v Ingram* [1949] 2 KB 397 and para **[7.15]**, where this intention was absent. Nonetheless, the apparent partner's state of mind regarding his status may in some cases be a factor in determining whether a holding out has occurred. Therefore, in the High Court case of *Smallman Limited v O'Moore and Newman* [1959] IR 220, while the question of holding out under s 36(1) of the 1890 Act does not appear to have been raised by the plaintiff, Davitt P took into account not simply the actions of the defendants, but also their intentions ie they believed that they were contracting as a company, rather than as a partnership. On this basis, he decided that there was no contract between the parties as they were not *ad idem*, the plaintiffs believing they were supplying goods to the partnership and the defendants believing the company was being supplied. Davitt P thought, obiter, that there was an arguable case (but he did not decide on the issue) for estopping the defendants, on the basis of their conduct, from pleading that they did not order goods as a partnership nor contract to pay for them.
34 See *Macken v Revenue Commissioners* [1962] IR 302 and para **[2.39]** et seq.
35 *Bourne v Freeth* (1829) 9 B & C 632; *Reynell v Lewis* (1846) 15 M & W 517; *Wyld v Hopkins* (1846) 15 M & W 517.
36 *Martyn v Gray* (1863) 143 ER 667.

him to be made and it was held that this was sufficient evidence for the defendant to be liable as a partner by holding out.[37]

If apparent partner is not aware of the identity of the recipient

[7.23] By the express terms of s 14(1), liability for holding out will ensue whether the representation to a particular third party is or is not made with 'the knowledge of the apparent partner'. Thus, provided that the representation is made by the apparent partner or by a third party and knowingly suffered by him, then the fact that he is unaware that it is actually communicated to a particular third party is irrelevant. Accordingly, a person whose name appears as a partner on a firm's notepaper may be liable under s 14(1) to third parties who receive the notepaper whether he is aware of this receipt or not.

Fraudulent inducement to hold oneself out as a partner

[7.24] The fact that an apparent partner was induced by fraud (such as a statement by the partners in the firm that he will not be liable as a result of his being held out) to hold himself out as a partner, will not prevent his being liable to a third party under s 14(1). Thus, the law supports the interests of third parties over the interests of a person who is fraudulently induced to represent himself as a partner. This can be justified on the basis that it achieves certainty for third parties who deal with partners by holding out. This rule is, of course, subject to the proviso that the third party, intending to rely on the holding out, had no part in the fraud.[38]

Relevance of Registration of Business Names Act 1963

[7.25] The Registration of Business Names Act 1963[39] will, in many cases, play an important, although not necessarily decisive, role in the question of whether a person is liable as a partner by holding out. This Act provides, inter alia, that a firm which carries on business under a name which is not that of all the partners is required to register this name as a business name and confirm the identity of the partners in the firm. Under ss 7 and 12(1) of the 1963 Act, a firm which has registered its business name is required to notify the Registrar of Business Names of any change in the particulars registered or if it ceases to use that name. For this reason, the details in the register of business names may constitute a representation that a person is a partner in two distinct situations. First, a former partner may be held out as still being a partner by his name continuing to be

---

[37] However, see the Australian case *Duke Group Ltd (in liq) v Pilmer* [1999] SASC 97 which indicates that while the person's name need not necessarily be mentioned, those holding themselves out or being held out as partners should be 'particular identified persons who are not in fact partners but who can be identified in the representation as holding themselves out or being held out as partners'. This interpretation has been criticised, notably by Keith Fletcher as the leading commentator on partnership law in Australia (see Fletcher, *Higgins and Fletcher on The Law of Partnership in Australia and New Zealand* (8th edn, 2001) and Fletcher, *The Law of Partnership in Australia* (9th edn, 2007)) and the view of the author and editor is that the decision in *Martyn v Gray* is preferred.

[38] *Collingwood v Berkeley* (1863) 15 CB (ns) 145; *Maddick v Marshall* (1864) 17 CB (ns) 829; *Ellis v Schmoeck* (1829) 5 Bing 521; *Ex p Broome* (1811) 1 Rose 69.

[39] See generally in the relation to the application of the Registration of Business Names Act 1963 to partnerships, para [3.70] et seq.

listed as a partner.[40] Second, a firm consisting of A and B, who use a firm name A, B & C, may not have registered this as a business name. Any person dealing with that firm will therefore assume that C is a partner, since otherwise the use of C's name as part of the firm name would require the firm name to be registered as a business name. In this way, the impression is given that C is in fact a partner in that firm.

[7.26] Unlike s 36(2) of the 1890 Act (in relation to the advertisement of a change in a partnership in *Iris Oifigiúil*),[41] the Registration of Business Names Act 1963 does not provide that registration of a business name is deemed to be notice to third persons of the details of the registration. Nonetheless, the register of business names is a public record and ensuring proper registration will lessen the risk of a person who is not a partner being held out to be one. In addition, it is likely that a court will take into account whether a former partner arranged for the notification of his departure to the Registrar of Business Names when it is deciding if he held himself out as continuing to be a partner. This point is illustrated by the English case of *Bishop v Tudor Estates*.[42] In that case, a partnership was dissolved but the English Registrar of Business Names was not notified that the business name was no longer being used by a two-man partnership as required by the English equivalent of s 12(1) of the 1963 Act.[43] One of the partners continued to carry on the firm's business after its dissolution and it was held the other partner was liable as a partner by holding out to a third party who, after the dissolution of the firm, had seen the registration certificate with both persons still listed as partners.

2. There Must be Reliance by the Third Party

[7.27] In order to establish liability under s 14(1) of the 1890 Act, the second requirement to be satisfied is that the third party must have relied on the holding out which occurred.[44] In the words of s 14(1), the third party must 'on the faith of any such representation' have given credit to the firm. For this reason, if the third party was unaware of the representation, there can be no holding out. In *Ford v Whitmarsh*,[45] it was held that a general representation to the public at large is not sufficient for there to be a holding out, unless the person claiming under s 14(1) heard the representation and acted upon it. Where a third party heard the representation, he will not be able to rely on s 14(1) if he would have given credit to the firm regardless of whether that person was a partner or not, since in that case there would have been no reliance on the representation. Similarly, a representation which was made after the credit was given by the third party to the firm does not give rise to a liability under s 14(1) since there is no reliance.[46] Further, the reliance must match the representation that is made.[47]

---

40 See for example *Bishop v Tudor Estates* [1952] CPL 807, para **[7.26]**.
41 See para **[11.71]**.
42 *Bishop v Tudor Estates* [1952] CPL 807.
43 Registration of Business Names Act 1916, s 13.
44 See generally Webb, 'Partnership by Estoppel and Reliance' (1998) NZLJ 446 and Webb, 'Partnership Letterheads – again' (1996) NZLJ 124.
45 *Ford v Whitmarsh* (1840) H & W 53.
46 *Baird v Planque* (1858) 1 F & F 344.
47 *UCB Home Loans Corp Ltd v Soni* [2013] EWCA Civ 62. (contd.../)

Where third party knows that an apparent partner is not a partner

[7.28] The state of mind of the third party is obviously crucial in determining whether he acted on the faith of the representation of the person as a partner. This is clear from the judgment of Lord Denman CJ in *Lake v Duke of Argyll*.[48] When discussing the liability of a partner by holding out, he observed that: '[e]ach case of this nature must depend on its own circumstances with reference to the effect of the defendant's language and conduct on the plaintiff's mind.'[49]

[7.29] An issue which may arise in modern professional partnerships is whether there is reliance on a holding out where a third party knows that the person being represented to him as a partner is not in fact a partner (eg if he knows him to be a salaried partner). In view of the importance of the state of mind of the third party, if he knows that the person he is dealing with is a salaried partner, he may, by virtue of his knowledge of the law, also be aware that he is entitled to sue a salaried partner under s 14(1) as a partner by holding out. In such a case it is contended that, even though the third party knew that the person was not a true partner, there would continue to be sufficient reliance by the third party under s 14(1), so as to entitle him to relief thereunder. On the other hand, if the third party is unaware of the law and knows simply that the apparent partner is not a real partner, it would seem that there is no 'reliance' within the meaning of s 14(1) and thus no liability as a partner by holding out.

Evidence of reliance

[7.30] It seems clear that the burden of proving that there has been a reliance on the holding out rests on the person seeking to establish liability under s 14(1) of the 1890 Act.[50] The question of whether reliance can be presumed in certain situations was the subject of English High Court and Court of Appeal decisions in *Nationwide Building Society v Lewis*.[51] That case concerned an action against a solicitor, Williams, who was a salaried partner in Lewis' firm.[52] The plaintiff sought to make Williams liable under s 14(1) of the 1890 Act for the negligent report on title which was prepared by Lewis. The plaintiff's action against Williams was met with the objection that at the time the negligent advice was acted upon by the plaintiff, there was no reliance, since there was no evidence that the plaintiff had any dealings with Williams or even knew of his existence. There was no evidence that the plaintiff had noticed Williams's name on

---

47 (...contd) In that case, the Court of Appeal found that UCB Home Loans had not advanced credit on the basis of a representation that a specific individual had made (or authorised or knowingly suffered to be made) that she was a partner in a particular firm by way of the form of letterhead used, but it had instead advanced credit on the basis of a representation made by her partner on forged certificates of title and forged letterhead which were not authorised by or knowingly suffered by her.

48 *Lake v Duke of Argyll* (1844) 6 QB 477.

49 *Lake v Duke of Argyll* (1844) 6 QB 477 at 480–481.

50 See for example the English case of *Nationwide Building Society v Lewis* [1998] 3 All ER 143 at 153.

51 *Nationwide Building Society v Lewis* [1998] 3 All ER 143.

52 The expression 'firm', though used in the report, is inappropriate as it was not a partnership, but rather it consisted of Lewis as the principal and Williams as his employee.

Lewis's notepaper. In the High Court, it was held that the plaintiff was entitled to assume that, on receipt of a report on title under cover of a letter which listed Lewis and Williams as partners, it was the report of a two-partner firm and that there was a presumption of reliance by the plaintiff on this fact. However, the Court of Appeal reversed this decision. It held that, as a general rule, direct evidence of the reliance must be produced and it was not prepared to presume that the plaintiff had relied on the holding out of Williams as a partner. Interestingly, it left open the question of whether in some circumstances it may be appropriate to infer that there was a reliance and Slade LJ indicated that if the plaintiff had dealt exclusively with a salaried partner, the court might presume that there was a reliance by a third party on that holding out.

[7.31] Since it will be difficult in some cases to prove an actual reliance by a third party, and in view of the possibility left open by the Court of Appeal, the Irish courts may in certain cases presume reliance where this is justified on the circumstances surrounding the representation. In this regard, it is worth noting that the Solicitor's Indemnity Fund was indemnifying Williams in relation to the action, but not Lewis, because of allegations of dishonesty against him. This may have influenced the court's decision in not wishing to make Williams liable for Lewis' actions. If this factor was not present, it is apprehended that the court might have presumed the necessary reliance in this case. In this regard, it is interesting to note that s 36(1) of the 1890 Act already operates in effect a presumption of reliance in the case of a former partner *vis-à-vis* existing customers of the firm who are unaware of the departure of the former partner.[53]

3. There Must be a Giving of Credit by the Third Party

[7.32] The third and final requirement for there to be a liability for a partner by holding out under s 14(1) of the 1890 Act is that the third party must have given credit to the firm. Care should be taken with this expression as it does not have a technical meaning. Instead, it must be taken to mean any situation where a third party alters his situation[54] on the faith of the holding out being true and in this sense, this requirement adds little to the previous requirement that the third party has relied on the holding out. Indeed, it is suggested that once the third party has acted on the understanding that the defendant is a partner, that will be sufficient to satisfy s 14(1). In *Nationwide Building Society v Lewis*[55] it was noted that as s 14(1) was simply an example of the wider doctrine of estoppel by conduct, the precise language of s 14(1) ('given credit to the firm') was not important once there was a reliance or acting on the faith of the representation as required for an estoppel by conduct to exist. In support of this non-technical meaning of the expression is the case of *Lynch v Stiff*[56] where the Australian High Court held that the entrusting of money to a firm of solicitors for investment purposes constituted the 'giving of credit' to the firm under the Australian equivalent of s 14(1).[57]

---

53   See para **[7.52]** et seq.
54   Note that this is in keeping with the requirement of estoppel by representation as stated by Viscount Simonds in *Tool Metal Manufacturing Co v Tungsten Electrical* Co [1955] 2 All ER 657 at 660 that the 'gist of the equity lies in the fact that one party by his conduct led the other to alter his position'.
55   Per Rimer J at *Nationwide Building Society v Lewis* [1997] 3 All ER 498. His ultimate decision was reversed by the Court of Appeal ([1998] 3 All ER 143) but there was no disagreement with this principle, see Gibson LJ at [1998] 3 All ER 143 at 147.
56   *Lynch v Stiff* [1943] 68 CLR 428.

[7.33] In *Heffernan & Anor v Murray & Ors*,[58] the first plaintiff, Mr Heffernan, claimed that he had given credit as a consequence of the thirteenth defendant, Mr Simpson, holding himself out as a partner in the Ballykisteen Development Partnership. Binchy J agreed that Mr Heffernan had given credit to the partnership as a result of the actions of Mr Simpson, but as he had not proven that Mr Simpson had held himself out to Mr Heffernan as a partner in his dealings with him, his claim under s 14(1) of the 1890 Act failed as all three elements of s 14(1) had not been met.

Torts may constitute a giving of credit

[7.34] The fact that the third party must have 'given credit to the firm', in the sense of having relied on the holding out as being true, means that some, but not all torts will fall within the scope of s 14(1). Thus, for example, a third party who has incurred loss as a result of negligent advice provided to him by a firm may be able to maintain an action against a partner by holding out on the grounds that he sought advice from the firm and understood that the partners listed on the headed notepaper were all partners in the firm. On this basis, he could maintain that he had altered his situation or relied on the holding out being true. In contrast, a partner by holding out is not likely to be responsible for the injury in a road accident to a third party by 'his' firm under s 14(1). The third party is likely to be outside the scope of s 14(1), since when he crossed the road, he could not be said to have altered his situation on the faith of the holding out that a person was a partner.

4. A Fourth Requirement – Must there be a Partnership?

[7.35] Although s 14(1) envisages three main requirements for the establishment of liability, it seems to contemplate a possible fourth requirement, namely that there should be a partnership in existence.[59] Section 14(1) talks of a person being liable as a partner where he represents himself as a partner 'in a particular firm' and it requires the third party to have given 'credit to the firm' before liability will arise. Prima facie, therefore, it would seem that where a sole trader represents that he is in partnership with another, he will not be liable as a partner by holding out under s 14(1). This is because he is not holding himself out as a partner in a particular firm and any credit given by the third party will not be to the firm, since none exists.[60] Nonetheless, such a person will not

---

57 Partnership Act 1862, s 14(1) of New South Wales.

58 *Heffernan & Anor v Murray & Ors* [2015] IEHC 195.

59 For a contrary view, see l'Anson Banks, *Lindley & Banks on Partnership* (20th edn, 2017) at para 5.35 (fn 172). Note also that the proviso in s 38 of the 1890 Act contemplates liability for a person who holds himself out as a partner of a bankrupt. But this does not necessarily support the view that there can be a holding out without there being a partnership, since under s 33(1) of the 1890 Act, a partnership can exist between a bankrupt and non-bankrupt if there is an agreement that the bankruptcy of a partner will not dissolve the partnership.

60 Note that in the English High Court case of *Nationwide Building Society v Lewis* [1997] 3 All ER 498, there was a successful claim of holding out under s 14(1) of the 1890 Act against one Williams who worked with, but was not a partner of, Lewis (a sole trader). Curiously, Williams's counsel does not appear to have pleaded the fact that there was no partnership in existence. However, on appeal the decision was reversed by the Court of Appeal [1998] 3 All ER 143, but not on the grounds that there was no partnership.

escape all liability for his actions. This is because, as has been noted, liability as a partner by holding out is an example of the wider doctrine of estoppel by conduct.[61] On this basis, it seems clear that where a sole trader represents that he is in partnership with another, he will be estopped from denying the truth of this representation to a person who has acted on that representation.

[7.36] A case which can be explained on this basis is that of *O'Connor v Woods*.[62] In that case, one partner, O'Connor, left the accountancy firm of John A Woods & Co. However after his departure, he continued to work for some clients of the firm. The bill which he furnished to one such client was in respect of work which he had done after his departure from the firm, yet he furnished this bill in the firm name rather than his own. Without giving a basis for his holding, Kenny J held that he was liable to account to his former firm for these fees since 'he claimed them in the name of John A Woods'.[63] This decision cannot be explained on the basis of s 14(1) of the 1890 Act since there was no issue of liability between O'Connor and the third party. Rather the case simply concerned a dispute between the partners inter se. The result might be explained under the general principles of estoppel by conduct, ie O'Connor had obtained fees from the client on the basis of a representation that the fees were due to the partnership rather than to him personally and therefore he was estopped from denying the truth of this claim when his former partners sought these fees. Yet this theory does of course suffer from the problem that the representation was not made to the firm but to a client of the firm and that the firm knew that it was incorrect.

[7.37] This also explains *McAleenan v AIG*,[64] in which the plaintiff was employed by a sole trader, Michael Lynn & Co, Solicitors, in November 2004. While she had not become a partner in that firm before her resignation in 2007, AIG sought to avoid the professional indemnity insurance policy that the firm held with it on the basis that Ms McAleenan had held herself out as a partner in the firm at all material times, and also sought to avoid the policy on the basis of material non-disclosure, misrepresentation or untrue statements. In considering whether Ms McAleenan had held herself out as a partner, Finlay Geoghegan J noted that Ms McAleenan had remained subject to PAYE at all times, while there were meetings regarding a proposed partnership agreement no agreement had been reached as to the terms on which a partnership would come into existence between Mr Lynn and Ms McAleenan or how profits would be shared between them (indeed, she was given a partnership agreement in July 2007 which she refused to sign), when the business name of the firm was changed, it was registered to Mr Lynn and not to a partnership, Ms McAleenan was given a P45 when she resigned, and the firm's bank account had remained in the sole name of Mr Lynn. However:

– in 2005 Ms McAleenan had indicated to the Law Society that she was a partner in the firm – she explained to the Court that she believed herself to be a 'named partner' and that she understood this to mean that she remained an employee, but was 'named' as a partner to clients pending formally entering into partnership with Mr Lynn;

---

61 See para **[7.05]**.
62 *O'Connor v Woods* (22 January 1976) HC.
63 *O'Connor v Woods* (22 January 1976) HC at p 18.
64 *McAleenan v AIG* [2010] IEHC 128.

- Ms McAleenan had ticked 'partner in a solicitor's practice' on her application for a practising certificate in both 2006 and 2007, albeit she struck out the section concerning accounts that was to be completed by partners, and instead completed the section that required completion by employees;

- in the proposal form for the professional indemnity insurance policy with AIG, the number of partners in the firm was listed as two (although the word 'partner' appeared directly after Mr Lynn's name, but not Ms McAleenan's); and

- Ms McAleenan's name was included on the firm's notepaper in 2007 – Ms McAleenan indicated to the Court that she had agreed to this as she understood that negotiations regarding her becoming a partner in the firm were close to complete.

Finlay Geoghegan J noted the complexities surrounding the concept of 'salaried partner',[65] and the distinction between 'true partners' and a person who holds himself out as, or is held out by the true partners to be, a partner in a partnership. She was satisfied that there was no partnership between Mr Lynn and Ms McAleenan, and that any partnership between them remained under negotiation, citing with approval the observation of Megarry J in *Stekel v Ellice*[66] that: '… the question whether or not there is a partnership depends on what the true relationship is, and not on any mere label attached to that relationship.' However, Finlay Geoghegan J was satisfied that Ms McAleenan had, on occasion, held herself out to be a partner in the firm, and that the misrepresentation by her in the AIG proposal form that she was a partner in the firm was material and made recklessly. AIG was therefore entitled to avoid the professional indemnity insurance policy against Ms McAleenan.

Companies holding themselves out to be partnerships

[7.38] Just as a person may hold himself out as being in partnership with another when no partnership exists, so too it is common for non-partnerships, such as limited liability companies, to use the expression '& Partners' as part of their name. The reason may be to give the enterprise a degree of standing that might otherwise not be present and such names may give the public the impression that the people who own the enterprise are personally liable for its obligations. However, as with individuals who represent that they are in partnership when none exists, these companies (or the shareholders thereof) will prima facie not be liable on the basis of holding out under s 14(1) since there never was a partnership in existence as required by that section. Nonetheless, as in the case of individuals, it would seem that liability might be established on general principles of estoppel by conduct. Thus, companies which represent themselves to be a partnership may be estopped from subsequently denying that the company is a partnership. For example a company which has a nominal share capital, but which uses the phrase '& Partners' as part of its name without any reference to limited liability, may have dealings with third parties who believe that the owners are in partnership, with consequent unlimited liability. In those circumstances, it is thought that the members of the

---

[65] As to which, see para **[6.18]** et seq.
[66] *Stekel v Ellice* [1973] 1 WLR 191.

company may be in danger of being estopped from denying that they have unlimited liability and in this way the corporate veil of a company may be pierced.[67]

III. CONSEQUENCES OF A FINDING OF HOLDING OUT

[7.39] It has been seen that the primary consequence of a finding of holding out is that the apparent partner is liable to a third party who relied on that holding out, as if he were a partner in the firm.[68] Other consequences of a finding that a person is liable as a partner by holding out will now be considered.

Partner by Holding Out is not a Partner Inter Se

[7.40] It is important to bear in mind that the doctrine of holding out is relevant only as an estoppel.[69] Therefore, it does not create the relationship of partnership but only prevents a person from denying that he is a partner. Thus, a person who is liable as a partner by holding out is not a partner in the firm and will not have the usual rights and duties of a partner, such as the right to share in the profits or be liable for the general losses of the firm. Similarly, he will not be bound by the acts of the true partners in the firm and the firm will not be bound by his actions under partnership law.[70] This is apparent from the express terms of s 14(1) itself which merely makes the partner by holding out 'liable as a partner' but does not make him a partner. Thus, as was stated by Richards B in *Greenham v Gray*:[71]

> '[t]rue it is, that persons may act so as to constitute themselves partners, and become liable to third persons, while they are not partners, nor liable inter se.'[72]

[7.41] In *Milliken v Milliken*,[73] there was a partnership agreement to run a bookshop at 115 Grafton Street in Dublin between Jane Milliken, Mr Grant and Mr Bolton. The agreement also contained a provision for the admission at a future time of Jane Milliken's son (Edward) who was to replace her as a partner in the firm. In addition, Jane Milliken was authorised by Mr Grant and Mr Bolton to hold Edward out as a partner in the firm. Edward brought an action to be admitted as a partner in the firm and he relied, inter alia, upon the fact that his mother was authorised to hold him out as a

---

67 See generally regarding the piercing of the corporate veil, Courtney, *The Law of Companies* (4th edn, 2016) at para [5.001] et seq; Hutchinson, Keane on *Company Law in the Republic of Ireland* (5th edn, 2016) at para [11.01] et seq; Forde and Kennedy, *Company Law* (5th edn, 2017) at para 4-51 et seq.
68 See para **[7.06]**.
69 See for example the judgment of Megaw LJ in *Hudgell Yeates & Co v Watson* [1978] 2 All ER 363 at 374.
70 See the judgment of Waller LJ in the English case of *Hudgell Yeates & Co v Watson* [1978] 2 All ER 363 at 373 in relation to the non-application of s 5 of the 1890 Act to a partner by holding out. Of course, the partner by holding out may bind the firm under general agency principles, but not as a 'partner'. See further para **[7.45]**.
71 *Greenham v Gray* (1855) 4 Ir CLR 501.
72 *Greenham v Gray* (1855) 4 Ir CLR 501 at 512. This paragraph (including the quote from the judgment of Richards B in *Greenham v Gray*) was quoted with approval by Binchy J in *Heffernan & Anor v Murray & Anor* [2015] IEHC 196.
73 *Milliken v Milliken* (1845) 8 Ir Eq R 16.

partner. However, since the 'holding out' of a partner only grants rights to third parties who rely on that fact and not to the person who was held out as a partner, Blackburne MR correctly rejected his application to be admitted as a partner.

[7.42] Another case which involved the question of whether a person is a partner inter se on the basis of a holding out was the High Court case of *Re Boyle*.[74] That case involved a solicitor, Boyle snr, who employed his son, Boyle jnr, as a solicitor in his firm. The names of the father and son both appeared on the notepaper of the firm, though there was nothing on the notepaper which indicated a partnership between them. If they were partners, the son would not have been entitled to charge a trust in which his father was a trustee, for legal advice.[75] Overend J noted that while a third party might believe that they were in partnership, it was clear that the act of having a person's name on the notepaper of a firm (perhaps the most common method of holding out) did not make them partners inter se.

Holding out Results in a Joint Liability

[7.43] While a partner by holding out does not become a partner inter se, s 14(1) does provide that he is liable 'as a partner'. For this reason, like all partners, he will be jointly (and in some cases, jointly and severally) liable[76] with the real partners for the partnership obligations.[77] Thus, a judgment which has been obtained against a firm in the firm name may be enforced against a person who is liable as a partner by holding out,[78] assuming of course there was a third party who relied on the holding out.

[7.44] Similarly, the liability of a partner by holding out under s 36(1) of the 1890 Act results in him being liable as a partner. This is because under that section, any apparent partners are treated as 'still being members of the firm'.

Liability of Firm for Apparent Partner's Acts

[7.45] Where a person is a partner by holding out, s 14(1) of the 1890 Act considers only his liability to third parties and it does not deal with the liability of the partnership for his actions as an apparent partner. This issue is determined by the general law of

---

[74] *Re Boyle* [1947] IR 61.
[75] See further para **[12.07]**.
[76] As to the situations in which a partner is jointly and jointly and severally liable, see para **[11.07]** et seq.
[77] In *Re McManus* (1858) 7 Ir Ch R 82, a claim of holding out was not considered in the bankruptcy court as it was held to be an inappropriate forum, but, obiter, Macan J indicated that if the creditors had been able to show a holding out he would have treated them 'constructively as joint creditors'. On this basis, he would have prevented the apparent partner from proving on the bankruptcy of his alleged co-partner, relying on the well-established principle of the administration of estates that a partner is not entitled to prove on the bankruptcy of his co-partners, if by so doing he reduces the surplus available for the joint creditors (as to this principle, see generally para **[27.124]**). It follows that in the application of this rule of the administration of estates, the apparent partner is treated as if he was a true partner. See also l'Anson Banks, *Lindley & Banks on Partnership* (20th edn, 2017) at para 27-116.
[78] *Davis v Hyman & Co* [1903] 1 KB 854.

agency, so that if a firm represents that a person is a partner in the firm, this is clearly a representation that the person is an agent of the firm.[79] It follows that the firm will be liable to third parties for the acts of the agent within the sphere of his agency. In order to determine whether the firm will be bound by a particular action of the apparent partner, it is apprehended that the principles which determine whether a firm is bound by the actions of a real partner, will apply to the position of an apparent partner.[80] Clearly, where the representation that a person is a partner in a firm is not authorised by the firm itself, but by a third party or by the apparent partner, these general principles of agency will have no application and the firm will not be bound by the actions of the apparent partner.

Minor Partner not Liable as a Partner by Holding Out

[7.46] Just as a minor partner is not liable for the debts of the firm or the acts of his co-partners,[81] so too a minor is not liable as a partner by holding out.[82]

IV. SPECIFIC INSTANCES OF HOLDING OUT

[7.47] In this section, a number of specific situations in which a person is held liable as a partner by holding out will be considered.

Salaried Partners

[7.48] The classic example of a partner by holding out is a salaried partner. A salaried partner is a person who is usually an employee of the partnership but allows himself to be held out as a partner in a firm. The position of a salaried partner is considered in detail elsewhere in this work.[83]

Replacement Partners

[7.49] Where a former partner is replaced in the firm by another partner, the application of the doctrine of holding out means that it is not possible to sue a former partner and his replacement partner jointly for the same debt. This could occur for example where in a firm consisting of A and B, A is replaced by C. If an obligation is incurred by the firm to an existing customer after that date, there is nothing to prevent that customer from suing B and C jointly as the partners in the firm or A and B jointly on the basis that A allowed himself to be held out as still being a partner (assuming the customer did not know of A's departure).[84] However, where the third party was unaware both of A's retirement and C's admission, under the rule in *Scarf v Jardine*,[85] he cannot sue A, B and C jointly, since A

---

79 Since under s 5 of the 1890 Act, every partner is an agent of the firm. See for example the judgment of Megarry J in *Stekel v Ellice* [1973] 1 All ER 465 at 472: '*Quoad* the outside world it often will matter little whether a man is a full partner or a salaried partner; for a salaried partner is held out as being a partner, and the partners will be liable for his acts accordingly.'

80 As to these principles, see para **[10.01]** et seq.

81 *Lovell and Christmas v Beauchamp* [1894] AC 607, see para **[4.04]**.

82 *Price v Hewitt* (1853) 8 Ex 146; *Johnson v Pye* (1665) 1 Sid 258. See further para **[4.13]**.

83 See generally in relation to salaried partners, para **[6.18]** et seq.

84 Under s 36(1) of the 1890 Act.

never held himself out as being a partner of C's. This rule can be justified, presumably, on the basis that the doctrine of holding out is designed to protect third parties from fraud arising out of a misrepresentation that a person is a partner. Where the third party can sue a person who is a partner *or* a person as if he were liable as a partner, then the third party is clearly protected and the rationale for the doctrine of holding out does not justify the third party being able to sue both.

Deceased Partner may not be a Partner by Holding Out

[7.50] Under s 14(2) of the 1890 Act, after the death of a partner, the use of a firm name or the deceased partner's name as part of the firm name does not amount to a holding out as regards the deceased partner. Section 14(2) states:

> Provided that where after a partner's death the partnership business is continued in the old firm-name, the continued use of that name or of the deceased partner's name as part thereof shall not of itself make his executors or administrators estate or effects liable for any partnership debts contracted after his death.

This rule is part of the wider principle that a partner (or more precisely his estate) is not liable for obligations incurred by the firm after his death.[86] This principle is grounded in the general rule of agency that the authority of a person to bind a principal is terminated on the death of the principal[87] and since death is a public event, third parties are deemed to be on notice of this fact. It follows that a representation that a deceased partner is still a partner in a firm, whether by the use of a firm name or otherwise, does not result in his estate being liable for post-death obligations on the basis of a holding out. Accordingly, it has been held that a deceased partner is not a partner by holding out even in relation to existing customers of the firm who are unaware of his death.[88]

'of itself'

[7.51] Section 14(2) of the 1890 Act provides that the use of the name of the deceased partner will not 'of itself' make his estate liable. The use of this phrase indicates that it is possible for a deceased partner's estate to be liable on the basis of a holding out in other circumstances. Thus, if the personal representative led third parties to believe that the deceased partner was still alive, or that the estate would be liable for obligations incurred after his death, then it is apprehended that the estate would be liable on the basis of a holding out.

Former Partners

[7.52] As has been noted,[89] when examining a claim that a former partner is liable as a partner by holding out, liability may be established under either s 14(1) or s 36(1) of the 1890 Act.[90] Some specific examples of holding out by former partners will now be

---

[85] *Scarf v Jardine* (1882) 47 LT 258.
[86] See further in relation to this principle, para **[11.53]** et seq.
[87] *Keon v Hart* (1867) 3 Ir CLR 138 and (1869) 2 Ir CLR 388. See further para **[24.43]**.
[88] *Devaynes v Noble, Houltons's Case* (1816) 1 Mer 529; *Vulliamy v Noble* (1817) 3 Mer 593.
[89] See para **[7.06]**.
[90] For a discussion of ways to reduce the chance of an inadvertent holding out by a former partner, see para **[11.76]**.

considered in the context of both s 14(1) and s 36(1). Before doing so, reference will be made to the remaining subsections of s 36 which provide that:

> (2) An advertisement in the London Gazette as to a firm whose principal place of business is in England or Wales, in the Edinburgh Gazette as to a firm whose principal place of business is in Scotland, and in *Iris Oifigiúil*[91] as to a firm whose principal place of business is in Ireland, shall be notice as to persons who had not dealings with the firm before the date of the dissolution or change so advertised.[92]

> (3) The estate of a partner who dies, or who becomes bankrupt, or of a partner who, not having been known to the person dealing with the firm to be a partner, retires from the firm, is not liable for partnership debts contracted after the date of the death, bankruptcy, or retirement respectively.

Section 36(3) operates from the date of departure

[7.53] Under s 36(3) of the 1890 Act, a former partner is not liable for post-departure obligations if he satisfies the description of 'not having been known to the person dealing with the firm to be a partner'. It is perhaps self-evident that the relevant time, for determining whether he is a known partner, is the date of departure or earlier. Thus, the test is whether at, or prior to, the date of departure, he was a known partner in the third party's eyes. If after the date of actual departure, he becomes a 'known' partner in the eyes of the third party, it is too late and the former partner will not thereby be liable for post-departure partnership obligations. This conclusion is justifiable on principle since the third party who does not know that a person is a partner when he is one, cannot, when he discovers that he *was* one, claim that he should be liable for obligations incurred after his departure. By that time, the third party will have no basis for believing that the partnership had authority to bind that former partner. Thus in the New Zealand case of *Elders Pastoral Ltd v Rutherford*,[93] the defendant was a partner in a firm until June of 1987 at which stage the firm had a current account with the plaintiff. She retired a month later, when the debt was $563, but no notice of retirement was given to the plaintiff. The plaintiff became aware of the defendant's existence in August of 1987. The plaintiff's action against the defendant for the outstanding sum was rejected under the terms of the New Zealand equivalent of s 36(3) of the 1890 Act[94] on the basis that she was not known to be a partner. In the New Zealand Court of Appeal, Somers J also noted that the use in the New Zealand equivalent of s 36(1)[95] of the expression 'he is entitled to treat all apparent members of the old firm as *still* being members of the firm' indicated that the creditor must have known that the former partner was a member of the partnership when he/she was in fact of a member of the firm.

Inconsistency between s 14(1) and s 36(3)

[7.54] There is a prima facie conflict between s 14(1) and s 36(3) of the 1890 Act. Section 36(3) provides that a former partner who, not having been known to the person

---

[91] This is a construction of the term 'Dublin Gazette' in s 36(2) as required by the Adaptation of Enactments Act 1922, s 4.

[92] For a more detailed analysis of s 36(2) of the 1890 Act see para **[11.70]** et seq.

[93] *Elders Pastoral Ltd v Rutherford* (1990) 3 NZBLC 99.

[94] New Zealand Partnership Act 1908, s 39(3).

[95] The New Zealand equivalent is s 39(1).

dealing with the firm to be a partner, is *not* liable for partnership debts contracted after his retirement.[96] On the other hand, s 14(1) makes no reference to unknown partners and under its terms, all former partners are liable for post-departure debts, if they are held out as still being partners. Section 36(3) is clearly intended to prevent a third party from fixing a former partner, whom he did not know to be a partner, with liability for partnership debts incurred after his retirement. The inconsistency arises because s 36(3) exempts all former partners who were unknown partners, but does not contemplate a situation where the third party did not know that a person was a partner at or prior to his departure, but nevertheless believes a person to be a partner after his departure *because* of a holding out. It is suggested that it cannot have been intended that s 36(3) would exempt all former unknown partners from liability for post-departure obligations, even those incurred by a holding out. For this reason, it is submitted that s 36(3) should be read as being subject to s 14(1) and that a former partner may be liable under s 14(1) on the basis of a holding out. In keeping with this view that s 36(3) is subject to s 14(1) is the decision in *Williams v Keats*,[97] albeit a pre-1890 Act case. There, a partner retired from a firm but allowed the firm to carry on business with a name which included his name. When his former partner accepted a bill of exchange in both their names from a new customer of the firm and one who does not appear to have known him as a partner,[98] it was held that he was liable on the bill of exchange, notwithstanding his departure.

Holding out on basis of firm name

[7.55] One of the most common ways in which a former partner is held out as still being a partner, is by reliance on the fact that no change was made to the firm name to indicate his departure from the firm. A number of situations are worthy of consideration.

Where firm name does not contain former partner's name

[7.56] The first situation to consider is where a partner departs from a firm whose name contains no reference to him. Thus, if Mr Grey retires from a firm called Black & White and he allows the firm to continue to use this name, clearly this will not per se constitute a holding out of Mr Grey under s 14(1) of the 1890 Act to new customers of the firm.[99] Mr Grey will of course be subject to the automatic holding out which applies in favour of pre-existing customers of the firm under s 36(1), unless those customers are on notice of his retirement.[100]

Where firm name contains former partner's name

[7.57] Another situation is where a partner departs from a firm which continues to use a firm name that contains his name. Thus, Mr Grey may retire from a firm called Black, White & Grey and allow the firm to continue to use this name. It is not possible to generalise about the effect of such a use, since in the circumstances of a particular case,

---

[96]   It is apprehended that by 'retirement' is meant any departure from the firm, see para **[11.60]**.
[97]   *Williams v Keats* (1817) 2 Stark 290.
[98]   It appears from the arguments of counsel in the case that the plaintiffs were new customers of the firm.
[99]   *Evans v Drummond* (1801) 4 Esp 89; *Farrar v Deflinne* (1844) 1 Car & K 580; *Scarf v Jardine* (1882) 47 LT 258.
[100] This issue is considered further at para **[11.85]**.

this use may or may not constitute a holding out of him as a partner under s 14(1) of the 1890 Act to *new* customers of the firm.[101] It is suggested that the presence of other circumstances will be crucial in determining whether a holding out exists in such a case. It is worth noting that a former partner is entitled to seek an injunction to restrain his former partners from using the firm name in such a way as to expose him to the risk of liability.[102]

[7.58] Mr Grey will, of course, be subject to the automatic holding out which applies to pre-existing customers of the firm under s 36(1), unless they are on notice of his retirement.[103]

Where firm name is former partner's name plus '& Co'

[7.59] A final situation is where a partner leaves a firm and the firm continues to use a firm name which consists of his surname only and the words '& Co'. If Mr Grey retires from a firm called Grey & Co and he allows the firm to continue to use this name, it has been held in a number of early twentieth century cases that this will not *by itself* constitute a holding out of Mr Grey as a partner under s 14(1) of the 1890 Act to *new* customers of the firm.[104] However, this is not to say that Mr Grey may not be liable under s 14(1), since the other circumstances of the case may justify a finding of a holding out.[105] Mr Grey will, of course, be subject to the automatic holding out which applies to pre-existing customers of the firm under s 36(1), unless they are on notice of his retirement.[106]

[7.60] One could perhaps take from this that the use of the term '& Co' alongside a former partner's name will be useful in reducing the likelihood of his being held out as a partner. The logic for this would seem to be that the use of the term '& Co' indicates that the firm represents more than just the named person who may have retired, but that there is a continuity to the firm. Whether at the beginning of the twenty-first century, the expression '& Co' has this effect is open to considerable doubt, especially in view of the modern practice of partnerships and sole traders to use that expression without any great thought. Accordingly, one should treat these authorities with caution.

Where ss 14(1) and 36(2) both apply

[7.61] The situation becomes somewhat more complicated if the former partner advertises his departure in *Iris Oifigiúil*. This is because s 36(2) of the 1890 Act provides that such an advertisement is deemed to be notice of his departure to persons who had no dealings with the firm before his departure (ie new customers). This may give rise to ss 14(1) and 36(2) both applying to the same fact situation. In such a case, it is contended that, where the *only* act of holding out by a former partner is the continued

---

101 See for example the case of *Re Fraser, ex p Central Bank of London* [1892] 2 QB 633, where the former partner was held not to be liable on the basis of a holding out. But contrast that with *Williams v Keats* (1817) 2 Stark 290, which is considered at para **[11.79]**.

102 *Gray v Smith* (1889) 43 Ch D 208; *Thynne v Shove* (1890) 45 Ch D 577.

103 This issue is considered further at para **[11.85]**.

104 *Townsend v Jarman* [1900] 2 Ch 698; *Burchell v Wilde* [1900] 1 Ch 551.

105 As to a holding out under s 14(1) generally, see para **[7.12]** et seq.

106 This issue is considered further at para **[11.85]**.

use of his name as part of the firm name, the terms of s 36(2) will take precedence over s 14(1). Therefore, once the former partner has advertised his departure in *Iris Oifigiúil,* new customers will be deemed to be on notice thereof, and the continued use of his name as part of the firm name will not constitute a holding out of him as a partner to new customers under s 14(1).[107]

[7.62] While advertising in *Iris Oifigiúil* may therefore entitle a former partner to leave his name in the firm name without fear of being liable on the basis of a holding out to new customers, it is thought that the former partner could not rely on such an advertisement where the acts of holding out are more extensive. Thus, if he flagrantly held himself out as a partner (for example by expressly permitting his former partners to state that he is a partner), it is thought that he could not defeat a claim of holding out by new customers on the grounds that they were on constructive notice of the advertisement of his departure. Otherwise, s 36(2) could be used as an instrument of fraud and it is thought that this would be prevented by the courts.[108]

---

[107] *Newsome v Coles* (1811) 2 Camp 617. But cf *Williams v Keats* (1817) 2 Stark 290. In the latter case, a partner retired from a firm and gave notice thereof in the English equivalent of *Iris Oifigiúil*. Thereafter, a bill of exchange was accepted by his former partner in the names of the two of them. No evidence was produced to show that the plaintiffs, who from the arguments of counsel appear to have been new customers, knew of the retirement of the partner. Both names still remained painted up over the premises and the only evidence produced that the retired partner authorised the continued use of the name was that he did not prevent it. It was held that the retired partner was still liable on the bill of exchange in spite of the advertisement of his retirement in the English equivalent of *Iris Oifigiúil*. However note that this decision was prior to the 1890 Act and in particular the deemed notice provisions of s 36(2) which, it is contended, render it of limited applicability today.

[108] See further para **[11.71]** and *Newsome v Coles* (1811) 2 Camp 617.

Chapter 8

Types of Partnerships

INTRODUCTION

[8.01] In this chapter, it is proposed to examine the following different types of partnerships:

    I.   Partnership at Will and Formal Partnership;

   II.   Partnership by Deed, by Agreement or Orally;

  III. Sub-Partnership;

  IV. Group Partnership;

   V. Parallel Partnership;

  VI. Firms with Partners in Common;

 VII. Corporate Partnership;

VIII. Quasi-Partnership;

  IX. Registered Farm Partnerships and Registered Succession Farm Partnerships.

It is important to note that these various categories are not necessarily mutually exclusive, so that one partnership may fall within more than one category, eg a partnership at will (which may be dissolved by any one partner) may also be a corporate partnership (since it may have at least one corporate partner). On the other hand, some of the categories of partnerships are mutually exclusive, so that a formal partnership cannot be a partnership at will. In the succeeding chapter, consideration will be given to a further type of partnership,[1] namely an illegal partnership.

Overview

[8.02] The most important categories of partnership are partnerships at will and formal partnerships (or as they are sometimes known, fixed term partnerships),[2] since every partnership will fall into one of these categories. However the great disadvantage of a partnership at will is that, unlike a formal partnership, it may be dissolved by any one partner at any time by simply giving notice to that effect to his co-partners. On such a dissolution, a partner in the firm is then entitled to have the firm wound up.[3] It follows that the consequences of having a partnership at will are potentially devastating.

---

[1]   In the broadest sense of the word, since an illegal partnership is not strictly a partnership since it is automatically dissolved, see para **[9.27]**.

[2]   As to why the term 'formal partnership' has been used rather than 'fixed term partnership' see para **[8.05]**.

[3]   Partnership Act 1890, s 39. Thus leading to a general dissolution of the firm, rather than simply a technical dissolution (which occurs when a firm continues after a change in membership). See further in relation to the distinction between a general and a technical dissolution of a firm, para **[23.07]**.

Nonetheless, a concerning aspect of the 1890 Act is that the default form of partnership thereunder is a partnership at will. This means that those successful trading or professional firms which are informally created are subject to winding up at the whim of one partner. Indeed, it is apprehended that there are many successful firms which are partnerships at will but in which the partners would be astonished to discover that they are subject to this risk. It is contended that giving one partner the right to wind up the partnership in this way is contrary to the reasonable expectations of business persons who are not versed in the law of partnership (and is probably contrary to the expectations of many professional advisers who might be expected to be aware of the legal position). These persons quite reasonably, it is argued, expect the law of partnership to map the law of other business enterprises, such as that of companies, where a vote of 75% is required to voluntarily wind up a company.[4] In this way, it is suggested that the law of partnership fails the reasonable expectations of the business community. Yet the rationale for this rule would appear to be that a person may not be forced to be a partner with another person against his will and, therefore, he may bring the association to an end at any time. However, the same purpose may be achieved by entitling the disaffected partner to leave the partnership, but not to wind up the firm. Instead, therefore, the default position could be changed so that a general dissolution would only arise on a vote of the majority of the partners and in the event of one partner giving notice of dissolution, the firm would be subject to a technical dissolution only.[5] In order to facilitate the departing partner, he should be entitled to receive the value of his share of the partnership as at the date of departure. In effect, it is suggested that the default position should change so as to allow the continuing partners to purchase the departing partner's share.[6]

I. PARTNERSHIP AT WILL AND FORMAL PARTNERSHIP

[8.03] Every partnership is either a partnership at will or a formal partnership, and different rights accrue to the partners depending on the classification of their partnership. The crucial difference between a partnership at will (or informal partnership) and a formal partnership is that a partnership at will is one which is informally created and so may be dissolved by the notice of any one partner at any time, while in a formal partnership the partnership is formally created in the sense that this right is either expressly or implicitly excluded. The right of a partner to dissolve a partnership by notice at any time is contained in ss 26(1) and 32(c) of the 1890 Act.[7] This right is a default, rather than a mandatory right and therefore applies to every

---

4   Companies Act 2014, s 579(2) and s 202(1)(a)(i).
5   Of course, if the firm consisted of just two partners, then of necessity the partnership would be generally dissolved if one partner left the firm.
6   The method of calculation of this value would ideally be set out in the partnership agreement. However in the absence of such an agreement, the 1890 Act could provide for the departing partner to receive the value of his partnership share as if the firm was wound up and the assets thereof sold. This figure would have to be agreed by the partners and in the absence of agreement fixed by the court. It is submitted that the uncertainty attaching to such a provision is outweighed by the benefit of preventing a disaffected partner from winding up a successful partnership.
7   See further para **[8.06]** et seq.

partnership, unless expressly or implicitly excluded by the partners. The rationale for having such a powerful default right is down to the fundamental nature of the right of every partner to decide with whom and for how long he wishes to be a partner. The importance of such an unfettered right is obvious when one considers that a partner is liable to an unlimited degree for the acts of his co-partner in the carrying on of the partnership business.[8] However, it is queried whether this right needs to be protected in such a potentially devastating manner.[9]

[8.04] It is appropriate, however, to first consider the use of this name 'formal partnership' since it is being used instead of the more usual term, fixed term partnership.

Use of the Term 'Formal Partnership'

[8.05] The textbooks and courts have traditionally used the name 'fixed term partnership' to describe a partnership which excludes the right of one partner to dissolve the partnership at any time. This is because the most common way in which this right is excluded is by the partnership being for a fixed term. In such a case, the right of one partner to dissolve the partnership at any time is said to be excluded by implication. However, the crucial difference between a partnership at will and other partnerships (whether one calls them formal partnerships or fixed term partnerships) is the presence or absence of the right of one partner to dissolve the partnership by notice. It is not the presence of absence of a fixed term, although this is the most common way in which the right to dissolve the partnership is excluded. This means that the use of the name 'fixed term partnership' can cause confusion since a partnership may be for an undefined term, yet it may exclude the right of one partner to dissolve the partnership by notice. Such a partnership for an undefined term is nonetheless confusingly categorised as a fixed term partnership.[10] The problem with categorising partnerships by emphasising the duration of the partnership, rather than the presence or absence of the right of a partner to dissolve the partnership, is highlighted by the English High Court case of *Walters v Bingham*.[11] This concerned the well-known London based law firm of Theodore Goddard & Co which had been regulated by a series of partnership deeds during its long history. At a partners' meeting it was resolved to hold over on the terms of the latest but expired partnership deed 'pending adoption of a new deed', which new deed was to last for an undefined time. The question arose as to whether one partner was entitled to dissolve the partnership by notice during this period.[12] Rather than examining whether

---

[8]   See generally para **[11.04]** et seq.

[9]   See para **[8.02]**.

[10] This partnership may have no right of dissolution, in which case it will be a partnership for joint lives, since it will come to an end on the death of one partner. Alternatively, it may have a right of dissolution for two or more partners, in which case it will be a partnership for an undefined time, but not a partnership at will (since no one partner has the right to dissolve the partnership by notice).

[11] *Walters v Bingham* [1988] 138 NLJ 7.

[12] During the interregnum it transpired that one partner, Bingham, had been involved in irregularities in the management of trust funds. Accordingly, the other partners sought to expel him. In an apparent bid to create a diversion, Bingham purported to unilaterally dissolve the partnership. Bingham maintained that the firm was a partnership at will for the period prior to the adoption of the new deed and that therefore he had the power to, and had duly dissolved the firm by notice.

one partner had a right to dissolve the partnership by notice, Browne-Wilkinson VC attempted to show that the partnership was a 'fixed term partnership' and thus not a partnership at will. He concluded that the partnership 'expressed to last until the new permanent deed was executed, was for a fixed term and not for an "undefined time"'.[13] It is submitted that the court forced itself into these knots by wrongly viewing the question of whether a firm is a partnership at will or not, solely in terms of its duration. This approach to categorising partnerships is exacerbated by the continued use of the term 'fixed term partnership' to indicate that a partnership is not a partnership at will. The conclusion in this case is the result of a preoccupation with the duration of the partnership as the determinative factor in categorising firms as partnerships at will or not. A better approach, it is thought, is to accept that the existence of a fixed term will exclude the right of one partner to dissolve a partnership, but that this right may also be excluded in other ways. Thus, a partnership for an undefined time will not be a partnership at will, if there is an express or implied agreement to exclude the right of a partner to dissolve the partnership. To highlight this fact, it is proposed to use the term 'formal partnership' to distinguish such firms from those partnerships at will (or informal partnerships) which have been informally created and therefore have not excluded the right of a partner to dissolve the partnership by notice. A fixed term partnership may then be considered as a type of formal partnership. Yet, since the majority of formal partnerships are in fact fixed term partnerships, much of the following analysis deals with this particular type of formal partnership and the references to fixed term partnerships should be construed accordingly.

The Nature of a Partnership at Will

[8.06] As noted, a partnership at will is one in which the partners have not varied the default right of a partner under the 1890 Act to dissolve a partnership by notice. Curiously, this right of any one partner to dissolve a partnership at will is set out in two different sections of the 1890 Act, ie s 26(1) and s 32(c). Section 26(1) of the 1890 Act states:

> Where no fixed term has been agreed upon for the duration of a partnership, any partner may determine the partnership at any time on giving notice of his intention so to do to all the other partners.

The margin note to this section describes it rather confusingly as 'Retirement from partnership at will', yet there is no retirement (in the normal sense of this word), but rather a dissolution of a partnership at will.

[8.07] Section 32(c) reads:

> Subject to any agreement between the partners, a partnership is dissolved ...
>
> (c)   If entered into for an undefined time, by the partner giving notice to the other or others of his intention to dissolve the partnership.

[8.08] It is to be noted that s 32(c), but not s 26(1), states that the right to dissolve a partnership at will by giving notice is subject to contrary agreement. However, it is thought that s 26(1) is also subject to a contrary agreement between the parties. This is because it would be senseless if a partner was entitled to exclude his right to dissolve the

---

13   *Walters v Bingham* [1988] 138 NLJ 7 at 8.

partnership by notice under the express terms of s 32, but not under s 26(1). Since there is no significant difference between these sections, and the legislature cannot have intended two sections of the 1890 Act to have completely opposite meanings, it is submitted that both must be interpreted in the same manner. It clearly does less violence to the language of the 1890 Act to interpret the sections as enabling them both to be excluded by agreement of the partners, as the contrary interpretation flies in the face of the express wording of s 32. Furthermore, this conclusion is in keeping with the general tenor of the 1890 Act which favours the parties' agreement overriding the terms of the Act[14] (save in exceptional circumstances)[15] and in particular s 19 of the 1890 Act which allows partners to vary their rights and duties set out in the Act.[16] It would of course be preferable if this apparent inconsistency between the two sections was obviated by having the right to dissolve clearly expressed in one section of the 1890 Act only.

The Nature of a Formal Partnership

[8.09] A partnership which expressly or implicitly excludes the right of a partner to dissolve the partnership at any time is a formal partnership. Most often, this will be done by means of an agreement between the partners that the partnership will last for a fixed term. Where the partners have agreed a term, there will be no power for any one partner to dissolve that formal partnership by notice and the only way to terminate the partnership before the expiry of the fixed term is by all the partners agreeing to the dissolution. Failing this, or a specific power of early dissolution in the agreement, each partner will remain a member of the firm until the end of the term, unless of course he leaves the partnership in breach of his agreement. If a fixed term is not expressly stated in the partnership agreement, it may be inferred from the other terms of the partnership agreement and the circumstances of the case. Accordingly, any provision in a partnership agreement which sets limits to the duration of a partnership may constitute that partnership as a formal partnership.

[8.10] It has already been noted that the right of a partner to dissolve the partnership by notice may also be excluded without the partners agreeing a fixed term.[17] For example a partnership which could be dissolved by 'mutual consent' was held not to be a partnership at will.[18] Such a partnership will be dissolved by the death of one partner and is therefore a partnership for the joint lives of the partners and may be regarded as a type of formal partnership.[19] However, any provision which excludes the right of any one partner to dissolve the partnership by notice renders the partnership a formal

---

14   See for example the Partnership Act 1890, ss 21, 22, 24, 25, 29(1), 30, 32, 33, 42(1), 43, 44.
15   These exceptions are thought to be (i) the right to a true account of partnership dealings under s 28 of the 1890 Act, see para **[21.88]**, and (ii) the right of a former partner to publicly notify the dissolution of the partnership under s 37 of the 1890 Act, see para **[26.07]**. It is argued that both provisions are incapable of exclusion since the former is so basic a right that it goes to the heart of the question of whether there is a real partnership, while the latter right is necessary in order to ensure that former partners are not prevented from eliminating their liability for obligations incurred by their former firms after their departure.
16   See generally in relation to variation, para **[5.14]**.
17   See para **[8.05]**.
18   *Neilson v Mossend Iron Company* (1886) 11 App Cas 298.
19   *Moss v Elphick* [1910] 1 KB 846. See further, regarding a partnership for joint lives not being a partnership at will, *Moore v Moore* [2016] EWHC 2202 (Ch).

partnership, eg, where the partnership is for an undefined time but where it has been agreed that it is subject to dissolution by the notice of two or more partners.

[8.11] In the context of main partnerships and sub-partnerships, it remains to be noted that just because a main partnership is a fixed term partnership does not mean that the sub-partnership[20] will also be a fixed term partnership.[21] Finally, there are some exceptional cases in which a formal partnership may be dissolved ahead of time. Thus, despite the agreement between the parties as to the duration of the agreement,[22] a right to an early determination of a formal partnership remains for repudiatory breach,[23] fraud or misrepresentation and the partnership may be dissolved by court order under s 35 of the 1890 Act.[24]

Formal Partnership or Partnership at Will?

[8.12] Every partnership must be either a formal partnership or a partnership at will. In most partnership disputes, it will be of obvious practical importance to determine whether the partnership is at will or a formal partnership. As noted, the key difference between the two types of partnerships is that a partnership at will may be dissolved by any one partner by giving notice to the other partner(s) at any time.[25] Accordingly, where a partnership either expressly or impliedly excludes this right, it will be a formal partnership. It has been noted that one of the main ways in which this right is excluded is by the partners agreeing to a fixed term for their partnership.

[8.13] In addition there is a presumption that a partnership is a partnership at will and thus terminable at any time by a single partner, unless there is an agreement to the contrary between the partners. In the words of Farwell J: 'the result of a contract of partnership is a partnership at will, unless some agreement to the contrary can be proved.'[26] The burden of proof lies on the party alleging the agreement to the contrary. As noted by Ronan LJ in the Irish Court of Appeal case of *Murphy v Power*,[27] 'the party who alleges an agreement to the contrary is bound to prove it'.[28] Effectively, that party will have to prove the existence of a term which is inconsistent with the right of a partner to dissolve the partnership by notice.[29]

[8.14] Where a partnership is to be terminated by mutual arrangement only, the presumption of a partnership at will is rebutted and the partnership is a formal partnership.[30] On the other hand, the fact that a partnership has entered into a lease for a

---

20 As to sub-partnerships, see para **[8.45]**.
21 *Frost v Moulton* (1856) 21 Beav 596.
22 *Syers v Syers* (1876) 1 AC 174.
23 Although as to the changing English law position in relation to the repudiation of partnership agreements, see para **[23.65]** et seq.
24 See generally in relation to the determination of a partnership on each of these grounds, para **[23.01]** et seq.
25 Partnership Act 1890, ss 26(1) and 32.
26 *Moss v Elphick* [1910] 1 KB 846 at 849 where he was quoting Lord Lindley from Lindley & Tomlin, *Lindley on Partnership* (7th edn, 1905) at p 142.
27 *Murphy v Power* [1923] 1 IR 68.
28 *Murphy v Power* [1923] 1 IR 68 at 75. See also *Burdon v Barkus* (1862) 4 De GF & J 42.
29 For an example of some of these terms, see para **[8.28]** et seq.

fixed term of years or purchased premises in fee simple does not rebut the presumption.[31]

Status of partnership for single adventure or undertaking

[8.15] Section 32(b) of the 1890 Act provides that:

> Subject to any agreement between the partners, a partnership is dissolved ...
>
> (b)   If entered into for a single adventure or undertaking, by the termination of that adventure or undertaking.

A partnership which is for a single adventure or undertaking will not be a partnership at will, since it is incapable of dissolution by the notice of one partner until the adventure or undertaking is completed. For this reason, it is a formal partnership. It may be argued that it should be viewed as a type of fixed term partnership even though no 'term' in the sense of a definite period of time is agreed, but rather the term lasts until the venture is completed.[32]

Fixed Term Partnership becoming a Partnership at Will

[8.16] The majority of formal partnerships will be fixed term partnerships and it is important to note that a fixed term partnership may become a partnership at will in two main ways. First, it may become a partnership at will by the continuation of the partnership after the expiry of the fixed term. In the case of a partnership for a single venture, it may become a partnership at will by its continuation after the end of the venture. Second, it may become a partnership at will by the continuation of the partnership's business after the technical dissolution of the partnership.[33]

Continuation of fixed term partnership after expiry of initial term

[8.17] The most common way in which a fixed term partnership becomes a partnership at will is when the firm's business is continued by the partners after the fixed term expires, without there being any agreement that they will continue for a further fixed term. In *Booth v Parks*[34] the legal effect of a partnership which continued after the expiration of the initial term was described by Hart LC as follows:

> '[A]fter the expiration of the term at first agreed upon, partnerships frequently continue without a new agreement: and the effect of that is, that the partners, after the expiration of the partnership term, continuing to carry on the trade without a new deed, all the old covenants are infused into the new series of transactions; with the single exception of the

---

30   See for example *Moss v Elphick* [1910] 1 KB 465 and on appeal [1910] 1 KB 846.

31   *Burdon v Barkus* (1862) 4 De GF & J 42; *Alcock v Taylor* (1830) Tam 506; *Jefferys v Smith* (1820) 21 RR 175.

32   Note that the current editor of l'Anson Banks, *Lindley & Banks on Partnership* (20th edn, 2017), appears to take a different view at para 24–23. He states that s 27(1), insofar as it applies to partnerships for a fixed term, does not apply directly to partnerships formed to complete a particular transaction since that section only applies to a partnership entered into 'for a fixed term', but he states that it may do so by analogy.

33   As to the distinction between a general and a technical dissolution of a partnership, see para **[23.07]**.

34   *Booth v Parks* (1828) 1 Mol 465.

covenant for duration; for either may instanter dissolve the prolonged partnership, but all the other original stipulations are continued.'[35]

[8.18] Thus, in the absence of any agreement as to the duration of the new partnership, it continues as a partnership at will. There is a statutory presumption that the fixed term partnership continues as a partnership at will which is now contained in s 27(1) of the 1890 Act. However, it is important to note that it is not correct to say, as Hart LC did, that 'all the other original stipulations' of the fixed term partnership continue. As shall be noted hereunder, these original stipulations may, in the words of s 27(1), be inconsistent with a partnership at will, in which case they will not survive.

Care when dealing with the continuation of a fixed term partnership

[8.19] The continuation of a fixed term partnership is an area in which considerable caution should be exercised. This is because it is often wrongly assumed that when a fixed term partnership continues after its term, the new partnership will be treated as a partnership which has been renewed for another term, as happens in the case of the overholding of leases.[36] However, the law of partnership applies different principles than those which apply to leases and a fixed term partnership which continues after its term will become a partnership at will and therefore terminable at any time by notice of any partner.

Section 27 of the 1890 Act

[8.20] Section 27 of the 1890 Act now governs the position of a fixed term partnership which continues after the expiry of its fixed term. It provides that:

(1) Where a partnership entered into for a fixed term is continued after the term has expired, and without any express new agreement, the rights and duties of the partners remain the same as they were at the expiration of the term, so far as is consistent with the incidents of a partnership at will.

(2) A continuance of the business by the partners or such of them as habitually acted therein during the term, without any settlement or liquidation of the partnership affairs, is presumed to be a continuance of the partnership.

While subsection (1) of s 27 provides that a continuation of the partnership leads to it being deemed a partnership at will, subsection (2) is a statutory presumption that there is such a continuation of the partnership between persons who continue in business together after the expiry of the fixed term, without a settlement of the firm's affairs.

[8.21] However this is subject to there being no 'express new agreement' between the partners. An express new agreement will not be deemed to come into being where a draft deed of partnership has been prepared by the parties, but not executed,[37] although the position may be different if it can be demonstrated that the partners have conducted

---

[35] *Booth v Parks* (1828) 1 Mol 465 at 466.

[36] The same mistaken assumption is often made that on the admission of a new partner to a fixed term partnership, a fixed term partnership continues without his agreement to be bound by that term. See para **[8.25]**.

[37] *Firth v Armslake* (1964) 108 SJ 198 (in which the new partnership agreement had not been signed because agreement had not been reached on certain key terms regarding seniority and holidays). (contd.../)

themselves in accordance with the terms of the new, unsigned, partnership agreement and not indicated their dissatisfaction with the terms of that draft following negotiations.

Section 27 applies to partnerships for a single venture

[8.22] By its express terms, s 27(1) deals with fixed term partnerships. It has been seen[38] that a partnership for a single adventure or undertaking may be regarded as a type of fixed term partnership. Thus, if such a partnership is continued after the joint adventure is concluded, it will also result in the formation of a partnership at will. Such a partnership will be subject to the same rights and duties as applied to the original partnership for a single adventure, so far as they are consistent with a partnership at will.

Technical dissolution of a formal partnership

[8.23] While the primary way in which a formal partnership becomes a partnership at will is on the expiry of the fixed term, it may also occur on the technical dissolution of a formal partnership. Since a partnership is not a separate legal entity, but an aggregate of all of its members, it follows that any change in its membership terminates the existing firm and creates a new firm. However, where the newly constituted firm continues the pre-existing partnership business, this is known as a technical dissolution. In contrast, a general dissolution involves the winding up of the firm's business.[39]

[8.24] In the case of a technical dissolution, the 'new' partnership that comes into being, like all partnerships, is presumed, in the absence of contrary agreement, to be a partnership at will.[40] Thus in *Cuffe v Murtagh*,[41] there was a partnership between six partners to carry on a flour milling business in Dublin and Athlone for a fixed term of seven years. Before the end of the seven years, two of the partners died. The death of the partners was not contemplated by the terms of the partnership agreement and the partnership business continued as before the deaths thus leading to a technical, rather than a general, dissolution of the partnership. Since the partnership agreement had not contemplated the continuation of the fixed term partnership after the death of any of the partners, the presumption that the new partnership was a partnership at will applied and, accordingly, it was held by Chatterton VC that a partnership at will came into existence on the death of the partners.

Addition of new partners to a formal partnership

[8.25] A change in the membership of a firm (and thus a technical dissolution) will occur on the admission of a new partner, as well as on the departure or death of a partner. For this reason, particular care should be taken with the admission of a new partner to a formal partnership. This is because if the new partner does not expressly

---

37 (\...contd) See also *King v Chuck* (1853) 17 Beav 325 (in which the new articles of partnership were not finalised as one partner had declined the proposal of the co-partner that the co-partner's son enter into the agreement in the co-partner's place).

38 See para **[8.15]**.

39 See further regarding the difference between a technical and a general dissolution, para **[23.07]**.

40 See para **[8.13]**.

41 *Cuffe v Murtagh* (1881) 7 LR Ir 411.

agree to enter into a formal or 'fixed term' partnership agreement with the existing partners (or has impliedly agreed to do so by his conduct), then the very act of admitting him will lead to the technical dissolution of the pre-existing partnership and the new partnership will be assumed to be a partnership at will.[42] In the case of a fixed term partnership, the duration of the 'new' partnership will no longer be fixed and instead the partnership may be dissolved by the notice of any one partner. This point is vividly illustrated by *Firth v Armslake*.[43] There, two doctors had a formal partnership agreement whereunder they agreed to carry on in partnership for their joint lives. They subsequently introduced a third doctor to the firm and a new partnership agreement was drawn up, but it was never executed by them. After a short period in partnership with the third doctor, the two original doctors sought to dissolve the partnership. In the English High Court, Plowman J held that the new partnership which had been created between the three was a partnership at will, since no agreement had been reached as to its duration. For this reason, it was held that it was validly dissolved by the two original doctors.

Principle in s 27 applies to business continued after technical dissolution

[8.26] By its express terms, s 27(1) of the 1890 Act only applies to the first method in which a formal partnership becomes a partnership at will, ie where the formal partnership continues after its term has expired. However, it is thought that the principle contained in s 27(1) is equally applicable to the second way in which a formal partnership becomes a partnership at will, ie a partnership which is technically dissolved (by a change in membership) continues its business after that dissolution.[44] Similarly, it is thought that the concept of an agreement to the contrary ('without any express new agreement') in s 27(1) applies to a formal partnership which is technically dissolved as it does to a fixed term partnership which continues after its term. Therefore, a formal partnership will not become a partnership at will if the original partnership agreement contemplates the technical dissolution by the departure of a partner, eg where the partnership agreement provides that the formal partnership will continue between the surviving partners notwithstanding the death of a partner. Similarly, the formal partnership will not become a partnership at will if the new partner expressly or impliedly agrees to be bound by the terms of the formal partnership. If he does not, then the 'new' partnership is a partnership at will and is subject only to those terms which are consistent with a partnership at will.[45] This is clear from *Cuffe v Murtagh*,[46] in which Chatterton VC noted:

---

[42] The current editor of *Lindley & Banks on Partnership* states that there is a second requirement for such a partnership to be converted into a partnership at will, ie that the fixed term partnership agreement must not contemplate the admission of further partners, see l'Anson Banks, *Lindley & Banks on Partnership* (20th edn, 2017) at para 9-14. However, it is conceived that, even where the partnership agreement contemplates the admission of new partners, where a new partner is admitted and he does not agree to be bound by the terms of the agreement, a 'new' partnership is created and none of the clauses in the original formal partnership agreement will automatically apply.

[43] *Firth v Armslake* (1964) 108 SJ 198.

[44] *Austen v Boys* (1857) 24 Beav 598 (aff'd (1858) 2 De G & J 626).

'The death of a partner effected in law a dissolution ... The partnership thenceforth carried on *de facto* was accordingly one at will, but subject to all the terms and conditions which by the deed of 1862, regulated the preceding partnership, so far as they were not inapplicable to a partnership at will.'[47]

Knowledge of partners irrelevant to existence of a partnership at will

[8.27] *Cuffe v Murtagh*[48] also highlights the fact that, in determining whether a partnership at will has come into existence, it is irrelevant that the partners themselves may believe that a formal partnership is still in existence. In that case, after the death of the two partners in the firm, the remaining four partners drew up an agreement which assumed that the fixed term partnership of seven years was still in existence and would see out its term. However, it was held that, at the time of the execution of this agreement, the partners were partners at will since their formal partnership had been dissolved on the death of the first partner. Chatterton VC noted:

'The death of a partner effected in law a dissolution ... The partnership thenceforth carried on *de facto* was accordingly one at will ... It appears, however, that the surviving partners did not look upon the partnership of 1862 as dissolved, but, on the contrary they regarded it as subsisting for the residue of the term of seven years ... This was a mistake on their parts.'[49]

Consistency of Clauses with a Partnership at Will

[8.28] Those clauses which have been held to be consistent and inconsistent with a partnership at will are now to be considered. This issue will be relevant first when determining whether a firm is or is not a partnership at will. Thus a partnership which excludes the power of one partner to dissolve the partnership by notice will not be a partnership at will but a formal partnership. The issue is also relevant in the context of a fixed term partnership which continues after its fixed term as a partnership at will or any other situation in which a formal partnership becomes a partnership at will. In particular, it will be necessary to consider which of the terms of the fixed term partnership are inconsistent with a partnership at will and are therefore not carried over into that partnership. However, in this latter respect, a word of caution should be observed before proceeding with this analysis. As noted by Molony CJ in the Irish Court of Appeal case of *Murphy v Power*,[50] only limited benefit is obtained from examining previous cases:

---

[45] The present position in England seems to be different, ie none of the terms of the original formal partnership apply to the new partnership at will, but instead the terms of the 1890 Act apply: *Firth v Armslake* (1964) 108 SJ 198, but note that in that case the incoming partner and the existing partners had negotiated a new agreement (which had not been perfected or signed) to replace the agreement between the existing partners. See also *Cheema v Jones* [2017] EWCA Civ 1706 in which Asplin LJ found that, in negotiating a new partnership agreement between two existing partners and three incoming partners, no reference had been made to the original agreement, and there was no evidence that the incoming partners had seen the final form of the original agreement. As such, the new partners were not bound by the terms of the original agreement.

[46] *Cuffe v Murtagh* (1881) 7 LR Ir 411.

[47] *Cuffe v Murtagh* (1881) 7 LR Ir 411 at 420.

[48] *Cuffe v Murtagh* (1881) 7 LR Ir 411.

[49] *Cuffe v Murtagh* (1881) 7 LR Ir 411 at 420.

'It is not at all necessary to examine into the particular cases in which it has been held that a particular term of a written contract did or did not go into the new unwritten contract, because every case has turned upon its own particular circumstances and upon the question as applied to the words of the particular instrument whether the old was or was not applicable to the new contract.'[51]

Clauses inconsistent with a partnership at will

[8.29] In this section, consideration will be given to clauses which are inconsistent with a partnership at will and therefore tend to indicate that the partnership is not at will. In addition, where a fixed term partnership is continued after the expiry of its term or a formal partnership otherwise becomes a partnership at will, such a clause will not survive.

Duration clause is inconsistent with a partnership at will

[8.30] As noted by Hart LC in *Booth v Parks*,[52] the covenant for duration is clearly inconsistent with a partnership at will and does not survive the change into a partnership at will. Instead, as has been noted, the partnership at will is for an indefinite term which may be brought to an end by the giving of notice by any one partner.[53]

Manner of dissolution of partnership is inconsistent with partnership at will

[8.31] Since the very basis of a partnership at will is that it may be dissolved by notice of a partner, it follows that clauses which govern the manner in which a partnership is to be dissolved so as to restrict this right have been held to be inconsistent with a partnership at will.[54] Thus, it has been held that a clause that the partnership should be dissolved if one partner assigned or mortgaged his share did not survive into the partnership at will.[55] However, clauses which simply deal with the position of the parties after the dissolution are not inconsistent with a partnership at will.

Other clauses which apply for a fixed number of years

[8.32] It may occur in a formal partnership that clauses, other than the duration clause, refer to the firm's duration. For example in *Murphy v Power*[56] the partnership agreement had a duration clause which provided that the partnership would last for 10 years, but the agreement also provided for the possibility of the purchase of one partner's share during 'the said period of ten years'. The partnership continued after the 10-year term and the issue arose as to whether this latter term was consistent with a partnership at will and so continued after the 10-year period. In the Irish Court of Appeal, Ronan LJ held that while the right to purchase a partner's share might survive into the partnership at will, if it had been expressed to apply 'during the term of the partnership', there was no case in

---

50   *Murphy v Power* [1923] 1 IR 68 at 72.
51   Quoting the words of Lord Selborne in *Neilson v The Mossend Iron Co* (1886) 11 App Cas 298 at 303.
52   *Booth v Parks* (1828) 1 Mol 465.
53   See para **[8.03]**.
54   *Campbell v Campbell* (1893) 6 R 137; *Neilson v Mossend Iron Co* (1886) 11 App Cas 298.
55   *Campbell v Campbell* (1893) 6 R 137.
56   *Murphy v Power* [1923] 1 IR 68.

which the terms of a fixed term partnership were held to apply to a subsequent partnership at will 'where a clause such as that in question is expressly limited to years numbered'. [57]

Where one alternative no longer exists

[8.33] *Murphy v Power*[58] is also authority for the principle that a clause which grants two alternatives will not be carried over into a partnership at will, where one of those alternatives is inconsistent with the partnership at will. The facts of that case were that John and Thomas Power entered a partnership agreement in which they agreed to carry on a grocery, wine and spirit business in Clonmel for a period of 10 years. The partnership agreement provided that in the event of Thomas predeceasing John, John should be entitled to purchase the share of Thomas or be entitled to have Thomas's share in the business continue for the 'remainder of the said period of ten years' without any interference from the personal representatives of Thomas. After the expiration of the 10-year term, both parties continued to carry on the business without any reference to a new term, and the partnership thus went from being a fixed term partnership to a partnership at will. It was admitted that the provision requiring Thomas's share of the partnership assets to be continued in the business for the 'remainder of the ten years' was only applicable during the 10 years and was not carried over into the partnership at will. However, it was claimed that John was entitled to exercise the alternative option, namely to purchase Thomas's share after the 10-year period. It has already been noted that the Irish Court of Appeal held that the right to purchase Thomas's share did not survive the partnership at will.[59] However, a second reason for not allowing John's claim was Molony CJ's holding that where, as in this case, alternative rights are given and one of those alternatives is inapplicable to a partnership at will by efflux of time, one cannot claim the benefit of the other alternative. He stated:

> 'I can find no authority for the proposition that when alternative rights are given to a person, and one of these alternatives is obviously inapplicable to a partnership at will, the person is entitled to claim the benefit of the other, when it was obviously the intention of the framers of the instrument that there should be two alternatives and the right to choose between them.'[60]

Expulsion clause is inconsistent with a partnership at will

[8.34] A power to expel a partner is clearly inconsistent with a partnership which may be dissolved by notice of any partner. As explained by Westbury LC in *Clark v Leach*:[61]

> 'there is good reason ... for holding that this particular stipulation in the written agreement is gone after the expiration of the term, from the fact that the new contract being for no

---

57   *Murphy v Power* [1923] 1 IR 68 at 76.
58   *Murphy v Power* [1923] 1 IR 68.
59   Paragraph **[8.32]**.
60   *Murphy v Power* [1923] 1 IR 68 at 73–74.
61   *Clark v Leach* (1863) 1 De GJ & SM 409. Cf the obiter comments of Browne-Wilkinson VC in *Walters v Bingham* [1988] 138 NLJ 7 that an expulsion clause is consistent with a partnership at will, which are, correctly it is submitted, disapproved of in l'Anson Banks, *Lindley & Banks on Partnership* (20th edn, 2017) at para 10-29.

specified time, but determinable at the will of either party, the power to determine the partnership is not wanted.'[62]

Clauses consistent with a partnership at will

[8.35] Consideration is now given to those clauses which are consistent with a finding that a partnership is a partnership at will. In addition, these clauses will survive the change in a formal partnership to a partnership at will.

Clause which refers to events happening 'during term' of partnership

[8.36] Clauses which refer to events happening during the term of a partnership are consistent with a partnership at will. In *Cuffe v Murtagh*,[63] Chatterton VC held that the expression 'during the continuance of the said partnership'[64] which had been used in the formal partnership did not prevent the clause in question from continuing to apply to the subsequent partnership at will. Similarly in *Murphy v Power*,[65] Ronan LJ referring to the rule that a provision of a fixed term partnership will apply to a subsequent partnership at will, observed that this rule applies to clauses which use the words 'during the term or during the partnership'.[66]

Right of pre-emption

[8.37] The right of the partners to acquire an outgoing or deceased partner's share can survive the expiration of a fixed term partnership.[67] In *Murphy v Power*[68] Molony CJ observed obiter that:

> 'an option to purchase the share of a deceased partner is applicable to the partnership at will constituted by the carrying on of the business without fresh articles after the expiration of the partnership term.'[69]

Option to nominate another person as partner

[8.38] The decision in *Cuffe v Murtagh*[70] is authority for the principle that the right to nominate a partner still applies where a partnership continues after the expiry of its fixed term. In that case, the fixed term partnership contained a clause which entitled a partner to nominate a person to succeed him on his death and to take his share in the

---

[62] *Clark v Leach* (1863) 1 De GJ & SM 409 at 415.
[63] *Cuffe v Murtagh* (1881) 7 LR Ir 411.
[64] He relied expressly on *Essex v Essex* (1855) 20 Beav 442.
[65] *Murphy v Power* [1923] 1 IR 68.
[66] *Murphy v Power* [1923] 1 IR 68 at 76.
[67] *Neilson v Mossend Iron Co* (1886) 11 App Cas 298, which was approved by Ronan LJ in *Murphy v Power* [1923] 1 IR 68; *Daw v Herring* [1892] 1 Ch 284; *Brooks v Brooks* (1901) 85 LT 453.
[68] *Murphy v Power* [1923] 1 IR 68.
[69] *Murphy v Power* [1923] 1 IR 68 at 72. This statement was obiter since on the facts of the case the right of pre-emption was inapplicable to the partnership at will, see para **[8.32]**. As authority for this principle, Molony CJ relied on *Cox v Willoughby* (1880) 13 Ch D 863; *Daw v Herring* [1892] 1 Ch 284; *Brooks v Brooks* (1901) 85 LTR 453; *McGown v Henderson* [1914] SC 839.
[70] *Cuffe v Murtagh* (1881) 7 LR Ir 411.

partnership. When the partnership became a partnership at will, Chatterton VC held that this clause continued since:

> 'I can see nothing insensible or repugnant in such a clause if inserted in a deed establishing a partnership at will. It amounts to this, and no more, that one partner may put a substitute for himself into the firm, who will have just the same rights as he would have had if he had continued a partner.'[71]

[8.39] Similarly, in *Murphy v Power*[72] the partnership agreement contained a clause which provided that if John Power pre-deceased Thomas Power, John would be entitled to grant his interest in the partnership to some other person.[73] Molony CJ noted obiter that it 'has been held in *Cuffe v Murtagh*[74] that a right to nominate a partner continued after the term of the partnership had expired',[75] and on this basis he held that this provision was not repugnant to a partnership at will.

Option to appoint a substitute for that nominee

[8.40] Under the terms of the fixed term partnership agreement in *Cuffe v Murtagh*,[76] a partner was entitled to appoint a person to succeed him in the firm, such nomination not to take effect until the nominee was 21. One of the deceased partners in that case appointed one of his nephews as his successor and another nephew as a substitute, in the event of his first nominee dying. It was held that the power to appoint a substitute nominee was implicit in the power to appoint a nominee and that this power was also applicable to the partnership at will which came into being.

Arbitration clause

[8.41] An arbitration clause has been held to be consistent with a partnership at will and thus survives into that partnership.[77]

Clauses dealing with post-dissolution matters

[8.42] It would seem to be particularly consistent with a partnership at will for it to have a clause governing the manner in which the partnership is to be wound up, since such a partnership may be dissolved at any time by any one partner without the consent of the others. On this basis, one may conclude that it is not in any way inconsistent with a partnership at will to provide how the partnership is to be wound up after it has been dissolved.[78]

---

71   *Cuffe v Murtagh* (1881) 7 LR Ir 411 at 422.
72   *Murphy v Power* [1923] 1 IR 68.
73   Failing such an appointment, Thomas was to be entitled to purchase John's share. Unlike the clause relating to Thomas dying first, as to which see para **[8.33]**, this clause did not have the right to compel John's share of the firm's assets to continue in the partnership for the remainder of the fixed term.
74   *Cuffe v Murtagh* (1881) 7 LR Ir 411.
75   *Murphy v Power* [1923] 1 IR 68 at 73.
76   *Cuffe v Murtagh* (1881) 7 LR Ir 411.
77   *Cope v Cope* (1885) 52 LT 607; *Gillet v Thornton* (1875) 44 LJ Ch 398.
78   See for example *Essex v Essex* (1855) 20 Beav 442.

II. PARTNERSHIP BY DEED, BY AGREEMENT OR ORALLY

[8.43] While strictly not a separate category of partnership, it should be observed that partnerships which are constituted by deed will not be treated any differently from other partnerships which are constituted by written or oral agreements. This is apparent from *Bolton v Carmichael*.[79] There, it was claimed that a partnership constituted by deed, unlike other partnerships, could not be dissolved by the conduct of the parties. However, Lord Chancellor Brady rejected this argument, holding that such a partnership was capable of being dissolved by the actions of one of the partners.

[8.44] It sometimes occurs that professional partnerships draw up a written partnership agreement, but do not sign it. There is little to be gained from this practice but uncertainty and a consequent increased likelihood of litigation in the event of a dispute between the partners. Clearly the partners in such a case have an oral partnership agreement, but there will exist a considerable doubt about the terms thereof. In the event of a dispute, a court may determine that some, and possibly all, of the terms of the draft agreement are incorporated into the oral partnership even though the agreement was never executed. Equally, the fact that the agreement was not signed may be taken as evidence of the fact the parties did not wish those terms to govern their relationship. This will lead to the unhappy situation in which the terms of the 1890 Act will apply unfettered to the partnership in question.[80] Any persons involved in such arrangements should be aware of the risks attached to it.

III. SUB-PARTNERSHIP

[8.45] A sub-partnership is a partnership within a partnership. This type of partnership arises where at least one member of a partnership (the main partnership) has a partnership with a third party to share the profits of the main partnership and so is in partnership with that third party (the sub-partnership). However, this type of arrangement is not that common today and indeed some professional partnerships will expressly prohibit the members from entering a sub-partnership with a third party. A sub-partnership may also be created where a partner in a main partnership purports to introduce a third party to the main partnership, without the authority of the partners in the main partnership. Instead of the third party becoming a partner in the main partnership, what may result is a sub-partnership between that partner and the third party.

[8.46] In sub-partnerships, the partner in the main partnership and the third party are partners inter se, but the third party is not a partner in the main partnership.[81] This is because of the principle that the 'partner of my partner is not my partner'.[82] Rather, for the third party to become a partner in the main partnership he must be admitted thereto with the consent of all the partners in that firm.[83] Thus, A, B, C and D may be partners in

---

[79]   *Bolton v Carmichael* (1856) 1 Ir Jur (ns) 298.

[80]   As to the unsuitability of these terms for modern partnerships, see further para **[21.01]** et seq.

[81]   *Bray v Fromant* (1821) 6 Madd 5; *Ex p Dodgson* (1830) Mont & M 445.

[82]   See the Roman law principle of *socius meisocii meus socius non est*: para 91 of Pothier, *Traité du Contrat du Société*. See also *Ex p Barrow* (1815) 2 Rose 255, *per* Lord Eldon.

[83]   Partnership Act 1890, s 24(7). See generally in relation to the admission of new partners, para **[13.22]**.

the main partnership and D may also have agreed to share the profits of the main partnership with E and thereby formed a sub-partnership of the main partnership. By virtue of this sub-partnership, E does not become a partner of A, B or C. E will be indirectly sharing the profits of the main partnership with A, B and C and this is prima facie evidence of partnership. However, it is noted elsewhere in this work that the sharing of the profits of a firm does not of itself make that person a partner.[84] As he is not a partner in the main partnership, E will not be liable for the losses of the main partnership.[85] Of course, indirectly, he may end up sharing these losses with D under the terms of the sub-partnership agreement.

[8.47] Despite the similarity between the two partnerships, the terms of the main partnership are not incorporated by implication into the terms of the sub-partnership, nor is the duration of the sub-partnership deemed to be the same as that of the main partnership.[86]

Partnership Agreement may Require Modification

[8.48] The provisions of the 1890 Act will apply to a sub-partnership as they do to any other type of partnership. Of course, the partners in a sub-partnership may, and should, provide by agreement for the modification of the general law to take account of the special circumstances of a sub-partnership. For example it may be appropriate for the sub-partnership agreement to reflect many of the terms of the main partnership agreement and for the sub-partnership to terminate on the termination of the main partnership agreement.

IV. GROUP PARTNERSHIP

[8.49] It has been noted earlier in this work that a partnership may exist between two or more firms.[87] The partnership so formed is termed a group partnership. In contrast to a sub-partnership, a group partnership is a partnership between two or more firms. Thus, where A and B are partners in a firm called X, and C and D are partners in a firm called Y, a partnership between the firms X and Y would be a group partnership. Unlike a sub-partnership, the members of all of the constituent firms, A, B, C and D are partners inter se (as neither firm X nor firm Y has separate legal personality) and a group partnership is treated the same way as any other partnership. Group partnerships may arise unintentionally, eg, where two or more firms begin to carry on business together without forming a company or drafting a partnership agreement to establish the terms of the venture. Since the two separate firms are carrying on business together with a view to profit,[88] they are in partnership.

[8.50] The existence of a group partnership was first recognised by the Irish courts in *McCalmont v Chaine*.[89] There, a group of Irish based consignees were being sued by a

---

84 See the Partnership Act 1890, s 2(3) and generally para **[2.95]** et seq.
85 See the Scottish case of *Fairholm v Marjoribanks* (1725) Mor 14558 and the Australian case of *Australia and New Zealand Banking Group v Richardson* [1980] Qd R 321.
86 *Frost v Moulton* (1856) 21 Beav 596.
87 See para **[2.36]**.
88 As required by the Partnership Act 1890, s 1(1), and see further para **[2.01]** et seq.
89 *McCalmont v Chaine* (1835) 3 Law Rec (ns) 215.

partner in a London firm which carried on business with a Mexican firm. The consignees used to ship goods for the London firm to the Mexican firm. The London firm consisted of McCalmont and Inglis, while the Mexican firm consisted of McCalmont, Inglis and Graves. In their defence, the consignees claimed that the two firms shared in the profits of the sale of the goods consigned and were in fact a group partnership and therefore the partners in the Mexican firm should have been joined as co-plaintiffs in the action.[90] The Irish Court of Common Pleas left the question of whether a group partnership existed to be decided by the jury.

Application of Registration of Business Names Act 1963

[8.51] There is no prohibition under the Registration of Business Names Act 1963[91] on two or more firms operating under the same business name. Therefore, the constituent firms of a group partnership, X and Y and the group partnership itself, X & Y may operate under the same business name, in which case they should each make a separate filing under that Act.

Application of s 1435(1) of Companies Act 2014

[8.52] Since the members of all of the constituent firms of a group partnership are partners inter se, care should be taken to ensure that any partnership between two or more firms does not contravene s 1435(1) of the Companies Act 2014. It will do so if the aggregate number of partners in the constituent firms exceeds 20.[92] This restriction on size does not apply to firms of solicitors where each partner is a solicitor,[93] firms of accountants where each partner is a statutory auditor,[94] limited partnerships formed for the purposes of thoroughbred horse breeding,[95] or limited partnerships with fifty members or less and formed for the purpose of providing investment and loan finance together with ancillary facilities and services to persons engaged in industrial or commercial activities.[96] Such partnerships may therefore form group partnerships without having regard to the restriction in s 1435(1). Both limited partnerships and investment limited partnerships are exempt from the 20 member limit set out in s 1435(1) by virtue of the fact that they are each 'formed in pursuance of some other statute,[97] however, s 4(2) of the Limited Partnerships Act 1907 restricts the number of partners in a limited partnership to 20 (this will be subject to the carve-outs at

---

[90] Note that it is no longer a requirement for all the partners in a firm to be named as plaintiffs, see para **[12.11]**.

[91] See generally in relation to the application of the Registration of Business Names Act 1963 to partnerships, para **[3.70]** et seq.

[92] See further on the restriction on the size of partnerships, para **[4.29]** et seq.

[93] Companies Act 2014, s 1435(1)(c)(i).

[94] Companies Act 2014, s 1435(1)(c)(ii).

[95] Companies Act 2014, s 1435(1)(c)(iii).

[96] Companies Act 2014, s 1435(1)(c)(iv).

[97] Companies Act 2014, s 1425(1)(b) (the Limited Partnerships Act 1907 and the Investment Limited Partnerships Act 1994 respectively). It remains to be seen whether further exemptions will be introduced in respect of legal partnerships, multi-disciplinary practices, and limited liability partnerships when these business models become available to the legal community in Ireland under the Legal Services Regulation Act 2015.

s 1435(1)(c)(iii) and (iv)) (or to ten in the case of a limited partnership carrying on banking business). There is no maximum number of partners for an investment limited partnership.[98]

Right of Partner in Constituent Firm to Manage Group Partnership

[8.53] As has been seen,[99] a group partnership is treated in the same way as any other partnership. Therefore, each partner in the constituent firm, as a partner in the group partnership, will be entitled to take part in the management of the group partnership.[100] In many cases, this will be too cumbersome and the group partnership agreement may instead provide for a committee consisting of partners from the constituent firms to manage the group partnership. This system is often used by group partnerships which have constituent firms throughout the country. Another alternative is for a bloc vote system, where each constituent firm is given one vote in the group partnership.

Modification of Partnership Agreement

[8.54] The provisions of the 1890 Act will apply to a group partnership as they do to any other type of partnership. Of course, the partners may, and should, provide by agreement for the modification of the general law to take account of the special circumstances of a group partnership. In addition to the management structure, which has already been referred to,[101] the partnership agreement might deal with such issues as:

- the automatic expulsion or retirement of the partners in a constituent firm, from the group partnership, when the constituent firm ceases to be a member of the group partnership;
- the manner in which the goodwill and assets of the constituent firms and those of the group partnership are to be owned, whether by the group partnership or the constituent firms or both;
- the terms upon which a constituent firm is expelled from the group partnership;
- the expulsion of a partner from a constituent firm leading to his automatic expulsion from the group partnership;
- the terms upon which the group partnership may use the assets of a constituent firm;
- the terms upon which a constituent firm may retire from the group partnership.

V. PARALLEL PARTNERSHIP

[8.55] A parallel partnership is a partnership which is run in parallel to another firm, but, unlike a group partnership, the members of the constituent firms remain separate and are not partners inter se. Where there is a sufficient distinction between the operations of the constituent firms, they will be regarded as operating as a parallel partnership, rather than as a group partnership.

---

[98] See para **[29.41]**.
[99] See para **[8.49]**.
[100] Partnership Act 1890, s 24(5) (assuming there is no contrary agreement between the partners), see generally para **[13.01]** et seq.
[101] See para **[8.53]**.

[8.56] Parallel partnerships were common in Ireland in the 1970s and 1980s as a means for large accountancy firms to avoid the prohibition in s 376 of the Companies Act 1963 (the predecessor to s 1435(1) of the Companies Act 2014) on firms having more than 20 partners.[102]

[8.57] The situation operated as follows: where an accountancy firm wished to admit more partners (which admission would make the number of partners in the firm exceed 20) it instead formed two partnerships which operated in parallel. Since the members of the constituent firms were not in partnership with each other, and assuming each constituent firm had less than 20 partners, the terms of s 376 of the Companies Act 1963 were not contravened. The partners in the separate firms were treated in practice as if they were partners in the same firm – this was achieved by providing for payments to be made by one partnership to the other in the form of an administration charge or management fee, and by the use of cross indemnities and the provision of services between the firms.[103] However, the need for such partnerships in the accountancy and legal professions was eliminated by the enactment of s 13 of the Companies (Amendment) Act 1982 which disapplied the 20-member restriction in s 376 of the 1963 Act to partnerships of accountants and partnerships of solicitors. Section 13 of the 1982 Act was then carried over into s 1435(1)(c) of the Companies Act 2014, and its scope expanded.[104] In Great Britain, the 20-member limit (in so far as it still applied) was removed in its entirety by the Regulatory Reform (Reform of 20 Member Limit in Partnerships etc) Order 2002 (SI 2002/3203) with effect from 21 December 2002 and later in Northern Ireland by The Partnerships etc (Removal of Twenty Member Limit) (Northern Ireland) Order 2003.

[8.58] Today, firms that do not benefit from an exemption from the limit on members under s 1345(1) of the Companies Act 2014 may have to consider using parallel partnerships as a possible means of overcoming the prohibition on partnerships of more than 20 persons. In addition, parallel partnerships might be considered in order to overcome a prohibition on partnerships between professionals and unqualified persons.[105] This might be achieved by having the unqualified person(s) in a parallel partnership with the main partnership. However in either case, it will not be an easy matter to ensure that that the parallel firms are sufficiently well defined to avoid them being held to be a partnership of two firms and thus a group partnership. The practice in the 1970s and 80s amongst the accountancy firms did not receive judicial scrutiny.

---

[102] As to this prohibition see para **[4.29]**. See generally Vollans, 'Parallel Partnerships' (1997) Professional Practice Management 86.

[103] These arrangements were never tested in the courts and it is queried whether they actually achieved their aim. This is because it is arguable that these parallel partnerships failed to eliminate the fact that more than twenty persons were de facto carrying on business in common with a view to profit, thus satisfying the definition of partnership in the 1890 Act, s 1(1).

[104] See generally in relation to the Companies Act 1963, s 376, the Companies (Amendment) Act 1982, s 13 and the Companies Act 2014, s 1345(1), para **[4.29]** et seq.

[105] To the extent that multi-disciplinary practices are introduced as a business model in Ireland under the Legal Service Regulation Act 2015, a parallel partnership may no longer be needed in certain cases however, at the time of writing, it is doubtful that multi-disciplinary practices will be introduced in Ireland in the near future, see para **[30.71]**.

However, were a parallel partnership to be subject to such scrutiny today, it is submitted that an Irish court would examine very closely not simply the documentation establishing the parallel partnerships, but more importantly the de facto relationship between the two partnerships and the individual partners, to determine whether there is a group partnership in existence.

VI. FIRMS WITH PARTNERS IN COMMON

[8.59] There is nothing to prevent a person from being a partner in more than one firm. Indeed the Rules of the Superior Courts envisage such a situation by providing that the leave of the court shall be required for the issue of an execution between firms with one or more members in common.[106] Firms which have partners in common may raise difficult issues, particularly for professionals, such as accountants and solicitors. For example say there are two firms, A and B, with one partner, C, in common. If firm A acts on one side of a transaction, while firm B acts on the other side of the transaction, C who is common to both firms will owe all of the partners in A and all of the partners in B a fiduciary duty and may be required to notify his partners in A of information which he has learned as a result of being a partner in B, or vice-versa. Similarly, he may be imputed with notice of some matter in firm B, as a result of his being a partner therein, and this may impact upon the discharge of his duties in firm A.[107]

VII. CORPORATE PARTNERSHIP

[8.60] The term corporate partnership refers to a partnership where some or all of the members are companies, whether limited or unlimited companies. It has been noted elsewhere in this work, that a partnership may consist of corporate partners since a company may be a 'person' for the purposes of the definition of partnership in s 1(1) of the 1890 Act and therefore may be a partner.[108] Indeed, corporate partnerships have been given statutory recognition[109] and have also been recognised by the courts.[110] Such partnerships have the advantage that they may be formed without formality and, for the corporate partners themselves, they have the advantage of being tax transparent.[111] A corporate partnership will commonly arise between companies which undertake a business venture together, without forming a separate joint venture company for that purpose and therefore such 'joint ventures' between companies will in fact be corporate partnerships.

---

106   Rules of the Superior Courts, Ord 14, r 10.
107   Note that under the 1890 Act, s 16, notice to a partner in a firm is taken as notice to all of the partners. See further in relation to the difficulties of a common partner in this context, para **[10.128]**.
108   See para **[2.35]** et seq.
109   For example the European Communities (Accounts) Regulations 1993 which apply, inter alia, to partnerships whose members are companies with limited liability.
110   For example *MacCarthaigh v Daly* [1985] IR 73, in which O'Hanlon J held that a partnership, in which one of its members was a limited company, was a valid partnership.
111   See further in relation to the tax transparency of partnerships, para **[3.18]**.

Corporate Partnership between Single Member Companies

[8.61] Under the Companies Act 2014, it is possible to form a private or a public company limited by shares with just one member. There is no reason in principle why a corporate partnership cannot be created between two single member companies which are owned by the same person. In this way, a de facto partnership of just one person is created, although the partnership is *de jure* between two legal entities.

Entering Partnership must be Intra Vires Corporate Partner

[8.62] Unlike an individual, a corporate partner is subject to the doctrine of ultra vires unless that corporate partner is a 'private company limited by shares'[112] which, by virtue of s 38 of the Companies Act 2014, is not required to have an objects clause by virtue of it being deemed to have full and unlimited corporate capacity.[113] Save in the case of such a 'private company limited by shares', it will be necessary to establish that the company has the corporate capacity to become a partner.[114] It is conceived that this should be relatively easy to establish in most cases, in view of the wide-ranging nature of modern day objects clauses.[115]

Use of Corporate Partner to Facilitate Large Partnerships

[8.63] The prohibition on partnerships of more than 20 partners in s 1435(1) of the Companies Act 2014 has been referred to already.[116] This prohibition may be circumvented by using a corporate partner, ie, by some of the partners becoming shareholders in a company which would itself constitute only one member of the firm for the purposes of s 1435(1) of the 2014 Act. However, the shareholders in the company would of course have the disadvantage of being one step removed from the firm.

---

112 As defined in the Companies Act 2014, s 2(1).

113 As to the doctrine of ultra vires generally, see Hutchinson, *Keane on Company Law* (5th edn, 2016) at para [12.20] et seq; Courtney, *The Law of Companies* (4th edn, 2016), para [7.003] et seq and para [30.047] et seq. As to the changes introduced by the Companies Act 2014 to the doctrine of ultra vires, see Courtney, *Bloomsbury Professional's Guide to the Companies Act 2014* (2015) at para [5.002] et seq; Forde and Kennedy, *Company Law* (5th edn, 2017) at para 4-27 et seq.

114 An interesting issue might arise under company law in the case of a company and its director becoming members of a partnership. In the event of a loan by a third party to the partnership, the argument could be made that because of the joint liability of partners for the debts of the firm, the company is effectively guaranteeing the director's obligation in contravention of the Companies Act 2014, s 239. However, it is thought that interpreting the term '*enter into a guarantee or provide any security*' in s 239 in this manner would only be justified if the partnership was entered into with the purpose of avoiding its provisions and not where the company and partner happen to also be in partnership in relation to a separate business venture. To the extent that any doubt arises, the 2014 Act, s 242 provides for a validation procedure which can be carried out by the company.

115 See for example the English case of *Newstead v Frost* [1980] 1 All ER 363, and see generally, para [4.16].

116 See para [4.29] et seq.

Modification of Partnership Agreement

[8.64] The provisions of the 1890 Act apply to a corporate partnership as they do to any other type of partnership. Of course, the partners may, and should, provide by agreement for certain provisions of the 1890 Act to be adapted in their application to corporate partners, eg, those sections of the Act which refer to the death or bankruptcy of a partner. This issue is discussed in detail elsewhere in this work.[117]

Charge on Corporate Partnership's Assets

[8.65] Section 409 of the Companies Act 2014 provides that certain charges which are created by a company are void, unless their particulars are delivered to the Registrar of Companies within 21 days of their creation.[118] Since s 409 refers expressly to a charge created by a company, it might at first seem that this section does not apply to a charge which is created by a corporate partnership over its assets, even where the partnership is composed entirely of companies. However, this view overlooks the crucial fact that a partnership is not a separate legal entity.[119] Thus, any charge which is given by a partnership will be given by the partners jointly and it is suggested that to be valid, it will have to comply with s 409 of the 2014 Act in the case of a corporate partner.

Accounts of Corporate Partnerships

[8.66] Certain corporate partnerships will be obliged to prepare and file accounts, namely those corporate partnerships where the members of the partnership which have unlimited liability, are themselves companies limited by shares or guarantee.[120] This obligation is contained in the European Communities (Accounts) Regulations 1993,[121] which require such corporate partnerships to prepare a profit and loss account,[122] a

---

117 See para **[21.23]**.

118 See s 408(1) of the Companies Act 2014 for the list of exceptions from the obligation to register particulars of a charge pursuant to s 409(1).

119 See generally para **[3.04]**. For this reason, it is impractical for partnerships to grant floating charges since a floating charge created by a partnership over '*personal chattels*' (within the meaning of the Bills of Sale (Ireland) Acts 1879–1883) will, unlike a floating charge created by a company, be a '*bill of sale*' and must therefore be registered within seven clear days of its execution to ensure that it is a valid security. However, some assets are excluded by the Bills of Sale Acts, ie interests in land, shares or interests in the stock, funds or securities of a government or an incorporated company, or choses in action, ships (under the Mercantile Marine Act 1955) and agricultural machines, stock and crops (under the Agricultural Credit Act 1978). See generally Courtney, *The Law of Companies* (4th edn, 2016) at para [4.093].

120 Or where the members of such corporate partnerships are themselves corporate partnerships so described.

121 SI 396/1993, implementing Directive 90/605/EC. Regulation 7 thereof applies the Companies (Amendment) Act 1986 (dealing with the accounts of public and private companies) to these partnerships as though they were companies. The Companies (Amendment) Act 1986 was repealed by the Companies Act 2014 and its provisions were incorporated (with some amendments) into Part 6 and Schedule 3 of the Companies Act 2014 and therefore those provisions apply to such a partnership in the same way as they do to a limited liability company.

122 European Communities (Accounts) Regulations 1993, reg 12(1).

balance sheet[123] and a partners' report[124] and to have an auditor's report prepared.[125] Subject to the provisions of the Companies Act 2014 regarding small companies,[126] each of these documents must be filed in the Companies Registration Office by the corporate partnership.

VIII. QUASI-PARTNERSHIP

[8.67] This section examines the quasi-partnership.[127] As the name suggests, a quasi-partnership is not in fact a partnership.

Meaning of a Quasi-Partnership

[8.68] Section 1(2)(a) of the 1890 Act provides that the relationship between members of a company is not a partnership.[128] Yet this has not meant that the courts will not apply partnership principles to the relationship between certain shareholders. As noted by Barron J in *Irish Press plc v Ingersoll*:[129]

'Where there are equal shareholdings in a company and where the reality is that the shareholders have entered into a partnership the Court will where necessary apply the principles of the Law of Partnership.'[130]

While a technical definition for the term 'quasi-partnership' does not exist, it may be described as a legal entity which is not a partnership in legal form, but is a partnership in substance. Charleton J, in *In the matter of Dublin Cinema Group*[131] stated that a quasi-partnership could exist in a company whose:

'... background is two or more friends, two or more family members, two or more business partners operating together through a limited liability or other corporate vehicle for the purpose of carrying on their business ...'.

---

123 European Communities (Accounts) Regulations 1993, reg 12(2).
124 European Communities (Accounts) Regulations 1993, reg 14.
125 European Communities (Accounts) Regulations 1993, reg 20.
126 See ss 358 and 360 of the Companies Act 2014 (as substituted by s 51 of the Companies (Accounting) Act 2017) which give an audit exemption to 'small companies'. See para **[14.64]**.
127 Courtney, *The Law of Companies* (4th edn, 2016) at para [11.036] et seq; Forde and Kennedy, *Company Law* (5th edn, 2017) at paras 11-81, 11-95 and 11-109-11.114; Hannigan, 'Section 459 of the Companies Act 1985 - a code of conduct for the quasi-partnership' [1988] Lloyd's Maritime & Commercial Law Quarterly 60; Prentice, 'The theory of the firm; minority shareholder oppression; sections 459–461 of the Companies Act 1985' (1988) 8 Oxford Journal of Legal Studies 55; Rider, 'Partnership law and its impact on 'Domestic Companies'' (1979) 38 Camb LJ 148; Fitzpatrick, 'Re Westbourne Galleries' [1971] 22 NILQ 60.
128 See further para **[2.29]**.
129 *Irish Press plc v Ingersoll* (15 December 1993) HC.
130 *Irish Press plc v Ingersoll* (15 December 1993) HC at p 70 of the transcript.
131 *In the matter of Dublin Cinema Group* [2013] IEHC 147.

For these reasons, principles of partnership law have been applied by the courts to such entities.[132]

The rationale for the quasi-partnership concept

[8.69] Company law, and particularly company legislation, is directed towards the classic corporate model which, under the Companies Act 2014 and its predecessor, the Companies Act 1963, involves the separation of the ownership of a company from its management. In this model, the owners (the shareholders) appoint managers (the directors) to run the company's business. In contrast, the partnership model is one in which there is no such separation of powers since the owners (the partners) of the firm are also its managers. The principles of partnership law which apply to firms reflect this fact, while company law principles reflect the separation of powers. Into this arena comes a company which, from a separation of powers perspective, more closely resembles the partnership model than the classic corporate model. This company is owned and managed by the same people, since the directors and shareholders are one and the same. Indeed, in many cases, such companies begin their lives as partnerships and choose to become companies solely to have 'a vehicle to secure a limited liability for possible losses'.[133] The rationale therefore in applying partnership law principles to such companies is that this accords with the reality of their existence, if not their appearance.

A quasi-partnership is not a partnership by holding out

[8.70] It should be noted that the quasi-partnership concept only came into common use in the late twentieth century[134] and therefore should not be confused with the nineteenth century use of that term[135] to describe a partnership by holding out.[136]

---

132 In *O'Connor v Atlantis Seafood Wexford Ltd & Ors* [2017] IEHC 589, Mrs O'Connor had not specifically pleaded that the respondent company was a quasi-partnership, but Keane J observed that there was a 'tenable' argument that this was an argument of law (which would not need to be pleaded) rather than a material fact, which would need to be pleaded. He did not, however, rule on the point.

133 Per Gannon J in *Re Murph's Restaurants* [1979] ILRM 141 at 150. See also *Ebrahimi v Westbourne Galleries* [1973] AC 360, where Mr Ebrahimi and Mr Nazar were originally partners and then incorporated their business.

134 The seminal quasi-partnership case is *Re Yenidje Tobacco Co Ltd* [1916] 2 Ch 426, but the principles enunciated therein only surfaced with regularity in the latter half of the twentieth century, ie *Re Expanded Plugs Ltd* [1966] 1 All ER 877; *Re K/9 Meat Supplies (Guildford) Ltd* [1966] 1 WLR 1112 and *Re Fildes Bros Ltd* [1970] 1 WLR 592. But note that in the Irish Queen's Bench case of *Forrester v Bell* (1847) 10 Ir LR 555, it was conceded by counsel for the defendant that a member of a provisional committee for a joint-stock company (which was never registered) was in fact a quasi-partner.

135 The term 'quasi-partnership' is used to mean a partnership by holding out in Scotland: see Brough, *Miller on Partnership* (2nd edn, 1994) at pp 54–57. This was also the meaning which for many years was used in Lord Lindley's textbook, eg Salt & Francis, *Lindley on Partnership* (11th edn, 1950), at p 4.

136 The concept of a partner by holding out is considered in detail at para **[7.01]** et seq.

Characteristics of a Quasi-Partnership

[8.71] Since there is no technical definition of a quasi-partnership, it is important to analyse the cases in which legal entities have been classified as quasi-partnerships so as to isolate their characteristics. In this way, one can more easily predict whether, in a particular case, the courts will apply the principles of partnership law to that entity. In considering these characteristics, it will be apparent that it is not necessary to have all of them, though obviously, the less that an entity has, the less likely that it will be treated as a quasi-partnership. However, it is not necessarily an easy matter to show that these characteristics are present so as to apply partnership law to an entity which was intended to be governed by company law. This is clear from the judgment of Murphy J in the High Court case of *Crindle Investments v Wymes*:[137]

> 'the presumption must be that parties who elect to have their relationship governed by corporate structures rather than, say, a partnership intend their duties – and where appropriate their rights and remedies – to be governed by the legal provisions relating to such structures and not otherwise. It would require, in my view, reasonably clear evidence to impose obligations on directors or shareholders above and beyond those prescribed by legislation or identified by long established legal principles.'[138]

[8.72] The characteristics which have been accepted as sufficient evidence of a quasi-partnership will next be considered.

Restricted to private companies?

[8.73] A quasi-partnership has been defined by legal commentators as applying exclusively to private companies.[139] In one sense, this is not surprising as the cases to date have dealt almost exclusively with such companies.[140] However, there would appear to be no reason in principle to restrict the application of this concept to private companies. Once the entity in question is in substance a partnership, it is suggested that the court may apply partnership law principles to it. Thus, a public company which has two controlling shareholders (and several minor shareholders) might be deemed to be a quasi-partnership between the controlling shareholders especially where these two shareholders are also directors of the company. Indeed, in *Irish Press plc v Ingersoll*,[141] a company, albeit a private company, with two shareholders was held to be a quasi-partnership, even though one of the two shareholders was a plc.[142] However, in the case of a listed public company with a large number of shareholders, it is highly unlikely that an argument as to the existence of a quasi-partnership could be successfully maintained.

---

137 *Crindle Investments v Wymes* (27 March 1997) HC, upheld on appeal to the Supreme Court, [1998] 2 ILRM 275.

138 *Crindle Investments v Wymes* (27 March 1997) HC at p 11 of the transcript.

139 See the definition in Fox and Bowen, *The Law of Private Companies* (1995) at p 187.

140 See, however, *Re A Company* [1986] BCLC 376, where an unquoted plc was involved in the case and the court favoured a finding of quasi-partnership between the owners of a private company (which was taken over by the plc) and the plc.

141 *Irish Press plc v Ingersoll* (15 December 1993) HC.

142 It is not, however, suggested that a company which is publicly quoted on the stock exchange would have the requisite relationship between the shareholders to be a quasi-partnership.

In *Connemara Minings Company plc & Companies Acts*,[143] Laffoy J commented that the concept of a quasi-partnership could not apply in the case of the holder of a 6.23% shareholding in a public listed company with over four hundred shareholders.

[8.74] Nonetheless, the key cases to date have involved private companies, the analysis which follows necessarily concentrates on those companies. However, this should not be seen as restricting in any way the scope of the principles discussed.

Type of shareholdings of the quasi-partners

[8.75] *Irish Press plc v Ingersoll*[144] also considered the type of shareholding in a company which gives rise to a quasi-partnership. In the High Court, Barron J stated that a quasi-partnership arises where 'there are equal shareholdings in a company and where the reality is that the shareholders have entered into a partnership'.[145] Despite the fact that Barron J restricted his description of quasi-partnerships to companies with equal shareholdings, it is apprehended that he did not intend this to be an all-inclusive description of quasi-partnerships. While equality of control is common in ordinary partnerships, it is not a requirement and therefore it is submitted that it should not be a requirement of quasi-partnership.[146] Support for this view is to be found in the English High Court case of *Re Bird Precision Bellows Ltd*,[147] where Nourse J observed that:

'The proposition ... that there can only be a quasi-partnership in a case where all the shareholders make similar contributions to the company is supportable neither on authority nor in principle.'[148]

[8.76] Another common characteristic of quasi-partnerships relates to the number of quasi-partners. Thus, the companies which have been found to be quasi-partnerships commonly have had only two shareholders.[149] However, just as it is possible to have an ordinary partnership with more than two partners, it is suggested that it is also possible to have a quasi-partnership with more than two quasi-partners. This was the case in *Re Murph's Restaurant Ltd*,[150] where, as will be noted hereunder,[151] the quasi-partnership in that case consisted of three shareholders in a private company.

---

143 *Connemara Minings Company plc & Companies Acts* [2013] IEHC 225.
144 *Irish Press plc v Ingersoll* (15 December 1993) HC.
145 *Irish Press plc v Ingersoll* (15 December 1993) HC at p 70 of the transcript.
146 While in *Horgan v Murray* [1999] IEHC 65, no quasi-partnership was found to exist, the fact that two of the shareholders had a 30% shareholding each and the third had a 40% shareholding was not the reason why no quasi-partnership was found to exist. See generally Glennon, 'The Residual Nature of the Minority Shareholder Remedy' (2000) 7 CLP 14.
147 *Re Bird Precision Bellows Ltd* [1984] 1 Ch 419. The line of authority on valuing minority shareholdings in quasi-partnership companies is predicated on a shareholder being able to have a minority, rather than an equal, interest in a quasi-partnership. See, further, para **[8.103]** below.
148 *Re Bird Precision Bellows Ltd* [1984] 1 Ch 419 at 433.
149 For example in *Irish Press plc v Ingersoll* (15 December 1993) HC. See also *Re Vehicle Buildings* [1986] ILRM 239.
150 *Re Murph's Restaurant* [1979] ILRM 141. See generally in relation to this case Ussher, 'Company Law – Oppression, Justice and Equity' (1979–80) DULJ 92.
151 Paragraph **[8.93]**.

Ownership and management of the company in the same people

[8.77] Perhaps the most important characteristic of quasi-partnership is that the ownership and management of the company are vested in the same people. This follows from the very rationale for the concept of quasi-partnership, ie applying partnership principles to companies which resemble the partnership model of both management and ownership being vested in the same people.[152] Indeed the classic quasi-partnership model is one in which all the quasi-partners are the sole shareholders and the sole directors of the company.[153] *Re Murph's Restaurant Ltd*[154] is one such case and there, Gannon J held that the company in that case should be treated as a quasi-partnership as it was, inter alia, 'a business in which all three [shareholders] engaged on the basis that all should participate in its direction and management'.[155]

[8.78] However, ownership and management of the company by the same people can be achieved even where there are other shareholders and other directors, provided that these other shareholders are minor shareholders[156] and the other directors are in a minority on the board.[157] Thus, a company which does not fully comply with the classic quasi-partnership model may still constitute a quasi-partnership, though clearly the closer one keeps to this model, the more likely this will be the case.[158] On the other hand, as one moves further away from the classic partnership model of control and management, a

---

152 The right of every partner to participate in the management of the firm is an important factor in most partnerships. This is because each partner is liable to an unlimited degree for the debts of the firm, so it follows that each partner is granted the right to participate in the firm's management: Partnership Act 1890, s 24(5). However, this right may be excluded by agreement, see generally para **[13.01]** et seq.

153 Eg *Re Vehicle Buildings* [1986] ILRM 239.

154 *Re Murph's Restaurant Ltd* [1979] ILRM 141.

155 *Re Murph's Restaurant Ltd* [1979] ILRM 141 at 155.

156 At a very minimum, the other shareholders in respect of whom a quasi-partnership is not being claimed should not have 25% or more of the shares in the company, but even shareholdings below this percentage may be such as to enable the holders thereof to exert too great an influence for the company to be viewed as being in reality a partnership. In *Fowler v Gruber* [2010] 1 BCLC 563, Lord Menzies formed the view that the three founding shareholders of Completion Products Limited (friends who had worked together for a number of years) had formed a company that was also a quasi-partnership, however, the sale by one of those shareholders of one-quarter of his shareholding to a third party, and the acquisition of further shares in the company by Aberdeen City Council, served to add two minority shareholders to the company, with the result that it ceased to be a quasi-partnership. Between them, those two minority shareholders only held 14.28% of the company's issued share capital. However, as they held their shares on a normal commercial basis, and as Lord Menzies saw no evidence that any agreement between the founding shareholders had been explained to or agreed to by the new minority shareholders, he found that the company had ceased to be a quasi-partnership.

157 It is, however, conceivable that the controlling shareholders might not have a *de jure* majority on the board but a de facto majority by virtue of the use of shadow directors.

158 In *Horgan v Murray* [1999] IEHC 65, a quasi-partnership was alleged to exist between three people who were the sole shareholders in the company and who, together with others, were the directors. While O'Sullivan J found that no quasi-partnership existed, the fact that there were other directors was not determinative.

court is less likely to hold that a quasi-partnership exists. The High Court case of *Feighery v Feighery*[159] concerned the relationship between the 10 shareholders in SIAC Construction Ltd. The 10 shareholders were the sole members of the company, but only two of the 10 were also on the board of directors of the company and they were in a significant minority on the board. This clearly militated against a finding of quasi-partnership between the 10.[160]

[8.79] Thus, it will be rare that a company will be held to be a quasi-partnership unless all the relevant shareholders are also directors or shadow directors of the company.[161] However, conceptually, it is not possible to state that a company will never be a quasi-partnership unless all of the shareholders in question are directors or shadow directors. This is because in an ordinary partnership, one may have a dormant partner,[162] and so it could be argued that a company may be a quasi-partnership where one or more of the shareholders does not take an active part in its management.

Equality, mutuality, trust and confidence is necessary

[8.80] An important characteristic for alleged quasi-partners is the presence between them of a relationship of 'equality, mutuality, trust and confidence'.[163] Without this element having at one time existed between the shareholders, it seems that the company will not be treated as a quasi-partnership. It is to be noted that 'equality' in this sense does not refer to an equality of control,[164] but to non-discriminatory treatment.

[8.81] It might be argued that the existence of such a relationship between the alleged quasi-partners should not be a requirement for quasi-partnership. This argument goes that an ordinary partnership can technically exist even where the parties never had confidence or trust in each other and therefore a quasi-partnership should be treated as existing even where this is absent. However, it is clear that an ordinary partnership without trust between the partners is both highly undesirable and unlikely to occur in view of the power of each partner to bind his co-partner to an unlimited degree.[165] Moreover, such a firm is likely to have a very limited future and be subject to claims that the partners have breached their fiduciary duties to each other.[166] It is therefore apprehended that a court will only ignore the legal form of a company and treat it as a quasi-partnership where the company is, or was at one time, akin to an ordinary

---

[159] *Feighery v Feighery* [1999] 1 IR 321.
[160] Note however that Laffoy J rejected the petitioner's application for a purchase order for shares under s 205 of the Companies Act 1963 (now s 212 of the Companies Act 2014) without ruling on whether the company was a quasi-partnership or not.
[161] As to the meaning of a shadow director, see the Companies Act 2014, s 221. See generally in relation to shadow directors, Courtney, *The Law of Companies* (4th edn, 2016) at para [13.065] et seq.
[162] As to dormant partners generally, see para **[6.04]**.
[163] Per Gannon J in *Re Murph's Restaurant Ltd* [1979] ILRM 141 at 151.
[164] Since equality of control is not a requirement for quasi-partnership, para **[8.75]**.
[165] As to the unlimited liability of a partner for the acts of his co-partner, see generally, para **[11.04]**.
[166] See generally in relation to fiduciary duties, para **[15.01]** et seq.

partnership, in the sense of having the requisite 'equality, mutuality, trust and confidence' between the members.

[8.82] The importance of the presence of 'equality, mutuality, trust and confidence' between the quasi-partners has been recognised by the High Court in *Re Murph's Restaurant Ltd*.[167] There, Gannon J expressly adopted the judgment of Lord Cross in the English case of *Ebrahimi v Westbourne Galleries Ltd*[168] that:

> 'People do not become partners unless they have confidence in one another and it is of the essence of the relationship that mutual confidence is maintained ... The relationship between Mr Rothman and Mr Weinberg was not, of course, in form that of partners: they were equal shareholders in a limited company. But the court considered that it would be unduly fettered by matters of form if it did not deal with the situation as it would have dealt with it had the parties been partners in form as well as in substance.'[169]

[8.83] Having recognised the importance of the quasi-partners having confidence in each other, Gannon J went on to hold that the breach of that confidence by two of the three quasi-partners in Murph's Restaurant Ltd justified him in ordering a winding up of the company. On the facts of that case, two of the quasi-partners sought to remove the third from his position as a director of the company and this was held to constitute a:

> 'deliberate and calculated repudiation by both of them of that relationship of equality, mutuality, trust and confidence between the three of them which constituted the very essence of the existence of the company.'[170]

The Supreme Court recognised the quasi-partnership doctrine in *McGilligan v O'Grady*[171] where Keane J observed:

> 'It is undoubtedly the case that, if there is a relationship between shareholders in a company indicating a degree of mutual confidence and trust, the court may order the winding up of the company on the just and equitable ground where one or more of the shareholders and/or directors exercise their powers in a manner which is inconsistent with that relationship. Specifically, this may arise where the right of the shareholders to participate in the management of the company is infringed, as for example by the removal of a director. These principles were laid down in *Ebrahimi v Westbourne Galleries* [1973] AC 360 and were adopted in this jurisdiction by Gannon J in *Re Murph's Restaurants Ltd* [1979] ILRM 141 at 144.'[172]

Where company provides livelihood

[8.84] While it is not necessary for the parties to be earning their livelihood from the venture for it to be a quasi-partnership, it is to be noted that a common characteristic of many quasi-partnership cases is that the companies are in fact vehicles through which the parties earn a livelihood. Indeed, this factor is undoubtedly important in the court's decision to depart from the company law rules and instead apply those rules which apply

---

[167] *Re Murph's Restaurant Ltd* [1979] ILRM 141. See generally regarding this case, Ussher, 'Company Law - Oppression, Justice and Equity' (1979–80) DULJ 92.

[168] *Ebrahimi v Westbourne Galleries Ltd* [1973] AC 360.

[169] *Ebrahimi v Westbourne Galleries Ltd* [1973] AC 360 at 383.

[170] *Re Murph's Restaurants Ltd* [1979] ILRM 141 at 151.

[171] *McGilligan v O'Grady* [1999] 1 ILRM 303.

[172] *McGilligan v O'Grady* [1999] 1 ILRM 303 at 343–44.

to partnerships. The fact that the directors/shareholders also earn their livelihood by working for the company arguably brings a company closer to the classic partnership model of management and control being vested in the same people. Thus in *Re Murph's Restaurant Ltd*,[173] Gannon J held that it was significant that by ceasing to be a director, the petitioner would have been deprived 'of a livelihood, and not simply of an investment'.[174] In contrast, in the High Court case of *Feighery v Feighery*,[175] the fact that of the ten shareholders in SIAC Construction Ltd, only two (including the petitioner) were employees of the company may have militated against a finding of quasi-partnership.[176]

Consequence of Treatment as a Quasi-Partnership

[8.85] Having considered the situations in which the courts have found that companies are quasi-partnerships,[177] it is now appropriate to examine the consequences of such a finding. The whole *raison d'être* for the concept of quasi-partnerships is to apply principles of partnership law to non-partnerships. Therefore, this is the primary consequence of the finding that a company is a quasi-partnership and in *Re Vehicle Buildings*,[178] Murphy J held that the company in question was a quasi-partnership and that 'in companies such as exist in the instant case it is appropriate to apply the analogy of partnership law'.[179] In *Neenan Travel Ltd v Minister for Social and Family Affairs*,[180] Laffoy J referenced Courtney's *Law of Companies*[181] when noting that the consequences of a finding of quasi-partnership are the entitlement of the quasi-partners to participate in the company's management, the expectation of each quasi-partner that their quasi-partners will act in good faith, and the entitlement of a quasi-partner to object to any fundamental change in the company's business activities.

[8.86] The remainder of this section is concerned with the principles of partnership law which have been applied to quasi-partnerships. In general terms, resort will be made to partnership law to prevent the otherwise lawful exercise of a right by the shareholders or

---

173 *Re Murph's Restaurants Ltd* [1979] ILRM 141.
174 *Re Murph's Restaurants Ltd* [1979] ILRM 141 at 151.
175 *Feighery v Feighery* [1999] 1 IR 321.
176 Note, however, that Laffoy J rejected the petitioner's application for a purchase order for shares under s 205 of the Companies Act 1963 (now s 212 of the Companies Act 2014) without ruling on whether the company was a quasi-partnership or not. In *Con Davis v Sean Walshe v and Plynth Limited t/a Dew Wholesale* [2003] 14 ELR 1, Murphy J commented that issues of quasi-partnership do not appear to arise in the context of employment by a company.
177 See also *Dublin Laundry Co Ltd v Clarke* [1988] ILRM 29, where the defendant engaged in the development of land with another person through limited liability companies. Costello J noted that it was the defendant's intention that he would undertake the venture 'in partnership with Mr Anglin through the medium of a company', though nothing turned on this point.
178 *Re Vehicle Buildings* [1986] ILRM 239.
179 *Re Vehicle Buildings* [1986] ILRM 239 at 241. He expressly relied on the seminal English decision on quasi-partnerships, *Re Yenidje Tobacco Co Ltd* [1916] 2 Ch 426, as authority for this proposition.
180 *Neenan Travel Ltd v Minister for Social and Family Affairs* [2011] IEHC 458.
181 Laffoy J quoted from Courtney, *The Law of Private Companies* (2nd edn, 2002) at para [1.131] (now at Courtney, *The Law of Companies* (4th edn, 2016) at para [11.040]).

directors in a company under the articles of association or company law. The exercise of this right (eg the right of the shareholders to remove a shareholder/director from his position as a director of the company)[182] may be challenged on the basis that while appropriate in a company, it is not appropriate where the person is a quasi-partner.

[8.87] Before examining these partnership law principles which have been applied to quasi-partnerships, the difficult decision of Laffoy J in *Feighery v Feighery*[183] must be considered since it challenges the notion that the doctrine of quasi-partnership allows a partner restrict a statutory power. In that case, the petitioner was one of 10 shareholders in a large construction company. The company had a turnover of over £60 million. The board of directors of the company consisted of a number of prominent non-executive directors and only two of the shareholders were directors of the company and they were in a significant minority on the board. In view of this clear distinction between the ownership and management of the company, the company in question was much closer in nature to a publicly quoted company than a partnership. Attempts were underway by the respondent shareholders to remove the petitioner as a director and he responded by seeking an order under s 205 of the Companies Act 1963[184] for his shares to be purchased by the respondent shareholders or for the respondents' shares to be purchased by him on the grounds that the company was a quasi-partnership and it was not open to the respondents to remove him as a director. Despite the clear distinction between the management and ownership of the company in this case, Laffoy J chose to assume that the company was a quasi-partnership. She then based her decision to dismiss the petition on the fact that the right of a quasi-partner was restricted to obtaining a winding-up order and did not extend to preventing or restricting a statutory power, which in this case was the statutory power to remove a director.[185] In order to support this rather broad principle that a quasi-partner is not entitled to interfere with a statutory right, Laffoy J relied on the decision in *Re Murph's Restaurant Ltd*.[186] However, it should be noted that although a winding-up order was granted in that case, this was the relief that was sought by the petitioner and neither the judgment of Gannon J nor of McWilliam J[187] supports the principle that quasi-partners are restricted to relief in the form of a winding-up order. While a winding-up order is the form of relief which is commonly granted in quasi-

---

182 See for example *Re Murph's Restaurant Ltd* [1979] ILRM 141. Cf *Feighery v Feighery* [1999] 1 IR 321 where the removal was allowed to go ahead.

183 *Feighery v Feighery* [1999] 1 IR 321.

184 Now s 212 of the Companies Act 2014.

185 Under s 182 of the Companies Act 1963 (now s 146 of the Companies Act 2014).

186 *Re Murph's Restaurant Ltd* [1979] ILRM 141. She also relied on the English High Court case of *Bentley-Stevens v Jones* [1974] 1 WLR 638 in which Plowman J held that there was nothing in the case of *Ebrahimi v Westbourne Galleries* [1973] AC 360 'which suggests that the plaintiff is entitled to an injunction to interfere with the defendant's statutory right to remove the plaintiff from its board'. Yet there have been a number of English cases which do not support such a restrictive view of quasi-partners' rights, see, for example, *Re a Company* [1986] BCLC 376 where Hoffmann J held that those who risk their capital in a private company may have legitimate expectations that they will not be deprived of their directorships or management rights in the company. See also *Re a Company (No 00330 of 1992) ex p Holden* [1991] BCC 241 in which Harman J granted an injunction restraining directors from activating a compulsory share transfer provision in the articles.

187 In the preliminary proceedings reported at [1979] ILRM 142.

partnership cases, it is another matter to restrict quasi-partners to such relief and it is contended that this is too broad a restriction on the form of relief which may be granted by the courts in true quasi-partnership cases. It is suggested that Laffoy J might not have enunciated such a principle if she had been faced with a true quasi-partnership rather than the company in that case which was more akin to a quasi-quoted company than a quasi-partnership.[188] Accordingly, one might seek to depart from Laffoy J's decision on the basis that her comments are obiter. It is clear that the petitioner in that case was not entitled to restrict the shareholders' rights to remove him as a director but this, it is submitted, was because the company was not a quasi-partnership and not because a quasi-partner is not entitled to restrict the statutory powers of a company in appropriate cases. Therefore, it is contended that Laffoy J's principle is without real authority and if adopted would severely restrict the very *raison d'être* for the doctrine of quasi-partnership which after all is to apply partnership law principles to statutory powers of companies which are in substance partnerships and where appropriate to restrict those statutory powers.[189] For the foregoing reason, one should welcome the implicit criticism of Laffoy J's decision in the Supreme Court case of *McGilligan v O'Grady*.[190] There Keane J stated that *Feighery v Feighery* and *Bentley v Jones*[191] (which had been relied upon by Laffoy J) should not be followed insofar as they suggested that an interlocutory injunction should not be granted to restrain a company from removing a director pending the hearing of a petition under s 205 of the Companies Act 1963.[192]

[8.88] Reference will next be made to the rights of quasi-partners which have been recognised by the courts. Since quasi-partnerships are those companies which are owned and managed more like the classic partnership model than the classic corporate model, it follows that many of the following partnership principles relate to the management of the company by quasi-partners.

Entitled to management participation

[8.89] One of the most basic rights of a partner in an ordinary partnership is the right under s 24(5) of the 1890 Act to take part in the management of the partnership business.[193] This principle is applied to quasi-partnerships, so that once a company has been deemed to be a quasi-partnership, each of the quasi-partners may not normally be denied the right to take part in the management of the firm. The importance of this right

---

[188] *Feighery v Feighery* [1999] 1 IR 321.
[189] See for example the English High Court case of *Re A Company* [1986] BCLC 376 where Hoffmann J held that the petitioner had an arguable case to prevent his removal as a director. See generally Bowen, *Fox and Bowen on The Law of Private Companies* (2nd edn, 1995) at p 187 et seq.
[190] *McGilligan v O'Grady* [1999] ILRM 303.
[191] *Bentley v Jones* [1974] 1 WLR 638.
[192] Now s 212 of the Companies Act 2014. In *McGilligan v O'Grady* [1999] 1 ILRM 303, the Supreme Court upheld an injunction restraining the defendant from removing the plaintiff as a director of Premier International Trading House Ltd. In particular, Keane J distinguished *Feighery v Feighery*, above on the basis that in that case the plaintiff relied on the understanding with his family members that he would remain as a director while in *McGilligan v O'Grady*, the plaintiff was to remain as a director of Premier International Trading House Ltd under the terms of an agreement between the investors in Premier International Trading House Ltd and the company itself.

in quasi-partnerships was recognised in *Re Murph's Restaurant Ltd*,[194] where Gannon J quoted Lord Wilberforce's description of this right as 'an obligation so basic that, if broken, the conclusion must be that the association must be dissolved'.[195] In that case, Gannon J observed that two of the three directors/shareholders in the company treated the third as an employee, by making:

> 'it clear that they did not regard [him] as a partner but simply as an employee. Their refusal to recognise any status of equality amounted to a repudiation of their relationship on which the existence of the company was founded'.[196]

On this basis, he held that the third director/shareholder was entitled to a winding up order of the company.[197]

Veto on change in business

[8.90] Another partnership principle which has been applied to quasi-partnerships is the right of a partner under s 24(8) of the 1890 Act to veto any change in the nature of the partnership business. The application of this right to quasi-partnerships has been recognised in Australia. In *Re Tivoli Freeholds*[198] a company was formed to run theatres. Subsequently, the company got involved in financially successful take-over raids on other companies. This activity was intra vires the company, yet the Supreme Court of Victoria held that the company should be wound-up in the light of the distinct interests of the founders, whose interest was not just purely financial but also somewhat vocational in character, since the company was formed for the purpose of running theatres.

---

[193] This right may be waived by the partners. See generally in relation to the management rights of partners, para **[13.01]** et seq. See also Clark, 'Unfair prejudice and the corporate quasi-partnership' (1989) 10 Company Lawyer 153.

[194] *Re Murph's Restaurant Ltd* [1979] ILRM 141.

[195] *Ebrahimi v Westbourne Galleries Ltd* [1973] 2 AC 360 at 380.

[196] *Re Murph's Restaurant Ltd* [1979] ILRM 141 at 155.

[197] *Horgan v Murray* [1999] IEHC 65 was another quasi-partnership case which was concerned with the right of a partner to management participation. Mr Horgan, Mr Milton and Mr Murray were the sole shareholders in Murray Consultants Limited, a well-known public relations company. They were also three (but not all) of the directors of the company. Mr Horgan claimed that notwithstanding that there were other directors, all business decisions were taken only with the agreement and consensus of the three, who held regular 'partners' meetings' between themselves. When Milton and Murray sought to replace Horgan with Murray as the managing director of the company and to fundamentally change the way in which the company was run, Horgan sought a number of declarations, including one that he was in partnership with Milton and Murray in Murray Consultants Limited. O'Sullivan J could find no basis for a finding that there was a partnership relationship between the three which was 'separate and anterior to their relationship as common shareholding members' in Murray Consultants Limited. Quoting from the decision of Murphy J in *Crindle Investments v Wymes* (27 March 1997), upheld on appeal to the Supreme Court, [1998] 2 ILRM 275*)*, he held that Murray Consultants Limited had been 'conceived and consciously promoted' as a company, and he saw no clear evidence that additional rights or obligations, beyond those arising as a matter of company law, were contemplated.

[198] *Re Tivoli Freeholds* [1972] VR 445.

Duty of good faith

[8.91] A partnership right which has been implicitly applied to quasi-partnerships is the duty of good faith.[199] This occurred in *Irish Press plc v Ingersoll*,[200] in which two joint venture companies formed between the Irish Press plc and Ingersoll were held to be quasi-partnerships.[201] The formation of the companies was based on the representations of Ingersoll to the Irish Press that it was a considerable organisation, from which personnel would be available to assist the two joint venture companies. This turned out not to be the case as personnel were not made available to the companies. In addition, Ingersoll placed its nominees on the boards of the companies for the purposes of Ingersoll's interests and not the companies. This was held to be evidence of *mala fides* and of the breakdown of trust between the parties. While Barron J did not explicitly rely on partnership law to reach his decision, it is clear that the absence of good faith on the part of Ingersoll was decisive in his decision to order the sale of Ingersoll's shares to the Irish Press.

Right to wind up the business

[8.92] One consequence of treating a company as a quasi-partnership is that it may be wound up on the same grounds upon which a partnership may be dissolved.[202] This can be explained, as it was by McWilliam J in *Re Murph's Restaurant Ltd*,[203] as follows:

> 'in substance, a partnership exists between the three persons carrying on the business of the company together and that, *prima facie*, the petitioner would have been entitled to a dissolution of the partnership if it were a partnership and not a company, and that, accordingly, he has a *bona fide* claim to have the company wound up.'[204]

[8.93] In that case, the quasi-partnership was a company which was owned equally by three men, who were also the sole directors. Two of the men were brothers and the company operated a successful restaurant business with branches in Lower Baggot Street and Suffolk Street in Dublin and also in Cork. The profits of the business were shared equally between them. Relations soured between the three and the two brothers sought to dismiss the third as a director. The latter applied for a court order to wind up the company on just and equitable grounds under s 213 of the Companies Act 1963.[205] Gannon J relied on the circumstances in which a partnership would be dissolved on 'just and equitable' grounds under s 35(f) of the 1890 Act. The reliance on s 35(f) of the 1890

---

199 See generally in relation to the fiduciary duties of partners, para **[15.01]** et seq.
200 *Irish Press plc v Ingersoll* (15 December 1993) HC.
201 *Irish Press plc v Ingersoll* (15 December 1993) HC at p 80 of the transcript, where Barron J noted that the relationship in the two joint venture companies was 'in effect partnership'.
202 In the Supreme Court case of *McGilligan v O'Grady* [1999] 1 ILRM 303 at 308, Barron J observed that '*Ebrahimi v Westbourne Galleries Ltd* [1973] 2 AC 360 and *Re Murph's Restaurant Ltd* [1979] ILRM 141 ... establish that it is just and equitable that a shareholder in a company which is a quasi-partnership should have the same right to dissolution as he or she would have had as a partner in a partnership.'
203 *Re Murph's Restaurant Ltd* [1979] ILRM 141.
204 *Re Murph's Restaurant Ltd* [1979] ILRM 141 at 144, where Gannon J relied on *Re Lundie Bros Ltd* [1965] 1 WLR 1051.
205 Now s 569 of the Companies Act 2014.

Act can in part be explained by the phrase 'just and equitable' which is common to s 213(f) of the Companies Act 1963[206] and s 35(f) of the 1890 Act. Gannon J expressly adopted the explanation which had been put forward by Lord Wilberforce for reliance on partnership law principles:[207]

> 'The same words "just and equitable" appear in the Partnership Act [1890, s 35][208] as a ground for dissolution of a partnership and no doubt the considerations which they reflect formed part of the common law of partnership before its codification. The importance of this is to provide a bridge between cases under s [213 of the Companies Act 1963] and the principles of equity developed in relation to partnerships.'[209]

[8.94] Having established the application of s 35(f) of the 1890 Act to the quasi-partnership, Gannon J expressly adopted the judgment of Lord Wilberforce in *Ebrahimi v Westbourne Galleries Ltd*[210] regarding the grounds for the dissolution of quasi-partnerships:

> 'The just and equitable provision nevertheless comes to his assistance if he can point to, and prove, some special underlying obligation of his fellow member(s) in good faith, or confidence, that so long as the business continues he shall be entitled to management participation, an obligation so basic that, if broken, the conclusion must be that the association must be dissolved. And the principles on which he may do so are those worked out by the courts in partnership cases where there has been exclusion from management (see *Const v Harris* [1824] Tur and Rus 496, 525) even where under the partnership agreement there is a power of expulsion (see *Blisset v Daniel* (1853) 10 Hare 493).'[211]

[8.95] Gannon J held that the attempt by the two shareholder directors to remove the third from the management of the company was a deliberate and calculated repudiation of that relationship of equality, mutuality, trust and confidence which constituted the very essence of the company. Accordingly, he granted the order to wind up the company on just and equitable grounds under s 213(f) of the Companies Act 1963.[212]

[8.96] The right of a quasi-partner to wind up a quasi-partnership was also at issue in *Re Vehicle Buildings*.[213] There, the quasi-partnership was a company which was owned equally by two shareholders who were also the sole directors. The company operated a successful repair and sales business of motor cars. However, relations between the two broke down leading to a high degree of animosity and allegations of fraud. This resulted in a complete state of deadlock in the management of the company. In the High Court, Murphy J granted an order for the winding up of the company on just and equitable grounds under s 205 of the Companies Act 1963.[214] In doing so, he relied on the

---

[206] Now s 569 of the Companies Act 2014, and s 569(1)(e) has retained the reference to 'just and equitable'.

[207] *Ebrahimi v Westbourne Galleries Ltd* [1973] AC 360.

[208] In the judgment, the reference is to the 'Partnership Act 1892, s 25', but this is clearly a typographical error.

[209] *Ebrahimi v Westbourne Galleries Ltd* [1973] AC 360 at 374.

[210] *Ebrahimi v Westbourne Galleries Ltd* [1973] AC 360.

[211] *Ebrahimi v Westbourne Galleries Ltd* [1973] AC 360 at 380.

[212] Now s 569(1)(e) of the Companies Act 2014.

[213] *Re Vehicle Buildings* [1986] ILRM 239.

[214] Now s 212 of the Companies Act 2014. An appeal to the Supreme Court was dismissed in an ex tempore judgment on 10 March 1986 and the order of Murphy J was upheld.

judgment of Lord Cozens-Hardy MR in *Re Yenidje Tobacco Company Ltd*[215] that dissolution of a partnership will be granted where there is deadlock:

'In those circumstances, supposing it had been a private partnership, an ordinary partnership between two people having equal shares, and there being no other provision to terminate it, what would have been the position? I think it is quite clear under the law of partnership, as has been asserted in this Court for many years and is now laid down by the Partnership Act, that that state of things might be a ground for dissolution of the partnership for the reasons which are stated by Lord Lindley in his book on Partnership at p 657 in the passage which I will read, and which, I think, is quite justified by the authorities to which he refers.'[216]

[8.97] Murphy J then went on to quote the instances of deadlock which justify the dissolution of a partnership as set out by Lord Lindley:

'Refusal to meet on matters of business, continued quarrelling, and such a state of animosity as precludes all reasonable hope of reconciliation and friendly co-operation have been held sufficient to justify a dissolution. It is not necessary, in order to induce the court to interfere, to show personal rudeness on the part of one partner to the other, or even any gross misconduct as a partner. All that is necessary is to satisfy the court that it is impossible for the partners to place that confidence in each other which each has a right to expect, and that such impossibility has not been caused by the person seeking to take advantage of it.'[217]

Since a partnership would be dissolved on the grounds of deadlock, Murphy J held that the quasi-partnership in that case should be wound up where its management was deadlocked.[218]

[8.98] Interestingly, the grounds listed by Lord Lindley are not those for the dissolution of a partnership under the 'just and equitable' ground in s 35(f), but rather those for the dissolution of a partnership under 35(d), ie on the basis of the wilful or persistent breach of the partnership agreement or other misconduct which renders the continuance of the partnership impractical.[219] Therefore, while Murphy J relied ostensibly on s 35(f) of the 1890 Act to justify the winding up of the quasi-partnership, in fact he relied on s 35(d) of the 1890 Act. Similarly, in *Re Murph's Restaurant Ltd*,[220] although ostensible reliance was placed on s 35(f) of the 1890 Act to justify the winding-up order, the loss of mutual confidence between the quasi-partners in that case would appear to fall more

---

215 *Re Yenidje Tobacco Company Ltd* [1916] 2 Ch 426.

216 *Re Yenidje Tobacco Company Ltd* [1916] 2 Ch 426 at 430.

217 *Re Yenidje Tobacco Company Ltd* [1916] 2 Ch 426 at 430.

218 Charleton J, in *In the matter of Dublin Cinema Group* [2013] IEHC 147 also noted that in a situation where deadlock exists in a company which is a quasi-partnership because it has, as its background, two or more friends, family members or business partners operating together through a company for the purpose of carrying on their business, a winding-up on 'just and equitable' grounds might be justified.

219 See generally in relation to this and the other grounds for the dissolution of a partnership under s 35 of the 1890 Act, para **[25.01]** et seq.

220 *Re Murph's Restaurant Ltd* [1979] ILRM 141.

appropriately under the grounds listed in s 35(d) of the 1890 Act, ie misconduct rendering the continuance of the partnership impractical.

[8.99] One can conclude therefore that a court, whether relying ostensibly on s 35(f) or not, is likely to take into account all of the subsections of s 35 of the 1890 Act in order to determine whether a quasi-partnership should be wound up. However, as signalled by Lord Hoffmann when delivering the House of Lords decision in *O'Neill v Phillips*,[221] considered by Binchy J in *Hamill v Vantage Resources Limited & anor*,[222] if it is possible for the business of the partnership to be continued, an order for dissolution of the partnership is unlikely to be granted – logically, the same approach would be taken in the case of a quasi-partnership.[223]

[8.100] Where the court forms the view that a quasi-partnership should be wound up on just and equitable grounds, Charleton J's comments in *In the matter of Dublin Cinema Group*,[224] where he noted the court's right under s 216 of the Companies Act 1963 (now s 572 of the Companies Act 2014) to make 'any other order that it thinks fit' when hearing a winding-up petition, should be borne in mind. In his decision, he signalled his view that if evidence exists that it is appropriate for a quasi-partner to leave a quasi-partnership in return for appropriate compensation, he would be empowered to make such an order.

Other consequences

[8.101] To date, the number of principles of partnership law which have been applied to quasi-partnerships has been relatively limited and the same principles tend to recur in different cases.[225] However, many other principles of partnership law would appear to be equally applicable to quasi-partnerships and in future cases, one would expect to see the application of these principles. For example in *Re Murph's Restaurant Ltd*,[226] there was a bid by two of the shareholder directors for property a number of months after the company had bid for it. Their bid was higher than the company's bid and the property was duly purchased by the quasi-partners. Although no allegation was made in the case, if the circumstances were different and the quasi-partners had made a private profit, reliance could, for example, have been placed on s 30 of the 1890 Act to support a claim by the other quasi-partner for a share thereof.[227] Similarly, one may see in future cases,

---

221 *O'Neill v Phillips* [1999] BCC 600.

222 *Hamill v Vantage Resources Limited & anor* [2015] IEHC 195.

223 In *Hamill v Vantage Resources Limited & Anor* [2015] IEHC 195, Binchy J quoted from the judgment of Lord Hoffmann in the House of Lords in *O'Neill v Phillips* [1999] BCC 600 (who had, in turn, quoted from the judgment of Lord Wilberforce in *In re Westbourne Galleries Ltd* [1973] AC 360 at 380.) Lord Hoffmann commented that: '… one should not press the quasi-partnership analogy too far: "[a] company, however small, however domestic, is a company not a partnership or even a quasi-partnership …".'

224 *In the matter of Dublin Cinema Group* [2013] IEHC 147

225 For example the right to wind up a quasi-partnership on the grounds upon which a partnership would be dissolved in both *Re Murph's Restaurant Ltd* [1979] ILRM 141 and in *Re Vehicle Buildings* [1986] ILRM 239, see para **[8.92]** et seq.

226 *Re Murph's Restaurant Ltd* [1979] ILRM 141.

227 See generally in relation to the making of a private profit by a partner, para **[15.27]**. (contd…/)

the application to quasi-partnerships of such rights as the right of a partner to be indemnified by his firm for liabilities incurred by him in the ordinary course of business,[228] the right of every partner to have access to partnership books[229] and accounts,[230] the right of a partner to publicly notify the dissolution of the firm,[231] etc.

But not extending to usual clauses in partnership agreements

[8.102] It is also interesting to note that in *Re Murph's Restaurant Ltd*,[232] Gannon J referred to the failure of the quasi-partners to devote their full time to the company.[233] As is noted elsewhere in this work, there is no obligation under partnership law on a partner to devote his full time to the partnership's business.[234] However, such a term is invariably contained in partnership agreements. Nonetheless, it is suggested that it is stretching the concept of quasi-partnership too far to suggest that quasi-partners are subject to terms which, although not implied by partnership law, are commonly contained in partnership agreements.

Valuation of interest

[8.103] The question of whether or not a company is a quasi-partnership will also affect the valuation of the shareholding held by a minority shareholder who is seeking the purchase of his shareholding by the other shareholders or by the quasi-partnership company. Laffoy J in *Skytours Travel Limited v Companies Acts: Doyle v Bergin*[235] commented that it was only in the case of a quasi-partnership company (or in other exceptional cases) that a minority shareholding would be valued on a non-discounted basis. Referring to the judgment of Costello J in *Colgan v Colgan*[236] in which he stated

---

[227] (\...contd) Note that under company law, the issue of private profits is now the subject of an express statutory duty on a director to avoid any conflict between his duties to the company and his other (including personal) interests (Companies Act 2014, s 228(1)(f)). However, s 29(1) of the 1890 Act is arguably of wider scope, since it does not require a conflict of interest, but simply requires every partner to account to the firm for any benefit derived by him from his use of the firm's business connection. As to a director's statutory duty to avoid such a conflict of interests, see generally, Hutchinson, *Keane on Company Law* (5th edn, 2016) at para [27.140]; Courtney, *The Law of Companies* (4th edn, 2016) at para [16.088] et seq and Forde and Kennedy, *Company Law* (5th edn, 2017) at para 7-54 et seq.

[228] Partnership Act 1890, s 24(2), but this is subject to any agreement to the contrary between the partners, see generally in relation to this indemnity, para **[14.40]** et seq.

[229] Partnership Act 1890, s 24(9), but this is subject to agreement between the partners to the contrary, see generally the right to partnership books, para **[14.85]** et seq.

[230] Partnership Act 1890, s 28, see generally in relation to the right to partnership accounts, para **[14.92]** et seq.

[231] Partnership Act 1890, s 38, see generally para **[26.06]**.

[232] *Re Murph's Restaurant Ltd* [1979] ILRM 141.

[233] In referring to the purchase by the quasi-partners of the property, he notes: 'In connection with this development both Kevin and Murph gave a lot of time which otherwise would have been devoted to the business of the company' [1979] ILRM 141 at 146.

[234] See para **[21.96]**.

[235] *Skytours Travel Limited v Companies Acts: Doyle v Bergin* [2011] IEHC 517.

[236] *Colgan v Colgan* (22 July 1993) HC.

that all of the authorities that he had reviewed indicated that a discount should not be applied when valuing a minority shareholding in a quasi-partnership company, Laffoy J also took account of the judgment of Nourse J in *In Re Bird Precision Bellows Ltd*[237] where he outlined the reasons for not applying a discount when carrying out such a valuation:

> 'Usually he will be a minority shareholder whose interests have been unfairly prejudiced by the manner in which the affairs of the company have been conducted by the majority. On the assumption that the unfair prejudice has made it no longer tolerable for him to retain his interest in the company, a sale of his shares will invariably be his only practical way out short of a winding up. In that kind of case it seems to me that it would not merely be not fair, but most unfair, that he should be bought out on the fictional basis applicable to a free election to sell his shares in accordance with the company's articles of association, or indeed on any other basis which involved a discounted price. In my judgment the correct course would be to fix the price *pro rata* according to the value of the shares as a whole and without any discount, as being the only fair method of compensating an unwilling vendor of the equivalent of a partnership share.'

While these cases, in acknowledging that there can be a minority shareholder in a quasi-partnership, indicate that equality of shareholding is not necessarily a prerequisite to the existence of a quasi-partnership, this view is not without its detractors. Laffoy J in *Neenan Travel Ltd v Minister for Social and Family Affairs*[238] commented, in concluding that she had been presented with no evidence of the existence of a quasi-partnership, that the shareholder in question did not have an equal shareholding (he held just over 16% of the company, with various members of a family group holding the remainder) and quoted from Courtney's *Law of Companies*: '... an inequality of shareholding is anathema to the mutuality that has consistently been found to be a requirement for a quasi-partnership company.'[239]

Sometimes no consequence

[8.104] In some cases where a court finds that a company is a quasi-partnership, there will be no consequence. This may be explained by the fact that partnership law will not have any particular principles which would be of assistance, or of relevance, to the issue before the court. Thus in the High Court case of *Holland v McGill and Ryan*,[240] Murphy

---

[237] *Re Bird Precision Bellows Ltd* [1984] 1 Ch 419.

[238] *Neenan Travel Ltd v Minister for Social and Family Affairs* [2011] IEHC 458.

[239] Laffoy J quoted from Courtney, *The Law of Private Companies* (2nd edn, 2002) at para 1.128. The statement remains in the current edition (Courtney, *The Law of Companies* (4th edn, 2016) at para [11.039]).

[240] *Holland v McGill and Ryan* (16 March 1990) HC. See also *Kennedy and Ors v Allied Irish Banks plc* (18 May 1995) HC (upheld on appeal (29 October 1996) SC) in which Murphy J treated the relationship between three companies and their shareholders as a partnership between the individuals for the purposes of the companies' claim against the defendant for breach of contract. See also *O'Flanagan v Ray-Ger Ltd* (28 April 1983) HC, where Costello J referred to the two shareholders in the company as 'partners' and stated that the 'partnership business would be carried on by the company', yet this finding of quasi-partnership did not lead to the application of partnership law to the relationship. See also *Dublin Laundry Co Ltd v Clarke* [1988] ILRM 29, para **[8.85]**.

J noted that the company in question consisted of 'three individuals [who] were equal shareholders or equal partners, which, I think, would be an adequate expression for them in this enterprise'.[241] The case concerned the issue of whether a disputed directors' meeting had been validly held and therefore it is perhaps not surprising that the principles of partnership law did not have any apparent effect or application to the decision.

The Next Frontier – a Quasi-Company?

[8.105] As has been seen, the concept of a quasi-partnership has led to a cross-fertilisation between company and partnership law by means of the application of partnership principles to certain closely-held companies. This cross-fertilisation only began in earnest in the latter half of the twentieth century. However, the fact that the cross-fertilisation has taken place in this direction, rather than the reverse, is somewhat ironic, in view of the more active developments in company law during this time. Indeed, the lack of legislative change to partnership law in recent times and the relative paucity of partnership caselaw, combined with the changing nature of today's professional firms, supports the view that partnership law is in greater need of fertilisation from the considerably more active field of company law, than vice versa. This possibility is worthy of investigation.

[8.106] It has been seen that a quasi-partnership is an entity which is in form a company, but is in substance a partnership, often its form as a company being the result solely of its desire to have limited liability.[242] Similarly, there are many examples of large professional partnerships which operate in reality as companies, but are prevented from being companies in form, by rules of their profession.[243] It is these partnerships in particular which one might term 'quasi-companies', that are ripe to have their reality recognised by being subject to certain company law principles.

[8.107] In the Irish context, these professional partnerships will have dozens of partners, hundreds of employees, may be members of international partnerships and will often have greater turnovers than some publicly quoted companies. In view of their size, it is impractical for these firms to operate according to the traditional partnership model, where ownership and management of a firm is vested in the same people. This is because it is not feasible to have decisions taken regarding the day-to-day business of the firm by the many dozens of partners that make up the firm. Instead, these firms mimic the traditional corporate model with its separation of management and ownership. This separation of powers is achieved in these firms by their being run by a management committee of a small number of partners (which one might term 'quasi-directors') who are elected by all the partners (which one might term 'quasi-shareholders'). Like a board of directors in a company, the management committee runs the firm's business on a day-to-day basis and reports to the quasi-shareholders at partners' meetings (quasi-general meetings) which are held on a monthly basis or less frequently, with one main partners' meeting being held each year (the quasi-annual general meeting).

---

[241] *Holland v McGill and Ryan* (16 March 1990) HC at p 3 of the transcript.

[242] See para **[8.69]**.

[243] See further para **[1.10]** et seq.

[8.108] If one takes this theory one step further, one must consider which principles of company law to apply to such quasi-companies. Clearly, the principles to apply will be those company law principles applicable to the management of companies according to the traditional corporate model. So, for example, if a partner (quasi-director)[244] is removed from his position on the management committee, he may argue that the company law principles which have been applied to the removal of directors from companies should be applicable to this situation.[245] More generally, there may be a case for treating the partners on the management committee (quasi-directors) as having duties to the quasi-shareholders, employees and creditors of the firm as if they were directors of a company.[246] Other areas of company law may also be of relevance to quasi-companies such as minority shareholder protection, protection of creditors, disqualification of directors, etc. Indeed, it is perhaps surprising that in view of the close historical ties between partnership and company law,[247] recourse to company law principles has not happened heretofore.

IX. REGISTERED FARM PARTNERSHIPS AND REGISTERED SUCCESSION FARM PARTNERSHIPS

[8.109] Farm partnerships were formally introduced in Ireland in 2015 following the end of milk quotas on 31 March 2015.[248] Farm partnerships are not a separate type of partnership; instead, they are ordinary partnerships, subject to the 1890 Act, in respect of which additional rules are in place. Registered farm partnerships benefit from various financial incentives, including enhanced stock relief. Succession farm partnerships are intended to promote the transfer of farms to the next generation of Irish farmers, while entitling the original farmer to retain a percentage of the farm assets (up to 20%). The registration of a succession farm partnership also entitles the partners to an annual tax

---

244 For a legislative application of company law principles to partnerships, see generally the application of the requirement that certain partnerships file accounts under the European Communities (Accounts) Regulations 1993 and see para **[14.66]** et seq. In particular note that under reg 24(4) of those regulations, a partner in a partnership the subject of those regulations, is deemed to be akin to an officer of a company for the purposes of those sections of the Companies Act 2014 that deal with breaches of obligations to annex particular documents to annual returns, to append auditors' reports and to publish financial statements (ie ss 356(5), 316(3), 340(7), 347(5), 355(7), 355(9) and 356(5)), while under reg 16 of the European Communities (Accounts) Regulations 1993 the partner is treated as akin to a shareholder for the purposes of the requirement that all the partners consent to the exemption of the partnership from the requirement to file accounts under s 357 of the Companies Act 2014.

245 See generally in relation to the removal of directors, Hutchinson, *Keane on Company Law* (5th edn, 2016) at para [27.35] et seq; Courtney, *The Law of Companies* (4th edn, 2016) at para [13.087] et seq; Forde and Kennedy, *Company Law* (5th edn, 2017) at para 6-72 et seq.

246 See generally in relation to the duties of directors, Courtney, *The Law of Companies* (4th edn, 2016) at para [16.004] et seq; Hutchinson, *Keane on Company Law* (5th edn, 2016) at para [27.81] et seq; Forde and Kennedy, *Company Law* (5th edn, 2017) at para 7-01 et seq.

247 See generally in relation to these historical links, para **[1.04]**.

248 Originally subject to the Registration of Farm Partnerships Regulations 2015 (SI 247/2015), farm partnerships and succession farm partnerships are now subject to the Registration of Farm Partnerships and Succession Farm Partnerships Regulations 2017 (SI 273/2017).

credit each year for five years, which is divided between them in accordance with their profit sharing ratio.[249]

[8.110] To become a registered farm partnership, the 'primary participant' (ie one of the partners) must submit a written application to the Minister for Agriculture, Food and the Marine together with a copy of the partnership agreement. The primary participant must also confirm that the farmland being used by the partnership is not more than 75 kilometres away from any other farmland used by the partnership, and provide the Minister with such other information or material as he may reasonably require.[250] To be added to the register of succession farm partnerships, a partnership must already be a registered farm partnership.[251]

The partnership agreement

[8.111] To qualify as a registered farm partnership, a farm partnership must have a written partnership agreement in place. To demonstrate compliance with s 667C(1A)(b) of the Taxes Consolidation Act 1997, the partnership agreement must comply with the 1890 Act and must:

- provide that the partnership exists only for the purpose of carrying on the trade of farming;
- set out information that identifies the partners, the farmland farmed by the partnership, the partners' respective shares in the partnership and how the partnership will be operated. If a partner co-owns the farmland that will be farmed by the partnership, his co-owner(s) must also be partners in the farm partnership;
- include a commitment from the partners listed in the partnership agreement to operate as a farm partnership for at least five years;
- provide for at least two but no more than 10 partners (a partner cannot be a partner in his own right, and at the same time be a director or shareholder of a corporate partner in the same farm partnership);
- have no 'non-active' partners (ie all partners in the partnership must work an average of at least 10 hours per week in the partnership business);
- have, as a partner, at least one person who has been engaged in the trade of farming on farmland (consisting of at least three hectares of usable farmland) owned or leased by that partner for at least two years immediately before the date that the farm partnership is formed;
- have at least one other partner (being an individual) who has either been engaged in the trade of farming on farmland (consisting of at least three hectares of usable farmland) owned or leased by him for at least two years immediately before the date that the farm partnership is formed, or has a

---

[249] Taxes Consolidation Act 1997, s 667D(6).
[250] In addition to the application form and partnership agreement, an 'on-farm' agreement is also required, setting out the key duties and responsibilities of each partner.
[251] Taxes Consolidation Act 1997, s 667D(1).

specific qualification[252] and is entitled to at least 20 per cent of the partnership's profits;

– provide that no partner can have an interest in any farm asset outside of the farm partnership at any time during the period of registration of the farm partnership;[253]

– provide that any payment that a partner receives from the trade of farming for the purposes of the farm partnership agreement must be paid by him to the farm partnership.

A partner can only be involved in one registered farm partnership at a time (whether directly, or whether as a shareholder or director of a corporate partner).

Registration

[8.112] On successful registration of a farm partnership, the partnership is entered on the Register of Farm Partnerships. Registration lasts for five years, and the registered farm partnership receives both a unique identifier and a certificate of registration. Registered farm partnerships benefit from certain financial incentives under s 667C of the Taxes Consolidation Act 1997, in particular enhanced stock relief and deductions against trading income.

Succession Farm Partnerships

[8.113] Certain registered farm partnerships may also apply to be entered on the Register of Succession Farm Partnerships provided that they comply with certain further conditions. As succession farm partnerships are designed to encourage the transfer of farm assets to the next generation, one of the requirements is that a legally-binding succession agreement is entered into whereby the farmer agrees to transfer at least 80% of the farm assets to his successor at a time during the period beginning three years after, and ending ten years after, the date of the application to be entered on the Register of Succession Farm Partnerships. Further, in addition to the provisions that must have been included in the partnership agreement to enable the farm partnership to be registered as a registered farm partnership, the partnership agreement in respect of a partnership that wishes to be entered on the Register of Succession Farm Partnerships must also include details of:[254]

– farm assets (as of the date of the application for registration);

– any conditions to which the transfer or sale will be subject;

---

[252] The acceptable qualifications are listed in the Schedule to SI 273/2017. Alternatively, Teagasc can deem a qualification to be equivalent. Confirmation of that qualification must be included with the application form.

[253] There are certain exclusions from this. One is for an 'excluded farm asset' (farmland, livestock or machinery used for pig farming, poultry farming, mushroom farming, forestry, bloodstock farming, intensive horticultural cropping, on-farm milk processing other than milking and storage of milk, or generation of fuel or electricity, provided that the activity is specifically excluded from the scope of the farm partnership by the partnership agreement). The other exclusion is for farmland owned or leased by a partner but licensed to the farm partnership.

[254] Taxes Consolidation Act 1997, s 667D(2)(e).

– the year in which the proposed transfer will take place; and
– any other terms agreed between the farmer and the successor(s) (including in relation to the farm assets, the manner in which the farming trade is carried on, or the creation of any rights of residence in the dwellings on the farmland).

Chapter 9

Illegal Partnerships

INTRODUCTION

[9.01] Like any other contract, a partnership contract may be illegal and as such it will be void and unenforceable.[1] Illegality of a partnership contract arises at common law where the partnership is formed for an illegal purpose,[2] and under statute where the partnership is formed in contravention of an express statutory prohibition.[3] In this chapter, consideration will be given to the situations in which a partnership is illegal and the consequences of such illegality under the following headings:

    I.   Illegal Partnerships Generally;

    II.   Partnerships Illegal under Statute;

    III.   Partnerships Illegal at Common Law;

    IV.   Consequences of Illegality.

Overview

[9.02] The fact that a firm is guilty of an unlawful act will not necessarily make the partnership illegal. Rather, the nature of the illegal act must be considered to determine whether the partnership itself will be deemed to be illegal. For example a statute may expressly prohibit the formation of certain partnerships, in which case it is clear that a partnership formed in contravention of this prohibition will be illegal. Alternatively, a

---

1   In relation to illegal contracts generally, see Clark, *Contract Law in Ireland* (8th edn, 2016) at para 14-01 et seq; McDermott and McDermott, *Contract Law* (2nd edn, 2017) at para [16.01] et seq; Friel, *The Law of Contract* (2nd edn, 2000) at p 276 et seq; Trietel, *The Law of Contract* (14th edn, 2015) at para 11-002 et seq; *Anson's Law of Contract* (30th edn, 2016) at p 409 et seq; *Chitty on Contracts* (32nd edn, 2015) at para 16-001 et seq; Enonchong, *Illegal Transactions* (1998). As regards illegal partnerships specifically, see Note, 'Partnerships for an Illegal Purpose' (1928) 41 Harv LR 650 and Rosenthal, 'Illegal Associations in English Law' (1975) 10 Israel LR 277.

2   For example where a partnership is formed to perpetuate a crime, see *Everet v Williams* (1725) 9 LQR 197 and para **[9.24]**.

3   For example the prohibition in s 59 of the Solicitors Act 1954 on solicitors acting in partnership with unqualified persons, see para **[9.10]**. Under the Legal Services Regulation Act 2015, it will shortly become possible to form 'legal partnerships' between practising barristers, and 'legal partnerships' between practising solicitors and practising barristers (and such legal partnerships may, in turn, together with firms of solicitors, apply to be authorised as limited liability partnerships). It appears, at the time of writing, less likely that the multi-disciplinary practice model also contemplated by the 2015 Act (partnerships providing both legal and non-legal services, at least one of the partners in which must be a practising solicitor or a practising barrister) will be introduced. See, further, in relation to the 2015 Act, para **[30.01]** et seq.

statute may require a partnership to register a business name,[4] but it is clear that the failure to do so will not render the partnership illegal. Once a partnership is illegal, whether because it contravenes a statutory provision or is contrary to the common law, s 34 of the 1890 Act provides that it is automatically dissolved. Even where the unlawful act is not such as to render the partnership illegal, the Irish courts have taken a strict view of illegal acts by partnerships, as evidenced by their refusal to permit innocent partners to benefit from the illegal act of a guilty partner.[5]

I.   ILLEGAL PARTNERSHIPS GENERALLY

[9.03] The question of whether a particular partnership is illegal must be determined on its facts, taking account of all the circumstances of the case. In general terms, if the illegality is merely an incident to the conduct of the firm's business, then the partnership will not be illegal. On the other hand, if the illegality is inherent in the purpose for which the partnership is entered into, the firm will be illegal. In the words of Lord Lindley:[6]

> '[I]n order to show that a partnership is illegal, it is necessary to establish either that the object of the partnership is one the attainment of which is contrary to law, or that the object being legal, its attainment is sought in a manner which the law forbids. But proof that a firm has been guilty of an illegal act is not sufficient to bring the firm within the class of illegal partnerships; for if this were enough, every partnership which does not pay its debts, or which commits any tort, or is guilty of culpable negligence would be illegal, which is obviously absurd. Neither does it by any means follow that because one or more clauses in a contract of partnership are illegal that the partnership is itself illegal.'[7]

[9.04] In addition to considering the surrounding circumstances of the illegal act, regard should be had to the intention of the partners and the nature of the illegal act when determining the legality of partnerships. Of crucial import is the nature of the business which is actually carried on by the partnership and the outside activities of the partners will not be relevant. This is clear from s 34 of the 1890 Act which is concerned primarily with the consequences of an illegal partnership, but which provides that:

> A partnership is in every case dissolved by the happening of any event which makes it unlawful for the *business of the firm* to be carried on or for the members of the firm to carry on in partnership. [Emphasis added.]

---

[4]   Under the Registration of Business Names Act 1963, s 3, considered at para **[3.70]** et seq.

[5]   See *Horgan v Baxter* (11 May 1982) HC, para **[9.36]**.

[6]   This statement is now to be found in l'Anson Banks, *Lindley & Banks on Partnership* (20th edn, 2017) at para 8-02.

[7]   See for example *McEllistrim v Ballymacelligott Co-operative Agricultural and Dairy Society* [1919] AC 548, wherein the House of Lords overturned a decision of the Irish Court of Appeal ([1919] 1 IR 313). The House of Lords held that a clause in the rules of a co-operative society was in restraint of trade and therefore illegal, but that the society was not illegal. Note also Lord Parmoor's comments in that case that the relationship between a co-operative society and its members is akin to that of the relationship between a partnership and its partners, [1919] AC 548 at 604–605.

The Intention of the Partners is Relevant

[9.05] An important factor in determining whether an unlawful act will render a partnership illegal is the intention of the partners in forming the partnership. For example a partnership which is formed with the express intention of carrying on a business without having a statutory licence to do so is likely to be an illegal partnership, since the partnership is formed with the very intention of deriving benefit from a illegal act. Such a partnership is likely to be illegal, even if the statute itself provides for the partners to be guilty of an offence where they carry on business without such a licence. In contrast, where the partnership is not formed with such an express intention and the licence is inadvertently not obtained, the court is more likely to take the view that the partnership is not illegal.

Nature of the Illegal Act

[9.06] While the intention of the parties is relevant in determining whether a partnership is illegal, it is by no means conclusive, and in some cases, even inadvertent illegal acts will render a partnership illegal. Thus, a breach of a provision which goes to the heart of a firm's business (such as a prohibition on a partnership with unqualified persons) would be regarded as sufficient to render the firm illegal, even if the breach was unintentional.[8]

[9.07] In contrast, a partnership will not be illegal where the partners intentionally breach the terms of a relatively minor provision,[9] such as the obligation under ss 3 to 6 of the Registration of Business Names Act 1963 to register a business name or the obligation under s 7 of that Act to register any change in previously-registered particulars relating to that business name.[10] In view of the ancillary nature of these provisions to the business of the firm, it is apprehended that even an intentional breach of this Act would not render such a partnership illegal.

[9.08] On the other hand, there will of course be illegal acts which will not fall neatly into either of these categories, so that it is conceived that, depending on the circumstances, a partnership which breaches the prohibition on anti-competitive agreements in s 4(1) of the Competition Act 2002 may be illegal while another partnership in breach of the same provision may not be illegal. This section provides that agreements between undertakings which have as their object or effect the prevention, restriction or distortion of competition in trade in any goods or services in the State (or

---

8   See *Hudgell Yeates & Co v Watson* [1978] 2 All ER 363, considered at para **[9.12]**.
9   See also *SCF Finance Co Ltd v Masri (No 2)* [1987] QB 1002; *Re Cavalier Insurance Co Ltd* [1989] 2 Lloyd's Rep 430; *Tinsley v Milligan* [1994] 1 AC 340; *Phoenix General Insurance Co of Greece SA v Halvanon Insurance Co Ltd* [1988] QB 216. See also the Australian cases of unlicensed builders in *Baxter & Sons v Chen* (1981) 27 SASR 74 and *Fong & Reck v Minoo* (1980) 1 SR (WA) 222. An example of a partnership which carried on an illegal gaming business is provided by *Collins and Byrne v Inspector of Taxes* [1956] IR 233.
10 See further in relation to the registration of business names, para **[3.70]** et seq. Under s 10 of the Registration of Business Names Act 1963 every partner is liable on summary conviction to a class C fine (at the time of writing, a class C fine is a fine not exceeding €2,500) where his firm makes default, without reasonable excuse, in registering a business name or a change in particulars. See, further, para **[3.84]**.

in any part of the State) are prohibited and void. Thus, for example, a partnership which has an anti-competitive term in its employment agreement with its employees will contravene s 4(1) of the 2002 Act, but it will clearly not be an illegal partnership since the presence of this clause in an employment agreement would not make it unlawful for the partnership business to be carried on or for the partners to carry on in partnership, but rather is merely an incident to the firm's business.[11] On the other hand, a partnership between competitors where the very *raison d'être* for the firm is to pass information between the members regarding pricing, would be clearly illegal since it goes to the heart of the partnership business (and s 4(1)(a) of the 2002 Act cites, by way of example, agreements which directly or indirectly fix purchase or other selling prices or any other trading conditions as agreements that will be prohibited and void under the 2002 Act).

II. PARTNERSHIPS ILLEGAL UNDER STATUTE

[9.09] In this section, regard will be had to partnerships which are illegal under statute by first examining two examples of specific statutory provisions concerning partnerships and the effect of contravening their terms, namely:

(i)   the prohibition on solicitors being in partnership with non-solicitors; and

(ii) the prohibition on partnerships of more than 20 partners (in respect of which there are now several exceptions).

Section 59 of the Solicitors Act 1954

[9.10] Sometimes statutory provisions will expressly prohibit the very formation of certain partnerships and in most cases a partnership which breaches such an express prohibition will be illegal. An example of an express statutory prohibition on the formation of certain types of partnership is contained in the Solicitors Act 1954.[12] Under s 59 of this Act, it is prohibited for a solicitor to carry on business as a solicitor in

---

11 In this regard, an illegal clause in a partnership agreement which does not taint the whole partnership may in some circumstances be severed from the partnership agreement under the doctrine of severance. As to which see further Clark, *Contract Law in Ireland* (8th edn, 2016) at para 14-94 et seq and McDermott and McDermott, *Contract Law* (2nd edn, 2017) at para [16.194] et seq. See also *John Orr Ltd v Orr* [1987] ILRM 703 in which Costello J severed part of a non-solicitation clause from a store purchase agreement.

12 Other statutory prohibitions which are not considered in detail in this chapter, but which may ground a claim of illegal partnership are:
  – s 52(1) of the Dentists Act 1985, which provides that registered dentists may only enter into partnership to act as dentists with other registered dentists;
  – s 54 of the Veterinary Practice Act 2005 under which veterinary practitioners may only partner with other veterinary practitioners; and
  – s 43 of the Medical Practitioners Act 2007 (together with the Medical Council's *Guide to Professional Conduct and Ethics for Registered Medical Practitioners* (8th edn, 2016) at para 54.1) under which registered medical practitioners are only allowed to partner with other registered medical practitioners.

partnership with a person who has not been admitted as a solicitor.[13] However, as mentioned above,[14] the Legal Services Regulation Act 2015 contemplates new business models whereby practising barristers may enter into 'legal partnerships' with one another, and practising solicitors may enter into 'legal partnerships' with practising barristers.[15] However, at the time of writing, the restriction in s 59 of the Solicitors Act 1954 remains in force.

[9.11] In *Gulliver v Brady & ors p/a Matheson Ormsby Prentice*,[16] a memorandum of understanding was entered into between Mr Gulliver (a tax advisor, but not a solicitor) and the law firm of Matheson Ormsby Prentice which provided that, subject to the fulfilment of certain conditions, Mr Gulliver would be admitted as a full equity partner in that firm. The memorandum provided inter alia that the parties would use:

> '... best endeavours to facilitate the establishment of a dedicated tax advisory group [within the firm] to complement and assist in the development of the existing taxation advisor service ... It is further agreed ... that subject to regulatory constraints an integral element of this agreement is the commitment of the parties hereto to put in place a mechanism by which [Mr Gulliver] will ... be admitted as a full profit sharing partner of [the firm] with effect from the 1st day of January 2003.'

The admission of Mr Gulliver as an equity partner in the firm would have breached s 59 of the Solicitors Act 1954, and so one of the 'regulatory constraints' to which the memorandum of understanding must be referring is s 59 of that Act. This point was not examined by the Court as the dispute was referred to arbitration, and later settled, with Mr Gulliver subsequently leaving the firm. In some firms, senior non-solicitors tend to be given the role of 'consultant' or 'director' and not that of 'partner' to avoid breaching the prohibition in s 59.

[9.12] The interesting case of *Hudgell Yeates & Co v Watson*[17] concerned a partnership which breached the English equivalent[18] of s 59 of the Solicitors Act 1954. It involved an action by the plaintiff law firm against one of its clients for unpaid fees. The defendant argued that the action against him should be struck out because one partner in the law firm inadvertently failed to renew his solicitor's practising certificate for a period of seven months. The defendant's case rested on his claim that the partnership was illegal, since it was a partnership between solicitors and an unadmitted person, in contravention of the English Solicitors Act.[19] As it was an illegal partnership, he claimed

---

13   Section 59(1) states that: 'A solicitor shall not wilfully – (a) act, in business carried on by him as a solicitor, as agent for an unqualified person so as to enable that person to act as a solicitor ...' Since every partner is an agent for his co-partners (see para **[10.07]**), a solicitor, who is in partnership with an unqualified person, is in breach of this section. Note also the prohibition on a solicitor being a partner, without the consent of the Law Society of Ireland, if he has less than three years' experience: s 37 of the Solicitors (Amendment) Act 1994.

14   See fn **3** above.

15   See, further, para **[30.01]** et seq.

16   *Gulliver v Brady & ors p/a Matheson Ormsby Prentice* [2003] IESC 68.

17   *Hudgell Yeates & Co v Watson* [1978] 2 All ER 363.

18   Ie s 39 of the English Solicitors Act 1974 which was later repealed by s 66(1) of the Courts and Legal Services Act 1990. As to the current position in England, see l'Anson Banks, *Lindley & Banks on Partnership* (20th edn, 2017) at para 8-53 et seq.

19   At that time, the Solicitors Act 1974. See, further, fn **18** above.

that the firm was automatically dissolved as required by s 34 of the 1890 Act.[20] Although the failure by the partner to renew his practising certificate was accidental, the Court of Appeal was left with no option but to uphold the defendant's claim that the firm was dissolved automatically on the failure of this partner to renew his practising certificate.[21] This case highlights the importance of professionals, who are restricted from acting in partnership with unqualified persons,[22] ensuring that their practising certificates are renewed on a timely basis. The failure to do so will render their partnership automatically dissolved even where the failure is inadvertent.[23]

[9.13] The only Irish case on this area supports the conclusion reached in *Hudgell Yeates & Co v Watson*.[24] That case is *Martin v Sherry*[25] and was heard before the enactment of s 59 of the Solicitors Act 1954, but it dealt with a related issue under the Solicitors (Ireland) Act 1898.[26] This Act prohibited the recovery of costs by a solicitor if he did not hold a practising certificate. The case concerned a claim that a solicitor in Armagh was not entitled to his costs from the unsuccessful litigant on the grounds that he was in partnership with his son who had failed to take out a practising certificate with the Incorporated Law Society. The Taxing Officer held that the costs were not payable on the grounds that during the time when such costs were earned, one 'member of the solicitors' firm' had not obtained his practising certificate. However, the Irish Court of Appeal decided that there was no partnership between the father and son and therefore the costs were properly chargeable. Interestingly, Holmes LJ indicated obiter that in the event of there being a partnership between the father and son, he would favour holding that the costs were not recoverable.[27]

Business arrangement between solicitors and other professionals

[9.14] In considering the application of s 59 of the Solicitors Act 1954, reference has been made to the situation where one of the solicitors in a firm omits to renew his practising certificate. The prohibition in s 59 of the 1954 Act is of course equally applicable to a partnership between a solicitor and somebody who has never held a

---

20   See further para [9.27].
21   The Court of Appeal did however hold that, on the dissolution of the partnership, his co-partners instantly comprised amongst themselves a new partnership by operation of law and for this reason, inter alia, the defendant's defence was unsuccessful. See para [9.28].
22   For example dentists, vets and registered medical practitioners, see further fn 12 above.
23   Indeed in order to avoid dissolution through inadvertence as happened in *Hudgell Yeates & Co v Watson* [1978] 2 All ER 363, above, partnership agreements amongst professionals who are prohibited from being in partnership with unqualified persons should contain a clause to the effect that, if a partner fails to renew his practising certificate then he is deemed to have retired from the partnership. In this way the lesser of two evils occurs ie a forced retirement of one of the partners, rather than an automatic dissolution of the firm. See also para [21.136].
24   *Hudgell Yeates & Co v Watson* [1978] 2 All ER 363.
25   *Martin v Sherry* [1905] 2 IR 62.
26   (61 & 62 Vict c 17), s 48.
27   In *Re Jackson* (1834) 3 Ir Law Rec 92, MacMahon MR considered, without deciding on the facts, the possibility that a solicitor-partner who had failed to renew his practising certificate under ss 66–68 of the Irish Stamp Duty Act of 1816 (56 Geo III, c 56), the predecessor of s 48 of the Solicitors (Ireland) Act 1898, would be unable to recover his fees.

practising certificate. Since a business arrangement need not be called a partnership to constitute a partnership[28] and may arise with no formality,[29] care must be taken in relation to any profit sharing or referral arrangement which law firms have with a person who is not a solicitor, eg a barrister, an accountant or an auctioneer.[30] Otherwise, such an arrangement may be held to constitute a partnership, in which case it will contravene s 59 and the whole partnership will be illegal. If the arrangement constitutes a partnership, a clause that a partnership shall not be deemed to exist between the parties will be to no avail.[31]

Business arrangement with a foreign lawyer

[9.15] A partnership between an Irish solicitor and a foreign lawyer who has not been granted a practising certificate or qualifying certificate by the Law Society of Ireland would also fall foul of the prohibition in s 59 of the Solicitors Act 1954. In England, the principal prohibition on partnerships between solicitors and foreign lawyers was removed in 1990.[32] However, as the requirement for an appropriate certificate from the Law Society still exists in Ireland, care should be taken about any referral arrangements or other associations between Irish law firms and foreign law firms (including firms in Northern Ireland),[33] to ensure that they do not constitute partnerships unless the required practising certificates or qualifying certificates have been obtained.

Partnerships between barristers not currently allowed

[9.16] Practising barristers are, at the time of writing, prohibited from entering into any professional partnership, whether with other practising barristers or others.[34] When the provisions of the Legal Services Regulation Act 2015 which will permit practising barristers to enter into 'legal partnerships' with other practising barristers or with practising solicitors (and to apply for such legal partnerships to be authorised as limited

---

[28] See para **[2.15]** et seq.

[29] See for example *Robinson v Anderson* (1855) 20 Beav 98 and 7 De GM & G 239 (appeal) and see generally, para **[1.09]** et seq.

[30] Note the power of the Law Society, with the concurrence of the Minister for Justice and Equality, to make regulations providing for fee-sharing by solicitors with non-solicitors under s 71(1)(a) of the Solicitors (Amendment) Act 1994. Note further that notaries are also restricted from entering into fee-sharing arrangements with persons who are not notaries (Public Notaries (Ireland) Act 1821, ss 11 and 14). As a notary is often also a partner in a law firm, care must be taken to ensure that fees received from his notarial work are managed separately.

[31] See para **[2.19]** et seq.

[32] Courts and Legal Services Act 1990, s 89 and Sch 14. See, further, l'Anson Banks, *Lindley & Banks on Partnership* (20th edn, 2017) at para 8-53 et seq.

[33] There have been a number of 'arrangements' between law firms in Ireland and law firms in Northern Ireland over the last 20 years. In this context, note the power of the Law Society of Ireland, with the concurrence of the Minister for Justice and Equality, to make regulations for the provision of fee-sharing by solicitors with members of the legal profession in another jurisdiction under s 71(1)(b) of the Solicitors (Amendment) Act 1994.

[34] *Code of Conduct for the Bar of Ireland* (version as adopted on 23 July 2014) at para 7.14. A breach by a practising barrister of that Code of Conduct can result in a complaint being made (whether by a client or by the Bar of Ireland) to the Barristers' Professional Conduct Tribunal.

liability partnerships) and which will also permit practising barristers to enter into multi-disciplinary practices offering both legal and non-legal services, the above-mentioned prohibition will cease to apply.[35]

Section 1435(1) of the Companies Act 2014

[9.17] Another express statutory prohibition on the creation of certain partnerships is contained in s 1435(1) of the Companies Act 2014[36] which prohibits the formation of partnerships with more than 20 members[37] and provides as follows:

> No company, association or partnership[38] consisting of more than 20 persons shall be formed for the purpose of carrying on any business (other than the business of banking), that has for its object the acquisition of gain by the company, association or partnership, or by the individual members thereof, unless:[39]
>
> (a) it is registered as a company under this Act;
>
> (b) it is formed in pursuance of some other statute;[40] or
>
> (c) it is a partnership formed for the purpose of—
>
>   (i) carrying on practice as accountants in a case where each partner is a statutory auditor;
>
>   (ii) carrying on practice as solicitors in a case where each partner is a solicitor;

---

35 See para **[30.01]** et seq. At the time of writing, however, it appears unlikely that a framework for multi-disciplinary practices will come into effect in the short term.

36 For a historical perspective of this section and its predecessors, see para **[4.29]**.

37 Note that any remaining statutory provisions limiting the number of partners in an ordinary partnership or in a limited partnership to 20 was removed in Great Britain by the Regulatory Reform (Reform of 20 Member Limit in Partnerships etc) Order 2002 (SI 2002/3203) and later in Northern Ireland by The Partnerships etc (Removal of 20 Member Limit) (Northern Ireland) Order 2003.

38 Note that s 1435(1) of the Companies Act 2014 does not apply to investment limited partnerships by virtue of (i) s 1435(4) of the 2014 Act which disapplies s 1435 to an investment limited partnership within the meaning of the Investment Limited Partnerships Act 1994; (ii) s 4(4) of the Investment Limited Partnerships Act 1994 (pursuant to the Companies Act 2014, Sch 6, s 11(1), the reference in the Investment Limited Partnerships Act 1994 to s 376 of the Companies Act 1963 is to be read as a reference to the equivalent provision (s 1435(1) of the 2014 Act)); and (iii) s 1435(1)(b) of the 2014 Act which excludes from the scope of the prohibition a partnership formed under another statute.

39 The exemptions from the restriction in s 1435(1) of the Companies Act 2014 are considered in more detail elsewhere in this work, see para **[4.31]** et seq.

40 Thus excluding limited partnerships since they are formed under the Limited Partnerships Act 1907. Limited partnerships are, however, governed by size restrictions contained in s 4(2) of the Limited Partnerships Act 1907 save where those limited partnerships are carrying on the business of thoroughbred horse breeding or providing certain investment and related services (s 1435(5) of the Companies Act 2014). See, further, para **[28.27]**. Legal partnerships and multi-disciplinary practices, as they will also be formed under another statute (the Legal Services Regulation Act 2015), should also fall outside the scope of s 1435(1), as will limited liability partnerships (to the extent that they are originally established as legal partnerships under the Legal Services Regulation Act 2015, see para **[30.18]** et seq).

    (iii)   carrying on or promoting the business of thoroughbred horse breeding, being a partnership to which, subject to subsection (5), the Limited Partnerships Act 1907 relates; or

    (iv)   the provision of investment and loan finance and ancillary facilities and services to persons engaged in industrial or commercial activities, being a partnership—

        (I)   that consists of not more than 50 persons; and

        (II)   to which, subject to subsection (5), the Limited Partnerships Act 1907 relates.

'acquisition of gain'

[9.18] For s 1435(1) to apply to a partnership, the firm must have as its object the 'acquisition of gain'. However, it seems clear from the Supreme Court case of *Deane v Voluntary Health Insurance Board*[41] that every partnership will satisfy this requirement. In that case, Finlay CJ (Hederman and Egan JJ, concurring) reversed a High Court decision that the term 'for gain' was equivalent to the term 'for profit'. The case was concerned with the use of the expression 'for gain' in the definition of 'undertaking' set out in s 3(1) of the Competition Act 1991.[42] To interpret this expression, the Supreme Court relied on the interpretation of the term 'acquisition of gain' in s 4 of the Companies Act 1862.[43] Finlay CJ adopted the definition of this term by Jessel MR in *Re Arthur Average Association for British, Foreign and Colonial Ships*[44] that 'gain is something obtained or acquired. It is not limited to pecuniary gain.'[45] Finlay CJ noted that the definition of Jessel MR:

> 'appears to me to be a satisfactory and in so far as is relevant to the section of the Companies Act with which it was dealing ... a complete definition of the word "gain".'[46]

On this basis, the Supreme Court held that although the Voluntary Health Insurance Board collected only such revenue as was necessary to cover its costs, the surplus going to the Central Fund, it was still an association formed for the acquisition of gain. Since the term 'acquisition of gain' is wider than the term 'view of profit', which every partnership must, by definition, have,[47] it follows that every partnership will at a minimum, have as its object the 'acquisition of gain' and will therefore be subject to s 1435(1) of the Companies Act 2014 unless expressly excluded from its scope.

Partnerships formed in contravention of s 1435(1)

[9.19] Since s 1435(1) of the Companies Act 2014 expressly prohibits, subject to the exceptions set out above, the formation of a partnership with more than 20 persons, it

---

41   *Deane v Voluntary Health Insurance Board* [1992] 2 IR 319.

42   Now s 3(1) of the Competition Act 2002.

43   The predecessor of both s 1435(1) of the Companies Act 2014 and its immediate predecessor, s 376 of the Companies Act 1963.

44   *Re Arthur Average Association for British, Foreign and Colonial Ships* (1875) LR 10 Ch App 542.

45   *Re Arthur Average Association for British, Foreign and Colonial Ships* (1875) LR 10 Ch App 542 at 546.

46   *Deane v Voluntary Health Insurance Board* [1992] 2 IR 319 at 330.

47   Partnership Act 1890, s 1(1) and see further para **[2.62]**.

seems clear that a partnership which is formed in contravention of the section is illegal.[48] *Re D*[49] concerned an association for mutual marine insurance which had over 20 members and was not registered as a company as required under the predecessor of s 1435(1).[50] In the High Court, Miller J held that the association was illegal, since it had over 20 members and was not registered as a company. The association had appointed an agent to underwrite policies on its behalf. As an illegal association, it was held that it could not appoint an agent to contract on its behalf and that the policy of insurance issued by its agent was void.

Banking partnerships

[9.20] Section 1435(1) of the Companies Act 2014 does not apply to banking partnerships which are instead subject to a separate restriction set out in s 1436 of the 2014 Act. Section 1436 provides that the number of partners in a banking partnership cannot exceed ten. This restriction is of limited practical significance since, at the time of writing, a partnership cannot apply for authorisation as a bank.[51]

Farm partnerships and succession farm partnerships

[9.21] While s 667C(1A)(b) of the Taxes Consolidation Act 1997 provides that, to be a 'registered farm partnership', a farm partnership must have between 2 and 10 partners, and to be added to the Register of Succession Farm Partnerships, a succession farm partnership must already be a 'registered farm partnership' (thereby implying that it must also have no more than 10 partners),[52] it is very unlikely that a failure to meet these requirements will render the partnership illegal (provided of course that there are at least two partners). Rather, it will instead leave the partnership unable to register as either a

---

48 See *Greenberg v Copperstein* [1926] Ch 657; *Smith v Anderson* (1880) 15 Ch D 247. In *Gurry v McNamee and McDonald* (1868) ILTR 265, a plea of an illegal partnership was unsuccessful on the facts of that case. There, Gurry sued McNamee and McDonald for the return of money lent to both of them. The defence was that all three of them and others were partners and the money had been expended in the business of the firm. The plaintiff replied that there was no deed of partnership and that the firm was illegal, but the Irish Court of Common Pleas rejected the plaintiff's argument since it did not show that the partnership was illegal by having more than 20 members.

49 *Re D* (1877) 2 ILTR 97.

50 Ie s 4 of the Companies Act 1862 (25 & 26 Vict, c 89) (the predecessor of both s 1435(1) of the Companies Act 2014 and its immediate predecessor, s 376 of the Companies Act 1963).

51 See ss 9 and 9F of the Central Bank Act 1971 which provide that the Central Bank of Ireland shall not propose that the European Central Bank (as the ultimate supervisory authority for banks in the euro area since the introduction of the Single Supervisory Mechanism in November 2014) grant a banking licence to an applicant for authorisation unless that applicant meets various conditions, including that it is a body corporate with its registered office and head office both located in the State. As a partnership is not a body corporate, a partnership cannot currently be a bank.

52 Section 667D of the Taxes Consolidation Act 1997 provides, at ss (2), that only a 'registered farm partnership' can apply to be a 'registered succession farm partnership'. While s 667D(2)(a) only provides that a 'registered succession farm partnership' needs to have at least two members, both of whom must be individuals, the fact that it must first be a 'registered farm partnership' means that it can have no more than 10 partners.

'registered farm partnership' or as a 'registered succession farm partnership', and to obtain the benefits that result from such registration.[53]

Non-statutory Rules

[9.22] It is perhaps self-evident that the failure of a partnership to comply with non-statutory rules is most unlikely to render the partnership illegal. Thus in *Hawkins v Rogers*[54] it transpired that a racehorse partnership was not registered under the Rules of Racing or the National Hunt Steeplechase Rules. Not surprisingly, Dixon J gave little credence to this omission and he held that it did not affect the legality of the firm.

III. PARTNERSHIPS ILLEGAL AT COMMON LAW

[9.23] The second category of illegal partnerships is those partnerships which are illegal under common law. There may be some overlap between statutory illegality and illegality at common law since in modern times many of the previous common law offences are now contained in statutes. Two specific examples of such partnerships which are illegal under common law are:

   (i)   partnerships formed for a criminal purpose, and

   (ii) partnerships which are contrary to public policy.

Criminal Purpose

[9.24] The most striking example of a partnership which is illegal at common law is one which is formed for a criminal purpose. A colourful example of a partnership which was held to be illegal under this heading is provided by the 18th century case of *Everet v Williams*.[55] In this case, an account of partnership dealings by one partner against his co-partner was rejected by the court on the grounds that it was an illegal partnership. The bill in equity which was filed by the plaintiff stated that he was experienced in commodities such as rings and watches and that it was agreed that he and the defendant would provide the necessary tools of their proposed trade together, namely horses, saddles and weapons. They also agreed to share equally in the costs of the venture, ie the expenses involved in staying at inns, alehouses and taverns. The bill stated that they had successfully 'dealt with' a gentleman for a gold watch, rings, swords, canes, cloaks and other goods and the plaintiff sought an account of these dealings which had realised some £2,000. Despite the plaintiff's (and his lawyers') best attempts to disguise the purpose of the partnership, the action was dismissed on the grounds that this was clearly a partnership for the business of highwaymen and was therefore illegal. To add insult to injury, the costs were ordered to be paid by the counsel who signed the bill and the solicitor for the plaintiff was attached and fined for contempt, while at a subsequent date the plaintiff and defendant were hanged.[56]

---

53   See further, para **[8.109]** et seq.

54   *Hawkins v Rogers* [1951] IR 48.

55   *Everet v Williams* (1725) 9 LQR 197 which case was referred to by O'Flaherty J in *Irish Rail v Ireland* [1996] 2 ILRM 500 at 507.

56   See Anon, 'The Highwayman's Case' (1893) 9 LQR 197.

Contrary to Public Policy

[9.25] Another type of partnership which is illegal at common law is one which is formed for a purpose that is contrary to public policy.[57] Under this heading would fall a partnership during a period of war with an alien enemy,[58] a partnership to subvert the course of justice[59] and a partnership in the profits derived from prostitution.[60] Thus, in *Herring v Walround*,[61] an enterprise to exhibit what appears to have been Siamese twins was held to be illegal.

IV. CONSEQUENCES OF ILLEGALITY

[9.26] Whether a partnership is illegal at common law or under statute, the consequences of that illegality will be the same. These consequences will now be considered.

Automatic Dissolution of Illegal Partnership

[9.27] It has been seen that under s 34 of the 1890 Act, dissolution of an illegal partnership takes place automatically and the knowledge of the partners of the event which makes the firm illegal is irrelevant. This is clear from *Hudgell Yeates & Co v Watson*.[62] In that case, the partners in the law firm were unaware of the failure by one partner to renew his practising certificate;[63] indeed, in a similar case it had been noted that one might be 'as little likely to enquire about his solicitor's stamped certificate as about his certificate of vaccination'.[64] Nonetheless, Waller LJ held that: 'knowledge or otherwise of partners does not affect the dissolution. It takes place by force of law.'[65]

Yet a new partnership may come into being

[9.28] In cases where the illegality is caused by the presence in the partnership of an unqualified person, the dissolution of the illegal partnership may lead to a new partnership coming into existence between the remaining qualified partners. This was the case in *Hudgell Yeates & Co v Watson*,[66] where the Court of Appeal held that a new

---

57 See for example *Lemenda Trading Co Ltd v African Middle East Petroleum Co Ltd* [1988] QB 448. As to the categories of public policy, and whether there is scope for those to be extended, see Clark, *Contract Law in Ireland* (8th edn, 2016) at para 14-04 et seq and McDermott and McDermott, *Contract Law* (2nd edn, 2011) at paras [16.07]–[16.08].

58 *R v Kupfer* [1915] 2 KB 321; *Hugh Stevenson & Sons v Aktiengesellschaft* [1918] AC 239; *Rodriguez v Speyer Bros* [1919] AC 59.

59 *Amalgamated Society of Railway Servants v Osborne* [1909] 1 Ch 163; *Kemp v Corporation of Glasgow* (1920) SC 73.

60 *Hamilton v Main* (1823) 2 S 356.

61 *Herring v Walround* (1682) 2 Cas in Ch 110.

62 *Hudgell Yeates & Co v Watson* [1978] 2 All ER 363.

63 Knowledge of the law being presumed, per Waller LJ, at 372.

64 *Martin v Sherry* [1905] 2 IR 62 at 68, per Holmes LJ, in which it was held on the facts that no partnership existed.

65 *Hudgell Yeates & Co v Watson* [1978] 2 All ER 363 at 372.

66 *Hudgell Yeates & Co v Watson* [1978] 2 All ER 363.

partnership came into existence between the other solicitors in a firm, when the errant partner's practising certificate was not renewed.

No Action May be Taken by an Illegal Partnership

[9.29] If a partnership is illegal, the firm cannot maintain an action in respect of any transaction which is tainted with illegality. Thus in *Biggs v Lawrence*[67] it was held that an illegal partnership, formed for the purposes of smuggling goods, could not recover the price of the smuggled goods it had sold.

Actions May be Taken against an Illegal Partnership

[9.30] While it is seen to be just that an illegal partnership should suffer from its own illegality, there would be no justice in allowing its illegality to be used as a defence against the claims of innocent third parties. Accordingly, where an illegal partnership is sued by a third party, the illegal partnership cannot use its illegality as a defence to the action. This is assuming that the third party is unaware of the illegality of the transaction or the partnership at the time of the performance by the third party of his part of the bargain.[68] If the third party is aware of the illegality, his claim is defeated by the rule *ex turpi causa non oritur actio.*[69]

No Action May be Taken by Members of an Illegal Partnership

[9.31] An illegal partnership will confer no right on either party as against the other.[70] In *Ottley v Browne*,[71] the plaintiff was a banker and a partner in two firms in Belfast importing sugar and hemp. At that time, the Bankers Act of 1755[72] prohibited bankers from having an interest in trading partnerships. However, the plaintiff divested himself of his interest in the two partnerships, but he did so by transferring his interest to the defendant on a secret trust for the plaintiff's benefit. When he sought to enforce this trust, Manners LC refused to do so, on the grounds that the partnership breached the prohibition in the Bankers Act.

[9.32] A partner who has met the liabilities of an illegal partnership cannot recover any contributions from his partners,[73] nor will damages be awarded for a breach of its terms,[74] nor will a court enforce an arbitrator's award in favour of one partner in an illegal partnership.[75] Similarly, a court will not specifically enforce an agreement for an illegal partnership, even where the agreement has been partly performed. Thus, in *Ewing v Osbaldiston*,[76] the plaintiff and defendant agreed to form a partnership to run a

---

[67] *Biggs v Lawrence* (1789) 3 TR 454. See also *Shaw v Benson* (1883) 11 QBD 563; *Jennings v Hammond* (1882) 9 QB 225.

[68] *Re South Wales Atlantic SS Co* (1876) 2 Ch D 763.

[69] An action does not arise from a base cause.

[70] *Armstrong v Lewis* (1834) 2 Cr & M 274.

[71] *Ottley v Browne* (1810) 1 Ball & Beatty 360.

[72] An Act for promoting Public Credit of 1755 (29 Geo 2, c 16).

[73] *Mitchell v Cockburn* (1794) 2 H Bl 380.

[74] *Duvergier v Fellows* (1828) 5 Bing 248, aff'd (1832) 1 Cl & Fin 39.

[75] *Aubert v Maze* (1801) 2 Bos & Pul 371.

[76] *Ewing v Osbaldiston* (1837) 2 M & Cr 53.

theatre which was illegal by virtue of the Plays Act 1736. The plaintiff subsequently sought to enforce the terms of the partnership agreement, but it was held that due to the illegality of the agreement, the court could not decree its specific performance.[77]

Position of a personal representative

[9.33] However, the liability of a personal representative of a deceased partner is treated differently and his liability to account to the creditors and beneficiaries of the estate is not affected by the deceased's illegal activities. His obligation to account to the creditors and beneficiaries of the estate is established by *Joy v Campbell*.[78] There Redesdale LC relied on a case where:

> 'a person who was executor to a smuggler, on being called on to account for the estate of the testator, endeavoured to avoid a considerable part of the account by saying that they were smuggling transactions on which the Courts would not allow any action to be maintained: the answer was, all that died with the smuggler; he could not have been sued himself, but his executor shall not set up that as a defence against his creditors and legatees.'[79]

[9.34] However, *Ottley v Browne*[80] is authority for the principle that if no account has been settled between the partners themselves before the death of a partner, the deceased partner's personal representative may rely on the illegality as a defence to a claim for a partnership account.

Illegality Does not Have to be Pleaded

[9.35] For a court to refuse to enforce an illegal partnership, it is not necessary for one of the parties to plead the illegality. Illegality will be raised by the court on its own motion if it is clear on the face of the pleadings or becomes apparent during the course of the trial.[81]

Illegal Acts of a Valid Partnership

[9.36] It has been seen that a partnership may commit an illegal act without rendering the partnership illegal. A partner who receives a benefit as a result of an illegal act, but where the partnership is itself legal, will not, it seems, be subject to an action by his partner for the recovery of that illegal benefit.[82] This is the case, even where the other partners are innocent of the illegal act and where the non-interference of the court will

---

[77] See also the Australian case of *Renowden v Hurley* [1951] VLR 13 in which a medical partnership was held to be illegal since it had failed to obtain the requisite State Medical Board registration. On this basis, one partner was refused specific performance and could not make a claim for a share of the profits.

[78] *Joy v Campbell* (1804) 1 Sch & Lef 328.

[79] *Joy v Campbell* (1804) 1 Sch & Lef 328 at 339.

[80] *Ottley v Browne* (1810) 1 Ball & Beatty 360.

[81] *Scott v Brown Doering & Co* [1892] 2 QB 724. See also *Chettiar v Arunsalam Chettiar* [1962] AC 924.

[82] *Horgan v Baxter* (11 May 1982) HC. As to the present position in England, see *Farmers' Mart Ltd v Milne* [1915] AC 106 at 113 per Lord Dunedin and *Close v Wilson* [2011] EWCA Civ 5.

lead to the guilty partner benefiting.[83] *Horgan v Baxter*[84] involved a dispute over the profits of a cattle exporting partnership. In the plaintiff's action for the winding up of the partnership, it transpired that the defendant partner had forged certain financial documents relating to the partnership business. These forgeries resulted in his receiving increased export payments for the cattle which the firm had exported. The legality of the partnership itself was not doubted and Carroll J accepted that the innocent partner was entitled to half of the profits of the venture. However she held that the innocent partner was only entitled to share in those export payments which were properly claimed by the defendant. In this way, the innocent partner could not benefit from the illegal act of his co-partner.[85] Costs were, however, awarded against the defendant.[86]

[9.37] However, where the guilty partner obtained money from his innocent partner, it is thought that the position would be different and that the court would allow the recovery of this money. This is because, unlike the principle that an innocent partner should not *benefit* from the illegal act, to allow the guilty partner retain the innocent partner's money would permit the innocent partner to *suffer* as a result of the illegal act of his partner.[87]

---

[83]   *Whiteman v Sadler* [1910] AC 514.

[84]   *Horgan v Baxter* (11 May 1982) HC.

[85]   Note, however, that there was some inconsistency in Carroll J's approach since she allowed the plaintiff partner share in the profits which resulted from the falsification by the defendant of documentation regarding the purchase price of cattle. This falsification allowed the defendant to get a greater sale price for the cattle. See further para **[15.30]**.

[86]   Costs were awarded against the defendant partner on the basis that, if the defendant had kept proper accounts and had not forged certain documents, the matter could have been disposed of by the Examiner: *Baxter v Horgan* (28 May 1990) HC, (7 June 1991) SC.

[87]   *Sykes v Beadon* (1879) 11 Ch D 170.

PART B
RELATIONS BETWEEN PARTNERS AND THIRD PARTIES

Chapter 10

Liability of a Partner for the Acts of his Co-Partners

INTRODUCTION

[10.01] In this chapter it is proposed to examine the manner in which liability arises under partnership law for the actions of partners. The liability of a firm for the acts of its partners is governed by numerous sections of the 1890 Act.[1] The most important of these sections is s 5, since it confirms[2] the general principle that a 'partner is an agent of the firm and his other partners for the purposes of the business of the partnership'. This principle is the cornerstone for the liability of a firm for the acts of its partners. Thus, since a partner is the firm's agent for the partnership business, it follows that the firm should be liable for the acts of that agent which are done as part of the firm's business.[3]

[10.02] As a partnership is not a separate legal entity but simply a collection of partners,[4] it should be noted that a finding that a firm is liable for the acts of its partners is equivalent to a finding that all the partners are liable for the acts of one partner. For this reason, nothing turns on the references throughout the 1890 Act to the liability of the firm in some sections, and at other times to the liability of the partners.[5] Each of these instances of liability under the 1890 Act will be considered in turn and this area will be analysed under the following headings:

    I.   General Principles of a Partner's Liability;

    II.   Within the Ordinary Course of Business of a Firm;

---

[1]   Other statutory instances of a firm's liability for the acts of a partner are to be found in the Rules of the Superior Courts (SI 15/1986 as amended) where there are two instances of that liability. First, under RSC, Ord 77, r 44(1), when money in Court is ordered to be paid to partners, it is stated that such money may be paid to any one or more of the partners or the survivor of them. Second, under RSC Ord 76, r 12(2), where a partnership is petitioning for the bankruptcy of one of its debtors, it is stated that the bankruptcy summons may be granted on the affidavit of just one partner.

[2]   Prior to the 1890 Act, this principle was accepted as correct: *Cox v Hickman* (1860) 8 HLC 268.

[3]   Partnership Act 1890, s 5, as noted by Kelly J in *AIB PLC v Higgins & Ors* [2010] IEHC 219, (3 June 2010) at p 36 of the judgment: '... it is important to recall that under s 5 of the Partnership Act 1890 every partner is an agent of the firm and his other partners for the purpose of the business of the partnership. The acts of every partner pertinent to normal carrying on of the business bind the other partners.'

[4]   As to the aggregate theory of a partnership, see para **[3.04]**.

[5]   See for example the Partnership Act 1890, ss 5 and 6, where the reference is to the liability of the firm and of the partners, while in ss 10, 11 and 38 there is a reference to the liability of the firm only.

III.   Ratification; and

IV.   Specific Instances of Liability under the 1890 Act.

Overview

[10.03] A significant issue in relation to every partnership is the type of acts for which partners are liable. This is particularly so when one considers that once liability is established for a certain act, the liability of the partner therefor is unlimited in financial terms.[6]

[10.04] The basic premise for the liability of a partner for the acts of his co-partner is that since a partnership is an aggregate of all the partners,[7] an act which is done on behalf of a partnership is, under general agency principles, an act of each partner and each partner is therefore bound by that act. To determine whether an act is being done *on behalf of* the partnership, one must ask is the act within the firm's ordinary course of business? Clearly, if the act is being done as part of the business for which the partnership was formed, it is being done on behalf of all the partners. As such, the partners are bound by that act and liable for its consequences.

[10.05] While the question of whether the act of a partner is within a firm's ordinary course of business is an objective test, the courts are undoubtedly influenced by the consequences of such a finding, ie the resultant liability to an unlimited degree on the 'innocent' partners in the firm. However, imposing vicarious liability on a firm for the actions of a partner can be justified, in principle, on the basis that it is the firm which can control a partner's actions in relation to the partnership business and it is the firm which is the economic beneficiary of those actions and therefore it must take responsibility when those actions cause loss to third parties.[8] This rationale should be borne in mind when determining whether the circumstances of a particular act are such as to justify it being deemed within a firm's ordinary course of business, so as to attach liability therefor to the 'innocent' partners. Thus, the further one moves from an act which is '... so closely connected with acts the partner ... was authorised to do that, for the purpose of the liability of the firm ... to third parties, the wrongful conduct may

---

6   See para **[11.04]**.

7   See further regarding the nature of a partnership, para **[3.04]**.

8   See generally in relation to vicarious liability, McMahon and Binchy, *Law of Torts* (4th edn, 2013) at para [43.01] et seq. Note the rationale for this liability as explained by Collins MR in *Hamlyn v John Houston & Co* [1903] 1 KB 81 at 85–86: '[t]he principal having delegated the performance of a certain class of acts to his agent, it is not unjust that he, being the person who has appointed the agent, and who will have the benefit of his efforts if successful, should bear the risk of his exceeding his authority in matters incidental to the doing of the acts the performance of which has been delegated to him.'

9   Per Lord Nicholls in *Dubai Aluminium Co Ltd v Salaam* [2003] 2 AC 366. Mr Salaam had dishonestly participated in a fraud against Dubai Aluminium and Mr Amherst had acted as Mr Salaam's solicitor in drafting documents wrongfully assisting the fraud. The firm in which Mr Amherst was a partner had settled Dubai Aluminium's claim of US$10,000,000 and sought a contribution from Mr Salaam under the Civil Liability (Contribution) Act 1978. The firm's claim for contribution depended on it showing that it was liable, under s 10 of the 1890 Act (firm liable for wrongful acts/ommissions of a partner), for the wrongful acts committed by Mr Amherst. (contd.../)

fairly and properly be regarded as done by the partner while acting in the ordinary course of the firm's business …',[9] the less likely this act will be within the firm's ordinary course of business.[10] So an unpredictable and non-recurring act of a partner is less likely to fall within the firm's ordinary course of business, since the other partners are not in a good position to prevent this act.[11] On the other hand, such an act is more likely to be regarded as being within the firm's ordinary course of business, if the firm is the economic beneficiary of the act, on the basis that it should therefore shoulder the economic loss caused to third parties by that act.

[10.06] Finally, reference must be made to the use by the courts of the doctrines of express, implied and ostensible authority as a means of establishing the liability of a partner for the acts of his co-partner. The use by some courts of these concepts and the use by other courts (and the 1890 Act) of the concept of 'within the ordinary course of business' may lead to a certain degree of confusion. Thus, it is suggested that in analysing existing caselaw, one should see these three doctrines of authority as simply a way of determining whether an act is within the ordinary course of business of the firm (by virtue of it being authorised either expressly, impliedly or ostensibly by the partners).[12] In general terms, it would be preferable if the courts stuck to the one concept, namely whether the act is within the ordinary course of business of a firm. Such an approach is in keeping with the approach in employment law regarding the liability of an employer for the acts of his employee which are within the 'course of his employment', where the courts succeed in avoiding mixing in issues of actual, implied

---

9   (\...contd) The House of Lords held that the firm was entitled to a contribution from Mr Salaam and that the 1890 Act did not restrict the application of vicarious liability to instances where a partner had committed a tortious wrong. In reaching its decision, the House of Lords needed to determine whether Mr Amherst's wrongful conduct could be seen to have been carried out in the ordinary course of the firm's business for the purposes of s 10.

10   See for example the decision in *Flynn v Robin Thompson & Partners and Wallen* (2000) 97(6) LSG 36, where a partner in a firm of solicitors assaulted his opposing counsel in the precincts of the court. The English Court of Appeal found that the assault was so extraordinary and so far removed from the ordinary conduct of an advocate that it could not be within the ordinary course of the firm's business. As a result, the firm was not liable under s 10 of the 1890 Act to the plaintiff for the assault. A scuffle over some papers had also taken place within the courtroom and the court seemed prepared to find that the firm could be liable under s 10 in respect of that scuffle, on the basis that it occurred 'in the development of the contentious exchanges'. However, for procedural reasons the case regarding the scuffle in the courtroom did not go to trial. See, further, 'Liability of a partnership for a partner's assault' J Crim L 2000, 64(4), 368–370.

11   See generally Fortney, 'Am I my Partner's Keeper? Peer Review in Law Firms' (1995) 66 U Col LR 329; DeMott, 'Our partners' keepers? Agency dimensions of partnership relationships' (1995) 58 Law and Contemporary Problems 221; Bromberg, 'Enforcement of Partnership Obligations – who is sued for the partnership?' (1992) 71 Nebraska LR 143.

12   Lord Nicholls (with whom Lord Slynn and Lord Hutton agreed), in *Dubai Aluminium Co Ltd v Salaam* [2003] 2 AC 366, commented that, as regards the meaning of 'acting in the ordinary course of the business of the firm' in s 10 of the 1890 Act, except where the wronged party is defrauded by a person acting within the scope of his apparent authority, authority is not the touchstone of what is done in the ordinary course of employment or business.

or ostensible authority[13] with the basic issue of whether the act in question is within the ordinary course of employment of the employee.

I.   GENERAL PRINCIPLES OF A PARTNER'S LIABILITY

Partners as Agents

[10.07] In considering the general principles of a partner's liability for the acts of his co-partner, it is useful to refer first to the provisions of the 1890 Act which deal with the liability of a firm/partners for the acts of a partner. There are eight sections of the 1890 Act under which liability may attach to a firm for the acts of a partner, ie s 5 (firm liable for general acts of a partner), s 6 (firm liable for acts/instruments executed by a partner), s 10 (firm liable for wrongful acts/omissions of a partner), s 11 (firm liable for misapplication of property by a partner), s 13 (firm liable for breach of trust by a partner), s 15 (firm liable for admission or representation by a partner), s 16 (notice to a partner is binding on firm) and s 38 (firm liable for post-dissolution acts of a partner). Each of these sections is an example of the wider principle that a partner is liable for the acts of his co-partner done as part of the ordinary course of business of the firm,[14] and each is considered in detail below.[15] For present purposes, it is sufficient to note that this liability flows from the fact that each partner is his co-partner's agent for the purposes of the partnership business.

[10.08] The agency position of partners and partnerships is similar to that which exists in the primary form of business enterprise, the registered company. Like a registered company, which carries on its business through its directors, a partnership carries on its business through its partners. For this reason, to establish the liability of a partnership for the acts of a partner, reliance has to be placed on the principles of agency. Thus in every case of the purported liability of the firm for the acts of a partner, the most important issue to be determined will be whether the partner in question was the agent of the firm for the relevant act. As noted by Lord Cranworth in *Cox v Hickman*:[16] '[t]he liability of one partner for the acts of his co-partner is in truth the liability of a principal for the acts of his agent.'[17] This principle is now contained in the opening statement of s 5 of the 1890 Act which states: '[e]very partner is an agent of the firm and his other partners for the purpose of the business of the partnership ...'.

[10.09] Since partners are agents for the firm for the purposes of the business of the partnership, under general agency law, the firm will be liable for acts which are done within the scope of that agency, in other words within the 'ordinary course of business of the firm' and thus s 5 of the 1890 Act goes on to state:

---

13   This is so, even though an employee, like a partner, is clearly a species of agent. See McMahon and Binchy, *Law of Torts* (4th edn, 2013) at para [43.10] et seq.

14   Partnership Act 1890, s 5.

15   Paragraph **[10.81]** et seq.

16   *Cox v Hickman* (1860) 8 HLC 268. See also *Shaw v Galt* (1863) 16 Ir CLR 357, in which the High Court relied expressly on *Cox v Hickman* and held that 'the existence of such partnership implies also the existence of such a relation between those persons as that "each of them is a principal and each an agent for the others"', per O'Brien J (at 374).

17   *Cox v Hickman* (1860) 8 HLC 268 at 304.

[T]he acts of every partner who does any act for carrying on in the usual way business of the kind carried on by the firm of which he is a member bind the firm and his partners, unless the partner so acting has in fact no authority to act for the firm in the particular matter, and the person with whom he is dealing either knows that he has no authority, or does not believe him to be a partner.

[10.10] Section 5 of the 1890 Act is seen as having two 'limbs', summarised by Chadwick LJ in *Bank of Scotland v Henry Butcher & Co*[18] where he observed that:

'The inquiry under the first limb of s 5 of the 1890 Act is whether the act of one partner, say partner A, is done for the purpose of the business of the partnership. If it is, then, in doing that act, A is the agent of the firm and the other partners are bound by A's act. There is no need, in such a case, for the persons seeking to rely on the act to invoke the second limb.

The hypothesis which underlies the second limb of s 5 is that A's act is not, in fact, done for the purpose of the partnership business – so that the first limb is not in point. The inquiry under the second limb – in a case where it is necessary to invoke that limb – is whether A's act is an "act for carrying on in the usual way business of the kind carried on by the firm". That requires consideration of two elements: (i) what business is "business of the kind carried on by the firm"; and (ii) is A's act "an act for carrying on in the usual way" that business. Where those two elements are present, the person with whom A is dealing is entitled to treat the act as done for the purpose of the business of the partnership unless he knows that A has in fact no authority, or does not know or believe A to be a partner.'

[10.11] In *Bank of Scotland v Henry Butcher & Co*,[19] the partnership agreement entered into by the defendants provided that one partner could not give a guarantee on behalf of the partnership without the consent of the other partners. The partnership entered into a consultancy agreement with a Mr Hopkins under the terms of which it would receive a share of profits from mutual business deals in return for providing a guarantee to Bank of Scotland in respect of Mr Hopkins' overdraft. The guarantee was then entered into by four of the partners in the firm 'as partners ... and individuals'. Bank of Scotland called in the guarantee following a default by Mr Hopkins, and the partnership argued that it was not bound by the guarantee as not all partners had consented to it. Bank of Scotland (with whom the Court of Appeal agreed) argued that the guarantee was given in the course of the partnership business and, as a result, the signature of the four partners was sufficient to bind the partnership in light of s 5 of the 1890 Act. Agreeing with the findings of fact made by the trial judge that the consultancy agreement was partnership business, with the guarantee given in respect of that business therefore being given in the course of the business of the partnership, Munby J stated that the key question was not whether the partnership had ratified the consultancy agreement but whether the partnership had adopted the provision of consultancy services as part of its business. As it had, the firm was found liable under s 5 of the 1890 Act.

[10.12] In addition, s 7 of the 1890 Act is a statement of the corollary of s 5, namely that a firm is not liable for acts of a partner which are outside a firm's ordinary course of business, albeit in the context of the pledging of the firm's credit:

---

[18] *Bank of Scotland v Henry Butcher & Co* [2003] 2 All ER (Comm) 557 at paras 87 and 88 of the transcript.

[19] *Bank of Scotland v Henry Butcher & Co* [2003] 2 All ER (Comm) 557 (CA).

Where one partner pledges the credit of the firm for a purpose apparently not connected with the firm's ordinary course of business, the firm is not bound, unless he is in fact specially authorised by the other partners: but this section does not affect any personal liability incurred by an individual partner.

[10.13] It is the requirement that an act be within the firm's ordinary course of business which underlies the liability of a firm for the acts of a partner and which will now be considered along with the two other requirements for a firm to be bound by the acts of a partner.

The Three Requirements for a Firm to be Bound by the Acts of Partner

[10.14] The liability of a firm for the acts of a partner in any particular case may be considered under the most appropriate section of the 1890 Act or under the general liability of a firm under agency principles for the acts of a partner. Whether one is attempting to establish liability under any of these eight sections[20] or under the general principle of agency, three basic requirements must be satisfied before liability will be established. These are that:

1. the act must be done by a partner;[21]
2. the act must be done *qua* partner;[22]
3. the act must be within the ordinary course of business of the firm.[23]

The first and second requirement are arguably self-evident and will generally be easy to establish, while the requirement that the act be within the firm's ordinary course of business has caused the most difficulty and much of this chapter will be spent analysing this notion.

1. The Act Must be Done by a Partner

[10.15] Before a firm will be bound by the act of its partner, it is clear that the act must be that of a partner. Thus, in each of the eight instances of liability of a firm for the acts of a partner in the 1890 Act referred to above,[24] the act which is binding on the firm[25] is expressly referred to as the act of a 'partner'. It follows that the actions of a salaried partner[26] and the actions of an intending partner[27] will not bind the firm under these sections or under the general principles of the liability of a firm for the acts of a partner. Nonetheless, the actions of such a person may be binding on the firm under the general principles of agency, eg a salaried partner may have ostensible authority to bind the firm.[28]

---

20 With the exception of s 16, see para **[10.126]**.
21 Partnership Act 1890, s 5 and see para **[10.15]**.
22 *Allied Pharmaceutical Distributors Limited v Walsh* [1991] IR 8, see para **[10.20]**.
23 Partnership Act 1890, s 5, see para **[10.26]**.
24 Paragraph **[10.07]**.
25 In the case of s 15 of the 1890 Act, the act of the partner is an admission or representation by a partner which is 'evidence against the firm' and may be rebutted, see para **[10.123]**.
26 See the judgment of Waller J in *Hudgell Yeates & Co v Watson* [1978] 2 All ER 363 at 373.
27 *Catt v Howard* (1820) 3 Stark 3; *Tunley v Evans* (1845) 2 Dow & L 747.
28 See the judgment of Megarry J in *Stekel v Ellice* [1973] 1 All ER 465 at 472 and see also para **[7.45]**.

Regardless of status of partner within the firm

[10.16] The fact that a partner in a firm is a junior partner does not in any way reduce his power to bind his partners. This is clear from *Morans v Armstrong*[29] where a partner in a Dublin firm of merchants claimed that a composition with creditors was not binding on the firm since it was approved only by a 'junior partner', who had nothing to do with the financial transactions of the firm. This argument was rejected by Brady CB who stated:

'The junior partner binds the others as much as any other partner, or as all the partners together. The world cannot know his department in the establishment, it is enough that he was partner at all.'[30]

[10.17] Similarly, the fact that a partner is a dormant partner will not affect his power to bind the firm. As noted previously,[31] a dormant partner is treated as a partner for all legal purposes, therefore his firm is equally bound by his actions as by the actions of any other partner and each of the references in ss 5 to 16 and 38 of the 1890 Act to 'partner' should be taken to include dormant partners.

The firm must have been in existence

[10.18] A consequence of the requirement that to bind the firm the act must be done by a partner is the fact that the act must have been performed at a time when the firm was in existence. If the firm does not yet exist, the partner cannot be said to have authority to bind it. This follows from the general principle of agency law that there can be no agency if the purported principal does not exist, as is clear from *Dublin Laundry Co Ltd v Clarke.*[32] That case concerned the purported agency between the defendant, a director in a company, and that company. The defendant, at the time of a contract for the purchase of land, intended that the obligations and benefits of the contract be taken over by that company. However, at the time of the contract the company had not yet been incorporated. As there was no principal in existence, Costello J held that the defendant could not have entered into the contract as an agent.

Where a third party does not believe that he is dealing with a partner

[10.19] It is clear from the foregoing that in determining whether a firm is bound to a third party by an act, it is important that the act in question is being done by a partner.[33] In cases where a partner in a firm does not have the authority to do acts within the ordinary course of business of a firm, the third party must believe that he is dealing with a partner. This is because, under s 5 of the 1890 Act, if the partner does not have authority to do an act which is within the firm's ordinary business, the firm will nonetheless be bound by that act, *unless* the third party did not know or believe that he

---

29   *Morans v Armstrong* (1840) Arm M & O 25.
30   *Morans v Armstrong* (1840) Arm M & O 25 at 26–27.
31   See generally para **[6.04]** et seq.
32   *Dublin Laundry Co Ltd v Clarke* [1988] ILRM 29.
33   We are referring exclusively to the liability of a firm for the acts of a partner. It is of course possible that a firm would be bound by the acts of person under a separate heading, eg the acts of an agent who is not a partner such as an employee.

was a partner. Where the third party does not believe that he is dealing with a partner, he must be taken to know that the first requirement for the firm to be bound has not been satisfied. If the third party subsequently discovers that the person is a partner, he cannot claim that the firm should be bound by that act since it is within the ordinary course of business of a firm.

2. The Act Must be Done *qua* Partner

[10.20] The second requirement to be satisfied for a firm to be bound by the actions of a partner is that the act in question must be done by the partner *qua* partner. It is important to distinguish between this requirement and the fact that the act must be done within the ordinary course of business of the firm. For example the act of a partner in an accountancy firm who becomes a company director for his own family's company may not be binding on his firm since, although done by a partner and constituting an act which is within the ordinary course of business of an accountancy firm, it may not have been done by him *qua* partner. This distinction was clearly made by Barron J in the High Court case of *Allied Pharmaceutical Distributors Ltd v Walsh*,[34] where he quoted with approval the following principle:

> 'The fact that the wrongful act is carried out by a partner does not necessarily make the partnership liable, even if what he does is within the ordinary course of business of the partnership ... [T]he words of the Act do not refer to the rights and liabilities of the partners *inter se* in the abstract, but only in relation to contracts made with or acts done to the detriment of third persons, and those third persons must be persons who are dealing with the partner as such, or who are in a position to elect to deal with the partner as such, or to treat his wrongful act as the act of a partner.'[35]

[10.21] Although Barron J was referring to s 10 of the 1890 Act, it is contended that this principle applies to all instances of liability of a firm for the acts of its partners.[36] The case itself involved one partner in the accountancy firm of Robert J Kidney & Co, who gave investment advice to clients of the firm. However, he also began to take deposits from clients of the firm which he used to lend to other clients via his own private company. When it transpired that this company was insolvent, a client of the firm sued all the partners for the loss he suffered. The other partners argued that the giving and taking of deposits was an independent transaction of the partner and thus the firm was not liable. This was rejected by Barron J, who held that the firm was liable for the acts of this partner. He held that the taking of deposits was done by the partner in his position as investment adviser to the clients. Thus, it was done by him *qua* partner.

[10.22] A case in which a partner was held not be acting *qua* partner is that of *British Homes Assurance Corp Ltd v Paterson*.[37] This dealt with a claim that a firm was liable for the misappropriation by one of its partners of client funds under s 11 of the 1890

---

[34] *Allied Pharmaceutical Distributors Ltd v Walsh* [1991] IR 8.

[35] *Allied Pharmaceutical Distributors Ltd v Walsh* [1991] IR 8 at 14, quoting in part from *British Homes Assurance Corporation Ltd v Paterson* [1902] 2 Ch 404 at 411.

[36] Note in particular that, while Barron J was referring to s 10 of the 1890 Act, the case upon which he relied, *British Homes Assurance Corporation Ltd v Paterson* [1902] 2 Ch 404, dealt with a claim under s 11 of the 1890 Act.

[37] *British Homes Assurance Corp Ltd v Paterson* [1902] 2 Ch 404.

Act. In that case, the plaintiff instructed a solicitor, Atkinson, to act on its behalf in relation to a mortgage. At that time, Atkinson practised under the name of 'Atkinson and Atkinson'. Soon after, he entered partnership with Paterson and he informed the plaintiff that he would in future carry on business under the name of 'Atkinson and Paterson'. The plaintiff ignored this and continued to deal with Atkinson as 'Atkinson and Atkinson' and on completion of the transaction, sent a cheque to him in the name of 'Atkinson and Atkinson or order'. When Atkinson absconded with this money, the plaintiff sued Paterson for the return of the money. Farwell J held that the defendant was not liable for the default and in a passage which was quoted with approval by Barron J,[38] he observed:

> 'In my opinion, the defendant does not come within the words of the Act, because I do not think that it is open to a third person to assert that the individual with whom he has intentionally contracted as an individual on his several contract, or with whom he has elected to continue a contract as with an individual, was acting in the ordinary course of business of the firm, or was acting within the scope of his ostensible authority. He knew that he was not acting or appearing to act, for the firm at all, and he preferred to have it so.'[39]

[10.23] This requirement that the partner be acting *qua* partner also explains the decision reached in the Australian case of *Chittick v Maxwell*.[40] There, it was held by the Supreme Court of New South Wales that the negligence of a partner in a law firm was not attributable to his co-partners when that partner negligently failed to protect his client's interest in a property. His co-partners were not liable because, although the work had been done in the firm's premises and for clients of the firm, the clients (who were the parents-in-law of the partner) had not requested the service.

Qua partner and written contracts

[10.24] The *Allied Pharmaceutical* case[41] involved the question of whether the advice of a partner was done *qua* partner. In other cases, a third party may be attempting to claim that a contract was executed by a partner *qua* partner rather than in a personal capacity, and in such a case, this issue will be determined, inter alia, by the terms of the contract. The case of *Dublin Laundry Co Ltd v Clarke*[42] will be of assistance in such instances although it involved a company rather than a partnership. It concerned a purported agency between a company and its director. The defendant claimed that when he entered a contract for the purchase of land, he intended that the obligations and benefits of the contract were to be taken over by a company which had not yet been incorporated. In the High Court, Costello J quoted with approval an earlier judgment of Budd J in *Lavan v Walsh*[43] that:

> 'The question as to whether an agent is to be deemed to have contracted personally in the case of a contract in writing depends on the intention of the parties as appearing from the

---

[38] *Allied Pharmaceutical Distributors Ltd v Walsh* [1991] IR 8 at 14.
[39] *British Homes Assurance Corp Ltd v Paterson* [1902] 2 Ch 404 at 411.
[40] *Chittick v Maxwell* (1993) 118 ALR 728.
[41] *Allied Pharmaceutical Distributors Ltd v Walsh* [1991] IR 8.
[42] *Dublin Laundry Co Ltd v Clarke* [1988] ILRM 29.
[43] *Lavan v Walsh* [1964] IR 87.

terms of the written agreement as a whole. The construction of the document is a matter of law for the Court.'[44]

Applying this principle to the fact that the contract in question named the defendant alone in the title as the purchaser, the fact that there was no reference to agency in the contract and that it was signed by the defendant and one other person (his future co-director in the company), Costello J held that the parties did not intend that he sign the contract in a representative capacity.

May be qua partner, even if firm is incapable of doing act

[10.25] An action by a partner may still be regarded as having been done *qua* partner even where the firm itself would not have been able to do such an act. This is clear from the *Allied Pharmaceutical* case.[45] In that case, the giving and taking of loans to and from clients by a partner in an accountancy firm was prohibited by the ethical guidelines of the accountancy profession. Nonetheless, Barron J stated:

> 'It is not open however to the remaining partners in a firm to assert that a third party dealt with the partner as an individual rather than as a partner because the nature of the work was such that it could not have been performed by the partnership.'[46]

Accordingly, Barron J held that the firm was bound by those loans and he relied expressly on the Scottish case of *Kirkintilloch Equitable Co-operative Society Ltd v Livingstone*.[47] There, the defendant accountancy firm sought unsuccessfully to avoid liability for the negligence of one of its partners on the grounds that audit work was not within the ordinary business of the firm since a firm was incapable of being appointed as an auditor.[48] Barron J quoted with approval the judgment of Lord Cameron in that case that:

> '"Authority," as the word is used in section 10 [of the Partnership Act 1890], appears to me to be used in the sense of control, direction, or knowing approval of the action or actions in question and the test is factual and objective. I see nothing in the Act which implies that co-partners cannot give authority to one of their number to perform, as a partner, acts which they themselves may not be legally qualified to perform.'[49]

3. The Act Must be Within the Firm's Ordinary Course of Business

[10.26] The third and final condition to be satisfied for a firm to be bound by the acts of its partners is the one which has received the most attention by the courts, namely that the act be within the ordinary course of business of the firm.[50] The importance of this

---

[44] *Dublin Laundry Co Ltd v Clarke* [1988] ILRM 29 at 38 quoting from *Lavan v Walsh* [1964] IR 87 at 96.

[45] *Allied Pharmaceutical Distributors Ltd v Walsh* [1991] IR 8.

[46] *Allied Pharmaceutical Distributors Ltd v Walsh* [1991] IR 8 at 14.

[47] *Kirkintilloch Equitable Co-operative Society Ltd v Livingstone* [1972] SC 111.

[48] Since an individual accountant, and not a firm, was entitled to be an auditor.

[49] *Allied Pharmaceutical Distributors Ltd v Walsh* [1991] IR 8 at 15 quoting from *Kirkintilloch Equitable Co-operative Society Ltd v Livingstone* [1972] SC 111 at 122.

[50] An interesting point of comparison is the requirement under s 14(2) of the Sale of Goods Act 1893 (inserted by s 10 of the Sale of Goods and Supply of Services Act 1980) that goods be sold in the course of business for certain warranties to be implied regarding those goods, (contd.../)

requirement is evident from the inclusion of the term 'within the ordinary course of business of the firm' or an approximation thereof[51] in each of the eight instances of liability of a firm for the acts of a partner under the 1890 Act. Thus, a firm is liable for the acts/omissions/contracts/representations, etc of a partner where:

- it constitutes 'the carrying on in the usual way business of a kind carried on by the firm' (s 5);
- it relates 'to the business of the firm' (s 6);
- it is 'within the ordinary course of business of the firm' (s 10);
- it is within the scope of a partner's 'apparent authority'[52] (s 11(a));
- it is in the 'course of its business' (s 11(b));
- it is used 'in the business or on the account of the partnership' (s 13);
- it is made in the 'ordinary course of its business' (s 15);
- it is 'necessary to wind up the affairs of the partnership', which must be taken as being within the ordinary course of business of a dissolved partnership.

Likewise, a firm is not liable for the pledging of the credit of the firm by a partner, where it is unconnected with the 'firm's ordinary course of business' (s 7).

[10.27] Whichever of these sections is relied upon, the test is the same – is the act something which is within the ordinary course of business of the firm?[53] It will therefore be seen that the classification of a particular act as being within the 'ordinary course of business of the firm' is crucial since the question of the liability of the firm for the acts of a partner generally or under a specific section of the 1890 Act is determined by this fact.

[10.28] For example a firm of doctors would be liable for the damage caused by the negligent driving of one of the partners where he is involved in a car accident on the way to see a patient. This is because the negligent driving of the partner is an act which is

---

[50]   (\...contd) see regarding the English equivalent of this requirement Lacy, 'Selling in the course of business under the Sale of Goods Act 1979' (1999) 62 Modern Law Review 776.

[51]   Clearly it would be preferable if the same wording was used in each section and this is an area that could be usefully revised in any future amendment of the 1890 Act.

[52]   It is noted at para **[10.32]** that an act which is apparently authorised is synonymous with saying that it is ostensibly authorised which, it is noted at para **[10.31]**, is equivalent to saying that it is within the firm's ordinary couse of business.

[53]   The current editor of *Lindley & Banks on Partnership* (20th edn, 2017) at para 12-91, takes the view that the expression 'carrying on in the usual way business of the kind carried on by the firm' in s 5 and 'in the ordinary course of business' in s 10 can be taken to both mean the same thing, ie was the partner 'acting in the ordinary course of business of the firm'? Further, in *JJ Coughlan v Ruparelia* [2002] EWHC 1733 (QB) (aff'd on appeal at [2003] EWCA Civ 1057) the trial judge, Mackay J, held that there was no material difference between 'the usual way of business of the kind carried on by the firm' for the purposes of s 5 of the 1890 Act and 'acting in the ordinary course of the business of the firm' for the purposes of s 10 of the 1890 Act. The same can, it is apprehended, be said of the other sections, so that for any act to be binding on the firm it must be 'within the ordinary course of business of the firm'. For a contrary view see Bennett, *An Introduction to the Law of Partnership in Scotland* (1995) at para 12.5.

committed by the partner while acting in the ordinary course of business of the firm.[54] On the other hand, the firm of doctors will not generally be liable for the damage caused by one of the partners, where on his way to see a patient he decides to take a detour and assault an innocent third party. This assault would not be regarded as being 'within the ordinary course of business of the firm' since the partner is acting in a completely unusual manner for his own purposes and not in order to benefit the firm.[55]

[10.29] In the following section, further detailed consideration will be given to the meaning of the phrase 'within the ordinary course of business' of a firm.

II. WITHIN THE ORDINARY COURSE OF BUSINESS OF A FIRM

An Act which is Authorised is within the 'ordinary business' of firm

[10.30] It has been noted that a partner is the agent of his firm. For this reason, partnership law has applied the rules, applicable to the question of the authority of an agent to bind his principal, to the issue of the authority of a partner to bind his firm. Thus, a partner may have actual authority or ostensible authority to bind the firm to a particular act.

Actual authority and ostensible authority

[10.31] The actual authority of a partner may be described as 'real' authority from the firm to the partner to do a certain act in the sense that, unlike ostensible authority, it results from a manifestation of consent from the firm to the partner to do the act.[56] Actual authority may be sub-divided into either express authority or implied authority. It may take the form of express authority, where this consent is based on the terms of the oral or written partnership agreement. Alternatively, actual authority may take the form of implied authority from the firm to the partner, where the very existence of a partnership implies a consent from the firm to a partner to do acts which would be regarded as incidental to that partnership, such as open a bank account for the firm, sign cheques in the name of the firm, etc.

[10.32] An important distinction must be made between the actual authority of a partner (whether express or implied) and the ostensible authority (which is sometimes called apparent authority) of a partner. Unlike actual authority, ostensible authority, as its name suggests, is not 'real' authority in the sense that it does not result from an express or implied agreement between the partner and the firm. Rather, ostensible authority is implied by law. It arises not as a result of any manifestation of consent between the firm and the partner, but rather from a representation by the firm (including representation by conduct) to a third party that there is such a consent in place. Thus, ostensible authority is the authority which a partner ostensibly or apparently has in the eyes of third parties as a result of a representation by the firm to that effect. By definition, ostensible

---

54   Partnership Act 1890, s 10.
55   See fn **10** above regarding the decision in *Flynn v Robin Thompson & Partners and Wallen* (2000) 97(6) LSG 36.
56   See generally Reynolds, *Bowstead & Reynolds on Agency* (20th edn, 2014) at para 3-001 et seq.

authority exists because there is no actual authority from the partnership to the partner to do the act in question and in this important way, ostensible authority differs from the confusingly similar term 'implied authority'. One may regard actual authority as being concerned with the internal mechanics of a partnership, while ostensible authority is concerned with the view of the partnership from the outside. Thus the question of whether an act is actually authorised is determined by a search for that authority in the relations between the partners inter se. With ostensible authority, one searches instead for the appearance of such an authority from the perspective of outsiders dealing with the firm. The nature of ostensible authority in the context of a partnership was summarised by Clarke J in *ACC Bank plc v Johnston p/a Brian Johnston & Co Solicitors*,[57] where he commented that:

> 'Ostensible authority is only relevant when there is no actual authority. If the relevant partner has actual authority then that is sufficient to bind the partnership. Ostensible authority is, therefore, concerned with circumstances where partners may be bound for each other's actions even though the partner actually committing the wrongful act may not have actual authority.'

[10.33] In this regard, ostensible authority is essentially a fiction which has been created by the courts to protect third parties who deal with agents by allowing the third parties to rely on representations by the principal that the agent is authorised to do the act in question. By imposing ostensible authority in this way, the law imposes liability on the principal for making this representation. Thus, ostensible authority is a form of estoppel, whereby as a result of his conduct, a principal is prevented from denying that a person is not his agent.[58]

Ordinary course of business and express, implied or ostensible authority

[10.34] Once a partner has either express, implied or ostensible authority to do a particular act, then it follows that the firm is bound by that act.[59] It is important to bear in mind that in dealing with the question of whether an act is within the ordinary course of business of a firm, one is essentially dealing with whether the act was expressly, impliedly or ostensibly authorised by the firm. This is because a finding of ostensible authority involves the conclusion that the act in question was such as to be reasonably regarded by third parties as being an ordinary part of the business of the firm and therefore something which the partners must be regarded as having ostensibly authorised. Similarly, a finding of implied authority involves a finding that certain powers are incidental to the business of partnership and thus must be implied under general partnership law for partners in all partnerships. Accordingly, an act which is impliedly authorised may be regarded as being part of the ordinary course of business of all firms. And in the case of an act which is expressly authorised, such an act must be regarded as being within the ordinary course of business of the firm on the grounds that it is expressly authorised by the partners. For this reason, the question of whether an act of a partner is within a firm's ordinary course of business has sometimes been

---

[57] *ACC Bank plc v Johnston p/a Brian Johnston & Co Solicitors* [2011] IEHC 108.

[58] See generally Wilken and Villiers, *The Law of Waiver, Variation and Estoppel* (3rd edn, 2012).

[59] See generally in relation to the authority of an agent to bind a principal, Reynolds, *Bowstead & Reynolds on Agency* (20th edn, 2014) at para [3-001] et seq.

determined by asking if that act was expressly, impliedly or ostensibly authorised. Thus, in analysing the requirement that an act be 'within the ordinary course of business' of a firm, reference will of necessity be made to these three different types of authority. It should be borne in mind that the essential question is whether the act was within the firm's ordinary course of business, and if this is the case, one need not be concerned as to whether it was expressly, impliedly or ostensibly authorised. After all, it is this requirement which is used as the rubric for establishing liability in each of the different sections on a firm's liability under the 1890 Act.[60]

Precise Meaning of 'within the ordinary course of business'

[10.35] It is difficult to formulate general rules regarding the meaning of the phrase 'within the ordinary course of business' as it applies to a particular firm, as each firm will, to a certain degree, be different. In this sense, the concept shares many similarities with the concept of 'within the course of employment' as a test for the liability of an employer for the actions of his employees.[61]

[10.36] However, some general observations may be made. It should be clear from the discussion which follows that in determining whether an act is within a firm's ordinary course of business, one should examine, inter alia, the manner in which the firm's business is described in the partnership agreement, the actual business carried on by the firm, the usual manner in which business of similar firms is transacted, the usual conduct of the partner who has committed the act, the knowledge of his co-partners of that conduct and the type of contact already existing between the firm and the third party who is making the claim that the act is within the firm's ordinary business.[62]

Not to be read literally

[10.37] If one were to interpret the expression 'within the ordinary course of business' literally, most claims against a partnership would be disallowed, since in most partnerships it is not within the ordinary course of business of a firm for a partner to commit wrongful acts or omissions. Thus, the expression must not be read as meaning that the wrongful act or omission is itself a part of the partnership business. Rather the wrongful act or omission must have been committed during the conduct by the partner of an activity which was within the ordinary course of business of the firm.[63] This

---

[60] See para **[10.26]**.

[61] See generally McMahon and Binchy, *Law of Torts* (4th edn, 2013) at para [43.38] et seq and such cases as *Boyle v Ferguson* [1911] 2 IR 489; *Kiely v McCrea & Sons Ltd* [1940] Ir Jur Rep 1; *Murphy v Ross* [1920] 2 IR 199; *Lawlor v O'Connor* (1929) 63 ILTR 103; *Lloyd v Grace, Smith & Co [1912] AC 716*.

[62] Lord Nicholls, in *Dubai Aluminium Co Limited v Salaam* [2002] UKHL 48, observed that: 'Clearly, the nature and scope of a business carried on by partners are questions of fact. Similarly, what the ordinary course of the business comprises, in the sense of what is the normal manner in which the business is carried on is also a question of fact. So is the scope of a partner's authority.'

[63] The liability of one partner for the acts of his co-partner involves the imposition of vicarious liability on the first partner, since the first partner may not have done the act in question, but is nonetheless liable therefor. See generally in relation to vicarious liability, McMahon and Binchy, *Law of Torts* (4th edn, 2013) at para [43-01] et seq.

distinction is vividly highlighted by the decision of the New Zealand Court of Appeal in *Proceedings Commissioner v Ali Hatem.*[64] There, one partner in a garage partnership, who was in charge of the firm's staffing, was held to have been guilty of sexual harassment of an employee of the firm. Clearly this act, which was a statutory tort under the Human Rights Commission Act 1977 in New Zealand, was not part of the ordinary course of business of a garage in a literal sense. However, it was held to be within the meaning of this term in the legal sense, since the partner was acting in the ordinary course of business when he performed this wrongful act or to put it another way, he was acting within the general scope of the authority created by the firm's business even though the particular conduct was tortious. On this basis his co-partners were held liable for this tort. From a policy perspective, this decision may be justified since if the sexual harassment of an employee by a partner is not the responsibility of the firm as a whole, then it is less likely to be vigorously policed. The words of Tipping J are instructive:

> 'Although sexual harassment cannot be regarded as part of the ordinary course of the firm's business, we are of the view that, when acting as he did, the perpetrator was acting in the ordinary course of the firm's business. The first acts of sexual harassment occurred when he was interviewing one of the complainants for a job. There were numerous instances of sexually loaded remarks ... In this case, the perpetrator was doing something within the ordinary course of business of the firm, ie dealing with staff members in the work environment. In so doing, he committed the statutory tort of sexual harassment. He thereby did tortiously something which he was generally authorised to do. The firm is liable for his conduct.'[65]

It includes an act which is contrary to the guidelines of a profession

[10.38] Since the expression 'ordinary course of business' is not to be interpreted literally, an act which is contrary to the ethical guidelines of a profession may nonetheless be within that firm's ordinary course of business as was the situation in the High Court case of *Allied Pharmaceutical Distributors Ltd v Walsh.*[66]

It includes an act which is negligent or fraudulent or an intentional wrong

[10.39] It is clear from *Proceedings Commissioner v Ali Hatem*[67] that it is unlikely that negligence or fraud will literally be part of a firm's ordinary course of business, yet if a partner is guilty of fraud or negligence during the conduct by him of an activity which is within the ordinary course of business of the firm, the firm will be liable therefor. This

---

[64] *Proceedings Commissioner v Ali Hatem* [1999] 1 NZLR 305. See also *Cricklewood Holdings Ltd v CV Quigley & Sons Nominees Ltd* [1992] 1 NZLR 463 in which a partner in a law firm, though acting dishonestly, was held to be acting in the ordinary course of business when he raised money on mortgages using clients' funds. See also the Canadian case of *McDonic v Hetherington* (1997) 31 OR (3d) 577 in which a law firm was held responsible for one partner's negligent dealings with client funds. In the Ontario High Court case of *Public Trustee v Mortimer* (1985) 16 DLR (4d) 404 it was held that a law firm was liable where one partner, who acted as a trustee and executor of a client's will, stole money from the estate.

[65] *Proceedings Commissioner v Ali Hatem* [1999] 1 NZLR 305 at 313.

[66] *Allied Pharmaceutical Distributors Ltd v Walsh* [1991] IR 8, see para **[10.25]**.

[67] *Proceedings Commissioner v Ali Hatem* [1999] 1 NZLR 305, see para **[10.37]**.

was also the case in *Rapp v Latham*.[68] There, a partner who had received money from a customer to purchase wine on his behalf, fraudulently represented to the customer that he had complied with the customer's instructions. When it transpired that he had misappropriated this money, his firm was held liable for the loss to the customer caused by the fraud.[69] Similarly in the Scottish case of *Welsh v Knarston*,[70] a firm of solicitors was liable for the negligence of a partner in failing to institute proceedings in a personal injuries case within the prescribed limitation period.

A change in the nature of a partnership business is not 'ordinary business'

[10.40] By virtue of the express terms of s 24(8) of the 1890 Act, a change in the nature of a firm's business is not within the ordinary course of a firm. Under s 24(8), a change cannot be made in the nature of the partnership business without the consent of all the existing partners. Thus, in the absence of express authority from each of the partners, it is outside the ordinary course of business of the firm for one partner to change the nature of the firm's business and therefore the firm will not be bound thereby.

A representation of authority is not 'ordinary business'

[10.41] Similarly, it is not within a firm's ordinary course of business for a partner to be authorised to represent to third parties the extent of his authority,[71] since otherwise a partner could extend his own authority by a representation to that effect. Accordingly, where a third party has relied on a partner's incorrect representation that he has authority to bind the firm, the partnership will not be bound by this representation. In *Hirst v Etherington*,[72] the defendant was a partner in a solicitors' firm with one other person. He arranged a loan of £30,000 for his client from the plaintiff and as part of the transaction, Etherington undertook to repay £36,000 to the plaintiff. The plaintiff's solicitor obtained an assurance from Etherington that this undertaking was given in the course of normal business of the firm. In this way, he assumed that he was binding Etherington's partner to this undertaking. In the English Court of Appeal, it was held first that this undertaking, which was given as security for a loan, was not given in the ordinary course of business of the firm and second that the representation by Etherington that his undertaking was within the normal business of the firm, was not binding on the firm, since it was not within the ordinary course of business of the firm to give such a representation in the first place.

'Ordinary business' is that of the firm, not of a partner

[10.42] In determining whether an act of a partner is within the ordinary course of business of a firm, the fact that it is, or is not, within the ordinary course of business of the partner in question is irrelevant. To determine whether the firm is bound, the test is whether the act is within the ordinary course of business of the firm. This point may be

[68] *Rapp v Latham* (1819) 2 B & A 795, which case was quoted with approval by Barron J in *Allied Pharmaceutical Distributors Ltd v Walsh* [1991] IR 8 at 17.

[69] The same situation exists under the doctrine of the vicarious liability of an employer for the fraud of his employee: *Lloyd v Grace, Smith & Co* [1912] AC 716.

[70] *Proceedings Commissioner v Ali Hatem* [1972] SLT 96.

[71] *Ex p Agace* (1792) 2 Cox 312.

[72] *Hirst v Etherington* [1999] 8 CLY 145.

particularly relevant in large firms where the work is departmentalised to a considerable degree as is illustrated *Morans v Armstrong.*[73] There it was argued that a composition with creditors was not binding on a Dublin firm of merchants, since it was approved by a partner who had nothing to do with the financial transactions of the firm. This defence was rejected by Brady CB who observed that the 'world cannot know his department in the establishment, it is enough that he was partner at all'.[74]

There should be a sufficient connection with what partner is authorised to do

[10.43] In *JJ Coughlan v Ruparelia,*[75] JJ Coughlan Ltd (a ground work contractor) alleged that it had been a victim of a fraud perpetrated by Mr Ruparelia, a partner in the defendant firm of solicitors. The firm's liability in the tort of deceit depended on whether statements made to induce JJ Coughlan Ltd to enter into the investment were made 'in the ordinary course of the business of the firm' for the purposes of s 10 of the 1890 Act. The firm's liability in relation to a claim for damages depended on whether the making of the agreement was 'an act for carrying on in the usual way business of the kind carried on by the firm' within the meaning of s 5 of the 1890 Act. In the High Court, the claims against the firm were dismissed on the grounds that the acts of Mr Ruparelia were not in the ordinary course of the business of the firm, with the judge, Mackay J, holding that there was no material difference between 'the ordinary course of the business' within the meaning of s 10, and 'the usual way of business of the kind carried on' within the meaning of s 5. JJ Coughlan Ltd appealed against the findings that the firm was not liable. Dyson LJ in the Court of Appeal agreed that there was no material difference between 'the ordinary course of the business' within the meaning of s 10, and 'the usual way of business of the kind carried on' within the meaning of s 5.

[10.44] Regarding whether the acts of Mr Ruparelia were the kind or class of acts that are carried out by solicitors in the ordinary course of their business, Dyson LJ stated that a:

> '... useful starting point is to ask whether the general description of the act falls within the scope of the ordinary business of solicitors. It is a necessary condition that the act should satisfy this requirement. Thus, for example, if the solicitor enters into a contract for the sale of double-glazing, he cannot bind his firm under section 5, nor will his firm be vicariously liable for any wrongful act in relation to the transaction under section 10. It is not the ordinary business of solicitors to sell double-glazing. The transaction is of a general nature that falls outside the scope of a solicitor's ordinary business. It is unnecessary to examine the transaction further to see that this is so. Whatever the terms of the contract of sale, it is not made by the solicitor as part of the ordinary business of a solicitor.'[76]

Dyson LJ did, however, caution that '... the issue of whether the acts of a solicitor are of the kind or class which fall within the ordinary business of a solicitor should always be determined without taking into account the nature or characteristics of those acts. There

---

[73]   *Morans v Armstrong* (1840) Arm M & O 25.
[74]   *Morans v Armstrong* (1840) Arm M & O 25 at 26–27.
[75]   *JJ Coughlan v Ruparelia* [2002] EWHC 1733 (QB) (aff'd on appeal at [2003] EWCA Civ 1057.
[76]   *JJ Coughlan v Ruparelia* [2002] EWHC 1733 (QB) at para 25 of the transcript.

is nothing in the authorities which compels such an approach to be adopted.'[77] He noted that motive is irrelevant, again using the analogy regarding the sale of double-glazing. If a solicitor carries out a conveyancing transaction in a dishonest manner, the firm will be liable; however, if the solicitor enters into a contract to sell double-glazing, the firm will not be liable under s 10 whether the solicitor's intentions are honest or dishonest. Dyson LJ held that the words, used by the judge in the High Court to describe the scheme into which Mr Ruparelia induced the plaintiff to enter ('preposterous' and 'abnormal and incredible'), were not inappropriate. Dyson LJ held that Mr Ruparelia's actions were not within the ordinary course of a solicitor's business and were not of a kind or class that it was in the ordinary course of a solicitor's business to do.

[10.45] Regarding liability under s 10 of the 1890 Act, Dyson LJ applied the broad test propounded by Lord Nicholls in the House of Lords in *Dubai Aluminium Co Ltd v Salaam*[78] (this House of Lords decision had been handed down after the High Court decision in *JJ Coughlan v Ruparelia*,[79] but before Dyson LJ delivered the decision of the Court of Appeal). Dyson LJ commented that the Court needed to evaluate, having regard to all the circumstances, whether the acts of Mr Ruparelia were sufficiently closely connected to what he was authorised to do that they could fairly and properly be regarded as having been done while he was acting in the ordinary course of the firm's business. The Court held that: 'the nature of this incredible scheme was so far removed from what Mr Ruparelia was authorised to do that what he did could not fairly and properly be regarded as having been done in the ordinary course of the defendant's business.'[80]

Care when relying on earlier precedents

[10.46] One must be cautious about using nineteenth and early twentieth century cases as authorities for what constitutes the ordinary course of business of modern partnerships. This is because of the rapid changes which have taken place in most types of partnership business since that time. The words of Staughton LJ in the English case of *United Bank of Kuwait Ltd v Hammoud*[81] are, it is suggested, equally applicable to all partnerships, and not just to solicitors' partnerships to which he directed them:

> 'That material should today be treated with caution, in my judgment; the work that solicitors do can be expected to have changed since 1888; it has changed in recent times

---

77   *JJ Coughlan v Ruparelia* [2002] EWHC 1733 (QB) at para 26 of the transcript.
78   *Dubai Aluminium Co Ltd v Salaam* [2003] 2 AC 366. In that case, a solicitor in a firm of solicitors drafted agreements on a dishonest basis to assist in a fraudulent transaction and the firm, which had no knowledge of that fraud, was held to be liable on the basis that drafting such agreements (for a proper, rather than for a dishonest, purpose) was within the ordinary course of the business of a firm of solicitors and the acts were so closely connected with what the solicitor was authorised to do, they were to be regarded as done by him while acting in the ordinary course of the firm's business.
79   The High Court decision in *JJ Coughlan v Ruparelia* was reported at [2002] EWHC 1733 (QB).
80   *JJ Coughlan v Ruparelia* [2002] EWHC 1733 (QB) at para 37 of the transcript.
81   *United Bank of Kuwait Ltd v Hammoud* [1988] 1 WLR 1051.

and is changing now. So I prefer to have regard to the expert advice of today in deciding what is the ordinary authority of a solicitor.'[82]

For this reason, expert evidence may play an important role in determining whether a particular act is within the ordinary course of business of a partnership. In that case an undertaking was given by a partner[83] in a solicitor's firm to the plaintiff bank as security for a loan being given by the bank to a client of the firm. After a consideration of expert evidence from the President of the English Law Society, it was held that the giving of an undertaking by a solicitor to a bank, which was lending to the solicitor's client, was within the ordinary course of business of a solicitors' firm. Accordingly, the firm was held liable when the undertaking was not honoured.

'Business of partnership' clause

[10.47] The classification of what is within the ordinary course of business of a firm may, to an extent, be achieved by the partners themselves. This is because partnership agreements will commonly define the business of the partnership. It follows that the wider the partners make the definition or description of the 'nature of business' in their partnership agreement, the more likely it is that the firm will be bound by the acts of one of the partners.[84]

Express Authority of a Partner

[10.48] As has been noted, an act of a partner will bind the firm if is within the firm's ordinary course of business, which will be the case if it is expressly authorised by the firm. The nature of express authority will now be considered. An expressly authorised act may be regarded as being within the firm's ordinary course of business by virtue of it being actually authorised by the firm.

[10.49] The question of whether a partner has the express authority of his co-partners to do a particular act is essentially a question of fact. It will be determined by the agreement reached between the parties regarding their authority to bind each other. For example the partners in a dental practice may expressly authorise one of the partners to give financial advice to a patient on their behalf. In such a case, the authority of the partner is clearly not ostensible or implied since it is neither a part of the ordinary course of business (in the strict sense) of a dentist to give financial advice, nor is it an implied power of a non-trading partnership to give such advice. However, the giving of such financial advice will be deemed to be within the ordinary course of business of the firm by virtue of it having been expressly authorised by the partners and in this way such an act will be binding on the firm.

---

82   *United Bank of Kuwait Ltd v Hammoud* [1988] 1 WLR 1051 at 1063F.
83   In fact, he is described as a salaried partner, but the status of the partner appears not to have been considered by the court.
84   In relation to the terms of such clauses, see further para **[21.36]** et seq.

Implied Authority of a Partner

[10.50] While, an act may be within a firm's ordinary course of business on the basis that it is expressly authorised by the firm, it is possible for an act to be within the firm's ordinary course of business by virtue of it being impliedly authorised by the firm.

[10.51] Just as, under company law, directors have the power under the Companies Act 2014 to manage the business of the company (subject to its constitution, the Companies Act 2014 itself, and any directions given by the company in general meeting),[85] so too a partner has the implied authority to do certain acts which are incidental to the partnership's business. Therefore, a partner may open a bank account in the firm name, sign cheques in the firm name, etc. While these powers may not be expressly contained in the terms of the partnership agreement, they are regarded as a necessary incident of every partnership and are implied into the partnership relationship, unless agreed to the contrary by the partners.[86] A statutory example of the implied authority of a partner is to be found in the Rules of the Superior Courts which provide that when money in court is ordered to be paid to a firm, any one partner is authorised to accept payment of such money.[87]

[10.52] Unlike the ostensible authority of a partner, for the most part, these implied powers apply regardless of the nature of the business of the firm, save that certain implied powers apply to trading partnerships (ie firms which buy and sell for a profit) but not to non-trading partnerships, such as professional partnerships.

Implied authority of a partner in every partnership

[10.53] An individual partner in a partnership, whether a trading or a non-trading partnership, has implied authority to:

(a) bring or defend legal proceedings in the firm-name or the joint names of all of the partners;[88]

(b) open a bank account in the name of the firm;[89]

(c) sign cheques on behalf of the firm;[90]

(d) enter contracts on behalf of the firm within the ordinary course of business of the firm;[91]

(e) sell goods belonging to the firm;[92]

---

85 Companies Act 2014, s 158(1). See also *Att Gen v Great Eastern Railway* (1880) 5 App Cas 473 at 478, per Selbourne LC. See generally Hutchinson, *Keane on Company Law* (5th edn, 2016) at para [27.81]; Courtney, *The Law of Companies* (4th edn, 2016) at para [13.161] et seq.

86 Even where these powers are excluded inter se, third parties may be able to rely on the ostensible authority of a partner to do these activities on the part of the firm. See generally in relation to ostensible authority para **[10.61]**.

87 RSC, Ord 77, r 44(1).

88 *Tomlinson v Broadsmith* [1896] 1 QB 386; *Whitehead v Hughes* (1834) 2 C & M 318; *Seal v Kingston* [1908] 2 KB 579.

89 l'Anson Banks, *Lindley & Banks on Partnership* (20th edn, 2017) at para 12-42.

90 *Backhouse v Charlton* (1878) 8 Ch D 444; *Laws v Rand* (1857) 27 LJCP 76.

91 Partnership Act 1890, s 6.

92 *Lambert's Case* (1614) Godb 244; *Fox v Hanbury* (1776) Cowp 445.

(f)   purchase goods (on credit[93] or otherwise) on behalf of the firm in the ordinary course of business;[94]

(g)   take on employees for the purposes of the partnership business[95] and dismiss such employees;[96]

(h)   appoint or remove agents;[97]

(i)   receive payment in respect of debts of the firm[98] both before[99] and after dissolution;[100] and

(j)   give releases in respect of such debts.[101]

[10.54] The implied authority of a partner to give a release of debts owed to the debtors of the firm is illustrated by *Crowe v Lysaght*.[102] In that case, Lysaght was indebted to four partners who worked as builders. One of the partners in the building firm, Crowe, accepted a surrender of Lysaght's interest in his house in Monkstown, Co Dublin in full satisfaction and discharge of the debt. Crowe's partners claimed that the settlement was entered into by Crowe without their authority and that they were not bound thereby. While Crowe had not the express authority of his partners to release the defendant in this manner, he had implied authority to do so and it was held that his partners were bound by his actions.

Authority not implied for partners in all partnerships

[10.55] An individual partner does not have implied authority from the firm, whether a trading or a non-trading partnership,[103] to:

(a)   enter into partnership on behalf of the firm;[104]

(b)   give a guarantee on behalf of the firm;[105]

(c)   submit to arbitration.[106] However, it seems clear that this restriction applies only to ad hoc submissions to arbitration since it seems clear that a partner does

---

93   But not the power to borrow: *Higgins v Beauchamp* [1914] 3 KB 1192, which a partner in a trading partnership has implied authority to do, see para **[10.57]**.

94   *Gardner v Childs* (1837) 8 Car & P 345; *City of London Gas v Nicholls* (1862) 2 Car & P 365.

95   *Beckham v Drake* (1841) 9 M & W 79 and aff'd (1843) 11 M & W 315.

96   *Donaldson v Williams* (1833) 1 Cromp & M 345.

97   *Ex p Mitchell* (1808) 14 Ves 597; *Ex p Hodgkinson* (1815) 19 Ves 291.

98   See for example the dicta of Budd J in *Re Shanahans Stamp Auctions Ltd* [1962] IR 386 at 424 that '[t]he law allows one partner to receive the whole debt on account of the firm to whom it is due,' where he relied on *Piddock v Burt* [1894] 1 Ch 343 as authority.

99   *Anon* (1701) 12 Mod Rep 447 (Case 777); *Jacaud v French* (1810) 12 East 317.

100   Partnership Act 1890, s 38.

101   *Crowe v Lysaght* (1861) 4 LR Ir 744.

102   *Crowe v Lysaght* (1861) 4 LR Ir 744.

103   Note that a partner in a firm of solicitors does not have implied authority to accept office as a trustee of a trust or constitute himself a trustee: *Re Fryer* (1857) 3 K & J 317; *Mara v Browne* [1896] 1 Ch 199; *Re Bell's Indenture* [1980] 3 All ER 425.

104   *Singleton v Knight* (1888) 13 App Cas 788; *Hawksley v Outram* [1892] 3 Ch 359.

105   *Brettel v Williams* (1849) 4 Ex 623.

106   *Antram v Chace* (1812) 15 East 209; *Stead v Salt* (1825) 3 Bing 101; *Adams v Bankart* (1835) 1 Cr M & R 681.

have implied authority to enter contracts on behalf of the firm which provide for the submission to arbitration in the event of a dispute between the parties;[107]

(d)   execute a deed on behalf of the firm,[108] regardless of whether the partnership is formed by deed,[109] unless it is a deed of arrangement[110] or a release.[111]

[10.56] However, where a deed is executed by one partner on behalf of the firm in the presence of all the other partners, it is deemed to have been expressly or actually authorised by the firm.[112] Even where a document is ineffective as a deed on the basis that the executing partner did not have implied authority to enter it, the document may operate to bind the partners to the underlying transaction. Thus, in the case of *Re Briggs & Co*,[113] the execution of a deed by a partner to effect a legal assignment of book debts of the firm was ineffective, since the execution of the deed had not been authorised by the firm. However, since an equitable assignment of book debts does not require to be done under seal, it was held that the document was effective in creating such an assignment.

Implied authority of a partner in every trading partnership

[10.57] An individual partner in a trading partnership has implied authority from the firm to:

– pledge partnership property as security for the borrowings of the firm;[114]

– draw, accept or endorse a bill of exchange and to draw or endorse a promissory note in the ordinary course of business;[115]

– borrow money on the credit of the firm in the ordinary course of business of the firm,[116] including overdrawing on the firm's bank account,[117] but not a personal loan of a partner even if used for the purposes of the partnership.

---

107   See also the views of the current editor of *Lindley & Banks on Partnership* (20th edn, 2017) at para 12-41.

108   *Harrison v Jackson* (1797) 7 TR 207; *Steiglitz v Egginton* (1815) Holt NP 141; *Marchant v Morton, Down & Co* [1901] 2 KB 829.

109   *Harrison v Jackson* (1797) 7 TR 207, see also para **[10.90]**.

110   *Dudgeon v O'Connell* (1849) 12 Ir Eq 566; *Morans v Armstrong* (1840) Arm M & O 25; see further para **[10.92]**.

111   *Hawkshaw v Parkins* (1819) 2 Swan 539; *Crawford v Stirling* (1802) 4 Esp 207; *Duncan v Lowdnes and Bateman* (1813) 3 Camp 478.

112   *Burn v Burn* (1798) 3 Ves Jr 573; *Orr v Chase* (1812) 1 Mer 729; *Brutton v Burton* (1819) 1 Chitty 707.

113   *Re Briggs & Co* [1906] 2 KB 209.

114   Per Murray J in *Northern Bank Ltd v McNeill* (14 February 1986) HC NI at p 34 of the transcript; *Ex p Howden* (1842) 2 Mont D & De G 574; *Gordon v Ellis* (1844) 7 Man & G 607; *Brownrigg v Roe* (1850) 5 Ex Ch 489.

115   *Dickinson v Valpy* (1829) 10 B & C 128; *Lewis v Reilly* (1841) 1 QB 349; *Stephens v Reynolds* (1860) 5 H & N 513. For a historical perspective, see Anon, 'Imperfect acceptance by one partner in fraud of the firm' (1878) 12 ILT & SJ 527.

116   *Lane v Williams* (1692) 2 Vern 277; *Ex p Bonbonus* (1803) 8 Ves Jr 540; *Denton v Rodie* (1813) 3 Camp 493.

117   *Looker v Wrigley* (1882) 9 QBD 397; *Blackburn Building Society v Cunliffe, Brooks & Co Works* (1884) 9 App Cas 857; *Re Wrexham, Mold & Connah's Quay Railway Co* [1889] 1 Ch 440.

[10.58] While a partner in a trading partnership has implied authority to borrow money on the credit of the firm, this is only the case if the loan is borrowed as part of the ordinary course of the firm's business. Thus, where borrowings are made to a partner for personal purposes, such as to finance his capital contribution to the firm, the firm will not be bound thereby. This is illustrated by the case of *Re Ferrar, ex p the Ulster Banking Co*,[118] which involved an attempt by the Ulster Banking Company to prove upon the bankrupt estate of Ferrar, the surviving partner of the firm of Simms and Ferrar. The firm ran the *Belfast Mercury* newspaper and the bank sought to prove upon Ferrar's estate in respect of a loan by it to Simms which Simms had used for the purposes of the partnership. During the course of the loan, the bank had attempted to treat the debt of Simms as the firm's debt. However, they were unsuccessful in their attempts to obtain Ferrar's consent to transfer money which was due to the firm to reduce Simms's loan account. Macan J dismissed the bank's action and he held that in order for the firm to be bound by a loan such as this, there must be a positive agreement or sufficient conduct of the other partner from which to infer that the debt was adopted by the firm. It is not sufficient simply that the loan was used by the partner for the purpose of the firm.[119]

[10.59] It is important to note that the implied authority of a partner to borrow, execute bills of exchange, pledge, etc does not apply to non-trading partnerships.[120] Thus in *Plumer v Gregory*,[121] a partner in a solicitors' firm borrowed money from a client without the knowledge of his co-partners, saying that the firm wanted it to lend to another client. The borrowing of money from a client for lending to another client was not impliedly authorised by the firm and was held not to be within the ordinary course of business of a solicitors' firm and so the innocent partners were held not to be liable for the loss to the client.

Trading partnership v non-trading partnership

[10.60] The distinction between the implied authority of a partner in a trading partnership and in a non-trading partnership is not contained in the 1890 Act. Rather, it results from a distinction which was made at common law between the different role of a partner in a firm which bought and sold goods (a trading firm) from the role of a partner in a non-trading firm. It was felt that since the borrowing of money and other financial powers of partners were open to abuse and could impose substantial liability on the partners, these powers should be restricted to those partnerships which were involved in trading. The distinction still exists, but it may be criticised on the grounds that it takes no account of the needs or practices of particular partnerships. In particular, it is queried whether it is justifiable for a partner in a professional partnership with numerous partners, hundreds of employees and international offices and which engages in sophisticated financial and tax transactions should be denied the foregoing implied

---

118 *Re Ferrar, ex p the Ulster Banking Co* (1859) 9 Ir Ch R 11.
119 Macan J observed that 'interest alone amounting to £801.9s.4d., all now sought to be charged against the partnership assets, as if applied to partnership purposes: which application, *even if clearly established*, would not in itself merely make the claim a partnership debt', *Re Ferrar, ex p the Ulster Banking Co* (1859) 9 Ir Ch R 11 at 15.
120 Though of course, it may be ostensibly or expressly authorised, See for example *Allied Pharmaceutical Distributors Ltd v Walsh* [1991] IR 8, considered at para **[10.66]**.
121 *Plumer v Gregory* (1874) LR 18 Eq 621.

power to borrow, pledge, execute bills of exchange, etc, in the firm name,[122] while a partner in a two-person trading firm would be able to rely on such powers. For this reason, it is suggested that in the twenty-first century, this distinction between trading and non-trading firms has outlived its usefulness and should be abandoned. Instead, if partners in certain firms wish to protect themselves from the abuse of powers by their co-partners, they should build in a system of controls to their partnership agreement, rather than relying on the question of whether the firm is a trading or a non-trading firm.

Ostensible Authority of a Partner

[10.61] The third type of authority is the ostensible authority of a partner to bind the firm to a certain act.[123] That act may be regarded as being within the firm's ordinary course of business by virtue of it being ostensibly authorised by the firm. Accordingly, a third party who wishes to establish that a firm is liable for the acts of a partner may attempt to prove that the act was ostensibly authorised by the firm. As has been noted, this type of authority is not actual authority since there is no real authority from the firm to the partner to do the act.[124] Rather, it is a form of estoppel which, in light of the firm's conduct, prevents the firm from denying that the partner was authorised to do the act.

There must be a representation that the act was authorised

[10.62] Before a partner is deemed to have been ostensibly authorised to do an act on behalf of his firm, there must have been a representation by the firm that the act was within the firm's ordinary course of business.[125] This is clear from Henchy J's adoption of the following statement on the nature of ostensible authority in the Supreme Court case of *Kett v Shannon*:[126]

> '[O]stensible authority is created by a representation by the principal to the third party that the agent has the relevant authority, and that the representation, when acted on by the third party, operates as an estoppel, precluding the principal from asserting that he is not bound. The representation which creates ostensible authority may take a variety of forms, but the most common is a representation by conduct, by permitting the agent to act in some way in the conduct of the principal's business with other persons, and thereby representing that

---

122 He could of course be granted by his partners the express power to borrow on behalf of the firm.

123 See Stone, 'Usual and Ostensible Authority One Concept or Two' (1993) Journal of Business Law 325. For the general liability of a principal for the acts of his agent, see *Fitzsimons v Duncan and Kemp & Co* [1908] 2 IR 483 (one company liable for a second company's defamatory report on the creditworthiness of the plaintiff, where the second company was the agent of the first).

124 See para **[10.32]**.

125 The representation must be by the principal: *Essford v Crown Shipping (Ireland) Ltd* [1991] ILRM 97.

126 Where he quoted from the judgment of Goff LJ in *Armagas Ltd v Mundogas SA* [1985] 3 All ER 1795. See also the statement of the law on ostensible authority by Diplock LJ in *Freeman & Lockyer v Buckhurst Park Properties (Mangal) Ltd* [1964] 2 QB 480, which was relied upon by Goff LJ. The second sentence of this passage was also quoted with approval by Barron J in *Allied Pharmaceutical Distributors Ltd v Walsh* [1991] IR 8 at 15.

the agent has the authority which an agent so acting in the conduct of his principal's business usually has.'[127]

There must be justification for implying authority

[10.63] This need for a justification for implying such authority was termed 'the bootlaces or bootstraps problem' by Clarke J in *ACC Bank plc v Johnston p/a Brian Johnston & Co Solicitors*,[128] where he cautioned that:

> '... it is important to note that, in order for any person to have the ostensible authority of another, the person relying on ostensible authority must be able to point to actions or omissions on the part of the person sought to be bound which justify implying authority. It is not possible to rely simply on the statements or actions of the person who is said to have implied authority. This is sometimes referred to as the bootlaces or bootstraps problem. A person cannot pull himself up by his own bootlaces. A person cannot create a situation where they have the implied authority of a third party simply by asserting or acting as if they have that authority. These general principles apply equally to the ostensible authority of employees or agents as much as they do to partners. In the context of partnership, therefore, the mere fact that someone says that they are a partner of a third party or acts in a way which implies that they are such a partner, does not give that person ostensible authority to bind the third party. The third party has done nothing to create the ostensible authority. It is necessary, therefore, that a person claiming the existence of such an implied authority must be able to point to some act or omission on the part of the alleged partner from which it is reasonable to imply the existence of the partnership and the entitlement of the putative partner to bind that partnership.'[129]

Whether the representation is made intentionally or negligently is irrelevant.[130]

Belief of third party per se is not sufficient

[10.64] While the belief of a third party that a partner has the authority of the firm to carry out the act is relevant in determining whether the partner has ostensible authority, a third party's belief is not in itself sufficient to establish liability.[131] It is necessary to show that there has been a representation by the firm. As stated by Barron J in *Allied Pharmaceutical Distributors Ltd v Walsh*:[132]

> 'It is necessary therefore for the plaintiff to establish an ostensible authority. This does not depend upon the belief of the person dealing with the partner, but requires evidence to establish some form of representation by the partnership to such person from which it is reasonable for that person to infer the existence of the authority.'[133]

---

127 *Kett v Shannon* [1987] ILRM 364 at 366, quoting from the judgment of Goff LJ in *Armagas Ltd v Mundogas SA* [1985] 3 All ER 1795.

128 *ACC Bank plc v Johnston p/a Brian Johnston & Co Solicitors* [2011] IEHC 108.

129 *ACC Bank plc v Johnston p/a Brian Johnston & Co Solicitors* [2011] IEHC 108 at para 5.3 of the judgment.

130 *Isabel Kenny v James Kelly* [1988] IR 457 (the misinterpretation of instructions given by a manager was held to grant ostensible authority). See also *Irish Permanent Building Society v O'Sullivan* [1990] ILRM 598.

131 Conversely, where the third party does not believe that the partner is authorised, in spite of a representation, the act will not be binding on the firm: *Kendal v Wood* (1870) LR 6 Ex 243.

132 *Allied Pharmaceutical Distributors Ltd v Walsh* [1991] IR 8.

133 *Allied Pharmaceutical Distributors Ltd v Walsh* [1991] IR 8 at 15. See also *Kett v Shannon* [1987] ILRM 364.

In that case, the defendants argued that the ordinary business of their accountancy firm did not include investment advice, since such work was within the ordinary course of business of a stockbroker or merchant banker. Barron J held that it was irrelevant that the firm did or did not give investment advice once there was a representation by the firm that Walsh, the partner who gave that advice, was authorised to do so.

[10.65] The Supreme Court enunciated the same principle in *Kett v Shannon*.[134] This involved the liability of an employer for the acts of an employee within the ordinary course of employment. There, Shannon had purchased a car from a garage and when the car developed problems, he returned it to the garage for repairs. A mechanic in the garage, who worked for the vendor of the car, gave Shannon another car while his own car was being repaired. The Supreme Court held that, although Shannon believed that the mechanic had ostensible authority, that was not sufficient and it was held that the mechanic did not in fact have ostensible authority to lend the car to Shannon. Henchy J observed:[135]

> '[T]he essence of ostensible authority is that it is based on a representation by the principal (the vendor) to a third party (the purchaser) that the alleged agent (the mechanic) had authority to bind the principal by the transaction he entered into. Such a representation, however, was absent in this case ... I have no doubt that in the eyes of the purchaser the mechanic had ostensible authority to lend him the [car]. But that is not enough to create ostensible authority in the law of agency. There should have been a representation of some kind by the vendor to the purchaser that the mechanic had authority.'[136]

Representation may be by conduct

[10.66] As noted by Barron J in *Allied Pharmaceutical Distributors Ltd v Walsh*:[137]

> 'The representation does not have to be made in writing or even orally. It is sufficient if it is made by conduct which is the normal way in which an ostensible authority is established.'[138]

In that case the conduct of the firm, in allowing a partner in an accountancy partnership to solicit loans from the plaintiff, a corporate client of firm, without any comment from the firm, was held to be a representation that the partner had authority to so act:

> 'Here the defendant firm was also the auditor of the plaintiff. As such it would have had to have been aware of the transactions with [the partner's private investment company]. At no time did it suggest to the plaintiff that there was anything unusual or improper in making the deposits. There was nothing to suggest to the plaintiff that it should not effect similar transactions in future. In my view, the absence of any comment[139] from the defendant firm was a sufficient representation by conduct that Mr Walsh has had the authority of the defendants to direct the making of such deposits.'[140]

---

134 *Kett v Shannon* [1987] ILRM 364.
135 Griffin and Hederman JJ concurring.
136 *Kett v Shannon* [1987] ILRM 364 at 366.
137 *Allied Pharmaceutical Distributors Ltd v Walsh* [1991] IR 8.
138 *Allied Pharmaceutical Distributors Ltd v Walsh* [1991] IR 8 at 17.
139 Although one approach was made by the partners to the errant partner to cease the activity. However he restarted and no further attempts were made by the partners.
140 *Allied Pharmaceutical Distributors Ltd v Walsh* [1991] IR 8 at 17.

[10.67] Barron J also relied on the case of *Mercantile Credit v Garrod*.[141] In that case, the partnership agreement between a dormant partner and an active partner for the running of a garage expressly excluded the active partner from selling cars on behalf of the garage. The active partner simply had authority on behalf of the partnership to repair cars. The dormant partner became aware that the active partner was selling cars and it was held that, in view of the dormant partner's inaction on discovering this fact, the selling of cars was within the ordinary course of business of the firm and the firm was bound by such sales.[142]

A question of fact in each case

[10.68] As noted by Clarke J in *ACC Bank plc v Johnston p/a Brian Johnston & Co Solicitors*,[143] it is important when reviewing any caselaw in the area of ostensible authority to carefully consider the precise set of facts with which the court is confronted in each case. In *ACC v Johnston*, Mr Mallon and Mr Traynor had been partners in a firm of solicitors. At a meeting on 30 March 2006, they agreed to dissolve their partnership with immediate effect, and Mr Mallon ceased his involvement in the management of the firm at that time. The financial terms of the dissolution were documented in an agreement entered into five months later, on 30 August 2006. The Law Society of Ireland was advised by Mr Traynor in October 2006 that the partnership had been dissolved with effect from 30 March 2006, but the firm's insurers were not notified until December 2006, the firm's existing banking arrangements had remained in place until August 2006 (meaning that Mr Mallon could have signed cheques on the firm's behalf during that period), no notice was published in *Iris Oifigiúil* of the dissolution of the firm, and clients of the firm were not otherwise notified of the change until after August 2006. Mr Traynor continued to conduct his business using 'Traynor Mallon' notepaper that listed both Mr Traynor and Mr Mallon as partners until early September 2007. This litigation stemmed from Mr Traynor, as solicitor for a borrower, giving various undertakings to ACC Bank after the agreement to dissolve the firm had been reached on 30 March 2006. The undertakings were not honoured, and when the solicitor who acted for ACC Bank was found guilty of negligence in the manner in which he dealt with various aspects of the secured lending transaction between ACC Bank and Mr Traynor's client, that solicitor then sought to recover from Traynor Mallon and the issue arose as to whether Mr Mallon was a partner in Traynor Mallon at the time that the key undertaking was given in August 2006. While Clarke J found that the partnership had been dissolved with effect from 30 March 2006, he then needed to consider whether Mr Traynor had the ostensible authority from Mr Mallon to carry on the business that they had previously carried on together at the time that the undertakings were given. Clarke J found that such ostensible authority did exist as no steps had been taken to inform the firm's clients, other firms with which it dealt, or the general public about the dissolution of the

---

141 *Mercantile Credit v Garrod* [1962] All ER 1103.

142 See also the following general agency cases referred to by Dunn in Ussher and O'Connor (eds), *Doing Business in Ireland* (1998) at para 11.01.[3]d et seq; *Kigobbin Mink Ltd v National Credit Co* [1980] IR 175; *Allied Irish Banks v Murnane* (21 December 1988) HC; *Woodman, Matheson & Co v Waterford Corporation* [1939] IR 93; *Brady v Igoe and Morris* [1939] Ir Jur Rep 1; *McGuill v Aer Lingus* (3 October 1983) HC.

143 *ACC Bank plc v Johnston p/a Brian Johnston & Co Solicitors* [2011] IEHC 108.

partnership. As the giving of undertakings was seen to be within the ordinary course of the business of a firm of solicitors, Clarke J found that Mr Mallon was responsible for the undertakings given by Mr Traynor and his lack of knowledge as to the undertakings given by Mr Traynor was no defence.

Easier to establish ostensible authority for partners than other agents

[10.69] In referring to other instances of the liability of a principal for the acts of its agents, one should bear in mind that ostensible authority between a partner and his firm will be more easily established than in other agent/principal relationships. This is because the relationship between partners is a closer one than that between other principals and agents and very little may be required to establish the required representation that the act is within the firm's ordinary course of business. Thus in *Allied Pharmaceutical Distributors Ltd v Walsh*,[144] Barron J referred to a principal/agent case, but noted that:

> 'In my view the position is stronger when the alleged agency arises between partners. The basis of partnership is mutual trust between the partners. When one partner is put into a position of trust with a client in my view that alone is a representation that the partnership trusts that partner and will stand over whatever he does.'[145]

Restrictions on Authority of a Partner

[10.70] It has been noted that the question of whether a firm is bound by the acts of a partner is determined primarily by whether the act in question is within the ordinary course of business of the firm.[146] Accordingly, a third party dealing with a partner need not enquire into that partner's specific authority, provided that the act in question is within the firm's ordinary course of business. The third party is entitled to assume that the firm will be bound by acts within the firm's ordinary course of business. The firm will be bound, even if the partner in question did not in fact have authority to bind the firm, provided that the third party was not aware of his lack of authority. When the third party is aware that a partner has no authority to bind the firm in general or to do a specific act, the third party will know that such an act is not within the firm's ordinary course of business and the firm will not be bound thereby. This principle underlies the rule in s 5 of the 1890 Act that:

> [T]he acts of every partner who does any act for carrying on in the usual way business of the kind carried on by the firm of which he is a member bind the firm and his partners, unless the partner so acting has in fact no authority to act for the firm in the particular matter, and the person with whom he is dealing either knows that he has no authority, or does not believe him to be a partner.

[10.71] Similarly, this principle is contained in s 8 of the 1890 Act, which provides that:

> If it has been agreed between the partners that any restriction shall be placed on the power of any one or more of them to bind the firm, no act done in contravention of the agreement is binding on the firm with respect to persons having notice of the agreement.

---

[144] *Allied Pharmaceutical Distributors Ltd v Walsh* [1991] IR 8.
[145] *Allied Pharmaceutical Distributors Ltd v Walsh* [1991] IR 8 at 17.
[146] See para **[10.26]**.

[10.72] Neither s 5 nor s 8 of the 1890 Act states whether the third party dealing with the partnership should have actual notice of the restriction on a partner's authority/his lack of authority or whether constructive notice may be sufficient. However, it seems that in some cases, the circumstances of the transaction between a third party and a partner will be such as to put the third party on notice that the partner is acting outside of his authority. In such a case, it is thought that the third party will not be allowed to rely on the fact that he did not have actual notice of this fact and the firm will not be bound by that act.[147]

[10.73] Section 5 of the 1890 Act also provides that a third party, who does not believe that he is dealing with a partner (which partner happens not to have authority to bind the firm), cannot claim that the firm should be bound by that act[148] on the grounds that he was unaware of the partner's absence of authority.

Authority of a Partner in General

Indemnity to non-acting partners

[10.74] Up to this, consideration has been given primarily to the liability of a firm (effectively, the non-acting partners) *to third parties* for the acts of an acting partner which are within the ordinary course of business of a firm (whether actually, impliedly or ostensibly authorised). The position of non-acting partners *vis-à-vis* the acting partner should also be noted, particularly if the act in question has caused a loss to the firm. Where the non-acting partners in a firm are held liable to third parties for the acts of an acting partner in the firm, they may also have recourse against that partner for their losses. This is because they are entitled to an indemnity from that partner, where the act involves a degree of culpability,[149] unless, of course, they authorised the act.[150]

Mental incapacity does not per se terminate authority

[10.75] The mental incapacity of a partner in a firm does not per se terminate his authority (whether actual, implied or ostensible) to bind the firm. Thus, a partner who becomes subject to a mental disorder which is not apparent or known, will continue to have power to bind the firm and will remain liable for the acts of his co-partners.[151] However, it is of course possible for the other partners, once they become aware of a partner's mental condition, to apply to court for the dissolution of the partnership under s 35(a) of the 1890 Act.[152]

---

147 See for example the case of *Kendal v Wood* (1870) LR 6 Ex 243.

148 See further in relation to this aspect of s 5 of the 1890 Act, para **[10.19]**.

149 *Bury v Allen* (1845) 1 Colly 589. As to the possibility of a partner being able to recover from his co-partner for partnership losses caused by the other's negligence, see para **[14.37]**. See also the views of l'Anson Banks, the current editor of *Lindley & Banks on Partnership* (20th edn, 2017) at para 20-13 et seq, where he explores the question of whether something more than mere negligence is required in light of recent English and Scottish caselaw.

150 *Bury v Allen* (1845) 1 Colly 589.

151 *Imperial Loan Co v Stone* [1892] 1 QB 599; *Baxter v The Earl of Portsmouth* (1826) 5 B & C 170; *Molton v Camroux* (1849) 4 Ex 17. See also *Kingsborough v Venables and Wilson* (1834) 2 Ir Law Rec (NS) 81.

152 The dissolution of a partnership by the court on the grounds of the mental incapacity of a partner is dealt with at para **[25.22]** et seq.

Law of agency is also of general application to partnerships

[10.76] It is important to bear in mind that quite apart from the principles contained in the eight sections of the 1890 Act,[153] the law of agency is of general application to partnerships. Thus, for example, the question of whether the actions of an employee of the firm[154] bind the firm will be determined by general agency principles, ie whether the employee had actual, implied or ostensible authority to bind the firm.[155]

III. RATIFICATION

[10.77] Having considered the issue of whether the act of a partner is within the firm's ordinary course of business, reference will now be made to those acts which do not satisfy this requirement, but which may subsequently bind the firm by virtue of the firm's ratification thereof. Under the doctrine of ratification, an act which was not binding on a principal at the time it was done by his agent because of the agent's lack of authority, may still bind the principal, if the principal subsequently authorises it.

[10.78] A case of partnership liability which can be explained[156] using this doctrine is that of *Dudgeon v O'Connell*.[157] In that case, a partner in a banking partnership, the National Bank of Ireland, executed a trust deed on behalf of the firm in favour of a debtor of the partnership in Drogheda. Since the deed was executed by an individual partner in the bank without the express authority of the other partners in the bank, it was claimed that it was ineffective in light of the rule that a deed must be executed by all the partners in a firm.[158] However, for seven years after the execution, the bank received money under the trust deed and did not object to the validity of the deed. In light of this ratification by the bank,[159] Brady LC rejected the claim that the deed was not binding on the bank.

There Must be Knowledge of the Act to be Ratified

[10.79] In order for the ratification to bind the firm, it is essential that the ratifying partners do the act of ratification in the knowledge of the act they are ratifying, since it

---

153 Paragraph **[10.07]**.

154 And in this regard, note that a salaried partner is an employee of the firm. See generally in relation to salaried partners, para **[6.18]**.

155 See for example the case of *Cullimore v Savage South Africa Co (No 1)* [1903] 2 IR 589 in which the plaintiff brought an action against the defendants (assumed by the court to be partners) for his false imprisonment by their employee. The Irish Court of Appeal dismissed the action on the grounds that the employee did not have implied authority to imprison the plaintiff.

156 The judgment of Brady LC in this case can be explained as either an example of a deed (ie a composition with creditors) which may be executed by one partner or as an example of the unauthorised act of a partner being ratified by the actions of the other partners.

157 *Dudgeon v O'Connell* (1849) Ir Eq R 566.

158 See paras **[10.55]** and **[10.56]**.

159 The other ground on which this decision can be explained is that, as a composition deed with creditors, it is an exception to the rule that one partner cannot bind the firm by deed, see para **[10.92]**.

is not possible to ratify in ignorance of the act being ratified.[160] In this regard, the general rule under s 16 of the 1890 Act that notice of a matter to a partner is deemed to be notice to the firm may not be used to impute knowledge to a partner of the unauthorised act. The knowledge of the unauthorised act must be actual knowledge.[161]

The Firm Must have Been in Existence at the Time of the Act

[10.80] It is a basic principle of the law of agency that in order for a principal to ratify an act which was purportedly done on his behalf, the principal must have been in existence at the time of the act.[162] Accordingly, if an act was done by a person on behalf of a partnership to be formed in the future, the firm which is then formed may not ratify that act. What the firm may, of course, do is to grant a fresh obligation to the relevant third party, whereby it agrees to adopt the transaction in question in place of the person who entered the transaction. Unlike the ratification of an unauthorised act, this involves the creation of a fresh obligation by the firm.

IV. SPECIFIC INSTANCES OF LIABILITY UNDER THE 1890 ACT

[10.81] Having considered the requirements for an act to be binding on the firm, ie that it is done by a partner, *qua* partner and as part of the ordinary course of business of the firm, it is now proposed to examine in detail each of the eight instances of the agency of a partner mentioned in the 1890 Act. In all but one of these sections,[163] these three conditions are the basic requirements which have to be satisfied. The other requirements, if any, of these sections are considered below. At the outset, it is useful to bear in mind the distinction between some of the sections that was drawn by Lord Millett in *Dubai Aluminium Co Ltd v Salaam*[164] where he noted that:

> 'Section 9 is not concerned with the liability of the firm at all but with the liability of the individual partners. It provides that every partner in a firm is liable jointly with the other partners for all debts and obligations of the firm incurred while he was a partner. Section 12 makes every partner jointly and severally liable for loss for which the firm was liable under sections 10 and 11 while he was a partner in the firm. Where section 10 makes the firm vicariously liable for loss caused by a partner's wrongdoing, therefore, section 12 makes the liability the joint and several liability of the individual partners. Sections 11 and 13 are not concerned with wrongdoing or with vicarious liability but with the original liability of the firm to account for receipts ... Section 11 deals with money which is properly received by the firm in the ordinary course of its business and is afterwards misappropriated by one of the partners. The firm is not vicariously liable for the misappropriation; it is liable to account for the money it received, and cannot plead the partner's wrongdoing as an excuse for its failure to do so. Section 13 deals with money which is misappropriated by a trustee who happens to be a partner and who in breach of trust or fiduciary duty afterwards pays it to his firm or otherwise improperly employs it in the partnership business. The innocent partners are not vicariously liable for the misappropriation, which will have occurred outside the ordinary course of the firm's

---

[160] Per Lord Russell of Kilowen CJ in *Marsh v Joseph* [1897] 1 Ch 213 at 246.
[161] See further para **[10.131]**.
[162] See Reynolds, *Reynolds & Bowstead on Agency* (20th edn, 2014) at para [2-060].
[163] Namely s 16 of the 1890 Act, see para **[10.126]** et seq.
[164] *Dubai Aluminium Co Ltd v Salaam* [2003] 2 AC 366.

business. But they are liable to restore the money if the requirements of the general law of knowing receipt are satisfied.'

1. Section 5 of the 1890 Act

[10.82] Section 5 of the 1890 Act sets out the basis of the liability of the firm for the actions of the partners. It provides that:

> Every partner is an agent of the firm and his other partners for the purpose of the business of the partnership; and the acts of every partner who does any act for carrying on in the usual way business of the kind carried on by the firm of which he is a member bind the firm and his partners, unless the partner so acting has in fact no authority to act for the firm in the particular matter, and the person with whom he is dealing either knows that he has no authority, or does not believe him to be a partner.

This section has two main goals, both of which have already been considered. First, it confirms the important general principle that every partner is an agent of the firm and that for an act to bind the firm, it must be done by a partner, *qua* partner[165] and in the ordinary course of business of the firm.[166] Second, it establishes that a firm is bound to a third party by an act of a partner which is outside that partner's authority, if it is within the firm's ordinary course of business and the third party is unaware of this absence of authority.[167]

Firm is not bound by some character references

[10.83] The provision of a character reference by a firm for clients or employees may be an act done in the ordinary course of business of a partnership. However, the giving of certain character references will still not bind the firm under the general liability of a firm for the acts of its partners or under a specific section of the 1890 Act, such as s 5 or 6. This is because the giving of certain character references on behalf of the firm is subject to the terms of s 6 of the Statute of Frauds Amendment Act 1828.[168] This section provides that a partnership is not liable for a false and fraudulent representation as to the character or solvency of any person, unless the representation is in writing and signed by all the partners. Thus, if one partner alone signs a fraudulent credit reference in the firm name, the other partners are not bound by that reference, but only the partner giving the reference.[169] Section 6 does not apply to negligent character references, so the firm may be liable for them even if they are not in writing and not signed by all the partners.[170]

---

165 It is contended that this requirement is implicit in s 5 of the 1890 Act. This is because an act done by a partner which is within the ordinary course of business of his firm, may be done by him in an individual capacity and not as a partner, in which case it should not bind the firm.

166 See para **[10.26]**.

167 See para **[10.70]**.

168 9 Geo 4, c 14. See generally in relation to this Act, Breslin, *Banking Law* (3rd edn, 2013) at para [6.19].

169 *Hirst v West Riding Union Banking Co* [1901] 2 KB 560; *Williams v Mason* (1873) 8 LT (ns) 232. See generally *Forshall v Walsh* (18 June 1997) HC at p 69 of the transcript, which decision was upheld on appeal, (31 July 1998) SC.

170 *Banbury v Bank of Montreal* [1918] AC 626.

2. Section 6 of the 1890 Act

[10.84] The second instance of the agency of a partner under the 1890 Act is to be found in s 6, which states that:

> An act or instrument relating to the business of the firm and done or executed in the firm-name, or in any other manner showing an intention to bind the firm, by any person thereto authorised, whether a partner or not, is binding on the firm and all the partners.
>
> Provided that this section shall not affect any general rule of law relating to the execution of deeds or negotiable instruments.

[10.85] Section 6 confirms that the three requirements[171] for a firm to be bound by the acts of a partner are equally applicable to a contract executed by a partner, whether oral or written, as they are to other acts of a partner. Thus, s 6 requires the contract (i) to be executed by a partner, (ii) relate 'to the business of the firm' (ie ordinary course of business) and (iii) be 'executed in the firm-name, or in any other manner showing an intention to bind the firm' (ie *qua* partner). Thus, a firm will not be bound by a contract entered into by a partner, even where the execution of such a contract is part of the ordinary course of business of the firm, if the contract is entered into by the partner in a personal capacity.[172] However, the fact that a contract is executed in a partner's sole name only does not necessarily mean that the contract was not executed *qua* partner. On the other hand, a contract which was initially entered into by a partner in a personal capacity may be subsequently adopted by his firm. *Stewart v Davis*[173] involved a personal contract with a partner which, on his death, was adopted by his co-partner. The case involved the plaintiff, who was apprenticed as an attorney to James Davis, a partner in the defendant firm in Belfast. His co-partner, William Davis, operated another branch of the firm in Great Brunswick Street in Dublin. The indenture of apprenticeship was made with James Davis as an apprentice attorney could not be apprenticed to a firm but only to an individual. The indenture provided for the plaintiff to serve James Davis and his partner, William Davis. A fee was paid by the plaintiff by means of a bill of exchange in the name of the firm. Upon the death of James Davis, William Davis's adoption of this indenture was clearly evidenced by a series of statements and letters by him to the plaintiff and his parents. However, it transpired that he had not room for another apprentice in Dublin and he refused to refund the portion of the apprentice's fee for the unexpired part of the contract. He claimed that all of the fee was received and retained

---

[171]   See further in relation to these requirements, para **[10.14]**.

[172]   In this context, note that the general principles of agency law regarding disclosed and undisclosed principals will apply to situations where a partner signs a contract. See generally Ussher and O'Connor, *Doing Business in Ireland* (1998) at para 11.01[3][e] et seq and see also Reynolds, *Reynolds & Bowstead on Agency* (20th edn, 2016), at para [8-001] et seq. Thus, if the partner discloses that he is an agent, whether he discloses the identity of the firm or not, liability under the contract attaches to the principal (the firm). This principle is also reflected in s 9 of the 1890 Act which provides for joint liability (and not joint and several liability) for the firm in respect of contracts (see para **[11.08]**). However, if the partner does not disclose the agency, liability under the contract will attach to him until the third party discovers the existence of the principal firm (eg see the case of *Dublin Laundry Co Ltd v Clarke* [1988] ILRM 29, a case concerning a company) when he may hold the firm and the principal liable under the contract.

[173]   *Stewart v Davis* (1847) 11 Ir LR 34.

by James Davis. Pigot CB held that there was a clear adoption by William Davis of the contract for his own benefit and, accordingly, he was liable to refund that part of the fee which had been received by James Davis for the unexpired part of the contract.

Incoming partners not bound by contract with old firm

[10.86] Although self-evident, it is worth emphasising that when partners enter a contract on behalf of a firm, they do so on behalf of the partners at the time of the execution of the contract. Accordingly, a partner who joins a firm after the execution of a contract by that firm will not prima facie be bound by the terms of that agreement. This issue is considered in detail elsewhere in this text.[174]

Bills of exchange

[10.87] One type of contract which may be executed by a partner on behalf of his firm is a bill of exchange, and it is deserving of separate treatment. As has been noted,[175] only partners in trading partnerships are impliedly authorised to bind the firm by executing bills of exchange.[176] However, the execution of a bill of exchange on behalf of a partnership is treated differently from other contracts and is subject to the terms of the Bills of Exchange Act 1882.[177] Section 23(2) of that Act provides as follows:

> No person is liable as drawer, indorser, or acceptor of a bill who has not signed it as such: Provided that ...
>
> (2) The signature of the name of a firm is equivalent to the signature by the person so signing of the names of all persons liable as partners in that firm.

[10.88] Thus, a bill of exchange will be binding on a partnership if it is signed by a partner in the firm name, provided of course it is signed by the partner within the ordinary course of business of the firm.[178] However, if the partner who signs the bill of exchange does not have authority to sign the bill on behalf of the firm and the recipient of the bill knows of this lack of authority, then the firm is not bound.[179] Where the firm name is also the name of one of the partners, there is a rebuttable presumption that bills signed by him in his own name will bind the firm.[180] If there are two firms of the same name with a common partner, the partners in both firms will be bound by a bill of exchange in the firm name, if the signatory has authority to use each firm's name.[181]

---

[174] The start and end of a partner's liability for partnership obligations is considered in detail at para **[11.01]** et seq.
[175] See para **[10.57]**.
[176] Note, however, that this does not include cheques, since partners in trading and non-trading partnerships may execute cheques on behalf of the firm, see para **[10.53]**.
[177] 45 & 46 Vict, c 61.
[178] *Dickinson v Valpy* (1829) 10 B & C 128; *Lewis v Reilly* (1841) 1 QB 349. See also the case of *Ringham v Hackett* (1980) 124 Sol J 221. See generally in relation to bills of exchange, Donnelly, *The Law of Credit and Security* (2nd edn, 2015) at para 5-34 et seq.
[179] Partnership Act 1890, s 5. See also *Ringham v Hackett* (1980) 124 Sol J 221.
[180] *Yorkshire Banking Co v Beatson* (1880) 5 CPD 109.
[181] *Swan v Steele* (1806) 7 East 210.

[10.89] *Malcomson v Malcomson*[182] involved the acceptance of a bill of exchange by a partner signing the firm name and his own name. The bill of exchange was drawn upon and addressed in the name of the firm only, the Milford Spinning Company, as the drawee. It was accepted by one of the partners, Frederick Malcomson, 'for Milford Spinning Co and self'. The drawer of the bill of exchange had first proved against the firm for the amount owed under the bill of exchange and then attempted to prove against Malcomson for the remainder of his claim. He contended that the effect of the form of acceptance was as an acceptance on behalf of the partnership and also by Malcomson personally as a promissory note. Chatterton VC held that this form of acceptance did not bind Malcomson separately on the grounds that there could not be two acceptances of a bill of exchange and the firm was bound by his acceptance on its behalf. The Vice-Chancellor also rejected the claim that the effect of the use of the words 'and self' was to create a guarantee by Malcomson that the firm would pay the bill in full.

Deeds

[10.90] By its express terms, s 6 of the 1890 Act does not purport to affect the general law regarding the execution of deeds. As has been seen, a partner does not have implied authority to bind the firm by deed.[183] However, he may be expressly authorised by his partners to bind the firm. Where a partner is expressly authorised to execute a deed, the firm will only be bound if he signs the deed in the firm name, even where the deed discloses that he is acting for the firm[184] and therefore he should never execute a deed in his own name. In order to ensure that the firm is bound by covenants contained in the deed, these should be expressed to be made by the firm rather than being made by a partner in the name of the firm.[185]

Powers of Attorney

[10.91] Where authority is given to a partner to execute a deed on behalf of the firm by means of a general power of attorney, the power of attorney is not required to be made under seal.[186] However, where the power of attorney purports to authorise the partner(s) who have been appointed as attorneys to execute particular categories of documents on behalf of the partnership, the documents executed by those attorneys as attorneys for the partnership must be within the scope of the power of attorney. In *Heffernan & Anor v Murray & Ors*,[187] a power of attorney was granted to two partners in the Ballykisteen Developments Partnership to execute all documents relating to or connected with the development business of the partnership and a related company, including any related security documents and guarantees. The two attorneys then executed a deed of release

---

[182] *Malcomson v Malcomson* (1878) 1 LR Ir 228.
[183] See para **[10.55]**.
[184] *Hall v Bainbridge* (1840) 1 Man & G 42.
[185] *Combe's Case* (1613) 9 Co Rep 75a; *Wilks v Back* (1802) 2 East 142; *John Bros Abergarw Brewing Co v Holmes* [1900] 1 Ch 188.
[186] Powers of Attorney Act 1996, ss 15(2) and 17(1). However, the power of attorney must be a general power of attorney in the form set out in the Third Schedule to that Act or in a form to the like effect and expressed to be made under that Act. See generally, Gallagher and O'Herlihy, *Powers of Attorney: A Statutory Annotation* (4th edn, 2016).
[187] *Heffernan & Anor v Murray & Ors* [2015] IEHC 196.

and indemnity on behalf of the partnership in favour of a retiring partner. In the High Court, Binchy J found that the power of attorney related to the partnership's development business, and not to the constitution of the partnership itself, and that the provision of an indemnity to a retiring partner could not be seen to be a transaction relating to a development by the partnership, or a matter ancillary to such a transaction. As a result, the partner who had retired from the partnership was not able to rely on the deed of indemnity from the continuing partners when the partnership was sued in respect of matters that took place while he was a partner.

Exception for a composition deed with creditors

[10.92] An exception to the rule that one partner may not execute a deed on behalf of a firm is where the deed is a composition deed with creditors. In *Dudgeon v O'Connell*[188] a banking partnership was held bound by a trust deed for the benefit of a creditor which was executed by one partner in the bank. Brady LC held that:

> 'He was ... a partner; and though there are some deeds which he could not execute so as to bind his co-partners, I much doubt whether this, being a composition deed, is one which he could not execute. He could release the whole debt; therefore it seems to follow that he could forego part of it by a composition deed.'[189]

[10.93] The case of *Morans v Armstrong*[190] did not involve the actual execution of a composition deed with creditors but rather an agreement to execute a composition deed. In that case, Brady CB held that a Dublin-based partnership was bound by the act of one partner who had agreed that his firm would execute a composition deed with creditors of the firm on the receipt thereof.

Authority of non-partners to execute deed on behalf of firm

[10.94] As previously noted,[191] the general law of agency applies to partnerships as it does to other natural and legal persons. This will be relevant to situations in which a third party is dealing with a non-partner who may be authorised to act on behalf of the firm. Most commonly, this will occur in the case of a salaried partner, who is legally an employee of the firm, but who, under general agency principles, will have ostensible authority to bind the firm.[192]

[10.95] In the context of the execution of deeds, the general rule was that an agent had to have authority under seal in order to execute a document under seal and this rule applied equally to partnerships.[193] Thus in *Corner v Irwin*,[194] WH Irwin was an agent of the defendant firm and when he executed a deed on behalf of the firm, Palles CB held that:

---

[188] *Dudgeon v O'Connell* (1849) 12 Ir Eq R 566. This case can also be explained by ratification of the deed by the other partners, see para **[10.78]**.

[189] *Dudgeon v O'Connell* (1849) 12 Ir Eq R 566 at 573.

[190] *Morans v Armstrong* (1840) Arm M & O 25.

[191] See para **[10.76]**.

[192] See generally in relation to salaried partners, para **[6.18]**.

[193] *Powell v London and Provincial Bank* [1893] 2 Ch 555 at 563 (per Bowen LJ); *Re Seymour* [1913] 1 Ch 475 at 481 (per Joyce J); *McArdle v Irish Iodine Co* (1864) 15 Ir CLR 146.

[194] *Corner v Irwin* (1876) 10 Ir CLR 354.

'It was proved at the trial that WH Irwin was the agent of the Defendant, but that he was not appointed by instrument under seal. His execution, therefore, of the power of attorney was insufficient to render that document the deed of the Defendant.'[195]

[10.96] Since the Powers of Attorney Act 1996, it is now the case that a general power of attorney is not required to be made under seal in order for the donee of the power to execute a document under seal.[196]

3. Section 10 of the 1890 Act

[10.97] The third statutory instance of a partner's authority to bind his firm is to be found in s 10 of the 1890 Act which provides that:

> Where, by any wrongful act or omission of any partner acting in the ordinary course of business of the firm, or with the authority of his co-partners, loss or injury is caused to any person not being a partner in the firm, or any penalty is incurred, the firm is liable[197] therefor to the same extent as the partner so acting or omitting to act.

[10.98] By its express terms, s 10 confirms that the three requirements for a firm to be bound by the acts of a partner are equally applicable to wrongful acts and omissions and reference should be made to the analysis which has previously been made of these requirements.[198] The wide terms of this section, applying as it does to 'any wrongful act or omission' causing 'loss or injury' should be noted. In its decision in *Dubai Aluminium Co Ltd v Salaam*,[199] the House of Lords considered whether s 10 extends beyond simply torts to a wide range of wrongful acts. Lord Nicholls held that there is nothing in the wording of s 10 that confines its application to common law torts.[200] While at first glance this is a wide interpretation of s 10, it is qualified by the requirement that any wrongful act must have taken place in the ordinary course of the firm's business.

'with the authority of his co-partners'

[10.99] The second part of s 10 deals with the liability of the firm for torts which are committed by a partner on the express authority of the firm. In such a situation the act is binding on the firm on the basis that it has been expressly authorised by the partners and for this reason, such an act may be deemed to be part of the ordinary course of business of the firm.[201]

---

[195] *Corner v Irwin* (1876) 10 Ir CLR 354 at 359.
[196] Powers of Attorney Act 1996, ss 15(2) and 17(1). However, the power of attorney must be a general power of attorney in the form set out in the Third Schedule to that Act or in a form to the like effect and expressed to be made under that Act.
[197] By virtue of s 12 of the 1890 Act, the liability under s 10 is joint and several. See generally in relation to the nature of a partner's liability, para **[11.01]** et seq.
[198] See para **[10.14]** et seq.
[199] *Dubai Aluminium Co Ltd v Salaam* [2003] 2 AC 366.
[200] *Dubai Aluminium Co Ltd v Salaam* [2003] 2 AC 366 at para 10 of the transcript.
[201] See further in relation to actual authority, para **[10.31]** et seq.

'any person not being a partner'

[10.100] Section 10 provides that for liability to arise under either the first or second part of that section, the loss must have been caused to any 'person not being a partner'. Therefore, s 10 does not apply to a situation in which one partner commits a wrong against another. This is based on the principle that a partner is a co-principal in the firm and therefore the negligence of one partner is imputed to all. However, it seems clear that this principle is not of general applicability and that while an action may not be maintainable under s 10 of the 1890 Act, it may be maintainable under general law.[202] Thus in *Hawkins v Rogers*[203] the High Court allowed an action by one partner against his co-partner for damages caused by his co-partner's interference with his personal property.[204] Support for this view is also provided by the Canadian case of *Geisel v Geisel*.[205] There, a two-partner farming partnership came to an end when one partner was killed in an accident on the farm. The deceased partner's estate sought to sue the other partner in connection with the accident. The defendant partner sought to rely on the Canadian equivalent of s 10 to support his contention that a partner may not sue his partners in tort. In the Manitoba Queen's Bench, Ferg J held that the purpose of s 10 was merely to make clear that a firm is liable for the actions of its partners. He held that it did not intend to alter the pre-existing rights of one partner to sue another in tort, as is clear from s 46 of the 1890 Act.[206]

'to the same extent'

[10.101] The vicarious liability of the firm under s 10 of the 1890 Act for the acts of its partner is stated to be 'to the same extent' as the liability of the partner. However, this expression does not in any way limit the liability of the firm, so that even if the partner who committed the wrongful act is not liable, eg by virtue of the availability of a defence, the other partners in the firm may be liable. In the English case of *Meekins v Henson*,[207] a firm of solicitors was sued for damages for publishing a defamatory letter which had been signed in the firm name by one partner. The writer of the letter was held not to be liable on the basis that he was not motivated by malice, but his partner was held liable for this wrongful act of his partner, since he had acted out of malice. Similarly, a firm is guilty of fraudulent misrepresentation, where a partner who knows the true facts intentionally allows his partner, who is ignorant of these facts, to make a false statement.[208]

---

[202] For this reason, one partner can sue his co-partner for contribution for losses under Civil Liability Act 1961, s 21, see further para **[11.23]**.

[203] *Hawkins v Rogers* [1951] IR 48.

[204] See further para **[20.15]**.

[205] *Geisel v Geisel* (1990) 72 DLR 245.

[206] See further in relation to s 46, para **[1.28]**.

[207] *Meekins v Henson* [1962] 1 All ER 899.

[208] *Ludgater v Love* (1881) 44 LT 694.

Malicious torts

[10.102] It used to be the case that the malicious tort of one partner was not binding on the firm, where the other partners did not concur in that act.[209] Thus, in the pre-1890 case of *Reid v Mitchell*,[210] an action against a Belfast banking partnership for the malicious prosecution and imprisonment of the plaintiff was not sustainable by simply showing that the public officer of the firm had acted with malicious intent. Doherty CJ held that:[211]

'[T]here must be evidence of previous authority, or subsequent adoption or assent, to involve persons who have not taken any part in the transaction, where malice forms a necessary ingredient.'[212]

Similarly in *Cantwell v Cannock*,[213] also a pre-1890 Act case, an action was brought by the plaintiff against the defendant firm for false imprisonment and malicious prosecution by a partner in connection with the plaintiff's alleged shop-lifting in the firm's store. No evidence was adduced against the other partners to establish their concurrence in the acts and in the High Court, Lefroy CJ held that they were not liable on the ground that they had not concurred in the acts.

[10.103] However, in so far as these cases are authority for the requirement that the other partners must concur in a malicious tort before the firm is liable, it is contended that this is no longer good law. Rather, it is contended that once the tort is committed as part of the firm's ordinary course of business, the firm is liable. The fact that the tort is wilful or malicious does not take the tort out of the ordinary course of business, though it will of course be a factor in determining whether it was done as part of the firm's ordinary course of business in the first place. Support for this view is to be found in the wording of s 10 itself, which refers baldly to 'any wrongful act or omission' and to the post-1890 caselaw which does not make a distinction between malicious torts and non-malicious torts.[214] Nonetheless, it is thought that a court will generally be reluctant to impose vicarious liability on innocent partners for the malicious torts of their co-partner, unless they are clearly done as part of the firm's ordinary course of business since such torts are usually unpredictable and non-recurring so that the innocent partners are not in a good position to prevent them.

---

[209] As regards the special position of references by a firm regarding the character or solvency of any person, see para **[10.83]**.

[210] *Reid v Mitchell* (1842) 4 Ir LR 322. See also the general agency case of *Kinahan v Malyn* (1853) 6 Ir Jur 76 (wrongful arrest continued by mistaken identification of employee, but employer not liable therefor).

[211] Doherty CJ relied expressly on *Arbuckle v Taylor* (1815) 3 Dow 160, an unsuccessful case against a firm for damages as a result of the malicious prosecution of the plaintiff by one of the partners.

[212] *Reid v Mitchell* (1842) 4 Ir LR 322 at 327.

[213] *Cantwell v Cannock* (1854) 6 Ir Jur (os) 155.

[214] *Hamlyn v John Houston & Co* [1903] 1 KB 81; *Janvier v Sweeney* [1919] 2 KB 316; *Citizens Life Assurance Co v Brown* [1904] AC 423; *Wright v Outram & Co* (1890) 17 R 596. This is also the position in the US: *K & G Oil Tool & Services Co v G & G Fishing Tool Service* (1958) 158 Tex 594, 314 SW 2d 782, 358 US 898, 79 S Ct 223, 3 Led 2d 149.

[10.104] In *Flynn v Robin Thompson & Partners and Wallen*,[215] a partner in a firm of solicitors assaulted his opposing counsel in the precincts of the court. The English Court of Appeal found that the assault was so extraordinary and so far removed from the ordinary conduct of an advocate that it could not be within the ordinary course of the firm's business. As a result, the firm was not liable under s 10 of the 1890 Act to the plaintiff for the assault. A scuffle over some papers had also taken place within the courtroom and the court seemed prepared to find that the firm could be liable under s 10 in respect of that scuffle, on the basis that it occurred 'in the development of the contentious exchanges'. However, for procedural reasons the case regarding the scuffle in the courtroom did not go to trial.[216]

[10.105] An interesting example of a case which imposed liability on partners for the intentional tort of their co-partner is provided by the American case of *Dresser Industries v Digges*.[217] In that case, the partners in a law firm were held liable for a co-partner's intentional over-billing of a major client of the firm over a three-and-a-half year period to the tune of $3 million. Undoubtedly, the fact that the other partners benefited from this intentional tort was a factor in the court's decision to hold them liable for it.

[10.106] Since criminal liability usually involves personal guilt, a partner is not usually guilty of a crime where the act is committed by his co-partner,[218] unless of course he has the requisite criminal intent.[219]

4. Section 11 of the 1890 Act

[10.107] The fourth instance of agency under the 1890 Act is contained in s 11 which provides that:

> In the following cases; namely –
>
> (a) Where one partner acting within the scope of his ostensible authority receives the money or property of a third person and misapplies it; and
>
> (b) Where a firm in the course of its business receives money or property of a third person, and the money or property so received is misapplied by one or more of the partners while it is in the custody of the firm;
>
> the firm is liable[220] to make good the loss.

---

215 *Flynn v Robin Thompson & Partners and Wallen* (2000) 97(6) LSG 36.
216 See further 'Liability of a partnership for a partner's assault' J Crim L 2000, 64(4), 368–370.
217 *Dresser Industries v Digges* (1989) WL 139243 (D Md).
218 See for example the American cases of *United States v Ward* (1948) 168 F 2d 236 (3rd Cir); *Sleight v United States* (1936) 65 App DC 203, 82 F 2d 459; *State v Maurisky* (1925) 102 Conn 634, 129 A 714.
219 See for example prosecutions under the Trade Descriptions Act 1968 in England, *Parsons v Barnes* [1973] Crim LR 537; *Clode v Barnes* [1974] 1 WLR 544. But cf the Australian case of *Bishop v Chung Brothers* (1907) 4 CLR 1262, 13 ALR 412. See generally regarding the position in New Zealand, Webb and Molloy, *Principles of the Law of Partnership* (6th ed, 1996) and also Webb, 'The Criminal Liability of Partners' [1976] NZLJ 340.
220 By virtue of s 12 of the 1890 Act, the liability under s 11 is joint and several, see generally para **[11.14]**.

[10.108] Section 11 clarifies the requirements to be satisfied for a firm to be bound by the misappropriation of a third party's money or property by a partner or a firm. Section 11(a) requires the money or property to have been received by a partner who was ostensibly authorised to receive it, while s 11(b) requires the money or property to have been received by the firm 'in the course of its business'. It has been noted already that an act which is ostensibly authorised may be regarded as being within the ordinary course of business of a firm,[221] and therefore there is a considerable degree of overlap between these sections and reference should be made to the analysis which has previously been made of this issue.[222] Yet there are some important distinctions between these sections. Under s 11(a) of the 1890 Act, the firm is liable if the money or property is received by a partner and then misapplied by *that* partner, while under s 11(b), the firm is liable if the money or property is received by the firm, and while it is in the custody of the firm, it is misapplied by any partner. For this reason, it may be more appropriate for an action against a firm for the misapplication of client funds to be taken under the general liability of a firm for the acts of its partners in the ordinary course of business, rather than having to concern oneself with the requirements of s 11.

[10.109] In the English High Court case of *Re Bell's Indenture*,[223] a partner in a law firm was liable as a constructive trustee when he assisted the trustees of a marriage settlement in dissipating the trust fund. However his co-partner, who had not known of the breach of the trust,[224] was held by Vinelott J not to be liable for the breach of trust even though the money had passed through the firm's account. This was because it was held not to be within the ordinary course of business of a law firm for a partner to constitute himself a constructive trustee or to accept the office of trustee.[225]

Money or property must have been received under s 11

[10.110] If no money or property is received, there will be no liability under either subsection of s 11. Under s 11(a) the money or property must be received *by a partner* while under s 11(b) it must be received *by the firm*. In practice very little may turn on this difference in wording, since under s 11(a), the property is received by a partner who is acting on behalf of the firm (ie within his ostensible authority). Similarly, under s 11(b) the money or property must be received *by the firm* in the course of its business. Since the firm will often act through its partners, this means that the property may be received by one partner on behalf of the firm. However, s 11(b) is wide enough to encompass a situation where an employee or other agent of the firm receives the money or property of a third party and in such a case the property would be regarded as having been received by the firm.

---

[221] See para **[10.34]**.

[222] See para **[10.26]** et seq.

[223] *Re Bell's Indenture* [1980] 3 All ER 425.

[224] And for this reason, he would not have been liable under s 13 of the 1890 Act, see para **[10.119]**.

[225] See *Mara v Browne* [1896] 1 Ch 199; *Re Fryer* (1857) 3 K & J 317. See also l'Anson Banks, *Lindley & Banks on Partnership* (20th edn, 2017) at para 12-114.

[10.111] *Willett v Chambers*,[226] although pre-dating the 1890 Act, is an example of a case where the firm was liable for the misapplication of money received by a partner pursuant to the principles underlying s 11(a). There, a partner in a two-man law firm received money from a client to invest on a mortgage. However, the partner misapplied the money and a bill for the supposed transaction was sent to the client in the firm name which the client paid to the innocent partner. It was held that the transaction was within the ordinary course of business of the firm and accordingly the innocent partner was held liable for the loss which resulted to the client. Similarly, in *Rhodes v Moules*,[227] a partner in a law firm was arranging a mortgage for a client and he deceived the client into believing that the bank required additional security. The client gave the partner some bearer share warrants which were then misappropriated by the partner. The solicitor had on previous occasions received bearer bonds from the client and the firm was in the habit of holding bearer bonds for clients. Accordingly, the court held that the request for the bearer bonds and the misappropriation by the partner was within the ordinary course of business of the firm and therefore the firm was held liable for the loss.

[10.112] In contrast, in *Harman v Johnson*[228] a partner in a law firm was given money by a client to invest on a mortgage when a good opportunity came along. The partner misapplied the money. The innocent partner was held not liable for the loss because it was held that it was not part of the business of solicitors' firms generally, or of that particular firm, to receive and hold money pending investment. The court indicated that if the money had been given to the solicitor to invest in a specific mortgage,[229] that would have been within the ordinary course of business of the firm and the innocent partner would have been liable for the loss occasioned.

[10.113] Similarly in *Cleather v Twisden*,[230] a client entrusted bearer bonds for safe-keeping to a partner in a solicitors' firm who misappropriated them. His partners, who were unaware of this transaction, were held not to be liable for the loss to the client, since it was held not to be part of the ordinary course of business of solicitors' firms to accept securities for safekeeping.[231]

Misapplication while in custody of firm under s 11(b)

[10.114] Under s 11(b), the misapplication of the money or property must take place while it is in the custody of the firm. This is not the case under s 11(a), where liability will be imposed on the firm where property is received by a partner and misapplied by him without placing it to the credit of the firm. The requirement that the property be in the custody of the firm explains the decision in *Sims v Brutton and Clipperton*.[232] This involved a firm of solicitors which accepted money from a client to invest in a particular

---

226 *Willett v Chambers* (1778) Cowp 814. See also *Blair v Bromley* (1847) 2 Ph 354.
227 *Rhodes v Moules* [1895] 1 Ch 236.
228 *Harman v Johnson* (1853) 2 E & B 61.
229 As was the case in *Willett v Chambers* (1778) Cowp 814, above.
230 *Cleather v Twisden* (1884) 28 Ch D 340.
231 See generally Anon, 'Liability of Solicitor for Partner's Misappropriation of Securities' (1884) 18 ILT & SJ 73.
232 *Sims v Brutton and Clipperton* (1850) 5 Ex 802.

mortgage. The investment was made and the money passed out of the custody of the firm to the mortgagor. Subsequently, one of the partners in the firm acted fraudulently and induced the mortgagor to repay the money to him rather than to the client. It was held that the firm of solicitors was not liable, as the misapplication of the money took place when the firm did not have it in its custody.

5. Section 13 of the 1890 Act

[10.115] The fifth example of the liability of the firm for the acts of its partners under the 1890 Act is provided by s 13; although in truth, this section has as its primary aim the exemption of partners from liability. A secondary consequence of this exemption is the fact that it fixes partners with liability in situations not covered by the exemption:

> If a partner, being a trustee, improperly employs trust-property in the business or on the account of the partnership, no other partner is liable for the trust-property to the persons beneficially interested therein:
>
> Provided as follows:-
>
> (1) This section shall not affect any liability incurred by any partner by reason of his having notice of a breach of trust; and
>
> (2) Nothing in this section shall prevent trust money from being followed and recovered from the firm if still in its possession or under its control.

Different from other instances of agency under the 1890 Act

[10.116] Section 13 is an important section since its primary aim is to provide an exemption for innocent partners in the firm who are unaware of a breach of trust by their co-partner. This exemption is out of step with the general application of vicarious liability on a partner for the wrongs of his co-partners, since it exempts partners for liability for the use by their co-partner of property in the partnership business in breach of trust. This approach has been justified on the basis that under the other sections of the 1890 Act, and particularly s 11, property reaches the firm in the ordinary course of its business, but this is not the case under s 13, since trust-property reaches the firm as a result of a breach of trust. For this reason, legal commentators have suggested that there is no basis for imposing liability on the firm and hence the exemption is justified.[233]

[10.117] In *Walker v Stones*,[234] a partner in a law firm agreed to become the trustee of a family trust. When he allegedly breached the trust by benefiting the father who had set up the trust, rather than the beneficiaries of the trust, the issue arose as to whether the partners were vicariously liable for the alleged breach of trust. In the Court of Appeal, Sir Christopher Slade considered both s 13, and also s 10 as it applies to breaches of trust. Section 10 provides that a firm is liable for the wrongs committed by a partner in the ordinary course of business of the firm, while s 13 deals with breaches of trust by a partner. Section 13 provides that where a partner is a trustee, liability does not attach to his co-partners if there is a breach of trust, unless the co-partners have notice of the breach of trust. On that basis, Sir Christopher Slade concluded that s 13 deals with a

---

233 See in particular Brough, *Miller on Partnership* (2nd edn, 1994) at p 373. See also l'Anson Banks, *Lindley & Banks on Partnership* (20th edn, 2017) at para 12-131 and Pollock, *Digest of the Law of Partnership* (15th edn, 1952) at p 48.

234 *Walker v Stones* [2000] 4 All ER 412.

situation where a partner agrees to be a trustee (a trustee partner) while s 10 would apply to a situation where a partner, not already being a trustee, conducts himself as an accessory to a breach of trust so as to constitute himself as a constructive trustee, ie s 10 and s 13 are mutually exclusive. Section 13 assumes that the individual trusteeship which a partner undertakes is not something undertaken in the ordinary course of business of the firm, since otherwise it would be inconsistent with s 11 (which provides for the firm to be liable where there is a misapplication of property received by a firm or a partner where the property is received within the ordinary course of business of the firm). He therefore concluded that s 10 has no application to breaches of trust committed by a partner who agrees to be a trustee (a trustee partner) on the basis that the legislature assumed in drafting the 1890 Act that breaches of trust committed by a trustee partner fell outside the ordinary business of a partnership and therefore did not give rise to liability on the part of the firm under s 10. He observed that s 10 applies to all partnerships, not just partnerships of solicitors, and for this reason one should not be surprised that individual trusteeship by a partner was not within the ordinary course of business of a firm. On this basis, he held that the innocent partners in the law firm could not be vicariously liable for the alleged breach of trust by the partner under s 10 or s 13 since the innocent partners were not aware of the alleged breach.

[10.118] While the exemption in s 13 is clearly part of Irish law, the basis for the distinction between the liability of a firm for a breach of trust and other misapplications of property must be questioned and it is suggested that the blanket exemption for innocent partners in s 13 may not always be justified. Clearly the exemption for innocent partners is justified in a case where a partner in a firm, who happens to be a trustee, improperly brings trust funds into the partnership business as part of his capital contribution without the knowledge of his co-partners. In such a case, he will clearly be improperly employing 'trust-property in the business or on the account of the partnership' under the terms of s 13 and his co-partners will not be liable therefor. However, the exemption in s 13 is prima facie wide enough to apply to a case where a partner in a solicitor's firm, who is a trustee of a client trust, uses that trust money for the partnership business. In such a case, his co-partners (who are unaware of the breach of trust) will be able to rely on the exemption contained in s 13. Yet in the case of a misapplication of a client's property under s 11 of the 1890 Act, partners who are unaware of the misapplication are liable therefor. It is difficult to justify partners being exempt from liability for their co-partner's misuse of a client's trust funds but not his misuse of other non-trustee client funds.[235] It would, it is contended, be preferable if the usual test for the liability of a firm for the acts of a partner applied, ie was the breach of trust carried out as part of the ordinary course of business of the firm?

---

[235] For a case which supports partners being vicariously liable for a breach of trust by their co-partners see *Agip (Africa) Ltd v Jackson* [1992] 4 All ER 385 in which the partners were held to be constructive trustees. It is interesting to note that in America, s 305(b) of the Uniform Partnership Act (1997) (Last Amended 2013) provides liability for a firm for the misapplication of the money or property of a third party in almost identical terms to s 11 of the 1890 Act. Unlike the 1890 Act, the American legislation does not provide any exemption for breaches of trust similar to that of s 13.

'notice of a breach of trust'

[10.119] Under s 13(1) of the 1890 Act, a partner will not be able to rely on the exemption in s 13 if he has notice of the breach of trust. On the other hand, if all of the partners in a firm are aware of the breach of trust, the firm is liable for the loss occasioned. Thus, in *Cummins v Cummins*,[236] two brothers in a Cork partnership of four brothers were appointed by their father as trustees of a fund for the benefit of their two sisters. Contrary to the terms of the trust deed, the fund was not secured by the trustees, but was left in the firm to the knowledge of all four partners. Subsequently, one of the non-trustee partners applied the fund to pay off the firm's debts. As all four partners were aware of the breach of trust, Sugden LC held that they were all liable for that breach.

Notice of breach of trust not imputed under s 16

[10.120] As noted hereunder,[237] s 16 of the 1890 Act provides that a firm is deemed to be on notice of a fact relating to the 'partnership affairs' where one partner in the firm is on notice of that fact. However, it seems that notice of a breach of trust will not be imputed to the firm under s 16 of the 1890 Act, since a breach of trust by a partner does not relate to the 'partnership affairs'.[238] It is, however, clear that where a partner ought to have known of the breach of trust, he will be treated as if he were aware of the breach.[239]

Breach of fiduciary duty as a company director

[10.121] The position of a director *vis-à-vis* his company is analogous to the position of a trustee *vis-à-vis* his trust, in the sense that both a company director and a trustee occupy fiduciary positions. For this reason, a partner who is a company director may be guilty of a breach of trust and thus fall within the terms of s 13. For example that partner may breach his fiduciary duty as a director by using that position to earn secret profits for himself. Under the terms of s 13 of the 1890 Act, it seems that the co-partners of such a director would be liable to account to the company for such profits, if they were aware of this breach of trust/fiduciary duty.[240]

---

236 *Cummins v Cummins* (1845) 8 Ir Eq R 723.
237 See para **[10.126]**.
238 See the statement of Lord Lindley which is to be found in l'Anson Banks, *Lindley & Banks on Partnership* (20th edn, 2017) at para 12-131. See also *Ex p Apsey* (1791) 3 Bro CC 265; *Ex p White, re Nevill* (1871) LR 6 Ch 397; *Ex p Heaton* (1819) Buck 386. This does however raise the issue which has already been considered at para **[10.118]** of the case of a breach of trust which is clearly within the ordinary course of the firm's business. It has been suggested that a firm should be liable for such breaches of trust and therefore it would be consistent with this contention that the firm would be deemed to be on notice of such breaches of trust within the firm's ordinary course of business, where one partner is on notice thereof.
239 *Keble v Thompson* (1790) 3 Bro CC 112; *Smith v Jameson* (1794) 5 TR 601; *Ex p Watson* (1814) 2 V & B 414; *Ex p Woodin* (1843) 3 MD & D 399; *Ex p Poulson* (1844) De Gex 79.
240 See *Falkner Bell & Company v Scottish Pacific Coast Mining Company Ltd* (1888) 15 R 290. See also Brough, *Miller on Partnership* (2nd edn, 1994) at p 380.

Remedy of tracing is available in respect of a breach of trust

[10.122] Section 13(2) of the 1890 Act confirms what is already the case, namely that the remedy of tracing is available to the beneficiary of a trust which has had its property improperly employed by a partner.[241] Thus, a beneficiary under a trust will be able to trace the trust-property, if it is still in the hands of the firm and the firm did not obtain it in good faith and for value.[242]

6. Section 15 of the 1890 Act

[10.123] The sixth instance of the statutory liability of a firm for the acts of its partners is contained in s 15 of the 1890 Act, which provides that:

> An admission or representation made by any partner concerning the partnership affairs, and in the ordinary course of its business, is evidence against the firm.

[10.124] The three requirements for a firm to be bound by the acts of a partner are equally applicable to the question of whether a representation or admission can be used as evidence against a firm.[243] It has been noted that an admission by a partner as to his own authority is not evidence against the firm under s 15, because representations as to a partner's own authority are not made within the ordinary course of business of a firm.[244]

Not conclusive evidence

[10.125] Under the express terms of s 15 of the 1890 Act, the representation or admission is simply 'evidence against the firm'. This evidence may be rebutted by the partners and is not therefore conclusive evidence of the facts.[245] Thus in *Luckie v Forsyth*,[246] Sugden LC observed that:

> '[I]t is clearly settled that the declaration of one partner respecting a partnership transaction, made after the dissolution of the partnership, is admissible as evidence against the other partners; not conclusive, but as an admission, which does not preclude the party against whom it is used, showing by other evidence that the admission was not correct.'[247]

Although this case related to the dissolution of a partnership, the same principle would clearly apply during the life of the partnership.

7. Section 16 of the 1890 Act

[10.126] The seventh instance of the liability of a firm for the acts of its partners under the 1890 Act is contained in s 16, which provides that:

---

[241] This is the case anyway under the law of tracing: Keane, *Equity and the Law of Trusts in Ireland* (3rd edn, 2017) at para 19.01 et seq and Biehler, *Equity and the Law of Trusts in Ireland* (6th edn, 2016) at p 889 et seq.
[242] See the Scottish case of *Dunlop's Trustees v Clydesdale Bank* (1891) 18 R 751.
[243] See further in relation to these requirements, para **[10.14]** et seq.
[244] See para **[10.41]**. See also the case of *Armagas Ltd v Mundogas SA* [1985] 3 All ER 1795 and the cases cited therein.
[245] *Newton v Belcher* (1848) 12 QB 921; *Hollis v Burton* [1892] 3 Ch 226.
[246] *Luckie v Forsyth* (1846) 3 Jo & Lat 388.
[247] *Luckie v Forsyth* (1846) 3 Jo & Lat 388 at 394.

Notice to any partner who habitually acts in the partnership business of any matter relating to partnership affairs operates as notice to the firm, except in the case of a fraud on the firm committed by or with the consent of the partner.

As a result of this section, a firm cannot in general claim to be ignorant of a matter which is known by a partner in the firm. In addition, where a third party is required to show that a firm is on notice of some fact, it is sufficient to show that notice was given to one of the partners who habitually acts in the firm's business.

Acting qua partner and within ordinary course of business?

[10.127] Unlike the other instances of liability under the 1890 Act, the three requirements for a firm to be bound by the acts of a partner are not applicable to the question of whether a notice is binding on the firm.[248] This, it is apprehended, is because the second and third requirements, ie that the partner be acting *qua* partner and in the ordinary course of business, do not apply in light of the different nature of s 16 *vis-à-vis* the other seven instances of liability under the 1890 Act. In those other instances, the partner is doing an act on behalf of the partnership, while under s 16 the role of the partner is completely passive since he is simply the recipient of notice. Accordingly, it is conceivable that the partner may not be acting *qua* partner or in the course of the partnership business when he receives notice from a third party. In addition, there is no reason why a third party should be required only to give notice to a partner while he is so acting. For this reason, it is suggested that notice may be given to a partner at a time when he is not working as a partner, eg after office-hours, and still be binding on the firm.

'relating to partnership affairs'

[10.128] It is important to note that a firm will only be on notice of matters which relate to the partnership affairs. The significance of this requirement is highlighted by the Scottish case of *Campbell v McCreath*,[249] which involved two firms of solicitors in two different towns in Scotland. The partners in each firm were the same, although they traded under different names in the two towns. In the sale of a farm, one firm acted for the purchaser of the farm and the other acted for the vendor. The seller repudiated the sale of the farm and he claimed that the firm acting for the buyer was imputed with knowledge that he did not wish to sell the farm by virtue of s 16 of the 1890 Act. It was held that s 16 was restricted to the affairs of the firm itself and not to those of its clients, and therefore the firm acting for the purchaser was deemed not to be on notice of these facts.[250]

---

248 See further in relation to these requirements, para **[10.14]** et seq.

249 *Campbell v McCreath* (1975) SC 81.

250 The deemed notice of a firm of information given to one partner will often arise in the context of an alleged conflict of interest created by different partners acting for clients with conflicting interests. See generally the New Zealand Court of Appeal decision in *Russell McVeagh v Tower Corporation* [1998] 3 NZLR 641. In that case, it was held that a law firm was not in a conflict of interest position so as to disqualify it from acting for a company intending to take-over another company which had received tax advice from one of the partners. The court was influenced in part by the fact that the New Zealand legal profession was relatively small and access to expert advice was therefore limited. (contd.../)

Meaning of 'firm'

[10.129] Under the terms of s 16 of the 1890 Act, it is the 'firm' which is deemed to be on notice of matters notified to a partner. It is important to note that the 'firm' is those persons who were members of the firm at the time of the notice. It does not include those persons who became members of the firm subsequently or those who had left the firm prior to such notice.[251]

'partner who habitually acts'

[10.130] Before the firm will be bound by a notice given to a partner, it must be established that the partner habitually acts in the partnership business. For this reason, notice to a dormant partner[252] will not bind the firm since, by his very nature, he will not habitually act in the partnership business.

Type of 'notice'

[10.131] Section 16 refers simply to 'notice' to a partner. Traditionally, the approach has been to conclude that this refers simply to actual notice, as the doctrine of constructive notice is not generally applicable to commercial transactions.[253] However, elsewhere in this work[254] it is doubted whether this approach is always justifiable and it is suggested that some reasonable limits should be placed by the courts on the requirement of 'actual notice', since such an approach would be more in keeping with the approach under general agency principles.[255]

---

250 (\...contd) Accordingly, the court did not wish to restrict access further by imposing sanctions which were not required in the interests of justice. See, however, the interesting dissenting judgment of Thomas J who considered that the fiduciary obligation of solicitors to their clients should not be diluted for this reason. Of note also is the decision of Birmingham J in *O'Connor v Byrne & Anor* [2014] IEHC 472 in which the first defendant (the founding partner of a firm of solicitors, but who no longer held a practising certificate, with the firm being run instead by his fiancée) engaged in property sub-sale transactions while the firm also advised the purchasers. Birmingham J criticised the practice, commenting that it was 'institutionalising conflicts of interest.'

251 Subject of course to s 36(1) of the 1890 Act, whereby a person who deals with a firm after a change in its constitution is entitled to treat all apparent members of the firm as still being members of the firm until he has notice of the change. See generally in relation to this section, para **[11.85]** et seq.

252 See generally as to such partners, para **[6.04]**.

253 See l'Anson Banks, *Lindley & Banks on Partnership* (20th edn, 2017) at para 12-29.

254 See para **[11.65]** et seq.

255 Ie a principal will not be bound if the third party knew or ought to have known from all the surrounding circumstances that the agent did not possess the ostensible authority in question: *Discount Kitchens Ltd v Crawford* [1989] Halsbury's Monthly Review, Jan, Q238. See also *Staveley v Uzielli* (1800) 2 F & F 30; *Aste v Montague* (1858) 1 F & F 264; *Marsden v City and County Assurance Co* (1865) LR 1 CP 232; *Dickinson v Lilwal* (1815) 4 Camp 279; *Blackburn v Scholes* (1810) 2 Camp 341; *Manser v Back* (1848) 6 Hare 443. See also Reynolds, *Reynolds and Bowstead on Agency* (16th edn, 1996) at para 8-052 quoting *Combulk Pty Ltd v TNT Management Pty Ltd* (1993) 113 ALR 214, *Alliance & Leicester BS v Edgestop Ltd* [1993] 1 WLR 1462, *Feuer Leather Corp v Frank Johnston & Sons Ltd* [1981] Com L Rep 251 and *Standard Bank v Bank of Tokyo* [1995] 2 Lloyd's Rep 167 at 175.

'except in the case of fraud'

[10.132] Under the terms of s 16 of the 1890 Act, notice will not be imputed to the firm, where there is a fraud committed on the firm by or with the consent of the partner in receipt of the notice. This may be supported in principle since it is not expected that a partner engaged in fraud will communicate to the partnership the fact that he is committing a fraud. So in *Bignold v Waterhouse*,[256] where a partner in a firm of carriers agreed to transport valuable parcels free of charge in fraud of his partners, it was held that the knowledge that these parcels were valuable could not be imputed to his partners.

8. Section 30 of the 1890 Act

[10.133] The final instance of agency under the 1890 Act is contained in s 38. This section clarifies that the power of a partner to bind his firm continues after the dissolution of the partnership in order to wind up its affairs:

> After the dissolution of a partnership the authority of each partner to bind the firm, and the other rights and obligations of the partners, continue notwithstanding the dissolution so far as may be necessary to wind up the affairs of the partnership, and to complete transactions begun but unfinished at the time of the dissolution, but not otherwise.
>
> Provided that the firm is in no case bound by the acts of a partner who has become a bankrupt; but this proviso does not affect the liability of any person who has after the bankruptcy represented himself or knowingly suffered himself to be represented as a partner of a bankrupt.

[10.134] The three requirements for a firm to be bound by the acts of a partner are equally applicable to the question of whether a firm is bound by post-dissolution acts.[257] For this purpose, s 38 simply clarifies that on the dissolution of a firm, its winding up is within the ordinary course of its business. Accordingly, any act of a partner in a dissolved firm which is necessary to wind up the affairs of the partnership will bind the firm.

Power to wind up includes power to settle accounts

[10.135] It is clear from *Luckie v Forsyth*[258] that the power to wind up a partnership includes a power to settle the accounts of the firm with third parties. That case was concerned with a dissolved partnership which had granted to one of the partners, Cameron, the power to receive and pay debts of the firm and to wind up the firm. It was claimed by the personal representatives of the other partners that Cameron was not authorised to settle the accounts of the firm with a third party so as to bind the other partners not to require an investigation of the accounts. Sugden LC held that a partner had such a power and, accordingly, that the accounts were binding on the firm.

Winding up by a bankrupt partner

[10.136] Under the proviso to s 38, the firm is not bound by the acts of a partner in winding up the firm, if that partner has become a bankrupt. This proviso also makes

---

256 *Bignold v Waterhouse* (1813) 1 M & S 255.
257 See generally in relation to these three requirements, para **[10.14]** et seq.
258 *Luckie v Forsyth* (1846) 3 Jo & Lat 388.

clear that if the partners of a bankrupt represent themselves to be partners of the bankrupt, they will liable as if they were his partner, and in this regard, it is irrelevant that a firm is not generally bound by the acts of a bankrupt partner.

Chapter 11

Nature and Duration of Liability

INTRODUCTION

[11.01] In the preceding chapter, consideration was given to the instances in which a partner is liable for the acts of his co-partners. It is now proposed to examine the nature and duration of that liability under the following headings:

    I.   Nature of a partner's liability; and

    II.   Duration of a partner's liability.

[11.02] Under the first heading, consideration will be given to the unlimited nature of a partner's liability, the nature of the joint liability of a partner for some partnership obligations[1] and the nature of the joint and several liability of a partner for other partnership obligations. In considering the duration of a partner's liability, reference will be made to the start of a partner's liability for partnership obligations when he joins a firm and to what extent that liability ends when he departs[2] from a firm. In recent times, there has been considerable mobility of partners between professional partnerships and for this reason, of considerable practical importance are those situations in which a former partner remains liable for partnership obligations, even where they are incurred after his departure. This liability and the ways in which it may be reduced will be considered in detail.

Overview

[11.03] Arguably, of most concern for partners will be the nature and duration of their liability for partnership obligations. The primary reason being that since partners are liable to an unlimited degree for the obligations of their firm, prospective, existing and former partners will naturally be concerned as to the duration of this liability. Therefore, much of the law concerning partnership liability deals with the start and especially the end of a partner's liability for the obligations of the firm. A particularly important aspect of this liability is the fact that there may be a time lag between the departure of a partner from a firm and the point in time when he is no longer liable for partnership obligations incurred after his departure. This period of potential liability arises because a former partner remains liable to a third party, who is unaware of his departure, for partnership obligations incurred by the firm in favour of that third party who dealt with the firm after the partner's departure. In this way, there is a twilight zone of liability for a former

---

[1]   Unless the context otherwise appears, the term 'obligations' is used in the sense of contractual and tortious obligations.

[2]   Here, as elsewhere in this text, this term is used, unless the context otherwise requires, in the sense of a partner's departure from the firm for whatever reason, eg expulsion, death, retirement, etc.

partner which only ends when all third parties, who dealt with the firm while he was a partner, are aware that he is no longer a partner in the firm. This twilight zone of liability has the effect of putting the onus on a former partner to ensure that third parties, who dealt with his firm, are made aware of his departure. This continued liability of a former partner can be justified on general principles since it stems from the fact that while he was a partner, that person thereby authorised the firm to make him liable for partnership obligations. Thus, third parties who dealt with the firm during the course of this agency are entitled to assume that future dealings will be on the same basis, until they are notified to the contrary. If this were not the case, it would place an intolerable burden on third parties who deal with partnerships to check before every transaction as to the identity of the partners who are bound by that transaction. In this regard, it is preferable that the burden be placed on the former partner to notify third parties of his departure. This is done by holding former partners liable for a post-departure partnership obligation incurred in favour of such third parties, even though this obligation will clearly not have been incurred by the firm on his behalf.

I.   NATURE OF A PARTNER'S LIABILITY

Extent of Liability

[11.04] As will be noted in detail hereunder, a partner may be jointly liable for the obligations of the firm or he may be jointly and severally liable for those obligations.[3] However, whether his liability is joint or joint and several, the extent of that liability is unlimited. In the words of Lord Lindley: 'every member of an ordinary partnership is liable to the utmost farthing of his property for the debts and engagements of the firm.'[4]

[11.05] For this reason, some partners seek effectively to limit their liability, by not becoming members of a partnership directly, but rather through the medium of a limited liability company.[5] While this option is not available to many professional partnerships,[6] where it is available it may be used to effectively cap an individual's liability to the share

---

3   See para **[11.07]** et seq.

4   See l'Anson Banks, *Lindley & Banks on Partnership* (20th edn, 2017) at para 13-14.

5   Although see, for example, the manner in which Bloxham Stockbrokers, a limited partnership, was restructured in 2011 when seven individual general partners each formed an unlimited liability company (owned and controlled by that partner). Those unlimited liability companies then became general partners in the limited partnership in place of those seven individuals (as detailed in McDermott J's judgment in *Danske Bank v Tinney* [2015] IEHC 770). The use of unlimited liability companies by those individual partners appeared to be more tax advantageous albeit that their liability remained unlimited.

6   For example in the case of the solicitors' profession, see the Solicitors Act 1954, s 64. Note, however, that under s 70 of the Solicitors (Amendment) Act 1994, the Law Society of Ireland has power (with the concurrence of the Minister for Justice and Equality, following consultation with the Minister for Business, Enterprise and Innovation) to make regulations providing for the incorporation of solicitors' practices. At the time of writing, no such regulations have been made. The Legal Services Regulation Act 2015 will, once the Legal Services Regulatory Authority has signed the relevant regulations into law, (contd.../)

capital of the company, since, save in the most exceptional circumstances,[7] individual shareholders in the company will not have to contribute to the losses of the company beyond the issued share capital.

[11.06] In view of a partner's unlimited liability, it is important for partners to ensure that they have adequate insurance to cover potential claims which may arise from the partnership's activities. In the light of large claims against professional firms,[8] professional partnerships have continued to look at possible means to limit the exposure of their partners.[9] As shall be seen hereafter, the limited partnership does not provide the solution for such professionals, since a limited partner is prohibited from taking any part in the management of the firm.[10] Although not a popular remedy, there is of course nothing to prevent a firm restricting the liability of the firm by means of a contract with its clients. This could provide for the liability of the firm to be fixed at a monetary amount or to the value of the partnership assets and it would thereby exclude the exposure of the personal assets of the partners.

Type of Liability

[11.07] Under the terms of the 1890 Act, the liability of a partner for the acts of his partners may be either joint or it may be joint and several. However, as noted hereunder, the distinction between these two different types of liability has effectively been eliminated by the terms of the Civil Liability Act 1961. Nonetheless, the distinction remains an integral part of the 1890 Act and it is proposed firstly to consider the joint liability of a partner for the contractual obligations of the firm, which liability is established by s 9 of the 1890 Act. As noted by Lord Millett in *Dubai Aluminium v*

---

6   (\...contd) enable firms of solicitors to apply for authorisation as limited liability partnerships, and will also enable practising solicitors to enter into legal partnerships (which can also be authorised as limited liability partnerships) with practising barristers. However, at the time of writing, the restriction in s 59 of the Solicitors Act 1954 remains in force.

7   See generally in relation to the exceptional cases in which the veil of incorporation is lifted, Hutchinson, *Keane on Company Law* (5th edn, 2016) at para [11.16] et seq; Courtney, *The Law of Companies* (4th edn, 2016) at para [5.001] et seq; Forde and Kennedy, *Company Law* (5th edn, 2017) at para 4-51 et seq.

8   This issue is most vividly highlighted by the £65 million award in the English case of *ADT Ltd v BDO Binder Hamlyn* [1996] BCC 808.

9   The limited liability partnership, which has existed in the United States since 1991, was introduced by the Limited Liability Partnerships Act 2000 to England and Wales, and to Scotland, and was introduced in Northern Ireland with effect from November 2004 by the Limited Liability Partnerships Act (Northern Ireland) 2002. In Ireland, the Legal Services Regulation Act 2015 makes provision for firms of solicitors, legal partnerships of barristers, and legal partnerships of solicitors and barristers, to apply for authorisation as limited liability partnerships (see further para **[30.01]** et seq). Regarding professional firms of accountants, the restriction on a company's statutory auditors being a body corporate was removed in 2010 by reg 6(b) of the European Communities (Statutory Audits) (Directive 2006/43/EC) Regulations 2010.

10   Limited Partnerships Act 1907, s 6, and see further regarding such limited partnerships, para **[28.01]** et seq.

Salaam, s 9 'is not concerned with the liability of the firm at all but with the liability of the individual partners'.[11]

Joint liability for contracts

[11.08] A partner who creates a contractual[12] responsibility subjects the firm to a single joint liability. This is set out in s 9 of the 1890 Act:

> Every partner in a firm is liable jointly with the other partners, and in Scotland severally also, for all debts and obligations of the firm incurred while he is a partner; and after his death his estate is also severally liable in a due course of administration for such debts and obligations, so far as they remain unsatisfied, but subject in England or Ireland to the prior payment of his separate debts.

This contrasts with the terms of s 12 of the 1890 Act which provide that a partner is jointly and severally liable for wrongful acts and omissions (under s 10) and the misapplication of property in the custody of the firm (under s 11).

Several liability of partner's estate for contracts

[11.09] Although s 9 of the 1890 Act is primarily concerned with establishing the joint liability of a partner for the firm's contractual obligations, it also provides that the estate of a deceased partner is severally liable for debts and obligations of the firm incurred while he was a partner. A creditor of the firm may therefore go against the estate of a deceased partner without having recourse to the firm's assets.[13] In the event of the deceased partner's estate being insufficient, the creditor may exercise his rights against the surviving partners for the balance of the debt. By the express terms of s 9, in any action against a deceased partner's estate for a partnership debt, the deceased partner's separate debts have priority as the partnership debt is postponed to the 'prior payment of his separate debts'.[14]

[11.10] It is to be noted that under the terms of s 9, a deceased partner's estate is liable for the debts and obligations of the firm 'so far as they remain unsatisfied'. However, the use in s 9 of this term refers simply to the fact that the debts and obligations have not been paid and it does not impose an obligation upon a creditor to go against the firm's assets first, before having recourse to a deceased partner's estate.[15]

Express assumption of liability by partners

[11.11] There is nothing to prevent the partners in a firm from expressly providing by contract that they will be jointly *and* severally liable for a particular contractual obligation. Indeed such assumptions of several liability are commonly contained in

11 *Dubai Aluminium v Salaam* [2003] 2 AC 366 at para 110 of the transcript.
12 The Partnership Act 1890, s 9 simply uses the expression 'debts and obligations'. However, as s 10 deals with 'wrongful acts and omissions', s 9 must be taken as referring to contractual obligations rather than tortious obligations.
13 See further in relation to the liability of a deceased partner's estate, para **[24.40]**.
14 This is in keeping with the general priority of the separate debts of a partner over the partnership debts when one is dealing with the separate estate of that partner. See generally para **[24.49]**.
15 *Wilkinson v Henderson* (1833) 2 LJ Ch 191.

contracts with partnerships and will override the terms of s 9.[16] Partners may also contractually agree, with third parties, limitations on their liability to third parties more generally.[17]

[11.12] Similarly, where the partners expressly assume joint liability under the terms of a contract, this fact may negative the several liability (which would otherwise apply) of the estate of a partner who dies. Thus in *Clarke v Bickers*[18] the partners gave a series of tenant's covenants under a lease jointly. The court refused to allow separate proceedings against the estate of one of the partners who subsequently died. This was because the separate liability of the deceased partner's estate was held to have been expressly negatived by the partners' covenants which were clearly joint in form.

[11.13] While the House of Lords decision in *AIB Group (UK) plc v Martin*[19] did not contain any significant new legal principles, it serves as a salutary lesson to those involved in property investment by way of partnership. Mr Martin, a property dealer, carried on business in three separate capacities: on his own account, with a Mr Gold, and with a Mr Shaw. As part of his business arrangement with Mr Gold, they purchased 14 investment properties and leased them out. The AIB Group provided the finance for each of those purchases. Mr Martin also owned a further 28 properties in his own right, in respect of which he had also received financing from the AIB Group. In respect of their jointly owned properties, Mr Martin and Mr Gold owed the AIB Group approximately Stg£1.7m, and provided a joint mortgage over those properties in favour of the AIB Group. When the joint debt of Mr Martin and Mr Gold reached Stg£2.3m, the AIB Group decided to enforce its joint mortgage. At that time, Mr Martin owed significant sums to the AIB Group in respect of the properties he owned in his own right. The joint mortgage provided by Mr Martin and Mr Gold over their jointly owned properties read as follows:

> 'The mortgagor hereby covenants with … the bank … that it will on demand pay or discharge to the bank … all sums of money … advanced to the mortgagor by the bank …'

The joint mortgage then provided that the term 'mortgagor' (where the mortgage was executed by more than one person) was to be construed

> '… as referring to all and/or any one of those persons and the obligations of such persons hereunder shall be joint and several.'

---

[16]   *Higgins v Senior* (1841) 8 M & W 834; *Ex p Wilson* (1842) 3 MD & D 57; *Ex p Harding* (1879) 12 Ch D 557.

[17]   See for example the arrangements entered into between The Birr Partnership and Ulster Bank Ireland Limited, as outlined in the judgment of Cooke J in *King & ors v Ulster Bank Ireland Limited* [2013] IEHC 250. Cooke J noted that the inclusion of a provision in a 2005 facility letter confirming that, once planning permission was received for a specific property, the bank's recourse to the partners would be for interest only, not for principal, was necessary as the default position under s 9 of the 1890 Act is that the partners are responsible for all of the debts of the partnership. In that case, that position was later superseded by a subsequent facility letter under which the bank's recourse to the partners was expressed to be for both capital and interest.

[18]   *Clarke v Bickers* (1845) 65 RR 657; see also *Sumner v Powell* (1816) 2 Mer 30 (joint indemnity by partners).

[19]   *AIB Group (UK) plc v Martin* [2002] 1 All ER 353.

AIB Group interpreted this provision as meaning that Mr Gold had covenanted to pay on demand not only the amounts advanced by the AIB Group to Mr Gold and Mr Martin jointly, but also the amounts advanced by the AIB Group to Mr Martin in his own right. In the Court of Appeal, Mr Gold's counsel noted that such an interpretation was:

> '... plain and obvious and frightening in its effects. Each partner is to be liable not only for partnership debts, but also for any separate debt his partner may have with the Bank, whether he knows of it or not.'

Despite this, three judges in the Court of Appeal and all five judges in the House of Lords found in favour of AIB Group's interpretation. While the judgment of Lord Millett did set out cogent reasons why the mortgage should be interpreted differently,[20] he did not dissent from the majority view.

Joint and several liability for torts

[11.14] Sections 10 and 11 of the 1890 Act provide for the liability of partners for the wrongful acts and omissions of the firm (s 10) and for the misapplication of money or property (s 11). Section 12 then goes on to provide for the type of liability which attaches to both these sections:

> Every partner is liable jointly with his co-partners and also severally for everything for which the firm while he is a partner therein becomes liable under either of the two last preceding sections.

It is to be noted that, while the misapplication of a third party's money or property may be a breach of contract as well as a tort, the liability of the partner therefor is joint and several as a result of s 12.

Express assumption of liability

[11.15] Just as there is nothing to prevent the partners in a firm from expressly providing by contract that they will be jointly and severally liable for a contractual obligation,[21] there would seem to be nothing to prevent a firm from agreeing that the partners will only be liable jointly in relation to a tortious liability, and thereby overriding the terms of s 12. Clearly, in order to be effective, the injured third party must be a party to this express or implicit agreement, something which will not always be the case in instances of tortious liability.[22]

Joint and several liability for breach of trust

[11.16] Unlike liability for contracts (s 9) and torts (s 12), s 13 of the 1890 Act, which deals with a breach of trust by a partner, does not specify the type of liability which attaches to that partner and his co-partners for a breach of trust. Accordingly, reference must be made to the general law of trusts, which provides that persons who are

---

[20] See further Twomey, 'Partnership law – unexpected liability for partner in property investment' (2002) DULJ, 24, 291–295.

[21] See para **[11.11]**.

[22] See the case of *British Homes Assurance Corporation v Paterson* [1902] 2 Ch 404, considered at para **[11.40]**, in which the firm was held not to be liable because the third party refused to treat the obligation as a joint obligation, but rather treated it as the several obligation of one partner.

implicated in a breach of trust are jointly and severally liable to the beneficiaries for the loss incurred.[23]

Nature of Joint Liability

[11.17] The basis of the joint liability of a firm (and thus of all the partners in the firm) for the acts of a partner, is that as a partner is the agent of the firm, the firm is liable for the acts of the partner within the ordinary course of its business.[24] Joint liability means that the firm is the primary obligant, but once the debt has been constituted against the firm, it may be enforced against any one partner. In the old Irish case of *Hayden v Carroll*,[25] Lord Carleton explained the rationale for allowing one partner in a firm to be sued for the whole of the joint debt as follows:

'As between the partnership-creditors and the partners, each partner is liable to the whole demand, and the whole fund is liable in the same manner; and either partner by being compelled to pay the entire debt, does not only discharge the debt of the other partner but also his own. Less public inconvenience arises from one partner's being liable to pay more than his proportion than would arise from placing any impediment in the way of the joint creditors resorting to the entire of that joint fund, which from the nature of the contract, is subject to the entire of the joint debt; the creditors are ignorant of the different proportions of the fund to which the several partners are intitled [sic], and also of the state of the account between the partners.'[26]

It is also important to note that joint liability does not limit the extent of the liability of a partner which remains unlimited.

[11.18] Historically, there were two significant distinctions between joint liability and joint and several liability. First, a judgment against one partner in a case where the partners were jointly liable precluded the bringing of a subsequent claim against his co-partner, but this was not the case if they were jointly and severally liable.[27] This principle

---

[23] *Alleyne v Darcy* (1854) 4 Ir Ch R 199 at 206 per Brady LC. See also *Fletcher v Green* (1864) 33 Beav 426 at 430; *Blyth v Fladgate* [1891] 1 Ch 337; *Re National Funds Assurance Co* (1878) 10 Ch D 118. The provisions of the Civil Liability Act 1961 also apply to a breach of trust, see s 2 of that Act, which defines a 'wrong' as including a breach of trust. See generally, Keane, *Equity and the Law of Trusts in Ireland* (3rd edn, 2017) at para 10.75; Biehler, *Equity and the Law of Trusts in Ireland* (6th edn, 2016) at p 537.

[24] See generally in relation to the liability of a partner for the acts of his co-partners, para **[10.01]** et seq.

[25] *Hayden v Carroll* (1796) 3 Ridg PC 545.

[26] *Hayden v Carroll* (1796) 3 Ridg PC 545 at 620.

[27] This rule could be explained by the theoretical basis of joint liability, namely that a partner (A), in a firm (A & B), is not liable personally on a contract which he has made with a third party in his capacity as a partner, but rather he is liable as a member of the firm. Thus, there was only one cause of action connecting the third party with A and his partner B. It followed that if a judgment was obtained against A personally in respect of the debt, the effect was that the debt merged in the judgment and the cause of action was severed, so that if A had no assets, the third party could not subsequently take an action against B since there was no longer any cause of action connecting them.

was known as the rule in *Kendall v Hamilton*.[28] However, this rule in *Kendall v Hamilton*[29] was reversed by s 18(1)(a) of the Civil Liability Act 1961 which states that:

Where damage is suffered by any person as a result of concurrent wrongs—

    (a)   Judgment recovered against any wrongdoer liable in respect of that damage shall not be a bar to an action against any other person, who would, if sued, have been liable as concurrent wrongdoer in respect of the same damage.

[11.19] Section 18(1)(a) is subject to the proviso that the plaintiff cannot recover more damages than he has suffered.[30] Even before the enactment of the Civil Liability Act 1961, the Rules of the Superior Courts allowed the difficulty in the case of *Kendall v Hamilton* to be avoided by permitting a partnership to be sued in the firm name.[31] These proceedings operate as an action against all the persons who were partners in that firm at the time of the accrual of the cause of action and for this reason, it is prudent to take proceedings against a partnership in this way.

[11.20] The second significant difference between joint liability and joint and several liability was the fact that the release of one partner who was jointly liable for a partnership obligation released his co-partners, but the release of a partner who was jointly and severally liable did not have the same effect. This difference has been effectively eliminated by s 17 of the Civil Liability Act 1961. This provides that the release[32] of, or accord with, a partner who is jointly liable for a partnership obligation will discharge his co-partner, only if the release or accord indicates an intention that the other partners are to be discharged.[33]

[11.21] In addition, the Civil Liability Act 1961 has categorised persons who are jointly liable and those who are severally liable as concurrent wrongdoers[34] and under the terms of s 12(1) of that Act, a concurrent wrongdoer is liable for the whole of the damage in respect of which he is a concurrent wrongdoer. An action against concurrent

---

[28]   *Kendall v Hamilton* (1811) 7 Ves Jr 514. In that case, the plaintiff made a loan to a firm in which W and M were partners. He sued both partners and he obtained judgment against them for the debt which was not satisfied because of their lack of resources. The plaintiff then discovered that a Mr Hamilton was also a partner in the firm and a man of means. However, when he sued him, it was held that as the liability of the partners was joint, the judgment in the first action extinguished Mr Hamilton's obligation. In addition, no relief was available in equity in cases such as these as equity regarded it as essential for all the parties to be joined to the proceedings so that all the issues could be settled between those who were jointly liable in the same proceedings.

[29]   *Kendall v Hamilton* (1811) 7 Ves Jr 514.

[30]   Civil Liability Act 1961, s 17(2).

[31]   The rule of court is now contained in the Rules of the Superior Courts, Ord 14, r 1 (SI 15/ 1986, as amended). See generally in relation to actions against a partner in the firm-name, para **[12.11]** et seq.

[32]   Similarly a satisfaction (ie a payment of damages, whether after judgment or by way of accord and satisfaction, or the rendering of any agreed substitution therefor) by one concurrent wrongdoer (which includes a partner who is jointly or jointly and severally liable) discharges all the other concurrent wrongdoers: Civil Liability Act 1961, s 16(1).

[33]   See the English Court of Appeal case of *Morris v Wentworth-Stanley* [1999] 2 WLR 470, para **[11.99]n** below.

[34]   A concurrent wrongdoer includes persons in breach of contract and in breach of trust as well as tortfeasors and it includes joint or several wrongdoers: Civil Liability Act 1961, s 11.

wrongdoers may be brought against all of them or against any one or more of them and if a judgment is obtained in an action against concurrent wrongdoers, it will take effect as if it were given against them separately.[35]

Nature of Joint and Several Liability

[11.22] While partners are jointly liable for the contractual obligations of other partners within the ordinary course of the partnership's business,[36] if those acts are tortious, the partners are jointly and severally liable.[37] It has been seen that prior to the Civil Liability Act 1961, the distinction between joint liability and joint and several liability was significant. Thus, while successive actions were not always available against partners who were jointly liable, successive actions could always be taken against partners who were jointly and severally liable.[38] So it was in *Re Clarkes*[39] which involved four partners in a building firm in Monaghan. The four partners entered a joint and several bond in favour of the Provincial Bank of Ireland securing the payment of any outstanding balances from the firm to the bank. Separate judgments were obtained against each of the partners by the bank and the bank also sought to obtain a judgment against the firm. The defendants claimed that the bank, by obtaining separate judgments, had elected to take the separate estate and that the bond was merged in the judgments which had been obtained by the bank. Sugden LC held that as the obligation was joint and several, the bank was entitled to prove against the joint estate of the firm for its debt and that the separate judgments did not destroy the joint estate.

Partner's Right to Contribution

[11.23] A partner who has paid more than his share of an award of damages in respect of a joint liability or a joint and several liability has a right to a contribution from his co-partners. Section 21 of the Civil Liability Act 1961 provides that where two or more persons are responsible for the same wrong, one person, who is sued in respect of a

---

[35]   Civil Liability Act 1961, s 14(1) and (2).

[36]   See *King & ors v Ulster Bank Ireland Limited* [2013] IEHC 250 (per Cooke J at para 27 of the judgment): '[the]…borrower is a partnership and, as such, all of the partners are jointly liable for their borrowing as a matter of law.'

[37]   Partnership Act 1890, ss 10 and 12. See generally in relation to joint and several liability, the '*Partnership Law Report on a Reference under Section 3(1)(e) of the Law Commissions Act 1965*' (Cm 6015) published in 2003 by The Law Commission and The Scottish Law Commission in which those Law Commissions recommended joint and several liability for partners more generally.

[38]   In contrast to the theoretical basis for joint liability (see fn **27** above), in a case where there is joint and several liability for the partners in the firm of A & B, there are three causes of action connecting the third party with A & B, A and B, ie two with each of the partners, since they are severally liable, and one with the firm. Accordingly, even if a judgment was obtained against A, who proves to have no assets, a successive action was always available against B since there remains a cause of action connecting B with the third party. It has been seen that this was not always the case in relation to a joint liability ie under *Kendall v Hamilton* (1811) 7 Ves Jr 514, considered at para **[11.18]** above and prior to the enactment of s 18 of the Civil Liability Act 1961.

[39]   *Re Clarkes* (1845) 2 Jo & Lat 212. The first instance decision of Macan C is reported at (1844) 7 Ir Eq R 39.

wrong, may recover such amount of contribution from his concurrent wrongdoer(s) as is deemed by the court to be just and equitable having regard to the contributor's fault.[40] However, if the partner against whom contribution is sought, is entitled to an indemnity[41] in respect of the damages from the partner seeking the contribution, then no contribution will be permitted.

[11.24] Under (the now repealed) s 5 of the Mercantile Law Amendment Act 1856,[42] where one of two partners who are jointly liable for a debt has paid that judgment debt, he is entitled, in order to enforce his right to contribution, to an assignment of the judgment and of all securities for the debt, subject to the equities subsisting between the debtors as partners. This principle of subrogation is also established by caselaw, so that it seems that despite the repeal of this Act, a partner may have the rights stated in s 5 under the common law.[43]

II. DURATION OF A PARTNER'S LIABILITY

General Rule

[11.25] The start and end of a partner's liability for the firm's obligations may be summarised in the form of a three-part general rule. This general rule is as follows.

A partner:

(1) is not liable for obligations incurred by his firm before he became a partner;

(2) is liable for obligations incurred by his firm while he was a partner;

(3) is not liable for obligations incurred by his firm after his departure, subject to important exceptions in respect of persons who dealt with the firm while he was a partner.

[11.26] Each of these will be examined in turn. Before doing so, a good illustration of the general rule is provided by the decision in *Minnit v Whinery*.[44] In that case, Thomas Minnit was a member of a sugar-boiling partnership in Dublin with Boles and Jopson. He decided to withdraw from the partnership and after his withdrawal, Boles and Jopson offered to purchase sugar from Whinery. Before Whinery accepted the offer, Thomas Minnit notified him that he was no longer interested in the partnership. Whinery indicated that he was satisfied with the security of Boles and Jopson and he got promissory notes in the names of those two only. Subsequently, Joshua Minnit joined the

---

40   See further para **[14.25]** et seq and see generally in relation to contribution between concurrent wrongdoers, McMahon and Binchy, *Law of Torts* (4th edn, 2013) at para [4.08] et seq and Kerr, *The Civil Liability Acts* (5th edn, 2017) .

41   For example under s 41(c) of the 1890 Act. See generally para **[20.82]**. See also McMahon and Binchy, *Law of Torts* (4th edn, 2013) at para [4.27] et seq.

42   19 & 20 Vict, c 97, repealed by the Statute Law Revision Act 1983.

43   See Breslin, *Banking Law in the Republic of Ireland* (1st edn, 1998) at p 628 where he quoted *Kennedy v Campbell* [1899] 1 IR 59 at 63. See also *Re 19th Ltd* [1989] ILRM 652; Doyle, 'Reason and Justice in the Law of Subrogation' (1994) ILT 10; Johnston, *Banking and Security Law in Ireland* (1998) at [9.57] et seq.

44   *Minnit v Whinery* (1721) 5 Bro PC 489.

partnership. When Whinery failed to get payment on the promissory notes from Boles and Jopson, he sought payment from Thomas Minnit and Joshua Minnit. It was held that Whinery was not entitled to payment from the new partner (Joshua Minnit) since the obligation to pay for the sugar was incurred by the firm before his admission (rule 1). Rather, Boles and Jopson were liable on the contract to supply sugar since it was incurred by their firm while they were partners (rule 2). It was also held that Whinery was not entitled to payment from the former partner (Thomas Minnit) since the obligation to pay for the sugar was incurred after his retirement from the firm and Whinery had full notice of his withdrawal from the partnership (rule 3).

Importance of date of admission and retirement

[11.27] It is perhaps clear from *Minnit v Whinery*[45] that it is important for the date of a partner's admission or departure to be clearly set out in the partnership agreement or in the dissolution agreement, as appropriate. In this regard, the date of the removal/addition of a partner's name from the register of business names, the firm's stationery or the date of the notice of a partner's departure in *Iris Oifigiúil* is likely to provide supporting evidence of the date of departure or admission.

1. Partner not Liable for Pre-admission Obligations

[11.28] The first part of the general rule regarding the duration of a partner's liability is in fact a corollary of the second part of the general rule (that a partner is liable for obligations incurred while he was a partner), ie a partner is not liable for obligations incurred by the firm before he joined it.

[11.29] When an incoming partner joins a firm, the pre-existing partnership between the original members is technically dissolved and the old firm is replaced by the newly constituted partnership between the increased group of partners. However, the members of the old firm remain liable for obligations incurred prior to that date and the incoming partner is not liable for those obligations.[46] The case of *Forester v Bell*[47] is authority for the principle that an incoming partner is not liable for obligations incurred prior to his admission to the partnership. In that case, the plaintiff had entered a contract with one member of the provisional committee of a company prior to its formation. When the company was never formed, he took an action on the contract against another member of the committee on the grounds that all of the members of the committee were liable to him as they were in partnership prior to the proposed formation of the company. However, the defendant was not a member of the provisional committee at the time the contract was entered into. In the High Court, Blackburne CJ held obiter that, assuming the members of the committee to be in partnership, the defendant was not liable on the contract, since at the time of the contract he was not a member of the committee and 'incoming partners are not liable for contracts made previously to their joining the partnership'.[48] The principle underlying this case is now set out in s 17(1) of the 1890 Act, which states that:

---

45   *Minnit v Whinery* (1721) 5 Bro PC 489.
46   *Minnit v Whinery* (1721) 5 Bro PC 489, considered at para **[11.26]**.
47   *Forester v Bell* (1847) 10 Ir LR 555.
48   *Forester v Bell* (1847) 10 Ir LR 555 at 558. Blackburne CJ relied on the authority of *Vere v Ashby* (1829) 10 B & C 288.

A person who is admitted as a partner into an existing firm does not thereby become liable to the creditors of the firm for anything done before he became a partner.

[11.30] It follows that where a partner joins a firm, and his co-partners state that an account of the old firm is a debt of the firm as newly constituted, this statement will not bind the incoming partner.[49] The incoming partner may of course agree, expressly or by implication, with his new partners to be responsible for the obligations incurred prior to his admission. An example of a situation in which such an agreement arises by implication is where an incoming partner allows the pre-existing debts of the firm to be discharged out of profits which arise after his admission. However, such an agreement is not binding on any creditor of the firm, unless entered into with that creditor, either expressly or by implication, and for sufficient consideration.[50]

[11.31] The rationale for an incoming partner not being liable for the pre-existing obligations of his new firm is clear, namely that at the time the obligations were incurred by the firm, there was no agency between the incoming partner and the firm and therefore he is not bound by those obligations. It does of course follow that the corollary is also true ie that a partnership is not liable for the acts of a partner which are done by him before he became a partner.[51]

'does not thereby'

[11.32] Section 17(1) of the 1890 Act expressly provides that a partner who joins a firm is not thereby liable for the pre-existing obligations of the firm. It follows that the incoming partner may be liable in other ways, such as by expressly or implicitly adopting these obligations.[52] Similarly, s 17(1) does not prevent an incoming partner being liable for debts which are incurred by his firm to a third party pursuant to a contract which was entered into prior to his admission, but where each obligation under the contract (such as a new delivery of goods) is really a new debt being incurred by the 'new' partnership of which he is a member.[53]

Liabilities which may pre-date or post-date admission to a partnership

[11.33] In *Lyons v Delaney*,[54] a dispute arose between the plaintiff (Mrs Lyons) and the defendants, her financial and tax advisors, in respect of an investment she had made in a hotel consortium. Leave to join O'Sullivan & Associates (a firm of solicitors) to the proceedings issued in 2014. Mr O'Kennedy (who had been a partner in O'Sullivan &

---

49 *French v French* (1841) 2 Man & G 644; *Lemere v Elliot* (1861) 6 H & N 656.

50 See the statement of Lord Lindley that 'if an incoming partner agrees with his co-partners that the debts of the old shall be taken by the new firm, this, although valid and binding between partners, is, as regards strangers, *res inter alios acta*, and does not confer upon them any right to fix the old debts on the new partner.' Lord Lindley relied on *Vere v Ashby* (1829) 10 B & C 288 at 298, *Ex p Peele* (1802) 6 Ves Jr 602 and *Ex p Williams* (1817) Buck 13. See l'Anson Banks, *Lindley & Banks on Partnership* (20th edn, 2017) at para 13-26.

51 These acts would not be 'within the ordinary course of business of the firm' and therefore not binding on the firm, see further para **[10.35]** et seq.

52 As to such adoptions of liability, see para **[11.30]**.

53 *Dyke v Brewer* (1849) 2 C & K 828.

54 *Lyons v Delaney* [2015] IEHC 685,

Associates) from April 2004 to September 2010 argued that he should not be joined to the proceedings for various reasons, including that he was not a partner in the firm when the liability to Mrs Lyons crystallised. Mrs Lyons's investment had been made in September 2003, and a related loan facility from Irish Nationwide Building Society was drawn down in October 2003 (Mrs Lyons claimed that this loan was drawn down by the defendants without her authority and that they had not advised her that her investment would involve a borrowing). Mr O'Kennedy argued that nothing had happened since October 2003 to affect Mrs Lyons's liability to Irish Nationwide Building Society. A power of attorney was also signed by Mrs Lyons in favour of the defendants at some time between 2006 and 2008. That power of attorney had been drafted by O'Sullivan & Associates at a time when Mr O'Kennedy was a partner in the firm. Binchy J noted that Mrs Lyons's allegations of negligence against the defendants spanned the period from 2003 to 2011, and it was not possible to say at that time that she would not succeed under one or more of the claims of negligence in respect of the period during which Mr O'Kennedy was a partner. As such, Mr O'Kennedy failed to have the third party notice set aside on that basis (although he did succeed in having it set aside due to a delay in that notice being served).

2. Partner Liable for Obligations Incurred while a Partner

[11.34] The second part of the general rule regarding the duration of the liability of a partner, is that a partner is liable for obligations incurred by the firm while he was a partner and remains liable therefor after his retirement from the firm. This rule is contained in s 17(2) of the 1890 Act which provides that:

> A partner who retires from a firm does not thereby cease to be liable for partnership debts or obligations[55] incurred before his retirement.

[11.35] Thus in *Cummins v Cummins*,[56] a four-partner firm in Cork owed money to a trust. One of the partners retired from the firm leaving ample assets in the partnership to pay the debt to the trust. However, after his retirement, the retired partner assisted in the misapplication of the money in breach of the terms of the trust. Sugden LC held that the retired partner remained liable for this obligation to the trust as the mere retiring and leaving sufficient assets was not sufficient to discharge his liability. In *Best & anor v Ghose & ors*,[57] an order was sought for the taking of an account of the dealings by a limited partnership (Bloxham Stockbrokers) in a fund on behalf of Mr Best. Baker J, having regard to s 17(2), accepted that partners who had retired from a limited partnership could have continuing liability for obligations incurred while they were partners. However, she accepted that certain partners (who had been general partners in Bloxham Stockbrokers at the time that it invested in the fund) had never, as a matter of fact, been involved in the management of the fund, and had no information or documents in relation to it. While Baker J accepted that this would not present a defence

---

55 Although the expression 'debts or obligations' which is used in s 17(2) is the same term as is used in s 9, it is clear that in s 17(2), it is not restricted to contractual debts and obligations, but refers to all obligations, including tortious obligations, cf the position in s 9, considered at para **[11.08]**.

56 *Cummins v Cummins* (1845) 8 Ir Eq R 723.

57 *Best & anor v Ghose & ors* [2018] IEHC 376.

in other causes of action, in this particular case, she refused relief against all partners other than the managing partner.[58] In *Stanton v Foley*,[59] the plaintiff's claim related to the actions of a partner in a firm of solicitors in 1983, who had since died. While the second defendant had been in partnership with him in 1983, all pre-2000 records of the firm had subsequently been destroyed. As only the deceased partner could have disputed the plaintiff's claim, and as the relevant files had been destroyed, Noonan J did not allow the plaintiff's claim against the second defendant to proceed, notwithstanding that he had been a partner in the partnership at the time of the conduct complained of, as he would not have been in a position to defend himself and could not have obtained a fair trial.

[11.36] It may, of course, be possible for a departing partner to obtain an indemnity from the continuing partners in respect of these liabilities.[60] However, such an indemnity will operate only *inter partes* and will not prevent the partner from being sued by a third party. Rather, the former partner will remain liable to third parties for these obligations, subject only to the relevant rules on the barring of claims under the Statute of Limitations 1957.[61]

[11.37] Of course, if a partner has guaranteed the debts of a partnership of which he is a member, and that partnership is later dissolved, depending on the manner in which the guarantee is drafted, the beneficiary may be able to continue to rely on it. In *Healy v Ulster Bank Ireland Ltd*,[62] Mr Healy had provided a guarantee to Ulster Bank of the loan obligations of a medical practice in which he was a partner with a Mr Cullen. The partnership was dissolved at the end of July 2007, with Mr Cullen paying a sum in excess of €2,000,000 to Mr Healy in consideration for Mr Cullen taking over the assets and liabilities of the partnership. However, a release of Mr Healy's guarantee was not procured from Ulster Bank. In August 2007, Mr Healy lodged the proceeds of the partnership dissolution with Ulster Bank. In August 2008, Ulster Bank enforced the guarantee by exercising a right of set-off in respect of Mr Healy's credit balance on his personal account against the debit balance then outstanding in respect of the loan to the partnership. Mr Healy was not able to demonstrate to the satisfaction of the court that he had been released from his guarantee, so Ulster Bank was not ordered to reverse the set-off.

---

58 The account sought in this case was, per Baker J at para 36 of the judgment, '…an account as long understood by the courts of equity, the giving of a narrative or an explanation in respect of transactions or events in the operation of the Fund.'

59 *Stanton v Foley* [2018] IEHC 675.

60 See for example the key features of the deed of indemnity and release in respect of a partner who retired from a partnership known as the Ballykisteen Developments Partnership, summarised at para 20 of Binchy J's judgment in *Heffernan & Anor v Murray & Ors* [2015] IEHC 196. However, in that case, the retiring partner was not permitted to rely on that indemnity as it had not been executed correctly on behalf of the continuing partners.

61 See generally in relation to the limitation of actions, Canny, *Limitation of Actions* (2nd edn, 2016).

62 *Healy v Ulster Bank Ireland Ltd* [2009] IEHC 360. The decision of the High Court was subsequently set aside by the Supreme Court ([2015] IESC 106) due to the High Court not having made a finding regarding the 'veracity or reliability' of one of the witnesses in the case. On the re-hearing of the case before Barrett J in the High Court ([2018] IEHC 12), the set-off by Ulster Bank was again not reversed.

'partnership debts or obligations'

[11.38] The continuing liability of a former partner under s 17(2) of the 1890 Act is expressed to be for partnership debts or obligations. For this reason, if a debt or obligation is not that of the partnership, the retiring partner will not be liable therefor under s 17(2). On this basis, a partner will not be liable for obligations which are not binding on the firm such as where they are incurred by intending partners where no partnership is in existence. This principle is also illustrated by the case of *Forester v Bell*.[63] That case concerned an action to recover money against a member of a provisional committee for the formation of The Irish West Coast Railway Company. The plaintiff had entered a contract with Campbell, one member of the provisional committee, to act as a clerk to the company. When the company was never formed, he took an action to enforce his contract against Bell, another member of the provisional committee on the grounds that Campbell and Bell were in partnership with the aim of forming the company. In the High Court, Blackburne CJ, held Bell was not liable on this contract since it was made with Campbell as an intending partner in the enterprise and not as a partner of Bell:

> 'The members of this provisional committee were not partners, nor had any of them a right to bind the others; so that the defendant cannot be visited with liability by any analogy to the case of partners. The committee can only be regarded as a number of individuals engaged in arranging measures for future co-partnership; and if any of them be sued, he must be shown to have entered into the contract which forms the cause of action.'[64]

[11.39] Just as persons, who intend to become partners together, will not be liable for each others' acts prior to the existence of the partnership, similarly, where an obligation is incurred by a future partner,[65] it will not be binding on the existing partners in the firm. This follows from the fact that at the time the obligation is incurred by the future partner, there is no agency between the future partner and the firm and therefore the obligation cannot be said to be an obligation of the partnership.

Did the third party treat it as a partnership obligation?

[11.40] *British Homes Assurance Corporation v Paterson*[66] illustrates that in determining whether something is a partnership obligation, it is important to consider the attitude of the third party who is claiming that the firm is liable for this obligation. In that case, the plaintiff company had instructed a solicitor, Atkinson, to act on its behalf in relation to a particular transaction. At that time, Atkinson practised under the name of 'Atkinson and Atkinson'. Soon after he entered partnership with Paterson and he informed the plaintiff that he would in future carry on business under the name of 'Atkinson and Paterson'. The plaintiff ignored this and continued to deal with Atkinson

63 *Forester v Bell* (1847) 10 Ir LR 555.
64 *Forester v Bell* (1847) 10 Ir LR 555 at 557–558.
65 It has been seen that if persons have not commenced carrying on business in common, they will not be partners (para **[2.39]** et seq) and therefore no liability will ensue under partnership law for the actions of those persons. Liability may of course arise under general principles of agency law.
66 *British Homes Assurance Corporation v Paterson* [1902] 2 Ch 404.

as 'Atkinson and Atkinson' and on completion of the transaction, sent a cheque to him in the name of 'Atkinson and Atkinson or order'. When Atkinson absconded with this money, the plaintiff sued Paterson for the return of the money. By its actions, the plaintiff elected to abide by its original arrangement with Atkinson and did not treat the transaction as a 'partnership obligation'. Accordingly, it was held that it could not hold Paterson jointly liable for this fraudulent act.

Position of a deceased partner

[11.41] The general rule that a partner remains liable for obligations incurred while he was a partner is equally applicable to the estate of deceased partners.[67] Thus, a partner who ceases to be a member of a firm by reason of his death will remain liable for obligations incurred while he was a partner. This is illustrated by the decision in *Harris v Farwell*.[68] There, a banking partnership was indebted to a third party creditor at the time of the death of one of the partners. The firm subsequently went bankrupt and the creditor received part of his debt on the bankruptcy. However, it was held that the creditor was entitled to claim the balance of his debt from the deceased partner's estate.

Situations where former partner is released from liability

[11.42] In a number of situations, the general rule that a former partner remains liable for obligations incurred while he was a partner does not apply. This will most commonly arise where the partner is released from this obligation.

By substitution of new firm for old firm

[11.43] When a partner departs from a firm and the firm continues as before, there is a technical dissolution of the partnership, since the old firm no longer exists and is replaced by a newly constituted partnership between the continuing partners.[69] The firm, as newly constituted, may, expressly or by implication, adopt the liabilities of the 'old' firm, in which case the retiring partner will not be liable for these liabilities. However, in order to be effective *qua* the firm's creditors, the adoption by the 'new' firm of the 'old' firm's liabilities must be agreed to by the creditors of the firm, which agreement may also be expressed or implied. This principle is reflected in s 17(3) of the 1890 Act:

> A retiring partner may be discharged from any existing liabilities, by an agreement to that effect between himself and the members of the firm as newly constituted and the creditors, and this agreement may be either express or inferred as a fact from the course of dealing between the creditors and the firm as newly constituted.

[11.44] Section 17(3) requires that there must some express or implied adoption by the creditor of the new firm in place of the old firm. This will not necessarily be an easy matter to prove as is illustrated by the case of *Cummins v Cummins*.[70] There, one of the partners in a Cork firm was held to be liable for a partnership debt which had been incurred by the firm during his membership. After his departure from the firm, the

---

[67] See further regarding the liability of a deceased partner's estate, para **[24.40]** et seq.
[68] *Harris v Farwell* (1851) 15 Beav 31.
[69] See generally in relation to the distinction between a technical dissolution (where the business of the firm continues) and a general dissolution (where the firm is wound up), para **[23.07]**.
[70] *Cummins v Cummins* (1845) 8 Ir Eq R 723.

newly constituted firm had not been distinctly adopted by the creditor in place of the old firm. In the words of Sugden LC:

> 'It is not so easy a matter for a man by leaving an old firm, and thus creating a new firm, to get rid of his own liability. There must be some acceptance by the creditor of the new firm as his debtors; some dealing with it, some discharge, or something amounting to a discharge, of the liability of the old firm; the mere act of retiring and leaving assets will not amount to a discharge.'[71]

Agreement must be supported by consideration?

[11.45] As with any agreement, to be effective it seems that an agreement by a creditor to release the 'old' firm and accept the newly constituted firm in its place must be supported by consideration. In *Lodge v Dicas*,[72] the creditor of a firm agreed to the retirement of one partner from the firm and to the continuing partners paying the debts of the firm. However, it was held that the retired partner still remained liable as the agreement was not supported by consideration.[73] Although there is some doubt about the continued applicability of this case,[74] it seems that on general principles, when dealing with the release by a creditor of a former partner's liability, it is prudent to provide for some alteration to be made in the payment conditions, eg the newly constituted firm might agree to a slightly earlier date for the payment of the debt.

By replacement partner assuming retiring partner's obligations

[11.46] Another way of releasing a former partner from his liability for the partnership obligations is where the partner replacing him in the firm, if there is one, assumes these obligations in his stead. However, the introduction of a new partner in place of a former partner does not per se discharge the departing partner from his liability for the debts of the firm incurred while he was a partner. The assumption of pre-existing liabilities by a replacement partner may be done by express agreement or it may be inferred from the conduct of the new partner. In the absence of the agreement of the creditors, such an agreement between the departing, incoming and continuing partners will only be binding inter se. To be effective in replacing the departing partner with the incoming partner *qua* creditors, the creditors must also, either expressly or by inference, accept the newly constituted firm in place of the old firm as being liable for the firm's obligations. Only if this occurs will the liability of the departing partner cease and will the incoming partner be liable for these obligations.

[11.47] The courts appear more open to finding an implied agreement on the part of a creditor to discharge a departing partner from liability for pre-existing obligations where there is an agreement for an incoming partner to be liable for those obligations[75] than

---

71 *Cummins v Cummins* (1845) 8 Ir Eq R 723 at 733.
72 *Lodge v Dicas* (1820) 3 B & A 611.
73 See also *David v Ellice* (1826) 5 B & C 196 and the New Zealand case of *Re Guthrie & Co, ex p Bank of Australasia* (1884) NZLR 2 SC 425 and at 429.
74 See *Thompson v Percival* (1834) 5 B & Ad 925 and *Lyth v Ault* (1852) 7 Ex 669. See also the statement of Lord Lindley in *Lindley on Partnership* now contained in l'Anson Banks, *Lindley & Banks on Partnership* (20th edn, 2017) at para 13-114.
75 See for example *Hart v Alexander* (1837) 2 M & W 484.

where there is no such agreement.[76] This attitude can be supported because, in general terms, the options of the creditor will not be altered by the replacement of a partner, whereas they will be limited where there is simply the departure of a partner. In addition, consideration for the release of the retired partner will be easily found ie the replacement of the former partner by the incoming partner. While it may be easier to establish the discharge of the departing partner where he is being replaced, it is still however necessary to find an express or implied agreement on the part of the creditor to the release of the retired partner. In the words of Lord Lindley:

> 'It by no means follows that a creditor who assents to an arrangement by which a new person becomes liable to him consents to abandon his hold on another person clearly liable to him already; and unless a substitution of liability can be established, the old liability remains.'[77]

By failing to claim against deceased partner's estate promptly

[11.48] The final way in which a former partner, or more precisely a deceased partner's estate, may be released from his liability for the partnership obligations is by the passage of time. As has been noted, a deceased partner's estate, like any former partner, remains liable for obligations of the firm incurred while he was a partner.[78] However, this principle is subject to the proviso that any such claim against the deceased partner's estate must be made within a reasonable time of the death. This is because if the creditor allows the administration of the estate to continue without any claim on his part, he will not subsequently be allowed to maintain such a claim.[79]

3. Partner not Liable for Post-Departure Obligations

[11.49] The third and final part of the general rule regarding the duration of a partner's liability is that a former partner is not liable for obligations incurred by his former firm after his departure. However, unlike the first and second parts of the general rule, this part is subject to significant exceptions. These exceptions arise principally where the obligation is incurred by the firm to a person who dealt with the firm prior to the departure of the partner, ie pre-existing customers.[80] Before dealing with these important exceptions, the general rule will be considered.

Application of general rule without exception

[11.50] The 1890 Act contains five situations in which the general rule, that a partner is not liable for obligations incurred after his departure from the firm, will apply without exception. These will be considered in turn and are as follows:

    (i)   a partner is not liable for obligations incurred after his death;

    (ii)   a partner is not liable for obligations incurred after his bankruptcy;

---

[76] See for example *Kirwan v Kirwan* (1836) 2 C & M 617.

[77] l'Anson Banks, *Lindley & Banks on Partnership* (20th edn, 2017) at para 13-120.

[78] See para **[11.41]**.

[79] *Oakeley v Pasheller* (1836) 10 Bli (ns) 548; *Brown v Gordon* (1852) 16 Beav 302; *Bilborough v Holmes* (1876) 5 Ch D 255.

[80] The expressions 'pre-existing customers' and 'new customers' are used throughout the remainder of this chapter to refer respectively to those persons who did have dealings or did not have dealings with the firm prior to a change in the membership of the firm.

(iii) a former partner is not liable where he was not known to be a partner;

(iv) a former partner is not liable to pre-existing customers on notice of his departure; and

(v) a former partner is not liable to new customers aware of his departure.

[11.51] The first three instances are where the former partner dies, becomes bankrupt or is not known to be a partner and these are contained in s 36(3) of the 1890 Act:

> The estate of a partner who dies, or who becomes bankrupt, or of a partner who, not having been known to the person dealing with the firm to be a partner, retires from the firm, is not liable for partnership debts contracted after the date of death, bankruptcy, or retirement respectively.

'partnership debts'

[11.52] Although s 36(3) provides that the former partner is not liable for 'partnership debts', it is contended that this expression should not to be interpreted in a restrictive manner as applying only to contractual debts incurred by the firm. This is because the principle underlying s 36(3), ie that the authority of a firm to bind a former partner terminates on the death, bankruptcy or retirement of an unknown partner, is equally applicable to torts as it is to contracts. For this reason, it is thought that the term 'partnership debts' refers to any obligation, whether contractual or tortious, which is incurred by the firm in favour of third parties.[81] Thus, under s 36(3) of the 1890 Act, a partner is not liable for obligations incurred by the firm after his bankruptcy or death or his retirement (provided he is not known to be a partner). Each situation will be examined in turn.

(i) A partner is not liable for obligations incurred after his death

[11.53] The principle that a partner (or more precisely his estate) is not liable for obligations incurred by the firm after his death is grounded in the general rule of agency, that the agency of an agent (in this case, the firm) to bind his principal (in this case, the partner) is terminated on the death of the principal.[82] Furthermore, since death is a public event, third parties are deemed to be on notice thereof. Thus, on the death of a partner, the firm does not have ostensible authority to bind the deceased partner's estate and no notice is required to be given of a partner's death to third parties to prevent his estate being liable for obligations incurred after the date of death.

[11.54] This principle is also reflected in the proviso to s 14(2) of the 1890 Act, which provides that the use of a deceased partner's name as part of a firm name does not make his estate liable for debts contracted by the firm after his death:

> Provided that where after a partner's death the partnership business is continued in the old firm-name, the continued use of that name or of the deceased partner's name as part

---

[81] Note that in the context of unknown partners, this interpretation is consistent with s 36(1) of the 1890 Act which does not restrict itself to contractual obligations. This section exempts unknown partners from its ambit since it applies only to apparent members of the firm and makes apparent partners liable for all obligations until pre-existing customers are aware of their departure from the firm.

[82] *Keon v Hart* (1867) 2 Ir CLR 138 and on appeal (1869) 3 Ir CLR 388. See further para **[24.04]**.

thereof shall not of itself make his executors or administrators estate or effects liable for any partnership debts[83] contracted after his death.

The principle that a deceased partner's estate is not liable for obligations incurred after his death does, of course, presuppose that the firm continues after his death and incurs obligations. Since s 33(1) of the 1890 Act provides that a partnership is automatically dissolved by the death of a partner, this will only occur if the partners have expressly or implicitly agreed that the firm will so continue despite that death.[84]

(ii) A partner is not liable for obligations incurred after his bankruptcy

[11.55] Like the death of a partner, the basis for the principle that a partner is not liable for obligations incurred by the firm after his bankruptcy is the fact that bankruptcy is a public event and third parties are deemed to be on notice thereof. Thus, on the bankruptcy of a partner, the firm does not have ostensible authority to bind the bankrupt's estate and no notice is required to be given of a partner's bankruptcy to third parties to prevent his estate being liable for obligations incurred after that date.[85] As with the death of a partner, the principle that a bankrupt partner is not liable for obligations incurred after his bankruptcy, presupposes that the firm continues after his bankruptcy. Since the default rule under s 33(1) of the 1890 Act is that a firm automatically dissolves on the bankruptcy of a partner, this will only occur if the partners expressly or implicitly agree that the firm will so continue.[86]

'Bankruptcy' does not prima facie include corporate insolvency

[11.56] It should be noted that the term 'bankruptcy' as it is used in s 36(3) of the 1890 Act is not adapted for partnerships which have corporate partners. Since a company cannot go into bankruptcy, the insolvency of a corporate partner does not constitute its 'bankruptcy' for the purposes of s 36(3). It might, however, be argued that the principle underlying the provision that bankrupt partners are not liable for partnership obligations incurred after their bankruptcy is equally applicable to insolvent companies. Thus, third parties may not be able to hold insolvent corporate partners liable for obligations incurred by their firm after their insolvency. This argument might be supported by the fact that just as the bankruptcy of a partner is a matter of public record, so too is the

---

[83] As with the use of the term 'partnership debts and obligations' in s 17(2) of the 1890 Act, it is apprehended that this term includes both tortious and contractual obligations, see further para **[11.52]**.

[84] See generally in relation to the exclusion by agreement of this term, para **[21.128]** and in relation to the dissolution of a partnership by death, see generally para **[23.32]** and para **[24.01]** et seq.

[85] Partnership Act 1890, s 36(3).

[86] See generally in relation to the exclusion by agreement of this term, para **[21.129]** and in relation to the dissolution of a partnership by bankruptcy, see generally, para **[23.39]**. Note that it would be technically possible, though practically difficult, for a bankrupt partner to remain a partner in a firm and thereby rely on the terms of s 36(3) of the 1890 Act to avoid being liable for partnership obligations incurred after his bankruptcy. See generally in relation to the practical difficulties of a bankrupt partner continuing in partnership, para **[27.62]** et seq.

winding up of an insolvent company,[87] so that third parties should not be allowed to rely on the partnership having ostensible authority for the insolvent corporate partners after the appointment of a liquidator.

[11.57] It is because of doubts such as this, regarding the application to corporate partners of certain provisions of the 1890 Act (which were clearly drafted with individuals in mind), that it is recommended that in a partnership for corporate partners, the 1890 Act be adapted. This area is considered in detail elsewhere in this work.[88]

(iii) A former partner is not liable where he was not known to be a partner

[11.58] Section 36(3) also states that a former partner, who not having been known to a person dealing with the firm to be a partner, is not liable for debts contracted by the firm after his departure. Thus, even where such an unknown partner has left the firm and failed to notify pre-existing customers of this fact[89] or failed to place an advertisement thereof in *Iris Oifigiúil*[90] he will not be liable for debts incurred by the firm after his departure. The rationale for such 'unknown partners' not being liable for post-departure obligations is that, in the eyes of the third party dealing with the firm, the firm never had any authority to bind that partner in the first place. For this reason, there is no basis for the third party to hold that partner liable for obligations incurred by the firm after he ceased to be a partner. In *Carter v Whalley*,[91] there was no evidence of the retired partner's involvement in the firm being known to the plaintiff or to the general public. Accordingly, the retired partner was held not to be liable for the debt which was incurred by the firm to the plaintiff after his retirement.[92]

[11.59] The principle that an unknown partner is not liable for partnership obligations incurred after his retirement is also to be found in s 36(1) of the 1890 Act. Section 36(1) sets out one of the exceptional cases in which pre-existing customers of a firm have a right to sue former partners for obligations incurred after their departure from the firm, and is considered below.[93] For present purposes, it need simply be observed that this section only applies this exception to former partners who were 'apparent members' of the firm. It is clear that unknown partners cannot, by their very nature, be apparent members of a partnership.

---

87 For example a creditors' winding up must be advertised in *Iris Oifigiúil*: Companies Act 2014, s 586. More generally, when a liquidator is appointed to a company, all invoices, business letters and orders issued on behalf of that company must contain a statement to the effect that the company is being wound up, and the company's website together with any electronic mail sent by or on behalf of that company must also contain that statement (Companies Act 2014, s 595). See generally Courtney, *The Law of Companies* (4th edn, 2016) at para [24.001] et seq, Hutchinson, *Keane on Company Law* (5th edn, 2016) at paras [36.01] and [38.01] et seq.
88 See para **[21.23]** et seq.
89 As envisaged by s 36(1) of the 1890 Act.
90 As envisaged by s 36(2) of the 1890 Act.
91 *Carter v Whalley* (1830) 109 ER 691.
92 See also *Heath v Sansom* (1831) 4 B & Ad 172; *Evans v Drummond* (1801) 4 Esp 89.
93 See para **[11.85]** et seq.

'retires from the firm'

[11.60] Section s 36(3) provides that the unknown partner is not liable for obligations incurred after he 'retires from the firm'. However, it is clear that this expression is not to be interpreted as applying only to retirement in the traditional sense of that word. This is because the basis of the unknown partner being exempt from liability is that when the partner left the firm, the third party was unaware that the was a partner and in this context, it is irrelevant how he came to leave the firm. Accordingly, it is apprehended that this expression refers to any departure from the firm by an unknown partner and therefore would include a non-traditional retirement, eg where the partner is expelled from the partnership.

Person not known to be a partner may be a dormant or active partner

[11.61] It is important to bear in mind that a person who is not known to be a partner is not synonymous with that person being a dormant partner. An unknown partner may not be actively involved in the partnership business (in which case, he is a dormant partner) but he may also be an active partner, who happens to be unknown to be a partner by the third party, for example, by virtue of working in a branch office of the firm.

(iv) Former partner is not liable to pre-existing clients on notice of departure

[11.62] A fourth instance of the general rule that a partner is not liable for post-departure obligations is provided by the corollary of s 36(1) of the 1890 Act. This section, as shall be seen below,[94] is the main exception to the general rule that a former partner is not liable for obligations incurred after his departure. Under this section, where a firm incurs a liability to a person who dealt with the firm while the former partner was a member of the partnership, then that former partner is liable therefor, unless the third party knew of his departure. Section 36(1) states:

> Where a person deals with a firm after a change in its constitution he is entitled to treat all apparent members of the old firm as still being members of the firm until he has notice of the change.

[11.63] The corollary of this section is obviously that where the obligations have been incurred by the firm in favour of third parties who are on notice of the partner's retirement, then that former partner is not liable for those obligations and the general rule applies. The rationale for this principle was explained by Davitt P in the High Court case of *Smallman Ltd v O'Moore and Newman:*[95]

> '[T]he purpose of a notice of dissolution of partnership is to inform the party sought to be affected that the authority of each partner, to act as agent for the other or others, has been withdrawn.'[96]

[11.64] It follows that the former partner will not be liable for obligations incurred by the firm in favour of that third party. In *Minnit v Whinery,*[97] which is considered above,[98]

---

94   See para **[11.85]**.
95   *Smallman Ltd v O'Moore and Newman* [1959] IR 220.
96   *Smallman Ltd v O'Moore and Newman* [1959] IR 220 at 223–224.
97   *Minnit v Whinery* (1721) 5 Bro PC 489.
98   See para **[11.26]**.

the third party, Whinery, was on notice of Thomas Minnit's departure since Thomas Minnit had visited him to tell him that he was no longer interested in the partnership. Therefore, when Whinery sought payment from Thomas Minnit for obligations incurred by the firm after this notice, this was rejected by the court.

What constitutes notice?

[11.65] There can be little doubt that actual notice, as was given in *Minnit v Whinery*,[99] will result in the former partner not being liable for obligations incurred by the firm to that third party. This does however raise the question of whether constructive notice of a partner's departure is sufficient to exempt the former partner from liability for post-departure obligations. It is noted hereafter that the advertisement in *Iris Oifigiúil* of a partner's departure is not notice to pre-existing customers of the firm who do not actually see the advertisement.[100] Nonetheless, this does not rule out the possibility of constructive notice being deemed to be sufficient in some circumstances and some support for this view is to be found in the High Court case of *Smallman Ltd v O'Moore and Newman*.[101] In that case the defendants were building contractors and had been in partnership under the name 'O'Moore and Newman'. During that partnership they had ordered building materials from the plaintiff. Subsequently, they formed a company for the purposes of carrying on the firm's business which they called 'O'Moore and Newman & Co Ltd'. They circularised their suppliers with notice of this change and advertised it in *Stubbs Gazette* and the *Merchant's Gazette*, both of which were taken by the plaintiff. After the formation of the company, business was continued in the partnership name of 'O'Moore and Newman', although cheques were paid to the plaintiff by the director and secretary of the company. A circular was also sent to the plaintiff advising it that the company was taking over the partnership's assets and liabilities. The plaintiff's bookkeeper had no recollection of receiving the circular or of noticing the change in the cheques. When the plaintiff was not paid for certain goods supplied to the defendants, it sued the defendants personally and not the company. The defendants claimed that the action against them personally should be dismissed since the goods ordered by the company and the action should have been taken against it.

[11.66] On the question of whether constructive notice of the change in the partnership was sufficient, it was argued by the defendants that the use of the company's cheques and the issuing of a circular was sufficient for the plaintiff to be on notice of the dissolution of the partnership. Reliance was placed on two nineteenth century decisions. In the first, *Barfoot v Goodall*,[102] a change in a banking partnership's cheques from 'Dickenson, Goodall and Fisher' to 'Dickenson, Goodall, and Co' and later to 'Dickenson, Goodall, and Dickenson' was held to be effective notice to a customer of that banking partnership, who drew many cheques on these forms, that Fisher was no longer a partner in the bank. Reliance was also placed on *Jenkins v Blizard*,[103] in which it was held that the publication of a notice of dissolution of a partnership in a newspaper, which paper was habitually taken by the party sought to be affected, was evidence of

---

99   *Minnit v Whinery* (1721) 5 Bro PC 489.
100   See the Partnership Act 1890, s 36(2), and para **[11.73]**.
101   *Smallman Ltd v O'Moore and Newman* [1959] IR 220.
102   *Barfoot v Goodall* (1811) 3 Camp 147.
103   *Jenkins v Blizard* (1816) 1 Stark 418.

notice sufficient to be left to the jury. Davitt P referred to both cases and gave judgment for the defendants, but not on the grounds of the plaintiff's constructive notice of the partnership's dissolution.[104] He dismissed the action against the defendants personally, on the basis that the defendants contracted on behalf of the company, while the plaintiff thought it was contracting with a partnership, and therefore the parties were not *ad idem*. On the constructive notice issue, he took the view that on the facts, the question of whether the plaintiff was on notice of the dissolution of the partnership was irrelevant. This is because, even if the plaintiff knew that the partnership was dissolved, it could still have believed that both of the defendants had joined personally in ordering the goods, in which case the parties would still not have been *ad idem*. For this reason, he did not decide the issue of whether the plaintiff had 'constructive notice' of the dissolution of the partnership.

[11.67] However, Davitt P does assume at one point in his judgment that the plaintiff had constructive notice of the dissolution and therefore seems to accept that constructive notice may be sufficient.[105] This is in keeping with the previous English decisions and on this basis, it is submitted that the receipt of a circular by a third party along with obvious changes to its letterhead,[106] name or cheques, should be regarded as notice to the third party of some change to the constitution of the partnership because these changes would require the third party to inquire as to the nature of the change.

[11.68] Thus, in general terms, it is thought that actual notice should not be required under s 36(1). So where a third party originally dealt with a firm where the partners were A, B and C, and if C left the firm, then, for example, if 10 years later, the third party began to deal with the firm again, it is thought that the third party could not reasonably seek to make C liable on the grounds that he was not actually aware of his

---

[104] Davitt P's sympathies appeared to clearly lie with the plaintiff since he suggested that the plaintiff might have a case in estoppel against the defendants, whereby the defendants would be estopped by their conduct from pleading that they did not order the goods: 'I come regretfully to the conclusion that the judgment must be for the defendants': *Smallman Ltd v O'Moore and Newman* [1959] IR 220 at 224.

[105] 'Assuming that the plaintiffs had effective notice of the ending of the partnership in this case the result would be that they must be presumed to know that O'Moore had no authority to act as Newman's agent and vice versa': *Smallman Ltd v O'Moore and Newman* [1959] IR 220 at 224.

[106] However, the change of letterhead on its own would not seem to be sufficient. See the Scottish decision of *Welsh v Knarston* [1972] SLT 96, where the change in the letterhead alone was not sufficient. There, a former partner claimed that since the entry in the register of business names for the firm-name did not contain his name (because, he had never been registered therein as a partner in the first place), a third party dealing with the firm should have been on notice that he had retired when he received the firm letterhead which no longer had his name. This claim was rejected by the Scottish court. See also the decision of the Supreme Court of Victoria in *Hammerhaven Pty Ltd v Ogge* [1996] 2 VR 488, where it was held that notice in the equivalent of s 36(1) of the 1890 Act (ie the Victoria Partnership Act 1958, s 40) was actual notice (but note that it interpreted this to mean that the respondent needed to produce evidence of facts from which knowledge of his retirement might be fairly inferred, which meant inferred by a tribunal of fact and not inferred by the third party). On this basis, it held that the change of the respondent's listing on the letterhead from 'partner' to 'consultant' was not sufficient notice to the third party.

departure from the firm. Rather, it is suggested that some reasonable limits will be placed by the courts on the requirement of notice and this is likely to be done by interpreting the term 'notice' to include constructive notice. In particular, it is contended that the proposition that constructive notice does not apply in commercial transactions cannot be supported in principle.[107] This approach is in keeping with general agency principles that a principal will not be bound if the third party knew or ought to have known from all the surrounding circumstances that the agent did not possess the ostensible authority in question,[108] which type of authority is the basis for the liability of a former partner for post-departure obligations.[109]

Notice as a result of examining Register of Business Names?

[11.69] Consideration has already been given to the application of the terms of the Registration of Business Names Act 1963 to partnerships and in particular the question of whether the filing of the details of a partner's departure from a firm is constructive notice to third parties.[110]

(v) A former partner is not liable to new customers aware of his departure

[11.70] The fifth and final instance of the general rule that a former partner is not liable for obligations incurred after his departure, is that a former partner is not liable to persons who only began dealing with the firm after his departure ('new customers') provided that they are aware that he is no longer a partner in the firm. Since these third parties will be on notice that a person is no longer a partner, they will be aware the firm no longer has authority to bind that former partner and thus they will not be able to claim that the former partner is liable to them for obligations incurred by the firm after his departure.

[11.71] Section 36(2) of the 1890 Act facilitates these new customers being put on notice of the departure of a partner. This is because under s 36(2), a notice[111] in *Iris*

---

[107] See *Manchester Trust v Furness* [1897] 2 QB 539.

[108] See for example *Discount Kitchens Ltd v Crawford* [1989] Halsbury's Monthly Review, Jan, Q238. See also *Staveley v Uzielli* (1800) 2 F & F 30; *Aste v Montague* (1858) 1 F & F 264; *Marsden v City and County Assurance Co* (1865) LR 1 CP 232; *Dickinson v Lilwal* (1815) 4 Camp 279; *Blackburn v Scholes* (1810) 2 Camp 341; *Manser v Back* (1848) 6 Hare 443. See also Reynolds, *Reynolds and Bowstead on Agency* (16th ed, 1996) at para 8-047 et seq quoting *Combulk Pty Ltd v TNT Management Pty Ltd* (1993) 113 ALR 214 and *Alliance & Leicester BS v Edgestop Ltd* [1993] 1 WLR 1462. Cf the Canadian case of *Rockland Industries Ltd v Amerada Minerals Corp of Canada* (1980) 108 DLR (3d) 513 and *Willis, Faber & Co Ltd v Joyce* (1911) 104 LT 576. In the context of partnerships, it has been noted (para **[10.72]**) that in some cases, the circumstances of the transaction between a third party and a partner will be such as to put the third party on notice that the partner is acting outside of his authority. In such a case, the third party will not be allowed to rely on the fact that the did not have actual notice of this fact and the firm will not be bound by that act: *Kendal v Wood* (1870) LR 6 Ex 243.

[109] Ie since the firm no longer has implied or express authority to do the act, it must bind the former partner under the doctrine of ostensible authority, see generally para **[10.61]**.

[110] See para **[3.82]**.

[111] It is to be noted that there is no prescribed format regarding the form of this notice.

Oifigiúil of the departure of a partner is deemed to constitute notice to persons who had no dealings with the firm before the departure, whether they saw the notice or not:

> An advertisement in the London Gazette as to a firm whose principal place of business is in England or Wales, in the Edinburgh Gazette as to a firm whose principal place of business is in Scotland, and in *Iris Oifigiúil*[112] as to a firm whose principal place of business is in Ireland, shall be notice as to persons who had not dealings with the firm before the date of the dissolution or change so advertised.

Where new customers are not aware of departure

[11.72] Where a former partner does not advertise in *Iris Oifigiúil*, new customers will not be deemed to be on notice of his retirement. If the new customers are not aware of that partner's departure from the firm, the liability of the former partner to them for post-departure obligations will be determined by whether the former partner allowed himself to be held out as still being a partner in the firm. The question of whether the former partner has continued to hold himself out as a partner is considered in detail hereunder.[113]

Effect of notice in Iris Oifigiúil on pre-existing customers

[11.73] It is worth emphasising that a notice in *Iris Oifigiúil* that a partner has departed from the partnership is of no effect on pre-existing customers, since they will not be deemed to have constructive notice of the advertised departure. This is because by the express terms of s 36(2) of the 1890 Act, the constructive notice only applies to persons who had no previous dealings with the firm. Of course, if a pre-existing customer happens to see the advertisement, he will be on actual notice of its contents and will not therefore be able to claim that the former partner is liable for obligations incurred by the firm after he was aware of his departure.[114]

Exceptions where former partner is liable for post-departure obligations

[11.74] Having considered the five examples of the general rule that a former partner is not liable for the obligations of the firm incurred after his departure, it is now proposed to consider three important exceptions to this rule. In each of the following situations, a former partner is liable for obligations incurred by his former firm, even though those obligations are incurred after his departure:

   (i)   continued holding out as a partner;
   (ii)   continuing authority of partners for the purposes of winding up;
   (iii)   pre-existing customers who are unaware of his departure.

(i) Continued holding out as a partner

[11.75] The first exception to the general rule arises when the former partner allows himself to be held out as a partner. Under s 14(1) of the 1890 Act, a person who represents himself or knowingly allows himself to be represented as a partner is liable as

---

[112] This is a construction of the term *Dublin Gazette* as required by the Adaptation of Enactments Act 1922, s 4.
[113] See para **[11.75]** et seq and see also para **[7.52]** et seq.
[114] See para **[11.62]**.

if he was a partner to anyone who relied on this representation.[115] This section applies both to persons who were never partners in the firm and to persons who were partners but who have left the firm. In this way, a former partner could end up being liable for debts which were incurred by his former firm after his retirement. The English High Court case of *Tower Cabinet Co Ltd v Ingram*[116] was concerned with the continued holding out of a former partner in a firm. The former partner was held out as still being a member of the firm by means of his name continuing to appear on the headed notepaper of the firm. This case highlights that the requirement in s 14(1) that a person 'knowingly suffer' himself to be held out as a partner requires more than mere carelessness. What is required is knowledge by the former partner that he is being represented as a partner. In that case, it was held that the former partner's carelessness in not destroying the headed notepaper of the firm was not sufficient to constitute him as a person who was 'knowingly suffering' himself to be held out as a partner.

Reducing the likelihood of a holding out by a former partner

[11.76] It is clear from *Tower Cabinet Co Ltd v Ingram*,[117] that in order to reduce the likelihood of third parties believing that he is still a partner, a former partner should remove his name from the firm's letterhead. Another way in which a former partner might reduce the likelihood of his being held out as a partner, is by notifying by circular all pre-existing customers of the firm of his retirement. In addition, he should notify all new customers of the firm of his departure by a notice to that effect in *Iris Oifigiúil*, since, as has been noted, s 36(2) of the 1890 Act provides that all new customers are deemed to be on notice of such an advertisement. He should also ensure that the necessary filings are made with the Registrar of Business Names to take account of his departure.[118] Similarly, he should ensure that his name is removed from the firm's brass plate or other publicity material. Finally, where a former partner's name is part of the firm name and that name is to be continued to be used by the partnership after that partner's departure, it may be prudent to have the words '& Co' added.[119]

[11.77] In *ACC Bank plc v Johnston p/a Brian Johnston & Co Solicitors*,[120] Mr Mallon and Mr Traynor had been partners in a firm of solicitors and agreed at a meeting on 30 March 2006 to dissolve their partnership with immediate effect. Mr Mallon ceased his involvement in the management of the firm at that time, and the financial terms of the dissolution were documented in an agreement entered into five months later, on 30 August 2006. Mr Mallon was, however, found to be liable in respect of undertakings subsequently given by Mr Traynor as various steps had not been taken regarding the dissolution of the partnership. For example while the Law Society of Ireland was advised by Mr Traynor in October 2006 that the partnership had been dissolved with effect from 30 March 2006, the firm's insurers were not notified until December 2006, the firm's existing banking arrangements remained in place until August 2006 (meaning that Mr Mallon could have signed cheques on the firm's behalf during that period), no

---

[115] See generally in relation to a partner by holding out, para **[7.01]** et seq.
[116] *Tower Cabinet Co Ltd v Ingram* [1949] 2 KB 397.
[117] *Tower Cabinet Co Ltd v Ingram* [1949] 2 KB 397.
[118] See generally in relation to this requirement, para **[3.80]**.
[119] However, see the reservations expressed regarding this principle, para **[7.60]**.
[120] *ACC Bank plc v Johnston p/a Brian Johnston & Co Solicitors* [2011] IEHC 108.

notice was published in *Iris Oifigiúil* of the dissolution of the firm, and clients of the firm were not otherwise notified of the change until after August 2006. Of particular importance was the fact that Mr Traynor continued to conduct his business using 'Traynor Mallon' notepaper that listed both Mr Traynor and Mr Mallon as partners until early September 2007.

Where partner advertises his departure but holds himself out as a partner

[11.78] It is possible that a former partner would advertise his departure as a partner in *Iris Oifigiúil* but yet, in some way, continue to hold himself out as a partner. On the one hand, new customers of the firm will be subject to s 36(2) of the 1890 Act. Thus, even though they may not have actually seen the advertisement of the departure of the partner in *Iris Oifigiúil*, they will be deemed to be on notice thereof.[121] However, on the other hand, these new customers may be led to believe that the former partner is still a partner by virtue of his actions in holding himself out as such. This raises the question of whether the fact that new customers are deemed to be on notice of a partner's advertised departure in *Iris Oifigiúil* under s 36(2) will take precedence over the liability of a former partner to new customers for holding himself out as a partner.[122] It is contended that in such a case, it would be inequitable to allow the former partner to hold himself out as a partner, but at the same time exempt himself from liability by relying on the fact that he has placed an advertisement in *Iris Oifigiúil*.[123] For this reason, it is submitted that s 36(2) of the 1890 Act must be read as being subject to s 14(1) of that Act, such that the placing of an advertisement in *Iris Oifigiúil* will be rendered ineffective by the subsequent holding out of the former partner.[124]

[11.79] This, it is contended, is the principle underlying the pre-1890 cases of *Williams v Keats*[125] and *Newsome v Coles*.[126] In the former case, a retired partner advertised his departure from his firm in the English equivalent of *Iris Oifigiúil*,[127] yet he allowed his name to continue to be painted over the firm's door. When his former partner accepted a bill of exchange in both their names from a new customer,[128] it was held that the retired

---

[121] Pursuant to s 36(2) of the 1890 Act, see para **[11.71]**.

[122] See also the question of whether s 14(1) of the 1890 Act takes precedence over s 36(3), para **[7.54]**.

[123] A comparison might be made with the principle of land law that a person may not derogate from his grant: 'A grantor having given a thing with one hand is not to take away the means of enjoying it with the other', per Bowen LJ in *Birmingham, Dudley & District Banking Co v Ross* (1888) 38 Ch D 295 at 313. See also *Griffen v Keane* (1927) 61 ILTR 177; *Kennedy v Elkinson* (1937) 71 ILTR 153 and see generally Elliot, 'Non-Derogation from Grant' (1964) 80 LQR 244 and Wylie, *Irish Land Law* (5th edn, 2013) at para [7.37] et seq.

[124] However, it is not suggested that where the holding out consists solely of the continued use of the firm-name, which contains that of the former partner, the notice in *Iris Oifigiúil* will be rendered ineffective, see para **[7.62]**.

[125] *Williams v Keats* (1817) 2 Stark 290.

[126] *Newsome v Coles* (1811) 2 Camp 617.

[127] Ie *The Gazette*.

[128] It appears from the arguments of counsel in the case, that the plaintiffs were new customers of the firm.

partner was liable on the bill of exchange, notwithstanding the advertisement of his departure.[129]

[11.80] Similarly, in *Newsome v Coles*,[130] three brothers had carried on business in partnership under the name Thomas Coles & Sons. After the partnership was dissolved, the business was carried on by one brother only under the same name. The dissolution of the partnership was advertised in the English equivalent of *Iris Oifigiúil*.[131] The plaintiff dealt with this entity after the dissolution and he had no dealings with the previous firm. However, he sought to make all three brothers liable on a bill of exchange which was accepted in the name of Thomas Coles & Sons by the brother who continued the business. As the other brothers had not held themselves out as partners in the business and did not know the old name was being used by their brother, they were held not to be liable on the bill of exchange.

(ii) Continuing authority of partners for the purposes of winding up

[11.81] The second important exception to the general rule that a partner is not liable for obligations incurred after his departure is that the partners in a dissolved partnership are authorised to bind the firm so far as necessary for the purposes of its winding up. This is clear from s 38 of the 1890 Act which provides that:

> After the dissolution of a partnership the authority of each partner to bind the firm, and the other rights and obligations of the partners, continue notwithstanding the dissolution so far as may be necessary to wind up the affairs of the partnership, and to complete transactions begun but unfinished at the time of the dissolution, but not otherwise.

> Provided that the firm is in no case bound by the acts of a partner who has become bankrupt; but this proviso does not affect the liability of any person who has after the bankruptcy represented himself or knowingly suffered himself to be represented as a partner of the bankrupt.[132]

'so far as may be necessary to wind up the affairs of the partnership'

[11.82] It is important to bear in mind that a former partner will only be bound by an obligation incurred on behalf of his former firm under s 38, if the act in question is necessary to wind up the affairs of the firm. This requirement is highlighted by *Bristow v Miller*.[133] There, the partnership of Maxwell, Miller and Company was between Matthew Maxwell and Mr Miller. The partnership was dissolved and Matthew Maxwell was empowered to settle the affairs of the firm. A circular to that effect was published and received by a supplier of the firm, James Maxwell, who was also a brother of

---

129 Note, however, that where the 'holding out' consists solely of allowing the name of the firm to remain unchanged, it is contended that this holding out under s 14(1) will not take precedence over the advertisement of a partner's departure in *Iris Oifigiúil* under s 36(2) and in this regard, *Williams v Keats* must be regarded as being superseded by s 36(2) of the 1890 Act. See para **[7.61]** et seq.

130 *Newsome v Coles* (1811) 2 Camp 617.

131 Ie *The Gazette*.

132 See l'Anson Banks, *Lindley & Banks on Partnership* (20th edn, 2017) at para 13-64 where the summary of principles applicable to s 38 of the 1890 Act as set out in *Boghani v Nathoo* [2011] 2 All ER (Comm) 743 is reproduced.

133 *Bristow v Miller* (1848) 11 Ir LR 461.

Matthew Maxwell. Subsequently, Matthew Maxwell sent an account which he signed in the firm's name to James Maxwell. This account indicated a balance was owing by the firm to James Maxwell. The debts which were the subject of this account had been incurred by the firm many years previously and were therefore outside the relevant limitation period under the Statute of Limitations.[134] However, James Maxwell relied on the fact that the account was issued within the limitation period to claim that he could sue Miller for these debts. Miller argued that the account was not binding upon him. In the High Court,[135] Crampton J held that 'after a partnership is dissolved, one of the late firm cannot by his act or admission involve his co-partner in any new legal liability'.[136]

[11.83] The question then arose as to whether the settling of debts which were owed by the firm, but which had been incurred outside the statutory limitation period, constituted the incurring of a new legal liability or the incurring of an obligation which was necessary to wind up the affairs of the firm. The Court held that Matthew Maxwell was seeking to create a new liability for Miller as the original liability had been extinguished by the Statute of Limitations and his actions in signing the account went beyond what was necessary to wind up the affairs of the partnership and thus did not bind Miller.[137]

'obligations of the partners, continue'

[11.84] Under s 38 of the 1890 Act, the obligations of the partners are said to continue notwithstanding the dissolution of the partnership as far as may be necessary to wind up the partnership affairs. For this reason, a partner who retires from a firm which is wound up, may be liable under s 38 for a liability incurred after his departure, if that liability stems from the firm's failure to complete an obligation incurred by the firm while he was a member of the firm. In such a case, the former partner cannot rely on the fact that the liability to a third party was technically incurred after his departure from the firm, since it is regarded as a continuing obligation of that partner. This is illustrated by the Scottish case of *Welsh v Knarston*.[138] There, a firm of solicitors was sued for negligence for failing to institute proceedings in a personal injuries case within the prescribed limitation period. Two partners in that firm retired before the expiration of the limitation period and the firm itself was dissolved soon after their departure and before the expiration of the limitation period. The plaintiff claimed that the two retired partners were liable for the loss suffered by him as a result of the firm's failure to institute proceedings in time. Since this liability was incurred on the expiry of the limitation period, which was after the date of retirement of the partners, they argued that they were not liable to the plaintiff for the damage caused to him. However, the court held that pursuing the personal injuries action was a continuing obligation of the two retired partners, since it was undertaken by the firm prior to their retirement and on the general

---

134 An Act for rendering a written Memorandum necessary to the Validity of certain Promises and Engagements of 1828 (9 G 4, c 14).

135 The judgment of the court was given by Crampton J. Concurring judgments were delivered by Perrin J and Moore J.

136 *Bristow v Miller* (1848) 11 Ir LR 461 at 472, Crampton J relied on *Kilgour v Finlyson* (1789) 1 H Bl 156.

137 For a criticism of this decision, see para **[26.18]**.

138 *Welsh v Knarston* [1972] SLT 96.

dissolution of the firm, they were required to pursue this action. They were thus liable for the loss suffered by the plaintiff in his action being statute-barred.

(iii) Pre-existing customers who are unaware of his departure

[11.85] Undoubtedly the most important exception to the general rule that a partner is not liable for obligations incurred by his firm after his departure is contained in s 36(1) of the 1890 Act. This section provides that:

> Where a person deals with a firm after a change in its constitution he is entitled to treat all apparent members of the old firm as still being members of the firm until he has notice of the change.

The rationale for this rule is that the customers of a firm, who deal with that firm on the basis of the liability of all the partners and/or their collective expertise, are not obliged to keep track of any changes in the constitution of the firm. Rather, it is up to the partners to notify the customers of any change in the authority of the firm to bind certain partners. This is because under normal agency rules, where a principal/agent relationship exists, the agent has authority to bind the principal and such authority will continue in the eyes of a third party until notice[139] of its revocation has been received by that third party.[140] Accordingly, in the absence of notification of the departure of a partner from a firm, the customers are entitled to assume that the firm had authority to bind all the partners who they believed to still be partners in the firm, even if one of them is no longer a partner. On this basis, a former partner is liable for obligations incurred by the firm to that customer.

'deals with a firm'

[11.86] Section s 36(1) of the 1890 Act provides that a former partner is liable for post-departure obligations in relation to an existing customer who 'deals with a firm'. This expression would prima facie appear to apply to contractual dealings between the firm and third parties. However, the principle underlying s 36(1), namely that the authority of a firm to bind a former partner continues until notice of the termination of this authority, is equally applicable to torts, as it is to contracts. For this reason, it is thought that this expression must be taken to refer to all dealings, whether contractual or tortious, between the firm and third parties.

'apparent members of the firm'

[11.87] By its express terms, s 36(1) only makes former partners liable for post-departure obligations where those partners are 'apparent members of the firm'. It follows that a person who is not known to be a partner will, by his very nature, not be an 'apparent member' of the firm. For this reason, s 36(1) will not have any application to such partners and there will be no need for unknown partners[141] to notify their departure to persons who had dealings with the firm before their departure. This can be supported in principle because the rationale for s 36(1) is that the agency of the firm to act on

---

139   This is thought to include constructive notice, see para **[11.65]**.

140   *Daniel Kelleher v Continental Irish Meat Ltd (In Receivership)* (9 May 1978) HC. See also *Scarf v Jardine* (1882) 47 LT 258.

141   See generally in relation to the liability of unknown partners, para **[11.58]**.

behalf of a partner continues in the eyes of a third party until he is notified of its termination. Thus, where the partner is unknown, third parties will not assume that the firm has authority to bind him in the first place and there will be no need for notice to be given to those customers of the partner's departure for him not to be liable for obligations incurred after his departure.

No need for reliance on continued presence of partner

[11.88] While the rationale for s 36(1) of the 1890 Act is that pre-existing customers are assumed to have relied on the fact that the former partner was still a member of the firm, there is no requirement on the third party to prove such reliance in fact. Under s 36(1), a pre-existing customer of the firm need only establish the following three conditions, ie that he:

(i) dealt with the firm while the former partner was a member of the firm;
(ii) knew the former partner was a member of the firm; and
(iii) was unaware of his departure.

[11.89] If the three conditions are satisfied, the former partner will be liable for obligations incurred by the firm to that third party after his departure. This is in contrast to the position under s 14(1) of the 1890 Act, where a third party, in order to establish liability on the part of a former partner by holding out, must prove that he has actually relied on the fact that the partner by holding out was a member of the firm. However, by analogy with the decision in *British Homes Assurance Corporation v Paterson*,[142] which is considered above,[143] it might be argued that the former partner can escape liability where he can show that the third party dealt with the other partners in such a way as to show that, although he believed that the former partner was a member of the firm at that time, he looked only to the other partners for the satisfaction of the post-departure obligation. In such a situation, the court may refuse to allow the third party to hold the former partner liable for the obligation.

[11.90] It should be remembered that, from a former partner's perspective, the crucial factor in determining his liability for post-departure obligations is the knowledge or lack of knowledge of pre-existing customers of the firm that he has departed. For this reason, it is prudent for a departing partner to notify pre-existing customers of his departure by whatever means are appropriate.[144]

Corollary of s 36(1) applies

[11.91] Although s 36(1) addresses only the liability of the former partner to pre-existing customers of the firm, it seems clear that the corollary of this principle also applies. Thus, just as a former partner is liable to pre-existing customers for the actions of the firm, so too is the firm liable to pre-existing customers for the actions of a former partner. This liability will last until the pre-existing customers are on notice[145] that the former partner is no longer a partner. This follows from the fact that the relationship between a partner and his firm is one of mutual agency. Thus, a partner may, at one and

---

142 *British Homes Assurance Corporation v Paterson* [1902] 2 Ch 404.
143 See para **[11.40]**.
144 For examples of the ways in which to this might be achieved, see para **[11.76]**.
145 The possibility that this notice may be constructive is considered at para **[11.65]**.

the same time, be acting as an agent and a principal since he will be an agent for the firm and, at the same time, he (and all his co-partners) will be the principal, for which each partner will be the agent. For this reason, pre-existing customers will also be entitled to assume that the agency of the former partner to bind the firm continues until notice of its revocation has been received by them. Failure to give such notice will result in a situation where the firm will be bound by the acts of former partners[146] to pre-existing customers who are unaware of their retirement. Of course, where the former partner is an unknown partner,[147] there will be no need to give such notice, since such a partner will never have had authority in the eyes of third parties to bind the firm and therefore it will not be necessary for the firm to revoke it by giving notice to those third parties.

Indemnity instead of notice to persons who dealt with firm

[11.92] In larger firms, where partners depart on a regular basis, it is considered impractical to notify these departures to all the pre-existing customers of the firm. In these situations, it is common for the departing partner to obtain sufficient comfort from the fact that he has an indemnity from the continuing partners in respect of any liabilities incurred after his departure. This is particularly so if the firm has considerable resources and adequate insurance.

Implied indemnity

[11.93] Even where an express indemnity is not given by the continuing partners to the departing partner, *Gray v Smith*[148] is authority for the proposition that a court will normally imply an indemnity in respect of the firm's debts and obligations, if the departing partner has relinquished his share of the partnership assets.[149] The rationale for this implied indemnity is that the assets of the firm, to which creditors are presumed to look for payment, are being assigned to the continuing partners and therefore they should discharge the obligations of the firm. In view of this rationale, it would seem that this implied indemnity should apply to partnership obligations incurred both before and after the partner's departure. Consequently, if for whatever reason, the continuing partners do not wish the former partner to have an indemnity from them for the obligations of the firm, this implied indemnity should be expressly excluded in the agreement governing the departure of the partner.

Indemnity does not affect primary liability

[11.94] Although self-evident, it is perhaps worth emphasising that any indemnity received by a former partner from the continuing partners does not affect his primary liability for the obligations of the firm to third parties. Thus in *Luckie v Forsyth*,[150] a

---

[146] These acts must of course be within the ordinary course of business of the firm to be binding, see para **[10.30]** et seq.

[147] As to which, see para **[11.58]**.

[148] *Gray v Smith* (1889) 43 Ch D 208.

[149] *Gray v Smith* (1889) 43 Ch D 208 (sale of outgoing partner's share to continuing partners); *Saltoun v Houston* (1824) 1 Bing 433 (outgoing partner received consideration for his share). Note that there is also an implied indemnity in favour of the vendor partner who sells to a third party, see *Dodson v Downey* [1901] 2 Ch 620 and see para **[19.24]**.

[150] *Luckie v Forsyth* (1846) 3 Jo & Lat 388.

retiring partner received an indemnity from the continuing partners in relation to the liabilities of the firm under the terms of a deed of dissolution. Under this deed, the continuing partners were given authority to wind up the firm and settle its accounts. The continuing partners settled an account with the plaintiff, one of the firm's creditors, in respect of debts which were incurred by the firm while the retired partner was a member of the firm. The retired partner argued that if the plaintiff was to have the benefit of the deed of dissolution whereby the continuing partners had authority to settle his account, he should also be bound by the indemnity and therefore the retired partner should not be liable on the account. Not surprisingly, Sugden LC rejected this defence, holding that the 'authority to wind up the concern is independent of the obligation to indemnify'.[151]

Right of a Partner to Notify Departure or Dissolution

[11.95] An important provision in relation to the liability of a former partner for post-departure obligations to pre-existing and new customers of the firm is contained in s 37 of the 1890 Act. This section gives a partner the express right to give notice of a dissolution of the firm or his retirement from the firm:

> On the dissolution of a partnership or retirement of a partner any partner may publicly notify the same, and may require the other partner or partners to concur for that purpose in all necessary or proper acts, if any, which cannot be done without his or their concurrence.

[11.96] The type of act of public notification which a departing partner may require his partners to concur in might, for example, be where he wishes to force the continuing partners to sign a notice of his retirement for inclusion in *Iris Oifigiúil*.[152] The issuing of a circular to all the firm's clients is clearly within the terms of the expression 'publicly notify' and the co-operation of the continuing partners may be required, and thus forced under the terms of s 37, in order for a former partner to compile a complete list of recipients. Another act of public notification is the removal of a partner's name from the Register of Business Names by filing a Form RBN2A.[153] The Form RBN2A must be signed by the 'partners' in the firm[154] and therefore it is something which cannot be done without the concurrence of the continuing partners. Accordingly, a former partner may have to rely on s 37 to force the continuing partners to file this form. Thus in the High Court case of *Larkin v Groeger and Eaton*,[155] the continuing partner was ordered[156]

---

151 *Luckie v Forsyth* (1846) 3 Jo & Lat 388 at 396.
152 See for example *Troughton v Hunter* (1854) 18 Beav 470 and *Hendry v Turner* (1886) 32 Ch D 355. Although this action does not need to be done pursuant to the powers in s 37 of the 1890 Act, since, unlike the case of notifying the Registrar of Business Names, an advertisement can be placed in *Iris Oifigiúil* even where it has been submitted by the departing partner only as the practice of *Iris Oifigiúil* is to treat such notices as advertising copy.
153 See generally in relation to the requirement to file a Form RBN2A, para **[3.80]** et seq.
154 The Registration of Business Names Act 1963, s 7 provides that the statement to be filed to notify a change in the details of the business name should be signed in the like manner as the statement required on registration, which under s 5 is to be signed by 'all the individuals who are partners' or if by one partner, then verified by statutory declaration.
155 *Larkin v Groeger and Eaton* (26 April 1988) HC.
156 The order was made by the arbitrator, John Gore-Grimes, solicitor and his award was approved by Barrington J in the High Court.

to file the necessary forms in order to notify the Registrar of Business Names that the retiring partners were no longer partners in the firm.

May not be excluded by contrary agreement

[11.97] Most of the rights of partners under the 1890 Act are default provisions, rather than mandatory, so that they may be excluded by contrary agreement between the partners.[157] However, it is argued elsewhere in this work that the right of a former partner to notify the general dissolution of the partnership or his departure from the firm is, because of its importance, one of the few mandatory rights and so may not be excluded by contrary agreement.[158]

Other Ways of Termination of Liability of a Partner

[11.98] Up to this, consideration has been given to the duration of a partner's liability for the obligations of the firm from the perspective of (a) his joining and leaving the firm, (b) a new firm taking over the obligations of the old firm and (c) an incoming partner taking over the obligations of a former partner. It is now proposed to consider the termination of a partner's liability for the firm's obligations as a consequence of:

    (i)   the release or discharge of a partner by a creditor;

    (ii)   the payment of a partnership debt;

    (iii) a judgment; and

    (iv) limitation of actions.

(i) The release or discharge of a partner by a creditor

[11.99] Under the terms of the Civil Liability Act 1961, a person may discharge a co-partner from a partnership obligation by means of a release of, or accord with, a partner provided that the release or accord indicates an intention that the co-partner be released.[159]

---

[157] See generally in relation to the exclusion of these default rights, para **[21.04]**.

[158] See generally para **[21.152]** et seq.

[159] Civil Liability Act 1961, s 17(1). See generally McMahon and Binchy, *Law of Torts* (4th edn, 2013) at para [4.08] et seq. Even where the release or accord does not indicate an intention to release the other partners, the injured party may not obtain in aggregate any more than the amount of damages to which he was justly entitled: Civil Liability Act 1961, s 17(2). Similarly a satisfaction (ie a payment of damages, whether after judgment or by way of accord and satisfaction, or the rendering of any agreed substitution therefor) by one concurrent wrongdoer (which includes a partner who is jointly or jointly and severally liable) discharges all the other concurrent wrongdoers: Civil Liability Act 1961, s 16(1). See the English Court of Appeal case of *Morris v Wentworth-Stanley* [1999] 2 WLR 470 in which it was held that the English equivalent of s 18(1)(a) (namely s 3 of the Civil Liability (Contributions) Act 1978) did not preclude a defence of accord and satisfaction where it would otherwise arise. In that case, it was held that, since the debts in question owed to the plaintiff by the defendant firm were joint obligations of the partnership requiring the issue of liability and the determination of a counterclaim (by the one of the partners) to be disposed of in a single action, the plaintiff could not, in the absence of an express reservation of right, rely on s 3 to preclude the defence of accord and satisfaction. Thus, when the plaintiff settled with the partner who had counter-claimed 'in full and final settlement of the judgment' and subsequently sued the other partner, this second action was dismissed on the basis of an accord and satisfaction.

(ii) The payment of a partnership debt

[11.100] Where a partner pays a partnership debt, his co-partners are released from liability in respect of that debt.[160] This is a consequence of the general principle that a joint obligation (or a joint and several obligation) of the partners will be discharged by its performance by one partner. Where the partner discharging the debt to the creditor is also a debtor of the creditor in his own right, it will be a question of fact whether the payment was intended by the partner to be made in discharge of the partnership debt or his own personal debt. However, if the payment is made out of partnership funds, it will be taken to be applied in discharge of the partnership debt.[161]

Rule in Clayton's Case and payments of partnership debts

[11.101] The rule in *Clayton's case*[162] will be of importance when one is dealing with the payment of partnership debts, particularly where the payment is made after the membership of the firm has changed by the addition or departure of a partner. This rule provides that where there is a single open current account between two parties then, in the absence of contrary evidence, it is presumed that the debtor intended to pay off the earliest item standing to the debit of the payer first. This rule will not apply where there are two or more distinct accounts, in which case the creditor may appropriate the payment as he wishes. However, the rule does apply where there is a continuous current account. The rule is of particular relevance where there is a change in the membership of a firm after which, instead of having a separate account for the old firm and the newly constituted firm, there may be just one continuous account. In such a case, any payment by the 'new' firm to its creditors which is not specifically designated as paying off the new firm's debts, will be presumed to pay off the older debts first.[163] As has been seen, a new partner is not liable for the obligations of the firm which were incurred prior to his admission.[164] Therefore, by allowing the firm to operate a continuous open account, the new partner may unwittingly be paying off debts for which he is not liable, to the prejudice of debts for which he is liable. As the rule in *Clayton's case* is based on the presumed intentions[165] of the parties, any evidence that the new partner intended to pay off the new firm's debt will disapply this rule.

---

[160] *Watters v Smith* (1831) 2 B & D 889; *Beaumont v Greathead* (1846) 2 CB 494; *Thorne v Smith* (1851) 10 CB 659. See also the Civil Liability Act 1961, s 16.

[161] *Thompson v Brown* (1827) Moo & M 40.

[162] *Clayton's case* (1816) 1 Mer 572. See also *Smurfit Paribas Bank Ltd v AAB Export Finance Ltd (No 2)* [1991] 2 IR 19; *Hennerty v The Governor and Company of the Bank of Ireland* (5 July 1988) HC and 26 May 1989; *Re the Estate of Chute and Kelly* [1914] 1 IR 180; *In the Matter of Daniel Murphy Ltd* [1964] IR 1. See generally, Breslin, *Banking Law in Ireland* (3rd edn, 2013) at para 8.38 et seq; Donnelly, *The Law of Credit and Security in Ireland* (2nd edn, 2015) at para 7-106 et seq. The judgment of Barrett J in *Allied Irish Banks plc v Gerard J Smith* [2015] IEHC 707 notes that the rule has its limitations when viewed in the context of the more sophisticated transactions that are entered into now, when compared with the types of transactions entered into in the early nineteenth century when the 'rule in *Clayton's case*' was developed.

[163] *Beale v Caddick* (1857) 2 H & N 326; *Scott v Beale* (1859) 6 Jur (ns) 559.

[164] See para **[11.28]**.

[165] *Re Hodgon's Trusts* [1919] 2 Ch 189; *Wilson v Hurst* (1883) 4 B & Ad 760; *Re Hallett's Estate* (1880) 13 Ch D 696; *Cory Brothers & Co v Owners of The Mecca* [1897] AC 286; *Deeley v Lloyds Bank* [1912] AC 756.

(iii) A judgment

[11.102] As has been seen,[166] where judgment is obtained against one partner in respect of a joint obligation of the firm, this no longer operates as a bar to a subsequent action against the other partners who are jointly liable on the obligation, provided that the plaintiff cannot recover more damages than he has suffered. Of course, where the judgment has been satisfied, the liability of the partners therefore will be terminated.[167]

(iv) Limitation of actions

[11.103] A partnership debt may also be terminated if the action therefor is instituted outside the relevant limitation period under the Statute of Limitations 1957.[168]

[11.104] An issue which has been considered by the Irish courts is the question of whether it is possible for the limitation period to be extended by an acknowledgement of a partnership obligation by a partner during the course of its winding up. On the basis of the pre-1890 Irish case of *Bristow v Miller*,[169] the answer to this question would appear to be in the negative. In that case, the debts had been incurred outside the relevant limitation period under the Statute of Limitations of 1828.[170] However, during the winding up, one partner acknowledged that the debt was owed by the firm by sending an account to the creditor. The High Court[171] held that after a partnership is dissolved, a partner cannot involve his co-partner in any new legal liability[172] and since the original liability had been incurred over six years since the institution of proceedings, the issuing of the account was not binding on the firm.

[11.105] This strict approach to acknowledging partnerships debts on the winding up of a partnership is queried elsewhere in this work.[173] However, when one is dealing with a partnership which is not being wound up, it would appear that a partner has implied authority to make part payments of a debt or acknowledge the debt, so as to extend the limitation period.

---

[166] See para **[11.18]**.
[167] Civil Liability Act 1961, s 16(1); *Higgen's Case* (1605) 6 Co 44b; *Lechmere v Fletcher* (1833) 1 C & M 623; *Field v Robins* (1838) 8 A & E 90; *King v Hoare* (1844) 13 M & W 494.
[168] See generally Canny, *Limitation of Actions* (2nd edn, 2016).
[169] *Bristow v Miller* (1848) 11 Ir LR 461.
[170] An Act for rendering a written Memorandum necessary to the Validity of certain Promises and Engagements of 1828 (9 G 4, c 14).
[171] The judgment of the court was given by Crampton J; Perrin and Moore JJ concurred.
[172] Crampton J relied on *Kilgour v Finlyson* (1789) 1 H Bl 156.
[173] See para **[26.18]** et seq.

Chapter 12

Litigation by and against Partners

INTRODUCTION

[12.01] The 1890 Act does not deal with the rules which apply to legal proceedings either by or against a partnership. This issue is dealt with in the Rules of the Superior Courts[1] (referred to in this chapter as the RSC), the Rules of the Circuit Court[2] (referred to in this chapter as the RCC) and the Rules of the District Court[3] (referred to in this chapter as the RDC) In this chapter, the rules applicable to litigation involving a firm and its partners will be considered under the following headings:

    I.   Litigation by and against Partnerships;

    II.   Litigation in Partners' Own Names; and

    III.   Set-Off.

Overview

[12.02] The importance of the nature of a partnership comes to the fore once again when one is dealing with litigation either by a firm or against a firm. It has been noted that the grand characteristic of partnerships is the fact that they do not have a separate legal existence, since each partnership is an aggregate of all of its members.[4] One would expect therefore that in any litigation involving the firm, all the partners in that firm should be made a party to the proceedings. Yet, in order to reduce the administrative burden of joining numerous parties every time a partnership is involved in litigation, the law chooses to treat partnerships involved in litigation as if they were separate legal entities. It does this by providing in the Rules of Court for actions to be taken by or against a firm in the firm name. However, it is crucial to bear in mind that this procedural rule is simply that, ie a rule of procedure which allows partnership litigation to be conducted *as if* the firm were a separate legal entity. It does not alter the fundamental nature of a partnership as an aggregate of its members and this issue will remain of relevance to the conduct of any such litigation. Arising from this aggregate nature is the fact that although the same firm name may be used in litigation by or against a firm, with each change in the membership of the firm, a new partnership is created.[5] It follows that one must 'look through' the firm name to see who is ultimately liable for or the beneficiary of the matter being litigated, namely those persons who were

---

[1]   SI 15/1986, as amended. See generally Ó Floinn, *Practice and Procedure in the Superior Courts* (2nd edn, 2008); Delany and McGrath, *Civil Procedure in the Superior Courts* (3rd edn, 2012).

[2]   SI 510/2001, as amended.

[3]   SI 93/1997, as amended.

[4]   See para **[3.04]**.

[5]   See for example the statement of Eichelbaum CJ in *Hadlee v Commissioner of Inland Revenue* [1993] AC 524 and para **[23.09]**.

partners in the firm at the time of the accrual of the cause of action.[6] It is for this reason that the Rules of Court also allow a party in partnership litigation to apply to court for a statement of the names of the partners in the firm at the time of the accrual of the cause of action. It follows that parties to an action against a firm may not dispense with the need to identify the correct parties to their action, since it is only these parties against whom a judgment may be executed.

[12.03] Therefore, in all issues of partnership litigation, other than the right of litigants to use the firm name in the proceedings in the first place, the aggregate theory of partnership remains paramount.

I.   LIGITATION BY AND AGAINST PARTNERSHIPS

General

[12.04] Formerly, actions against a partner in a firm were subject to the rule that a judgment against one partner in a case where the partners were jointly liable precluded the bringing of a subsequent claim against his co-partner.[7] This principle was known as the rule in *Kendall v Hamilton*.[8] However, this rule was reversed by s 18(1)(a) of the Civil Liability Act 1961[9] which states:

> Where damage is suffered by any person as a result of concurrent wrongs –
>
> (a)   judgment recovered against any wrongdoer liable in respect of that damage shall not be a bar to an action against any other person who would, if sued, have been liable as concurrent wrongdoer in respect of the same damage.

---

6   In *Honohan McInerney Construction Ltd* [2018] IEHC 311, Murphy J held that the balance of justice favoured the dismissal of the plaintiff's claims (arising out of mapping discrepancies relating to the purchase of a site) against McInerney Construction Limited and various solicitors for several reasons, notably including the fact that they failed to name the solicitor defendants in their capacity as partners in a particular firm, and had instead sued them in their capacity as principals in firms which had never dealt with the plaintiffs. Further, the plaintiffs attempted to sue the sixth defendant as a partner in a firm in which she was instead an employee. The decision in this case underscores the importance of carefully establishing those who were partners in a firm when the cause of action accrued, and naming those parties correctly in the proceedings. See also *Stanton v Foley* [2018] IEHC 675.

7   This was not the case if they were jointly and severally liable, see para **[11.22]**.

8   *Kendall v Hamilton* (1811) 7 Ves Jr 514. In that case, the plaintiff made a loan to a firm in which W and M were partners. He sued both partners and he obtained judgment against them for the debt which was not satisfied because of their lack of resources. The plaintiff then discovered that a Mr Hamilton was also a partner in the firm and a man of means. However, when he sued him, it was held that, as the liability of the partners was joint, the judgment in the first action extinguished Mr Hamilton's obligation. Even before the Civil Liability Act 1961, the applicability of the rule in *Kendall v Hamilton* was in doubt in view of *Montgomerie v Ferris and Brown* (1887) 20 LR Ir 282 and *Pim v Coyle and Coyle* [1903] 2 IR 457. In both cases, the court held that a plaintiff does not abandon his rights against one partner by reason of his having entered judgment in default of appearance against the other (whether execution had issued or not). See also *Lindsay v Crawford* (1910) 45 ILTR 52.

9   See generally McMahon and Binchy, *Law of Torts* (4th edn, 2013) at para [4.08] et seq. See also s 2 of the Tortfeasors Act 1951 which was repealed by s 5 and the Schedule to the Civil Liability Act 1961.

[12.05] Section 18(1)(a) is subject to the proviso that the plaintiff cannot recover more damages than he has suffered.[10] Even before the enactment of the Civil Liability Act 1961, the RSC allowed the difficulty in the case of *Kendall v Hamilton* to be avoided, by permitting a partnership to be sued in the firm name. This is because proceedings in the firm name operate as an action against all the persons who were partners in that firm at the time of the accrual of the cause of action. The rules applicable to actions by and against partners in the superior courts are now[11] to be found in Ord 14, r 1 of the RSC and the terms of this order are considered in detail below.

Authority to bring or defend proceedings

[12.06] As is noted elsewhere in this work,[12] a partner has authority to bring proceedings on behalf of his firm or to defend proceedings on behalf of his firm, since these actions are within the implied authority of a partner. It should be remembered that this authority only extends to partnership matters. This principle is illustrated by the case of *Fairlie v Quin and Lewis*.[13] There, an application was made to deem service on Quin, a partner in a firm in Newry, as good service on his co-partner, Lewis, who was out of the jurisdiction. Doherty CJ rejected the application, since the applicant did not establish that the cause of action was a partnership one and therefore Quin did not have authority to accept the proceedings on behalf of Lewis.

Disability of partner affecting firm

[12.07] An issue which may arise in litigation either by or against a firm is the possibility of the firm being affected by the disability of a partner in the firm. The principle that the disability of a partner affects the firm[14] results from the agency basis for partnership law[15] and the aggregate nature of a partnership.[16] A partner is at one and the same time a principal and an agent – he is the principal, for whom his co-partners act, and at the same time, he acts as agent for his co-partners. It has long been recognised that a principal, who has a disability, cannot circumvent this disability by using an agent to do the act on his behalf[17] and equally that a principal will be affected

---

10 Civil Liability Act 1961, s 17(2).
11 For previous versions of these rules see, the Rules of the Supreme Court (Ireland) 1905, the Rules of the Supreme Court Ireland 1891 and the General Orders of 1872.
12 See para **[10.53]**.
13 *Fairlie v Quin and Lewis* (1839) Smythe 189.
14 See for example *Crowe v Lysaght* (1861) 4 LR Ir 744.
15 As to the agency basis for partnership law, see para **[2.71]**.
16 Ie, a firm is not a separate legal entity, but an aggregate of its members and each partner is a mutual agent for his co-partners. See generally para **[3.04]**.
17 *Collins v Carey* (1839) 2 Beav 128. The following statement of Lord Cranworth in *Broughton v Broughton* (1854) 5 De GM & G 160 at 164, was quoted with approval by Overend J in the High Court case of *Re Boyle* [1947] 1 IR 61 at 75: '[t]he rule really is, that no one who has a duty to perform shall place himself in a situation to have his interests conflicting with that duty: and a case for the application of the rule is that of a trustee himself doing acts which he might employ others to perform, and taking payment in some way.'

by the disability of an agent. This latter point was noted by Overend J in the High Court case of *Re Boyle*:[18]

> 'What is the law when a principal, who can lawfully make a profit, employs an agent, who could not be allowed to make a profit, to do all the work? In my opinion a principal who acts by an agent, who is under a disability, cannot claim to be in any better situation than his agent. So far as I know this is a new proposition and I propound it with some diffidence.'[19]

[12.08] That case involved the classic example of the disability of a partner affecting a firm, namely that a firm is prevented from receiving payment for services to a trust, where one of the partners in the firm is a trustee. This is because the prohibition on a trustee charging his own trust for services provided by him extends to services provided by the firm, of which he is a partner. However, on the facts of that case, there was an agency relationship between the parties, but not a partnership. It involved a solicitor in Dublin who agreed to act as agent for his son, also a solicitor, in relation to the son's practice, while his son was fighting in the Second World War. During this time, the father was appointed as an executor and trustee of a trust and his son was appointed as the solicitor to the trust. The trust deed did not entitle the trustee to charge for any professional services and thus the father would not have been entitled to charge for his legal services to the trust. However, the legal services were provided by the father to the trust in the name and on behalf of his son. The High Court held that the disability of the agent (the father) affected his principal (the son) so that the son was not entitled to be paid for these legal services.

[12.09] Before leaving this area, reference should be made to the exceptional case of *Re De Courcenay*,[20] which was not considered in *Re Boyle*.[21] There, Atkinson and Bridge were partners in a firm of land agents. Atkinson was a trustee under a settlement for the vendor of some property. There was no clause in the deed of settlement enabling trustees to charge for their services. The firm worked for the settlement and the majority of work done by the firm for the settlement was done by the non-trustee partner, Bridge. It was, however, admitted that Atkinson was to get half of the fee for this work, as a partner in the firm. In the High Court, Wylie J held that Atkinson, as the trustee, should not be entitled to charge for his services as there was no provision in the trust deed entitling such payments to be made. When he came to consider the claim of the firm and in particular the claim of Bridge, Wylie J acknowledged that:

> '[S]ome of the cases would appear to go the length of deciding that, where a firm of which the trustee is a member does the work, the firm can make no claim unless there is an express stipulation that the trustee is to derive no benefit.'[22]

---

18 *Re Boyle* [1947] 1 IR 61.
19 *Re Boyle* [1947] 1 IR 61 at 74–75.
20 *Re De Courcenay* [1912] 1 IR 341.
21 *Re Boyle* [1947] 1 IR 61.
22 *Re De Courcenay* [1912] 1 IR 341 at 343.

However, he went on to hold that:

> 'But in order to meet the justice and merits of the case as regards Mr Bridge, I think I am justified by the decision of Stirling J, in *In Re Doody*[23] in making an order for the payment of his share.'[24]

[12.10] The later decision in *Re Boyle*[25] suggests that *Re De Courcenay*[26] is now confined to its own peculiar facts and in particular the fact that the vendor of the property did not object to the payment of the full fee to the firm. However, it is clear that as a general rule the inability of a partner to charge a trust for professional services will affect his firm.[27] Modern partnership agreements attempt to circumvent this restriction by providing that, where a partner in a firm advises a trust of which his co-partner is a trustee and which does not entitle the co-partner to charge the trust, the non-trustee partner is entitled to retain fees paid to him or the firm for his services for his exclusive benefit and not for the benefit of the firm.[28] In this way, the fees are due to the non-trustee partner in his own right and not as a partner in the firm and the disability of the firm arising from the disability of his co-partner will have no application to this payment.

Proceedings in Firm Name

[12.11] Order 14, r 1 of the RSC[29] provides that a partnership may sue or be sued in its firm name.[30] Although there is no need to set out in the proceedings the names of the individual partners, where a partnership is sued in the firm name the partners are sued individually as definitively as if they had their names set out.[31] As is noted hereunder these proceedings may be served on one partner.[32] This rule is a natural consequence of the mutual agency of partners,[33] ie a partner who has the authority to contract in his partners' names and on their behalf should be capable of becoming the medium of affixing his own and his partners' legal liability and thus proceedings may be served in the firm name on one partner. Therefore, in order to avoid the injustice which could be caused by delaying a plaintiff until he serves the partners whose whereabouts are difficult to find, the first part of Ord 14, r 1 states:

---

23   *Re Doody* [1898] 1 Ch 129. In this case, an exception was made regarding a trustee charging for his legal services in the case of litigation, which was not the case in *Re De Courcenay*.

24   *Re De Courcenay* [1912] 1 IR 341 at 343.

25   *Re Boyle* [1947] 1 IR 61.

26   *Re De Courcenay* [1912] 1 IR 341.

27   *Broughton v Broughton* (1854) 5 De GM & G 160, relied on by Overend J in *Re Boyle* [1946] IR 61; *Collins v Carey* (1839) 2 Beav 128; *Christopher's v White* (1847) 10 Beav 523. See also *Re Gates* [1933] 1 Ch 913.

28   For an example of such a clause, see *Re Gates* [1933] 1 Ch 913.

29   The corresponding rule in the Circuit Court is RCC, Ord 8, r 1, and in the District Court is RDC, Ord 43, r 18.

30   See generally Anon, 'Service on Partners and Firms' (1879) 13 ILT & SJ 131 for a criticism of the previous law which did not allow for actions to be taken in the firm-name and a call for the introduction of this procedural rule which by that time had been introduced into England.

31   *Western National Bank v Perez* [1891] 1 QB 304.

32   See para **[12.24]** et seq.

33   See generally in relation to this agency, para **[10.07]**.

Any two or more persons claiming or being liable as co-partners and carrying on business within the jurisdiction, may sue or be sued in the name of the respective firms, if any, of which such persons were co-partners at the time of the accruing of the cause of action ...

[12.12] It must be remembered that Ord 14, r 1 is simply a rule of procedure and it does not impact upon the nature of a partnership as an aggregate of its members.[34] In this regard, in the Supreme Court case of *Re A Debtor Summons*[35] Fitzgibbon J observed in relation to the predecessor of Ord 14, r 1 that:

'[A] firm as such has no existence; partners carry on business both as principals and as agents for each other within the scope of the partnership business; the firm-name is a mere expression, not a legal entity, although for convenience under Ord XLVIII A it may be used for the sake of suing and being sued.'[36]

[12.13] The major exception to the general rule that a firm may be sued in its firm name, is that an order of adjudication for the bankruptcy of a firm must not be made in the firm name, but it must be made against the partners individually with the addition of the firm name.[37]

'persons claiming'

[12.14] Since Ord 14, r 1 applies to 'any two or more persons *claiming* or being liable' as co-partners, it is clearly envisaged that, even where a partnership is subsequently shown not to actually exist between the parties, the court will allow the action to proceed against the proper parties, if the parties acted in the belief that there was a real partnership.[38]

'being liable as co-partners'

[12.15] The use of the phrase 'liable *as* co-partners' in r 1 and throughout Ord 14 is a clear reference to the possibility of a person, who is not in fact a partner, being liable as a partner by holding out under s 14(1) of the 1890 Act. This area is considered in detail elsewhere in this work.[39] However, it is clear that the rules of procedure regarding partners are equally applicable to a person who is liable as a partner by holding out.

'at the time of the accruing of the cause of action'

[12.16] Ord 14, r 1 states that partners, who were members of the firm at the time of the accrual of the cause of action, may sue or be sued in the firm name. It is important to bear in mind that Ord 14, r 1 is simply a rule of procedure and does not alter the rights and liabilities of the partners in a firm inter se or *vis-à-vis* third parties.[40] If, for example, 20 partners are members of a partnership at the time proceedings are taken against that firm in the firm name, these proceedings are deemed to refer only to those, say 15 partners, who were members of that firm at the time of the accrual of the cause of

---

[34]   See generally in relation to the nature of a partnership, para **[3.04]**.
[35]   *Re A Debtor Summons* [1929] IR 139.
[36]   Quoting from Farwell LJ in *Sadler v Whiteman* [1910] 1 KB 868 at 889.
[37]   RSC, Ord 76, r 34. See generally in relation to this area, para **[27.35]** et seq.
[38]   See for example *Noble Lowndes & Partners (a firm) v Hadfields Ltd* [1939] Ch 569.
[39]   See para **[7.01]** et seq.
[40]   *Meyer & Co v Faber (No 2)* [1923] 2 Ch 421.

action. It is irrelevant that the five new partners were members of the firm at the time the proceedings were issued or indeed at the time the case was heard. The liability of the five new partners is not affected by this rule of procedure. The important issue remains, who was a member of the firm at the time of the accrual of the cause of action? Thus in *Pentland v Gibson*,[41] the estate of a deceased partner (Gibson) was being sued by a partnership called the Saint Patrick Assurance Company of Ireland for outstanding sums due to the firm by Gibson. The action was taken on behalf of the partnership by Pentland who was not a member of the firm at the time of the issue of the proceedings. For this reason, Gibson's personal representative claimed that Pentland was not entitled to bring the action. However, this claim was rejected by Bushe CJ on the grounds that Pentland had been a member of the firm at the time of the accrual of the cause of action.[42]

'carrying on business within the jurisdiction'

[12.17] Before a partnership may sue or be sued in its firm name, Ord 14, r 1 requires it to be carrying on business within the jurisdiction. If the partnership, which is being sued or which is suing, does not satisfy this requirement, then the proceedings must be in the names of each of the partners. Thus, it has been held that where a partnership carries on business outside the jurisdiction, the service of a summons in that firm name has no effect.[43] On the other hand, if the firm carries on business within the State, it is irrelevant that some of the partners are abroad when the proceedings are served in the firm name.

Disclosure of Partners' Names

[12.18] Whether a partnership is the plaintiff or the defendant in court proceedings, the other party to those proceedings will have an interest in ascertaining the identity of the members of the firm. In view of the importance of this information to a third party, the right to it is recognised by the second part of Ord 14, r 1.[44] This states that any party to an action by or against a partnership may:

> apply to the Court for a statement of the names of the persons who were, at the time of the accruing of the cause of action, co-partners in any such firm, to be furnished in such manner, and verified on oath or otherwise, as the Court may direct.

The application for the partners' names is made by motion[45] before the Master of the High Court.[46]

---

41   *Pentland v Gibson* (1833) Alc & Nap 310.
42   Similarly in *Hunter v Morgan* (1828) 2 Hud & Bro 119, in another action on behalf of the Saint Patrick Assurance Company of Ireland, it was held by Bushe CJ that a bond which was entered into by the defendant in favour of three partners in that firm, but for the benefit of the whole partnership, could be enforced by the plaintiff, another partner in the firm, even though he was not a party to the bond.
43   *Western National Bank of City of New York v Perez, Triana & Co* [1891] 1 QB 304.
44   The corresponding rule in the Circuit Court is RCC, Ord 8, r 1, and in the District Court is RDC, Ord 43, r 19.
45   RSC, Ord 52.
46   RSC, Ord 63, r 1(4) and it may be heard *ex parte*: RSC, Ord 63, r 4. Note that one counsel only is allowed, unless the Court shall otherwise order: RSC, Ord 52, r 17(1).

[12.19] For a defendant in an action brought by a partnership, there is no necessity for him to apply to court for the disclosure of the members of the partnership. This is because Ord 14, r 2[47] grants a defendant, in a case where a partnership sues in its firm name, the right to receive on demand from the plaintiff firm, the names and places of residence of each of the partners on whose behalf the action is brought. Once the identity of the partners is disclosed, the proceedings continue in the firm name with the same consequences as if those named partners had been listed as plaintiffs in the action.[48] If the plaintiff firm fails to comply with such a request, the defendant may make an application to court[49] and the court may stay the action upon such terms as it may choose.

Person Carrying on Business in Jurisdiction under Another Name

[12.20] Reference might also be made at this juncture to a situation where a person is carrying on business in the jurisdiction, not in partnership, but under a business name other than his own. Order 14, r 11[50] regulates the circumstances in which a person carrying on business within the jurisdiction under a name or style other than his own name may be sued under that business name, as if it were a firm name. It provides that the rules of court regarding proceedings against a partnership apply to such a case, so far as the nature of the case permits. The fact that the owner of the business has registered his business name under the Registration of Business Names Act 1963 would appear to be irrelevant in determining whether a third party may still sue in the business name, as if it were a partnership.[51]

[12.21] By its express terms Ord 14, r 11 only applies to a 'person'. The question of whether this includes a company was considered in *Re A Debtor's Summons*.[52] There, a partnership business had 40 years previously been acquired by a company. Nonetheless, proceedings were issued against the partnership name, under which the business had continued to be carried on, rather than against the company. In the Supreme Court, Kennedy CJ rejected the claim that the predecessor of Ord 14, r 11[53] applied, observing that:[54]

> '[Ord 14 r 11] of the Order, which it was suggested met the present case, must be read in its context, and is not, in my opinion, to be read as referring to incorporated companies, an

---

[47]   The corresponding rule in the Circuit Court is RCC, Ord 8, r 2, and in the District Court is RDC, Ord 43, r 20(1).

[48]   RSC, Ord 14, r 2.

[49]   By way of motion on notice: RSC, Ord 52.

[50]   The equivalent rule in the Circuit Court is RCC, Ord 8, rr 7–9, and in the District Court is RDC, Ord 43, r 24. Under RCC, Ord 8, r 7 and RDC, Ord 43, r 24(1), the person must not have registered the business name under the Registration of Business Names Act 1963.

[51]   This approach seems to be consistent with the general approach to the Registration of Business Names Act 1963, insofar as third parties are not deemed to be on constructive notice of filings in respect of the departure of partners in the register of business names, see para **[3.82]**.

[52]   *Re A Debtor's Summons* [1929] IR 139.

[53]   Ie Ord XLVIIIA, r 11 of the Rules of the Supreme Court (Ireland) 1905.

[54]   See also the judgment of Murnaghan J.

interpretation which would appear to me to override the statutory provisions and the ordinary law as to incorporated companies.'[55]

[12.22] In *Irwin v Austin & Sons*,[56] the sole owner of a business carried it on under the name of 'Austin & Sons'. The manager of the business, who was an employee of the sole owner, was served with a summons in the name of 'Austin & Sons' pursuant to the predecessor of Ord 14, r 11.[57] Since all the rules in Ord 14 relating to firms also apply to the situation in which a business name is used, it was held that the manager should have been notified, by notice in writing at the time of the service, of the capacity in which he was served.[58] Since this was not done, the Irish Court of Appeal held that proper service had not been effected.[59]

A Partnership as a Defendant

[12.23] Having considered the principles which are applicable to actions both by and against partnerships, this section analyses the principles which are only applicable to cases in which a partnership is the defendant.

Service of proceedings on a firm

[12.24] It has been noted that a firm may be sued in its firm name.[60] The next issue to consider is the manner in which these proceedings may be served on the firm. The service of proceedings on a firm is dealt with by Ord 14, r 3 of the RSC.[61] This provides that where persons are sued as partners in the firm name, service may be effected by serving[62] a summons on:

(a)   any one or more partner, or

(b)   at the principal place of business[63] of the partnership within the State on the person having control or management of the partnership business there.[64]

---

[55]   *Re A Debtor's Summons* [1929] IR 139 at 144. However, see the Interpretation Act 2005, s 18(c) which provides that any reference in an 'enactment' (which includes a statutory instrument) to a 'person' includes a reference to a body corporate. The Rules of the Superior Courts are contained in an 'enactment' (SI 15/1986 as amended).

[56]   *Irwin v Austin & Sons* (1907) 41 ILTR 190.

[57]   Ord XLVIIIA, r 11 of the Rules of the Supreme Court (Ireland) 1905.

[58]   As required in the case of partnerships under the predecessor of Ord 14, r 4 (Ord XLVIIIA, r 4 of the Rules of the Supreme Court (Ireland) 1905), see para **[12.25]**.

[59]   Walker LC (Fitzgibbon and Holmes LJJ, concurring).

[60]   See para **[12.11]**.

[61]   The corresponding rule in the Circuit Court is RCC, Ord 8, r 3, and in the District Court is RDC, Ord 41, r 7. For the situation prior to RSC, Ord 14, r 3, see *Smith v Smith and Neill* (1878) 11 Ir CLR 535. See also Anon, 'Service on Partners and Firms' (1879) 13 ILT & SJ 131, where the inconvenience of the previous law is discussed.

[62]   Service is made personally: RSC, Ord 9, r 2. See also Ó Floinn, *Practice and Procedure in the Superior Courts* (2nd edn, 2008) at p 58 et seq; Delany and McGrath, *Civil Procedure in the Superior Courts* (3rd edn, 2012) at para 3-02 et seq.

[63]   As to what constitutes a principal place of business, see *Weatherley v Calder & Co* (1889) 61 LT 508.

[64]   See for example *Cullimore v Savage South Africa* [1903] 2 IR 589, in which proceedings were served on the manager of the business pursuant to Ord IX, r 9 of the Rules of the Supreme Court Ireland 1891, which corresponds to the existing RSC, Ord 14, r 3.

Amendment to Ord 14, r 4 required

[12.25] Order 14, r 4 provides that every person served must be informed by notice in writing at the time of service 'whether he is served as a partner or as a person having the control or management of the *partnership, business,* or in both characters'. The comma between the word 'partnership' and 'business' should be deleted from this rule since the reference should be to 'partnership business'. This is clear since that is the phrase used in Ord 14, r 3, (to which Ord 14, r 4 is secondary). In addition Ord 14, r 4 clearly envisages two options (ie service on a person as a partner or as a manager of the partnership business) by its reference to 'both characters' and not three options which is arguably the case with the comma (ie service on a person as a partner, as a manager of the partnership or as manager of the business).

Persons on whom service is effected

[12.26] Where no notice of the manner in which someone is served is given, the person served is deemed to be served as a partner.[65] Accordingly, it seems that where a person is served as a partner only, no notice need be given. However where a person, who is in control or management of the partnership business, is served without notice to that effect, it would seem that the firm might not have been properly served. The person, who is so served, is not required to enter an appearance, unless he is also a partner.[66]

[12.27] A person, such as an employee, who does not have control or management[67] of the partnership business may not be properly served under this rule, unless of course the partnership has authorised the employee to accept service.[68]

[12.28] Under the express terms of Ord 14, r 3, service of proceedings on a partner or the person having control or management of the firm is 'deemed good service upon the firm so sued' so that each partner in the firm is treated as if he were personally served.[69] As observed by Fitzgibbon LJ in the Irish Court of Appeal '[i]t is the clear effect of this rule that service in accordance with its terms is equivalent to personal service upon each and every member of the partnership'.[70]

---

[65]   RSC, Ord 14, r 4.

[66]   RSC, Ord 14, r 6, which is considered at para **[12.37]**.

[67]   As to what constitutes a 'person having control or management', see *Grant v Anderson* (1892) 1 QB 108. In the exceptional English Court of Appeal case of *Willmott v Berry Brothers* (1982) 126 SJ 209, a person having control of the former partnership business was held to have been validly served under the English equivalent of RSC, Ord 14, r 1 even though, unknown to the plaintiff, the partnership business was by that stage being carried on by a limited company and the person served had never been an employee of the firm.

[68]   See *Kenneth Allison Ltd v AE Limehouse & Co* [1991] 4 All ER 500 (service on a partner's personal assistant).

[69]   *Heydon v Hammond and Murray* (1848) 10 Ir LR 201, where Doherty CJ ordered that service on Hammond in Drogheda, the partner of Murray, should be deemed good service on Murray who was in England. Cf *McCann v Thomson* (1847) 11 Ir LR 201; *Thompson v Haughton* (1848) 11 Ir LR 201; *Oldham v Shaw* (1841) 4 Ir LR 1; *McKenny v Mark* (1839) 2 Ir LR 161; *Moore v Johnston* (1892) 26 ILTR 92; *Nolan v Fitzgerald* (1851) 2 Ir CLR 79.

[70]   *Cullimore v Savage South Africa* [1903] 2 IR 589 at 640 commenting on the predecessor of RSC Ord 14, r 3, namely Ord IX, r 9 of the Rules of the Supreme Court Ireland 1891.

[12.29] Where the service is effected under Ord 14, r 3, it will be deemed to be good service upon the firm, even if some or all of the partners are out of the jurisdiction and no leave to issue a summons against these partners is required. However, as noted below,[71] if judgment is subsequently obtained against the firm, it will not affect a partner out of the jurisdiction when the summons was issued, unless he has made an appearance in the proceedings, has been subsequently served[72] or has been made a party to the action.[73] Where it is sought to serve a partner who is out of the jurisdiction, leave to do so may be obtained under RSC Ord 11 and 11A,[74] but where the partner is within a country which is party to Regulation (EU) No 1215/2012 of the European Parliament and of the Council on jurisdiction and the recognition and enforcement of judgments in civil and commercial matters (recast) (known as the Recast Brussels Regulation) or the Convention on Jurisdiction and the Enforcement of Judgments in Civil and Commercial Matters signed at Lugano on 30 October 2007 (known as the Lugano Convention),[75] then no leave is required to serve that partner.[76]

Substituted service

[12.30] Where it is not possible to effect personal service, an application can of course be made to court for substituted or other service or for the substitution for service of notice by advertisement or otherwise under Ord 10, r 1.[77]

---

71 See para **[12.48]**.
72 See for example *Lindsay v Crawford* (1910) 45 ILTR 52.
73 He may be made a party to the action under RSC, Ord 11.
74 See for example *Lindsay v Crawford* (1910) 45 ILTR 52. In that case, a partner who it was sought to make liable was out of the jurisdiction. Judgment was entered in default against his firm and leave was given under Ord IX, r 1 of the Rules of the Supreme Court (Ireland) 1905, the predecessor of RSC, Ord 11, r 1, to issue a concurrent writ and serve it on the partner out of the jurisdiction. The partner so served acknowledged service of the concurrent writ, and the plaintiff proceeded against him and obtained judgment to enable execution under Ord XLVIIIA, r 8 of the Rules of the Supreme Court (Ireland) 1905, the predecessor of RSC, Ord 14, r 8. For a criticism of this decision, see *West of England Steamship Owners Protection and Indemnity Association Ltd* [1957] 3 All ER 421 per Roxburgh J.
75 The Recast Brussels Regulation is directly effective in Ireland. The Lugano Convention is applied in Ireland by the Jurisdiction of Courts and Enforcement of Judgments Act 1988 (as amended).
76 RSC, Ord 11A, r 2. See Ó Floinn, *Practice and Procedure in the Superior Courts* (2nd edn, 2008) at p 84 et seq; Delany and McGrath, *Civil Procedure in the Superior Courts* (3rd edn, 2012) at para 9-49 et seq.
77 As already noted, under RSC, Ord 14, r 3, partners who are out of the jurisdiction are deemed to have been properly served where the summons is served on one of the partners or at the principal place of business of the partnership upon the person having control or management of the partnership business there. For this reason, the cases which deal with the substitution of service on a partner out of the jurisdiction are largely of historical interest only. See para **[12.57]**.

Exception for service on a dissolved partnership

[12.31] It has been noted elsewhere in this work[78] that a partner's liability for partnership obligations does not cease on the dissolution of the partnership. In this regard, Ord 14, r 3 permits service to be effected against a dissolved partnership in the firm name. However, it provides that where persons are being sued in the firm name and the plaintiff is aware, before the commencement of the action, that the firm is dissolved, then the summons must be served on each partner within the jurisdiction who it is sought to make liable.[79] This aspect of Ord 14, r 3 is stated simply to apply to a 'dissolved' partnership, which, as has been noted elsewhere,[80] is capable of two separate meanings. However, in this context, it seems clear that a 'dissolved partnership' is a reference to a partnership which is generally dissolved (in the sense of being subject to a winding up of the firm's business), rather than one which is technically dissolved (in the sense of simply having undergone a change of membership in the firm).[81]

[12.32] Although only a procedural rule, and therefore not affecting the liability of a partner in a firm, Ord 14, r 3 may render proceedings in a firm name ineffective against a partner in a dissolved firm who is within the jurisdiction. This will occur where the plaintiff knows that the partnership has been dissolved and he fails to have a summons served upon that partner.

Service on a company under Ord 14

[12.33] Although RSC Ord 14 is concerned primarily with litigation by and against partnerships, *Cullimore v Savage South Africa Co*[82] is authority for the principle that in certain circumstances, the service of proceedings on a company, as if it were a partnership, will be allowed. Such service may be deemed sufficient where the mistaken belief by the plaintiff, that the enterprise being sued was not a company, was caused by the actions or omissions of the company. In that case, the plaintiff brought an action for false imprisonment when he attended a wildlife show called 'Savage South Africa' on Jones' Road in Dublin. A company called 'Shows, Limited' had put on the show. However, the company had failed to comply with its company law obligations to have its name affixed outside its place of business.[83] Accordingly in the Court of Appeal, FitzGibbon LJ held that the plaintiff was justified in assuming that the business of 'Savage South Africa' was not carried on by a company. For this reason, he held that the

---

[78] See para **[11.74]**.

[79] See for example the decision in *Chohan Clothing Co (Manchester) Ltd v Fox Brooks Marshall (a firm)* Court of Appeal, (1997) The Times, 9 December.

[80] See para **[23.07]**.

[81] Otherwise every time there is a change in the firm (whether by the addition or departure of a partner), it would be necessary to serve each partner personally. Quite apart from rendering Ord 14, r 1 of dubious benefit by virtue of its non-application to many partnerships, this interpretation of Ord 14, r 3 would be inconsistent with the implicit intention of Ord 14, r 1, namely to apply to partnerships which have had a change in membership. This intent can be garnered from the reference therein to service in the firm-name applying to the persons who 'were co-partners at the time of the accruing of the cause of action'.

[82] *Cullimore v Savage South Africa Co* [1903] 2 IR 589.

[83] As required, at that time, by the Companies Act 1862, s 41. This obligation is now contained in the Companies Act 2014, s 49(1)(a).

plaintiff was justified in suing the enterprise as a partnership under the predecessor of Ord 14, r 1[84] by serving proceedings in the 'firm name' (ie Savage South Africa) at the principal place of business of the 'partnership' upon any manager thereof.[85] The application of this case is limited to the issue of service of proceedings. It is not authority for the principle that a judgment could be obtained against a company when a business is served as a partnership since in the subsequent Supreme Court case of *Re A Debtor Summons*,[86] FitzGibbon J noted that:

> 'It was never suggested in *Cullimore's Case* [1903] 2 IR 589 at 604, that the appearance and defence of the managing director of Shows, Limited, the company which "ran" the show called and sued as "Savage South Africa" could enable a judgment against either himself or Savage South Africa to be executed against "Shows, Limited", and there are passages in some of the judgments which seem to imply that it could not.'[87]

[12.34] In *Re A Debtor Summons*,[88] the proceedings were issued against, inter alia, 'Sealy, Bryers and Walker', which had been the name of a partnership, whose business had been taken over 40 years earlier by a company called 'Alex Thom and Company, Limited'. The action was unsuccessful and costs were awarded to the defendants. The enforcement of this award was sought by means of a debtors summons under the bankruptcy legislation. However in the Supreme Court,[89] FitzGibbon J noted that if the plaintiff had recovered judgment in the action, it would have been impossible for him to execute the judgment since:

> '[a] judgment against a name, which is not that of any existing firm, in an action in which no individual has been served as, has appeared as, has admitted that he is, or has been adjudged to be, a partner, is, in my opinion, absolutely null and void and unenforceable; and especially must this be the case where the party whose liability in such a case is alleged is a limited company which has never been connected with the proceedings.'

[12.35] Kennedy CJ noted that:

> 'The only question which might arise would be that of amending the proceedings in favour of Alex Thom and Company, Limited, by inserting the name of the company as a defendant, a course which would require the amendment of every single step in the action from writ to the judgment. I cannot imagine any Court in its discretion acceding to that request after judgment.'[90]

[12.36] Of course the more usual option will be for the court to amend the proceedings before judgment is issued, as happened in *Kent Adhesive Products Company v Ryan*,[91] where individuals were sued, instead of a company, through the failure of the individuals

---

84 Order XVI, r 14 of the Rules of the Supreme Court Ireland 1891.
85 Order IX, r 9 of the Rules of the Supreme Court Ireland 1891.
86 *Re A Debtor Summons* [1929] IR 139.
87 *Re A Debtor Summons* [1929] IR 139 at 148.
88 *Re A Debtor Summons* [1929] IR 139.
89 Kennedy CJ and Fitzgibbon J. Murnaghan J dissented on the grounds that he would allow this error of mis-description to be corrected.
90 *Re A Debtor Summons* [1929] IR 139 at 145.
91 *Kent Adhesive Products Company v Ryan* (5 November 1993) HC.

concerned to ensure that their stationery complied with the Registration of Business Names Act 1963.[92]

Appearance by a partnership being sued

[12.37] Once the partners have been served as partners in the firm name, Ord 14, r 5 requires them to make an appearance[93] in their own name and not in the firm name.[94] However, after such appearances have been made, the proceedings continue in the firm name.[95] Where a summons is served on a person who had control or management of the partnership business, he need not make an appearance, unless he is a partner in the firm.[96]

Appearance by putative partner

[12.38] Order 14, r 7(1) provides that where a person is served as a partner, but he denies that he is such, he may enter an appearance which states that he is making the appearance as:

> a person served as a partner in the defendant firm but who denies that he was a partner at any material time ...

[12.39] This appearance is treated as an appearance for the firm, until it is set aside on the application[97] of either the plaintiff, on the ground that the person entering the appearance is a partner, or on the application of the putative partner, on the ground that he is not a partner.[98]

[12.40] Pursuant to Ord 21, r 7, a person, who denies the alleged constitution of any partnership is required to deny it specifically in his defence.

Appearance by person who is not personally served and denies partnership?

[12.41] Only a person who is served as a partner should appear and, as has been noted, Ord 14, r 7 permits that person to appear and at the same time deny that he was a partner at the material time. As a general rule, a person who denies that he is a partner in an enterprise should not enter an appearance, if he is not personally served in the proceedings. This is because a person, who is not served as a partner, but who enters an

---

[92] In that case, the defendants failed to put their company name on the stationery of the company. See generally in relation to the amendment of proceedings, RSC, Ord 28 and Ó Floinn, *Practice and Procedure in the Superior Courts* (2nd edn, 2008) at pp 267 et seq; Delany and McGrath, *Civil Procedure in the Superior Courts* (3rd edn, 2012) at para 5-153 et seq.

[93] As to appearances generally see RSC, Ord 12. A managing partner of a partnership may authorise the firm's solicitor to enter an appearance for all the partners in the firm: *Tomlinson v Broadsmith* [1896] 1 QB 386.

[94] The equivalent rule in the Circuit Court is RCC, Ord 8, rule 4, and in the District Court is RDC, Ord 43, r 22.

[95] RSC, Ord 14, r 5.

[96] RSC, Ord 14, r 6.

[97] Such an application is by way of motion on notice to the other parties to the action: RSC, Ord 52.

[98] RSC, Ord 14, r 7(1).

appearance, may be held to have thereby admitted partnership. This is clear from *Cullimore v Savage South Africa Co.*[99] There, the plaintiff brought an action for false imprisonment in connection with his attendance at a show called 'Savage South Africa'. A company called 'Shows, Limited' had put on the show. Fillis was the director, shareholder and manager of this company and Hardacre was its managing director. However, the plaintiff assumed that the business of 'Savage South Africa' was not carried on by a company and he sued the enterprise 'Savage South Africa' as a partnership in the firm name under the predecessor of RSC Ord 14, r 1.[100] Although it was not a partnership, it has already been noted that the service of proceedings (at the principal place of business of the enterprise upon any manager thereof) was deemed to be sufficient service under the predecessor of RSC Ord 14, r 3.[101] The plaintiff served the proceedings personally on Fillis.[102] Hardacre, although not personally served, entered an appearance. The observations of FitzGibbon LJ in the Irish Court of Appeal on the decision by Hardacre to enter an appearance are equally applicable today to a person who denies being a partner and who is not personally served or deemed[103] to be served as a partner:

> '[A] person who is not a partner, or who alleges that he is not a partner, should not enter an appearance, because appearance admits service, and Hardacre cannot have been served unless Fillis was either a co-partner with him, or was the person who had the management of a business in which Hardacre was a partner. I therefore cannot agree ... that the defence was open to Hardacre of denying that he was a member of a partnership which carried on business under the name of "Savage South Africa".'[104]

Waiver of defective appearance by defendant firm

[12.42] Even where the partners in a firm fail to appear in their own names as required by Ord 14, r 5, the plaintiffs may, by their own conduct, be estopped from subsequently relying on this defective appearance. This was the case in *Brown Brothers & Co v*

---

99   *Cullimore v Savage South Africa Co* [1903] 2 IR 589. Note that the reliance in that case by the Irish Court of Appeal on *Davies & Co v André* (1890) 24 QBD 598 must now be treated with caution in view of the terms of RSC, Ord 14, r 7. See fn **102** below.

100   Order XVI, r 14 of the Rules of the Supreme Court Ireland 1891.

101   Order IX, r 9 of the Rules of the Supreme Court Ireland 1891.

102   Now, under RSC Ord 14, r 7, where a person is 'served as a partner' or deemed to be so served, he is permitted to challenge the validity of the proceedings by entering an appearance, denying that he is a partner at the material time. In this case, this possibility was not open to Fillis as no equivalent of RSC, Ord 14, r 7 existed at that time. Note that reliance was placed on the case of *Davies & Co v André* (1890) 24 QBD 598, which has since been overruled in part by the introduction of RSC, Ord 14, r 7. However the principle underlying *Davies & Co v André* is still applicable to the case of a person who is not personally served or deemed to be served as a partner and who enters an appearance. For example this would be the case, where a firm is sued, not in its firm name, but in the name of some of the partners. Applying FitzGibbon LJ's logic, a person who was not so served who is claimed to be a partner should not enter an appearance to deny this fact.

103   Note that a person who is a member of a partnership will be *deemed* to have been personally served by service in the firm name: RSC, Ord 14, r 3.

104   *Davies & Co v André* (1890) 24 QBD 598 at 641.

Ballantine Brothers.[105] There, the plaintiff served proceedings on the firm of Ballantine Brothers in the firm name. However, an appearance was made in the firm name, rather than individually in the partners' own names as required by the predecessor of Ord 14, r 5.[106] Subsequently the solicitor for the firm wrote to plaintiff's solicitor, claiming certain credits on behalf of his client which were rejected by the plaintiff's solicitor. The plaintiff claimed that the appearance was made contrary to the predecessor of RSC Ord 14, r 5 and that it should be set aside. In the High Court, Fitzgerald J held that the irregularity in the appearance was waived by the subsequent correspondence and that the defendants should be allowed to amend the appearance.

Judgment against a firm

[12.43] The proceedings which have been taken against a partnership in the firm name may result in a judgment or order against the firm in the firm name,[107] which judgment or order will apply to those persons who were partners in the firm at the time of the accrual of the cause of action. Although the judgment is in form against the firm, rather than the partners individually, it is in substance a judgment against all the partners individually.[108]

Execution against a firm

[12.44] If the judgment or order against the firm[109] is not satisfied by the firm, RSC Ord 14, r 8(1) provides that it may be enforced against:

(1)   partnership property within the jurisdiction;

(2)   any person who appeared in his own name as required by Ord 14, rr 5 and 6;

(3)   any person who admitted on the pleadings that he is a partner;

(4)   any person who was adjudged to be a partner; and

(5)   any partner individually served as a partner,[110] but who did not enter an appearance.

Accordingly, execution[111] may be levied against the property of the individual partners without having to levy execution first against the partnership property.

[12.45] The power of a court to make a charging order in favour of a judgment creditor against the interest of a partner in a partnership under s 23(2) of the 1890 Act is considered in detail elsewhere in this work.[112]

---

[105]   *Brown Brothers & Co v Ballantine Brothers* (1878) 12 ILTR 70.

[106]   Ie Ord XI, r 3 of the General Orders of 1872.

[107]   RSC, Ord 14, r 8(1).

[108]   *Re Handford* [1899] 1 QB 566; *Western National Bank of City of New York v Perez, Triana & Co* [1891] 1 QB 304; *Clark v Cullen* (1882) 9 QBD 355.

[109]   It has been noted (para **[19.38]** et seq) that s 23(1) of the 1890 Act prohibits execution against partnership property, except where there is a judgment against the firm.

[110]   This would not include a partner in a firm which was served under RSC, Ord 14, r 1 by service in the firm name: *Re Ide* (1886) 17 QBD 755.

[111]   See generally in relation to execution, RSC, Ord 42, rr 10, 11, 25 and 35 and Ó Floinn, *Practice and Procedure in the Superior Courts* (2nd edn, 2008) at p 393 et seq.

[112]   See para **[19.38]** et seq.

Execution against persons who deny being partners

[12.46] A situation may arise where the plaintiff claims that he is entitled to issue execution against any other person 'as being a member of the firm', but who does not fall within the previous categories, often because the person denies being a partner. In such a case, the plaintiff may apply to court for leave to issue execution against such a person under RSC Ord 14, r 8(2). If the person disputes his liability, the court may order that his liability be determined in any manner in which any issue or question in an action be tried and determined.

[12.47] It is noteworthy that unlike the wording of RSC Ord 14, r 1 which applies to persons who are 'liable as co-partners' the reference in RSC Ord 14, r 8(2) is to 'a member of the firm' and not to any person being liable as a partner. For this reason, this rule has no application to persons who are alleged to be partners by holding out, since they are not members of the firm.

Restriction on execution against partners outside jurisdiction

[12.48] While RSC Ord 14 gives considerable assistance to plaintiffs seeking to enforce a judgment against a firm, there is a significant restriction on the application of these provisions to partners outside the jurisdiction. Order 14, r 8(2) provides that a partner, who was out of the jurisdiction when the summons issued, is not affected by any judgment against the firm,[113] provided that:

(1)   he was not served in the jurisdiction, or

(2)   he did not make an appearance, or

(3)   he was not made a party to the action under RSC Ord 11.

This does not, however, impact upon the execution against partnership property in which a partner, who is out of the jurisdiction, has an interest.

[12.49] The High Court decision in *Lindsay v Crawford*[114] is an example of a case where execution was successfully issued against a non-resident partner under the predecessor of RSC Ord 14, r 8.[115] There, two of the partners in a three-man firm lived in Newtonwards and Banbridge, while the third partner, Lindsay, was in London, but he had property in Ireland. As the plaintiff wished to make this property liable for the firm's debts, he applied for and got leave to serve Lindsay out of the jurisdiction and Lindsay made an appearance. No appearance was entered by the firm and judgment was entered by default against it. The court also granted judgment against the defendant alone. In doing so, it rejected Lindsay's contention that a judgment already existed in

---

113   This position appears not to be affected by the terms of the Recast Brussels Regulation (which is directly effective in Ireland) or the Lugano Convention (which is applied in Ireland by the Jurisdiction of Courts and Enforcement of Judgments Act 1988 (as amended)). Note that under art 8(1) of the Recast Brussels Regulation, the execution of a judgment against the assets of individual partners under Ord 14, r 8 is possible if the partners are domiciled in a state which is party to the Regulation *and* are joined under art 8(1) in the action against the firm.

114   *Lindsay v Crawford* (1910) 45 ILTR 52.

115   Order XLVIIIA, r 8 of the Rules of the Supreme Court (Ireland) 1905.

respect of the firm which he alleged was equivalent to a judgment against each of the partners, thereby precluding a separate judgment against him.

Where firms have common partners and actions between firms and partners

[12.50] Order 14, r 10 provides that Ord 14, rr 1–9 are equally applicable to actions between a firm and one or more of its members and to actions between firms having one or more partners in common. However, when it comes to enforcing the judgment or order in such cases, Ord 14, r 10 provides that execution is only allowed with the leave of the court[116] and before granting such leave, the court may direct an account or inquiry to be taken or such other direction as may be just.[117] Any action between a firm and one of its partners will of course be subject to the general reluctance of a court to entertain an action between a partner and his firm and where such an action is permitted, the court will usually require an action for account between the partners to be included.[118]

Garnishee order against a firm

[12.51] A garnishee order is a means by which a creditor, who has a judgment against a debtor, may obtain satisfaction for his debt. It does this by allowing the creditor to get an attachment order against third parties who owe money to the judgment debtor. RSC, Ord 45, r 1 provides for the issue of such garnishee orders.[119] The garnishee order may be obtained against 'any other person' who owes money to the debtor to answer the creditor's judgment or order. By virtue of RSC Ord 45, r 3, the term 'any other person' *includes* a partnership, where at least one of the partners is resident in Ireland. However, RSC, Ord 14, r 9 provides that a garnishee order may be obtained against a firm, even where one or more of the partners are resident abroad, provided that a person having control and management[120] of the firm *or* a partner within the jurisdiction is served with the garnishee order.[121] Any appearance by a partner is sufficient appearance by the firm.[122] Under Ord 45, r 3, the garnishee order against the partnership may be made in the firm name.

Garnishee order not available against co-partner

[12.52] While a garnishee order may be obtained against a firm in respect of monies owed by the firm to a third party debtor, it may not be possible to get a garnishee order in relation to the monies owed by a firm to a partner in that firm. This follows from the High Court case of *Foley v Toomey*.[123] There, the plaintiff was a creditor of Philip Toomey, who had no goods to answer the judgment or execution order which the plaintiff had obtained against him. The plaintiff sought a garnishee order against Philip

---

116 The court application is made by way of notice of motion to the other parties to the action: RSC, Ord 52.

117 RSC, Ord 14, r 10. The equivalent rule in the Circuit Court is RCC, Ord 8, r 6.

118 See generally in relation to actions between partners, para **[20.01]** et seq.

119 See generally in relation to garnishee orders, Ó Floinn, *Practice and Procedure in the Superior Courts* (2nd edn, 2008) at p 427 et seq.

120 As to what constitutes a 'person having control or management', see *Grant v Anderson* (1892) 1 QB 108.

121 RSC, Ord 14, r 9. The equivalent rule in the Circuit Court is RCC, Ord 8, r 5.

122 RSC, Ord 14, r 9.

123 *Foley v Toomey* (1953) 87 ILTR 141.

Toomey's partner, Denis Toomey. He claimed an attachment against so much of the debt which was due by the firm to Philip Toomey, as would answer the plaintiff's judgment and execution order. This application suffered from two defects, first it was based on the wrongful assumption that a firm and a partner may be in creditor/debtor relationship,[124] and second the correct procedure for the charging of a partner's share is an order under s 23 of the 1890 Act.[125] Accordingly, Murnaghan J rejected the application for the garnishee order against Denis Toomey and instead he amended the application by treating it as a summons under s 23 of the 1890 Act.[126]

II. LITIGATION IN PARTNERS' OWN NAMES

[12.53] Up to this, consideration has been given primarily to the ability of a firm to sue or be sued in its firm name. It is important to note that this facility, which is granted by RSC Ord 14, r 1, is optional and it is always possible for proceedings to be commenced in the partners' own names, but in such a case, all the partners should be made defendants or plaintiffs.[127]

[12.54] Whether proceedings are taken in the firm name or not, some general observations may be made about the different types of proceedings. An action in contract, where the firm is the principal to the contract,[128] or an action in tort, where the firm has suffered joint damage[129] or caused damage (in which case the partners are

---

124 See generally in relation to the nature of the partnership relationship, para **[3.05]**.

125 See generally in relation to the charging of a partner's share, para **[19.38]** et seq.

126 The order granted by Murnaghan J is stated to refer to 'Patrick' Toomey, but this must be taken to be a typing error and to mean Philip Toomey. He awarded costs to Denis Toomey.

127 In such a case, service would be effected under RSC Ord 9, r 2. See generally Ó Floinn, *Practice and Procedure in the Superior Courts* (2nd edn, 2008) at p 58 et seq.

128 See *McCalmont v Chaine* (1835) 3 Ir Law Rec (ns) 215, para **[12.56]n** et seq. See also *Corner v Irwin* (1876) 10 Ir CLR 354. That case involved an unincorporated mutual association rather than a partnership, and Palles CB (Fitzgerald, Deasy and Dowse BB, concurring) held that the manager of the association could not sue in his own name on a contract made with him as manager for his undisclosed principals. See also *Phelps v Walker* (1838) 1 Cr & Dix 141, in which Joy CB refused to allow an action on a bill of exchange in the name of the secretary of the Saint Patrick Insurance Company of Ireland, since the proceedings did not clarify that the action was been taken as secretary to that firm, rather than in a personal capacity. See also l'Anson Banks, *Lindley & Banks on Partnership* (20th edn, 2017) at paras 14-27–14-38.

129 See for example *Turkington and Ors v Telegraph Group Ltd* (13 November 1998) HC NI in which a solicitors' firm sued for defamation. Note, however, the effect of suing as a firm rather than individually since Sheil J held that '[a]s the plaintiffs have sued as a partnership, as they are entitled to do, they may recover for damage done to the reputation of the firm as a body, but not for any damage done to the reputation of individual partners ... the measure of damages is the extent to which compensation should be paid for the lowering of the standing of the firm in the eyes of right thinking members of the public and the injury to the feelings of the partners, but the fact that one partner may have been particularly affected by the libel is not material for it is the effect on the partners jointly which is to be the subject of compensation' (at p 6 of the transcript). See the statement of Lord Lindley set out in l'Anson Banks, *Lindley & Banks on Partnership* (20th edn, 2017) at para 14-39 that: 'where a joint damage accrues to several persons from a tort, they ought all to join in an action founded upon it', where he relied on *Cabell v Vaughan* (1699) 1 Wms Saund 291, *Addison v Overend* (1796) 6 TR 766 and *Sedgworth v Overend* (1797) 7 TR 279.

jointly and severally liable for that damage)[130] is usually taken by, or against all the partners in the firm. On the other hand, an action in respect of land is often brought in the names of the partners in whom the legal estate is vested.[131] Criminal proceedings are not usually instituted in the firm name, since a conviction in the firm name will be treated as a nullity.[132]

Where a Change in the Membership of the Firm

[12.55] Where the partners in a firm are being named as defendants, consideration may have to be given to including partners who have joined or left the firm since the accrual of the cause of action. This issue should be determined on the basis of the liability of the incoming and outgoing partners for the obligations of the firm which issue is considered in detail elsewhere in this work.[133]

Misjoinder or non-joinder of partners

[12.56] In this context, RSC Ord 15, r 13 provides that a claim against or by a partnership cannot be defeated by the misjoinder or non-joinder of partners to the proceedings. This principle is equally applicable to dormant partners[134] and partners by holding out.[135] Indeed, since proceedings may be commenced in the firm name, this issue will not even arise in many cases.[136] Order 15, r 13 simply reflects the pre-existing common law position in Ireland and, of course, the RSC, as procedural rules, could not affect the common law position. Thus in *McBirney v Harran*[137] the firm of McBirney, Collis & Co were the drawers of a bill of exchange and Harran was the drawee. On an action by the firm to enforce the bill, Harran claimed that, at the time that the bill was drawn, a person called Fowler was a partner in the firm and he should have been joined in the proceedings. In the Irish Court of Common Pleas, Doherty CJ refused to nonsuit the case on this basis.[138]

---

130   Partnership Act 1890, ss 10 and 12. See further para **[11.14]** et seq.
131   l'Anson Banks, *Lindley & Banks on Partnership* (20th edn, 2017) at para 14-42.
132   *R v Harrison & Co* (1800) 8 TR 508.
133   See para **[11.25]** et seq. See for example *Grantham v Redmond* (1859) Ir Ch R 449.
134   *McBirney v Harran* (1843) 5 Ir LR 428. See also *Leveck v Shafto* (1796) 2 Esp 468; *Lloyd v Archbole* (1810) 2 Taunt 324; *Stracey v Deey* (1789) 2 Esp 469.
135   *Spurr v Cass* (1870) 23 LT 409.
136   RSC, Ord 14, r 1.
137   *McBirney v Harran* (1843) 5 Ir LR 428.
138   But cf *McCalmont v Chaine* (1835) 3 Ir Law Rec (ns) 215 which concerned an alleged group partnership between two firms. The action, which was taken against the defendants, was instituted by one firm alone and the defendants claimed that the proceedings were defective since all the partners in the group partnership should have been joined as co-plaintiffs. The Irish Court of Common Pleas held that there was sufficient evidence of the existence of a group partnership for this issue to be left to the jury. See also *Sandes v Dublin United Tramways and Cruise* (1883) 12 LR Ir 206 & 424. Sandes took an action against Dublin United Tramways for money owed to his firm without joining his partner, Cruise, as a co-plaintiff. In his amended pleadings he named his partner as a co-defendant and in his statement of claim he stated that Cruise had assigned all benefit of the claim to him. (contd.../)

Service of Proceedings

[12.57] Related to the issue of joinder and non-joinder is the question of the service of proceedings on partners who are being sued in their own names. The principles applicable to service on individuals are applicable to partners who are being sued in their own names and reference should be made to the standard works on this area.[139]

III. SET-OFF

[12.58] In an action by or against a firm, the right of set-off may be raised as a defence. The right of set-off in a bankruptcy situation is considered elsewhere in this work.[140] In this section, brief reference will be made to set-off between firms, partners and third parties in non-bankruptcy situations.

[12.59] Before the right to set-off debts arises, there must be a mutuality of debts,[141] ie they must be owed by and to the same person in the same right. Thus, if the debt in question is not owed to and by the firm, but, for example, to a partner personally, that debt cannot be set off by the firm against a debt owed by the firm.[142] In *McCully v*

---

138 (\...contd) An objection by Cruise to being named as a defendant was allowed by the Irish Court of Appeal since the statement of claim did not contain any allegation that Cruise was interested in the subject matter of the case nor did it aver that Cruise had refused to join Sandes as a co-plaintiff and no relief was claimed against Cruise. In *Mulcahy v McCarthy* (24 July 2014) HC, the Court agreed that if a partner refuses to join his fellow partner as a plaintiff in legal proceedings, the plaintiff partner can overcome this issue by joining his partner as a defendant, Such joinder would take place under RSC, Ord 15, r 13. This judgment cited with approval the decision in *Cullen v Knowles* [1898] 2 QB 380.

139 See RSC, Ord 9 and generally Ó Floinn, *Practice and Procedure in the Superior Courts* (2nd edn, 2008) at p 58 et seq. The following cases, which deal with the substitution of service on a partner out of the jurisdiction, are of limited relevance since this issue is now governed by RSC, Ord 14, r 3 (which now deems service on a firm in the firm name as good service upon the firm, whether any members are out of the jurisdiction or not (see para **[12.30]**)): *Nolan v Fitzgerald* (1851) 2 Ir CLR 79; *McCann v Thomson* (1847) 11 Ir LR 201; *Thompson v Haughton* (1848) 11 Ir LR 201; *Fairlie v Quin and Lewis* (1839) Smythe 189; *Flaherty v Grierson* (1834) 2 Ir Law Rec (ns) 124; *Grant v Prosser and Prosser* (1824) Sm & Bat 95; *Nugent v Williams* (1835) 3 Ir Law Rec (ns) 275; *Murray v S Moore and D Moore* (1835) 1 Jones Ir Ex R 129; *Re Scott Brothers* (1852) 19 LTOS 149; *Murphy v Crewsdon and Swainston* (1845) 8 Ir LR 161; *Moore v Johnston* (1892) 26 ILTR 92; *Re Bell and Bell* (1836) 5 Ir Law Rec (ns) 200; *McKenny v Mark and Mark* (1839) 2 Ir LR 161; *Seymour v Donnelly* (1857) 2 Ir Jur (ns) 186; *Oldham v Shaw* (1841) 4 Ir LR 1; *Bradley v Alder* (1829) 2 Ir Law Rec 348.

140 See para **[27.84]**.

141 *In the matter of Irish Shipping* [1986] ILRM 518; *Incorporated Law Society of Ireland v O'Connor* (24 June 1994) HC, aff'd (25 November 1994) SC. See generally Breslin, *Banking Law* (3rd edn, 2013) at para 8-13 et seq; Johnston and Werlen, *Set-Off Law and Practice* (2nd edn, 2010) at Chapter 18.

142 If the debt is owed jointly and severally by the partners, there will be a mutuality of debts and it may be set off against the separate debt of one partner: *Owen v Wilkinson* (1858) 28 LJCP 3. Note, however, that a plaintiff may not prevent a firm from raising set-off as a defence by choosing to sue only one of the partners, since the partner sued may require his partners to be joined as parties: *Robinson v Geisel* [1894] 2 QB 685 and see also RSC Ord 15.

Green,[143] the plaintiff brought an action for monies which were due to him from the defendant firm. The defendant firm claimed a set-off in respect of monies owed by the plaintiff to one of the partners. The set-off was rejected by FitzGibbon J who observed that:

> 'This set-off cannot be maintained. It is clearly law that where an action is brought against a partnership, one of the partners cannot come in with a debt which is due by the plaintiff to him privately, outside of the partnership, and by setting it off claim thus to defeat the claim against the firm.'[144]

[12.60] Similarly in *Jackson v Yeats*,[145] an executor sought to retain a legacy which had been bequeathed to the legatee, in satisfaction of sums owed by the legatee, not to the testator, but to the Sligo firm of Pollexfen & Co, in which the testator was a partner. In the High Court, Barton J rejected the application for set-off on the grounds of the absence of mutuality since the legatee was not indebted to the testator.

[12.61] The right of set-off by and against partnerships is of considerable practical importance for banks which hold partnership accounts on the one hand and accounts for the partners personally on the other hand. In the absence of any agreement, it is clear that any sum due to the bank by the firm on the partnership account cannot be set-off against sums due by the bank to the partners on their personal accounts or vice versa.[146]

[12.62] Regarding a right of set-off between former partners following the dissolution of a partnership, *Hurst v Bennett*[147] concerned a claim by four partners in a dissolved law firm, who were trustees of the firm's lease of a property in Covent Garden, against one of the former partners (Mr Hurst) under the terms of an indemnity given by all the partners to the trustees of the lease. The key clause of the partnership agreement provided as follows:

> 'The legal estate in all freehold or leasehold property acquired for the purpose of the partnership ... shall be vested in the partners upon trust for sale or in some of the partners as trustees for all the partners and the net proceeds of sale and the rent and profits until sale shall form part of the partnership assets and the trustees shall be entitled to be indemnified by the partnership against the rent and all outgoings in respect of the said property and the costs and expenses of observing the covenants relating thereto.'

Mr Hurst alleged that he should be entitled to set off sums which were owed to him on the taking of a partnership account against that claim. The High Court held that the trustees' claim was *qua* trustees holding property in trust for the partnership, and not *qua* partners, and therefore Mr Hurst did not have a valid counterclaim or cross-demand to that claim in respect of amounts he claimed were owed to him by the partnership. Mr Hurst appealed and the Court of Appeal unanimously dismissed the appeal. Both Arden LJ and Gibson LJ shared the view that set-off was only available when there was a mutuality of debts and that there was no mutuality in this case. However, Sir Christopher Staughton was unconvinced on the question of mutuality. His view was that the trustees

---

143 *McCully v Green* (1897) 32 ILTR 14.

144 *McCully v Green* (1897) 32 ILTR 14 at 15.

145 *Jackson v Yeats* [1912] 1 IR 267.

146 *Cavendish v Greaves* (1857) 27 LJ Ch 314; *Watts v Christie* (1849) 18 LJ Ch 173.

147 *Hurst v Bennett* [2001] BPIR 89 (HC) (Mr Justice Ferris), [2001] EWCA Civ 182.

were not claiming trust money, but were instead seeking compensation for a loss that they had suffered, and would pocket that compensation themselves. He did, however, also hold that Mr Hurst should not be allowed to claim set-off, but his finding was on the grounds that as no partnership account had been taken, there was no reason to believe that Mr Hurst would be owed money by the other partners.[148]

[12.63] Finally, it remains to be observed that a set-off may be allowed in a situation in which there is technically no mutuality of debts. This arises in a partnership where there is a dormant partner, but the active partner has led a third party to believe that he is acting as a principal and not as a partner. In such a case, the third party may be owed money by the active partner personally and at the same time owe the active partner money. The active partner cannot defeat the third party's claim to a set-off by subsequently disclosing that he has a dormant partner and thereby relying on the fact that the money which is owed to the third party is owed by the partner personally and cannot be set off against the money which is owed by the third party to the firm.[149]

---

[148] As to the taking of partnership accounts, see para **[20.14]** et seq.
[149] *Stracey v Deey* (1789) 2 Esp 469.

PART C
RELATIONS BETWEEN PARTNERS INTER SE

Chapter 13

Management Rights of Partners

INTRODUCTION

[13.01] It has been noted previously that before a partnership can be said to exist, there must be at least two persons who are 'carrying on a business'.[1] In this chapter, the rights of the partners to manage that partnership business will be analysed. In particular, consideration will be given to the right of a partner to participate in the management of the firm's business and to the manner in which management decisions are taken in partnerships. This area will be considered under the following headings:

    I.   The Right to Participate in a Firm's Management;

    II. The Decision-Making Process.

Overview

[13.02] Part C of this work considers the rights of partners inter se. The aptness of the description of the 1890 Act as a 'default partnership agreement' becomes obvious in dealing with the first of these rights (the management rights of partners). This area is governed by no less than five separate provisions of the 1890 Act. First, the right to manage the firm is established by s 24(5) of the 1890 Act. Then the exercise and extent of this right is clarified by s 24(8) (majority voting on ordinary matters), s 24(7) (consent of all partners required for the admission of a new partner), s 24(6) (partners not entitled to be paid for acting in the partnership business) and s 25 (the expulsion of a partner is not permitted without an express power to do so). Although this chapter considers the extent of these default provisions, it must always be remembered that each of them may be modified by express or implicit agreement amongst the partners in a particular case.[2]

I. THE RIGHT TO PARTICIPATE IN A FIRM'S MANAGEMENT

Right of Every Partner to Management Participation

[13.03] A basic principle of partnership law is that unless otherwise agreed, all partners are equal. Therefore, rights and duties of partners will only be different where such differences have been expressly or implicitly agreed to by the partners.[3] In the context of financial rights, this principle of equality has been recognised by the Supreme Court, where O'Byrne J stated that '[i]n law, and subject to the express terms of the partnership deed as to the distribution of profits and otherwise all the partners are equal'.[4]

---

[1]   Partnership Act 1890, s 1(1), and see generally para **[2.38]**.

[2]   See further regarding the variation of the rights of partners, para **[5.14]**.

[3]   See the Partnership Act 1890, ss 24 and 19 and para **[14.05]**.

[4]   In *O'Dwyer, Inspector of Taxes v Cafolla & Co* [1949] IR 210 at 241.

[13.04] However, this rule of equality is also applicable to non-financial rights and in particular to the right of a partner to manage the firm. Section 24(5) of the 1890 Act provides that, subject to express or implied agreement to the contrary between the partners, '[e]very partner may take part in the management of the partnership business'. Thus, in the absence of a contrary agreement, regardless of his seniority, his relative share of the profits or contribution to capital, each partner may participate in the management of the business of the firm.[5]

Management Participation is a Basic Right

[13.05] It has been noted previously that a partner is liable to 'the utmost farthing of his property' for the obligations of his firm.[6] It follows that a partner should be entitled to have a say in the management of the firm and this also explains why the courts regard management participation as a basic right which is to be jealously protected. In *Shaw v O'Higgins*,[7] the management rights of one partner in a firm were infringed by his co-partner who removed partnership money from the common fund to his own separate fund for safe-keeping. Accordingly, MacMahon MR granted an injunction to prevent either partner from excluding the other from the management of the firm.

[13.06] In *Re Murph's Restaurant Ltd*,[8] there was a quasi-partnership[9] between the petitioner and two brothers for the running of a number of restaurants in Dublin and Cork. However, the two brothers began to undermine the petitioner's position in the business. They did this by refusing to treat him as an equal and instead they treated him as an employee rather than as a partner. In the High Court, Gannon J held that the petitioner's right to participate in the management of a quasi-partnership was breached

---

5   The presumption of equality among partners in relation to the management of the firm was originally to be reinforced by the terms of the Equal Status Bill 1997. However, that Bill was declared unconstitutional by the Supreme Court (*Re Article 26 and The Equal Status Bill 1997* [1997] 2 IR 387). The Bill, among other matters, had purported to outlaw discrimination in relation to the admission of partners to a firm, a partner's right to manage the firm and the expulsion of partners. However, the re-drafted Equal Status Act 2000 contained no reference to partnerships as the then Department of Enterprise, Trade and Employment was advised that the partnership provisions in the earlier draft of the Bill had presented constitutional difficulties and were not required to transpose Directive 86/613/EEC on the application of the principle of equal treatment between men and women engaged in an activity in a self-employed capacity. The Department also felt that further consultation in the area would be necessary and disagreed with the views of certain members of the opposition that anti-discrimination provisions in relation to partnerships could instead be incorporated into company law. In 2004, s 7 of the Equality Act 2004 inserted a new s 13A into the Employment Equality Act 1998 with the result that partnerships are now prohibited (irrespective of the terms of any partnership agreement) from treating some partners differently to others on any of nine grounds: gender, civil status, family status, sexual orientation, religion, age, disability, race, or membership of the Traveller community. See, further, O'Mara, 'Equal Partners' Law Society Gazette, April 2004.

6   Per Lord Lindley, see para **[11.04]**.

7   *Shaw v O'Higgins* (1829) 3 Ir Law Rec 104.

8   *Re Murph's Restaurant Ltd* [1979] ILRM 141.

9   The quasi-partnership was a company, in which three individuals were the sole shareholders/directors. As to quasi-partnerships generally, see para **[8.67]** et seq.

by the two others and he approved Lord Wilberforce's view of the importance of the right of a partner to management participation, ie that:[10]

> 'so long as the business continues [the partner] shall be entitled to management participation, an obligation so basic that, if broken, the conclusion must be that the association must be dissolved.'[11]

Accordingly, Gannon J ordered that the quasi-partnership should be wound up.[12]

Management participation is a right, not an obligation

[13.07] Under s 24(5) of the 1890 Act, a partner has a right, rather than an obligation, to participate in the management of his firm. Accordingly, there is no requirement that a partner devote his full time or indeed any time to the management or business of the firm, in the absence of any agreement between the partners to that effect.[13] Rather, the amount of time which a partner devotes to the management of the firm is at his discretion. For this reason, it is common to have a term in the partnership agreement requiring the partners to devote their full attention to the firm's affairs, whether to its management or the general business of the firm.[14] However, it must be remembered that a partner who opts out of management participation may not rely on this fact to escape

---

10   From *Ebrahimi v Westbourne Galleries Ltd* [1973] AC 360 at 380.
11   *Re Murph's Restaurant Ltd* [1979] ILRM 141 at 154.
12   *Horgan v Murray* [1999] IEHC 65 was another quasi-partnership case which was concerned with the right of an alleged partner to management participation. Horgan, Milton and Murray were the sole shareholders in Murray Consultants Limited, a well-known public relations company. They were also three of the directors of the company but Horgan alleged that while there were other directors, all business decisions were taken only with the agreement and consensus of the three, who held regular 'partners' meetings' between themselves. When Milton and Murray sought to replace Horgan with Murray as the managing director of the company and to fundamentally change the way in which the company was run, Horgan sought a number of declarations, including one that he was in partnership with Milton and Murray in Murray Consultants Limited. Horgan also claimed that Milton and Murray had breached the partnership agreement which, he claimed, existed independently of, and prior to, the formation of the company. However, as there was no written agreement regarding any partnership between Horgan, Murray and Milton that existed separately from the relationship between them as co-shareholders in the company, counsel for Milton and Murray argued that all individuals who come together to form a company make some form of prior agreement between themselves to form that company, but such prior agreement is not necessarily a partnership agreement. Finding in favour of Milton and Murray, O'Sullivan J held that he did not see a basis to infer a partnership relationship separate to their relationship as common shareholders.
13   See further regarding dormant or sleeping partners and the right to take part in the management of a firm, para **[6.09]**. See also *Hodson v Hodson* [2009] EWHC 430 (Ch) in which Arnold J in the High Court of England and Wales noted that it is not a prerequisite to the existence of a partnership that a particular partner be involved in the management of the partnership (Arnold J's decision was affirmed by the Court of Appeal in *Rowlands v Hodson* [2009] EWCA Civ 1042).
14   See further regarding such terms, para **[21.96]**.

liability for the acts of the active partner. The misconduct of his co-partner is the misconduct of the partnership and for which he is jointly liable.[15]

Position of Large Firms

[13.08] In contrast to companies, in partnerships there is no separation between the owners of the business and its managers.[16] Thus in partnerships, the partners both own and manage the firm. However, in firms with numerous partners, it becomes unwieldy to have a situation where each of the partners takes an active role in the management of the firm. Accordingly, in larger firms, it is common to find structures which restrict the right of each partner to participate in the management of the firm. These structures are akin to those found in companies and usually involve the management of the partnership being delegated to a handful of the partners. Commonly, this is done by entrusting the management of the firm to the equivalent of a board of directors, known as a management committee, which is made up of a small number of the partners in the firm and which will often appoint a 'managing partner'.[17] This committee is entrusted with the day-to-day management of the firm, while more important issues of management are left to be decided by meetings of all of the partners.[18] In order to have such management structures, those partnerships must have a provision in their partnership agreement which expressly or implicitly excludes the right of every partner under s 24(5) of the 1890 Act to be a member of the management committee.

Where Right to Manage is Modified or Excluded

[13.09] Although an important right, it is clear from the terms of s 24(5) of the 1890 Act that the right of a partner to management participation is a default right, rather than mandatory. Accordingly, it may be excluded by agreement of the partners. It should be borne in mind that restrictions on a partner's right to management participation will not be effective with respect to any third party who deals with the firm, unless those third

---

15 See for example the judgment of Maguire CJ in *Re O'Farrell and the Solicitors Act 1954* [1960] IR 239 at 252–253 (which was overturned on appeal by the Supreme Court on constitutional grounds, [1960] IR 261).

16 See further in relation to the conceptual difference between the management of partnerships and companies, para **[8.69]**.

17 In *Best & anor v Ghose & ors* [2018] IEHC 376 an order was sought for the taking of an account of the dealings by a limited partnership (Bloxham Stockbrokers) in a fund on behalf of Mr Best. The account sought was, per Baker J at para 36 of her judgment, '...an account as long understood by the courts of equity, the giving of a narrative or an explanation in respect of transactions or events in the operation of the Fund.' Baker J, having regard to the 1890 Act, s 17(2) (see para **[11.34]** et seq), accepted that general partners who had retired from a limited partnership could have continuing liability for obligations incurred while they were partners, but noted that certain partners (who had been general partners in Bloxham Stockbrokers at the time that it invested in the fund) had never been involved in the management of the fund, and had no information or documents in relation to it. While Baker J accepted that this would not present a defence in other causes of action, in this particular case she refused relief against all partners other than the managing partner.

18 It has been suggested earlier that these partnerships might be regarded as quasi-companies and thus subject to certain principles of company law, see para **[8.105]**.

parties are aware of the restriction.[19] Where for example a third party is unaware of the restriction on a partner from signing large cheques, the firm will be bound by such a cheque, since it is within the implied authority of the partner to sign such a cheque.[20]

Remuneration for Management

[13.10] In the absence of any agreement or custom to that effect, there is no right for a partner, whether a managing partner or not, to receive remuneration for his management of the firm. In *Hutcheson v Smith*,[21] it was alleged that the managing partner of a distillery firm in Armagh should be entitled to an allowance for his management of the firm. Brady CB rejected this contention, observing that:

> 'The first exception is as to the sum of £200 per annum, claimed by the defendant as resident partner, for managing the business and treating the customers. There is no evidence of any agreement to that effect as between the partners; but it is contended that this sum ought to be allowed to the defendant, as coming under the description of just and fair allowances mentioned in the decree. But there is no evidence that such an allowance is usual in the trade ... and I know of no principle which would authorise me to say that a partner is to have a separate charge upon the partnership funds for the management of the concern, where there is no agreement for the purpose.'[22]

[13.11] This remains the position today and while 'nothing is more common than a managing partner, and nothing unusual in an arrangement that he should receive something additional for his management',[23] if it is intended that a partner should receive remuneration for his management of the firm, this should be expressly agreed upon by the partners. Otherwise the default position under s 24(6) of the 1890 Act, that '[n]o partner shall be entitled to remuneration for acting in the partnership business' will apply. Thus in *Moore v Moore*[24] Master Ellison relied on s 24(6) to reject one partner's claim for a contribution for her additional work in running the partnership business during a period when her workload increased due to tensions between the other two partners.

II. THE DECISION-MAKING PROCESS

[13.12] Having established the right of a partner to participate in the management process, it is proposed to consider the nature of this management right and, in particular, the manner in which decisions are taken by partners. This issue is governed by s 24(8) of the 1890 Act which provides that, subject to express or implied agreement between the partners to the contrary:

> Any difference arising as to ordinary matters connected with the partnership business may be decided by a majority of the partners, but no change may be made in the nature of the partnership business without the consent of all existing partners.

---

19 Partnership Act 1890, s 8 and see generally para **[10.70]**.
20 See generally in relation to implied authority, para **[10.50]**.
21 *Hutcheson v Smith* (1842) 5 Ir Eq R 117.
22 *Hutcheson v Smith* (1842) 5 Ir Eq R 117 at 123.
23 Per Greene B in *Greenham v Gray* (1855) 4 Ir CLR 501 at 509.
24 *Moore v Moore* (27 February 1998) HC NI.

Section 24(8) contemplates two distinct situations, the first is where the partners are faced with decisions on ordinary matters and the second concerns partnership decisions which would change the nature of the partnership business.

Deciding on Ordinary Matters

[13.13] Under s 24(8) of the 1890 Act, differences as to ordinary matters may be decided by a majority of the partners.

'majority of the partners'

[13.14] By the expression 'majority of the partners' is meant a majority in number of the partners. It is important to bear in mind that it is not a majority on the basis of capital contribution, profit share, seniority or otherwise, but simply a majority in number. Similarly, 'a majority of the partners' means a majority of all the partners in the firm and not a majority of just those who are present at a particular meeting of the partners. However, since s 24(8) is a default provision, it is possible to exclude or modify its application to a particular partnership. For example a partnership agreement could provide that decisions may be taken by a majority of the partners who are *present* at a partners' meeting or that a decision may be taken by a majority of partners in terms of their percentage share of the profits.

[13.15] Where a resolution is passed by a group of partners which does not constitute a majority of the partners, whether under the partnership agreement or under the default rule in s 24(8), that decision will be invalid.[25]

Exercise of management powers in good faith

[13.16] Like the exercise of any power by a partner, the right to manage the firm should be exercised by a partner in accordance with his overriding fiduciary duty to his co-partners.[26] A partner will be in breach of this fiduciary duty if he does not exercise his management rights for a bona fide purpose and in a bona fide manner.[27] Thus, the partners who form the majority in relation to a particular decision must give all the other partners the opportunity of being heard and an agreement by the majority, in advance of hearing the minority opinion, to ignore those views would be a breach of this duty of good faith.[28] In *Taylor v Hughes*[29] Sugden LC expressly adopted the following statement of Lord Eldon:[30]

---

[25] *Re London and Southern Counties Freehold Land Co* (1885) 34 WR 163; *Howbeach Coal Co v Teague* (1860) 120 RR 518; *Ex p Morrison* (1847) De Gex 539; *Young v Ladies' Imperial Club Ltd* [1920] 2 KB 523.

[26] See generally in relation to a partner's fiduciary duties, para **[15.01]** et seq.

[27] *Heslin v Fay (1)* (1884) 15 LR Ir 431. See also *Blisset v Daniel* [1853] 10 Hare 493 and generally para **[15.12]** et seq.

[28] *Great Western Railway Co v Rushout* (1852) 5 De G & Sm 290.

[29] *Taylor v Hughes* (1844) 7 Ir Eq R 529.

[30] *Taylor v Hughes* involved the plaintiff, a partner in the Agricultural and Commercial Bank of Ireland, who had sold his interest in the firm but the continuing partners had attempted to authorise a creditor of the firm, who only began dealing with the firm after the plaintiff left the firm, to enforce his judgment against the plaintiff.

'I call that the act of all which is the act of the majority, provided all are consulted, and the majority are acting bona fide, meeting, not for the purpose of negativing, what any one may have to offer, but for the purpose of negativing, what, when they are met together, they may, after due consideration, think proper to negative: For a majority of partners to say; We do not care what one partner may say, we, being the majority, will do what we please, is, I apprehend, what this Court will not allow.'[31]

[13.17] On the other hand, it is to be noted that the minority should not be merely obstructive, since after reasonable discussion, they may be overruled.[32]

'may be decided'

[13.18] The language used in s 24(8) (any differences 'may be decided' by a majority) is permissive in nature. Nonetheless, it is clear that, in the absence of any agreement to the contrary between the partners, this is the default rule which will apply and differences arising as to ordinary matters *must* be decided by a majority of the partners.[33]

'ordinary matters connected with the partnership business'

[13.19] Pursuant to s 24(8), it is 'ordinary matters' of the partnership that may be decided by a majority of the partners. What constitutes an ordinary matter will be determined as a matter of fact in each case, taking into account the manner in which that particular firm's business is run and how the business of firms of that nature are generally run. For example in *Highley v Walker*,[34] the taking on of a partner's son as an apprentice in a fabric spinning business was regarded as an ordinary matter within the terms of s 24(8) of the 1890 Act and therefore it only required a decision of the majority of the partners.

Unilateral termination of a partner's authority

[13.20] In view of s 24(5) of the 1890 Act (entitling every partner to take part in the management of the firm in the absence of contrary agreement) and s 19 (allowing for a change to the rights of partners only where all partners agree), it seems clear that a partner's authority to bind the firm cannot be removed against his wishes by his co-partners, unless such action would be an 'ordinary matter' and thus removable by a majority under s 24(8). It is contended that in most firms, it is unlikely that it would be an ordinary matter for a majority of the partners to be entitled to restrict the authority of a partner to bind the firm. Support for this view is to be found in the famous American partnership case of *Nabisco v Stroud*,[35] although in that case, the attempt to restrict a partner's authority was made by one of the two partners, rather than a majority. Nonetheless, the principle in that case would seem to be equally applicable to an attempt by a majority of the partners to unilaterally terminate a partner's authority to bind the firm. There, Freeman and Stroud were involved in a grocery store partnership and regularly ordered bread from the plaintiff. However, at one stage during the partnership

---

[31] *Const v Harris* (1824) T & R 496 at 525.
[32] *Wall v London and Northern Assets Corporation* [1898] 2 Ch 469.
[33] See for example *Highley v Walker* (1910) 26 TLR 685.
[34] *Highley v Walker* (1910) 26 TLR 685.
[35] *Nabisco v Stroud* 249 NC 467, 106 SE 2d 692 (1959).

Stroud went to the plaintiff and advised it that he would no longer be liable for any bread which was sold thereafter to the firm. Nonetheless, at the request of Freeman, the plaintiff continued to supply bread to the partnership and when the firm failed to pay, it sued Stroud. It was held that Stroud was liable to pay for the bread, on the grounds that he was a partner in the firm which ordered the bread and his actions in approaching Nabisco did not affect his liability, since it was not possible for him to unilaterally restrict the authority of Freeman to bind the partnership. While, the result achieved in this case may appear at first unjust, it can be supported in principle, ie it is better to have a situation where third parties have certainty in their dealings with partners who are acting in the ordinary course of business, than to permit a partner or the majority of partners to restrict at any time the authority of his co-partner to bind the partnership. For the 'innocent' partner, who does not wish to be bound by his partner, the obvious solution is to dissolve his partnership and notify the third party of the dissolution.

[13.21] However it has been suggested[36] that one situation in which a restriction on the authority of a partner in a firm may constitute an ordinary matter, and thus could be done with the approval of a majority of the partners, is restricting the signing of partnership cheques to at least two partners.

Admission of new partners and expulsion of existing partners

[13.22] One important aspect of the management of a firm is the recruitment of new partners.[37] This area is dealt with separately by s 24(7) of the 1890 Act and therefore cannot be considered to be an ordinary matter of the partnership. Section 24(7) states that, subject to any express or implied agreement between the partners to the contrary, '[n]o person may be introduced as a partner without the consent of all existing partners.' As a default rule, this right is usually modified in large partnerships, where it is common for the senior partners or a majority of all the partners to appoint new partners to the firm.

[13.23] Similarly, the expulsion of existing partners may not be considered an ordinary matter of the partnership since s 25 of the 1890 Act provides that '[n]o majority of the partners can expel any partner unless a power to do so has been conferred by express agreement between the partners'. This default rule will commonly be replaced by a right granted to a stated majority of the 'innocent' partners to expel another partner for stated misbehaviour.[38]

Same meaning as 'within the ordinary course of business'?

[13.24] Under the terms of s 24(8), matters are decided on a majority vote if they are 'ordinary matters connected with the partnership business'. It has been noted previously that third parties dealing with a firm are entitled to assume that the firm is bound by the actions of one partner who does something which is 'within the ordinary course of

---

[36]   See the comments of the current editor of l'Anson Banks, *Lindley & Banks on Partnership* (20th edn, 2017) at para 13-32.

[37]   See further in relation to the admission of new partners, para **[21.105]**.

[38]   See further in relation to such clauses, para **[23.83]**.

business of the firm'.[39] It is contended that the term 'within the ordinary course of business' and the term 'ordinary matter connected with the partnership business' are synonymous, since otherwise this would lead to the unjustifiable position where a transaction could be deemed to be sufficiently 'ordinary' to be passed by a decision of a majority of partners, but not sufficiently ordinary for a third party to assume that it was binding on the firm. Such a conclusion would lead to a situation where different tests would be applied to the internal management of the firm than apply to its external relations with third parties and this cannot be justified in principle.[40] Therefore it is apprehended that, in order to determine whether a particular matter may be decided by a majority of the partners, it must be an ordinary matter connected with the partnership business which is synonymous with the term 'within the ordinary course of business' of the firm. The meaning of this phrase is analysed in detail elsewhere in this work.[41]

Where there is deadlock in voting

[13.25] It may happen in a partnership vote that there is a complete deadlock on a particular issue between the partners. In such a situation, the status quo will be preserved on the basis of the principle that those who oppose a change are entitled to outweigh those who seek to alter the existing state of affairs.[42] Thus in *Donaldson v Williams*,[43] it was held that in a partnership of two members, one partner could not dismiss an employee of the firm where the other partner objected. However, where there is deadlock, not just on one issue but in relation to all management decisions of the partnership, it will not be possible for the partners to continue in business together. In such a situation, a dissolution of the partnership may be granted by the High Court under s 35 of the 1890 Act.[44]

'change may be made in the nature of the partnership business'

[13.26] The second part of s 24(8) of the 1890 Act provides that, subject to contrary agreement between the partners, no change may be made in the nature of the partnership business without the consent of all the existing partners. No definition is provided of what constitutes a change in the nature of the partnership business. It is thought that examples of such a change in the nature of the partnership business would be a merger

---

39 See generally as to the meaning of the term 'within the ordinary course of business of a firm', para **[10.35]**.
40 For a diverging view, see the comments of the present editor of l'Anson Banks, *Lindley & Banks on Partnership* (20th edn, 2017) at para 15-05, where he states that emphasis is placed on the connection to the partnership business in s 24(8), rather than on what is needed to carry on the partnership business 'in the usual way', although he concedes that the use of either test may give rise to the same result.
41 See para **[10.35]**.
42 This principle can be traced back to the principle of Roman law, *in re communi, neminem dominorum jure facere quicquam, invito altero, posse*: Digest X: 3:28 (in a common matter none of the principals can legally do anything if any of the others are unwilling). See also *Clements v Norris* (1878) 8 Ch D 129.
43 *Donaldson v Williams* (1833) 1 Cromp & M 345.
44 See *Re Vehicle Buildings* [1986] ILRM 239 and para **[25.55]** et seq.

of the firm with another,[45] a change of a professional firm to a multi-disciplinary practice, or a sale of a substantial part of the business of a firm. Lord Lindley, in discussing a change in the nature of a partnership business, put the matter thus, 'no majority, however large, can lawfully engage the partnership in such matters against the will of even one dissentient partner'.[46]

[13.27] The Australian case of *Re Tivoli Freeholds*[47] is an example of one where there was a change in the nature of the business against the wishes of a minority of the members of a quasi-partnership.[48] The quasi-partnership was a company whose shareholders had more than a financial interest in the company, but also a somewhat vocational interest, since the company was formed for the purposes of running theatres. However, the company subsequently got involved in financially successful take-over raids of other companies. This activity was intra vires the company, yet the Supreme Court of Victoria ordered that the company be wound up in the light of the distinct interests of the founders.

[13.28] Similarly in *Bissell v Cole*,[49] the English Court of Appeal held that a switch from the business of a travel agency to a tour operator was a change in the nature of the partnership business and thus required the consent of all the partners.

If not ordinary business nor change in partnership business

[13.29] Section s 24(8) of the 1890 Act could have been expressed in more precise terms, since it is not clear what is required to take a decision on a matter which is not an ordinary matter connected with the partnership business, but is also not a change in the nature of the partnership business. To take an example, a decision in a law firm to convert a partnership asset into the ownership of one partner only is clearly not an ordinary matter connected with the business of a law firm. However, it is also not a change in the nature of the partnership business, since the partnership business will remain unaffected by the transfer of the asset. It is submitted that the conversion of an ordinary partnership of solicitors, or a legal partnership of barristers, or a legal partnership of solicitors and barristers, to a limited liability partnership under the Legal Services Regulation Act 2015, while involving a change in the liability of the partners in the partnership, will not of itself cause a change in the nature of the underlying business of the partnership.[50] It is suggested that situations such as these, which although not a 'change ... in the nature of the partnership business' may nonetheless not be ordinary matters connected with the partnership business, in which case they must logically be

---

[45] In any event s 24(7) of the 1890 Act provides that unless there is a contrary provision in the partnership agreement, no partner may be introduced into a firm without the consent of all the partners, see para **[13.22]**.

[46] l'Anson Banks, *Lindley & Banks on Partnership* (20th edn, 2017) at para 15-09, relying on *Attorney-General v Great Northern Railway Company* (1860) 1 Dr & Sm 154.

[47] *Re Tivoli Freeholds* [1972] VR 445.

[48] See generally in relation to quasi-partnerships, para **[8.67]** et seq.

[49] *Bissell v Cole* [1998] CLY 1443.

[50] Unlike the position in the UK, the Irish limited liability partnership will continue to be a 'partnership' for the purposes of the 1890 Act, rather than a body corporate with separate legal personality as it is in the UK. (contd.../)

thought of as extraordinary matters. It is explicit in s 24(8) that such matters cannot be decided by a majority vote. Even though it does not constitute a change in the nature of the partnership business, it is apprehended that it is implicit in s 24(8) that such extraordinary matters require unanimity, in the absence of any other agreement. This conclusion is in keeping with basic principles of contract, ie each partner became a partner for the definite purpose agreed at the commencement of the partnership and it is not possible for the other partners to force one partner to do something against his will which is not ordinarily connected therewith.[51] However, a legislative clarification of this section would be helpful.

---

[50] (\...contd) See l'Anson Banks, *Lindley & Banks on Partnership* (20th edn, 2017) at para 10-116 where it is noted that the change from a partnership to an LLP in the UK usually necessitates a dissolution of the firm, and the transfer of its assets and liabilities to a new third party (ie the LLP). As such, absent provision to the contrary in the partnership agreement, it would seem that a decision to change a business from one carried out by a UK partnership to one carried out by a UK LLP is likely to require the consent of all existing partners.

[51] See also Lord Lindley's statement, set out in l'Anson Banks, *Lindley & Banks on Partnership* (20th edn, 2017) at para 15-09, relying on *Attorney-General v Great Northern Railway Company* (1860) 1 Dr & Sm 154, that: '[e]ach partner is entitled to say to the others, 'I became a partner in a concern formed for a definite purpose, and upon terms which were agreed upon by all of us, and you have no right, without my consent, to engage me in any other concern, nor to hold me to any other terms ...'''.

Chapter 14

Financial Rights of Partners

INTRODUCTION

[14.01] Since the purpose of a partnership, by its very definition, is the making of a profit,[1] an important issue in every partnership will be the right of a partner to his financial entitlements from the firm. The importance of this right is reflected in the number of provisions in the 1890 Act which supplement this right, such as the right of access to the accounts of the firm[2] and the right to interest on any loan made by a partner to the firm.[3] In this chapter it is proposed to examine each of the financial rights of a partner and the consequent financial duties of his co-partners under the following headings:

    I.   Sharing of Profits and Losses;

    II.   Outlays and Advances by Partners;

    III. Payment by Firm for Services from Partner;

    IV. Payment of Interest; and

    V.   Partnership Books and Accounts.

Overview

[14.02] The financial rights of a partner are characterised by the fact that they are almost all default, rather than mandatory, rules which are implied into the partnership relationship by the 1890 Act. As such, they are subject to contrary agreement by the partners. The rights set out in this chapter will therefore apply untrammelled to partners who do not have a written partnership agreement and who rely exclusively for their protection on the terms of the 1890 Act. What pervades these financial rights is the view that partners are to be treated equally, since if they had intended it to be otherwise, they could have provided a term to that effect in a written partnership agreement. Thus, the default position is that partners share profits and losses equally and will not be entitled to interest on capital contributions, even where one partner has contributed substantially more capital than the others.

---

1   Partnership Act 1890, s 1(1): 'Partnership is the relation which subsists between persons carrying on a business in common with a view of profit'; see generally in relation to this requirement, para **[2.62]**. For an interesting analysis of the partnership bank account and the bank's legal relationship with the firm see, Jones, 'Joint Accounts and Partnership Accounts' (1948) 51 Journal of Institute of Bankers of Ireland 131. See generally Gilson and Mnookin, 'Sympsoium on the law firm a social institution: sharing among the human capitalists: An economic inquiry into the corporate law firm and how partners split profits' (1985) 37 Stan LR 313.

2   Partnership Act 1890, s 28, see para **[14.92]**.

3   Partnership Act 1890, s 24(3), see para **[14.53]**.

[14.03] While partnership law allows these default rules to be varied or excluded by the partners, it is contended hereunder that it will not allow the partners to exclude one financial right which is so basic that its exclusion would deprive the arrangement of its very existence as a partnership, namely the duty of each partner to render each other true accounts and full information regarding the partnership.

I.   SHARING OF PROFITS AND LOSSES

[14.04] Since partnerships are formed to make profits, perhaps the most important financial right of a partner is his right to share in the profits and his most important duty is his obligation to share in the losses of his firm. This is expressly dealt with by s 24(1) of the 1890 Act which states:

> The interests of partners in the partnership property and their rights and duties in relation to the partnership shall be determined, subject to any agreement express or implied between the partners, by the following rules:
>
> > (1) All the partners are entitled to share equally in the capital and profits of the business, and must contribute equally towards the losses whether of capital or otherwise sustained by the firm.

Assumption that all Partners are Equal

[14.05] It is to be noted that s 24(1) of the 1890 Act assumes, in the absence of contrary agreement between the partners, that all partners are equal. This statutory assumption reflects the pre-1890 common law, know as the rule in *Peacock v Peacock*.[4] One of the first Irish cases in which this rule surfaced is *Stuart v Ferguson*.[5] This case concerned one Thomas Ledlie who joined an existing two-partner brewery in Co Antrim. No formal agreement was reached regarding his share in the firm and Joy CB held that:

> 'In the absence also, of all evidence as to the amount of Thomas Ledlie's share at that period, we must, according to the rule in *Peacock v Peacock*, fix it at one-third.'[6]

[14.06] In *Horgan v Baxter*,[7] the High Court relied implicitly on the assumption of equality underlying the principle in s 24(1). There, the plaintiff and defendant were involved in a partnership which exported cattle to Italy. The defendant had not paid certain moneys to one of the customers of the firm and as a result of the failure of the customer to claim this sum within the limitation period, his claim had become statute barred. The defendant had not informed the plaintiff of the fact that he had retained the funds or that the claim was time barred. There appears to have been no agreement by the parties regarding the proportion in which profits of the firm were to be shared. Therefore, in implicit reliance on s 24(1), Carroll J held that the plaintiff, as a partner in the concern, was entitled to half of these funds.

---

4   *Peacock v Peacock* (1809) 16 Ves 49.
5   *Stuart v Ferguson* (1832) Hayes 452.
6   *Stuart v Ferguson* (1832) Hayes 452 at 466. See also *Walmsley v Walmsley* (1846) 3 Jo & La T 556 and para **[14.82]**.
7   *Horgan v Baxter* (11 May 1982) HC.

[14.07] This important rule that partners share profits and losses equally is a default, rather than a mandatory, rule so, as is clear from the introductory words of s 24(1), it is subject to any express or implied agreement between the partners.[8]

Rationale for presumption of equality

[14.08] The presumption of equality in s 24(1) applies regardless of the level of capital contribution of the respective partners and even where one partner makes no capital contribution. This presumption can be justified on the basis that even where partners contribute unequally to the capital of the firm, in the absence of contrary agreement, it is reasonable for them to share profits and losses equally, since they may bring other skills to the firm, such as client contacts, specialist skills, a greater work-rate, etc. There is no ready means of calculating the value of these attributes and in these circumstances, while an assumption of equality will not always be equitable, there is no other rule which suggests itself as being more equitable and in this sense 'equality is equity'.[9] Thus, even where one partner does considerably more work than another, the rule of equality applies in the absence of express or implicit agreement to the contrary.[10] The court operates on the basis that if the partners wished to share the profits (or losses) of the firm other than equally, they could have agreed in their partnership agreement to different proportions. In the absence of an express agreement, the courts will look to the other terms or the course of dealing to determine whether there is an implied agreement between the partners. The burden of proof is on the partner alleging the inequality of sharing.[11]

[14.09] In the English Court of Appeal case of *Joyce v Morrissey*,[12] a dispute arose between the four members of the rock band 'The Smiths' regarding their sharing of profits. The lead singer (Morrissey) and the lead guitarist (Johnny Marr) were the prime movers behind the band and alleged that they were entitled to 40% of the profits each, with 10% each going to the drummer and bass guitarist. They relied also on the fact that the group's accountants, Ossie Kilkenny & Co, had sent accounts to the drummer

---

8   And an agreement to the contrary regarding how profits and losses are to be shared will not result in a finding that a partnership does not exist: see *M Young Legal Associates Ltd v Zahid* [2006] EWCA Civ 613 in which Wilson LJ commented that, when one says that participation in profits and losses is not determinative as to the existence of a partnership, this does not mean that such participation is even necessary. See also *Hodson v Hodson* [2009] EWHC 430 (Ch), in which one of the defendants denied that she was a partner in a partnership (notwithstanding that she had signed a deed of partnership) and claimed that while she was entitled to 1% of the partnership's profits, this was a nominal amount that she had not received (although she acknowledged that she had benefitted from her association with the firm in other ways). Arnold J held that the sharing of profits is not a prerequisite to the existence of a partnership.

9   Per Sir Frederick Pollock, *A Digest of the Law of Partnership* (11th edn, 1920), p 81. This principle also explains s 24(4) of the 1890 Act, which provides that, even though capital contributions may be unequal, interest is not payable on capital in the absence of an agreement between the partners to that effect. See para **[14.53]**.

10   *Webster v Bray* (1849) 7 Hare 159; *Robinson v Anderson* (1855) 20 Beav 98 aff'd 7 De GM & G 239.

11   *Robinson v Anderson*, above.

12   *Joyce v Morrissey* [1998] TLR 707.

showing this split of 40/40/10/10. Waller LJ held that s 24(1) of the 1890 Act applied and the equality of profit-sharing could not be achieved by sending partnership accounts to one's partner and assuming that his silence constituted acceptance of the new terms, particularly where the partner might not be expected to understand the accounts without some explanation. With considerable understatement, Waller LJ observed that:

> 'Mr Morrissey undoubtedly felt that because of the more major contribution which he and Mr Marr were making, he ought to be able to dictate the terms on which the partnership continued. But he might not have appreciated certain fundamentals of partnership law.'[13]

Equality of profit-sharing even where a single venture

[14.10] The default rule that partners share profits and losses equally is also applicable in the case of partnerships formed for one-off ventures. In *Robinson v Anderson*,[14] two solicitors, who were not in partnership, were jointly retained by the same client to undertake litigation on his behalf. A dispute arose as to the division of the fees and it was held that, for the purposes of this litigation, they were partners, and the rule of equality was applied by the court to that case. What is curious about this case is the fact that the court did not find the default rule of equal sharing was varied by implication between the partners, since in that case the amount of work which was done by them was not equal and they had been paid separate and different amounts by the client. Accordingly, this aspect of the case might not necessarily be followed today, especially since s 19 of the 1890 Act expressly provides for the rights contained in the 1890 Act to be varied by the consent of the partners, which consent may be inferred from a course of dealing between them.

Where a firm enters into partnership

[14.11] Where a firm enters into partnership with an individual, the question arises as to whether the firm will be treated as one partner, so that the firm gets one half of the profits and the individual gets one half. The other possibility is that each of the partners in the firm is treated as being a partner in the larger partnership, so for example if it is a two-man firm, the two partners in the firm and the individual would get a one-third share of the profits each. In one case, it has been held that the presumption of equality will apply so that the firm and the individual will receive a half share each and the firm's half share must then be sub-divided between the partners of that firm.[15] However, it would be surprising if in a similar case today, the sharing of the profits were not subject to an express or implied agreement of the partners. Nonetheless, in view of the default rule, care should be taken in any partnerships between a firm and an individual to carefully set out the precise profit-sharing ratios.

Unequal sharing ratios do not revert to equality on departure of partner

[14.12] Where the partners have agreed to share the profits and losses of a firm unequally, the fact that one of the partners then leaves the firm will not result in the default position under s 24(1) of the 1890 Act applying between the continuing partners

---

13 *Joyce v Morrissey* [1998] TLR 707 at 708.
14 *Robinson v Anderson* (1855) 20 Beav 98, aff'd (1855) 7 De GM & G 239.
15 *Warner v Smith* (1863) 1 De GJ & S 337.

as regards the departing partner's share. Rather, if there is no agreement as to how a departing partner's entitlement to a share of the profits is to be divided between the continuing partners (other than it is to be shared between them), that entitlement will be taken by the continuing partners in the ratio in which they were interested in the profit share on the date of departure.[16] Again of course, it seems clear that this principle is equally susceptible to evidence of an implicit contrary agreement between the partners.

Income and Capital Profits Treated the Same

[14.13] The profits of a firm may be profits of income, which will be the normal profits of a trading or professional partnership, or profits of a capital nature, which may arise on the sale of a capital asset or on a revaluation of the capital of the firm.[17] Where the partners agree to share the profits of an income nature unequally, it is assumed that unless there is a contrary agreement between the partners, capital profits will also be shared in the same proportion.[18] Otherwise, if the equality of sharing in s 24(1) of the 1890 Act were to apply to the sharing of capital profits, one would have the situation, where income profits would be shared as agreed, for example 60:40, yet s 24(1) would require capital profits to be shared 50:50. The problem with this approach is that on a dissolution, s 44 of the 1890 Act requires the ultimate residue (which includes capital profits) to be divided 'in the proportion in which profits are divisible'. In this example, this would lead to the situation in which capital profits are shared 50:50 while the partnership continues but 60:40 on its dissolution. To avoid such an absurd situation, capital profits are assumed to be shared in the same proportion as profits of income, unless otherwise agreed.[19]

'share equally in the capital'

[14.14] It is important to note that while s 24(1) of the 1890 Act states that each partner shall 'share equally in the capital', this does not entitle a partner, in the event of a dissolution, to receive an equal share of the capital of the firm, if he is not otherwise entitled to it. Thus a partner in a two-partner firm, who has contributed only 10% of the capital of £1,000 of a firm, is only entitled to that £100 back. Section 24(1) of the 1890 Act, when it speaks of sharing equally in the capital, does not entitle him to an equal share (£500) of this capital on a dissolution, since s 44(b)(3) of the 1890 Act takes precedence over s 24(1). Section 44(b)(3) requires the firm to pay to each partner rateably what is due to him in respect of capital. This issue is considered elsewhere in this text in more detail.[20]

Equality of Profits is 'subject to any agreement' to the Contrary

[14.15] By the express terms of s 24(1) of the 1890 Act, the partners may either expressly or implicitly agree to a profit and/or loss share which is not equal. In the New

---

16   *Robley v Brooke* (1833) 7 Bli (ns) 90.
17   See for example the English Court of Appeal decision in *Popat v Schonchhatra* [1997] 3 All ER 800 at 805 per Nourse LJ.
18   See l'Anson Banks, *Lindley & Banks on Partnership* (20th edn, 2017) at para 19-21.
19   See l'Anson Banks, *Lindley & Banks on Partnership* (20th edn, 2017) at para 19-21.
20   See para **[26.116]**.

Zealand High Court case of *Brenssell v Brenssell*[21] Tipping J held in relation to the New Zealand equivalent of this section[22] that:

'[F]or there to be an implied agreement it must, in my view, have been something so obvious that no dispassionate observer could have been left in any doubt about what was intended on both sides.'[23]

[14.16] Thus, for example, the contribution by partners of capital to a firm in unequal proportions is not deemed to be an implicit agreement to the contrary so as to negative the assumption in s 24(1) that the profits will be shared equally. In such a situation, the profits will not be shared in accordance with the rate of capital contributions, but will still be shared equally. This point is worthy of emphasis since the natural assumption might be to share these profits in the proportion in which capital was contributed, in light of the practice under company law of shareholders sharing in the assets of a company on a liquidation in proportion to their share capital.[24] If the partners wish to share all the firm's profits (or just the firm's capital profits) in the same proportion as they contributed capital, a provision to this effect should be inserted in the partnership agreement.

Meaning of Profits

[14.17] Although s 24(1) refers to the sharing of 'profits', the 1890 Act does not contain a definition of what constitutes a 'profit'. However, the Supreme Court considered this issue in *Meagher v Meagher*.[25] In that case, Kingsmill Moore J adopted the classic common law definition of the term 'profit':

'If the total assets of the business at the two dates be compared, the increase which they shew at the later date as compared with the earlier date (due allowance ... being made for any capital introduced into or taken out of the business in the meanwhile) represents in strictness the profits of the business during the period in question.'[26]

[14.18] The High Court considered the meaning of 'profit' further in *Irish Life and Permanent PLC & Companies Acts*[27] by reference to the definition adopted by Kingsmill Moore J in *Meagher v Meagher*, with Clarke J stating that:

---

[21] *Brenssell v Brenssell* [1995] 3 NZLR 320 aff'd by the New Zealand Court of Appeal at [1998] NZFLR 28.

[22] Partnership Act 1908, s 27.

[23] *Brenssell v Brenssell* [1995] 3 NZLR 320 at 324.

[24] This mistake was made by the English High Court Judge, Neuberger J in *Popat v Schonchhatra* [1995] 4 All ER 646, as noted by Nourse J at [1997] 3 All ER 800 at 804.

[25] *Meagher v Meagher* [1961] IR 96.

[26] *Meagher v Meagher* [1961] IR 96 at 111, where he quoted from the judgment of Fletcher Moulton LJ in *Re Spanish Prospecting Co Ltd* [1911] 1 Ch 92 at 99. The case itself concerned the increase in the value of a number of the houses owned by a partnership of builders. Relying on the definition of profit in *Re Spanish Prospecting Co Ltd*, Kingsmill Moore J concluded that: '[i]t appears to me, therefore, that any increase in value of the assets of the business between the date of the dissolution and the date of realisation, which is attributable to the use of the assets ... is properly to be regarded as profits.'

[27] *Irish Life and Permanent PLC & Companies Acts* [2009] IEHC 567.

'As is clear from the authorities to which I have referred,[28] the general meaning of the word profit is that a company, partnership or the like has had an improvement in its assets, not explicable by a change in the amount of capital invested.'

[14.19] Thus, profits are most usefully considered as the difference between the receipts and expenses of a business for a particular period of time, and in calculating the expenses, account is not taken of extraordinary expenses such as capital and borrowings.[29]

[14.20] Despite the central role of 'profits' in the very existence of a partnership[30] and its continued life,[31] the meaning of partnership profits has received little consideration in this or other jurisdictions.[32] This is presumably because the partners will themselves agree on what constitutes profits and in the absence of any express agreement, generally accepted accounting principles will be the basis for determining what is meant by that term.[33] In general, therefore, it is preferable for the partners themselves to be as precise as possible in the drafting of their agreement regarding when, what and how these profits are to be shared. It is particularly helpful if at the time of the creation of the partnership, the partners enlist the services of their accountant to determine, for example, whether extraordinary expenses are to be paid out of ordinary income or out of borrowings or capital, whether work in progress is to be taken into account in determining the profit share of each partner, the value to be attributed to doubtful debts, the amount of depreciation of fixed assets, etc.

Profits may exceptionally include a partner's separate business interests

[14.21] Section 30 of the 1890 Act provides that a partner who, without the consent of the other partners, carries on any business of the same nature as and competing with the

---

28   *Meagher v Meagher* [1961] IR 96, together with *Buckley on the Companies Acts* (14th edn, 1981) and the judgments in *Re Spanish Prospecting Company* [1911] CH 92; *Drown v Gaumont-British Picture Corporation* [1937] Ch 402; *McClelland v Hyde* [1942] NI 1; *Rushden Heel Company Limited v Keane* [1946] 2 All ER 141 and *Wilson v Dunnes Stores (Cork) Limited* (22 January 1976) HC.

29   Since if account was taken of such extraordinary items, payment of the profits of the business could not be made until these items were paid off. Thus, there is no requirement to replace lost capital (ie where the capital contributions have been spent and are not represented by saleable assets) prior to payment of the profits: l'Anson Banks, *Lindley & Banks on Partnership* (20th edn, 2017) at para 21-03.

30   Partnership Act 1890, s 1(1).

31   Partnership Act 1890, s 24(1).

32   Although in former times, there was some debate amongst commentators about the meaning of profits: Story, *Commentaries on the Law of Partnership* (6th edn, 1868) at p 30, fn 1.

33   There is old authority for the view that profit is, in the absence of an agreement to the contrary, the net profit of a firm for a given year on the basis of the money which has been actually received by the firm during that year less any money which has been actually paid out during the same period: *Maclaren v Stainton* (1861) 3 De GF & J 202; *Badham v Williams* (1902) 86 LT 191. However, as noted above it seems likely that a court today would have regard to the approach of modern accountancy techniques to the meaning of the term 'profit'. It is also to be noted that this cash basis was rejected in the US, where it has been held that the accrual method of determining profits was to be used in the absence of contrary agreement: *McDonald v Fenzel* (1996) 638 NYS 2d 15.

firm, must account for and pay over to the firm all profits made by him in that business. Thus, if the other partners do not consent to such profits, they become part of the firm's profits. For this reason, where there is any likelihood of a partner receiving 'personal' fees for something which could be done by him in his capacity as a partner, he may wish to expressly exclude these 'personal' profits from forming part of the firm's profits. For example in accountancy and legal partnerships, where it is common to have the partners act as directors for client companies, the partners may wish to exclude from the partnership profits, any fees they receive from family directorships, since otherwise they will fall within the terms of s 30.

[14.22] Similarly under s 29 of the 1890 Act, in the absence of an agreement between the partners, a partner must account to the firm for any benefit derived by him from any transaction concerning the partnership or from the use by him of the partnership property, name or business connection. Thus, if the other partners do not consent to such profits, they become part of the firm's profits. For this reason, a partner may wish to exclude from the partnership profits any 'personal' profit which he makes from the use of business connections of the firm, since if he fails to do so, he may be required to pay them into the partnership profits.

Sharing of anticipated profits

[14.23] It is usual for partnership agreements to provide that drawings may be taken by partners on a periodic basis, normally monthly, in anticipation of future profits.[34] However, in the absence of such an agreement, the partners will be required to wait to take any money from the business until the profit of the firm has been ascertained at the end of the financial year.

Undrawn profits

[14.24] Unless agreed to the contrary by the partners, the profits of the firm which have been allocated to a partner, but not withdrawn by him, may be withdrawn by him at any time. A contrary agreement might arise where the partnership agreement provides for the undrawn profits to be used, for example, to fund a retirement annuity pension for the partners or to cover future tax expenses, by means of a reserve tax account.[35]

Obligation to Contribute to Losses Equally

[14.25] In addition to dealing with profits, s 24(1) of the 1890 Act also establishes that, subject to contrary agreement, partners are liable to contribute equally to the losses of the firm. A consequence of the equality of sharing of losses is that if one partner alone pays the creditors of the firm, he is entitled to a contribution from his co-partners. In *McOwen v Hunter*,[36] McOwen, who was a member of a firm called the Saint Patrick Insurance Company of Ireland, was sued by creditors of the firm for a partnership debt. He lost the case and had to pay the creditors of the firm the amount of the judgment. He

---

[34]   See further regarding such clauses, para **[21.66]**.

[35]   See also *Hopper v Hopper* [2008] EWCA Civ 1417 in which the Court of Appeal found that signed accounts clearly indicated that the partners had intended to add undrawn profits to capital.

[36]   *McOwen v Hunter* (1838) 1 Dr & Wal 347.

sought to be reimbursed out of the funds of the partnership and in view of the obligation of partners to share losses equally, Conyngham LC awarded him the sum which he had paid the creditors and his legal costs in resisting the creditors' claim.

'subject to any agreement'

[14.26] It is important to bear in mind that, while the presumption of equality applies to the sharing of losses, it is displaced under the express terms of s 24(1) by 'any agreement express or implied between the partners'. An implicit agreement to the contrary arises where the partners agree the ratio of profit share, but do not refer to the ratio in which they will share losses. In such a case, it is assumed that the partners also agreed to share the losses in the same proportion as the profits, rather than equally in accordance with s 24(1). As noted by Jessel MR in *Re Albion Life Assurance Society*:[37]

> 'It is said, as a general proposition of law, that in ordinary mercantile partnerships where there is a community of profits in a definite proportion, the fair inference is that the losses are to be shared in the same proportion. I entirely assent to that proposition, although it seems that no positive authority can be adduced in support of it.'[38]

[14.27] Support for this principle is now to be found in the terms of s 44(a) of the 1890 Act. This section, which is admittedly concerned only with the sharing of losses on the dissolution of a firm, states that losses on a dissolution are to be paid by the partners in the proportion in which they were entitled to share profits. It would not make sense for losses to be shared differently during the life of the partnership than on the dissolution of a partnership. This rule can also be supported in principle, since a partner who gains most by a greater profit share when the partnership is successful should also be liable for a greater share of the losses when the partnership is less successful.

Agreement as to capital contribution is not agreement to contrary

[14.28] The contribution by partners of capital to a firm in unequal proportions is not deemed to be an implicit agreement to the contrary so as to negative the assumption in s 24(1) that the losses will be shared equally. The losses will not be shared in accordance with the rate of capital contributions, but will still be shared equally.

Income and Capital Losses Treated the Same

[14.29] Just as income profits and capital profits are treated the same in the absence of contrary agreement,[39] so too capital losses are assumed to be shared in the same proportion as income losses in the absence of contrary agreement.[40] As has been seen, the income losses are assumed to be shared, in the absence of agreement, in the same proportion as the income profits.[41] It follows that where there is agreement only as to profit share, the capital losses will be shared in the same proportion as the sharing of income profits.[42] However if there is an agreement between partners to share losses of income in a certain proportion,[43] this is taken to be an implicit agreement to share losses of capital in the same proportion, thereby overriding the equality of sharing in s 24(1).

---

37   *Re Albion Life Assurance Society* (1880) 16 Ch D 83.
38   *Re Albion Life Assurance Society* (1880) 16 Ch D 83 at 87.
39   See para **[14.13]**.
40   Per Jessel MR in *Re Albion Life Assurance Society* (1880) 16 Ch D 83 at 87.
41   See para **[14.26]** and *Re Albion Life Assurance Society* (1880) 16 Ch D 83.

Losses are shared equally where no agreement as to profit share

[14.30] Where there is no agreement regarding the sharing of profits, there is no implicit agreement to the contrary within the terms of s 24(1) and the proportion in which partners share their losses is determined by s 24(1), ie equally. *Lefroy v Gore*[44] is an example of a case where there was no agreement as the ratio in which profits (or losses) would be shared. The case concerned the efforts of 25 individuals to connect Dublin to the West of Ireland by train. The intention had been to incorporate a company for this purpose, but no company was ever incorporated as the project was abandoned shortly after its inception. However, an engineer, who had advised on the venture, took an action for his fees against Lefroy, as one of the partners in the venture. Lefroy paid the engineer and then sought a contribution from the other individuals involved in the project. Sugden LC held that Lefroy was entitled to an equal contribution from each of his co-partners to the engineer's bill and his legal costs in defending the action.

Where partner gets indemnity from his co-partners

[14.31] In some instances, a partner may be indemnified by his co-partners in respect of his liability for the losses of the firm. Such an indemnity will not affect a partner's primary liability to third parties for the firm's debts.[45] However, when it comes to the internal sharing of losses between the partners, the effect of the indemnity will be that the indemnified partner will not have to contribute to the firm's losses. In this way, the indemnified partner may end up not having to share in the losses of the firm. This commonly occurs in the case of salaried partners,[46] who are indemnified in respect of any losses which they might incur as a result of being held out as partners.[47]

Where one partner is unable to meet his share of the loss

[14.32] If one of the partners in a firm is unable to pay his share of the losses of the firm, by reason of bankruptcy or otherwise, the other partners will have to make up this loss in proportion to their share of the losses.[48] This principle is also illustrated by *Lefroy v Gore*.[49] In that case, one member of the firm, Sir James Murray, was lawfully[50]

[42] It is apprehended that where there is an agreement to share losses in a specific proportion, different from the profit sharing ratio, on a dissolution the capital losses will be shared in this proportion rather than in accordance with the agreed profit sharing ratio and thus s 44(a) of the 1890 Act will not apply (capital losses shared in same proportion as profit share) but will have been overridden by the contrary agreement of the partners as envisaged by that section. See also para **[17.17]** et seq.

[43] It has been seen that where there is not express agreement regarding the proportion in which losses of income are to be shared, they are shared in the same proportion as income profits, see para **[14.26]**.

[44] *Lefroy v Gore* (1844) 7 Ir Eq R 228.

[45] *Luckie v Forsyth* (1846) 3 Jo & Lat 388, see para **[11.94]**.

[46] Of course, a salaried partner will invariably not be a real partner, see para **[6.18]**.

[47] See generally in relation to a partnership by holding out, para **[7.01]** et seq.

[48] *Lowe v Dixon* (1886) 34 WR 441; *Dering v Winchelsea* (1787) 1 RR 41; *Hole v Harrison* (1673) 1 Ch Ca 246; *Peter v Rich* (1629) 1 Rep Ch 34.

[49] *Lefroy v Gore* (1844) 7 Ir Eq R 228, see para **[14.30]**.

[50] The release was given in return for his agreement to testify in the litigation brought by the engineer, see para **[14.45]**.

released from his obligation to contribute to the firm's debt to the engineer who sued the firm. Sugden LC held that, in view of the fact that Sir James Murray was not liable for the firm's debts, Lefroy was entitled to ask the other members of the firm to rateably cover Sir James Murray's share.

[14.33] Where on a winding up of the partnership, one partner is insolvent and unable to pay his share of capital losses, the position is more complex and is considered elsewhere in this work.[51]

Where losses caused by one partner

[14.34] The fact that the losses of a firm are primarily caused by the actions of one partner will not prevent him from claiming a contribution towards that loss from his co-partners. This principle is illustrated by *Pim v Harris*.[52] In that case, the parties entered into a partnership for the purchase and sale of guano and they agreed to share profits and losses equally. A loss was suffered by the firm and Pim sought an equal contribution from his co-partner, Harris. The loss had been caused by Pim's purchase of guano at a higher price than he obtained on its resale and Harris alleged that since the loss was caused by Pim's default and negligence, he was not liable to contribute to loss. Chatterton VC held that the plaintiff had not been negligent and that although the loss was caused primarily by the actions of Pim, this fact did not prevent him from recovering from the defendant in respect of the defendant's share of the loss.[53]

Where one partner morally culpable

[14.35] While a partner will not be alleviated from his obligation to contribute to the losses of the firm on the basis that those losses were primarily caused by another partner in the firm, there is authority for the principle that where the loss was the result of recklessness,[54] wilful misconduct[55] or fraud,[56] an innocent partner will not be required to contribute to the loss, unless he has ratified the act in question.[57] Indeed, it seems that the guilty partner may have an obligation to compensate or indemnify the firm.[58] It is important to remember that one is concerned here with the rights of partners inter se, namely the right of a partner to seek contribution from his co-partners for a loss caused by him. The 'innocent partner' remains liable to third parties for the wilful misconduct of his co-partners.[59] It is only in relation to the issue of contribution to his co-partners that he may be exempt.

---

[51] See para **[26.118]**.

[52] *Pim v Harris* (1876) 10 Ir Eq R 442.

[53] On appeal, the case was also dismissed by Ball LC: (1876) 10 Ir Eq R 445.

[54] *Bury v Allen* (1845) 1 Colly 589 at 604; *Thomas v Atherton* (1878) 10 Ch D 185.

[55] *Re Webb* (1818) 8 Taunt 443.

[56] *Robertson v Southgate* (1848) 6 Hare 536.

[57] *Cragg v Ford* (1842) 1 Y & C Ch 280. As to the requirements to be satisfied for an act to be ratified see para **[10.77]**.

[58] *Bury v Allen* (1845) 1 Colly 589 at 604.

[59] This is because he is bound by the acts of his partners, regardless of whether they constitute gross negligence, wilful misconduct or fraud, if they are within the ordinary course of business of the firm. See para **[10.35]**.

[14.36] Where the innocent partner is the one seeking the contribution, it would follow from the foregoing principle that he can claim a 100% contribution from the guilty partner or, in the event of this being impossible, a contribution from the other innocent partners.

[14.37] The situation is less clear where the loss is caused by the simple negligence of a partner. For example what is the position of a partner who has suffered a loss because of his co-partner's negligence resulting in the firm being successfully sued? Is the innocent partner liable to make a contribution to the guilty partner, or where he has already paid damages to the third party, is he entitled to be indemnified by the guilty partner? There is no clear authority on this point in Ireland. It might be argued that once a partner agrees to carry on business in common with another partner, he accepts the possibility of mistakes being made and he cannot then turn around and seek damages from the negligent partner, if the act of negligence was carried out in good faith on behalf of the firm.[60] However, under general principles, there would seem to be no reason in principle why an innocent partner could not maintain an action for damages on the basis that the guilty partner was negligent *vis-à-vis* the innocent partner or that he breached the terms of their partnership agreement. After all, the innocent partner may argue that he owes him a duty of care not to be negligent and cause loss to the partnership as a whole. Therefore, once third parties are protected, as they are by virtue of the fact that all of the partners are primarily liable to them for the acts of a partner, it could be argued that there is no reason to prevent an innocent partner seeking to be indemnified by the guilty partner in this manner.[61] Support for this view is to be found in the New Zealand case of *Gallagher v Schulz*[62] in which the plaintiff and defendant were partners in the building of two flats owned by the plaintiff who was unskilled while the defendant was a professional property valuer with considerable experience of this type of project. The defendant encouraged the plaintiff to leave the organisation of the development project to the defendant and this resulted in a financial disaster. Williamson J awarded damages to the plaintiff for the defendant's negligence which resulted in his failure to ensure the

---

[60] Authority for this view can be found in the American cases of *Wirum & Cash Architects v Cash* (1992) 837 P 2d 692 (partner not liable for mere mismanagement); *Johnson v Weber* (1990) 803 P 2d 939 (general partner in a limited partnership not liable for mere negligence in connection with failure of partnership business); *Northen v Tatum* (1909) 51 So 17 (partner liable only for losses caused by fraud, bad faith or culpable negligence); *Snell v De Land* (1891) 27 NE 183 (partner only liable for loss resulting from wilful disregard of duty); and *Thomas v Milfelt* (1949) 222 SW 2d 359 (partner only liable for losses caused by fraud, culpable negligence or bad faith).

[61] This would appear to be consistent with the right of a court to determine the rate of contribution between wrongdoers on the basis of what is just and equitable under s 21 of the Civil Liability Act 1961, see para **[14.39]**. See the related area of indemnification of a partner for expenses incurred on behalf of the partnership (para **[14.40]** et seq) and the American cases of *Bras v Bras* (1972) 463 F 2d 413 (no reimbursement for improvement to partner's own land which benefited adjoining partnership property, without approval of other partners and *Ledbetter v Ledbetter* (1996) 476 SE 2d 626 (partner not entitled to be reimbursed for expenses that were allegedly attributable to the partnership business but that were incurred in violation of a clear provision in the partnership agreement that required the approval of his partners).

[62] *Gallagher v Schulz* (1988) 2 NZBLC 103.

timely completion of the flats and his obtaining mortgages at higher levels than were necessary. The only possible grounds for distinguishing this case from a typical negligence action against a professional partnership might be the fact that in this case, one party was clearly unskilled and arguably required the court's protection. Yet, it is thought that a skilled professional is just as entitled to expect a duty of care from his fellow skilled professional, particularly when all his assets are at risk from his co-partner's negligence. In the English case of *Tann v Herrington*,[63] Herrington (a chartered surveyor) entered into partnership with Tann (an architect). Herrington assumed responsibility for dealing with the firm's professional indemnity insurance and delayed notifying the insurers of a claim. The court found that Herrington owed a duty to the firm to exercise reasonable skill and care, adopting an objective approach to assessing that duty. As a result, Herrington was solely responsible for the losses suffered and could not recover a portion of these from Tann.[64]

Illegal partnerships

[14.38] When considering the right of a partner to seek contributions from his co-partners for a partnership loss, a distinction must be drawn between an act which is illegal and an illegal partnership. As has been noted elsewhere in this work,[65] in an illegal partnership (eg one formed for the purpose of highway robbery)[66] the courts will not countenance an action between the partners for a contribution or otherwise. This is because the partnership relationship itself is tainted with illegality. However, where the act which has caused the partnership loss is an illegal act (eg failure to comply with the Registration of Business Names Act 1963),[67] which does not taint the partnership, a contribution action may be maintained between the partners.[68]

---

[63]   *Tann v Herrington* [2009] EWHC 445 (Ch).

[64]   See l'Anson Banks, *Lindley & Banks on Partnership* (20th edn, 2017) at para 20-10 et seq for a discussion of the three potential categories of claims arising from a partner's breach of duty: (1) a firm incurs a potential liability because a partner breaches a duty to a third party, (2) a firm incurs a potential liability without any breach of duty to a third party, and (3) a partner takes responsibility for a particular aspect of the firm's business but does not show the required degree of skill and care in doing so (thereby causing loss to the firm as was the case in *Tann v Herrington*). Notwithstanding that an objective standard was applied in *Tann v Herrington* and also in the case of *Winsor v Schroeder* (1979) 129 NLJ 1266, as both of those cases would seem to fall within the third class, the current editor of *Lindley & Banks on Partnership* submits that a subjective standard should continue to be applied in each of these potential categories, save perhaps where a partner has a very particular skill in respect of which a higher, objective, standard is warranted.

[65]   See para **[9.03]**.

[66]   As in the case of *Evert v Williams* (1725) 9 LQR 197.

[67]   For example under the Registration of Business Names Act 1963, s 10, every partner in a firm which fails to register its business name, if required to do so by s 4, is liable on summary conviction to a Class C fine. See para **[3.84]**.

[68]   *Ramskill v Edwards* (1885) 34 WR 96; *Ashurst v Mason* (1875) 23 WR 506; *Baynard v Woolley* (1855) 109 RR 548; *Lingard v Bromley* (1812) 12 RR 195.

Civil Liability Act 1961

[14.39] The Civil Liability Act of 1961 places on a statutory basis the right to contribution between wrongdoers (including partners) in respect of an award of damages against one wrongdoer alone. Section 21 of that Act provides that where two or more persons are responsible for the same wrong, one person, who is sued in respect of the wrong, may recover such amount of contribution from his concurrent wrongdoer(s) as is deemed by the court to be just and equitable having regard to the contributor's fault. The court also has power under s 21(2) of the Civil Liability Act 1961 to exempt any person from liability to make a contribution or to direct that the contribution to be recovered from any contributor shall amount to a complete indemnity.[69]

II.   OUTLAYS AND ADVANCES BY PARTNERS

[14.40] As has been noted, s 24(1) of the 1890 Act establishes the principle that each partner is equally liable for the losses of the firm. A consequence of this is that if one partner pays more than his share of the firm's expenses, he is entitled to be reimbursed by his colleagues.[70] This principle, while implicit in s 24(1), is also explicitly stated in s 24(2) of the 1890 Act which states that subject to express or implied contrary agreement between the partners:

> The firm must indemnify every partner in respect of payments made and personal liabilities incurred by him –
>
> (a) In the ordinary and proper conduct of the business of the firm; or
>
> (b) In or about anything necessarily done for the preservation of the business or property of the firm.

Like the other provisions in s 24, this is a default rule rather than a mandatory one and therefore it may be varied by the partners.

'ordinary and proper conduct of the business of the firm'

[14.41] Under s 24(2)(a), payments or liabilities are only recoverable if they have been incurred in the 'ordinary and proper conduct of the business of the firm'. In cases of dispute as to whether expenses are incurred within the ordinary and proper conduct of the firm's business, recourse will likely be had to, inter alia:

(a) the description of the nature of the firm's business in the partnership agreement;

(b) the actual business carried on by the firm at the time the expenses were incurred; and

(c) whether such expenses are normally reimbursed by firms in the same business.[71]

---

[69] See generally in relation to contribution between concurrent wrongdoers, McMahon and Binchy, *Law of Torts* (4th edn, 2013) at para [4.01] et seq and Kerr, *The Civil Liability Acts* (4th edn, 2011) at p 43 et seq.

[70] See para [14.25].

[71] See *Hutcheson v Smith* (1842) 5 Ir Eq 117, considered at para [14.44].

[14.42] It is contended that the expression 'ordinary and proper conduct of the business of the firm' as used in s 24(2) is synonymous with the term 'in the ordinary course of the business of the firm', which is used throughout the 1890 Act[72] and particularly in relation to determining which acts of a partner are binding on the firm. In this context, the expression has been subject to considerable judicial analysis.[73] To decide otherwise would lead to the unjustifiable position where a transaction was deemed to be sufficiently 'ordinary' to be paid for out of the firm's funds but not sufficiently ordinary for the firm to be bound thereby. This would result in a different test being applied to the internal management of the firm than that which applies to its external relations with third parties, which cannot be justified in principle.[74] For this reason, for a discussion of the meaning of the term 'ordinary and proper conduct of the business of the firm', reference should be made to the discussion, elsewhere in this work, of the meaning of the term 'within the ordinary course of business of a firm'.[75]

Right to indemnity extends beyond technical dissolution

[14.43] On the technical dissolution of a firm,[76] s 42 of the 1890 Act entitles a former partner to the share of the profits made since his departure which are attributable to the use of his share of the partnership assets.[77] It is clear that the right of a partner in s 24(2) to an indemnity from his firm for his incurring of business expenses extends to business which is carried on after such a technical dissolution. For the purposes of apportioning these expenses between the partners, the former partner, who is claiming a share of partnership profits under s 42, is treated as a member of the firm. Accordingly, the former partner's share of the post-dissolution profits is adjusted to reflect any moneys which are owed to the continuing partners in this regard. The Supreme Court confirmed this in *Meagher v Meagher*.[78] This case involved a claim by a former partner for post-dissolution profits under s 42, and Kingsmill Moore J, delivering the judgment of the court, held that a deduction must be taken from the post-dissolution profits of a firm for:

> '(a) such portion of the sum realised as is attributable to any expenditure on the assets by the surviving partners out of their own assets and not out of partnership property.'[79]

Right to indemnity may include client entertainment expenses

[14.44] A type of outlay which may be incurred by a partner and which is likely to fall under the terms of s 24(2) is client entertainment expenses, an increasingly common expense in modern partnerships. The nineteenth century case of *Hutcheson v Smith*[80] is an example of a case where the client entertainment expenses were held not to have been

---

72 Most notably in s 10 of the 1890 Act, but for a list of the sections in which this term, or a variation of it, appears, see para **[21.38]**.
73 As to this caselaw, see para **[10.35]** et seq.
74 A similar argument has been made elsewhere in this text in relation to the meaning of 'ordinary matters connected with the partnership business' in s 24(8), see para **[13.24]**.
75 See para **[10.35]** et seq.
76 As to the distinction between a general dissolution and a technical dissolution, see para **[23.07]** et seq.
77 See generally in relation to s 42 of the 1890 Act, para **[26.63]**.
78 *Meagher v Meagher* [1961] IR 96.
79 *Meagher v Meagher* [1961] IR 96 at 112.
80 *Hutcheson v Smith* (1842) 5 Ir Eq 117.

incurred in the ordinary and proper conduct of the firm's business. In that case, Brady CB held that a partner in a distillery partnership in Armagh was not allowed to recover from his co-partners the costs which he had incurred in what was described as 'treating the customers' of the firm. He held that these entertainment expenses were not 'usual in the trade' at that time nor was there any agreement between the partners to allow them. This case might, it is suggested, be decided differently today in view of the modern approach of partnerships to client entertainment. In this context, the cautionary words of Staughton LJ[81] regarding reliance on nineteenth century cases are instructive. Although he was dealing with the question of whether an activity was within the ordinary course of business of a modern solicitors' firm, his comments are equally applicable to the question of whether the payment of certain expenses by a partner are reimbursable by the firm:

> 'That material should today be treated with caution, in my judgement; the work that solicitors do can be expected to have changed since 1888; it has changed in recent times and is changing now. So I prefer to have regard to the expert advice of today in deciding what is the ordinary authority of a solicitor.'[82]

'preservation of the business or property of the firm'

[14.45] Section 24(2) also provides for the firm to indemnify a partner in respect of payments made or liabilities incurred for the preservation of the business or property of the firm. Thus, any expenses incurred by a partner for the benefit of the firm's property or business may be recoverable under s 24(2). In *Lefroy v Gore*,[83] the release by a partner of a debt due to the firm, for the overall benefit of the firm, was regarded as being a liability incurred for the preservation of the firm's business or property. In that case, Lefroy was the partner who was sued by an engineer for his professional fees for his work on an abandoned railway project. In defending the action, Lefroy arranged for one of his co-partners, Sir James Murray, to give evidence at the trial in return for a release from Lefroy in respect of any obligation to contribute to any resulting judgment. As a result of the evidence of Sir James Murray, the engineer's claim against Lefroy was substantially reduced. Nonetheless, the other partners disputed Lefroy's claim that they should bear rateably Sir James Murray's share of the loss. However, Sugden LC held that, assuming that there was nobody else to call as a witness other than Sir James Murray, Lefroy was entitled to ask the members to rateably cover Sir James Murray's share.

Improvement by firm of a partner's property

[14.46] The contrary position to the incurring of expenses by a partner preserving partnership property or business is the status of improvements which are made by a firm to property used by it but owned by one partner in the firm. This matter is considered in detail elsewhere in this work, though it is to be noted that there is some support for the view that such improvements are deemed to be the property of the firm.[84] However, it

---

[81]   In *United Bank of Kuwait Ltd v Hammoud* [1988] 1 WLR 1051.
[82]   *United Bank of Kuwait Ltd v Hammoud* [1988] 1 WLR 1051 at 1063F.
[83]   *Lefroy v Gore* (1844) 7 Ir Eq R 228.
[84]   See *Burdon v Barkus* (1862) 4 De GF & J 42 and para **[16.44]** et seq.

could be argued that, applying the corollary of the principle underlying s 24(2)(b), the improvements should remain the property of the partner, with him indemnifying the firm for such improvements.

III. PAYMENT BY FIRM FOR SERVICES FROM PARTNER

[14.47] A related question to that of the repayment by a firm of expenses incurred by one of its partners in the course of the partnership business is that of the remuneration by a firm for services provided to it by a partner. This issue is covered in s 24(6) of the 1890 Act which states that, subject to express or implied contrary agreement between the partners, '[n]o partner shall be entitled to remuneration for acting in the partnership business'. Again this is a default rather than a mandatory rule, and in some partnerships, it is common for partners to be paid remuneration before becoming entitled to a share of the profits. If this is intended, s 24(6) of the 1890 Act must be excluded by having an express or implied provision to that effect in the partnership agreement.

Prohibition Extends to Allowance for Managing the Firm

[14.48] It is clear that the term 'remuneration for acting in the partnership business' includes managing the firm, so that there is no right for a managing partner to receive remuneration for his management provided to the firm, in the absence of an agreement or a custom to that effect. In *Hutcheson v Smith*,[85] it was alleged that the managing partner of a distillery should be entitled to an allowance for his management of the firm. There was no evidence of such an agreement between the parties nor of any custom in the distillery trade for the granting of such an allowance. Accordingly, Brady CB rejected this claim and held that:

> 'The first exception is as to the sum of £200 per annum, claimed by the defendant as resident partner, for managing the business and treating the customers. There is no evidence of any agreement to that effect as between the partners; but it is contended that this sum ought to be allowed to the defendant, as coming under the description of just and fair allowances mentioned in the decree. But there is no evidence that such an allowance is usual in the trade ... and I know of no principle which would authorise me to say that a partner is to have a separate charge upon the partnership funds for the management of the concern, where there is no agreement for the purpose.'[86]

Prohibition does not Extend to Acting in Firm after Dissolution

[14.49] There are, however, two instances in which a partner is entitled to remuneration for acting in the partnership business and managing the firm. The first situation is where the partnership business has been carried on by some of the partners after its dissolution. This principle has been recognised by the Irish courts in the context of claims by former partners under s 42 of the 1890 Act.[87] Under this section, a former partner, who has let his share of the partnership assets remain with the firm, is entitled to that proportion of the profits of the firm which are attributable to the use of his share. The courts have held that in calculating what is due to the former partner under s 42, account must be taken of the time and work of the continuing partners in earning those profits.[88] In the High

---

[85] *Hutcheson v Smith* (1842) 5 Ir Eq R 117.
[86] *Hutcheson v Smith* (1842) 5 Ir Eq R 117 at 123.

Court case of *Barr v Barr*,[89] one partner in a family grocery partnership in Donegal died and his personal representative took an action against the three continuing partners for the deceased partner's share of the post-dissolution profits under s 42. Barron J held that:

> 'Clearly in considering what profits the assets of the deceased in the Partnership produced it would be necessary to give credit to those working Partners for their labours in obtaining those profits.'[90]

[14.50] Similarly, in the Supreme Court case of *Meagher v Meagher*,[91] Kingsmill Moore J, delivering the judgment of the court, held that a deduction must be taken from the post-dissolution profits of a firm for:

> 'such amount of the total sum as is properly allowable in respect of the personal superintendence, management and exertions in regard to the partnership business by [the surviving partners].'[92]

Prohibition does not Extend to Breach of Duty to Devote Full Time

[14.51] The second situation in which a partner is allowed remuneration for acting in the partnership business is where the partners agree to devote their whole time to the partnership, and one partner is left to run the business on his own because of the breach by the other partner of this duty. In such a situation, the courts have held that the remaining partner is entitled to remuneration for his services.[93]

IV. PAYMENT OF INTEREST

[14.52] Under the law of lending, interest is generally not payable on sums advanced by one party to another in the absence of a statutory provision or an agreement to that effect (although, in some cases, an obligation to pay interest may be inferred, most usually in respect of an overdraft).[94] In considering the question of whether interest is payable by the firm to a partner for capital, advances or otherwise, one must refer to the 1890 Act

---

87   It has also been recognised by the English courts, and not just in respect of s 42 of the 1890 Act – see, for example, *Emerson (Emerson's Executrix) v Emerson's Estate* [2004] 1 BCLC 575 in which two brothers had carried on a farming partnership and, following the death of one partner, the surviving partner carried on the business and received a compensation payment following a livestock cull arising out of the spread of foot and mouth disease. It was held that this amount was a capital profit made after the dissolution of the partnership (to be divided equally) under s 24(1) of the 1890 Act, subject to payment of an allowance to the surviving partner in respect of the carrying on of the farming business.

88   See generally in relation to claims under s 42 of the 1890 Act, para **[26.63]** et seq.

89   *Barr v Barr* (29 July 1992) HC.

90   *Barr v Barr* (29 July 1992) HC at p 6 of the transcript.

91   *Meagher v Meagher* [1961] IR 96.

92   *Meagher v Meagher* [1961] IR 96 at 112.

93   *Airey v Borham* (1861) 4 LT 391.

94   *Shaw v Picton* (1825) 4 B & C 715; *Calton v Bragg* (1812) 15 East 223; *Gwyn v Godby* (1812) 4 Taunt 346; *Tew v Earl of Winterton* (1792) 1 Ves Jr 451. See generally in relation to interest, Breslin, *Banking Law* (3rd edn, 2013) at para 8-16; Donnelly, *The Law of Credit and Security* (2nd edn, 2015) at para 7-75 et seq.

and the terms of the partnership agreement. In the absence of any agreement in relation to capital or advances between the partners, the default position is set by the terms of the 1890 Act.

Interest Payable on Capital?

[14.53] Section 24(4) of the 1890 Act states that, subject to express or implied contrary agreement between the partners, '[a] partner is not entitled, before the ascertainment of profits, to interest on the capital subscribed by him'. Thus, even where the partners contribute capital unequally to the partnership (or where one partner fails to pay his capital contribution), no interest is payable on the capital contributed by the partners,[95] unless this is specifically agreed by them. For this reason, it is common to have a provision in partnership agreements that interest will be payable on the capital.[96]

'before the ascertainment of profits'

[14.54] A partner is not entitled to interest on his capital in the absence of an agreement to that effect. In this regard, s 24(4) of the 1890 Act codifies the pre-existing caselaw.[97] The drafting of this section is somewhat confusing and in particular the use of the phrase 'before the ascertainment of profits'. The section does not mean that a partner is entitled to interest on capital after the ascertainment of profits, regardless of whether the partners have an agreement to that effect.[98] The position is that interest is only payable on capital if the partners agree to that effect and where they agree, it is payable after the ascertainment of profits.[99] This position is consistent with the general assumption of partnership law that in the absence of contrary agreement, the partners are treated equally, even where they contribute unequal capital to the firm.[100]

Interest not payable on undrawn profits

[14.55] Where the partners in a firm have agreed that interest is to be payable on capital, it will only be payable on capital which is properly classified as such. Therefore, it will

---

95 See *Millar v Craig* (1843) 6 Beav 433; *Hill v King* (1863) 3 De GJ & Sm 418. The rationale for this principle is the same as that for the equal sharing of profits: see para **[14.08]**. For easier ascertainment of capital gains, the partnership agreement might set out the proportion of capital attributable to each partner initially and, if relevant, their respective shares in a particular partnership asset.

96 See generally in relation to such clauses, para **[21.74]**.

97 *Millar v Craig* (1843) 6 Beav 433; *Hill v King* (1863) 3 De GJ & Sm 418; *Cooke v Benbow* (1865) 3 De GJ & Sm 1; *Rishton v Grissel* (1870) LR 10 Eq 393.

98 The American Uniform Partnership Act (1914) provided that interest was not payable on capital (s 18(d)); however that reference was removed when the American Uniform Partnership Act 1997 (Last Amended 2013) was developed – that Act is silent as to whether interest is payable on capital – as such, it would appear that the partner can agree that interest may be paid on capital.

99 There would however appear to be nothing to stop the partners from agreeing that interest is to be payable on capital and that it is to be payable before the ascertainment of profits.

100 For example see the equal sharing of profits under s 24(1) of the 1890 Act and discussed at para **[14.04]** et seq.

not be payable on undrawn profits of the firm, unless such profits have been capitalised.[101]

Implied agreement to pay interest

[14.56] Under the terms of s 24(4), the agreement that interest is to be payable on capital may arise expressly or by implication. In *Pim v Harris*,[102] an implied agreement to pay interest was found, although in that case the funds in question were in the form of an advance rather than a capital contribution.[103] There, the plaintiff and defendant formed a partnership for the purchase of guano and its subsequent sale. The plaintiff made advances to the partnership for the purposes of paying the purchase price for the guano and the defendant agreed to keep the plaintiff in funds as to half the net invoice value of the guano which the partnership had left unsold. On the dissolution of the partnership, a balance was owing from the defendant to the plaintiff. Chatterton VC held that interest was payable on the advances which had been so made by the plaintiff to the partnership. The court based its decision on the existence of an implied contract between the parties as shown by their subsequent dealings whereby they seem to have provided funds and if the funds were not provided on time, to pay interest on those funds.[104]

Payment of interest on benefits wrongly obtained by a partner

[14.57] The general rule that interest is not payable on capital is subject to the exception that the court will allow interest on the restitution of money belonging to the firm which has been expended for the personal benefit of the partner or withheld by a partner or on a private profit[105] made by a partner in breach of his fiduciary duty.[106]

Interest Payable on Advances?

[14.58] The issue of whether interest is payable on an advance by a partner to a firm over and above his capital contribution is addressed by s 24(3) of the 1890 Act which provides that, subject to any express or implied agreement between the partners:

> A partner making, for the purpose of the partnership, any actual payment or advance beyond the amount of capital which he has agreed to subscribe, is entitled to interest at the rate of five per cent. per annum from the date of the payment or advance.

Since this is a default rule, if the partners do not want interest to accrue on advances beyond the capital agreed in the partnership agreement, this provision should be excluded by the terms of the partnership agreement.[107]

---

101 See further regarding the capitalisation of profits, para **[17.18]**.

102 *Pim v Harris* (1876) 10 Ir Eq R 442.

103 As it was a pre-1890 case, it was not subject to the terms of s 24(3) of the 1890 Act, which is considered at para **[14.58]**.

104 This is the implication of Chatterton VC's judgment but no details of those subsequent dealings are contained in the report.

105 As to private profits, see para **[15.27]**.

106 *Moore v Moore* (27 February 1998) HC NI, see para **[15.67]**.

107 See also para **[21.69]**. Note that an 'advance' and additional capital are treated the same for the purposes of the payment of interest under s 24(3), but an advance is paid-off ahead of capital on the distribution of assets on a general dissolution under s 44(b) of the 1890 Act.

Does corollary apply?

[14.59] An issue may arise as to whether interest accrues on moneys which are held by a partner, but which belong to the firm. It seems that interest is not payable by the partner to the firm on these sums,[108] unless the partner in question is guilty of fraud. In *Hutcheson v Smith*,[109] one partner was appointed a receiver by the court to wind up the partnership and collect in the assets of the firm. However, he misled his partner and the court as to the amount of partnership money which he had collected. Accordingly, Brady CB held that:

> 'Considering these circumstances, and looking at the position in which he was placed with respect to the Court, I think this is a clear case to make him pay interest on the balance in his hands belonging to the plaintiff.'[110]

Interest on Post-Dissolution Profits

[14.60] Section 42(1) of the 1890 Act deals with the situation where surviving partners continue the business of the partnership after one or more of the partners departs from the firm. It entitles the former partner to such share of the post-dissolution profits as are attributable to the use of his share of the partnership assets, or to interest at the rate of 5% per annum on the amount of his share of the partnership assets.[111] This issue is considered in detail elsewhere in this text.[112]

Interest on a Partnership Account

[14.61] On the basis that interest is not generally chargeable at common law in the absence of express agreement,[113] it would seem to follow that where an account of partnership dealings is taken on the departure of a partner, interest is not payable on that account between the date it is agreed and the date of payment. In *Graves v Davies*,[114] it was held by Walsh MR that a sum of money owing by a two-man firm of stockbrokers on the date of its dissolution (which dissolution was caused by the death of one partner) was not subject to interest since it was a simple contract debt. Whether this principle should be followed today has, however, been doubted.[115]

Interest Awarded by a Court

[14.62] While interest may not be payable without express agreement, a court may award interest on a judgment for any sums owing between partners. Under s 22 of the Courts Act 1981, such an award of interest may be made for the period between the date

---

108 *Evans v Coventry* (1857) 8 De GM & G 835.
109 *Hutcheson v Smith* (1842) 5 Ir Eq R 117.
110 *Hutcheson v Smith* (1842) 5 Ir Eq R 117 at 125.
111 See for example *Pilsworth v Mosse* (1863) 14 Ir Ch R 163, considered at para **[26.73]**.
112 See generally in relation to s 42 of the 1890 Act, para **[26.63]**.
113 See para **[14.52]**.
114 *Graves v Davies* (1866) 17 Ir Ch Rep 227.
115 See Breslin, *Banking Law* (3rd edn, 2013) at paras 8-28 and 8-29 where he refers to *Provincial Bank of Ireland v Reilly* (1890) 26 LR Ir 313 and *Stewart v Stewart* (1891) 27 LR Ir 351. See also Donnelly, *The Law of Credit and Security* (2nd edn, 2015) at para 7-73 (also in relation to *Provincial Bank of Ireland v Reilly* (1890) 26 LR Ir 313).

the cause of action arose and the date of judgment and, at the date of writing, the rate is 2%.[116]

[14.63] Under s 22(2)(b) of the Courts Act 1981, the court may not award interest in relation to a debt, upon which 'interest is payable as of right whether by virtue of any agreement or otherwise'. Since the right to interest under s 42 of the 1890 Act at the rate of 5% per annum is at the option of the partner, rather than being 'as of right', it would seem that the court is not precluded from making an award of interest greater than 5% in a situation to which s 42 of the 1890 Act would otherwise apply (if, at that time, the relevant interest rate was higher than 5% which is not the case at the time of writing).[117]

V.   PARTNERSHIP BOOKS AND ACCOUNTS

No Obligation to File Accounts

[14.64] Unlike limited liability companies[118] and, since 2017, certain unlimited liability companies,[119] which are required to file financial statements with the Companies Registration Office, there is no obligation on partnerships to file statutory financial statements in the Companies Registration Office or elsewhere.[120] The reason will be understood if one considers the rationale for imposing the requirement on limited liability companies to file financial statements in the first place. This obligation derives from the decision to restrict the liability of the shareholders in limited liability companies to the amount, however small, of their capital contribution to the company. Thus, third parties who deal with a limited liability company must assess the business risk involved in dealing with that company solely on the basis of the company's assets and not those of its shareholders. In order to enable third parties to assess this business

---

[116] Originally set by s 26 of the Debtors (Ireland) Act 1840, the rate can be varied from time to time by Ministerial Order. The most recent Ministerial Order was the Courts Act 1981 (Interest on Judgment Debts) Order 2016 (SI 624/2016) which reduced the rate from 8% to 2% with effect from 1 January 2017. See generally in relation to interest awarded by the court, Breslin, *Banking Law* (3rd edn, 2013) at para 8.30; Donnelly, *The Law of Credit and Security* (2015) at para 20-33.

[117] See also l'Anson Banks, *Lindley & Banks on Partnership* (20th edn, 2017) at para 20-41 in relation to the equivalent provision for the granting of court interest in England.

[118] See generally in relation to the requirement upon limited companies to file accounts, Courtney, *The Law of Companies* (4th edn, 2016) at para [18.001] et seq and Hutchinson, *Keane on Company Law* (5th edn, 2016) at para [29.01] et seq. But note that under ss 358 and 360 of the Companies Act 2014, a 'small company' does not have to have its accounts audited where it meets two of three 'qualifying conditions' (a turnover not exceeding €12 million, a balance sheet total not exceeding €6 million and an average employee number of 50 or less) in its first financial year, and also where it meets two of those conditions in certain other cases, generally for two consecutive years.

[119] Since the commencement of the Companies (Accounting) Act 2017, unlimited liability companies which are owned or controlled (directly or indirectly) by limited liability companies now have obligations to file financial statements with the Companies Registration Office in respect of financial years beginning on or after 1 January 2017. See, further, Courtney and Curtis, *Bloomsbury Professional's Company Law Guide 2017* (2017) at para [5.01] et seq.

[120] See however the obligation on investment limited partnerships to file accounts with the Central Bank, para **[29.177]**.

risk, the limited liability company is required to make its financial position public by filing its financial statements. The Companies (Accounting) Act 2017 extended the filing requirement to unlimited liability companies that are directly or indirectly owned or controlled by limited liability companies. This change was to address concerns that corporate structures were being set up to circumvent the requirements to file financial statements by interposing a limited liability company (often based outside the EEA) between the unlimited company and its ultimate beneficial owners with the intention of shielding those owners from unlimited liability and making it more difficult to identify those owners.

[14.65] However, in the case of a partnership, these rationales for filing accounts are absent since all the partners are liable to an unlimited degree for the obligations of the firm. This also explains why, under the European Communities (Accounts) Regulations 1993,[121] in those cases in which all the members of a partnership have effective limited liability, the partnership is required to file accounts.

European Communities (Accounts) Regulations 1993

[14.66] Under Regulation 6 of the European Communities (Accounts) Regulations 1993, where all of the members of a partnership[122] which have unlimited liability, are themselves limited liability companies or their equivalent,[123] the partnership (hereinafter referred to as a 'Regulation 6 partnership') must file accounts.[124] The rationale behind this exception is that a Regulation 6 partnership has effective limited liability. This is because the liability of a partner, which is a limited liability company, is effectively limited to the share capital of that company. Since the exemption from the requirement to file accounts is reserved for partnerships which truly have unlimited liability, a Regulation 6 partnership is not allowed to benefit from this exemption. The 1993 Regulations were introduced to counter the issue of 'off-balance sheet' accounting whereby companies took advantage of the confidentiality of partnership accounts by forming corporate partnerships in order to conceal the true state of their finances. A similar rationale underpinned the decision to introduce the Companies (Accounting) Act

---

[121] SI 396/1993. These Regulations were introduced to implement Council Directives 90/604/EEC and 90/605/EEC.

[122] Note that the term 'partnership' is defined in the interpretation section of the Regulations (reg 3(1)) incorrectly as having the same meaning as in the 'Partnerships Act, 1890', rather than the 'Partnership Act, 1890'.

[123] Regulation 6 provides that it applies to (1) unlimited companies and partnerships where those members who do not have a limit on their liability are either companies limited by shares or guarantee, or equivalent bodies not governed by the law of the State, or any combination thereof and (2) unlimited companies and partnerships where those members who do not have a limit on their liability are either unlimited companies or partnerships of the type referred to in (1) that are governed by the laws of a Member State or comparable bodies governed by the laws of a Member State, or any combination of the foregoing and the bodies listed in (1).

[124] Note however that these accounts need not be audited if the partnership has a turnover not exceeding €12 million, a balance sheet total not exceeding €6 million and an average employee number of 50 or less: Companies Act 2014, ss 358 and 360. The Companies Registration Office form to be used by a partnership filing accounts is a Form P1, which is set out in the European Communities (Accounts) (Form) Regulations 1995 (SI 178/1995).

2017 to counter companies setting up unlimited liability companies directly owned by offshore limited liability companies to limit the liability of their ultimate beneficial owners and to make those owners more difficult to identify.

[14.67] A Regulation 6 partnership is subject to the same requirements as a limited liability company regarding the filing of accounts. This is because Regulation 7 of the European Communities (Accounts) Regulations 1993 provides that the Companies (Amendment) Act 1986 (dealing with the accounts of public and private companies) applies to these partnerships as though they were companies. The Companies (Amendment) Act 1986 was repealed by the Companies Act 2014 and its provisions were incorporated (with some amendments) into Part 6 and Schedule 3 of the Companies Act 2014, and therefore those provisions apply to a Regulation 6 partnership in the same way as they do to a limited liability company.[125]

Modification of company accounts provisions for partnerships

[14.68] In view of the structural differences between companies (with their directors and shareholders) and partnerships, certain provisions needed to be enacted to allow for the application to Regulation 6 partnerships of the requirements in the Companies (Amendment) Act 1986 (now contained in Part 6 of the Companies Act 2014), regarding the filing of accounts.

Appointment of auditors

[14.69] A Regulation 6 partnership is required to appoint auditors who shall make a report on the accounts examined by them, and on the firm's profit and loss account and balance sheet, and, if relevant, the firm's group accounts.[126]

Signing of balance sheet, etc

[14.70] The balance sheet and the profit and loss account of a Regulation 6 partnership must be signed on behalf of the partners by two partners authorised to do so,[127] and the copy of the auditor's report must be certified by two of the partners to be a true copy thereof.[128] Similarly, where the Regulation 6 partnership is required to file a copy of the balance sheet and the profit and loss account with the Registrar of Companies, both documents must be certified by two of the partners authorised by the partners so to do.[129]

[14.71] Any group accounts forwarded to the Registrar of Companies must be certified to be a true copy by two of the partners, authorised by the partners to do so.[130]

---

125   Note that by virtue of the Companies Act 2014, Sch 6, s 11(1), the reference in the European Communities (Accounts) Regulations 1993 to the Companies (Amendment) Act 1986 is to be read as a reference to the equivalent provisions of the Companies Act 2014. For further detail on these obligations, see Courtney, *The Law of Companies* (4th edn, 2016) at para [18.001] et seq and Courtney and Curtis, *Bloomsbury Professional's Company Law Guide 2017* (2017).
126   European Communities (Accounts) Regulations 1993, reg 22(1).
127   European Communities (Accounts) Regulations 1993, reg 10(1).
128   European Communities (Accounts) Regulations 1993, reg 13(6).
129   European Communities (Accounts) Regulations 1993, reg 20(1).
130   European Communities (Accounts) Regulations 1993, reg 20(2).

Partners' report

[14.72] Rather than a directors' report having to be attached to the balance sheet, a Regulation 6 partnership must have a report of the partners attached which must be signed by two of the partners authorised to do so.[131] Regulation 14(1) provides that the partners' reports must contain the following information:

(a)   a fair view of the development of the business of the partnership and of its subsidiary undertakings, if any, during the financial year ending with the relevant balance sheet;

(b)   particulars of any important events affecting the partnership or any of its subsidiary undertakings, if any, which have occurred since the end of that year;

(c)   an indication of likely future developments in the business of the partnership and any of its subsidiary undertakings, if any;

(d)   an indication of the activities, if any, of the partnership and any of its subsidiary undertakings, if any, in the field of research and development; and

(e)   an indication of the existence of branches (within the meaning of Council Directive 89/ 666/EC)[132] of the partnership outside the State and the country in which each such branch is located.

Section 357 guarantees

[14.73] Another modification of company accounts provisions in their application to reg 6 partnerships, concerns the exemption of certain Regulation 6 partnerships from filing accounts, where they have filed s 357 guarantees (formerly known as 'section 17 guarantees'). This exemption will only apply if all the partners have consented in writing to the exemption and a certified copy of the guarantee must be forwarded to all the partners.[133]

Publication of information regarding subsidiaries and associates

[14.74] Like a company, a Regulation 6 partnership may publish information regarding its subsidiaries and associates in a separate statement pursuant to s 316 of the Companies Act 2014. Such a statement must be signed on behalf of the partners by two partners and a copy of the statement must be certified, by two of the partners, to be a

---

131   European Communities (Accounts) Regulations 1993, reg 14(2). The information to be included in this report was not a copy-out of that required in respect of companies by s 13 of the Companies (Amendment) Act 1986 and remains different to the information now required in the directors' report to be furnished under s 325 of the Companies Act 2014 by most companies.

132   OJ L395, 21-12-1989, pp 36-39 (Eleventh Council Directive 89/666/EEC of 21 December 1989 concerning disclosure requirements in respect of branches opened in a Member State by certain types of company governed by the law of another State). This Directive was repealed with effect from 20 July 2017 by Directive (EU) 2017/1132 relating to certain aspects of company law (OJ L 169, 30.6.2017, pp 46–127) which codifies a number of EU Directives relating to company law into one Directive.

133   European Communities (Accounts) Regulations 1993, reg 16 and s 357 of the Companies Act 2014.

true copy thereof, when filed with the Registrar of Companies with the partnership's accounts for the relevant financial year.

Offences and penalties

[14.75] Many of the accounts-related provisions of the Companies Act 2014, which replaced the Companies (Amendment) Act 1986, apply to 'officers'. These provisions are modified in their application to Regulation 6 partnerships by Regulation 24(4) of the European Communities (Accounts) Regulations 1993. This provides that a partner in a Regulation 6 partnership shall be deemed to be an officer for the purposes of the sections which impose penalties on officers for the failure to comply with the accounts requirements.

Implicit Obligation on Partnerships to Keep Accounts

[14.76] Although a partnership, unless it is a Regulation 6 partnership, is not required to file accounts,[134] it is required to keep accounts. This obligation is not expressly stated in the 1890 Act but is a necessary incident of the partnership relationship, since it facilitates the taking of an account between the parties.[135] The right to an account between partners is well-settled and a crucial right of every partner. Thus in *Murphy v Keller*,[136] Brady LC noted that a partner: 'would, as a matter of course, be entitled of common right to have an account of the partnership taken in this Court.'[137]

[14.77] In order to ensure that this right to an account has any meaning, the partners themselves must keep an account of the firm's financial dealings. The obligation upon a firm to keep accounts was implicitly recognised in the Supreme Court case of *Baxter v Horgan*.[138] This case concerned a partnership dispute between two members of a cattle trading partnership. The partnership bought and sold cattle and the plaintiff sought a share of partnership funds which had not been disclosed by the defendant. The plaintiff was successful in the action and the costs were awarded against the defendant in the High Court. On appeal to the Supreme Court, Egan J upheld this award of costs. He held that as the defendant partner used to buy the cattle on behalf of the partnership, he was under a duty to keep accurate records and accounts. This he had failed to do and the costs of the action were mainly incurred by the defendant's failure to keep such accounts.

[14.78] The obligation to keep an account is also implicit in a number of provisions of the 1890 Act, eg s 28, which requires a partner to render true accounts of all things affecting the partnership to his co-partners and s 24(9), which entitles a partner to inspect the partnership books. In addition, a partnership will, in many instances, be required to submit its accounts to the Revenue Commissioners for the purposes of assessing the liability of the partners to tax.[139]

---

134 As to such Regulation 6 partnerships, see para **[14.66]** et seq.
135 See generally as to taking of an account between the partners, para **[20.14]**.
136 *Murphy v Keller* (1851) 2 Ir Ch R 417 and 1 Ir Ch R 24 & 104.
137 *Murphy v Keller* (1851) 2 Ir Ch R 417 at 421.
138 *Baxter v Horgan* (28 May 1990) HC, (7 June 1991) SC.
139 See the Taxes Consolidation Act 1997, s 880 and see generally para **[21.92]**.

[14.79] Quite apart from this obligation to keep an account of the partnership dealings, it is common for partnership agreements to require the partners to keep a profit and loss account and a balance sheet made up to a certain date each year.[140]

Where Certain Partners are Obliged to Keep Accounts

[14.80] Where the parties in a trading partnership have not agreed between themselves as to who should keep accounts, the partner who does the purchasing on behalf of the firm has a duty to keep accounts. Thus in *Baxter v Horgan*,[141] Egan J held that as the defendant partner used to buy the cattle on behalf of the partnership, he was under a duty to keep accurate records and accounts.

[14.81] Similarly, after a change in a firm, it is the duty of the continuing partners in the firm to keep the accounts so as to show the change in the financial position of the firm.[142]

Where Partner Refuses to Produce the Firm's Accounts

[14.82] A court will have no sympathy for a partner who refuses to produce the accounts of the firm and will make presumptions against such a partner in estimating the profits or losses of the firm. This is clear from the decision in *Walmsley v Walmsley*.[143] In that case, the parties were partners in a firm in which they had contributed capital of £4,000 in equal proportions. On a court application by the plaintiff for an account of the partnership dealings, the defendant refused to produce the accounts of the partnership transactions to the court. The Master held that the plaintiff should be entitled to half of the net profits of the firm. However, as the Master had no accounts upon which to base his estimate of the profits of the firm, he estimated them to be 10% per annum of the capital of the firm for each year of operation. On appeal, Sugden LC upheld this decision and noted obiter that, in view of the defendant's behaviour, even if the Master had estimated these profits at 20% of the capital, he would have upheld that decision.

Types of Accounts

[14.83] Although there is an obligation upon a firm to keep an account of its financial dealings, the firm has a considerable discretion as to the form and number of accounts which it may maintain. This is in contrast to the position of companies which are subject to detailed regulation regarding the form and content of their accounts.[144] It is noted elsewhere in this work, that it is desirable that a firm keep a separate capital account and a current account[145] so as to reduce the likelihood of confusion between the true amount of capital attributable to each partner and other sums such as undrawn profits of that partner or proceeds from the sale of partnership property. When a profit or loss is

---

140 See further in relation to such clauses in partnership agreements, para **[21.92]**.

141 *Baxter v Horgan* (28 May 1990) HC, (7 June 1991) SC.

142 *Toulmin v Copland* (1836) 2 Y & C 625; *Ex p Toulmin* (1815) 1 Mer 598.

143 *Walmsley v Walmsley* (1846) 3 Jo & La T 556.

144 See generally Courtney, *The Law of Companies* (4th edn, 2016) para [18.001] et seq; Hutchinson, *Keane on Company Law* (5th edn, 2016) at para [30.01] et seq. Unless of course it is a Regulation 6 partnership, see para **[14.66]**.

145 See para **[17.09]**.

declared by the firm, such amount should be debited or credited, as appropriate, to the partners' current accounts. If the partners wish to capitalise undrawn profits standing to the credit of their current account, these sums should be transferred to the capital account.

[14.84] In this regard, other types of partnership accounts to which the partners may transfer some of the firm's profits are a tax reserve account and a retirement annuity fund, both of which are self-explanatory.

Access to Partnership Books

[14.85] It has been seen that partners are under an implicit obligation to keep accounts.[146] Section 24(9) of the 1890 Act, although it refers simply to partnership books, contains the right of a partner to have access to those accounts (since it is argued that the term 'partnership books' includes the accounts of the partnership).[147] It states that, subject to any express or implied agreement between the partners to the contrary:

> The partnership books are to be kept at the place of business of the partnership (or the principal place, if there is more than one), and every partner may, when he thinks fit, have access to and inspect and copy any of them.

[14.86] This right of access to the partnership books will be enforced by the courts. In *Shaw v O'Higgins*,[148] one partner had removed partnership money from the common fund of the firm to his own fund for safe keeping. MacMahon MR granted an injunction to prevent the partners acting contrary to the partnership agreement and, in particular, to prohibit either partner from excluding the other from having access to the partnership books.[149]

'when he thinks fit'

[14.87] The right of a partner in s 24(9) of the 1890 Act to inspect the partnership books is stated to be exercisable when a partner thinks fit. It is apprehended that this expression must be read as being subject to the reasonable demands of the firm to those books. In the pre-1890 case of *Mallet v Boileau*,[150] the plaintiff was a member of a partnership called The Dublin and London Steam Marine Company, which operated a ferry between Dublin and London. Under the terms of the partnership agreement, the plaintiff was granted the right to inspect the partnership books, yet when he sought to do so, he was prevented from examining them. When the matter came before McMahon MR, he held that the refusal of access was justifiable since the request was made at an

---

146 See para **[14.76]**.
147 See para **[21.91]**.
148 *Shaw v O'Higgins* (1829) 3 Ir Law Rec 104.
149 The rule in s 24(9) that access to partnership books can be excluded by agreement to the contrary between the partners is based on the common law position prior to the 1890 Act. Thus in *Sugrue v Hibernian Bank* (1829) 2 Law Rec 285, an application was made for access to the partnership books and the Master of the Rolls refused the application on the grounds that the access was excluded under the terms of the partnership agreement: '[t]hat follows, you will find, from the constitution of the partnership', at 288.
150 *Mallet v Boileau* (1835) 3 Ir Law Rec (ns) 264.

improper time since the accounts were being used at that time in preparation for the general meeting of the firm.

Removal of partnership books

[14.88] If, as part of the inspection process, a partner wishes to remove the partnership books from the place of business of the firm, an explicit right to this effect should be included in the partnership agreement. Without such a provision, the express wording of s 24(9) of the 1890 Act precludes it.

Inspection of partnership books by an agent

[14.89] The right in s 24(9) to inspect the partnership books may be delegated by a partner to his agent but the agent may be required to give an undertaking to use the information so gleaned for that purpose alone. This is clear from the High Court case of *Healy v Healy Homes Ltd*[151] which concerned the identical right of a director to inspect the books of account of his company under s 147(3) of the Companies Act 1963.[152] This section tracks the wording of s 24(9) of the 1890 Act and undoubtedly owes its origin to s 24(9). Accordingly, Kenny J relied on the partnership case of *Bevan v Webb*[153] as authority for the principle that a partner may appoint an agent who may attend with the partner or on his own, to examine the books of account of the firm. This right of the agent is subject to his giving an undertaking to use the information acquired by him from such inspection only for the purpose of advising the partner in relation to the matter for which the agent was retained. As noted by Kenny J, the rationale for entitling a director (or a partner) to have his agent inspect the books of account, is that directors (and partners) will often times not have any accountancy training and therefore will require the assistance of an accountant to interpret the books of account.

Partnership Books to be Kept at Place of Business

[14.90] Under s 24(9), and subject to express or implied agreement to the contrary, the partnership books are to be kept at the place of business of the partnership or at its principal place of business, if there is more than one. It is for this reason that partnership agreements usually contain a statement of the firm's place of business or its principal place of business.[154] If the partnership does not want to keep the partnership books at its place of business, or if the partners wish to be entitled to remove them temporarily for inspection purposes, this should be expressly provided for in the partnership agreement.

No right for assignee to inspect partnership books

[14.91] The right of a partner in s 24(9) to inspect the partnership books does not extend to the assignee of a partner's share. This is clear from the terms of s 31(1) of the 1890 Act which states that:

---

[151] *Healy v Healy Homes Ltd* [1973] IR 309.

[152] Access by a director to a company's accounting records is now governed by the Companies Act 2014, s 284(1).

[153] *Bevan v Webb* [1901] 2 Ch 59.

[154] See further regarding such clauses, para **[21.39]**.

An assignment by any partner of his share in the partnership, either absolute or by way of mortgage or redeemable charge, does not, as against the other partners, entitle the assignee, during the continuance of the partnership, to ... inspect the partnership books.

Access to Partnership Accounts

[14.92] As has been seen, s 24(9) deals with the right of a partner to have access to the partnership books. In contrast, s 28 of the 1890 Act deals with the partnership accounts and it provides that '[p]artners are bound to render true accounts and full information of all things affecting the partnership to any partner or his legal representatives'.

[14.93] Unlike the right of access to partnership books in s 24(9), this section is not stated to be subject to any agreement to the contrary between the partners. Since the right of access to partnership books can be excluded, while access to partnership accounts is not expressed to be subject to contrary agreement, it is important to consider the difference between the expression the 'books of a partnership' and the 'accounts of a partnership' and this area is considered in detail elsewhere in this work.[155]

[14.94] It is noted elsewhere in this text that the right of a partner to have access to the firm's accounts is so basic a right that it cannot be varied by the terms of the partnership agreement[156] and so must be regarded as a mandatory, rather than a default rule. This is because the whole purpose of a partnership is to make a profit and if a partner is allowed to be deprived of his right to have access to the information which details how much, if any, profit has been made, this deprives him of his *raison d'être* as a partner.

Signing of Cheques

[14.95] As has been noted elsewhere in this work,[157] in the absence of agreement to the contrary, each partner is authorised to sign cheques on behalf of the firm.[158]

---

155 See para **[21.91]**.
156 See para **[21.88]**. But for a contrary view, see l'Anson Banks, *Lindley & Banks on Partnership* (20th edn, 2017) at para 22-13.
157 See para **[10.53]**.
158 *Backhouse v Charlton* (1878) 8 Ch D 444; *Laws v Rand* (1857) 27 LJCP 76.

Chapter 15

Fiduciary Duties of Partners

INTRODUCTION

> '[T]he mere existence of a partnership creates a fiduciary relationship between the partners.'
>
> Per McWilliam J, *Williams v Harris.*[1]

[15.01] As is clear from this statement of McWilliam J, partners are in a fiduciary relationship with each other.[2] As such, they owe each other a fiduciary duty and in this chapter, the nature and extent of this fiduciary duty will be examined. The rationale for imposing a fiduciary duty upon partners is clear. In the words of Bacon VC: '[i]t is because they trust one another that they are partners in the first instance; it is because they continue to trust each other that the business goes on.'[3] Being in this position of trust, the partners are required not to abuse this trust and this duty between fiduciaries is the primary control of partners' behaviour inter se.

[15.02] A partner's fiduciary duty has two aspects; fiduciary duties which are recognised at common law and fiduciary duties which are recognised by statute. These two types of fiduciary duties will be examined under the following headings:

    I.   Common Law Instances of Fiduciary Duty;

    II.   Statutory Instances of Fiduciary Duty;

    III. Characteristics of a Partner's Fiduciary Duty.

Overview

[15.03] The fiduciary duty of a partner towards his co-partner arises because of the nature of the partnership relationship, ie where two persons agree to be partners they agree to be bound by the acts of the other in relation to the partnership business and, most significantly, they are thereby liable to an unlimited degree for those acts. For this relationship to work, the parties need to be truthful and honest to a very high degree, in

---

1   *Williams v Harris* (15 January 1980) HC at p 12 of the transcript.

2   See also the comments of Ryan P in *ADM Londis plc v Ranzett Ltd & ors* [2016] IECA 290 in which he differentiated between the fiduciary duties owed in a partnership from those owed in a trust or corporate structure, commenting that '[in] many established classes of fiduciary relationships one person acts as the fiduciary of another eg trustee/beneficiary and director/company but it is not reciprocal. Only one person in the relationship owes fiduciary obligations to the other. Partnership is different, having mutual duties; each partner owes fiduciary obligations to the other.' Baker J, in her judgment in *Best & Anor v Ghose & Ors* [2018] IEHC 376, examined the nature of a fiduciary relationship generally and, in particular, the key characteristics of that relationship (at paras 67 and 68 of the judgment).

3   *Helmore v Smith* (1886) 35 Ch D 436 at 444.

the words of Cardozo J not 'honesty alone, but the punctilio of an honor the most sensitive'.[4] This fiduciary duty involves not simply the duty of good faith, but that standard of behaviour which one would expect from persons in this relationship of trust.

[15.04] One of the criticisms that may be made of the 1890 Act is that it fails to contain an express recognition of a partner's general fiduciary duty to his co-partner, especially since that Act was a codification of the common law[5] which had for long acknowledged the existence of this duty.[6] However, the 1890 Act does recognise a number of instances of this fiduciary duty, such as the duty on a partner to render true accounts and information on the partnership to his co-partner[7] and the obligation of a partner to account to the firm for any benefit derived by him from any transaction concerning the partnership or using the partnership property, name or business connection.[8] Although the 1890 Act did not recognise a partner's general fiduciary duty, as is noted hereunder, the existence of this duty has been consistently recognised by the courts since that time. Accordingly, it is standard for partnership agreements to expressly state that 'the partners shall be just and faithful to each other', so as to remind partners of this basic obligation upon which the partnership relationship is founded. It is because of the importance of a partner's fiduciary duty to the partnership relationship that it is argued below that the duty may not in general be excluded by the partners by inserting a term to the contrary in their partnership agreement.[9] It is suggested that, as the 1890 Act operates as a default partnership agreement for partners, it is particularly important that the very existence of this fiduciary duty be recognised expressly by its provisions, ideally in terms which would ensure that it cannot be excluded by contrary agreement.[10]

I.   COMMON LAW INSTANCES OF FIDUCIARY DUTY

[15.05] In this section, consideration will be given to those instances of a partner's fiduciary duty which have been recognised by the courts, as distinct from those fiduciary duties which have been recognised by the 1890 Act. While the distinction between common law fiduciary duties and statutory fiduciary duties is maintained for convenience, the distinction is not of any legal significance, since in many cases, a statutory fiduciary duty will simply be the codification of the common law position prior to the 1890 Act.[11] Reference will be made first to the treatment of a partner's fiduciary duty by the Supreme Court in *Meagher v Meagher*[12] and *Williams v Harris*.[13]

---

4   *Meinhard v Salmon* (1928) 164 NE 545 at 546. See para **[15.20]**.
5   See generally, para **[1.23]**.
6   *Chandler v Dorsett* (1679) Finch 431; *Helmore v Smith* (1886) 35 Ch D 436 at 444 per Bacon VC; *Blisset v Daniel* (1853) 10 Hare 493.
7   Partnership Act 1890, s 28.
8   Partnership Act 1890, s 29.
9   Although, as is clear from the terms of the 1890 Act itself (eg s 29(1): every partner must account to the firm for any benefit derived by him *without the consent of the other partners* from any transaction concerning the partnership) and *Williams v Harris* [1980] ILRM 237 (para **[15.54]**), specific instances of the fiduciary duty may be excluded by the partners.
10   Ie a statement that the implied term is outside the ambit of s 19 of the 1890 Act.
11   As to the role of the 1890 Act as a codification of the common law of partnership, see para **[1.23]**.
12   *Meagher v Meagher* [1961] IR 96.
13   *Williams v Harris* (15 January 1980) HC, [1980] ILRM 237 (SC).

Recognition of Fiduciary Duty by the Supreme Court

[15.06] The first recognition by the Supreme Court of a partner's fiduciary duty was in *Meagher v Meagher*.[14] That case concerned the fiduciary duties which existed between continuing partners in a firm and a deceased partner's estate, but, as is clear from that case, the fact that the duty was owed to a deceased partner's estate does not affect the nature of the fiduciary duty. It involved three brothers who had been partners in a firm which bought and renovated houses for re-sale. They had no written partnership agreement and when one of the brothers died, an issue arose as to whether his share of the partnership assets was to be taken as one third of the value of the houses owned by the firm as of the date of death, or the value of those houses when they were realised by the firm, which was a number of years later. There was a substantial difference in the value of the deceased partner's share depending on which date was taken, due to a rise in the value of the houses as a result of a general rise in property prices at that time. The personal representatives of the deceased partner claimed to be entitled to this increase in the value of his share in the partnership assets. In the High Court, Dixon J held, without reference to fiduciary duties, that the personal representatives were entitled to the value of the deceased partner's share in the assets as of that date of death. However, in the Supreme Court, Kingsmill Moore J (Ó Dálaigh and Maguire JJ concurring) reversed this decision, by relying on the fiduciary nature of a partner's position *vis-à-vis* his co-partner. He held that:

> 'The claim made in this case is that the representatives of the deceased have no right to take the benefit of a general rise in prices occurring between the dissolution and sale, but that the whole advantage of such rise should go to the surviving partner. This appears to me to be contrary to the principles of equity and the provisions of the Partnership Act. Surviving partners stand in a fiduciary relationship to the representatives of a deceased partner: *Stevenson's Case*[15] *per* Lord Dunedin at p 248; per Lord Atkinson at pp 250, 251, 252 ... A person in a fiduciary position cannot make a profit out of his trusteeship by appropriating to himself the rise in value of assets which he holds as trustee.'[16]

[15.07] While the Supreme Court could have reached its decision solely on the basis of s 42 of the 1890 Act,[17] it chose to rely also on the presence of a fiduciary duty between the partners, and on this basis, held that the deceased partner's estate was entitled to share in the increase in value of the partnership assets.

[15.08] The nature of the fiduciary duty of partners was subsequently examined by the High Court and the Supreme Court in *Williams v Harris*[18] which also concerned the existence of a fiduciary duty between continuing partners in a firm and former partners.

---

14   *Meagher v Meagher* [1961] IR 96.
15   *Stevenson's Case* [1918] AC 239.
16   *Meagher v Meagher* [1961] IR 96 at 110. As noted by Kingsmill Moore J, the same result is arrived at by the application of s 42 of the 1890 Act.
17   Ie the right of an outgoing partner to share in post-dissolution profits, see para **[15.51]**. Note that this aspect of a partner's fiduciary duty, namely the prohibition on his making a personal profit from the use of the partnership assets, is also dealt with by the 1890 Act in s 29(1) (accountability of a partner for private profits), see para **[15.28]**.
18   *Williams v Harris* (15 January 1980) HC, [1980] ILRM 237 (SC).

Unlike *Meagher v Meagher*,[19] the partners in *Williams v Harris*[20] had executed a partnership deed which dealt with their respective rights on retiring from the firm. The deed provided that in the event of the retirement of a partner from the partnership, the continuing partners would purchase the retiring partner's share. There was almost a two-year time lapse between the date of retirement of two of the partners from the firm and the date of payment by the continuing partners for their share. The retired partners claimed that they should be paid interest on the purchase price for this period on the grounds that they were owed a fiduciary duty by the continuing partners which prevented the latter from having the benefit of both the purchase price and the retired partners' share for this two-year period.[21] In the High Court, McWilliam J awarded interest to the former partners on the basis of this fiduciary duty, but his decision was reversed in the Supreme Court. However, the existence of a fiduciary duty between partners was not doubted by the Supreme Court; rather it held that on the facts of that case, this duty had been excluded by the parties. In the High Court, McWilliam J had observed that:

> 'One of the results of a fiduciary relationship is that interest may be awarded on money misused by any person in a fiduciary position, on the ground that a person in a fiduciary position is not allowed to make a profit out of his trust and, if he does, he is liable to account for that profit or to pay interest in lieu thereof.'[22]

[15.09] However on appeal, Kenny J (Griffin J[23] and O'Higgins CJ, concurring) held that the partners had excluded the application of this fiduciary duty to the payment of interest by the express terms of their partnership deed and so the continuing partners were not liable to pay interest on the purchase price. Kenny J was influenced by the fact that the partnership deed provided that the continuing partners were to be the owners of all the assets and capital of the firm as and from the date of retirement and be liable for all the firm's liabilities as and from the same date. He concluded that as the continuing partners were the owners of the retired partners' share from the date of retirement, they were trading after that date, not with the assets of the retired partners but with assets which belonged to them solely. In addition, Kenny J held that it was relevant that no provision was made as regards the payment of interest, even though a delay in the payment for the retiring partner's share was contemplated by the terms of the deed. He distinguished the case of *Meagher v Meagher*[24] on the grounds that there was no partnership agreement of any kind in that case and therefore there could have been no exclusion of the fiduciary duties of the continuing partners.

[15.10] Although the High Court decision was overturned on the facts, the Supreme Court was in agreement with McWilliam J regarding the existence of a fiduciary duty between partners. Indeed, in the Supreme Court, Kenny J quoted with approval from the same judgment of Lord Atkinson in *Stevenson's Case*[25] as McWilliam J had done:

---

19   *Meagher v Meagher* [1961] IR 96.
20   *Williams v Harris* (15 January 1980) HC, [1980] ILRM 237 (SC).
21   Unlike the case of *Meagher v Meagher* above, the retiring partners were precluded from relying on s 42 of the 1890 Act because their partnership agreement constituted an 'agreement to the contrary' within the meaning of s 42.
22   *Williams v Harris* (15 January 1980) HC at pp 9–10 of the transcript.
23   While agreeing with Kenny J, Griffin J also delivered a separate judgment.
24   *Meagher v Meagher* [1961] IR 96.

'The [partnership] relation is a fiduciary relation. If that be so, the authorities show that equity will never permit the person standing in that relation to another to trade with the property of that other for his own gain. He must hold the profits he is making in trust for the owner of the property the use of which produced them.'[26]

[15.11] While the Supreme Court in *Meagher v Meagher*[27] and in *Williams v Harris*[28] confirmed the existence of this fiduciary duty between partners in the context of continuing and former partners, it is clearly also applicable to relations between continuing partners.

Partner Must Act in Firm's Interest

[15.12] One of the basic elements of a partner's fiduciary duty is the requirement to act in the firm's interest and where a partner acts in his own interest, this will constitute a breach of fiduciary duty.[29] This aspect of a partner's fiduciary duty was considered in the quasi-partnership[30] case of *Irish Press plc v Ingersoll*.[31] This case involved a 50:50 shareholding in two separate joint venture companies by Irish Press plc and the Ingersoll Group of companies. This relationship was held by Barron J to be 'in effect a partnership',[32] and he noted that the decision by Irish Press plc to pursue the venture was based on representations by the Ingersoll Group that it was a considerable organisation from which personnel would be available to assist this quasi-partnership. Personnel were not in the event available from Ingersoll to assist the quasi-partnership. This fact, combined with the placing by Ingersoll of its nominees on the board of the two joint venture companies for the purposes of Ingersoll's interests and not the company's, was held to be evidence of *mala fides* and of the breakdown of trust between the parties. Barron J held that this constituted a breach of Ingersoll's fiduciary duty to Irish Press which justified the ordering of a sale of Ingersoll's shares in the quasi-partnership to Irish Press plc under s 205 of the Companies Act 1963 (the predecessor to s 212 of the Companies Act 2014).[33]

[15.13] While a partner has a duty to act in the overall interests of the firm, the argument might be made that a particular breach of a partner's fiduciary duty was justified on the grounds that it was in the firm's overall interests. However, such an argument is unlikely to be successful in instances of clear breaches of fiduciary duty as is illustrated by the

---

25   *Stevenson's Case* [1918] AC 240, aff'g [1917] 1 KB 842.
26   *Williams v Harris* [1980] ILRM 237 at 241 quoting from *Stevenson's Case* [1918] AC 239 at 250.
27   *Meagher v Meagher* [1961] IR 96 at 110.
28   *Williams v Harris* (15 January 1980) HC, [1980] ILRM 237 (SC)
29   *Reilly v Walsh* (1848) 11 Ir Eq R 22. This case, which is considered hereunder, involved one partner in a building venture who wrote to potential lenders to the venture discouraging them from lending to his partner for the purposes of the venture. See further para **[15.57]**.
30   See further regarding quasi-partnerships, para **[8.67]** et seq.
31   *Irish Press plc v Ingersoll* (15 December 1993) HC.
32   *Irish Press plc v Ingersoll* (15 December 1993) HC at p 80 of the transcript.
33   Similarly in the Scottish case of *Finlayson v Turnbull* [1997] SLT 613, it was held that the removal of clients' files from a partnership by the departing partners in a partnership at will, was a breach by them of their fiduciary duty to the continuing partners and damages were awarded to the continuing partners for the damage caused to the firm's goodwill. (contd.../)

colourful[34] American case of *Beasley v Cadwalader, Wickersham & Taft*.[35] There, a
partner in one of the oldest law firms in the United States was expelled by the firm as a
result of an aggressive push from hungrier, younger and more productive partners for a
greater share of the profits. The expulsion of the plaintiff was the result of an all-day
clandestine meeting between some, but not all, of the partners. Remarkably, the firm's
partnership agreement had no provision for the expulsion of a partner and the plaintiff
alleged that his expulsion from the firm was a breach of the fiduciary duties owed to
him by his co-partners. In their defence, the partners in the firm claimed that the
expulsion of less productive partners was in the overall interests of the firm.[36] This was
rejected by the court which held that 'it was a gross breach of fiduciary duty for some
partners to throw others overboard for the expediency of increased profits'.[37] In view of
the motive for this flagrant breach of fiduciary duty, the court awarded punitive damages
against the defendant firm.

Partner Must Act in Good Faith and not Abuse his Powers

[15.14] One of the most important requirements of partners' fiduciary duties is that they
act with the utmost good faith in their dealings with each other.[38] Indeed, many of the
instances of a partner's fiduciary duty to be found in this chapter will involve a partner's
duty of good faith. The duty of good faith of a partner means that his powers under the
partnership agreement or under the 1890 Act should not be exercised for an ulterior

---

33 (\...contd) Cf *DB Rare Books Ltd v Antiqbooks (a limited partnership)* [1995] 2 BCLC 306,
     where it was alleged that one partner in a limited partnership materially breached the
     partnership agreement so as to justify a buy-out by the innocent partner. The term which was
     allegedly breached was that the partners should be just and faithful to each other and at all
     times act in the interests of the partnership. It was alleged that one partner breached this term
     by notifying the Revenue Commissioners that there was a shortfall in the payment of VAT
     which was due to the actions of the other partner. The English Court of Appeal held that the
     sending of this letter to the Revenue Commissioners was not a material breach of the
     partnership agreement and instead ordered the dissolution of the partnership. See the case
     comment 'Breach of partnership agreement' (1996) In House Lawyer 39.
34 For a discussion of this case, see Twomey, 'Firing your partner the American way' (1998) Law
     Society Gazette, Vol 92, No 3 at 22. Interestingly, the court added an American refinement to
     the maxim of equity that he who comes to equity must do so with clean hands, by noting that
     there were degrees of cleanliness. Cook J stated: 'if Beasley had dirt under his fingernails,
     Cadwalader Wickersham & Taft was up to its elbows in the dung heap' (1996) WL 438777 at
     6. See generally Martin, 'Duties of Care under the Revised Uniform Partnership Act' (1998)
     U Chi LR 1307.
35 *Beasley v Cadwalader, Wickersham & Taft* (1996) WL 438777, No CL-94-8648 AJ.
36 The chairman of the partnership put the matter thus: '[t]here was a fear, there is a fear, there
     always will be a fear, that highly productive partners ... can leave, go to another place and get
     more money. And life is not made up of love, it is made up of fear and greed and money – how
     much you get paid in large measure. Unless we didn't get Cadwalader's profitability to where
     it was with our competitors' firms, my great fear was that people were going to leave and that
     we would not be able to sustain ourselves.' *Beasley v Cadwalader, Wickersham & Taft* (1996)
     WL 438777, No CL-94-8648 AJ at 7.
37 *Beasley v Cadwalader, Wickersham & Taft* (1996) WL 438777, No CL-94-8648 AJ.

motive, such as for that partner's own benefit as distinct from the benefit of the firm. This is illustrated by the decision in *Blisset v Daniel*.[39] In that case, there was a wide power of expulsion contained in the partnership agreement and the partners in the firm wished to get rid of the plaintiff partner. They wished to do so for the ulterior motive that he objected to one of the other partners, Vaughan, being appointed as a manager in the firm. Vaughan had issued an ultimatum to the other partners that if the plaintiff remained, he would leave and thereby prevailed on the other partners to expel the plaintiff. Before doing so, the partners persuaded the plaintiff to sign the firm's accounts, and in this way they ensured that they would acquire the plaintiff's share at a reasonable value. The exercise of the right to expel the plaintiff was held to be a breach of good faith by the other partners and the expulsion was held to be void.

[15.15] Another instance of a partner's duty of good faith is provided by the decision in *Heslin v Fay (1)*.[40] There, the partnership agreement for a grocery store in North King Street in Dublin gave one partner, Fay, the power to increase the capital of the firm, if it was necessary for carrying on the business of the firm. The agreement also entitled each partner to withdraw the amount of any surplus capital paid by him to the partnership. When one of the partners, Heslin, called on his co-partners to repay the surplus capital which he had paid to the firm, Fay responded by raising the capital of the firm, so as to reduce the amount of the surplus owed to Heslin. Sullivan LC held that Fay had no right to use his power of increasing the capital for the purpose of resisting the plaintiff's demand for a return of his surplus capital and for this reason, Heslin was granted a dissolution of the partnership.

Partners Must Treat Each Other as Equals

[15.16] Another aspect of the fiduciary duties owed by one partner to another is the requirement that partners treat each other as equals. However, as is obvious from the terms of the 1890 Act itself,[41] this is an aspect of a partner's fiduciary duty which may be excluded by agreement between the partners, since partners may for example share profits unequally or have differing voting rights.[42] However, where this aspect of a partner's fiduciary duty is not excluded, a partner is obliged to treat his partner as an

---

[38]   In *Yam Seng PTE Ltd v International Trade Corp Ltd* [2013] 1 CLC 662, Leggat J remarked that '[u]nder English law a duty of good faith is implied by law as an incident of certain categories of contract, for example contracts of employment and contracts between partners or others whose relationship is characterised as a fiduciary one'. The existence of a generally recognised principle of *uberrimae fidei* in partnership was expressly acknowledged by Hogan J in the Court of Appeal in *Flynn & anor v Breccia & anor* [2017] IECA 74 and by Finlay Geoghegan J in the same case, where she commented that partnership agreements are in the category of agreements and contracts to which a duty of good faith applies. See also *Golstein v Bishop* [2014] Ch 131 where one partner in a firm of solicitors acted unilaterally in deciding to represent a particular client without consulting his co-partner (who had asked him not to represent that client in light of the perceived risk that his business affairs could pose to the firm). Christopher Nugee QC (sitting as a deputy High Court judge) held that this unilateral action was a breach of the duty of good faith.

[39]   *Blisset v Daniel* (1853) 10 Hare 493.

[40]   *Heslin v Fay (1)* (1884) 15 LR Ir 431.

[41]   See for example the opening words of s 24 and s 19 of the 1890 Act.

equal. This is clear from the decision in *Bolton v Carmichael*.[43] That case concerned a law partnership between Carmichael and his nephew, Bolton. However, Carmichael treated Bolton more as a clerk than a partner, keeping him ignorant of the affairs of the firm and denying him access to the firm's books or communications with clients. In addition, he had:

> 'throughout the existence of the partnership an assumption of superiority which may have been natural enough considering the relationship or rather connection between them, but which was very inconsistent with that equality which should exist between partners. When he is desirous of dissolving it he does not communicate directly with his partner, but he writes to the young man's father, treating the petitioner more like an apprentice than a partner, and as if his voice in the matter was quite a secondary consideration.'[44]

Brady LC held that these actions on the part of Carmichael led to the dissolution of the partnership.

Equality does not mean identical treatment

[15.17] It is clear that the requirement that partners treat each other equally does not mean that they must treat each other identically and there is nothing to prevent a partner from negotiating a partnership agreement whereby he will be in an inferior position to his co-partner. This is made clear from the terms of the partnership agreement in *O'Dwyer, Inspector of Taxes v Cafolla & Co*.[45] Indeed, it is doubted elsewhere in this book whether the conclusion that the parties were in fact partners on the extreme facts of that case would necessarily be followed today.[46] That case involved a father and his sons who carried on a well-known fish and chip business in partnership in O'Connell Street and Capel Street in Dublin. The business had previously been run by the father as a sole trader and when he entered partnership with his sons he was, in the words of O'Byrne J, in 'a commanding position in the partnership'.[47] The father had almost complete control of the business since he retained ownership of the premises in which the business was being carried on, of all the capital, the assets and the goodwill and was the only signatory on the bank account. In addition, he had the right at any time to deal in any way with the assets of the partnership by way of loan, mortgage, compromise, etc, and he alone was entitled to employ and dismiss staff and enter into contracts on behalf of the firm. The other partners were entitled to draw on the partnership account at any time, but only by cheque drawn by the father and for amounts approved by him. He also had the right at any time to bring the partnership to an end and instead to resume carrying on the business for his sole benefit. Nonetheless, the High Court and Supreme Court accepted that a valid partnership was in existence.[48]

---

42   See para [15.56] et seq for a discussion of those fiduciary duties which may not be excluded by agreement between the partners.

43   *Bolton v Carmichael* (1856) 1 Ir Jur (ns) 298.

44   *Bolton v Carmichael* (1856) 1 Ir Jur (ns) 298 at 302.

45   *O'Dwyer, Inspector of Taxes v Cafolla & Co* [1949] IR 210.

46   See para [2.79].

47   *O'Dwyer, Inspector of Taxes v Cafolla & Co* [1949] IR 210 at 239.

48   The Commissioner for the Special Purposes of the Income Tax Acts had held that a valid and subsisting partnership was in existence. This was not challenged on appeal and in the High Court, Maguire J noted that '[t]here was abundant evidence on which the Special Commissioner could come to this conclusion' *O'Dwyer, Inspector of Taxes v Cafolla & Co* [1949] IR 210 at 222).

Partners Owe Each Other a Duty of Honesty

[15.18] It is perhaps self-evident that an integral part of a partner's fiduciary duty is his duty to be honest in his partnership dealings with his partners. This principle is illustrated by *Hutcheson v Smith*.[49] In that case, the defendant partner had been appointed to collect in the firm's assets as part of its winding up. However, he had not been candid in his statements to his partner or to the court regarding the amount of partnership funds in his possession. Accordingly, Brady CB ordered that the defendant pay interest to his partner on his share of that money from the date the defendant had it in his possession.[50]

[15.19] In the Australian case of *Johnson v Snaddon*,[51] the management committee of a firm of solicitors concluded that the number of partners in the firm was no longer sustainable. With a view to increasing the net earnings per equity partner, each partner was asked to fill out a questionnaire indicating whether each fellow partner should remain as an equity partner, become a non-equity partner, become a consultant of the firm, or leave the firm. Only one partner, and Mr Johnson himself, considered that Mr Johnson should be an equity partner. Two indicated that he should be a non-equity partner, eight thought that he should be a consultant and three thought that he should not be in the firm in any capacity. On the question of trust and respect, Mr Johnson was rated as either average or below average. Mr Johnson was advised that the result of the survey was that his fellow partners did not wish him to remain as an equity partner. Mr Brown, the chief executive of the firm (who was not a partner) offered him a consultancy position in the firm, but Mr Johnson stated that he could not work for the partners who had treated him in this fashion, that he was leaving the firm and that he was considering himself expelled by the partners. In the ensuing litigation, Mr Johnson alleged that the conduct of the other partners amounted to conduct designed to make his position intolerable so as to expel him from the partnership and that in so acting, the partners breached their fiduciary duty to him. The Supreme Court of Victoria held that there was no breach of fiduciary duty – the decision of the other partners that they no longer wanted Mr Johnson as a partner was not itself a breach by them of their fiduciary duty towards Mr Johnson. While partners are required to be honest with each other and not pursue their own interests to the detriment of the firm, it is not the case that partners cannot fall out with each other without breaching their fiduciary duties. Buchanan JA stated:[52]

> 'While partners must be worthy of each other's trust and faith, they are not obliged to continue to trust and have faith in each other's abilities. Equally they are not obliged to continue to respect each other and to wish to remain in partnership. Rectitude is demanded of a partner, but not good manners or sympathy. A partnership is a commercial undertaking, the principal object of which is to make profits, and the partners are entitled

---

49 *Hutcheson v Smith* (1842) 5 Ir Eq R 117.
50 The duty of honesty can also extend to prospective partners: see *Conlon v Simms* [2008] 1 WLR 484, a case involving a firm of solicitors, where Parker LJ in the Court of Appeal confirmed that prospective partners have a duty to disclose material matters (in that case, matters which could have affected Mr Simms' status as a solicitor).
51 *Johnson v Snaddon* [2001] VSCA 91.
52 At paras 27 and 28 of his judgment.

to pursue that objective robustly provided that they act honestly with each other and do not act in their own interests where to do so conflicts with the interests of the partnership ... If the partners determine that one of their number is no longer an asset to the partnership, so that they consider it is in the best interests of the partnership that the partner leave, they may embark upon negotiations for his departure without breaking any fiduciary obligation owed to him.'

Other Instances of a Partner's Fiduciary Duty at Common Law

[15.20] Some legal commentators have expressed doubt as to whether a partner's fiduciary duty extends beyond his obligation to exhibit good faith in his dealings with his partners.[53] However, it is contended that a partner's fiduciary duty should not be so restricted. Rather, it is thought that the term a 'partner's fiduciary duty' encompasses more than simply good faith[54] and indeed that the instances of fiduciary duties set out in this chapter are not exhaustive, but merely examples of the higher duties of conduct which are owed by persons in special relationships, such as that of partners. These duties have been developed by the courts in the exercise of its equitable jurisdiction and include not only the duty of good faith, but also duties such as that of honesty, loyalty,[55] a duty to avoid conflicts of interest, a duty to avoid profiting personally from partnership opportunities/information, a duty to provide full accounts of all information and assets in one's possession or control and to account for benefits obtained in breach of these duties.[56] The Companies Act 2014 codified, for the first time, the eight key fiduciary duties of a company's directors, one of which is the duty to act in good faith in what the director believes to be in the best interests of the company.[57] Arguably, partners are in

[53] See Halsbury's *Laws of England* (4th edn, 1994) Vol 35, para 93, fn 1, where it is stated that partners owe each other a duty of good faith but that the 'issue as to whether partners also owe each other a fiduciary duty is less clear'. Note also that in l'Anson Banks, *Lindley & Banks on Partnership* (20th edn, 2017) at para 16-01 et seq, reference is made only to a partner's duty of good faith and other instances of a partner's fiduciary duty are not examined.

[54] This is the case in America: *Hurt, Smith, Bromberg & Ribstein on Limited Liability Partnerships, the Revised Uniform Partnership Act, and the Uniform Limited Partnership Act* (2018 edn). See generally Feldman, 'Your Partner's Keeper: the duty of good faith and fair dealing under the Revised Uniform Partnership Act' (1995) 48 SMU Law Review 1931; Keeley, 'Whose Partnership is it Anyway?' (1994) 63 Fordham LR 609; DeMott, 'Fiduciary obligation under intellectual siege: contemporary challenges to the duty to be loyal' (1992) 30 Osgoode Hall LJ 471.

[55] In *Best & Anor v Ghose & Anor* [2018] IEHC 376 (at para 53 of her judgment) Baker J noted the suggestion of Professor Biehler in *Equity and the of Law of Trusts in Ireland* (6th edn, 2016) at p 234 that the requirement of loyalty must be present in all fiduciary relationships.

[56] See generally in relation to fiduciary duties, Keane, *Equity and the Law of Trusts in Ireland* (3rd edn, 2017) at para [10.53] et seq, para [13.07] et seq and para [22.02]; Biehler, *Equity and the Law of Trusts in Ireland* (6th edn, 2016) at p 234 et seq.

[57] See generally Courtney, *The Law of Companies* (4th edn, 2016) at para [16.042] et seq; Hutchinson, *Keane on Company Law* (5th edn, 2016) at para [27.84] et seq. Note in particular Courtney's comment at para [16.042] that the duty on a director to act in good faith in what the director believes to be in the best interests of the company (set out in the Companies Act 2014, s 228(1)(a)) is 'the sub-structure on which all other duties are built. In a real sense, the duty in s 228(1)(a) defines all other duties owed by directors, which could be described as mere elaborations of this, the very epitome of a fiduciary duty'.

more need of a higher standard of conduct from their co-partners than shareholders and directors of companies in view of their personal liability for the partnership debts. Support for the view that partners' fiduciary duties should not be restricted to a duty of good faith may be gleaned from the expansive view of a partner's fiduciary duty contained in the Supreme Court judgments in *Williams v Harris*[58] and *Meagher v Meagher*.[59] In both cases, the Supreme Court recognised the existence of a fiduciary duty based on the nature of the relationship between the partners, without restricting its application to simply that of good faith. By doing so, the Court has retained the flexibility to extend the duty owed by partners to each other beyond that of good faith as the circumstances require, in the same way as the duties of directors in a company have been extended.[60] Since the parties to a partnership agreement cannot anticipate all the problems that may arise during the life of the partnership, this approach allows the courts to supply general terms to fill in the gaps in the partnership agreement. Therefore, it is apprehended that the courts will require a partner to exhibit that standard of behaviour which one would expect to exist between persons who are in a relationship of 'equality, mutuality, trust and confidence'.[61] This is considerably more than one expects from parties dealing at arm's length. In the eloquent terms of Cardozo J, the eminent American jurist:

> 'Joint adventurers, like co-partners, owe to one another ... the duty of finest loyalty. Many forms of conduct permissible in a workaday world for those acting at arm's length, are forbidden to those bound by fiduciary ties. A trustee is held to something stricter than the morals of the market place. Not honesty alone, but the punctilio of an honor the most sensitive is then the standard of behaviour. As to this there has developed a tradition that is unbending and inveterate. Uncompromising rigidity has been the attitude of courts of equity when petitioned to undermine the rule of undivided loyalty by the "disintegrating erosion" of particular exceptions ... Only thus has the level of conduct for fiduciaries been kept at a level higher than that trodden by the crowd. It will not unconsciously be lowered by any judgment of this court.'[62]

---

58   *Williams v Harris* [1980] ILRM 237.
59   *Meagher v Meagher* [1961] IR 96.
60   Note for example that the duties of a director in a company are not restricted to the duty of good faith, and the fiduciary duties of directors were codified for the first time by the Companies Act 2014. Eight fiduciary duties are listed, six of which have effect in place of common law rules and equitable principles, while the remaining two (the duty to act honestly and responsibly in relation to the conduct of the company's affairs, and the duty to have regard to the interests of the company's members) are not stated to replace existing common law and equitable principles, as they are derived from existing statutory rules. See Hutchinson, *Keane on Company Law* (5th edn, 2016) at para [27.84] et seq; Courtney, *The Law of Companies* (4th edn, 2016) at para [16.038] et seq.
61   To use a term coined by Gannon J in *Re Murph's Restaurant Ltd* [1979] ILRM 141 at 151, in his description of the essence of a quasi-partnership relationship. See also the Privy Council case of *Rama v Miller* [1996] 1 NZLR 257 (one partner was held to have breached his fiduciary duty to his co-partner by entering into a deed of settlement of the firm's failed transactions without his co-partner's approval and against his known wishes).
62   *Meinhard v Salmon* (1928) 164 NE 545 at 546.

II.   STATUTORY INSTANCES OF FIDUCIARY DUTY

[15.21] In addition to the fiduciary duties of a partner which have been recognised by the courts, there are four statutory instances of a partner's fiduciary duty, all of which are contained in the 1890 Act. These are the duties of a partner:

1.   to render true accounts and full information (to each other) (s 28);
2.   to account for private profits (s 29(1));
3.   to account for profits of a competing business (s 30);
4.   to share post-dissolution profits (s 42(1)).

Each of these statutory fiduciary duties will be examined in turn.

1. Duty to Render True Accounts and Full Information

[15.22] The first instance of a partner's fiduciary duty under the 1890 Act is a partner's duty to provide his co-partners with full information and accounts regarding the partnership. This is contained in s 28 which states that: '[p]artners are bound to render true accounts and full information of all things affecting the partnership to any partner or his legal representatives.'[63]

[15.23] The Scottish case of *Ferguson v MacKay*[64] provides a good example of this fiduciary duty. It concerned a solicitor who was retiring from his firm and who was negotiating the terms of his retirement package with his partners. Before finalising these terms, his partners failed to disclose that three substantial conveyancing instructions had been received by the firm. After the retirement package was agreed, the retiring partner discovered that his co-partners had been less than frank in relation to these lucrative instructions. The court held that his co-partners had breached their fiduciary duty to give him full information on all things affecting the partnership and granted damages to the retiring partner for this breach. The more recent Scottish case of *William Sim v David Howat*[65] considered the extent of a partner's duty under s 28, with Lord Hodge noting at para 40 of his judgment that:

> 'The duty under section 28 is not a duty which is owed at all times. Partners are not obliged to inform their colleagues of everything which occurs in the course of partnership business as otherwise one could not delegate management powers to a managing partner while allowing others to concentrate on earning income for the firm. The duty arises in specific circumstances. Examples of those circumstances include when a partner seeks information from another or when in the context of negotiations between the partners, one partner has information relating to the partnership which is material to the subject matter of the negotiation. In the latter case section 28, which falls to be interpreted in the context

---

63   In *Inversiones Frieira SL v Colyzeo Investors II LP* [2012] Bus LR 1136, while the proceedings involved a limited partnership, Norris J observed (at paras 23(b) and (c) of his judgment) that the right of a partner to full information and true accounts from his co-partners under s 28 is as much a right of a limited partner in a limited partnership as it is the right of an ordinary partner.

64   *Ferguson v MacKay* [1985] SLT 1994.

65   *William Sim v David Howat* [2012] CSOH 171.

of the obligation of the utmost good faith, places the partner under an obligation to disclose that information to his partners ...'

Exclusion of partner's right to receive full information?

[15.24] Unlike the other three fiduciary duties set out in the 1890 Act (namely, ss 29(1), 30 and 42(1)) which are considered hereunder, the right to true accounts and information is not stated to be subject to contrary agreement amongst the partners. This raises the difficult question of whether this right may be varied or excluded by the parties to a partnership agreement, particularly in view of the terms of s 19 of the 1890 Act which states that 'the rights and duties of partners, whether ascertained by agreement or defined by this Act, may be varied by the consent of all the partners'.[66]

[15.25] While as a matter of contract it is arguable that the partners can agree to whatever terms they desire, it is difficult, if not impossible, to imagine a true partnership existing where the partners are not required to render true accounts or full information to each other. Such persons would not, it is contended, be carrying on business in common, in the sense of having the requisite proximity in their relationship as required by the definition of a partnership.[67] Furthermore, without having true accounts and information on the partnership, a partner would not be in a position to monitor any abuses by his co-partners of their positions. This ability to monitor abuses is of particular significance in partnerships, since each partner is liable to an unlimited degree for the partnership obligations. For these reasons, it is contended that the right of a partner to true accounts and partnership information in s 28 of the 1890 Act and the corresponding duty of his co-partner to provide that information is so basic in every partnership that it is not possible for the partners to exclude it.[68] It is suggested that this may be why the drafters of the 1890 Act did not provide that s 28 was to be subject to contrary agreement.

[15.26] However, it seems clear that a term in a partnership agreement clarifying the parameters of the right to receive full information is acceptable, provided that it is not so restrictive as to deprive the right of any true effect. For example it is thought that a court would enforce an agreement that imposed restrictions on the time and place in which information could be obtained, so as to prevent difficult partners abusing this right. Similarly, the court might enforce a restriction on access to sensitive information which was not necessary to protect the interests of the affected partner.

---

[66] Note that s 19 is not without exceptions, for example an agreement between partners which purports to vary the liability of a partner to third parties under ss 9 and 10 of the 1890 Act would clearly be unenforceable.

[67] See the definition of a partnership in s 1(1) of the 1890 Act and see generally, para **[2.68]**.

[68] Note that in America, s 105 of the Uniform Partnership Act (1997) (Last Amended 2013) provides that certain implied terms in that Act are not capable of being varied by the partners, save (in some cases) in limited circumstances. One of these is the reasonable right of access to the books and records of the partnership under s 408 of that Act which cannot be unreasonably restricted. It is also to be noted that, unlike the position in Ireland, the obligation of good faith and fair dealing, the duty of loyalty, and the duty of care, are statutory rights in America and under the Uniform Partnership Act (1997) (Last Amended 2013), they may not be eliminated or altered by the terms of the partnership agreement, save to the limited extent set out in that Act.

2. Duty to Account for Private Profits

[15.27] In the High Court case of *Williams v Harris*,[69] McWilliam J applied to partners the principle that 'a person in a fiduciary position is not allowed to make a profit out of his trust and, if he does so, he is liable to account for that profit'.[70] This aspect of a partner's fiduciary duty is also to be found in s 29(1) of the 1890 Act, which states that:

> Every partner must account to the firm for any benefit derived by him without the consent of the other partners from any transaction concerning the partnership, or from any use by him of the partnership property name[71] or business connexion.

Unlike the fiduciary duty in s 28, this fiduciary duty is capable of exclusion by the partners since it is expressed to be subject to the 'consent of the other partners'.

A secret or private profit?

[15.28] Since the benefit with which s 29(1) is concerned is one which is obtained by a partner without the consent of his co-partners, it is commonly referred to as a 'secret profit'. However, it should be noted that this description is not completely accurate as the duty to account arises whether the partner conducts the business openly or secretly.[72] Of course, if all his co-partners are aware of his activities, he may claim that they impliedly consented to the activity, so as to negative the duty to account. The term 'private profit' is used by the 1890 Act in the margin to s 29(1) and this, it is contended, is a more accurate term. Thus, while the term 'secret profit' is commonly used by the courts,[73] in the interests of accuracy, reference should be made to 'private profit'.

Sale of partner's goods to firm at sale price is a private profit

[15.29] A classic example of a private profit is where a partner sells goods to the partnership at the sale price of those goods, rather than the price at which he acquired them. The difference between these two prices is obviously a profit accruing to the partner, and if not approved by his co-partners is a private profit. The partnership in *Burton v Wookey*[74] was between two parties who had agreed to deal in gems. The

---

69 *Williams v Harris* (15 January 1980) HC. McWilliam J's judgment was reversed by the Supreme Court on the facts, [1980] ILRM 237, but not as to the principle regarding the application of fiduciary duties to partners. See further para **[15.08]**.

70 *Williams v Harris* (15 January 1980) HC, pp 9–10 of the transcript. In this way, a partner is treated like a trustee, since a trustee is obliged not to place himself in a position where his duty as a trustee and his self-interest might conflict. It is a basic principle of equity that a trustee, who is under a fiduciary duty to his beneficiary, may not make a profit from his position as a trustee: *Re De Courcenay* [1912] 1 IR 341, which concerned a trustee who was also a partner. See generally, Keane, *Equity and the Law of Trusts in Ireland* (3rd edn, 2017) at para 10.53 et seq; Biehler, *Equity and the Law of Trusts in Ireland* (6th edn, 2016) at p 236 et seq.

71 This clause would clearly benefit from the insertion of a comma between the words 'property' and 'name'.

72 *Glassington v Thwaites* (1833) 1 Sim & St 124.

73 See for example Carroll J's reference to 'secret profit' in *Horgan v Baxter* (11 May 1982) HC at p 11 of the transcript, and Kelly J's reference to 'the making of a secret profit [being] wholly inconsistent with the notion of partnership ...' in *Daly & ors v Killally & anor* [2009] IEHC 172.

74 *Burton v Wookey* (1882) 6 Mad 367. This case was expressly approved by Brady LC in *Lock v Lynam* (1854) 4 Ir Ch R 188.

defendant partner was also a shopkeeper and had agreed to be the active partner in the partnership and purchase the gems from miners in his neighbourhood. Some time after the formation of the partnership, the defendant, instead of paying the miners in cash for the gems, paid them with goods from his shop. In his account with the plaintiff partner, the defendant partner treated those goods as having been purchased by the miners for an amount equal to their sale price, rather than their cost price. By charging the firm the sale price of those goods, the defendant clearly breached his duty to avoid making a private profit. It was held that the plaintiff was entitled to an equal division of the profit made by the defendant in his dealings in those shop goods.

Retention by a partner of increased margin or statute-barred sums

[15.30] If a partner makes a greater profit on a sale of the partnership goods than was expected or agreed by his partner, whether due to his own negotiating skills or otherwise, he is not entitled to keep this increase in profit, since this will be a private profit. This principle is highlighted by the High Court case of *Horgan v Baxter*.[75] In that case, the parties were involved in a cattle-exporting partnership. They sold cattle to Italian based customers at a 4% margin on the cost at which they acquired the cattle. It appeared from the evidence that in his dealings with the firm's customers, the defendant partner falsified documentation in order to claim a greater acquisition price and hence a greater profit when he sold the cattle. However, the increased margin which he received on the sale of the cattle was not declared by him to his partner. Carroll J held that if, as was likely on the evidence, a private profit was so made by the defendant, he would be accountable therefor to his partner.[76]

[15.31] Also in that case, the defendant had retained certain sums of money which were owed by the firm to one of its customers. With the passage of time, these sums had become statute barred and the customers were no longer entitled to claim them. However, the defendant had not informed his partner that he had retained these funds. Accordingly, these sums also constituted a private profit and Carroll J held that the plaintiff was entitled to half of these funds.

Renewal of leases by partner is private profit

[15.32] A common situation in which there may arise a private profit is where a partner renews a lease of partnership property in his own name, rather than in the firm's name. In such a case, the partner will not be allowed to treat the renewed lease as one in which his co-partners have no interest.[77] In *Clegg v Edmondson*,[78] the managing partners of a firm gave notice to their co-partners of their dissolution of a partnership at will. At the

---

[75] *Horgan v Baxter* (11 May 1982) HC.
[76] But note that where state aid for cattle export was improperly claimed by the defendant, Carroll J indicated that the plaintiff would not have been entitled to claim his share of this illegal profit, see further para **[9.36]**.
[77] See for example *Featherstonhaugh v Fenwick* (1810) 17 Ves Jr 298; *Clegg v Fishwick* (1849) 1 Mac & G 294; *Keech v Sandford* (1726) Sel Cas Ch 61. See also the comment of Arden LJ in *Woodfull v Lindsley* [2004] EWCA Civ 165 that '... it is obvious that if ... a fiduciary holds trust property at the cesser of his fiduciary relationship, he remains accountable for it. His duty is to hand it back to the person or persons to whom the fiduciary duty was owed.'
[78] *Clegg v Edmondson* (1856) 8 De G & J 173.

same time, they announced that they intended to renew the lease of the partnership premises in their own name. It was held that they were not permitted to acquire the lease for their own benefit, even where the landlord objected to renewing the lease to any of the partners, other than them. A distinction should however be drawn between the purchase of the reversion of a lease by a partner and the renewal of a lease by a partner in his own name, where the lease was held by his firm. The former case does not involve a private profit, since the partner who purchases the reversion does not do so by virtue of any existing interest in the lease.[79]

Sale by one partner of his share to another

[15.33] The acquisition by a partner of another partner's share in the firm for his own benefit would prima facie appear to be a 'transaction affecting the partnership' and therefore subject to s 29(1), if there is any benefit deriving to the firm. It would also prima facie fall under the fiduciary duty of a partner to give full information to his co-partners regarding all things affecting the partnership under s 28. However, *Cassels v Stewart*[80] is authority for the principle that the purchase by one partner of another partner's share is not something which needs to be notified to his co-partners, so as to give them an opportunity to join in the purchase.[81]

Use of the 'partnership property name or business connexion'

[15.34] The reference to the use of the partnership property,[82] name or business connection in s 29(1) will apply to the use of partnership opportunities, ie where a partner benefits from an opportunity which was offered to the partnership or which he learned of through the partnership and which might have been used to benefit the partnership. This principle is illustrated by the lease renewal cases referred to already. The concept underlying such cases is that these opportunities are regarded as partnership property and therefore may not be appropriated by one partner for his exclusive benefit.[83] It will however sometimes be a difficult issue to decide whether an opportunity is that of a partner personally or of the partnership. In this regard, the nature of the partnership business will of course be crucial. In the New Zealand case of *Parkin v Alabaster*,[84] the parties ran an apartment letting business together. Alabaster was employed as the manager of the business and Parkin denied that any partnership existed

---

79 See for example *Griffith v Owen* [1907] 1 Ch 195.

80 *Cassels v Stewart* (1881) 6 App Cas 64. See also the Australian case of *Birtchnell v Equity Trustees, Executors and Agency Co Ltd* (1929) 42 CLR 384. In the Canadian case of *Hogar Estates Ltd in Trust v Shebron Holdings Ltd* (1979) 25 OR (2d) 543, the agreement was set aside as one partner did not disclose that an obstacle to planning had been removed which made the partnership interest more valuable.

81 Note that the purchase of another partner's share was not governed by the partnership agreement in that case, nor was the purchase of a partner's share part of the firm's business.

82 See for example *Moore v Moore* (27 February 1998) HC NI, where one partner used partnership funds for his own personal benefit.

83 See for example the American case of *Stark v Reingold* (1955) 113 A 2d 679 which found that a partner in a rental car firm could not acquire for himself a similar opportunity which he was offered in the course of the partnership business for franchises in neighbouring counties.

84 *Parkin v Alabaster* (1998) Butterworths Current Law (NZ) 509.

between them. However, the Court of Appeal found that the relationship between the parties was that of partnership. At issue then became the accounting between the partners on the dissolution of this partnership and in particular whether it extended to Parkin's involvement with a third party in a proposal to acquire and re-locate a hotel to another site. However, it was held that the business opportunity to acquire and relocate the hotel was taken outside the scope of the business of providing accommodation as undertaken by the partnership. For this reason, Alabaster was not entitled to an accounting in relation to the hotel project.

Use of the partnership name or business connection

[15.35] By its express terms, s 29(1) requires a partner to account for any transaction concerning the partnership or for any use by him of the partnership property or business connection. Unlike the use of partnership property, it is not always so easy to identify a use of the partnership name or business connection by a partner which is a private profit under s 29(1). This is because in many partnerships and particularly professional partnerships, the partners will be closely identified with their partnership and therefore the business connection of the partnership will be partly due to the personal connections of the partners. It follows that business may come to a former partner because of his personal attributes, rather than because of his role as a partner in the firm and therefore will not involve a use by him of the partnership connection or name under s 29(1). This is illustrated by the unsuccessful claim for damages in the High Court case of *O'Connor v Woods*.[85] There, the plaintiff, a former partner in the accountancy firm of John A Woods & Co had come to know certain clients of the firm while he was a partner. When the plaintiff left the firm, these clients continued to use his services and the continuing partners in the firm claimed that the fees received by the plaintiff from these clients should be paid to the continuing partners, on the basis that the plaintiff had only come to know the clients 'through his association with the partnership'.[86] This was rejected by Kenny J who only countenanced granting damages if the plaintiff had enticed the clients away from the firm:

'There was no enticement by him in connection with this work and there was no obligation on him to leave work with the partnership which he could do ... This case illustrates the view of the first named defendant that the plaintiff is liable for enticement when a company, firm or individual who had been clients of the partnership took their business away when the plaintiff left. The plaintiff never entered into a covenant or agreement that he would not practise as an accountant after he terminated the partnership and if the parties to the [partnership agreement] wished to provide that a retiring partner should not practise,[87] they should have inserted such a clause in the agreement ... It does not follow that because a company or individual took any part of their business away from the partnership when the plaintiff left it, that the plaintiff is liable for the fees.'[88]

---

[85] *O'Connor v Woods* (22 January 1976) HC.

[86] *O'Connor v Woods* (22 January 1976) HC at p 14 of the transcript.

[87] It seems clear that Kenny J means that the continuing partners could have prevented him from practising as an accountant 'in competition with the firm' and not prevented him from practising as an accountant anywhere.

[88] *O'Connor v Woods* (22 January 1976) HC at pp 10–2 of the transcript.

[15.36] Since a breach of s 29(1) will be difficult to establish in a situation where a partner deals with clients of his previous firm, many partnership agreements attempt to deal with this possibility by means of a restrictive covenant on the outgoing partner.[89]

If private profit is made outside of firm's ordinary course of business

[15.37] An issue which needs to be addressed under s 29(1) is whether the profit in question must arise from a transaction which is within the firm's ordinary course of business for it to be a private profit? As will be noted hereunder, this is the case with a partner's fiduciary duty under s 30 of the 1890 Act which provides that a partner must account for all profits, where he carries on any 'business of the same nature as and competing with that of the firm'. Indeed, in some cases ss 29(1) and 30 will both apply to the same fact situations. However, the wording of s 29(1) states simply that there is a duty to account for a private profit made from any transaction concerning the partnership, *or* from any use of the partnership property name or business connection. While the term 'any transaction concerning the partnership' would seem to imply that the transaction in question is of the same nature as carried on by the firm, the use of the firm's business connection, name or property does not, on the face of the section, need to be done by the partner in a business of the same nature as the firm's business. Thus, should a partner in an accountancy firm be made to account for his use of the firm's client list and the firm's offices to sell his private antique collection, if he does so without the consent of his partners? Commentators have suggested that the partner will not be required to account for the private profit made from an activity that is not within the firm's ordinary course of business.[90] Support for this proposition is based on the pre-1890 case of *Aas v Benham*,[91] in which one partner in a firm of *shipbrokers* used information which he had acquired while a member of the firm, to set up a *shipbuilding* company, for which he received monetary compensation. His co-partners' action to recover a share of this compensation failed, since it was held that this business was outside the ordinary course of business of the firm.

[15.38] However, it is apprehended that an Irish court may not necessarily adopt this view. Instead it may take the view that a partner must account for any secret profit using the firm's name or business connection, even where it arises from an activity which is outside the firm's ordinary course of business. Such an approach can be supported by the clear wording of s 29(1) which (save in relation to 'any transaction concerning the partnership'), does not require the use of the partnership property, name or business connection to be used in the same business as carried on by the firm, before the partner has to account for the profits derived thereby. In addition, the duty to account for a secret profit is an aspect of the duty of fiduciaries not to benefit from their positions and this latter principle is not restricted by the requirement that the benefit arise from a certain area of business. Rather, the rationale behind the principle in s 29(1) is to avoid a situation where the fiduciary/partner would be encouraged not to act in the firm's

89 See further in relation to such covenants para **[22.24]** et seq.
90 See l'Anson Banks, *Lindley & Banks on Partnership* (20th edn, 2017) at para 16.39. The position appears to be the same in Scotland, see Brough, *Miller on Partnership* (2nd edn, 1994) at p 162 quoting *Fuller v Duncan* (1891) 7 TLR 305.
91 *Aas v Benham* [1891] 2 Ch 244. Note that the case was heard prior to the enactment of the 1890 Act and without reference to that Act.

interests.[92] Accordingly, it is irrelevant whether the benefit obtained is in an area which is within the ordinary course of business of the firm or otherwise. Indeed, English caselaw, albeit in the company law field, would appear to support this interpretation. Thus, *Broadman v Phipps*[93] involved a director, who was held to be in a fiduciary position *vis-à-vis* his company, being held to account for the private profit which he had made, even where it was derived from a business which was not carried on by the company. Furthermore, it is a basic principle of the law of agency that an agent is not allowed to make a private profit out of his position, whether it is made outside the ordinary course of business of his principal or not.[94] Since partners are agents for their co-partners, it is difficult to see why a partner can, but an agent cannot, benefit from his position, where the use of the partnership property, name or business connection is outside the firm's ordinary course of business.

[15.39] For these reasons, it is apprehended that the Irish courts should take the more liberal interpretation of s 29(1). Accordingly, it would be prudent for any partner, who proposes to use the property, name or business connection of his firm, even in a venture which is outside the firm's ordinary course of business, to first obtain the consent of his partners thereto.

Duty not to make private profit applies after the firm's dissolution

[15.40] Section 29(2) of the 1890 Act clarifies that s 29(1) applies also after the dissolution of a partnership which is caused by the death of a partner:

> This section applies also to transactions undertaken after a partnership has been dissolved by the death of a partner, and before the affairs thereof have been completely wound up, either by any surviving partner or by the representatives of the deceased partner.

[15.41] Although s 29(2) only contemplates the existence of the duty during the winding up of a partnership which has been dissolved by the death of a partner, there would seem to be no reason in principle for the duty not to apply after the technical or general dissolution of a partnership, howsoever caused, until the end of its winding up. Otherwise a partner could on dissolution attempt to appropriate the firm's assets and goodwill.[95] Support for this contention can be found in *Meagher v Meagher*,[96] since the Supreme Court did not distinguish between the application of fiduciary duties to partners when the business went through a technical dissolution on the death of the first

---

[92]   See eg *Burton v Wookey* (1882) 6 Mad 367, which was quoted with approval by Brady LC in *Lock v Lynam* (1854) 4 Ir Ch R 188.

[93]   *Broadman v Phipps* [1967] 2 AC 46.

[94]   *Murphy v O'Shea* (1845) 1 Ir Eq R 329; *Chariot Inns v Assicurazioni Generali SpA* [1981] IR 199; *Sherrard v Barron* [1923] 1 IR 21; *Reading v Attorney General* [1951] AC 5107.

[95]   See l'Anson Banks, *Lindley & Banks on Partnership* (20th edn, 2017) at para 16-34. See also the Privy Council decision in *Pathirana v Pathirana* [1967] 1 AC 233 which concerned a two-person partnership. The defendant gave notice dissolving his partnership with the plaintiff in a petrol station. Before the notice had expired, the defendant renewed, in his own name, certain petrol supply agreements. After the dissolution of the partnership, he carried on trading from the same premises in his own name. He was held to be accountable to the plaintiff for a share of the profits from these new agreements.

[96]   *Meagher v Meagher* [1961] IR 96 at 110. See also *Williams v Harris* (15 January 1980) HC, [1980] ILRM 237 (SC).

of the three brothers and a general dissolution on the death of the second brother. However, s 29(1) does not apply after the winding up of a partnership is complete. In such a situation all the former partners can use the business connection and partnership name for their own benefit, in the absence of a contrary agreement.[97]

[15.42] In *Sew Hoy v Sew Hoy*,[98] a family partnership was dissolved in 1977. Land, which was the sole asset of the partnership, had been sold to the Crown in 1976. In 1992, the Crown no longer required that land and, as required by the relevant compulsory purchase legislation, offered the land back to the person from whom it was acquired or his successors. Since the partnership had been dissolved, the issue to be decided was whether any fiduciary duties were owed by the former partners to one another. The issue arose in the context of a claim by four of the former partners that one of the successors of another former partner had taken up the offer without fully consulting with them and without revealing certain information about the land. Reliance was placed, in particular, on s 41 of the New Zealand Partnership Act, the equivalent of s 29(2) of the 1890 Act, which provides that the rights and obligations of partners remain so far as may be necessary to wind up the affairs of the partnership and complete transactions begun but unfinished. The New Zealand Court of Appeal held that s 41 did not apply to an inchoate right to purchase property (if offered back by the state) in this case. When the offer was made in 1992 to sell back the property, it was to the former partners as individuals and not to the dissolved partnership.

'consent of the other partners'

[15.43] Section 29(1) permits a partner in a firm to earn profits for his own benefit, where they are not 'private', ie where the consent of the other partners has been obtained thereto. There must have been full disclosure of all the facts to the partners giving their consent in order for this consent to be regarded as valid. This principle is illustrated by *Dunne v English*,[99] in which the defendant and plaintiff had agreed to buy a mine for £50,000 with a view to its resale for £60,000. The mine was resold by the defendant for in excess of £60,000 to a company in which the defendant had an interest. When the plaintiff sought his share of the extra profit made by the defendant, it was argued that the plaintiff had some knowledge that the defendant had an interest in the purchase beyond his share of the £10,000 profit. However, it was held that since the plaintiff did not know the precise extent of the benefit, he was entitled to share in this private profit.

3. Duty to Account for Profits of a Competing Business

[15.44] Section 30 of the 1890 Act provides the third statutory instance of a partner's fiduciary duty. It establishes the duty of a partner to account to the firm for any profits earned by him in a business which competes with the firm:

> If a partner, without the consent of the other partners, carries on any business of the same nature as and competing with that of the firm, he must account for and pay over to the firm all profits made by him in that business.

---

97   See para **[18.18]** et seq.
98   *Sew Hoy v Sew Hoy* [2001] NZLR 391 (CA).
99   *Dunne v English* (1874) LR 18 Eq 524.

[15.45] It is to be noted that the side margin note to this section describes it as a 'duty of partner not to compete with the firm'. However, there is no such duty imposed by this section. Rather the duty on a partner under this section is simply to account to the firm for the profits made by him from a competing business. As with s 29(1), the partner is accountable to his co-partners, whether the partner conducts the business openly or secretly.[100] Although, if all his co-partners are aware of his activities, he may claim that they impliedly consented to the activity, so as to negative the duty to account. As noted by Brady LC in *Lock v Lynam*,[101] one of the primary reasons why a partner is discouraged from competing with the firm is because he would be able to use his position as a partner to commit a fraud on his co-partners, by siphoning off business opportunities from the firm for his own benefit:

> 'If two persons make such an arrangement as the petitioner and respondent did here, the fact of either of them entering into other contracts of the same kind, without the knowledge and assent of his partner; gives a direct motive for the commission of fraud on his first partner, and one can easily see how such a fraud might be accomplished.'[102]

[15.46] In that case, the parties had agreed to enter a partnership for the purpose of obtaining contracts for the supply of meat to British troops based in Ireland. During the operation of this partnership, Lynam entered into similar arrangements with third persons, whereby he was to share in the profits of similar contracts, if obtained by them. Lock sought an account of the profits of these contracts which Lynam had with third parties. Lynam argued that there was no agreement with Lock that he would not enter into similar contracts with third parties. Nonetheless, Brady LC held that such conduct by Lynam was a breach of his duty of good faith to his partner and he ordered that an account of those contracts be taken:[103]

> 'If the respondent had requested the petitioner to join in these other contracts, and Mr Lock had refused so to do, it might have been different; but when, without such an offer, he entered into this secret bargain, I must repeat that at all events, it seems a breach of faith as between man and man, as well as a contravention of the principles which govern this Court.'[104]

Competing with firm after technical dissolution

[15.47] A partner who leaves a firm which continues in business after his departure[105] is not subject to the terms of s 30 of the 1890 Act. As a former partner, he is not a partner for the purposes of that section and therefore the prohibition in s 30 does not extend to him, unless of course he is using partnership property, ie the partnership name or connection under s 29(1). It will be a separate issue, of course, if he is subject to the

---

100 *Glassington v Thwaites* (1833) 1 Sim & St 124.
101 *Lock v Lynam* (1854) 4 Ir Ch R 188.
102 *Lock v Lynam* (1854) 4 Ir Ch R 188 at 189–90.
103 Subsequently, he withdrew somewhat from that position by relying less on the fiduciary duty and instead looking at the dealings between the parties to see if those dealings raised an express or implied term that neither of them would enter into competing arrangements. In view of the subsequent enactment of s 30 of the 1890 Act, this subsequent withdrawal is of little significance.
104 *Lock v Lynam* (1854) 4 Ir Ch R 188 at 190.
105 Ie on a technical dissolution of the firm.

terms of a restrictive covenant which forbids him from competing with the firm after his departure.[106] Where there is no such restrictive covenant, the former partner will not have to account for profits made in a competing business. Thus in *O'Connor v Woods*,[107] the plaintiff, a former partner in an accountancy firm, had come to know certain clients of the firm while he was a partner. When he left the firm, these clients continued to use his services and Kenny J rejected the continuing partners' claim that the fees received by the plaintiff from these clients should be paid to the continuing partners.

Competing with firm after general dissolution

[15.48] As noted below[108] fiduciary duties continue to apply during the winding up of a partnership. Accordingly, where a partner competes with his firm while it is being wound up,[109] he will be required to account for any profit thereby earned by him without his partners' consent, since he may be reducing the value of the firm's goodwill by his actions. However, once the firm has been wound up, s 30 has no application to a partner in the former firm.

'consent of the other partners'

[15.49] By the express terms of s 30, the duty of a partner to account to the firm for the profits of a competing business is subject to contrary agreement with his partners. The consent of the other partners may be indirect consent, such as where the partners refuse an offer to participate in a competing venture. This is clear from *Lock v Lynam*,[110] where Brady L noted, obiter, that if Lynam, the errant partner, had first requested Lock to join in the contracts which he had with third parties and Lock had refused, it might not have been a breach of duty for Lynam to subsequently enter the contracts. In the context of a partner's private profits, it has been noted[111] that *Dunne v English*[112] is authority for the principle that to be valid, a partner's consent must have been obtained after the full disclosure of all the facts by the partner seeking the consent. This principle is clearly also applicable to any consent obtained under s 30.

'of the same nature as and competing with that of the firm'

[15.50] Section 30 of the 1890 Act only applies where the business is of the same nature as the firm's business and competes with the firm's business. Therefore, s 30 has no application for example to a partner in a dentistry partnership who gets involved in a property speculation business. For this reason, and as a partner is not required to devote his full time to the firm, it is common for partnership agreements to provide that a partner will not be involved in any other business, without the consent of his partners and will devote his full time to the firm.[113]

---

106   See generally in relation to such restrictive covenants, para **[22.24]** et seq.
107   *O'Connor v Woods* (22 January 1976) HC.
108   See para **[15.58]**.
109   Ie during a general dissolution of the firm.
110   *Lock v Lynam* (1854) 4 Ir Ch R 188.
111   See para **[15.43]**.
112   *Dunne v English* (1874) LR 18 Eq 524.
113   As to such terms, see para **[21.96]**.

4. Duty to Share Post-dissolution Profits

[15.51] The final instance of a partner's fiduciary duty under the 1890 Act is the duty of continuing partners to account to a former partner for profits made in the partnership business after his departure by the use of his share of the partnership assets. This is contained in s 42(1) which provides that:

> Where any member of a firm has died or otherwise ceased to be a partner, and the surviving or continuing partners carry on the business of the firm with its capital or assets without any final settlement of accounts as between the firm and the outgoing partner or his estate, then, in the absence of any agreement to the contrary, the outgoing partner or his estate is entitled at the option of himself or his representatives to such share of the profits made since the dissolution as the Court may find to be attributable to the use of his share of the partnership assets, or to interest at the rate of five per cent. per annum on the amount of his share of the partnership assets.

[15.52] This section is analysed in detail elsewhere in this work.[114] However, it remains to be observed that by its express terms, s 42(1) clarifies that this aspect of a partner's fiduciary duty may be excluded by the terms of an agreement between the parties (ie, 'in the absence of any agreement to the contrary'). The effect of such a provision in the partnership agreement was considered by the Supreme Court in *Williams v Harris*.[115] In that case, the partnership agreement provided that upon retirement, the share of a retiring partner shall 'as and from the time of his death or ceasing to be a partner ... be purchased and belong to the remaining partners'. However, the retiring partners only received the purchase price for their share two years after their retirement, due to the delay in having a valuation fixed by arbitration. Accordingly, they claimed interest for this two-year period at the rate of 5% under s 42. Both the High Court and the Supreme Court rejected the claim for interest under s 42 on the basis that the terms of the partnership agreement constituted an agreement to the contrary within the terms of s 42(1) and therefore prevented that section from applying.[116]

III. CHARACTERISTICS OF A PARTNER'S FIDUCIARY DUTY

[15.53] Having considered some of the instances of a partner's fiduciary duty at common law and under statute, the remainder of this chapter is concerned with the characteristics of these duties. As a general point, it should be noted that a partner's fiduciary duty is of general application since it arises out of the fiduciary relationship between partners. Yet this fiduciary relationship between the partners does not affect the relationship between a partner and a third party. Thus the fact that a partner receives partnership money from a third party does not automatically mean that the payment will

---

114 See para **[26.63]** et seq.

115 *Williams v Harris* [1980] ILRM 237.

116 Although, in the High Court, McWilliam J held that the retiring partners were entitled to interest on the basis that the continuing partners were in a fiduciary position. He therefore held that they could not have the benefit of both the purchase money and the retiring partner's share. In the Supreme Court, it was held that the terms of the partnership agreement excluded the application of this fiduciary duty.

be regarded as having been received by the partner from the third party in a fiduciary capacity.[117]

Fiduciary Duty may be Excluded by Agreement

[15.54] As is clear from *Williams v Harris*,[118] it is possible for a partner's fiduciary duty to be excluded by agreement between the partners. The fiduciary duty in that case was the obligation of the continuing partners to account to a former partner for the use of his share in the assets of the firm. Referring to this fiduciary duty as 'general equitable principles', Kenny J observed in the Supreme Court that:

> 'The defendants do not dispute the existence of these general equitable principles but say that the terms of the partnership deed prevent them applying to this case. A passage in the speech of Viscount Haldane in *Stevenson's Case* [1918] AC 239 and the terms of s 42 of the Partnership Act, 1890, show that the terms of the partnership deed may override these general principles. The passage reads:
>
> "In the absence of a special agreement to the contrary, and there is none such in the contract before us, the rule is that on a dissolution of partnership, all the property shall be converted into money by a sale and that the proceeds of the sale, after discharging all the partnership debts and liabilities, shall be divided among the partners according to their shares."'[119]

[15.55] In addition, it has been seen that the 1890 Act itself recognises that certain fiduciary duties may be excluded. In three of the four statutory instances of a partner's fiduciary duty, these duties are expressed to be subject to contrary agreement between the partners (ie ss 29(1), 30 and 42).

But some fundamental fiduciary duties may not be excluded

[15.56] However, it is not suggested that *Williams v Harris*[120] is authority for the principle that all fiduciary duties may be excluded. Rather, the fourth instance of fiduciary duties contained in the 1890 Act, namely the duty in s 28 to render true accounts and full information, may not be excluded by the terms of any agreement between the parties. This is because, as has been noted, this fiduciary duty is so basic an incident of partnership that it is thought to be impossible to conceive that a relationship without such a duty would constitute a partnership.[121] On the same basis, it is apprehended that other fiduciary duties, which are fundamental to the parties being partners in the first place, may not be excluded.[122] Thus for example, the duty of a partner to be honest and truthful in his dealings with his co-partners is thought to be

---

117 *Piddock v Burt* [1894] 1 Ch 343, which was quoted with approval by Budd J in *Re Shanahans Stamp Auctions Ltd* [1962] IR 386.
118 *Williams v Harris* (15 January 1980) HC, [1980] ILRM 237 (SC).
119 *Williams v Harris* [1980] ILRM 237 at 241 quoting from *Stevenson's Case* [1918] AC 239 at 246.
120 *Williams v Harris* [1980] ILRM 237 at 241.
121 See para **[15.25]**.
122 Note that in America, s 105 of the Uniform Partnership Act (1997) (Last Amended 2013) gives statutory footing to the obligation of good faith and fair dealing, and to the duty of loyalty and the duty of care, and those obligations and duties may not be eliminated or altered by the terms of the partnership agreement save to the limited extent set out in that Act.

essential for this relationship to exist and therefore cannot be excluded by the partners, particularly since the partners are agreeing to be bound to an unlimited degree by the acts of the firm.[123]

Fiduciary Duty is Reciprocal

[15.57] The fiduciary duty owed by one partner to another is reciprocal. It follows that where one partner refuses to carry out his part of his duty towards his partners, he does not have a cause of action against the other partner if they fail to comply with their fiduciary duty to him.[124] In *Reilly v Walsh*,[125] two brothers, Oliver and Edward Walsh, agreed to take a lease of land in Suffolk Street in Dublin from Archdeacon Barton and build some houses thereon. The lease was not partnership property, but was to be taken by them at a future time as joint tenants, thus ensuring that on the death of either, the survivor would be entitled to the entire property. However, during the project, not only did Oliver not join or assist Edward in the building or make any financial contributions toward it, but he showed clear *mala fides* by writing to potential lenders to discourage them from lending to Edward for the purposes of the venture. Yet, after Oliver's death, his personal representatives sought the assistance of the court of equity to prevent the legal right of survivorship from applying to partnership property, so as to prevent Edward being entitled to the whole property. Richards B noted that 'from the very commencement [Oliver's] conduct was the very opposite of what it should have been if he intended to act as a partner fairly'[126] and for this reason, he refused to invoke equitable principles to prevent the rule of survivorship from operating in favour of Edward.

Application of Fiduciary Duty to Dissolved Partnerships

[15.58] The fiduciary duty of a partner exists not simply between partners during the term of a partnership, but also between former partners in a partnership which is in general dissolution, ie a dissolution which results in the firm's winding up.[127] This is

---

123   *Quaere* the position where all the partners are limited liability entities. See the interesting debate in the US regarding whether partners should be able to exclude their fiduciary duties by contract: Vestal, '"Assume a Rather Large Boat": The Mess We Have Made of Partnership Law' (1997) 54 Wash & Lee LR 487; Vestal, 'The Disclosure Obligations of Partners Inter Se Under the Revised Uniform Partnership Act of 1994: Is the Contractarian Revolution Failing?' (1995) 36 William & Mary LR 1559; Hynes, 'Fiduciary Duties and RUPA: An Inquiry into Freedom of Contract' (1995) 58 Law & Contemporary Problems 29; Ribstein, 'Fiduciary Duty Contracts in Unincorporated Firms' (1997) 54 Wash & Lee LR 537.

124   *McLure v Ripley* (1850) 2 Mac & G 274. This is also the position in Australia: *Chan v Zacharia* (1984) 154 CLR 178 and *Metlej v Kavanagh* [1981] NSWLR 339.

125   *Reilly v Walsh* (1848) 11 Ir Eq R 22.

126   *Reilly v Walsh* (1848) 11 Ir Eq R 22 at 28.

127   This is consistent with the treatment by the 1890 Act of the winding up of a firm, ie under s 39 of the 1890 Act, the partners are allowed to continue to bind the firm for the purposes of the winding up. See also *Clegg v Fishwick* (1849) 1 Mac & G 294; *Clements v Hall* (1858) 2 De G & J 173. As regards the distinction between a general dissolution and a technical dissolution, see para **[23.07]** et seq.

clear from the judgment of McWilliam J in the High Court case of *Williams v Harris*,[128] where he held that the:

> 'fiduciary relationship ... continues until the partnership has been wound up or, as here, until the terms of the partnership agreement with regard to the retirement of a partner or partners have been completely carried out.'[129]

Including technical dissolutions

[15.59] Just as fiduciary duties continue after the general dissolution of a partnership, they normally[130] also continue after the technical dissolution[131] of a firm. Accordingly, a fiduciary relationship exists between continuing partners in a firm and retired partners or their personal representatives.[132] Thus in the Supreme Court case of *Williams v Harris*,[133] Kenny J gave two instances of the fiduciary duty of a partner, both of which were on the technical dissolution of the partnership:

> '[W]hen a partnership was dissolved and one of the partners continued to trade with all the assets of the partnership, then, in the absence of agreement to the contrary, he was liable to account to the former partner for the profits which he made by the use of the former partner's share of the assets. Another principle was that the relationship between partners and between the partner or partners who continued the business and the personal representative of a deceased partner was a fiduciary one so that those partners who continued the business were, in the absence of an agreement to the contrary, liable to account for the profits which they earned with the share of a retiring or deceased partner.'[134]

[15.60] In addition, s 28 of the 1890 Act (duty of partners to render true accounts and full information to each other) s 29 (accountability of partner for private profits) and s 42(1) (right of outgoing partner to share of post-dissolution profits) either expressly or implicitly provide that those fiduciary duties apply after the technical dissolution of the partnership.[135] Since these sections are simply examples of the broader fiduciary duty of

---

128 *Williams v Harris* (15 January 1980) HC; McWilliam J's judgment was reversed by the Supreme Court on appeal on the facts of the case, [1980] ILRM 237 (SC), but not as to the principle regarding the application of fiduciary duties to partners.

129 *Williams v Harris* (15 January 1980) HC at p 12 of the transcript. It is worth noting that under s 38 of the 1890 Act, a partner is only authorised to bind the firm 'as far as may be necessary to wind up the affairs of the partnership, and to complete transactions begun but unfinished at the time of the dissolution but not otherwise'.

130 It has been noted that one exception to this rule is that the fiduciary duty of a partner not to compete with the partnership business ceases on the technical dissolution of the firm in relation to that outgoing partner, see para **[15.47]**.

131 See generally 'Symposium on withdrawals and expulsions from law firms: the rights and duties of partners and their firms' (1998) 55 Wash & Lee LR 997.

132 See for example *Moser v Cotton* (1990) 140 NLJ 1313.

133 *Williams v Harris* [1980] ILRM 237.

134 *Williams v Harris* [1980] ILRM 237 at 240–241.

135 Thus, s 28 of the 1890 Act provides for information to be given to a partner or 'his personal representatives', while s 29(2) provides for partners to account for secret profits from 'transactions undertaken after a partnership has been dissolved by the death of a partner'. Section 42 of the 1890 Act provides for a share of the profits of the firm to be paid in respect of post-dissolution profits to the outgoing partner or his estate.

every partner, it is clear that all fiduciary duties of a partner are also owed by former partners in a technically dissolved partnership.

Application of Fiduciary Duty to Prospective Partnerships

[15.61] *Fawcett v Whitehouse*[136] is authority for the proposition that a prospective partner owes a fiduciary duty to his prospective partners.[137] In that case, a party to a proposed partnership who negotiated the purchase of property for the intended firm, received a commission in respect of the sale. He was held liable to account to the subsequent partnership for this commission. This approach can be justified on principle since the existence of a partner's fiduciary duty arises not simply by virtue of his being labelled a partner, but rather on the grounds that he is in a relationship of trust with his co-partner and therefore if this relationship arises before the partnership has been agreed or finalised, it seems that the fiduciary duties may also arise.

Effect of a Breach of a Fiduciary Duty

[15.62] In the case of some fiduciary duties, the 1890 Act itself provides a remedy for their breach, namely the obligation upon the partner to account for any profit made. This is the case in relation to the duty not to make private profits (s 29(1)), the duty not to compete with the firm (s 30) and the duty not to use a former partner's share in the firm for the continuing partners' exclusive benefit (s 42(1)). In other instances of a partner's fiduciary duty, reliance will have to be placed on the common law for a remedy.

Action for breach of duty should be taken as part of a partnership action

[15.63] Before considering the effect of a breach of fiduciary duty, reference should be made to the form of an action for a breach of fiduciary duty. It is noted elsewhere in this book that the courts are reluctant to deal with isolated partnership actions (such as one for a breach of fiduciary duty), since they prefer to deal with disputes between partners as part of an action for an account of partnership dealings.[138] This is clear from *Hawkins v Rogers*.[139] That case concerned a horse named 'Lonely Maid' which was owned by a partnership between the parties. The horse had been entered to run in three prestigious races (the 1,000 Guineas, the Oaks and the Curragh Foal Plate). Each of the entries for the races was made by the defendant in his own name, but the plaintiff was debited in the accounts between them with half the entry fees paid. After the dissolution of the partnership, the horse was bought by the plaintiff from the partnership, the parties having agreed prior to the auction that the sale should be with these race engagements. However, after the sale, the defendant struck the horse out of its engagements. An action was taken by the plaintiff against the defendant as a personal action (rather than a partnership action) for interference with the property of the plaintiff. In the High Court,

---

[136] *Fawcett v Whitehouse* (1829) 1 Russ & M 132. See also *Conlon v Simms* [2008] 1 WLR 484.

[137] See also *Central Railway of Venezuela v Kisch* (1867) 16 LT 500; *New Brunswick Railway v Muggeridge* (1860) 3 LT 651; *Hichens v Congreve* (1828) 4 Russ 562. This is also the position in Australia: *United Dominions Corp v Brian Pty Ltd* (1985) 157 CLR 1.

[138] See further in relation to the principles which are applicable to partnership actions, para **[20.01]** et seq.

[139] *Hawkins v Rogers* [1951] IR 48.

Dixon J held obiter that, if the plaintiff had alleged a breach of trust by the defendant, it would have been a breach of trust of:

> 'the fiduciary relationship and mutual duties subsisting between partners, and the action would in effect be a partnership action. In the case of an action founded on the partnership relation, it is well settled, and is indeed inherent in the nature of the partnership, that one isolated partnership transaction cannot be investigated by itself, but that the proper remedy and only way of disposing of the matter is to take a full and mutual account of all the partnership dealings.'[140]

Damages will be the usual remedy

[15.64] As with the actions for a breach of a fiduciary duty under ss 28, 29(1), 30 or 42(1) of the 1890 Act, the usual remedy for the loss which has been caused by a breach by a partner of his fiduciary duty is damages or an account of profits. Thus, in the Scottish case of *Ferguson v MacKay*,[141] the partners breached their duty of disclosure of information to a retiring partner under s 28 of the 1890 Act and the court awarded the retiring partner damages in respect of the loss suffered by him as a result of this breach. Similarly, in *Horgan v Baxter*,[142] the defendant, unbeknownst to his partner, had retained certain sums of money which were owed by the firm to one of the customers of the firm and these sums had, with the passage of time, become statute barred. Carroll J held that the plaintiff was entitled to an account of these profits, namely, half of these funds.

Sometimes dissolution will be ordered

[15.65] However, damages or an account of the profits will not always be the most appropriate remedy for a breach of fiduciary duty and the court may grant an order of dissolution of the partnership in appropriate circumstances. This was the case in the pre-1890 decision of *Heslin v Fay (1)*.[143] There, Sullivan LC held that Fay had abused his powers as a partner by increasing the capital of the firm not for the stated purpose of this power but for the purpose of resisting the plaintiff's demand for a return of his surplus capital. Accordingly, Heslin was granted a dissolution of the partnership.[144]

Repudiation of partnership agreement by breach of fiduciary duty

[15.66] Another possible consequence of a breach by a partner of his fiduciary duty is that the breach, if it is sufficiently serious, may have repudiated the partnership agreement. This possibility is implicitly envisaged by the terms of the 1890 Act itself, ie s 35(d) which allows a court to dissolve a partnership, where a partner wilfully commits a breach of the partnership agreement or his conduct makes it unreasonable to carry on the partnership. This possibility was first recognised by the Irish courts in the previously referred to case of *Reilly v Walsh*.[145] In that case, Edward contended that the partnership

---

[140] *Hawkins v Rogers* [1951] IR 48 at 54.
[141] *Ferguson v MacKay* [1985] SLT 1994.
[142] *Horgan v Baxter* (11 May 1982) HC.
[143] *Heslin v Fay (1)* (1884) 15 LR Ir 431.
[144] Such an order for dissolution could now be granted under either s 35(d) of the 1890 Act (not reasonably practicable for the partners to carry on partnership) or s 35(f) (just and equitable for partnership to be dissolved).
[145] *Reilly v Walsh* (1848) 11 Ir Eq R 22. See para **[15.57]**.

agreement was repudiated by Oliver's conduct, since Oliver showed clear *mala fides* by writing to third parties to discourage them from giving Edward a loan for the purposes of their joint venture. Richards B held that there was an intention to form a partnership, but that none subsequently existed on the basis that the partnership had either never come into existence or that it was repudiated by the actions of Oliver. More recently, in the High Court case of *Larkin v Groeger and Eaton*,[146] Barrington J appeared to accept the application of the principle of repudiatory breach to partnership agreements. There, the question arose as to the precise date upon which a partnership was dissolved. The partners had submitted their dispute to arbitration, the arbitration award had not specified the date of dissolution, but the award provided that none of the partners had:

> 'acted during the terms of the partnership with due regard to the provisions and intentions of the partnership agreement or partnership agreements and that *de facto* such agreements had effectively ceased to operate by April 1983.'[147]

Barrington J confirmed the validity of that award and thus implicitly accepted that the breach of duties had led to a repudiation of the agreement.[148]

Payment of interest on firm's funds where partner breaches fiduciary duty

[15.67] As is noted elsewhere in this work, the normal rule regarding the retention by a partner of the firm's money is that the partner is not charged interest thereon.[149] However, this will not be the case where there has been a breach of fiduciary duty by that partner in relation to the funds. This principle is illustrated by *Hutcheson v Smith*.[150] In that case, the defendant partner had been appointed to collect in the firm's assets as part of its winding up. However, he had not been candid in his statements to his partner or to the court regarding the amount of partnership assets in his possession. Accordingly, Brady CB ordered that the defendant pay interest to his partner on his partner's share of that money, as and from the date he had it in his possession. Similarly in *Moore v Moore*[151] Master Ellison allowed interest of 5% on capital expenditure by one partner out of the firm's funds for his own personal gain. In that case, the partner had used funds due to the farming partnership to purchase a vehicle for his own personal farming interests and to modernise his home. Master Ellison observed that while the general rule is that interest is not payable on capital, 'the Court allows interest on the restitution of

---

[146] *Larkin v Groeger and Eaton* (26 April 1988) HC.
[147] *Larkin v Groeger and Eaton* (26 April 1988) HC at p 9 of the transcript.
[148] 'It appears to me that the arbitrator's problem was that because all partners had at some stage begun to ignore their duties under the partnership it was difficult to say by what precise date the partnership has ended,' *Larkin v Groeger and Eaton* (26 April 1988) HC at p 15 of the transcript. However, there has been a shift in the English position towards a view that the doctrine of repudiation could not, of itself, bring about a dissolution of the partnership relationship, beginning with the obiter comments of Lord Millet in *Hurst v Bryk* [2002] 1 AC 185. See further para **[23.65]** et seq.
[149] *Webster v Bray* (1849) 7 Hare 159; *Stevens v Cook* (1859) 5 Jur (ns) 1415; *Turner v Burkinshaw* (1867) LR 2 Ch App 488. See para **[14.59]**.
[150] *Hutcheson v Smith* (1842) 5 Ir Eq R 117.
[151] *Moore v Moore* (27 February 1998) HC NI.

money of the firm which has been expended or withheld by a partner, and of secret profits made by a partner in breach of good faith towards his partners'.[152]

Payment of costs where partner is in breach of fiduciary duty

[15.68] Where an account of partnership dealings is taken, it is usual for the costs of the preparation of partnership accounts to be paid out of the partnership assets.[153] However, where one of the partners breaches his fiduciary duty to the others, he may be fixed with those costs. This was the case in *Baxter v Horgan*.[154] There, the Supreme Court upheld Murphy J's decision to award costs against just one of the partners, since that partner had been in clear breach of his fiduciary duty to his partner by his forging of certain documents.

---

[152]   He was quoting from Halsbury's Law of England (4th edn, 1994) Vol 35 at para 121.
[153]   See para **[20.115]**.
[154]   *Baxter v Horgan* (28 May 1990) HC, (7 June 1991) SC.

Chapter 16

Partnership Property

INTRODUCTION

[16.01]

> 'As I understand the law of partnership it does not necessarily follow from the carrying on of a business by two or more persons in partnership on certain premises, the property of the partners, that these premises become partnership property.'

Per O'Connor MR in *Re Christie*.[1]

The observations of O'Connor MR, made in the context of partnership premises, are equally applicable to all property which is used by a partnership. In this chapter, the principles applicable to determining which property is partnership property will be considered and in so doing, reference will also be made to the different types of partnership property. The consequences of finding that certain property is partnership property will also be considered. Thus, this chapter is divided up into the following three sections:

    I.   Determining What is Partnership Property;

    II. Specific Types of Partnership Property; and

    III. Characteristics of Partnership Property.

Overview

[16.02] In every partnership it will be important to determine which property is owned by the partnership and which property, although it may be used by the partnership, is the property of a partner or partners individually or of some third party.[2] This is because partnership property, unlike the personal property of a partner which is used by the firm, must be used for the purposes of the partnership and so, for example, any increase in its value will accrue to the firm and not to an individual partner. In the case of the personal property of a partner, that partner will be entitled to use it as he wishes and on the bankruptcy of the firm or on his bankruptcy, the property is available for the benefit of his separate creditors, in priority to the firm's creditors.

[16.03] This crucial question of whether property is partnership property is determined by the agreement and intention of the partners, whether express or implied. If the partners intend that property is to be partnership property, then the fact that it happens to be vested in one partner's name will be irrelevant to a finding that the property belongs to the firm. For this reason, each case must be determined according to its own set of circumstances. However, the 1890 Act assists in this inquiry by providing two rebuttable

---

[1]   *Re Christie* [1917] 1 IR 17 at 32.

[2]   See generally Hanbury, 'Partnership Property' (1927) 43 LQR 392.

presumptions regarding the status of property. Thus, it is presumed that property which is acquired for the purposes and in the course of the partnership business is partnership property[3] and it is presumed that property which is purchased with partnership funds is partnership property.[4] However, one must not lose sight of the overriding importance of the intentions of the partners and these presumptions may therefore be rebutted in appropriate circumstances. It follows that much of this chapter will be taken up with a consideration of the factors which have been used by the courts to find that an asset was or was not intended to be partnership property. It should be remembered that these factors, such as the use to which the property was put, the identity of the person in whom the property is legally vested, the treatment of the proceeds from its sale, the treatment by the partners inter se of the asset, etc, are not crucial factors in themselves but are important only as manifestations of the partners' intentions.

I.   DETERMINING WHAT IS PARTNERSHIP PROPERTY

[16.04] The question of whether a particular piece of property is partnership property or not falls to be considered under the 1890 Act and the principles which emerge from the decisions of the courts from both before and after that Act.[5] Three separate sections of the 1890 Act deal directly with the classification of property as partnership property; these are ss 20(1), 20(3) and 21. Section 20(3) deals with a rather specialised situation, ie the status of property purchased by a firm out of the profits of land where the land is not itself partnership property. Accordingly, reference will be made to that section after first dealing with the general issue of whether property used by a firm is partnership property.[6] Sections 20(1) and 21 of the 1890 Act aim to assist in this determination by raising two rebuttable presumptions regarding property which is used or purchased by the partnership.

---

[3]   Partnership Act 1890, s 20(1).

[4]   Partnership Act 1890, s 21.

[5]   Note that under the Partnership Act 1890, s 46 the rules of equity and common law applicable to partnerships from pre-1890 continue unless they are inconsistent with the 1890 Act. See also para [1.28] et seq.

[6]   A summary of this analysis may be presented in the following manner, ie positive answers to the following questions would be strongly indicative of partnership property:

– did the parties intend the property to be partnership property?
– is the property registered in the firm's name or in a partner's name?
– is the property held on trust for the firm?
– is the property used by the firm for its business?
– does the use of the property earn profits and if so, how are these profits treated in the accounts of the partnership?
– did the firm pay for the property or did a partner pay for it?
– is the property treated as partnership property in the firm's accounts?
– do the partners treat it as partnership property inter se?
– do the partners treat the property as partnership property *vis-à-vis* third parties?

Sections 20(1) and 21 of the 1890 Act

[16.05] Section 20(1) describes partnership property as follows:

> All property and rights and interests in property originally brought into the partnership stock or acquired, whether by purchase or otherwise, on account of the firm, or for the purposes and in the course of the partnership business, are called in this Act partnership property, and must be held and applied by the partners exclusively for the purposes of the partnership and in accordance with the partnership agreement.

[16.06] Thus, property which is brought into the partnership stock is partnership property. It is suggested that the term 'stock' must be taken to mean all the assets used in the business, as it would have meant in 1890, rather than be given its modern meaning of inventory or stock-take of a firm. Also under this section, any asset acquired on account of the firm or for the purposes and in the course of the partnership business is partnership property. Although this section does not on its face contemplate any exceptions to this principle, it is in fact subject to contrary agreement.[7] This is because virtually all[8] of the sections of the 1890 Act are subject to the terms of s 19 of that Act which entitles the partners to vary any of the provisions of the Act. It follows that even where property is acquired for the purposes of the firm, the question of whether that property is partnership property will be subject to the express or implied intention of the partners regarding that property.[9]

[16.07] Section 21 adds to the description of partnership property in s 20(1) by providing a presumption that if the firm's funds are used to purchase property, that property is deemed to be partnership property:

> Unless the contrary intention appears, property bought with money belonging to the firm is deemed to have been bought on account of the firm.

In spite of the use of the word 'deemed', the presumption raised by this section is clearly rebuttable.[10]

'property' in ss 20(1) and 21

[16.08] The term property, as used in ss 20(1) and 21, is not defined by the 1890 Act. Giving the term its ordinary meaning,[11] it will include all items of property including such items as the goodwill of the partnership, patents, trade marks, copyright, etc.

Onus on party alleging partnership property

[16.09] The onus of proving that property is partnership property is upon the person who alleges it. This is clear from *Re Christie*,[12] where O'Connor MR stated that:

---

7   See for example *Re Christie* [1917] 1 IR 17 and para **[16.14]**.
8   But not, it is thought, the Partnership Act 1890, ss 28 or 37, see paras **[15.25]** and **[26.09]** respectively.
9   See *Re Christie* [1917] 1 IR 17, para **[16.14]**.
10 Since the section itself uses the term 'unless the contrary intention appears'. See also *Re Little* (1843) 6 Ir Eq R 197 aff'd at (1847) 10 Ir Eq R 275 and *Morris v Barrett* (1829) 3 Y & J 384.
11 See *Inspector of Taxes v Kiernan* [1982] ILRM 13 at 15 per Henchy J as to when it is appropriate to give a statutory term its ordinary meaning.
12 *Re Christie* [1917] 1 IR 17.

'[T]he premises must be brought into the common stock of the partnership. They may or they may not so be, according to the agreement of the partners, and any person asserting such an agreement must prove it, either by giving direct evidence of the agreement, or proving a course of dealing from which the inference is to be drawn. This was the law before the Partnership Act, 1890, and in this respect the law was not altered by the Act but confirmed.'[13]

Presumption that Property used in Firm's Business is Firm Property

[16.10] Perhaps the most important factor in determining whether property is partnership property or not is the presumption that property is partnership property if it is acquired 'for the purposes and in the course of the partnership business'.

[16.11] *Re Ryan*[14] illustrates the self-evident principle that in deciding whether an asset was acquired for the purposes and in the course of the partnership business, regard will be had to the actual use of the property by the firm after its acquisition. In that case, premises in Abbey Street in Dublin were purchased by two partners for the purposes of extending their business as dealers in spirits. Although this case was decided prior to the 1890 Act, since that Act is a codification statute,[15] the same principles applied to the determination of partnership property both before and after the enactment of s 20(1). Harrison J applied the principles which later were to be found in s 20(1) and held that, as the premises in Abbey Street were acquired for the partnership business, they were partnership property. A more difficult issue arises when an asset, which is paid for by one partner, is used by the firm and treated as the property of the firm. One such case is that of *Moore v Moore*,[16] where one brother in a farming partnership introduced a number of cattle to the business. Master Ellison noted the presumption in s 20(1) of the 1890 Act but found that this presumption was rebutted on the evidence:

'[T]he crucial question is always: was the asset both used and treated as partnership? Mere use in itself is usually insufficient to bring about a change in the status of such an asset[17] ... Although there is a presumption that a partner who pays for an asset and introduces it into "the common stock" – as, in the instant case, the dairy herd would have been – is not lending it but rather contributing it to the partnership. I find that in the instant case such a presumption is rebutted by the first defendant's acknowledgment that four of the cattle which had been introduced by the plaintiff were returned to him in 1991 around the time of the dissolution of the partnership.'

In contrast in the same case, Master Ellison rejected the plaintiff's claim for compensation for the value of the pig slurry which he used to fertilise the partnership lands but which came from his private pig breeding business. He held that the pig slurry was brought into the common stock of the partnership and it was used and treated as partnership property and there was no basis upon which to refund any of its value to the plaintiff.

---

13 *Re Christie* [1917] 1 IR 17 at 32, quoting *Davis v Davis* [1894] 1 Ch 393 as authority for this principle.
14 *Re Ryan* (1868) 3 Ir Eq R 222.
15 See generally para **[1.23]**.
16 *Moore v Moore* (27 February 1998) HC NI.
17 Quoting in part from I'Anson Banks, *Lindley & Banks on Partnership* (17th edn, 1995) at para 18-14 (now at para 18-13 of the 20th edn (2017)).

[16.12] *Murtagh v Costello*[18] illustrates that the courts do not take a restrictive approach to the meaning of the s 20(2) phrase 'for the purposes of and in the course of the partnership business'. In that case, the partnership agreement provided for six individuals to become partners as flour merchants and 'in all other matters in which the majority of them should agree to trade or deal'.[19] During the course of the partnership, the partners acquired two pieces of freehold land in Athlone which were purchased using partnership money and were conveyed into the name of two of the partners in trust for the firm. One piece of land, Ballykeerin, was farmed by one of the partners, and the second piece of land, Annadonnell, was occupied by tenants. The profits from the farming and the rent from the tenants were brought into the profit and loss account of the firm. In addition, both pieces of land were used by the firm as security for borrowings to the firm. It was argued that neither piece of land was partnership property since farming and renting of property were not part of the trade of flour merchants. This argument was rejected by Chatterton VC who held that the rule in determining what property constituted partnership property was that it was partnership property if:

'paid for out of partnership money, and held as part of the stock of the firm, though the premises purchased may not have been actually used for carrying on upon them, or with them, the trade or business of the firm.'[20]

He held that both properties were part of the stock of the firm since the improvements thereon were paid for out of partnership money; the profits therefrom were entered into the profit and loss account; and the lands themselves were entered in the balance sheet. It is clear from *Murtagh v Costello*,[21] that the term 'partnership business' as used in s 20(1) of the 1890 Act is not to be interpreted restrictively but rather includes a situation where property is not strictly within the description of partnership business as set out in the partnership agreement, provided that it is held for the benefit of, or on behalf of, the partnership business.[22]

The overriding importance of the intention of the partners

[16.13] It is important to bear in mind that the presumption in s 20(1) is simply that. The fact that s 20(1) is not mandatory is clear from the terms of s 19 of the 1890 Act which expressly provide that the rights of partners defined by the Act may be varied by the consent of all the partners, which consent may be inferred from a course of dealing. For example where it was never the intention of the partners for property to be partnership property, it will be irrelevant that it may have been acquired for the purpose of the partnership.[23]

---

18 *Murtagh v Costello* (1881) 7 LR Ir 428.
19 *Murtagh v Costello* (1881) 7 LR Ir 428 at 429.
20 *Murtagh v Costello* (1881) 7 LR Ir 428 at 436.
21 *Murtagh v Costello* (1881) 7 LR Ir 428.
22 This contrasts with the importance of the description of the partnership business in other contexts, for example when one is dealing with the liability of a partner for the acts of his co-partner, see para **[21.37]**.
23 Of course, it is open to partners to change their minds. In *Sandhu v Gill* [2005] EWCA Civ 1297, Lord Neuberger noted that the original partnership deed between Sandhu and Gill had provided that, in respect of property purchased by Gill for use in the partnership business of running a home for the elderly, it would become partnership property after Sandhu paid a £70,000 contribution to Gill. (contd.../)

[16.14] *Re Christie*[24] concerned the question of whether a family farm in Co Antrim was partnership property. While it is thought that the wrong conclusion was reached on the facts,[25] the case is relevant for its discussion of the principles applicable to the issue of whether an asset is partnership property. In determining whether the farm was partnership property, O'Connor MR noted the overriding importance of the agreement of the parties, when he observed that:

> 'As I understand the law of partnership it does not necessarily follow from the carrying on of a business by two or more persons in partnership on certain premises, the property of the partners, that these premises become partnership property. To make them such the premises must be brought into the common stock of the partnership. They may or may not so be, according to the agreement of the partners.'[26]

[16.15] In *Smith v Earl of Howth*,[27] Atkins and Harman agreed with the Earl of Howth to quarry for green whinstones on part of his lands on the Hill of Howth. The agreement was for a three-year period for the purpose of supplying Dublin Corporation with stones for street repairs. This agreement was held to be either a lease or licence to quarry those lands for three years. Atkins alone subsequently entered into partnership with Smith to work the quarries. After Atkins left the country, Smith claimed to be entitled to Atkins' interest in the lands by virtue of his having been Atkins' partner. However, there was no evidence of any intention on the part of the partners that the lease/licence would become partnership property and significantly the partnership agreement was only between one co-owner (Atkins, but not Harman) and Smith.[28] Therefore in the Irish Court of Common Pleas, Monahan LCJ dismissed Smith's claim, observing that the agreement to enter a partnership to work the quarries was not sufficient to transfer an interest in the lands to Smith.[29]

---

23   (\...contd) That contribution was not paid in full before the dissolution of the partnership. At the outset of the winding-up proceedings, a consent order agreed to by both parties included an agreement that the property was to constitute a partnership asset. Lord Neuberger observed that the natural meaning and effect of that agreement was that the parties had intended that, as part of the winding-up, the property would be treated as owned equally.

24   *Re Christie* [1917] 1 IR 17.

25   See further para **[16.24]**.

26   *Re Christie* [1917] 1 IR 17 at 32. O'Connor MR relied on *Davies v Games* (1879) 10 Ch D 813 and *Davis v Davis* [1894] 1 Ch 393 where he quoted from North J's statement that "[i]t is not the law that partners in business, who are the owners of the property by means of which the business is carried on, are necessarily partners as regards that property."

27   *Smith v Earl of Howth* (1859) 10 Ir CLR 125.

28   In this regard, the property could not be said to be subject to the presumption in s 20(1) since it does not appear to have been acquired for the purposes *and* in the course of the partnership business.

29   '[T]he agreement between Atkins and the plaintiff, as deposed to by the latter, that Atkins and he should be in partnership for working the quarries, did not transfer to or vest in the plaintiff any legal estate in the quarries' (1859) 10 Ir CLR 125 at 128–129. Monahan LCJ also held that if Atkins' right was a licence and thus an incorporeal right, it was revocable and was revoked by the Earl of Howth when he sought to remove Smith from the lands. Insofar as this implies that Smith would have acquired an interest in Atkins' property if it was a licence but not if it was a lease, this aspect of the judgment is inconsistent with the earlier part of his judgment and must be doubted.

[16.16] An Australian case that highlights the importance of the intention of the partners is *Harvey v Harvey*.[30] This case involved two brothers, Harold and Lyonel Harvey. Harold, the owner of a farm, went into partnership to work the farm with both his brother Lyonel and Lyonel's sons. During the negotiations, it was considered that Harold's son, who was then only six, would be entitled to the farm when he grew up. It was agreed that Harold would contribute some sheep and implements to the partnership, but he was not to work the farm, while the others were to contribute their skill and labour. Profits and expenses, including the cost of improving the farm, were to be shared equally. There was no express agreement that the land was to be treated as partnership property and it was not treated as such in the partnership books. During the life of the partnership, the land was improved by substantial areas being cleared and cultivated. After over 20 years, the partnership was dissolved and Lyonel's sons (Lyonel having died) claimed that the farm was partnership property and therefore should be sold on the dissolution of the firm with the proceeds being divided between the partners. The High Court of Australia held that the farm was not contributed by Harold as partnership property and never became such.

Importance of treatment of property in firm's accounts

[16.17] The treatment or non-treatment of property in the partnership accounts will also be relevant in determining the question of whether it is partnership property. Thus in *Re Littles*[31] the non-treatment in the accounts of the firm of a share in a banking company was regarded by Macan C as providing strong evidence against the bank's claim that the share was partnership property. He observed that 'it cannot be said that the absence of all mention of this share, is not a strong argument in contradiction of the allegation made by the [bank]'.[32] Further support for the finding that the share was not partnership property was the fact that when one partner retired from the partnership the dissolution agreement provided for him to release all his interest in the partnership property, but no reference was made to his releasing his interest in the share. In addition, despite having released all his interest in the partnership property, subsequent accounts of the firm provided for this former partner to receive dividends in respect of the share in the bank.[33]

[16.18] The importance of the treatment or non-treatment of the property in the accounts is also apparent from *Murtagh v Costello*.[34] There, a piece of freehold land at Ballykeerin was purchased out of the partnership assets and was conveyed into the name of one partner in trust for the firm. The land was held to be partnership property and it is

[30] *Harvey v Harvey* (1970) 120 CLR 529.
[31] *Re Littles* (1843) 6 Ir Eq R 197 and aff'd at (1847) Ir Eq R 275.
[32] *Re Littles* (1843) 6 Ir Eq R 197 at 198.
[33] See also *Jack v Jack* [2016] CSIH 75 in which the absence of any reference to farmland in the accounts of a partnership was held to be a strong indication that the parties involved did not intend it to be treated as partnership property. The fact that the land had been included in the accounts of the father when he was a sole trader, but was not subsequently included in the accounts of the partnership when he entered into a family partnership, coupled with the evidence of the partnership's accountant that to bring an asset from a sole trader into a partnership could have disadvantageous tax consequences, also influenced the court's finding that the farmland was not partnership property.
[34] *Murtagh v Costello* (1881) 7 LR Ir 428.

useful to consider the reasoning of Chatterton VC in reaching his decision. It was farmed by one of the partners and he lived there in a house built using partnership funds. The accounts of the farming of the land were entered in the profit and loss account of the firm and the lands were also entered as partnership assets in the balance sheet. Chatterton VC held that these lands were partnership property and noted that:

> 'If these lands were to be considered as the property of the persons comprising the partnership individually, and not as partners, the receipts and expenditures ought to have been carried to their personal accounts.'[35]

[16.19] However, it is not suggested that the failure to produce partnership accounts with the property included therein will inevitably result in property not being partnership property. Thus in *Re Ryan*,[36] Harrison J held that the premises in Abbey Street in Dublin, which were used by two partners for the purpose of their partnership business, were partnership property even though no 'partnership books were produced'.[37]

[16.20] In this context, it is to be noted that the exclusion of goodwill from the accounts of a partnership should not be regarded as indicative of the status of goodwill as a partnership asset, since goodwill is commonly omitted from partnership balance sheets.[38]

Importance of clarifying intentions of partners in agreement

[16.21] The importance of the intention of the partners in determining the status of property used by the partnership is also clear from the terms of s 20(3) ('in the absence of an agreement to the contrary') and s 21 ('unless the contrary intention appears'). For this reason, the question of which property is partnership property should be clarified where practicable in the partnership agreement. Sometimes of equal importance is a provision indicating which property is not partnership property.[39] Otherwise, a court may have to decide this issue by examining the intentions of the parties as disclosed by

---

35   *Murtagh v Costello* (1881) 7 LR Ir 428 at 437. See *O'Dwyer, Inspector of Taxes v Cafolla* [1949] IR 210 for a case in which the property used by the partnership was the personal property of one partner.

36   *Re Ryan* (1868) 3 Ir Eq R 222.

37   Cf *Re Christie* [1917] 1 IR 17, where there were never any accounts kept and the property was held not to be partnership property, see para **[16.24]**. See also *Ham v Bell* [2016] EWHC 1791 in which a farm and milk quota had been included in draft partnership accounts for a number of years before being removed from accounts prepared from 2004 onwards on the basis that those assets had been mistakenly included by the partnership's accountant in the pre-2004 draft accounts. The fact that, had the intention been that those assets would be partnership property, advice from the partnership's advisors on the capital gains tax implications of those assets being brought into the partnership as partnership property would most likely have been needed (and was not given) also influenced the court's decision. See also *Barton v Morris* [1985] 2 All ER 1032, where a guest house was listed in draft accounts as partnership property, but was held not to be such, discussed at para **[16.40]**. However, this must be regarded as an exceptional case in which the inclusion of an asset as partnership property in the accounts is not held to be partnership property.

38   See generally in relation to goodwill, para **[18.01]** et seq.

39   See further in relation to such clauses in partnership agreements, para **[21.41]**.

the facts of the case. In the High Court case of *Barr v Barr*,[40] a wholesale grocery partnership in Donegal stored some of its goods in a garage which adjoined the home of one of the defendant partners. The garage appeared in the balance sheet of the firm and was held to be partnership property. However, the other partners claimed that the defendant's home was also partnership property. The judgment does not provide the evidence to support such a claim which was, nevertheless, rejected by Carroll J. Such problems could, however, have been avoided by a provision in the partnership agreement clearly delineating which property was and which property was not partnership property.[41]

Intention of the parties, though relevant, is not always decisive

[16.22] Although the intention of the partners is an important consideration in determining whether property belongs to the partnership, it will not always be decisive. For example if the property in question cannot become partnership property, it is irrelevant that the partners may have so intended it. This is illustrated by the High Court case of *Larkin v Groeger and Eaton*.[42] In that case, three accountants went into partnership together and each transferred office equipment into the partnership at its commencement. However, some of the office equipment transferred by one of the partners, Larkin, into the partnership was on lease. Although the intention was that this equipment would be transferred into the partnership, clearly on the basis of the principle *nemo dat quod non habet*,[43] this could not be done, as Larkin could not assign property of which he was not the owner. Nonetheless, the partnership used this office equipment for the duration of the partnership. However Larkin, rather than the partnership, remained obligated to the lessor of the equipment under the terms of the lease. For this reason, on the dissolution of the partnership, it was ordered that the other two partners pay Larkin in respect of their use of the office equipment.[44]

Where property produces partnership profits

[16.23] Property which produces profits for the partnership is likely to have been acquired for the partnership business (as is clear from the express terms of s 20(1) of the 1890 Act) and will therefore be presumed to be partnership property. Again, however, the overriding importance of the intentions of the parties is illustrated by the caselaw in this area. In *O'Dwyer, Inspector of Taxes v Cafolla & Co*,[45] a father and members of his family carried on a fish and chip business in partnership in Dublin. Although the profits

---

40   *Barr v Barr* (29 July 1992) HC.
41   The decision of Roger Wyland QC in *Goldup v Cobb* [2017] EWHC 526 (Ch) underscored the importance of having an express or implied agreement as to whether a particular asset is partnership property. In that case, the parties were in partnership as a firm of solicitors and the defendant partner had a pension by virtue of her separate role as a local coroner. The court held that there was no rule of law that such a pension was automatically a partnership asset. The defendant claimed that the pension was a personal entitlement, and had never been an asset of the partnership as there was no agreement to that effect between the partners. The court found in her favour.
42   *Larkin v Groeger and Eaton* (26 April 1988) HC.
43   No one can give what he does not have.
44   The order of the arbitrator, John Gore Grimes, solicitor, was upheld by Barrington J.
45   *O'Dwyer, Inspector of Taxes v Cafolla & Co* [1949] IR 210.

were shared between the partners, the property which produced the profits, namely the premises, the capital, the equipment and stock, remained in the absolute ownership of the father under the terms of the partnership agreement. Under the terms of that agreement, the father was entitled to regain exclusive use of that property from the partnership at any time.[46] Thus, this property was not partnership property but the property of the father and although challenged by the Revenue Commissioners, the validity of the arrangements was upheld by the Supreme Court.[47]

The anomalous decision of Re Christie

[16.24] Reference has briefly been made to the decision of *Re Christie*.[48] The case involved two brothers, John and Joseph Christie, who held two fifths of a family farm in Co Antrim as tenants-in-common (acquired on the intestate death of their father). The remaining three-fifths was acquired by them down through the years under the Statute of Limitations on the deaths of their brothers and sister and was therefore acquired by them as joint tenants (and accordingly subject to the right of survivorship). It was admitted that there was a partnership between the brothers in the farming stock and the profits of the farm. Both brothers 'worked the farm together, they lived together, supported themselves out of the profits, and they treated the profits as equally divisible between them'.[49] The question arose as to whether the land which was acquired by them for the purposes of this partnership was partnership property. On the death of John, another brother, William, (who was also his next-of-kin) claimed that the farm was partnership property and thus that the joint tenancy in the three-fifths of the farm was severed. In this way, John's share would not have devolved to Joseph, but to his next-of-kin, William. Joseph disputed this claim as he contended that he was entitled to the three-fifths by survivorship. It is significant to note that William had emigrated 40 years earlier, and only on the death of John did he return to Ireland to assert a claim to his share of the farm on the grounds that it was partnership property. In determining whether the farm was partnership property, O'Connor MR noted the overriding importance of the agreement or intention of the parties, and held that:

> 'Now, I see nothing in the present case which leads to the conclusion that the two brothers, who jointly farmed the lands, ever agreed that they should bring them into the common stock of partnership between them. There is no direct evidence that they did so, and there is no such inference to be drawn from necessity or convenience. I know no case in which it was decided that the mere fact of farming lands by two or more persons, who divided the profits between them made the lands partnership property.'[50]

---

46   Another example of a case where there was a partnership in the profits of property but not a partnership in the property is *Re Christie* [1917] 1 IR 17, considered at para **[16.24]**.

47   See, however, the doubts expressed about the finding that it was a partnership, considered at para **[2.79]**.

48   *Re Christie* [1917] 1 IR 17.

49   *Re Christie* [1917] 1 IR 17 at 19, although there never was any actual division of profits or any accounts kept.

50   *Re Christie* [1917] 1 IR 17 at 32.

[16.25] It is difficult to distinguish the facts of *Re Christie*[51] from those in *Re Ryan*,[52] which also involved two brothers in business together, or indeed from *Murtagh v Costello*.[53] While the presumption in s 20(1) that property used for partnership purposes is partnership property is subject to the contrary intention the partners, it is submitted that there was insufficient evidence for such an inference in *Re Christie*.[54] Rather, it is suggested that O'Connor MR's decision was unduly influenced by the effect of a finding that it was partnership property, ie if the farm was deemed to be partnership property, William, who had emigrated 40 years earlier would deprive Joseph of part of the farm which he had farmed for his lifetime. It is apprehended that if John had had children and the same claim was being made by them, a different conclusion would have been reached. Accordingly this case should be treated with caution.[55]

Business efficacy test

[16.26] A refinement of the 'intention' principle is provided by the business efficacy test which was used in the English Court of Appeal case of *Miles v Clarke*.[56] There, the defendant entered into a partnership at will[57] to run a photography business with the plaintiff. The plaintiff was well known in the field and he brought his goodwill into the firm, while the lease, furniture and studio equipment belonged to the defendant. No agreement existed between the partners except as to the division of profits, although it was originally intended that all the property contributed by them would become partnership property. When the partnership came to an end, the test used by Harman J to determine which assets constituted partnership property was expressed as follows:

> 'In my judgment, no more agreement between the parties should be supposed than is absolutely necessary to give business efficacy to that which has happened, and that, I think is the only safe way to proceed.'[58]

[16.27] Applying this test, Harman J held that only the stock in trade and consumable items (in this case, photographic film) were partnership property, while the lease of the premises which was in the plaintiff's name and the goodwill which the defendant had brought into the business remained the separate property of each partner. It is apprehended that the test used by Harman J is not of general applicability, but will particularly suit an informal partnership in which the partners contribute their own property and which then comes to a premature end as in that case. Of general application, however, is the view that property which is consumed or sold by the partnership in the ordinary course of business is presumed to be partnership property, in the absence of any contrary agreement.

---

51   *Re Christie* [1917] 1 IR 17.
52   *Re Ryan* (1868) 3 Ir Eq R 222, considered at para **[16.11]**.
53   *Murtagh v Costello* (1881) 7 LR Ir 428, see para **[16.12]**.
54   *Re Christie* [1917] 1 IR 17.
55   Note also the reluctance of the court in some cases to hold that a partnership exists between family members who work a farm together, see *Walsh v Walsh* [1942] IR 403, discussed at para **[2.53]**.
56   *Miles v Clarke* [1953] 1 All ER 779.
57   And thus terminable by any one partner by notice, see further para **[8.03]**.
58   *Miles v Clarke* [1953] 1 All ER 779 at 782.

Presumption that Property Purchased by Firm is Firm Property

[16.28] The second important rebuttable presumption in this area is to be found in s 21 of the 1890 Act, ie that property which is bought with money belonging to the firm is partnership property. It seems clear that this presumption is stronger and therefore more difficult to rebut than the presumption in s 20(1). This is because it is contended that the purchase of an asset using partnership funds is a stronger indication of an intention that the asset be partnership property, than where an asset is acquired for the purposes of the partnership business, since in the latter case it may be provided out of one partner's personal property.[59]

[16.29] *Re Ryan*[60] is an illustration of the presumption in s 21, since in that case the premises in Abbey Street in Dublin in which the two partners operated their spirit dealership were purchased out of partnership funds. Harrison J held that these premises were partnership property.[61]

[16.30] Where the legal title to that property which has been purchased using partnership funds is not vested in all the partners, the presumption that the property is partnership property rests on the equitable concept of resulting trusts. This concept requires property which is purchased out of joint funds, but placed in the name of one person only, to be held on a resulting trust in favour of the joint owners of the funds.[62] In the context of partnerships, where partnership funds are used to purchase the property, then regardless of the identity of the person or persons in whom the property is legally vested,[63] there is a presumption that the partners are the beneficial owners of the

---

59 See for example the Australian case of *Harvey v Harvey* (1970) 120 CLR 529, para **[16.16]**.

60 *Re Ryan* (1868) 3 Ir Eq R 222, considered at para **[16.11]**.

61 See also the comments made in the Scottish decision of *Longmuir v Moffat* [2009] CSIH 19 that if property purchased with partnership funds could not be presumed to be partnership property (even if legal title is held in the name of an individual partner), and if the court was not entitled to examine the beneficial ownership of that property, the provisions of s 21 of the 1890 Act, as they apply to property such as lands and buildings, would be unworkable.

62 Unless the persons are married or have entered into a civil partnership, in which case different principles will apply. See generally in relation to resulting trusts, Keane, *Equity and the Law of Trusts in Ireland* (3rd edn, 2017) at para [12.01] et seq and Biehler, *Equity and the Law of Trusts in Ireland* (6th edn, 2016) at p 143 et seq. Note that in *Walsh v Walsh* [1942] IR 403, the High Court held that a resulting trust arose in the context of a farm which was run by family members as a common undertaking, but was not run as a partnership. All family members were held to be beneficiaries of a resulting trust created when moneys resulting from the labour of the family were deposited in the name of some only of the family members. The family members, in whose names the deposit was in, were held to be 'fiduciary owners' of the moneys.

63 Thus in *Murtagh v Costello* (1881) 7 LR Ir 428, in a six person firm, one piece of land was vested in one partner (on trust for the firm), while another piece of land was vested in two of the partners (on trust for the firm). In both cases, it was held that the property was partnership property. See also *Nadeem v Rafiq* [2007] EWHC 2959 (Ch) in which property was purchased in the name of one of the two partners and his wife for use by the partnership using a deposit paid for out of partnership funds and the balance financed by a mortgage over one property belonging to the partner and his wife – the purchased property was held to be partnership property.

property. In *Carter Bros v Renouf*,[64] a life insurance policy was taken out by R who was in partnership with his brother. At that time, the firm was in financial difficulties and the policy was mortgaged to a creditor of the firm. On R's death, there was a surplus available on the policy and the question arose as to whether this was partnership property or the personal property of R. The Australian High Court held that, as the policy premiums had been paid out of the firm's funds and as there was no evidence of an intention that R was to personally benefit from the policy, the policy was partnership property.

[16.31] However in some cases, where an intention to that effect can be deduced from the surrounding circumstances, property which has been purchased using partnership funds may be deemed to be the separate property of one partner. This was the situation in the New Zealand High Court case of *Brenssell v Brenssell*.[65] There, a husband and wife were partners in a farming partnership, Mrs Brenssell contributing capital of $180,000 and Mr Brenssell contributing $8,000. During the course of the partnership, the sum of $50,000 was withdrawn from the partnership account to enable Mrs Brenssell purchase 'A' shares in a company from her brother. The company in question was also involved in farming and was owned by the wife's family. In addition, under the terms of the wife's family trust, such of her father's children who held the 'A' shares were to be entitled on the father's death to his holding of 'B' shares. Accordingly, on her father's death, these 'B' shares became Mrs Brenssell's property. The marriage and subsequently the partnership between Mr and Mrs Brenssell dissolved and a dispute arose as to whether the 'A' shares were partnership property or Mrs Brenssell's personal property. Tipping J noted that under the New Zealand equivalent of s 21 of the 1890 Act,[66] the shares would constitute partnership property since they were bought with partnership funds, unless there was a contrary intention. He did however find such an intention in the fact that the contract for the acquisition of the shares was between Mrs Brenssell personally and her brother and that the purchase was financed by Mrs Brenssell's capital contribution. This latter conclusion was supported by the fact that at the time of the payment, the revenues of the partnership were not sufficient to pay out the purchase price and must, therefore, have been in substantial part a payment of capital, of which Mrs Brenssell had contributed over 95%. In these circumstances, Tipping J held that the 'A' shares were never intended to be partnership property but rather constituted a return of capital to Mrs Brenssell. Although not referred to explicitly, his finding of an intention that the property was not partnership property was no doubt influenced by the nature of the property in question, ie shares in a family company to which was attached the right to receive further shares under a family trust.

Rebutting the presumption in s 21: the importance of intention

[16.32] The express terms of s 21 indicate that the presumption that property purchased with firm money is partnership property may be rebutted by evidence of a contrary

---

[64] *Carter Bros v Renouf* (1962) 111 CLR 140.
[65] *Brenssell v Brenssell* [1995] 3 NZLR 320 aff'd by the New Zealand Court of Appeal at [1998] NZFLR 28.
[66] Partnership Act 1908, s 24.

intention of the partners.[67] In *Re Littles*,[68] the share in the Fife Banking Company was in the name of one partner but was paid for out of partnership money, thus giving rise to the presumption that the shares were partnership property. However, this presumption was rebutted by the fact that there was no mention of the shares in the accounts of the firm or in the agreement dealing with the retirement of one partner from the firm, which agreement listed all the partnership property. For this reason, the share was held not to be partnership property, but rather to be co-owned by the partners.

Corollary of s 21 does not apply

[16.33] While property which is purchased with partnership funds is presumed to be partnership property, it should be emphasised that the corollary of s 21 does not apply. Thus, property may be partnership property, even if it has been financed by one partner only. Clearly, the source of the purchase money is a factor in determining the status of the property but it must be considered in conjunction with the intentions of the parties.

Conflict between s 21 and s 20(3) of the 1890 Act

[16.34] Section 20(3) of the 1890 Act supplements the presumptions in ss 21 and 20(1) by providing a further rebuttable presumption, ie where partners own real property as co-owners, rather than as partners, and have made profits from the use of that real property, any purchase by them of more real property using those profits will belong to them as co-owners and will not be partnership property. Section 20(3) states:

> Where co-owners of an estate or interest in any land, or in Scotland of any heritable estate, not being itself partnership property, are partners as to profits made by the use of that land or estate, and purchase other land or estate out of the profits to be used in like manner, the land or estate so purchased belongs to them, in the absence of an agreement to the contrary, not as partners, but as co-owners for the same respective estates and interests as are held by them in the land or estate first mentioned at the date of purchase.

This presumption may conflict with the presumption in s 21 that property which is purchased with partnership money is partnership property. *Re Christie*[69] establishes that in the event of a conflict, s 20(3) takes precedence over s 21. Therefore, any property purchased with partnership funds is subject first to the presumption in s 20(3), which arises where the purchase is made out of profits of land and that land is co-owned by them, but not as partners. If this presumption is inapplicable, then s 21 will apply and it will be presumed to be partnership property.

[16.35] Under the express terms of s 20(3), the presumption therein is rebuttable, since it is stated to be subject to contrary agreement. It is also clear from the wording of s 20(3) that the presumption only applies to the purchase of land, although it is thought that the principle should also apply by analogy to improvements of the land.[70]

---

[67] See for example *Murtagh v Costello* (1881) 7 LR Ir 428, in which Chatterton VC noted obiter that the presumption that property purchased with the firm's funds was partnership property, would have been rebutted if the regular payments and receipts by the firm in respect of this property had been carried to each partner's personal accounts.

[68] *Re Littles* (1843) 6 Ir Eq R 197 aff'd at (1847) 10 Ir Eq R 275.

[69] *Re Christie* [1917] 1 IR 17.

[70] See the case of *Davis v Davis* [1894] 1 Ch 393, in which it was stated that this principle was applicable to improvements of the original property paid for out of the profits generated by the land.

Where land is held in mixed estates?

[16.36] The problems which arise when s 20(3) of the 1890 Act is applied to a case where the partners hold the land in mixed estates were also considered in the previously referred to case of *Re Christie*.[71] The issue arose in relation to the purchase by the two brothers of additional land[72] which was bought with the profits earned by their partnership. Since the original family farm was held as tenants-in-common as to two-fifths (acquired on the intestate death of their father) and as joint tenants as to three-fifths (acquired under the Statute of Limitations on the death of their siblings), the question arose as to whether the additional land was held by the brothers as joint tenants or as tenants in common. Under the terms of s 20(3), the rule is that the purchased land is held in the same estate as the existing land out of which the profits arise. However the section does not countenance the possibility, as happened in this case, that the land held by the co-owners prior to the purchase of the two pieces of land would be held in mixed estates. O'Connor MR concluded that:

> 'I do not think that [s 20(3)] can be applied at all, and therefore I feel obliged to fall back on the old law that lands purchased with partnership profits are partnership property, and are held on a tenancy in common.'[73]

[16.37] While O'Connor MR felt obliged to revert to the old law (which was reflected by the terms of s 21 of the 1890 Act) he did not consider the other possibility open to him, ie to hold that the acquired lands were held in mixed estates in the same proportions as the original farm. Indeed, it is contended that in a case where the partners choose to hold land in mixed estates, they should be presumed to acquire any additional land in the same estates and in the same proportions as their original holding, rather than presume that they intended to acquire the additional land solely as tenants in common. The former approach does less violence to the intention of s 20(3) and is in keeping with the partners' decision to hold the existing land in mixed estates. For this reason, it is suggested that O'Connor MR's reasoning is not of general application. Nonetheless, it is contended that it was justified on the facts of that case. This is because that part of the original farm which was held as joint tenants, was only held in this manner by operation of law rather than by the choice of the partners (since it had been acquired under the Statute of Limitations). Therefore, it is suggested that there was not a sufficient justification for affixing the estate of joint tenancy (with its requirement of

---

71   *Re Christie* [1917] 1 IR 17. See para **[16.24]**.

72   Four pieces of land in all were acquired by the brothers. Two of the pieces of land were purchased by the brothers out of partnership funds after the passing of the 1890 Act, while two of the pieces of land were purchased with partnership funds prior to the passing of that Act. In relation to the latter, O'Connor MR relied on *Morris v Barrett* (1829) 3 Y & J 384 as authority for the proposition that property purchased with partnership moneys becomes partnership property and that those two pieces of land, bought before the 1890 Act, were acquired by the brothers as tenants in common in equal shares, having been purchased out of partnership profits.

73   *Re Christie* [1917] 1 IR 17 at 36.

survivorship)[74] to part of the land which was subsequently acquired by the partners for partnership purposes.

Partnership Property v Joint Property of Partners

[16.38] Having considered the major presumptions regarding the status of property used by a partnership, it is useful to refer to one of the more difficult distinctions to make, ie between partnership property and property which, although not partnership property, is co-owned by the partners. The 1890 Act recognises that partners may co-own property, but not as partners, yet share the profits therefrom as partners. The opening clause of s 20(3) states that:

> Where co-owners of an estate or interest in any land ... not being itself partnership property, are partners as to profits made by the use of that land or estate...

[16.39] In addition it has been noted previously in this work[75] that s 2(1) of the 1890 Act recognises that co-ownership by persons of property does not imply that the persons sharing the profits thereof are partners:

> Joint tenancy, tenancy in common, joint property, common property, or part ownership does not of itself create a partnership as to anything so held or owned, whether the tenants or owners do or do not share any profits made by the use thereof.

One may, therefore, speak of property which is not partnership property although it is co-owned by persons who happen to be partners, but it is not co-owned by them as partners. As is clear from *Re Christie*,[76] the distinction between property which on the one hand is simply co-owned by partners and partnership property on the other hand is a particularly fine one to draw when the business of the firm is carried on using that jointly held property. This distinction was made by Macan C in *Re Littles*:[77]

> 'As to the distinction which I have taken between partnership property, and property belonging to the partners, it may be considered by those who are not professional men, as too refined; but let me take an example which will prove how different the two things are. Suppose then, there are three persons carrying on trade as wine merchants, and that they consider it advisable at the commencement of the summer to speculate in American flour, and that they said "Here is £1,000 lying idle, and we will take our chances, sharing the profits of the speculation, should it be successful, or bearing the loss of a failure"; that flour would belong to the partners, but would not constitute partnership property.'[78]

[16.40] In order to find that the co-owned property is partnership property, there must be something more than mere co-ownership. In other words there must be evidence of an intention by the partners that the property will become part of the partnership stock. The mere use of co-owned property is not sufficient in itself. A decision in which there was not this 'something extra' is that of *Barton v Morris*.[79] That case involved two co-

---

[74] Under this right, the surviving partner would acquire the share of the deceased partner in the land so held. As to the right of survivorship and joint tenancies, see Wylie, *Irish Land Law* (5th edn, 2013) at para [8.03] et seq.

[75] Paragraph **[2.89]**.

[76] *Re Christie* [1917] 1 IR 17, see para **[16.24]**.

[77] *Re Littles* (1843) 6 Ir Eq R 197 aff'd at (1847) 10 Ir Eq R 275.

[78] *Re Littles* (1843) 6 Ir Eq R 197 at 200.

[79] *Barton v Morris* [1985] 2 All ER 1032.

habitees who purchased a guesthouse in their joint names as joint tenants, which was thus subject to the rule of survivorship on the death of either co-owner. Ms Barton provided the majority of the funds for the purchase and the guesthouse was operated by them as a partnership until Ms Barton's death. In the draft accounts kept by Ms Barton, the guesthouse had been listed as a partnership asset for tax purposes 'for the sake of completeness'.[80] Ms Barton's personal representative claimed that the joint tenancy was severed by virtue of the guesthouse becoming partnership property. In the English High Court, Nicholls J held that there was no evidence of an intention on the part of the partners that the guesthouse was to be partnership property so as to sever the joint tenancy. However, in *Bathurst v Scarbarrow,*[81] Rix LJ observed that the presumption that partnership property is held in common can be displaced by evidence of an agreement to the contrary – in this case, he found that there was clear evidence that the parties had agreed to take ownership of a property for use in their darts business as joint tenants in the full knowledge of the implications of holding property in that manner.

[16.41] It is, of course, easier to make the distinction between partnership property and property which is co-owned by the partners where the property, which is co-owned by the partners, is not used for the purpose of carrying on the partnership business. This was the case in *Re Littles.*[82] This distinction was particularly important in that case, since it involved the bankruptcy of all of the partners in a River Bann salmon fishing partnership. On the bankruptcy of the partners in a firm, the joint estate (ie the partnership property) is first available to the creditors of the firm, while the separate property of each partner is first available to the separate creditors of that partner.[83] In this case, on the bankruptcy of the partners, the question arose as to whether a share of £500 in the Fife Banking Company was partnership property or the joint property of the partners in the firm. This share in the bank had been taken in the name of one of the partners. After his death, it was taken in the name of another partner. However, during the partnership, dividends on the share were divided between the partners in the firm and calls on the shares were paid for by the firm. Nonetheless, this evidence was not sufficient to support a finding that the share was partnership property, Macan C holding that:

> 'No distinction has been taken by Counsel between property that may belong jointly to the members of a firm, and property that constitutes part of the partnership assets. I think the two things are very distinct, and it appears to me, that the share was never partnership property;[84] although from the commencement it might have been understood to be the joint property of the partners.'[85]

---

80 *Barton v Morris* [1985] 2 All ER 1032 at 1035.
81 *Bathurst v Scarbarrow* [2005] 1 P&CR 58 (CA).
82 *Re Littles* (1843) 6 Ir Eq R 197 aff'd at (1847) 10 Ir Eq R 275.
83 See generally in relation to the administration of the estate of bankrupt partners, para **[27.94]** et seq.
84 As to the other factors which influenced the finding that it was not partnership property, see para **[16.17]**.
85 *Re Littles* (1843) 6 Ir Eq R 197 at 199.

Relevance of Manner in which Property is Registered or Owned?

[16.42] Other relevant factors in determining the status of property used by a partnership will be the manner in which it is registered and the manner in which it is legally owned. It goes without saying that the fact that property is legally owned by all the partners in a firm favours a finding that it is partnership property. However, it is quite clear that this fact alone does not mean that the property is partnership property. Equally, the fact that property is legally owned or registered in the name of some or only one of the partners does not prevent the property being held to be partnership property.[86] In the High Court case of *Hawkins v Rogers,*[87] a horse called 'Lonely Maid' was owned by a partnership between the plaintiff and defendant. The engagements of the horse to run in a number of prestigious races, including the Irish Oaks and the Irish 1,000 Guineas, were made by the defendant partner in his own name only. Nonetheless, Dixon J regarded the engagements as partnership property.[88] In *Stuart v Ferguson,*[89] the legal ownership of mills and premises in Antrim, where a partnership was carried on, were vested in one partner only. It was held that the mills were nonetheless partnership property and that this partner was a trustee as to one-half of this partnership property for his co-partner.[90]

Where property is not owned by any of the partners

[16.43] It is perhaps self-evident that it will be even more difficult to prove that property is partnership property where none of the partners has a legal interest therein but where the property is legally owned by a third party. This was the case in *Re Ryan,*[91] where the two brothers, John and Thomas Ryan, operated part of their partnership business from a premises in Parnell St in Dublin, which premises were registered in the name of Mary Ryan, the mother of both men. After the death of John, she transferred the property to Thomas. It was alleged by a creditor of the firm that the mother held the premises on trust for both brothers. Harrison J held that, although the property was used by the

---

86   In *Re Ryan* (1868) 3 Ir Eq R 222, two partners ran a spirits business from premises in Abbey St in Dublin and in determining whether the premises were partnership property, Harrison J held that 'the form of conveyance to the brothers becomes immaterial' (at 232) although, on the facts of the case, the conveyance was in fact made in favour of both of them, but as joint tenants, rather than as tenants in common.

87   *Hawkins v Rogers* [1951] IR 48.

88   The question of whether the engagements were partnership property was not expressly considered by Dixon J, since he held that this would have to be done between the partners as part of a full and mutual account of all partnership dealings and not the instant proceedings which were for damages for the striking out of the engagements.

89   *Stuart v Ferguson* (1832) Hayes 452.

90   In *Re Littles* (1843) 6 Ir Eq R 197 aff'd at (1847) Ir Eq R 275, a share in a company was in the name of one partner in a firm, yet it was held to be jointly owned by the partners, although not partnership property.

91   *Re Ryan* (1868) 3 Ir Eq R 222.

brothers for the purposes of carrying on business, it was not partnership property and remained the property of Mary Ryan.[92]

Status of Improvements by a Firm of a Partner's Personal Property

[16.44] Quite often partners will contribute personal property to the partnership when they join the firm. Such property becomes partnership property and any improvement to the property will belong to the firm.[93]

[16.45] Where property remains in the ownership of one or more of the partners, but is used by the partnership, an issue may arise as to the status of improvements to that non-partnership property, where they are financed from partnership funds. There is no clear authority on this point but support for the view that any such improvement may be partnership property is to be found in *Burdon v Barkus*.[94] There, a partner, with the knowledge of his co-partner, used partnership money to sink a pit on his co-partner's land for the purposes of their partnership business. However, this expenditure was made by the partner on the misapprehension that his partnership was for a fixed term rather than a partnership at will.[95] Thus, the partner who had made the expenditure was surprised to find that his co-partner could validly dissolve the partnership soon after the sinking of the pit. An inquiry was permitted to determine whether any allowance should be made in respect of the outlay in sinking the pit. Some support for this view is also to be found in *Re Ryan*.[96] In that case, the premises used by the firm in Parnell St in Dublin were not partnership property as they belonged to the mother of the two partners in the firm. In attempting to establish that the property was partnership property, it was alleged that the partners spent a substantial amount of partnership funds on refurbishing the premises as a 'grocery store and gin palace'.[97] Although not argued in the case, Harrison J did not rule out the possibility that the sons had a charge or lien on the property for improvements which were alleged to have been carried out on those premises.

[16.46] In *Harvey v Harvey*,[98] the facts of which have been outlined already,[99] one brother's farm (that of Harold Harvey) had been improved by the use of the labour and skill of the other partners and of considerable partnership funds. The High Court of Australia held that the dissolution accounts of the firm should be adjusted to take account of the fact that Harold had not been charged in the partnership accounts with the cost of making the improvements but that no adjustment should be made in respect of

---

92   Although not argued in the case, Harrison J did not rule out the possibility that Mary Ryan and her sons were jointly interested in the property, or that she was a partner with them in the business or indeed that the sons had a charge or lien on the property for improvements which were alleged (though not proven) to have been done to the premises.
93   *Robinson v Ashton* (1875) LR 20 Eq 25.
94   *Burdon v Barkus* (1862) 4 De GF & J 42.
95   See generally in relation to fixed term partnerships and partnerships at will, para **[8.03]** et seq.
96   *Re Ryan* (1868) 3 Ir Eq R 222.
97   *Re Ryan* (1868) 3 Ir Eq R 222 at 225.
98   *Harvey v Harvey* (1970) 120 CLR 529.
99   Paragraph **[16.16]**.

the labour expended by the other partners in the improvements. Somewhat confusingly, Menzies J stated:

> 'In a case where a property does not become an asset of the partnership but is intended to be retained by one partner, after the determination of the partnership, it follows that there can be no basis for treating the difference between the value of the property as it was when made available for partnership use, and the higher value of the property at the end of the partnership due merely to improvements made by the partnership as a profit divisible among the partners.' [100]

[16.47] It is suggested that this part of his judgment should be strictly interpreted as stating that the increase in value in the property due to improvements cannot be regarded as profits in the strict sense of that term, ie profits of income or capital which are available for division between the partners. [101] To give this statement a wider meaning flies in the face of the decision itself which charges Harold with the cost of the improvements.

[16.48] It is to be noted that in the reverse situation, ie where a partner has 'preserved' partnership property using his own funds, he is entitled under the express terms of s 24(2)(b) of the 1890 Act to an indemnity from the firm in respect of his expenditure on the partnership property. [102] It might be argued that in light of the mutual agency of partners for each other [103] and the fact that a partnership is not a legal entity, but an aggregate of the partners, [104] the principle underlying s 24(2)(b) should also apply to the case of a firm using its funds to improve the personal property of a partner, so that if the improvements are not deemed to become partnership property, the partner who owns them may be required to indemnify the firm for such improvements. Thus, it may be that where a firm uses partnership funds to improve a partner's personal property, the firm will have an interest therein. This interest would, at the very least, be a right to an indemnity from the partner in respect of that expenditure, which may, as contemplated in *Re Ryan* [105] constitute a lien in respect of the expenditure. In certain cases, the circumstances in which the improvement was made may be such as to justify a finding that the firm has a right to have the improvement itself regarded as partnership property. [106] Indeed, this has been held to be the case in a number of states in the United States of America. [107]

---

[100] *Harvey v Harvey* (1970) 120 CLR 529 at 556.

[101] As to this meaning of profits, see further para **[14.17]**.

[102] See generally in relation to the right of a partner to such an indemnity, para **[14.40]** et seq.

[103] Ie a partner is at one and the same time a principal and an agent, since he is a principal for his co-partners and the agent of his co-partners.

[104] See generally para **[3.04]**.

[105] *Re Ryan* (1868) 3 Ir Eq R 222.

[106] See for example the obiter statement of Chadwick J in *Faulks v Faulks* [1992] 15 EG 82 at 95.

[107] *Marston v Marston* (1931) 177 NE 862; *Taber-Prang Art Co v Durant* (1905) 75 NE 221 (improvements belonged to partnership except those for which the firm was reimbursed); *Gauldin v Corn* (1980) 595 SW 2d 329.

Rights of Non-owning Partner to Property used by Partnership

[16.49] As should be obvious at this stage,[108] the property which is used by a firm will not by virtue of that fact be partnership property. While a partner will not become a part-owner of the property of his partner by using that property, it has been noted that he may in certain circumstances be entitled to a charge or lien on this separate property for improvements which were financed by him or the partnership.[109] In addition, it seems that a partner who has no legal interest in the property will have an implicit licence to use the property for the duration of the partnership.[110] A licence was inferred in favour of a partner in *Lee v Crawford*.[111] In that case the property in question was partnership property (rather than the exclusive property of one partner) and a licence was inferred in respect of one partner's right to reside in the partnership premises. There, the plaintiff and defendant were partners and they acquired certain property for the partnership business. Under a verbal arrangement between the parties, Crawford resided in part of the property and he paid £20 a year 'rent' for the property. This amount was debited against him in the partnership books and described as rent, although no money actually passed from Crawford to the firm. After his death, his widow remained in the property and claimed that there was a tenancy in the property. In the High Court, Cherry LJ held that there was no tenancy, but that there was a mere arrangement that one partner should have exclusive use of part of the partnership property for partnership purposes. Since this arrangement or licence had come to an end, the surviving partner was entitled to take ejectment proceedings against the deceased partner's wife.[112]

II. SPECIFIC TYPES OF PARTNERSHIP PROPERTY

[16.50] Having considered the principles which are applicable to determining whether property is partnership property or not, it is now proposed to consider some examples of partnership property of a particular character.

Property Acquired by a Partner in Breach of Fiduciary Duty

[16.51] It has already been observed[113] that under s 29(1) of the 1890 Act every partner must account to the firm for private profits, namely profits earned from a transaction concerning the firm or his use of the firm's partnership property or business connection.[114] Similarly, under s 30 of the 1890 Act, a partner must account to the firm for profits made from a competing business.[115] Since both these sections of the 1890 Act require the errant partner to 'account to the firm', the property in question is treated as having been acquired for the benefit of the firm. It follows that secret profits which are

---

108 See further, para **[16.01]**.
109 Paragraph **[16.45]** et seq.
110 *Harrison-Broadley v Smith* [1964] 1 WLR 456.
111 *Lee v Crawford* (1912) 46 ILTR 81.
112 See generally in relation to licences, Wylie, *Irish Land Law* (5th edn, 2013) at para [22.02] et seq.
113 Paragraph **[15.27]**.
114 Unless he obtains the consent of the firm: Partnership Act 1890, s 29(1).
115 Unless he obtains the consent of the firm: Partnership Act 1890, s 30. See para **[15.44]** et seq.

earned under s 29 and profits from a competing business which are earned under s 30 may be regarded as beneficially owned by the partnership.[116]

Files

[16.52] Invariably in partnerships the files of the firm will constitute partnership property since they will have been created 'for the purposes and in the course of the partnership business'.[117] Their status as partnership property was considered in the High Court case of *O'Connor v Woods*.[118] In that case, the client files of the accountancy firm of John A Woods & Co were clearly regarded as partnership property by Kenny J:

> 'On the day he left he took a number of files relating to the business of clients of the partnership and they remained in his possession until May 1972. The first named defendant was furious at this removal of files. When he discovered it, he telephoned the plaintiff and demanded the immediate return of them. A number of meetings were held at which the plaintiff offered to return the files but the first named defendant refused this offer. The plaintiff's reason for removing the files was that they related to the business of companies with which he was closely associated and whose accounts he had prepared or to individuals who were friends of his and who were charged nominal fees only by him for his work. The plaintiff, however, had no right to remove these files and when he discovered that the first named defendant objected to this, his obligation was to return the files to the defendants. He did not discharge this obligation by offering to return them. He should (as he now admits) have returned them to the firm.'[119]

[16.53] In the Scottish case of *Finlayson v Turnbull*,[120] it was held that the removal of clients' files by the departing partners in a partnership at will was a breach by them of their fiduciary duty to the continuing partners. Accordingly, damages were awarded to the continuing partners for the resultant damage caused to the firm's goodwill.

Fees Received after the Technical Dissolution of the Firm

[16.54] It almost goes without saying that fees which are received by a professional firm during the life of the firm are partnership property. In addition, fees which are received for work done by the firm, although received after the technical dissolution of the partnership, remain partnership property. Thus, in the High Court case of *O'Connor v Woods*,[121] one partner, O'Connor, left an accountancy firm and subsequently received fees from clients of the firm in respect of work which he had undertaken prior to his

---

[116] See the decision of the Privy Council in *A-G for Hong Kong v Reid* [1994] 1 AC 324 and see also the statement of Lord Lindley, now to be found in l'Anson Banks, *Lindley and Banks on Partnership* (20th edn, 2017) at para 18-14, fn 62. See also para 18-14 of that work regarding any property acquired in breach of the duty of good faith being treated as an asset in the hands of the acquiring partner from acquisition, rather than from the time that it is accounted for to the partnership.

[117] Partnership Act 1890, s 20(1), and see para **[16.05]** et seq.

[118] *O'Connor v Woods* (22 January 1976) HC.

[119] *O'Connor v Woods* (22 January 1976) HC at pp 4–5 of the transcript.

[120] *Finlayson v Turnbull* [1997] SLT 613.

[121] *O'Connor v Woods* (22 January 1976) HC.

departure. Kenny J held that he was liable to repay those fees to the partnership.[122] In the same case, but in relation to another client of the firm, O'Connor continued to work for that client after his departure from the firm. The bill which he furnished was therefore in respect of work which he alone had done for the client after his departure from the firm. However, he furnished this bill in the firm name, rather than his own. Kenny J held that 'he is liable for these fees as he claimed them in the name of John A. Woods'.[123] By providing the bill in the firm's name, the fee became the firm's property, although the work thereon had been done solely by O'Connor.[124]

Capital Contributions

[16.55] Where the disputed property forms part of a partner's capital contribution to the firm, that property will be partnership property since, by its very nature, the capital of a firm is partnership property.[125]

Proceeds of Sale of Partnership Property

[16.56] If partnership property is sold, it is clear that the proceeds of the sale will also constitute partnership property. Where the property which is sold forms part of the capital of the firm, the proceeds will also form part of the firm's capital but any profit element in the sale forms part of the firm's current account rather than its capital account.[126]

Company Shareholdings

[16.57] Although a partnership is not a legal entity,[127] a firm may be registered under its firm name in a company's register of members as the holder of shares in the company.[128] On the basis of the general authority of a partner to act as agent for the firm, it seems clear that in such a situation, one partner may vote on behalf of the firm at shareholders' meetings of the company.[129]

---

122 It is worth noting that in that case, no deduction was made for the fact that O'Connor would have been entitled to a share of these fees since they were earned during his time as a partner. This is because in this case, the partnership agreement provided that the 'surviving partners or partner shall become the sole owner of the partnership business, goodwill and other assets' on the payment of a lump-sum to a retiring partner. Clearly, in the absence of such a provision, O'Connor would have been entitled to his share of these fees. (*O'Connor v Woods* (22 January 1976) HC at p 3 of the transcript, and Clause 14(d) of the partnership agreement.)

123 *O'Connor v Woods* (22 January 1976) HC at p 18 of the transcript.

124 Kenny J does not give the basis for his conclusion, but arguably it may be justified on the basis of estoppel by conduct, ie that by his conduct O'Connor lead others to believe that the work was that of the firm and he was therefore estopped from denying that fact, but see para **[7.36]**.

125 See generally in relation to capital, para **[17.01]** et seq.

126 As to the distinction between capital and current accounts, see para **[17.09]**.

127 See generally regarding the nature of a partnership, para **[3.04]**.

128 *Re Land Credit Co of Ireland - Weikersheim's Case* (1873) 8 Ch App 831.

129 See generally in relation to the authority of a partner to bind his firm, para **[10.01]** et seq. It has been held in *Ex p Mitchell* (1808) 14 Ves 597 that one partner may vote on behalf of the firm at meetings of creditors of a bankrupt debtor of the firm.

Offices held by Partners

[16.58] Where a partner is appointed to an office or appointed to some other position during his time as a partner in his firm, the question arises as to whether this office or appointment is the 'property' of the firm, in the sense of whether the partner is obliged to hold it and the fees therefrom on behalf of the firm. The issue is also likely to be of relevance where a partner leaves the firm and continues to receive fees from this position. A common example of such an office is where a partner in a firm of accountants is appointed as a liquidator to a company before his departure from the firm. In the absence of any agreement amongst the partners, it is likely that an office or appointment held by a partner will not be regarded as being held on behalf of the firm. This was the case in *O'Connor v Woods*[130] where the departing partner in a four-person partnership had been the secretary of a client company and was asked by the client to continue as such after his departure. In the High Court, the continuing partners claimed for loss of fees in respect of this position. This claim was rejected by Kenny J who held that there was no obligation on the departing partner to resign his position as secretary. In large multi-national firms, where the appointment of a partner is as much due to the fact that he is a member of that renowned partnership as it is to his own reputation, a stronger case may be made that the office is held on behalf of the firm. In such circumstances, a case may be made for distinguishing the decision in *O'Connor v Woods*.[131]

Chose in Action

[16.59] Like any other property, a chose in action can be partnership property,[132] and in *Don King Productions v Warren*[133] the question arose as to whether the benefit of non-assignable choses in action could be transferred to a partnership. That case involved a partnership between the well-known boxing promoters Don King and Frank Warren. Their partnership agreement provided that each was to assign to the partnership certain boxing promotion contracts to which they were separately a party. However, these contracts, being contracts for personal services and containing non-assignment provisions, could not be assigned. In the English High Court, Lightman J held that effect could be given to their agreement in equity as a declaration of trust of those contracts for the benefit of the partnership and in this way the contracts were held to be partnership property. Frank Warren appealed on the grounds that the boxing promotion contracts were not property within the meaning of s 20 of the 1890 Act and, even if they were, they could not be 'brought into the partnership stock' or 'acquired … on account of the firm' so as to become partnership property within the terms of s 20. The Court of Appeal rejected this claim and upheld the decision of the High Court, finding that property that was not capable of assignment could still be partnership property for the purposes of s 20 of the 1890 Act. Further, Frank Warren had also claimed that boxing promotion contracts concluded by him and Don King between the time of the dissolution and the winding up of the partnership were not partnership property. This

[130] *O'Connor v Woods* (22 January 1976) HC.
[131] *O'Connor v Woods* (22 January 1976) HC.
[132] *McLean v Kennard* (1874) LR 9 Ch App 336; *Kemp v Andrews* (1691) Carth 170.
[133] *Don King Productions v Warren* [1998] 2 All ER 608.

argument was also rejected by the Court of Appeal, which held that such contracts were also to be held on trust for the partnership.[134]

Partnership Opportunities

[16.60] The status of business opportunities of the partnership as items of partnership property is considered elsewhere in this work.[135]

Milk Quotas

[16.61] Prior to the abolition of EU milk quotas on 31 March 2015,[136] a potential issue for farming partnerships was the question of whether a milk quota was partnership property. In this regard, it was seen as significant that a milk quota was incapable of existing independently of the land to which it related.[137] In *Faulks v Faulks,*[138] lands were farmed in partnership by two brothers, John and Harry Faulks, but they were legally owned by John Faulks. Their partnership agreement provided for the land to be held on trust for the firm only during the continuance of the partnership. The quota, which was allocated to the firm, was held to attach to those lands as it was incapable of independent existence. Therefore, on the dissolution of the partnership, which was caused by the death of Harry Faulks, it was held that the land, along with the quota, passed to John Faulks. Thus, in that instance the milk quota was not regarded as partnership property.[139]

Post-dissolution Letters between Partners

[16.62] *Palmer v Mahony*[140] concerned the question of whether letters written between partners after the dissolution of the partnership are partnership property. The plaintiff and defendant were partners and the plaintiff relied on letters sent to him by the defendant to support his allegation that they had agreed on the extent to which accounts should be taken between them on a dissolution. The defendant sought copies of the letters on the basis they were partnership documents and therefore the common property of both parties. On technical grounds, Blackburne MR refused to order the discovery of the letters;[141] however, obiter, he held that as the defendant denied that the letters formed an agreement (as to the basis on which the accounts were to be taken), it was impossible for him at the same time to claim that they were the common property of the partners. The question of whether this aspect of the decision would be followed today is open to

---

134 *Don King Productions v Warren* [1999] 2 All ER 218.

135 Paragraph **[15.27]** et seq.

136 The 2003 Mid Term Review of the European Common Agricultural Policy proposed that milk quotas be abolished across the EU at the end of March 2015. That deadline was then formalised by Council Regulation (EC) No 1788/2003 of 29 September 2003 establishing a levy in the milk and milk products sector.

137 European Communities (Milk Quota) Regulations 1995 (SI 266/1995), s 4(1). The High Court decision in *Lawlor v The Minister for Agriculture* [1991] IR 356 is notable in that Murphy J ruled that the fact that the quota attached to land was not unconstitutional.

138 *Faulks v Faulks* [1992] 15 EG 82.

139 See also *Davies v H & R Ecroyd Ltd* [1996] 30 EG 97.

140 *Palmer v Mahony* (1844) 6 Ir Eq R 504.

141 Ie the defendant did not file a cross-bill in order to enforce this discovery.

doubt. The correspondence clearly concerned partnership affairs, albeit after the dissolution of the firm,[142] and therefore would appear to satisfy the terms of s 20(1) of the 1890 Act, namely, that property is partnership property if it has been brought into the partnership for the purposes and in the course of the partnership business. It is submitted that it is irrelevant to the question of whether property is partnership property that one of the partners agrees or disagrees with the contents thereof.

III. CHARACTERISTICS OF PARTNERSHIP PROPERTY

[16.63] In this final section, consideration is given to the consequences of categorising property as partnership property.

Partnership Property is held as Tenants in Common

[16.64] Perhaps the most important characteristic of partnership property, as noted by O'Connor MR, is that 'lands purchased with partnership profits are partnership property, and are held on a tenancy in common'.[143] Since partnership property is held as tenants in common,[144] there is no right to survivorship, so that on the death of a partner, his co-partner does not become entitled to the deceased partner's share. The treatment of partnership property is based on the long-established rule in equity of *jus accrescendi inter mercatores locum non habet*, ie the right of survivorship does not apply as between business men. In the context of the business of partnerships, this approach is clearly justified since a right of survivorship would be inconsistent with the fact that partnership property must be 'held and applied by the partners exclusively for the

---

[142] Note that a firm is treated as if it continues during its winding-up: s 38 of the 1890 Act. Cf *Nerot v Burnand* (1827) 4 Russ 247, aff'd at (1828) 2 Bli (ns) 215, where it was not automatically assumed that all assets acquired by a partner, while the partnership was being wound up, were partnership property. Instead, an inquiry was ordered as to whether the assets were partnership property.

[143] *Re Christie* [1917] 1 IR 17 at 36. In some cases, whether property is classified as partnership property or not may make no difference to the eventual outcome of the case. For example in *Walsh v Walsh* [1942] IR 403, the High Court held that members of a family who worked their deceased father's farm were not partners. Rather, they were held to be co-owners of the common undertaking as tenants in common. Yet, as regards the devolution of the share of a member of the undertaking on his death or departure, the result achieved was much the same as if the property was held to be partnership property. Thus, on the departure of a member, a new family group came into being, the share of the former member, when not paid to him, being held on a separate trust from the rest of the property for his benefit.

[144] Note that the rule that equity treats partners as tenants in common applies to other joint undertakings which fall short of partnership: *Walsh v Walsh* [1942] IR 403 at 411, where Gavin Duffy J noted: 'I hold that the true relationship, as a matter of law, was that of co-owners of the common undertaking, and that this co-ownership constituted no partnership. But the parties were tenants in common; the rule has been established for more than 200 years that 'in all cases of a joint undertaking or partnership, either in trade or in any other dealing, two or more persons who make a joint purchase will be considered in equity as tenants in common': *Lake v Gibson* (1729) 1 Eq Cas Abr 294.' In that case, Gavin Duffy J extended this principle to apply to property acquired other than by purchase. See generally in relation to tenancy in common, Wylie, *Irish Land Law* (5th edn, 2013) at para [8.12] et seq.

purposes of the partnership and in accordance with the partnership agreement'.[145] Similarly a right of survivorship would be inconsistent with the requirement that partnership property be applied on a dissolution in paying off the firm's debts and liabilities, repaying advances and capital and dividing any residue amongst the partners in the proportion in which they were entitled to share profits.[146]

Where legal estate in partnership property is held as joint tenants

[16.65] While it will be more usual for partnership property to be held by the partners as tenants in common, it is of course possible that the legal estate in partnership property will be held by the partners as joint tenants. In such a case, equity will require the beneficial interest in the property to be held as tenants in common, ie exclusively for the purpose of the partnership and in accordance with the partnership agreement. As observed by Richards B in *Reilly v Walsh*:[147]

> '[I]f the intention was that the property should be managed and enjoyed as a partnership matter, a Court of Equity will control and prevent what would otherwise be the legal effect, the right of survivorship.'[148]

[16.66] In *Re Ryan,*[149] the partnership of John and Thomas Ryan owned the business premises at Abbey St in Dublin and, after the death of John, Thomas mortgaged this property to secure his own personal debts. Harrison J observed that:

> '[T]he form of conveyance to the brothers becomes immaterial, the well-known principle of partnership law expressed in the maxim *jus accrescendi inter mercatores locum non habet*,[150] preventing (so far as the beneficial interest is concerned) the ordinary result of the doctrine of survivorship as between joint tenants applying to such a case; and although the recital contained in the deed of mortgage of the 21st of February, 1867, that upon the death of John Ryan, in 1860, all the estate and interest of the said John Ryan in said premises became legally vested in the said Thomas Ryan, by survivorship, as one of the joint tenants in said premises, is true as regards the legal estate therein, yet Thomas Ryan became thereupon, as regards the equitable and beneficial interest therein, a trustee for the minor children of his brother John.'[151]

Partnership does not per se sever joint tenancy

[16.67] It has been seen that if property is partnership property, there will be a severance of the joint tenancy at equity.[152] However, it has also been noted[153] that persons may be partners as to the profits of land, but not as to the land itself. It follows that partners who own property as joint tenants will not necessarily have their joint tenancy severed by virtue of their becoming partners, since the property can remain outside the partnership.

---

145 Partnership Act 1890, s 20(1). However, see *Bathurst v Scarbarrow* [2005] 1 P&CR 58 (CA) and para **[16.40]**.
146 Partnership Act 1890, s 44.
147 *Reilly v Walsh* (1848) 11 Ir Eq R 22 and para **[16.69]**.
148 *Reilly v Walsh* (1848) 11 Ir Eq R 22 at 28.
149 *Re Ryan* (1868) 3 Ir Eq R 222.
150 Ie the right of survivorship among merchants, for the benefit of commerce, does not exist.
151 *Re Ryan* (1868) 3 Ir Eq R 222 at 232.
152 Paragraph **[16.65]**.
153 Paragraph **[16.38]**.

This concept is illustrated by *McCarthy v Barry*.[154] That case concerned land in Caherdaniel in Co Kerry which had been demised by Daniel O'Connell, the renowned statesman, to two individuals, Trant and Barry. The two believed they had acquired the land as joint tenants and shortly after the land was demised, they entered into a partnership as millers and bakers. It was claimed that as the land was acquired for partnership purposes, it was partnership property and that this caused a severance of the joint tenancy, so that both held the land as tenants in common. As it turned out, due to an oversight by the lawyers involved in the case, the land had actually been demised to them in the first place as tenants in common. Accordingly, it was not necessary for the court to decide on the question of severance, although Smith MR observed that the severance of the joint tenancy would not have occurred simply by virtue of the existence of the partnership.[155]

Corollary of severance of joint tenancy does not apply

[16.68] While partnership property is held by partners as tenants in common, it is important to note that property which is held by partners as tenants in common is not necessarily partnership property.[156] This is apparent from the terms of s 2(1) of the 1890 Act:

> In determining whether a partnership does or does not exist, regard shall be had to the following rules:
>
>> (1) Joint tenancy, tenancy in common, joint property, common property, or part ownership does not of itself create a partnership as to anything so held or owned, whether the tenants or owners do or do not share any profits made by the use thereof.

Nonetheless, it is thought that the fact that property is held by persons as tenants in common is stronger evidence of a partnership than if the property were held as joint tenants.

Partner seeking equitable relief must have 'clean hands'

[16.69] The rule that a joint tenancy of partnership property is severed at equity is, like all rules of equity, subject to equitable principles. Therefore, the person seeking equitable relief, must, inter alia, have 'clean hands'.[157] It follows that a person who is claiming the benefit of this equitable rule must not himself be guilty of inequitable conduct. In *Reilly v Walsh*,[158] two brothers, Oliver and Edward Walsh, agreed to take a lease of land in Suffolk Street in Dublin from Archdeacon Barton and build some

---

154 *McCarthy v Barry* (1859) 9 Ir Ch R 377.
155 He relied on *Phillips v Phillips* (1832) 1 M & K 649; *North Eastern Railway Co v Martin* (1848) 2 Phil 762; *Padwick v Hurst* (1854) 18 Beav 577; *McMahon v Burchell* (1846) 2 Phil 134.
156 See for example *Moore v Moore* (27 February 1998) HC NI in which a farm that was the subject of the partnership was held by two brothers as tenants in common, but was not partnership property.
157 See generally regarding recourse to equitable relief, Keane, *Equity and the Law of Trusts in Ireland* (3rd edn, 2017) at para [3.01] et seq and Biehler, *Equity and the Law of Trusts in Ireland* (6th edn, 2016) at p 15 et seq.
158 *Reilly v Walsh* (1848) 11 Ir Eq R 22.

houses thereon. They agreed that they would take the lease as joint tenants, thus giving rise to the right of survivorship. However, during the project, not only did Oliver not join or assist Edward in the building, nor make any financial contributions towards it, but also he showed clear *mala fides* by writing to potential lenders to discourage them from lending to Edward for the purposes of the venture. Yet after Oliver's death, his personal representatives sought a share in the property and for this purpose relied on the equitable rule that the legal right of survivorship does not apply to partnership property. Richards B noted that 'from the very commencement his conduct was the very opposite of what it should have been if he intended to act as a partner fairly'[159] and on this basis, he refused to invoke equitable principles and held that the right of survivorship operated in favour of Edward.

All Partnership Property is Personal Estate not Real Estate

[16.70] The share of a partner in a partnership is, in fact, simply his proportion of the partnership property after that property has been turned into money and applied to pay off the partnership debts.[160] This follows from the terms of s 44 of the 1890 Act, which provides that partnership property is to be used, on the dissolution of the firm, to pay off the firm's liabilities, advances and the partners' capital contributions and the surplus is to be divided amongst the partners.[161] No distinction is made between real property and personal property for this purpose. For this reason it is said that real property, which forms part of the partnership property, is converted into personal estate for this purpose. This doctrine of conversion involves the application of the equitable principle that 'equity regards as done what ought to be done'. Thus, all parties have their rights determined according to matters as they should stand and not as they actually stand. As noted by Chatterton VC in *Murtagh v Costello*:[162]

'The rule of law by which this question is to be decided appears to me to be that, real estate purchased by a firm out of partnership money, and for partnership purposes, is personal estate, not only for the purpose of the administration of the partnership assets, but for all intents and purposes, including the purpose of ascertaining the relative rights of the real and personal representatives of deceased partners.'[163]

---

[159] *Reilly v Walsh* (1848) 11 Ir Eq R 22 at 28.

[160] This sentence was quoted by Keane J in *Bloxham v Companies Act* [2017] IEHC 664, together with the judgment of Joy CB in *Stuart v Ferguson* (1832) Hayes 452 (see para **[16.85]**, the statement by Lord Lindley (now at l'Anson Banks, *Lindley & Banks on Partnership* (20th edn, 2017) at para 19-05) that '[what] is meant by the *share* of a partner is his proportion of the partnership assets after they have all been realised and converted into money, and all the debts and liabilities have been paid and discharged ...' and the comment by the current editor of *Lindley & Banks on Partnership* (again at para 19-05 of the current edition of that work (20th edn, 2017)) that it 'would be more accurate to speak of a partner's entitlement to a proportion of the *net proceeds of sale* of the assets'. See generally in relation to the meaning of a partnership share, para **[19.03]** et seq.

[161] See also s 20(1) of the 1890 Act which requires partnership property to be used for the purposes of the partnership.

[162] *Murtagh v Costello* (1881) 7 LR Ir 428.

[163] *Murtagh v Costello* (1881) 7 LR Ir 428 at 435–436.

This principle of the doctrine of conversion is now to be found in s 22 of the 1890 Act:

> Where land or any heritable interest therein has become partnership property, it shall, unless the contrary intention appears, be treated as between the partners (including the representatives of a deceased partner), and also as between the heirs of a deceased partner and his executors or administrators, as personal or moveable and not real or heritable estate.

[16.71] Prior to 1965, when a person died intestate his realty devolved on his heir-at-law and his personalty devolved on his next-of-kin. However, as a result of the passing of the Succession Act 1965,[164] this is no longer the case and the importance of s 22 of the 1890 Act has been reduced accordingly. However, it will still be important where a testator leaves his realty to one person and his personalty to another,[165] since under s 22, land which is partnership property is treated as personalty.

[16.72] Under the express terms of s 22 of the 1890 Act, the conversion of real partnership property into personal estate is subject to there being no contrary agreement between the partners. Thus, where the partners either expressly or implicitly agree that land which is partnership property shall not be sold, this will exclude the application of the doctrine of conversion.[166]

Purpose for which Partnership Property must be Used

[16.73] Once it has been determined that property is partnership property, the 1890 Act contains a number of provisions which will determine the purpose for which that property is to be used. Most important of these provisions is s 20(1) which states that partnership property is to be applied by the partners exclusively for the purposes of the partnership and in accordance with the partnership agreement. It goes without saying therefore that a partner will not be allowed take partnership property for his own use.[167]

[16.74] In *O'Connor v Woods*,[168] a case in which O'Connor was in partnership with three other accountants, the partnership agreement provided that on the dissolution of a partnership by the departure of a partner, the continuing partners were to operate the business as before that departure. On his departure, O'Connor took files relating to the business of clients of the firm. In the High Court, Kenny J held that the plaintiff had no right to take those files and when he discovered that his co-partners objected to his taking of them, his obligation was to return the files to the firm. As the removal of these files prevented the firm from recovering fees from the clients in question, damages were awarded to the defendants.

---

164 Succession Act 1965, ss 10 and 66.
165 See generally in relation to the doctrine of conversion, Wylie, *Irish Land Law* (5th edn, 2013) at para [3.113] et seq; Biehler, *Equity and the Law of Trusts in Ireland* (6th edn, 2016) at p 913 et seq; Keane, *Equity and the Law of Trusts in Ireland* (3rd edn, 2017) at para [22.01] et seq.
166 See *Steward v Blakeway* (1869) LR 4 Ch App 603; *Re Wilson* [1893] 2 Ch 340.
167 But as regards the special position of the treatment of a firm's goodwill on its dissolution, see para **[18.22]** et seq.
168 *O'Connor v Woods* (22 January 1976) HC.

[16.75] Whether property is partnership property or not is also of considerable significance on the general dissolution of the partnership. Section 39 of the 1890 Act entitles the partners to sell the partnership property and to use the proceeds to pay off the partnership debts and liabilities.[169] Under s 44 of the 1890 Act, the surplus is required to be divided amongst the partners.[170] The classification of property as partnership property will have particular significance to the creditors of the firm and the separate creditors of the partners on the bankruptcy of the firm or of a partner. In general terms, partnership property is part of the joint estate of the firm and is therefore available first to the creditors of the firm, with the surplus, if any, being available to the separate creditors of the partners. In contrast, if the property is the personal property of a partner, it is available first to pay off his separate creditors, with the surplus, if any, being available to the creditors of the firm.[171]

Partner must account for private use of partnership property

[16.76] Another consequence of property being deemed to be partnership property is that a partner who uses partnership property for his own purposes may be required to account to his partner for that use. In a situation where one partner leaves a firm and the partnership business is still carried on, this principle is specifically recognised by the terms of s 42 of the 1890 Act.[172] This section provides that in the absence of contrary agreement, the continuing partners must pay the outgoing partner such a share of the profits as is attributable to the use by the firm of his share of the partnership assets. In *Walmsley v Walmsley*,[173] the parties had contributed capital of £4,000 in equal proportions to their partnership. The partnership was dissolved by the death of the plaintiff. However, the defendant continued in possession of the partnership property between the date of the dissolution of the partnership and the date of the appointment of a receiver. Accordingly, Smith MR held that the defendant was liable to pay the plaintiff's estate half of the rent of the firm's premises, between the date of dissolution of the firm and the date of the appointment of a receiver. This rent was estimated as equivalent to what the receiver actually obtained when he subsequently leased the premises.

[16.77] The principle that a partner must account to the firm for his use of partnership property for his own benefit is also applicable during the term of the partnership. This is clear from s 29 of the 1890 Act which provides that a partner must account to the firm for any benefit derived by him from any transaction concerning the partnership, the firm's business connection or the use of partnership property, without the consent of his partners.[174]

---

169 The Partnership Act 1890, s 39 is considered in detail at para **[26.28]** et seq.
170 The Partnership Act 1890, s 44 is considered in detail at para **[26.106]**.
171 This area is considered in detail at para **[27.94]** et seq.
172 See generally in relation to this duty to account to a former partner, para **[26.63]** et seq.
173 *Walmsley v Walmsley* (1846) 3 Jo & La T 556.
174 See generally in relation to the obligation to account during the partnership, para **[15.27]** et seq.

Position of Third Party Dealing with Property used by Firm

[16.78] As observed earlier,[175] property which is used in a partnership business usually (though not necessarily) constitutes partnership property. From the perspective of a third party such as a mortgagee or purchaser, it will be important to determine whether the property is the separate property of the partner or whether it is partnership property, in which case, all the partners will have a beneficial interest therein.

[16.79] *Re Ryan*[176] illustrates that a third party who deals with property which was used in a partnership may be deemed to be on notice that the property is partnership property. In that case, after the death of one partner (John Ryan), the other partner (Thomas Ryan) granted a mortgage over the partnership premises at Abbey St to secure his separate debts. Significantly, the mortgagee had transacted business with the two partners at the premises and the name 'Ryan, Brothers' was publicly posted on the premises. In addition, after the death of John, Thomas had discussed with the mortgagee the issue of whether the premises, if sold, would cover the liabilities of the partnership. On this basis, it was held that the mortgagee was on notice that the premises were partnership property and Harrison J held that the mortgagee was only entitled to half of the property.[177]

Partner may Purchase Property from the Firm

[16.80] It is clear from the High Court case of *Hawkins v Rogers*,[178] that there is no impediment to a partner purchasing property from his own firm. In that case, the plaintiff was a partner in a firm which was selling a horse at auction. It was accepted that the horse was owned by the partnership. At the auction, the plaintiff successfully bid for the horse. Dixon J, while noting the legal difficulty involved in a partner suing his own firm,[179] held that 'this legal difficulty does not however prevent him from becoming the purchaser of partnership property'.[180] While the purchase in this case was made by the plaintiff after the firm's dissolution, it is clear that a partner can purchase property from his firm at any time.

What is the Value of Partnership Property?

[16.81] The value of partnership property is an important issue, especially on the dissolution of a partnership, when the assets of the firm are being shared between the partners. In some cases, the partners themselves will put a value on partnership property in the balance sheet of the firm, but, unless expressly provided for in the partnership agreement, this value will not be taken on the technical or general dissolution of the

175 Paragraph **[16.10]**.
176 *Re Ryan* [1868] 3 Ir Eq R 222. As is the position generally, the mortgagee in that case was held to know the law, ie that if it was partnership property, Thomas Ryan would be a trustee as to one half of the premises for his brother's estate.
177 Note that the headnote to this case is misleading, since it states that in relation to the second premises, at Parnell St, which was owned by the mother of both men, the mortgagee did not have distinct notice that these premises were partnership property. However, this was never held by Harrison J and could not have been so held, since Harrison J had found that the premises at Parnell St was not partnership property in the first place.
178 *Hawkins v Rogers* [1951] IR 48.
179 See generally in relation to a partner suing his own firm, para **[20.07]**.
180 *Hawkins v Rogers* [1951] IR 48 at 60.

partnership[181] to be the real value of the property. This is clear from the High Court case of *Barr v Barr*,[182] where the premises used by the firm was held to constitute partnership property and was valued in the balance sheet of the firm at over £1,000. However, for the purposes of calculating the entitlement of a deceased partner's estate, Barron J held that its real value was £5,000. This case clearly indicates that if partners wish to use the balance sheet values for the purpose of calculating a departing partner's share, this should be expressly stated by them in their agreement, since this assumption will not be made by the courts.

Partnership Property need not be Vested in all the Partners

[16.82] It is possible for partnership property, including real property, to be held in the names of all the partners, regardless of how numerous.[183] However, for practical reasons, it is common for partnership property to be held by some only of the partners. This is particularly so in the case of large partnerships, where it would be impractical for all the partners to be the legal owners of the partnership property. It has been noted that property which is not held by all the partners may be partnership property[184] and it will be held by the legal owners (usually, some of the partners) on trust for all the partners.[185]

[16.83] If a partner, in whom the partnership property is vested, dies, the partnership property will devolve on his co-partners as surviving trustees for sale. In the absence of a contrary agreement, these co-partners must account to his estate for the deceased's share of the partnership property.

Assets Transferred in and out of Partnership

[16.84] Reference has been made in this chapter to both partnership property and the separate property of some or all of the partners. In this context, it is worth noting that there is nothing to prevent the partners in a firm converting an item of partnership property into the separate property of one or more of the partners.[186] Thus, if a firm is solvent[187] and all the partners agree,[188] partnership property may be removed from the

---

[181] See generally in relation to provisions in a partnership agreement for the valuation of a departing partner's share in the firm, para **[21.145]**.

[182] *Barr v Barr* (3 November 1983) HC.

[183] Cf the position in England, where there is a requirement that land be vested in no more than four partners: Law of Property Act 1925, s 34(2) and the Trusts of Land and Appointment of Trustees Act 1996.

[184] Para **[16.42]**.

[185] See for example *Re Ryan* (1868) 3 Ir Eq R 222 and *Reilly v Walsh* (1848) 11 Ir Eq R 22 and generally, para **[16.65]** et seq.

[186] *Ex p Rowlandson* (1811) 1 Rose 416, which was approved by Joy CB in *Stuart v Ferguson* (1832) Hayes 452. See also *Ex p Williams* (1805) 11 Ves Jun 3; *Ex p Fell* (1805) 10 Ves Jr 348; *Ex p Ruffin* (1801) 6 Ves 119 at 127.

[187] As regards the position when the firm is not solvent, see generally para **[27.01]** et seq, ss 57–59 of the Bankruptcy Act 1988 and s 74(3) and 74(4) of the Land and Conveyancing Law Reform Act 2009.

[188] The consent of all the partners would be required if the conversion of partnership property into the separate property of the firm would not be regarded as an ordinary matter connected with the partnership business, (contd.../)

firm and the capital of the firm may be reduced.[189] Indeed, the flexibility of a partnership regarding the use of its capital is one of the main advantages of a partnership over a limited liability company. In contrast, limited liability companies may not reduce their capital as a general rule.[190] This can be justified in principle since creditors of a company rely on the existence of the company's capital to satisfy their claims. With a partnership, the partners have unlimited liability, and therefore the creditors of the partnership look to the partners themselves and not just to the capital of the partnership.

Creditors cannot prevent transfer of partnership property

[16.85] Since the partners may move assets freely in and out of the partnership, the creditor of a partnership has no lien on the firm's property. Thus, the creditors of a firm cannot prevent the partners from bona fide changing its character, provided that it takes place prior to bankruptcy.[191] This is illustrated by *Stuart v Ferguson*.[192] This case involved the creditor of an Antrim-based milling partnership who claimed that, as a joint creditor of the firm, he had a lien on the joint estate for a debt owed to him by the partnership. Joy CB dismissed this claim, observing that:

> '[T]he share of each partner is only the share of the clear surplus which would remain after the payment of all the debts. That may be quite correct, as between the partners themselves; but the doctrine does not apply to a disposition of the joint estate by them. Creditors have no equity against the joint effects, save what they claim through the partners themselves. If a creditor does not proceed at law against the joint effects, he has no lien upon them, except in cases of death or bankruptcy. This has been established by so many cases, that it is only necessary to refer to a few of them, *Ex parte Peake* (1816) 1 Madd 346, *Ex parte Rowlandson* (1811) 1 Rose 416, *Campbell v Mullett* (1819) 2 Swan 551 ... They have no lien; but something approaching to lien, that is, a right to sue, and, by judgment and execution, to obtain possession of the property: but, till then, they cannot prevent the partners from effectually transferring it by *bona fide* alienation.'[193]

On dissolution, converted separate property is subject to partners' liens

[16.86] A separate issue to that of a creditor having a lien over partnership property is the existence of a partner's lien. A partner's lien is the term given to the right of a partner to have the partnership property used to pay off partnership debts and in this respect it is

---

[188] (\...contd) but rather as a change in the nature of the partnership business as contemplated by s 24(8) of the 1890 Act. This was recognised by Keane J in *Bloxham v Companies Act* [2017] IEHC 664 at para 39 of his judgment. This is of course in the absence of a contrary provision in the partnership agreement. See generally regarding s 24(8), para **[13.12]** et seq.

[189] This sentence was referred to by Keane J in *Bloxham v Companies Act* [2017] IEHC 664 at para 39 of his judgment. As regards the reduction in capital, this requires the consent of all the partners, see para **[17.13]** et seq.

[190] See generally in relation to the situations in which a private company may reduce its capital, Courtney, *The Law of Companies* (4th edn, 2016) at para [10.001] et seq.

[191] As to which, see generally para **[27.01]** et seq.

[192] *Stuart v Ferguson* (1832) Hayes 452.

[193] *Stuart v Ferguson* (1832) Hayes 452 at 473, quoting in part from the decision of *Campbell v Mullett* (1819) 2 Swan 551 at 575.

for the indirect benefit of creditors of the firm.[194] This right is set out in s 39 of the 1890 Act:

> On the dissolution of a partnership every partner is entitled, as against the other partners in the firm, and all persons claiming through them in respect of their interests as partners, to have the property of the partnership applied in payment of the debts and liabilities of the firm...

[16.87] Sometimes, partnership agreements provide that partnership property is to become the separate property of one partner on the dissolution of the partnership.[195] It is important to bear in mind that such a conversion of the joint property into the separate property is subject to a partner's lien. Therefore, the assets of the partnership on a dissolution, although converted into the separate property of one of the partners will be held for the benefit of the creditors of the firm and in this regard, will technically still remain partnership property.

Still partnership property if agreement to transfer remains executory

[16.88] An agreement to convert partnership property into the separate property of one partner will be of no effect if it remains executory, ie if the transfer of the property is dependant on some action which has not been taken. This is illustrated by *Re Fox*.[196] This case concerned a partnership deed between Fox and Doyle for the running of a hotel. Article 12 of their partnership deed provided that on the death of a partner, the share of the deceased partner should, as from the first of the month following his death, belong to the surviving partner. The deed also provided for the surviving partner to pay to the personal representatives of the deceased partner such sum as may be due to him on an account being taken. Doyle died, leaving Fox as the sole survivor and two months later Fox died. Nothing was done to effect the provisions of the partnership deed regarding the transfer of Doyle's share to Fox and it was held that the property remained partnership property. O'Connor MR stated:

> 'It occurs to me that the assets of the hotel venture never lost their character of partnership assets. They would have done so if the procedure set forth in article 12 of the partnership deed, to be adopted in the case of the death of a partner, had been carried out. But no such procedure was carried out or any account taken between the deceased and surviving partner. There is nothing in what has occurred to deprive the assets of the hotel of their character of partnership property.'[197]

---

[194] See generally in relation to a partner's lien, para **[19.50]**.
[195] See for example *Re Fox* (1915) 49 ILTR 224.
[196] *Re Fox* (1915) 49 ILTR 224.
[197] *Re Fox* (1915) 49 ILTR 224 at 225.

Chapter 17

Partnership Capital

INTRODUCTION

[17.01] Although a firm's capital may properly be regarded as part of the partnership property, it is proposed to deal with partnership capital separate from other partnership property. This is being done to emphasise the distinct nature of a firm's capital, which distinction is often blurred because of its treatment in practice by the partners themselves[1] and because of its treatment under accountancy principles.[2] The capital of a partnership will be considered under the following headings:

    I.   The Nature of Capital;

    II.   Profits of Capital and Losses of Capital.

Overview

[17.02] The capital of a partnership is the source of more confusion than most other areas of partnership law. This is caused in part by the confusion between the assets or other property of a partnership on the one hand and its capital. This confusion will be avoided if the capital of a firm is thought of as the sum which is contributed by the partners to establish the firm. Where capital is contributed in the form of assets, a potential confusion between assets and capital should be avoided by having these assets valued and the value inserted in the accounts as the partner's capital contribution. Any increase or decrease in the value of the underlying asset will then constitute a capital profit or loss as appropriate. This profit or loss is shared between the partners equally in the absence of any agreement regarding the sharing of profits or losses.

[17.03] On the dissolution of a partnership, it is important to note that capital contributions are repaid to the partners. The confusion surrounding the treatment of partnership capital is increased by s 24(1) of the 1890 Act since it rather simplistically states that all the partners are entitled to share equally in the capital of the business. This principle of equal sharing between the partners applies to capital profits and losses, but not to capital contributions. Thus, in much the same way as the capital of a company is repaid to shareholders on the winding up of the company,[3] so too, the capital contributions of the partners are repaid to them on the dissolution of the firm.

[17.04] Another cause of confusion is the fact that it is sometimes difficult to relate partnership capital as a legal concept with its treatment under accountancy conventions.

---

[1]   Commonly, partners will treat all the firm's underlying assets as the firm's capital.

[2]   It is a common accountancy practice to maintain one account for both a partner's capital contributions and his undrawn profits and this account is confusingly termed the 'capital account'.

[3]   Companies Act 2014, s 618.

In general terms, partnership law may be criticised for taking an unrealistic single accounting view of the partnership, in which the financial condition of the firm is accounted for only on the dissolution of the partnership rather than on a periodic basis. Thus, capital when referred to in s 44(b)(3) of the 1890 Act refers to capital contributions, but this contrasts with the dynamic nature of the capital account which changes to reflect profit, loss and withdrawal. It is for this reason that it is recommended that firms have separate capital and current accounts.[4]

I.   THE NATURE OF CAPITAL

[17.05] There is no definition of the term 'capital' in the 1890 Act. It may be regarded as the amount contributed by the partners to establish the firm or to continue the business of the firm and which is agreed by the partners to be the capital of the firm.[5] In contrast to the assets or property of the firm, which will vary from day to day, the capital will not vary with the trading fortunes of the firm. Instead, it will be represented by the amounts credited to the partners' capital accounts. The only time the capital will vary is if the partners decide to increase or reduce their capital contributions. In the words of Andrews LCJ in the Northern Ireland Court of Appeal:[6]

> 'Whilst the assets and liabilities of a partnership are subject to constant fluctuation, and, accordingly, the value of the share of each partner must also constantly fluctuate, this does not affect the amount of the agreed capital of the partnership business. In truth, the capital of a partnership is something different from its property or its assets.'[7]

---

[4]   In the US, an attempt was made to deal with this confusion by providing in s 401 of the Uniform Partnership Act (1997) (adopted in approximately three-quarters of US states in place of its predecessor, the Uniform Partnership Act (1914) by providing that that each partner has an 'account' which is credited with partner contributions and shares of profits and charged with distributions and a partner's shares of losses. However, this approach was later dispensed with and does not appear in the current Uniform Partnership Act 1997 (Last Amended 2013). Instead, that Act only provides for a default rule for sharing in distributions: see Hurt, Smith, Bromberg and Ribstein, *Bromberg & Ribstein on Limited Liability Partnerships, the Revised Uniform Partnership Act, and the Uniform Limited Partnership Act* (2018 edn). As to the problems which may arise where there is just one account for capital and revenue, see the New Zealand High Court case of *Brenssell v Brenssell* [1995] 3 NZLR 320 (aff'd by the Court of Appeal at [1998] NZFLR 28 (CA)).

[5]   In *Reed (Inspector of Taxes) v Young* [1984] STC 38 at 57, Nourse LJ stated that: '[t]he capital of a partnership is the aggregate of contributions made by the partners, either in cash or in kind, for the purpose of commencing or carrying on the partnership business and intended to be risked by them therein. Each contribution must be of a fixed amount. If it is in cash, it speaks for itself. If it is in kind, it must be valued at a stated amount. It is important to distinguish between the capital of a partnership, a fixed sum, on the one hand and its assets, which may vary from day to day and include everything belonging to the firm, having any money value, on the other.'

[6]   *McClelland v Hyde* [1942] NI 1.

[7]   *McClelland v Hyde* [1942] NI 1 at 7. Later in the same case, Babington LJ states that '[g]enerally speaking, capital is the money, lands, goods or other property with which the company or partnership commences business', at 12.

[17.06] The capital which has been contributed by the partners should be attributed to each of the partners in a separate account in the firm's books, known as the capital account. The capital so contributed should be represented as a cash sum, even where the capital contribution itself is in a non-cash form. This will require a valuation being put on certain assets such as goodwill or property, which are contributed by partners at the commencement of the partnership.[8] By having the capital contribution of each partner stated as a cash sum, the repayment of capital on the technical or general dissolution[9] of the firm is made considerably easier. Similarly, if interest is to be paid on a firm's capital, this will be facilitated by having it stated as a cash sum.[10] If the underlying assets which were contributed by a partner change in value, this will be represented by a profit or loss of capital, as the case may be. If the partners wish, they may re-value the asset which has been contributed and credit any increase or debit any reduction to the capital account of the partner.

No Obligation to Contribute to Capital

[17.07] Although it is usual for a partnership to have capital, there is no legal requirement for there to be capital and a partnership may exist between two or more persons, even where they have not contributed any capital. The only exceptions to this rule in Ireland are limited partnerships and investment limited partnerships. In the case of limited partnerships,[11] the limited partners must contribute some capital to the firm before it is deemed to exist.[12] Similarly, in the case of investment limited partnerships,[13] the limited partners must contribute or agree to contribute some capital to the firm before it will come into existence. In the UK, however, limited partners in a private fund limited partnership are not obliged to contribute capital.[14]

Indirect Capital Contribution

[17.08] The possibility of a partner making an indirect capital contribution to a firm is raised by the interesting case of *Larkin v Groeger and Eaton*.[15] In that case, three accountants went into practice together and each transferred office equipment into the partnership at its commencement as part of their capital contributions. However, some

---

8   Note that under s 4(2) of the Limited Partnerships Act 1907, where capital is contributed in the form of property, the value of this property is required to be assessed and stated. This is not required by the 1890 Act.

9   As to the distinction between a general and a technical dissolution, see para **[23.07]** et seq.

10   The partners may agree to pay interest on the capital contributed by the partners, see s 24(4) of the 1890 Act which is subject to contrary agreement.

11   Limited Partnerships Act 1907, s 4(2). See generally in relation to limited partnerships, para **[28.01]** et seq.

12   For an example of a case where the limited partners did not satisfy this requirement and did not therefore constitute a limited partnership, see *MacCarthaigh v Daly* [1985] IR 73, and para **[28.65]**.

13   Investment Limited Partnerships Act 1994, s 3 (definition of a limited partner). See generally in relation to investment limited partnerships, para **[29.01]** et seq.

14   Legislative Reform (Private Fund Limited Partnerships) Order 2017, art 2(3). See also para **[28.11]**.

15   *Larkin v Groeger and Eaton* (26 April 1988) HC.

of the office equipment transferred by one of the partners, Larkin, was leased by him from an office equipment company. Although the intention was that this equipment would be transferred into the partnership, this could not be done as he was not the legal owner of the equipment. The partnership used this leased property for its term and on his departure from the firm, Larkin claimed that the other two partners should relieve him of his obligations to the office equipment company under the terms of the lease. On the dissolution of the partnership, the arbitrator[16] ordered the other two partners to pay Larkin in respect of their use of the office equipment. On appeal to the High Court, Barrington J refused to vary the award. On a first reading, it might seem harsh that one partner is paid for the use by the firm of his capital, while another partner receives no such payment, the only difference between the two being that the first partner's capital is leased while the other partner's capital is not leased. However, this decision can be explained on the basis that when he contributed his capital to the firm, Larkin would have been credited in the capital account with the value of the leased assets, even though these did not belong to the firm. When this fact became apparent, Larkin's capital would have been reduced by the value of the leased assets. Therefore on the dissolution of the partnership, he would have received back no capital, assuming that the leased equipment was his only capital contribution. Thus, while Larkin made payments to the leasing company during the term of the partnership, he would have received no return of capital in respect of this lease. Although Barrington J did not go into the basis for his decision, it is contended that one should view these lease payments as an indirect capital contribution by Larkin. In this way, the payment by the other partners to Larkin on the dissolution may be seen as a repayment of Larkin's indirect contribution of capital to the firm. On this basis, this decision is of application to all instances of a partner contributing indirectly to the capital of the firm.

Importance of Having a Separate Capital and Current Account

[17.09] In order to avoid any confusion between the capital of the firm and its assets and profits, it is useful to have a separate capital account and a separate current account for each partner. While the capital account sets out the capital contribution of each partner, the current account shows the profits which each partner is entitled to draw from the firm, his actual drawings and his undrawn profits. However, it is common to find firms showing this information along with the partners' capital contributions in one account, which is often incorrectly termed a 'capital account'. This should be avoided as it gives rise to the common misapprehension that undrawn profits form part of the capital of a firm.[17] It is important to note that this is not the case, since the undrawn profits of a partner may be withdrawn by a partner at any time during the life of the partnership. In contrast, the capital contributed by a partner may only be withdrawn during the life of the partnership, if all the other partners agree.[18] Of course, if all of the partners wish, these undrawn profits may be converted into capital by transferring them from the current account to the capital account of that partner.

---

[16] John Gore Grimes, solicitor.

[17] For a case which highlights the difficulties created by consolidating the revenue and capital of a firm in one current account, see the New Zealand case of *Brenssell v Brenssell* [1998] NZFLR 28 (CA).

[18] See para **[17.13]**.

Importance of Distinction between Capital and an Advance

[17.10] Care should be taken to distinguish between those contributions that are made by partners to the firm and which are intended to form part of the capital of the firm on the one hand, and those which are made by way of an advance to the firm on the other. This distinction is important because the 1890 Act treats an advance preferentially to a capital contribution in two instances, namely on a winding up and as regards the payment of interest thereon.

[17.11] On a winding up, s 44(b) of the 1890 Act provides that, subject to contrary agreement, a partner who has made a contribution to the firm by way of an advance will be paid off ahead of his co-partner who has made a contribution to the firm by way of capital. For this reason, a partner making a 'contribution' to an ailing firm may be well advised to do so by way of advance. Alternatively in such a case, this rule in s 44(b), which is a default rather than a mandatory rule, should be varied.

[17.12] As regards the payment of interest on advances and on capital contributions, s 24(3) of the 1890 Act provides that in the absence of agreement between the partners, the default position is that a partner is entitled to interest of 5% per annum on any advance made by him to the firm. In contrast, s 24(4) of the 1890 Act states that, subject to contrary agreement, a partner is not entitled[19] to interest on the capital subscribed by him. For this reason, if a partner wishes to receive interest on his capital or wishes not to receive interest on advances, this default position should be varied in the partnership agreement.

Increase or Reduction of Capital

[17.13] In the absence of a contrary agreement between the partners, the capital of a firm cannot be increased or reduced without the consent of all the partners.[20] Accordingly, where a partner contributes capital to a firm, he will not be able to withdraw any part thereof while he continues to be a member of the firm, unless all his partners agree. For this reason, it is common for partnership agreements to allow some (usually a majority) of the partners to increase the capital of the firm. *Heslin v Fay (1)*[21] is authority for the proposition that this power to increase the capital of the partnership may not be exercised in a *mala fides* manner. That case involved a grocery partnership in North King Street in Dublin. The partnership agreement gave one of the partners, Fay, the power to increase the capital of the firm, if it was necessary for the carrying on of the business of the firm. The agreement also entitled each partner to withdraw from the

---

19 The use of the term 'before the ascertainment of profits' in s 24(4) does not imply that interest is payable after the ascertainment of profits in the absence of any agreement, see para [14.54].

20 *Bouche v Sproule* (1887) 57 LT 345; *Re Bridgewater Navigation Co* [1891] 64 LT 576. *Heslin v Fay (No 1)* (1884) 15 LR Ir 431 is authority for the principle that where a partnership agreement entitles one partner to increase the capital of the firm he must do so for bona fide reasons, but it is not, it is submitted, authority for the principle that the capital of a firm may not be increased or reduced without the authority of all the partners, as was claimed in *McLelland v Hyde* [1942] NI 1 at 6 per Andrews LCJ and in l'Anson Banks, *Lindley & Banks on Partnership* (20th edn, 2017) at para 17-10.

21 *Heslin v Fay (No 1)* (1884) 15 LR Ir 431.

firm the amount of any capital paid by him which was surplus to the firm's business. Heslin called on the partners in the firm to repay to him the surplus capital which he had paid. Fay responded by raising the capital of the firm so as to reduce the amount of the surplus owed to Heslin. In the Irish Court of Appeal, Sullivan LC held that the exercise by Fay of his power of increasing the capital of the firm for the purpose of resisting the plaintiff's demand for a return of his surplus capital was invalid as it was exercised in a *mala fides* manner.

II.   Profits of Capital and Losses of Capital

Nature of a Capital Profit or a Capital Loss

[17.14] Commonly, partners will contribute property such as premises or office equipment to a firm as part of their capital contribution. In such a case, the partners' capital account should be credited with the cash value of the property at the time of the contribution. However, the market value of the property which has been contributed will normally fluctuate with time. Nonetheless, any increase or reduction in the property value will not form part of the partners' capital contributions which will remain at the original figure. Instead, the increase or reduction in the value of this partnership property will constitute potential capital profits or capital losses which will be realised on the sale or revaluation of the property.[22] It is of course possible for the partners to decide to capitalise these profits or losses of capital by transferring them to the partners' capital account. Assuming that such a capitalisation is not made, this increase/decrease in the value of this property is a potential capital profit/loss. The treatment of a capital profit and a capital loss during the life of the partnership and on its dissolution will next be considered.

Division of Capital Profits and Losses during Life of Partnership

[17.15] Profits and losses of capital of a firm are treated in the same way as profits and losses of income of a firm. The profits or losses of a capital nature during the life of the partnership are divisible between the partners in accordance with the terms of their partnership agreement. If the profit or losses of income have been agreed by the partners to be shared unequally, the profits and losses of capital, in the absence of a specific agreement, will be shared in that proportion.[23] For this reason, where the intention is that the partners will share profits and losses of capital in a different proportion to the manner in which they share profits and losses of income, it is imperative that this is stated in the partnership agreement.

[17.16] If the partners have not agreed on a rate of division of the profits and losses (whether of income or capital), all partners are obliged to share equally in the profits of

---

22   Commonly, a capital profit will result on the dissolution of a partnership by virtue of the absence of a provision for goodwill in the accounts of the firm. This capital profit is realised when the goodwill is sold on the general dissolution of the firm.

23   See para [14.13] et seq in relation to capital profits and para [14.29] et seq in relation to capital losses. See also the Partnership Act 1890, s 44(a) and 44(b)(4) in relation to the approach on the dissolution of the partnership and *Robinson v Ashton* (1875) LR 20 Eq 25.

capital[24] and contribute equally to the losses of capital of the firm.[25] This follows from the terms of s 24(1) of the 1890 Act which provides that, subject to any express or implied agreement between the partners:

> All the partners are entitled to share equally in the capital and profits of the business, and must contribute equally towards the losses whether of capital or otherwise sustained by the firm.

Therefore, in the absence of agreement, the capital profits or capital losses will be divided equally between the partners.

[17.17] It is important to note that even where the partners have contributed to the capital of the firm *unequally*, in the absence of agreement, any capital profit (or loss) will be divided between the partners *equally* under s 24(1). The rationale behind s 24(1) is that in many cases capital, in the broad sense of that term, will be contributed in a manner which is difficult to quantify. For example it is common for partners to contribute capital in the form of goodwill, business connections, skill, assets, etc. Thus, while it has been noted that the legal meaning of capital is money or property contributed at the commencement or for the firm to continue, it also has a commercial meaning as including the skill and labour of the partners. Since it is difficult to quantify all these factors, in the absence of an agreement to the contrary, the appropriate default position is equality between the partners (regardless of the inequality of money or property contributed by them) and the capital profits and losses are therefore shared equally. As noted by Sir Frederick Pollock, the drafter of the 1890 Act: '[e]quality is equity, not as being absolutely just, but because it cannot be known that any particular degree of inequality would be more just.'[26] The resulting equality of capital profits and capital losses may come as a surprise to a partner who contributes all of the capital. For this reason and in order to avoid potential disputes, it is useful to have a provision in the partnership agreement specifically agreeing the rate at which profits and losses of capital will be shared between the partners.

Revaluation of current account on a technical dissolution

[17.18] Because of the possibility that property contributed by partners as capital may increase in value, there is often a revaluation of that property before the admission of new partners. This revaluation usually provides for the increase in the value of the underlying assets to be credited to the existing partners' capital accounts. Failing such a revaluation and capitalisation, the increase in the value of the assets underlying the capital contributions of each partner will be regarded as a capital profit and thus part of the current account and therefore distributable to new as well as existing partners on a general dissolution or on a sale of those assets.[27] By re-valuing the assets and

---

24 *Robinson v Ashton* (1875) LR 20 Eq 25. See also the Partnership Act 1890, s 44(b)(4) in relation to the sharing of capital profits on a dissolution.

25 See also the Partnership Act 1890, s 44(a) in relation to the sharing of losses on the dissolution of partnerships: ie '[l]osses, including losses and deficiencies of capital, shall be paid first out of profits, next out of capital, and lastly, if necessary, by the partners individually in the proportion in which they were entitled to share profits.'

26 Pollock, *A Digest of the Law of Partnership* (11th edn, 1920) at p 81.

27 This distribution will be in accordance with the Partnership Act 1890, s 24(1), unless of course, there is a contrary agreement between the partners.

capitalising the profit, the existing partners will get the exclusive benefit of this increase in value. Alternatively, the existing partners may agree with the new partner that all capital profits prior to his admission will belong to the existing partners.

Division of Capital Profits and Losses on a Dissolution

[17.19] The distribution of capital profits and losses on a dissolution of the firm is dealt with by the default rules in s 44(a) and 44(b)(4) of the 1890 Act. This section provides that in the absence of a contrary agreement, capital losses (ie 'including losses and deficiencies of capital') and capital profits (ie the 'residue') are distributed in the proportion in which the partners were entitled to share the profits of the firm.

[17.20] These subsections are traps for the unwary as this sharing of the capital losses or capital profits applies irrespective of the manner in which the partners have contributed to the capital of the firm.[28] Therefore, in the absence of any agreement to the contrary a partner who contributes all of the capital of the firm but shares the profits of the firm evenly with his co-partner, will share evenly with his co-partner any capital profit or capital loss on the winding up of the firm. An example will highlight the effect of s 44 in the context of capital profits. A and B contribute €1,000 and €4,000 respectively as capital, but share profits in their firm equally. That capital is used by the firm to purchase premises for €5,000. When the partnership is dissolved the premises are sold for €55,000, giving a €50,000 profit. The agreement is silent as regards the sharing of capital profits on a dissolution and accordingly after the capital contributions of €1,000 and €4,000 are paid back to each partner, A and B will share the €50,000 profit equally, even though they contributed unequally to the purchase of the premises.[29]

[17.21] If the partners wish to share the profits or losses of capital on a dissolution in the same proportion as they contributed capital to the firm, rather than in the manner in which they share profits, it will be necessary to have a provision to that effect in the partnership agreement. This provision will then override the default rules in ss 44(a) and 44(b)(4) of the 1890 Act, which are expressly stated to be 'subject to any agreement'. For example a provision that the 'losses' of the firm are to be shared in a different proportion to the profits, will be taken to refer to losses of capital. Accordingly, this provision will override the default rule in s 44(b)(4) that capital losses are to be divided according to profit share. Even where it is the parties' intention to share profits and losses of a capital nature on a dissolution in the same manner as profits and losses of income, it is useful to spell this out in the partnership agreement so as to avoid any subsequent misunderstanding between the parties.

[17.22] The application of the rules on the sharing of capital losses (as distinct from capital profits) is illustrated by the following example. A, B and C contributed capital of €2,000 to their firm in the following proportions €1,000, €500 and €500 respectively. They agreed that they would share profits and losses equally. On a winding up, there is residual capital of only €1,000, thus leaving a capital loss of €1,000. Under the default

---

[28]   See also the Partnership Act 1890, s 24(1) and see *Ex p Maude* (1867) 16 LT 577; *Re Weymouth Steam Packet Co* [1891] 1 Ch 66; *Re Wakefield Rolling Stock Co* [1892] 3 Ch 165.

[29]   The rationale for this rule is the same as for the equality of sharing of capital profits and capital losses during the life of the firm, see para **[17.17]**.

rules in the 1890 Act, this capital loss is shared in the same proportion as the profit shares.[30] Thus, A, B and C will share this capital loss equally and are therefore required to contribute a third each.[31] This approach is justifiable since such a shortfall in the capital is as much a loss of the firm as any other partnership loss and therefore it is made up by the partners in the same way as any other loss. Therefore, A, B and C each notionally contributes €333 to the firm so as to return the firm to a notional capital of €2,000. The notional capital is then repaid to the partners in accordance with their capital contributions, since s 44(b)(3) of the 1890 Act requires the capital contribution of each partner to be repaid to partners 'rateably'. Therefore A will notionally receive €1,000 and B and C will receive €500 each. To get the actual amount received by A, one must deduct his notional contribution of €333 from his capital of €1,000 to give €666. Similarly, for B and C, one must deduct their notional contribution of €333 from their capital of €500 to give €166 each. Thus A, B and C suffer varying degrees of losses, so highlighting the principle that:

> 'When the Act says losses are to be borne equally[32] it means losses sustained by the firm. It cannot mean that the individual loss sustained by each partner is to be of equal amount.'[33]

Section 44(b) takes precedence over s 24(1) on a winding up

[17.23] This example also highlights the fact that, although the default rule is that partners share the capital profits or capital losses in proportion to their profit sharing ratios, any capital (or advances) contributed by partners to the firm is treated as a debt from the firm to the partners which is postponed to third party creditors. As a debt to the partners, it is paid off rateably (as required by s 44(b)(2) and 44(b)(3) of the 1890 Act) so that it is paid to the partners in the proportion in which it was contributed (in the above example in the ratio 2:1:1) and not equally.[34] Yet s 24(1) of the 1890 Act appears prima facie to apply to this situation since it states that all 'the partners are entitled to share equally in the capital and profits of the business'. However, it is important to note that this does not mean that the capital which was contributed unequally by partners is treated as an aggregate fund to be divided between the partners in equal shares. Rather, this reference to 'capital' must be read as being first subject to the requirement in s 44(b)(2) that capital contributions are repaid to the partners *rateably* to the amount of their respective contributions.[35] The prima facie conflict between s 44(b)(2) and s 24(1)

---

30 Partnership Act 1890, s 44(a). See for example *Binney v Mutrie* (1886) 12 App Cas 160.
31 Where one partner is insolvent and unable to pay his share of a capital loss, the rule in *Garner v Murray* [1904] 1 Ch 57 will apply, see further para **[26.118]**.
32 Ie assuming that profits are shared equally, Partnership Act 1890, s 44(a).
33 Per Joyce J in *Garner v Murray* [1904] 1 Ch 57.
34 In this regard, it has been seen (para **[17.05]**) that the important monetary figure in relation to a partner's capital contribution is the agreed value of his capital contribution. Accordingly, the fact that the assets which represent his capital contribution increase or decrease in value will not affect his claim and the differential will be regarded as a capital profit or capital loss as appropriate.
35 This conclusion is in keeping with the common law position prior to the 1890 Act, ie that each partner is entitled, after payment of the firm's creditors, to a return of capital contributions before a surplus was available for distribution: *Darby v Darby* (1856) 15 Ves Jr 218.

has caused considerable confusion amongst legal commentators and judges[36] and it is suggested that this area would benefit from an amendment which clarifies that capital contributions are not shared equally between the partners on a dissolution but are repaid rateably to them.

---

[36] The Australian case of *Kelly v Tucker* (1907) 5 CLR 1 is unhelpful since the High Court simply expresses puzzlement at the apparent conflict between s 24(1) and s 44(b), rather than attempting to resolve the issue. More recently in *Rowella Pty Ltd v Abfam Nominees Pty Ltd* (1989) 64 ALJR 121, the High Court of Australia rejected obiter the suggestion that capital contributions should be shared equally. In Scotland, legal commentators have taken a different approach to reconciling the reference to 'capital' in s 24(1) and the terms of s 44(b)(2). There, it has been argued that the term 'capital' when used in s 24(1) should be interpreted as meaning the assets of the firm, rather than capital contributions, see Bennett, *An Introduction to the Law of Partnership in Scotland* (1995), para 15.3 et seq. See also Brough, *Miller on Partnership* (2nd edn, 1994) at p 417 et seq. This approach has a certain appeal as regards a possible amendment to the 1890 Act, but not as an interpretation of the plain meaning of s 24(1). This is because this approach does considerable violence to the wording of the 1890 Act since it suggests that the term 'capital' should be interpreted to mean assets of the firm in s 24(1), but capital contribution in every other section of the Act. Note that in l'Anson Banks, *Lindley & Banks on Partnership* (20th edn, 2017) at paras 17-08 et seq, reference is made to an earlier editor's attempt to classify 'capital' in s 24(1) as meaning partnership property, though the present editor's views are that: '"capital" should be given its normal meaning throughout [s 24] so that, if the partners contribute capital in unequal proportions but do not agree to share it in those proportions, they will each be entitled to an equal share of the firm's capital.'

Chapter 18

The Goodwill of a Partnership

INTRODUCTION

[18.01] In many partnerships, the firm's goodwill will be one of its most valuable assets. For this reason and in view of the uncertainty which sometimes attaches to the value and status of goodwill in a partnership, it is proposed to consider it as a separate item of partnership property. Much of the analysis deals with the right of partners to use the firm name, since in many partnerships and particularly in professional partnerships, the goodwill of a firm will be synonymous with the right to use the firm name. This chapter will consider:

    I.   The Nature of Goodwill;

    II.   Use of Goodwill after Dissolution; and

    III.   Valuation of Goodwill.

Overview

[18.02] One of the omissions of the 1890 Act is its failure to refer to the goodwill of a partnership. This omission has undoubtedly exacerbated the uncertainties surrounding the nature of goodwill and it is only in relatively recent times that goodwill has been accepted as being as much an item of partnership property as any other asset.[1] This uncertainty could be reduced by a number of clear provisions clarifying the status of goodwill and its treatment on the technical and general dissolution of the partnership. Thus, the 1890 Act could be usefully amended to confirm the present common law position, namely that the goodwill of a firm is partnership property, that on the dissolution of the partnership, a partner may have the goodwill sold for the common benefit of all the partners and that prior to the affairs of a firm being wound up, a partner may not attempt to appropriate the goodwill by using the firm name. If one considers the nature of goodwill, one will realise that these principles simply follow from the fact that goodwill, as something which is normally 'acquired ... for the purposes and in the course of the partnership business,'[2] constitutes partnership property. The insertion of such clear provisions in the default partnership agreement which is the 1890 Act would also have the added benefit of raising prospective partners' awareness of the importance of goodwill and more significantly alerting them to whether these default provisions are suitable for their partnership.

---

[1]   As regards the previous position see *Wilson v Williams* (1892) 29 LR Ir 176. See also the Scottish case of *Mackenzie v Macfarlane* (1934) SN 16 where Lord Wark opined that a firm of law agents had no realisable goodwill and that the firm-name was not an asset which must be sold on dissolution.

[2]   Partnership Act 1890, s 20(1).

[18.03] It will be seen that in some instances, the goodwill of a firm is not treated in the same way as other items of partnership property. For example on a dissolution of the partnership and assuming that no partner exercises his right to have the goodwill sold under s 39 of the 1890 Act for the benefit of the firm, each of the partners may use the firm name and attempt to appropriate the goodwill of the business for their own benefit.[3] This different treatment can be explained by the fact that unlike any other partnership asset, the goodwill of a firm is not a true group asset since it will often be due to the partners individually rather than the partnership.

I. THE NATURE OF GOODWILL

[18.04] The term 'goodwill' is not defined by the 1890 Act. Indeed, as the term 'goodwill' is regarded as a commercial rather than a legal term, it does not have any precise legal definition. One of the most used definitions describes the goodwill of a firm as the probability that all existing customers of a firm will wish to continue to deal with that firm.[4] Yet this definition fails to take account of other elements of a firm's goodwill, such as the probability of potential customers dealing with the firm because of the firm's marketing, neither does it take account of the firm's relationship with non-customers, such as its suppliers, which contributes to the firm's goodwill. For this reason, it is suggested that a more appropriate description of goodwill is that given by Lord Macnaghten in *Trego v Hunt*[5] as:

> '[T]he whole advantage, whatever it may be, of the reputation and connection of the firm, which may have been built up by years of honest work or gained by lavish expenditure of money.'[6]

[18.05] In his judgment in *Castledine v RSM Bentley Jennison (a firm)*,[7] Cooke J also examined 'that most elusive of assets, partnership goodwill', and took a similar view to that expressed in *Trego v Hunt*,[8] noting that:

> 'Although goodwill may be referred to as if it is a single asset, it may also be considered as a parcel of factors which could increase the opportunities of a successor to the business to enjoy ... The "right" to use the business name is obviously one important factor ... Other factors may consist of ownership of assets associated in the minds of customers with the

---

3   In the case of any other partnership asset, it is not open to the partners to attempt to appropriate it for their own benefit in this way. See for example how a partner is not allowed take the files of the partnership (which are partnership property) on his leaving the firm: *O'Connor v Woods* (22 January 1976) HC.

4   Per Lord Eldon in *Cruttwell v Lye* (1810) 17 Ves 335 at 346. See also Peelo, 'Come Together' (December 2011) Law Society Gazette.

5   *Trego v Hunt* [1896] AC 7.

6   *Trego v Hunt* [1896] AC 7 at 23.

7   *Castledine v RSM Bentley Jennison (a firm)* [2011] EWHC 2363 (Ch).

8   *Trego v Hunt* [1896] AC 7; however, Cooke J in *Castledine v RSM Bentley Jennison (a firm)* made no reference to the decision in that case, and instead quoted from the 19th edition of l'Anson Banks, *Lindley & Banks on Partnership* at para 10-193 (now para 10-223 of the 20th edition (2017)), which quoted Lord Lindley's explanation that: 'The term goodwill can hardly be said to have any precise signification. It is generally used to denote the benefit arising from connection and reputation; and its value is what can be got for the chance of being able to keep that connection and improve it.'

business itself, such as premises, registered trademarks or other intellectual property rights, even if those assets could be sold independently of any sale of the business. Others may relate to the involvement of particular individuals with the business, either in a positive sense in that they continue to work in the business under the ownership of the successor, or in the negative sense that they are prevented from offering services in competition with him.'

Goodwill is part of Partnership Property

[18.06] The early approach of the courts to the status of goodwill as an item of partnership property is illustrated by *Wilson v Williams*.[9] There, Chatterton VC doubted whether the goodwill of a Dublin stockbroking firm was partnership property per se, observing that:

> 'In order to constitute the goodwill an asset it must be saleable, for it is only by converting it into money that, on a dissolution, it is capable of being divided between the different persons entitled.'[10]

In that case, none of the partners was prohibited by the partnership agreement from carrying on the same business as carried on by the firm or from using the name of the firm and soliciting the firm's customers after the dissolution of the partnership. For this reason, Chatterton VC held that the goodwill was not saleable and thus not a partnership asset.[11] However, the approach taken by the Vice Chancellor has been rightly discredited,[12] and it is clear that the requirement that goodwill be saleable before it constitutes partnership property is no longer part of Irish law. Indeed, even prior to *Wilson v Williams*,[13] in *Dickson v McMaster & Co*,[14] Brady LC assumed that the goodwill of the firm in that case was partnership property. Requiring goodwill to be saleable is too simplistic an approach, since there may be instances where a firm will have a very valuable goodwill and thus a partnership asset, even where there are no restrictive covenants in place. The same logic dictates that goodwill, which for accountancy or tax purposes is valued in the firm's accounts as value-less, will still constitute partnership property and be capable of protection. In general terms, therefore, unless the partners agree otherwise, the goodwill of a firm will constitute partnership property.[15]

---

9   *Wilson v Williams* (1892) 29 LR Ir 176.
10 *Wilson v Williams* (1892) 29 LR Ir 176 at 181.
11 Chatterton VC also supported his conclusion that goodwill was not a partnership asset by reference to the fact that there was no mention of goodwill in the clause dealing with the valuation of assets on a dissolution.
12 See for example *Gargan v Ruttle* [1931] IR 152; *McClelland v Hyde* [1942] NI 1; *Burchell v Wilde* [1900] 1 Ch 551; *Fitch v Dewes* [1921] 2 AC 15.
13 *Wilson v Williams* (1892) 29 LR Ir 176.
14 *Dickson v McMaster & Co* (1866) 11 Ir Jur 202.
15 See for example the High Court case of *Gargan v Ruttle* [1931] IR 152, in which it was assumed that the firm's goodwill was partnership property, since under the terms of the arbitrator's award, one partners's interest therein was sold on the dissolution of the partnership to his co-partner. (contd.../)

Goodwill can be Partnership Property if Excluded from Accounts

[18.07] It is common for the goodwill of a firm to be stated in the accounts as having a nil value or indeed to be excluded from the accounts of a firm.[16] However, it is important to bear in mind that this does not mean that the goodwill in such a case is not partnership property or that it is valueless as there is a clear distinction to be made between the accountancy treatment of an asset and its status as partnership property or its real value under partnership law. In *Bloxham v Companies Act,*[17] Keane J observed that:

> '... it is important to acknowledge that the goodwill of a partnership may be treated entirely differently for accountancy and partnership law purposes, just as partnership assets generally may be treated differently for the purposes of tax law and partnership law.'

Accordingly, a partner leaving such a firm who is receiving payment for his share of partnership property may be entitled to the value of his share of the goodwill in the firm, and the nominal value of the goodwill in the accounts may be irrelevant in determining the value of his share.[18]

[18.08] Of course, this is not to say that the treatment by the partners of goodwill in the accounts will not be a factor in determining whether there is an implied agreement between them, eg, that the outgoing partner is not to receive any payment for his share of the goodwill. This is because the courts will naturally take account of the treatment by partners of matters in their accounts in helping to determine the precise nature of the agreement. This is illustrated by *McClelland v Hyde,*[19] which considered the question of whether the goodwill of a firm was part of its capital or assets.[20] There, the Northern Ireland Court of Appeal considered the status of the premises, vehicles and stock of a

---

[15] (\...contd) Note the unsatisfactory decision in *Heslin v Fay (1)* (1884) 15 LR Ir 431, where goodwill was treated as if it were part of the firm's net profits. There, the partnership agreement provided for goodwill of the firm to be sold by a departing partner to a continuing partner at a price equal to one year's profits of the firm. In ordering that an account be taken, Sullivan LC ordered that, in calculating the firm's net profits, there should be added thereto one year's profits in respect of the firm's goodwill. In *Cronin v Kehoe* [2012] IEHC 373, the partnership agreement entered into between Drs Cronin and Kehoe in respect of a general medical practice provided that while, at the start of the partnership, Dr Cronin (as incoming practitioner) would pay £40,000 to Dr Kehoe (as senior practitioner) in consideration of the goodwill that Dr Kehoe was bringing to the partnership, ownership of that goodwill would remain with Dr Kehoe as senior practitioner throughout the term of the partnership.

[16] In this way, if the goodwill passes to the continuing partners on the death or departure of a partner, it may not give rise to capital gains tax. See further the case of *Attorney-General v Boden* [1912] AC 1 KB 539.

[17] *Bloxham v Companies Act* [2017] IEHC 664 at para 80 of the judgment.

[18] *Wade v Jenkins* (1860) 2 Giff 509.

[19] *McClelland v Hyde* [1942] NI 1.

[20] In the Australian case of *Public Trustee v Schultz* (1964) 111 CLR 482, the partnership agreement provided for the accounts to be prepared on an annual basis and to include a statement of the partnership assets, including goodwill. These accounts never contained a value for goodwill and the partnership agreement provided that a deceased partner's share was to be valued by reference to the accounts. Accordingly, it was held that the price to be paid did not have to include an amount for goodwill.

partner's pre-existing business (called Anderson and Company), which had been contributed by one partner to the partnership. Andrews LCJ noted:

> 'We know nothing as to the value, if any, of the goodwill of the business of Anderson and Company immediately prior to the formation of the partnership; but this we do know, that, whether the business had any goodwill of value or not, it was treated by the parties as of no value, as it was in no way included in the capital of the business. The Annual Accounts of the business were prepared on this basis, goodwill never being introduced as a capital item.'[21]

Having established that the goodwill was not part of the capital, the Court held that the purchase price paid for it was not part of the capital and therefore not divisible between the partners in accordance with their agreement as to the division of capital.[22]

[18.09] It follows that the best route for prospective partners is to be as precise as possible about the treatment of the firm's goodwill.[23] If the partners intend that an outgoing partner is to receive no compensation for his share of the goodwill, this should be expressly stated in the partnership agreement, eg by a statement not simply that the goodwill is to be of no value but that it is to be of no value for the purposes of calculating an outgoing partner's share in the firm, and the agreement should expressly provide for the purchase of the outgoing partner's share of the goodwill by the continuing partners.

Goodwill is not Normally Part of a Firm's Capital

[18.10] As is clear from the Northern Ireland case of *McClelland v Hyde*,[24] the goodwill of a firm, although forming part of the partnership property, does not per se form part of the firm's capital. In the words of Andrews LCJ:

> '[I]n truth, the capital of the partnership is something different from its property or its assets. The latter necessarily includes everything of value which belongs to the partnership firm, and, accordingly, its goodwill, whilst the capital only includes goodwill when it is brought into the partnership as such.'[25]

Clearly, therefore, if goodwill is introduced by the partners as part of their capital contribution, it will constitute capital.

Goodwill only exists in Connection with a Business

[18.11] Goodwill can only exist in connection with a business and so in the case of a partnership, there must be a partnership business to which the goodwill attaches. In the High Court case of *Hopkins v Shannon Transport Systems Ltd*,[26] Hopkins and Gorman formed a partnership (called 'The Shannon Ferry') for the purposes of acquiring a number of ferry vessels in order to establish a ferry service across the river Shannon. The two and Hopkin's wife also formed a second partnership (called 'Killadysert

---

[21] *McClelland v Hyde* [1942] NI 1 at 7.
[22] See further para **[18.10]**.
[23] See fn **15** above regarding *Cronin v Kehoe*.
[24] *McClelland v Hyde* [1942] NI 1.
[25] *McClelland v Hyde* [1942] NI 1 at 7.
[26] *Hopkins v Shannon Transport Systems Ltd* (10 January 1972) HC. See generally O'Dowd, 'Company Law – Who pays the ferryman? – A neglected Irish case' (1989) 11 DULJ 120.

Estates') for the acquisition of land and options over certain land which was required for the ferry terminal. Hopkins and Gorman entered into negotiations with local authorities and other statutory bodies for the purposes of the project and as they required some capital for the venture they incorporated the defendant company and sought investors. An agreement was entered into between the company and the partnerships whereby the company would purchase the goodwill of 'The Shannon Ferry' partnership, two of the vessels owned by that partnership for £9,000 and the land and options owned by the 'Killadysert Estates' partnership at a profit to that partnership of £4,000. Hopkins sought to enforce the terms of this agreement by seeking his half share of the goodwill sold by 'The Shannon Ferry' partnership and his third share of the profit made by the 'Killadysert Estates' partnership. As regards the goodwill issue, Pringle J held that as a general principle, goodwill could only exist in connection with some existing business,[27] and in this case, when the agreement between the partnership and the company was entered into, there was no such business. However, he did accept that Hopkins and Gorman had established a co-operative relationship with local authorities and other statutory bodies which was sufficient and therefore held that Hopkins was entitled to a share of the goodwill. Pringle J held that he was entitled to only £500 of the sum paid for the goodwill, since the arrangements were entered into by him in breach of his fiduciary duty as a promoter of a company to make full disclosure to the company of his interest in the arrangements and therefore any element of profit was excluded. For the same reason, his share of the profits made by the 'Killadysert Estates' partnership was not recoverable by him.

Goodwill exists independently of firm's premises

[18.12] While it has been noted that the goodwill of a partnership only exists in connection with a business, it exists independently of the premises from which the business is carried on and can be transferred with or without those premises. In *Dennehy v Jolly*,[28] the defendant claimed to be entitled to carry on the business of a law stationer and stamp distributor at 74 Dame St in Dublin, which business had previously been carried on by a firm in which she and the plaintiff were partners. Her claim was based on the fact that the premises in which the business had been carried on was her property and the licence to carry on the business was in her name. On this basis, she argued that there was no separate goodwill in the firm's business. The partnership agreement was silent as to whether either partner could carry on the business after the dissolution. Sullivan MR rejected her claim that there was no goodwill in the business and observed that: 'the good-will may exist utterly independent of the premises; in many cases the possession of the premises is the merest feather-weight in the estimation of the good-will.'[29]

---

[27] He relied on *Inland Revenue Commissioners v Muller* [1901] AC 217 at 224 per Lord Macnaghten.

[28] *Dennehy v Jolly* (1875) 9 ILTR 3.

[29] *Dennehy v Jolly* (1875) 9 ILTR 3 at 4.

Nature of Purchase Price for Goodwill

[18.13] The nature of the purchase price which is paid for a firm's goodwill was considered by the Northern Ireland Court of Appeal in *McClelland v Hyde*.[30] The question arose as to whether money paid for the goodwill was part of the assets of the firm, part of the profits or part of the capital. In that case, a furniture removal partnership in Portadown sold its business and as part of the sale received a substantial sum for the goodwill of the firm. Under the terms of the partnership agreement, the profits of the business were shared equally between the partners and on a dissolution of the firm, the capital was to be repaid in the proportion in which it was contributed which was in unequal shares. It therefore was of significance whether the purchase price received for the goodwill was in the nature of capital (and divisible unequally) or in the nature of profits (and divisible equally) or indeed assets (and divisible equally pursuant to s 44 of the 1890 Act[31]). The Court of Appeal held that the compensation for goodwill was not in the nature of capital, but was either assets or profits since the goodwill is not part of the capital, but part of the assets of the firm, Babington LJ noting that:

> 'Generally speaking, capital is the money, lands, goods or other property with which the company or partnership commences business. Anything acquired or earned over and above this in the course of business is not capital but profit ... whether it be earnings in money or kind or accretions to capital or goodwill, it is *profit* as distinguished from *capital*.'[32]

[18.14] That case involved a partnership which was commenced by one partner contributing £500 as capital, while the other partner contributed £2,200, being the value of the premises and stock which had been used by him in the business up to that point. No reference was made to any goodwill being contributed by the partners. This was crucial since, in the words of Andrews LCJ, 'the capital only includes goodwill when it is brought into the partnership as such'.[33] It follows that a different conclusion would have been reached if the goodwill had been part of the partners' capital contribution to the partnership. However, even in that situation, it seems that the eventual purchase price for the goodwill should not be regarded as being 100% capital. This is because it would have to reflect the fact that the goodwill had increased in value during the course of the partnership and therefore would be part capital and part profits/assets, the latter being divisible by the partners in accordance with their agreed profit-share.

Express Reference Should be Made to 'Goodwill'

[18.15] In view of the potential value of a firm's goodwill, considerable caution should be taken to describe in a firm's partnership agreement whether the firm's goodwill is to be partnership property, whether it is the personal property of one or more partners, whether it is to have a value for the purposes of the partners inter se, whether an outgoing partner is to receive payment for his share of the goodwill from the continuing partners and whether on the general dissolution of the partnership, all or some only of

---

[30] *McClelland v Hyde* [1942] NI 1.

[31] Since surplus assets under s 44 of the 1890 Act are distributable in the same way as profits, which in this case meant equally under the terms of the partnership agreement.

[32] *McClelland v Hyde* [1942] NI 1 at 12.

[33] *McClelland v Hyde* [1942] NI 1 at 7.

the partners are to be entitled to the firm's goodwill. In *Cronin v Kehoe*,[34] the partnership agreement entered into between Drs Cronin and Kehoe in respect of a general medical practice provided that while, at the start of the partnership, Dr Cronin (as incoming practitioner) would pay £40,000 to Dr Kehoe (as senior practitioner) in consideration of the goodwill that Dr Kehoe was bringing to the partnership, ownership of that goodwill would remain with Dr Kehoe as senior practitioner throughout the term of the partnership.

[18.16] The question of whether all the partners are to be entitled to the firm's goodwill on a dissolution will be particularly relevant in the context of the use of the firm name, where some or all the partners' names are part of the firm name. This issue should be dealt with in the partnership agreement.

[18.17] When referring to a firm's goodwill in the partnership agreement, it is preferable to make express reference to the term 'goodwill'. Nonetheless, in *Dennehy v Jolly*,[35] O'Sullivan MR contemplated that the term 'all moneys, stock etc' included a reference to the firm's goodwill, and in *Dickson v McMaster & Co*,[36] Brady LC held that the expression 'all the stock in trade, goods, chattels, and effects of said partnership'[37] did include the firm's goodwill. In more recent times, the goodwill of a firm has been accepted as being part of the partnership property in the absence of any contrary indication and therefore it seems clear that a reference to 'partnership property' or 'partnership assets' will include goodwill.[38]

II. USE OF GOODWILL AFTER DISSOLUTION

[18.18] Having considered the nature of goodwill, it is now proposed to consider the use of the firm's goodwill on the dissolution of the partnership.[39] A crucial aspect of a firm's goodwill is usually the right to use the firm's name, and most of the cases in this area involve the right of a partner to continue to use the firm name after its dissolution.[40]

---

34 *Cronin v Kehoe* [2012] IEHC 373.
35 *Dennehy v Jolly* (1875) 9 ILTR 3.
36 *Dickson v McMaster & Co* (1866) 11 Ir Jur 202.
37 *Dickson v McMaster & Co* (1866) 11 Ir Jur 202 at 212.
38 *McClelland v Hyde* [1942] NI 1 at 7.
39 See generally Morse, 'Partnership Dissolution and Goodwill' (1972) 35 Modern LR 315; Jeremiah, 'What's in a name? The value of goodwill in a law firm' (1995) 6 Int Company and Commercial LR 419.
40 There has been a considerable amount of recent English caselaw in relation to the goodwill associated with the name of a music group, such as *Byford v Oliver* [2003] EWHC 295 (Ch), a trade mark case heard by Laddie J, in which he agreed that both the name of the band, 'Saxon', and the goodwill associated with it, were partnership assets. As a result, all partners had an interest in them (but did not own those assets themselves), and absent express provision to the contrary in the partnership agreement, the partners had an interest in the realised value of those assets, but none of them actually 'owned' the partnership assets such as the name or the goodwill in that name. (contd.../)

Sale of Partnership Business by Partners

[18.19] The position regarding the use of the firm's goodwill after the sale of the partnership business by the partners is founded on the principle that the seller of the goodwill of a business cannot afterwards destroy the value of what he has sold.[41] Thus, the partners who sell the partnership business to a purchaser may not solicit the customers of the partnership business[42] or carry on the business under the firm name[43] or represent themselves to be carrying on the business of the firm.[44] The purchaser of the goodwill may use the firm name, even if it contains the former partners' names, provided that it does not expose them to an appreciable risk of continuing liability.[45] Clearly, these principles are equally applicable whether the sale of the partnership business is to third parties or to another partner or partners.

[18.20] The High Court case of *Gargan v Ruttle*[46] concerned a partnership under the name of Gargan & Co, which dealt in buttered almonds,[47] confectionery, chewing-gum, tobacco and cigarettes.[48] At first instance, an arbitrator held that the partnership between Gargan and Ruttle had dissolved. As there was no partnership agreement between them, the arbitrator held that the goodwill, stock-in-trade and assets should belong to the plaintiff, while the defendant should receive a sum of money for his share of the goodwill, stock and other assets of the business. Although he had received a sum of money for his share of the goodwill, Ruttle continued to solicit the customers of the former firm. In the High Court, Meredith J held that the arbitrator's decision was to be treated the same way as if there was a partnership agreement between them which provided for the plaintiff to be entitled to the goodwill of the firm on a dissolution. He

---

40 (\...contd) In *Gill v Frankie Goes To Hollywood Ltd* [2008] ETMR 4, the court indicated that ownership of a firm's name, and ownership of the goodwill deriving from that name, could be owned by different parties – in that case, the name of the group was originated by one of its members prior to the group being formed, but the goodwill was viewed as having been created by the later use of that name in connection with the group's activities. In *McPhail v Bourne* [2008] EWHC 1235 (Ch), Morgan J found that that there was no goodwill in the name of the group 'Busted' – as a result, had a partnership been found to exist between the members of the group, that name would not have been partnership property.

41 *Gargan v Ruttle* [1931] IR 152, para **[18.20]**. For a historical perspective see Anon, 'Retiring Partner soliciting Customers of Old Firm' (1884) 18 ILT & SJ 367.

42 *Gargan v Ruttle* [1931] IR 152. See also *Jennings v Jennings* [1898] 1 Ch 378.

43 See *O'Connor v Woods* (22 January 1976) HC, where the departing partner was ordered to account to the firm for fees which he had billed in the former firm's name to a client of the firm who had continued to deal with him.

44 *Gargan v Ruttle* [1931] IR 152, para **[18.20]**. See also the New Zealand case of *Davidson v Wayman* [1984] 2 NZLR 115.

45 *Thynne v Shove* (1890) 45 Ch D 577; *Burchell v Wilde* [1900] 1 Ch 551; *Townsend v Jarman* [1900] 2 Ch 698. Note that this risk will be reduced by advertising the departure of the partners from the partnership business in *Iris Oifigiúil* and by notifying existing customers of the departure of the partners, see generally para **[11.62]** et seq.

46 *Gargan v Ruttle* [1931] IR 152.

47 Which Meredith J regretted not being given an opportunity to taste.

48 Described by Meredith J as a strange but very common mixture which for some inexplicable reason was rendered even stranger by the addition of walking sticks.

held that this was akin to the sale of goodwill between a vendor and purchaser of a business and that:

> 'when a man sells the goodwill of his business he cannot afterwards destroy the value of what he has sold by soliciting his old customers. Subject, however, to this restriction, the vendor is not precluded from setting up a rival business with which the old customers may deal on their own initiative.'[49]

Thus, Meredith J granted an injunction against Ruttle that so long as he should carry on business in the sale of the goods sold by the firm at the date of its dissolution, he was prohibited from soliciting customers of the firm at the date of dissolution. He was also prohibited from encouraging such customers not to deal with Gargan.[50]

Vendor partner may set up in competition with former firm

[18.21] While a partner who receives payment for his share of the firm's goodwill is not entitled to solicit customers of his former firm, it was noted by Meredith J in *Gargan v Ruttle*[51] that, in the absence of contrary agreement, he is entitled to set up business in competition with the firm and to deal with any customers who choose to deal with him. This is also clear from the High Court case of *O'Connor v Woods*.[52] There, the plaintiff took voluntary retirement from the accountancy firm of John A Woods & Co. Under the terms of the partnership agreement, a retiring partner received a payment for his share of the partnership (although in calculating this amount, the agreement provided that 'no valuation shall be placed on the goodwill of the partnership').[53] However, the partnership agreement provided that the surviving partners were to become the sole owners of the partnership business, goodwill and other assets. In this way, the outgoing partner's share in the goodwill was transferred, rather than sold,[54] to the continuing partners. After his departure, O'Connor set up in business as an accountant and a number of the clients of his former firm continued to deal with him. The surviving partners argued that O'Connor should be liable to them for the profits made by him from these clients, on the basis that he came to know them through his association with the partnership. This was rejected by Kenny J who held that:

---

[49]   *Gargan v Ruttle* [1931] IR 152 at 157, relying on the House of Lords case of *Trego v Hunt* [1896] AC 7.

[50]   Meredith J held that this injunction only applied while the defendant used the name Ruttle or any name introducing Ruttle. It is doubted whether this condition is supportable in principle, since the key issue is not the name which is used, but whether customers of the firm are being solicited so as to destroy the goodwill sold. Since, it is equally possible for Ruttle to destroy the value of what he has sold without using his name, the general applicability of this principle is doubted. See also *Darby v Meehan* (1998) TLR 733 where the English High Court granted the plaintiff an injunction to prevent his former partners from destroying the goodwill of an accountancy partnership by their soliciting of clients of practice, the plaintiff being entitled to that goodwill under the terms of their agreement for his departure from the firm.

[51]   *Gargan v Ruttle* [1931] IR 152.

[52]   *O'Connor v Woods* (22 January 1976) HC.

[53]   *O'Connor v Woods* (22 January 1976) HC at p 2.

[54]   It is clear from this case that a departing partner who transfers his share of the firm's goodwill, without receiving therefor a separate purchase price, is subject to the same restriction, as if he had sold his share.

'This case illustrates the view of the first named defendant that the plaintiff is liable for enticement when a company, firm or individual who had been clients of the partnership took their business away when the plaintiff left. The plaintiff never entered into a covenant or agreement that he would not practice as an accountant after he terminated the partnership and if the parties to the [partnership agreement] wished to provide that a retiring partner should not practice, they should have inserted such a clause in the agreement ... It does not follow that because a company or individual took any part of their business away from the partnership when the plaintiff left it, that the plaintiff is liable for the fees. To make him liable the first and third named defendants have to prove that he enticed the client away from the firm.'[55]

General Dissolution of the Firm

[18.22] The position regarding the use of the firm's goodwill after the general dissolution of a partnership (ie a dissolution which leads to the firm's winding up, rather than simply a change in the membership of the firm) is subject to the requirement that the affairs of the partnership may need to be wound up. If the firm is being wound up, the combined effect of s 30 of the 1890 Act (duty of partner to account for profits of a competing business with the firm)[56] and s 38 (continuing authority of partners to bind the firm for the purposes of its winding-up),[57] will prevent a partner from attempting to compete with the firm while it is being wound up.[58] In effect, the law treats all the partners as remaining as partners in the firm until the winding-up is complete and thus they may not use the goodwill or other partnership property for their own benefit.[59] In addition, on a general dissolution the goodwill of the partnership (assuming it has a marketable value) must be sold unless the partners agree to the contrary.[60] This is because under s 39 of the 1980 Act, each partner (or his estate, in the case of a deceased partner)[61] is entitled to insist that all the partnership property be sold for the common benefit of all the partners.[62]

---

55 *O'Connor v Woods* (22 January 1976) HC at pp 11–12.
56 See generally in relation to the Partnership Act 1890, s 30, para **[15.44]** et seq.
57 See generally in relation to the Partnership Act 1890, s 38, para **[26.11]** et seq.
58 See for example the Australian case of *Turner v Major* (1874) 5 AJR 61 and the New Zealand case of *Gray v Sladden* [1935] NZLR 35.
59 Note that in Western Australia, s 52 of the Partnership Act of 1895, as amended, reflects this position by providing that: '[a]fter a dissolution every partner in the dissolved firm, or his representatives, may, in the absence of any agreement to the contrary, restrain any other partner, or his representative, from carrying on the same business under the firm-name until the affairs of the firm have been wound up, and the partnership property disposed of.'
60 Note that in Western Australia, s 51 of the Partnership Act of 1895, as amended, provides statutory recognition for this right: 'On the dissolution of a partnership every partner shall be entitled, in the absence of any agreement to the contrary, to have the goodwill of the business sold for the common benefit of all the partners.'
61 See the New Zealand case of *Grey v Sladden and Stewart* [1935] NZLR 35 at 41–43 and the Australian case of *Perpetual Trustee Co v Federal Commissioner of Taxation* [1954] ALR 252.
62 See also *Burdon v Barkus* (1862) 4 De G F & J 42; *Crawshay v Collins* (1808) 15 Ves Jr 218; *Hill v Fearis* [1905] 1 Ch 466; *Hugh Stevenson & Sons v Aktiengesellschaft für Cartonnagen Industrie* [1917] 1 KB 842, aff'd [1918] AC 239.

[18.23] If the right to sell the goodwill on a general dissolution is not exercised or waived, then any of the partners may use the firm name,[63] provided that they do not hold themselves out as carrying on the new business in partnership with their former partners.[64] In addition, they may solicit customers of the former partnership business.[65] This may raise logistical difficulties in the break-up of a partnership with each partner using the firm name and soliciting the firm's clients. This may not be the most satisfactory way to deal with the general dissolution of a firm and it arguably encourages the partners to come to some arrangement whereby they sell the goodwill attaching to the use of the firm name to a third party for the benefit of all the partners or they agree that one of the partners will buy it from the others. Another possibility is that the partners sign a letter to the clients of the firm indicating that the firm is dissolving and that the clients are free to approach any of the partners to deal with their affairs.

Use of firm name which contains former partner's name

[18.24] It has been noted that on a general dissolution, all the partners may use the firm name, provided that this does not have the effect of holding themselves out as carrying on business with their former partners.[66] It should be noted, however, that where the dissolution of the partnership is caused by the death of a partner, the surviving partner(s) may use the firm name which includes that partner's name without being concerned about holding the deceased partner out as still being a partner. This is because under the terms of s 14(2) of the 1890 Act, the use of a firm name after the death of a partner does not constitute a holding out. The same principle would seem to apply to a case where the general dissolution is caused by the bankruptcy of one partner, since by virtue of s 36(3) of the 1890 Act, the estate of a bankrupt partner is not liable for partnership debts contracted after the date of bankruptcy.

Technical Dissolution of a Firm

[18.25] Where a partner departs from a firm (whether by retirement, expulsion, death or otherwise) and that firm continues as before the partner's departure, there is a technical dissolution of the partnership. If the partners have not agreed between themselves on how such a departing partner's share of the goodwill is to be dealt with, he will be entitled to the value, if any, of his share of the goodwill as of the date of his departure.[67] Where the firm continues to use his share of the goodwill to earn profits without any final settlement of accounts between the partners, then under the terms of s 42(1) of the 1890 Act, the outgoing partner is entitled to that share of those profits which are attributable to the use of his share of the partnership assets (including goodwill), or to 5% interest on his share of the partnership assets.[68]

---

63   *Wilson v Williams* (1892) 29 LR Ir 176.
64   *Troughton v Hunter* (1854) 18 Beav 470; *Bullock v Chapman* (1848) 2 De G & Sim 211; *Routh v Webster* (1847) 10 Beav 561. See also *Gray v Smith* (1889) 43 Ch D 208; *Jennings v Jennings* [1898] 1 Ch 378; *Churton v Douglas* (1859) Johns 174.
65   *Banks v Gibson* (1865) 34 Beav 566.
66   See further para **[7.52]** et seq for an analysis of situations where there may be a possible holding out of a former partner as still being a partner in a firm.
67   Partnership Act 1890, s 44.
68   See generally in relation to the right under the Partnership Act 1890, s 42(1), para **[26.63]**.

[18.26] If the use of the firm name by the continuing partners is not addressed in the partnership agreement, the outgoing partner may compete with the partnership business and use the firm name, provided that the other partners are not thereby exposed to the risk of liability on the basis of holding out.[69] In addition, assuming there has been no express or implied sale[70] by the outgoing partner of his share in the firm's goodwill to the continuing partners,[71] he may solicit clients of the firm to any new business which he decides to open.[72] In *O'Connor v Woods*,[73] there was a technical dissolution of the partnership when the plaintiff left the firm and the firm continued in business, Kenny J noting that:

> 'The plaintiff never entered into a covenant or agreement that he would not practise as an accountant after he terminated the partnership and if the parties to the [partnership agreement] wished to provide that a retiring partner should not practise,[74] they should have inserted such a clause in the agreement.'[75]

[18.27] In this regard, goodwill may be seen as an exception to the general rule that partnership property is to be used only for the benefit of the partnership and may not be appropriated by the outgoing partner for his own benefit.[76] This exception may be justified by the nature of goodwill, ie it will often not be a true group asset in the sense that it may be due to the partners individually, rather than to the firm.[77]

[18.28] In many cases, the technical dissolution of the partnership will arise in an ad hoc fashion and may not be subject to any agreement regarding the transfer of the firm's

---

[69] *Gray v Smith* (1889) 43 Ch D 208; *Jennings v Jennings* [1898] 1 Ch 378; *Churton v Douglas* (1859) Johns 174. In this regard, it is worth noting that any such risk will be reduced by compliance with the requirements of the Registration of Business Names Act 1963 where the firm has a registered business name (see further para **[3.70]** et seq) and by advertising the change in *Iris Oifigiúil* and notifying clients of the change (see para **[11.62]** et seq).

[70] The fact that the continuing partner may be entitled to the goodwill absolutely may be implied as happened in *Scott v Scott* (1903) 89 LT 582. There, the value of a deceased partner's share was to be paid for by the continuing partner and was to be ascertained according to the last balance sheet which did not include goodwill and for this reason, no payment was made for the goodwill. But in each case this is a matter of construction of the partnership agreement: *Smith v Nelson* (1905) 92 LT 313.

[71] As to the position where the outgoing partner has transferred his share of the goodwill to his co-partners, see para **[18.31]**.

[72] *Dawson v Beeson* (1882) 22 Ch D 504.

[73] *O'Connor v Woods* (22 January 1976) HC.

[74] It seems clear that by 'practise' Kenny J means that the continuing partners could have prevented him from practising as an accountant 'in competition with the firm' and not prevented him from practising as an accountant anywhere.

[75] *O'Connor v Woods* (22 January 1976) HC at pp 11–12.

[76] See generally regarding the purposes for which partnership property is used, para **[16.73]**.

[77] In recent years, considerable litigation has resulted from the break-up of music groups, with the future ownership of groups' goodwill proving to be a divisive issue, underscoring the importance of including express provision in a partnership agreement as to how goodwill (in particular, the name of the partnership) is to be dealt with on a dissolution of the group. See, further, Fields, 'Don't let me be misunderstood ... Appointed Person rejects trade mark application for THE ANIMALS by former drummer' (Ent LR 2014, 25(1), 27–28) examining the decision in *Burdon v Steel* 9 September 2013 (App Person).

goodwill. This was the case in *Wilson v Williams*,[78] and in such a case, there will be a right on the part of all the partners to use the firm name as is the case on a general dissolution.[79] There, a three-man firm carried on a stockbroking business at 38 Dame Street, Dublin and used the name 'Richard Williams and Sons'. The partnership was dissolved as regards the plaintiff partner by notice served upon him by the two other partners who continued to use the firm name for the stockbroking business. As there was no prohibition in the partnership agreement on the use of the firm name, Chatterton VC noted that:

> 'On a dissolution any of the partners may, unless expressly prohibited by contract from doing so, carry on the same business as before, and use the old name of the firm, and solicit the customers to deal with them.'[80]

[18.29] Therefore, in the absence of a restrictive covenant, any of the partners may attempt to acquire the firm's goodwill and this will have a consequent negative impact on the sale price of the firm's business. Indeed, in some firms, the absence of a restrictive covenant may render the goodwill in the firm almost valueless. In that case, Chatterton VC also noted that:

> '[U]nless the goodwill can be sold with the premises in which the business has been carried on, or unless it is preserved by restrictive covenants preventing the old partners from carrying on the business within certain limits or from using the partnership name, the goodwill would not be saleable. It would be valueless to any purchaser who did not also purchase the business premises or get the protection of such a covenant.'[81]

Thus, the value of having a non-compete provision becomes obvious. A non-compete restriction is usually regarded as incidental to a firm's goodwill and this will pass with an assignment of the goodwill.[82]

[18.30] While an outgoing partner may, in the absence of contrary agreement, attempt to attract the firm's clients on a technical dissolution, he is not entitled to take clients' files with him on his leaving the partnership.[83] Thus, in the Scottish case of *Finlayson v Turnbull*,[84] it was held that the removal of clients' files from a partnership by the outgoing partners in a partnership at will was a breach by them of their fiduciary duty to the continuing partners and damages were awarded to the continuing partners.

[18.31] In practice however, where there is an agreement for a continuing partnership, the partnership agreement will either expressly or by necessary implication[85] have a right on the part of the continuing partners to use the firm name after the departure of a partner. Where there is an express agreement between the continuing partners and the former partner, there will often be a transfer of the goodwill in the partnership by the

---

78   *Wilson v Williams* (1892) 29 LR Ir 176.
79   For the position on a general dissolution, see para **[18.22]** et seq.
80   *Wilson v Williams* (1892) 29 LR Ir 176 at 181–182.
81   *Wilson v Williams* (1892) 29 LR Ir 176 at 181.
82   *Townsend v Jarman* [1900] 2 Ch 698; *Showell v Winkup* (1889) 60 LT 389; *Jacoby v Whitmore* (1883) 49 LT 335.
83   *O'Connor v Woods* (22 January 1976) HC and see further para **[16.52]**.
84   *Finlayson v Turnbull* [1997] SLT 613.
85   For example where the goodwill is vested in the continuing partners as happened in *O'Connor v Woods* (22 January 1976) HC.

outgoing partner to the continuing partners and therefore the outgoing partner will not be entitled to use the former firm name. In *O'Connor v Woods*,[86] the plaintiff had agreed in his partnership agreement that the goodwill would be retained by his former partners in the firm of John A Woods & Co. After he set up in business in competition with the firm, he billed one of the former clients of the firm, who had continued to deal with him, and the bill was sent in his former firm's name. Accordingly, Kenny J held that he was liable to account for these fees to his former partners.

[18.32] Where a partner has transferred his interest in the goodwill to the other partners, he cannot then claim that the use of the firm name has the effect of holding him out as a partner. *Dickson v McMaster & Co*[87] concerned a linen manufacturing firm in County Down which operated under the names 'Dunbar, McMaster & Co' and 'Dunbar, Dickson & Co'. Under the partnership agreement, at the end of the term, an account was to be taken of the value of each partner's share in the firm[88] and McMaster was to pay the other partners the value of their shares. After the dissolution of the firm, McMaster continued in business with one of his former partners. One of the other partners, Dickson, brought an action to prevent their use of the firm name 'Dunbar, McMaster & Co' and the expression 'William Spotten & Co as successor to Dunbar, Dickson & Co'. This application was refused, Brady LC holding that the payment by McMaster for Dickson's share of the firm operated to transfer the goodwill of the partnership to him and thus entitled him to use the firm's names.[89]

[18.33] However, an outgoing partner who has transferred his interest in the firm's goodwill where the firm name is identical to his own, may, in the absence of contrary agreement, use this name, provided that he does not use it so as to give the impression that he is carrying on the business of the old firm. This might be the case if he were to carry on business in the same neighbourhood as his former firm.[90]

Applicability of s 29(1) of the 1890 Act

[18.34] When considering a partner's ability to use the goodwill of his former firm after either a general or a technical dissolution of the partnership, one is dealing with his

---

86 *O'Connor v Woods* (22 January 1976) HC.

87 *Dickson v McMaster & Co* (1866) 11 Ir Jur 202.

88 The expression used was each partner's share of the 'partnership, stock and capital' which was held to include goodwill.

89 It was noted obiter, by Brady LC at p 212, that McMaster 'cannot use the name of the Messrs Dickson'. This must be taken to mean that he cannot start using Mr Dickson's name, ie Benjamin Dickson, rather than preventing him from using the name 'Dunbar, Dickson & Co', since if as is contended by Brady LC, McMaster acquired all of the firm's goodwill, there is no reason why he could not use the firm's two names. See *Wilson v Williams*, para **[18.28]** which is authority for the proposition that, unless otherwise agreed, the firm name is the property of all the partners, even where it contains the surname of some or all of the partners (subject to it not having the effect of holding an outgoing partner as still being a partner in the firm). If a partner wishes to ensure that his surname is not used after the dissolution of the firm by his former partners, he should provide for this in the partnership agreement.

90 *Churton v Douglas* (1859) Johns 174.

ability to use the 'business connection' of the firm. This issue is also governed by s 29(1) of the 1890 Act which provides that:[91]

> Every partner must account to the firm for any benefit derived by him without the consent of the other partners from any transaction concerning the partnership, or from any use by him of the partnership property name or business connexion.

[18.35] In *O'Connor v Woods*,[92] the defendants, although not expressly relying on s 29(1), claimed that the former partner had come to know certain clients of the firm who had continued to use his services after he left. It was claimed that the fees received by the plaintiff from these clients should be paid to the defendants since he had only come to know the clients 'through his association with the partnership'.[93] Kenny J rejected this claim without analysis. This decision can however be supported on the basis that by its express terms, s 29(1) only applies while a person is a partner in a firm and does not apply to former partners, save during the firm's winding-up.[94] Accordingly, a former partner may not be prevented from benefiting from the firm's introductions and other business connections on the basis of s 29(1). To prevent a former partner from using the firm's business connection in this manner, there would have to be a restrictive covenant to this effect.

Applicability of s 30 of the 1890 Act

[18.36] One cannot leave the area of partners competing with their former firm on a technical or a general dissolution, without referring to s 30 of the 1890 Act, which provides that:[95]

> If a partner, without the consent of the other partners, carries on any business of the same nature as and competing with that of the firm, he must account for and pay over to the firm all profits made by him in that business.

[18.37] However, a partner who leaves his firm on its technical dissolution is not subject to the terms of s 30. As a former partner, he is not a partner for the purposes of that section and therefore the prohibition in s 30 does not extend to him. Where there is no restrictive covenant affecting him, the former partner will not have to account for profits made in a competing business.[96]

[18.38] However, on a general dissolution, as noted elsewhere in this work,[97] fiduciary duties, of which ss 30 and 29(1) are examples, continue to apply during the winding-up of a partnership. Accordingly, where a partner competes with his firm while it is being

---

91 See further in relation to the Partnership Act 1890, s 29(1), para **[15.27]** et seq.

92 *O'Connor v Woods* (22 January 1976) HC.

93 *O'Connor v Woods* (22 January 1976) HC at p 14.

94 The same point is made in relation to the Partnership Act 1890, s 30, para **[18.37]**.

95 See further in relation to the Partnership Act 1890, s 30, para **[15.44]** et seq.

96 Thus, in *O'Connor v Woods* (22 January 1976) HC, a former partner in an accountancy firm had come to know certain clients of the firm while he was a partner. When he left the firm, these clients continued to use his services and Kenny J rejected the continuing partners' claim that the fees received by the plaintiff from these clients should be paid to the defendant.

97 See para **[15.58]**.

wound up,[98] he will be required to account for any profit thereby earned by him, since he may be reducing the value of the firm's goodwill by his actions. However, once the firm has been wound up, s 30 has no application to a partner in the former firm.

III. VALUATION OF GOODWILL

Where Goodwill is Stated to Have a Nil Value

[18.39] It has been noted that it is common for partnership agreements or partnership accounts to provide for the goodwill of the firm to be valueless.[99] However, care should be taken with such provisions, since they do not necessarily mean that the goodwill will be treated as valueless as a matter of partnership law. The reason for such a provision is usually to facilitate the departure and introduction of partners. Thus, by providing that the goodwill is valueless, no amount will have to be paid for an outgoing partner's share of the goodwill, thereby facilitating the admission of new partners who will not be expected to buy a share of the goodwill to be admitted to the partnership.[100] However, if this is the intention, the partnership agreement should expressly state that the goodwill is to have no value for these purposes.

[18.40] Where the partners expressly agree that there is to be no payment made for goodwill, this fact does not mean that the goodwill does not exist, that it is not partnership property or that it has no value. It is simply an agreement by the partners that they shall not pay for a partner's share of the firm's goodwill on his departure.

Values and Valuation Mechanisms

[18.41] In some cases, the partners will have to value the goodwill, for example to pay an outgoing partner the value of his share therein. If a value is placed upon the goodwill in the accounts of a firm, this is not necessarily indicative of its likely value as a matter of law.[101] This is highlighted by the High Court case of *Barr v Barr*,[102] in which the partnership property in question was not the goodwill of the firm, but the partnership premises. The premises were valued in the balance sheet of the firm at £1,423.50.

---

[98] Ie a general dissolution of the firm.

[99] See para **[18.06]**.

[100] See generally regarding the different ways to value goodwill, Peelo, *The Valuation of Businesses and Shares – A Practitioner's Perspective* (2nd edn, 2016); McCarthy, 'Buying or Selling an Accountancy Practice' (2009) Accountancy Plus Magazine (available from www.cpaireland.ie) at pp 37–38, and McCarthy, 'Merging Accountancy Practices' (2009) Accountancy Plus Magazine (available from www.cpaireland.ie) at pp 32–33; O'Neill, 'Buying and Selling an Accountancy Practice in the 21st Century' (2004) Accountancy Plus Magazine (available at www.cpaireland.ie); Russell, 'Valuation of a Practice' (1995) Law Society Gazette Issue No 3 January 1995 and contained in Appendix 1 to the *Guidelines for solicitors retiring or ceasing to practise as sole practitioners or sole principals and for solicitors purchasing practices from them* published by the Guidance and Ethics Committee of the Law Society of Ireland (Revised March 2005).

[101] See for example the New Zealand case of *Davidson v Wayman* [1984] 2 NZLR 115, in which the Court of Appeal held that an arbitrator was wrong to use the book value of the goodwill, rather than its market value.

[102] *Barr v Barr* (3 November 1983) HC.

However, for the purposes of calculating the entitlement of a former partner to his share of the partnership property, Barron J held that its real value was £5,000. Similarly in *Cruickshank v Sutherland*,[103] the partnership agreement provided that the share of a deceased partner was to be made by reference to the accounts prepared up to April 30 next after his death. The accounts had been prepared consistently using book values, but the House of Lords held that this did not require a departing partner to accept the book values but rather a real value of the assets should be taken.

[18.42] Alternatively, the partners may provide a mechanism for its valuation, eg it may be valued at one to two times the average annual profits of the firm over a three-year period or a multiple of the gross annual recurring fees. In such a case, the courts will give effect to such valuation mechanisms.[104]

---

103 *Cruickshank v Sutherland* (1923) 128 LT 449.

104 In *Heslin v Fay (1)* (1884) 15 LR Ir 43, Sullivan LC gave effect to a clause which provided on a dissolution, for one of the partners to have the right to purchase the business and goodwill of the firm from the other partners, the goodwill to be valued at a sum equal to the firm's profits for one year.

Chapter 19

Shares in a Partnership

INTRODUCTION

[19.01] This chapter is concerned with the special nature of a partner's interest in his firm, which may be termed his share in the partnership, and some of the consequences which result from this special nature. This area will be considered under the following headings:

    I.   General Nature of a Partnership Share;

    II.   Assignment of a Partner's Share;

    III.   Execution against a Partner's Share for his Separate Debts; and

    IV.   Partner's Lien over Partnership Property.

Overview

[19.02] In an earlier chapter, consideration is given to the nature of the partnership relationship.[1] That chapter deals with the totality of the relationship between the partners and it was noted that in essence, the relationship is dictated by the fact that a partnership is not a separate legal entity but an aggregate of its members. This chapter may be regarded as a natural continuation of that analysis, but rather than looking at the partnership as a whole, the emphasis here is on each partner's interest in the partnership and how the aggregate nature of the partnership relationship impacts upon dealings with that interest, eg a partner's assignment of that share, the execution by a creditor against that share and the enforcement by a partner of the rights attaching to his partnership share by means of a partner's lien. It will be seen that the nature of a partnership as a whole remains relevant to this analysis. Thus, in the context of a creditor's rights against a partner's share in a firm, it follows from the aggregate nature of a firm that partnership property is the common property of all the partners. One might, therefore, expect that a separate creditor of a partner would be entitled to seek an execution order against that common property which is jointly owned by his debtor. However, to deal with the impracticality of allowing separate creditors levy execution against partnership property, s 23 of the 1890 Act treats the partnership as if it were a separate legal entity by prohibiting such execution. Instead, s 23 allows the separate creditor to levy execution against the debtor partner's share in the partnership by obtaining a charging order against it. The following analysis of the nature of a share in a partnership highlights the tensions between the strict legal theory of a partnership as an aggregate on the one hand and the commercial view of a firm as a entity on the other hand and how the 1890 Act resolves these tensions. As in the other instances of these tensions between the strict

---

[1]   Paragraph **[3.01]** et seq.

515

legal theory and the commercial view,[2] the result is the use of a legal fiction whereby the partnership is treated for that specific purpose as if it were a separate legal entity. In this context, it should not, therefore, be surprising to see the very close similarities between a share in a company, the archetypal separate legal entity, and a share in a partnership. Like a share in a company,[3] a share in a partnership confers no direct interest in the partnership assets; it is in the nature of personalty, it is a chose in action and it confers certain implied rights and obligations.[4]

I.   GENERAL NATURE OF A PARTNERSHIP SHARE

[19.03] The reference to a partner's 'share' in a partnership is somewhat misleading since, in the absence of any agreement, a partner is not entitled to a share in the partnership, in the sense of being entitled to any particular item of partnership property.[5] However, this distinction is sometimes blurred by the use by the courts and the 1890 Act

---

[2]   A similar tension is involved on the bankruptcy of a firm. There, the fiction of a firm constituting a separate legal entity is created, since the property of each partner on the one hand and of the partners as a whole on the other hand is distinguished (as if the firm was a separate legal entity) with a view to effecting justice between creditors of the firm and the separate creditors of the partners. See para **[27.94]** et seq. See also the fiction of a partnership as a separate legal entity in the context of persons being permitted to sue a firm in a firm name (para **[12.11]**) and a firm registering a business name (para **[3.70]**). See also para **[3.04]** et seq.

[3]   See Courtney, *The Law of Companies* (4th edn, 2016) at para [8.006] et seq. However, unlike a share in a company (which can have an open market value if transferred), a partnership share cannot have such an open market value on a technical dissolution of the firm (per Keane J in *McCormack v McCormack* [2017] IEHC 733 at para 277 of the judgment when criticising the plaintiff's attempt to attribute an open market value to the partnership business on a technical dissolution.

[4]   This final sentence was quoted with approval by Keane J in *Bloxham v Companies Act* [2017] IEHC 664 at para 37 of his judgment. In analysing the interest held by a partner in a partnership, he also referred to the decision of Hoffmann LJ in *Inland Revenue Commissioners v Gray* [1994] STC 360, where Hoffmann LJ observed that: '[as] between themselves, partners are not entitled individually to exercise proprietary rights over any of the partnership assets. This is because they have subjected their proprietary interests to the terms of the partnership deed which provides that the assets shall be employed in the partnership business, and on dissolution realised for the purposes of paying debts and distributing any surplus. As regards the outside world, however, the partnership deed is irrelevant. The partners are collectively entitled to each and every asset of the partnership, in which each of them therefore has an undivided share.' Keane J also referred to l'Anson Banks, *Lindley & Banks on Partnership* (19th edn, 2010) at paras 19-04 (regarding the essential nature of a partner's proprietary interest) and 19-08 (regarding the precise nature of a partner's beneficial interest in partnership assets) (the numbering of those sections remains the same in the 20th edn of that work (2017)).

[5]   In *Bloxham v Companies Act* [2017] IEHC 664, Keane J noted (at para 64) that the terms 'interest' or 'share' in connection with the transfer of assets and liabilities of a partnership should be given their natural and ordinary meaning ie a partnership interest or share in those assets and liabilities, but 'not the vested ownership of a portion of them equivalent to the relevant partnership share'.

of the phrase 'a partner's share of the partnership property'.[6] So in the Supreme Court case of *O'Dwyer, Inspector of Taxes v Cafolla & Co*,[7] Black J noted that taxation legislation:[8]

'recognises that the partners have separate interests or shares in the partnership property, and that, in respect of those shares, they are respectively entitled to the same allowances and deductions as if they were sole owners thereof without any partnership.'[9]

In *Bloxham v Companies Act*,[10] Keane J also commented that:

'the position of partnership dealings in assets for the purpose of tax law is significantly different from the position of such dealings for the purpose of both contract law and partnership law.'

[19.04] While taxation legislation refers to a partnership share in this manner for convenience, in truth, a partner cannot be said to be entitled to any particular item of partnership property. Instead, each partner has a beneficial interest[11] in the entirety of the partnership property and in this sense a partnership share is a bundle of the different property rights included within the assets of the firm, such as real property, personal property, choses in action, etc. However, a partner does not have a right to any particular partnership asset, to the exclusion of the other partners.[12] This is reflected in the fact that during the life of the partnership, each partner is entitled to require the partnership assets to be applied for partnership purposes and not for the exclusive use of one partner.[13] Similarly, when the partnership comes to an end, the partnership assets must be used to pay off the firm's debts and liabilities, with the surplus being shared between the partners.[14] Thus, in addition to his being entitled to the entirety of the partnership property, a partner's share can be described, as it was by Joy CB in *Stuart v Ferguson*,[15]

---

6   This sentence was referred to by Keane J in *Bloxham v Companies Act* [2017] IEHC 664 at para 32 of his judgment.

7   *O'Dwyer, Inspector of Taxes v Cafolla & Co* [1949] IR 210.

8   The legislation in question was the Income Tax Act 1918, now to be found in the Taxes Consolidation Act 1997.

9   *O'Dwyer, Inspector of Taxes v Cafolla & Co* [1949] IR 210 at 242.

10 *Bloxham v Companies Act* [2017] IEHC 664.

11 Although see the High Court of Australia judgment in the case of *Commissioner of State Taxation v Cyril Henschke Pty Ltd* [2010] HCA 43 where it was observed that the concept of a partner's share in partnership assets '... is not sufficiently or accurately expressed merely by use of the term "beneficial interest" ...'.

12 Acknowledged by Keane J in *Bloxham v Companies Act* [2017] IEHC 664 at para 32 of his judgment.

13 The Partnership Act 1890, s 20(1) provides that all partnership property 'must be held and applied by the partners exclusively for the purposes of the partnership and in accordance with the partnership agreement'. See generally para **[16.05]** et seq.

14 The Partnership Act 1890, s 39 provides that on the dissolution of the partnership, every partner is entitled to 'have the property of the partnership applied in payment of the debts and liabilities of the firm'. The Partnership Act 1890, s 44 states that the debts and liabilities of the firm are to be paid off with the partnership assets and provides for the residue to be 'divided amongst the partners in the proportion in which profits are divisible'.

15 *Stuart v Ferguson* (1832) Hayes 452.

as follows: 'the share of each partner is only the share of the clear surplus which would remain after the payment of all the debts.'[16]

[19.05] The following description given by Nourse LJ in the Court of Appeal to a partner's 'share' in *Popat v Shonchhatra*[17] was accepted as representing a correct statement of the law by Keane J in *Bloxham v Companies Acts*[18]:

> 'Although it is both customary and convenient to speak of a partner's "share" of the partnership assets, that is not a truly accurate description of his interest in them, at all events so long as the partnership is a going concern. While each partner has a proprietary interest in each and every asset, he has no entitlement to any specific asset and, in consequence, no right, without the consent of the other partners or partner, to require the whole or even a share of any particular asset to be vested in him. On dissolution the position is in substance not much different, the partnership property falling to be applied, subject to sections 40 to 43 (if and so far as applicable), in accordance with sections 39 and 44 of the Act of 1890. As part of that process, each partner in a solvent partnership is presumptively entitled to payment of what is due from the firm to him in respect of capital before division of the ultimate residue in the shares in which profits are divisible: see section 44(b). It is only at that stage that a partner can accurately be said to be entitled to a share of anything, which, in the absence of agreement to the contrary, will be a share of cash.'[19]

Position of Partnership Share on a Technical Dissolution

[19.06] The definition of a partner's share, as his proportion of the net proceeds of the partnership property after paying off the firm's liabilities, is equally applicable during the life of the partnership as it is on its general dissolution.[20] However, on the technical dissolution of a firm, ie where the firm continues in spite of the departure or admission of a partner, it is inappropriate to convert all of the partnership assets into money and to pay off all of the firm's liabilities. In these circumstances, it is more appropriate to view a partner's share as his share of the beneficial interest in the entirety of the partnership property and the manner in which this is to be valued and paid to the departing partner is usually contained in the partnership agreement. In such a situation, the partnership agreement will override the default provisions of s 39 of the 1890 Act, which would

---

16. *Stuart v Ferguson* (1832) Hayes 452 at 472. In New Zealand, the question has arisen as to whether a spouse's interest in a partnership is matrimonial property for the purposes of dividing the matrimonial property on a separation. In *Z v Z (No 2)* [1997] 2 NZLR 258, the New Zealand Court of Appeal held that a husband's interest as a partner an international accounting firm was matrimonial property as it was acquired after the marriage, since he had become a partner during the marriage and since this interest included his retirement benefit. Although the goodwill in the firm had a nil-value, it was held that the husband's interest was to be valued by taking account of the fact that he had access to, rather than ownership of, the firm's goodwill, which meant that he obtained an income as a partner in excess of professional fees which he earned for the firm. See also *Maw v Maw* [1981] 1 NZLR 25 (CA).

17. *Popat v Shonchhatra* [1997] 1 WLR 1367. Neuberger J also remarked, in *Sandhu v Gill* [2006] Ch 456 that, at any time before the completion of the winding-up of a partnership, the concept of a partnership share is 'conceptually somewhat opaque'.

18. *Bloxham v Companies Acts* [2017] IEHC 664.

19. At p 1372 of the judgment.

20. As to the distinction between a general and a technical dissolution, see para **[23.07]**.

otherwise entitle a departing partner to have his partnership share ascertained, by forcing the sale of the partnership assets and paying off the partnership liabilities.

[19.07] Where there is an implied agreement that the firm will continue on the departure of a partner, but there is no agreed mechanism regarding the valuation and payment for the departing partner's share, it seems that the court will order that his share be acquired at a valuation.[21] Even where there is no implied agreement that the firm will continue, in certain cases[22] the courts have exercised their discretion to refuse to order the sale of the partnership assets under s 39 of the 1890 Act, and instead have allowed the continuing partners to buy the departing partner's share at a valuation.[23]

Doctrine of Conversion Results from Nature of Partnership Share

[19.08] The doctrine of conversion of real partnership property into personal estate owes its existence to the nature of a partnership share.[24] As has been noted, a partner's share can be viewed as his proportion of the net proceeds of the partnership property, after that property has been turned into money and applied to pay off the partnership debts. However, no distinction is made in this regard between real property and personal property. For this reason it is said that partnership property that is real property is converted into personal estate. Thus, in *Murtagh v Costello*,[25] Chatterton VC held that:

> '[R]eal estate purchased by a firm out of partnership money, and for partnership purposes, is personal estate, not only for the purpose of the administration of the partnership assets, but for all intents and purposes.'[26]

[19.09] This principle is also to be found in the terms of s 22 of the 1890 Act:

> Where land or any heritable interest therein has become partnership property, it shall, unless the contrary intention appears, be treated as between the partners (including the representatives of a deceased partner), and also as between the heirs of a deceased partner and his executors or administrators, as personal or moveable and not real or heritable estate.

Partnership Share Creates a Relationship of Tenancy in Common

[19.10] While a partner's share gives him an interest in the entirety of the partnership assets, in technical terms he is entitled to partnership property as a tenant in common.[27] Thus, there is no right of survivorship for the continuing partners on the death or departure of a partner.[28]

---

21 See for example the English case of *Sobell v Boston* [1975] 2 All ER 282.
22 For example when the departing partner's share is small or where it is in a professional firm and the sale of the firm's assets and goodwill would be impractical: l'Anson Banks, *Lindley & Banks on Partnership* (20th edn, 2017) at para 19-11.
23 *Syers v Syers* (1876) 1 App Cas 174; *Rivett v Rivett* (1966) 200 EG 858.
24 See further regarding the doctrine of conversion, para **[16.70]**.
25 *Murtagh v Costello* (1881) 7 LR Ir 428.
26 *Murtagh v Costello* (1881) 7 LR Ir 428 at 435–436.
27 See generally in relation to the legal estate in which partnership property is held, para **[16.64]**.
28 Although see *Bathurst v Scarbarrow* [2005] 1 P&CR 58 (CA) regarding the possibility that partnership property can be held as joint tenants in limited circumstances. (contd.../)

Partnership Share may be Held upon Trust

[19.11] A share in a partnership, like any other asset, may be held upon trust for a third party. This is clear from the case of *O'Dwyer, Inspector of Taxes v Cafolla & Co*,[29] where the validity of a trust of a partner's share was upheld. In this case, a partner in well-known Dublin fish and chip restaurant executed a deed of trust. Under the terms of the trust, she assigned all her rights in the partnership to the managing partner, who was also her son-in-law, upon trust for his four children, all of whom were minors. In this way, each of the children's tax free allowance was used to reduce the income tax payable from partnership profits. The trust was challenged by the Inspector of Taxes on the basis that the managing partner controlled the firm. On this basis, the Inspector of Taxes alleged that the income attributable to the share which the managing partner held on trust should be treated as his personal income, rather than that of his children.[30] The Supreme Court rejected this contention and held that there was a valid trust of the partnership share and that the managing partner held the partnership income on trust for his four children.

II.   ASSIGNMENT OF A PARTNER'S SHARE

[19.12] Like any other asset, a share in a partnership[31] may be transferred by a partner to a third party, subject to any agreement to the contrary amongst the partners. Although shares in a partnership are not commonly assigned outright, the 1890 Act specifically deals with the rights of the assignee of the share *vis-à-vis* the continuing partners. However, since the share of a partner in a successful partnership may be a right to a valuable income stream, it is possible that it could be the subject of an assignment by way of security or a mortgage and the mortgagee of the partnership share would have the rights of an assignee considered below. It should be noted, however, that partnership agreements commonly restrict the right of a partner to assign or mortgage his share in the partnership.[32]

---

28   (\...contd) Rix LJ observed that the presumption that partnership property is held in common can be displaced by evidence of an agreement to the contrary – in that case, he found that there was clear evidence that the parties had agreed to take the particular property as joint tenants in full knowledge of the implications of holding property in that manner.

29   *O'Dwyer, Inspector of Taxes v Cafolla & Co* [1949] IR 210.

30   Reliance was placed on s 2(1) of the Finance Act 1937. This section provided that where as a result of a settlement (including a trust) any income was paid to benefit a child (under 21) of a settlor, such income was to be treated for income tax purposes to be the income of the settlor for that year. It was argued unsuccessfully in that case, that the partnership agreement and the trust deed should be regarded as one transaction so that the father would be deemed to be the settlor of his mother's share. Anti-avoidance provisions of the tax legislation have since been introduced concerning the admission of children into partnerships, see Taxes Consolidation Act 1997, s 798. See also Maguire, *Irish Income Tax 2017* (2016) at para [15.409].

31   And in a dissolved partnership per the Court of Appeal in *Harwood v Harwood* [1991] 2 FLR 274.

32   See further para [21.83].

[19.13] *Bloxham v Companies Act*[33] concerned Bloxham Stockbrokers, a stockbroking business which was placed into liquidation in mid-2012; a limited partnership, seven of its general partners were unlimited liability companies. It also had one limited partner. In 2011, the then seven individual general partners in Bloxham had each formed one of those unlimited liability companies, and had each transferred his interest in Bloxham to the corporate general partner owned by him. Those corporate general partners had each borrowed from Danske Bank A/S to finance their investment, and Danske Bank appointed receivers to each of those companies in October 2012 under debentures granted by each of those companies to Danske Bank. Keane J held that each corporate general partner held no more than a partnership share in Bloxham (and not an ownership interest in any partnership asset) and that the only asset that each corporate general partner could have secured in favour of Danske Bank under the debentures was the benefit of that partnership share. A general restructuring of Bloxham's partnership structure had taken place in 2011 and some correspondence issued by financial advisors as part of that process referred to proposed sales by individual partners of their respective portions of various partnership assets (rather than of their partnership shares in those assets). Keane J found that this was a result of the financial advisors approaching the restructuring from a tax perspective, rather than from a partnership law perspective, and that such correspondence was simply background information on the restructuring proposal, rather than reflecting what was actually taking place from a partnership law perspective.[34]

[19.14] It is important to bear in mind that a completely separate issue from the assignment of a partnership share is the question of whether the transferee of that share will become a partner in the firm. This is because a basic tenet of partnership law is that no person may become a partner with another person or persons, without their consent. This principle is contained in s 24(7) of the 1890 Act which simply states that '[n]o person may be introduced as a partner without the consent of all existing partners'. As a consequence of this basic principle, the transfer or assignment of a partner's share will operate as an assignment of the share in the partnership but does not entitle the assignee to become a member of the firm,[35] nor does it result in the assignor ceasing to be a partner. As explained by Smith MR in *Re Tipperary Joint-Stock Bank*:[36]

> '[I]n cases of partnership, one partner could not transfer his interest to a stranger, on this obvious principle – the members of the partnership might have confidence in each other,

[33] *Bloxham v Companies Act* [2017] IEHC 664.

[34] As part of the 2011 restructuring of Bloxham, certain documents were also furnished to the Central Bank of Ireland, including diagrams referring to 'shareholdings' in the partnership. Keane J commented that it was difficult to accept that the Central Bank would not have been aware of the nature of a partner's share as a matter of partnership law.

[35] Contrast the position under s 6(5)(b) of the Limited Partnerships Act 1907 (see generally para **[28.103]**), and under s 18(2) of the Investment Limited Partnerships Act 1994 (see generally para **[29.120]**), where in both instances the assignee of a limited partner's share becomes a limited partner in the limited partnership and investment limited partnership, respectively.

[36] *Re Tipperary Joint-Stock Bank* (1856) 6 Ir Ch R 72. The case was overturned on appeal by Brady LC at (1857) 6 Ir Ch R 524, but not in relation to this point of principle.

but they might not have confidence in the person to whom any of them might choose to assign his interest.'[37]

[19.15] The importance of each partner consenting to be in partnership with another is clear when one considers that a partner is liable to an unlimited degree for the acts of his co-partner done in the ordinary course of business of the partnership[38] and the rule is justified by the need for partners to have the degree of trust and confidence in each other which is necessary between partners.[39]

[19.16] The rights which an assignee of a partner's share in the partnership does and does not acquire are set out in s 31 of the 1890 Act:

(1) An assignment by any partner of his share in the partnership, either absolute or by way of mortgage or redeemable charge, does not, as against the other partners, entitle the assignee, during the continuance of the partnership, to interfere in the management or administration of the partnership business or affairs, or to require any accounts of the partnership transactions, or to inspect the partnership books, but entitles the assignee only to receive the share of profits to which the assigning partner would otherwise be entitled, and the assignee must accept the account of profits agreed to by the partners.

(2) In case of a dissolution of the partnership, whether as respects all the partners or as respects the assigning partner, the assignee is entitled to receive the share of the partnership assets to which the assigning partner is entitled as between himself and the other partners, and for the purpose of ascertaining that share, to an account as from the date of dissolution.

[19.17] Thus, the assignee of a partner's share is not entitled to:

- interfere in the management or administration of the partnership business or affairs;
- require any accounts of the partnership transactions; or
- inspect the partnership books.

[19.18] He is only entitled to:

- receive the share of the profits to which the assigning partner is entitled, though he is obliged to accept the account of profits agreed to by the partners in the firm; and
- insist on an account being taken in order to determine the amount which is owed to him on the dissolution of the firm.

In view of these restrictive rights of an assigning partner, it has been held in the New Zealand case of *Johnstone v Commissioner of Inland Revenue*[40] that, in relation to the New Zealand equivalent of s 31 of the 1890 Act,[41] a partner cannot assign his fixed capital in the partnership.

---

37   *Re Tipperary Joint-Stock Bank* (1856) 6 Ir Ch R 72 at 78, quoted with approval by Keane J in *McCormack v McCormack* [2017] IEHC 733 at para 277 of the judgment.
38   See generally in relation to this liability, para [10.30] et seq.
39   See generally in relation to this trust and confidence, para [15.01] et seq.
40   *Johnstone v Commissioner of Inland Revenue* [1996] NZLR 833.
41   Partnership Act 1908, s 34.

Assignee's Rights on a Dissolution

[19.19] Section 31(2) of the 1890 Act sets out the rights of an assignee on a dissolution of the partnership 'as respects all the partners or as respects the assigning partner'. The reference to a 'dissolution as respects all the partners', is clearly a reference to a general dissolution of the partnership, while the reference to a dissolution as respects the assigning partner is clearly a reference to a technical dissolution (where the assignor leaves the firm and the continuing partners remain in business). In either case, the assignee's rights are greater than when the assignor remains a member of the firm. In both cases, he is not restricted to the assignor's share of the profits, but is entitled to the assignor's share of the partnership assets and has a right of accounting from the date of dissolution of the firm. For example if the assignor of a partnership share dies or is declared bankrupt, the partnership will be immediately dissolved under the general law of partnership.[42] In such a case, the assignee will be entitled to the assignor's share of the partnership assets and is entitled to receive an accounting from the other partners from the date of death or bankruptcy.

Irrevocable right of assignee

[19.20] The right of an assignee under s 31(2) of the 1890 Act to the assignor's share in the partnership and to an account from the other partners is a statutory right of the assignee and, as such, it may not be waived by the terms of the partnership agreement. This is because the partnership agreement is a contract solely between the partners to which the assignee is not privy. Thus, while s 19 of the 1890 Act allows for the variation by the partners of their mutual rights and duties, this section would appear to have no application where the rights in question are not the 'mutual rights and duties of partners' but the rights of a third party assignee.[43]

Assignee takes Share subject to Rights of Partners

[19.21] The assignee of a partnership share takes that share subject to the equities between the assigning partner and his partners. He does not acquire a right to the assignor's share as it was when it was assigned; instead, he is subject to these equities, whether they arise before or after the assignment.[44] By the express terms of s 31(1) of the 1890 Act, the assignee must accept the account of profits agreed to by the partners.

[19.22] In contrast, the right of an assignee to an account on a dissolution of the firm is a statutory right under s 31(2). As such, once the partners have notice of the assignment,

---

[42] Unless there is a contrary agreement between the partners: Partnership Act 1890, s 33(1). As to the dissolution of a partnership by the death or bankruptcy of a partner, see generally para **[23.32]** et seq.

[43] In contrast, s 19 of the 1890 Act permits the variation of the rights of the partners under s 31(1) of the 1890 Act to prevent an assignee from being involved in, inter alia, the management and administration of the firm, since it is a variation of the 'rights' of the partners.

[44] See *Re Garwood's Trusts* [1903] 1 Ch 236 and para **[19.23]**. See also *Bergmann v McMillan* (1881) 17 Ch D 423; *Cavander v Bulteel* (1873) LR 9 Ch 79.

they cannot agree amongst themselves new terms which will prejudice that statutory right.[45]

Assignee may not interfere in 'management and administration' of firm

[19.23] Under the terms of s 31(1) of the 1890 Act, the assignee may not interfere in the management and administration of the firm. This is the case even where management decisions impact upon the share of the profits to which he is entitled. This is highlighted by the decision in *Re Garwood's Trusts*,[46] where the partners implemented a bona fide arrangement whereby they received salaries in return for the provision by them of additional services to the firm. The mortgagee of a partner's share in the firm suffered financially as result of this arrangement, since there was a consequent reduction in the share of profits to which he was entitled. Nonetheless, the court held that since the arrangement was bona fide, it formed part of the 'management and administration' of the firm and thus was outside the control of the assignee.

Section 31 does not Deal with Rights between Assignee and Assignor

[19.24] It is to be noted that s 31 of the 1890 Act deals with the relationship between the assignee and the other partners but does not deal with the legal relationship between the assignee and assignor. Accordingly, this is left to be governed by the general law. It is possible that the terms of the assignment (in particular where it is by way of security) will require the assignor to act in accordance with the assignee's instructions when the assignee exercises his right to participate in the management of the firm. Under the terms of s 31(1), direct liability is not imposed upon an assignee of a partnership share for the liabilities of the firm and it seems clear that the assignor is not relieved of any of his obligations to the firm.[47] However, indirect liability may be imposed upon the assignee. This is because it seems that as the assignee for value stands in the shoes of the

---

[45]   *Kelly v Hutton* (1868) LR 3 Ch App 703; *Watts v Driscoll* [1901] 1 Ch 294.

[46]   *Re Garwood's Trusts* [1903] 1 Ch 236.

[47]   Note that s 18(3) of the Investment Limited Partnerships Act 1994, in the context of a limited partner assigning his partnership share, clarifies this matter by stating that the assignment shall not 'relieve the assignor of any of its partnership obligations and s 31 of the Act of 1890 shall apply to any such assignment'. As regards the tax position, see the decision of the Privy Council in the New Zealand case of *Hadlee v Commissioners of Inland Revenue* [1993] AC 524 to the effect that an active partner in an accountancy firm, who makes an assignment of his partnership interest, is not thereby divested of liability to pay tax on the assigned income since he was assigning an expectancy, not an income-producing property, of future profits which flowed from his obligations under the partnership agreement. See also *Hocking v Western Australian Bank* [1909] 9 CLR 738 at pp 743–744 where Griffith CJ agreed with the contention that a person who agrees to buy part of a partner's share in a partnership does not become a partner and the partner, while remaining a partner in the partnership, becomes a trustee of the interest that he agreed to sell to the buyer. That judgment was given by reference to s 42 of the Partnership Act 1895 of Western Australia, which corresponds to s 31 of the 1890 Act.

assignor, he is required to indemnify the assignor in respect of the liabilities of the firm unless there is an agreement to the contrary between them.[48]

Assignment of Part only of a Partnership Share

[19.25] Section 31 of the 1890 Act refers to the assignment of a 'share in the partnership'. No reference is made to the assignment of part of a partnership share. Nonetheless, it is apprehended that s 31 is equally applicable to the assignment of part of a partnership share as there is no reason in principle why a partner could not assign all, but not part, of a partnership share. Indeed, support for this view is to be found in the Investment Limited Partnerships Act 1994. Section 18(3) of that Act expressly recognises the right of a limited partner to assign 'the whole or any part' of his partnership interest.[49]

Form of Assignment of a Partnership Share

[19.26] Since the right to receive money under the terms of a partnership agreement is a chose in action,[50] in order to have a legal assignment thereof, s 28(6) of the Supreme Court of Judicature Act (Ireland) 1877 requires the assignment to be in writing, to be absolute (although an assignment by way of security is acceptable) and for the persons from whom the assignor would have been entitled to receive the debt (ie the other partners) to be expressly notified. An assignment which fails to meet these requirements will operate as an equitable assignment only.

[19.27] It has been seen that a partnership share is the *beneficial* interest of that partner in all of the partnership assets.[51] Thus, any assignment of a share in a firm which has an interest in real property will involve the transfer of a beneficial interest in real property. It follows that the assignment must be in writing in order to satisfy s 2 of the Statute of Frauds (Ireland) 1695.[52] This would appear to be the position notwithstanding the fact that s 22 of the 1890 Act provides that land which is partnership property shall be treated as personal estate. This is because s 22 expressly provides that this treatment is to apply only 'as between the partners'. This conclusion is in keeping with the rationale

---

48   *Dodson v Downey* [1901] 2 Ch 620, in which the assignee was a purchaser for value of the share. In *Bloxham v Companies Act* [2017] IEHC 664, Keane J commented that it did not seem illogical to him that the assignor of a partnership share should take the precautionary step of seeking a contractual indemnity in this regard. See generally, Fletcher, *Higgins and Fletcher on The Law of Partnership in Australia and New Zealand* (8th edn, 2001).

49   See also the Australian High Court case of *Federal Commissioners of Taxation v Everett* (1980) 143 CLR 440 and see generally Rees, 'Partnership: Assignee's Liability to Assignor following Everett' [1981] Aust Current Law 23.

50   Since it is one of the 'personal rights of property which can only be claimed or enforced by action, and not by taking physical possession': *Torkington v Magee* [1902] 2 KB 427 at 430 (case reversed at [1903] 1 KB 644 but the reversal did not relate to that particular point). See generally in relation to the assignment of choses in action, Breslin, *Banking Law* (3rd edn, 2013) at para 11-42 et seq.

51   Paragraph **[19.04]**.

52   (7 Will 3, c 12). See generally in relation to compliance with s 2 of this statute, Wylie and Woods, *Irish Conveyancing Law* (3rd edn, 2005) at para [6.06] et seq and Clark, *Contract Law in Ireland* (8th edn, 2016) at para 4-01 et seq.

for s 22, namely that all partnership property is available for conversion into cash to pay off partnership debts, whether it is real or personal property and it does not conflict with the rationale for the Statute of Frauds, namely to prevent fraud in relation to alleged oral transfers of property.

Restriction on Right to Assign

[19.28] In some cases, the right of a partner to assign his share may be restricted by rules which govern the business or profession of which he is a member. For example solicitors are prohibited from sharing the profits or fees of their business with non-solicitors by s 59 of the Solicitors Acts 1954. Accordingly a partner in a law firm is likely to be prohibited from assigning (or mortgaging) his share in the firm to a non-solicitor, since this may involve him in the sharing of the profits or fees in contravention of this section.

[19.29] In addition to such controls imposed on businesses or professions as a whole, it is noted elsewhere that partnership agreements may prohibit partners from assigning their share in the partnership without the consent of all the partners.[53] Such a prohibition may be seen as attempting to counter the perceived threat to the independence of the firm where a partner assigns or mortgages his share and is then required to exercise his management powers on the instructions of the assignee or mortgagee.

Modification of s 31 to Allow for a Right of Nomination

[19.30] It is also possible for the partners to modify the operation of s 31 of the 1890 Act so as to allow for the 'complete' assignment of a partner's share, ie a right of the assignee to become a partner or it may be described as the right of the outgoing partner to nominate his successor.[54] While the presence of such a power is not commonly found in partnership agreements, it may be appropriate in family firms where the founder wishes to retain the power to appoint a successor.[55] This can only be achieved if the partnership agreement provides that *all* the partners in the firm are bound to accept the person nominated by the outgoing partner as a partner in the firm. This is because of the basic principle of partnership law that a person may only become another person's partner if the latter agrees to that change.[56] In the case of a nomination, this consent is obtained in advance by means of a provision in the partnership agreement and may be termed 'anticipatory consent'.

[19.31] In addition, the terms of s 31 of the 1890 Act which would otherwise prevent the assignee from acting as a partner, are automatically varied by the provision in the partnership agreement that the assignee be admitted to the partnership. Unlike a variation of the 'rights of an assignee' under s 31(2) of the 1890 Act,[57] this variation is permitted by the terms of s 19 of the 1890 Act, since it is a variation of the 'rights of the

---

[53] Paragraph **[21.83]**.
[54] Like all powers of a partner, this power is subject to the partner's fiduciary duty to his co-partners. See further in relation to a partner's fiduciary duty, para **[15.01]** et seq.
[55] See for example *McCarthy v Cunningham* (3 October 1979) HC NI.
[56] Paragraph **[19.14]**.
[57] As to which, see para **[19.20]**.

partners' to prevent an assignee from being involved in, inter alia, the management and administration of the firm.

Nature of power to nominate

[19.32] A power on the part of one partner to nominate his successor is a contractual right between partners which gives the nominee the right to be admitted as a partner to the firm. In *Cuffe v Murtagh*,[58] the partnership agreement contained a power on the part of each of the partners to nominate a successor on his death. It provided that the nominee should become and be accepted as a partner in respect of the deceased partner's share. Chatterton VC held that such a right of nomination was effective in entitling the nominee to 'attain an absolute right to be admitted a partner'.[59]

[19.33] In *Beamish v Beamish*,[60] the partners were entitled in their will to appoint a successor to their position as partners. In his will, one partner bequeathed 'in pursuance of every power enabling him' the residue of his estate to his son. It was held that this bequest did not involve the nomination of the son as his successor in the firm, on the grounds, inter alia, that the expression 'in pursuance of every power' referred to powers of appointment[61] in the technical sense and, as noted by Chatterton VC, the power to nominate a successor to a firm is:

> 'not a power in the technical sense, nor can it be treated upon the rules properly applicable to powers. It is rather a right to bind all the other partners to admit any one fulfilling the description of [the nominee]. The testator's share in the partnership was, properly speaking, his property, and not the subject matter of a power of appointment, which implies that the subject of it is not the property of the donee of the power.'[62]

Implicit right to nominate a substitute in place of nominee

[19.34] Implicit in the power to nominate a successor is the power to appoint a substitute in place of the original nominee. This is clear from *Cuffe v Murtagh*.[63] There, a partner exercised his power to nominate a successor by appointing his nephew as his successor and his other nephew as a substitute, should the first nephew die. Chatterton VC held that as the first nephew died, the second nephew was entitled to be appointed as the partner's successor:

> 'There is nothing in the deed inconsistent with a right in any of the parties to appoint another person to succeed him, in place of one who should not live to attain an absolute right to be admitted as a partner.'[64]

The same logic applies to substitution for reasons other than the death of the first nominee and it is apprehended that the power to nominate a substitute applies in any situation where the nominating partner wishes to replace his original nominee.

---

58   *Cuffe v Murtagh* (1881) 7 LR Ir 411.
59   *Cuffe v Murtagh* (1881) 7 LR Ir 411 at 426.
60   *Beamish v Beamish* (1869) 4 Ir Eq R 120.
61   As to powers of appointment generally, see Wylie, *Irish Land Law* (5th edn, 2013) at para [11.06] et seq.
62   *Beamish v Beamish* (1869) 4 Ir Eq R 120 at 139–140.
63   *Beamish v Beamish* (1869) 4 Ir Eq R 120.
64   *Beamish v Beamish* (1869) 4 Ir Eq R 120 at 426.

Right of nomination should be explicit

[19.35] Section 24(7) of the 1890 Act provides that no person may be admitted as a partner without the consent of all the existing partners. It therefore is important to ensure that the language in the partnership agreement should explicitly require all the partners in a firm to accept the nominee as a partner. *Milliken v Milliken*[65] concerned the right of a nominee (who, although a party to the partnership agreement, was not a partner) to take his mother's share in a firm of booksellers in Grafton St in Dublin. His acceptance as a partner was subject to his performance as an employee being to the reasonable satisfaction of the other partners. Since the other partners alone were the judges of whether the nominee had performed to their reasonable satisfaction, Blackburne MR refused the nominee's request for an order to appoint him as a partner.

[19.36] Where, as happened in that case, the language is not sufficiently explicit to bind all the other partners to accept the nominee as a successor, the nomination will usually operate as an assignment of the share of the profits to which the nominating partner is entitled.[66] In the Scottish decision of *Thomson v Thomson*,[67] it was agreed that on the death of either of two brothers in a bakery partnership, the business would be controlled by the surviving partner provided that either partner might nominate his widow to his share. When one partner died leaving all his estate to his widow, it was held that this provision was not sufficiently explicit to operate as a nomination of the widow as a partner.

Exercise of right of nomination should also be explicit

[19.37] As well as ensuring that the right to nominate a successor is explicitly stated in the partnership agreement, one should also ensure that the actual exercise of the right is done explicitly in pursuance of its terms. A failure to do so will result in the proposed nominee only obtaining the share of the profits to which the nominating partner is entitled. This is illustrated by *Beamish v Beamish*.[68] There, the well-known Cork brewing firm of Beamish & Crawford had a partnership agreement which allowed a partner to bequeath his share to legitimate male descendants of the founder of the firm, one William Beamish. By his will, Charles Beamish devised and bequeathed, and 'in pursuance of every power enabling' him the residue of his property to his son. However, he made no specific reference to his being a member of the firm or to his power to bequeath his partnership share. For this reason, Chatterton VC held that this bequest of the residue of his property was not a nomination of his son as a partner, but instead operated as a bequest of the profit share to which he was entitled.

III. EXECUTION AGAINST A PARTNER'S SHARE FOR HIS SEPARATE DEBTS

[19.38] Prior to the enactment of s 23 of the 1890 Act, a separate judgment creditor of a partner was entitled to levy execution, not only against that partner's own property, but

---

65   *Milliken v Milliken* (1845) 8 Ir Eq R 16.
66   See *Beamish v Beamish* (1869) 4 Ir Eq R 120, considered at para **[19.37]**.
67   *Thomson v Thomson* (1961) SC 255, aff'd (1962) SC (HL) 28.
68   *Beamish v Beamish* (1869) 4 Ir Eq R 120.

also against the property of the partnership. In principle, this position was justifiable, since the partnership property was owned by the judgment debtor partner (albeit jointly with his co-partners) and therefore there was no reason why the judgment creditor could not levy execution against the partnership property. However, this had obvious commercial difficulties for the innocent partners and for this reason s 23 of the 1890 Act was introduced. Instead s 23 treats the partnership property as if it were the property of the firm as a separate legal entity.[69] Indeed, s 23 is one of the few provisions of the 1890 Act which is not simply a codification of the existing common law. Section 23(1) prohibits in very broad terms the issue of writs of execution against the firm, save in respect of firm debts.[70] Section 23(2) then goes on to introduce alternative remedies for separate creditors of a partner, namely a charging order or the appointment of a receiver over that partner's share of the profits. Accordingly, this section is of considerable practical significance for the creditors of partners.

Section 23 of the 1890 Act

[19.39] Section 23 allows a judgment creditor of a partner to obtain an order against that partner, charging his interest in the firm with payment of the debt, and the creditor may enforce the charge by either obtaining an order for the sale of the partner's interest or for the appointment of a receiver. Section 23 states:

(1) ...[71] a writ of execution shall not issue against any partnership property except on a judgment against the firm.

(2) The High Court,[72] or a judge thereof, or the Chancery Court of the county palatine of Lancaster,[73] or a county court,[74] may, on the application by summons of any judgment creditor of a partner, make an order charging that partner's interest in the partnership property and profits with payment of the amount of the judgment debt and interest thereon, and may by the same or a subsequent order appoint a receiver of that partner's share of profits (whether already declared or accruing), and of any other money which may be coming to him in respect of the partnership, and direct all accounts and inquiries, and give all other orders and directions which might have been directed or given if the charge had been made in favour of the judgment creditor by the partner, or which the circumstances of the case may require.

(3) The other partner or partners shall be at liberty at any time to redeem the interest charged, or in case of a sale being directed, to purchase the same.

---

[69] Paragraph **[19.02]**. See generally Collins, *Enforcement of Judgments* (2014) and Markson, 'Partnership: Equitable Execution' (1981) 125 Sol Jo 109.

[70] Thus, the British Columbia Supreme Court has held that a judgment creditor cannot garnishee a debt owing to the partnership firm: *Houn v Maloff* (1964) 32 DLR (2d) 770. See also the English Court of Appeal decision in *Hirschorn v Evans* [1938] 2 KB 801.

[71] The introductory words 'After the commencement of this Act' were repealed by the Statute Law Revision Act 1908 (8 Edw 7 c 49).

[72] The original reference is to the High Court, which must be taken to mean the Irish High Court by virtue of s 8 of the Courts (Supplemental Provisions) Act 1961.

[73] The words 'or the Chancery Court of the county palatine of Lancaster' were repealed in England by the Courts Act 1971, Sch 11, Pt II and are clearly inapplicable in Ireland.

[74] This term must be taken to refer to the Circuit Court, in which the defendant resides as a result of the Courts (Supplemental Provisions) Act 1961, s 22(3)(b), 4th Sch, ref 46.

(4) This section shall apply in the case of a cost-book company[75] as if the company were a partnership within the meaning of this Act.

(5) This section shall not apply in Scotland.

Applicable rules of the Superior Courts

[19.40] The procedures for obtaining a s 23 charging order are set out in Ord 46 of the Rules of the Superior Courts. These provide that an application for a s 23 charging order shall be by motion[76] served on the judgment debtor partner and on all the other partners within the jurisdiction. Such service shall be deemed to be good service on all the partners.[77]

[19.41] Under s 23(3) of the 1890 Act, the partners of the judgment debtor are at liberty to redeem the share of the judgment debtor or, where a sale has been directed, purchase that share. For such purpose or for any application to court as result of an application to charge their partner's share, they may apply by motion served on the judgment debtor, the judgment creditor and such of the other partners who do not concur in the application and who are within the jurisdiction. Such service shall be deemed to be good service on all the partners.[78]

Section 23 order should not be first resort of creditor

[19.42] It seems that a s 23 charging order will be viewed as a remedy of last resort. Accordingly, the court is not likely to grant a charging order against a debtor partner, where the judgment creditor's only attempt to recover payment was to apply to the court for a charging order. Rather the court is likely to require direct evidence that all other means of enforcement of the debt have been exhausted.[79] This approach is justified in view of the drastic consequences of a charging order, in particular the right of the other partners to dissolve the partnership as regards the partner against whom the charging order has been obtained.[80]

Application for garnishee order amended to become s 23 application

[19.43] Although the application in *Foley v Toomey*[81] was for a garnishee order, a s 23 charging order was granted by the High Court in that case. There, the plaintiff was a creditor of Philip Toomey who had no goods to answer the judgment or execution order

---

[75]   This part of the section is of little application in Ireland, since cost-book companies are partnerships formed for the purpose of working a mine and where the agreement between the partners is entered in a book called a cost book. See *Geake v Jackson* (1867) 36 LJCP 109 at 109.

[76]   Rules of the Superior Courts, Ord 46, r 3. See generally in relation to such motions RSC, Ord 52.

[77]   Rules of the Superior Courts, Ord 46, r 3.

[78]   Rules of the Superior Courts, Ord 46, r 4.

[79]   As occurred in the New Zealand case of *Franklin v Ruck* (1900) 2 GLR 45.

[80]   Partnership Act 1890, s 33(2). See generally in relation to dissolution in these circumstances, para **[23.56]**.

[81]   *Foley v Toomey* (1953) 87 ILTR 141. The order granted by Murnaghan J refers to 'Patrick' Toomey, but this must be taken to be a typing error and to mean Philip Toomey.

which the plaintiff had obtained against him. The plaintiff sought a garnishee order against Philip Toomey's partner, Denis Toomey. Under the terms of this order, the plaintiff claimed an attachment against so much of the debt which was due by the firm to Philip Toomey as would answer the plaintiff's judgment and execution order. In the High Court, Murnaghan J amended the application by treating it as a summons under s 23 of the 1890 Act to charge the interest of Philip Toomey in the firm. On this basis, he charged that interest with the debt and ordered an account to be taken of what was due to Philip Toomey from the firm.

Section 23 order against a foreign firm

[19.44] Section 23 of the 1890 Act applies to foreign partners with assets in the State and carrying on business in the State, whether through a branch or an agent. This is clear from the decision of the High Court in *Scott and Horton v Godfrey*.[82] In that case, judgment had previously been obtained in England against Godfrey, a partner in a Belgian partnership. The judgment was registered in Ireland as goods belonging to the Belgian firm were in the hands of its agent in Belfast, though the agent did not constitute a branch of the firm.[83] The goods were samples of the firm's products since the agent procured orders for these items but the goods ordered were sent and invoiced directly by the firm to the purchasers. Johnson J held that as the firm was carrying on business in Ireland, albeit through an agent, and that it had assets here, he granted a charging order and appointed a receiver to Godfrey's share of the firm's assets in Ireland.

[19.45] Despite the impression from the judgment of Johnson J, there is nothing in the wording of s 23 which requires a firm to be carrying on business before a charging order will be made. Therefore, it is conceived that a s 23 order would be granted if a partner has assets in the State, even if the firm does not carry on business here.[84]

Rights of creditor pursuant to charging order

[19.46] Section 23(2) equates the position of a judgment creditor who has obtained a charging order with that of an assignee of partner's share. Section 23(2) does this by providing that the court may give such orders as might have been directed, if the charge had been made by the debtor partner, rather than by the court. Thus, like an assignee,[85] a creditor under a charging order is not entitled to have an account taken of partnership dealings during the life of the partnership, unless directed by the court. Nor is he entitled to inspect the partnership books or interfere in the management or administration of the partnership.[86]

---

[82] *Scott and Horton v Godfrey* (1901) 36 ILTR 81.

[83] The Partnership Act 1890, s 23 has been held to be equally applicable to the branch of a firm in the country: *Brown, Janson & Co v A Hutchinson & Co* [1895] 1 QB 737.

[84] This would be consistent with the practice in the case of Mareva injunctions, see generally Kirwan, *Injunctions Law and Practice* (2nd revised edn, 2015).

[85] Partnership Act 1890, s 31 and para **[19.16]**.

[86] Partnership Act 1890, s 31 and para **[19.16]**.

[19.47] By analogy with the position of an assignee of a partner's share *vis-à-vis* the other partners,[87] it is thought that a creditor who is granted a charging order over a partner's share may have his interests prejudiced by the bona fide actions of the partners in the firm, including the debtor partner. For example the profit share which is ultimately paid to the judgment creditor may be reduced by paying increased 'salaries' to the partners if this is part of a bona fide arrangement pursuant to the firm's normal management powers.[88]

[19.48] Under the terms of s 23(2), the basic right of a creditor under a charging order is to the debtor partner's 'interest in the partnership property and profits' and he is restricted to those rights which the partner had at the date of the order.[89] Implicit in the wording of s 23(3) ('in the case of a sale being directed') is the right of the judgment creditor to get a court order for the sale of the partner's share in the first place.

Rights of the partners of the judgment debtor

[19.49] The partners of the judgment debtor are entitled under the terms of s 23(3) to redeem their partner's share at any time. In addition, s 33(2) of the 1890 Act entitles the partners of a judgment debtor to dissolve the partnership since it expressly allows for such a dissolution where a partner 'suffers his share of the partnership property to be charged under this Act for his separate debt'.[90]

IV. PARTNER'S LIEN OVER PARTNERSHIP PROPERTY

[19.50] A partner's lien is the expression given to the right of a partner on the general dissolution of the firm to have the assets of the firm applied in payment of the firm's debts and liabilities and to have the surplus used to pay what may be due to the partners.[91] It is a very important right of every partner, since it may be the only means by which a departing partner can realise his investment in the firm, assuming the continuing partners do not wish to buy out his share. This right is contained in s 39 of the 1890 Act although the term 'lien' is not in fact used in that section. Section 39 states:

> On the dissolution of a partnership every partner is entitled, as against the other partners in the firm, and all persons claiming through them in respect of their interests as partners, to have the property of the partnership applied in payment of the debts and liabilities of the firm, and to have the surplus assets after such payment applied in payment of what may be due to the partners respectively after deducting what may be due from them as partners to the firm; and for that purpose any partner or his representatives may on the termination of the partnership apply to the Court to wind up the business and affairs of the firm.

The primary effect of s 39 is that, on the dissolution of the partnership, it entitles any partner to apply to court to have the affairs of the partnership agreement wound up and

---

87   As to which, see para **[19.21]**.
88   See *Re Garwood's Trusts* [1903] 1 Ch 236. See also *Watts v Driscoll* [1901] 1 Ch 294; *Kelly v Hutton* (1868) 16 WR 1182.
89   *Howard v Sadler* [1893] 1 QB 1; *Cooper v Griffin* [1892] 1 QB 740; *Gill v Continental Gas Co* (1872) LR 7 Ex 332.
90   As to such a dissolution, see para **[23.56]**.
91   See generally, Raeburn, 'The So-called Lien of a Partner' (1949) 12 Modern LR 432.

this right is considered elsewhere in this work.[92] This right, like almost all of the rights under the 1890 Act, is subject to the terms of s 19 of the 1890 Act and thus may be varied by agreement between the partners.[93]

Lien Attaches to 'the property of the partnership'

[19.51] Section 39 establishes a lien in respect of the partnership property, but only as regards the residue of that property after the obligations of the firm have been discharged.[94] It should also be noted that s 39 applies a partner's lien to the property of the partnership and the substitution of new stock for old stock will not lead to a loss of the lien.[95] Since the lien attaches only to partnership property, if a firm consists of persons who are partners as to the profits only and the property from which those profits are earned is not owned by the firm, the lien will attach only to the profits of the firm and not to this property. Also, where the partnership property is converted into the separate property of one or more of the partners, the other partners will have no lien against that property. This may arise for example on the dissolution of a partnership, where all the partners agree to divide some of the partnership property *in specie*. Once this has been done, the other partners lose their lien over this property.[96]

[19.52] On the dissolution of the partnership, the lien only attaches to property which was partnership property at the date of dissolution and it does not extend to after-acquired assets. Accordingly, if the continuing partners decide to carry on business and acquire other assets, these assets will not be subject to the departing partner's lien.

Lien Continues on Death or Bankruptcy of a Partner

[19.53] On the death (or bankruptcy) of a partner, that partner's lien does not terminate but remains in existence until his share is paid back to him (or his estate) or is bought out by the continuing partners. Obviously, the right of any person claiming through a deceased or bankrupt partner can be no greater than that of that former partner.[97] Even where it is agreed that the share of a bankrupt or deceased partner will be purchased by the continuing partners, the agreement must be implemented, since if it remains executory the lien will continue. This was the case in *Re Fox*.[98] There, the partnership

---

[92] Paragraph **[26.28]**. Note that it has been suggested that the lien may be used during the life of a partnership, where partnership assets are transferred to a third party who is on notice that they are partnership assets and who subsequently becomes insolvent: l'Anson Banks, *Lindley & Banks on Partnership* (20th edn, 2017) at para 19-25.

[93] See for example the New Zealand case of *Davidson v Wayman* [1984] 2 NZLR 115. See generally in relation to the variation of the rights of partners under the 1890 Act and the exceptional cases in which variation may not be possible, para **[21.88]**.

[94] See for example the Australian case of *United Builders Pty Ltd v Mutual Acceptance Ltd* (1980) 144 CLR 673.

[95] *Stocken v Dawson* (1845) 9 Beav 239; aff'd at (1848) 17 LJ Ch 282; *Skipp v Harwood* (1747) 2 Swan 586.

[96] *Holroyd v Griffiths* (1856) 3 Drew 428; *Re Langmead's Trust* (1855) 24 LJ Ch 237; *Lingen v Simpson* (1824) 1 Sim & St 600.

[97] See the New Zealand Court of Appeal decision in *Re Ward* [1985] 2 NZLR 352 (a bankrupt partner).

[98] *Re Fox* (1915) 49 ILTR 224.

agreement between Fox and Doyle was for the running of a hotel business. It provided for a partner's share in the hotel on his death to belong to and be purchased by the survivor as and from the first day of the next month following the death. The agreement provided also for the payment to be made within six months of the death to the personal representatives of the deceased partner. Doyle died and exactly two months later Fox died. Up to the date of the death of Fox, nothing had been done to give effect to the transfer of Doyle's share in the hotel to Fox. The personal representative of Doyle relied on s 39 of the 1890 Act to support his claim that Doyle's lien over the partnership property, ie the hotel, continued in their favour and that the hotel did not become the property of Fox. O'Connor MR agreed and he held that nothing had occurred to deprive the assets from continuing to be partnership property and thus the partner's lien continued.

'after deducting what may be due from them as partners'

[19.54] Section 39 of the 1890 Act states that the lien may be enforced in respect of 'what may be due to the partners respectively after deducting what may be due from them as partners to the firm'. It is important to bear in mind that the sums which may be deducted, as sums owing by the partners to the firm, must be sums which are owed by them in their capacity as partners. Thus, a partner who has borrowed money which is not partnership money from his partners for his own personal use is entitled to his share of the partnership assets without a deduction of this amount.[99]

'persons claiming through them in respect of their interests'

[19.55] Section 39 of the 1890 Act also provides that the lien may be enforced against the persons claiming through a partner, such as a personal representative or the Official Assignee in bankruptcy. Thus in *Re Ritson*,[100] it was held that a partner in a firm could have enforced his lien against the personal representatives of his deceased partner. In that case the deceased partner had charged his own real estate as security for a partnership debt. On his death he left this real estate to his son and the residue of his estate, including his share in the firm, to his four other children. The assets of the firm were used to pay off all the liabilities of the firm, including the secured debt. However, the four other children, but not the son, claimed that the partnership debt should have been discharged out of the real estate which was charged with it. The court rejected this claim on the grounds that the surviving partner in the firm could have enforced his lien (and so have the assets of the firm applied in payment of the firm's debts) against the personal representative of the deceased partner.

Position of purchasers

[19.56] In addition to a partner being entitled to enforce his lien against the personal representatives of his partner, he is entitled to enforce it against purchasers of partnership property from his co-partner. Such purchasers will also constitute 'persons claiming through' partners within the meaning of s 39 of the 1890 Act. However, a partner cannot enforce a lien over the trading stock which has been purchased in good

---

99   *Ryall v Rowles* (1749) 1 Ves Sen 348; *Croft v Pyke* (1733) 3 P Wms 180.
100   *Re Ritson* [1899] 1 Ch 128.

faith by a third party purchaser from a partner in the firm. Rather, the purchaser will acquire good title to that property.[101] If it were otherwise, the situation would be completely impractical, since the consent of all the partners would be required for the sale of the firm's stock.[102] The situation may be different in relation to the fixed assets of the partnership where the purchaser is aware that it is a fixed asset of the firm.[103]

[19.57] There is, however, a clear distinction to be made between the purchase of partnership property from a partner and a purchase of a partner's share in a firm. Where a purchaser is acquiring a partner's share in the firm, he will necessarily be acquiring it subject to the other partners' liens, regardless of his state of mind.[104]

Position of persons claiming through partner enforcing lien

[19.58] The right of a partner to enforce the lien against the representatives of his co-partners has been noted. Elsewhere in this work, it is noted that the representative of a partner is entitled to enforce this lien on behalf of the partner he represents.[105]

Loss of Lien

[19.59] Under the express terms of s 43 of the 1890 Act, the amount due to a departing partner from a firm is a 'debt accruing at the date of dissolution or death'. This section, in the words of Kingsmill Moore J in the Supreme Court case of *Meagher v Meagher*,[106] is 'directed to limitation of actions'.[107] Since it is a debt, the right which the lien is designed to enforce may be barred under s 11 of the Statute of Limitations 1957, by the lapse of a period of six years from the date of dissolution or death. Therefore, the lien will be unenforceable after this time.

[19.60] It remains to be noted that under the principle of *ex turpi causa non oritur actio*,[108] if a partnership is illegal, the partners have no lien upon the partnership property.[109]

Comparison with Lien under s 41(a) of the 1890 Act

[19.61] In addition to the lien under s 39, there is a lien under s 41(a) of the 1890 Act which arises when the partnership agreement is rescinded on the ground of fraud or misrepresentation of a co-partner. This section states:

> Where a partnership contract is rescinded on the ground of the fraud or misrepresentation of one of the parties thereto, the party entitled to rescind is, without prejudice to any other right, entitled—

---

[101] *Re Langmead's Trust* (1855) 24 LJ Ch 237.
[102] See l'Anson Banks, *Lindley & Banks on Partnership* (20th edn, 2017) at para 19-29.
[103] See l'Anson Banks, *Lindley & Banks on Partnership* (20th edn, 2017) at para 19-30.
[104] *Cavander v Bulteel* (1873) LR 9 Ch 79.
[105] See *Creagh v Creagh* (1862) 13 Ir Ch R 28 and para **[24.25]**.
[106] *Meagher v Meagher* [1961] IR 96.
[107] *Meagher v Meagher* [1961] IR 96 at 112. See para **[24.36]** et seq.
[108] Ie an action does not arise from a base cause.
[109] *Ewing v Osbaldiston* (1837) 2 Myl & C 53.

(a) to a lien on, or right of retention of, the surplus of the partnership assets, after satisfying the partnership liabilities, for any sum of money paid by him for the purchase of a share in the partnership and for any capital contributed by him ...

It is to be noted that this lien is without prejudice to a partner's other rights, such as damages. This lien is narrower than the lien under s 39 of the 1890 Act, in the sense that it applies only to the surplus of the partnership assets, but wider in the sense that there is no deduction for what may be due by the partner to the firm.

Chapter 20

Litigation between Partners

INTRODUCTION

[20.01]

'Partnership actions always take a long time and, indeed, are one of the most expensive and unsatisfactory types of action which we have.'

Kenny J in *O'Connor v Woods*.[1]

If encouragement was needed to try and resolve differences between partners without resorting to litigation, this is provided by Kenny J's opening words in that case of an 'acrimonious and undignified dispute between four well known accountants'.[2] This view of partnership disputes was reiterated by the Supreme Court, albeit in the context of quasi-partnerships,[3] when Murphy J observed that partnership disputes were similar to matrimonial proceedings in that:

'They both involve an examination of the conduct of the parties over a period of years and usually a determination by them to assert rights rather than solve problems. It may well be that the disparate forms of litigation are frequently fuelled by a bitterness borne of rejection: matrimonial or commercial. In neither discipline can the courts persuade the parties that it is in their best interests to direct their attention to solving their problems rather than litigating them.'[4]

[20.02] While repeating the observations of the Irish judiciary on this subject may persuade some partners to try and solve their problems by mediation or other non-adversarial methods,[5] actions between partners will often be considered by parties to those disputes. The procedural rules applicable to litigation by and against a partnership have been considered elsewhere in this work.[6] In this chapter, actions between the

---

1   *O'Connor v Woods* (22 January 1976) HC, at p 7 of the transcript. See generally regarding partnership disputes, Stoakes, 'Trouble a' t mill (partnership disputes)' (1999) 143 SJ 439; Day, 'An effective new law for the resolution of partnership disputes' (1998) 148 NLJ 838; Payne, 'Partners behaving badly' (1997) 18 Co Law 210; Kennan, 'Partners in dispute' (1993) 112 Accountancy 102.

2   *O'Connor v Woods* (22 January 1976) HC.

3   This case involved an action under the Companies Act 1963, s 205 (the predecessor to the Companies Act 2014, s 212) by a quasi-partner.

4   *Re Murray Consultants Ltd* [1997] 3 IR 23 at 42. See also *Rickard v Rickard* [2016] IECA 158 in which a dispute regarding the sale of partnership land, referred to by Irvine J as a 'difficult and tragic saga' continued for five years after a court order for sale was originally granted in favour of the plaintiff following the dissolution of the partnership.

5   It has been suggested at para **[21.166]**, that partners include a compulsory mediation clause in their partnership agreement.

6   See para **[12.01]** et seq.

partners themselves will be considered. This will involve a consideration of the different types of action, defences to those actions and the instances in which the court will not interfere. This will be done under the following headings:

 I.   General;
 II. Action for an Account of Partnership Dealings;
 III. Specific Performance;
 IV. Injunctions;
 V.   Receivers and Managers;
 VI. Actions for Misrepresentation;
 VII. Arbitration;
 VIII. Damages;
 IX. Where the Court will not Interfere between Partners; and
 X.   Costs of a Partnership Action.

Overview

[20.03] Disputes between partners may involve a wide variety of potential actions ranging from a claim for damages to an application for the appointment of a receiver to the firm. However, regardless of the form of action, two important characteristics of the partnership relationship should be borne in mind, as they will commonly influence the outcome of the litigation.

[20.04] First, one of the grand characteristics of a partnership is the fact that it is not a separate legal entity, but an aggregate of all the partners. For this reason, the partners are not treated as debtors or creditors of the firm while the partnership continues, since to do so would involve a person owing himself a debt. It is only on a final settlement of accounts between the partners on the firm's dissolution that they are regarded as debtors and creditors. It is for this reason that the courts are reluctant to allow a partner sue his co-partners in respect of a single partnership obligation. Instead, the courts lean in favour of all partnership obligations being determined as part of the general settlement of accounts on the dissolution of the firm.

[20.05] Another important characteristic of the partnership contract is that it requires a high degree of confidence and trust between the partners.[7] It is therefore understandable that the courts would be reluctant to compel an unwilling person to be another person's partner and it follows that the specific performance of partnerships, while not unheard of, is certainly not granted as a matter of course. For the same reason, the courts favour granting other remedies such as injunctions and appointing receivers/managers only as part of the dissolution of partnerships rather than during their life. This judicial attitude can be easily justified since the very fact that a court application is being made in the first place indicates that the degree of trust and confidence necessary for the partnership to continue may be absent. Thus, any court order which is intended to apply during the life of the partnership may turn out to be futile and clearly the court does not wish to involve itself in making such orders.

---

[7]   See generally regarding the fiduciary duties of partners, para **[15.01]** et seq.

I.   GENERAL

[20.06] Before considering each of the different types of partnership action, reference will be made to certain concepts which are of general application to litigation between partners, regardless of the type of action.

Action by Partner Against his own Firm

[20.07] Before the passing of the Supreme Court of Judicature Act (Ireland) 1877, proceedings could not be brought between a firm and one of the partners. Indeed, the general leaning against such actions continues today, since as noted by Dixon J in the High Court case of *Hawkins v Rogers*,[8] 'by so doing [the partner] would be the plaintiff and also the defendant in the same action'.[9] This is because, as a partner is jointly liable with his co-partners for the firm's obligations,[10] if he were allowed to sue his firm, this is akin to suing himself. In *Heffernan & Anor v Murray & Ors*,[11] the plaintiffs, a husband and wife, took legal action against the Ballykisteen Developments Partnership. Twelve of the members of that partnership were listed as defendants (together with a thirteenth defendant against whom a claim of holding out under s 14(1) of the 1890 Act by Mr and Mrs Heffernan was unsuccessful), but Mrs Heffernan, the second-named plaintiff, was also a member of that partnership (but was not named as one of the defendants). The dispute related to a contract for sale entered into by the partnership (including Mrs Heffernan) and Binchy J considered whether Mrs Heffernan could issue proceedings against the other members the partnership to compel them to complete the obligations of the partnership under a contract for sale entered into by it with Mrs Heffernan and her husband. He found that if Mrs Heffernan could seek damages against a partnership in which she was a partner by simply not listing herself as a defendant, it would be open to a partner in a partnership to be awarded damages without a full account of the partnership's dealings being taken, which could lead to the unjust enrichment of the partner to whom damages had been awarded.

[20.08] However, notwithstanding the above, this general leaning against such actions is no more than that. Accordingly, Ord 14, r 10[12] of the Rules of the Superior Courts[13] contemplates: 'actions between a firm and one of its members, and…actions between firms having one or more members in common.' Clearly, where two firms, with a common partner, sue each other this will technically involve the common partner being a plaintiff and a defendant in the same action. However, the general distaste of the courts for actions between a partner and his own firm, is still to be found in Ord 14, r 10, which provides that no execution shall be issued in such actions without the leave of the court. In granting such leave, the court may direct the taking of accounts and inquiries.

---

[8]   *Hawkins v Rogers* [1951] IR 48.

[9]   *Hawkins v Rogers* [1951] IR 48 at 60.

[10]   See further regarding a partner's liability for the obligations of his partners, para **[10.01]** et seq.

[11]   *Heffernan & Anor v Murray & Ors* [2015] IEHC 196.

[12]   See further para **[12.11]** et seq and see *Bradley v Alder* (1829) 2 Ir Law Rec 348.

[13]   SI 15/1986 (as amended).

[20.09] In light of the foregoing, the more usual action in a dispute between partners is for a partner to sue his co-partners, rather than the firm, and it is this action with which we are primarily concerned in this chapter.

[20.10] It remains to be observed that where the partnership in question is a partnership at will, the service of the proceedings by a partner for the firm's dissolution will itself dissolve the partnership.[14]

Parties to the Partnership Action

[20.11] As a general rule, all partners should be parties to a partnership action. The effect of this general rule is illustrated by *Sugrue v Hibernian Bank*.[15] There, a partner sought an injunction and the appointment of a receiver to a partnership, called the Hibernian Bank, which had over 800 members. In spite of the size of the partnership, MacMahon MR refused the order on the grounds that all the partners were not parties to the action.[16] However the effect of the principle that all partners should be parties to a partnership action has been modified considerably by the fact that a firm may now be sued in its firm-name,[17] and this is the case, even where the action is taken by a partner in the firm.[18] Furthermore, as has been noted elsewhere in this work, the failure to join a partner to a partnership action is no longer fatal.[19]

[20.12] In addition, in the context of disputes between partners, the availability of representative actions under Ord 15, r 9 of the Rules of the Superior Courts[20] will be of significance, particularly in those accountancy and legal firms which have well in excess of 20 partners.[21] In such cases, it may be useful to join partners to the action as representative plaintiffs or defendants. Such representative proceedings are only appropriate where the represented group of partners shares the same interest in the proceedings. If the interest of each partner is distinct from and in conflict with his partners, then representative proceedings will be inappropriate and each partner should be joined to the action.[22] A judgment or order resulting from the representative proceedings binds all the partners represented.[23]

---

[14]   *Unsworth v Jordan* [1896] WNP 2(5).

[15]   *Sugrue v Hibernian Bank* (1829) 2 Ir Law Rec 285.

[16]   The Master of the Rolls seemed to recognise the merit in having a different rule, since he states that: 'All this might be a good reason for adopting a new principle; but how can I act as you require in the face of decisions and recent ones too, quite the other way?' (1829) 2 Ir Law Rec 285 at 294. See also *Mallet v Boileau* (1835) 3 Ir Law Rec (ns) 264 where the Master of the Rolls refused to grant an injunction or appoint a receiver where, however numerous the members of the firm, they were all not parties to the action. In both cases the Masters of the Rolls expressed themselves bound by the decision in *Van Sandau v Moore* (1826) 1 Russ 441.

[17]   Rules of the Superior Courts, Ord 14, r 1, see para **[12.11]**.

[18]   This is implicit in the terms of the Rules of the Superior Courts, Ord 14, r 10.

[19]   See para **[12.56]** and see the Rules of the Superior Courts, Ord 15, r 13.

[20]   See for example *Smith v The Cork and Bandon Railway Co* (1869) 3 Ir Eq R 356. See also *Bruce v Donaldson* (1918) 53 ILTR 24 (action against an unincorporated association). See generally in relation to representative actions, Ó Floinn, *Practice and Procedure in the Superior Courts* (2nd edn, 2008) at pp 158–159.

[21]   As to such firms, see generally, para **[4.29]** et seq.

[22]   See *Re Hart* (1896) 2 Ch 788.

Forum for Actions

[20.13] The jurisdiction of the courts to deal with partnership actions[24] is vested in the High Court.[25] This is subject to the limited jurisdiction of the Circuit Court.[26] Thus under s 22 of the Courts (Supplemental Provisions) Act 1961,[27] proceedings for the dissolution of a partnership or the taking of partnership or other accounts are vested in the Circuit Court, save where the property of the partnership consists of land with a market value in excess of €3,000,000.[28] At the election of the plaintiff, the Circuit Court in question may be the judge of the circuit where the partnership business is or was carried on, or the judge of the circuit where the defendant or one of them resides or carries on business.[29] Where the partnership action is a claim for damages of €75,000 or less, it should be taken in the Circuit Court.[30]

---

23 Rules of the Superior Courts, Ord 15, r 22(2).

24 As regards an action for dissolution under Partnership Act 1890, s 35, see para **[25.11]** et seq.

25 Under s 36(5) of the Supreme Court of Judicature Act (Ireland) 1877 and by virtue of s 8 of the Courts (Supplemental Provisions) Act 1961, the 'dissolution of partnerships or the taking of partnership or other accounts' is vested in the High Court. See *Rainford v Newell-Roberts* [1962] IR 95 for an example of a case where a judgment in an action for account between the partners in a medical partnership (which had been given by the English High Court) was not enforced by Davitt P for want of submission to jurisdiction by the Irish resident partner.

26 Note that the District Court does not have jurisdiction since disputes between partners are equitable actions and as such are heard in the Circuit Court or the High Court (on appeal to the Court of Appeal), see also para **[25.12]**. See also the statement of Lord Millet in *Hurst v Bryk* [2000] 2 WLR 740 at 747–48 that: '[d]isputes between partners and the dissolution and winding up of partnerships, however, have always fallen within the jurisdiction of the Court of Chancery. This is because, while partnership is a consensual arrangement based on agreement, it is more than a simple contract ... it is a continuing personal as well as commercial relationship.'

27 Under s 22 and the Third Sch, ref 18 of the Courts (Supplemental Provisions) Act 1961 as amended by s 2(1)(d) of the Courts Act 1981 and by s 45(2) of the Civil Liability and Courts Act 2004 (s 45(2) was eventually commenced on 11 January 2017 by the Civil Liability and Courts Act 2004 (Commencement) Order 2017 (SI 2 of 2017)).

28 A definition of the term 'market value' was inserted into s 2 of the 1961 Act by s 45(1) of the 2004 Act (again with effect from 11 January 2017) as follows: 'market value' means, in relation to land, the price that would have been obtained in respect of the unencumbranced fee simple were the land to have been sold on the open market, in the year immediately preceding the bringing of the proceedings concerned, in such manner and subject to such conditions as might reasonably be calculated to have resulted in the vendor obtaining the best price for the land.'

29 Courts (Supplemental Provisions) Act 1961, Fourth Sch, ref 46. This provision adapts the reference to a 'court' in s 45 of the 1890 Act to include such a Circuit Court judge.

30 Courts of Justice Act 1924, s 77A, as most recently amended by the Courts and Civil Law (Miscellaneous Provisions) Act 2013.

II.   ACTION FOR AN ACCOUNT OF PARTNERSHIP DEALINGS

[20.14] Since the very *raison d'être* for partnerships is to make a profit,[31] it is not surprising that the most common action instituted between partners is the action for an account of partnership dealings, since this is the means by which partners claim a share of the profits made by their co-partners.[32] The right to have an account of the partnership's dealings and transactions is enshrined in s 28 of the 1890 Act which states that: '[p]artners are bound to render true accounts and full information of all things affecting the partnership to any partner or his legal representatives.' The right to an account has long been recognised by the Irish courts, Brady LC noting that they 'would, as a matter of course, be entitled of common right to have an account of the partnership taken in this court'.[33]

[20.15] In view of the importance of profits to the very existence of a partnership,[34] in many cases a court will only contemplate an action between partners if it is brought as part of an account of partnership dealings.[35] However, where the action between the partners is not a partnership action, then there will be no need for an account of partnership dealings to be taken. *Hawkins v Rogers*[36] involved a partnership which was selling by auction a horse called 'Lonely Maid' with its engagements in a number of prestigious Irish races, namely the Curragh Foal Plate, the 1,000 Guineas and the Irish Oaks. One of the partners in the firm, Hawkins, purchased 'Lonely Maid' at the auction. However, the other partner, Rogers, struck the horse out of these prestigious engagements subsequent to the sale. Hawkins took a personal action against Rogers for the damage caused by the defendant's actions. The defendant claimed that the plaintiff could not sue the defendant as a partner for damages and that his only action was for an

---

[31]   Partnership Act 1890, s 1(1) and see para **[2.62]** et seq.

[32]   See for example *Heslin v Fay (1)* (1884) 15 LR Ir 431, where Sullivan LC ordered the dissolution of the partnership and an account of the value of the stock, property, credits and effects of the partnership, an account of the profit and loss and an account of all sums advanced or paid to or to the use of the partnership by the plaintiff or defendants, as well as undrawn profits and he ordered that all proper credits be given to the partners.

[33]   *Murphy v Keller* (1851) 2 Ir Ch R 417 at 421.

[34]   The definition of partnership requires the parties to be carrying on business 'with a view of profit': Partnership Act 1890, s 1(1).

[35]   See however *Headly v Luby* (1868) 2 ILTR 302 where the parties had agreed to share the profits and losses of the firm equally. Luby had acquired cattle for the partnership but had not paid for them and the seller of the cattle successfully sued Headly for the purchase price. Headly sought a declaration that Luby owed him half of the purchase price which Headly had paid. There was an objection to the court's jurisdiction on the grounds that it related to a partnership account and should not be dealt with as an isolated matter. The court held that while this was a matter to be settled in taking partnership accounts, it was prepared to declare that the money was paid on Luby's behalf and thus gave a decree for the sum claimed. This can perhaps be explained on the basis of it being a declaratory judgement which goes no further than dealing with this disputed item between the partners. See also *Rickard v Rickard* [2016] IECA 158 in which accounts and enquiries were directed to be carried out after an order for the sale of partnership lands had been granted in 2011 following the dissolution of a partnership – once those accounts and enquiries were carried out, the plaintiff re-applied for, and obtained, a further order for partition and sale.

[36]   *Hawkins v Rogers* [1951] IR 48.

account of partnership dealings. However, Dixon J held that the action was not a partnership action, but a personal one and he awarded damages. In addition, Hawkins attempted to amend the pleadings, in order to claim that the defendant's actions also constituted a breach of trust by him as a partner. However, Dixon J held that such an amendment would mean that the proceedings would become a partnership action and as such would have to be dealt with by means of partnership account:

> 'In the case of an action founded on the partnership relation, it is well settled, and indeed is inherent in the nature of a partnership, that one isolated partnership transaction cannot be investigated by itself, but that the proper remedy and only way of disposing of the matter is to take a full and mutual account of all the partnership dealings.'[37]

[20.16] For this reason, a court will rarely[38] grant an order for a liquidated sum between partners, without ordering an account of partnership dealings. This principle was stated by Sullivan MR in *Norris v Sadleir*:[39]

> 'It is a settled principle that no partner can sue another in a Court of Law without an express stipulation to that effect in the partnership deed; for this reason, that before the action can be maintained, the partnership accounts must be taken.'[40]

[20.17] The rationale for this approach to the taking of a partnership account is that while the partnership continues, partners are not deemed to be debtors and creditors as regards their partnership dealings and will not be so deemed until the firm is wound up or there has been a final settlement of accounts between them.[41] On this basis, the courts will only in the rarest circumstances[42] allow a partner a right of action against his partner for a balance owing between them or for money advanced by one partner to the firm, if they have not agreed on a final settlement of accounts. However, the position is different in relation to a partner who departs from a continuing partnership, since in such a situation his former partners are his creditors in relation to any amount owed to him.

[20.18] The application for an account of partnership dealings is made pursuant to Ord 33 of the Rules of the Superior Courts.[43]

---

[37] *Hawkins v Rogers* [1951] IR 48 at 54.

[38] In *O'Connor v Woods* (22 January 1976) HC, there was a technical dissolution of the partnership caused by the plaintiff's departure and he sought a return of his capital from the firm. The defendants counter-claimed that they were owed moneys by the plaintiff as a result of his taking files from the firm and the High Court ordered a full account of partnership dealings to be taken by the Examiner. For this reason it is apprehended that *Dodd v White* (1892) 26 ILTR 402 is no longer good law. There, Dodd and White were solicitors in partnership in Dublin and Dodd claimed that he was owed certain sums by White under the terms of their partnership agreement. White claimed that he was entitled to set-off sums which he claimed to have advanced to Dodd. A decree was granted for some of the money claimed and it was held that set-off had no application to the suit in dispute. See further regarding the right to damages for a breach of the partnership agreement, para **[20.96]**.

[39] *Norris v Sadleir* (1872) 6 Ir Eq R 580. Note that this case was decided prior to the Supreme Court of Judicature Act (Ireland) 1877.

[40] *Norris v Sadleir* (1872) 6 Ir Eq R 580 at 586.

[41] *Carr v Smith* (1843) 5 QB 128; *Richardson v Bank of England* (1838) 4 My & Cr 165; *Bovill v Hammond* (1827) 6 B & C 149.

[42] See para **[20.27]**.

[43] SI 15/1986. See generally Ó Floinn, *Practice and Procedure in the Superior Courts* (2nd edn, 2008) at p 312 et seq.

Persons Entitled to an Account

[20.19] The partners themselves, their personal representatives and trustees in bankruptcy are entitled to an account against each other.[44] However, as noted elsewhere in this work,[45] under s 31 of the 1890 Act an assignee of a partner's share is not entitled to an account from the other partners during the life of the partnership, but is entitled to an account from the date of dissolution of the firm.

Compelling a partner to account without application to court

[20.20] A partner who wishes to compel his co-partner to account for partnership dealings should initiate an action for account. It is perhaps self-evident that he should not use self-help remedies to persuade his partner to account for partnership dealings. In *Re Jackson*,[46] a solicitor sought to compel his partner to account to him for the profits of the firm by withholding the papers of a particular client. Not surprisingly, MacMahon MR refused to allow the client to be mixed up with the settlement of the partnership accounts in this manner and did not permit a solicitor's lien[47] to be used in this way.

Cases in which Account will be Ordered without a Dissolution

[20.21] Originally, it was the case that an 'account could not be prayed for without a dissolution'.[48] It has been noted,[49] that under the terms of s 31(1) of the 1890 Act, this is still the case as regards an assignee of a partner, who is not entitled to an account of partnership dealings, unless the partnership is dissolved.

[20.22] However, as regards an action between partners, there is no good reason in principle to deny a partner the right to have an account taken of the partnership dealings because the partnership is not dissolved. Accordingly, it is no longer correct to say that an account will only be ordered as part of a dissolution of the partnership, and actions for account have been ordered without a dissolution in the following situations:

(a)   where a partner seeks to withhold private profits,[50] in which his co-partners are interested;[51]

(b)   where there is a fixed term partnership and one partner seeks to exclude or expel a partner or to force him to seek a dissolution of the partnership;[52] and

(c)   where the existence of the partnership is denied.[53]

---

[44]   For example in *Creagh v Creagh* (1862) 13 Ir Ch R 28, the account was granted in favour of a deceased partner's children against the personal representative of his co-partner.

[45]   See para **[19.16]** et seq.

[46]   *Re Jackson* (1834) 3 Ir Law Rec 92.

[47]   See further regarding solicitor's liens, para **[3.101]**.

[48]   Per Brady LC in *Bolton v Carmichael* (1856) 1 Ir Jur (ns) 298 at 299.

[49]   See generally para **[19.17]**.

[50]   See generally as regards such private profits, para **[15.27]** et seq.

[51]   *Beck v Kantorowicz* (1857) 3 K & J 230; *Hichens v Congreve* (1828) 4 Russ 562.

[52]   *Fairthorne v Weston* (1844) 3 Hare 387; *Harrison v Armitage* (1819) 4 Madd 143.

[53]   *Knowles v Haughton* (1805) 11 Ves Jr 168.

[20.23] In *Bradley v Alder*,[54] it was alleged that the defendant partners made every effort to encourage the plaintiff partner to sell his interest in the firm. They did this by holding all the partnership meetings in London, where they resided rather than in Dublin, by falsifying the accounts and by manufacturing a large debt in order to make the business appear ruinous. In these circumstances, MacMahon MR ordered an account of partnership dealings without requiring a dissolution.

[20.24] It is perhaps self-evident that where the partnership is in dissolution, an action for account will be granted almost as a matter of course.[55]

[20.25] An account may be taken as a general account (usually with a view to winding up the partnership) or a limited account of a particular transaction (such as where a partner is required to account for private profits).[56]

Defences to an Action for Account

[20.26] An action for an account of partnership dealings is an equitable remedy and will be subject to the general defences to equitable remedies which are considered hereafter.[57] In addition, there are a number of defences which are specific to the action for account.[58]

Parties agree to action without account

[20.27] It was established in *Norris v Sadleir*[59] that partners may agree that an action can be maintained between themselves without the necessity for an account to be taken. In such a case, the partners' agreement will be a good defence to a claim that the issue should be resolved by a partnership account. This issue was of particular relevance in banking partnerships, since it allowed the firm to pursue a partner for outstanding loans, without having to have an account of moneys which were owed by the banking partnership to the partner. The partnership in *Norris v Sadleir*[60] was a bank and Sullivan MR stated that:

> '[P]artners may make any contract they like, and one of the fairest contracts that can be made between partners, in the case of a Bank, is that each partner shall, in certain cases, be liable to the firm, or to a trustee for the firm, to repay the sums he *prima facie* owes the firm for advances, without having the partnership accounts taken; provided of course a stipulation to that effect may be contained in any partnership deed.'[61]

---

54   *Bradley v Alder* (1829) 2 Ir Law Rec 348.
55   See *Murphy v Keller* (1851) 2 Ir Ch R 417. See also *Bolton v Carmichael* (1856) 1 Ir Jur (ns) 298.
56   *Beck v Kantorowicz* (1857) 3 K & J 230; *Hichens v Congreve* (1828) 1 R & M 150.
57   See para **[20.99]**.
58   There may also be circumstances in which an action for account is unnecessary: see the comments of Peart J in *Boylan v McNulty and (by order) McGuinness, as personal representative of the late O'Herlihy* (13 February 2014) HC.
59   *Norris v Sadleir* (1872) 6 Ir Eq R 580.
60   *Norris v Sadleir* (1872) 6 Ir Eq R 580.
61   *Norris v Sadleir* (1872) 6 Ir Eq R 580 at 586. In that case, the receiver claimed against the assets of the deceased partner under the deed of partnership in respect of sums advanced by the firm to the deceased partner, even though no demand had been made upon the partner during his lifetime. (contd.../)

Existence of a settled account

[20.28] If the partners have previously agreed an account between them, this is known as a 'settled account' and provides a defence to a claim by one of the partners for an account of matters covered by the settled account.[62] In order to constitute a settled account, it should be in writing and all the items therein should have been acquiesced to by all the parties.[63] Thus, merely rendering an account to a partner is not a defence to the latter seeking an action for an account of partnership dealings.[64]

[20.29] The case of *Sim v Sim*[65] concerned a partnership between two corn merchants in Co Sligo. Eight years after the dissolution of the partnership, an account was drawn up by the plaintiff partner in his handwriting which omitted certain debts due to the partnership, since it was not certain if these debts would be paid. On the basis of this account, the defendant partner paid the stated balance to the plaintiff. It was held that the account was a settled account, even though it omitted these doubtful items. Cusack MR held that '[t]he law, as well as the act of the parties, provides that accounts settled shall not be set aside'.[66] At first instance, the Master's Court had held that the account was not a settled account since it did not contain a capital account, a profit and loss account and a balance sheet. However, this was rejected on appeal where Cusack MR noted that the Master:

> 'considers (adopting the opinion of the accountant) that, unless an account between partners be drawn up in precise form he suggests, that it is no account. I cannot concur in that proposition, which was never, up to the present time, decided in any case.'[67]

---

[61]   (\...contd) Under the terms of the deed, a demand was required to be made of 'him' and one was made of his personal representative. On this basis the claim was not allowed. It was held that as the demand would alter the status of the partner, the partner could not be turned into a debtor, unless a demand was made during his lifetime.

[62]   It is important to bear in mind that, while a settled account may be used as a defence to an action for an account, there is no obligation on partners to settle an account on the dissolution of their partnership. Their failure to do so will not prevent them from claiming against each other for any amounts outstanding. *Re McManus* (1858) 7 Ir Ch R 82 involved a grocery partnership between McManus and Middleton in Mullingar. On the dissolution of the partnership, there was no settlement of accounts between the partners, but Middleton received a bond from McManus for £300. On the bankruptcy of McManus, Middleton sought to prove this debt. It was alleged by the assignees in bankruptcy that Middleton should not be allowed to prove in the bankruptcy on the grounds that there was no settled account between McManus and Middleton. It was held by Macan J that just because there was no settlement of account as part of the dissolution did not mean that Middleton should not be entitled to prove on the separate estate of the bankrupt partner.

[63]   *Clancarty v Latouche* (1810) 1 Ball & Beatty 420 per Manners LC which involved the Dublin banking partnership of Latouche Bank.

[64]   *Clements v Bowes* (1853) 1 Drew 684.

[65]   *Sim v Sim* (1861) 11 Ir Ch R 310.

[66]   *Sim v Sim* (1861) 11 Ir Ch R 310 at 325, quoting Lord Eldon in *Chambers v Goldwin* (1805) 9 Ves 265.

[67]   *Sim v Sim* (1861) 11 Ir Ch R 310 at 322.

Cusack MR's decision must be supported since if the approach of the Master's Court was followed, partners would effectively not be able to settle an account between themselves, without going to the expense of employing an accountant, which cannot be supported in principle.

Settled account may be set aside for fraud or error

[20.30] However, it should be noted that settled accounts may be set aside in certain circumstances. As noted by Cusack MR in *Sim v Sim*,[68] settled accounts 'shall not be set aside but for fraud, or surcharged and falsified but for error'.[69] Similarly in *Drew v Power*,[70] Redesdale LC observed the following rule regarding the opening of settled accounts by the courts:

> 'One rule material to observe in all cases of account, is, that where there has been a settlement of account, and either the account has been signed, or a security taken on the footing of the account, a Court of Equity does not open this transaction and throw it again between the parties, as if no such transaction had happened, unless the evidence which is produced (and that evidence founded on charges in the bill) shews the whole transaction to be so iniquitous that it ought not to be brought forward at all to affect the party sought to be bound.'[71]

[20.31] In *Moore v Moore*,[72] a settled account between the members of a family involved in a farming partnership was opened because of the use by the defendant partner of the partnership funds for his own personal business interests. The Chancery Master, Master Ellison, observed:

> 'Although a settled account between the partners is a good ground of defence to an action for an account, in special circumstances the court may reopen the accounts or give liberty to surcharge and falsify. Settled accounts are not usually reopened *in toto* except upon the ground of fraud, or numerous and important errors, or mistakes affecting the whole account; otherwise the court will not usually do more than give liberty to surcharge and falsify. In the absence of fraud, accounts are not reopened in favour of a party who had stood by and acquiesced in them; but acquiescence in the principle of keeping an account does not amount to acquiescence in the accuracy of the items.'[73]

Since the plaintiff partner had nothing to do with the accounts of the partnership, he was unaware that the partnership funds were being siphoned-off by the defendant and it was therefore held that he was not a 'party who has stood by and acquiesced' and combined with the defendant's fraud. This justified the accounts being re-opened.

---

68 *Sim v Sim* (1861) 11 Ir Ch R 310.
69 *Sim v Sim* (1861) 11 Ir Ch R 310, quoting Lord Eldon in *Chambers v Goldwin* (1805) 9 Ves 265.
70 *Drew v Power* (1803) 1 Sch & Lef 182.
71 *Drew v Power* (1803) 1 Sch & Lef 182 at 192.
72 *Moore v Moore* (27 February 1998) HC (NI).
73 Master Ellison relied on *Gething v Keighley* (1878) 9 Ch D 547 and *Halsbury's Laws of England* (4th edn, 1994) Butterworths.

Denial of partnership

[20.32] It goes without saying that a possible defence to an action for account is a denial of the existence of a partnership between the parties.[74]

Arbitration

[20.33] Another defence to an action for account is that the subject matter of the dispute has previously been settled by an arbitration award which award is binding on the applicant partner.[75] However, where moneys are received on account of the partnership after the arbitration award, the award is not a defence to an action for an account of these moneys.[76]

[20.34] Where there is simply an agreement to refer a disputed matter to arbitration, this will not constitute a defence to an action for account.

Personal action between partners does not require taking of an account

[20.35] Although, not strictly a defence to an action for an account, the case of *Hawkins v Rogers*[77] illustrates that if the action between partners is not a partnership action, but a personal one, then the partner taking the action need not seek a partnership account.[78]

Illegality of partnership

[20.36] Although not specific to an action for an account of partnership dealings, the illegality of the partnership will clearly offer a defence to such an action. In the famous case of *Everet v Williams*,[79] an account of partnership dealings by one partner against the other was rejected by the court, as it concerned a partnership of highwaymen. The bill in equity filed by the plaintiff stated that he was experienced in commodities such as rings and watches and it was agreed that they both would provide the necessary tools of the trade namely horses, saddles and weapons. They also agreed to share equally in the costs of the venture, ie the expenses involved in staying at inns, alehouses and taverns. The bill stated that they had successfully 'dealt with' a gentleman for a gold watch and other goods and the plaintiff sought an account of these dealings. This case may have discouraged a line of partnership actions between highwaymen, since not only was the action dismissed on the grounds that the partnership was illegal,[80] but in addition, the costs were ordered to be paid by the counsel who signed the bill, the solicitor for the plaintiff was attached and fined, and the plaintiff and defendant were hanged.[81]

---

[74] In *Sim v Sim* (1861) 11 Ir Ch R 310, there was a second application for an account in relation to a second business relationship between the parties. This application was met with the successful defence that there was no partnership between the parties but rather an agency relationship.

[75] *Routh v Peach* (1795) 3 Anstr 637; *Tittenson v Peat* (1747) 3 Atk 529.

[76] *Spencer v Spencer* (1827) 2 Y & J 249.

[77] *Hawkins v Rogers* [1951] IR 48.

[78] See para **[20.15]**.

[79] *Everet v Williams* (1725) 9 LQR 197.

[80] See generally in relation to illegal partnerships, para **[9.01]** et seq.

[81] See Anon, 'The Highwayman's Case' (1893) 9 LQR 197.

Manner in which Account is Taken

[20.37] In ordering the taking of an account, the court should order that regard be had to the financial standing between the partners inter se, between the partners and third parties, and that account be taken of such items as advances made by partners to the firm and that just allowances be granted to the partners.[82] In addition, the court should order that all cross-claims between the partners be settled and it should provide for the apportionment of profits and losses between partners in accordance with their agreement or the 1890 Act.[83]

[20.38] The court, in ordering the taking of an account, has a discretion as to the basis upon which the account is to be taken. Indeed, in exercising this discretion, the court may decide to reserve its position until after it receives details of the account. In *Creagh v Creagh*,[84] in ordering an account to be taken, Smith MR stated that:

> 'It is not a convenient course to call upon this Court, on this appeal, to decide the principle on which the account should be taken. It will, I think, be more satisfactory that the account should be taken, before the court should offer an opinion ... a Court should not bind itself by a declaration previous to the accounts being taken.'[85]

[20.39] The court is likely to take account of the terms of the partnership agreement between the parties in exercising this discretion. Thus, in *Heslin v Fay (1)*,[86] Sullivan LC used a clause of the partnership agreement between the parties as the basis for his direction on the manner in which the accounts were to be taken. The partnership agreement provided for the goodwill of the firm to be sold by a departing partner to a continuing partner at a price equal to one year's profits of the firm. Thus, Sullivan LC ordered that in calculating the firm's net profits, there should be added thereto, one year's profits in respect of the firm's goodwill.[87]

[20.40] In taking the partnership account, regard should be had to the following matters.

Period of account

[20.41] The partnership account will normally be taken from the date of the commencement of the partnership or the date of the last settled account, if there is one.[88] The account will extend at least to the date of dissolution of the partnership, but in many cases it should extend beyond this date until the firm is fully wound up. This is implicit

---

82 *West v Skip* (1749) 1 Ves Sen 239. In relation to such allowances between partners, see generally para **[14.40]** et seq.

83 In relation to the sharing of profits and losses, see generally para **[14.04]** et seq.

84 *Creagh v Creagh* (1862) 13 Ir Ch R 28.

85 *Creagh v Creagh* (1862) 13 Ir Ch R 28 at 47–48.

86 *Heslin v Fay (1)* (1884) 15 LR Ir 431.

87 Although clearly goodwill is not part of a firm's net profits and this should not be interpreted as an appropriate way to approach all partnership accounts. See para **[18.06]**.

88 See for example *Heslin v Fay (1)* (1884) 15 LR Ir 431 at 449, where Sullivan LC ordered that an account be taken from the date of the last settled account (30 June 1880): '[a]nd, the Defendants in open Court so consenting, it is ordered that the settled account of the 30th day of June, 1880, be taken as binding on the parties, and that no account or inquiry previous to that date be taken.'

in the terms of the 1890 Act, ie s 38 of the 1890 Act (the continuing authority of the partners after the firm's dissolution for the purposes of winding up the firm) and s 42 of the 1890 Act (the right of an outgoing partner to a share of profits made after the firm's dissolution using his share of the firm's assets). In addition, in *Walmsley v Walmsley*,[89] a partner continued in possession of the partnership premises after the death of his co-partner. On a taking of an account of partnership dealings, Sugden LC upheld the Master's order that half of the market rent of those premises, for the period post-dissolution, should be paid to the deceased partner's estate.

[20.42] However, where the surviving partner actually continues the trade which had been carried on by the firm, the profits thereby created will not be the subject of a partnership account. This is because there is no longer a partnership with the former partner and, therefore, there can be no account of partnership dealings. Thus in *Booth v Parks*,[90] Hart LC[91] refused to order an account of partnership dealings where a surviving partner continued the business of the firm after the death of his partner. Of course, to the extent that the surviving partner is using the deceased partner's share of the partnership assets, the deceased partner's estate will be able to claim the share of the profits of the business which are attributable to this use under s 42 of the 1890 Act.[92]

Estimated profits in the absence of books

[20.43] Where a partner refuses to produce the firm's books for the purposes of the taking of an account, the court will estimate the profits of the firm and presumptions may be made against the guilty partner.[93] In *Walmsley v Walmsley*,[94] the personal representative of William Walmsley took an action against the defendant for an account of partnership dealings. The defendant, who had possession of the partnership books, wilfully and fraudulently refused to produce them in court. In the absence of other evidence, the court was forced to estimate the profits of the firm during its lifetime. It did so by holding that William Walmsley should be entitled to one half of the original capital which he had subscribed, plus 10% per annum for each year of business of the partnership. On appeal, Sugden LC upheld this decision, rejecting the defendant's claim that he had not been given credit for payments made by him and noting, obiter, that he would have supported an estimate of the profits based on 20% per annum of the original capital.

---

89 *Walmsley v Walmsley* (1846) 3 Jo & La T 556.

90 *Booth v Parks* (1828) 1 Mol 465.

91 This case is also interesting for Hart LC's strong opinions on the values of cross-examination: 'for as cross-examinations are at present, they are mere random hits in the dark. When I was very young at the bar, I used to cross-examine; but I soon gave it up. For the last thirty years I hardly recommended it. I may say I left it off as hopeless. I abandoned it in despair.' (1828) 1 Mol 465 at 467.

92 See further regarding this right under s 42, para **[26.63]**.

93 See *Moore v Moore* (27 February 1998) HC (NI) where Master Ellison relied on l'Anson Banks, *Lindley & Banks on Partnership* (17th edn, 1995) at para 22-31 (now at para 22.15 of the 20th edition of that work (2017)). This case also lists the types of items which one would expect to receive from a discovery related to the taking of a partnership account.

94 *Walmsley v Walmsley* (1846) 3 Jo & La T 556.

Partnership books are prima facie evidence

[20.44] In taking an account of partnership dealings, the court will treat the partnership books as prima facie evidence of their contents.[95] However, as such they are just prima facie evidence and in *Hutcheson v Smith*,[96] where one partner made incorrect entries into the accounts without the knowledge of his co-partner, the accounts were held not be to be evidence thereof.

Costs of taking the account

[20.45] The costs of preparing the accounts will normally be paid out of the partnership assets. In the case of *Hutcheson v Smith*,[97] Brady CB held that: 'upon partnership inquiries, bona fide on both sides, it is fair that there should be no costs on either side.'[98] This must be taken to mean that the costs are paid out of the partnership assets. More recently, this was confirmed by the Supreme Court in *Baxter v Horgan*,[99] where Egan J stated that: 'it is usual that in partnership actions the cost of accounts after dissolution[100] are directed to be paid out of partnership assets.'[101]

Where partner's misconduct increases costs of taking account

[20.46] However, where the actions of one partner are responsible for additional costs in the taking of a partnership account, the courts will order the costs to be paid by that partner. *Baxter v Horgan*[102] involved a dispute over the profits of a cattle-exporting partnership. The defendant partner had forged certain financial documents relating to the partnership business and had failed to keep proper books of account. In the High Court, Murphy J held that, as the defendant used to buy the cattle on behalf of the partnership, he was under a duty to keep accurate records and accounts. In the Supreme Court, it was acknowledged that usually the costs of the preparation of accounts were paid out of partnership assets. However, the Supreme Court upheld Murphy J's decision to award costs against the defendant, since if he had kept proper accounts and had not forged certain documents, the matter could have been disposed of by the Examiner.

Applicable Rules of the Superior Courts

[20.47] The procedural rules governing the taking of an account are to be found in Ord 33 of the Rules of the Superior Courts.[103]

---

95   Thus in *Heslin v Fay (1)* (1884) 15 LR Ir 431 at 449, Sullivan LC held that 'the books of the said partnership be taken as *prima facie* evidence as between the parties'.
96   *Hutcheson v Smith* (1842) 5 Ir Eq R 117.
97   *Hutcheson v Smith* (1842) 5 Ir Eq R 117.
98   *Hutcheson v Smith* (1842) 5 Ir Eq R 117 at 125.
99   *Baxter v Horgan* (7 June 1991) SC.
100 It is conceived that in actions for account without a dissolution, the costs will follow the event, see para **[20.115]**.
101 *Baxter v Horgan* (7 June 1991) SC at p 4.
102 *Baxter v Horgan* (28 May 1990) HC, (7 June 1991) SC.
103 SI 15/1986. See generally, Ó Floinn, *Practice and Procedure in the Superior Courts* (2nd edn, 2008) at p 312 et seq.

Ancillary Matters to the Taking of an Account

[20.48] A number of ancillary matters will arise in connection with the taking of a partnership account. Thus, a partner who has or had partnership money in his possession may be ordered to make a payment into court.[104] It is clear from the case of *Hutcheson v Smith*[105] that a partner, who applies for an order that his co-partner bring in and lodge partnership funds in court, will have his application rejected, if he also has partnership funds for which he does not offer to account.[106]

[20.49] A court will also grant an order of discovery to a partner in order to enable him discover all relevant aspects of the partnership transactions of which he is seeking an account. This right of a partner to such discovery is grounded in s 24(9) of the 1890 Act, which states that:

> The partnership books are to be kept at the place of business of the partnership (or the principal place, if there is more than one), and every partner may, when he thinks fit, have access to and inspect and copy any of them.

III.   SPECIFIC PERFORMANCE

[20.50] In keeping with the general principles governing the granting of an order of specific performance,[107] the courts will not, as a matter of course, order the specific performance of a partnership agreement.[108] This is because in many cases damages will be an adequate remedy;[109] and if the partnership is a partnership at will, an award of specific performance is likely to be futile, since the partnership may be dissolved immediately after the order is given.

---

[104] *Hutcheson v Smith* (1842) 5 Ir Eq R 117. See also *Freeman v Cox* (1878) 8 Ch D 148.

[105] *Hutcheson v Smith* (1842) 5 Ir Eq R 117.

[106] In partnership litigation, it is perhaps self-evident that a claim that a payment had been received by the firm must be proved by the party relying on that claim. In *O'Connor v Woods* (22 January 1976) HC, the defendant partners, in an action for an account of partnership dealings, alleged that their accountancy firm had lost fees because of the removal by the plaintiff partner of certain client files. The plaintiff, in his defence, alleged that these fees had been paid to the partnership prior to his removal of the files. In a statement of general application, Kenny J noted that a 'person who relies on payment must prove it and there has been no proof that the fees were paid to the partnership' (at p 9 of the transcript).

[107] See generally in relation to the remedy of specific performance, Farrell, *Irish Law of Specific Performance* (1994); Clark, *Contract Law in Ireland* (8th edn, 2016) at para 19-01 et seq; McDermott and McDermott, *Contract Law* (2nd edn, 2017) at para [24.02].

[108] As regards the dissolution of a partnership however, see *O'Connor v McNamara* [2009] IEHC 190 in which McGovern J granted an order against the defendant for specific performance of a dissolution agreement in respect of which there had been part performance by each of the plaintiff and the defendant, on the basis that the defendant was not unable to complete the agreement.

[109] See *Bagnell v Edwards* (1875) 10 Ir Eq 215, considered at para **[20.51]** and *Crowley v O'Sullivan (No 2)* [1900] 2 IR 478, considered at para **[20.53]**.

No Specific Performance where Damages are an Adequate Remedy

[20.51] *Bagnell v Edwards*[110] is an example of a case where specific performance was refused by the court as damages were regarded as an adequate remedy. There, the plaintiff and defendant had formed a partnership for the purposes of building a railway line from Enfield to Edenderry. However, contrary to the terms of the partnership agreement, the defendant failed to contribute his share of the capital. The plaintiff therefore was obliged to make certain advances to the firm to finance its operations. Under the partnership agreement (Clause 9), the plaintiff was entitled to receive from the defendant half of the amount of any advances he made to the firm plus interest. The plaintiff sought specific performance of the terms of the partnership agreement. Chatterton V-C held that:

> 'The relief actually sought is nothing but the payment of money, for which an action at law can be maintained by one partner against the other, and the 9th clause measures the damages so to be recovered. The principle of this Court is not to decree specific performance in such a case.'[111]

However, where damages are inadequate, an order of specific performance[112] or an injunction preventing the breach of the terms of a partnership agreement will be granted.[113]

Specific Performance of a Partnership at Will

[20.52] An order of specific performance for a partnership agreement will also be refused if the court feels that it would be futile. This may be the case in a partnership at will, since any one partner in a partnership at will may dissolve the partnership[114] even after the order for specific performance is made. Yet, if the order of specific performance is not likely to be futile, then it will be granted by the courts, even where the partnership is a partnership at will.[115] This is illustrated by the case of *Cuffe v Murtagh*.[116] That case considered a provision in a partnership agreement which entitled one partner to nominate a third party to take his place in the firm. Chatterton V-C stated:

> 'It was sought to apply to this question the principle that this Court will not decree specific performance of an agreement for a tenancy at will or a partnership at will, as it might be put an end to as soon as it was thus created. But that does not appear to me to govern this case; for there[117] the necessity for instituting the suit shows that the party

---

110 *Bagnell v Edwards* (1875) 10 Ir Eq 215.

111 *Bagnell v Edwards* (1875) 10 Ir Eq 215 at 218.

112 See, however, l'Anson Banks, *Lindley & Banks on Partnership* (20th edn, 2017) at para 23-45, where the general rule is stated to be that a court will not order a specific performance of a partnership agreement, relying on *Byrne v Reid* [1902] 2 Ch 735, but cf *CH Giles Y Co v Morris* [1972] 1 WLR 307.

113 See further para **[20.56]** et seq.

114 See generally regarding the dissolution by notice of a partnership at will, para **[23.12]** et seq.

115 *Floyd v Cheney* [1970] 1 All ER 446.

116 *Cuffe v Murtagh* (1881) 7 LR Ir 411.

117 The Vice-Chancellor seems to be referring to the facts of *Hercy v Birch* (1804) 9 Ves 357, which was pleaded as authority for the proposition that a partnership at will is not enforceable by specific performance.

resisting would at once relieve himself from the consequences of a decree, by putting an end to the relation: and this Court will not do anything futile, but will leave the party to his action for damages. Here, however, it does not at all follow that the other partners will dissolve the partnership because of such nomination; and on the contrary, it is to be presumed that they will perform the contract on their part, which they entered into as one for their mutual benefit.'[118]

Specific Performance of a Formal Partnership

[20.53] It should be an easier matter to obtain specific performance of a formal partnership[119] (which will usually be a fixed term partnership) than a partnership-at-will, since the court will not be faced with the possibility of making a futile order. In *Crowley v O'Sullivan (No 2)*,[120] the plaintiff abstained from bidding for a business premises in Bantry on the basis of his agreement with O'Sullivan. They had agreed that O'Sullivan would purchase the premises for the benefit of a partnership to be entered into between them for at least three years. O'Sullivan duly purchased the premises and they carried on business for seven months but at that stage O'Sullivan refused to execute a partnership deed. Crowley sought damages and in his defence, O'Sullivan claimed that their agreement was unenforceable under the Statute of Frauds 1695[121] as there was no evidence in writing of the agreement. At first instance, the defendant's argument was rejected and damages were awarded to the plaintiff on the basis that the agreement had been part performed and was therefore outside the Statute of Frauds. On appeal to the High Court,[122] Palles CB upheld this decision and accepted obiter that he could have ordered the specific performance of this fixed-term partnership.[123]

Specific Performance in Favour of Third Parties

[20.54] The courts have also considered the specific performance of a partnership agreement where the beneficiary of the order is not a partner in the firm. In *Milliken v Milliken*,[124] the plaintiff sought to take his mother's share in a firm of booksellers at 115 Grafton St pursuant to the terms of her partnership agreement with two others. The plaintiff, although not a partner in the firm, had been a party to the partnership agreement. Under the terms of the agreement, the partnership was for nine years and the plaintiff was entitled to take his mother's place as a partner after a three-year period.

118 *Cuffe v Murtagh* (1881) 7 LR Ir 411 at 422–423. The Vice-Chancellor relied on the case of *Featherstonhaugh v Turner* (1858) 25 Beav 382, where in a partnership at will, the partnership agreement provided that the surviving partner had first option on a deceased partner's share, and if he declined to purchase it, the share could be purchased by any other person. A sale was ordered or failing that, the surviving partner was ordered to pay to the deceased partner's estate, the value of the share and interest.
119 See further as to such partnerships, para **[8.09]** et seq.
120 *Crowley v O'Sullivan (No 2)* [1900] 2 IR 478.
121 7 Will 3, c 12.
122 Andrews and Johnson JJ concurring.
123 He relied on the decision in *England v Curling* (1844) 8 Beav 129, in which the court ordered the execution of a formal partnership agreement between persons who had been partners for 12 years under initialled heads of agreement.
124 *Milliken v Milliken* (1845) 8 Ir Eq R 16.

This was, however, subject to his performance as an employee of the firm being to the reasonable satisfaction of the other two partners. Blackburne MR had no objection in principle to granting an order of specific performance to the plaintiff. However on the facts, ie the other two partners alone were the judges of whether the plaintiff had performed to their reasonable satisfaction, he refused to order the specific performance of the provision in the partnership agreement entitling Milliken to be introduced as a partner.

Specific performance where no privity of contract

[20.55] While in *Milliken v Milliken*,[125] the plaintiff was a party to the agreement, in some cases the party seeking specific performance of the terms of the partnership agreement may not be a party to the partnership agreement.[126] This was the situation in *Drimmie v Davies*,[127] where the beneficiaries of an annuity contained in a partnership agreement wished to enforce this right. It involved a dentistry partnership between a father and a son at 27 Westmoreland St in Dublin. Under the terms of the partnership deed, the son agreed to pay an annuity to his siblings after the father's death. However, after his father died, he refused to honour this commitment. When he was sued by his siblings, he alleged that their claim was unenforceable as they were not parties to the partnership deed. Chatterton V-C noted that this rule of privity of contract did not prevail in equity:

> 'The equitable rule was that the party to whose use or for whose benefit the contract had been entered into has a remedy in equity against the person with whom it was expressed to be made. The Court deems the latter a trustee for the former, and would compel him to execute his trust according to the apparent intention of the contracting parties.'[128]

The Vice-Chancellor's decision was upheld by the Irish Court of Appeal,[129] which held that the son was a trustee for the children in respect of the annuities and it granted a decree for the specific performance of the partnership agreement.[130]

IV.   INJUNCTIONS

[20.56] The court may grant an injunction in all cases in which it appears to the court to be just and convenient to so do.[131] For example an injunction will be granted to a partner against his co-partner where the latter is in breach of his duty of good faith or where he acts in contravention of the terms of the partnership agreement. However injunctions,

---

125 *Milliken v Milliken* (1845) 8 Ir Eq R 16.
126 See generally regarding privity of contract, Clark, *Contract Law in Ireland* (8th edn, 2016) at para 17-001 et seq; Friel, *The Law of Contract* (2nd edn, 2000) at p 136 et seq; McDermott and McDermott, *Contract Law* (2nd edn, 2017) at para [19.01] et seq.
127 *Drimmie v Davies* [1899] IR 176.
128 *Drimmie v Davies* [1899] IR 176 at 182.
129 Fitzgibbon, Walker and Holmes LJJ.
130 The Irish Court of Appeal relied on *Page v Cox* (1851) 10 Hare 163 and *Murray v Flavell* (1863) 25 Ch D 89. However cf *Clitheroe v Simpson* (1879) 4 LR Ir 59, a case in which there was no partnership and it was held that no trust was created. But see *Cadbury Ireland v Kerry Co-Op* [1982] ILRM 77 regarding the use of trusts to surmount privity issues.
131 Supreme Court of Judicature Act (Ireland) 1877, s 28(8).

like other equitable remedies, are discretionary and will not be granted where the applicant partner is himself guilty of misconduct.[132]

[20.57] As with the equitable remedy of specific performance,[133] it is not a bar to the granting of an injunction that the partnership in question is a partnership at will, provided that the court is satisfied that the granting of such an order would not be futile.[134]

Initial Reluctance to Grant Injunctions without a Dissolution

[20.58] Initially, the courts showed a reluctance to grant injunctive relief other than with a view to dissolving the firm. Thus in *Sugrue v Hibernian Bank*,[135] an application for an injunction by a partner to restrain his co-partners from using the capital of the firm was refused by MacMahon MR on the grounds that the bill did not seek a dissolution of the firm. However, this requirement is no longer part of Irish law.[136] Thus in *Bradley v Alder*,[137] the defendant partners used oppressive methods in order to encourage the plaintiff partner to sell his interest in the firm[138] and accordingly, MacMahon MR granted an injunction to allow the plaintiff access to the partnership books and accounts.

[20.59] Nonetheless, the courts will not interfere between partners lightly and will therefore not grant an injunction to deal with minor squabbles or disagreements.[139] However, where the court feels its involvement is necessitated, it will grant an injunction and a breach of a partner's duty of good faith is one such instance where the court will interfere. Thus in *Anderson v Wallace*,[140] two partners were involved in a courier service whereby they contracted to deliver mail for the Irish post-office using horse-drawn coaches. Both Anderson and Wallace supplied horses for the venture. However, the post-office had several times suspended the contract and finally terminated it because of the bad horses which had been supplied by Wallace and because of his improper conduct. In these circumstances, Anderson obtained an injunction from MacMahon MR restraining Wallace from interfering in the management of the firm.

[20.60] Injunctions have also been granted to restrain a partner from breaching the terms of the partnership agreement[141] and to prevent him from carrying on business in the firm

---

132 See generally, para **[20.99]** et seq.

133 See para **[20.52]**.

134 See *Cuffe v Murtagh* (1881) 7 Ir LR 411, which dealt with an order of specific performance of a partnership at will, considered at para **[20.52]**. See also the English case of *Floyd v Cheney* [1970] 1 All ER 446, in which Megarry J indicated that he would have granted an injunction, even if the partnership was a partnership at will.

135 *Sugrue v Hibernian Bank* (1829) 2 Ir Law Rec 285.

136 See eg *Anderson v Wallace* (1826) 2 Mol 540, where an injunction was granted without an order for the firm's dissolution. See also *Fairthorne v Weston* (1844) 3 Hare 387; *Richardson v Hastings* (1844) 7 Beav 301.

137 *Bradley v Alder* (1829) 2 Ir Law Rec 348.

138 As to the tactics used by the defendants, see para **[20.23]**.

139 See para **[20.102]**.

140 *Anderson v Wallace* (1826) 2 Mol 540.

141 *Morris v Colman* (1812) 18 Ves Jr 437.

-name on his own account.[142] But they have also been refused in cases where a plaintiff sought to prevent his business partner from terminating an alleged partnership agreement, where the plaintiff failed to prove that damages would not be an adequate remedy: *Bradshaw v Murphy*.[143]

Injunctions in Dissolution Actions

[20.61] While there was an initial reluctance by the courts to grant injunctions in non-dissolution actions, the Courts of Equity had always granted injunctions in dissolution actions in order to ensure the smooth winding up of the firm.[144]

[20.62] In *O'Brien v Cooke*,[145] on the dissolution of a partnership between the parties, Cooke destroyed some of the firm's books and did not answer the interrogatories filed by O'Brien. Sullivan MR granted an injunction restraining Cooke from collecting the firm's debts on its dissolution and entitling O'Brien to do so, provided he indemnified the defendant for any losses incurred in the collection process.[146]

Injunction to restrain damage to goodwill on a dissolution

[20.63] A common concern on the dissolution of a partnership will be the desire to ensure as little impact as possible on the firm's goodwill on the part of those partners who wish to continue the firm's business. The courts have been willing to grant injunctions against partners or former partners in a firm in order to protect the firm's goodwill. This is highlighted by the High Court case of *Gargan v Ruttle*.[147] At first instance, an arbitrator held that a partnership between Gargan and Ruttle for the sale of confectionery had dissolved. As there was no partnership agreement between them, the arbitrator held that the goodwill, stock-in-trade and assets should belong to the plaintiff, while the defendant should receive a sum of money for his share of the goodwill, stock and other assets of the business. Although he received this sum of money, Ruttle continued to solicit the customers of the former firm. In the High Court, Meredith J held that the arbitrator's decision was to be treated the same way as if there was a partnership agreement between them which provided for the plaintiff to be entitled to the goodwill of the firm on a dissolution. On this basis, he granted an injunction against Ruttle, that so long as he should carry on business in the sale of the goods sold by the firm at the date of its dissolution, he was prohibited from soliciting those people who were

---

142 *Aas v Benham* [1891] 2 Ch 244.
143 *Bradshaw v Murphy* [2014] IEHC 146.
144 See for example *Investment and Pensions Advisory Service Ltd v Gray* [1990] BCLC 38, where a firm's provisional liquidator obtained a mareva injunction against a partner of the insolvent firm in order to preserve sums that had allegedly been wrongly paid to the partner during the partnership.
145 *O'Brien v Cooke* (1871) 5 Ir Eq R 51.
146 See also *Hutcheson v Smith* (1842) 5 Ir Eq R 117, where Brady CB granted an injunction against Smith (who was charged with collecting the firm's assets on its dissolution) restraining him from issuing bills of exchange in the name of the firm.
147 *Gargan v Ruttle* [1931] IR 152.

customers of the firm at the date of dissolution. He was also prohibited from encouraging such customers not to deal with Gargan.[148]

V. RECEIVERS AND MANAGERS

[20.64] Another equitable remedy which is often sought by partners is the appointment of a receiver or a manager to the firm. It is important to distinguish between the two officers; a receiver takes the assets of the partnership under his protection and in this way, the assets remain under the protection of the court; a manager has the additional role of carrying on the partnership business under the direction of the court. For this reason, it is perhaps more useful for a manager to be appointed.[149]

Appointment of a Receiver or Manager

[20.65] The court may appoint a receiver or manager[150] in all cases in which it appears to be just and convenient to so do[151] on the application of any partner or other person interested in the preservation of firm's assets, such as the personal representative of a deceased partner.[152]

Appointment of a receiver/manager without a dissolution

[20.66] As has been noted,[153] there is a general reluctance by the courts to interfere in partnership disputes, other than as part of the dissolution of the firm. This is especially so when the remedy which is being sought is as drastic as the appointment of a receiver/manager. Thus in *Sugrue v Hibernian Bank*,[154] an application for the appointment of a receiver was refused by MacMahon MR since the bill did not pray for the dissolution of the partnership. Similarly in *Shaw v O'Higgins*,[155] a conditional order for the appointment of a receiver had been obtained in a case where one partner had removed partnership money from the common fund to his own fund for safe-keeping. The conditional order for the appointment of the receiver was discharged, MacMahon MR instead granting an injunction to prevent the partners acting contrary to the partnership agreement.

[20.67] While there remains a reluctance to get involved in partnership disputes other than as part of a dissolution action, it is clear that where the circumstances demand it, the courts will appoint a receiver without the need for a dissolution[156] and it is

---

[148] Cf *Dickson v McMaster & Co* (1866) 11 Ir Jur 202 (injunction against former partner to prevent use of firm's name refused, where the applicant partner did not have exclusive rights to the firm's goodwill). See generally in relation to the goodwill of a partnership, para **[18.01]** et seq.

[149] See for example *Taylor v Neate* (1888) 39 Ch D 538.

[150] *Sargant v Read* (1876) 1 Ch D 600; *Lee v Jones* (1857) 3 Jur (ns) 954.

[151] Supreme Court of Judicature Act (Ireland) 1877, s 28(8); Rules of the Superior Courts, Ord 50, r 6.

[152] *Davis v Amer* (1854) 3 Drew 64.

[153] See para **[20.05]**.

[154] *Sugrue v Hibernian Bank* (1829) 2 Ir Law Rec 285.

[155] *Shaw v O'Higgins* (1829) 3 Ir Law Rec 104.

[156] *Const v Harris* (1824) T & R 496.

apprehended that the courts will appoint a manager without the need for a dissolution,[157] although this has yet to be done by the courts.[158] Accordingly *Sugrue v Hibernian Bank*[159] should be viewed as no longer representing the law in this area. In exercising its discretion to appoint a receiver or manager, the court will take into account the nature of the partnership business[160] and may be more inclined to appoint a receiver or manager to a small firm where fewer persons are affected.[161]

Appointment of a receiver/manager as part of a dissolution

[20.68] In contrast to an ongoing partnership, the courts are more inclined to appoint either a receiver or a manager to a partnership in dissolution.[162] However, it should be borne in mind that the appointment of a receiver or a manager, unlike the granting of an injunction, will affect all the partners since the partnership assets will be under the receiver's or the manager's control. For this reason, the appointment of a receiver or manager may not always be the most appropriate remedy for partnership disputes. Thus in *Toker v Akgul*,[163] the English Court of Appeal overturned the High Court's ruling that a receiver should be appointed 'almost as a matter of course'. There, the partnership had been dissolved and there was a dispute between the partners regarding the share to which the plaintiff was entitled. The Court of Appeal noted that the power to appoint a receiver was discretionary and there was no presumption in favour of the appointment just because the partnership was dissolved. Since the assets in that case were not in danger, the appointment by the High Court was revoked, the court favouring an inquiry into the partnership's assets by an independent arbitrator in order to settle the accounts. The decision in *Toker v Akgul* was followed by Laffoy J in *Haughey v Synnott*,[164] a case which concerned the dissolution of a two-partner firm of solicitors. The defendant sought an order under s 28(8) of the Supreme Court of Judicature Act (Ireland) 1877 and Ord 50, r 6 of the Rules of the Superior Courts for the appointment of a receiver or receiver/manager in respect of the partnership's assets, an order conferring certain

---

[157] See for example the Australian case of *Barrett v Snowball* (1870) 1 AJR 8, where a receiver was appointed over property of the partnership in Melbourne (which had been managed by a troublesome partner) whilst leaving the property of the partnership in Tasmania in the hands of the plaintiffs.

[158] Note that *Const v Harris* (1824) T & R 496 concerned receivers and not receivers and managers. Yet, there is no reason why in appropriate circumstances a court should not appoint a receiver or manager without the need for a dissolution (eg in the event of short term managerial difficulties in the firm) analogous to the appointment of an examiner to a company (albeit to companies who are unlikely or unable to pay their debts) without the need for the dissolution of the company. For a contrary view regarding the appointment of a manager, see l'Anson Banks, *Lindley & Banks on Partnership* (20th edn, 2017) at para 23-161. Note also that there have been no reported instances of a manager being appointed in England in the case of an ongoing partnership.

[159] *Sugrue v Hibernian Bank* (1829) 2 Ir Law Rec 285.

[160] See in particular, para **[20.73]** in relation to professional firms.

[161] *Hall v Hall* (1850) 3 Mac & G 79.

[162] See *Re a Company (No 00596 of 1986)* [1987] BCLC 133, where partnership principles were applied to a quasi-partnership.

[163] *Toker v Akgul* [1996] CLY 1733.

[164] *Haughey v Synnott* [2011] IEHC 467.

powers on the receiver or, in the alternative, an order under s 39 of the 1890 Act appointing a receiver to wind up the business or affairs of the partnership. Laffoy J quoted from the judgment of Evans LJ in *Toker v Akgul* where he commented that:

> 'Why then, one asks, should a receiver and manager with a power of sale be appointed as distinct from requiring a proper valuation of the partnership assets and a proper settlement of the partnership account? The appointment of a receiver and manager is bound to be cripplingly expensive and, as the learned judge observed, the cost had to be assumed to be wholly disproportionate to the nature of the business.'

While Synnott had, in his grounding affidavit, initially claimed that he was concerned that his former partner was misappropriating the partnership's assets, his final affidavit indicated that he wanted Haughey to account to the partnership for the value of the tangible partnership assets she had taken over, and in respect of the intangible partnership assets, that those be valued, in each case so as to determine Synnott's cash entitlement on dissolution. As such, Laffoy J (who had earlier noted Evans LJ's comment in *Toker v Akgul* regarding the appointment of a professional accountant as the receiver and manager of a partnership business as being a 'nuclear weapon') held that to appoint a receiver at interlocutory stage in this particular case would not be the appropriate mechanism to enable that account, valuation and determination to take place. Instead, Laffoy J noted that various options were open to the parties, including the appointment of an experienced accountant to value to the assets, or the agreement by the parties to refer the valuation to arbitration.[165]

Circumstances Justifying Appointment of Receiver or Manager

[20.69] Whether dealing with a dissolved or a continuing partnership, the courts are more inclined to appoint a receiver or manager where it is required to prevent non-partners from interfering with the firm's business, such as personal representatives, trustees in bankruptcy or assignees.[166]

[20.70] When dealing with an order between partners, the courts have appointed a receiver without the dissolution of the partnership in the following situations:[167]

    (a)   where the misconduct of a partner put the firm's assets in jeopardy.[168]

    (b)   where one partner fraudulently induced another to enter into partnership.[169]

---

[165] Indeed, the appointment of an arbitrator to resolve matters could enable the dissolution of the partnership to be resolved more quickly. In *Ryan & Ors v Ryan & Ors* [2014] IEHC 675, White J commented, in respect of a dissolved partnership where a receiver had been appointed, that the five-year duration of that receivership was 'far too long to finalise the dissolution of a partnership by way of official receivership'.

[166] *Philips v Atkinson* (1787) 2 Bro CC 272.

[167] See further in relation to these circumstances, l'Anson Banks, *Lindley & Banks on Partnership* (20th edn, 2017) at para 23-167 et seq.

[168] *Evans v Coventry* (1854) 3 Eq R 545; *De Tastet v Bordieu* (1805) 2 Bro CC 272; *Estwick v Conningsby* (1682) 1 Vern 118; *Harding v Glover* (1810) 18 Ves Jr 281; *Madgwick v Wimble* (1843) 6 Beav 495.

[169] *Ex p Broome* (1811) 1 Rose 69.

(c) where a partner wrongfully excluded his co-partner from the management of the partnership or from enjoying the firm's assets.[170]

[20.71] In relation to (c), in *Bradley v Alder*[171] the holding of partnership meetings out of the jurisdiction was not a sufficient reason for the court to appoint a receiver. That case concerned the Hibernian Gas Lighting Company, a firm which sold gas lighting to consumers in Dublin. An application to appoint a receiver was made by one partner, because of the behaviour of the defendant partners who made every effort to encourage the plaintiff partner to sell his interest in the firm by holding all the meetings in London and by falsifying the accounts. However, the application for a receiver was rejected by MacMahon MR, who instead granted an injunction to allow the plaintiff access to the partnership books and accounts.

[20.72] It remains to be observed that if the partnership is illegal, the court will not appoint a receiver or manager, since an illegal partnership confers no right on either party as against the other.[172]

Appointment of a receiver/manager to a professional practice

[20.73] The reluctance of courts to appoint a receiver or manager to a continuing firm is even more marked when one is dealing with a professional firm rather than a trading firm. This is because of the greater damage to the professional standing of such a firm which will be caused by the appointment. In this context, it is contended that the well-observed comments of Megarry J in the English High Court case of *Floyd v Cheney*[173] are equally relevant in this jurisdiction:

> 'I do not think that it can be denied that news that a receiver of a business or a professional practice has been appointed is news that may well cause members of the general public to hesitate in resorting to that business or practice. It may well indeed be that some of the inferences that the public would draw from the appointment of a receiver would be quite wrong: but one cannot expect the public to have a precise appreciation of every aspect of the institution of receivership. One must remember that a professional's man's reputation is a delicate blossom, which, once injured, can never be fully restored.'[174]

Partner may be Appointed a Receiver or Manager

[20.74] It is clear from the case of *Hutcheson v Smith*[175] that a partner may be appointed a receiver (or manager) to his own firm and generally the court will accede to such applications. The possibility of a partner being a receiver/manager can be justified by his personal right under s 38 of the 1890 Act to wind up the affairs of the partnership. Indeed, the courts will commonly appoint a partner as a receiver or manager of the firm and this may also be justified on the practical ground that he is most likely to be the person who is best acquainted with the firm's business. However, the appointment of

---

170 *Goodman v Whitcomb* (1820) 1 J & W 589; *Wilson v Greenwood* (1818) 1 Swan 481.

171 *Bradley v Alder* (1829) 2 Ir Law Rec 348.

172 *Armstrong v Lewis* (1834) 2 Cr & M 274. See generally in relation to illegal partnerships, para **[9.01]** et seq.

173 *Floyd v Cheney* [1970] 1 All ER 446. See also *Sobell v Boston* [1975] 2 All ER 282.

174 *Floyd v Cheney* [1970] 1 All ER 446 at 451.

175 *Hutcheson v Smith* (1842) 5 Ir Eq R 117.

one partner as a receiver does not put him in a stronger position *vis-à-vis* his co-partners, as the court will continue to treat all the partners equally. Thus in *Hutcheson v Smith*,[176] Brady CB[177] held that the partner receiver was not entitled to insist that the share of the partnership assets held by the other partner be impounded to answer the outstanding demands against the firm, unless the partner receiver brought the share of the partnership assets which he held into court for the same purpose.

Powers and Liabilities of a Receiver or Manager

[20.75] The court, in appointing a receiver or manager, cannot confer any greater powers on him than a partner has under the partnership agreement and the law of partnership.[178] A receiver or manager appointed by the court is an officer of the court and is not the agent of the applicant partner.[179] Once appointed, the receiver or manager is prima facie personally liable on contracts entered into by him *qua* receiver or manager,[180] but he is entitled to be indemnified for such liabilities out of the firm's assets in priority to the claims of the firm's creditors[181] and he is not entitled to an indemnity from the partners personally.[182]

VI. ACTIONS FOR MISREPRESENTATION

[20.76] The next action between partners to consider is where a partner claims that his entry into the partnership was induced by misrepresentation. Where a partner has been induced by the misrepresentation of his co-partner to enter into partnership, he may be entitled to damages for the loss thereby suffered and to rescind the partnership agreement.

---

[176] *Hutcheson v Smith* (1842) 5 Ir Eq R 117.

[177] Richards B concurring.

[178] *Niemann v Niemann* (1889) 43 Ch D 198. See also the Australian case of *Murray v King* [1986] FSR 116.

[179] *Moss SS Co v Whinney* [1912] AC 254; *Boehm v Goodall* [1911] 1 Ch 155; *Burt, Boulton and Hayward v Bull* [1895] 1 QB 276. See also *Evans v Clayhope Properties* [1988] 1 WLR 358.

[180] *Burt, Boulton and Hayward v Bull* [1895] 1 QB 276; *Re Flowers* (1897) 45 WR 118; *Re Glasdir Copper Mines Ltd* [1906] 1 Ch 365; *Boehm v Goodall* [1911] 1 Ch 155; *Moss SS Co v Whinney* [1912] AC 254.

[181] *Re Boynton Ltd* [1910] 1 Ch 519; *Re British Power Traction and Lighting Co Ltd* [1906] 1 Ch 497 and [1907] 1 Ch 528; *Batten v Wedgewood Coal Co* (1884) 28 Ch D 317. See also *Ryan & ors v Ryan & ors* [2014] IEHC 675 in which White J noted that the general principles set out in certain cases opened to the Court regarding the appointment of examiners and administrators could be applied to the appointment of a receiver in a partnership dissolution: *Wood and Ors v Gorbunova* [2013] EWHC 1935 (regarding a receiver's right to be indemnified from the relevant assets); *Boehm v Goodall* [1911] 1 Ch 155 (a court-appointed receiver is not an agent for the parties and can incur expenses or liabilities without the parties having a say in the matter); *Capewell v Revenue & Customs Commissioners* [2007] 1 WLF 386 (a receiver is entitled to be remunerated out of the relevant assets); *In Re Sharmane Ltd* [2009] IEHC 377 (there are no statutory criteria by reference to which reasonable remuneration should be considered but factors such as the nature, complexity and value of the work should be considered).

[182] *Boehm v Goodall* [1911] 1 Ch 155. See also *Evans v Clayhope Properties* [1988] 1 WLR 358.

Damages for Misrepresentation

[20.77] An action for damages will be available to the innocent partner in respect of the loss he has suffered as a result of the fraudulent[183] or negligent[184] misrepresentation of his partner which induced him into partnership, but not in respect of an innocent misrepresentation.[185] Thus in *Austin v Power*,[186] the plaintiff was induced by the fraudulent representation of the defendant to enter into partnership with him and it was held that he was entitled to damages for false representation and to a partnership account of the profits.

[20.78] Where a partner is induced to enter a partnership by misrepresentation, he may choose either to rescind the agreement or affirm it and sue for damages. He will not be entitled to do both. In the New Zealand case of *Wills and Brownie v Williams*,[187] the defendant was induced to join the plaintiffs in partnership on the basis of a misrepresentation by them regarding their net profits. The Court of Appeal held that once the defendant elected to affirm his partnership agreement he was entitled to damages for the misrepresentation but he was not also entitled to a refund of the price paid for goodwill by him.

Rescission

[20.79] As with all contracts, a partnership agreement may be rescinded by the partner who has entered into the agreement as a result of the fraudulent, negligent or innocent misrepresentatio of his partner,[188] provided that it is possible to achieve *restitutio in integrum*.[189] Thus, where the partnership is subsequently incorporated, such restoration is not possible and rescission will not be granted in such a case.[190] Reference should be made to the standard works on rescission.[191]

---

183   See generally the action for deceit in *Leyden v Malone* (13 May 1968) SC and see also McMahon and Binchy, *Law of Torts* (4th edn, 2013) at para [35.01] et seq. See also *Archer v Brown* [1985] QB 401.

184   *Securities Trust Ltd v Hugh Moore & Alexander Ltd* [1964] IR 417; *Hedley Byrne v Heller & Partners Ltd* [1963] 2 All ER 575 and see generally in relation to negligent misrepresentation, McMahon and Binchy, *Law of Torts* (4th edn, 2013) at para [10.71] et seq.

185   *Heilbut, Symonds & Co v Buckleton* [1913] AC 30.

186   *Austin v Power* (1898) 32 ILTR 8.

187   *Wills and Brownie v Williams* (1999) Butterworths Current Law (NZ) 832.

188   *Redgrave v Hurd* (1881) 20 Ch D 1; *Adam v Newbigging* (1888) 13 App Cas 308. The rescission of the partnership agreement will also result in the dissolution of the partnership, see para **[23.72]**.

189   Similar principles will also be applied by the courts to an action to rescind a dissolution agreement entered into by partners on a technical dissolution of a partnership – see the obiter comments of Keane J in *McCormack v McCormack* [2017] IEHC 733 at para 294 of the judgment that, even if a material misrepresentation had existed in that case, he did not think that it would have been open to order the remedy of rescission as, on the facts, *restitutio ad integrum* would not have been possible.

190   *Clarke v Dickson* (1858) E B & E 148.

191   Biehler, *Equity and the Law of Trusts in Ireland* (6th edn, 2016) at p 780 et seq; Keane, *Equity and the Law of Trusts in Ireland* (3rd edn, 2017) at para [17.01] et seq; Clark, *Contract Law in Ireland* (8th edn, 2016) at para 11-38 et seq; Friel, *The Law of Contract* (2nd edn, 2000) at p 348; McDermott and McDermott, *Contract Law* (2nd edn, 2017) at [14.129] et seq.

[20.80] This common law right to rescind is supplemented by the terms of s 41 of the 1890 Act which sets out the rights of the innocent partner where the partnership agreement is rescinded for fraud or misrepresentation. Although the wording of the section itself is unqualified, the principle of *restitutio in integrum* still applies to s 41, which reads:

> Where a partnership contract is rescinded on the ground of the fraud or misrepresentation of one of the parties thereto, the party entitled to rescind is, without prejudice to any other right, entitled –
>
> (a) to a lien on, or right of retention of, the surplus of the partnership assets, after satisfying the partnership liabilities, for any sum of money paid by him for the purchase of a share in the partnership and for any capital contributed by him, and is
>
> (b) to stand in the place of the creditors of the firm for any payments made by him in respect of the partnership liabilities, and
>
> (c) to be indemnified by the person guilty of the fraud or making the representation against all the debts and liabilities of the firm.

[20.81] Thus, s 41 provides a partner who has been induced by fraud or misrepresentation to enter a partnership agreement, with certain rights against both the partnership property and the partnership. He is granted a lien over the surplus partnership assets in respect of any sum paid for his partnership share and his capital contribution and he is granted a right to stand in the place of the firm's creditors in respect of any payments he has made to the creditors for the firm's liabilities. Each of these rights is available to the innocent partner, even if he had the means available of learning the truth and did not avail himself of them at the time of joining the firm.[192]

[20.82] Perhaps the most important of the rights of the innocent partner under s 41 is the right to an indemnity against the liabilities of the firm. Yet this indemnity is only available from the partner who is guilty of the fraud or of making the representation. The right to an indemnity is important because the rescission of the partnership agreement will leave the innocent partner liable to third parties for the obligations of the firm which were incurred while he was a partner. It will not avail the innocent partner to claim that he should not be liable to the third party because he was induced to become a partner by a misrepresentation. This issue is illustrated by the case of *Howard v Shaw*.[193] There, a mining partnership had executed promissory notes in favour of a third party, Levason, who had endorsed the notes over to another third party, Howard. Howard sought to enforce the notes against Shaw, one of the partners in the firm. Shaw alleged that he had been induced to enter into the partnership by Levason's fraudulent claims that the land, which was purchased by the firm, was good mining land. In the High Court, Blackburne CJ held that it was not open to Shaw in this action by Howard to deny or impeach the validity of the partnership deed which he had executed and he was held liable on the promissory note.

[20.83] In addition to being liable to third parties for the obligations of the firm which were incurred during the partnership, the innocent partner may also be liable for

---

[192] *Rawlins v Wickham* (1853) 3 De G & J 304.

[193] *Howard v Shaw* (1846) 9 Ir LR 335. Note that this case was decided prior to the Supreme Court of Judicature Act (Ireland) 1877.

obligations which were incurred by the firm to third parties after the dissolution of the partnership by rescission. Thus, if these third parties, who had previously dealt with the firm while he was a partner, were unaware of his departure, he will be liable for these subsequent obligations.[194] By its express terms (ie 'without prejudice to any other right'), s 41 is not exhaustive of the other rights, such as damages,[195] which are available to a partner who is induced by a misrepresentation to join the partnership.

Misrepresentation which Induces Dissolution Agreement

[20.84] Similar principles as apply to a misrepresentation which induces a partner to enter a partnership agreement also apply to misrepresentation between partners in connection with the dissolution of the partnership.[196] In the absence of misrepresentation, the dissolution agreement will bind the partners and their trustees in bankruptcy or personal representatives.[197] However in *Blisset v Daniel*,[198] the partners in a firm were acting with clear *mala fides* when they persuaded one partner to sign the firm's accounts and as soon as he did so, they expelled him from the firm. When they sought to use these accounts as the basis for a valuation of his share, it was held that they were not binding on the expelled partner.

VII. ARBITRATION

[20.85] Since arbitration clauses are standard in most partnership agreements, it is important to consider the judicial treatment of the arbitration of disputes between partners. For a more detailed treatment of arbitration, reference should be made to the standard textbooks in this area.[199] As a preliminary point, it should be noted that when a formal partnership (most often a fixed term partnership) continues in business after the expiry of its agreed term, it becomes a partnership at will and any arbitration clauses in the original fixed-term partnership are, in general, carried over into the partnership at will.[200]

Powers of Arbitrator

[20.86] There is nothing in the law of partnership which affects the basic principle of arbitration law that the powers of an arbitrator are determined by the terms of the arbitration clause and the terms of the parties' reference to arbitration. Assuming that the arbitration clause is an 'all disputes' category, the arbitrator will have a wide range

---

[194] See further regarding the liability of partners for post-dissolution obligations, para **[11.74]** et seq.

[195] See for example *Austin v Power* (1898) 32 ILTR 8, para **[20.77]**.

[196] *Law v Law* [1905] 1 Ch 140; *Spittal v Smith* (1829) Taml 45; *Chandler v Dorsett* (1679) Finch 431.

[197] *Luckie v Forsyth* (1846) 3 Jo & Lat 388 at 396.

[198] *Blisset v Daniel* (1853) 10 Hare 493.

[199] Dowling-Hussey, Dunne and Tackaberry, *Arbitration Law* (2nd edn, 2014); Mansfield, *Arbitration Act 2010 and Model Law* (2012). See also Clark, *Contract Law in Ireland* (8th edn, 2016) at paras 15-05 to 15-06.

[200] *Gillet v Thornton* (1875) 44 LJ Ch 398. See generally in relation to such partnerships, para **[8.09]** et seq.

of powers, including such basic powers as the power to take an account of partnership dealings,[201] to order and make payments between the parties[202] and to make an order as to the costs of the arbitration.[203] In addition, the arbitrator will have the following powers.

Power to dissolve the partnership

[20.87] An arbitrator, who is appointed to resolve a dispute between partners, has the power to dissolve the partnership.[204] This was established by the case of *Hutchinson v Whitfield*.[205] There, a dispute arose between two partners in an Armagh based distillery and they submitted all matters in dispute between them to arbitration. The arbitrator was not given the express power to dissolve the partnership, yet his award provided for the assets of the partnership to be vested in one partner for the purposes of the winding-up of the firm. The award was objected to on the grounds that the arbitrator was not granted the power to dissolve the partnership, which objection was rejected by Brady CB. In addition, an objection was made to the dissolution of the partnership on the grounds that the partnership deed itself provided that any dissolution of the partnership should only be by deed. However, Brady CB held that the fact that both the submission to arbitration and the award of the arbitrator were under seal was sufficient to satisfy this requirement.

[20.88] An arbitrator with power to dissolve a partnership is also entitled, as part of the order for dissolution, to order the return of a portion of any premium[206] which has been paid by a partner.[207] In addition to the power to dissolve a partnership, the High Court case of *Larkin v Groeger and Eaton*[208] is authority for the principle that, where a partnership is dissolved prior to the arbitration proceedings, but it is not clear upon what date the dissolution took effect, the arbitrator has power to determine the date of dissolution.

[20.89] It seems clear that, once the question of dissolution has been referred to arbitration, an application cannot be made to court to dissolve the partnership under s 35 of the 1890 Act.[209]

---

201   *Larkin v Groeger and Eaton* (26 April 1988) HC.
202   *Larkin v Groeger and Eaton* (26 April 1988) HC. See also *O'Cathain v O'Cathain* [2012] IEHC 223. In his judgment, Hedigan J was critical of the applicant partner's failure to partcipate in the arbitration in a meaningful manner, and refused his application to set aside the arbitral award.
203   Arbitration Act 2010, s 21.
204   See *Belfield v Bourne* (1894) 69 LT 786. See also the Scottish decision of *Hackston v Hackston and Another* (1956) SLT (Notes) 38, the New Zealand case of *Re a Deed of Partnership* (1914) 33 NZLR 1461 and the English case of *Phoenix v Pope* [1974] 1 All ER 512.
205   *Hutchinson v Whitfield* (1830) Hayes 78.
206   As to the return of premiums generally, see para [26.51].
207   *Belfield v Bourne* (1894) 69 LT 786.
208   *Larkin v Groeger and Eaton* (26 April 1988) HC.
209   *Phoenix v Pope* [1974] 1 All ER 512. As to the right of a partner to apply for a dissolution of the partnership under the Partnership Act 1890, s 35, see generally para [25.01] et seq.

Power to wind up the partnership

[20.90] The question of whether an arbitrator has power to wind up the partnership was considered in *Dennehy v Jolly*.[210] This case concerned a law stationery partnership at 74 Dame Street in Dublin. An application was made by one partner to court to wind up the partnership, in spite of a term in the partnership agreement that differences between the partners were to be referred to arbitration.[211] The defendant brought a motion to stay the plaintiff's application to wind up the partnership in view of this arbitration clause. However, Sullivan MR held that winding up the partnership was not within the terms of an arbitration clause. He reasoned that the winding up of a partnership is not a matter in dispute so as to be referred to arbitration, as there is the additional question of the terms upon which the partnership is to be wound up, the taking of accounts and the subsequent receiving of profits by the parties, which the arbitrator does not have power to do. It is contended that Sullivan MR's premise for denying the arbitrator the power to wind up a partnership is no longer valid in view of the extensive powers of arbitrators which have been recognised by the Irish courts.[212] On this basis, it is apprehended that *Dennehy v Jolly*[213] is no longer good law and that just as an arbitrator has power to dissolve a partnership, he also has power to wind up a partnership.

Power to divide assets between partners

[20.91] A useful power which has been used by arbitrators is the power to divide up the partnership assets as part of the dissolution of the partnership. Thus in *Gargan v Ruttle*,[214] a dispute between the plaintiff and defendant was referred to an arbitrator who held that the partnership had been dissolved. As part of his order, he effectively ordered the sale of the partnership by one partner to another, since he ordered that the goodwill, stock and all other assets of the firm belong to one partner and that the other partner should be entitled to a sum of money for his share of these partnership assets.[215]

Power to make ancillary orders

[20.92] One power of an arbitrator which may be of considerable practical significance is the power to order the partners to do ancillary matters in connection with the dissolution, such as signing forms, transferring title to partnership assets, etc. Thus in *Larkin v Groeger and Eaton*,[216] the arbitrator ordered the continuing partner in a firm to sign forms to notify the Registrar of Business Names that the former partners were no

---

[210] *Dennehy v Jolly* (1875) 9 ILTR 3.

[211] The clause provided that differences relating to the agreement or the partnership business or the rights and duties of the partners should be referred to arbitration.

[212] See for example the taking of accounts, and the orders to sign Companies Registration Office forms in *Larkin v Groeger and Eaton* (26 April 1988) HC. Similarly, in *Gargan v Ruttle* [1931] IR 152, the High Court upheld the award of an arbitrator that the partnership had been dissolved and that the goodwill, stock and all other assets of the firm belong to one partner and that the other partner be entitled to a sum of money for his share of these partnership assets.

[213] *Dennehy v Jolly* (1875) 9 ILTR 3.

[214] *Gargan v Ruttle* [1931] IR 152.

[215] This order was not varied on appeal to Meredith J in the High Court.

[216] *Larkin v Groeger and Eaton* (26 April 1988) HC.

longer carrying on business under the partnership name.[217] In this way, the possibility of those former partners being liable to third parties as partners by holding out was reduced.[218] The arbitrator also ordered the retiring partner to sign a surrender form with the insurance company in relation to an insurance policy which was part of the partnership arrangements[219] and to sign forms notifying the Companies Registration Office of his resignation as a director of a client company.[220]

If the Arbitrator Behaves Unfairly

[20.93] If, in the conduct of arbitration proceedings, the arbitrator behaves unfairly, the proper course of action is to invoke the assistance of the court at that stage. Any delay in seeking court assistance will be looked on unfavourably as happened in *Larkin v Groeger and Eaton*,[221] where the period of delay was seventeen months from the end of the arbitration and this influenced Barrington J in his refusal to interfere with the arbitrator's decision. The converse also applies: if a partner fails to engage meaningfully in the arbitration and seeks to delay matters, the court will also view this unfavourably, as was the case in *O'Cathain v O'Cathain*[222] where the applicant partner was found by Hedigan J to have engaged in repeated correspondence requesting documentation in relation to the partnership's accounts that demonstrated 'a clear pattern of obstructive behaviour', in particular as the requested documentation had already been provided to him.

Staying of Court Proceedings which are Within Arbitration Clause

[20.94] An agreement to refer a dispute to arbitration will not constitute a defence to an action in relation to the matter to be referred. However, the courts have the power to stay court proceedings where the parties have previously agreed to determine the dispute by arbitration.[223] Thus in *Sugrue v Hibernian Bank*,[224] MacMahon MR held that the

---

217 As required by s 7 of the Registration of Business Names Act 1963, see further in relation to business names and partnerships, para **[3.70]** et seq.

218 See generally in relation to partnership by holding out, para **[7.01]** et seq.

219 A well-drafted partnership agreement should avoid the necessity for such an order by having a 'further assurance' clause. See para **[21.155]**.

220 Also in that case, one partner objected to the arbitrator admitting in evidence, photocopies of the firm's cash receipts book which the defendants claimed had been lost. On appeal to the High Court, Barrington J held that once the arbitrator believed there had been a bona fide mistake and that the cash receipts book had been lost, he was entitled to admit photocopies of the book.

221 *Larkin v Groeger and Eaton* (26 April 1988) HC.

222 *O'Cathain v O'Cathain* [2012] IEHC 223.

223 Article 8(1) of the UNCITRAL Model Law on International Commercial Arbitration as given force of law in Ireland by the Arbitration Act 2010, s 6. See also *W Bruce v J Strong* [1951] 2 KB 447 and *Olver v Hillier* [1959] 2 All ER 220; *Channel Tunnel Group v Balfour Beatty Construction Ltd* [1993] AC 334. In *Dimsdale v Robertson* (1844) 7 Ir Eq R 536, Sugden LC refused to entertain a suit after an agreement to refer to arbitration (naming the arbitrators and containing a covenant not to sue) had been entered into. The case concerned the grant by the Governor of the New Plantation in Ulster of slobs in Lough Swilly and Lough Foyle to the plaintiff for reclamation. See also the Scottish case of *Roxburgh v Dinardo* (1981) SLT 291.

224 *Sugrue v Hibernian Bank* (1829) 2 Ir Law Rec 285.

plaintiff's action against his partners should be dismissed since, inter alia, he had not submitted his dispute to arbitration as required by the terms of his partnership agreement:

> 'Is it not decided, that the Court will insist on an experiment being made first with the tribunal created by the deed, I admit, you are not deprived of the jurisdiction here, if even that is not done; but will not the Court in its discretion say, you must first try your own domestic tribunal.'[225]

Of course, if the subject-matter of the court proceedings is not within the terms of the arbitration clause, a motion to have the court proceedings stayed will be rejected as happened in *Dennehy v Jolly*.[226]

Arbitrator's Award as a Bar to Court Proceedings

[20.95] Just as court proceedings may be stayed if the dispute is within the terms of an arbitration clause, so too court proceedings will not be allowed in connection with a dispute between partners where an arbitrator has already made an award concerning the dispute.[227] However, where the award of an arbitrator does not comply with the formalities set out in the submission to arbitration, it will be void and therefore will not be a bar to court proceedings. This was the situation in *Murphy v Keller*,[228] where a submission to arbitration was made by partners in a dissolved partnership for an account of their dealings as corn merchants. The submission provided that the award should be made within a given time and be under seal. The award which was made was not under seal and was not made within the time period. Subsequently, one of the partners sought to have the court take an account of partnership dealings. The other two partners alleged the account of partnership dealings which was done by the arbitrator was a bar to this court application. However, Brady LC held that the arbitrator's award was a nullity as it was not under seal and was not given within the time limit.

VIII. DAMAGES

[20.96] Since a partnership agreement is like any other contract, an action for damages may be taken for a breach of its terms.[229] Thus in *Greenham v Gray*,[230] the plaintiff was awarded damages against the defendant, when in contravention of their partnership agreement to carry on business as millers of cotton in Drogheda for five years, the defendant forcibly expelled him from the mills and refused to allow him to conduct the

---

[225] *Sugrue v Hibernian Bank* (1829) 2 Ir Law Rec 285 at 291.

[226] *Dennehy v Jolly* (1875) 9 ILTR 3, although as noted at para **[20.90]** et seq it is thought that the court erred in its conclusion on the facts, ie in its conclusion that the matter (the winding up of the partnership) was not within the terms of the arbitration clause.

[227] *Murphy v Keller* (1851) 2 Ir Ch R 417. The question of appealing the arbitrator's award is of course a separate issue. Dowling-Hussey, Dunne and Tackaberry, *Arbitration Law* (2nd edn, 2014); Mansfield, *Arbitration Act 2010 and Model Law* (2012). See also Clark, *Contract Law in Ireland* (8th edn, 2016) at paras 15-05 to 15-06.

[228] *Murphy v Keller* (1851) 2 Ir Ch R 417.

[229] See the English case of *Hitchman v Crouch Butler Savage Associates Services Ltd* (1983) 127 Sol Jo 441.

[230] *Greenham v Gray* (1855) 4 Ir CLR 501.

firm's business.[231] In *Mughal v Sher*,[232] the plaintiff (Mr Mughal) and defendant (Mr Sher) had worked together in a medical practice in Dooradoyle, Limerick. Mr Mughal sought a declaration that they had been in a 50:50 partnership together, and also sought damages in respect of various amounts due to him in respect of payments made by the HSE to the medical practice, and a loss of cash earnings. Mr Sher conceded that a partnership had existed, so Murphy J was only required to assess Mr Mughal's case for damages. Part of Mr Mughal's claim was for loss of cash earnings which arose following medical advice that he stop working in September 2014 due to concerns that he might be suffering from tuberculosis. In December 2014, Mr Mughal's doctor certified that he was fit to return to work, following which he informed Mr Sher, but received no response, and did not return to work until 22 weeks later, in May 2015. Part of Mr Mughal's claim for damages was a claim of €80,000 for loss of earnings in respect of that 22 week period. Mr Sher argued that the medical certificate that Mr Mughal was fit to return to work stipulated that he should wear a surgical mask when treating patients with compromised immune systems, and that this could put a walk-in medical practice in a compromising position. Hogan J awarded the full €80,000 to Mr Mughal on the basis that an arrangement could have been agreed to by Mr Sher to allow Mr Mughal to return to work in December 2014, but that Mr Sher had instead used Mr Mughal's illness to 'oust him from the practice'.

[20.97] However, in view of special nature of the partnership contract and in particular the likelihood of counter claims by the defendant partner, a court will often refuse to assess damages for a breach of contract in isolation, but will require an account to be taken of all partnership dealings between the partners.[233]

[20.98] However, where the circumstances of the case require, a full partnership account may be avoided by a court giving a declaratory judgement regarding one disputed item between the partners, without the necessity of having a full account.[234] In addition, as an ancillary matter to the granting of damages, the court may order the return of a premium which has been paid by one partner for his admission to the partnership.[235]

---

231 On the basis of the judgment of Neuberger J in *Mullins v Laughton* [2003] EWHC 2761 (Ch), it appears that damages may also be sought for loss of reputation.

232 *Mughal v Sher* [2015] IEHC 675.

233 See generally para **[20.14]** et seq. See l'Anson Banks, *Lindley & Banks on Partnership* (20th edn, 2017) as to slightly conflicting approaches taken by the Court of Appeal in England.

234 This may in fact be the explanation for *Headly v Luby* (1868) 2 ILTR 302 where the parties had agreed to share the profits and losses of the firm equally. Luby had acquired cattle for the partnership but had not paid for them and the seller of the cattle successfully sued Headly for the purchase price. Headly sought a declaration that Luby owed him half of the purchase price which Headly had paid. There was an objection to the court's jurisdiction on the grounds that it related to a partnership account. However, the court held that while this was a matter to be settled in taking partnership accounts, it was prepared to declare that the money was paid on Luby's behalf and thus gave a decree for the sum claimed.

235 Thus in *Bolton v Carmichael* (1856) 1 Ir Jur (ns) 298, although this case was in fact an action for a partnership account, Master Henn held that since the acts of Carmichael had caused the dissolution of the partnership, Bolton was entitled to a return of part of the premium which he had paid to become a partner. See generally in relation to the return of a premium, para **[26.51]** et seq.

IX. WHERE THE COURT WILL NOT INTERFERE BETWEEN PARTNERS

[20.99] In most cases, the relief which will be sought by a partner will be equitable in nature[236] and equitable principles will govern the granting of such relief and may preclude its availability. Accordingly, reference should be made to the standard works on equity for a detailed analysis of these principles.[237] Most of the following instances of occasions in which the court will not interfere in a partnership dispute correspond to these equitable principles.

Reluctance to Grant Remedy in Absence of Dissolution

[20.100] It has been noted throughout this chapter that there is a general reluctance on the part of the courts to grant a remedy in a partnership dispute which does not involve the dissolution of the partnership. Thus in *Sugrue v Hibernian Bank*,[238] an injunction and the appointment of a receiver was sought by a partner against the Hibernian Bank, but was refused on the grounds, inter alia, that the bill did not request the dissolution of the firm.[239] This judicial reluctance can be justified on the grounds that the very fact that an application is being made by a partner for such a remedy indicates the absence of confidence and trust between the parties. Since this confidence and trust is required for the continuation of the partnership, the more appropriate remedy is oftentimes a dissolution of the partnership.

[20.101] However, it is important to bear in mind that this is a general reluctance rather than an inflexible rule and the courts will not allow an errant partner to force his co-partners to submit to his wrongful conduct, on the basis that their only remedy is the dissolution of a profitable partnership.[240]

Trivial Disputes between Partners

[20.102] The courts expect partners to show a certain degree of flexibility and tolerance in the running of the partnership business. Accordingly, the court will not interfere in trivial partnership disputes or squabbles.[241] For example where the partners in a firm have entrusted the management of the firm to a managing partner, the court will be reluctant to interfere with this management, unless it is an improper exercise of these powers.[242]

---

236 For example specific performance; injunction; appointment of a receiver; rescission; an account of partnership dealings.

237 Keane, *Equity and the Law of Trusts in Ireland* (3rd edn, 2017) at para [3.01] et seq; Biehler, *Equity and the Law of Trusts in Ireland* (6th edn, 2016) at p 15 et seq.

238 *Sugrue v Hibernian Bank* (1829) 2 Ir Law Rec 285.

239 See also *Davis v Foreman* [1894] 3 Ch 655; *Kirchner & Co v Gruban* [1909] 1 Ch 413.

240 *Fairthorne v Weston* (1844) 3 Hare 387.

241 *Lawson v Morgan* (1815) 1 Price 303; *Anderson v Anderson* (1857) 25 Beav 190.

242 *Lawson v Morgan* (1815) 1 Price 303.

Laches

[20.103] An important equitable principle, which will bear on a partner's application for the court's assistance, is the question of whether he has been guilty of laches in applying to court.[243] Thus, a claim for equitable relief may be rejected by virtue of the passage of time combined with circumstances which render it inequitable to grant relief. In this context, *laches* should be distinguished from actions which are time-barred. Thus, delay per se is not sufficient to establish *laches*, although this may be sufficient to bar the action under the Statute of Limitations 1957.[244]

[20.104] *Reilly v Walsh*[245] is an example of a partnership case where the passage of time and inequitable conduct deprived a partner of equitable relief. In that case, two brothers, Oliver and Edward Walsh agreed to take a lease of land in Suffolk St in Dublin from Archdeacon Barton to build some houses thereon. However, after this agreement was reached, Oliver did not assist Edward or make any financial contributions to the building project. On the contrary, he showed clear *mala fides* by writing to third parties to prevent Edward getting a loan for the purpose of the venture. Time was stipulated to be important under the terms of the agreement with the Archdeacon and unless Edward had stepped in to undertake the business alone, the houses would never have been built. The agreement with the Archdeacon provided that the land would be leased by the brothers as joint tenants. For this reason, the rule of survivorship applied and on the death of Oliver, his share would be acquired by Edward. Oliver's personal representative unsuccessfully sought the assistance of the court to establish that that the land was held as tenants in common on the grounds that the partnership between the brothers severed this joint tenancy. Richards B held that:[246]

> 'From the very commencement [Oliver's] conduct was the very opposite of what it should have been if he intended to act as a partner fairly. He cannot be allowed to play fast and loose ... Time was important, for that was so stipulated in the contract; and unless Edward had stepped forward and undertaken this business himself, no benefit would have derived from it, but the contrary. Edward then came forward, and by Oliver's letters we find that he not only did not join with or assist Edward, but actually wrote to prevent a loan being made to him ... All we decide is, that after such conduct his representative has no equity to call on the Court to prevent the operation of the rule of law.'[247]

This case highlights the possible application of the defence of *laches* to a situation where a person delays entering into a partnership, invariably in order to see if a speculative venture will be profitable or loss-making and on seeing its profitability seeks specific performance of the terms of the agreement. It is clear that the courts will not reward such inequitable conduct.[248]

---

243   See for example the English case of *John v James* [1991] FSR 397.
244   See para **[20.110]**.
245   *Reilly v Walsh* (1848) 11 Ir Eq R 22.
246   Jackson and Moore JJ concurring.
247   *Reilly v Walsh* (1848) 11 Ir Eq R 22 at 28.
248   See also *Cowell v Watts* (1850) 2 H & Tw 224.

[20.105] It should of course be borne in mind that, where a defendant partner relies on *laches* as a defence, he must not himself be guilty of improper conduct which has contributed to the plaintiff's delay.[249]

Acquiescence

[20.106] Similar to the defence of laches, is the defence of acquiescence whereby a partner will be denied equitable relief because of his acquiescence in the behaviour of which he complains. Equity regards it as inequitable that such a partner should be permitted to be successful in his complaint. This principle is highlighted by the case of *Heslin v Fay (1)*.[250] There, the parties agreed to enter a grocery retail partnership and their agreement provided for the firm's grocery business in North King St in Dublin to be run as a sepaerate concern from another grocery business belonging to Fay in Thomas St in Dublin. However this did not happen in practice and the plaintiff acquiesced in the mingling of the two businesses from the beginning of the partnership. Sullivan LC held that the plaintiff was estopped by his conduct from complaining about this breach of the partnership agreement:

> 'One most extraordinary thing is that Heslin, who complains of this, was a party to the confusion from the beginning; and, so far as any grounds of relief go on this point, we think that he has no reason to complain, and that a case of acquiescence is brought home to him. He undid the deed by his own act, and acquiesced in its being disregarded for ten years, and he cannot now complain.'[251]

[20.107] Similarly, in *Mallet v Boileau*[252] a partner in the Dublin and London Steam Marine Company sought an injunction and the appointment of a receiver on the grounds that the firm had been mismanaged, that its funds had been blended with another firm's and that the firm had been rendered subservient to this other firm's interests. MacMahon MR refused to grant an injunction or appoint a receiver as he held that the concurrence of the plaintiff in these acts displaced any equity which the plaintiff originally had.

[20.108] As with the defence of *laches*,[253] where a defendant partner relies on acquiescence as a defence, he must not himself be guilty of improper conduct which has contributed to the plaintiff's delay.

Applicant Partner Must Have 'Clean Hands'

[20.109] The defences of *laches* and acquiescence are examples of the broader equitable principle that he who comes to equity must do so with clean hands. Thus, a partner who seeks an equitable remedy must show that he is not guilty of improper conduct, such as a breach of the duty of good faith to his co-partners or of a breach of the terms of the partnership agreement, but must be willing to perform his partnership obligations. For example in *Hutcheson v Smith*,[254] the plaintiff applied for an order that his co-partner

---

[249] See the Canadian case of *Blundon v Storm* (1971) 20 DLR (3d) 413.

[250] *Heslin v Fay (1)* (1884) 15 LR Ir 431.

[251] *Heslin v Fay (1)* (1884) 15 LR Ir 431 at p 445.

[252] *Mallet v Boileau* (1835) 3 Ir Law Rec (ns) 264.

[253] See para **[20.103]**.

[254] *Hutcheson v Smith* (1842) 5 Ir Eq R 117 at 119 where reference is made to the refusal of this order in an earlier court decision in that case.

pay the firm's debts which he had collected into court. The order was refused on the grounds that the plaintiff had also collected some of the firm's debts for which he did not offer to account.

Statute of Limitations 1957

[20.110] Actions for account between partners will not become time barred during the life of the partnership. This is because for actions for an account of partnership dealings, it is only on the dissolution of a partnership that time begins to run under the Statute of Limitations 1957.[255] It follows that a claim for an account between partners cannot become time-barred whilst the partnership continues. However, as soon as the partnership dissolves, the debt will become time-barred after six years,[256] and after twelve years if the claim is pursuant to a partnership deed.[257] Thus in *Loughnan v Sullivan*,[258] an action was taken by the assignees in bankruptcy of Loughnan against his former partner for a partnership account to be taken. The account was for the period up to the date of the bankruptcy of Loughnan. McMahon MR held that, as the action was taken after the expiry of six years from that date, it was statute barred.

[20.111] Section 43 of the 1890 Act will be of application to any claims between partners which relate to 'amounts due from surviving or continuing partners to an outgoing partner'. This section states that:

> Subject to any agreement between the partners, the amount due from surviving or continuing partners to an outgoing partner or the representatives of a deceased partner in respect of the outgoing or deceased partner's share is a debt accruing at the date of the dissolution or death.

[20.112] The fact that s 43 provides that any sums owing to a former partner are 'a debt accruing at the date of dissolution' is a reference to the date of dissolution being the relevant date for the purposes of the Statute of Limitations 1957. In the Supreme Court case of *Meagher v Meagher*,[259] the defendant relied on this section to support his claim that a departing partner was not entitled to any increase in the value of the partnership property, between the date of dissolution and the date of the realisation of those assets. Kingsmill Moore J held that s 43 supported such a conclusion, since this section was solely concerned with the limitation of actions:[260]

> 'The section does not say that a valuation is to be made as of the date of death, but that the sum due is a debt accruing at the date of death. When the sum is ascertained, it ranks for the purpose of limitation as a sum accruing at the date of death.'[261]

---

[255] *Betjemann v Betjemann* [1895] 2 Ch 474; *Knox v Gye* (1872) LR 5 HL 656. See also *Miller v Miller* (1869) LR 8 Eq 499; *Noyes v Crawley* (1878) 10 Ch D 31; *Barton v North Staffs Ry* (1887) 38 Ch D 458; *The Pongola* (1895) 73 LT 512.

[256] Statute of Limitations 1957, s 11(1)(a). See generally Canny, *Limitation of Actions* (2nd edn, Round Hall, 2016) at Appendix 1.

[257] Statute of Limitations 1957, s 11(5). See generally Canny, *Limitation of Actions* (2nd edn, Round Hall, 2016) at Appendix 1.

[258] *Loughnan v Sullivan* (1834) 3 Ir Law Rec (ns) 36.

[259] *Meagher v Meagher* [1961] IR 96.

[260] He relied on Lord Lindley's treatment of this section, now to be found at para 23-34 of l'Anson Banks, *Lindley & Banks on Partnership* (20th edn, 2017).

[261] *Meagher v Meagher* [1961] IR 96 at 112.

[20.113] It is important to note that this section only applies to a technical dissolution (in the sense of a change in the membership of the partnership), since on a general dissolution (in the sense of a winding up of the partnership), there are no continuing or surviving partners.[262]

[20.114] It remains to be observed that under the terms of the Statute of Limitations 1957, fraud on the part of the defendant partner or disability on the part of the plaintiff partner may postpone the accrual of the limitation period.[263] Similarly, part payment of the debt[264] and an acknowledgement of the debt[265] will result in the accrual of a fresh cause of action against the defendant partner.

X. COSTS OF A PARTNERSHIP ACTION

[20.115] Having considered a variety of possible actions between partners, it is now proposed to refer to the costs of such actions. In the words of Kenny J in *O'Connor v Woods*:[266] 'the general rule in a partnership action is that the costs of all the parties are paid out of the assets.'[267] This is very much a general rule and is of obvious application in cases where one partner's actions alone have not led to the court proceedings, eg dissolution proceedings, actions for an account on a dissolution[268] and the appointment of a receiver.[269] However, where the action is for damages, specific performance, an injunction or an account without a dissolution, the costs are likely to follow the event.[270]

[20.116] It is clear that the court will depart from the general rule, where to do so is justified on the merits of the case. For example this will occur where one of the partners has been joined to the proceedings on the grounds that he is a partner in the firm, but without any other involvement in the dispute between the other partners. *O'Connor v Woods*[271] was such a case and it involved a dispute in a four-person firm, where one partner had issued proceedings against his three partners, although he had no dispute with the second-named defendant. The action was for an account of partnership dealings

---

[262] Cf the Scottish decision in *Duncan v The MFV Marigold PD 145* [2006] SLT 975 (OH) in which Lord Reed held that s 43 applied to all dissolutions.

[263] See generally Canny, *Limitation of Actions* (2nd edn, 2016).

[264] Statute of Limitations Act 1957, s 65 and see generally Canny, *Limitation of Actions* (2nd edn, 2016) at para 7-27 et seq.

[265] Statute of Limitations Act 1957, s 56 and see generally Canny, *Limitation of Actions* (2nd edn, 2016) at para 7-12 et seq. See the obiter comment of HH Judge Kirkham in *Manning v English* [2010] Bus LR D89 that agreeing to the taking of a partnership account on dissolution does not equate to an acknowledgment of a debt.

[266] *O'Connor v Woods* (22 January 1976) HC.

[267] *O'Connor v Woods* (22 January 1976) HC at p 22 of the transcript. See eg *O'Brien v Cooke* (1871) 5 Ir Eq R 51.

[268] See the statement of Egan J in *Baxter v Horgan* (7 June 1991) SC at p 4 of the transcript that: 'it is usual that in partnership actions the cost of accounts after dissolution are directed to be paid out of partnership assets.'

[269] See generally *Cummins v Murray* [1906] 2 IR 509; *In re Morelli* [1968] IR 11.

[270] *Norton v Russell* (1875) LR 19 Eq 343; *Hamer v Giles* (1879) 11 Ch D 942; *Warner v Smith* (1863) 8 LT 221.

[271] *O'Connor v Woods* (22 January 1976) HC.

and it was met with a counter-claim for damages against the plaintiff by the first and third named defendants relating to the plaintiff's decision to take files from the firm. In the High Court, Kenny J noted that if the costs of the action were paid out of the partnership assets, the innocent second-named defendant would have had his share of the assets of the firm reduced considerably. Therefore, Kenny J ordered that the costs would be payable out of the capital share of the plaintiff, the first-named defendant and the third-named defendant only. In the New Zealand case of *Draper v Souster*[272] the High Court dealt with a situation where two accountants were unable to agree the financial consequences of the dissolution of their partnership. Costs were awarded against Souster since Williams J held that:

> '[T]he difficulties which the parties had in settling dissolution accounts and in dealing with outstanding partnership issues made it reasonable for [Draper] to have sued for an account. In those circumstances costs should follow the event because the proceeding was one to resolve disputed claims between partners and, in the event, [Souster] was unsuccessful. He did not even make a payment into court to limit his exposure to costs.'[273]

[20.117] Obviously, where one partner's misconduct is responsible for the incurring of additional costs in the partnership action, the courts will order the costs to be paid by that partner. This was the case in *Baxter v Horgan*[274] which involved a dispute over the profits of a cattle-exporting partnership after its dissolution. In the plaintiff's action for the winding up of the partnership, it transpired that the defendant partner had forged certain financial documents relating to the partnership business and had failed to keep proper books of account. The Supreme Court upheld Murphy J's decision to award costs against the defendant on the basis that, if the defendant had kept proper accounts and had not forged certain documents, the matter could have been disposed of by the Examiner.[275]

---

[272] *Draper v Souster* [1999] Butterworths Current Law (NZ) 729.
[273] *Draper v Souster* [1999] Butterworths Current Law (NZ) 729.
[274] *Baxter v Horgan* (28 May 1990) HC, (7 June 1991) SC.
[275] Cf *O'Brien v Cooke* [1871] 5 Ir Eq R 51 which is scarcely consistent with the more recent High and Supreme Court decisions and must be considered as no longer good law. That case was an action for the dissolution of the partnership. The defendant had destroyed some of the firm's books and did not answer the interrogatories filed by the other partner. The Master of the Rolls granted an order entitling the plaintiff alone to recover the debts of the firm and the costs of the order were held to be costs of the dissolution. Similar doubts must exist about *Hutcheson v Smith* (1842) 5 Ir Eq R 117, where costs were not awarded against the defendant partner (who had given an 'uncandid and evasive statement' of the firm's assets) on the grounds that he was insolvent, nor against the plaintiff, since it was the defendant who was at fault. Thus costs were ordered to be paid out of the partnership assets.

Chapter 21

The Terms of the Partnership Agreement

INTRODUCTION

[21.01] It has been observed[1] that the partnership relationship is based in contract and that this contract may be oral or in writing.[2] By having a written agreement, there will be increased certainty amongst the partners regarding the terms of their arrangement which should reduce any fears, distrust or ambiguity which might otherwise exist. In addition, this document provides concrete evidence of the terms which govern the partnership.[3]

[21.02] In considering each of the sections of a typical partnership agreement, reference will be made to the implied terms of the 1890 Act applicable to that section, the possible exclusion or variation of those terms and what terms might otherwise be included by the partners. This analysis will be done under the following main headings:

    I.   Interpretation of Partnership Agreements;

    II.   Typical Terms of a Partnership Agreement; and

    III. Where Partners have No Written Agreement.

Overview

[21.03] In addition to providing certainty as to the terms of the partnership, a written partnership agreement is crucial because of the shortcomings of the 1890 Act. In negotiating a partnership agreement, the Court of Appeal of England and Wales has held that the principle of caveat emptor does not apply, with each prospective partner owing a duty to the other prospective partners with whom he is negotiating to disclose all material facts of which he has knowledge, and of which the other prospective partners may not be aware.[4]

---

[1]   See para **[2.10]**. See generally regarding the drafting of partnerships agreements, Worcester, 'The drafting of partnership agreements' (1950) 63 Harv LR 985.

[2]   Save in the case of registered farm partnerships and registered succession farm partnerships, see para **[8.109]** et seq and investment limited partnerships, see para **[29.43]**. Partnerships applying for authorisation as regulated financial services providers by the Central Bank of Ireland would also be expected to supply a written partnership agreement with their application for authorisation. Legal partnerships and multi-disciplinary practices, which will be capable of formation when the remaining provisions of the Legal Services Regulation Act 2015 are commenced, will also be required to have written partnership agreements (see paras **[30.27]** and **[30.73]**).

[3]   See Goodman and Gahan, 'How a Partnership Agreement helps your practice' (July 2016) Veterinary Ireland Journal, Volume 6 Number 7 at pp 353–354.

[4]   *Conlon v Simms* [2006] EWCA Civ 1749, citing with approval the judgment of Lord Atkin in *Bell v Lever Brothers Ltd* [1932] AC 161 at 227.

[21.04] The 1890 Act implies a considerable number of terms into every partnership. However, these terms were drafted over a century ago and therefore many of them are inappropriate for modern partnerships. Yet, s 19 of the 1890 Act allows these terms to be varied or excluded by the terms of the partnership agreement between the parties. Thus, the first reason for having a written partnership agreement is to allow the partners to expressly exclude or vary those terms which otherwise would be implied by the 1890 Act into their partnership. While the 1890 Act implies a considerable number of terms into the partnership relationship, it fails to imply terms which in modern commercial agreements would be regarded as essential. Accordingly, the second reason for having a written partnership agreement is to allow partners to include important terms into their partnership relationship which are not implied by the 1890 Act.

[21.05] While having a written partnership agreement to counter these shortcomings of the 1890 Act provides a short-term solution to the problem, a more far-sighted approach would be the amendment of the 1890 Act, so that those partnerships which do not have written agreements are not stuck with terms which are plainly inappropriate for modern partnerships. To take but one example of such inappropriate terms, the 1890 Act fails to imply a right on the part of partners to expel their co-partner from the firm for intentional misconduct or fraud. On the contrary, s 25 of the 1890 Act provides that a majority of the partners cannot expel a partner unless a power to do so is conferred by the partnership agreement. Faced with a partner with whom the other partners no longer wish to be associated, and in the absence of a right to expel, the only option available to the innocent partners is to dissolve the partnership by notice (if it is a partnership at will)[5] or to apply to court for its dissolution under s 35 of the 1890 Act[6] (if it is a formal partnership). Exacerbating the problem is the fact that the court is granted the right to dissolve a partnership, but not the power to expel a partner. As the dissolution of a profitable firm is not the ideal way to deal with a partner who is guilty of misconduct, the default rule under the 1890 Act should be changed to entitle a majority of the partners to expel a partner for stated acts of misconduct and fraud. In addition, the court should be given the additional power under s 35 to expel a partner and to provide for his share to be bought by the other partners where it considers it just and equitable to do so, similar to the way it is done under company law.[7]

I.   INTERPRETATION OF PARTNERSHIP AGREEMENTS

[21.06] In this section, the general principles of construction which have been applied by the courts to the interpretation of partnership agreements will be examined. A

---

5   Partnership Act 1890, ss 26(1) and 32(c). See generally in relation to such a dissolution, para **[23.13]**.

6   See generally in relation to court dissolution of a partnership, para **[25.01]** et seq.

7   The Companies Act 2014, s 212 under which the court can make such order or orders as it sees fit where it finds that conduct oppressive or in disregard of a shareholder's interests exists, including an order for the purchase of the shares of any shareholder(s) in the company by other shareholder(s) in the company. Although clearly the comparison is less than perfect, since s 212 applies to oppression of a minority shareholder, while here the issue is oppression by a minority partner.

partnership agreement, like any contract, is subject to the normal rules on the interpretation of contracts.[8]

[21.07] Cooke J, in *King & ors v Ulster Bank Ireland Limited*[9] (a case involving borrowings by The Birr Partnership from Ulster Bank), identified certain essential points in relation to the construction of ambiguous provisions in contracts. While *King v Ulster Bank* concerned the interpretation of the terms of a facility letter, the principles set out below[10] are of more general application:

'–   The starting point in the construction of any written agreement where its meaning is in dispute is the actual text of the provision in question;

–   The task of the Court is to ascertain objectively the intention of the parties by reference to the meaning to be taken from the words they have used;

–   The meaning should be assessed by reference to the language employed, but taking into account the surrounding circumstances including the purpose and context of the contract as known to the parties at the time - the so-called "factual matrix";

–   The content of earlier negotiations and declarations by the persons concerned as to what their intention had been are irrelevant;

–   The Court should ask itself what the reasonable person possessed of relevant information as to the surrounding circumstances would understand the parties to have meant by the words in which they have expressed their agreement;

–   Where the wording used is capable of more than one meaning, that which gives commercial sense in the context of the contractual purpose should be preferred.

–   Where the wording is ambiguous and capable of more than one meaning, the provision should be construed against the interest of the party responsible for the drafting and presentation of the document.'

In addition to these general rules, the following principles have been held to apply specifically to partnership agreements.

---

8   For example the rules on *contra preferetem* and *ejusdem generis*. For a consideration of the general rules on the interpretation of contracts, see Lewison, *The Interpretation of Contracts* (6th edn, 2015); Clarke, *Contract Law in Ireland* (8th edn, 2016) at para 5-07 et seq; McDermott and McDermott, Contract Law (2nd edn, 2017) at para [10.01] et seq; Friel, *The Law of Contract* (2nd edn, 2000) at p 167 et seq. See also the judgment of O'Donnell J in *The Law Society of Ireland v The Motor Insurers' Bureau of Ireland* [2017] IESC 31 (at para 7) in which he noted that the judges in that case (Denham CJ, and O'Donnell, McKechnie, Clarke, MacMenamin, Charleton, and O'Malley JJ), and both parties to the proceedings, were in agreement that the operative principles of contractual interpretation at the time that the judgment was delivered were those set out in the judgment of Lord Hoffmann in *Investors Compensation Scheme Ltd v West Bromwich Building Society* [1998] 1 All ER 98 at pp 114–115. See also the judgment of Barrett J in *Hayes v Kelleher & Ors* [2015] IEHC 509 where, at Appendix C (Some Principles of Contractual Interpretation) to his judgment, he summarises various principles of contractual interpretation based on both Irish and English caselaw (*Hayes v Kelleher* was a dispute between shareholders in the Blarney Woollen Mills Group).

9   *King & ors v Ulster Bank Ireland Limited* [2013] IEHC 250.

10 *King & ors v Ulster Bank Ireland Limited* [2013] IEHC 250 at para 25 of the judgment.

Partnership Agreement is not Exhaustive

[21.08] A partnership agreement may be comprehensive in the sense that it may set out all the implied rights which the parties have decided to incorporate from the 1890 Act and any additional terms which are appropriate. In interpreting such an agreement, one must bear in mind that, although comprehensive, such an agreement will not be exhaustive, since quite apart from the 1890 Act, other rights and duties are implied by general partnership law. Accordingly, recourse will have to be made to the general law of partnership to determine the rights and duties of the partners. For example terms which are not contained in the 1890 Act and may not be contained in a typical partnership agreement, but which apply to a partner under partnership law, are the right of a partner to withdraw his share of the undrawn profits of the firm at any time[11] and the duty of a partner to exercise the powers under the partnership agreement in good faith.[12]

Partnership Deed interpreted like Partnership Agreement

[21.09] It is hardly necessary to observe that a court will interpret a partnership agreement executed under seal in the same manner as a partnership agreement which is executed under hand. The fact that the agreement is executed under seal does not alter the nature of the transaction nor its interpretation. As noted by McWilliam J in the High Court hearing in *Williams v Harris*:[13]

> 'To have any partnership there must, of necessity, be an agreement, be it implied, by parol, in writing under hand or, as here, by deed. The fact that the terms of the agreement are embodied in a deed does not alter the nature of the transaction.'[14]

Court refers to other Clauses of Agreement to aid Interpretation

[21.10] As with all contracts, a court will not interpret a clause in a partnership agreement in isolation. Rather, the court will refer to other clauses in the partnership agreement to aid in its interpretation of the clause in question. In *Williams v Harris*,[15] the shares of two partners in a partnership were sold on their retirement to the continuing partners in the firm pursuant to the terms of clause 26(a) of their partnership agreement. The retiring partners claimed interest on the purchase price for the period between the date they retired and the date they received the purchase money. A separate clause, 26(b), allowed the continuing partners a period of six months from the date of the retirement in which to exercise an option to wind up the partnership instead of purchasing the retiring partners' shares. The option to wind up the firm was not exercised by the continuing partners. However in the High Court, McWilliam J held that the fact that the continuing partners did not exercise their option under clause 26(b) 'does not mean that the provisions of clause 26(b) do not have any bearing on the

---

11   See para **[21.66]**.
12   See para **[21.14]** and see generally in relation to a partner's fiduciary duty, para **[15.01]** et seq.
13   *Williams v Harris* (15 January 1980) SC.
14   *Williams v Harris* (15 January 1980) SC at p 12 of the transcript. The decision of McWilliam J was overturned on appeal to the Supreme Court (reported at [1980] ILRM 237) but not in relation to this issue.
15   *Williams v Harris* (15 January 1980) SC.

construction of the deed'.[16] Rather, he relied on the terms of this clause to support his interpretation of clause 26(a) that interest should be paid for the period between the date of retirement and the date of payment.[17]

Duty of Court to give Full Meaning to Every Word in Agreement

[21.11] Another general rule of interpretation of contracts,[18] which is equally applicable to partnership agreements, is that a court may not ignore certain terms or words which have been inserted by the partners in their agreement. In the words of Andrews LCJ in *Best v McKay*,[19] it is the duty of the court to 'give as full a meaning as possible to every word'[20] of the partnership agreement. In that case, the partnership agreement provided for one partner to 'exercise *his* right' to terminate the partnership agreement. However there was no previous reference in the partnership agreement to the partner having a right to terminate the partnership agreement. Accordingly, it was argued that there was no such right to terminate the agreement. Rather than deleting the reference to the right to terminate, the Northern Ireland Court of Appeal substituted the word 'a' for 'his' so as to give full meaning to this clause and thereby allow the partner a right to terminate the partnership agreement.

[21.12] The obligation on the court to give a full meaning to the words of the partnership agreement applies even if the parties are inconvenienced by that full meaning. This is clear from the case of *Norris v Sadleir*,[21] which involved a partnership agreement for a banking partnership called The Tipperary Joint Stock Bank. The agreement provided that if a partner in the bank was also a customer of the bank and was indebted to it, then if the bank served the partner with a demand for that debt, the usual right of a partner to have an account taken between him and his partners would not apply[22] and the debt would be payable immediately by the partner to the bank. In this case, no demand was served on one partner, Sadlier, yet it was argued that the requirement that a demand be served on a partner should be ignored as it would make it difficult to work the partnership, since it would be necessary for the partnership to be perpetually serving demands on the partners. However, the Master of the Rolls rejected this contention, stating:

> 'If the contract is clear, the Court cannot put on it a different construction because the parties may be inconvenienced by it ... The parties must lie down under the contract which they have entered into between themselves, and which is to be interpreted according to the ordinary meaning of the language used.'[23]

---

[16] *Williams v Harris* (15 January 1980) SC at p 11 of the transcript.

[17] His conclusion that interest should be paid for this period, though not his reliance on clause 26(b), was overturned by the Supreme Court at [1980] ILRM 237.

[18] See *Re Jodrell* (1890) 44 Ch D 590. See generally Lewison, *The Interpretation of Contracts* (6th edn, 2015) at para 3.01 et seq.

[19] *Best v McKay* (1940) 74 ILTR 125.

[20] *Best v McKay* (1940) 74 ILTR 125 at 126.

[21] *Norris v Sadleir* (1872) 6 Ir R Eq 580.

[22] See generally in relation to the right to an account of partnership dealings, para **[20.14]** et seq.

[23] *Norris v Sadleir* (1872) 6 Ir R Eq 580 at 588.

But not too technical a meaning

[21.13] While the courts are thus obliged to give the ordinary meaning to the terms of the partnership agreement, they will not give too technical a meaning to them where this conflicts with the apparent intentions of the parties. Thus, in English Court of Appeal case of *Hitchman v Crouch Butler Savage Associates Services Ltd*,[24] Harman J held that a provision in a partnership agreement which required the signature of the senior partner on all expulsion notices being given to partners in the firm, did not apply to an expulsion notice served on the senior partner himself by his co-partners. Similarly in *Northern Bank v Manning*,[25] the Northern Ireland High Court considered a clause in a partnership agreement which contemplated payments to the widow of a deceased partner in a two person firm. The clause incorrectly referred to the 'net profits of the firm' after the death of one of the two partners. Murray J pointed out that this was legally impossible since there could not be a firm of one partner.[26] Nonetheless, he refused to hold the clause void for uncertainty since the partners' intentions were clear.

Agreement is Interpreted so as to Prevent Abuse of Power

[21.14] A partner's powers, under either the express terms of the partnership agreement or implied by the 1890 Act, may not be abused. Thus in *Heslin v Fay (1)*,[27] the partnership agreement for a grocery partnership in North King Street in Dublin gave one of the partners, Fay, the power to increase the capital of the firm if it was necessary for carrying on the business of the firm. Also under the terms of the partnership agreement, a partner was entitled to call at any time for a return of his surplus capital in the firm. When Heslin called for the return of his surplus capital, Fay used his power to increase the capital of the firm with the sole intention of 'swamping' Heslin's surplus. The Irish Court of Appeal held that Fay was not permitted to use this power in this mala fide manner.

Partnership Agreement is subject to Express or Implied Variation

[21.15] The right to vary the terms of a written or oral partnership agreement has for long been recognised by the courts and is considered in detail elsewhere in this text.[28] For this reason, when reading a partnership agreement, one should bear in mind that the express terms thereof may not represent the complete picture and regard must always be had to the conduct of the parties.[29] However, before any variation will be effective, s 19 requires that it be consented to either expressly or implicitly by all the partners.[30]

---

24   *Hitchman v Crouch Butler Savage Associates Services Ltd* (1983) 127 Sol Jo 441.
25   *Northern Bank v Manning* (December 1976) HC NI.
26   He relied on *Ex p Harper* (1857) 44 ER 692.
27   *Heslin v Fay (1)* (1884) 15 LR Ir 431.
28   See para **[5.14]** et seq.
29   *Heslin v Fay (1)* (1884) 15 LR Ir 431.
30   *Heslin v Fay (1)* (1884) 15 LR Ir 431.

Where Partnership Agreement is Executed Containing Blanks

[21.16] With the common use of standard precedent partnership agreements, one may come across partnership agreements which have been executed containing a number of spaces which were unintentionally left blank. Such agreements will be binding upon the parties, provided that the whole agreement (as distinct from a clause) is not thereby rendered illusory or meaningless. This is clear from *Heslin v Fay (1)*.[31] In that case, the partnership agreement provided for Heslin to contribute £2,000 to the capital of the firm, while the other three partners, who had already been partners together, were jointly to contribute £8,000, in part out of the partnership assets of their pre-existing partnership. This was stated in the partnership agreement as follows:

> 'The said £8,000 worth of capital to be contributed by the said Patrick McCabe Fay, Patrick J Kehoe and William F Moloney, shall be composed of (1) £ , being the costs and expenses of obtaining the houses Nos. 68 and 69, North King-street, Dublin, and in fitting, painting and repairing the warehouses and buildings erected thereon. Secondly of £ ___, being the cost price of stock-in-trade, machinery, implements and plant, brought into the premises by the said Patrick McCabe Fay, Patrick J Kehoe and William F Moloney. And thirdly, of £___ , cash contributed by the said Patrick McCabe Fay, Patrick J Kehoe and William F Moloney; and that the share of the said Christopher Heslin shall be £2,000, and shall be contributed in cash.'[32]

The agreement was executed by the partners without filling in the blanks and after a number of years of trading, the partners ended up in court. The capital had been contributed by the partners substantially in line with this clause and, not surprisingly, the Irish Court of Appeal accepted the validity of the partnership agreement, notwithstanding the presence of these blanks.

II. TYPICAL TERMS OF A PARTNERSHIP AGREEMENT

[21.17] In this section, consideration will be given to some of the terms which one typically finds in a partnership agreement. Since the terms in the 1890 Act are implied into every partnership agreement, unless expressly or implicitly excluded, particular regard will be paid to these implied terms. Where appropriate, reference will be made to those terms which, although not implied by the 1890 Act, might be considered for inclusion by the parties to a partnership agreement. The terms will be considered under the following headings:

1. Preliminary terms;
2. Partnership property;
3. Sharing of profits and losses;
4. Other financial rights of partners;
5. Partnership books and accounts;
6. Management rights of partners;
7. Retirement, expulsion and suspension of a partner;
8. Dissolution of the partnership;
9. Purchase of a departing partner's share;

---

[31]   *Heslin v Fay (1)* (1884) 15 LR Ir 431.
[32]   *Heslin v Fay (1)* (1884) 15 LR Ir 431 at 434.

10.   Position of a departing partner;
11.   Anti-competitive provisions;
12.   Final terms.

1. Preliminary Terms[33]

Form of agreement

[21.18] Partnership agreements are commonly executed under seal, but this is not legally necessary since in most cases the agreement will be supported by consideration.[34] If the partnership agreement contains a power of attorney, there is no longer any requirement for the agreement to be under seal.[35]

Repeat certain terms of the 1890 Act

[21.19] If the partners in the firm are satisfied with the implied terms of the 1890 Act, there is no requirement that those terms be contained in the partnership agreement. However, most partners, including lawyers, will not necessarily be familiar with the terms of the 1890 Act. For this reason, it is suggested that all the terms which are applicable to the partnership should be contained in the one document, namely the partnership agreement. By repeating in the partnership agreement those implied terms of the 1890 Act which are applicable to the partnership, misunderstandings amongst the partners should be reduced. This partnership agreement will then constitute a charter of the rights and duties of the partners which may then be safely used by the partners as a set of directions for the conduct of the firm's business. Nonetheless, it is important to bear in mind that such a document will not be exhaustive[36] and that the partners may have varied the application of some of the terms of this charter by their conduct.[37]

The parties

[21.20] The parties to the partnership agreement should obviously be stated in the parties clause of the agreement. In addition, where there are different types of partners, the partners may be described as such in the parties clause.[38] Thus, where a person is a senior or junior partner[39] or a dormant partner,[40] this should be stated. In limited

---

[33]   It is useful to have a definitions section as part of the partnership agreement in order to ease drafting issues in the body of the agreement.

[34]   See para **[5.10]** et seq. In the unlikely (and inadvisable) event of the partnership agreement purporting to convey an interest in land it should be under seal, See generally regarding the requirement to have a deed to convey an interest in land, Wylie, *The Land and Conveyancing Law Reform Act 2009: Annotations and Commentary* (2nd edn, 2017) at para [107].

[35]   Powers of Attorney Act 1996, s 15(2). See generally Gallagher and O'Herlihy, *Powers of Attorney: A Statutory Annotation* (4th edn, 2016).

[36]   See para **[21.08]**.

[37]   Partnership Act 1890, s 19, see para **[21.15]**.

[38]   Clearly the rights attaching the different categories of partners should be contained in the main body of the agreement.

[39]   Usually, there will be no distinction between partners who are senior (in terms of service) and those who are relatively recent partners. If there is a distinction between their respective rights, then clearly a distinction could be drawn between them in the parties clause. See also para **[6.35]**.

[40]   See generally in relation to dormant partners, para **[6.04]** et seq.

partnership agreements and investment limited partnership agreements, the limited partners should be clearly distinguished from the general partners, in view of the differing rights and duties of these two types of partners.[41] Since 'salaried partners' are not partners as a matter of law, they are not required to sign the partnership agreement and should not do so.[42] If they do sign the partnership agreement, this fact may be used to support a claim that they were in fact partners.

[21.21] It should be noted that the order in which the partners are listed in the partnership agreement might be significant for tax purposes. This is because the partner who is first named in the partnership agreement might, in the absence of any other agreement, be the 'precedent partner'. The 'precedent partner' is the partner who may be required by the Revenue Commissioners to file a return of the partnership's sources of income, the amount of that income, and such other information, accounts, statements and other information required of him by the Inspector of Taxes in respect of the relevant year of assessment.[43] The precedent partner must also, when required by notice from the Revenue Commissioners to do so, file a written statement of the profits or gains arising from each chargeable source in respect of such period as may be specified in the notice.[44] The precedent partner is deemed to be the 'chargeable person' for self-assessment purposes and must file a partnership return in respect of each year of assessment, whether or not he receives a request from the Inspector of Taxes to do so.[45] A failure by the precedent partner to make such a return will leave him liable to pay a surcharge in respect of any income or gains in respect of which he is chargeable as precedent partner,[46] and under s 1084 of the Taxes Consolidation Act 1997, that surcharge can be between 5% and 10% of the amount of tax, subject to certain caps. The role of the precedent partner is considered elsewhere in this work.[47] For this reason, the partnership agreement could usefully provide for the precedent partner to be indemnified by his co-partners in respect of any such charge.

[21.22] In large partnerships, it is useful to have the partners listed in a schedule to the agreement rather than having the first page of the agreement taken up with a list of names.

Special provisions for corporate partners

[21.23] A look at the provisions of the 1890 Act illustrates quite clearly that the Act was drafted from the perspective of individuals as partners and not companies. For this reason, it is prudent in any partnership involving a corporate partner to tailor the

---

[41] See generally in relation to limited partnerships, para **[28.01]** et seq and in relation to investment limited partnerships, para **[29.01]** et seq.

[42] See generally in relation to salaried partners, para **[6.18]** et seq. In particular, care should be taken to determine whether a person is a true partner or a salaried partner.

[43] Taxes Consolidation Act 1997, ss 880(2) and 1007(1).

[44] Taxes Consolidation Act 1997, s 880(5).

[45] Taxes Consolidation Act 1997, s 959M.

[46] Until 2007, the precedent partner could also be chargeable to income tax in the (albeit unlikely) event of there being unexhausted partnership profits not allocated among the partners.

[47] See para **[6.37]**.

provisions of the 1890 Act to the needs of that partner. The provisions which clearly contemplate an individual as a partner are:

- accountability of a partner for private profits after the dissolution of a partnership on the 'death' of a partner (s 29(2));
- dissolution of a partnership on the 'death' or 'bankruptcy' of a partner (s 33(1));
- partner not liable for partnership debts after his 'death or bankruptcy' (s 36(3)).

[21.24] Both ss 29(2) and 33(1) may be excluded by the partners in their partnership agreement. If these sections are not excluded, the agreement should clarify what the partners intend by the 'death' and 'bankruptcy' of a corporate partner. In the case of s 36(3), this is a statement of the law applicable to partnerships and its application to a corporate partner will be decided by the courts. However, the interpretation put upon these sections by the parties in their partnership agreement is likely to be used by a court in reaching its decision and, therefore, it would be useful if the partnership agreement addressed this issue.

[21.25] In addition, provision ought to be made in the partnership agreement for the consequences for the firm of certain events which are peculiar to a corporate partner, such as the appointment of a receiver, liquidator or examiner to the corporate partner.[48] Perhaps the most useful clause in the case of the insolvency of a corporate partner is one which entitles the unaffected partners to expel the corporate partner from the partnership, with an option to acquire its share in the partnership at a valuation.[49]

[21.26] It is generally inadvisable for an individual to enter a partnership with a limited liability company, unless the company has considerable resources. Otherwise, such a partnership may not have a 'level playing field', since the individual is liable to an unlimited degree for the liabilities of the firm, while the company, although *de jure* liable to the same degree, is de facto liable only to the limit of its share capital which may be nominal. In such a case, since the individual is jointly liable with the company for the firm's liabilities,[50] if the company does not meet these liabilities, the individual will end up having a disproportionate share of the firm's liabilities.

Consideration

[21.27] The usual consideration for a partnership agreement is the mutual agreement of the partners to be bound by the terms of the agreement. This is sufficient consideration as a matter of law.[51]

---

[48] Other events which are not exclusive to corporate partners are an inability to pay debts, an encumbrancer taking possession, distress, execution and sequestration. Although note that the Draft General Scheme of Landlord and Tenant Reform Bill 2011, published by the Department of Justice in 2011, provides (at head 41) that '[in] so far as it survives, the remedy of distress for rent is abolished'.

[49] This is of course subject to the general rules on fraudulent dispositions of property by companies and unfair preference of creditors. See generally, Courtney, *The Law of Companies* (4th edn, 2016) at para [26.087] et seq. Note the restrictions on dealings with companies in examinership: Companies Act 2014, s 520.

[50] Partnership Act 1890, s 9.

[51] See generally in relation to consideration para **[5.10]** et seq.

Commencement date

[21.28] It is essential to have a commencement date stated in the partnership agreement because it is from this date that each partner has the authority to bind his co-partners with unlimited liability.[52] It is possible for the partnership agreement to provide for a commencement date in the future. If no commencement date is stated in the partnership agreement, it is presumed to have commenced on the date of execution, ie the date of actual execution of the partnership agreement and not the date which is shown on the face of the agreement.[53]

Retrospective effect?

[21.29] The partnership agreement may provide that the partnership actually commenced at an earlier date than the date of execution of the partnership agreement, provided that this was actually the case. Thus in *Best v McKay*,[54] the partnership commenced on 16 August 1938. However, the partnership agreement, which was not signed until February 1939, provided that the agreement commenced on 16 August 1938 and this clause was upheld by the Northern Ireland Court of Appeal.

[21.30] However, if the partnership did not actually commence on the earlier date, such a clause will be of no effect. Thus in *Macken v Revenue Commissioners*,[55] the partnership agreement which was executed in April 1954 provided that 'the partnership shall be deemed to have commenced on 1st day of January 1954'.[56] In the High Court, Teevan J held that this clause was of no effect since the partnership did not commence on 1 January 1954 as the parties were not in fact carrying on business in common as of that date.

Duration

[21.31] The duration of a partnership, if known, should be stated in the partnership agreement. A partnership which excludes the right of any one partner to dissolve the partnership by notice at any time[57] is a formal partnership (as distinct from a partnership at will). Where this right is excluded by having a fixed term (such as for a fixed number of years) it is known as a fixed term partnership.[58]

[21.32] If the partners fail to expressly or implicitly exclude the right of one partner to dissolve the partnership, it is a partnership at will and the partnership may be dissolved at any time by any one partner.[59] In a formal partnership, the partnership may be dissolved in accordance with the terms of the agreement regarding dissolution, eg

---

52   See generally in relation to the liability of a partner for the acts of his co-partners, para **[10.01]** et seq.

53   *Steele v Mart* (1825) 4 B & C 272; *Hall v Cazenove* (1804) 4 East 477; *Goddard's Case* (1584) 2 Co Rep 4b.

54   *Best v McKay* (1940) 74 ILTR 125.

55   *Macken v Revenue Commissioners* [1962] IR 302.

56   *Macken v Revenue Commissioners* [1962] IR 302 at 308.

57   Partnership Act 1890, s 26(1) and s 32(c).

58   See further regarding fixed term partnerships, para **[8.09]**.

59   See further regarding partnerships at will, para **[8.06]**.

partnership agreements will commonly provide for the agreement to be for an undefined term and to be subject to dissolution on the vote of a majority of the partners.[60] If there are no provisions regarding the firm's dissolution, but simply an agreement for the partnership to last for a fixed term, the partnership may not be dissolved before the expiry of the fixed term unless *all* the partners agree to the dissolution.

Formal partnership should contemplate new partners

[21.33] In formal partnerships, as distinct from partnerships at will, the partners have expressly or implicitly agreed that the right of a partner to dissolve the partnership by notice is disapplied.[61] Most commonly, this is achieved by the partners agreeing a fixed term for their partnership. However, in such formal partnerships, it is advisable that the partnership agreement expressly requires new partners to be bound by the terms of the partnership agreement. This is because the very act of admitting a new partner who does not expressly agree to be bound by terms of the partnership agreement will lead to the conversion of the formal partnership into a partnership at will. In the absence of the new partner signing a supplemental partnership agreement or deed of admission, in order to show that the new partner is bound by the original partnership agreement, the original partners will have to show conduct on the part of the new partner which indicates his unequivocal intention to be bound by the original partnership agreement.[62] Where this is not proved, the original partners may be surprised to learn that although their original partnership was for a fixed term, their 'new' partnership is a partnership at will and therefore may be dissolved by the notice of any one partner. This was the case in the English High Court case of *Firth v Armslake*,[63] where two doctors had an agreement to carry on business in partnership for their joint lives. It was thus a formal partnership since it could not be dissolved by any one partner. They subsequently introduced a third doctor to the firm and a draft deed was drawn up but it was never executed by the three of them. During this new partnership, the two original doctors sought to dissolve it and Plowman J held that the formal partnership which had been created between the two doctors was converted into a partnership at will on the admission of the third doctor, since no agreement had been reached as to its duration. For this reason, it was validly dissolved by the two original doctors.

The name of the firm

[21.34] The firm name should be stated in the partnership agreement as should the manner in which the name may be amended. The choice of firm name will be important as often a considerable amount of goodwill will attach to it. The name chosen by the firm should not be such as to amount to a passing off by the firm of its goods or services as that of another.[64] If the name does not contain the surnames of all the partners of the firm, it is useful to provide in the partnership agreement that the firm name must be registered as a business name under the Registration of Business Names Act 1963.

---

60 See para **[8.05]** where the reason for using the term 'formal partnership' is explained.
61 See generally in relation to such partnerships, para **[8.09]**.
62 See the decision of the Ontario Court of Appeal in *Zamikoff v Lundy* (1970) DLR (3d) 637.
63 *Firth v Armslake* (1964) 108 SJ 198.
64 See para **[3.67]** et seq in relation to such passing off, and see generally McMahon and Binchy, *Law of Torts* (4th edn, 2013) at para [31.01] et seq.

Although such registration is required in any event by the terms of the Registration of Business Names Act 1963, such a provision will operate as a reminder to the partners to register, since it is an offence to fail to do so.[65]

[21.35] The partnership agreement should address whether, after a partner leaves the firm, the continuing partners and/or the retiring partner will be entitled to continue to use that firm name. This is important because unless governed by the partnership agreement, any of the partners may use the firm name after the technical[66] or general dissolution[67] of the firm.

Nature of firm's business

[21.36] One of the more important clauses in the partnership agreement is one which is often either overlooked or drafted without much consideration, ie the description of the firm's business. This clause is important because the term 'business of the partnership' appears in many crucial sections of the 1890 Act. Accordingly, the scope of the application of those sections to a particular partnership will be determined in part by the description of the firm's business in the partnership agreement. This is because, in determining the nature of a firm's business, a court will undoubtedly be influenced by the description the parties themselves put upon it.[68]

[21.37] When describing the nature of a firm's business, a draftsman's initial reaction might be to take a similar approach to the one which is taken when drafting objects clauses for companies, ie to draft the clause widely enough to cover as many areas of business as possible. The rationale for this approach is that it will not be necessary to amend the agreement if the firm decides to expand its area of business at a later stage. However, while this might be a suitable approach for companies, this is not necessarily the best approach for partnerships. To take an example, under s 5 of the 1890 Act, a partner is bound by the acts of his co-partners who carry on the 'business of the partnership'. Thus, the wider the firm's business, the more extensive the liability of a partner under s 5 for the actions of his co-partners.

[21.38] Section 5 is but one of 19 sections[69] of the 1890 Act whose scope is dependant on the 'business of the partnership' and thus indirectly on the definition given to that

---

[65] Registration of Business Names Act 1963, s 18, see generally para **[3.70]** et seq.

[66] *Wilson v Williams* (1892) 29 LR Ir 176 and see generally para **[18.18]** et seq.

[67] Provided that it does not involve a holding out by the partner in question that he is carrying on business with his former partners, see further para **[18.26]**. As to the distinction between a technical and general dissolution, see para **[23.07]**.

[68] Although it goes without saying that the courts will also take into account the actual business carried on by the partners where this is different from the definition of that term in the partnership agreement.

[69] Section 6 – an act or instrument relating to the 'business of the firm' executed in firm-name is binding on firm; s 7 – a pledge of credit not connected with firm's 'ordinary course of business' is not binding on firm; s 10 – firm is liable for wrongs of partner committed in 'ordinary course of business'; s 13 – the misapplication of trust property in the 'business of partnership' by trustee partner does not make other partners liable; s 15 – where a partner makes a representation concerning the firm's affairs this representation will bind the firm if it is made 'in the ordinary course of its business'; (contd.../)

term by the partners.[70] Accordingly, these sections should be taken into account before deciding on the breadth of the description of a firm's business to be used in the partnership agreement.

Implied term that partnership books kept at place of business

[21.39] The place of business of the firm should be stated in the partnership agreement. This is because, in the absence of a contrary agreement between the partners, s 24(9) of the 1890 Act implies a term into every partnership agreement that the partnership books are to be kept at the place of business of the partnership. If there is more than one place of business, the partnership agreement should state the principal place of business, since in such a situation the partnership books must be kept there.[71] If the partners do not wish to keep the firm's books at its place of business or its principal place of business, s 24(9) should be expressly excluded by the partnership agreement or there should be a provision setting out where the books are to be kept.

2. Partnership Property

[21.40] One of the most contentious issues on the dissolution of partnerships is often the question of partnership property and, accordingly, considerable care should be taken over the provisions of the partnership agreement which deal with this matter.

Clarify which property is partnership property

[21.41] It is useful to indicate in the partnership agreement the legal ownership of property which is used by, or associated in any way with, the partnership. Assets which are intended to be partnership property should be clearly stated as such in the partnership agreement.[72] If this is not done, the question of which property is

---

69   (\...contd) s 16 – a notice to a partner who acts in the 'partnership business' is notice to the firm; s 20(1) – property acquired for the purpose of and in course of 'partnership business' is partnership property; s 24(2) – unless otherwise agreed, a firm indemnifies a partner for liabilities incurred by him in the conduct of the 'business of firm'; s 24(5) – unless otherwise agreed, every partner is entitled to take part in the management of the 'partnership business'; s 24(6) – unless otherwise agreed, no partner is entitled to remuneration for acting in the 'partnership business'; s 24(8) – unless otherwise agreed, any differences arising as to ordinary matters connected with the 'partnership business' are decided by a majority of the partners and the 'nature of the partnership business' may only be changed with the unanimous consent of all the partners; s 27(2) – a continuance of the 'business' by the partners without any settlement is a continuance of the partnership; s 30 – a partner must account to firm if carrying on 'business' of the same nature as that of firm; s 31 – an assignee of a partner's share may not interfere in 'partnership business'; s 34 – a firm is dissolved if it is unlawful for the 'business of the firm" to be carried on; s 35(c) – a court may dissolve a partnership where there has been misconduct by a partner, the court having regard to the 'nature of business' of the firm; s 35(d) – a court may dissolve a partnership where a partner is guilty of misconduct in matters relating to the 'partnership business'; and s 35(e) – a court may dissolve a partnership where 'business of partnership' can only be carried on at a loss.

70   See the wide interpretation placed upon the term 'partnership business' in s 20(1) of the 1890 Act in the case of *Murtagh v Costello* (1881) 7 LR Ir 428, para **[16.12]**.

71   Partnership Act 1890, s 24(9).

72   See generally in relation to which property is partnership property, para **[16.01]** et seq.

partnership property will have to be decided by examining the intention of the parties as disclosed by the facts of each particular case. Problems most commonly arise in relation to the premises which are used by firms but whose status is not clearly stated. It often happens that one partner assumes that the premises occupied by the firm are part of the partnership capital, while the registered owner of the premises has no such intention. For this reason, there is considerable value in having a partnership agreement which sets out specifically not only those items which form part of the partnership property, but also those items which are excluded.[73]

[21.42] Where the premises which are used by the partnership are in fact owned by one of the partners in his personal capacity, the right of the firm to use the premises should be governed by a separate lease between the firm and that partner. However, in view of the doubts about whether a person can grant a lease to himself and another party jointly,[74] this lease should be granted by a company controlled by the partner, rather than the partner himself. So for example, a company which is incorporated by the partner might take a lease of the property with a view to sub-leasing it to the firm. Where the premises are an important factor in the partnership's business, this lease should ideally provide for the continued use by the firm of the property during the continuance of the partnership. A situation where real or personal property is owned by one partner yet is used by the partnership without a written agreement for its continued use is particularly dangerous. This is especially so in relation to the partnership premises, as a considerable amount of the firm's goodwill may attach to that premises. However, it is also important in the case of other types of property, such as machinery, computers, trade marks, patents, etc.

Indicate which property is not partnership property

[21.43] In the absence of any agreement to the contrary, s 20(1) of the 1890 Act implies a term that any property which is acquired on account of the firm or for the purposes and in the course of the partnership business is partnership property.[75] It is common for s 20(1) or a similar term to be contained in the partnership agreement so as to ensure that, unless otherwise indicated, all property used by the partnership is partnership property. In these circumstances, if some property is not intended to become partnership property, it should be specifically excluded. In *Barr v Barr*,[76] a Donegal grocery partnership stored some of the firm's goods in a garage which adjoined the home of one of the partners. The garage was accepted by the parties to be partnership property. However, a dispute then arose between the partners as to whether the home of the partner was also partnership property.[77] The claim was rejected by Carroll J in the High Court. The case does, however, highlight the usefulness of expressly stating the status of property which is associated in any way with the partnership.

---

[73] As to the value of stating which items are not partnership property, see para **[16.21]**.

[74] This results from the principle that one cannot contract with oneself, see *Rye v Rye* [1962] AC 496 at 513 per Lord Denning. See generally Wylie, *Landlord and Tenant Law* (3rd edn, 2013) at para [2.13].

[75] See further para **[16.10]** et seq.

[76] This decision of Carroll J from 3 November 1983 is unreported but is referred to in *Barr v Barr* (29 July 1992) HC at p 2 of the transcript.

[77] However, it is not clear from the judgment what the basis for this allegation was.

Increase in value of property owned by one partner or by firm?

[21.44] An asset which is in the ownership of one or more partners, but is used by the firm, may increase in value due to expenditure of the firm's money. This might happen, for example, where the firm replaces or repairs part of the premises used by the firm (which is owned by one partner only), but where the premises is not subject to a lease.[78] In order to avoid subsequent disputes, the partnership agreement should address in the partnership agreement the question of whether the partner or the firm will be the beneficiary of this increase in value. This is because partnership disputes have arisen in which the firm has claimed a charge or lien in respect of the increase in value of the asset and it is not clear whether a court would hold that the firm is to be indemnified for the expenditure or is entitled to a lien or some other interest in the property.[79]

[21.45] Where the situation is in reverse, ie the firm owns an asset and one partner expends his own money on improving or repairing that asset, there is an implied term under s 24(2) of the 1890 Act that the partner must be indemnified by the firm, if the payment is made in the ordinary course of business of the firm or if necessarily done for the preservation of the business or the property of the firm.[80]

Whether goodwill is partnership property

[21.46] The partnership property clause should also deal with the question of whether the goodwill in the firm is partnership property or not.[81] Usually the goodwill belongs to the firm but in some firms, the goodwill belongs to just one or more of the partners. In such a case, the agreement should determine whether any increase in its value as a result of the work of the other partners will also belong to those partners alone.

[21.47] It is important to bear in mind that even where the partnership agreement provides that the goodwill is to have a nil value or where the accounts of the firm value the goodwill at a nil value, this does not mean that there is no goodwill. Rather, in the absence of a contrary agreement, each of the partners is entitled to his share of the goodwill. Therefore, on a dissolution of the firm, the outgoing partner may obtain the value of his share of the firm's goodwill whether the goodwill is sold on a distribution of the firm's assets or the remaining partners continue to carry on the business.[82]

Offices and appointments held by partners

[21.48] In professional firms, the appointment of a partner as an inspector, receiver, liquidator or examiner to a company may be a particularly lucrative position and thus a valuable piece of partnership property. For this reason, partnership agreements will often provide that offices or appointments which are held by partners are held on the

---

78 If the property is subject to a lease, reference should be made to the right of a tenant to obtain compensation for improvements under landlord and tenant law. See generally Wylie, *Landlord and Tenant Law* (3rd edn, 2014) at para [32.03] et seq.
79 In relation to such claims, see generally para **[16.44]** et seq.
80 See further para **[14.40]** et seq.
81 It is common for firms to provide in their balance sheet that no value shall be placed on goodwill. See generally in relation to goodwill, para **[18.01]** et seq.
82 Partnership Act 1890, s 39.

firm's behalf so that the partners are required to account to the firm for any fees or salary received in respect of such positions.

[21.49] In addition, it is also useful to deal with the possibility of the appointed partner leaving the firm during the course of his appointment. It may not always be appropriate to require the outgoing partner to resign from his position,[83] since there is no guarantee that another partner in the firm would be appointed to that position in his stead.

Where partner is a trustee

[21.50] If a partner accepts a position as a trustee and the trust document does not expressly grant him the power to charge the trust for his professional services, he will not be entitled to so charge.[84] In addition, that disability will affect his firm and so the firm will also not be able to charge for any professional services provided to the trust by non-trustee partners in the firm. It is common for partnership agreements to attempt to circumvent this prohibition. This is done by providing that where a partner in a firm advises a trust of which his co-partner is a trustee (and which does not entitle the trustee co-partner to charge the trust), the non-trustee partner is entitled to retain for his exclusive benefit any fees received from the trust for his professional services.[85] In this way, the fees become due to that partner in his own right and the inability of the firm to charge for its services does not affect him.

3. Sharing of Profits and Losses

Implied term that equal sharing of profits and losses

[21.51] Section 24(1) of the 1890 Act provides that, subject to any contrary agreement between the partners, each partner is entitled to an equal share of the profits of the firm and must contribute equally towards the losses of the firm. Thus, for example, where there is no profit sharing agreement, a dormant partner who devotes no time to the firm will be entitled to the same share of the profits as an ordinary partner who devotes his full time to the firm.

Unequal sharing of profits and losses

[21.52] Since in many firms it will be inappropriate to have such an equality of sharing, one of the most important reasons for having a partnership agreement is to exclude the implied term in s 24(1).[86] This is done by the partners setting out a different sharing of

---

83   But see for example the English High Court case of *Re Sutton (Removal of Liquidator)* [1997] LS Gaz R 29, in which a partner in a firm which had day to day conduct of the liquidation of a number of companies, successfully applied for the removal of one of the liquidators who had ceased to be a member of the firm.

84   See generally in relation to partners as trustees, para **[12.08]** et seq.

85   See *Re Boyle* [1947] IR 61, *Re De Courcenay* [1912] IR 341 and *Re Gates* [1933] 1 Ch 913. See further para **[12.10]**.

86   In *Heffernan & Anor v Murray & ors* [2015] IEHC 196, a mother had negotiated the terms of her adult children joining a partnership. When the partnership became involved in litigation in relation to a contract for sale of certain property, the children claimed that, when the partnership was formed, it had been agreed that they would not share in liabilities connected with that contact for sale, and would not be subject to any cash calls or other liabilities associated with the partnership. (contd.../)

the profits and losses in their partnership agreement. Commonly partnership agreements use percentages and they will sometimes provide for a review of the percentages on a regular basis. One of the problems with percentages is that every time a new partner joins the firm, the percentages of the existing partners are reduced. In particular, this may raise the sometimes contentious issue of whether each of the existing partners' percentages should be reduced equally or in proportion to their existing percentage. Under a points system each partner has a given number of points which in relation to the aggregate points of all the partners represents his fractional share of the profits and losses. The use of the points system has the aesthetic advantage over percentages that the existing partners' points are not reduced each time a partner joins the firm and therefore this issue does not arise. Another perceived advantage of the points system over percentages is that on the retirement of a partner, the points of the existing partners remain the same, while using a percentage system, an issue arises as to whether the departing partner's percentages should be shared equally between the continuing partners or in proportion to their existing percentage. The points method of dividing profits and losses is commonly encountered as part of the lockstep system of sharing partnership profits and losses.

The lockstep system

[21.53] One of the more common forms of profit sharing in modern professional partnerships is the 'lockstep' system of sharing profits and losses. Under this system, the profits and losses of the firm are shared proportionately to the number of points held by each partner relative to the aggregate of all the partners' points. As part of this system, a partner acquires a set number of points upon admission to the firm and with each passing year (for the first 10 or so years), he acquires more points (and accordingly more profits), at which stage his number of points remain static for say the next 10 years or so until he reaches a certain age (usually 55). At that stage, the partner begins to lose points with each passing year until he reaches retirement age. This system is used in larger professional firms since it encourages early retirement by senior partners so as to make way for the admission of younger partners.[87] The lockstep system aims to keep the partnership vibrant by encouraging older partners on maximum points to retire under early retirement provisions. This retirement of one senior partner financially facilitates the introduction of two new partners since it will often transpire that the combined points of those two new partners, plus the cost to the firm of a pension to the retired partner, will be about the same as the amount which the retired partner had been withdrawing in profits from the firm.

---

[86] (\...contd) However, these terms were not included in the final partnership agreement, and Binchy J held that it would not be possible to exonerate those partners from the partnership's liabilities without an amendment to the partnership agreement. Accordingly, those partners were also bound by the terms of the partnership agreement entered into by the partnership.

[87] To be effective in encouraging retirement, firms which use the lockstep system commonly provide generous pension arrangements, though in view of the increased income tax relief of up to 40% (under s 787 of the Taxes Consolidation Act 1997, as amended) which is available for persons making pension arrangements, it may be that there will be a move to put the onus on partners to look after their own pension arrangements rather than looking to the firm.

[21.54] In some firms, there have been moves away from the lockstep system in favour of systems of profit sharing based on merit, contribution and fee-income. These methods of profit sharing will often rely on the views of the managing partner and a committee of partners in determining the partners' respective profit shares.

Profits and losses of capital treated in the same manner as income

[21.55] Profits and losses of capital are treated in the same way as profits and losses of income. Therefore, under s 24(1) of the 1890 Act, unless otherwise agreed between the partners, all partners are obliged to share equally in the profits of capital[88] and contribute equally to the losses of capital of the firm.[89] Similarly, if the profits and losses of income have been agreed to be shared unequally, the profits and losses of capital will be shared in that proportion. For this reason, where the intention is that the partners will share profits and losses of capital in a different proportion to the manner in which they share profits and losses of income, it is imperative that this is stated in the partnership agreement.

[21.56] This issue is particularly relevant where the partners have contributed to the capital of the firm unequally, but share profits of income equally. If the capital has increased in value so as to result in a capital profit, eg due to an increase in property prices, then in the absence of agreement, that capital profit will be divided between the partners equally and not in proportion to their original capital contributions. Accordingly, it is useful to deal in the partnership agreement with the sharing of profits and losses of capital separately from the sharing of profits and losses of income in order to concentrate the partners' minds on this distinction and to reduce the likelihood of subsequent disputes.

Where only the rate of profit-share is stated

[21.57] Sometimes partnership agreements will, somewhat idealistically it must be said, only provide for the proportion in which profits are to be shared and make no mention of the sharing of losses. Extreme care should be taken with such provisions. This is because s 24(1) of the 1890 Act provides that in the absence of agreement, profits and losses are shared equally. Thus, it might be thought that where there is no reference to the sharing of losses, that they are shared equally between the partners. This is not in fact the case. Instead, it has been held that losses are shared in the same proportion as profits.[90] This common law principle is also reflected in the 1890 Act, but only in s 44(a) in relation to the dissolution of the firm. This section provides that on the dissolution of a firm, the losses are paid by the partners in the proportion in which they were entitled to share profits. Therefore, if it is envisaged that the partners would share the losses in a different proportion to the sharing of profits, this should be expressly stated in the partnership agreement, since otherwise the rate of profit share will be taken also to be

---

[88]   *Robinson v Ashton* (1875) LR 20 Eq 25; See also the Partnership Act 1890, s 44(b)(4).

[89]   See also the Partnership Act 1890, s 44(a) in relation to the dissolution of partnerships: ie 'Losses, *including losses and deficiencies of capital*, shall be paid first out of profits, next out of capital, and lastly, if necessary, by the partners individually in the proportion in which they were entitled to share profits' (emphasis added).

[90]   *Re Albion Life Assurance Society* (1880) 16 Ch D 83.

the rate of loss share. While it would be most unusual for a partnership agreement to provide for the rate of loss share only,[91] the logic underlying this rule is equally applicable in reverse. Thus, it is contended that the rate of profit share in such a case would be taken to be the same as the agreed rate of loss share.

Position of salaried partners

[21.58] Since a salaried partner is not a partner as a matter of law,[92] he is not liable for the losses of the firm. However, he may be held liable to third parties for the obligations of the firm on the basis that he has allowed himself to be held out as a partner.[93] For this reason, it is common for the partners in a firm to indemnify the salaried partners in respect of any liability incurred by them as a result of their being held out as partners. This indemnity should be contained in a salaried partner's agreement (an agreement between the firm and the salaried partner) and not in the partnership agreement, as the salaried partner should not be a party to the partnership agreement since he is not a partner.[94]

Treatment of profits and losses on a dissolution

[21.59] Previously, consideration has been given to the sharing of profits and losses under s 24(1) of the 1890 Act which deals with the firm as a going concern. Section 44 of the 1890 Act also deals with the sharing of profits and losses by the firm, but on its dissolution. On the dissolution of a firm, the debts and liabilities of the firm are first paid off and then the advances and capital contributions of each partner are repaid.[95]

Sharing of capital profits and income profits on a dissolution

[21.60] After these matters have been dealt with, s 44(b)(4) of the 1890 Act requires all of the partners to share the 'ultimate residue' in the manner in which profits are divided. As previously noted, in the absence of agreement between the partners, the manner in which profits are divided is deemed to be equally.[96] The 'ultimate residue' will consist of capital profits and/or residual income profits. Under this section, the profits of income and the profits of capital are both distributed on a dissolution in the manner in which profits are divided. The capital profits on a dissolution represent a hidden fund of profits in the firm often resulting from the assets in the partnership accounts appearing at their written down value or they may result from the absence of a provision in the accounts for goodwill. This capital profit may be realised when the assets or goodwill are sold on the general dissolution of the firm.

---

91 And indeed the arrangement may not thereby constitute a partnership, since it may not have a 'view of profit' as required by the definition of partnership in s 1(1) of the 1890 Act, see further para **[2.62]** et seq.

92 See generally regarding salaried partners, para **[6.18]** et seq.

93 Partnership Act 1890, s 14(1). See generally in relation to liability as a partner by holding out, para **[7.01]** et seq.

94 See para **[21.20]**.

95 Partnership Act 1890, s 44(b)(1)–(3).

96 By virtue of s 24(1) of the 1890 Act, see also para **[21.51]**.

Sharing of losses of income and losses of capital on a dissolution

[21.61] It has been noted that in the absence of contrary agreement between the partners, the capital profits are shared on a dissolution in the same proportion as income profits.[97] Similarly, in the absence of any agreement, losses of capital and losses of income are shared on a dissolution in that same proportion. This follows from s 44(a) of the 1890 Act which provides that on a dissolution, the '[l]osses, including losses and deficiencies of capital' will be shared in the same proportion as the profits. Thus, if the partners agree to share profits in unequal proportions but the agreement is silent as regards the sharing of losses, capital losses are shared on a dissolution in the same unequal proportions.

[21.62] Consideration has been given already to the situation in which the partners may wish to separately provide for the sharing of capital profits and capital losses while the firm is a going concern.[98] The same principles apply to the sharing of profits of capital and losses of capital on a dissolution. Therefore, a provision in the partnership agreement will be imperative where the partners have, for example, contributed capital to the firm in unequal contributions but share profits equally, yet wish to receive the capital profits or capital losses on a dissolution in the same proportion as their capital contributions. An example will highlight the type of situation in which this may be relevant – A and B contribute €1,000 and €4,000 respectively as capital, but share profits in their firm equally. That capital is used by the firm to purchase premises for €5,000. When the partnership is dissolved the premises are sold for a €50,000 profit. The agreement is silent as regards the sharing of capital profits on a dissolution and accordingly after the capital contributions of €1,000 and €4,000 are paid back to each partner, A and B will share the €50,000 capital profit equally even though they contributed unequally to the purchase of the premises. The rationale for such a rule is that in any partnership, the capital which is contributed by a partner will not be restricted to money, but will encompass expertise, work-rate, business contacts etc. Thus, the capital profit is, in the absence of a contrary agreement, assumed to be divided equally between them rather than in proportion to the rate of 'financial' capital contributed by the partners.[99]

[21.63] If the partners wish to share the capital profits or losses of capital on a dissolution in the same proportion as they contributed capital to the firm, rather than in the manner in which they share profits, it will be necessary to have a provision to that effect in the partnership agreement. This provision will then override the terms of s 44(a) and 44(b)(4) of the 1890 Act. Even where it is the parties' intention to share capital profits and capital losses on a dissolution in the same manner as profits and losses of income, it is useful to spell this out in the partnership agreement so as to avoid any subsequent misunderstanding between the parties.

---

97   Partnership Act 1890, s 44(b)(4).

98   See para **[21.56]**.

99   The fairness of the rule is clear when one considers that if the capital which is contributed is dissipated, there will be a capital loss of €5,000 which is also shared equally between A and B. The €1,000 and €4,000 contributions are treated as deferred debts due by the firm to A and B, and A will in effect be liable for half of the €5,000 capital loss.

Compensation for goodwill is not capital but assets or profits

[21.64] Under general partnership law, the amount of money received by a partnership for the sale of its goodwill is not capital and therefore not repayable to the partners in the proportion in which they agreed to share capital.[100] Instead, it has been held to be either 'assets' or (capital) 'profits'. If it is assets, it is distributable on a dissolution, in the absence of agreement between the partners, according to s 44 of the 1890 Act as part of the ultimate residue (ie 'in the proportion in which profits are divisible'). If it is profits, it is distributable on a dissolution, in accordance with the terms of the partners' agreement or where there is no such agreement, equally.[101] However, if the parties wish to share the compensation for goodwill in the same proportion as they contributed capital to the firm, this should be stated expressly in the partnership agreement, since otherwise it will be distributed in the same manner as profits are shared.

Implied term that advances paid off in priority to capital on dissolution

[21.65] Under s 44(b) of the 1890 Act, unless otherwise agreed between the partners, advances which are paid by the partners to the firm are repaid to the partners, on the dissolution of the partnership, in priority to repayments of capital to the partners. It should be obvious therefore, that it will be significant whether a partner contributes additional funds to an ailing partnership in the form of an 'advance' or in the form of a further 'capital contribution'. If the partners do not wish to give priority to repayments of advances over capital, this priority, which is granted to advances by s 44(b), should be expressly excluded by the terms of partnership agreement.

Include right of a partner to make drawings

[21.66] It is usual for partnership agreements to provide for the firm's annual accounts to be signed by all the partners once they have been finalised. In addition, the agreement usually provides that the profits (or losses) of the firm are to be calculated every year on the basis of those signed accounts. Since this will only occur once a year, it is useful to have a provision entitling each partner to a certain amount of drawings on a monthly basis in anticipation of his end of year profit-share, with a provision for repayment in the event of the partners drawing more than their end of year entitlement.

Undrawn profits may be withdrawn at any time

[21.67] As a matter of general partnership law, the undrawn profits in a firm may be withdrawn at any time, unless there is a contrary provision in the partnership agreement.[102] The undrawn profits of a partner should be transferred to that partner's current account in the partnership accounts, from which they may be withdrawn at any time by that partner.

[21.68] If a firm wishes to use undrawn profits for a certain purpose, for example, to fund a retirement annuity pension for the partners or to create a reserve account to deal

---

[100] See the Northern Ireland Court of Appeal decision in *McClelland v Hyde* [1942] NI 1, paras **[18.08]** and **[18.10]**.

[101] Partnership Act 1890, s 44(b)(4) and s 24(1).

[102] l'Anson Banks, *Lindley & Banks on Partnership* (20th edn, 2017) at para 17-06.

with future tax assessments on the partners, this should be explicitly stated in the partnership agreement.

4. Other Financial Rights of Partners

Implied term that interest is payable on advances to the firm

[21.69] Section 24(3) of the 1890 Act provides that where a partner makes an advance to his firm beyond the amount of capital which he has agreed to subscribe under the terms of the partnership agreement, he is entitled to interest at the rate of 5% per annum on that advance. In some partnerships, the partners may wish to exclude or vary the application of this term, and if so, this should be done by the express disapplication of s 24(3) or the inclusion of a contrary term in the partnership agreement.

State capital as an amount of money

[21.70] It is common for partners to contribute capital to their firm in the form of non-cash assets.[103] In such a case, it is important that a value be put upon these assets and that this value be attributed to the contributing partner in the accounts of the firm. By so doing, the firm's capital structure and future changes thereto will be easier to discern than if the capital contributions are represented only by the relevant assets.

[21.71] From a capital gains tax perspective, it is also useful if the partnership agreement sets out at the commencement of the partnership the interest of each partner in the firm's capital and in a particular partnership asset, where it is introduced to the firm by more than one partner. In order to discern easily the capital of the firm, the capital clause in the partnership agreement should provide for the partnership accounts to contain a separate capital account for each partner.[104]

Manner in which capital contributions are repaid on a dissolution

[21.72] It is noted elsewhere in this work,[105] that on the dissolution of a partnership, s 44(b)(3) of the 1890 Act takes precedence over s 24(1). This means that the capital contributions of the partners are repaid to the partners 'rateably' in accordance with s 44(b)(3) and not 'equally' as might otherwise appear from the wording of s 24(1).[106]

[21.73] If the partners do not wish to receive back their capital contributions rateably, but to have them divided equally, this may be provided for in the partnership agreement, since s 44 is expressly stated to be subject to any contrary agreement between the partners.

---

[103] As to the distinction between partnership capital and partnership assets, see para **[17.05]**.

[104] As under s 30 of the Taxes Consolidation Act 1997, capital gains tax accruing to partners on the disposal of any partnership assets is to be assessed on each of them separately, and partnership dealings in assets are treated as dealings by the partners themselves, and not by the partnership. See further in relation to capital and current accounts, para **[17.09]**.

[105] See para **[26.116]**.

[106] Although any surplus capital is divided equally between them as required by s 44(b)(4) of the 1890 Act.

Indicate whether interest is to be payable on capital?

[21.74] In cases where the partners contribute capital unequally, they may wish to have a provision in their agreement that interest will be payable on capital contributions. In the absence of a specific provision, no interest is payable on the capital contributed by the partners. This is because s 24(4) of the 1890 Act provides that a partner is not entitled, before the ascertainment of profits, to interest on capital. Despite the use of the phrase 'before the ascertainment of profits', this section does not mean that a partner is entitled to interest on capital after the ascertainment of profits, he is only entitled to such interest if there is an express provision in the partnership agreement.[107]

[21.75] Where payment of interest on capital is allowed under the terms of the partnership agreement, it will be made out of the firm's profits and thus is said to constitute a payment of profits to the relevant partners[108] and it should be credited to each partner's current account before the profit for the year is ascertained. Where interest is payable on an advance and on capital, it is contended that interest will be payable on an advance in priority to interest on capital on the basis of the general priority accorded to advances over capital by the 1890 Act.[109]

Include right to increase or reduce capital?

[21.76] As a matter of general partnership law, in the absence of any contrary agreement between the partners, the capital of the firm cannot be increased or reduced without the consent of all the partners.[110] Thus, even if the firm will not survive without a further contribution of capital, a partner cannot be required to contribute additional capital against his will. Therefore, in those partnerships where there is a need for a further injection of capital, it may be useful to have a provision in the partnership agreement allowing for the increase or reduction of the capital where a majority of the partners so decide.

Is contribution of capital to be a condition precedent?

[21.77] If it is intended that a partner's right to participate in the partnership is to be conditional on his making his capital contribution, this should be expressly stated in the partnership agreement, as the courts will not readily infer such a precondition.[111]

---

107 *Millar v Craig* (1843) 6 Beav 433; *Hill v King* (1863) 3 De GJ & Sm 418; *Cooke v Benbow* (1865) 3 De GJ & Sm 1; *Rishton v Grissel* (1870) LR 10 Eq 393. See also I'Anson Banks, *Lindley & Banks on Partnership* (20th edn, 2017) at para 17-12.

108 I'Anson Banks, *Lindley & Banks on Partnership* (20th edn, 2017) at para 10-71.

109 This priority is evident from ss 24(3) and 44(b)(2) of the 1890 Act.

110 *Bouche v Sproule* (1887) 12 AC 385 at 405; *Re Bridgewater Navigation Co* [1891] 2 Ch 317 at 327 and para **[17.13]**.

111 This is apparent from the case of *Kemble v Mills* (1841) 9 Dow 446. In that case, the partners agreed that one partner would contribute £2,000 and do certain things for the benefit of the partnership, while the other would contribute £5,000. It was held that the first partner could maintain an action against the second partner in respect of the £5,000, even though the first partner did not prove that he had carried out his part of the bargain.

Implied term that no right of a partner to remuneration

[21.78] Section 24(6) of the 1890 Act provides that a partner is not entitled to remuneration for acting in the partnership business unless this is agreed to by all the partners.[112] It has been held that a managing partner of a firm is not entitled to an allowance for carrying on the partnership trade where there is neither an agreement nor a custom between the partners to have such an allowance.[113] Accordingly, if, as is sometimes the case, it is intended to pay the managing partner an additional share of the profits (sometimes incorrectly referred to as a 'salary') for managing the firm, this should be stated in the partnership agreement in order to circumvent the implied term in s 24(6) of the 1890 Act.

Implied term that partner has right to repayment of expenses

[21.79] Section 24(2) of the 1890 Act provides that, subject to contrary agreement between the partners, a partner is entitled to be reimbursed costs incurred by him in the ordinary and proper conduct of the business of the firm or in or about anything necessarily done for the preservation of the business or property of the firm.[114] Since this implied term is one which would be common amongst most partners, it might be useful to have this provision or some provision equivalent to it repeated in the partnership agreement.[115] In addition, it would be helpful to list those expenses which are regarded by the partners as reimbursable, so as to avoid any subsequent misunderstanding between the partners. In the nineteenth century case of *Hutcheson v Smith*,[116] there was no agreement between the partners in a distillery firm in Armagh for the reimbursement of expenses incurred by a partner in entertaining clients. For this reason, and as there was no evidence that such allowances were usual in the trade, Brady CB held they were not reimbursable. However, this decision should be treated with caution since today, client entertainment is likely to be viewed as being 'usual in the trade' in view of its integral role in modern business.

Implied term that each partner is entitled to sign cheques

[21.80] As a matter of general partnership law, each partner is authorised to sign cheques of the firm.[117] In many instances, a firm may wish to restrict the rights of certain partners to sign cheques or to sign cheques over a certain amount and to do so, a provision should be inserted in the partnership agreement to that effect. This provision should of course be duplicated in the bank mandate form. It is also common practice to state the name of the firm's bank in the partnership agreement, but this is not strictly

---

112 See generally in relation to s 24(6) of the 1890 Act, para **[14.47]**.
113 *Hutcheson v Smith* (1842) 5 Ir Eq R 117.
114 See generally in relation to s 24(2) of the 1890 Act, para **[14.40]**.
115 In this way, the partnership agreement will contain all the rights and duties of partners in one document, without having to have recourse to the 1890 Act. See para **[21.19]**.
116 *Hutcheson v Smith* (1842) 5 Ir Eq R 117.
117 *Backhouse v Charlton* (1878) 8 Ch D 444; *Laws v Rand* (1857) 27 LJCP 76.

necessary as a decision regarding the identity of the bank can be taken after the agreement is executed.[118]

Payment of premium

[21.81] In contrast to earlier times, modern partnership agreements do not usually provide for the payment of a premium by an incoming partner as a form of consideration for his being admitted as a partner. However, in the unlikely event of a partnership agreement providing for the payment of such premiums, the agreement should outline the circumstances in which the premium will be returned. Under s 40 of the 1890 Act, where such a partnership is dissolved before the end of the fixed term, otherwise than by death, the court has a discretion to order the repayment of the premium or part thereof to the paying partner.[119] In addition, under s 41(a) of the 1890 Act, where a partnership contract is rescinded on the ground of the fraud or misrepresentation of one of the parties thereto, the party entitled to rescind is entitled to a lien on the surplus of the partnership assets for any sum of money paid by him for any premium, or, in the words of that section, 'money paid by him for the purchase of a share in the partnership'.

[21.82] In modern professional firms, the antithesis of a premium, the payment of 'hello money', is more likely to occur than the payment of a premium. This payment is designed to encourage a new partner to join a firm on the assumption often that he will bring not only his professional reputation but also his pre-existing clients with him to the new firm.

Implied right to assign partnership share

[21.83] Under s 31(1) of the 1890 Act, a partner is entitled to assign his share in the partnership to a third party. The assignee does not thereby become a partner in the firm but instead becomes entitled to receive the assignor's share of the profits.[120] In addition, the assignee is not entitled to interfere in the partnership business. Nonetheless, it is common for partnership agreements to expressly exclude the right to assign a partnership share by providing that a partner may not do so, or only do so with the consent of the other partners.

[21.84] In limited partnerships[121] and investment limited partnerships,[122] it is more common for the limited partners to be entitled to assign their shares to third parties, since the assignee of a limited partner in either of these partnerships is entitled to become a partner in the firm in place of the assignor.

---

118 This decision would fall to be taken by the partners, in the absence of contrary agreement between the partners, under the general decision-making power of partners under s 24(8) of the 1890 Act.

119 See further regarding premiums and their repayment, para **[26.51]**.

120 See generally in relation to the assignment of a share in a partnership, para **[19.12]** et seq.

121 See the Limited Partnerships Act 1907, s 6(5)(b). This right is subject to the consent of the general partners and is subject to contrary agreement between the partners. See generally para **[28.117]** et seq.

122 See the Investment Limited Partnerships Act 1994, s 18. This right is subject to the consent of the general partners, but is not subject to the contrary agreement of the partners. See generally para **[29.126]**.

Annuity clauses

[21.85] The payment of pensions by firms which use the lockstep system has already been referred to.[123] The payment of annuities by firms to the family of former partners, although popular in former times, is no longer that common in modern partnership agreements. If the partnership agreement is to contain a provision for the payment of an annuity, it should be clear as to whether the annuity is only payable out of profits or whether it is payable regardless of the profits of the firm. As noted earlier in this work,[124] s 2(3)(a) of the 1890 Act provides that the receipt by a widow or a child of a deceased partner of a share of the profits of a firm by way of annuity does not per se make the recipient a partner.

Enforcement of annuity by beneficiaries

[21.86] In cases in which annuities are being paid, the beneficiary of the annuity will usually be a family relation of a deceased partner in the firm and the partnership agreement will require the continuing partners to pay the annuity. Despite the absence of any privity of contract between the beneficiaries and the continuing partners, the courts have allowed beneficiaries to enforce the payment of such an annuity against the continuing partners, by either allowing the personal representative of the deceased partner to take the action or by construing the grant of the annuity as the creation of a trust. In *Drimmie v Davies*,[125] Davies senior carried on a dental practice at 27 Westmoreland St in Dublin. He took his son, Davies junior, into the practice as a partner. The terms of the deed of partnership provided that should Davies senior die during the partnership, Davies junior would pay annuities to the other children of Davies senior. Davies senior died during the partnership but Davies junior refused to pay the annuities and was sued by his brothers and sisters and by the executor of Davies senior. Davies junior argued that his brothers and sisters were not entitled to sue since they were not party to his partnership agreement with Davies senior. In the Irish Court of Appeal, it was held that the personal representative was entitled to bring the action for the benefit of the children and if he failed to do so, the court would allow an action by the children by construing the grant of the annuity as the creation of a trust in their favour.[126]

5. Partnership Books and Accounts

Implied right of access to partnership books

[21.87] Under s 24(9) of the 1890 Act, each partner has a right of access to, and a right to inspect and copy, the partnership books. This right is subject to contrary agreement amongst the partners.[127]

---

123 See para **[21.53]**.
124 See para **[2.108]**.
125 *Drimmie v Davies* [1899] 1 IR 176.
126 See in particular the judgments of Fitzgibbon LJ and of Walker LJ.
127 See the introductory words of s 24 of the 1890 Act. See also, regarding contractual rights of access provided for in a partnership agreement, *Inversions Frieira SL v Colyzeo Investors II LP* [2012] Bus LR 1136 (a limited partnership case – see further para **[28.79]**).

Irrevocable right to partnership accounts

[21.88] Unlike the right of access to partnership books under s 24(9), the obligation on partners to render to each other true accounts and information in relation to the partnership under s 28 of the 1890 Act is not stated to be subject to contrary agreement between the partners. Indeed, it is apprehended that the right of a partner to true partnership accounts and information in relation to the partnership is irrevocable. This conclusion does, however, run counter to the express terms of s 19 of the 1890 Act which allows the partners to agree to a variation of their rights and duties set out in the Act. However, it is contended that some rights in the 1890 Act are of such importance as to be inalienable and that the right of a partner to a true account of partnership dealings is one of these rights. This conclusion is supported by the fact that, unlike practically all of the other implied rights in the 1890 Act,[128] s 28 is not stated to be subject to contrary agreement.

[21.89] However, more significant support for this conclusion is to be found in the nature of the right itself, namely access to the most basic information regarding the firm of which the partner is a member. If one partner was allowed to prevent the other partner from knowing the true state of affairs of the business, it is apprehended they would not be 'carrying on a business in common' in the true sense of that expression and therefore would not satisfy the definition of partnership in s 1(1) of the 1890 Act. It has been noted previously that to constitute a partnership, the partners must intend to make a profit.[129] Therefore, if one partner is deprived of his right to true accounts, the *raison d'être* of the partnership for that partner is arguably missing. In such a situation, it is contended that there would be no 'real' partnership.[130] Furthermore, without having true accounts and information on the partnership, a partner would not be in a position to monitor any abuses by his co-partners of their positions. This is of particular significance in partnerships, since each partner is liable to an unlimited degree for the partnership obligations. For this reason, it is contended that the right of a partner to true accounts and partnership information in s 28 of the 1890 Act is so basic a right in every partnership that it is not possible for the partners to agree that one partner will be deprived of this right.[131] However, a term in the partnership agreement clarifying the

---

128   Namely ss 21, 22, 24, 25, 29(1), 30, 32, 33, 42(1), 43 and 44 of the 1890 Act.

129   See para [2.62] et seq.

130   See for example *Horgan v Murray Consultants Ltd* [1997] 3 IR 23, in which the defence by the directors that they were not quasi-partners was based on the fact that they did not receive the company's accounts from the quasi-partners. When the petition was heard by O'Sullivan J in the High Court in 1999, he found that no quasi-partnership existed, but did not consider the point regarding the company's accounts in reaching his decision.

131   Note that in America, s 105 of the Uniform Partnership Act (1997) (Last Amended 2013) provides that certain terms implied by that Act into the partnership relationship are not capable of being varied by the partnership agreement, one of which is the reasonable right of access to the books and records of the partnership under s 408 of that Act. It is also to be noted that, unlike the position in Ireland, the obligation of good faith and fair dealing, the duty of loyalty and the duty of care are statutory rights in America and under the Uniform Partnership Act (1997) (Last Amended 2013), may not be eliminated or altered by the terms of the partnership agreement, save to the limited extent set out in that Act.

parameters of this right is acceptable, provided that it is not so restrictive as to deprive the right of any true effect.

[21.90] If it is intended that the partnership agreement constitute a comprehensive charter of the rights and duties of partners, without the necessity to refer to the 1890 Act,[132] the right of each partner to render each other true accounts should be set out in the written partnership agreement.

Difference between partnership books and accounts

[21.91] It has been seen that the right in s 24(9) of the 1890 Act of a partner to have access to partnership books may be excluded, but that the right of a partner in s 28 of the 1890 Act to have access to true partnership accounts may not be excluded. This raises the question of what is the substantive difference between a firm's books under s 24(9) and its accounts under s 28. It is suggested that the accounts of the firm are limited to that information which an auditor would prepare, namely the turnover, gross profit, net profit, etc. On the other hand the concept of partnership books is wider and is likely to include this same financial information, but also more general, and oftentimes more sensitive, information such as a detailed breakdown of the billings of the firm, eg by client type, by the work type, by the level of partner billings, by marketing information, etc. Therefore, if the partners in a firm wish to prevent a new partner or a junior partner from exercising his right of access to such sensitive information, this, it is suggested, can be done by the express exclusion in the partnership agreement of the type of information which may not be accessed.

Preparation of accounts

[21.92] Although partnerships are not required by law to prepare audited accounts,[133] it is advisable that partnerships (save for accounting firms, for obvious reasons) should have their accounts audited. Accordingly, the partnership agreement should make specific provision for the keeping of accounts and of a balance sheet, since there is no statutory obligation on a partnership to prepare or file accounts.[134] This clause should set out the date up to which the accounts of the firm are to be prepared and any special provisions regarding the preparation of the accounts, eg if goodwill is to be excluded[135] or how work in progress is to be treated.[136] It is also common practice to state the name

---

132 See para **[21.19]**.

133 Save in exceptional circumstances, see para **[14.66]** et seq. Note that the Revenue Commissioners may require accounts from the firm, see s 880(2) of the Taxes Consolidation Act 1997.

134 There is, however, the obligation of each partner to render true accounts to each other under s 28 of the 1890 Act. Note, however, that if the partners are limited liability companies they would be subject to the European Communities (Accounts) Regulations 1993, see further para **[14.66]** et seq. In addition, a partnership is required to deliver a return of income for the partnership: Taxes Consolidation Act 1997, s 880(2). This return must contain details of the amount of income from all sources of income of the partnership for the year of assessment and clearly for this purpose reference should be made to the accounts of the firm. See further Maguire, *Irish Income Tax* 2018 (2018) at para 4.50 et seq.

135 See generally in relation to goodwill, para **[18.01]** et seq.

136 See further para **[14.20]**. If the partners so wish, they may use an accounting method which allows for work in progress to be included in the calculation of the net profits.

of the firm's auditors in the partnership agreement, but this is not strictly necessary as a decision regarding their identity can be taken after the agreement is executed.[137]

[21.93] It is advisable for the partnership agreement to provide for all the partners to sign the accounts once they have been approved. In addition, in order to avoid minor disputes, it is useful to provide that the accounts thus signed are binding on all the partners in the absence of 'manifest errors'.[138]

6. Management Rights of Partners

Implied right of every partner to manage the firm's business

[21.94] Under s 24(5) of the 1890 Act, every partner may participate in the management of the business of the firm unless otherwise agreed. In large partnerships, this right will be inappropriate in light of the size of the firm. In such firms, management of the firm is usually entrusted to the managing partner and a managing committee, often comprising the head of each of the departments in the firm. The committee and/or the managing partner are usually entitled to take all day-to-day management decisions of the firm, while more important decisions are reserved for full partners' meetings. In addition, it is common in such larger partnerships to have a provision entitling the partners to delegate management issues to an office manager or chief executive, who will often not be a partner.

[21.95] Where it is intended to have such a management structure, the right of every partner to participate in the management of the firm, which is granted by s 24(5) of the 1890 Act, should be either expressly or implicitly modified by the terms of the partnership agreement.

Partners to devote full time to firm

[21.96] The 1890 Act does not imply a term requiring a partner to devote his full time to the firm. Accordingly, if there is no provision in the partnership agreement to that effect, the amount of time which a partner devotes to the firm is at his discretion. For this reason, it is vital to have a term in most partnership agreements requiring each partner to devote his full time to the firm or specifying the amount of time which he is required to devote to the firm's business. Without such a clause, it will not be an easy matter for the partners in a firm to prove that their co-partner, who carries on his outside interests to an excessive degree, is acting contrary to partnership law or to the partnership agreement.

[21.97] In conjunction with the requirement to devote full time to the firm's business, it is usual to find a clause prohibiting a partner from competing with the firm. Even without such an express provision, s 30 of the 1890 Act implies an obligation upon a

---

[137] Pursuant to the general decision making power of partners in s 24(8) of the 1890 Act.

[138] As regards the meaning of this expression, note the statement of Lord Lindley that '[w]here, however, all parties act *bona fide*, such clauses are operative; but the usual provision as to manifest errors applies only to errors in figures and obvious blunders, not to errors in judgment, eg in treating as good debts which ultimately turn out to be bad, or in omitting losses not known to have occurred': l'Anson Banks, *Lindley & Banks on Partnership* (20th edn, 2017) at para 10-79.

partner to account to the firm for any profits derived from a competing business.[139] Indeed in some partnerships, the partners may wish to have an even greater restriction on a partner's outside activities, on the basis that these might reflect badly on the firm's reputation. For example the partnership agreement may have a prohibition on partners obtaining any outside office or appointment, whether in a competing business or not, without the consent of the other partners.

[21.98] From a practical perspective, it is useful also to deal in the partnership agreement with the right of partners to take holidays, as this issue can often give rise to difficulties in busy partnerships. Such clauses will often provide that all the partners are not permitted to take holidays at the same time, in which case the clause should also address the sometimes difficult issue of whether certain partners will have a first choice regarding their dates for holidays.

Implied term as to decision making

[21.99] Under s 24(8) of the 1890 Act, all differences arising as to ordinary matters regarding the partnership business are decided by a majority of the partners. In addition, no change may be made in the nature of the partnership business without the consent of all the existing partners. Both these implied terms are subject to any contrary agreement between the partners.

Alternative voting structures

[21.100] It is important to bear in mind that a 'majority' in the context of s 24(8) of the 1890 Act means a majority in number and not a majority on the basis of capital contribution, profit share or otherwise. It follows that an express provision should be contained in the partnership agreement if the partners wish to vote on the basis of financial interest, rather than on a *per capita* basis. It is also possible to have partnership agreements which provide for a weighted voting system or for voting based on the number of points held by a partner in the lockstep system.[140]

[21.101] In addition, the partners may wish to change the voting structure to take account of the particular needs of the firm, so that, for example, during the holiday season, a decision may be taken by a majority of the partners attending the relevant partners' meeting rather than a majority of all the partners of the firm. Alternatively, there is nothing to prevent a partnership from using voting structures which are used by companies, such as allowing for written resolutions[141] or proxy voting.[142] In this regard,

---

[139] This is considered at para **[15.44]** et seq.

[140] As to the lockstep system generally, see para **[21.53]**.

[141] As regards the situation for companies, see Companies Act 2014, s 193 (in respect of unanimous written resolutions) and s 194 (in respect of majority written resolutions). See generally regarding such resolutions in companies, Courtney, *The Law of Companies* (4th edn, 2016) at para [14.103] et seq; Hutchinson, *Keane on Company Law* (5th edn, 2016) at para [25.34] et seq.

[142] As regards the situation for companies, see Companies Act 2014, s 183. See generally regarding proxy voting in companies, Courtney, *The Law of Companies* (4th edn, 2016) at para [14.062] et seq; Hutchinson, *Keane on Company Law* (5th edn, 2016) at para [25.55] et seq.

it is common for the larger partnerships to have adaptations of the company voting provisions from the Companies Act 2014, such as the provisions regarding the giving of notice of partners' meetings, the quorum necessary, etc. Indeed, as large professional partnerships begin more and more to resemble companies in their management, it is thought that the courts may apply company law principles to them, in the same way as the courts have adopted partnership principles to those companies which resemble partnerships.[143] In these larger partnerships, it would be inappropriate to expect unanimity on management decisions and usually important issues (such as a change in the nature of the firm's business, a merger with other firm(s), the expulsion of a partner[144] or the dissolution of the firm) will require 75% or greater of the votes, while other decisions will require only a majority of the votes.

[21.102] One issue is deserving of special mention, namely the admission of new partners. The general rule regarding the admission of a partner to the firm is contained in s 24(7) of the 1890 Act, ie that, unless otherwise agreed, it may only be done with the consent of all the partners.[145] However, where the partnership agreement provides for the admission of a partner on a less than unanimous vote, it must be remembered that the new partnership agreement with the incoming partner must be signed by all the partners and, therefore, there should be a mechanism providing for the exclusion of a partner who refuses to sign the new partnership agreement.[146]

[21.103] A similar issue arises in the case of a firm which wishes to be able to amend its partnership agreement with less than a unanimous vote. Under general principles of contract, a partner cannot be forced to accept an amendment of the partnership agreement against his will. Accordingly, to enable the partnership agreement to be amended successfully by a majority of the partners, it is essential that the partnership agreement provides a mechanism for the exclusion of a partner who refuses to sign the amended partnership agreement. In this context, an important distinction should be drawn between an amendment of the partnership agreement which will under normal principles require unanimity and a decision pursuant to the partnership agreement which may not necessarily require unanimity. For example if the partnership agreement states that the business of the partnership is stockbroking, it will require a unanimous decision of the partners to amend the business of the firm. On the other hand, if the partnership agreement provides that the business of the firm is stockbroking or such other business as may be decided by a majority of the partners, this will clearly not require unanimity. The importance of careful drafting in relation to partnership matters which may require to be changed over time should therefore be clear.

---

[143] See generally in relation to quasi-partnerships, para **[8.67]** et seq.

[144] This issue is also governed by s 25 of the 1890 Act which provides that a majority of the partners may only expel a partner if this power in contained in the partnership agreement.

[145] Whatever the provisions in the partnership agreement, they should be strictly complied with for the admission to be valid. Thus in *Re Ginger* (1856) 5 Ir Ch R 174, a number of people were admitted as members of the Tipperary Joint-Stock Bank without complying with the strict terms of the partnership deed. For this reason, Smith MR held that the admission was null and void.

[146] This overcomes the principle that a person cannot become another person's partner against his will, which is due to the *delectus personae* nature of the partnership contract.

Prohibition on sub-partnerships

[21.104] A sub-partnership arises where one partner in a firm is himself in partnership with a third party in relation to his role as a partner in the main firm.[147] This gives rise to complications as the partners in the main firm are dealing with one partner, who is in fact acting not just on behalf of himself, but also on behalf of a sub-partner. In order to avoid such complications, it is common to find a prohibition in partnership agreements on any of the partners entering sub-partnership agreements without the consent of all the partners.

Implied term governing admission of new partners

[21.105] Section 24(7) of the 1890 Act provides that, unless otherwise agreed by the partners, the admission of a new partner requires the consent of all the existing partners in the firm. In larger firms, the possibility of one partner being able to veto the admission of a new partner is often inappropriate and as has been noted, it is common for this implied term to be excluded from such partnerships.[148]

[21.106] Elsewhere in this work it has been noted that an incoming partner is not liable to third parties for the obligations of the firm incurred prior to his admission.[149] In practice, new partners will often become entitled to fees which were generated prior to their admission but they also agree to share in the liabilities of the firm which were incurred before that date. On the other hand, when a partner retires, he will usually cease to have any interest in the work in progress and is indemnified by the firm against liabilities of the firm. In this way, the arrival and departure of partners is facilitated. An exception to this practice might occur where the incoming partner does not wish to be liable for a specific liability which is known and he may wish to seek an indemnity from the continuing partners in relation thereto.

[21.107] Care should be taken on the admission of new partners to ensure that any variation of the written terms of the partnership agreement which had been made by the pre-existing partners, whether expressly or by conduct, are brought to the attention of the new partners. A failure to do so will result in the incoming partner not being bound by such variations.[150]

[21.108] When admitting new partners to a formal partnership (usually a fixed term partnership), care should be taken to ensure that the incoming partner agrees to be bound by the existing formal partnership agreement. Otherwise, the resulting partnership between the existing partners and the new partner may be deemed to be a partnership at will.[151]

---

[147] See generally in relation to sub-partnerships, para **[8.45]** et seq.

[148] See para **[21.102]**.

[149] See para **[11.28]** et seq.

[150] See generally para **[5.24]** et seq.

[151] See *Firth v Armslake* (1964) 108 SJ 198, where the existing partners had a written fixed term partnership agreement and the incoming partner did not sign a new partnership agreement, see para **[8.25]**.

Right to nominate a successor to the firm

[21.109] Although no longer commonly found in partnership agreements, in some cases, eg family partnerships, the right of an outgoing partner to appoint a successor to the firm may be relevant.[152] To enable a partner nominate a successor, a specific provision should be inserted in the partnership agreement which will bind all the partners to accept the nominee as a partner[153] and presumably expel any partner who refuses to sign a new partnership agreement with the nominee.[154] Without such a provision, any attempt by a partner to nominate a third party in his place will simply operate as an assignment to that person of the profits of the firm to which the existing partner is entitled.[155]

[21.110] Since this whole area of parents attempting to either have their offspring appointed as partners in their place or as new partners can be divisive, partnership agreements sometimes seek to avoid this issue by providing that a son or daughter of a partner may not be admitted as a partner in the firm.

Power to nominate a partner includes power to nominate substitute

[21.111] Where a partnership agreement provides a power to nominate a successor, there is implied into the partnership agreement a power to nominate a substitute for the nominee, should the first nominee die or otherwise be unavailable. This is clear from the case of *Cuffe v Murtagh*.[156] There, an agreement governing a partnership of flour millers in Athlone provided that a partner could nominate a successor to his position in the firm, such nomination not to take effect until the nominee reached 21. By his will, one partner in that firm appointed Edward Heffernan, or should he die, Matthew Heffernan, to succeed him.[157] Chatterton VC upheld the power of a partner to appoint a successor and held that when this power is contained in a partnership agreement, it includes by implication a power to nominate a substitute when, as in this case, the first nominee died before reaching 21. In principle, there is no reason why the power to nominate a substitute would not apply in any situation where the nominating partner wishes to replace his original nominee, and not just on the death of the original nominee.

Incapacity of a partner

[21.112] It is common for partnership agreements to deal with the contingency of one or more of the partners becoming incapacitated. In smaller partnerships the firm is likely to be less well able to deal with the financial loss caused by one partner being incapacitated. For this reason, it may be appropriate to provide for a deduction to be made from a partner's profit share if he is incapacitated for more than a stated period, eg

---

152 See generally regarding the power to nominate a successor, para **[19.30]** et seq.
153 *Cuffe v Murtagh* (1881) 7 LR Ir 411.
154 See the reference to a similar mechanism being used in relation to the admission of new partners, para **[21.102]**.
155 See generally in relation to the assignment of a partner's share, para **[19.12]** et seq.
156 *Cuffe v Murtagh* (1881) 7 LR Ir 411.
157 The court held that the words 'in case the said Edward Heffernan should die' which were contained in the will, referred to death under 21.

six months, with a provision for that deduction to be used to employ a *locum* in his absence.

Implied fiduciary duty of a partner

[21.113] Although there is an implied fiduciary duty on a partner toward his co-partners in his partnership dealings,[158] it is useful nonetheless to expressly state this duty in the partnership agreement. In this way, the partners are reminded of this duty and the partnership agreement resembles a detailed charter of one's rights and duties as a partner.

7. Retirement, Expulsion and Suspension of a Partner

[21.114] A partner may leave his firm in a number of situations and these will next be considered. They may be categorised as follows: first, retirement by a partner at any time ('voluntary retirement'); second, retirement by a partner when he reaches a certain age, usually 65 ('compulsory retirement'); third, there may be circumstances where the partner, through his own misconduct, should be required to leave the partnership ('fault expulsion'); and fourth where a partner should be required through unfortunate circumstances, such as illness or incapacity, to leave the firm ('no-fault expulsion'). In general terms, these clauses will deal with such matters as the former partner's right to compete against the firm, his entitlement to accrued but unpaid profits, his capital contributions and a pension. The first two categories fall broadly within the right of a partner to retire as that term is generally used and will be considered first.

Inclusion of a right to retire

[21.115] There is no power under general partnership law or under the 1890 Act for a partner to retire from his firm, regardless of his age. Accordingly, the only possibility for a partner who wishes to retire, in the absence of a retirement provision or the agreement of his partners, is for him to dissolve the partnership by notice if it is a partnership at will,[159] or to apply to court for a dissolution under s 35(f) of the 1890 Act if it is a formal partnership.[160] The only other alternative for a partner in a formal partnership is for him to leave the firm in breach of the terms of his partnership agreement. Since each of these possibilities represent drastic solutions, it is important to have a provision allowing a partner to retire. Indeed, this is one of the main reasons for having a written partnership agreement.

[21.116] From a practical perspective, a voluntary retirement clause should allow for retirement to be generally available only at the end of the firm's accounting year, in order to facilitate the calculation of what is owed to the retiring partner. The retirement clause should provide for the share of the retiring partner to be purchased by the continuing partners.[161]

---

[158] See generally in relation to this duty of good faith, para **[15.01]** et seq.

[159] Partnership Act 1890, ss 26(1) and 32(c). See generally in relation to such a dissolution, para **[23.13]** et seq.

[160] See generally in relation to the court dissolution of a partnership, para **[25.01]** et seq.

[161] See generally in relation to retirement, para **[23.76]** and in relation to the purchase of an outgoing partner's share, para **[21.141]**.

[21.117] If the partnership agreement contains only a bare provision for retirement, and no provision for the sale of the retiring partner's share, then the retiring partner may claim that on his retirement the firm is generally dissolved, and not just technically dissolved.[162] On this basis, he may claim that he is entitled to have the affairs of the partnership wound up under s 39 of the 1890 Act. However, this claim can be avoided by ensuring that the retirement clause provides for the purchase of the retiring partner's share by the continuing partners.[163] Similarly, the retirement clause should state that the retirement of a partner will not dissolve the partnership as regards the continuing partners. This ensures that a general dissolution of the partnership will be avoided on the retirement, though there will of course be a technical dissolution.

[21.118] Even where the retirement clause is drafted as a bare right to retire, with no reference to the non-dissolution of the firm or to the purchase of the retiring partner's share by the continuing partners, the firm is likely to be held to be technically dissolved only. This is because the very concept of 'retirement' envisages a continuation of the firm and would therefore strongly indicate a technical rather than a general dissolution of the firm.[164] Finally, it should be noted that the power to retire should be carefully drafted and should consider the possibility of more than one partner seeking to retire at the same time as is highlighted by the Northern Ireland case of *McCarthy v Cunningham*.[165] There, Lowry LCJ considered a clause in a partnership agreement between two partners which entitled "either partner" to retire by giving notice to the other whereupon the other partner was required to purchase the retiring partner's share. When both partners attempted to retire at the same time, Lowry LCJ held that this was not open to the partners since such mutual dissolution was not available to them. Since the partnership was for the joint lives of the partners, he granted a declaration that the partnership was still in existence.

Compulsory retirement and no-fault expulsion

[21.119] In large professional partnerships and particularly as part of the 'lockstep system',[166] it is usual to have provisions requiring partners to retire from the firm at a certain age. As with voluntary retirement clauses, these compulsory retirement clauses should provide for the forced sale of the retiring partner's share to the continuing partners and that the retirement does not dissolve the partnership as between the continuing partners.

---

[162] As to the distinction between a general and a technical dissolution, see para **[23.07]**.

[163] The agreement should set out the valuation mechanism for valuing the share of the retiring partner in the firm and in the interests of the continued cash flow of the continuing firm, it is useful to provide that any payment for that share will be made in instalments, see further para **[21.141]** et seq.

[164] See *Sobell v Boston* [1975] 2 All ER 282. However, in the case of a two-person partnership, the retirement of one will cause the dissolution of the partnership. In *Tann v Herrington* [2009] EWHC 445 (Ch), the 'outgoing partner' terms of the partnership agreement were held to apply on the retirement of Tann from the partnership, notwithstanding that his departure had also caused the dissolution of the partnership.

[165] *McCarthy v Cunningham* (13 October 1979) HC.

[166] See further para **[21.53]**.

[21.120] Since the expulsion of a partner for illness or incapacity is similar to his compulsory retirement, these matters will often be dealt with together, so that a partner is also required to retire (ie subject to a no-fault expulsion) in the event of him being incapacitated for a set period of time.

Inclusion of a right to expel a partner or fault expulsion

[21.121] In addition to voluntary and compulsory retirement, there may be circumstances where a partner should be required to leave the partnership because of his misconduct.

[21.122] When considering fault expulsion, it is crucial to realise the shortcomings of the 1890 Act in this regard. Indeed, one of the major omissions of the 1890 Act is the fact that it does not imply a right on the part of partners to expel their co-partner from the firm for gross misconduct or fraud. On the contrary, s 25 of the 1890 Act provides that no majority of the partners can expel a partner unless a power to do so is conferred by the partnership agreement. Faced with a partner with whom the other partners no longer wish to be associated, and in the absence of a right to expel, the only option available to the innocent partners is to dissolve the partnership by notice if it is a partnership at will[167] or to apply to court for its dissolution under s 35 of the 1890 Act[168] if it is a formal partnership. A second drawback of the 1890 Act is the fact that the court is simply granted the right to dissolve a partnership, but not the power to expel a partner. As the dissolution of a profitable firm is not the ideal way to deal with a partner who is guilty of misconduct, it is imperative for partnership agreements to include a right to expel a partner for misconduct.

[21.123] The expulsion clause should list the activities which will justify the expulsion of a partner, such as his adjudication as a bankrupt, criminal behaviour, conduct which prejudices the business of the firm, etc. In this context, some expulsion clauses allow for the expulsion of a partner who is 'insolvent'. It has been held that this term does not require the partner to be bankrupt, but would occur when the partner is unable to pay his debts when due and demanded, even if on a realisation of all his assets, he might be able to meet all his liabilities in full.[169] This conclusion is in keeping with the general meaning of that term in the company law context.[170]

---

167 Partnership Act 1890, s 26(1) and s 32(c). See generally in relation to such a dissolution, para **[23.13]**.

168 See generally in relation to court dissolution of a partnership, para **[25.01]** et seq.

169 *Bayly v Schofield* (1813) 1 M & S 338.

170 The Companies Act 2014 (at s 570) deems a company to be unable to pay its debts in various circumstances, most notably if it does not pay a debt in excess of a specified amount for three weeks after demand has been made. Under s 570(d) of the Companies Act 2014, a company will also be deemed to be unable to pay its debts if the court determines that it is unable to do so on the basis of proof provided to it, and the court is permitted to take account of the company's contingent and prospective liabilities. Interestingly, Laffoy J noted in *Re Connemara Mining Company plc* [2013] IEHC 225 that there is no Irish authority which directly considers the criteria that must be applied by the court in making its determination. On the facts of that particular case, Laffoy J stated that it was not necessary for her to express a view on the relevant merits of the cash flow test or the balance sheet test in determining insolvency.

[21.124] As with retirement clauses, expulsion clauses should provide that the expulsion of a partner will not dissolve the partnership between the continuing partners and it should also provide for the forced sale by the expelled partner of his share to the continuing partners.[171] Unlike the situation where a partner retires (voluntarily or compulsorily), it is common for partnership agreements to provide that the value of an expelled partner's share is to be calculated without taking into account the value of the firm's goodwill. This is justified on the basis that to be expelled, the partner is usually guilty of conduct which may damage the firm's goodwill and therefore he should not be rewarded for this conduct by obtaining the full value of his share.[172]

[21.125] Each time a partner joins or leaves a firm, the old partnership is technically dissolved and a new partnership is constituted as a matter of law.[173] This may raise difficulties in relation to an attempt to expel a partner from a 'new' partnership on the basis of his conduct in the 'old' partnership. To avoid such an issue, the terms of the expulsion clause should provide that the technical dissolution of the firm will not affect the right to expel a partner for his conduct prior to that technical dissolution.

Power to suspend a partner

[21.126] For public relations reasons, a firm may wish to suspend, rather than expel, a partner who is suspected of involvement in misconduct. In cases where the alleged misconduct of a partner appears in the media, this procedure has the advantage of providing a swift response, without the need for a full inquiry by the firm. This power should be expressly contained in the partnership agreement, since it is not implied by the 1890 Act or under general partnership law.

Exercise of power of expulsion or suspension must be bona fide

[21.127] It has already been noted that the powers of a partner must be exercised bona fide.[174] This principle is equally applicable to the power of expulsion or suspension as is illustrated by the case of *Blisset v Daniel*.[175] There, a majority of the partners were given a wide power of expulsion, since that power did not require any reason to be given for the expulsion. Blisset was expelled from the firm by his co-partners as he had objected to a proposal that the firm would appoint one of the other partners, Vaughan, and his son as managers of the firm. Vaughan had delivered an ultimatum to the other partners that he would leave the partnership if Blisset remained. Before the expulsion notice was served on Blisset, he was prevailed upon to sign the accounts of the firm, thereby ensuring that the continuing partners would obtain his share in the firm at a favourable price. It was held that the power of expulsion was not therefore used bona fide but rather for an ulterior motive and that its exercise in these circumstances was invalid.

---

[171] As regards the valuation mechanism for valuing the share in the firm, see further para **[21.145]**.

[172] Similarly, the power to expel a partner usually takes effect straight away and not at the end of the firm's accounting year, which may be the case with a voluntary or compulsory retirement.

[173] See generally as to such technical dissolutions, para **[23.07]** et seq.

[174] *Heslin v Fay (1)* (1884) 15 LR Ir 431, see also para **[21.14]**. See generally in relation to partners' fiduciary duties, para **[15.01]** et seq.

[175] *Blisset v Daniel* (1853) 10 Hare 493.

8. Dissolution of the Partnership

Implied dissolution on death of a partner

[21.128] Section 33(1) of the 1890 Act provides that in the absence of any contrary agreement between the partners, a partnership is dissolved by the death of a partner. On such a dissolution, the personal representatives of the deceased partner are entitled to have the assets of the firm sold, the liabilities of the firm paid off and the surplus divided amongst the partners.[176] It seems clear that in most successful partnerships of three or more members, the partners, if asked, would indicate their desire to continue in business in the event of the death of one of the members of the firm. For this reason, it is usually essential to have a clause in the partnership agreement that the death of one partner will not dissolve the partnership between the surviving partners.[177] This clause should also include an automatic right for the surviving partners to acquire the deceased partner's share, since otherwise they will have the uncertainty of having to enter negotiations with the deceased partner's estate for the purchase of this share. [178]

Implied dissolution of firm on bankruptcy of a partner

[21.129] Section 33(1) of the 1890 Act also provides that, in the absence of a contrary agreement between the partners, the bankruptcy of a partner dissolves the firm. It is usual to exclude the application of this implied term from most partnerships, since the bankruptcy of one partner may relate exclusively to his financial position and therefore should not automatically dissolve the firm as regards the other partners.[179] The exclusion of s 33(1) in its application to the bankruptcy of a partner is normally achieved by providing in the partnership agreement for the expulsion of the bankrupt partner. This clause should also include an automatic right for the continuing partners to acquire the bankrupt partner's share,[180] since otherwise they will have the uncertainty of having to enter negotiations with the Official Assignee for its purchase.

[21.130] If the continuing partners purchase the share from the bankrupt partner prior to his adjudication as a bankrupt, care should be taken to ensure that full value is paid for the share, since payment at undervalue may be attacked as a fraudulent conveyance or

---

[176] Partnership Act 1890, s 39. See generally Shayne, 'Addressing Dissolution Issues in Partnership Agreements' (1997) 43 The Practical Lawyer 15.

[177] While a provision that the death of a partner will not dissolve the firm will prevent the general dissolution of the firm, it will not prevent a technical dissolution of the firm. This is because, as with any change in the constitution of a partnership, on the death of a partner, the continuing firm will be a 'new' firm as a matter of law and the 'old' firm will have therefore been technically dissolved. See generally in relation to the technical and general dissolution of a firm, para [23.07] et seq.

[178] As regards the valuation mechanism for valuing the share in the firm, see further para [21.145].

[179] As with the death of a partner, the exclusion of s 33(1) of the 1890 Act in relation to the bankruptcy of a partner will prevent the general dissolution of the firm, but it will not prevent a technical dissolution of the firm. See generally in relation to general and technical dissolutions, para [23.07] et seq.

[180] As regards the valuation mechanism for valuing the share in the firm, see further para [21.145].

preference under bankruptcy law.[181] If full value is paid for the share, such a transaction will be binding on the Official Assignee of the bankrupt partner.[182]

Implied right of partner to dissolve a partnership at will

[21.131] Both s 26(1) and s 32(c) of the 1890 Act entitle a partner in a partnership at will to dissolve the partnership by notice. Thus, regardless of the number of partners in the partnership at will, any partner, and thus even a dormant partner, may dissolve the partnership by simply arriving at a partners' meeting and giving notice orally to his co-partners that the firm is dissolved. Surprisingly, s 32 is stated to be subject to contrary agreement, while s 26(1) is silent in this regard. However, it has been argued elsewhere in this book that both sections are in fact subject to contrary agreement since it would be senseless if a partner was entitled to exclude his right to dissolve the partnership by notice under the express terms of s 32, but not under s 26(1).[183] On this basis, the parties in a partnership may exclude the right of a partner to dissolve the partnership by notice, by having a term to the contrary in their partnership agreement.

Implied dissolution of fixed term partnership

[21.132] Under s 32(a) of the 1890 Act, unless otherwise agreed, a fixed term partnership is dissolved on the expiry of the term. It has been observed that a fixed term partnership which continues after the expiry of its term is converted into a partnership at will, with the consequence that any one partner may dissolve the 'new' partnership by notice.[184] This may not suit the partners involved. Accordingly, in order to avoid the fixed term partnership becoming a partnership at will, the partnership agreement might usefully provide that the fixed term partnership will continue after the expiry of the fixed term for the same period again, for a shorter period or will continue until dissolved by a majority of the partners.

Implied dissolution of a partnership for a single venture

[21.133] Under s 32(b) of the 1890 Act, a partnership which is entered into for a single adventure or undertaking is dissolved by the termination of that undertaking or adventure, unless otherwise agreed by the partners. Thus care should be taken with partnerships which are formed for one-off events, as will often be the case for large sporting events. Thus, for example, a partnership which is formed for the purposes of a large sporting event and which does not provide for a specific duration or otherwise exclude the application of s 32(b), will immediately be dissolved on the termination of that event.

Implied right to dissolve firm on charging of a partner's share

[21.134] Under s 33(2) of the 1890 Act, a partnership may, at the option of the other partners, be dissolved if a partner suffers his share of the partnership property to be

---

[181] See generally in relation to fraudulent preference and fraudulent conveyances, Sanfey and Holohan, *Bankruptcy Law and Practice* (2nd edn, 2010).

[182] *Borland's Trustee v Steel Bros & Co Ltd* [1901] 1 Ch 279.

[183] See para **[8.08]**.

[184] See para **[8.16]**.

charged under that Act for his separate debt. This right is not expressed to be subject to an agreement to the contrary, yet it seems clear that it may be excluded by the terms of the partnership agreement.[185] Rather than exclude this term, it may be more useful to obviate the need to dissolve the partnership. This could be done by providing that a partner is prohibited from charging his share or interest in the partnership and that a partner who suffers his share to be charged for his separate debt may be expelled from the partnership.

Automatic dissolution of an illegal firm

[21.135] Section 34 of the 1890 Act provides that a partnership is dissolved by the happening of any event which makes it unlawful to carry on its business. Unlike many of the implied terms discussed previously, it is not possible to exclude the application of s 34 pursuant to s 19 of the 1890 Act. This is because s 19 of the 1890 Act provides that partners may vary their 'rights and duties' set out in the Act. However, in no sense is s 34 a right or a duty of a partner, but rather it is a statement of the effect of illegality on a partnership. Accordingly, s 34 may not be varied by the agreement of the partners.

[21.136] However, it is possible to avoid its worst effects. For example it has been noted earlier in this work that where one of the partners in a law firm accidentally fails to renew his practising certificate, the partnership is in contravention of a statutory prohibition on solicitors being in partnership with unqualified persons.[186] It follows that the partnership is deemed to be unlawful and is immediately dissolved.[187] However, the dissolution of the partnership may be avoided by having a provision in the partnership agreement that, on the failure of a partner to renew his practising certificate, he will be automatically expelled from the firm until such time as he obtains a new certificate. In this way, one ensures that the partnership itself remains lawful and the automatic dissolution of the firm is avoided.

Implied right of departing partner to profits after "technical" dissolution

[21.137] Where a firm continues after the departure of a partner, the continuing firm will have the use of the departing partner's share in the partnership for the period of time between the date of departure and the date the departing partner receives payment in respect of his share. Section 42(1) of the 1890 Act addresses the use by the continuing partners of the departing partner's share in the firm. Under that section, a departing partner or his estate is entitled to the share of the firm's profits made since his departure

---

185 This approach is in line with the general tenor of the 1890 Act which favours the partners' agreement taking precedence over the implied terms of that Act save in exceptional cases, and is in line with s 19 of the 1890 Act which allows all the partners to agree to a variation of their rights and duties set out in that Act, see para **[5.14]** et seq. It is contended that the right to dissolve the partnership on one partner having his interest charged is not so basic a right as to be incapable of exclusion by agreement between the partners. Cf the right to a true account of partnership dealings under s 28 of the 1890 Act (see para **[21.88]**) and the right of a former partner to publicly notify his retirement or the dissolution of the partnership (see para **[26.06]**).

186 Solicitors Act 1954, s 59.

187 See the Court of Appeal case of *Hudgell Yeates & Co v Watson* [1978] 2 All ER 363, discussed at para **[9.12]** et seq.

and attributable to the use of his share of the partnership assets, or to 5% of his share of the partnership assets.[188] Section 42(1) provides that this right may be expressly excluded by contrary agreement between the partners.[189]

No interest for period between departure and payment

[21.138] Under s 42(2) of the 1890 Act, the right of a departing partner to a share of the profits will be excluded by implication where there is an option for the continuing partners to purchase the departing partner's share and the terms of that option are duly complied with in all material respects. Thus, even where there is a delay between the date of the departure of a partner and the date of receipt of the purchase money for the share under this option to purchase, the departing partner will not be entitled to interest for this period, unless expressly agreed by the partners. This is because s 42(2) of the 1890 Act provides that where an option is given to the continuing partners to purchase the interest of the departing partner and that option is duly exercised, then the right under s 42(1) to any 'further or other share of the profits' is excluded.[190]

[21.139] In the Supreme Court case of *Williams v Harris*,[191] there was almost a two-year period between the retirement of two partners from a partnership and their receipt of the purchase money for the sale of their shares to the continuing partners. Because of the delay, the retiring partners claimed a share in the profits of the firm from the date of retirement to the date of receipt. The Supreme Court held that the provision in this case for the sale of the partnership share rendered inapplicable the right of a retiring partner to a share in the profits of a firm from the date of dissolution.

[21.140] It follows that if an outgoing partner wishes to obtain interest on the purchase price between the date of departure and the date he receives his purchase money, he should expressly provide for it in the partnership agreement.

9. Purchase of a Departing Partner's Share

[21.141] In considering the terms of the partnership agreement up to this point, reference has been made to a number of situations in which a partner will leave the firm, namely as a result of death,[192] bankruptcy,[193] expulsion[194] or retirement.[195] Assuming that the other partners wish to continue with the partnership business, the question of the purchase of that departing or deceased partner's share will arise. This section of the

---

188 See generally in relation to this right, para **[26.63]** et seq.
189 For an example of a case where there was a contrary agreement, see *Williams v Harris* [1980] ILRM 237, para **[26.99]**.
190 Although the reference is to 'share of the profits' only, it is contended that there is an implicit reference to interest under s 42(1) of the 1890 Act, see para **[26.101]**.
191 *Williams v Harris* [1980] ILRM 237.
192 See para **[21.128]**.
193 See para **[21.129]**.
194 See para **[21.121]** et seq.
195 See para **[21.115]** et seq.

chapter considers this area.[196] The expression 'departing partner' is used to describe a partner who ceases to be a member of a firm for whatever reason, including death.

Option to purchase or automatic vesting of departing partner's share

[21.142] It is important in most partnership agreements to have a clause which either gives the continuing partners an option to purchase a departing partner's share in the firm (including his share of the goodwill) or provides for that share to automatically vest in the continuing partners on the payment of the agreed purchase price.[197] Without such a clause, the departing partner or his estate may argue that the partnership has been generally dissolved (as distinct from technically dissolved only) by the departure and should be wound up under s 39 of the 1890 Act and the assets of the firm sold and any surplus distributed amongst the partners.

[21.143] While the automatic vesting of a departing partner's share in the continuing partners is appropriate for larger partnerships, in small partnerships such a forced sale may be financially very onerous for the continuing partners. For this reason, it may be appropriate in those partnerships to grant the continuing partners the option to refuse to buy the departing partner's share. Similarly, if the continuing firm is small, it is advisable to provide for the purchase of any departing partner's share to be made in instalments so as to ensure that the firm's cash flow is protected.

Interest on payment in instalments

[21.144] It has been noted that in small firms, it may be useful to have a provision that the purchase price for a departing partner's share will be paid in instalments, so as to reduce the impact upon the firm's cash-flow. Where this is the case, the agreement may provide for interest to be payable on the instalments. In *Beater v Murray*,[198] it was agreed that a departing partner's share in the Dublin firm, Arnott & Co, was to be purchased by the continuing partners. Under the terms of the partnership deed, payment was to be made as follows:

> '[T]he amount of his share in said firm ... together with interest thereon, at the rate of £10 per cent per annum, shall be paid to his personal representatives by four annual consecutive equal instalments.'[199]

---

[196] As regards the capital acquisitions tax issues which may arise, see Bohan and McCarthy *Capital Acquisitions Tax* (4th edn, 2013) at para 15.05 et seq.

[197] In *Pentland v Gibson* (1833) Alc & Nap 310, the partnership agreement provided that in the event of the death of a partner in Saint Patrick Assurance Company of Ireland, his share was to vest in his personal representative provided that the personal representative should within 12 months sign the partnership agreement, failing which the partners were entitled to sell the share, the proceeds to be held on trust for the personal representative. Bushe CJ held that the effect of this clause was that the deceased partner's share vested in the personal representative immediately on his death and the requirement to sign the partnership agreement was simply a condition subsequent, rather than precedent and that the partners simply had an option to require the personal representative to become a member, failing which, they were entitled to sell the shares for the benefit of the personal representative.

[198] *Beater v Murray* (1870) 4 ILTR 532.

[199] *Beater v Murray* (1870) 4 ILTR 532.

The question arose as to whether this meant that on the four payment dates, the partner's estate was entitled to interest of 10% on the instalment being paid or on the entire residue of his capital which was unpaid at the time. It was held that interest was payable on the instalment only. The decision taken by the court in this pre-1890 case is questionable. It is somewhat inequitable to allow the firm to use all of the partner's capital and only pay interest on part thereof. This runs counter to the principles now contained in s 42 of the 1890 Act which favours a former partner obtaining the benefit of the totality of his interest in the partnership. Accordingly, in a similar fact situation, it is thought that a court would favour an interpretation that interest is payable on the total capital outstanding. For this reason, where a partnership agreement states that interest is payable on instalments, it should be clearly stated whether the interest relates to the instalment or the entire purchase price outstanding.

Manner of valuation of departing partner's share

[21.145] The manner in which the share of a departing partner is to be valued should also be addressed in the partnership agreement. One option is to have it valued by the firm's auditors, or alternatively to simply value it on the basis of the book values contained in the most recent accounts of the firm prior to the partner's date of departure. In either case, the method of valuation should be expressed in the partnership agreement, since the balance sheet value will not be taken to be the real value of the property on the technical or general dissolution of the partnership. Indeed the courts are reluctant to stick to the book value in the absence of agreement to that effect, since the book value will often be less than the real value of the assets. This is clear from the High Court case of *Barr v Barr*,[200] where the premises used by the firm were held to constitute partnership property and were valued in the balance sheet of the firm at over £1,000. However, for the purposes of calculating the entitlement of a deceased partner's estate, Barron J held that their real value was £5,000. Accordingly, if partners wish to use the balance sheet values for the purpose of calculating a departing partner's share, this should be expressly stated by them in their agreement. Similarly in *Cruickshank v Sutherland*,[201] the partnership agreement provided that the share of a deceased partner was to be made by reference to the accounts prepared up to April 30 next after his death. The accounts had been prepared consistently using book values but the House of Lords held that this did not require a departing partner to accept the book values but rather a real value of the assets should be taken.[202]

[21.146] Consideration should be given to whether the work in progress of the firm is to be included in the valuation of the departing partner's share. Where partners agreed that the valuation of the departing partner's share was to be determined on the basis of the

---

200 *Barr v Barr* (3 November 1983) HC.

201 *Cruickshank v Sutherland* (1923) 128 LT 449.

202 See l'Anson Banks, *Lindley & Banks on Partnership* (20th edn, 2017) at para 10-180 regarding recent English and Scottish cases on the valuation of the share of a departing partner, in particular: *Re White* [1999] 1 WLR 2079; *Drake v Harvey* [2012] 1 All ER (Comm) 617; *Ham v Ham* [2014] WLTR 255; *Gadd v Gadd* [2002] 08 EG 160. The emphasis in *Re White* (which was endorsed in *Drake v Harvey* and *Ham v Ham*) on the inappropriateness of formulating a general rule, and the importance of the terms of the partnership agreement regarding valuation, should be borne in mind.

partnership accounts, yet the firm was a number of years in arrears in relation to its accounts, the courts have intervened to order accounts to be drawn up to a date closer to the retirement so as to avoid a situation in which the departing partner is prejudiced.[203]

[21.147] Where there is no agreement between the partners to the contrary, a departing partner will be entitled to his profit share up to the date of his retirement, any undrawn profits which he has accumulated during his membership of the firm and the amount standing to his credit in his capital account.[204] However, in larger professional partnerships, it is common to find an express provision that the capital profits (including any increase in the value of the goodwill) of the firm will benefit only those partners for the time being of the firm, and that no payment is to be made to departing partners in respect of either item. Such a provision is seen to be for the greater good of such partnerships as a whole, since it eases the entry and exit of partners to and from them. Instead of receiving a payment for goodwill, partners who leave larger firms are often entitled to a pension from the firm.[205]

Valuation of goodwill

[21.148] The question of whether an outgoing partner is to receive a payment in respect of the firm's goodwill should be expressly dealt with in the partnership agreement. This is because a generic reference to his receiving payment in respect of his share of the firm's assets, or of his share of the 'stock in trade, goods, chattels and effects'[206] may include the firm's goodwill.

[21.149] On the other hand, if goodwill is to be excluded from the valuation of a partner's share, this should be done by means of an explicit statement that the firm's goodwill is to have a nil-value,[207] that an outgoing partner is to receive no payment in respect of the goodwill and that the goodwill will accrue for the benefit of the continuing partners.

[21.150] Where goodwill is to be valued as part of the partnership agreement, consideration should be given to the manner of the valuation, eg as a multiple of the firm's average profits or whether a fixed value is to be attached to it.

10. Position of a Departing Partner

Implied indemnity in favour of departing partner

[21.151] It has been observed earlier in this work[208] that where a partner leaves his firm, he continues to be directly liable to third parties for obligations incurred by the firm while he was a partner. In some cases, the continuing partners in the firm may

---

203   *Simmons v Leonard* (1844) 3 Hare 581; *Pettyt v Janeson* (1819) 6 Madd 146; *Lawes v Lawes* (1881) 9 Ch D 98.

204   See generally in relation to a partner's capital account and his current account, para **[17.09]**.

205   Paying a partner in respect of his share of the firm's increased goodwill (after say 30 years of service) would also be likely to lead to a large capital gains tax bill for the departing partner.

206   See *Dickson v McMaster & Co* (1866) 11 Ir Jur 202 where this expression was held not to include goodwill and see generally in relation to goodwill, para **[18.01]** et seq.

207   But it is important to bear in mind that such a statement on its own is not sufficient.

208   See para **[11.34]** et seq.

indemnify the departing partner in respect of these obligations. However, even where there is no such express indemnity, it seems that an indemnity will be implied in favour of the departing partner in respect of the firm's debts and obligations if the departing partner has relinquished his share of the partnership assets.[209] The rationale for this implied indemnity is that the assets of the firm, to which creditors are presumed to look for payment, are being assigned to the continuing partners and therefore they should discharge the obligations of the firm. If, on the departure of such a partner, the continuing partners do not intend to indemnify him in respect of obligations incurred by the firm while he was a partner, then this should be expressly stated in the partnership agreement or in the agreement which assigns his share to the continuing partners.

Implied right of all partners to notify dissolution

[21.152] Under s 37 of the 1890 Act every partner, and not just a departing partner, has an implied right to publicly notify the retirement of a partner or the dissolution of the partnership and to require the other partners to do any necessary acts in relation thereto. Section 37 states:

> On the dissolution of a partnership or retirement of a partner any partner may publicly notify the same, and may require the other partner or partners to concur for that purpose in all necessary or proper acts, if any, which cannot be done without his or their concurrence.

[21.153] This implied term is not expressed to be subject to contrary agreement and it is apprehended that this right is of such importance (since it will end the liability of a former partner for the future debts of the firm),[210] that it may not be excluded by the terms of the partnership agreement.[211] Nonetheless, it is apprehended that a firm is entitled to have a say in the exercise of this right by, for example, controlling the content of the advertisement in *Iris Oifigiúil* or the contents of circulars to clients, provided that this input is not so extensive as to deprive the notice of its intention.[212]

Other forms to be completed on departure of a partner

[21.154] Section 37 of the 1890 Act does not give any guidance on what is meant by the right of a partner to require the other partners to concur in 'necessary or proper acts' for

---

[209] *Gray v Smith* (1889) 43 Ch D 208 (sale of outgoing partner's share to continuing partners); *Saltoun v Houston* (1824) 1 Bing 433 (outgoing partner received consideration for his share). See also para **[11.93]**. There is also an implied indemnity in favour of the vendor partner who sells to a third party, see *Dodson v Downey* [1901] 2 Ch 620 and see para **[19.24]**.

[210] This arises because under s 36(1) of the 1890 Act, a person who deals with a firm after a change in its constitution is entitled to treat all apparent members of the firm as still being members until he has notice thereof. See further in relation to the continuing liability of a former partner, para **[11.74]** et seq.

[211] See further para **[26.06]**. But for a contrary view, cf l'Anson Banks, *Lindley & Banks on Partnership* (20th edn, 2017) at para 13-45.

[212] Under the Partnership Act 1890, s 36(2), an advertisement in *Iris Oifigiúil* operates as a notice to all persons, who had no dealings with the firm, of the fact that the retired partner is no longer a member of the firm. Thus he is not liable for obligations incurred by the firm after that date to such persons. See generally para **[11.62]** et seq. Under s 36(1) of the 1890 Act, actual notice to pre-existing clients of firm will ensure that the outgoing partner is not liable to them for obligations incurred after the date of the notice, see generally para **[11.85]** et seq.

the purposes of notifying a dissolution or a retirement. For this reason, it is useful for the partnership agreement to specifically require partners to sign forms such as the Form RBN2A (to notify the Registrar of Business Names of a change to the firm's registered business name),[213] and notifications required under insurance contracts, leases, resignations as a director of shelf companies, etc. In *Larkin v Groeger and Eaton*,[214] there was no such provision in the partnership agreement, and on its dissolution, reliance does not appear to have been placed on s 37 of the 1890 Act. Accordingly, it was necessary for the arbitrator[215] to order the continuing partner[216] to sign the Form RBN2A,[217] and order the departing partner to sign a surrender in relation to the firm's insurance policy and a Form B10[218] (notifying the Companies Registration Office of his resignation as a director of a company controlled by the partnership).

[21.155] In addition to specifying the forms and documents to be completed by the continuing and former partners, it may be useful to have a 'further assurance' clause to require the partners to execute such other documents as are necessary in connection with the departure of a partner, eg his retirement as a trustee of partnership assets or as a director. If widely drafted, such a clause may include acts which are not covered by the expression 'necessary or proper acts' in s 37 of the 1890 Act.

[21.156] It might also be useful to provide in this clause for the departing partner to give up all the firm's books and documents and any documents belonging to clients of the firm which are in his possession on the date of his departure.

11. Anti-Competitive Provisions

Implied duty of partner to account for profits in competing business

[21.157] Section 30 of the 1890 Act requires a partner to account to the firm for any benefit derived by him from any business carried on by him of the same nature or in competition with the firm,[219] without the consent of his partners. In some firms, it may be appropriate to have a provision entitling a partner to carry on a competing business with the firm, without having to account for profits.[220] For example in accountancy or

---

[213] See generally as regards registration of business names, para **[3.70]** et seq.

[214] *Larkin v Groeger and Eaton* (26 April 1988) HC.

[215] John Gore Grimes, solicitor, whose decision was upheld by Barrington J in the High Court, *Larkin v Groeger and Eaton* (26 April 1988) HC.

[216] Note that Larkin was the continuing partner in relation to his own business of Michael Larkin and Associates which merged with Groeger and Eaton to form the partnership in the first place. Thus, he was also an outgoing partner in relation to the firm of Groeger, Eaton and Larkin.

[217] Then known as a Form RBN 5. It was necessary for this order to be made, as the obligation to make a filing under the Registration of Business Names Act 1963 is on the firm and not the outgoing partner: Registration of Business Names Act 1963, s 7.

[218] Then known as a Form 9.

[219] Note that the margin note in the 1890 Act for s 30 is misleadingly termed 'Duty of a partner not to compete with firm', yet this section does not prohibit a partner from competing with his firm, but rather requires him to account for any profit made.

[220] Such a provision in the agreement should also exclude the application of s 29(1) of the 1890 Act, para **[21.158]**.

legal firms, the business of the firm may include the payment of fees for the services of a partner for acting as a director of a client company. Therefore, if a partner in the firm also happens to have a family or private directorship, he is likely to be carrying on business of a nature carried on by the firm. The partner will be required by s 30 of the 1890 Act to account to the firm for the payments received by him from such a directorship, unless it is expressly excluded by him in his partnership agreement.

Implied accountability of partners for private profits

[21.158] While s 30 of the 1890 Act is concerned with profits derived from a competing business to that of the firm, s 29(1) deals with profits from the use of the firm's name or business connection. This section requires a partner to account for any profit made by him, without the consent of the other partners, from any transaction concerning the partnership, or from any use by him of the partnership property, name or business connection. In some partnership agreements, it may be appropriate to exclude the application of s 29(1) to certain appointments, eg a part-time academic or a State appointment held by a partner. In this way, the partner will be entitled to keep the fees derived therefrom or to do such work for free,[221] even though it involves the use of the firm's property, name or business connection.

Non-compete provisions

[21.159] It is usual for a partnership agreement to contain a provision which restrains a partner from competing with the firm after he leaves the partnership. Any such clauses will have to comply with the Competition Act 2002 and in the case of large partnerships, Article 101 of the Treaty on the Functioning of the European Union. The application of these provisions to non-compete clauses is considered in detail elsewhere in this work.[222]

[21.160] In general terms, where the restriction is on a departing partner from competing with the firm, it will not generally contravene the Competition Act 2002 if it does not exceed what is necessary, in terms of duration, geographic coverage and subject matter, to secure the transfer of any goodwill from the departing partner to the continuing partners.[223] The principle that a restriction must not exceed what is necessary to transfer the goodwill of the partnership is clearly highlighted by the English High Court case of *Peyton v Mindham*.[224] That case involved a partnership between two medical general practitioners. Their agreement provided that if the partnership should come to an end in certain circumstances, the departing partner would be prohibited from professionally advising, attending, prescribing or treating any person who was, or had at any time been, a patient of the firm, or a member of the household of such patient. The clause was struck down by Plowman J as being unreasonable since it prevented the

---

[221] Although if the work is done for free, there will be no profit so as to bring it within the terms of s 29(1). Nonetheless, an express provision entitling the partner to do such work without charging therefor, will have the additional advantage of excluding any possibility that the partner will be accused of being in breach of his fiduciary duty to his co-partners by so doing. See generally in relation to fiduciary duties, para **[15.01]** et seq.

[222] See para **[22.01]** et seq.

[223] See generally in relation to such clauses, para **[22.29]** et seq.

[224] *Peyton v Mindham* [1971] 3 All ER 1215.

departing partner from acting as a consultant to patients of the practice and not merely as a general practitioner.

[21.161] On the other hand, a restriction on a partner competing with the firm while he remains a member of the partnership will not contravene the Competition Act 2002. This is because a necessary incident of the agreement to work in partnership is the requirement that the partners will not compete with each other while the partnership continues.[225]

12. Final Terms

Arbitration and mediation clauses

[21.162] Most modern partnership agreements contain an arbitration clause which provides for the settlement of disputes between the parties by arbitration. In view of the personal, as well as business, relationship which usually exists between partners, arbitration is often a better option than litigation. In order to avoid subsequent disputes about the extent of the arbitration clause, it should specify whether it applies only to disputes which arise while the firm is continuing or whether it also applies to disputes which arise after the firm's dissolution. Any arbitration proceedings between partners will be governed by the Arbitration Act 2010 and for a consideration of this area, reference should be made to the treatment thereof elsewhere in this work.[226]

Winding up or dissolution is 'dispute' within arbitration clause

[21.163] Elsewhere in this work, it has been noted that the parties to a widely drafted arbitration clause may seek the dissolution of the partnership from the arbitrator and will therefore be precluded from applying for a court dissolution under s 35 of the 1890 Act.[227] Similarly, it is contended that a petition for the winding up of a partnership[228] may be a 'dispute' within the terms of a widely drafted all-disputes[229] arbitration clause. Thus, where the arbitration clause covers the dispute in issue, the application to wind up or dissolve the partnership must be dealt with by the arbitrator.

[21.164] This is thought to be the case despite the decision to the contrary in the pre-1890 case of *Dennehy v Jolly*.[230] That case concerned a law stationery partnership at 74 Dame St in Dublin and the plaintiff's application to court to wind up the partnership in spite of the arbitration clause in the partnership agreement. This clause provided that differences between the partners relating to the agreement or the partnership business or the rights and duties of the partners were to be referred to arbitration. The defendant

---

[225] *Scully Tyrrell & Co/Edberg*, Competition Authority, Dec No 12, 29 January 1993; *United States v Addyston Pipe & Steel Company et al* 85 Fed 271 (6th Cir 1898). See generally in relation to the treatment of such non-compete provisions, para **[22.24]** et seq.
[226] See generally, para **[20.85]** et seq. For a treatment of arbitration generally, see Dowling-Hussey, Dunne and Tackaberry, *Arbitration Law* (2nd edn, 2014); Mansfield, *Arbitration Act 2010 and Model Law* (2012).
[227] See para **[20.89]** and para **[25.14]**.
[228] As to such petitions for the winding up of partnerships generally, see para **[27.06]** et seq.
[229] Ie, where the partners agree to refer all disputes between them to arbitration.
[230] *Dennehy v Jolly* (1875) 9 ILTR 3.

brought a motion to stay the plaintiff's application to wind up the partnership in view of this arbitration clause. However, Sullivan MR held that the winding up of the partnership was not within the terms of the arbitration clause. He reasoned that the winding up of a partnership is not a matter in dispute so as to be referred to arbitration, as there is the additional question of the terms upon which the partnership is to be wound up, the taking of accounts and the subsequent receiving of profits by the parties and the arbitrator does not have power to do these things. Sullivan MR's premise for denying the arbitrator the power to wind up a partnership is no longer valid in view of the extensive powers of arbitrators which have been recognised by the Irish courts.[231]

[21.165] Thus, it is thought that *Dennehy v Jolly*[232] is no longer good law and just as an arbitrator may be exclusively granted the power to dissolve a partnership,[233] he also may be granted the exclusive power to wind up a partnership.

Mediation as a pre-requisite to arbitration

[21.166] While arbitration has the advantage over litigation of being quicker and less procedural, it is nonetheless an adversarial process and in many cases will lead to further acrimony between the partners, damage to the firm's goodwill and oftentimes the general dissolution of the partnership. This is particularly true in smaller partnerships, where the comparison of partnership to a marriage is sometimes appropriate and the closeness of the relationship can exacerbate the difficulties which arise during a dispute. In an attempt to avoid the acrimony which usually attaches to adversarial proceedings, it is recommended that the partnership agreement require the partners to engage a mediator in an attempt to resolve their dispute.[234] Only if this approach is unsuccessful, should they resort to arbitration or litigation.

Winding up clause

[21.167] Where the parties wish to distribute the assets of the partnership *in specie* on the firm's winding up, this should be expressly stated in the partnership agreement. In the absence of such an agreement between the partners, s 39 of the 1890 Act dictates that the assets of the firm are sold and any surplus money is divided between the partners.[235]

---

[231] See for example the taking of accounts and the orders to sign Companies Registration Office forms in *Larkin v Groeger and Eaton* (26 April 1988) HC. Similarly, in *Gargan v Ruttle* [1931] IR 152, the arbitrator held that the partnership had been dissolved and he ordered that the goodwill, stock and all other assets of the firm belong to one partner and that the other partner be entitled to a sum of money for his share of these partnership assets.

[232] *Dennehy v Jolly* (1875) 9 ILTR 3.

[233] See *Hutchinson v Whitfield* (1830) Hayes 78 and para **[20.87]**.

[234] A suggested mediation clause might provide for the dispute between the partners to be referred to a mediator to be appointed by the partners, or in the absence of agreement to be appointed by the President of the Law Society of Ireland.

[235] See *Cook v Collingridge* (1822) Jac 607; *Rigden v Pierce* (1822) 6 Madd 353.

III. WHERE PARTNERS HAVE NO WRITTEN AGREEMENT

[21.168] Despite its inadvisability, some partners carry on business without having their own written partnership agreement. These partners may be surprised to discover that they do in fact have a 'written' partnership agreement and that its terms are contained in the 1890 Act. Throughout the various sections of a typical partnership agreement discussed in this chapter, reference has been made to these implied terms. However, when one is dealing with a partnership without a written agreement, it is useful to have all of the terms implied by the 1890 Act set out *in toto*. Accordingly, each of these terms is set out below[236] and as has been noted, they may be varied or excluded from the partnership by an express or implicit agreement (including an oral agreement) by the partners to the contrary.[237]

Financial Rights

[21.169] The implied financial rights of a partner are:

- each partner shares equally in the profits and losses of income and capital;[238]
- a partner is not entitled to interest on capital;[239]
- a partner is entitled to interest at 5% from the firm on capital or an advance paid by him beyond the amount he agreed to subscribe;[240]
- a partner is not entitled to remuneration for acting as a partner;[241] and
- the partnership must indemnify a partner in respect of payments and liabilities incurred by him in the ordinary and proper conduct of the partnership business and in relation to the preservation of the partnership business or property.[242]

Management Rights

[21.170] The implied management rights of a partner are:

- all partners may take part in the management of the firm;[243]
- a partner may not be admitted into the firm without the consent of all the partners;[244]

---

[236] Note that the listed terms are not exhaustive of the terms which apply to a partnership, but are those implied terms which one would expect to be addressed in a typical partnership agreement. In addition to these terms, reference could be made to the general provisions of the 1890 Act, eg the liability of a partner for the acts of his co-partner under s 5 or the right of a partner to apply for a court dissolution of the partnership under s 35 and to general partnership law, eg the fiduciary duty of a partner to his co-partners (see *Williams v Harris* [1980] ILRM 237). These provisions, though relevant to a partnership, are not the type of terms which one would find in a typical partnership agreement.

[237] Partnership Act 1890, s 19.

[238] Partnership Act 1890, s 24(1).

[239] Partnership Act 1890, s 24(4).

[240] Partnership Act 1890, s 24(3).

[241] Partnership Act 1890, s 24(6).

[242] Partnership Act 1890, s 24(2).

[243] Partnership Act 1890, s 24(5).

[244] Partnership Act 1890, s 24(7).

- differences arising as to ordinary matters are decided by a majority vote of partners, but no change may be made to the partnership business without the consent of all the partners;[245]
- partnership books are to be kept at the place of business of the firm (or its principal place of business, if more than one) and every partner may, when he thinks fit, have access to them and may inspect and copy them;[246] and
- a majority of the partners may not expel a partner.[247]

Duties of Partners

[21.171] The implied duties of a partner are:

- a partner must account to the firm for profits which he has earned from carrying on a competing business with the firm;[248] and
- a partner must account to the firm for benefits derived by him from any transaction concerning the partnership or from his use of the partnership property, name or business connection.[249]

Dissolution of the Partnership

[21.172] The implied rights regarding the dissolution of the partnership are:

- the partnership is dissolved, if entered into for a fixed term, by the expiration of that term;[250]
- the partnership is dissolved, if entered into for a single venture or undertaking, by the termination of that venture or undertaking;[251]
- the partnership is dissolved, if entered into for an undefined time, by one partner giving notice to the other(s) of his intention to dissolve the partnership;[252]
- the partnership is dissolved by the death of a partner;[253]
- the partnership is dissolved by the bankruptcy of a partner;[254]
- the partnership may be dissolved at the option of the other partners, where a partner suffers his share of the partnership property to be charged under the 1890 Act for his separate debts;[255]
- a departing partner from a continuing firm, where there was no settlement of accounts, is entitled to the share of the post-dissolution profits which are attributable to the use by the firm of his share of the partnership assets or to 5%

---

245   Partnership Act 1890, s 24(8).
246   Partnership Act 1890, s 24(9).
247   Partnership Act 1890, s 25.
248   Partnership Act 1890, s 30.
249   Partnership Act 1890, s 29.
250   Partnership Act 1890, s 32(a).
251   Partnership Act 1890, s 32(b).
252   Partnership Act 1890, s 32(c) and s 26(1).
253   Partnership Act 1890, s 33(1).
254   Partnership Act 1890, s 33(1).
255   Partnership Act 1890, s 33(2).

interest on the amount of his share of the partnership assets,[256] unless an option by the continuing partners to purchase the departing partner's share has been duly exercised;[257]

- the profits and losses of income and of capital of the firm on a dissolution are shared in the proportion in which profits are shared;[258] and

- in repaying the assets of the firm on a dissolution, advances by partners to the firm are re-paid in priority to the repayment of capital contributions.[259]

Implied Terms which may not be Excluded

[21.173] The following terms implied by the 1890 Act may not be excluded by an agreement to the contrary between the partners and thus will apply to all partnerships, whether the partners have a written partnership agreement or not:[260]

- a partnership is dissolved by the happening of any event which makes it unlawful for the business of the firm to be carried on or for the members of the firm to carry it on in partnership;[261]

- partners must render to each other true accounts and full information of all things affecting the partnership;[262] and

- on the dissolution of a partnership any partner may publicly notify the same and require the other partners to concur in the doing of all necessary and proper acts.[263]

---

[256] Partnership Act 1890, s 42(1).

[257] Partnership Act 1890, s 42(2).

[258] Partnership Act 1890, s 44.

[259] Partnership Act 1890, s 44(b).

[260] Note that there are other rights contained in the 1890 Act which may not be varied by the partners inserting a contrary term in their partnership agreement. These terms are not ones which one would find in a typical partnership agreement and therefore are not listed here. For example it is apprehended that the right of a partner to apply to court for the dissolution of the partnership under s 35 of the 1890 Act is not subject to variation by the partners, albeit that it can be replaced by a right to apply to an arbitrator for a winding-up (see para **[25.14]**). This is because the power of a partner set out in s 19 of the 1890 Act to vary the 'mutual rights and duties' set out in the Act, does not, it is contended, extend to s 35. Section 35 sets out, not so much a 'mutual' right within the terms s 19 of the 1890 Act, but rather a separate right granted to each of the partners by that section. Since this right was not granted by the partners to each other, it can be argued that it is not a mutual right and that it is not possible for them to vary it by agreement between themselves.

[261] Partnership Act 1890, s 34. See also para **[9.27]**. It could be argued that this is not a 'mutual right' in any case and so would not be subject to variation pursuant to s 19 in the first place.

[262] Partnership Act 1890, s 28. It has been noted elsewhere, (para **[21.88]**) that this right although a 'mutual' right within the terms of s 19 of the 1890 Act is not variable by the partners, since it is not stated to be subject to a contrary agreement and because of its importance to the very existence of a partnership.

[263] Partnership Act 1890, s 37. This right although a 'mutual' right within the terms of s 19 of the 1890 Act is thought not to be subject to variation by the partners since, unlike most of the implied terms, it is not stated to be subject to contrary agreement and also because if it were subject to variation, a former partner could be exposed to an indefinite liability to future creditors of a firm of which he is no longer a partner. See further para **[26.06]**.

Chapter 22

Anti-Competitive Provisions

INTRODUCTION

[22.01] In this chapter, consideration will be given to the status of the terms of agreements involving partners which actually or potentially restrict competition. These terms will most commonly appear in both the partnership agreement itself and in the terms of any agreement for the sale of a partnership business between the vendors of the business (the partners) and the purchaser. Both types of agreement are governed by the terms of the Competition Act 2002 and the validity of such potentially anti-competitive provisions will be considered under the following headings:

I.   Competition Law Principles Applicable to Partnerships;

II.   Anti-Competitive Terms in Partnership Agreements;

III. Anti-Competitive Terms in Partnership Sale Agreements;

IV. Article 101 of the Treaty on the Functioning of the European Union.

Overview

[22.02] The basis for the regulation of agreements under Irish competition law is now set out in s 4(1) of the Competition Act 2002. This section prohibits agreements if they have as their object or effect the distortion, prevention or restriction of competition. Underlying this prohibition is the principle that anything which restricts free competition is regarded as being contrary to the public interest. Yet, in some instances a restraint on competition will be justifiable; for example, by allowing a business person to take on a third party as his partner and allowing the third party to validly promise not to compete with the firm for a period after his departure, joint enterprises are encouraged for the overall benefit of the economy. Indeed, where an outgoing partner receives a payment for his share of the goodwill, it would be unfair to allow him to destroy the goodwill that he has sold by permitting him to set up in competition with the firm. Similarly, it would be unfair to allow partners in a firm, who have sold a partnership business to a third party, to destroy the firm's goodwill, by competing with the purchaser of the business. Competition law is concerned with reconciling the public interest in free enterprise and free competition on the one hand and the property interests of partners, partnerships and purchasers of partnership businesses on the other hand. The general principles of competition law which have been established in reconciling these competing interests in a business enterprise will, in general, be the same, whether the business is that of a partnership or some other form of business enterprise. In some instances, however, the special nature of a partnership will justify the special treatment of such a business enterprise under competition law.[1]

---

[1]   Reference should be made to the most recent works in this area: Andrews, Gorecki & McFadden, *Modern Irish Competition Law* (2015); Eaton and O'Brien, *Competition Law in Ireland* (2015).

I. COMPETITION LAW PRINCIPLES APPLICABLE TO PARTNERSHIPS

[22.03] The compatibility with competition law of all agreements involving partners, whether agreements between partners inter se, between firms inter se or between partners/partnerships and third parties, must be assessed in the light of the Competition Act 2002.[2] The most important provision of that Act is s 4(1).

Anti-Competitive Provisions are Prima Facie Prohibited and Void

[22.04] Section 4(1) of the Competition Act 2002 provides that:

> Subject to the provisions of this section, all agreements between undertakings, decisions by associations of undertakings and concerted practices which have as their object or effect the prevention, restriction or distortion of competition in trade in any goods or services in the State or in any part of the State are prohibited and void, including in particular, without prejudice to the generality of this subsection, those which–
>
> (a) directly or indirectly fix purchase or selling prices or any other trading conditions,
>
> (b) limit or control production, markets, technical development or investment,
>
> (c) share markets or sources of supply,
>
> (d) apply dissimilar conditions to equivalent transactions with other trading parties thereby placing them at a competitive disadvantage,
>
> (e) make the conclusion of contracts subject to acceptance by the other parties of supplementary obligations which by their nature or according to commercial usage have no connection with the subject of such contracts.

A non-compete restriction will not be prohibited if it either comes within a category of agreements that is the subject of a declaration under s 4(3) of the Competition Act 2002 or complies with the conditions set out in s 4(5) of the Competition Act 2002.[3]

[22.05] By virtue of s 4(2) and 4(5) of the Competition Act 2002, a non-compete restriction will not be prohibited under s 4(1) if, taking into account all relevant market conditions, it:

> contributes to improving the production or distribution of goods or provision of services or to promoting technical or economic progress, while allowing consumers a fair share of the resulting benefit and does not –
>
> (a) impose on the undertakings concerned terms which are not indispensable to the attainment of those objectives,
>
> (b) afford undertakings the possibility of eliminating competition in respect of a substantial part of the products or services in question.[4]

---

[2] The Competition Act 2002 has been amended on several occasions, most notably by the Competition (Amendment) Act 2006, the Competition (Amendment) Act 2010, the Competition (Amendment) Act 2012 and, most recently, the Competition and Consumer Protection Act 2014. The latter Act merged the Competition Authority with the National Consumer Agency to form the Competition and Consumer Protection Commission. Note that under s 6 of the Competition Act 2002, breaches of s 4(1) of the 2002 Act, or of its European equivalent, art 101(1) of the Treaty on the Functioning of the European Union (formerly art 81(1) of the Treaty of Rome) (see, further, para **[22.68]** et seq), constitute criminal offences.

[3] Competition Act 2002, s 4(2).

So, provided that it does not impose terms which are not indispensable to those aims, and does not eliminate all competition, a non-compete restriction will not be prohibited under s 4(1) if it contributes to the improvement of the production or distribution of goods, or the provision of services, or the promotion of technical or economic progress. These are often referred to as the 'efficiency conditions' and there is a high bar to reach when invoking them. Whether they are met in a given case must be determined following a 'self-assessment' approach (rather than the 'notification' approach that applied under the predecessor to the 2002 Act, the Competition Act 1991). That means that, unless an agreement is the subject of a declaration under s 4(3),[5] the partnership itself (and its advisers) must decide whether the agreement meets the conditions set out in s 4(5) and is therefore safe from the prohibition in s 4(1). If ever challenged, the partners must be able to demonstrate that the efficiency conditions are met.

[22.06] Throughout this chapter, reference is made to the Competition and Consumer Protection Commission in respect of developments in this area from 2014 onwards and to its predecessor, the Competition Authority, in respect of pre-2014 matters.

[22.07] Under the Competition Act 1991, category certificates could be issued by the Competition Authority to the effect that certain agreements, decisions or concerted practices, or categories thereof, did not contravene s 4(1) of the 1991 Act (s 4(1) of the 1991 Act was worded in very similar terms to s 4(1) of the 2002 Act). The most relevant to the matters considered in this chapter was the 'Certificate in respect of Agreements involving Merger and/or a Sale of Business'.[6] That certificate was revoked when Part 2 of the 2002 Act came into force, and was briefly replaced by a 'Notice in respect of agreements involving a merger and/or sale of business' which was itself revoked in 2003. While no longer in force, the terms of that category certificate and the decisions made by reference to it may be instructive when self-assessing whether a term of a partnership agreement or of a partnership sale agreement could be prohibited and void under s 4(1) of the 2002 Act. Further, as detailed below, the practice of the Competition and Consumer Protection Commission is to take account of particular paragraphs contained in the European Commission's 'Commission Notice on restrictions directly related and necessary to concentrations'[7] in assessing non-compete clauses.

[22.08] Under s 4(3) of the Competition Act 2002, the Competition and Consumer Protection Commission can make a declaration that a specific category of agreements complies with s 4(5). If such a declaration is made, then an agreement within that category will not be prohibited and void under s 4(1). At the time of writing, only one

---

4   These conditions are set out in the Competition Act 2002, s 4(5).

5   As to which, see para **[22.08]** below.

6   Dec No 489, 2 December 1997. This category certificate applied to all sales of a business and therefore included the sale of part or all of a partnership business by one or all of the partners in a firm. If the terms of the sale of a partnership business came within the provisions of that category certificate, the sale did not require to be notified to the Competition Authority under the Competition Act 1991. Of particular relevance were arts 4 and 5 of that certificate which set out the type of post-sale restrictions on vendors which were not notifiable to the Competition Authority and these are referred to later in this chapter.

7   (2005/C 56/03).

such declaration is in force, entitled a 'Declaration in respect of Vertical Agreements and Concerted Practices'.[8]

Partners and partnerships as undertakings

[22.09] To fall within the ambit of s 4(1) of the Competition Act 2002 in the first place, an agreement must be between undertakings, and s 3(1) of the 2002 Act defines an undertaking as:

> a person being an individual, a body corporate or an unincorporated body of persons engaged for gain in the production, supply or distribution of goods or the provision of a service and, where the context so admits, shall include an association of undertakings.[9]

[22.10] When the Competition Authority was first established after the enactment of the Competition Act 1991, the first case heard by it involved two partners. This was the case of *Nallen/O'Toole*.[10] Curiously, the Competition Authority did not hold that the arrangement was one between undertakings on the grounds that the parties were partners. Rather, it held that this arrangement was one between undertakings on the basis that they were both individuals and thus would satisfy the terms of s 3(1) of the 1991 Act. However, since a partner will usually be either an individual[11] or a body corporate, it follows that arrangements between existing or former partners will invariably satisfy the terms of s 3(1) of the Competition Act 2002 on the grounds that they are individuals or bodies corporate.

[22.11] One of the requirements of the definition of an undertaking in s 3(1) of the Competition Act 2002 is that the person be 'engaged for gain'.[12] This will invariably be the case for a partner, since to be a partner in the first place, s 1(1) of 1890 Act requires a person to be carrying on business with 'a view of profit'. *Doyle/Moffitt*[13] involved both a partnership agreement between the two parties to carry on business for a period of 10 years and a partnership sale agreement, whereby one partner agreed to purchase the other partner's share over the 10-year period. The Competition Authority held that both the partnership agreement and the partnership sale agreement were agreements between undertakings for the purposes of the Competition Act 1991:

---

[8]   Competition Authority, Dec No D/10/001, 1 December 2010. It is available on the website of the Competition and Consumer Protection Commission (www.ccpc.ie). The Commission's concerns regarding vertical agreements relate mainly to resale price maintenance so this declaration is not particularly relevant to a non-compete clause in a partnership agreement or in a partnership sale agreement.

[9]   The definition of 'undertaking' in s 3(1) of the Competition Act 1991 was broadly similar: 'a person being an individual, a body corporate or an unincorporated body of persons engaged for gain in the production, supply or distribution of goods of the provision of a service.'

[10] *Nallen/O'Toole* Competition Authority, Dec No 1, 2 April 1992, Notif CA/8/91.

[11] However note that a partner could also be a group of individuals, since it has been seen that a firm may be a partner, see para **[2.36]**.

[12] Note that the term 'gain' is wider than the term 'profit', since it includes non-pecuniary gain: *Deane v The Voluntary Health Insurance Board* [1992] 2 IR 319 which is considered at para **[2.65]**.

[13] *Doyle/Moffitt* Competition Authority, Dec No 333, 10 June 1994, Notif CA 1133/92.

'The parties to the present agreement are ... engaged as partners in the provision of veterinary services for gain and are therefore undertakings within the meaning of the [Competition] Act.'[14]

[22.12] Since individual partners may be undertakings, it follows that a partnership may also be an undertaking, since a partnership is simply an aggregate of partners, rather than a separate legal entity.[15] This is clear from *Scully Tyrrell & Co/Edberg*,[16] in which the notified arrangement was a merger of a partnership with a company, which arrangement was held to be between undertakings and therefore subject to the terms of the Competition Act 1991.

'Undertaking' or employee? – vendor partner who becomes an employee of purchaser

[22.13] As a matter of competition law, an agreement between an employer and his employee is not an agreement between separate undertakings, since the employee and the employer form an integral part of the same economic undertaking.[17] A situation may arise where a partner, who is clearly a separate undertaking to start, sells his share of the partnership business to a third party and as part of the sale agreement becomes an employee of the purchaser. In this case, the question arises as to whether that partner remains an 'undertaking' for the purposes of the Competition Act 2002, even though he is thereby becoming an employee.

[22.14] In *Scully Tyrrell & Co/Edberg*[18] the partners in a firm of loss adjusters sold the partnership business to Edberg Ltd. However, as part of the sale, the partners acquired a 38% shareholding in Edberg Ltd and they agreed to become directors and employees of Edberg Ltd. For this reason, the partners argued that they should be treated like employees under competition law and therefore as not constituting separate undertakings from Edberg Ltd. However, the Competition Authority held that, at the time of agreement for the sale of the business, the partners were separate from Edberg Ltd and on that basis, it held that the sale agreement was an agreement between

---

14 *Doyle/Moffitt* Competition Authority, Dec No 333, 10 June 1994, Notif CA 1133/92. at para 18.

15 See generally as to the nature of a partnership, para **[3.04]**.

16 *Scully Tyrrell & Co/Edberg* Competition Authority, Dec No 12, 29 January 1993, Notif CA/ 57/92. The partners in the firm of loss adjusters argued that the agreement for the purchase of its business by Edberg Ltd was a concentration and thus outside the terms of the Competition Act 1991, s 4(1). Edberg Ltd had its own loss adjusting business which it carried on through a subsidiary company. The Competition Authority held that the acquisition by Edberg Ltd of Scully Tyrell combined with its existing loss adjusting business would constitute a merger and thus come within the terms of Competition Act 1991, s 4(1). It relied on its earlier decision in *Woodchester Bank Ltd/UDT Bank Ltd*, Competition Authority, Dec No 6, 4 August 1992, Notif CA/10/92.

17 This was set out in the 'Notice of Competition Authority, Employee Agreements and the Competition Act', *Iris Oifigiúil* 18 September 1992 at p 632–633 (in force at that time, but no longer in place). See *Peter Mark/Majella Stapleton*, Competition Authority, Dec No 13, 18 February 1993, Notif CA 1011/92E.

18 *Scully Tyrrell & Co/Edberg* Competition Authority, Dec No 12, 29 January 1993, Notif CA/ 57/92.

undertakings. It follows that a partner, who negotiates the sale of his partnership share and at the same time agrees to become an employee of the purchaser, will remain subject to the terms of s 4(1) of the Competition Act 2002 and will not be able to avoid its terms on the basis that he is an employee. This position can be justified since at the time of the sale, which is the relevant time for assessing the nature of the potentially anti-competitive provisions, the partner and the purchaser are separate economic entities, unlike the situation with an employer and employee, since the employee normally acts on behalf of the undertaking (the employer) and therefore does not constitute a separate undertaking.

Market Power of Professional Partnerships

[22.15] Once a partnership arrangement is considered to be within the terms of the Competition Act 2002, the market power of the partners or the partnership will often be a crucial factor in assessing whether an agreement or arrangement between partners or partnerships would lead to a distortion of competition law, so as to contravene s 4(1) of the Competition Act 2002. This is particularly so, when one is dealing with a merger of firms which together would have a large market share.[19] In many cases, a high market share may be indicative that the merger of those partnerships would lead to a diminution of competition.[20] However, when one is dealing with partnerships, it is sometimes difficult to obtain information on market share because, unlike companies, partnerships are not generally required to publish accounts.[21] For this reason, the approach which was taken in the past by the Competition Authority[22] was to estimate the market share of a partnership on the basis of the number of professionals engaged by the firm, as a percentage of the total number of professionals in the country or in the region in question. While the Competition and Consumer Protection Commission might use this method for determining the market share of the firm in question if faced with a merger involving a professional firm today, it has more significant information gathering powers now under the Competition Act 2002. It can require the parties to an agreement or arrangement, as well as third parties, to provide it with information, including

[19] Where the turnover generated by the partnerships exceed certain thresholds, the merger control regime under the Competition Act 2002 will likely be triggered. In such cases, the parties to the merger will have to seek the approval of the Competition and Consumer Protection Commission before they may implement the merger transaction. The thresholds are relatively high (aggregate turnover in Ireland of all of the undertakings involved is not less than €50 million; *and* the turnover, in Ireland, of each of at least two of the undertakings involved is not less than €3 million). Where the merger control regime is not triggered, s 4(1) remains relevant.

[20] While market share remains an important indicator of market power in the assessment of most mergers, the Competition and Consumer Protection Commission will also look at other indicators of market power and competition in the relevant market(s), such as the existence of barriers to entry and expansion and whether the merged entity's customers would be able to exercise countervailing buyer power (eg by switching their custom to another provider) in the face of any attempt by the merged entity to raise prices or otherwise restrict competition.

[21] See generally in relation to partnership accounts, para **[14.64]** et seq.

[22] In a case involving a partnership of loss adjusters: *Scully Tyrell & Co/Edberg* Competition Authority, Dec No 12, 29 January 1993, Notif CA/57/92.

confidential information such as estimates of market share, when it is conducting investigations under the Competition Act 2002.

Will the Anti-competitive Provision Result in Efficiency Gains?

[22.16] Under s 4(1) of the Competition Act 2002, anti-competitive agreements involving partnerships are prima facie prohibited and void. However, as mentioned above, s 4(2) of the 2002 Act provides that an anti-competitive agreement will not be prohibited under s 4(1) if it meets the conditions set out in s 4(5), ie if, taking into account all relevant market conditions, the agreement:

> contributes to improving the production or distribution of goods or provision of services or to promoting technical or economic progress, while allowing consumers a fair share of the resulting benefit and does not –
>
> (a) impose on the undertakings concerned terms which are not indispensable to the attainment of those objectives,
>
> (b) afford undertakings the possibility of eliminating competition in respect of a substantial part of the products or services in question.

So, an agreement that would otherwise be considered anti-competitive will not be prohibited under s 4(1) if it is indispensable to the improvement of the production or distribution of goods, or the provision of services, or the promotion of technical or economic progress.

[22.17] In general terms, if the restriction is designed to protect legitimate interests and does not exceed what is necessary to do so, it will not be struck down as contrary to s 4(1). Thus, if the anti-competitive restriction is excessive as regards geographic coverage, duration or subject matter,[23] it is unlikely to benefit from s 4(2) as it will not meet the conditions set out in s 4(5). An example of a case where the restriction on a partner went further than was necessary is provided by the English High Court case of *Peyton v Mindham*.[24] This involved a partnership between two doctors in general practice. Their agreement provided that if the partnership should be dissolved by notice, the recipient of the dissolution notice would be prohibited from professionally advising any patient of the firm. Plowman J struck down the clause as being excessively restrictive of competition, since it prevented the defendant partner from acting as a consultant to patients of the practice and not merely as a general practitioner.

Each restrictive covenant must be considered on its own facts

[22.18] In order to determine whether a restrictive covenant is reasonable, it is perhaps self-evident that the surrounding circumstances of the case must be carefully considered

---

23   See for example *Doyle/Moffitt*, Competition Authority Dec No 333, 10 June 1994, Notif CA/ 1133/92, in which the non-compete provision for a period of five years went beyond what was necessary to secure the transfer of the goodwill of the business from the retiring partner to the continuing partner and the Competition Authority held that these non-compete provisions were not indispensable to the attainment of the objectives of the agreement so as to satisfy the requirements for a licence under s 4(2) of the Competition Act 1991.

24   *Peyton v Mindham* [1971] 3 All ER 1215.

and in particular the nature of the partnership business. As noted by Meredith J in the High Court case of *Gargan v Ruttle*:[25]

> "'What 'goodwill' means ... must depend on the character and nature of the business to which it is attached." The same remark applies certainly with no less force, to protective obligations imposed on a particular class of persons, such as vendors, in respect of particular classes of business.'[26]

[22.19] Accordingly, when one is dealing with a loss adjusting business where the customers (ie the insurers) deal with the firm frequently, a two-year restrictive covenant was regarded as a sufficient restriction on the vendor-partner of that business in order to ensure that the goodwill was transferred to the purchaser.[27] In contrast, where the business of the partnership was the sale of electrical goods to the public and where customers tend to purchase the products infrequently, a restriction on a partner of longer than two years was contemplated by the Competition Authority as being justifiable.[28]

Combined effect of agreements

[22.20] Although a non-compete provision in a partnership agreement may be valid on its own, one should bear in mind that the combined effect of this restriction with another agreement, which also contains a non-compete provision, may offend against s 4(1) of the Competition Act 2002. This is highlighted by *Doyle/Moffitt*,[29] where two vets signed a partnership agreement for a period of ten years. At the same time, they signed a partnership sale agreement, whereby one partner was to purchase the other partner's share over the course of the ten years. Under the partnership agreement, there was a restriction on each of the partners competing with the firm for five years after the date of his retirement. Under the sale agreement, there was a restriction on the vendor partner from competing with the purchaser partner for five years from the date of the completion of the sale which was to take place ten years after the commencement of the partnership. The combined effect of both these restrictions was that, if the vendor partner retired during the first few years of the partnership, he would be subject to a five-year restriction period and he could have a further five-year restriction period imposed on him on the completion of the sale. This latter restriction could not be justified as being required to secure the transfer of the goodwill to the other partner, since the transfer of the goodwill in the business would have been secured a number of years previously. For this reason, the Competition Authority held that the combined effect of these two non-compete provisions offended against s 4(1) of the Competition Act 1991 (the predecessor to s 4(1) of the 2002 Act).

---

25 *Gargan v Ruttle* [1931] IR 152.
26 *Gargan v Ruttle* [1931] IR 152 at 158, quoting with approval the judgment of Lord Macnaghten in *Trego v Hunt* [1896] AC 7 at 23.
27 *Scully Tyrell & Co/Edberg* Competition Authority, Dec No 12, 29 January 1993, Notif CA/57/92.
28 *Nallen/O'Toole* Competition Authority, Dec No 1, 2 April 1992, Notif CA/8/91.
29 *Doyle/Moffitt Competition Authority*, Dec No 333, 10 June 1994, Notif CA/1133/92.

Importance of mutuality of restriction

[22.21] By the very nature of partnership agreements as distinct from other arrangements involving partners or partnerships (such as partnership sale agreements or mergers),[30] the potentially anti-competitive restrictions contained in them, will commonly apply to all partners. This is because they usually apply to any partner who leaves the partnership. This fact increases the likelihood of these restrictions being acceptable under s 4(2) of the Competition Act 2002 by virtue of meeting the conditions set out in s 4(5). This is because an important consideration in determining whether a non-compete clause is reasonable is the issue of whether the provision applies equally to all partners, regardless of their age or seniority in the firm.[31] Thus in *Coolmoyne and Fethard Cooperative Creamery v Bulfin*,[32] O'Brien LC, in treating a co-operative as 'little more than an ordinary partnership',[33] held that the prohibition on a member from supplying milk to any other co-operative was not in restraint of trade for the following reason:

> 'If, after this man had ceased to be a member of the society, the regulations bound him to supply milk to the creamery and to no one else even in the district, then the case might be totally different. But no such restriction is imposed, and both the duties which they owe to him, and which are reciprocal, continue for their mutual benefit, and there is no unreasonableness.'[34]

[22.22] As explained by Mason J in the Australian High Court case of *Geraghty v Minter*:[35]

> 'The fact that the covenant is entered into by each of the partners and may become binding on any of them, depending upon the events which happen, is a factor which is to be taken into account in assessing whether it is reasonable between the parties.'[36]

II.   ANTI-COMPETITIVE TERMS IN PARTNERSHIP AGREEMENTS

[22.23] Having briefly considered some of the relevant terms of the Competition Act 2002, this section considers the application of these provisions to potentially anti-competitive terms in partnership agreements. In the next section of this chapter, their application to potentially anti-competitive terms in partnership sale agreements will be considered.

---

30 Most agreements for the sale of a partnership business do not provide for the restriction on competition to apply mutually to a purchaser and a vendor. But see the case of *Doyle/Moffit* Competition Authority, Dec No 333, 10 June 1994, Notif CA/1133/92, where the vendor partner was restricted from competing in relation to the veterinary part of the practice and the purchaser partner was restricted from competing in relation to the equine part of the practice. This was treated by the Competition Authority as a general dissolution of a partnership, where the business is divided *in specie* between the partners

31 *Bridge v Deacons* [1984] 1 AC 705.

32 *Coolmoyne and Fethard Co-operative Creamery v Bulfin* [1917] 2 IR 107.

33 *Coolmoyne and Fethard Co-operative Creamery v Bulfin* [1917] 2 IR 107 at 123.

34 *Coolmoyne and Fethard Co-operative Creamery v Bulfin* [1917] 2 IR 107 at 127.

35 *Geraghty v Minter* (1979) 142 CLR 177.

36 *Geraghty v Minter* (1979) 142 CLR 177 at 198.

Provision that Existing Partners will not Compete with Firm (Non-compete Restrictions)

[22.24] The basis of most partnerships is that two persons who previously had worked separately will henceforth work together. Accordingly by its very nature, the partnership agreement could be considered to be anti-competitive, since both partners will usually, either expressly or implicitly, agree not to work in competition with the firm. Indeed s 30 of the 1890 Act recognises this fact by implying into every partnership a term that each partner must account to the firm for any profit derived by him, without the consent of the other partners, from his carrying on of any business which competes with the firm.[37] For this reason, it would be contrary to the very nature of a partnership if such an express or implicit anti-competitive agreement were to be treated as contrary to the terms of s 4(1) of the Competition Act 2002. This principle has been accepted by the Irish courts for many years in considering such clauses under the doctrine of restraint of trade. Thus in *Coolmoyne and Fethard Co-operative Creamery v Bulfin*,[38] Ronan LJ treated the relationship between the members of a co-operative as akin to a partnership and he noted that the law looked jealously at restraints of trade on former partners, but took a very different attitude to restraints on partners while they remained members of the firm:

> '[P]artners are free to enter into combination to carry on a trade or a business for their own interest together, provided it is not with a view to injure others; and the law regards them as the best judges of what is reasonable as between themselves.'[39]

[22.25] In 1994 this principle was accepted by the Competition Authority in *Doyle/ Moffitt*,[40] when it adopted the following reasoning:[41]

> 'Again, when two men become partners in a business, although their union might reduce competition, this effect was only an incident to the main purpose of a union of their capital, enterprise, and energy, to carry on a successful business, and one useful to the community. Restrictions in the articles of partnership upon the business activity of the members, with a view to securing their entire effort in the common enterprise, were, of course only ancillary to the main end of the union, and were to be encouraged.'[42]

On this basis, the Competition Authority held that it:

> 'does not regard partnerships as being in contravention of the [Competition] Act *per se*. In certain circumstances, however, partnership agreements may be in breach of section 4(1).'[43]

---

[37] See also s 29(1) of the 1890 Act which implies a term that every partner will account to the firm for any benefit derived by him, without the consent of his partners, from any transaction concerning the partnership or from his use of the partnership property, name or business connection. See further para **[15.27]** et seq.

[38] *Coolmoyne and Fethard Co-operative Creamery v Bulfin* [1917] 2 IR 107.

[39] *Coolmoyne and Fethard Co-operative Creamery v Bulfin* [1917] 2 IR 107 at 133.

[40] *Doyle/ Moffitt* Competition Authority, Dec No 333, 10 June 1994, Notif CA/1133/92.

[41] Quoting Taft J in *United States v Addyston Pipe & Steel Company* (1898) 85 Fed 271.

[42] *United States v Addyston Pipe & Steel Company* (1898) 85 Fed 271 at 280.

[43] *Doyle/ Moffitt* Competition Authority, Dec No 333, 10 June 1994, Notif CA/1133/92 at para 23 quoting from *Nallen/O'Toole* Competition Authority, Dec No 1, 2 April 1992, Notif CA/8/91 at para 23.

[22.26] Thus, the express or implicit requirement that partners will not compete with the firm while they are partners is not in breach of s 4(1) of the Competition Act 2002. The circumstances in which other terms of the partnership agreement will be deemed to be contrary to s 4(1) will be considered next.

Each Partner to Devote Full Time and Attention to Firm

[22.27] A provision that partners will devote their full time and attention to the firm is simply an affirmation of the fact that they will not compete with each other so long as they remain in business together. Therefore, it is also not contrary to s 4(1) of the Competition Act 2002. As noted by the Competition Authority in *Scully Tyrrell & Co/ Edberg*:[44]

> 'An agreement between parties to engage in business together could not operate if the parties were free to compete with the business or with each other. The Authority believes that individuals could not jointly engage in business together if they were free to compete with each other. It is clear, even if it is not explicitly stated, that an agreement between parties to carry on business together, implies that they will not compete against the business or against each other so long as they remain in business together ... Indeed such arrangements may be pro-competitive in that the combined entity may be in a better position to compete with other undertakings in the relevant market.'[45]

Notice to Retire and Requirement to Hand over Correspondence

[22.28] Also common in partnership agreements is a provision which requires each partner to give to the firm notice of his intention to retire from the firm and to hand over correspondence and information which belongs to the partnership. While such provisions may be regarded as a restriction on a partner's withdrawal from the partnership, they have as their object the orderly management of a partner's departure and not the distortion of competition. For this reason in *Doyle/Moffit*,[46] the Competition Authority held that such provisions were not contrary to s 4(1) of the Competition Act 1991 (the predecessor to s 4(1) of the Competition Act 2002).

Non-compete Restriction on Departing Partner

[22.29] An important provision in many partnership agreements is a restriction on departing partners from competing with the firm, since such activity may be very damaging to the business of the continuing firm. In considering the principles which apply to such non-compete clauses, the Competition Authority held that a restriction on competition on the retirement of a partner is to be treated in the same way as a non-compete provision on the sale of a business.[47] This is because generally on the departure of a partner, there will be a transfer by the departing partner of the firm's goodwill to the

---

[44] *Scully Tyrrell & Co/Edberg* Competition Authority, Dec No 12, 29 January 1993, Notif CA/57/92.

[45] *Scully Tyrrell & Co/Edberg* Competition Authority, Dec No 12, 29 January 1993, Notif CA/57/92 at para 74–75.

[46] *Doyle/Moffit* Competition Authority, Dec No 333, 10 June 1994, Notif CA/1133/92.

[47] *Doyle/Moffit* Competition Authority, Dec No 333, 10 June 1994, Notif CA/1133/92 at para 22.

continuing partner, while on the sale of a business, there will also be a transfer of the firm's goodwill by the vendor to the purchaser. In either case, the same question must be asked: is the restriction necessary in order to achieve the transfer of goodwill? The validity of some kind of restriction on the transferor of goodwill was recognised by the Competition Authority in *Nallen/O'Toole*,[48] where it quoted with approval the judgment of Taft J in *United States v Addyston Pipe & Steel Company*[49] that:

> 'It was equally for the good of the public and trade, when partners dissolved, and one took the business, or they divided the business, that each partner might bind himself not to do anything in trade thereafter which would derogate from his grant of the interest so conveyed.'[50]

[22.30] Since the Competition Authority has held that the principles applicable to a non-compete restriction on a departing partner are the same as those applicable on the sale of a business, regard must now be had to decisions of the Competition and Consumer Protection Commission and its predecessor, the Competition Authority, generally regarding restrictions on vendors on the sale of a business.

Commission Notice on restrictions directly related to and necessary to concentrations

[22.31] The Competition and Consumer Protection Commission has indicated in a number of recent decisions (albeit not relating to partnerships) that, when assessing whether a restrictive covenant such as a non-compete clause (often referred to as an 'ancillary restraint') is directly related, and necessary, to the proposed sale and whether the maximum duration of the restriction is acceptable, it has followed the approach of the European Commission in paragraphs 20 and 26 of its 'Commission Notice on restrictions directly related to and necessary to concentrations'.[51]

Paragraph 20 of the Commission Notice

[22.32] Paragraph 20 of the Commission Notice provides that non-compete clauses are justified:

– for up to three years where the sale of the business includes the transfer of 'customer loyalty in the form of both goodwill and know how';

– for up to two years where the sale of the business only includes the transfer of goodwill.

Paragraph 26 of the Commission Notice

[22.33] Paragraph 26 of the Commission Notice provides that non-solicitation and confidentiality clauses will be evaluated in the same way as non-compete clauses as they

---

48 *Nallen/O'Toole Competition Authority*, Dec No 1, 2 April 1992, Notif CA/8/91 at para 41.
49 *United States v Addyston Pipe & Steel Company* (1898) 85 Fed 271.
50 *United States v Addyston Pipe & Steel Company* (1898) 85 Fed 271 at 280.
51 Commission Notice on restrictions directly related and necessary to concentrations (2005/C 56/03). See for example M/14/010 – *Irish Wind / SWS*; M/17/024: *UPS/Eirpost*; M/16/052 – *Halstonville / Travelodge Hotels*; M/17/048 *Canada Pension Investment Board/Shell E&P Ireland Limited*.

have a 'comparable effect'. It should be noted that the Competition and Consumer Commission requires the parties to demonstrate substantively that a non-compete restriction involves the transfer of goodwill and know how before it will accept the restriction as necessary to the transfer of the business.[52]

Revocation of Category Certificate

[22.34] As mentioned above, the Competition Authority's Category Certificate for Agreements involving a Merger and/or a Sale of Business[53] was revoked in 2002 but may still be useful when self-assessing (under s 4(2) of the Competition Act 2002) whether an agreement is not prohibited and void under s 4(1) of that Act by virtue of meeting the 'efficiency' conditions set out in s 4(5). As such, the decisions made by the Competition Authority both before that Category Certificate came into effect, and while it was in effect (in its original form or as its successor, the Competition Authority's 'Notice in respect of agreements involving a merger and/or sale of business') are noted below insofar as relevant to partnership agreements and partnership sale agreements.

Pre-Category Certificate Decisions

[22.35] In 1992, the Competition Authority noted that s 4(1) of the Competition Act 1991 (the predecessor to s 4(1) of the Competition Act 2002) would be breached if the restraint on competition exceeded what was necessary in terms of its duration, geographic coverage and subject matter to secure the transfer of any goodwill involved.[54]

[22.36] The 1994 case of *Doyle/Moffit*[55] involved an arrangement between two vets which provided for Moffit to gradually acquire Doyle's partnership share over the life of the partnership and their partnership agreement restricted Doyle, for five years from the date of his retirement and within 20 miles of the practice, from:

- acting for any person who had been a client of the firm in the previous two years;
- seeking or holding any professional veterinary appointment capable of being held by a veterinary surgeon for which the continuing partner had applied; and
- doing anything to damage the firm's goodwill.

[22.37] The Competition Authority held that in terms of geographic coverage (20 miles) and subject matter (veterinary surgeon) the restriction was reasonable but in terms of duration (five years) it was excessive since, in general, non-compete clauses of more

---

52   See, most recently, the decision of the Competition and Consumer Protection Commission in the *Loughnane/Crinkle Merger case*, Case M/17/036, proposed acquisition by Sean Loughane (Galway) Limited of certain business assets of Crinkle Fine Foods Unlimited Company, 3 October 2017.

53   Dec No 489, 2 December 1997.

54   *Nallen/O'Toole* Competition Authority, Dec No 1, 2 April 1992, Notif CA/8/91 at para 43. See generally *John Orr Ltd v Orr* [1987] ILRM 703 which concerned a restraint of trade clause on the owner of a company when he sold his shares in the company. The non-compete clause was held to be excessively restrictive since it sought to restrain the vendor from trading in wall coverings (which was outside the company's business) and applied world-wide.

55   *Doyle/Moffit* Competition Authority, Dec No 333, 10 June 1994, Notif CA/1133/92.

than two years are longer than necessary to secure the transfer of the goodwill and therefore offended against s 4(1) of the Competition Act 1991.[56]

[22.38] However the Competition Authority was of the view that, in certain circumstances, a non-compete clause of longer than two years would be justified.[57] Thus in *Doyle/Moffit* itself,[58] the Competition Authority indicated that while the five-year restriction was excessive, it might be prepared to accept a non-compete clause of longer than two years in the circumstances of that case.[59] The circumstances in question were that Doyle, the founder of the veterinary practice, took his assistant, Moffit, into partnership for a ten-year period and over this period he agreed to sell his share in the partnership to Moffit. Of relevance was the fact that Doyle had operated the practice for 28 years, was well-known in the locality and closely identified with the practice, and for these reasons, the Competition Authority would have looked favourably on a non-compete provision of longer than two years.[60]

Category Certificate decisions

[22.39] In the Category Certificate for Agreements involving a Merger and/or a Sale of Business, the Competition Authority noted that some restraint on a party disposing of all or part of his interest[61] in a business was essential for the proper transfer of goodwill, but that it would contravene s 4(1) of the Competition Act 1991, if the restraint on competition exceeded what was necessary in terms of its duration, geographic coverage and subject matter to secure the transfer of any goodwill involved. The Category Certificate also set out limits on non-compete restrictions that were not to be exceeded, on the sale of a business that included goodwill, if the parties wished to rely on the existence of the Category Certificate to avoid having to notify their agreements to the Competition Authority. Those limits were that any post-sale non-compete restriction could not exceed two years from the date of the completion of the sale; could not apply

---

56 See also *GI/General Semiconductor Industries* Competition Authority, Dec No 10, 23 October 1992, Notifs CA/51/92 and CA/52/92.

57 In the decision on the Category Certificate for Agreements involving a Merger and/or a Sale of Business (No 489, 2 December 1997), the Competition Authority (in reliance on the European Commission decision in the *Nutrica Case* [1984] 2 CMLR 165) noted that the length of time necessary to transfer the goodwill will vary from business to business and some of the factors involved in assessing this time were (i) how frequently consumers in the relevant market change brands and type (in relation to the degree of brand loyalty shown by them) and (ii) for how long, after the sale of the business, the seller, without a restrictive clause, would be able to make a successful comeback to the market and regain his old customers.

58 *Doyle/Moffit* Competition Authority, Dec No 333, 10 June 1994, Notif CA/1133/92.

59 The Competition Authority indicated in a letter to the parties that it accepted that a non-compete clause of longer than two years might be necessary in this case, but that five years was not justified. It did not receive a response to this letter.

60 Although in this case and in *Nallen/O'Toole* Competition Authority, Dec No 1, 2 April 1992, Notif CA/8/91, one is dealing with the sale of a partnership business, rather than the departure of a partner, it has been noted (para [22.29]) that the same principles apply.

61 Thus encompassing the position of a departing partner who sells his share of the partnership business to the continuing partners.

to any location outside the territory where the products[62] concerned were manufactured or purchased or sold by the vendor at the time of the agreement; and could not apply to goods or services other than those manufactured, purchased or sold by the vendor at the time of the agreement. A requirement to notify the Competition Authority if the limits set out in the Category Certificate were exceeded did not, however, mean that s 4(1) of the 1991 Act was automatically breached, but rather that a decision was needed from the Competition Authority as to whether the non-compete restrictions were necessary to secure the transfer of the goodwill involved.

[22.40] Until the revocation of the Category Certificate, in the absence of special circumstances, the prudent approach was for partners to have a non-compete clause on a departing partner which complied with Article 4 of the Category Certificate and in this way to avoid having to notify the agreement.

[22.41] Other potentially anti-competitive restrictions on departing partners such as a restriction on their use or disclosure of confidential information and know-how are considered in the context of partnership sale agreements[63] while non-solicit restrictions on departing partners are considered next.

Express non-solicit restrictions on partner selling his share

[22.42] In addition to general non-compete restrictions, partners who sell their interest in the partnership goodwill to the continuing partners will often undertake not to solicit employees and customers of the business. As noted above,[64] para 26 of the 'Commission Notice in respect of agreements involving a merger and/or sale of business' provides that such non-solicitation clauses should be evaluated in the same way as non-compete restrictions as they have 'comparable effect'.[65]

Non-compete and non-solicit restrictions in a departmentalised firm

[22.43] The Privy Council in *Bridge v Deacons*[66] considered whether a non-compete or non-solicit restriction on a departing partner from a departmentalised firm should be treated differently from a restriction on a partner in a non-departmentalised firm. This case concerned a dispute between the law firm Deacons, one of the oldest and largest law firms in Hong Kong, and the plaintiff, one of its former partners. When Bridge was

---

62   Although services were not expressly mentioned, it is likely that that the same applied to the provision of services.

63   See para **[22.65]** et seq.

64   See para **[22.33]**.

65   This was also recognised by the Competition Authority in its 'Category Certificate in respect of Agreements involving a Merger and/or Sale of Business'. Accordingly, Article 4(a) thereof also applied to a post-sale restriction on the departing partner (who sold his share to the continuing partners) from soliciting customers or employees of the business and it was not regarded as offending s 4(1) of the Competition Act 1991 if it did not: (a) exceed two years from the date of completion of the sale; (b) apply to any location outside the territory where the products concerned were manufactured, purchased or sold by the vendor at the time of the agreement; or (c) apply to goods or services other than those manufactured, purchased or sold by the vendor at the time of the agreement.

66   *Bridge v Deacons* [1984] AC 705.

a partner in the firm, Deacons had 29 partners and was divided up into a number of
different departments. Bridge had only worked in one of those departments, the
intellectual property department. However, the restrictive covenant in the partnership
agreement restrained a former partner from competing against the business of the firm
as a whole. Bridge claimed that this was an unreasonable restraint of trade, as he
claimed that the restrictive covenant should have applied only in respect of the clients of
the intellectual property department. However, the Privy Council held that the restriction
was reasonable. It justified its decision on the basis that Bridge was entitled to a share of
the goodwill of the firm as a whole while he was a partner and not just the goodwill
attaching to the intellectual property department and on the basis that while he was a
partner, he had the benefit of this restraint of trade clause. In these circumstances, it is
submitted that the Privy Council was correct in not allowing Bridge to compete against
the other departments. It is possible that the same approach would be taken by the
Competition and Consumer Protection Commission and the Irish courts, since a partner
who enters a partnership agreement and acquires the benefit of the firm's goodwill on
the basis of accepting the terms of a restrictive covenant should not subsequently be
allowed to derogate from his grant back of the goodwill. That said, the Irish courts have
traditionally been reticent to uphold broad non-compete restrictions that would prevent a
person from earning a livelihood.[67]

Non-solicit Restriction Implied on Partner Selling his Share

[22.44] This chapter is primarily concerned with potentially anti-competitive provisions
which have been expressly agreed by partners. However, even where a partner has not
signed a non-compete agreement, he will be subject to an implied non-solicit restriction
where he sells his share of the goodwill in the firm to his co-partner(s). This implied
obligation, on a seller of the goodwill of a business not to solicit customers of the
business being sold, arises by virtue of the principle that a person is not allowed to
destroy what he has sold.

[22.45] This principle is illustrated by the High Court case of *Gargan v Ruttle*.[68] There, a
partnership dispute between the parties ended up in arbitration. The arbitrator's award
provided that the partnership had dissolved and that the goodwill, stock-in-trade and
assets should belong to the plaintiff and that the defendant should receive a sum of
money for his share thereof. However, there was no express restriction placed on the
defendant under the terms of the arbitrator's award and the defendant continued to solicit
the customers of the former firm. The plaintiff sought an injunction to restrain him from
so doing. In the High Court, Meredith J regarded the plaintiff as being in the same
position as a partner who comes before the court after he has purchased the goodwill in
the firm from his co-partner under the terms of their partnership agreement. On this
basis, he held that the following general principle applied to the defendant:

> '[W]hen a man sells the goodwill of his business he cannot afterwards destroy the value of
> the goodwill of what he has sold by soliciting his old customers. Subject, however, to this

---

[67] See for example the judgment of Laffoy J in *Hernandes v Vodafone Ireland Ltd* [2013]
      IEHC 70.

[68] *Gargan v Ruttle* [1931] IR 152.

restriction, the vendor is not precluded from setting up a rival business with which the old customers may deal on their own initiative.'[69]

[22.46] Accordingly Meredith J held that even though the defendant had not signed a non-solicit provision, he was subject to an implied restriction not to solicit the customers of his former firm. Therefore, he granted an injunction against the defendant prohibiting him from soliciting the customers of the firm at the date of dissolution to either deal with him or not to deal with the plaintiff.

[22.47] It should be borne in mind that the fact that customers of a partner's former firm decide to follow the outgoing partner does not constitute soliciting by the outgoing partner. In the High Court case of *O'Connor v Woods*,[70] the partnership agreement provided that on a technical dissolution,[71] the goodwill in the firm was to remain with the continuing partners and the departing partner was to receive an annuity of £1,000 for 10 years, as well as the amount standing to the credit of his capital account. When the plaintiff left the firm, the continuing partners in the firm alleged that he had enticed away clients of the firm and they sought damages for loss of earnings. On the facts of the case, Kenny J held that there was no enticement. He noted that the plaintiff was not liable for enticing clients as:

> 'It does not follow that because a company or individual took any part of their business away from the partnership when the plaintiff left it, that the plaintiff is liable for the fees. To make him liable the first and third named defendants have to prove that he enticed the client away from the firm.'[72]

[22.48] He noted that in many cases O'Connor was asked by clients to do the work and 'there was no obligation on him to leave work with the partnership which he could do'.[73] However, to the extent that any fees which he received from these clients were attributable to work done by the firm, he was of course obliged to account to the firm for this amount.

Non-compete Provisions on a General Dissolution of the Partnership

[22.49] Unlike a technical dissolution of a partnership (in which the firm continues despite a change in its membership), on a general dissolution there are no continuing partners and the partnership business comes to an end and is usually wound up. In such situations, the partners may, instead of winding up the firm, decide to divide the firm's business *in specie* and any such division will be treated as a sale of a partnership share by one partner to the other. This is clear from *Doyle/Moffit*.[74] Although that case involved a partnership sale agreement, the Competition Authority noted that the arrangement amounted to a general dissolution of the partnership, with the business

---

69 *Gargan v Ruttle* [1931] IR 152 at 157, where he relied on the authority of *Trego v Hunt* [1896] AC 7.
70 *O'Connor v Woods* (22 January 1976) HC.
71 Ie a change in membership of a firm which does not lead to the firm's winding up but where the business of partnership continues as before.
72 *O'Connor v Woods* (22 January 1976) HC at p 12 of the transcript.
73 *O'Connor v Woods* (22 January 1976) HC at p 10 of the transcript.
74 *Doyle/Moffit* Competition Authority, Dec No 333, 10 June 1994, Notif CA/1133/92.

being divided *in specie* between the two partners.[75] This is because the partners agreed that Moffit would gradually acquire Doyle's partnership share over the life of the partnership. The agreement restricted Doyle from competing with the firm in relation to veterinary matters, while it prohibited Moffit from providing equine and equestrian services. This restriction on Moffit allowed Doyle to continue in practice in the equine and equestrian services area and in this way, a certain element of the partnership, with its associated goodwill, was retained by him and the remainder of the goodwill was retained by Moffit. The Competition Authority held that this general dissolution of the partnership with a division *in specie* should be considered in the same manner as it considers anti-competitive provisions on a vendor of the goodwill of a business.

[22.50] Accordingly, one may conclude from this that a restriction on partners on a general dissolution of the firm does not offend against s 4(1), if it does not exceed what is necessary to secure the transfer of any goodwill involved, in terms of its duration, geographic coverage and subject matter.[76]

Restrictions on Withdrawal from Partnerships

[22.51] A restriction on a partner from withdrawing from the partnership is potentially restrictive of competition, since it restricts a partner from setting-up in competition with the firm. However, like a provision requiring a partner to devote his full time and attention to the firm,[77] reasonable restrictions will be regarded as a necessary incident of the partnership relationship and not in contravention of the Competition Act 2002. Indeed, it seems that the absence of a clause in the partnership agreement entitling a partner to withdraw from the firm or a clause in the agreement that a partner will be bound for life will not per se render the agreement contrary to s 4(1)[78] since as noted obiter by O'Brien LC in *Coolmoyne and Fethard Co-opertive Creamery v Bulfin*:[79]

> 'An ordinary contract between two, or twenty, or a hundred individuals binding themselves in merely commercial relations for the term of their lives would not, I conceive, be illegal.'[80]

---

[75] At para 22, the Competition Authority noted: 'In effect the sale involves the dissolution of the partnership with each party retaining a part of the business previously carried on jointly.'

[76] As previously noted, the Competition Authority held that in terms of geographic coverage (20 miles) and subject matter (veterinary services and equestrian services), the restriction was reasonable but in terms of duration (five years), it was excessive since in general, non-compete clauses of longer than two years offended against s 4(1) of the Competition Act 1991, see further para **[22.37]**.

[77] See para **[22.27]**.

[78] See *Tipperary Creamery Society v Hanley* [1912] 2 IR 586 (where the clause was held to be unenforceable as an unreasonable restraint of trade since it required the defendant to sell all the milk from his cows, regardless of what part of the country they were situated in, to the plaintiff co-operative in Tipperary). See also *Athlacca Co-operative Creamery Ltd v Lynch* (1915) 49 ILTR 233. There, co-operative rules were held not be in restraint of trade where the prohibitions on the sale of milk applied only to cows in certain townlands even though those rules made no provision for the withdrawal of a member otherwise than by the transfer of his shares with the consent of the Committee of the Co-operative.

[79] *Coolmoyne and Fethard Co-operative Creamery v Bulfin* [1917] 2 IR 107.

[80] *Coolmoyne and Fethard Co-operative Creamery v Bulfin* [1917] 2 IR 107 at 125.

[22.52] However, this will not be the case if the restrictions on withdrawing from the partnership go further than necessary for the proper administration or management of the firm or the transfer of the goodwill to the continuing partners. In *Scully Tyrrell & Co/ Edberg*,[81] the partners in Scully Tyrell, a firm of loss adjusters, were selling their interest in the firm to Edberg Ltd, a subsidiary of RHL (which was a competitor of Scully Tyrell's). As part of the sale, they acquired a 38% shareholding in Edberg Ltd and they also entered into a shareholders' agreement with RHL. The Competition Authority held that the shareholders' agreement could be viewed as similar to the creation of a partnership between the vendor-partners and RHL. Treating the shareholders' agreement as a partnership, the Competition Authority held that:

> 'there is a case for not regarding such arrangements, of themselves, as offending against Section 4(1). Indeed such arrangements may be pro-competitive in that the combined entity may be in a better position to compete with other undertakings in the relevant market. The position changes, however, if the parties are prevented from withdrawing from such arrangements. If a party wishes to withdraw from such arrangements, then measures designed to prevent him doing so may restrict competition. In the event that one of the parties to such an arrangement decides to withdraw then, given the Authority's views in *Nallen/O'Toole*,[82] where one partner bought out the other partner's share in the business, a provision which restricts the vendor from competing with the business for a time may be justified in order to allow the purchaser obtain the goodwill of the business for which he had paid.'[83]

[22.53] In that case, the non-compete clauses did not merely prevent the vendor-partners in Scully Tyrell from competing with the business while they remained involved in it,[84] the clauses also sought to tie the partners to the business for a minimum period of three years after the sale of their interest in Scully Tyrell. This three-year period was in excess of the generally approved period of two years.[85] This was achieved by providing that if the partners terminated their employment (they were employees and shareholders in Edberg Ltd) with the acquiring company before the expiry of three years, their shares in the acquiring company could be acquired at a knock down price. In addition, once they sold the shares at the end of the three-year period, they were prevented from competing with the business for a further six months,[86] giving a minimum of a three-and-a-half-

---

[81]   *Scully Tyrrell & Co/ Edberg* Competition Authority, Dec No 12, 29 January 1993, Notif CA/ 57/92.

[82]   *Nallen/O'Toole* Competition Authority, Dec No 1, 2 April 1992, Notif CA/8/91.

[83]   *Scully Tyrrell & Co/ Edberg* Competition Authority, Dec No 12, 29 January 1993, Notif CA/ 57/92 at para 75.

[84]   Which restriction would have been acceptable, in the same way as a non-compete restriction during the course of a partnership is acceptable, see para [22.24].

[85]   Under the Category Certificate in respect of Agreements involving a Merger and/or a Sale of Business (Dec No 489, 2 December 1997), Article 4(a). See also *GI/General Semiconductor Industries* Competition Authority, Dec No 10, 23 October 1992, Notif CA/51/92 and CA/52/ 92, see para [22.37].

[86]   The Category Certificate in respect of Agreements involving a Merger and/or a Sale of Business (Dec No 489, 2 December 1997), later went on to provide in Article 5(b) for a restriction to be acceptable for a period of up to two years after the sale of a retained shareholding of at least 10% by the vendor, thus giving an aggregate restriction of greater than two years from the date of the sale of the business, see fn **104**.

year restriction from the time of the sale of their share in the firm to RHL. On this basis it was held by the Competition Authority that these restrictions on the withdrawal of a partner from this 'partnership arrangement' were void under s 4(1) of the Competition Act 1991.

Non-compete Provisions and Salaried Partners

[22.54] Unlike the situation with agreements between vendors and purchasers of a partnership business or with agreements between partners inter se,[87] an employee has a relatively reduced bargaining power in negotiating the terms of his agreement with his employer. For this reason, competition law looks more carefully at restrictive covenants in employment agreements[88] than in partnership agreements or partnership sale agreements. Since a salaried partner is in legal terms an employee,[89] non-compete provisions on salaried partners will be treated in the same manner as restrictions on employees and therefore will be more carefully examined than agreements in which there is an equality of bargaining power. Indeed, it is noted elsewhere in this work[90] that salaried partners may be viewed as worse-off than employees, since not only do they not share in the profits of the firm, but they also are potentially liable for the firm's losses on the basis of their being held out as partners. A strong argument may, therefore, be made for salaried partners to be treated *at least* as favourably as employees under competition law.[91]

Non-compete Provisions and Incoming Partners

[22.55] The inequality of the bargaining power of the parties may also be a factor in assessing a non-compete provision which is imposed on a partner who is joining a large well-established firm. This is because in some cases, the incoming partner will be in a weak bargaining position regarding the other partners.

[22.56] Thus in *Craig v Cole*,[92] the Supreme Court of Western Australia held that the relationship between one partner and his co-partners in a firm of eight specialist radiologists was more consistent with that of an employer/employee relationship. There, a restrictive covenant in the medical partnership agreement provided a power of expulsion whereby a partner could be expelled. On his expulsion, there would be a payment to him for his share of the goodwill and a covenant by him not to practice within 20 miles of the practice for six years. The plaintiff was duly expelled by his co-partners, yet D'Arcy J held that the validity of the restrictive covenant was to be considered as if the relationship was that of employer and employee. This resulted from

---

87 Since restrictive covenants between partners are looked on in the same way as restrictive covenants between vendors and purchasers, see para **[22.29]**.
88 See *Lyne-Pirkis v Jones* [1969] 3 All ER 783; *Ronbar Enterprises v Greeen* [1954] 1 All ER 266. See generally in relation to restrictions in employment agreements, Regan and Murphy, *Employment Law* (2nd edn, 2017) at para [11.01] et seq.
89 See generally in relation to salaried partners para **[6.18]** et seq.
90 See para **[6.26]**.
91 See further in relation to restrictive covenants on the sale of a business, Clark, *Contract Law in Ireland* (8th edn, 2016) at para 15-45 et seq.
92 *Craig v Cole* [1964] WAR 257.

D'Arcy J's conclusion that the plaintiff never really owned the goodwill in the partnership like a real partner, but simply 'acquired an interest' in it since this was a prerequisite to his working in the practice. He supported his finding that the plaintiff had never really owned the goodwill by virtue of the fact that the plaintiff had been employed by the firm as a young radiologist before being admitted to the partnership, that the partnership business was carried on by the firm under the name the 'Perth Radiological Clinic', the telephones were listed under that name and work was referred by general practitioners to the clinic, rather than to the individual partners. Thus, he concluded that the plaintiff's expulsion from the partnership was as effective as any discharge from employment and for this reason he held that the restrictive covenant should be considered as if it was between employers and employees, rather than that of the vendor and purchaser of the goodwill which would normally be the case between partners. In these circumstances, he held that the restrictive covenant was more than was required to protect the continuing partners.

III. ANTI-COMPETITIVE TERMS IN PARTNERSHIP SALE AGREEMENTS

[22.57] As well as partnership agreements, agreements for the sale of a partnership business may also contravene s 4(1) of the Competition Act 2002. Thus, the sale itself may be such as to cause a distortion of competition, or the partnership sale agreement may contain clauses restricting the vendor partners from competing with the purchaser.

Partnership Sale Agreements

[22.58] The sale of a partnership business has the potential to breach s 4(1) of the Competition Act 2002, since it may, for example, result in diminishing the number of competitors in that business.[93] This was not the case in *Nallen/O'Toole*[94] in which the Competition Authority considered the sale of a television and video business in Belmullet by one partner to his co-partner in the context of s 4(1) of the Competition Act 1991. At the time of the sale, there were four competitors in the relevant market. On the facts of that case, therefore, the Competition Authority concluded that the sale of the business did not per se contravene s 4(1) of the 1991 Act, since it would not diminish the number of competitors, as the purchaser of the business would continue the business. In general, therefore, any sale by one partner of his share to the continuing partners is unlikely to per se breach s 4(1) of the 2002 Act.

[22.59] However, where one partnership business is being bought by another competitor or where two partnerships merge, the partnership sale agreement or merger agreement may breach s 4(1) of the Competition Act 2002, since it could lead to a diminution of

---

[93] As discussed in para **[22.15]** above, an agreement for the sale of a partnership business may trigger the merger control regime under the Competition Act 2002, in which case s 4(1) is not relevant as the assessment of whether the transaction results in a diminution of competition will be assessed under the merger control rules.

[94] *Nallen/O'Toole* Competition Authority, Dec No 1, 2 April 1992, Notif CA/8/91.

competition in the relevant market.[95] In such a case, if the agreement meets the 'efficiency' conditions set out in s 4(5), it will not be prohibited or void.

Non-compete Restriction on Vendor Partners

[22.60] The status of non-compete restrictions on vendor partners has already been considered since non-compete restrictions on departing partners are treated in the same way as non-compete restrictions on vendor partners.[96] In particular, it has been noted that in general, a two-year limit applies to a non-compete provision on the sale of a partnership business.[97] Thus in *Scully Tyrrell & Co/ Edberg*,[98] the vendor-partners were restricted from competing with the purchasers of the business for a minimum of three-and-a-half years by the combined effect of a number of agreements. The Competition Authority held that this was excessive and offended against s 4(1) of the Competition Act 1991 and that a period of two years was sufficient for the new owners to acquire the goodwill, since the Competition Authority 'would generally consider a non-competition clause exceeding two years in a sale of a business agreement to offend against s 4(1)'.[99]

[22.61] However, it should be remembered that restrictions which exceed the terms set out in para 20 of the European Commission's 'Notice on restrictions directly related and necessary to concentrations'[100] may nonetheless not offend against s 4(1) of the Competition Act 2002 if they meet the 'efficiency' conditions set out in s 4(5) of the Competition Act 2002 and decisions made by the Competition Authority in respect of notifications made to it under the Competition Act 1991 will be helpful in making that assessment.[101]

---

[95] See para [22.15] above in respect of the types of factors taken into consideration by the Competition and Consumer Protection Commission when assessing whether the sale of a partnership business to a competitor (or potential competitor) could result in a diminution of competition.

[96] See para [22.29].

[97] See para [22.37]. In *Doyle/Moffitt* Competition Authority, Dec No 333, 10 June 1994, Notif CA/1133/92, the Competition Authority refused to issue a certificate under s 4(4) of the Competition Act 1991 for a five-year restriction on a vendor partner from competing with the business being sold. The Competition Authority noted that protection against competition was only acceptable so long as it was necessary to secure the transfer of the goodwill and since the duration of the restriction exceeded two years, which the Authority generally considered sufficient, the provision was held to be invalid.

[98] *Scully Tyrrell & Co/ Edberg* Competition Authority, Dec No 12, 29 January 1993, Notif CA/57/92.

[99] *Scully Tyrrell & Co/ Edberg* Competition Authority, Dec No 12, 29 January 1993, Notif CA/57/92 at para 72, citing *GI/General Semiconductor Industries* Competition Authority, Dec No 10, 23 October 1992, Notifs CA/51/92 and CA/52/92.

[100] (2005/C 56/03).

[101] Regarding know-how and confidential information clauses in the context of the Competition Act 1991, see *ACT/Kindle* Competition Authority, Dec No 8, 4 September 1992, Notif CA/11/92 and *GI Corporation/ General Semi-Conductor Industries*, Competition Authority, Dec No 10, 23 October 1992, Notifs CA/51/92 and CA/52/92 and para [22.65] et seq. See generally Cahill, 'Vendor Restrictions on the Sale of a Business – The Impact of Irish Competition Law' (1997) Conveyancing and Property Law Journal 35.

[22.62] In *Nallen/O'Toole*[102] the Competition Authority found that a three-year non-compete restriction on the vendor partner in favour of the purchasing partner of the partnership business did not offend against s 4(1) of the Competition Act 1991. The Authority held that this time was necessary for the transfer of the goodwill in the business to the purchaser, as customers tended only to purchase the products (electrical goods) infrequently,[103] close personal contact was a major factor in the business and the vendor partner was remaining in business in the locality. Where the Competition Authority took the view that a restraint which attempted to do no more that ensure the transfer of the goodwill to the purchaser, it tended to conclude that it did not have as its object or effect the distortion of competition and so did not contravene s 4(1) of the Competition Act 1991.[104]

Non-solicitation on Vendor Partners

[22.63] It has also been seen that non-solicit restrictions are simply another type of non-compete restriction which the Competition Authority has recognised are necessary to ensure the proper transfer of goodwill to the purchaser of a business.[105] Indeed, such a non-solicitation agreement regarding the customers of a business will be implied on the sale of the goodwill of that business,[106] and the rules applicable to non-solicitation clauses on the sale of a partnership business are the same as those which apply to the sale of any other business.[107] Thus, an agreement not to solicit customers of a partnership for a minimum of five years was held by the Competition Authority to

---

[102] *Nallen/O'Toole* Competition Authority, Dec No 1, 2 April 1992, Notif CA/8/91.

[103] Cf *Scully Tyrell & Co/Edberg* Dec 12, 29 January 1993, Notif CA/57/92 above, where a two-year restriction was regarded as sufficient in view of the fact that the clients of the business (a small number of insurance companies) had frequent contact with the business (loss adjusting).

[104] When the Category Certificate for Agreements involving a Merger and/or a Sale of Business was in force, where a vendor partner remained engaged in the partnership business being sold as a shareholder, director or employee, a restriction on such a person from competing with the business for so long as that engagement continues, would have fallen within the terms of that Category Certificate, even though the restriction might have been for longer than the generally accepted period of two years from the first sale of the interest in the business. That would not have been the case where the interest in the business was merely that of a passive investor or where it was done as an artificial construction to obtain a longer restraint. Where the vendor partner retained a shareholding of not less than 10% of the business following completion of the sale agreement, a restriction which prevented him from competing with the business for a period of up to two years from the date of a future sale of those shares would have fallen within the terms of the Category Certificate, even though that restriction may have been for longer than the generally accepted period of two years from the original sale of the interest.

[105] See para **[22.42]**.

[106] *Gargan v Ruttle* [1931] IR 152.

[107] See generally *Woodchester Bank/UDT Bank* Competition Authority, Dec No 6, 4 August 1992, Notif CA/10/92; *GI/General Semiconductor Industries* Competition Authority, Dec No 10, 23 October 1992, Notif CA/51/92 and CA/52/92; *Phil Fortune/Budget Travel Ltd* Competition Authority, Dec No 9, 14 September 1992, Notif CA/1/92.

contravene s 4(1) of the Competition Act 1991, since it exceeded the generally accepted period of two years.[108]

Unlimited Duration Restriction on Use of Firm Name after Sale

[22.64] A common restriction on the sale of a partnership business will be on the use of the firm name by the vendor partners. Even though these restrictions are usually of unlimited duration, they do not in general offend against s 4(1) of the Competition Act 2002, since they are necessary to prevent the vendors from passing themselves off as carrying on the business of the firm being sold. This can be supported in principle since clearly a use of a firm's name by the vendor partner is likely to lead to a passing off by the vendor partner of himself as still carrying on the business of that firm and is likely to lead to an appropriation of the firm's goodwill, even if done many years after the sale. Therefore, in *Scully Tyrrell & Co/Edberg*,[109] the Competition Authority held that a restriction of unlimited duration on the partners in the firm of 'Scully Tyrell & Company' from using the words 'Scully', 'Tyrell' or 'Scully Tyrell' as a trade name or mark in the relevant market, was necessary to prevent the partners from passing themselves off as Scully Tyrell & Company and therefore did not offend against s 4(1).

Restriction on Use/Disclosure of Confidential Information

[22.65] Partnership sale agreements will commonly restrict the vendor partners from using or disclosing the trade secrets and other confidential information relating to the firm.[110]

[22.66] However in *Scully Tyrrell & Co/Edberg*,[111] the Competition Authority made clear that such clauses would have been contrary to s 4(1) of the Competition Act 1991, if they were intended as a means of preventing the vendor partners from competing with the firm, after the expiry of the non-compete provision. However, if as in that case, the restriction on the use or disclosure of confidential information was not intended or designed to impede the re-entry into the market by the vendor partners once the non-compete clauses had expired, then such restrictions, even if of unlimited duration, did

---

[108]   *Scully Tyrrell & Co/Edberg* Competition Authority, Dec No 12, 29 January 1993, Notif CA/ 57/ 92. See generally *John Orr Ltd v Orr* [1987] ILRM 703 which concerned a non-solicitation clause on the owner of a company when he sold his shares in the company. The non-solicitation clause was held to be excessively restrictive since it sought to restrain the vendor from soliciting not only the customers of the company being sold but also the customers of the purchaser, its subsidiaries or associated companies. Accordingly, Costello J held that this aspect of the non-solicitation clause could be severed.

[109]   *Scully Tyrrell & Co/Edberg* Competition Authority, Dec No 12, 29 January 1993, Notif CA/ 57/ 92.

[110]   Under s 6(31) of the Category Certificate in respect of Agreements involving a Merger and/or a Sale of Business, such restrictions were generally not considered as anti-competitive, since they were seen as merely designed to prevent the vendor partner from using commercial information which was the property of the business being sold.

[111]   *Scully Tyrrell & Co/Edberg* Competition Authority, Dec No 12, 29 January 1993, Notif CA/ 57/92.

not offend against s 4(1) of the 1991 Act.[112] In that case, the Competition Authority was satisfied by the assurances of the parties that the restriction on the disclosure or use of confidential information was not intended as a means of preventing the vendor partners from competing with the firm after the expiry of the non-compete provision. One approach, when drafting confidential information clauses, is to explicitly provide that they are without prejudice to the vendor's ability to compete with the purchasers (at the expiry of the general non-compete provision, if there is one).[113]

Restriction on Use of Technical Know-how

[22.67] The technical know-how of a business is that body of technical information, if any, that is secret, substantial and identified in an appropriate form, over and above the knowledge of a particular line of business.[114] Where the confidential information consists of know-how, a restriction of unlimited duration on its use by the vendor partner will not fall within the terms of s 4(5) of the Competition Act 2002 because a vendor would be at a disadvantage in re-entering the market if he could not make use of such know-how and thus an unlimited restriction on use or disclosure of know-how would be tantamount to an unlimited restriction on competing in the relevant market.[115] Accordingly, the rule allowing for unlimited duration restrictions on the use of confidential information does not apply. Rather, para 20 of the Commission Notice on restrictions directly related to and necessary to concentrations provides that on the sale of a business which involves the use of know-how, a post-sale non-compete or non-solicitation provision of up to three years' duration is acceptable.

---

112 See generally in relation to restrictions on the use of non-technical know-how on the sale of a business, *Phil Fortune/Budget Travel* Competition Authority, Dec No 9, 14 September 1992, Notif CA/1/92.

113 Article 4(c) of the Category Certificate for Agreements involving a Merger and/or a Sale of Business provided that post-sale restrictions on vendors which restricted the vendor from using or disclosing confidential information regarding the business for an unlimited duration still fell within the terms of the Category Certificate.

114 Competition Authority Category Certificate in respect of Agreements involving a Merger and/or a Sale of Business (Dec No 489, 2 December 1997), Article 4(b). See also the definition of the terms 'secret', 'substantial' and 'identified' in the European Commission Block Exemption for Franchise Agreements, Regulation No 4087/88.

115 For its previous Category Certificate in respect of Agreements involving a Merger and/or a Sale of Business (Dec No 489, 2 December 1997), s 6(32), the Competition Authority relied on the decision of the European Commission in *Reuter/BASF* [1976] 2 CMLR D44 in which it was noted that in determining the duration of a non-compete clause, the factors particularly to be taken into account are the nature of the transferred know-how, the opportunities for its use and the knowledge possessed by the purchaser and that a non-compete clause extending to existing know-how may be longer than in respect of new or further developments of know-how.

IV. ARTICLE 101 OF THE TREATY ON THE FUNCTIONING OF THE EUROPEAN UNION

[22.68] Article 101(1)[116] of the Treaty on the Functioning of the European Union prohibits and renders void the following:

> '[A]ll agreements between undertakings, decisions by associations of undertakings and concerted practices which may affect trade between Member States and which have as their object or effect the prevention, restriction or distortion of competition within the internal market and, in particular those which:
>
> (a) directly or indirectly fix purchase or selling prices or any other trading conditions;
>
> (b) limit or control production, markets, technical development, or investment;
>
> (c) share markets or sources of supply;
>
> (d) apply dissimilar conditions to equivalent transactions with other trading parties, thereby placing them at a competitive disadvantage; and
>
> (e) make the conclusion of contracts subject to acceptance by the other parties of supplementary obligations which, by their nature or according to commercial usage, have no connection with the subject of such contracts.'

Accordingly, partnership agreements will fall within the ambit of art 101(1) insofar as they are anti-competitive, but only if they affect or aim to affect competition within the internal market. For this reason, many anti-competitive restrictions concerning partners and partnerships relating to businesses in Ireland only will fall outside the terms of art 101(1) particularly because of the de minimis provisions.[117]

[22.69] For those few partnerships that fall within the terms of this article, they will be required to comply with the terms of the Competition Act 2002 and art 101(1). It is worth bearing in mind that Irish competition law is based on art 101(1) and, accordingly, compliance with s 4 of the Competition Act 2002 will, in most cases, ensure compliance

---

116 Originally art 85 of the Treaty of Rome. Renumbered by the Treaty of Amsterdam as art 81 of the Treaty of Rome on 1 May 1999, and then renumbered as art 101 of the Treaty on the Functioning of the European Union by the Treaty of Lisbon which came into force on 1 December 2009.

117 Many partnership arrangements would not meet the criteria that they would affect competition within the internal market. In addition, if art 101(1) were triggered, the European Commission's de minimis Notice may be relevant and 'save' otherwise anticompetitve arrangements (European Commission Notice on agreements of minor importance which do not appreciably restrict competition under Article 101(1) of the Treaty on the Functioning of the European Union (2014/C 291/01)). While agreements which have as their 'object' the restriction of competition will not benefit from this Notice, the Notice provides a safe harbour for agreements which could have, as their effect (and not their object) the prevention, restriction or distortion of competition by viewing them (by reference to market share thresholds) as not appreciably restricting competition under art 101(1). Where the agreement is between undertakings that are competitors, their aggregate market share must not exceed 10% to benefit from the safe harbour. Where they are not competitors, the market share held by each of them must not exceed 15%. Where it is difficult to classify the undertakings as competitors or non-competitors, the 10% threshold is used. See also *Völk v Vervaecke* (1969) ECR 295 regarding this requirement that the effect on trade be appreciable.

with art 101(1). However, where both European and Irish competition law apply, in the unlikely event of a conflict, European competition law will prevail.

[22.70] In addition, like a declaration under s 4(3) of the Competition Act 2002, under the terms of art 101(3), an exemption may apply to an agreement which prima facie breaches Article 101(1). Article 101(3) allows for art 101(1) to be disapplied to such an agreement where it 'contributes to improving the production or distribution of goods or to promoting technical or economic progress, while allowing consumers a fair share of the resulting benefit', and does not impose restrictions on the undertakings concerned which are not indispensable to the achievement of these objectives, and does not afford those undertakings the possibility of eliminating competition in respect of a substantial part of the market for the products in question. If the agreement meets those conditions, it will not be prohibited under art 101(1) and no prior agreement from the European Commission will be needed for that to happen.[118] It is also possible for block exemptions from art 101(1) to be granted in respect of particular categories of agreements.[119]

[22.71] Finally, it remains to be noted that, just as the Competition Authority held that an outgoing partner is an undertaking for the purposes of s 4(1) of the Competition Act 1991, so too the European Court of Justice has held that an outgoing partner is an undertaking for the purposes of the predecessor of art 101(1) (art 81(1) of the Treaty of Rome).[120]

---

[118] Council Regulation (EC) No 1/2003 of 16 December 2002 on the implementation of the rules on competition laid down in arts 81 and 82 of the Treaty, art 1(2). Before this Regulation came into force, an agreement would need to be notified to the European Commission for an exemption to be granted. As with the position in Ireland following the introduction of the Competition Act 2002, there was a move to self-assessment under the EU competition regime.

[119] See for instance Commission Regulation (EU) No 330/2010 of 20 April 2010 on the application of art 101(3) of the Treaty on the Functioning of the European Union to categories of vertical agreements and concerted practices and the related European Commission Guidelines on Vertical Restraints 2010/C 130/01. Block exemptions have also been granted in respect of specialisation agreements and technology transfer agreements.

[120] *Gottfried v Reuter v BASF AG* [1976] 2 CMLR D 44.

PART D
DISSOLUTION OF PARTNERSHIPS

Chapter 23

Causes of Dissolution

INTRODUCTION

[23.01] A partnership may be dissolved in two ways; either by court order or in circumstances which do not require a court order. In Chapter 25, the circumstances in which a court will order a dissolution of a partnership are considered. This chapter is concerned with the circumstances in which a partnership is dissolved without the necessity for a court order. These causes of dissolution may be said to be automatic, in the sense that the occurrence of these events will per se lead to the dissolution of the partnership and a court order is not required. The instances in which this occurs may be divided into the following 10 events:

1. Dissolution of a partnership at will by notice;
2. Dissolution by death of a partner;
3. Dissolution by bankruptcy of a partner;
4. Dissolution by expiration of a fixed term partnership;
5. Dissolution by termination of an adventure or undertaking;
6. Dissolution by agreement;
7. Dissolution as a result of a charging order;
8. Dissolution by illegality of the partnership;
9. Dissolution by repudiation; and
10. Dissolution by rescission.

[23.02] These events of dissolution are default rules since, save for the illegality of a partnership, it is within the power of the partners to agree that their partnership will continue notwithstanding the occurrence of any of these events. These 10 causes of dissolution are considered under the following headings:

I. Concepts Applicable to All Dissolutions;
II. Events which Per Se Cause Dissolution; and
III. Events which do not Per Se Cause Dissolution.

Overview

[23.03] It has been seen that the terms of the 1890 Act may be regarded as providing the terms of a default partnership agreement which applies to all partnerships, save insofar as the partners agree to the contrary. This is particularly apparent when one is dealing with the dissolution of a partnership since seven separate provisions of that Act imply terms regarding a firm's dissolution. For example this so-called default partnership agreement provides that the firm is dissolved when notice of dissolution is given by a partner or on the death/bankruptcy of a partner or on the expiration of a fixed term/single venture, etc.

[23.04] The most important of these implied terms is the right in ss 26(1) and 32(c) of the 1890 Act on the part of a partner in a partnership at will to dissolve the partnership by giving notice of dissolution to his fellow partners. This implied term will often be inconvenient to the fortunes of a firm since it allows a successful partnership to be dissolved and wound up at the whim of one partner. Yet, it is arguably a necessary inconvenience, since the other option, namely a default provision preventing a partner from leaving the firm (by dissolving it) could not possibly be supported, in view of the sacrosanct right of a partner to choose with whom he shall enter partnership and for what period. The importance of this right becomes clear when one considers that a partner has unlimited liability for the actions of his co-partners and dissolving the partnership may be the only way to terminate this liability. An alternative would be for the 1890 Act to have a default right entitling the other partners to buy the departing partner's share at a valuation.

[23.05] Similarly, the implied term in s 33(1) of the 1890 Act that a partnership is dissolved on the death or bankruptcy of a partner may be inconvenient for the fortunes of the firm. This implied term means that in a successful partnership of three or more partners, the partnership is automatically dissolved and may be wound by a personal representative or Official Assignee on the death or bankruptcy of a partner. It is for this reason that in nearly all modern partnership agreements this implied term in s 33(1) is excluded. Undoubtedly, a better approach to the death or bankruptcy of a partner would be to adopt the same approach that is taken by s 33(2) of the 1890 Act to the charging by a partner of his share of the partnership property. Section 33(2) provides that the 'innocent partners' have the right to dissolve the partnership where one partner suffers his share of the partnership property to be charged. Adopting this approach, it is suggested that the automatic dissolution of the partnership should be replaced with a right on the part of the 'innocent' partners to dissolve the partnership or to acquire the dead or bankrupt partner's share at a valuation. In this way, the unnecessary winding up of successful partnerships is avoided. Further support for this proposal is to be found in the terms of the Investment Limited Partnerships Act 1994, which provides that the death or bankruptcy of a partner in an investment limited partnership[1] does not dissolve the partnership in the absence of any agreement of the partners.

[23.06] Whether the consequences of the death or bankruptcy of a partnership are reformed or not, the precise application of these consequences to corporate partners should be clarified. This is because, despite the fact that the 1890 Act has been held to apply to corporate partners, no attempt has yet been made to clarify the events in the life of a corporate partner to which it applies. Until this is done, the effect on a partnership of the winding up, receivership, liquidation, examinership, etc of a corporate partner will remain in a legal limbo.

---

[1] Provided that there is more than one general partner: Investment Limited Partnerships Act 1994, s 37(1). See generally regarding such partnerships para **[29.01]** et seq and, on this specific point, para **[29.201]** et seq.

I.   CONCEPTS APPLICABLE TO ALL DISSOLUTIONS

General Dissolution v Technical Dissolution

[23.07] When one talks of the instances in which a partnership may be dissolved (whether by a court order or not), one is generally referring to the general dissolution of a partnership, as distinct from its technical dissolution. It is important to distinguish between these two concepts.

[23.08] Since a partnership is not a separate legal entity, but rather an aggregate of the partners which make up the firm, it follows that a firm is dissolved anytime there is a change in the aggregate, ie any time a partner arrives or departs. Whether this dissolution is a general dissolution or a technical dissolution depends on what happens after that change in the membership. A general dissolution is a dissolution of the firm which leads to its winding-up. Unless agreed otherwise, a partnership which is subject to a change in membership is dissolved and therefore may be wound up on the demand of any one partner. This is because the right to force a winding up of a partnership on its dissolution is granted to every partner by s 39 of the 1890 Act.[2]

[23.09] In contrast, a technical dissolution of a firm will take place where there is a change in the membership of the firm, but the right of a partner under s 39 to wind up that firm is expressly or implicitly waived by the partners. Instead, on the arrival or departure of a partner, the business of the firm is continued as it was before that change. Therefore a technical dissolution may be described as a change in the membership of the firm which does not lead to the winding up of the firm.[3] As explained by Eichelbaum CJ in the New Zealand case of *Hadlee v Commissioner of Inland Revenue*:[4]

> 'In law, the retirement of a partner, or the admission of a new partner, constitutes the dissolution of the old partnership and the formation of a new one. Here, upon the happening of such events there was no overt signs of dissolution; the partnership's financial structure and arrangements were such that none was required but that does not alter the underlying legal significance of any retirement or new admission ... Nor, in my opinion, is it possible to avoid these legal propositions by the terms of the partnership agreement.'[5]

[23.10] The confusion surrounding the use of the term 'dissolution' is caused in part by the fact that the 1890 Act itself uses the term to mean in different sections, a technical dissolution only,[6] a general dissolution only[7] and a technical or a general dissolution.[8]

---

2   See generally in relation to this right, para **[26.26]** et seq.
3   See for example *Cuffe v Murtagh* (1881) 7 LR Ir 411, where a six-man partnership was dissolved by the death of two partners. After this change in the composition of the firm, the remaining partners continued to carry on business and it was held by Chatterton VC that a new partnership came into existence on this technical dissolution of the old partnership. See also *McCormack v McCormack* [2017] IEHC 733 at para 243 of the judgment.
4   *Hadlee v Commissioner of Inland Revenue* [1993] AC 524. This decision was affirmed without reference to this specific point by the Privy Council, [1993] 2 NZLR 385. See also the Scottish case of *Jardine-Paterson v Fraser* (1974) SLT 93 at 97.
5   *Hadlee v Commissioner of Inland Revenue* [1989] 2 NZLR 447 at 455.
6   Partnership Act 1890, s 42.
7   Partnership Act 1890, s 44.
8   Partnership Act 1890, s 31(2).

This confusion is not helped by the different use of the term 'dissolution' under company law, ie when a company is dissolved, it is the final act of its winding-up – it is therefore the date upon which the company ceases to exist as a legal entity.[9] In contrast, the date of dissolution for a partnership is the date upon which there is a change in the membership of a firm, which firm may continue to carry on business (in the case of a technical dissolution) or it may be wound up (in the case of a general dissolution). Considerable benefit would result from the use of completely different terms to differentiate between these two stages in the life of a partnership. Thus, one might talk instead of the disassociation of a partnership where a partner joins or leaves the firm and the termination of the partnership when the firm ceases to carry on business or carries on business only with a view to winding up. However until such time, one is left with the term dissolution to describe these different situations.

General Dissolution may be Avoided by Terms of Agreement

[23.11] Since a general dissolution of a partnership leads to the firm's winding up, it is common for partnership agreements to be drafted so as to prevent this drastic consequence from arising every time there is a change in the membership of the firm. Indeed, one of the main reasons to have a partnership agreement is to have a clause which prevents the general dissolution and forced winding up of a successful partnership, for example on the death of a partner.[10] In the Supreme Court case of *Williams v Harris*,[11] the partnership agreement[12] provided that if 'a partner retires from the partnership, the partnership shall be dissolved *so far only as regards that partner*'[13] and his share 'should be purchased by and belong to the remaining partners'[14] at a price to be calculated in accordance with the partnership agreement. In this way, the departure of a partner, which might otherwise lead to the firm's general dissolution, led only to the firm's technical dissolution and the departing partner was not entitled to force a winding up of the partnership under s 39 of the 1890 Act.

II.   EVENTS WHICH PER SE CAUSE DISSOLUTION

[23.12] In this section of the chapter, each of the 10 causes of dissolution of a partnership which have been noted will be considered in turn.

---

9   Companies Act 2014, ss 704 (Dissolution of company by court), 705 (Final meeting and dissolution in members' voluntary winding up) and 706 (Final meeting and dissolution in creditors' voluntary winding up).

10 See generally in relation to clauses which exclude the automatic dissolution of a partnership, para **[21.128]**.

11 *Williams v Harris* [1980] ILRM 237.

12 The partnership agreement was, for reasons, which are not contained in the case report, drafted by English lawyers.

13 *Williams v Harris* [1980] ILRM 237 at 239.

14 *Williams v Harris* [1980] ILRM 237 at 239.

1. Dissolution of a Partnership at Will by Notice

[23.13] Unless the partners in a firm have agreed otherwise, any one partner[15] in a partnership at will[16] may dissolve the partnership by giving notice of dissolution to his partners. The right to dissolve a partnership at will by notice is contained in two different sections of the 1890 Act, ss 26(1) and 32(c). Section 26(1) provides that:

> Where no fixed term has been agreed upon for the duration of a partnership, any partner may determine the partnership at any time on giving notice of his intention so to do to all the other partners.

[23.14] Section 32(c) states that:

> Subject to any agreement between the partners, a partnership is dissolved ...
>
> (c)   If entered into for an undefined time, by any partner giving notice to the other or others of his intention to dissolve the partnership.
>
> In the last mentioned case the partnership is dissolved as from the date mentioned in the notice as the date of dissolution, or, if no date is so mentioned, as from the date of the communication of the notice.

[23.15] The right in s 32(c) to dissolve a partnership at will by notice is stated to be subject to contrary agreement. However, s 26(1) is not so restricted. Yet, it is thought that s 26(1) is also subject to contrary agreement. This conclusion avoids a conflict between the two sections and is in keeping with the general tenor of the 1890 Act which favours the parties' agreement overriding the terms of the Act.[17] It is also in keeping with s 19, which provides that the rights and duties of partners under the 1890 Act may be varied with the consent of all the partners.

[23.16] The right of any one partner in a partnership at will to dissolve the partnership by giving notice to his co-partners is one of the rights of partners under the 1890 Act which is of most potential harm to successful partnerships. The risk of allowing all partners to retain this right is that one of them may use the threat of dissolution, and the consequent damage to the firm's goodwill and reputation, as a negotiating weapon in any dispute between the partners. For this reason, in most firms, it is essential that this right be excluded and the exclusion of ss 26(1) and 32(c) is an important term of most partnership agreements.[18] A partnership in which the power to dissolve the partnership by notice is excluded is a formal partnership.[19]

---

[15]   And this would include a dormant partner or a junior partner, but not a salaried partner, who is not a true partner.

[16]   See generally in relation to such partnerships, para **[8.03]** et seq.

[17]   See for example the Partnership Act 1890, ss 21, 22, 24, 25, 29(1), 30, 32, 33, 42(1), 43 and 44. See also *Moss v Elphick* [1910] 1 KB 465. But cf the right to an account under s 28 of the 1890 Act and the right of a former partner to publicly notify the dissolution of the partnership under s 37 of the 1890 Act. Both appear to be exceptions to this rule, see para **[21.88]** and para **[26.09]**. It is thought that both rights are so basic as not to be capable of exclusion by the parties. Similarly, although not a right in the strict sense, the automatic dissolution of a partnership due to its illegality under s 34 of the 1890 Act may not be excluded by the terms of a partnership agreement, see para **[23.60]**.

[18]   See further para **[21.131]**.

[19]   See further in relation to such partnerships, para **[8.09]** et seq.

The form of the notice of dissolution

[23.17] The form of the notice of dissolution of a partnership at will is addressed by s 26(2) of the 1890 Act, though in a somewhat unsatisfactory manner. It states that:

> Where the partnership has originally been constituted by deed, a notice in writing, signed by the partner giving it, shall be sufficient for this purpose.

[23.18] In *ACC Bank plc v Johnston p/a Brian Johnston & Co Solicitors,*[20] one of five separate judgments arising out of breaches of undertaking by a firm of solicitors, Traynor Mallon, Clarke J had to consider whether a letter of 14 March 2006 from the solicitors acting for Mr Mallon to Mr Traynor brought the partnership to an end. While the letter itself was not effective to dissolve the partnership,[21] Clarke J commented that the absence of a date from a letter purporting to dissolve a partnership '... is not, of itself, fatal'. In delivering this part of his judgment, Clarke J[22] quoted from *Halsbury's Laws of England*[23] which addressed the circumstances in which the dissolution of a partnership by notice can occur as follows:

> 'Subject to any agreement between the partners, a partnership for which no fixed term has been agreed, and for no fixed adventure or undertaking, may be dissolved by any partner by giving notice of his intention so to do to the others. The Partnership Act 1890, does not require the notice to be in writing. The firm is dissolved from the date mentioned in the notice as the date of dissolution or, if no date is so mentioned, as from the date of the communication of the notice. The notice must amount to an unambiguous intimation of a final intention to dissolve the partnership and must be given to all partners unless the articles otherwise provide.'

[23.19] By its express terms, s 26(2) applies only to partnerships constituted by deed and it states that written notice is 'sufficient' rather than a necessary requirement. Since this is the only section of the 1890 Act which deals with the form of the dissolution notice, two questions remain unanswered: is oral notice sufficient for a partnership not constituted by deed and is oral notice sufficient for a partnership constituted by deed?

Oral notice

[23.20] It is apprehended that oral notice of dissolution is sufficient to dissolve a partnership at will. This conclusion is supported by the fact that s 26(2) of the 1890 Act is simply an enabling provision and in any event applies only to partnerships at will which are constituted by deed. In addition, s 32 makes no reference to the form the notice of dissolution should take. Therefore, it is argued that, just as a partnership at will may be created[24] or varied[25] orally, it may also be dissolved by oral notice of dissolution, whether that partnership is constituted by oral or written agreement.[26]

---

[20] *ACC Bank plc v Johnston p/a Brian Johnston & Co Solicitors* [2011] IEHC 108.

[21] See further para **[23.22]**.

[22] *ACC Bank plc v Johnston p/a Brian Johnston & Co Solicitors* [2011] IEHC 108 at para 4.1 of the judgment.

[23] *Halsbury's Laws of England* Vol 35, para 164.

[24] See para **[2.11]**.

[25] See para **[5.14]** et seq.

[26] *Halsbury's Laws of England/Partnership* (Vol 79 (2014)) at para 173 notes that, subject to any agreement between the partners to the contrary, notice from a partner of his intention to dissolve a partnership at will is not required to be in writing. (contd.../)

[23.21] Applying the same logic, it is apprehended that a partnership at will which is constituted by deed may be dissolved by oral notice.[27] Support for this conclusion can be found in *Bolton v Carmichael*.[28] There, it was claimed that a partnership constituted by deed, unlike other partnerships, could not be dissolved by the conduct of the parties. However Master Henn rejected the claim that special rules applied to the dissolution of partnerships by deed. For this reason, it is thought that when s 26(2) of the 1890 Act talks of written notice being sufficient to dissolve a partnership by deed, it means just that and this section does not *require* notice of the dissolution of a partnership at will constituted by deed to be under seal, nor does it prohibit such a partnership from being dissolved by the oral notice of one partner.

Notice must be unambiguous

[23.22] In *ACC Bank plc v Johnston p/a Brian Johnston & Co Solicitors*,[29] Clarke J commented that a notice of dissolution must be an 'unambiguous intimation of a final intention to dissolve the partnership'.[30] The key section of the letter considered by Clarke J read as follows:

> 'Dear Mr Traynor, We are instructed by ... [Mr Mallon] in respect of regularising matters regarding the determination of the partnership practising under the style and/or title of Traynor Mallon & Company, Solicitors ... Finally we have been instructed, in the absence of your consent to dissolve the partnership, to apply to Court pursuant to Section 35(c) and 35(d) of the [1890 Act] to dissolve the Partnership on the grounds of your professional misconduct ...'

As the letter intimated that the dissolution might take place on foot of a court process, Clarke J found the letter to be ambiguous as regards the proposed end-date of the partnership – was it to be dissolved immediately, or following a court process? In light of that ambiguity, he found the letter to be insufficient to dissolve the partnership between Mr Mallon and Mr Traynor.

Notice to all partners?

[23.23] In the English High Court case of *Walters v Bingham*,[31] Browne-Wilkinson VC considered the requirement that notice of the dissolution be given to the other partners. He stated obiter that the term 'notice' in s 26(1) and s 32(c) should not be construed too literally since to do so would make the section unworkable in certain circumstances, such as in large firms where it would be impossible to communicate with all the partners at the one time. Support for this practical view of the workings of partnerships can be derived from the 1890 Act itself which provides in s 16 that notice to a partner who habitually acts in the partnership business of any matter relating to partnership affairs

---

26 (\...contd) It must, however, amount to 'an unambiguous intimation of a final intention to dissolve the partnership, and must be given to all partners unless the partnership agreement otherwise provide'. (See Clarke J in *ACC Bank plc v Johnston p/a Brian Johnston & Co Solicitors* [2011] IEHC 108).

27 See for example the English case of *Walters v Bingham* [1988] 138 NLJ 7.

28 *Bolton v Carmichael* (1856) 1 Ir Jur (ns) 298.

29 *ACC Bank plc v Johnston p/a Brian Johnston & Co Solicitors* [2011] IEHC 108.

30 Quoting from *Halsbury's Laws of England* Vol 35 para 164. See fn **26** above for the equivalent paragraph in the current edition.

31 *Walters v Bingham* [1988] 138 NLJ 7.

operates as notice to the firm. Thus, once the partners are left in no doubt as to the intention of the partner giving the notice, this should be sufficient.[32] On the facts of that case, Browne-Wilkinson VC held that the service of the correct number of envelopes containing copies of the notice at the firm's offices was sufficient notice.

Subject to agreement of partners

[23.24] The manner in which a partnership may be dissolved and the form of any notice of dissolution is, like most of the rights and duties of partners, subject to the agreement of the partners. Therefore, where the partners themselves provide that a dissolution of the partnership will only be effective if done by deed, then this requirement must be satisfied. This was the case in *Hutchinson v Whitfield*,[33] where the partnership deed for a Limerick-based firm of woollen merchants provided that the partnership could only be dissolved by deed. A dispute arose amongst the partners and an arbitrator was appointed to resolve the dispute. The arbitrator ordered all the partnership assets to be vested in one partner for the purposes of winding up the concern. The other partner claimed that this award did not operate as a dissolution of the partnership, since the partnership could only be dissolved by deed. However, Smith B held that since the submission to arbitration and the award of the arbitrator were both by deed, the requirement that the dissolution be under seal was in fact satisfied.

Notice may be given by partner's agent

[23.25] It seems clear that an agent of a partner may dissolve the partnership by notice on behalf of that partner. Thus in *Hawkins v Rogers*,[34] a letter had been written by one partner's solicitor to the other partner which purported to terminate the partnership and in the High Court, Dixon J favoured a finding that the partnership was dissolved, observing that:

> 'There was never any written partnership agreement nor any arrangement as to the length of dissolution necessary and, accordingly, I would be prepared, if necessary, to hold the letter effectual for its declared purpose.'[35]

Notice inferred from conduct

[23.26] Notice of a dissolution of a partnership may be effective even though terms such as 'I hereby dissolve the partnership' are not used. This is because notice of dissolution of a partnership may be inferred from the conduct of the partners.[36] The clearest example of this is the fact that the service by one partner on his co-partner of

---

[32] *Syers v Syers* [1876] AC 174 at 183. See also Hardcastle, 'Partnership Law in Transition' (1989) 41 Sol J at 1282.

[33] *Hutchinson v Whitfield* (1830) Hayes 78.

[34] *Hawkins v Rogers* [1951] IR 48.

[35] *Hawkins v Rogers* [1951] IR 48 at 51–52.

[36] This conclusion can also be drawn from the terms of s 19 of the 1890 Act which allows the rights and duties of partners to be varied expressly or inferred from a course of dealing. See, for instance, *Chahal v Mahal* [2005] 2 BCLC 655 where it was noted that the transfer of a partnership's business to a limited company would usually cause the dissolution of the partnership (although, on the facts, the partnership in that case was not dissolved).

proceedings for a court dissolution of a partnership at will, is deemed to be a notice to dissolve the partnership.[37]

[23.27] While *Larkin v Groeger and Eaton*[38] is primarily an example of the dissolution of a partnership by repudiation,[39] it may also be viewed as an example of the notice of dissolution being implied from partners' conduct to each other. In that case, the partnership agreement between a number of accountants provided for the partnership to be dissolved by three months' notice in writing of any partner. Certain disputes arose between the partners and soon after the partners began to ignore their obligations and duties to each other under the partnership agreement. The disputes were referred to arbitration. The arbitrator held that the partnership had not been dissolved in accordance with the terms of the partnership agreement, but had been dissolved by the conduct of the parties and had therefore ceased de facto as a partnership. On appeal to the High Court, Barrington J upheld the arbitrator's decision.[40]

When notice is effective

[23.28] Under s 32 of the 1890 Act, the date of dissolution of a partnership at will is the date mentioned in the notice or, where there is no date on the notice, it is the date the notice is communicated. There would seem to be no reason in principle why a notice should not be prospective, in which case, it may be superseded by another dissolution event, such as the death of a partner.[41]

[23.29] Once the notice of dissolution is communicated, the partnership is immediately dissolved. It is not necessary for a partner to give his co-partners a reasonable period before the notice takes effect.[42] Thus, a partner can arrive at a partners' meeting and state it 'is my pleasure on this day to dissolve the partnership'[43] and this notice will take immediate effect. Once the notice has been given, it can only be withdrawn with the

---

[37]   *Unsworth v Jordan* [1896] WNP 2(5). Clarke J in *ACC Bank plc v Johnston p/a Brian Johnston & Co Solicitors* [2011] IEHC 108 also commented (at para 4.4 of the judgment) that where a dissolution takes place by way of a court process, the dissolution takes effect when the court process begins, although it is questionable whether this is in fact correct, and whether the start of the court process signifies the intention to dissolve the partnership, with actual dissolution taking place when the court delivers its judgment.

[38]   *Larkin v Groeger and Eaton* (26 April 1988) HC.

[39]   As to dissolution by repudiation, see para **[23.65]**.

[40]   It is unclear from the report whether the partnership was dissolved by the inferred notice of dissolution of the parties or the repudiation of the partnership agreement by the parties, but Barrington J does appear to favour a finding of dissolution by repudiation, see para **[23.68]**. See also *Bolton v Carmichael* (1856) 1 Ir Jur (ns) 298, where Master Henn held that the partnership was dissolved by the exchange of three letters between the partners, see para **[23.49]**. See also, regarding dissolution by conduct, the Scottish case of *Gray v Dickson* [2007] GWD 31-540 (Sheriff's Court).

[41]   As in *McLeod v Dowling* (1927) 43 TLR 655, see para **[23.29]**.

[42]   *Featherstonhaugh v Fenwick* (1810) 17 Ves 298; *Crawshay v Maule* (1818) 1 Swan 495; *Ex p Nokes* (1801) 1 Mont Part 108.

[43]   *Featherstonhaugh v Fenwick* (1810) 17 Ves 298 at 307.

consent of all of the partners.[44] *McLeod v Dowling*[45] vividly illustrates the fact that the notice is only effective when it is communicated to the recipient. In that case, McLeod posted a notice of dissolution to his sole partner, Dowling, that as and from the date of the notice, namely 23 March, the partnership was dissolved. The notice was received by Dowling on 24 March at 10 am, but McLeod had died at 3 am on that same day. Accordingly, in the English High Court, Russell J held that the partnership was dissolved not on the purported effective date (23 March), nor at the time that it was received (at 10 am on 24 March), but at the time of death of McLeod, at 3 am on 24 March.

[23.30] It will not always be the case that it will be possible to specify with such precision the date or indeed time of the dissolution of a partnership. This will be particularly so where notice to dissolve the partnership is inferred from the conduct of the parties. Such a difficulty will not, however, be an obstacle to a finding that the partnership was dissolved, as is illustrated by *Larkin v Groeger and Eaton*.[46] In that case, the arbitrator held that the partnership, which had been dissolved by the actions of the partners in ignoring their obligations and duties to each other as partners, was no longer operating by a certain date. However, he did not attempt to isolate a date upon which the partnership was actually dissolved. On appeal to the High Court, Barrington J held that the arbitrator was not obliged to specify the date that the partnership was dissolved, since it was difficult on the facts of that case to isolate such a date.

No duty on partner giving notice to act reasonably

[23.31] There is no duty on a partner giving a notice of dissolution to act reasonably in reaching his decision to dissolve the partnership.[47] This is because individuals involved in business should be allowed make and break their business arrangements as they see fit. Nonetheless, since a partner owes his co-partners a fiduciary duty,[48] the decision must not be made with *mala fides* or with a fraudulent intent.[49]

2. Dissolution by Death of a Partner

[23.32] The second cause of dissolution of a partnership is the death of a partner. Section 33(1) of the 1890 Act provides that:

> Subject to any agreement between the partners, every partnership is dissolved as regards all the partners by the death or bankruptcy of any partner.

As death is a public event, no further notice is required to be given to the partners for the dissolution to take effect and the partnership dissolves as of the time of death.[50] Section s 36(3) of the 1890 Act provides that the estate of a deceased partner is not liable for

---

[44] *Jones v Lloyd* (1874) 30 LT 487; *Finch v Oake* [1896] 1 Ch 409; *Glossop v Glossop* [1907] 2 Ch 370.
[45] *McLeod v Dowling* (1927) 43 TLR 655.
[46] *Larkin v Groeger and Eaton* (26 April 1988) HC.
[47] *Russell v Russell* (1880) 14 Ch D 471.
[48] See generally in relation to the fiduciary duties of partners, para **[15.01]** et seq.
[49] *Daw v Herring* [1892] 1 Ch 284; *Neilson v Mossend Iron Co* (1886) 11 App Cas 298.
[50] See for example *McLeod v Dowling* (1927) 43 TLR 655, considered at para **[23.29]**.

partnership debts contracted after the date of death and no notice of the partner's death need be given to creditors of the firm in this regard.[51]

'every partnership'

[23.33] Unlike a dissolution by notice which applies only to partnerships at will, it is clear from the use of the phrase 'every partnership' in s 33(1) of the 1890 Act that a partnership is dissolved by the death of a partner, whether it is a partnership at will or a formal partnership. Thus in *Cuffe v Murtagh*,[52] there was a partnership for a fixed term of seven years between six flour merchants in Athlone, and during that term two of the partners died. After these deaths, the other partners continued to operate the business as before. Before the end of the seven years, they drew up an agreement which assumed that the fixed term partnership was still in existence and would see out its term. However, as noted by Chatterton VC, this was based on a misapprehension of the effect of the partners' deaths on the partnership:

> 'It appears, however, that the surviving partners did not look upon the partnership as dissolved, but, on the contrary they regarded it as subsisting for the residue of the term of seven years ... This was a mistake on their parts, as they did not take into account the rights of the personal representatives of the deceased partners, or the fact of dissolution by death.'[53]

[23.34] Clearly, therefore, the fact that the partners themselves believe and conduct themselves as if the partnership is still in existence is irrelevant in determining whether the partnership is dissolved or not.

'Subject to any agreement between the partners'

[23.35] The dissolution of a partnership by death may be avoided by an agreement between the partners to the contrary, as is clear from the terms of s 33(1) of the 1890 Act. Indeed, an important clause in most partnership agreements is one which excludes the application of this section, so as to allow the firm to continue as before the death. This is often done by means of a clause requiring the surviving partners to purchase the deceased partner's share in the firm. As observed by Chatterton VC in *Cuffe v Murtagh*:[54]

> 'The death of a partner effected in law a dissolution, unless his share was purchased under the terms of the partnership deed by the survivors: and this as I have stated, was not done by them.'[55]

The 'death' of a corporate partner?

[23.36] Although it is possible for a company to be a partner in a firm,[56] the 1890 Act, in setting out the various contingencies for partnerships during their existence, does not appear to contemplate a partnership with corporate partners. Therefore, while the death

---

[51]   See generally in relation to the effect of death of a partner, para **[24.04]** et seq.
[52]   *Cuffe v Murtagh* (1881) 7 LR Ir 411.
[53]   *Cuffe v Murtagh* (1881) 7 LR Ir 411 at 420.
[54]   *Cuffe v Murtagh* (1881) 7 LR Ir 411.
[55]   *Cuffe v Murtagh* (1881) 7 LR Ir 411 at 420.
[56]   See para **[2.35]**.

of an individual partner dissolves the partnership, the 1890 Act is silent as to the effect on the partnership of the 'death' of a corporate partner, which would approximate to the dissolution of a corporate partner since that is its final act, upon which it ceases to exist as a legal person.[57] This issue is of greater relevance in recent years as result of the wholesale dissolution of companies by their being struck-off due to their failure to file accounts.[58]

[23.37] It is suggested that the dissolution of a corporate partner should be treated by the courts as equivalent to the 'death' of an individual partner, so as to result in the application of s 33(1) of the 1890 Act to that partnership. This can be justified on two grounds. First, on the dissolution of a company, the company ceases to exist as a legal person in the same way as on the death of an individual, he or she ceases to exist as a legal person. Indeed, in the case of a company, a dissolution is even more drastic, since the liquidator does not have authority to act on behalf of the company after this point, while a personal representative still acts on behalf of the deceased. The second reason for treating the death of an individual as synonymous with the death of an individual for the purposes of s 33(1) is for very practical reasons, ie since the corporate partner ceases to exist on its dissolution, it will not be possible for it to continue as a partner. In particular, it will not have any representative (akin to a personal representative) as the role of the receiver, liquidator or examiner (if any existed) would have ceased on that date.[59] While the 1890 Act does not contemplate companies being partners, more recent partnership legislation has done so and further support for the view that s 33(1) should apply to the dissolution of a corporate partner is to be found in the Investment Limited Partnerships Act 1994. This Act contemplates a partnership (albeit an investment limited partnership) having corporate partners and, significantly, s 37(2)(a) of that Act equates the death of a partner who is an individual, with the dissolution, inter alia, of a corporate partner,[60] since under that section, both events may lead to the dissolution of the partnership.[61]

[23.38] Even if a court were not prepared to interpret the phrase 'death of a partner' in s 33(1) as equivalent to the dissolution of a corporate partner, the court might achieve a similar result by the application of the doctrine of frustration. This doctrine would

---

57 Companies Act 2014, ss 704 (Dissolution of company by court), 705 (Final meeting and dissolution in members' voluntary winding up) and 706 (Final meeting and dissolution in creditors' voluntary winding up). See generally in relation to the dissolution of a company, Courtney, *The Law of Companies* (4th edn, 2016) Ch 24; Hutchinson, *Keane on Company Law* (5th edn, 2016) at para [36.22] and paras [38.55] et seq.

58 Under the Companies Act 2014, s 726. According to the Companies Registration Office Annual Report for 2017, 5,420 companies were involuntarily struck off the register of companies in 2017.

59 *Salton v New Beeston Cycle Co* [1900] 1 Ch 43.

60 In fact it equates 'incapacity, retirement, bankruptcy, removal, resignation, insolvency, dissolution or winding-up' of a partner with 'death' of a partner, in the sense that if any of these events apply to the sole general partner, the partnership is dissolved: Investment Limited Partnerships Act 1994, s 37(2)(a). As regards the effect of the winding up or insolvency of a corporate partner under s 33(1), see para **[23.40]** et seq.

61 If the partner in question is the sole general partner: Investment Limited Partnerships Act 1994, 37(2)(a).

appear to be equally applicable to a partnership contract as it is to any other contract. On this basis, it could be argued that the dissolution of a corporate partner may result in the discharge of the partnership agreement by frustration and the consequent dissolution of the partnership.[62]

3. Dissolution by Bankruptcy of a Partner

[23.39] As has been seen,[63] s 33(1) of the 1890 Act also provides that, subject to contrary agreement between the partners, a partnership is dissolved by the bankruptcy of a partner. Although the 1890 Act does not specify when the dissolution is effective, the High Court has held that it is effective from the date of the adjudication of the bankrupt. Thus in *Provincial Bank of Ireland v Tallon*,[64] a husband and wife carried on business in partnership and when the husband was declared a bankrupt, Johnston J observed that under s 33 of the 1890 Act the 'partnership became dissolved when the adjudication took place'.[65]

The 'bankruptcy' of a corporate partner?

[23.40] Although the 1890 Act provides that the bankruptcy of an individual partner dissolves the partnership, it is silent as to the effect on the partnership of the insolvency of a corporate partner, the passing of a winding up resolution for a corporate partner and the appointment of a receiver, liquidator or examiner to the corporate partner. A distinction should be drawn between the appointment of an examiner, receiver or a winding up with a view to a corporate re-organisation where the corporate partner is not insolvent[66] on the one hand, and the insolvency of a corporate partner in sense of an inability to pay its debts as they fall due on the other hand.

[23.41] First, in relation to the former events, it is thought that the passing of a resolution to wind up a corporate partner (whether as part of a re-organisation or as part of a creditors' or members' winding-up) and the appointment of an examiner or receiver to a corporate partner will not activate s 33(1) of the 1890 Act. This view may be supported not simply on the basis that s 33(1) refers only to bankruptcy, but more importantly because the bankruptcy of an individual partner is quite distinct from all of

---

62 For an alternative view, see l'Anson Banks, *Lindley & Banks on Partnership* (20th edn, 2017) at para 24-19 where the current editor takes the view that the doctrine of frustration does not apply to partnership agreements. See generally regarding the discharge of a contract under the doctrine of frustration, Clark, *Contract Law in Ireland* (8th edn, 2016) at para 18-79 et seq; McDermott and McDermott, *Contract Law* (2nd edn, 2017) at para [21.01] et seq; Friel, *The Law of Contract* (2nd edn, 2000) at p 323 et seq.

63 See para **[23.32]**.

64 *Provincial Bank of Ireland v Tallon* [1938] IR 361.

65 *Provincial Bank of Ireland v Tallon* [1938] IR 361 at 365.

66 Under the Companies Act 2014, s 509(1), an examiner can be appointed to a company that is 'likely to be' unable to pay its debts, as well as to a company that 'is … unable to pay its debts'. A company does not need to be insolvent for a receiver to be appointed to its assets or business – the ability of a secured creditor to appoint a receiver may result from a breach of covenant, rather than a non-payment. The Companies Act 2014, s 569(1) sets out a range of circumstances in which a company may be wound-up, and an inability to pay its debts is just one of those.

these events which may occur to a corporate partner. This contrasts sharply with the similarity between the death of an individual partner and the dissolution of a corporate partner, which similarity supports the contention[67] that s 33(1) should apply to the dissolution of corporate partners as it does to the death of individual partners. There is not the same clear-cut similarity between the bankruptcy of an individual and the winding up, receivership, or examinership of a corporate partner. In addition, unlike the dissolution of corporate partner, in any of these events, it remains possible for the business of the corporate partner to continue to operate through its receiver or examiner. For this reason, it is submitted that insofar as s 33(1) refers to bankruptcy, there is no justification for deeming the reference to bankruptcy to include a reference to the appointment of an examiner, receiver or the winding up of a corporate partner.[68]

[23.42] On the other hand, in the case of the insolvency of a corporate partner (in the sense of its inability to pay its debts as they fall due) and the appointment of a liquidator to wind up an insolvent company, there is a very close similarity with the bankruptcy of an individual partner. The rationale for dissolving a partnership on the bankruptcy of a partner is the fact that the bankrupt partner is unable to perform his part of the partnership bargain since all his property is divested of him and passes to the Official Assignee.[69] This rationale is equally applicable to the insolvency of a corporate partner, where the liquidator's role is to realise and distribute the company's assets.[70] For this reason, it is apprehended that a court should interpret the term bankruptcy of a partner as referring to such situations. Support for treating the insolvency of a corporate partner as equivalent to the bankruptcy of an individual partner is to be found in the approach taken in the Investment Limited Partnerships Act 1994. Unlike the 1890 Act, this Act contemplates a partnership, albeit an investment limited partnership, having corporate partners. Of significance is that fact that it equates the bankruptcy of an individual partner with the insolvency of a corporate partner, since it provides that both events lead to the dissolution of the partnership, if they occur to the last surviving general partner in an investment limited partnership.[71] Interpreting bankruptcy as including corporate insolvency may also impact upon the process of winding up the partnership. This is because s 38 of the 1890 Act provides that on the dissolution of a partnership, the partners have authority to bind the firm for the purposes of its winding up, but the firm

---

[67]   See para **[23.37]**.

[68]   In addition note that in *Re K/9 Meat Supplies (Guildford) Ltd* [1966] 1 WLR 1112, a company which was a quasi-partnership was the subject of an winding up petition. Pennycuick J held that the bankruptcy of one of three quasi-partners did not, by analogy with s 33(1) of the 1890 Act, constitute grounds for the winding up of the company.

[69]   See generally regarding the bankruptcy of a partner, para **[27.01]** et seq.

[70]   See generally Courtney, *The Law of Companies* (4th edn, 2016) at para [25.001] et seq.

[71]   Investment Limited Partnerships Act 1994, 37(2)(a). See also the European Court of Justice decision in *Gourdain v Nadler* [1979] ECR 733, regarding the scope of Article 1 of the Brussels Convention on Jurisdiction and Enforcement of Judgments in Civil and Commercial Matters 1968 (OJ 1978 304/37) which article 'exempts bankruptcy proceedings for the winding up of insolvent companies or other legal persons and analogous proceedings'. That exemption is now at Article 1(2)(b) of the Recast Brussels Regulation (Regulation (EU) No 1215/2012 of the European Parliament and of the Council of 12 December 2012 on jurisdiction and the recognition and enforcement of judgments in civil and commercial matters.

is not bound by the acts of a bankrupt partner.[72] Therefore, this interpretation would mean that where a firm is dissolved by the insolvency of a corporate partner, the firm would not be bound by the acts of that insolvent corporate partner in its winding up.

[23.43] In *Anderson Group Pty Ltd (In liquidation) v Davies,*[73] the effect of the winding-up of a corporate partner on a hotel partnership was considered. The New South Wales equivalent of the 1890 Act, the Partnership Act 1892, also does not refer to the effect of a winding-up of a corporate partner on the partnership, and there was no written partnership agreement in place. The only relevant section of the Partnership Act 1892 equates to s 33(1) of the 1890 Act and provides '[s]ubject to any agreement between the partners, every partnership is dissolved as regards all the partners by the death or bankruptcy of any partner'.[74] All parties accepted that, on the facts of this particular case, the partnership had been dissolved, but disagreed as to the date of that dissolution. The plaintiff (the corporate partner) claimed that the partnership had been dissolved by the service of a notice of dissolution of the partnership by one of the partners under the New South Wales equivalent of s 32 of the 1890 Act.[75] This section allows a partnership entered into for an undefined time to be dissolved by one partner giving notice of his intention to dissolve the partnership to his co-partners. However, the defendants claimed that, 11 months before this notice was delivered, the corporate partner was wound-up, and that this had caused the dissolution of the partnership. The defendants relied on s 33(1) of the Partnership Act 1892[76] (set out above) and claimed that it was implicit in that subsection, which provides for the bankruptcy of an individual partner to cause the dissolution of a partnership, that the winding-up of a corporate partner would also cause a dissolution of a partnership. Barrett J held that the term 'bankruptcy' in s 33(1) of the Partnership Act 1892 did not include the winding-up of a company. He pointed out that, on a bankruptcy, an individual divests himself of his property, while on a winding-up of a company this does not occur since the assets of the company on a winding-up remain intact, but there is simply a change in the identity of the corporate controller, which change is inherent in the nature of a company and therefore does not cause the partnership interest to become vested in a stranger. Barrett J did acknowledge that the underlying cause of the winding-up might afford some separate ground on which the court could order dissolution under the equivalent of s 35 of the 1890 Act. He concluded by holding that the winding-up per se did not dissolve the partnership and that s 33(1) of the Partnership Act 1892 only applies to partners who are capable of suffering bankruptcy, namely natural persons. It is submitted that this is not the correct view.[77]

[23.44] It should, of course, be remembered that where a corporate partner is subject to winding up, receivership, liquidation, insolvency or examinership, the other partners in the firm may apply to court for the dissolution of the partnership under s 35 of the 1890 Act on the grounds that this has rendered the continuance of the partnership

---

[72] See generally in relation to the restriction on a bankrupt partner from winding up the firm, para **[27.62]** et seq.

[73] *Anderson Group Pty Ltd (In liquidation) v Davies* [2001] NSWSC 1482.

[74] Partnership Act 1892, s 33(1).

[75] Partnership Act 1892, s 32.

[76] The equivalent of the s 33(1) of the 1890 Act.

[77] See para **[23.40]** et seq.

impossible.[78] As noted hereafter, the courts do not have a power to force the expulsion or sale of such a partner's share to the continuing partners, although the usefulness of legislation which would grant the courts such a power is clear.[79]

[23.45] Finally, in view of the uncertainties under general partnership law caused by having corporate partners in a firm, it is suggested that the partners themselves should legislate for such contingencies by clearly providing for the consequences of any of these corporate events occurring.[80] This is because of the damage which could be done to a firm by having as a partner therein a company which is insolvent. Often, this is done by giving the unaffected partners a right to force the expulsion of that corporate partner and to buy its share in the firm.

Legislating for corporate partners

[23.46] It is clear from the foregoing analysis of the dissolution of a partnership by the bankruptcy or death of a partner that a major shortcoming of the 1890 Act is its failure to legislate for corporate partners. The result is a high degree of uncertainty as to the precise legal status of a partnership involving corporate partners where those partners are subject to events such as resolutions to wind up the company (with a view to a re-organisation), the appointment of a receiver, examiner or liquidator or the dissolution of the company. At the very least, this area could be clarified by providing that the dissolution and insolvency of a corporate partner result in the dissolution of the partnership in the absence of contrary agreement under s 33(1) of the 1890 Act, and that the reference to a bankrupt partner in s 38 of the 1890 Act is to be taken as referring to an insolvent corporate partner.[81]

4. Dissolution by Expiration of a Fixed Term Partnership

[23.47] The next cause of dissolution to be considered is contained in s 32(a) of the 1890 Act, which provides that:

> Subject to any agreement between the partners, a partnership is dissolved –
>
> (a) If entered into for a fixed term, by the expiration of that term.

---

78 For example on the grounds that the affected partner is incapable of performing his part of the partnership contract (Partnership Act 1890, s 35(b)) or on just and equitable grounds (Partnership Act 1890, s 35(f)).

79 See para **[23.81]** et seq.

80 For a list of possible contingencies which should be considered by the draftsman of an agreement for a partnership which includes corporate partners, see para **[21.23]** et seq.

81 A more comprehensive reform of this area would involve the amendment of the default partnership agreement (which is contained within the provisions of the 1890 Act) to provide that on the death or bankruptcy of an individual partner or the dissolution or insolvency of a corporate partner, the partnership would not be automatically dissolved but rather that the other partners would have the right to acquire the affected partner's share in the firm at a valuation to be agreed or fixed by an independent valuer. In this way, the default position would no longer be one which automatically dissolves the partnership and gives the personal representative or Official Assignee the right to force the winding up of a successful partnership (see generally in relation to this right, para **[26.26]** et seq) due to the death or financial difficulties of that partner.

Thus, a fixed term partnership[82] automatically dissolves at the end of the term. However, s 32(a) is expressly stated to be subject to contrary agreement between the partners. As noted elsewhere,[83] the agreement to the contrary may be express or implied, such as where a fixed term partnership is continued by the partners after the expiration of the term. This is clear from the terms of s 27(2) of the 1890 Act which states that:

> A continuance of the business by the partners or such of them as habitually acted therein during the term, without any settlement or liquidation of the partnership affairs, is presumed to be a continuance of the partnership.

In the absence of any agreement as to the duration of this continued partnership, it continues as a partnership at will.[84]

5. Dissolution by Termination of an Adventure or Undertaking

[23.48] Another cause of dissolution of partnerships is the automatic dissolution of a partnership for a single adventure or undertaking, on the termination of that adventure or undertaking. Section 32(b) of the 1890 Act provides that:

> Subject to any agreement between the partners, a partnership is dissolved –
>
> (b) If entered into for a single adventure or undertaking, by the termination of that adventure or undertaking:

Like s 32(a), this provision is subject to contrary agreement between the partners which may be implicit, such as where a partnership for a single venture is continued by the partners after the end of the venture.[85] In the absence of any agreement as to the duration of that continued partnership, it continues as a partnership at will.[86]

6. Dissolution by Agreement

[23.49] Regardless of the provisions of the partnership agreement regarding the duration of the partnership, the partners may unanimously agree to dissolve the partnership at any time.[87] This proposition is implicit in the terms of s 19 of the 1890 Act, which provides that the rights and duties of partners, whether ascertained by agreement or by the 1890 Act, may be varied by the consent of all the partners. Thus in *Bolton v Carmichael*,[88] Bolton had entered into a solicitors' partnership with Carmichael for seven years, but after one year and two months, differences began to arise between them. There was an

---

[82] It has been noted previously that all partnerships are either formal partnerships or partnerships at will, and that the majority of formal partnerships are fixed term partnerships, see para **[8.09]**.

[83] See para **[8.16]** et seq.

[84] *Booth v Parks* (1828) 1 Mol 465, see para **[8.17]**.

[85] Partnership Act 1890, s 27(2). Although, s 27(1) refers to fixed term partnerships and s 27(2) refers to 'the term' of a partnership, it is thought that a partnership for a single venture is within the ambit of s 27(2), even though the 'term' agreed is for the duration of the venture rather than a time period.

[86] *Booth v Parks* (1828) 1 Mol 465, see para **[8.17]**.

[87] For a more recent case involving the enforcement of a dissolution agreement see *Hylands v McClintock* [1999] NI 28 involving a café business in Belfast.

[88] *Bolton v Carmichael* (1856) 1 Ir Jur (ns) 298.

exchange of letters between them and Master Henn held that the dissolution of the partnership took place at this time in spite of the agreed term of seven years:

'I cannot come to any other conclusion than that it was virtually dissolved by this correspondence, the dissolution originating with the respondent, acquiesced in by the petitioner's father, and subsequently confirmed by the petitioner.'[89]

Form of agreement to dissolve

[23.50] The agreement to dissolve a partnership may be made orally or in writing, but must be between all the partners. In the Circuit Court case of *O'Neill v Whelan*,[90] a partnership was dissolved by oral agreement between the partners, Connolly J noting that:

'I have no evidence that any of the terms of the dissolution of partnership were expressed in writing. It is not necessary that the agreed terms should be reduced to writing.'[91]

[23.51] Although it is not necessary to have a written dissolution agreement, in order to avoid any dispute about the date of dissolution, it is of course prudent to have one. This will be of particular importance in establishing whether a contentious liability was incurred before or after the date of dissolution. In *Re Pim*,[92] Walsh J held that the dissolution of the partnership in that case was effective on 31 March, since there was a written dissolution agreement with that date, there was an advertisement of the dissolution on 4 April and there was an execution of a deed on 3 April transferring property in accordance with the dissolution agreement. Careful attention should be paid to the drafting of the dissolution agreement – the case of *O'Connor v McNamara*[93] included an action for an order for specific performance of a dissolution agreement in respect of which one partner had not informed the other partner that there were time sensitivities around procuring the release of a particular piece of property from security granted in favour of the bankers to the partnership, and had also omitted to include a provision that time was to be of the essence (when that partner was under time-pressure that he had not adequately disclosed to his former partner).

Partners can agree to dissolve partnership before agreeing final financial terms

[23.52] In *ACC Bank plc v Johnston p/a Brian Johnston & Co Solicitors*,[94] Clarke J accepted that at a meeting between two partners in a firm of solicitors on 30 March 2006, it had been agreed to dissolve the partnership between them with immediate effect. While the two partners did not agree the final financial terms applicable to the dissolution of the partnership at that time, Clarke J held that this did not affect the conclusion that the partnership was dissolved with effect from that meeting as the parties' intention to do so was unambiguous. The date by reference to which the partnership should be valued and financial terms agreed is the dissolution date,

---

[89]   *Bolton v Carmichael* (1856) 1 Ir Jur (ns) 298 at 301.

[90]   *O'Neill v Whelan* (1951) 85 ILTR 111.

[91]   *O'Neill v Whelan* (1951) 85 ILTR 111 at 113.

[92]   *Re Pim* (1881) 7 LR Ir 458.

[93]   *O'Connor v McNamara* [2009] IEHC 190.

[94]   *ACC Bank plc v Johnston p/a Brian Johnston & Co Solicitors* [2011] IEHC 108.

notwithstanding that the final financial terms might not be agreed for some time after the dissolution date. Clarke J noted that the final written agreement documenting the dissolution of the partnership and the related financial terms was dated 30 August 2006. Clause 18 of that agreement provided that '[u]pon the signing hereof Seamus Mallon shall no longer be a partner of the firm ...' and Clause 19 provided that '[a]s and from the date of the signing hereof Seamus Mallon shall have no responsibility whatsoever to the clients of the firm ...'. Clarke J held that such wording should not be viewed as having retrospectively revived the partnership. Those provisions were regarded as 'unfortunate drafting' but did not alter the fact that the two partners had unambiguously accepted at their 30 March 2006 meeting that the partnership between them was at an end.

[23.53] In some cases, the partnership agreement itself will provide a mechanism for the dissolution of the partnership. In order to dissolve the partnership, those terms should be followed but the courts will take a pragmatic approach to compliance therewith, as is evidenced by *Hutchinson v Whitfield*.[95] As has been noted,[96] in that case the partnership deed provided that the partnership could only be dissolved by deed. Yet, Smith B held that an arbitrator's award to the effect that all the partnership assets be vested in one partner for the purposes of winding up the concern was effective in dissolving the partnership; the fact that the submission to arbitration and the award of the arbitrator were both by deed was sufficient to satisfy the requirement that the dissolution be by deed.

[23.54] A written dissolution agreement will commonly contain a non-compete restriction on some of the partners and the status of these agreements is considered elsewhere in this text.[97]

Mere intention to dissolve is insufficient

[23.55] It is perhaps self-evident that the mere intention on the part of the partners to dissolve the partnership is insufficient. There must be an agreement between all the partners to dissolve. Thus in *Milliken v Milliken*,[98] a partnership agreement to run a bookshop at 115 Grafton St allowed for the partnership to be dissolved by the mutual consent of the parties. Blackburne MR held that, while there was evidence of an intention to dissolve on the part of all the partners, there was not sufficient evidence of the 'mutual consent' of the partners for the dissolution of the partnership.[99]

6. Dissolution as a Result of a Charging Order

[23.56] Another possible cause of the dissolution of a partnership is provided by s 33(2) of the 1890 Act which provides that:

> 'A partnership may, at the option of the other partners, be dissolved if any partner suffers his share of the partnership property to be charged under this Act for his separate debt.'

---

95   *Hutchinson v Whitfield* (1830) Hayes 78.
96   See para **[23.24]**.
97   See para **[22.49]** et seq.
98   *Milliken v Milliken* (1845) 8 Ir Eq R 16.
99   '[C]ertain facts are charged that are evidence of their intentions or agreement to dissolve it, but none of them amount to an averment that the partnership has, by the mutual consent of all been actually dissolved' *Milliken v Milliken* (1845) 8 Ir Eq R 16 at 26.

Where the option to dissolve is exercised under this section, it must be exercised within a reasonable time of the charging order.[100] While s 33(2) is not expressed to be subject to the contrary agreement of the partners, it is apprehended that the partners may vary or exclude the application of this section to their partnership.[101] Commonly, the need to dissolve the partnership, in the case of a partner's share being charged for his separate debt, is obviated by having a provision to the effect that such a partner may be expelled from the partnership.

'the other partners'

[23.57] It is not immediately clear whether the use of the term 'the other partners' in s 33(2) entitles any one partner to dissolve the partnership, or whether all the partners (apart from the partner whose share is charged) must consent to the dissolution. Since it is in the plural, it is suggested that this expression means all the other partners. If it was intended that just one partner could dissolve the partnership, it would have been appropriate to use the expression 'any partner' which is used elsewhere in the 1890 Act, eg in ss 26(1) and 32(c).

Date of dissolution

[23.58] Unlike s 32 of the 1890 Act which states that the date of dissolution is the date mentioned in the dissolution notice or the date of communication of the notice, s 33(2) is silent as regards the effective date of dissolution. However, by analogy with s 32, it is thought that the date of dissolution under s 33(2) is the date mentioned as the date of dissolution in the exercise by the other partners of their option to dissolve the partnership or, if no date is mentioned, it is the date of communication of the option to dissolve the partnership to the partner whose share is charged.

'under this Act'

[23.59] The reference in s 33(2) to a charging order against a partner's share is expressed to be to a charging order 'under this Act'. This must be taken to mean proceedings under s 23 of the 1890 Act, ie where an application may be made by a judgment creditor to court for an order charging a partner's interest.[102] It follows that only such a charging order against a partner's share will entitle the other partners to dissolve the partnership.

7. Dissolution by Illegality of the Partnership

[23.60] Another cause of the dissolution of a partnership is to be found in s 34 of the 1890 Act, which provides that:

> A partnership is in every case dissolved by the happening of any event which makes it unlawful for the business of the firm to be carried on or for the members of the firm to carry it on in partnership.

---

[100] *Scarf v Jardine* (1882) 47 LT 258.
[101] Partnership Act 1890, s 19. See para **[21.134]**.
[102] For a consideration of the procedure for the charging of a partner's share under s 23 of the 1890 Act, see para **[19.38]** et seq.

The circumstances in which a partnership may be illegal and the consequences, aside from dissolution, of such illegality have been considered in detail elsewhere in this work.[103]

Knowledge of facts giving rise to dissolution is irrelevant

[23.61] It is clear from *Hudgell Yeates & Co v Watson*[104] that the knowledge of the partners of the event which makes the firm illegal is irrelevant to a finding that the firm is dissolved. In that case, the partners in a law firm were unaware of the failure by one partner to renew his practising certificate.[105] It was unlawful at that time under English law for a solicitor to be in partnership with an unqualified person.[106] Although, as noted by Holmes LJ in an earlier Irish case, one might be 'as little likely to enquire about his solicitor's stamped certificate as about his certificate of vaccination',[107] the English Court of Appeal held that the firm was dissolved on the happening of this event. As noted by Waller LJ, the 'knowledge or otherwise of partners does not affect the dissolution. It takes place by force of law.'[108]

'in every case'

[23.62] It has been seen that in some instances the 1890 Act provides for certain rights and obligations of partners, without specifying that these can be avoided by agreement to the contrary between the partners, eg, the right of the partners to dissolve the partnership where a partner's share is subject to a charging order under s 33(2) of the 1890 Act. Although this right in s 33(2) is not stated to be subject to contrary agreement, it may be excluded by agreement between the partners, by virtue of s 19 of the 1890 Act which allows the mutual rights and duties of partners under the 1890 Act to be varied by the 'consent of all the partners'.[109]

[23.63] However, it is clear that the same does not apply to the dissolution of a partnership under s 34 of the 1890 Act. It has been noted that the dissolution of an illegal partnership takes place by 'force of law' and for this reason it is automatic and may not be avoided by a term to the contrary in the partnership agreement. In this regard, the dissolution of a partnership by illegality is not one of 'the mutual rights and duties' referred to in s 19 of the 1890 Act which may be varied by the consent of all the partners. The use of the expression 'in every case' in s 34 of the 1890 Act underlines this fact.[110]

---

103 See para **[9.01]** et seq.

104 *Hudgell Yeates & Co v Watson* [1978] 2 All ER 363.

105 Knowledge of the law is to be presumed, ie that a solicitors' firm with an unqualified partner is illegal, *Hudgell Yeates & Co v Watson* [1978] 2 All ER 363 at 372 per Waller LJ.

106 That position began to change with the Courts and Legal Services Act 1990, s 89 and Sch 14. See further l'Anson Banks, *Lindley & Banks on Partnership* (20th edn, 2017) at para 8-53 et seq.

107 *Martin v Sherry* [1905] 2 IR 62 at 68.

108 *Hudgell Yeates & Co v Watson* [1978] 2 All ER 363 at 372.

109 Note however that s 19 of the 1890 Act is thought not to be applicable to the rights in ss 28 or 37 of the 1890 Act, see para **[21.88]** and **[21.152]**.

110 The partners may, however, attempt to avoid the partnership being deemed illegal in the first place, see para **[9.12]** et seq.

'the business of the firm'

[23.64] Section 34 of the 1890 Act provides that a partnership is dissolved where it is unlawful for the 'business of the firm' to be carried on. It is not clear whether a firm with more than one business will be saved dissolution, if only one of these businesses is unlawful. One commentator[111] has suggested that this is the case. Yet on the face of s 34, it is difficult to see how it may be interpreted to permit the partnership to survive. By its express terms, the only outcome under s 34 is for the partnership to be dissolved. Therefore if only part of the partnership business is illegal, there seems to be no half-way measure, either the partnership may continue doing this illegal business, which it plainly cannot, or it must be dissolved. Accordingly, it is apprehended that the illegality of part of the partnership business will taint the whole relationship.[112]

9. Dissolution by Repudiation

[23.65] While previously, there did not seem to be any reason in principle why the doctrine of repudiation could not apply to a partnership agreement, as it does to other types of contract, in recent years the position in England has shifted, starting with obiter comments made by Lord Millet in *Hurst v Bryk*.[113] Historically, the basis for the dissolution of a partnership by repudiation was that a partner, by his misconduct, may be regarded as repudiating his agreement with his co-partners and thereby dissolving the partnership, and that this conclusion was in keeping with the terms of s 35(d) of the 1890 Act, since thereunder a partner's misconduct is sufficient grounds for a court to order a dissolution of a partnership, ie where a partner wilfully commits a breach of the partnership agreement or his conduct makes it unreasonable to carry on the partnership. However, we are concerned here with the automatic dissolution of the partnership, rather than dissolution by court order, which is considered later.[114]

[23.66] In Ireland, support for the view that a partnership may be dissolved by repudiation can be found in *Reilly v Walsh*.[115] There, Oliver and Edward Walsh agreed to take a lease of land in Suffolk St in Dublin from Archdeacon Barton and build some houses thereon. However, not only did Oliver not join or assist Edward in the project or make any financial contributions to it, but he also showed clear *mala fides* by writing to

---

[111] See l'Anson Banks, *Lindley & Banks on Partnership* (20th edn, 2017) at para 24-51.

[112] Note that in America, the Revised Uniform Partnership Act (1997) (Last Amended 2013) (s 801(4)(A)) provides for the dissolution of a partnership where it is unlawful for all or substantially all of the business of the partnership to be continued. *Quaere* whether the doctrine of severance would apply to a partnership agreement, ie the possibility of that part of the business of the partnership which is illegal being of an incidental nature to the overall business so that it might be severed from the rest of the partnership agreement. As to the doctrine of severance see generally Clark, *Contract Law in Ireland* (8th edn, 2016) at para 14-94 et seq; Friel, *The Law of Contract* (2nd edn, 2000) at p 299 et seq; Peel, *Treitel – The Law of Contract* (14th edn, 2015) at para 11-153 et seq; *Chitty on Contracts* (32nd edn, 2015) at para16-211 et seq; McDermott and McDermott, *Contract Law* (2nd edn, 2017) at para [16.194] et seq. See also *Carney v Herbert* [1985] AC 301.

[113] *Hurst v Bryk* [2002] 1 AC 196.

[114] See para **[25.01]** et seq.

[115] *Reilly v Walsh* (1848) 11 Ir Eq R 22.

third parties to prevent Edward getting a loan from them for the purposes of the venture. After Oliver's death, his estate sought his share of the venture's profits. Edward rejected this claim on the grounds that Oliver had repudiated the partnership agreement. Richards B[116] found for Edward, holding that, while there was an original intention to form a partnership, it had either never come into existence or was repudiated by the actions of Oliver.

[23.67] More recently, the application of the doctrine of repudiation to partnership agreements was again recognised in Ireland by the High Court in the quasi-partnership[117] case of *Re Murph's Restaurant Ltd*.[118] There, Gannon J held that the treatment by two quasi-partners of a third quasi-partner as if he were an employee was contrary to the principles which apply to a quasi-partnership. The two had:

> 'made it clear that they did not regard [the third quasi-partner] as a partner but simply as an employee. Their refusal to recognise any status of equality amounted to a repudiation of their relationship on which the existence of the [quasi-partnership] was founded.'[119]

Since this case did not involve an ordinary partnership, but a company, it was not dissolved by repudiation, but instead Gannon J ordered the company to be wound up under s 213 of the Companies Act 1963.[120]

[23.68] *Larkin v Groeger and Eaton*[121] involved an ordinary partnership between a number of accountants. During the partnership, the partners began ignoring their duties to each other under their partnership agreement. An arbitrator[122] was appointed to resolve their dispute and he held that this conduct had brought the partnership to an end.[123] On appeal to the High Court, Barrington J upheld the decision of the arbitrator and in so doing implicitly accepted that a partnership may be dissolved by repudiation, when he observed that:

> '*Lindley on Partnership*[124] accepts that repudiation of the partnership by one of the partners accepted by the other, dissolves the partnership ... It also cites *Bothe v Amos* [1975] 2 All ER 321 as authority for the proposition that the conduct of the partners in acting in a way which is inconsistent with the continuance of the partnership dissolves the partnership.'[125]

---

116 Jackson and Moore JJ, concurring.
117 As to quasi-partnerships generally, see para **[8.67]** et seq.
118 *Re Murph's Restaurant Ltd* [1979] ILRM 141.
119 *Re Murph's Restaurant Ltd* [1979] ILRM 141 at 155.
120 The predecessor to s 569(1) of the Companies Act 2014.
121 *Larkin v Groeger and Eaton* (26 April 1988) HC.
122 John Gore Grimes, solicitor.
123 It has already been noted that this case may also be viewed as an example of a dissolution by notice, the notice being inferred from the conduct of the partners, see para **[23.27]**.
124 The reference by Barrington J is to the 14th edition of *Lindley on Partnership*. See further para **[23.69]** et seq below regarding the evolution of the English position.
125 At p 15 of the transcript.

The evolution of the English position

[23.69] In *Hurst v Bryk*,[126] all the partners in a law firm, save for the plaintiff, agreed to the dissolution of the firm. The other partners signed an agreement terminating the practice in breach of the terms of their written partnership agreement, since thereunder the partnership could only be terminated by the service of retirement notices which would come into effect a number of months subsequently. The English Court of Appeal[127] held that this act constituted a repudiation of the partnership agreement which was accepted by the plaintiff, thereby bringing the partnership to an end. The plaintiff was entitled to damages for the repudiatory breach of the partnership agreement, but it was held that he was also obliged, along with his partners, to contribute to certain unperformed liabilities of the firm, such as payments under the partnership lease and any winding-up obligations incurred by a partner pursuant to his power under s 38 of the 1890 Act to wind up the firm. Since these obligations related to the fact that there was at one time a lawful partnership in existence, the plaintiff was obliged to contribute to them. The plaintiff would, of course, have been entitled to damages insofar as the repudiation caused or accelerated these obligations. This was not so in this case, since the dissolution would have occurred anyway, albeit a number of months later. While the decision of the Court of Appeal was upheld in the House of Lords,[128] obiter comments made by Lord Millet signalled a shift in the English position towards a view that the doctrine of repudiation could not of itself bring about the dissolution of the partnership relationship. He stated that:

> 'By entering into the relationship of partnership, the parties submit themselves to the jurisdiction of the court of equity and the general principles developed by that court in the exercise of its equitable jurisdiction in respect of partnerships. There is much to be said for the view that they thereby renounce their right of unilateral action to bring about the automatic dissolution of their relationship by acceptance of a repudiatory breach of the partnership contract, and instead submit the question to the discretion of the court.'[129]

[23.70] Views have differed as to the merits of Lord Millet's obiter comments in *Hurst v Bryk*. In *Mullins v Laughton*,[130] Neuberger J endorsed the comments of Lord Millet, concluding that:

> 'While the point is plainly difficult, I have reached the conclusion that, on the basis of the written material, and the brief oral argument on the topic, Lord Millett's provisional view should prevail. First, although he expressly left the point open, his characteristically thorough and careful analysis plainly favours the view that dissolution of a partnership by accepted repudiation is not possible. Indeed, the fact that he devoted three pages of close argument and analysis to question whether a partnership could be dissolved by acceptance of a repudiatory breach, when it had been assumed on all sides, is of significance in itself, as is the fact that none of the other four members of the House of Lords disagreed with

---

126 *Hurst v Bryk* [1997] 2 All ER 283. In *Doyle v Irish National Insurance Co plc* [1998] 1 ILRM 502, Kelly J relied on the Court of Appeal decision in *Hurst v Bryck* [1997] 2 All ER 283 as authority for the principle that a repudiatory breach did not extinguish a contract completely.

127 Brown and Gibson LJJ, Hobhouse LJ dissenting.

128 *Hurst v Bryk* [2002] 1 AC 185.

129 *Hurst v Bryk* [2002] 1 AC 185 at p 196.

130 *Mullins v Laughton* [2003] Ch 250.

him. Secondly, apart from the sole decision of Harman J[131] (which, as I have mentioned, was reversed on another point by the Court of Appeal), the weight of previous authority, at least as considered and analysed by Lord Millett, is against the view that a partnership could be dissolved by an accepted repudiation. Thirdly, the reasons advanced in the Law Commission Paper[132] and in the current edition of Lindley & Banks for questioning Lord Millett's provisional view do not appear to me to be particularly convincing, and, indeed, the main reason each gives seems to me to be undermined by the other.'[133]

The views expressed by Lord Millet and by Neuberger J were followed in *Golstein v Bishop*[134] in which Christopher Nugee QC (sitting as a deputy judge of the High Court) also held that the doctrine of acceptance of repudiation did not apply in partnership law. The Court of Appeal in *Golstein v Bishop*[135] was more cautious on the point – Briggs LJ expressed his personal view as being that Lord Millet, Neuberger J and Christopher Nugee QC were all correct on the point, but as that part of the High Court decision was not challenged on appeal, he did not express a more formal view. Of interest is his comment[136] that a potentially interesting question exists as to whether there are any exceptions to Lord Millet's analysis, such as the case of a two-partner firm, in respect of which '… some but by no means all his objections to the recognition of dissolution by accepted repudiation fall away'. That point remains open for further consideration.[137]

Effect of repudiation on partnership obligations

[23.71] The general rule under contract law is that once a contract is repudiated, the performance of unperformed primary obligations under a repudiated contract cease.[138] However, the effect of a repudiatory breach is not to extinguish the contract altogether, and on the repudiation of a partnership agreement, certain unperformed obligations continue, notwithstanding the dissolution of the partnership.[139]

---

[131] Neuberger J was referring to *Hitchman v Crouch Butler Savage Associates* (1982) 80 LS Gaz 550 in which Harman J held that the doctrine of accepted repudiation did apply to a partnership (his decision was reversed by the Court of Appeal on a different point).

[132] Neuberger J was referring to the Law Commission Consultation Paper No 159 (2000) in which the Law Commission, at para 6.29, 'respectfully question[ed] Lord Millett's view'. Neuberger J's view was that the Law Commission seemed to have assumed that Lord Millett had held that the partnership agreement could be terminated by accepted repudiation, so that the unterminable partnership would merely be 'a partnership at will which the accepting parties may then terminate immediately' and Neuberger J felt that this interpretation was not correct.

[133] *Mullins v Laughton* [2003] Ch 250 at p 273.

[134] *Golstein v Bishop* [2013] EWHC 881 (Ch).

[135] *Golstein v Bishop* [2014] Ch 455.

[136] *Golstein v Bishop* [2014] Ch 455 at p 461.

[137] See further, l'Anson Banks, *Lindley & Banks on Partnership* (20th edn, 2017) at para 24-05 et seq and in particular para 24-08 regarding the current approach in New South Wales, British Columbia and Scotland.

[138] *Photo Productions Ltd v Securicor* [1980] 2 WLR 283; *Heyman v Darwins Ltd* [1942] 1 All ER 337. See generally Clark, *Contract Law in Ireland* (4th edn, 1998) at p 428 et seq; McDermott and McDermott, *Contract Law* (2nd edn, 2017) at para [22.106] et seq; Friel, *The Law of Contract* (2nd edn, 2000) at p 311 et seq.

[139] Based on the Court of Appeal judgment in *Hurst v Bryk* [1997] 2 All ER 283. See however the interesting dissent of Hobhouse LJ at p 297.

10. Dissolution by Rescission

[23.72] As with all contracts, a partnership agreement is subject to the doctrine of rescission. Thus, it may be rescinded by the partner who has entered into the agreement as a result of the fraudulent, negligent or innocent misrepresentation of his partner,[140] provided that it is possible to achieve *restitutio in integrum*. Since a rescinded contract places the parties in the position as if the contract had not happened, it is clear that the rescission of a partnership agreement will lead to its automatic dissolution. Where *restitutio in integrum* is not possible, eg where the partnership is subsequently incorporated, rescission will not be granted to a partner.[141] Since the general law of contract controls the exercise of the right of rescission, reference should be made to the standard works on this area.[142] The 1890 Act simply deals with the consequences of rescission, rather than expressly authorising it. It does this by setting out in s 41 the rights of a partner who has rescinded a partnership where he entered that partnership by reason of the fraud or misrepresentation of his co-partner. That section provides that where a partnership contract is rescinded on those grounds, the innocent partner is entitled to a lien on the surplus partnership assets for any sum paid by him or capital contributed by him. He is also entitled to stand in the place of the creditors of the firm for any payments made by him in respect of the partnership liabilities and to be indemnified against all the debts and liabilities of the firm.

[23.73] The application of the doctrine of rescission to partnerships is considered elsewhere in this work.[143]

III.   EVENTS WHICH DO NOT PER SE CAUSE DISSOLUTION

[23.74] The ten causes of dissolution of a partnership which have been considered in this chapter may be termed circumstances which lead to the automatic dissolution of a partnership, since the event per se leads to the dissolution of the firm and no court order is required. In addition, there are three other events in the life of a partnership which might appear to cause the automatic dissolution. These are:

1.   Mental incapacity of a partner;

2.   Retirement of a partner; and

3.   Expulsion of a partner.

These events do not automatically cause the general dissolution of a partnership, although they may eventually give rise to a general dissolution of the partnership and for this reason will next be considered.

---

140   *Redgrave v Hurd* (1881) 20 Ch D 1; *Adam v Newbigging* (1888) 13 App Cas 308. See further para **[20.76]** et seq and see generally Clark, *Contract Law in Ireland* (8th edn, 2016) at para 11-40 et seq; Friel, *The Law of Contract* (2nd edn, 2000) at p 254 et seq.

141   *Clarke v Dickson* (1858) EB & E 148.

142   See for example Clark, *Contract Law in Ireland* (8th edn, 2016) at para 11-38 et seq; Friel, *The Law of Contract* (2nd edn, 2000) at p 348 et seq; McDermott and McDermott, *Contract Law* (2nd edn, 2017) at para [14.129] et seq; *Chitty on Contracts* (32nd edn, 2015) at para 22-025 et seq.

143   See para **[20.79]** et seq.

1. Mental Incapacity of a Partner

[23.75] While permanent mental incapacity is a ground for a court dissolution of a partnership under s 35(a) of the 1890 Act,[144] the supervening mental illness of a partner in a firm does not per se dissolve the firm. This is clear from *Re Ferrar, ex p Ulster Banking Co.*[145] In that case, the Ulster Bank sought to prove upon the joint estate of the Belfast firm of 'Simms and Ferrar' on the firm's bankruptcy. The firm consisted of just two partners, Mr Simms and Mr Ferrar. During the course of the partnership, Simms had become of unsound mind. The fact that his mental incapacity did not per se dissolve the partnership, is clear from Macan J's statement that '[d]uring a considerable time, while Simms was totally incapable, and when Ferrar had the power to bind the partnership assets, as sole active partner ...'.[146] It would seem, therefore, that rather than dissolving the partnership, the mental incapacity of a partner may render the incapacitated partner a dormant partner.[147]

2. Retirement of a Partner

[23.76] Another event which does not per se lead to the general dissolution of a partnership is the retirement of a partner from the firm.[148] However, the desire of a partner to leave a partnership may eventually lead to the firm's general dissolution. This is because there is no general right to retire under partnership law, regardless of whether the partner in question has reached a normal age of retirement or not. Where the firm does not have a right to retire, the options which are available to a partner who wishes to retire will vary depending on whether the partnership is a partnership at will or a formal partnership.[149] Depending on which option is taken, the partnership may in fact end up in general dissolution and the usefulness of having a right on the part of a partner to retire in every partnership agreement, should therefore be clear.[150]

[23.77] For this reason, it would be helpful if, at the very least, the fact that a partner is not entitled to retire from a partnership in the absence of an agreement, was spelt out in the 1890 Act so as to bring prospective partners' attention to the fact that they should provide for an exit mechanism. The only reference to 'retirement' in the 1890 Act is somewhat misleading, ie the margin note to s 26(1) describes that section as 'retirement from partnership at will', yet that section deals only with the dissolution of a partnership at will. Alternatively and in view of the 1890 Act's role as a default partnership agreement, that Act could provide a default right to retire whereby the outgoing partner's share is purchased by the continuing partners at a price to be agreed or fixed by valuation in the absence of agreement. After all, the failure of partners to provide for a right to retire is often due to a simple failure by them to consider future contingencies

---

144 See generally in relation to a court dissolution under the 1890 Act, s 35(a) and para **[25.01]** et seq.

145 *Re Ferrar, ex p Ulster Banking Co* (1859) 9 Ir Ch R 11.

146 *Re Ferrar, ex p Ulster Banking Co* (1859) 9 Ir Ch R 11 at 15.

147 See further in relation to the possibility of such a partner being a dormant partner, para **[6.11]**.

148 See generally, 'Symposium on withdrawals and expulsions from law firms: the rights and duties of partners and their firms' (1998) 55 Wash & Lee Law Review 997.

149 See generally in relation to partnerships at will and formal partnerships, para **[8.12]** et seq.

150 See generally in relation to such clauses, para **[21.115]** et seq.

and not a positive intention to require a partner to stay in the firm until death. Such a default provision would avoid the unnecessary winding up of successful partnerships where one partner desires to retire.

Retirement from a partnership at will

[23.78] In a partnership at will, the only option available to a partner who wishes to retire (in the absence of a right to retire or his partners agreeing to his retirement) is for him to give notice dissolving the partnership.[151] This notice will cause a general dissolution of the firm and unless already waived, the retiring partner will have a right to force a sale of the partnership assets under s 39 of the 1890 Act. A partner may have waived this right for example, where the partnership agreement provides for his share in the firm to be purchased by the continuing partners.[152]

Retirement from a formal partnership

[23.79] The position is somewhat more complicated in a formal partnership, ie a partnership in which the right of a partner to dissolve the partnership at any time is excluded. The right to dissolve the partnership by notice is usually excluded by a provision that the partnership will be for a fixed term. Where a partner wishes to retire from a formal partnership before the end of the term, he must obtain the agreement of his partners. In the absence of any agreement with his partners, he has two options. He may seek a dissolution of the partnership from the court under s 35 of the 1890 Act, probably under subsection (f), on the grounds that it is 'just and equitable'.[153] The only other alternative is for him to retire from the firm in breach of the formal partnership. Where a partner walks out on the partnership in breach of his obligations under the agreement and against the wishes of the continuing partners, they may seek an injunction to restrain him,[154] continue to treat him as a partner (in which case, they may be entitled to seek the profits he makes from a competing business)[155] or seek damages for breach of contract.

Retirement from an insolvent firm

[23.80] Where a partner has a right to retire under the terms of his partnership agreement, the fact that the firm from which he wishes to retire is insolvent[156] does not affect his right to retire therefrom. However, his retirement does not relieve him of his

---

151 See generally in relation to dissolution of partnerships at will by notice, para **[23.13]**.

152 See for example the English case of *Sobell v Boston* [1975] 2 All ER 282.

153 See generally in relation to s 35(f) of the 1890 Act and para **[25.55]** et seq.

154 See *England v Curling* (1844) 8 Beav 129. Note, however, the general reluctance of courts to specifically enforce partnership agreements: *Bagnell v Edwards* (1875) 10 Ir Eq 215 and see generally, para **[20.56]** et seq.

155 Under the Partnership Act 1890, ss 29 and 30, see generally in relation thereto, para **[15.27]** et seq.

156 In this context, an insolvent firm is taken to be one in which the joint assets are less than the joint liabilities, regardless of the separate assets of the partners: *Ex p Carpenter* (1826) Mont & MacA 1.

liability for the obligations of the firm which were incurred while he was a partner.[157] Furthermore, it seems that a sale by a partner of his share in a insolvent firm cannot be set aside as a fraud on the creditors of the firm, unless there is clear evidence of fraud.[158] However, if he withdraws money from his insolvent firm on his retirement, this transaction may be impeached by the Official Assignee of the continuing firm.[159]

3. Expulsion of a Partner

[23.81] A third event during the life of a partnership which does not per se cause the dissolution of a partnership is the expulsion of a partner.[160] However, like the desire to retire, the desire to expel a partner may lead to the general dissolution of the firm.

[23.82] There is no right under the 1890 Act to expel a partner. Indeed, this fact is expressly stated by s 25 of the 1890 Act which provides that '[n]o majority of the partners can expel any partner unless a power to do so has been conferred by express agreement between the partners'.

[23.83] The absence of a right under general partnership law to expel a partner is an important reason for having a written partnership agreement expressing that right, since no matter how unprofessional, negligent or belligerent a partner becomes, the other partners are not entitled to expel him from the firm in the absence of such a right. The desire of the partners in a firm to expel their co-partner (in the absence of a right to expel) may lead to a general dissolution of that firm. This is because the only recourse for the 'innocent' partners is to apply to court under s 35 of the 1890 Act for a general dissolution of the partnership on the grounds of the partner's misconduct.[161] In the case of successful firms, this may be too drastic a way to deal with the problem of one difficult partner, yet dissolution is the only recourse, since the court does not have the power to expel a partner, regardless of the misconduct of the partner in question.[162] The court's only power is to order the dissolution of the partnership.[163] Clearly, this is an area which would benefit from reform. There would appear to be no reason in principle why a court should not have a power to order the sale of an errant partner's share in the firm to the other partners. Such a power has proved to be of considerable assistance in resolving shareholders' disputes under s 212 of the Companies Act 2014 (formerly

---

157 See further in relation to the continuing obligations of former partners in firms, para **[11.34]** et seq.

158 *Ex p Carpenter* (1826) Mont & MacA 1; *Parker v Ramsbottom* (1824) 3 B & C 257; *Ex p Peake* (1816) 1 Madd 346.

159 Per Lord Lindley: see l'Anson Banks, *Lindley & Banks on Partnership* (20th edn, 2017) at para 24-108. See also *Anderson v Maltby* (1793) 4 Bro CC 422; *Re Kemptner* (1869) 21 LT 223; *Billiter v Young* (1856) 25 LJQB 169. See generally para **[27.71]** et seq.

160 See generally, 'Symposium on withdrawals and expulsions from law firms: the rights and duties of partners and their firms' (1998) 55 Wash & Lee Law Review 997; Fletcher, 'Partnership – multiple expulsions' (1998) 72 Aus LJ 506; Wiley, 'Taxation – multi-partner firm – payment of removal expenses to partner' (1990) 49 Camb LJ 32.

161 For example under the Partnership Act 1890, s 35(c) or (d), as to which see generally para **[25.34]** et seq.

162 *Fairthorne v Weston* (1844) 3 Hare 387.

163 Partnership Act 1890, s 35.

s 205 of the Companies Act 1963).[164] Entitling the court to order the sale of a partner's share would help eliminate the dilemma, in which 'innocent' partners are placed in dealing with errant partners – on the one hand they do not wish to dissolve a successful partnership, but at the same time, they cannot continue in partnership with the errant partner.

[23.84] Similarly, the 1890 Act could be usefully amended by including a right to expel a partner for stated misbehaviour. After all, one of the primary purposes of the 1890 Act is to provide a default partnership agreement for partners who do not have a written partnership agreement. However, it is suggested that the 1890 Act falls down in this task by its failure to provide a right of expulsion for stated misbehaviour by a partner. Such a clause would, it is contended, be expected in any normal partnership agreement. As a protection for innocent partners, the proposed default power of expulsion might provide that it may only be exercised in good faith with a view to benefiting the firm and the partner whom it is sought to expel must be given an opportunity of being heard.

[23.85] Where the partnership agreement does contain an express right to expel a partner, the expulsion will normally not result in the general dissolution of the partnership, but simply a technical dissolution. This is because the expulsion clause will usually provide for a forfeiture of the right of the expelled partner to force a sale of partnership assets (under s 39 of the 1890 Act). This is commonly done by the expulsion clauses providing for a forced sale of the expelled partner's share to the continuing partners.[165]

Does right of expulsion apply to a partnership at will?

[23.86] Earlier in this work, it was noted that a fixed term partnership becomes a partnership at will where the business of the firm is continued after the expiry of the fixed term.[166] It was also seen that all the terms of a fixed term partnership will continue to apply to the partnership at will, save in so far as they are inconsistent with the incidents of a partnership at will.[167] An issue which may arise in such partnerships is the question of whether an expulsion clause in a fixed term partnership survives so as to apply to the partnership at will. Despite some commentators' views to the contrary,[168] it is apprehended that in modern commercial agreements, which most partnership agreements now tend to be, there is nothing inconsistent in having a power of expulsion survive and apply to the subsequent partnership at will.[169] Since it was agreed by all the partners as being applicable to their fixed term partnership, it is suggested that it also should apply to the subsequent partnership at will.

---

[164] See generally Courtney, *The Law of Companies* (4th edn, 2016) at para [11.007] et seq; Hutchinson, *Keane on Company Law* (5th edn, 2017) at para [26.44] et seq; Forde and Kennedy, *Company Law* (5th edn, 2017) at p 354 et seq.

[165] See generally in relation to expulsion clauses, para **[21.121]**.

[166] See para **[8.16]**.

[167] Partnership Act 1890, s 27(1), see further para **[8.20]**.

[168] See l'Anson Banks, *Lindley & Banks on Partnership* (20th edn, 2017) at para 24-113.

[169] In support of this view is the judgment of Browne-Wilkinson VC in the English case of *Walters v Bingham* [1988] 138 NLJ 7.

Exercise of a power of expulsion

[23.87] The exercise of a power of expulsion will have serious repercussions for the expelled partner and may often lead to a loss of livelihood. For this reason, a court will strictly construe the right to expel a partner and any conditions which have to be met to exercise that right.[170] Yet the courts will take a practical approach to the interpretation of expulsion clauses, as is illustrated by *Hitchman v Crouch Butler Savage Associates.*[171] There, an expulsion clause which required the senior partner in a firm to sign all expulsion notices was interpreted by the English Court of Appeal as not requiring the senior partner's signature, when it came to his own expulsion notice.

[23.88] Where there is an express right to expel a partner without cause, there is no requirement for the partners to give reasons for the expulsion to the partner being expelled.[172] Nonetheless, the right to expel a partner must be exercised *bona fide*, as is clear from *Blisset v Daniel.*[173] In that case, there was a wide power of expulsion which entitled the partners to expel one of their number without cause. The partners wished to get rid of Blisset, not because it was in the firm's interest, but for the ulterior motive that he objected to one of the other partners, Vaughan, being appointed as a manager in the firm. Vaughan had issued an ultimatum to the other partners that if Blisset remained, he would leave and thereby prevailed on the partners to expel Blisset. Before doing so, the other partners persuaded Blisset to sign the firm's accounts, and in this way the continuing partners would acquire Blisset's share at a reasonable value. In these circumstances, it was held that the expulsion of Blisset was void.

[23.89] Although there is no Irish authority on the issue of whether a partner who is to be expelled pursuant to an express power of expulsion should be a given a fair hearing before the exercise of such a power, prudence would indicate that the other partners should do so in order to strengthen the expelling partners' hand in the event of the expulsion being subsequently challenged. This is particularly so where the partner in question is earning his livelihood through the partnership, which will often be the case.[174]

[23.90] In this context, it is to be noted that there have been some New Zealand cases which support the view that the partner to be expelled should be given a chance to put forward his case.[175] However, it must be remembered that partners are not in an

---

170 *Smith v Mules* (1852) 9 Hare 556; *Clark v Hart* (1858) 6 HL Cas 633; *Russell v Russell* (1880) 14 Ch D 471. In relation to those clauses which provide for cause to be shown for the right to arise, see *Carmichael v Evans* [1904] 1 Ch 486; *Green v Howell* [1910] 1 Ch 495.

171 *Hitchman v Crouch Butler Savage Associates* (1983) 127 Sol Jo 441.

172 *Re Gresham Life Assurance Society, ex p Penney* [1861–73] All ER 903.

173 *Blisset v Daniel* (1853) 10 Hare 493.

174 Compare the situation in which a trade union official was expelled from the trade union in the Supreme Court case of *Glover v BLN Ltd* [1973] IR 388 where it was held that he was entitled to have notice of the charges against him and an opportunity to refute them. See generally Hogan and Morgan, *Administrative Law in Ireland* (4th edn, 2010) at para 14-183 et seq and Bradley, *Judicial Review* (2000). See also Webb and Molloy, *Principles of the Law of Partnership* (6th edn, 1996) at para 2.54 et seq regarding the position in New Zealand.

175 See for example *Malborough Harbour Board v Goulden* [1985] 2 NZLR 378; *Re Northwestern Autoservices Ltd* [1980] 2 NZLR 302; *Jackson v Moss* [1978] NZ Recent Law 20. (contd.../)

employer/employee relationship and the concept of unfair dismissal does not and should not apply to partners, since partners are entitled to carry on business with whomever they choose. Therefore, the partners are free to choose to have a 'no-cause' expulsion provision in order to avoid the consuming and costly process of having to prove misconduct on the part of a partner and instead to allow for the immediate and surgical removal of a troublesome partner. For this reason, where the expulsion clause is clearly worded, a partner who is expelled in accordance with its terms is unlikely to have the expulsion overturned by a court.

[23.91] In the Australian case of *Hanlon v Brookes*[176] the Victoria Court of Appeal considered the expulsion of two partners from a law firm. Under the terms of the partnership agreement, a 75% vote was sufficient to expel a partner and this vote was at the absolute discretion of the partners. The partner to be expelled was not entitled to be present at the meeting at which the decision was to be taken. The Court of Appeal held that the expulsion clause was to be strictly interpreted. However, even with such an interpretation, it held that the partner to be expelled was not entitled to be present at the meeting or to vote on the issue and that the failure to accord natural justice did not provide a basis for invalidating the expulsion. This case is also interesting in that it appears to be the first case in partnership law which confirms that two partners may be expelled by the one resolution.[177] The court held that the following clause in the expulsion provision, ie 'expel a partner from the partnership', could be interpreted to mean more than one partner, in light of another clause in the agreement to the effect that the singular included the plural and *vice versa*.

[23.92] In contrast, in the English High Court case of *Re A Solicitor's Arbitration*,[178] the expulsion clause was not as explicit, but simply provided that if 'any partner' should be guilty of misconduct, he could be expelled from the firm by the 'other partners'. Russell J held that this expulsion clause was not sufficiently explicit to authorise one partner in a three partner firm to expel both of his co-partners.

Bankruptcy as a ground for expulsion

[23.93] It is common to find partnership agreements which contain a power to expel a partner who becomes bankrupt.[179] In this way, the automatic dissolution of a partnership on the bankruptcy of a partner under s 33(1) of the 1890 Act is excluded and instead, the partnership continues between the non-bankrupt partners.

---

[175] (\...contd) Note also that s 35(2) of the Western Australia Partnership Act of 1895 (as amended) provides that where a power of expulsion is exercised it may be done so 'only in good faith with a view to the benefit of the firm, and the partner whom it is sought to expel must have an opportunity of being heard'.

[176] *Hanlon v Brookes* (1997) 15 Australian Company Law Cases 1626.

[177] Cf the comments of Street J in *Bond v Hale* (1969) 89 WN 404 at 409 aff'd (1969) 90 WN 119. See also the Australian case of *Russell v Clarke* [1995] 2 Qd R 310 where the Queensland Supreme Court held that for an expulsion to be valid under a clause allowing 'the other partners' to expel a partner guilty of misconduct, all the other partners must agree to the expulsion. See also Fletcher, 'Partnership – multiple expulsions' (1998) 72 Aus LJ 506

[178] *Re A Solicitor's Arbitration* [1962] 1 WLR 353.

[179] See generally in relation to such clauses, para **[21.129]**.

Expulsion of a partner after technical dissolution

[23.94] It has been noted already that there is a technical dissolution of a partnership each time a partner joins or leaves the firm.[180] As and from the date of the change in membership, a 'new' firm is constituted. This is significant when it is proposed to expel a partner from such a 'new' firm if the misconduct for which he is being expelled took place when he was a member of the 'old' firm. In such circumstances, it could be argued that it is not possible to expel a partner from the 'new' partnership for his conduct as part of the 'old' firm. This argument may be successful, unless the continuity of the firm for this purpose is expressly or implicitly contemplated by the terms of the partnership agreement.

---

[180] See para **[23.07]** et seq.

Expulsion of a partner after technical dissolution

Chapter 24

Death of a Partner

I. INTRODUCTION

[24.01] Since the only certainty in life is death,[1] of all the causes of dissolution of a partnership, death is one which will commonly occur and is deserving, on this ground alone, of separate consideration. The death of a partner gives rise to a variety of rights and duties between the deceased partner's estate on the one hand and the surviving partners and the creditors of the deceased partner on the other hand. These rights and duties will be considered in this chapter under the following headings:

I.   Effect of the Death of a Partner;
II. Position of Personal Representatives;
III. Liability of Deceased Partner's Estate;
IV. Position of a Surviving Partner; and
V.   Bequest of a Partnership Share.

Overview

[24.02] The most significant effect of the death of a partner under partnership law is that in the absence of contrary agreement between the partners, it leads to the automatic dissolution of the partnership and its winding up at the behest of the deceased's personal representative (or indeed any other partner).[2] Therefore, death is a catastrophic event for most partnerships (and particularly those with three or more members). Furthermore, even if the partnership is not wound up, the right of the personal representative to wind up the firm may be used by him as a negotiating weapon in discussions with the partners regarding the sale to them of the deceased partner's share. For these reasons, partnerships are advised to have a written partnership agreement which avoids this consequence and instead provides for the partnership to continue and usually for the deceased partner's share to be purchased by the surviving partners at a fair valuation.

[24.03] However, the issue remains for those many informal partnerships which do not have a written partnership agreement. Indeed, like the role of the statutory default provisions in the Companies Act 2014 for a company that prefers to have a short-form constitution,[3] the 1890 Act is primarily designed for such informal partnerships. Yet, on the death of a partner the 1890 Act fails these partnerships. For example if the parties had happened to carry on business through a company rather than a partnership, then the

---

[1]   For this reason, it is common for partnership agreements to require each of the partners to take out life insurance.

[2]   Partnership Act 1890, ss 33(1) and 39. For this reason, clauses which provide for the partnership to continue despite the death of a partner are common, see generally 'Partnership Continuation Agreements' (1959) 72 Harv LR 1302.

[3]   See further Courtney, *The Law of Companies* (4th edn, 2016) at para [1.141].

death of one of the shareholders would not lead to the winding up of the company.[4] It is difficult to justify the present situation whereby one partner may force a business, which is carried on through a partnership, to be wound up on the death of a partner. Therefore, it is suggested that, just as has been done for investment limited partnerships by the Investment Limited Partnerships Act 1994,[5] the default rule for ordinary partnerships should be changed to provide that the death of a partner does not lead to the automatic dissolution of the partnership. If the partners wish to have such an arrangement, it is suggested that this proposed new default rule should be subject to variation by the partners. By changing the default rule in this way, it is apprehended that the unnecessary winding up of successful partnerships would be avoided as well as the 'manifest loss' referred to by Chatterton VC.[6] To supplement this proposed change, the continuing partners should have the option to purchase the deceased partner's share at a valuation to be agreed by the partners, or in the absence of agreement to be determined by a valuation mechanism or by an independent valuer. Only if this option is not exercised should the death of a partner lead to the dissolution of the firm.

I.   EFFECT OF THE DEATH OF A PARTNER

Death Prima Facie Dissolves a Partnership

[24.04] Perhaps the most important consequence of the death of a partner is that it dissolves[7] the partnership, though this consequence may be avoided by agreement to the contrary between the partners.[8] Thus, as observed by Chatterton VC in the pre-1890 Act case of *Beamish v Beamish:*[9]

---

4   On the death of a shareholder, the default position under s 96(2) of the Companies Act 2014 is that his personal representative acquires those shares (although a company's constitution will frequently contain provisions that place limitations on this) and if the deceased shareholder was a director, he may be replaced on the board of directors, if desired, by the other shareholders or by the other directors, depending on how the statutory default provisions of the Companies Act 2014 have been dealt with in the company's constitution.

5   Section 37(1), see further para [29.201] et seq.

6   See para [24.04].

7   The term dissolution is used here to mean the general dissolution of the partnership, in the sense of a dissolution which leads to the firm's winding up. As to the distinction between a general and technical dissolution of a partnership, see para [23.07].

8   See for example the provisions of the partnership agreement in *Cullinan v Keogh* [2013] IEHC 400 as referred to by Laffoy J in her judgment of 6 September 2013: 'Clause 15(2) was headed "Death". Clause 15(2)(a) provided, in essence, that on the death of any of the partners the partnership would not be automatically dissolved. Significantly for present purposes, under Clause 15(2)(b) the surviving partners would have the option of purchasing the Deceased partner's share in the partnership on the terms set out in the Schedule thereto. There was a time limit in respect of the exercise of the option. If the option was not exercised, the affairs of the partnership would be "wound up in accordance with the provisions of the Partnership Act (as amended or extended)".' See generally in relation to the dissolution of a partnership by death, para [23.32] et seq.

9   *Beamish v Beamish* (1869) 4 Ir Eq R 120. See also *Creagh v Creagh* (1862) 13 Ir Ch R 28, where Smith MR quoted with approval the judgment of Lord Eldon in *Crawshay v Collins* (1808) 15 Ves Jr 218 that 'another mode of determination is, not by effluxion of time, but by the death of one partner'. (contd.../)

'The death of a partner is, in the absence of provision to the contrary, a dissolution of a partnership, upon which the business ought to be wound up, and the assets realized and divided among the surviving partners and the representatives of the deceased partner, according to their respective interests in the business. But to guard against the manifest loss that such a course would in most cases involve in partnership deeds, there are usually agreements between the parties that death is not to operate as a dissolution ... by empowering the surviving partners to buy the share of the deceased partner, at a price to be ascertained in some specified manner.'[10]

[24.05] The fact that the partnership is entered into for a term of years, during which term the partner dies, does not displace the rule that that partnership is dissolved on his death.[11] The principle that death dissolves a partnership is now contained in s 33(1) of the 1890 Act which states that: '[s]ubject to any agreement between the partners, every partnership is dissolved as regards all the partners by the death or bankruptcy of any partner.'

Death of corporate partners

[24.06] A corporate partner, being an artificial person, is not capable of dying. This raises the question of whether a corporate partner which is wound up or struck off the register of companies,[12] might be considered to have 'died' for the purposes of s 33 of the 1890 Act, so as to lead to the dissolution of the partnership. This issue is considered elsewhere in this work.[13]

Date of dissolution

[24.07] While s 33(1) of the 1890 Act states that a partnership is dissolved by the death of a partner, it omits to state the date upon which the dissolution is effective. However, it seems clear that the dissolution takes effect at the moment of death. In *McLeod v Dowling*,[14] the two parties were in partnership together and McLeod wished to dissolve the partnership. To do so, he sent a notice of dissolution by post to Dowling. This notice was received by Dowling on 24 March at 10 am, but McLeod had died at 3 am on that same day. In the English High Court, Russell J held that the partnership was not dissolved by notice (at 10 am), but rather by the death of McLeod at 3 am on 24 March.

---

9   (\...contd) For a more recent example of a case where a partnership was dissolved by the death of a partner, see *Meagher v Meagher* [1961] IR 96 at 105, where Kingsmill Moore J noted that a partnership at will between three brothers was dissolved by the death of one of them. See also *Pilsworth v Mosse* (1863) 14 Ir Ch R 163.

10 *Beamish v Beamish* (1869) 4 Ir Eq R 120 at 138–139.

11 See for example *Murtagh v Costello* (1881) 7 LR Ir 428, where a partnership for a term of seven years was held to have been dissolved after five years on the death of one of the partners.

12 As to winding up of companies and the striking off of companies, see generally Courtney, *The Law of Companies* (4th edn, 2016) at para [24.001] et seq; Hutchinson, *Keane on Company Law* (5th edn, 2016) at paras [36.01] et seq and [38.01] et seq.

13 See para **[23.36]**.

14 *McLeod v Dowling* (1927) 43 TLR 655.

Death may also terminate other partnership arrangements

[24.08] The decision in *Lee v Crawford*[15] illustrates that the death of a partner, as well as dissolving the partnership, is also likely to terminate other ancillary agreements between the deceased partner and the firm. In that case, Lee and Crawford were partners and Crawford resided in part of the property which was used by the partnership. Crawford paid £20 a year 'rent' to the firm as this sum was debited against him in the partnership books. After Crawford's death, his wife continued to reside in the premises and his personal representative claimed that there was a continuing tenancy in the personal representative. In the High Court, Cherry LJ held that if there was any tenancy, it was one which was to continue only during the continuance of the partnership and therefore came to an end on the death of Crawford.

No Right of Survivorship on Death of a Partner

[24.09] It is well settled that upon the death of a partner, there is no automatic right of survivorship and thus the surviving partners are not entitled to the deceased partner's share in the partnership.[16] In *Cuffe v Murtagh*,[17] there was a partnership between six persons and two of the partners died. The surviving partners carried on the business on the assumption that they were entitled to the deceased partners' shares by survivorship. Chatterton VC noted that this:

'was a mistake on their parts, as they did not take into account the rights of the personal representatives of the deceased partners, or the fact of the dissolution by death.'[18]

Surviving Partner is not Entitled to Acquire Deceased Partner's Share

[24.10] As well as there being no right of survivorship on the death of a partner, the surviving partners do not have an implied right to purchase a deceased partner's share. As noted by Kingsmill Moore J[19] in the Supreme Court case of *Meagher v Meagher*:[20]

'It is an almost universal rule in winding up a partnership on dissolution that, unless there is a provision to the contrary in the articles, a partner, or the representatives of a deceased partner, cannot be forced to accept a valuation of the assets. Any partner, or the representatives of a deceased partner, has a right to insist that the assets be sold in the open market.'[21]

---

15   *Lee v Crawford* (1912) 46 ILTR 81.
16   *Lake v Gibson* (1729) 1 Eq Cas Abr 294; *Lake v Craddock* (1732) 3 PW 158; *Jefferys v Small* (1683) 1 Vern 217; *Buckley v Barber* (1851) 20 LJ Ex 114.
17   *Cuffe v Murtagh* (1881) 7 LR Ir 411.
18   *Cuffe v Murtagh* (1881) 7 LR Ir 411 at 420.
19   Ó Dálaigh and Maguire JJ concurring.
20   *Meagher v Meagher* [1961] IR 96.
21   *Meagher v Meagher* [1961] IR 96 at 108. Kingsmill Moore J relied on *Stevenson and Sons v Aktiengesellschaft für Cartonnagen Industrie* [1918] AC 239 at 246 per Lord Haldane, *Burdon v Barkus* (1862) 4 De GF & J 42 at 49, *Darby v Darby* (1856) 15 Ves Jr 218 at 226, 227 and *Featherstonhaugh v Fenwick* (1810) 17 Ves Jr 298 at 309.

[24.11] Therefore, if the surviving partners wish the firm to continue, they will have to enter negotiations with the personal representative to purchase the deceased partner's share. Without an express term allowing for such a purchase, or providing that the firm will not be dissolved by the death of a partner, s 33(1) of the 1890 Act will apply untrammelled and the partnership will be dissolved. In such a situation, the personal representative of the deceased partner is entitled to apply to court to wind up the firm.[22] This is one of the reasons why, in most partnerships, it is prudent to have a written partnership agreement which provides that the death of a partner will not dissolve the partnership, but that the deceased partner's share is to be acquired by the surviving partners at a valuation[23] or otherwise.

Where there is a provision for the sale of share on death

[24.12] As noted by Chatterton VC in *Beamish v Beamish*,[24] the usual way in which partners depart from the default position under s 33(1) of the 1890 Act is by agreeing that a deceased partner's share will be acquired by the surviving partners. As is clear from *Re Fox*,[25] the terms of such a provision should be strictly complied with in order to ensure that the deceased partner's share is transferred to the surviving partners. In that case, the partnership agreement between Fox and Doyle provided that the share of a deceased partner in a hotel partnership would go and belong to the surviving partner and be purchased by the surviving partner within six months of the death of the other partner by means of a payment to the estate of the deceased. Fox died two months after Doyle had died and nothing was done during the two-month period to give effect to the transfer of Doyle's share to Fox. On the administration of Fox's estate, he proved to be insolvent and an issue arose as to whether the assets of the hotel were to be used to satisfy the creditors of the partnership or Fox's separate creditors. In the High Court, O'Connor MR held that the partnership assets never vested in Fox and remained partnership property. Since this case concerned a two-person partnership, it would not have been possible for the dissolution of the partnership, on the death of one partner, to have been prevented.[26] For this reason, O'Connor MR's reference to the property remaining partnership property is strictly incorrect. This reference should be not taken as implying that the partnership was not dissolved, but rather a reference to the fact that the property remained available for the payment of partnership debts, rather than the separate debts of Fox.[27]

[24.13] In the Scottish case of *Moffat v Longmuir*,[28] a mother and son were in a farming partnership with one another. The mother died. Under the terms of the partnership agreement, on the death of a partner the surviving partner was entitled to acquire the

---

22 Partnership Act 1890, s 39. See further in relation to the rights of the personal representative of the deceased partner to wind up the partnership, para **[24.23]**.
23 See generally regarding such clauses para **[21.141]** et seq.
24 *Beamish v Beamish* (1869) 4 Ir Eq R 120, considered at para **[24.04]**.
25 *Re Fox* (1915) 49 ILTR 224.
26 Since to be a partnership there must be two or more persons, Partnership Act 1890, s 1(1). See generally para **[2.28]**.
27 See generally regarding the priority of the debts of the firm and the debts of a partner on the dissolution of a partnership, para **[27.94]** et seq.
28 *Moffat v Longmuir* [2001] SC 137 (Court of Session).

deceased partner's share at book value if he gave notice to the representative of the deceased partner within three months of the death. The mother died intestate and nobody was appointed as her executor during the three-month period following her death (the son and his three sisters were entitled to be appointed as executors). During the three-month period, the son purported to give notice to himself of his intention to purchase his mother's share in the partnership and did so by making an entry in the farm diary to the effect that he thereby gave notice of his intention to purchase his mother's share. It was held that since his three sisters stood in the same position as him to the deceased, he alone would not answer the description of the term 'representative' in the partnership agreement. Therefore, it was held that the entry in the farm diary did not constitute notice to the representative of the deceased partner for the purposes of the partnership agreement.

Surviving Partner May act on Behalf of Dissolved Firm

[24.14] Although under s 33 of the 1890 Act a partnership is, in the absence of contrary agreement between the partners, dissolved by the death of a partner, the surviving partner(s) are entitled to act on behalf of the firm for the purposes of its winding up. This is clear from the terms of s 38 of the 1890 Act. The authority of a surviving partner to act on behalf of the firm is also recognised in the context of payments of money into court. Thus, when money in court is ordered to be paid to partners, Ord 77, r 44(1) of the Rules of the Superior Courts authorises such money to be paid to the survivor of those partners.

[24.15] The authority of a surviving partner to act on behalf of a firm arose in the High Court case of *Leech v Stokes Brothers & Pim*.[29] There, Mr Leech and Mr Fetherstonhaugh were partners in a firm of solicitors and the case involved an action by Mr Leech against the firm's accountants.[30] The action alleged negligence on the part of the accountants in their preparation of the law firm's accounts. The accountants had been engaged by the other partner in the firm, Mr Fetherstonhaugh, to prepare the accounts. However, the accountancy firm had failed to discover the embezzlement of money from the law firm by one of the employees. After Mr Fetherstonhaugh's death, Mr Leech initiated an action against the accountants. In light of the right of a partner to wind up the firm's affairs, Hanna J correctly observed that:

> 'Mr Leech, though suing in his own name, admits that he is seeking to recover damages on behalf of the firm, as the last surviving partner. This would seem to be his right under law, and no question was raised by the defendants on this point.'[31]

[24.16] Where the partnership has been dissolved by agreement between the partners and one partner is authorised by agreement to wind up the firm, the post-dissolution death of one of the partners does not revoke this authority. Thus in *Luckie v Forsyth*,[32] a four-person partnership operated a business which shipped goods from Ireland to and from India. The partnership was dissolved and one of the partners, Cameron, was

---

[29] *Leech v Stokes Brothers & Pim* [1937] IR 787.
[30] The defendant partnership was the precursor of the Irish branch of the well-known firm of accountants, KPMG.
[31] *Leech v Stokes Brothers & Pim* [1937] IR 787 at 789.
[32] *Luckie v Forsyth* (1846) 3 Jo & Lat 388.

authorised to wind up the firm and collect its debts under the terms of a dissolution agreement between the four partners. During the winding-up, one of the partners died and soon after Cameron settled the terms of an outstanding bill owed by the firm to one of its creditors. The personal representative of the deceased partner claimed that he was not bound by the settlement but Sugden LC held that: '[i]t has also been said that one of the partners died before the settlement of the accounts; but that cannot affect the authority given to Mr Cameron.'[33]

[24.17] It should be noted that the right to bind the firm for the purposes of its winding-up is vested exclusively in the surviving partners. The personal representative of a deceased partner is not entitled to interfere in the partnership business.[34] His only right in this regard is the right, under s 39 of the 1890 Act, to apply to court for the firm to be wound up.

II. POSITION OF PERSONAL REPRESENTATIVE

[24.18] While the default rule under s 33(1) of the 1890 Act is that a partnership is dissolved by the death of a partner, in practice the personal representative[35] may have little or no involvement with the deceased partner's firm. This is because it is usual for the partnership agreement to exclude the application of s 33(1) by providing for the partnership not to dissolve on the death of a partner and for the deceased partner's share to be acquired by the surviving partners. Where the partnership share of the deceased partner does not automatically pass to the surviving partners, the following issues will be of importance.

No Right of Personal Representative to Become a Partner

[24.19] Where a firm is not dissolved on the death of a partner[36] and the surviving partners in a firm continue the partnership business after the death of a partner, it is well-settled that the personal representative of a deceased partner is not entitled to interfere in the business of the firm or become a partner.[37] However, the personal representative may become a partner if all the surviving partners consent to his becoming a partner.[38] Although the personal representative is not entitled to interfere in

---

33   *Luckie v Forsyth* (1846) 3 Jo & Lat 388 at 396.

34   *Fraser v Kershaw* (1856) 25 LJ Ch 445; *Freeland v Stansfeld* (1854) 23 LJ Ch 923; *Ex p Finch* (1832) 1 D & Ch 274. As to the position when all the partners are dead, see *Philips v Atkinson* (1787) 2 Bro CC 272.

35   Note that reference is made throughout this chapter to a personal representative, which expression is deemed to include an executor and an administrator. See generally in relation to personal representatives, Brady, *Succession Law in Ireland* (2nd edn, 1995) at para [9.01] et seq. As regards the position in Northern Ireland, see Grattan, *Succession Law in Northern Ireland* (1996) at p 211 et seq.

36   For example where there is a term in the partnership agreement expressly excluding s 33(1) of the 1890 Act, or the surviving partners simply continue the business without the personal representative seeking a winding up order under s 39 of the 1890 Act.

37   *Pearce v Chamberlain* (1750) 2 Ves Sen 33.

38   *Pearce v Chamberlain* (1750) 2 Ves Sen 33; *McLean v Kennard* (1874) LR 9 Ch App 336. (contd.../)

the business of the firm, the share of the deceased partner in the firm vests in the personal representative on his death.[39] This share encompasses the interest of the personal representative in the moneys owed to and by the deceased partner's firm. Thus, the personal representative has an interest in debts owed to the firm which were incurred prior to the death and which are paid to the surviving partners.[40] On the other hand, the surviving partners have a right of reimbursement from the personal representative for payments by them which reduce the deceased's share of the debts of the firm.[41]

Personal representative treated in some respects as a partner

[24.20] Although the personal representative is not entitled to become a partner in the deceased's firm, in some respects the personal representative is treated as a partner. Some of these instances are expressly recognised by the terms of the 1890 Act. For example as will be noted hereafter, s 39 of the 1890 Act provides that, on the dissolution of a partnership, a partner 'and all persons claiming through them in respect of their interests' are entitled to have the partnership property sold to pay off the debts and liabilities of the firm and to apply to court for the winding up of the firm. Similarly, under s 42 of the 1890 Act, an outgoing partner 'or his estate' is entitled to the share of the firm's profits which are attributable to the use by the firm of that partner's share of the partnership assets.

[24.21] Other instances of a personal representative being treated as if he were a partner have been recognised by the courts. In *Luckie v Forsyth*,[42] the court recognised the right of an executor to intervene in the winding-up if he felt it was not being run properly. In that case, one of the partners in a dissolved firm, Mr Cameron, was authorised to wind up the firm and collect its debts. During the winding-up, one of the other partners, Mr Faloon, died and Sugden LC noted that:

> 'Though Mr Faloon had died, yet he had a personal representative, whose duty it was to have intervened if Mr Cameron did not act properly; but instead of doing so, all the

---

38   (\...contd) See also *Cullinan v Keogh* [2013] IEHC 400 (an application for an interlocutory injunction) in which Laffoy J noted that the question of whether the defendant (the personal representative of the deceased partner) was a partner in the partnership would fall to be determined in accordance with the terms of the partnership agreement.

39   In *Pentland v Gibson* (1833) Alc & Nap 310, the partnership agreement provided that in the event of the death of a partner in the Saint Patrick Assurance Company of Ireland, his share was to vest in his personal representative, provided that the personal representative should within 12 months sign the partnership agreement, failing which the partners were entitled to sell the share, the proceeds to be held on trust for the personal representative. Bushe CJ held that the effect of this clause was that the deceased partner's share vested in the personal representative immediately on his death and the requirement to sign the partnership agreement was simply a condition subsequent, rather than precedent and that the partners had an option to require the personal representative to become a member, failing which, they were entitled to the sell the shares for the benefit of the personal representative.

40   *Lees v Laforest* (1851) 14 Beav 250.

41   *Musson v May* (1814) 3 V & B 194.

42   *Luckie v Forsyth* (1846) 3 Jo & Lat 388.

partners left the plaintiffs to deal with Mr Cameron, and never took any step to put an end to his authority.'[43]

[24.22] Similarly, the courts have held that the fiduciary duties which partners owe each other do not cease on the death of a partner, but continue in favour of the personal representatives until the affairs of the firm are wound up or the deceased partner's share has been purchased by the surviving partners.[44] This was recognised by the Supreme Court first in *Meagher v Meagher*[45] where Kingsmill Moore J held[46] that surviving 'partners stand in a fiduciary relationship to the representatives of a deceased partner'[47] and subsequently in the Supreme Court case of *Williams v Harris*,[48] where Kenny J noted that:

> '[T]he relationship between partners and between personal representatives of a deceased partner was a fiduciary one so that those partners who continued the business were, in the absence of an agreement to the contrary, liable to account for the profits which they earned with the share of a retiring or deceased partner.'[49]

Right and Duty of Personal Representative to Wind up the Firm

[24.23] Reference has already been made in passing to the right of a personal representative to bring an action to wind up the firm where it has been dissolved by the death of a partner.[50] This right is set out in s 39 of the 1890 Act, which states that:

> On the dissolution of a partnership every partner is entitled, as against the other partners in the firm, and all persons claiming through them in respect of their interests as partners, to have the property of the partnership applied in payment of the debts and liabilities of the firm, and to have the surplus assets after such payment applied in payment of what may be due to the partners respectively after deducting what may be due from them as partners to the firm; and for that purpose any partner or his representatives may on the termination of the partnership apply to the Court[51] to wind up the business and affairs of the firm.

[24.24] In most cases, it should not be necessary for the personal representative of a deceased partner to apply to court to wind up the firm. Often, the personal representative may decide to allow the partnership business to continue or may sell the

---

[43] *Luckie v Forsyth* (1846) 3 Jo & Lat 388 at 395.
[44] In relation to such fiduciary duties generally, see para [15.01] et seq.
[45] *Meagher v Meagher* [1961] IR 96.
[46] Ó Dálaigh and Maguire JJ concurring.
[47] *Meagher v Meagher* [1961] IR 96 at 110, where he quoted *Hugh Stevenson & Sons v Aktiengesellschaft für Cartonnagen Industrie* [1918] AC 239 as authority for this principle.
[48] *Williams v Harris* [1980] ILRM 237.
[49] *Williams v Harris* [1980] ILRM 237 at 241. Like fiduciary duties which are owed between living partners, the fiduciary duties owed by a partner to the personal representative of his deceased partner may be excluded by a provision to that effect in the partnership agreement. See generally in relation to the exclusion of these fiduciary duties, para [15.54] et seq.
[50] Note that the proceedings by the personal representative to wind up the partnership may be consolidated conveniently with the administration suit: *Re Pilkington* (1933, No 1351) which was consolidated with *Hughes v Pilkington* (1934, No 325P).
[51] This reference must be interpreted as a reference to the Circuit Court in actions in which the partnership property does not exceed a market valuation of €3,000,000, and otherwise to the High Court, see para [25.12].

deceased partner's share to the other partners. Where this is not done, it is clear from the Supreme Court case of *Meagher v Meagher*,[52] that it is not only the right of a deceased partner's personal representative to wind up the affairs of the firm, but it is also his duty. There, Kingsmill Moore J observed[53] that it 'was the duty of the partners and executors to wind up the affairs of the [firm]'.[54] Furthermore, as previously noted,[55] where a partnership is not being wound up properly by a partner or a third party, the personal representative of a deceased partner will have a duty to intervene in the winding up. Like most rights conferred on partners by the terms of the 1890 Act, the right of a partner or his personal representative to wind up a firm in s 39 may be excluded by an agreement to the contrary between the partners.[56]

Right of personal representative to have partnership assets sold as part of winding up

[24.25] Under the terms of s 39 of the 1890 Act, the personal representative of a deceased partner is entitled to have the partnership property 'applied in the payment of the debts and liabilities of the firm'. Implicit in this right is the entitlement of the personal representative to have the partnership assets sold in the open market. This right is critical since it may be the only way for the personal representative to recover the value of the deceased partner's share, especially as there is no obligation upon the surviving partners to buy the deceased partner's share. The right of a personal representative to sell the partnership assets was considered in *Creagh v Creagh*[57] which concerned a Mr Creagh who had been involved in a milling partnership in Doneraile Co Cork with a Mr Stawell. On Creagh's death, a quantity of wheat formed part of the firm's stock in trade which was subsequently ground into flour and sold at a loss. If the wheat had not been ground into flour and instead sold as wheat within a reasonable time of the death of Creagh, it would have been sold at a profit. Accordingly, it was claimed that Stawell's estate was chargeable with the value of the wheat at the date of death of Creagh. Smith MR appeared to support this claim by ordering an account to be taken to determine the value of the wheat at the time of the death of Creagh. He adopted the following principle:[58]

> 'The question then is, whether the surviving partners ... can take the whole property, do what they please, and compel the executor to take the calculated value? That cannot be, without a contract for it with the testator. The executor has a right to have the value ascertained, in the way in which it can be best ascertained, by sale.'[59]

---

52   *Meagher v Meagher* [1961] IR 96.
53   Ó Dálaigh and Maguire JJ concurring.
54   *Meagher v Meagher* [1961] IR 96 at 105.
55   See *Luckie v Forsyth* (1846) 3 Jo & Lat 388, considered at para **[24.21]**.
56   Partnership Act 1890, s 19. As to two exceptional rights (ie ss 28 and 37 of the 1890 Act) which may not, it is apprehended, be excluded, see paras **[21.88]** and **[21.152]**.
57   *Creagh v Creagh* (1862) 13 Ir Ch R 28.
58   This extract is from the judgment of Lord Eldon in the *Crawshay v Collins* (1808) 15 Ves 218 at 227 which was quoted with approval by Smith MR.
59   *Creagh v Creagh* (1862) 13 Ir Ch R 28 at 47.

[24.26] The right to have the partnership assets sold in the open market to the best bidder has been recognised by the Supreme Court[60] in *Meagher v Meagher* where Kingsmill Moore J stated that:[61]

'[I]n default of agreement, either the surviving partners or the representatives of a deceased partner are entitled to have the value of the partnership assets ascertained by a sale in open market and not by a valuation.'[62]

[24.27] In order to avoid a situation where the personal representative of a deceased partner can force the sale of partnership assets, partnership agreements commonly grant the surviving partners a right to purchase the deceased partner's share at a value to be fixed using an agreed valuation mechanism.[63] Even where there is no such right, the personal representative may of course decide to sell the deceased partner's share to the surviving partners as an alternative to winding up the firm.

Where Personal Representative Allows Share to Remain in Firm

[24.28] If the surviving partners do not acquire the deceased partner's share, the personal representative may decide to allow the deceased partner's share to remain in the business, rather than winding up the partnership. To do this, the personal representative must be so authorised by the deceased partner or obtain the consent of the beneficiaries of the deceased partner's estate.[64]

Risk of personal representative being a partner

[24.29] Where a personal representative does not actually enter partnership with the surviving partners, but allows the deceased partner's share to continue in the firm, he should be conscious of the risk that he may be deemed to be, or that he may be held out as, a partner *qua* personal representative, with the attendant liability.[65] *Y v O'Sullivan*[66] is an example of a case where an executor was held to be a partner by virtue of his involvement in the deceased's business. What is unusual about this case is that the original business of the testator was not a partnership but a sole proprietorship. Yet, the High Court held that after the death of the testator, the executor (who was also a legatee) in continuing the testator's business for several years for the benefit of himself and the other legatees was in partnership with those legatees. The executor during all of this time had carried on the business alone, but the profits were divided amongst the legatees. Maguire J held that it was 'not open to doubt that, since the death of the

---

60 Ó Dálaigh and Maguire JJ concurring.
61 *Meagher v Meagher* [1961] IR 96.
62 *Meagher v Meagher* [1961] IR 96 at 109.
63 See generally in relation to such clauses, para **[21.141]** et seq.
64 *Kirkman v Booth* (1848) 11 Beav 273.
65 See for example *Ex p Garland* (1804) 1 Smith 220; *Ex p Holsworth* (1841) 1 MD & D 475; *Wightman v Townroe* (1813) 1 M & S 412. See also the statement of Jebb J in *Barklie v Scott* (1827) 1 Hud & Bro 83 at 94 that: 'the case where investments have been made in partnerships, by executors, of the property to which infants are entitled under the wills of their testators; there the legal interest is in the executors, and the persons beneficially entitled, cannot be affected by their act or made liable to any loss.'
66 *Y v O'Sullivan* [1949] IR 264.

deceased, a partnership business has been carried on, by the executor for the benefit of the partners'.[67]

Risk of beneficiaries being partners

[24.30] In *Y v O'Sullivan*,[68] there were no surviving partners since the testator was a sole trader. Thus, the only partnership which the court could have found was one between the executor and the beneficiaries. Where there are surviving partners, the courts have not looked beyond a partnership between the personal representative and the surviving partners. However, this case does raise the added danger for beneficiaries who allow a personal representative to retain a deceased partner's share in the firm, that they will be deemed to be partners with the surviving partners. In such a case, the beneficiaries would be in the position of dormant partners who do not take an active role in the partnership.[69] This conclusion can be supported in principle since the business is being carried on for the benefit of the beneficiaries and they are in a position to control the continued operation thereof and so they may be regarded as carrying on the business in common[70] with the personal representative, albeit as dormant partners. In these circumstances, it is justifiable that they be fixed with liability for any losses which may occur.[71]

Liability of estate and of personal representative

[24.31] The fact that a personal representative of a deceased partner's estate is at law a trustee, does not prevent him from being held personally liable if he is deemed to have become a partner in the firm.[72] If he is held personally liable, he will not be entitled to an indemnity out of the estate for such liability, unless he carried on the partnership business pursuant to a direction under the will or with a view to a realisation of the partnership assets or with the consent of the beneficiaries.[73] In such a case, the liability of the estate will, as a general rule, not exceed the amount authorised by the testator to be used in the partnership business.[74]

[24.32] Before a personal representative will be regarded as having been authorised by the deceased to allow the deceased partner's share to remain in the business or to carry on the partnership trade, there should be an express power to that effect in the will.[75] In

---

67   *Y v O'Sullivan* [1949] IR 264 at 273.
68   *Y v O'Sullivan* [1949] IR 264.
69   See generally in relation to dormant partners, para **[6.04]** et seq.
70   See generally in relation to the meaning of this expression, para **[2.68]** et seq.
71   *Quaere* the position of a beneficiary who does not (explicitly or implicitly) agree to the continued use of the deceased partner's share in the firm.
72   *Muir v City of Glasgow Bank* (1879) 4 App Cas 337.
73   *Ex p Garland* (1804) 1 Smith 220; *Dowse v Gorton* [1891] AC 190; *Labouchere v Tupper* (1857) 11 Moo PC 198.
74   *Cutbush v Cutbush* (1839) 8 LJ Ch 175; *Strickland v Symons* (1884) 53 LJ Ch 582; *Re Johnson* (1880) 15 Ch D 548.
75   Note that where the personal representative is authorised to carry on the partnership trade, he may wish to do so through a company rather than as a partner. *Geraghty v Geraghty* (3 December 1970) HC involved a testator who had bequeathed his joinery (a sole trader's business) to trustees who were empowered under the terms of the will to carry on the business. (contd.../)

Hall v Fennell,[76] a case concerning a pawnbroking business[77] in Fenian St in Dublin, Sullivan MR adopted the following passage:

'I think it is, and it has been admitted to be, a rule without exception, that to authorise executors to carry on a trade, or to permit it to be carried on with the property of a testator held by them in trust, there ought to be the most distinct and positive authority and direction given by the will itself for that purpose.'[78]

[24.33] Where such an express power is present, the estate will be liable for the actions of the personal representative in carrying out his duty, since as noted by the Sullivan MR:

'If a testator authorises his executors to carry on a trade with trade assets existing at the time of his death, those assets are liable to the trade debts subsequently incurred, in other words, this particular class of assets is put in peril with the trading which the testator has directed.'[79]

[24.34] Where the deceased partner's share in the firm is authorised to be continued in the business, an issue arises as to the priority of debts incurred by the business before and after the death. The general rule is that the liability of the deceased partner's estate to creditors after the death is subject to the liability of trade creditors at the date of death being discharged first. However this priority is lost where the trade creditors at the time of the death know that the business is being carried on otherwise than for the purposes of selling it and they take no steps to prevent it. *Re Hodges*[80] concerned the creditors of an iron-monger's business[81] in Westmoreland St in Dublin which was continued after the death of the owner. Porter MR held that the trade creditors of the deceased at the time of death were aware that the business was being carried on not simply for the purpose of selling it as a going concern but in general. Accordingly, he held that the trade creditors after the death should be paid off in priority to the trade creditors at the time of death.[82]

Account of profits or interest where share is left in firm

[24.35] Where a deceased partner's share in a partnership is left in the firm and the partnership business is carried on as before, the personal representative is entitled to an

---

75   (\...contd) Kenny J granted the trustee's application to form a limited liability company for the purposes of acquiring the partnership business.

76   *Hall v Fennell* (1875) 9 Ir Eq R 406 and 615.

77   Note that the business was not in fact a partnership business, but that of a sole trader.

78   Sullivan MR was quoting from the judgment of Lord Langdale in *Kirkman v Booth* (1848) 11 Beav 273 at 280. He also relied on *Travis v Milne* (1851) 20 LJ Ch 665; *Ex p Butterfield* (1847) 1 De G 319 and *Owen v Delamere* (1872) LR 15 Eq 134. On appeal, Ball LC overruled the Master of the Rolls only in relation to the application of this principle to the facts of that case and not as to the principle itself, see (1875) 9 Ir Eq R 615.

79   *Hall v Fennell* (1875) 9 Ir Eq R 406 at 410.

80   *Re Hodges* [1899] 1 IR 480.

81   Note that it was not a partnership business.

82   He relied on *Dowse v Gorton* [1891] AC 190 and *Re Brooke* [1894] 1 Ch 604. Cf *Re Oxley* [1914] 1 Ch 604. See l'Anson Banks, *Lindley & Banks on Partnership* (20th edn, 2017) at para 26-29 (fn 116) in which the current editor expresses a contrary view, ie that it is insufficent to show that the creditors of the deceased knew that the business was being carried on but took no steps to prevent it.

account of the profits which are attributable to the deceased partner's share. Alternatively, he is entitled to interest at the rate of 5% on the amount of this share. Prior to the 1890 Act, this right was recognised by the common law. Thus in *Booth v Parks*,[83] the personal representative of a deceased partner sought such an account of the post-dissolution profits and Hart LC held that if the surviving partner:

'continues it as a trade, it is at his own risque, liable to the option of accounting for profits, or being charged with interest upon the deceased partner's share of the surplus, as taken at his death.'[84]

This right of a personal representative is now contained in s 42(1) of the 1890 Act and is considered in detail elsewhere in this work.[85]

Deceased Partner's Share in the Partnership is a Debt

[24.36] The nature of a deceased partner's share in the partnership is dealt with by s 43 of the 1890 Act and was considered in the case of *Meagher v Meagher*.[86] Section 43 provides that:

Subject to any agreement between the partners, the amount due from surviving or continuing partners to an outgoing partner or the representatives of a deceased partner in respect of the outgoing or deceased partner's share is a debt accruing at the date of the dissolution or death.

[24.37] In *Meagher v Meagher*,[87] three brothers carried on a house building partnership. There was no partnership agreement between them and when one partner died, the question arose as to the share of the deceased in the stock of houses belonging to the firm. It was argued that the effect of s 43 was that the share of the deceased partner must be ascertained by a valuation made as of the date of his death. In this way, the deceased partner's estate would not have been entitled to the rise in property prices which increased the value of the houses considerably since the date of death. This argument was rejected by Kingsmill Moore J in the Supreme Court (Ó Dálaigh and Maguire JJ concurring), who held that s 43 is simply 'directed to limitation of actions'[88] and that once the valuation of the assets has been ascertained (for example by their sale), this sum ranks, for the purpose of limitation, as a sum accruing at the date of death.[89]

---

83 *Booth v Parks* (1828) 1 Mol 465.
84 *Booth v Parks* (1828) 1 Mol 465 at 466.
85 See para **[26.63]** et seq.
86 *Meagher v Meagher* [1961] IR 96.
87 *Meagher v Meagher* [1961] IR 96.
88 *Meagher v Meagher* [1961] IR 96 at 112.
89 As to whether s 43 applies in circumstances where the death of a partner brings about a general, rather than a technical, dissolution of a partnership, see l'Anson Banks, *Lindley & Banks on Partnership* (20th edn, 2017) at para 26-03 where the current editor notes his view (shared with Lord Lindley) that s 43 does not apply in such a case. Interestingly, in the US, the American Uniform Partnership Act (1914) provided (in s 43) a term which appears to mirror this interpretation of s 43 of the 1890 Act, ie that the right of an outgoing partner shall 'accrue to any partner, or his legal representative ... at the date of dissolution'. This was reversed by s 410(c) of the current American partnership legislation, the Uniform Partnership Act (1997) (Last Amended 2013) to avoid a situation where partners would '"...sit on their claims" waiting for the partnership to dissolve' (Uniform Partnership Act (1997) (Last Amended 2013) with prefatory note and comments (19 August 2015) at p 125.

Personal Representative Becoming a Partner in his own Right

[24.38] It has been seen that a personal representative who allows the deceased partner's share to be used in the partnership is in danger of being deemed a partner in the firm *qua* personal representative.[90] A separate issue is the question of whether a personal representative may become a partner *in his own right* in the partnership in which the deceased was a partner.[91] *Re Johnston's Estate*[92] is authority for the proposition that a personal representative can do so.[93] In *Re Johnston's Estate*,[94] the executor of a deceased partner actually entered into partnership with the deceased partner's former partner. She also obtained funding for the business by mortgaging the deceased partner's interest in the partnership premises at 14 O'Connell St in Dublin. The executor had not been so authorised by the terms of the will and when the mortgagee sought to enforce the mortgage, Hargreave J held that he could not, since:

> 'Nothing in the law disables an executor from entering into a trading partnership; but he must not use his testator's assets in such business, nor pledge them to raise money for it. [The executor] was perfectly entitled to enter into partnership with [the surviving partner], after [the deceased partner's] death; but she was not entitled to use, for any of the purposes of that business, her testator's assets; nor could she legitimately raise capital for that business by pledging [the deceased partner's] property.'[95]

However, it should be obvious that the admission of the personal representative as a partner in his own right does not impose any liability on the deceased partner's estate and any profits accruing to the personal representative remain his personal property.[96] As noted hereunder, this does have complications in light of the conflict between the interests of a personal representative and those of a partner.

[24.39] A similar situation is where a surviving partner is appointed a personal representative for his co-partner. This is a common situation especially in family firms. However, this situation should in general be avoided since there will be a clear conflict between that person's interest as a surviving partner and his duty as a personal representative.[97] The conflict of interest is most apparent where the personal representative is faced with the question of whether to seek to wind up the firm, sell the deceased partner's share to the surviving partners or allow the share to continue in the business. In particular, any sale of a deceased partner's share in a firm by a personal representative (who is himself a surviving partner) to the surviving partners is

---

90 See para **[24.29]**.
91 For an example of a case where the personal representative of a deceased partner entered into partnership, see *Collins and Byrne v Inspector of Taxes* [1956] IR 233.
92 *Re Johnston's Estate* (1864) 15 Ir Ch R 260.
93 *Re Johnston's Estate* (1864) 15 Ir Ch R 260 at 265 per Hargreave J.
94 *Re Johnston's Estate* (1864) 15 Ir Ch R 260.
95 *Re Johnston's Estate* (1864) 15 Ir Ch R 260 at 265.
96 *Simpson v Chapman* (1853) 4 De GM & G 154.
97 As to the personal representative's role as a trustee, see the Succession Act 1965, s 10(3) and see generally Brady, *Succession Law in Ireland*, (2nd edn, 1995) at para [9.68] et seq. As regards the position in Northern Ireland, see Grattan, *Succession Law in Northern Ireland* (1996) at p 276 et seq.

vulnerable to being set aside.[98] However, in such a situation, the surviving partner who is the personal representative is entitled to retain out of the deceased partner's estate any amount which is due to the firm by the deceased.[99] It should also be noted that any account finalised between the personal representative and the surviving partners will not be regarded as settled.[100]

III. LIABILITY OF DECEASED PARTNER'S ESTATE

Obligations Incurred Prior to Death of Partner

[24.40] The liability of a partner for the debts and obligations of his firm is examined in detail elsewhere in this work.[101] There it is noted that in general, the estate of a deceased partner is liable for obligations which were incurred by the firm while the deceased was a partner. Section 9 of the 1890 Act sets out the liability of the deceased partner's estate in the following terms:

> Every partner in a firm is jointly liable with the other partners, and in Scotland severally also, for all debts and obligations of the firm incurred while he is a partner; and after his death his estate is also severally liable in a due course of administration for such debts and obligations, so far as they remain unsatisfied, but subject in England or Ireland to the prior payment of his separate debts.

[24.41] The rationale for this preservation of liability was considered in the case of *Pentland v Gibson*.[102] There, it was held that the estate of a deceased partner, who had been a partner in The Saint Patrick Assurance Company of Ireland, was liable for obligations incurred by the firm for which the partner would have been liable had he still been alive. Bushe CJ observed that holding the deceased partner's estate liable was justified because:

> 'Any other construction would be unjust to the public, who dealt with the [partnership] on the faith that their security for the capital being made good, would extend to the assets of each deceased member; and would also be unjust on surviving members who entered into a contract, by which the assets of all the members were pledged ... and upon whom would fall ... the loss which must be occasioned by the death of every member, if his assets be not held responsible.'[103]

[24.42] It is clear from the terms of s 9 of the 1890 Act that it reserves joint and several liability for the estate of a deceased partner for debts and obligations of the firm which were incurred while the deceased was a partner. In contrast, the living partners are jointly, but not severally, liable for the debts and obligations of the firm. The exceptional nature of the several liability of a deceased partner's estate does not appear ever to have

---

98 See for example *Cook v Collingridge* (1822) Jac 607.
99 *Morris v Morris* (1874) LR 10 Ch App 68. See also s 46(2)(a) of the Succession Act 1965. In England and Northern Ireland, the right of retainer was abolished by s 10(1) of the Administration of Estates Act 1971 and by s 3(1) of the Administration of Estates Act (NI) 1971.
100 *Wedderburn v Wedderburn* (1836) 2 Keen 722; aff'd (1838) 4 My & Cr 41.
101 See para **[10.01]** et seq and para **[11.01]** et seq.
102 *Pentland v Gibson* (1833) Alc & Nap 310.
103 *Pentland v Gibson* (1833) Alc & Nap 310 at 326.

been questioned, although no convincing reason appears therefor.[104] One possible explanation is that it might be seen as a corollary of the principle of non-survivorship,[105] namely, that as the deceased partner's estate does not belong to the surviving partners, it follows that the creditors of the firm should be allowed go against this estate severally, before all its assets are disbursed. However, it might be more in keeping with this rationale if it was restricted to situations in which the surviving partners are insolvent and not to every situation in which a partner dies. Nonetheless, as s 9 of the 1890 Act presently stands, a creditor of a firm, whose debt was incurred while the deceased partner was a member of the firm, is entitled to proceed against the deceased partner's estate alone,[106] although an action against the surviving partners and the deceased partner's estate is, for obvious reasons, a better option.

Not Liable for Obligations Incurred after Death of Partner

[24.43] While s 9 of the 1890 Act is concerned with obligations incurred by a partner prior to his death, a separate issue to consider is the liability of a deceased partner's estate for obligations incurred by the firm after his death. It is noted elsewhere in this work that under s 36(1) of the 1890 Act, all persons who had dealings with a firm are entitled to assume that all members of the firm remain as such until they have been notified to the contrary.[107] For this reason, when the dissolution of a partnership is caused by the departure of a partner, it is important to notify third parties of this fact. In this way, that partner will not be liable for debts incurred after the notification of the dissolution to such third parties. However, where the dissolution of the partnership is caused by the death of a partner, there is no need to notify third parties of this fact. This follows from the express wording of s 36(3) of the 1890 Act[108] which provides that the 'estate of a partner who dies ... is not liable for partnership debts contracted after the date of death'. This section takes precedence over s 36(1) of the 1890 Act. This can be justified in principle, since death is a public fact and it is well settled under the laws of agency that the authority of an agent terminates on the death of his principal, whether the third party knew it or not.[109] Thus, even where a third party mistakenly believes a partner to be still alive, the deceased partner's estate will not be liable for any obligations incurred by the firm in favour of that third party.

---

[104] Note that the reason put forward by the famous American jurist, Joseph Story, in *Commentaries on the Law of Partnership* (1841) p 514, was that in equity all partnership debts are deemed to be joint and several. However, Lord Lindley does not appear to accept this as sufficient reason, since he notes that in bankruptcy, equitable principles are also recognised, yet there, the joint debts are not treated as several, see l'Anson Banks, *Lindley & Banks on Partnership* (20th edn, 2017), para 13-06, fn 21, where Lord Lindley's comments are reproduced. See also *Note* (1958) 11 Oklahoma LR 229.

[105] See further in relation to non-survivorship, para **[24.09]**.

[106] *Wilkinson v Henderson* (1833) 2 LJ Ch 191; *Re Doetsch, Matheson v Ludwig* [1896] 2 Ch 836. See generally regarding actions against partners and firms, para **[12.01]** et seq.

[107] See further regarding s 36(1) of the 1890 Act, para **[11.85]** et seq.

[108] See generally in relation to the liability of a deceased partner's estate for obligations incurred after his death, para **[11.53]** et seq.

[109] *Keon v Hart* (1867) 2 Ir CLR 138 and on appeal (1869) 3 Ir CLR 388.

[24.44] The effect of the general rule regarding the liability of a deceased partner's estate for post-dissolution obligations of the firm is vividly illustrated by *Bagel v Miller*.[110] This case involved the death of a partner in a two-person firm of boot-sellers. Before his death, the firm had ordered certain boots from the plaintiff, some of which were delivered before and some after the death. The plaintiff sought to recover the price of both sets of goods. It was held that the deceased partner's estate was liable for the goods which were ordered and delivered before the death, but that it was not liable for the goods delivered after the death, as the obligation to pay only arose when the goods were delivered.

Where deceased partner's share of partnership assets is left in firm

[24.45] The principle that a deceased partner's estate is not liable for obligations incurred after his death seems to apply even where the personal representative leaves his share of the partnership assets continue in the business. In such circumstances, s 42(1) of the 1890 Act entitles the estate to a share of the profits attributable to the use of the deceased partner's share of the partnership assets or to interest at 5%.[111] Nonetheless, the estate will not be liable for obligations incurred during this period of trading since, as noted by the Hart LC in the pre-1890 case of *Booth v Parks*,[112] a surviving partner who continues to trade does so 'at his own risque'.[113] In this regard, the deceased partner's estate might be said to have the benefit of trading without the burden of being liable for any obligations thereby incurred since the public notice of the death is regarded as taking precedence over any possible liability on the part of the deceased partner's estate.[114] This conclusion may be seen to be in keeping with the general approach of s 42(1) of the 1890 Act, since that section allows the personal representative to choose interest at 5%, even where the use of the deceased partner's share of the partnership assets has led to a loss.[115]

Deceased partner's estate liable for winding up of firm

[24.46] It has been seen that a deceased partner's estate is not liable to third party creditors for obligations incurred after his death. However, it seems clear that where the death of a partner leads to the general dissolution of the firm and thus its winding up, the deceased partner's estate will be liable for the obligations incurred as part of the winding up of the firm, even though these will strictly speaking have been incurred after the death. This follows from the terms of s 38 of the 1890 Act, since this section grants continuing authority to the partners, notwithstanding the dissolution of the firm, to wind

---

110 *Bagel v Miller* [1903] 2 KB 212.

111 See para **[24.35]**.

112 *Booth v Parks* (1828) 1 Mol 465.

113 *Booth v Parks* (1828) 1 Mol 465 at 466.

114 Unless of course, the testator authorised the continued use of his partnership assets in the business, in which case, these assets would be available to meet the partnership debts: see *Ex p Garland* (1804) 1 Smith 220 and para **[24.31]**. In addition, the deceased partner's estate might be liable in certain circumstances for holding itself out as liable for the partnership obligations incurred after the date of death, para **[24.47]**.

115 See further para **[26.63]** et seq.

up the partnership business. This approach can be justified in principle, since there is no reason why the deceased partner's estate should escape from his share of these liabilities.

Obligations incurred by holding out

[24.47] Reference is made elsewhere in this work to the fact that a non-partner may be liable as a partner where he allows himself to be held out as a partner and that this principle is equally liable to former partners.[116] The general principle that a partner is not liable for obligations incurred after his death is subject therefore to a claim that a deceased partner's estate may be liable on the basis of a holding out. However, s 14(2) of the 1890 Act provides that the use of the old firm's name after a partner's death 'does not of itself' make his estate liable for debts contracted after his death.[117]

[24.48] The use of this phrase ('does not of itself') indicates that this section does not rule out the possibility of a deceased partner's estate being liable on the basis of a holding out in other circumstances. Thus, it is apprehended that if the personal representative led third parties to believe that the deceased partner was still alive or that the estate would be liable for obligations incurred after the death, then the estate would be liable on the basis of holding out.

Position of Separate Creditors of a Deceased Partner

[24.49] A basic principle of the administration of estates is that the separate creditors of a deceased partner, as distinct from the joint creditors of his firm, do not have any rights against the deceased partner's share in the firm until the debts of the partnership have been satisfied.[118] The principle that separate creditors of a deceased partner are only concerned with the separate estate of that partner, and not his interest in the partnership, is also reflected in the general rule that the personal representative of the deceased partner, and not the separate creditors, can seek an account of partnership dealings from the surviving partners.[119] However, it is clear that a full account of a deceased partner's estate can only be taken by having a full account of his share in the partnership and therefore the separate creditors have an indirect interest in the deceased partner's share in the partnership. This indirect interest has been recognised by the courts in some circumstances. Thus, at the behest of the separate creditors,[120] the courts have ordered an account to be taken against the surviving partners, where the personal representative is also a surviving partner,[121] where the personal representative has refused to seek an

---

116 See s 14(1) of the 1890 Act and see further para **[7.01]** et seq.
117 This is also in keeping with the prohibition on a personal representative of a deceased partner from interfering in the business of the firm, as to which, see para **[24.19]**.
118 See generally in relation to the administration of estates, para **[27.94]** et seq.
119 *Clegg v Fishwick* (1849) 1 Mac & G 294; *Stainton v The Carron Company* (1853) 18 Beav 146. See generally in relation to the right of a partner (and his personal representative) to an account of partnership dealings, para **[20.14]** et seq.
120 The same logic would appear to apply to an application by a legatee or a next-of-kin of a deceased partner for an account to be taken and so it is apprehended that this principle is equally applicable to them.
121 *Beningfield v Baxter* (1886) 56 LT 127; *Travis v Milne* (1851) 20 LJ Ch 665; *Cropper v Knapman* (1836) 6 LJ Ex Eq 9.

account from the surviving partners[122] and where the surviving partners and the personal representative are in collusion.[123]

IV.   POSITION OF A SURVIVING PARTNER

[24.50] Reference in this section will be made to the rights and duties of the surviving partners *vis-à-vis* the deceased partner's estate.

Surviving Partners may use Firm name

[24.51] It has been noted that on the dissolution of a partnership by death, the default position under s 39 of the 1890 Act entitles the personal representative of the deceased partner to have all the assets, including the goodwill, of the partnership sold.[124] Where the right to sell the goodwill is not exercised or waived,[125] the surviving partners may continue the business of the partnership and for this purpose use the firm name after the death of one of the partners.[126] It has been seen that any concern that the deceased partner might be liable as a result of being held out as still being a partner by the use of the same firm name is dispelled by s 14(2) of the 1890 Act.[127]

Actions by Surviving Partners against Deceased's Estate

[24.52] It seems that a surviving partner may institute proceedings against the estate of a deceased partner as a creditor of the deceased partner or in order to seek an account of partnership dealings.[128] In an action for an account of partnership dealings by the surviving partners, the personal representative of the deceased partner must be joined as a party.[129]

[24.53] A surviving partner or partners may also institute proceedings against the personal representative of a deceased partner where there is a dispute regarding entitlement to a particular asset on the death of a partner. In *Cullinan v Keogh*,[130] a dispute arose regarding the beneficial ownership of the €1,300,000 proceeds of a life policy taken out by Geraldine Cullinan, who had been in partnership (known as the Renmore Partnership) with her two brothers. The surviving partners claimed that the proceeds belonged to the partnership and were to be used to purchase the partnership share of the deceased. The personal representative of the deceased partner, who was also her husband, claimed that the proceeds formed part of the deceased's estate. Irish Life had paid out the proceeds to the defendant as her personal representative. The surviving

---

122   *Burroughs v Elton* (1805) 11 Ves Jr 29; cf *Yeatman v Yeatman* (1877) 7 Ch D 210.
123   *Gedge v Traill* (1823) 2 LJ (os) Ch 1; *Alsager v Rowley* (1802) 6 Ves Jr 748; *Doran v Simpson* (1799) 4 Ves Jr 651.
124   See para **[24.25]**.
125   See para **[18.25]**.
126   *Wilson v Williams* (1892) 29 LR Ir 176, see further para **[18.18]** et seq.
127   See para **[24.47]**.
128   *Addis v Knight* (1817) 2 Mer 117; *Robinson v Alexander* (1834) 2 Cl & F 717. See also l'Anson Banks, *Lindley & Banks on Partnership* (20th edn, 2017) at para 26-08.
129   *Rawlings v Lambert* (1860) 1 J & M 458.
130   *Cullinan v Keogh* [2013] IEHC 400.

partners were not making a claim against the estate of the deceased, but were instead contesting the beneficial ownership of the €1,300,000 paid by Irish Life to the defendant. The surviving partners sought an injunction preventing the defendant from dealing with the proceeds; however, Laffoy J refused that relief on the basis that there were no grounds to believe that the proceeds would be dissipated by the defendant pending a full hearing of the case. The case was later settled before it reached a full hearing.

Liability of Surviving Partners

[24.54] It has been observed that the surviving partners are jointly liable (with the deceased partner's estate) for obligations incurred by the firm during the ordinary course of business of the firm prior to the death of the partner.[131] Obviously, the surviving partners will not be liable for personal contracts entered into by the deceased partner while he was a member of the firm, even if such a contract benefits the firm. Thus, where a partner, prior to his death, borrows money in order to fund his capital contribution to the firm, the surviving partners will not be liable for these borrowings, since they constitute the personal obligation of the deceased partner. Of course, were the surviving partners to adopt this personal obligation of the deceased partner, as happened in *Stewart v Davis*,[132] they would become liable for the obligation. In that case, James Davis and William Davis were partners in a solicitors' firm[133] which had branches in Belfast and Dublin. The petitioner was an apprentice solicitor and his indenture of apprenticeship was made with James Davis, since at that time a person could only be apprenticed to an individual and not to a firm. The indenture of apprenticeship provided for the petitioner to serve James Davis and his partner, William Davis. A fee was paid by the petitioner by means of a bill of exchange which was drawn in the name of the firm. Upon the death of James Davis, William Davis claimed the benefit of the indenture of apprenticeship. However, he had no room for an apprentice and when the petitioner sought to be transferred to another solicitor, William Davis refused to refund the portion of the apprentice's fee for the unexpired part of the contract as he claimed that all of the fee was received and retained by the deceased partner. Pigot CB held that there was a clear adoption by William Davis of the contract for his own benefit on the death of his partner. Accordingly, he was ordered to refund that part of the fee which was attributable to the unexpired part of the contract.

V.   BEQUEST OF A PARTNERSHIP SHARE

[24.55] A partner is entitled to bequeath his share in the firm as he wishes. However, as noted elsewhere in this work,[134] a bequest of a partner's share does not operate as a power of nomination of a partner. Therefore, the beneficiary of the bequest of a partnership share does not thereby become a partner. Rather, he is entitled to receive the amount due to the testator at the time of death in respect of his share and to post-

---

131   See para **[24.40]**.
132   *Stewart v Davis* (1847) 11 Ir LR 34.
133   Or as it was then known, a firm of attorneys.
134   See *Beamish v Beamish* (1869) 4 Ir Eq R 120 and see generally para **[19.33]** et seq.

dissolution profits where appropriate.[135] If the testator wishes to appoint another person as a partner in his stead, all of the other partners in the firm must agree to accept the deceased partner's nominee as their partner. [136]

Form of Bequest

[24.56] The preferred wording of a bequest of a partnership share is one which bequeaths 'all the capital, assets and profits' of the firm to the beneficiary and, where relevant, makes a specific reference to goodwill. It is thought that undrawn profits of a partner will be covered by the term 'profits' but would not necessarily fall within the term 'capital', unless those profits had first been capitalised.[137]

[24.57] It has been observed previously that a partner's right to partnership property is an identical and equal right with his partners to the firm's assets.[138] For this reason, it is not possible for a partner to claim a specific item of partnership property to the exclusion of his co-partners and therefore it is not possible for him to bequeath a specific item of partnership property under the terms of his will.

Share of Deceased Partner in Land is Personalty

[24.58] The share of a partner in a partnership is in fact simply his proportion of the partnership property after that property has been turned into money and applied to pay off the partnership debts.[139] No distinction is made between real property and personal property for this purpose. For this reason, real property which forms part of the partnership property is said to be converted into personal estate. This involves the application of the doctrine of conversion[140] which is considered elsewhere in this work.[141] Thus in *Murtagh v Costello*,[142] the share of a deceased partner in partnership lands in Athlone and Carlow was held to be personal property. Under the rules of succession law which applied at that time, this share passed to the deceased partner's personal representative and not his heir:

'The rule of law by which this question is to be decided appears to me to be, that real estate purchased by a firm out of partnership money, and for partnership purposes, is personal estate, not only for the purpose of the administration of the partnership assets,

---

135 See generally regarding the entitlement to post-dissolution profits, s 42(1) of the 1890 Act which applies to the outgoing partner, his estate or his representatives, and see generally, para **[26.63]** et seq.

136 See generally regarding the right to nominate a successor, para **[19.30]** et seq.

137 However for a contrary view see l'Anson Banks, *Lindley & Banks on Partnership* (20th edn, 2017) at para 26-47. As to the distinction between a capital account and a current account, see para **[17.09]**.

138 See generally regarding the rights of a partner to a share of partnership property, para **[19.03]**.

139 See generally in relation to the meaning of a partnership share, para **[19.03]** et seq.

140 See generally in relation to the doctrine of conversion, Wylie, *Irish Land Law* (5th edn, 2013) at para [3.113] et seq; Wylie, *A Casebook on Equity and Trusts in Ireland* (2nd edn, 1998) at p 145 et seq; Biehler, *Equity and the Law of Trusts in Ireland* (6th edn, 2016) p 913 et seq; Keane, *Equity and the Law of Trusts* (3rd edn, 2017) at para [22.01] et seq.

141 See para **[16.70]**.

142 *Murtagh v Costello* (1881) 7 LR Ir 428.

but for all intents and purposes, including the purpose of ascertaining the relative rights of the real and personal representatives of deceased partners.'[143]

[24.59] This principle is now to be found in s 22 of the 1890 Act:

> Where land or any heritable interest therein has become partnership property, it shall, unless the contrary intention appears, be treated as between the partners (including the representatives of a deceased partner), and also as between the heirs of a deceased partner and his executors or administrators, as personal or moveable and not real or heritable estate.

[24.60] However, as a result of the passing of the Succession Act 1965,[144] the distinction between personalty and realty is no longer of such importance. Now, when a person dies intestate, his realty no longer devolves on his heir-at-law and his personalty no longer devolves on his next-of-kin. However, s 22 of the 1890 Act may still be important; for example where a testator leaves his realty to one person and his personalty to another.

Legacy to a Partner Whose Firm is Indebted to Testator

[24.61] Under the law of the administration of estates, a legatee who is indebted to a testator's estate must make good this indebtedness before he can claim from the testator's estate. Thus in *Jackson v Yeats*,[145] Barton J noted that: '[i]t is well settled that a legatee, indebted to the testator, can receive nothing from the testator's bounty until he has brought into account the amount of the debt.'[146] The logic behind the rule is clear, namely that a legatee who has assets belonging to the testator in his hands must increase the estate before receiving anything out of it. In the context of partnerships, the question has arisen as to the position of a legatee under a will who is a partner in a firm which owes money to the testator's estate. Does the firm have to make good this indebtedness before the partner can receive his legacy? It was held in *Turner v Turner*[147] that the firm does not have to pay the debt before the partner is entitled to his legacy, on the grounds that the debt is not due from the legatee, but from a firm of which he happens to be a member. However, where the firm is in essence controlled by the legatee,[148] it is apprehended that the firm may be required to make good the indebtedness before receiving the legacy.

Legacy to a Person who is Indebted to Testator's Firm

[24.62] A related situation to that of a legatee whose firm is indebted to a testator, is that of a legatee who is indebted not to the testator, but to the testator's firm. This was the situation in the High Court case of *Jackson v Yeats*.[149] In that case, the legatee owed

---

143 *Murtagh v Costello* (1881) 7 LR Ir 428 at 435–436.
144 Succession Act 1965, ss 10 and 66.
145 *Jackson v Yeats* [1912] 1 IR 267.
146 *Jackson v Yeats* [1912] 1 IR 267 at 270. He relied on the authority of *In re Akerman* [1891] 3 Ch 212; *In re Wheeler* [1904] 2 Ch 66 and *Turner v Turner* [1911] 1 Ch 716.
147 *Turner v Turner* [1911] 1 Ch 716.
148 To take an extreme example of a partnership which is controlled by one person, consider a partnership between two single member companies which are both owned by the legatee. As to such a partnership, see para **[8.61]**.
149 *Jackson v Yeats* [1912] 1 IR 267.

money to the Sligo partnership of Pollexfen & Co, of which the testator was a partner. It was argued that the legacy from the testator to the legatee should be retained by the executor until the legatee paid his debt to Pollexfen & Co, on the basis of the corollary of the rule in *Turner v Turner*.[150] However, Barton J held that the legatee did not have to settle the debt with the testator's firm before receiving his legacy, since he did not have any of the testator's assets in his hands:

'[I]n order to be assets in hand, the debt must be due to the estate; and this debt, which was due to the firm of which testator was a partner, does not come within that description.'[151]

[24.63] It is however arguable that the testator will be an indirect beneficiary of payment to his former firm because his return from the partnership will normally be increased by the amount of the payment. Accordingly, it is doubtful whether this rule is without exception and Barton J himself did not rule out circumstances existing in which a debt due to a testator's firm might be regarded as a debt due to the separate estate of the deceased partner:

'It may be possible to suppose circumstances under which a debt due to a partnership might, for the purposes of this rule of retainer, be, or might have become, or might have to be regarded as a debt due, or involving ascertainable liability, to the separate estate of a deceased partner. But it has not been suggested that there are any such circumstances here.'[152]

Such circumstances, it is conceived, would exist where the firm is in essence controlled by the legatee.[153]

Ademption

[24.64] Where a bequest cannot be made due to the extinction of the item bequeathed, the bequest is said to be revoked under the equitable doctrine of ademption.[154] The doctrine of ademption will have application to partnership law where a partner bequeaths his partnership share, subsequently leaves the partnership and is paid for his share. In such a situation, the partnership share will not exist at the time of the testator's death and the bequest of that share may be said to have been adeemed.

---

[150] *Turner v Turner* [1911] 1 Ch 716.

[151] *Jackson v Yeats* [1912] 1 IR 267 at 271.

[152] *Jackson v Yeats* [1912] 1 IR 267 at 271–272.

[153] For example a partnership which is controlled by two single member companies which are both owned by the legatee. As to such a partnership, see para **[8.61]**.

[154] See generally, Brady, *Succession Law in Ireland* (2nd edn, 1995) at para [6.56] et seq; Wylie, *Irish Land Law* (5th edn, 2013) at para [3.138] et seq; Keane, *Equity and the Law of Trusts* (3rd edn, 2017) at para [25.02] et seq; Wylie, *A Casebook on Equity and Trusts in Ireland* (2nd edn, 1998) at p 178 et seq. As regards the position in Northern Ireland, see Grattan, *Succession Law in Northern Ireland* (1996) at pp 163 et seq.

Chapter 25

Dissolution by the Court

INTRODUCTION

[25.01] In Chapter 23, consideration was given to the instances in which a partnership is automatically dissolved by the actions of one or more of the partners, such as the giving of notice by a partner in a partnership at will or the occurrence of some other event, such as the death or bankruptcy of a partner and in Chapter 24 one of these issues, the death of a partner, was examined in detail.

[25.02] In this chapter, consideration will be given to the dissolution of a partnership by court order. Section 35 of the 1890 Act sets out the main instances in which a partnership may be dissolved by court order. Each of these will be analysed in turn under the following headings:

    I.   Section 35 of the 1890 Act;
    II.   Mental Incapacity of a Partner;
    III. Permanent Incapacity of a Partner;
    IV. Conduct Prejudicial to the Partnership Business;
    V.   Wilful or Persistent Breach of the Partnership Agreement;
    VI. Misconduct Rendering Continuance Impractical;
    VII. Partnership Carried on at a Loss;
    VIII. Dissolution on Just and Equitable Grounds.

Overview

[25.03] In a formal partnership (ie, where the partners have excluded the right of a partner to dissolve the partnership by notice),[1] the partners commonly agree to remain in partnership together for a fixed term. It will often occur that some of the partners may wish to bring the partnership to a premature end for a variety of reasons ranging from personality clashes to wrongful conduct by a partner. Unfortunately, there is no automatic right under the 1890 Act for the partners to expel a partner guilty of misconduct and for this reason, these types of situations will often result in an application to court for a dissolution of the partnership under s 35 of the 1890 Act. The only other option open to the partner(s) wishing to end the partnership with a difficult partner is to breach the partnership agreement by walking out, which is most unsatisfactory.[2]

---

[1]   See further para [8.09].

[2]   Quite apart from the fact that he may be sued for breach of contract, this option is also unsatisfactory because it may leave the departing partner liable as a partner for obligations incurred by his former firm after his departure under s 36(1) of the 1890 Act, see further para [11.74] et seq.

[25.04] A number of general aspects of s 35 are worthy of mention at this juncture. It provides for the dissolution of a partnership in six separate instances. The court has an absolute discretion to order a dissolution in any of the six cases listed in that section. This should encourage potential litigants to make every effort to resolve their differences amicably, since there is no requirement on a court to order or not to order a dissolution, regardless of the conduct of the partners. However, since the courts generally lean against ordering the specific performance of a partnership agreement between unwilling partners,[3] the result of an application to court to dissolve a partnership will often, but not always, be a court dissolution.[4] Partnership disputes will usually end up in dissolution because a court in a partnership dispute, unlike the situation in a company dispute,[5] does not have a statutory power to order the expulsion of a partner or the sale of one partner's share to his co-partners.[6] It follows that the parties to a partnership dispute have the added knowledge that a dissolution of their firm is more likely than not to result from an application to court under s 35. In general terms therefore, there should be a very great incentive for partners in dispute to attempt to agree to dissolve amicably rather than going to court to obtain an order which is likely to be to the same effect.

[25.05] Although s 35 has six separate headings under which a dissolution of a partnership may be claimed, more often than not, a dissolution will be sought under s 35(f) on the grounds that it is just and equitable to dissolve the partnership. Such an application obviates the need for the petitioner to satisfy the pre-conditions of the other subsections of s 35, such as incapacity, breach of partnership agreement, etc.[7] Furthermore, the courts, in making an order under this section, rely quite readily on grounds which would fall more easily under the other subsections of s 35. It follows that one may expect this trend of applying for court dissolutions under s 35(f) to continue, certainly until the courts are granted a statutory power to expel partners or order the sale of one partner's share to his co-partners.

I.   SECTION 35 OF THE 1890 ACT

[25.06] In the remainder of this chapter each of the instances in which a partnership may be wound up is considered in detail. First, however, consideration will be given to s 35

---

3   See para **[20.50]** et seq.

4   Indeed in the New Zealand case of *Smith v Baker* [1977] 1 NZLR 511, the court declined to order a dissolution of the partnership since in the circumstances of the case, a dissolution had already taken place. In *Mullins v Laughton* [2003] Ch 250, Neuberger J commented that the wording of s 35 of the 1890 Act makes it clear that the court may decline to make an order dissolving the partnership '… if another course would achieve a more just result' and that even if the court does make an order dissolving the partnership under s 35, it may order a sale of the partnership's assets, rather than simply winding up the partnership 'in the normal way'.

5   Companies Act 2014, s 212.

6   See, however, the exceptional case of *Syers v Syers* (1876) AC 174, considered at para **[26.36]**.

7   For example in *Barber v Rasco International Ltd* [2012] EWHC 269 (QB), as all partners were in agreement that the relationship between them had irretrievably broken down and that it would be just and equitable to dissolve their partnership, the court did not see any need to look at issues regarding the conduct of the partners, or to question whether dissolution under another subsection of s 35 (in this case, s 35(c) or s 35(d)) would be more appropriate.

as a whole and a number of general concepts in relation to court proceedings for the dissolution of a partnership. Section 35 states that:

> On application by a partner the Court may decree a dissolution of the partnership in any of the following cases:
>
> (a) When a partner is found lunatic by inquisition, or in Scotland by cognition, or is shown to the satisfaction of the Court to be of permanently unsound mind, in either of which cases the application may be made as well on behalf of that partner by his committee or next friend or person having title to intervene as by any other partner:
>
> (b) When a partner, other than the partner suing, becomes in any other way permanently incapable of performing his part of the partnership contract:
>
> (c) When a partner, other than the partner suing, has been guilty of such conduct as, in the opinion of the Court, regard being had to the nature of the business, is calculated to prejudicially affect the carrying on of the business:
>
> (d) When a partner, other than the partner suing, wilfully or persistently commits a breach of the partnership agreement, or otherwise so conducts himself in matters relating to the partnership business that it is not reasonably practicable for the other partner or partners to carry on the business in partnership with him:
>
> (e) When the business of the partnership can only be carried on at a loss:
>
> (f) Whenever in any case circumstances have arisen which, in the opinion of the Court, render it just and equitable that the partnership be dissolved.

'On application by a partner'

[25.07] Under the express terms of s 35 of the 1890 Act, the application for the court dissolution of a partnership may only be made by a partner in the firm or on his behalf. However, this provision has been supplemented by two other statutory provisions which grant the Central Bank of Ireland the right to apply to court for the dissolution of certain types of partnerships.[8] These provisions are now contained in the European Union (Markets in Financial Instruments) Regulations 2017[9] and the Investment Intermediaries Act 1995 and will be considered first.

Where the partnership is an authorised investment firm or market operator of a regulated market under the European Union (Markets in Financial Instruments) Regulations 2017

[25.08] In the case of a partnership which is an authorised investment firm or a market operator of a regulated market[10] under the European Union (Markets in Financial

---

8   Regulation 29 of the European Communities (Electronic Money) Regulations 2002 (SI 221/2002) also extended s 35 of the 1890 Act to enable the Central Bank to petition for the court dissolution of an electronic money institution that was a partnership if it failed to comply with a direction from the Central Bank, or if its authorisation was withdrawn and it had ceased to carry on the business of issuing electronic money. However, those Regulations were revoked by the European Communities (Electronic Money) Regulations 2011 (SI 183/2011) and the 2011 Regulations did not contain an equivalent provision.

9   SI 375/2017.

10 See further para **[3.41]** in relation to what constitutes an investment firm or a market operator of a regulated market under the European Union (Markets in Financial Instruments) Regulations 2017.

Instruments) Regulations 2017, reg 148(10) allows the Central Bank to petition the High Court for a decree of dissolution in respect of the partnership, and extends s 35 of the 1890 Act to the Central Bank so that, under s 35, the Central Bank may seek the dissolution of that partnership on the following grounds:

- in the opinion of the Central Bank, the partnership is unable, or may be unable, to meet its obligations to its clients or creditors;
- the partnership's authorisation has been withdrawn or revoked and it has ceased to carry on business as an investment firm or has ceased to operate a regulated market;
- the Central Bank considers the partnership's winding-up is in the interest of the proper and orderly regulation and supervision of investment firms or regulated markets or is necessary for the protection of investors; or
- the partnership has failed to comply with any direction given by the Central Bank under the Regulations.

Where the partnership is an authorised investment business firm under the Investment Intermediaries Act 1995

[25.09] Section 22(8) of the Investment Intermediaries Act 1995 is almost identical to reg 148(10) of the European Union (Markets in Financial Instruments) Regulations 2017. Thus, in the case of a partnership which is an authorised investment business firm (or a former authorised investment business firm), s 22(8) of the 1995 Act entitles the Central Bank to petition the High Court for its dissolution under s 35 of the 1890 Act. Like reg 148(10) of the 2017 Regulations, s 22(8) of the 1995 Act extends the grounds upon which the Central Bank may seek such a dissolution to include grounds that are almost identical to those which are applicable to an authorised investment firm or market operator of a regulated market under the 2017 Regulations and set out above.[11]

Partnership at Will

[25.10] It has been noted previously that any one partner in a partnership at will may dissolve the partnership by giving a notice of dissolution to the other partners.[12] The service of the proceedings in a dissolution action will constitute such a notice of dissolution, so as to automatically dissolve a partnership at will.[13] It follows that a partner in a partnership at will who wishes to dissolve the partnership should, save in exceptional cases,[14] do so by notice to his partners rather than by petitioning the court under s 35 of the 1890 Act.[15] Otherwise, it could be argued that the petitioner was abusing the court process.

---

[11] These grounds are set out in s 22(1) of the Investment Intermediaries Act 1995.
[12] See generally in relation to the dissolution of a partnership at will by notice, para **[23.13]** et seq.
[13] *Unsworth v Jordan* [1896] WN 2(5).
[14] For example where he is also seeking ancillary relief.
[15] In *ACC Bank plc v Johnston p/a Brian Johnston & Co Solicitors* [2011] IEHC 108, Clarke J commented that a notice of dissolution must be an 'unambiguous intimation of a final intention to dissolve the partnership'. (contd.../)

'the Court may decree a dissolution'

[25.11] Section 35 of the 1890 Act states that the court 'may' decree a dissolution in the instances set out therein. It should therefore be borne in mind that the court is not bound to order a dissolution of a partnership, even if the terms of s 35 clearly apply to the circumstances in question.

Jurisdiction to Grant Dissolution

[25.12] Under the terms of s 35 of the 1890 Act, a dissolution of a partnership may be decreed by 'the Court'. Section 45 of the 1890 Act provides that this expression includes every court and judge having jurisdiction in the case.[16] While jurisdiction to hear dissolution actions is vested in the High Court,[17] the Circuit Court also has limited jurisdiction regarding proceedings for the dissolution of a partnership, save where the property of the partnership consists of land with a market value in excess of €3,000,000.[18] This is, of course, subject to the monetary limit of €75,000 applicable to Circuit Court actions at the time of writing.[19] Where the dissolution proceedings are to issue in the Circuit Court, the plaintiff may choose the circuit where the partnership

---

15 (\...contd) The key section of the letter considered by Clarke J read as follows: 'Dear Mr Traynor, We are instructed by … [Mr Mallon] in respect of regularising matters regarding the determination of the partnership practising under the style and/or title of Traynor Mallon & Company, Solicitors … Finally we have been instructed, in the absence of your consent to dissolve the partnership, to apply to Court pursuant to Section 35(c) and 35(d) of the [1890 Act] to dissolve the Partnership on the grounds of your professional misconduct …' As the letter intimated that the dissolution might take place on foot of a court process, Clarke J found the letter to be ambiguous as regards the proposed end-date of the partnership – was it to be dissolved immediately, or following a court process? In light of that ambiguity, he found the letter to be insufficient to dissolve the partnership between Mr Mallon and Mr Traynor.

16 Note that Ord 66, r 27(6) of the Rules of the Circuit Court which deal with the taxation and measurement of costs provides that all suits for the taking of any partnership account or for the dissolution of any partnership are deemed to be equity proceedings and that the District Court does not have jurisdiction to deal with equitable proceedings. See para **[20.13]**.

17 Section 36(5) of Supreme Court of Judicature Act (Ireland) 1877 vested exclusively in the High Court the jurisdiction to hear actions for the 'dissolution of partnerships or the taking of partnership or other accounts'.

18 Under the Courts (Supplemental Provisions) Act 1961, s 22, Sch 3, ref 18 as amended by s 2(1)(d) of the Courts Act 1981 and by s 45(2) of the Civil Liability and Courts Act 2004 (s 45(2) was eventually commenced on 11 January 2017 by the Civil Liability and Courts Act 2004 (Commencement) Order 2017 (SI 2/2017)). A definition of the term 'market value' was inserted into s 2 of the 1961 Act by s 45(1) of the 2004 Act (again with effect from 11 January 2017) as follows: '"market value" means, in relation to land, the price that would have been obtained in respect of the unencumbranced fee simple were the land to have been sold on the open market, in the year immediately preceding the bringing of the proceedings concerned, in such manner and subject to such conditions as might reasonably be calculated to have resulted in the vendor obtaining the best price for the land'.

19 Courts of Justice Act 1924, s 77A, as most recently amended by the Courts and Civil Law (Miscellaneous Provisions) Act 2013.

business is or was carried on, or the circuit where the defendant or one of them resides or carries on business.[20]

Parties to the action

[25.13] As a general rule, all of the partners in a firm should be joined as parties to an action for the dissolution of the partnership. This is because all partners will be interested in the firm's affairs and all issues between the partners can only be safely wound up and settled if the partners are all parties to the action.[21]

Arbitration

[25.14] The inter-relation between an arbitration clause and the right of a partner to seek the dissolution of the partnership under s 35 of the 1890 Act deserves consideration. Where the partnership agreement contains an arbitration clause, it is not immediately clear whether a partner who wishes to dissolve the partnership on the grounds set out in s 35 is required to seek redress from the arbitrator, rather than applying to court to dissolve the partnership under s 35 of the 1890 Act. In the context of general disputes between the partners, where they have agreed to refer the matter to arbitration,[22] Article 8(1) of the UNCITRAL Model Law on International Commercial Arbitration (given force of law in Ireland by s 6 of the Arbitration Act 2010) entitles a party to that arbitration agreement to apply to have the matter in dispute between the parties referred to arbitration unless the court finds that the arbitration agreement 'is null and void, inoperative or incapable of being performed'. The party applying to have the matter so referred must do so no later than the time that he submits his first statement on the substance of the dispute between the parties and, unless the court finds that the arbitration agreement is 'null and void, inoperative or incapable of being performed', the court must refer the dispute to arbitration. If a dispute between the partners (which is subject to an arbitration agreement) is already before the court, the partners may themselves refer the matter to arbitration, and an arbitral award can be made, before the matter is determined by the court.[23] Therefore, when dealing with general disputes between partners, an arbitration clause will normally provide that the parties agree to any decision of the arbitrator being 'full and final' or 'final and binding', thereby precluding recourse to court for a resolution of the dispute.[24]

---

[20] Courts (Supplemental Provisions) Act 1961, s 22, Sch 3, ref 18. Note that since the District Court is a creature of statute, the rule is that its jurisdiction is restricted to those situations where jurisdiction has been expressly conferred on it.

[21] *Richardson v Hastings* (1844) 7 Beav 301.

[22] Such an arbitration clause is referred to in Article 7(1) of the UNCITRAL Model Law on International Commercial Arbitration as an 'arbitration agreement' as follows: 'an agreement by the parties to submit to arbitration all or certain disputes which have arisen or which may arise between them in respect of a defined legal relationship, whether contractual or not. An arbitration agreement may be in the form of an arbitration clause in a contract or in the form of a separate agreement.'

[23] Article 8(2) of the UNCITRAL Model Law on International Commercial Arbitration.

[24] But see *Winterthur Swiss Insurance Co v ICI* [1990] ILRM 159 and *McCarthy v Joe Walsh Tours Ltd* [1991] ILRM 813. (contd.../)

[25.15] However, when the dispute in question involves one partner seeking the dissolution of the partnership, one must be satisfied that the dissolution is covered by the terms of the arbitration clause. In particular, one must take account of the wording of s 35 of the 1890 Act. Since s 35 expressly confers on the court the power to dissolve a partnership, the argument could be made that the parties cannot preclude the express jurisdiction of the court in this way.[25] However, it is contended that there should be no difference in approach to preferring the jurisdiction of an arbitrator over that of the courts, whether the jurisdiction of the court is conferred by the 1890 Act or by other legislation or the common law. In the English High Court case of *Olver v Hillier*,[26] Roxburgh J observed, in reference to the effect of an arbitration contract on s 35 of the 1890 Act, that 'it may be that the contract has ousted that section altogether as a matter of pure construction'.[27] Furthermore, the dissolution of partnerships by arbitrators has been recognised by the Irish courts on a number of occasions.[28] Accordingly, it is apprehended that where an arbitration clause is clearly drawn so as to expressly or implicitly grant the arbitrator the power to dissolve the partnership, the courts will refuse to hear an application from one of the partners for the dissolution of the partnership under s 35.[29]

---

[24]   (\...contd) See generally Dowling-Hussey, Dunne and Tackaberry, *Arbitration Law* (2nd edn, 2014); Mansfield, *Arbitration Act 2010 and Model Law* (2012). See also Clark, *Contract Law in Ireland* (8th edn, 2016) at paras 15-05–15-06. See *Sugrue v Hibernian Bank* (1829) 2 Ir Law Rec 285 for a decision given prior to the Arbitration Act 2010. This case involved an application by one partner for an injunction to prevent his co-partners from using the firm's capital, the Master of the Rolls noting in relation to the arbitration clause that: '[i]s it not decided, that the Court will insist on an experiment being made first with the tribunal created by the deed, I admit, you are not deprived of the jurisdiction here, if even that is not done; but will not the Court in its discretion say, you must first try your own domestic tribunal.' See generally in relation to the attitude of the courts to staying proceedings between partners where the dispute is governed by an arbitration clause, para **[20.94]**.

[25]   In the absence of an arbitration alternative, it seems clear that the parties could not oust the court's jurisdiction by an agreement between the partners to that effect since this is contrary to public policy: *Mansfield v Doolin* (1868) 4 IRCL 17; *Gregg & Co v Fraser & Sons* [1906] 2 IR 545. See generally Clark, *Contract Law in Ireland* (8th edn, 2016) at paras 15-05 and 15-06.

[26]   *Olver v Hillier* [1959] 2 All ER 220.

[27]   *Olver v Hillier* [1959] 2 All ER 220 at 221. Although recognising this possibility, on the facts of the case, Roxburgh J queried whether this was the best choice for the parties and he exercised his discretion by not granting the stay: '[T]he dissolution of a partnership which involves the exercise of a judicial discretion under s 35(f) and which may involve the appointment of a receiver and manager, is again a matter which perhaps is more conveniently left in the hands of the court' [1959] 2 All ER 220 at 222. However, it is doubted whether this part of the case establishes a principle of general application. See l'Anson Banks, *Lindley & Banks on Partnership* (20th edn, 2017) at para 10-309.

[28]   See *Hutchinson v Whitfield* (1830) Hayes 78; *Larkin v Groeger and Eaton* (26 April 1988) HC; *Gargan v Ruttle* [1931] IR 152. See generally para **[20.87]**. Cf *Dennehy v Jolly* (1875) 9 ILTR 3 which, it is argued, is no longer good law, para **[20.90]**.

[29]   See also the Scottish case of *Roxburgh v Dinardo* (1981) SLT 291 and the New Zealand case of *Re Deed of Partnership between Arnold and Hutchinson* (1914) 33 NZLR 1461 in support of this view.

[25.16] Where the partners have actually referred the dispute to an arbitrator and granted him the power to dissolve the partnership under his power of appointment,[30] there can be no doubt that a court will not countenance an application to dissolve the partnership under s 35 of the 1890 Act.[31]

Where partnership agreement sets out causes of dissolution

[25.17] Related to the issue of an arbitrator being granted the power to dissolve a partnership, is the effect of the partners setting out in their partnership agreement the circumstances in which a partner may dissolve or seek the dissolution of the partnership. Unlike conferring upon an arbitrator the power to dissolve the partnership, such a provision will not restrict the jurisdiction of the court to order a dissolution under s 35 of the 1890 Act. In *Sugrue v Hibernian Bank*,[32] it was alleged that a dissolution could not have been granted by the court as the circumstances of the case did not fall within the list of causes of a dissolution set out in the partnership agreement.[33] However, MacMahon MR noted that:

'[t]hat may be the dissolution contemplated by the contract of the parties, but that does not affect the right to dissolve, founded on the misconduct of the parties.'[34]

It is apprehended that the same principle applies not just to misconduct but to all of the situations in which a court grants a dissolution under s 35 of the 1890 Act. Thus, the power of a court to dissolve a partnership is not restricted by the terms of the partnership agreement.[35]

[25.18] However, it is perhaps self-evident that the court will take account of the terms of the partnership agreement in exercising its discretion to order a dissolution under s 35. In *Heslin v Fay (1)*,[36] clause 29 of the partnership deed contained various terms regarding the manner in which the assets were to be valued and divided on 'any dissolution' of a grocery partnership in North King St in Dublin. One of the partners sought a court dissolution of the partnership on the basis that the other partner had abused his powers under the partnership agreement.[37] In granting a dissolution, the Irish Court of Appeal held that clause 29 should apply to a dissolution by court order.

---

[30] See *Hutchinson v Whitfield* (1830) Hayes 78, where Smith B held that an arbitrator may be expressly entrusted by the partners with the power to dissolve the partnership. See para **[20.87]**.

[31] See for example the case of *Phoenix v Pope* [1974] 1 All ER 512.

[32] *Sugrue v Hibernian Bank* (1829) 2 Ir Law Rec 285. Since this case was pre-1890, the court considered its inherent jurisdiction to dissolve partnerships rather than the power of a court to dissolve a partnership under s 35 of the 1890 Act.

[33] This was the reason put forward by the petitioner for not seeking a dissolution from the court, but rather an injunction. Accordingly the comments are obiter.

[34] *Sugrue v Hibernian Bank* (1829) 2 Ir Law Rec 285 at 292.

[35] Save insofar as the partners may confer this jurisdiction upon an arbitrator.

[36] *Heslin v Fay (1)* (1884) 15 LR Ir 431.

[37] The case was pre-1890 and therefore did not rely on s 35 of the 1890 Act, but rather on the inherent jurisdiction of the court to dissolve a partnership on the grounds of the conduct of the respondent partners.

Date of Dissolution

[25.19] Where there is a provision in a partnership agreement for the partnership to dissolve on the occurrence of a certain event such as death, bankruptcy or incapacity, it goes without saying that the partnership dissolves as of that date. However, s 35 of the 1890 Act is silent regarding the date of dissolution of a partnership dissolved by court order. While there is authority for the view that the date of dissolution is the date of the court's judgment,[38] Clarke J in *ACC Bank Plc v Johnston p/a Brian Johnston & Co Solicitors*[39] indicated that the date that court proceedings are issued could be the relevant date, commenting that 'it is, of course, open to a partner to go down the route of applying to court for a dissolution of the partnership. Where dissolution occurs as a result of a court process the dissolution is normally taken to date from the issue of proceedings'. Notwithstanding that obiter comment, it is submitted that the correct date of dissolution is the date of the court's judgment, whereas the issue of the proceedings instead signifies a partner's intention to have the partnership dissolved by the court. In practice in a court application for the dissolution of a partnership on the grounds of a partner's misconduct, the court may hold that the partnership was actually dissolved prior to the court hearing by the conduct of the partner. This happened in *Bolton v Carmichael*,[40] where an application was made for the court dissolution of a solicitors' partnership by Bolton on the grounds of Carmichael's conduct. Brady LC held that the partnership had been dissolved prior to the court hearing by the misconduct of Carmichael. Similarly in the High Court case of *Larkin v Groeger and Eaton*,[41] Barrington J upheld the award of an arbitrator[42] that an accountancy partnership had been dissolved by the actions of the partners in ignoring their duties to each other prior to the issue of proceedings.

---

[38] In *Besch v Frolich* (1842) 1 Ph 172, a distinction was drawn beween the date on which dissolution is treated as having occurred as between the partners themselves, and the date on which the dissolution takes place as regards third parties, with the court holding (following 'some doubt') that the date of dissolution of a partnership by the court should be the date of the decree of dissolution but that there was no reason why, as between the partners themselves, dissolution could not be treated as having taken place from the date that proceedings were taken. In *Lyon v Tweddell* (1881) 44 LT 785, that distinction was not drawn, with the Court of Appeal holding (per Jessell MR) that a partnership exists until judgment is pronounced and (per James LJ) that where the dissolution results from the partners not getting along, dissolution must be from the date of the Court's judgment (James LJ acknowledged that dissolution could take effect from an earlier date in the case of misconduct or breach, the finding of Lush LJ echoed that point). See also l'Anson Banks, *Lindley & Banks on Partnership* (20th edn, 2017) at paras 24-101-24.102.

[39] *ACC Bank Plc v Johnston p/a Brian Johnston & Co Solicitors* [2011] IEHC 108 at para 4.4 of the judgment.

[40] *Bolton v Carmichael* (1856) 1 Ir Jur (ns) 298.

[41] *Larkin v Groeger and Eaton* (26 April 1988) HC.

[42] John Gore Grimes, solicitor.

Costs of Dissolution Order

[25.20] The costs of a dissolution under s 35 of the 1890 Act are in general paid out of the partnership assets.[43] Where the application is unsuccessful, it is likely that costs will follow the award and be granted against the partners applying for the dissolution.

Other Statutory Provisions for the Dissolution of Partnerships

[25.21] While s 35 of the 1890 Act is the main statutory provision under which a partnership may be dissolved by court order, a partnership may also be wound up as an unregistered company under Part 22, Chapter 3 of the Companies Act 2014. Section 1326 of that Act defines an 'unregistered company' as including those partnerships which have eight or more members. Under the terms of Part 22, Chapter 3 of the Companies Act 2014, such a partnership may be compulsorily wound up by the court. The compulsory winding up of a partnership as an unregistered company is primarily of use to partnerships which are unable to pay their debts and accordingly this area is considered in the chapter on bankruptcy.[44]

II.   MENTAL INCAPACITY OF A PARTNER

[25.22] Having considered the terms of s 35 of the 1890 Act in general terms, it is now proposed to examine each of the instances in s 35 in which a court may grant a dissolution of the partnership, beginning with the mental incapacity of a partner.

Section 35(a) of the 1890 Act

[25.23] The mental incapacity of a partner does not of itself dissolve the partnership. However, under s 35(a) of the 1890 Act, when a partner is of unsound mind, a court application may be brought to have the partnership dissolved:[45]

> On application by a partner the Court may decree a dissolution of the partnership in any of the following cases:
>
> (a)   When a partner is found lunatic by inquisition, or in Scotland by cognition, or is shown to the satisfaction of the Court to be of permanently unsound mind, in either of which cases the application may be made as well on behalf of that partner by his committee or next friend or person having title to intervene as by any other partner.

Before the Court will decree a dissolution of the partnership on grounds of insanity, it must be satisfied that the insanity exists and is permanent.[46]

---

[43]   See *Jones v Welch* (1855) 1 Jur (ns) 994 (following *Besch v Frolich* (1842) 1 Ph 172) which dealt with an application under s 35(a) of the 1890 Act).

[44]   See para [27.06] et seq.

[45]   Note that the Lunacy Act 1890 (53 Vict, c 5) did not extend to Ireland. Section 35(a) of the 1890 Act was repealed in England by the Mental Health Act 1959 and there is now no express statutory power in England to dissolve a partnership on the basis of the mental incapacity of a partner – see further l'Anson Banks, *Lindley & Banks on Partnership* (20th edn, 2017) at 24-56.

[46]   See also *Kirby v Carr* (1838) 3 Y & C Ex 184.

[25.24] In addition to this power under s 35(a), s 73 of the Lunacy Regulation (Ireland) Act 1871[47] provides for the dissolution of a partnership involving a person of unsound mind. However, the Assisted Decision-Making Capacity Act 2015, when the relevant provisions of that Act are commenced in full, will repeal the 1871 Act.[48] The 2015 Act provides for various supports for individuals experiencing difficulties with mental capacity, by providing for the appointment of 'decision-making assistants', 'co-decision makers' and 'decision-making representatives'. The 2015 Act also contemplates a possible recovery of mental capacity. Given the absolute nature of the requirement in s 35(a) of the 1890 Act that a person be of 'permanently unsound mind' before the court will grant an order for dissolution under s 35(a), while the 2015 Act contemplates a more case-by-case approach to the assessment of a person's decision-making capacity, the appointment of persons to assist with decision-making, and the possibility of a recovery of mental capacity, it is apprehended that applications to court for the dissolution of a partnership under s 35(a) will now rarely, if ever, be made. Rather, the court may instead be asked to consider a dissolution on just and equitable grounds under s 35(f) where issues as to mental capacity arise.

[25.25] In the context of partners who experience issues with decision-making capacity, one should also bear in mind the potential application of the Powers of Attorney Act 1996 (in respect of enduring powers of attorney made prior to the commencement of Part 7 of the Assisted Decision-Making Capacity Act 2015) and the 2015 Act itself (in respect of enduring powers of attorney made after the commencement of Part 7 of that Act).[49] Under these provisions, an enduring power of attorney can operate when the donor of the power lacks capacity in respect of one or more decisions referred to in that power of attorney. Thus, where a partner has granted an enduring power of attorney over his partnership interest (which power of attorney has been duly registered under the relevant Act)[50] and that partner subsequently lacks capacity in respect of one or more decisions referred to therein, such a power of attorney may obviate the need for the unaffected partners to make an application to court to dissolve the partnership, since they will be able to deal with the donee of the power of attorney rather than the partner. While theoretically the unaffected partners may still apply for a court dissolution in such a case and may view a dissolution order as being important for example where the incapacitated partner is incapable of performing his obligations under the partnership agreement, it should be noted that a court is less likely to order a dissolution of the partnership on the grounds of mental incapacity where the partner in question is a dormant partner (since his incapacity should have less impact on the firm) and in view of the fact that the 2015 Act contemplates a possible return to capacity, and not a 'permanent' incapacity.[51]

---

[47] (34 & 35 Vict, c 22). Note also the possibility that a mentally unsound partner may have previously executed an enduring power of attorney under the Powers of Attorney Act 1996, see para **[25.25]**.

[48] See further para **[4.19]** in relation to the Assisted Decision-Making Capacity Act 2015.

[49] At the time of writing, Part 7 of the Assisted Decision-Making Capacity Act 2015 has not yet been commenced.

[50] Powers of Attorney Act 1996, s 10; Assisted Decision-Making Capacity Act 2015, s 69.

[51] See para **[6.10]** and para **[25.27]**.

'application ... on behalf of that partner'

[25.26] Section 35(a) of the 1890 Act allows an application to be made for the dissolution of the partnership not only by the 'innocent' partners but also on behalf of the mentally incapacitated partner. This contrasts with sub-ss (b), (c) and (d) of s 35, where the application may only be made by the 'innocent' partner. In general, when the court dissolves a partnership on the grounds of insanity, the costs of the application are paid out of the partnership assets.[52]

Effect of s 35(b) on Interpretation of s 35(a)

[25.27] Section 35(b) of the 1890 Act states that a court may also dissolve a partnership when a partner becomes 'in any other way' permanently incapable of performing his part of the partnership contract. In contrast, s 35(a) does not expressly require the mentally incapacitated partner to be 'permanently incapable of performing his part of the partnership contract', but instead requires the court to be satisfied that his incapacity is permanent. The implication of the use of the expression 'in any other way' in s 35(b) is that s 35(a) deals with mental incapacity leading to a partner being permanently incapable of performing his part of the partnership contract, while s 35(b) deals with other forms of incapacity which have the same effect. Thus, s 35(a) may be seen as an example of the general principle in s 35(b). On this basis, it seems that s 35(a) must be interpreted as requiring not just permanent mental incapacity of the partner, but also that the incapacitated partner is incapable of performing his part of the partnership contract. It is submitted that, having regard to the requirement that incapacity under s 35(a) be 'permanent', applications under s 35(a) will be rare when the Assisted Decision-Making Capacity Act 2015 is commenced in full.[53] Further, as regards a dormant partner, his mental incapacity may have no such consequence since he will have no duties to perform in the partnership. For this reason, it is contended that the mental incapacity of a dormant partner may not have led to the firm's dissolution before the Assisted Decision-Making Capacity Act 2015, and is even less likely to do so now. Support for this view is to be found in the Scottish case of *Eadie v McBean's Curator Bonis*.[54] There, the court refused to order the dissolution of the partnership where the incapacitated partner had no active duties in the management of the firm but had merely provided the capital and where the *curator bonis* of the insane partner opposed the application.[55]

---

52 *Jones v Welch* (1855) 1 Jur (ns) 994.

53 See para [25.24] above.

54 *Eadie v McBean's Curator Bonis* (1885) 12 R 660.

55 In the event that an application for dissolution under s 35(a) is taken, the rule that the date of the court order will in general be the precise date of dissolution of a partnership when it is dissolved by court order will apply equally to the dissolution of a partnership as a result of mental incapacity (regardless of the date the partner becomes of unsound mind) (*Besch v Frolich* (1842) 1 Ph 172; *Sander v Sander* (1845) 2 Coll 276; *Jones v Welch* (1855) 1 Jur (ns) 994). Of course, if the partnership agreement itself provides for the automatic dissolution of the partnership on the mental incapacity of a partner, this is a separate issue as the dissolution will derive from the agreement and not from any court order. Accordingly, a subsequent order of the court regarding such a dissolution will date from the actual dissolution of the partnership and not from the date of the court order. (*Bagshaw v Parker* (1847) 10 Beav 532; *Robertson v Lockie* (1846) 15 Sim 285).

Conflict between Agency Law and Partnership Law

[25.28] Under general agency law, the mental incapacity of a principal terminates the agency.[56] However, it has been seen that under partnership law, the mental incapacity of a partner does not ipso facto dissolve the partnership.[57] Since the partnership continues, the agency of one partner to act on behalf of his mentally incapacitated partner continues. In this respect, the partnership relationship is an exception to this general rule of agency law. This perhaps can be justified on the basis that it is possible for a partner to be dormant and thus have no active role in the partnership. Accordingly, it follows that the agency relationship can continue despite his supervening mental incapacity. Where the incapacitated partner is an active partner, the unaffected partner may apply to court for a dissolution of the partnership under s 35(a).

III. PERMANENT INCAPACITY OF A PARTNER

[25.29] Section 35(b) states that:

> On application by a partner the Court may decree a dissolution of the partnership in any of the following cases ...
>
> (b) When a partner, other than the partner suing, becomes in any other way permanently incapable of performing his part of the partnership contract.

'other than the partner suing'

[25.30] Unlike the case of a person who is found to be mentally incapacitated under s 35(a), where a person is otherwise incapacitated, an application under s 35(b) may not be made on behalf of the affected partner. The application may only be made by the unaffected partners.

Why not allow incapacitated partner to petition court?

[25.31] The issue of permitting an incapacitated partner to petition court is deserving of further consideration. There would appear to be no reason in principle for allowing an affected partner to petition for a court dissolution in the case of a mental incapacity, but not in the case of a general incapacity. The rationale for preventing the affected (or guilty) partner from petitioning for a dissolution is clear in the case of a wilful breach of the partnership agreement (s 35(d)), ie otherwise a partner who wishes to seek a court dissolution of the partnership would have an incentive to wilfully breach the agreement. However, this is hardly applicable in the case of non-mental incapacity. Just as it is impossible to envisage a partner, who wishes to dissolve the partnership, intentionally suffering a mental incapacity, it is almost as difficult to envisage a situation in which such a partner would intentionally cause his own non-mental incapacity.[58] It is hard to

---

[56] *Yonge v Tonybee* [1910] 1 KB 215.

[57] See para [25.23].

[58] Especially when one is dealing with a physical incapacity. In the case of a non-physical incapacity, such as the loss of a practising certificate, it may be possible for the partner to intentionally cause this incapacity. However, even in such a situation, what is being suggested is simply that the incapacitated partner be allowed to petition the court for the dissolution of the partnership. Once the petition is made, the court has a complete discretion as to whether to grant the dissolution, see para [25.11].

find any justification for the discriminatory treatment of generally incapacitated partners especially when one considers that the granting of a dissolution is in any event subject to the court's discretion. Rather than being treated in the same manner as a partner with a mental incapacity, a partner with a general incapacity is treated in the same way as a partner who has committed a wilful breach of the agreement under s 35(d) or who is guilty of misconduct calculated to prejudicially affect the partnership business under s 35(c). To take an example, a partner in a professional firm who becomes blind, and who can no longer carry out his part of the partnership contract, is treated the same way as if he was guilty of misconduct. He is not entitled to petition for the dissolution of the partnership under s 35(b),[59] yet his co-partners may do so. This differing treatment is even more difficult to justify when one considers that a partner who causes a partnership loss, intentionally, recklessly or otherwise, is not prevented from petitioning for the firm's dissolution on the grounds that the business may only be carried on at a loss under s 35(e). This discriminatory treatment of physical and other non-mental incapacity is a relic of the Victorian perspective of such illness and should, it is contended, be abandoned.

Types of Incapacity

[25.32] While s 35(a) deals expressly with mental incapacity, s 35(b) is broad enough to cover any type of incapacity, other than mental incapacity. This is clear as s 35(b) refers to a partner becoming 'in any other way' permanently incapable of performing his part of the partnership contract, obviously referring to something other than mental incapacity in s 35(a). Thus s 35(b) would, for example, cover any physical incapacity such as loss of hearing, loss of vision, paralysis, etc, which in many partnerships would render it impossible for the affected partner to continue in business. However, the term is not restricted to physical incapacity and it would be broad enough to cover an application to dissolve a partnership on the basis of a non-physical incapacity which rendered him incapable of performing his part of the partnership contract, eg the permanent loss by a partner in a professional practice of his practising certificate.[60]

'permanently incapable'

[25.33] By its express terms, s 35(b) requires the incapacity to be of a permanent nature. In *Whitwell v Arthur*,[61] an attack of paralysis prevented a partner from performing his partnership duties. However, since medical evidence indicated that the paralysis might only be temporary, the petition for the dissolution of the partnership was refused.

---

[59] He could of course argue that he is entitled to a dissolution on just and equitable grounds under s 35(f) of the 1890 Act.

[60] This is one instance of non-mental incapacity where it could be argued that the affected partner was at fault. However, it is doubted that this exceptional type of case justifies denying all partners affected by non-mental incapacity the right to petition the court under s 35(b) of the 1890 Act.

[61] *Whitwell v Arthur* (1865) 35 Beav 140.

IV. CONDUCT PREJUDICIAL TO THE PARTNERSHIP BUSINESS

[25.34] Section 35(c) of the 1890 Act states that:

> On application by a partner the Court may decree a dissolution of the partnership in any of the following cases ...
>
> (c) When a partner, other than the partner suing, has been guilty of such conduct as, in the opinion of the Court, regard being had to the nature of the business, is calculated to prejudicially affect the carrying on of the business.

'other than the partner suing'

[25.35] Like s 35(b) and (d), an application under s 35(c), may not be made on behalf of the guilty partner, but only by the innocent partners.

'in the opinion of the court'

[25.36] By its use of the phrase 'in the opinion of the court', s 35(c) requires the court to form a subjective view of whether the conduct was calculated to prejudicially affect the carrying on of the firm's business. The Court must take into account the nature of the partnership business in reaching this conclusion. However, there is no requirement that this conduct be connected with the partnership business, though it must be calculated to prejudicially affect the partnership business. Thus, a partner's criminal actions may have been committed completely separate from his partnership, but yet may fall within the terms of s 35(c).

'guilty of such conduct ... calculated'

[25.37] The use in s 35(c) of the phrase 'guilty of such conduct ... as is calculated to prejudicially affect' connotes a strong degree of culpability on the part of the partner. Accordingly, it is thought that the conduct in question must be done with the intention of causing harm to the partnership and not simply that it has a possibility of harming the partnership business.[62] Where the requisite intent is absent, it may be more appropriate for an application to be made under the second limb of s 35(d) of the 1890 Act, since that limb does not require an intent to harm the partnership.

V. WILFUL OR PERSISTENT BREACH OF THE PARTNERSHIP AGREEMENT

[25.38] Section 35(d) of the 1890 Act states that:

> On application by a partner the Court may decree a dissolution of the partnership in any of the following cases ...
>
> (d) When a partner, other than the partner suing, wilfully or persistently commits a breach of the partnership agreement, or otherwise so conducts himself in matters relating to the partnership business that it is not reasonably practicable for the other partner or partners to carry on the business in partnership with him.

---

[62] For a contrary view see l'Anson Banks, *Lindley & Banks on Partnership* (20th edn, 2017) at para 24-86 and Brough, *Miller on Partnership* (2nd edn, 1994) at p 483–284.

First Limb of s 35(d)

[25.39] Section 35(d) may be divided into two limbs. Under the first limb, a court may dissolve the partnership where one partner has been guilty of a wilful or persistent breach of the partnership agreement. While the drafting of the section is far from clear on the point, it is contended that the first limb requires the wilful or persistent breach of the partnership agreement to be of such a nature so as to make it reasonably impracticable for the other partners to continue in partnership. Otherwise, wilful or persistent breaches of a minor nature would entitle the innocent partners to petition for a dissolution.[63] An example of such a minor breach might be the failure of a partner to comply with the common requirement in partnership agreements that partners have their own separate life insurance cover.

'other than the partner suing'

[25.40] Like s 35(b) and (c), an application under the first limb of s 35(d) may not be made on behalf of the guilty partner, but only by the innocent partners.

'wilfully or persistently'

[25.41] Since the breach of the terms of the partnership agreement must be either wilful or persistent, an application under s 35(d) may not be made in the case of either an accidental or isolated breach of the partnership agreement by a partner. *Heslin v Fay (1)*[64] provides an example of a case where a dissolution order was made as a result of the wilful breach of the terms of the partnership agreement. There, the partnership deed for a grocery partnership in North King Street in Dublin provided that each partner was entitled to withdraw any surplus capital in the firm which had been advanced by him. When Heslin called on his partners to repay him his surplus capital, they refused to do so and instead claimed that they had raised the capital of the firm by admitting another partner and this had the effect of swamping Heslin's surplus capital.[65] This claim was unsubstantiated and it was held by the Irish Court of Appeal that the decision by the other partners to refuse to return the capital was a wilful breach of the partnership agreement which justified an order for the dissolution of the partnership. In *Golstein v Bishop*,[66] Christopher Nugee QC[67] found that Mr Bishop had been persistently obstructive when the partnership's accounts were being prepared, had made unilateral decisions regarding staff, clients and the premises of the partnership, and had regularly undermined his co-partner, Mr Golstein. While this case was not an application for dissolution under s 35(d) of the 1890 Act, the judge commented that had it been, he would have found that the grounds for such a dissolution had been met.

---

63 For a contrary view see l'Anson Banks, *Lindley & Banks on Partnership* (20th edn, 2017) at para 24-92.

64 *Heslin v Fay (1)* (1884) 15 LR Ir 431. See also *Bolton v Carmichael* (1856) 1 Ir Jur (ns) 298.

65 The allegation that they raised the capital by admitting another partner was unsubstantiated. Even if this claim could have been substantiated, the Court of Appeal held that the capital was not raised in bona fide manner and on this basis it could also have been argued that the terms of the partnership agreement were breached.

66 *Golstein v Bishop* [2014] Ch 131.

67 Sitting as a deputy judge of the High Court.

Petitioner should not Acquiesce in Misconduct

[25.42] It goes without saying that a petitioner who seeks a dissolution of the partnership should not have acquiesced in the conduct which he alleges justifies the dissolution. In *Heslin v Fay (1)*,[68] the partnership agreement provided that the partnership business in North King Street in Dublin was to be operated separately from Fay's own business in Thomas Street. Heslin claimed, inter alia, that the partnership should be dissolved on the basis of Fay's failure to comply with this term of the partnership agreement. However in the Irish Court of Appeal, Sir Edward Sullivan C held that this 'misconduct' had been acquiesced in by Heslin and he observed that 'he undid the deed by his own act, and acquiesced in its being disregarded for ten years, and he cannot now complain'.[69]

VI. MISCONDUCT RENDERING CONTINUANCE IMPRACTICAL

Second Limb of s 35(d)

[25.43] The second limb of s 35(d) of the 1890 Act allows for a dissolution of a partnership where the misconduct of a partner relating to the partnership business makes it impractical to carry on the business in partnership. This is broader than the first limb, since it applies, not just to breaches of the partnership agreement, but to all misconduct.

'other than the partner suing'

[25.44] Like s 35(b) and (c), an application under the second limb of s 35(d) may not be made on behalf of the guilty partner, but only by the innocent partner(s). In many cases of internal disagreement between partners, no partner will be completely innocent. For this reason, the more appropriate application in cases of internal feuding may be an application for dissolution on just and equitable grounds under s 35(f).[70]

'relating to the partnership business'

[25.45] The second limb of s 35(d) requires the misconduct to relate to the partnership business. In this regard it is distinguishable from s 35(c) where the misconduct need not relate to the business. However, unlike s 35(c), there is no requirement under s 35(d) that the conduct be calculated to prejudicially affect the carrying on of the partnership business.

Degree of Misconduct

[25.46] What is envisaged by the second limb of s 35(d) is an irretrievable breakdown of relations between the partners. The court will not order a dissolution of a partnership on the basis of minor partnership squabbles or personality clashes. Rather, the misconduct must be such as to contravene the principles of equality, trust and confidence which should exist between partners.

---

[68] *Heslin v Fay (1)* (1884) 15 LR Ir 431.
[69] *Heslin v Fay (1)* (1884) 15 LR Ir 431 at 445.
[70] See for example the quasi-partnership case of *Re Vehicle Buildings* [1986] ILRM 239, considered at para **[25.58]** et seq where both partners were at fault for the deadlock.

Repudiation of equality, trust and confidence

[25.47] An early example of a case where there was such a repudiation of equality, trust and confidence between the partners is *Bolton v Carmichael*.[71] There, Bolton joined Carmichael as a partner in his solicitor's practice. The partnership deed provided for Carmichael to provide Bolton with half-yearly accounts, but this was never done. Although the case concerned a petition by Bolton for the partnership to be dissolved by court, Brady LC held that the partnership had in fact been dissolved by the actions of Carmichael. It was held that the actions of Carmichael towards his partner, who was also his nephew, were in contravention of the principles of equality and mutual cordiality and confidence which one expects in a partnership:

> '[T]here was throughout the existence of the partnership an assumption of superiority which may have been natural enough considering the relationship or rather connection between them, but which was very inconsistent with that equality which should exist between partners. When [Carmichael] is desirous of dissolving it he does not communicate directly with his partner, but he writes to the young man's father, treating the petitioner more like an apprentice than a partner, and as if his voice in the matter was quite a secondary consideration, whilst his last letter to the petitioner is calculated to irritate, and to convince the petitioner that the partnership could not be carried on upon those terms on which alone it could have been carried on satisfactorily, namely, equality and mutual cordiality and confidence.'[72]

[25.48] *Re Murph's Restaurant Ltd*[73] is another example of one where there was a repudiation of this relationship of equality and confidence between the partners. That case involved a quasi-partnership. As has been noted elsewhere in this work, a quasi-partnership is an entity which is in form a company, but in substance a partnership such that it is appropriate to apply the principles of partnership law to it.[74] There, two brothers and the petitioner were equal shareholders and the sole directors in a company. The two brothers treated the petitioner as if he was their employee and sought to dismiss him as a director of the company. Gannon J held that this was a 'repudiation of the relationship of equality, mutuality, trust and confidence'[75] which constituted the very essence of their business relationship. By analogy with s 35(d) of the 1890 Act, the petition to wind-up the company was granted since as a result of the misconduct of the two brothers, it was not reasonably practicable for the petitioner to carry on in business with them.

[25.49] The absence of any continued confidence between the partners was also an important factor in the winding up of the quasi-partnership in *Re Vehicle Buildings*.[76] The quasi-partnership in this case was a private company which was owned by a Ms Fitzpatrick and a Mr Howley in equal proportions and in which they were the sole

---

71   *Bolton v Carmichael* (1856) 1 Ir Jur (ns) 298. The case was framed as an application for the dissolution of the partnership, but the court held that the partnership had been previously dissolved by the actions of the defendant.
72   *Bolton v Carmichael* (1856) 1 Ir Jur (ns) 298 at 302.
73   *Re Murph's Restaurant Ltd* [1979] ILRM 141.
74   See generally in relation to quasi-partnerships, para **[8.67]** et seq.
75   *Re Murph's Restaurant Ltd* [1979] ILRM 141 at 151.
76   *Re Vehicle Buildings* [1986] ILRM 239. An appeal to the Supreme Court was dismissed in an ex tempore judgment on 10 March 1986 and the order of Murphy J was upheld.

directors. The relationship between the two broke down leading to a state of deadlock in the management of the company. Murphy J granted an order for the winding up of the company on just and equitable grounds under s 213(f) of the Companies Act 1963.[77] Although the winding up was ostensibly granted by analogy with s 35(f) of the 1890 Act (dissolution of a partnership on just and equitable grounds), a close reading of the case shows that Murphy J relied extensively on the provisions of s 35(d) of the 1890 Act.[78] Murphy J expressly adopted the judgment of Lord Cozens-Hardy MR in *Re Yenidje Tobacco Co Ltd*[79] regarding the effect of a state of deadlock on a quasi-partnership:

> 'I think it is quite clear under the law of partnership, as has been asserted in this Court for many years and is now laid down by the Partnership Act, that that state of things might be a ground for dissolution of the partnership for the reasons which are stated by Lord Lindley in his book on Partnership.'[80]

[25.50] Murphy J goes on to quote Lord Lindley's reasons for the winding up of a partnership under s 35(d) of the 1890 Act:

> 'Refusal to meet on matters of business, continued quarrelling, and such a state of animosity as precludes all reasonable hope of reconciliation and friendly co-operation have been held sufficient to justify a dissolution. It is not necessary, in order to induce the court to interfere, to show personal rudeness on the part of one partner to the other, or even any gross misconduct as a partner. All that is necessary is to satisfy the court that it is impossible for the partners to place that confidence in each other which each has a right to expect, and that such impossibility has not been caused by the person seeking to take advantage of it.'[81]

Applying these principles to the state of deadlock between Ms Fitzpatrick and Ms Howley, Murphy J granted the winding up order.

VII. PARTNERSHIP CARRIED ON AT A LOSS

[25.51] It has been seen elsewhere in this work that a partnership will only exist if it is formed with a 'view of profit'.[82] It should not be surprising, therefore, that under s 35(e) of the 1890 Act, a court may dissolve a partnership when its business can only be carried on at a loss.

Any Partner may Petition

[25.52] Unlike s 35(b), (c) and (d), under s 35(e) of the 1890 Act, any partner in the firm may petition the court for the firm's dissolution. Thus, even where the partner's reckless trading has caused the loss in question, he may petition the court for the firm's dissolution. Allowing all partners to petition for a dissolution on the basis that the

---

77 The predecessor to s 569(e) of the Companies Act 2014.
78 It is interesting to note that if the company had in fact been a partnership, the petitioner would not have been able to bring an action under s 35(d) of the 1890 Act since she was not innocent of any misconduct herself as required by that section, see para **[25.40]**.
79 *Re Yenidje Tobacco Co Ltd* [1916] 2 Ch 426.
80 *Re Yenidje Tobacco Co Ltd* [1916] 2 Ch 426 at 430.
81 *Re Yenidje Tobacco Co Ltd* [1916] 2 Ch 426 at 430.
82 Partnership Act 1890, s 1(1) and see further para **[2.62]** et seq.

partnership can only be carried on at a loss, is obviously based on the reasonable assumption that a partner is unlikely to cause a loss to his own partnership, and indirectly to himself, in order to ground a claim for the firm's dissolution.

'can only be carried on at a loss'

[25.53] The requirement that the partnership 'can only be carried on at a loss' means that the partnership business must have no prospect of profit.[83] If the losses incurred by a firm are attributable to special and temporary circumstances, rather than an inherent defect in the business, then the court will not order the firm's dissolution.[84] It is not necessary that the firm be insolvent. Indeed, it may even have considerable cash reserves, but if the business can only be carried on at a loss, the court may dissolve the firm under s 35(e). On the other hand, the court may not dissolve a firm which is temporarily insolvent or making heavy trading losses but where there is a prospect of future profit. This is because what is envisaged by s 35(e) is not simply that the firm is temporarily running at a loss, but that the firm's business is irretrievably unprofitable. Thus in *Jennings v Baddeley*,[85] the capital of the firm had been exhausted and for the business to return to profit, further capital was required from the partners. This capital was not forthcoming and accordingly the court ordered the firm's dissolution.

[25.54] It is hardly surprising that the corollary of s 35(e) does not apply, ie a partnership which is profitable is obviously not immune from a dissolution order under the other sub-sections of s 35.[86]

VIII. DISSOLUTION ON JUST AND EQUITABLE GROUNDS

[25.55] The final subsection of s 35 of the 1890 Act allows the dissolution of a partnership on just and equitable grounds.[87] Section 35(f) is in almost identical terms to s 569(e) of the Companies Act 2014 which provides for the winding up of companies on just and equitable grounds. By analogy with the cases decided under s 569(e) of the 2014 Act,[88] it seems clear that s 35(f) should not be restricted in its scope by the previous sections of s 35, but is to be interpreted *sui generis*.[89] This is confirmed by the

---

83   *Handyside v Campbell* [1901] 17 TLR 623.
84   *Handyside v Campbell* [1901] 17 TLR 623 at 624 per Farwell J.
85   *Jennings v Baddeley* (1856) 3 Jur (ns) 108.
86   See for example the quasi-partnership of *Re Vehicles Buildings* [1986] ILRM 239 where Murphy J ordered the winding up of a profitable company on the basis of the deadlock between the two shareholders. An appeal to the Supreme Court was dismissed in an ex tempore judgment on 10 March 1986.
87   See generally Webb, 'Dissolving Partnerships: "just and equitable"' (1996) NZLJ 445; Sammon, 'Winding up on the "just and equitable" ground - an untrammelled discretion' (2014) 32(7) ILT 101-104).
88   And its predecessor, s 213(f) of the Companies Act 1963.
89   See *Re Amalgamated Syndicate* [1897] 2 Ch 600; *Re Yenidje Tobacco Co Ltd* [1916] 2 Ch 426. For an early Irish example of a liberal interpretation of the just and equitable ground for winding up a company, see *Re Newbridge Sanitary Laundry Ltd* [1917] 1 IR 237. For a detailed treatment of the cases decided under s 213(f) of the Companies Act 1963, see Courtney, *The Law of Companies* (4th edn, 2017) at para [24.119] et seq.

judgment of Gannon J in *Re Murph's Restaurant Ltd,*[90] where he quoted with approval from the statement of Lord Wilberforce in *Ebrahimi v Westbourne Galleries*[91] on the meaning of 'just and equitable':[92]

> 'For some 50 years, following a pronouncement by Lord Cottenham LC [*Spackman, ex parte* (1849) 1 Mac and G 170, 174] in 1849, the words "just and equitable" were interpreted so as only to include matters *ejusdem generis* as the preceding clauses of the section, but there is now ample authority for discarding this limitation.'[93]

Although Gannon J was dealing with a quasi-partnership, rather than a partnership, there can be little doubt that the same principles apply to a partnership.

Refer to s 569(e) of Companies Act 2014

[25.56] In view of the similarity between s 569(e) of the Companies Act 2014 and s 35(f) of the 1890 Act, the principles applied by the courts in s 569(e) cases (and cases under its predecessor, s 213(f) of the Companies Act 1963) will be of assistance in determining the likely approach of the courts in partnership cases. In the High Court case of *Re Murph's Restaurant,*[94] a case under s 213(f) of the 1963 Act, Gannon J relied on the principles enunciated by the courts in the s 35(f) cases. This approach was justified since:[95]

> 'The same words "just and equitable" appear in the Partnership Act 1892 s 25[96] as a ground for dissolution of a partnership and no doubt the considerations which they reflect formed part of the common law of partnership before its codification. The importance of this is to provide a bridge between cases under [s 569(e)][97] and the principles of equity developed in relation to partnerships.'[98]

Clearly this bridge is not one-way so that the cases on which it is just and equitable to wind up a company under s 569(e) will provide assistance in determining the situations in which a court will dissolve a partnership on just and equitable grounds under s 35(f).

[25.57] The two seminal Irish quasi-partnership cases which relied on the just and equitable grounds of s 35(f) (ie *Re Murph's Restaurant Ltd*[99] and *Re Vehicle Buildings*[100]) involved a loss of confidence amongst the partners which could have been dealt with under s 35(d) of the 1890 Act. This illustrates that in deciding whether it is just and

---

90   *Re Murph's Restaurant Ltd* [1979] ILRM 141.
91   *Ebrahimi v Westbourne Galleries* [1973] AC 360 at 374.
92   He was referring to the use of the phrase 'just and equitable' in the English equivalent of s 569(e) of the Companies Act 2014 at that time, namely s 222(f) of the Companies Act 1948.
93   *Re Murph's Restaurant Ltd* [1979] ILRM 141 at 153.
94   *Re Murph's Restaurant Ltd* [1979] ILRM 141.
95   Quoting from the judgment of Lord Wilberforce in *Ebrahimi v Westbourne Galleries Ltd* [1973] AC 360 at 374.
96   This is obviously a typing error and should refer to 'the Partnership Act 1890, s 35'.
97   The English equivalent of s 569(e) of the Companies Act 2014 at that time was s 222(f) of the Companies Act 1948.
98   *Re Murph's Restaurant Ltd* [1979] ILRM 141 at 153.
99   *Re Murph's Restaurant Ltd* [1979] ILRM 141.
100   *Re Vehicle Buildings* [1986] ILRM 239.

equitable to grant a dissolution of a partnership, the court will attach importance to factors which would fall to be considered under ss 35(a) to (e) of the 1890 Act. For this reason, any future applications for the dissolution of a partnership are likely to be brought under s 35(f) so as to ensure that all possible factors are considered by the court.

Any Partner may Petition?

[25.58] Unlike ss 35(b), (c) and (d), a partner who is guilty of misconduct is not prevented from applying for a dissolution of the partnership under the express terms of s 35(f) of the 1890 Act. This is clear from *Re Vehicle Buildings*.[101] As has been noted,[102] the company at the centre of this case was a quasi-partnership and therefore the court applied principles of partnership law to it. As there was complete deadlock between the two sole shareholders/directors in the company, it was argued that the company should be wound-up on the grounds that if it were a partnership it would be just and equitable to dissolve it. The respondent defended the petition on the basis that a petitioner who relies on the 'just and equitable' ground must come to court with clean hands[103] and as the breakdown in relations between the two was due partly to the petitioner's conduct, the application should be refused. In the High Court, Murphy J stated:

> 'whilst I am not by any means prepared to exculpate the petitioner from any wrong-doing I do not feel that I would be justified either in concluding that she was guilty of such misconduct as would dis-entitle her in the particular circumstances of this case to have an order made which seems to be required not only in her interest but in the interests of the creditors of the company.'[104]

[25.59] Thus a partner who is implicated in some way in the problems which ground an application for the partnership to be wound up on just and equitable grounds will not be prevented by this fact from petitioning for the dissolution. However, a court will not order a dissolution of a partnership under s 35(f) if the conduct of the petitioning partner was the primary or sole cause of the problems justifying the dissolution. Thus, in *Re Murph's Restaurant Ltd*,[105] Gannon J quoted with approval from the judgment of Lord Cross in *Ebrahimi v Westbourne Galleries Ltd*:[106]

> 'If neither [partner] has any longer confidence in the other so that they cannot work together in the way originally contemplated then the relationship should be ended – unless, indeed, the party who wishes to end it has been solely responsible for the situation which has arisen.'[107]

[25.60] Therefore, a petitioner under s 35(f) of the 1890 Act who has been guilty of some misconduct will not be deprived of a dissolution of the partnership on this ground

---

Re Vehicle Buildings [1986] ILRM 239.
102 See para **[25.49]**.
103 See generally in relation to this maxim of equity, Keane, *Equity and the Law of Trusts in Ireland* (3rd edn, 2017) at para 3.18 et seq and Biehler, *Equity and the Law of Trusts in Ireland* (6th edn, 2016) at p 21 et seq.
104 *Re Vehicle Buildings* [1986] ILRM 239 at 243. The decision of the High Court was upheld by the Supreme Court on appeal in an ex tempore judgment on 10 March 1986.
105 *Re Murph's Restaurant Ltd* [1979] ILRM 141.
106 *Ebrahimi v Westbourne Galleries Ltd* [1973] AC 360 at 384.
107 Quoted at *Re Murph's Restaurant Ltd* [1979] ILRM 141 at 153.

alone, provided that his misconduct is not the sole or primary cause of the circumstances justifying the dissolution.

Shifting Onus of Proof in Deadlock Cases

[25.61] The presence of deadlock between partners is a classic example of a case where a court will order the dissolution of a partnership on the grounds that is just and equitable to do so, as happened in the quasi-partnership case of *Re Vehicle Buildings*.[108] In cases of deadlock, no management decisions can be taken because of an even division of power between diametrically opposed views and thus 'no business which deserves the name of business in the affairs of the company can be carried on'.[109] *Re Vehicle Buildings*[110] is also authority for the proposition that, once the petitioner has established deadlock in the relations between the partners, the onus is then shifted to the respondent partner(s) to show some means by which the deadlock can be solved. In the absence of such evidence, the court will order the dissolution of the partnership. Murphy J stated:

> 'Essentially – or so it would seem-this argument relates to the onus of proof. I accept that the petitioner must establish the case in relation to deadlock. However, in a case such as the present where the petitioner establishes equality of shareholding and equality of management and a complete unwillingness of each party to co-operate with each other it seems to me that to put it at its lowest that the onus shifts to the respondent or the company to show some means by which this apparently insoluble problem may be resolved.'[111]

Can the business be continued?

[25.62] However, Lord Hoffmann, in delivering the House of Lords decision in *O'Neill v Phillips*,[112] indicated that if it is possible for the business of the partnership to be continued, an order for dissolution of the partnership is unlikely to be granted:

> 'There are cases, such as *In re A Company*[113] ... in which it has been said that if a breakdown in relations has caused the majority to remove a shareholder from participation in the management, it is usually a waste of time to try to investigate who caused the breakdown. Such breakdowns often occur (as in this case) without either side having done anything seriously wrong or unfair. It is not fair to the excluded member, who will usually have lost his employment, to keep his assets locked in the company. But that does not mean that a member who has not been dismissed or excluded can demand that his shares be purchased simply because he feels that he has lost trust and confidence in the others. I rather doubt whether even in partnership law a dissolution would be granted on this ground in a case in which it was still possible under the articles for the business of the

---

108 *Re Vehicle Buildings* [1986] ILRM 239.
109 Per Lord Cozens-Hardy MR in *Re Yenidje Tobacco Company Ltd* [1916] 2 Ch 426 at 431. The reference is to 'company' since this case involved a quasi-partnership.
110 *Re Vehicle Buildings* [1986] ILRM 239.
111 *Re Vehicle Buildings* [1986] ILRM 239 at 242. The decision of the High Court was upheld by the Supreme Court on appeal in an ex tempore judgment on 10 March 1986.
112 *O'Neill v Phillips* [1999] BCC 600, considered by Binchy J in *Hamill v Vantage Resources Limited & anor* [2015] IEHC 195.
113 *In re A Company* [1989] 5 BCC 218.

partnership to be continued. And as Lord Wilberforce observed in *In re Westbourne Galleries Ltd*[114]… one should not press the quasi-partnership analogy too far: "A company, however small, however domestic, is a company not a partnership or even a quasi-partnership …".'

---

[114]   *Ebrahimi v Westbourne Galleries Ltd* [1973] AC 360.

Chapter 26

Post-Dissolution and Winding Up of a Partnership

INTRODUCTION

[26.01] In the preceding chapters, consideration is given to the separate ways in which a partnership may be dissolved, namely dissolution by court order and dissolution without the need for court intervention. It is now proposed to deal with the consequences of a dissolution of a partnership and in particular the winding up of a firm. These matters are considered under the following headings:

I. General Consequences of a Firm's Dissolution;
II. Winding up of Firm's Business;
III. Return of Premiums;
IV. Post-Dissolution Profits; and
V. Distribution of Assets.

Overview

[26.02] The dissolution of a partnership raises a number of different issues, some of which have been considered earlier in this work, such as the appointment of a receiver to a partnership[1] and the entitlement of the partners to the firm's goodwill on a dissolution.[2] In this chapter, reference is made to the remaining issues on the dissolution of a partnership, ranging from the general consequences of the dissolution of a partnership, such as the right of the partners to publicly notify the dissolution, to the distribution of firm's assets as part of its winding up.

[26.03] As was done in Chapter 23, it is important to draw the distinction between a technical and a general dissolution of a partnership, in light of the confusion surrounding this area. It has been noted that this confusion is attributable in part to the term 'dissolution' being used to describe both a technical and a general dissolution. Indeed, considerable benefit would result from the use of a different nomenclature.[3] That chapter deals with the causes of dissolution of a partnership and in particular the events in the life of a partnership which cause the technical dissolution of the firm (ie a dissolution in the sense of a change in the membership of the firm which does not necessarily lead to its winding up). Yet each of those events has the potential to lead to the general dissolution of the firm (ie a dissolution which leads to the firm's winding up)

---

[1] See para [20.64] et seq.

[2] See para [18.18] et seq. As to the tax considerations in respect of goodwill where it is to pass to the continuing partners on the departure of a partner, see the case of *Attorney-General v Boden* [1912] 1 KB 539.

[3] See para [23.10] in which it is suggested that more appropriate terms would be a disassociation of the partnership and a termination of the partnership.

since on any dissolution of a firm,[4] a partner has the right under s 39 of the 1890 Act to have the partnership wound up. Chapter 25 considers the dissolution of a partnership by court order and in most cases this will involve the winding up of the partnership.[5]

[26.04] While this chapter considers the winding up of a partnership, it is important to note that this chapter is of relevance to technical as well as general dissolutions.[6] This is because of the difficulty in drawing a clear line between a technical dissolution and a general dissolution as the same events that lead to a general dissolution also lead to a technical dissolution. Thus, the death of a partner may lead to the firm continuing as before the death (a technical dissolution) or it may lead to the firm being wound up and sold by the surviving partners (a general dissolution). It follows that it is only with the benefit of hindsight that one can say whether a certain event causes a technical or a general dissolution of a firm. Furthermore, even where an event such as the death of a partner does cause a general dissolution, there will often be a grey area in the life of the firm after the death of a partner during which the future of the firm is unclear, since there is no clear point at which a dissolution ceases to be a technical dissolution and becomes a general dissolution. Indeed, any attempt to isolate such a point would of necessity be artificial.

[26.05] For these reasons, this chapter is also of relevance to technical dissolutions, and, indeed, some of the issues considered hereunder, such as the right of a partner to publicly notify the dissolution of the partnership, are equally relevant to a partner who leaves a continuing firm as they are to a partner in a firm which is being wound up.

I.   GENERAL CONSEQUENCES OF A FIRM'S DISSOLUTION

Authority of Partner to Publicly Notify Dissolution

[26.06] An important consequence of the dissolution of a firm is the right of a partner to notify the public of that fact. The notification of the public of a firm's dissolution is important on the technical dissolution of a firm since it helps to terminate the liability of a partner for the acts of a firm which continues in business after his departure.[7] Such a notification is of equal importance in the case of the general dissolution of a partnership because a third party who had dealings with the firm is entitled to treat the firm as still existing until he is notified of the dissolution.[8] In relation to third parties who had no

---

4   In the sense of a change in the membership of a firm which may lead to a technical or a general dissolution.
5   However, s 35 of the 1890 Act refers only to the court decreeing a dissolution of the partnership and it is conceivable that a bare order of dissolution by a court with no ancillary orders regarding winding up could amount in effect to an order to disassociate, since there is the possibility that some of the partners would be able to continue the partnership business as if it was a technical dissolution.
6   Indeed, the issue of post-dissolution profits made by a firm (para **[26.63]** et seq) is concerned with technical dissolutions only.
7   Partnership Act 1890, s 36(1); *Minnit v Whinery* (1721) 5 Bro PC 489. See generally, para **[11.70]**.
8   This issue is dealt with in more detail, para **[11.85]** et seq. See for example *Smallman Ltd v O'Moore and Newman* [1959] IR 220 which involved the general dissolution of a firm.

dealings with the firm, an advertisement of the dissolution of the firm in *Iris Oifigiúil* is deemed to be notice of the departure of a partner or of the firm's dissolution to such persons.[9]

[26.07] As noted by Davitt P in the High Court case of *Smallman Ltd v O'Moore and Newman*:[10]

'The purpose of a notice of dissolution is to inform the party sought to be affected that the authority of each partner, to act as agent for the other or others, has been withdrawn.'[11]

Thus, once the third party is actually notified or deemed to be notified of the dissolution, a partner in that firm is no longer liable for the acts of his former co-partners, subject (in the case of a winding up) to the continuing authority of the winding up partner(s) under s 38.[12]

[26.08] The importance of notifying third parties of the dissolution of a partnership is evident from the terms of s 37 of the 1890 Act, which not only grants a partner the right to publicly notify the firm's dissolution but also to require the other partners to concur for that purpose. Section 37 states:

On the dissolution of a partnership or retirement of a partner any partner may publicly notify the same, and may require the other partner or partners to concur for that purpose in all necessary or proper acts, if any, which cannot be done without his or their concurrence.

[26.09] Thus, under the terms of this section, a partner may force his co-partners to sign a notice of dissolution for its publication in *Iris Oifigiúil*.[13] It is to be noted that unlike most of the other provisions in the 1890 Act, s 37 is not stated to be subject to contrary agreement amongst the partners. Although the general tenor of the 1890 Act, and in particular s 19, favours the partners being able to contract out of the rights and duties contained in the Act, it is submitted that certain rights under the Act are of such import as to be inalienable. It has already been suggested that a partner's right to a true account of partnership dealings is one of these inalienable rights.[14] It is now contended that the right of a former partner to publicly notify his departure or the dissolution of his firm is also inalienable. Support for this conclusion is based first on the fact that the section is not stated to be subject to contrary agreement and second on the crucial nature of this right, ie, it ends the liability of a former partner for the future debts of a firm of which he is no longer a partner.[15] On this basis, it is contended that this right should not be capable of being excluded by the terms of the partnership agreement.[16] If this right could be alienated, a former partner would be liable for the future obligations incurred by his

---

9   Partnership Act 1890, s 36(2) and see generally, para **[11.70]** et seq.
10 *Smallman Ltd v O'Moore and Newman* [1959] IR 220.
11 *Smallman Ltd v O'Moore and Newman* [1959] IR 220 at 223–224.
12 As to this authority, see para **[26.11]** et seq.
13 *Hendry v Turner* (1886) 32 Ch D 355.
14 See para **[21.88]**.
15 This arises because under s 36(1) of the 1890 Act, a person who deals with a firm after a change in its constitution is entitled to treat all apparent members of the firm as still being members *until he has notice thereof*. See further in relation to the continuing liability of a former partner, para **[11.74]** et seq.
16 But for a contrary view, see l'Anson Banks, *Lindley & Banks on Partnership* (20th edn, 2017) at para 13-45.

former firm to third parties who were unaware of his departure, yet he would not have the right to publicly notify them of his departure. It is hard to see any justification for such a situation. A third reason for s 37 to be inalienable is that s 19 of the 1890 Act provides that the partners may vary the 'mutual rights and duties of partners' contained in the Act. However, its non-application to s 37 may be justified not only on the basis of the importance of the right, but also on the basis that one is dealing here with the rights of a former partner and not the 'mutual rights and duties of partners'.[17]

[26.10] While the right to publicly notify a dissolution or a retirement is thought to be inalienable, it is nonetheless apprehended that a firm is entitled to have a say in the exercise of this right by, for example, controlling the content of the advertisement or the circular notifying the dissolution. Thus, it is suggested that a provision in a partnership agreement which allows all the partners to have a say in the form of public notification is permissible, so long as that input is not such as to deprive the notice of its effect as a notice of dissolution.

Authority of Partners to Bind Firm on a Dissolution

[26.11] When a partnership is subject to a general dissolution, the business of the firm must be wound up. This winding up must be done by somebody and, for this reason, s 38 of the 1890 Act provides that after dissolution each partner's authority to bind the firm continues, but only for the purposes of completing the firm's transactions and winding up the firm.[18]

> After the dissolution of a partnership the authority of each partner to bind the firm, and the other rights and obligations of the partners, continue notwithstanding the dissolution so far as may be necessary to wind up the affairs of the partnership, and to complete transactions begun but unfinished at the time of the dissolution, but not otherwise.
>
> Provided that the firm is in no case bound by the acts of a partner who has become bankrupt; but this proviso does not affect the liability of any person who has after the bankruptcy represented himself or knowingly suffered himself to be represented as a partner of the bankrupt.

Proviso to s 38

[26.12] The rule that a partner winding up a firm has authority to bind that firm is subject to the exception that the firm is not bound by the acts of a bankrupt partner. Therefore, a third party, who is dealing with a bankrupt partner acting on behalf of a firm being wound up, will not be able to claim that the firm is bound by the acts of that partner. This proviso will not, however, prevent a person (whether a former partner or

---

17 Unlike other post-dissolution rights of partners (eg the right of a partner to force a sale of partnership assets under s 39), the potential liability arising from a failure to exercise the right of public notification of dissolution is limitless. Thus, while the application of s 19 to s 39 may be justified, it is thought that the same cannot be said of its application to s 37.

18 For a pre-1890 Act decision, see the judgment of Walsh MR in *Graves v Davies* (1866) 17 Ir Ch R 227 where at 235 he relies on the authority of *Butchart v Dresser* (1853) 4 De GM & G 542, to state that the third party 'seems to have dealt, as regards this account, with William Davies only for the purpose of winding it up, which was within his authority as surviving partner'.

not) from being liable as a partner by holding out under s 14(1) of the 1890 Act, where he allows himself to be held out as in partnership with a bankrupt partner.[19]

Breadth of authority of winding up partner

[26.13] Section 38 of the 1890 Act has two limits on the authority of the winding up partner to bind the firm; the act must either be necessary to wind up the firm or it must be necessary to complete unfinished transactions of the firm. Since there is a large degree of overlap between these two requirements, they will be considered together.

[26.14] In general terms, the surviving partners have the right to complete all unfinished operations necessary to fulfil contracts of the firm which were still in force when the firm was dissolved.[20] Examples of matters which are within the authority of a winding up partner are the power to bind the firm in the sale of its assets,[21] to secure a debt incurred by the firm prior to its dissolution[22] and to withdraw sums on deposit at the firm's bank.[23] Where a third party doubts the authority of the winding up partner to do a given act, the prudent course of action is to join all the partners in the dissolved firm to the act.

Winding up partner has authority to institute proceedings on behalf of firm

[26.15] Another act which the winding up partner is authorised to do as part of the winding-up process is to institute proceedings on behalf of the firm to protect the firm's property or recover damages owing to the firm. In *Hutchinson v Whitfield*,[24] a Limerick partnership of woollen merchants was dissolved and all the partnership effects were vested in one of the partners, Hutchinson, for the purposes of winding up the firm. Smith B held that Hutchinson was entitled to maintain an action on behalf of the firm against a third party for wrongful conversion of the firm's goods. Similarly in *Leech v Stokes*,[25] the sole surviving partner of a Dublin firm of solicitors took an action for negligence against the accountants who had advised the firm during its existence. In the High Court, Hanna J held that the plaintiff 'though suing in his own name, admits that he is seeking to recover damages on behalf of the firm, as the last surviving partner. This would seem to be his right under the law.'[26]

Power to settle debts on behalf of the firm

[26.16] One of the principal reasons for granting a partner the authority to wind up the firm is to allow him to settle debts owed by the firm to third parties and to collect debts owed to the firm. Accordingly, the power to settle debts must be regarded as being

---

[19] See generally regarding a partner by holding out, para **[7.01]** et seq.

[20] Per Lord Reid in *IRC v Graham's Trustees* (1971) SLT 46 at 48.

[21] *Morgan v Marquis* (1853) 9 Ex 145. See also *Crean v Quin* (21 June 1976) HC, in which Kenny J deals with the surrender of a tenancy by a partner on behalf of the dissolved partnership.

[22] *Re Clough, Bradford Commercial Banking Co v Cure* (1885) 31 Ch D 324.

[23] See the Scottish case of *Dickson v National Bank of Scotland* (1917) SC (HL) 50.

[24] *Hutchinson v Whitfield* (1830) Hayes 78.

[25] *Leech v Stokes* [1937] IR 787. Hanna J's judgment was affirmed on appeal by the Supreme Court ([1937] IR 817).

[26] *Leech v Stokes* [1937] IR 787 at 789.

within the authority of the winding up partner. In *Luckie v Forsyth*,[27] it was held that a partner was bound by the settlement reached by the winding up partner with a creditor of the firm. Indeed the court indicated, obiter, that the admissions of the winding up partner are prima facie binding on the firm. Sugden LC observed that:

> 'It is clearly settled that the declaration of one partner respecting a partnership transaction, made after the dissolution of the partnership, is admissible as evidence against the other partners; not conclusive, but as an admission, which does not preclude the party against whom it is used, showing by other evidence that the admission was not correct.'[28]

[26.17] The case itself involved a partner, Cameron, in a dissolved partnership being authorised to wind up the firm and collect its debts under the terms of a dissolution agreement between the partners. During the winding up, Cameron settled the terms of a bill with a creditor of the firm in respect of one of these transactions. Cameron went bankrupt and it was held that the other partner in the firm was bound by the settlement since Sugden LC held that: 'if one of the late partners in a dissolved partnership, be authorized to wind up the concern, he is authorized to bind the other partners by a stated and settled account.'[29]

[26.18] In this context, one must consider the perplexing decision in *Bristow v Miller*.[30] There, the partnership between Mathew Maxwell and Mr Miller was dissolved by agreement and Mathew Maxwell was empowered to settle the affairs of the firm. A circular to that effect was published and received by Maxwell's brother in Belfast, James Maxwell, a creditor of the firm. Subsequently, Mathew Maxwell sent an account which he signed in the firm's name to James Maxwell. This account indicated a balance was owing by the firm to James Maxwell. The debts which were the subject of this account had been incurred outside the relevant limitation period under the Statute of Limitations.[31] However, James Maxwell sought to enforce the debt against Miller on the grounds that the account had been issued by Mathew Maxwell within the limitation period and that this account was binding upon Miller. In the High Court, Perrin J held that:

> 'Maxwell had no authority to bind Miller by creating a new debt or making a new contract. He had authority to liquidate the debts of the old firm, but the account furnished by him was furnished not in his capacity as partner, but in his new capacity of manager to wind up the concern.'[32]

---

27 *Luckie v Forsyth* (1846) 3 Jo & Lat 388. Cf *Smallman Ltd v O'Moore and Newman* [1959] IR 220, considered at para **[11.63]** et seq where the contract was held not to be with the dissolved firm, since although the plaintiff believed he was contracting with the firm, the former partners believed the contract was with the newly incorporated company which had taken over the firm's business.

28 *Luckie v Forsyth* (1846) 3 Jo & Lat 388 at 394.

29 *Luckie v Forsyth* (1846) 3 Jo & Lat 388 at 395.

30 *Bristow v Miller* (1848) 11 Ir LR 461.

31 The relevant Statute of Limitations at that time was An Act for rendering a written Memorandum necessary to the Validity of certain Promises and Engagements of 1828 (9 G 4, c 14).

32 *Bristow v Miller* (1848) 11 Ir LR 461 at 472–474.

[26.19] It was held that in signing the account, Mathew Maxwell went beyond what was necessary to wind up the affairs of the partnership by creating a new cause of action as the original liability had been extinguished by the Statute of Limitations. Accordingly, Miller was not bound by this account. However, it is questioned whether this pre-1890 case would be followed today since the very *raison d'être* for s 38 is to allow for the settling of accounts with creditors of the firm and this purpose would be defeated if such settlements could be avoided where the settlement operates as an acknowledgement of a debt for the purposes of the Statute of Limitations 1957.[33] It is thought that the decision may have been overly influenced by the fact that the third party creditor was in fact the winding up partner's brother and the desire to avoid a preference to him.[34] Rather it is thought that a partner winding up a firm is generally authorised to bind his firm by admitting liability for a debt which was constituted against the firm while the partnership still subsisted and before its dissolution.[35]

Indemnity to non-winding up partners does not affect liability

[26.20] It is perhaps self-evident that the primary liability of a partner to third parties for the acts of the winding up partner is unaffected by the existence of any indemnity which may exist between the partners. In *Luckie v Forsyth*,[36] Sugden LC held that the existence of an indemnity from Cameron, the winding up partner, in favour of his co-partner, did not relieve the co-partner from liability to a creditor in respect of a bill which was settled by Cameron with that creditor.

Effect of Dissolution on Contracts with Employees

[26.21] When a firm is dissolved the question arises as to the effect of the dissolution on the firm's contracts with employees and the authority of the winding up partner to maintain those contracts. It is contended that these contracts continue unless terminated since it is only on the completion of the winding up of a firm (rather than on the actual dissolution of the partnership) that the firm's contracts with employees will terminate. At that stage there may be a claim for redundancy.[37] This conclusion is in keeping with

---

[33] *Bristow v Miller* (1848) 11 Ir LR 461 may also be distinguished on the ground that it rests on the precise terms of An Act for rendering a written Memorandum necessary to the Validity of certain Promises and Engagements of 1828 (9 G 4, c 14). This Statute provided that in any account stated or settled, it must be signed by the party to be charged and not his agent, which clearly influenced the court in that case.

[34] In addition, the question of whether the settlement of an account operates as an acknowledgement of a debt for the purposes of the Statute of Limitations 1957 will depend on whether an action is brought within the limitation period. If it is brought within the time period, the subsequent acknowledgement will not create a new liability, whereas if is it not brought within the limitation period, it will create a new liability. Thus if one were to adopt the approach in *Bristow v Miller* (1848) 11 Ir LR 461 the question of whether the winding up partner is authorised to make the settlement is determined by outside circumstances, ie whether the third party brings an action within the limitation period, which approach is difficult to justify.

[35] See for example the Scottish case of *McNab v Lockhart* (1843) 5 D 1014.

[36] *Luckie v Forsyth* (1846) 3 Jo & Lat 388.

[37] As to redundancy generally, see Regan and Murphy, *Employment Law* (2nd edn, 2017) at para [19.001] et seq. See also Redmond, *Dismissal Law in Ireland* (2nd edn, 2007) at para [17.01] et seq.

s 38 of the 1890 Act, since that section contemplates the partners having authority to continue the firm's affairs after its dissolution until the completion of the winding up, for which purpose the employees will no doubt be necessary.[38]

[26.22] Of course, where the firm suffers a technical dissolution, the contracts with the employees are not terminated but are regarded as having been adopted by the newly constituted partnership.

On a Technical Dissolution, a Former Partner's Share is a Debt

[26.23] A common consequence of the departure of a partner is that the firm continues and the outgoing partner will have his share in the partnership purchased by the continuing partners and may be owed moneys by the firm in respect of this share. The 1890 Act specifically refers to such debts in s 43 which provides that:

> Subject to any agreement between the partners, the amount due from surviving or continuing partners to an outgoing partner or the representatives of a deceased partner in respect of the outgoing or deceased partner's share is a debt accruing at the date of the dissolution or death.

[26.24] In the Supreme Court case of *Meagher v Meagher*,[39] Kingsmill Moore J held that the purpose of this section is to clarify the date upon which money is deemed to be owing to a former partner for the purposes of the limitation of actions.[40] Thus, once the valuation of the partnership assets has been ascertained for the purpose of determining the former partner's share, this sum ranks for the purpose of limitation as a sum accruing at the date of dissolution.[41] As a simple contract debt, the claim by an outgoing partner to recover this sum will be barred after the lapse of six years from the date of dissolution.[42]

---

[38] See also l'Anson Banks, *Lindley & Banks on Partnership* (20th edn, 2017) at para 25-03 and the Court of Appeal in *Rose v Dodd* [2005] ICR 1779, but cf the decision of the English Employment Appeals Tribunal in *Tunstall v Condon* [1980] ICR 786 and the decision of the English High Court in *Briggs v Oates* [1991] 1 All ER 407.

[39] *Meagher v Meagher* [1961] IR 96.

[40] *Knox v Gye* (1872) LR 5 HL 656. This is also the position in New Zealand, see *Re Bloomfield* (1978) 2 TRNZ 587 and *Smith v Smith* [1926] NZLR 311 in relation to the equivalent section of the New Zealand Partnership Act of 1908. See also the Australian case of *Cameron v Murdoch* [1983] WAR 321 and on appeal (1986) 63 ALR 575. In America, this issue is dealt with by the Uniform Partnership Act (1997) (Last Amended 2013), s 503(c) which provides that the right to an account of the partnership's transactions accrues at the date of dissolution. In the Supreme Court case of *Williams v Harris* [1980] ILRM 237, the defendants argued that by virtue of s 43 of the 1890 Act, the amount due to the retiring partner was a debt accruing as and from the date of retirement and therefore a retiring partner no longer had an interest in the partnership and was not entitled to interest for the two years between the date of retirement and the date the valuation was finalised by arbitration. Although the Supreme Court found for the defendants, reliance was not placed on this aspect of their argument.

[41] In *Meagher v Meagher*, above, the date of dissolution was the date of death of a partner.

[42] Statute of Limitations 1957, s 11(1)(a).

Third Parties Dealing with Dissolved Firm

[26.25] On the general dissolution of a partnership, the position of third parties *vis à vis* the firm is the same as the position of third parties *vis à vis* a firm on its technical dissolution. This area is considered in detail elsewhere in this work.[43] Thus, in general terms, a third party who dealt with the firm prior to the general dissolution is entitled to treat the firm as continuing until receipt by him of actual notice of the dissolution.[44] In a case where the third party is not on notice of the departure of the partner, the former partner is bound by post-dissolution acts of his co-partners, as if the firm was not dissolved. On the other hand, third parties who only begin dealing with a firm after its dissolution, are deemed to be on notice of an advertisement of the dissolution in *Iris Oifigiúil*[45] and, therefore, the former partner is not bound by post-dissolution acts of his co-partners with these third parties.

II.   WINDING UP OF FIRM'S BUSINESS

[26.26] The formal winding up of a firm's business will be considered first in relation to the forced sale of partnership assets and then in relation to the winding up process.

Forced Sale of Partnership Assets

[26.27] On the general dissolution of a partnership and in the absence of any agreement to the contrary between the partners, all the partnership assets should be sold. As noted by Kenny J:

> 'In the absence of a special agreement to the contrary ... the rule is that on a dissolution of partnership all the property shall be converted into money by a sale and that the proceeds of the sale, after discharging all the partnership debts and liabilities, shall be divided among the partners according to their shares.'[46]

[26.28] The right of a partner to have the partnership assets sold is perhaps the most important right of a partner on the dissolution of his firm. From a financial perspective, it is critical, since it may be the only way for a partner to recover the value of his share in the firm.[47] This right, which amounts to an equitable lien over the partnership property, has a statutory basis in s 39 of the 1890 Act:

---

43   See para **[11.25]** et seq.
44   Partnership Act 1890, s 36(1).
45   Partnership Act 1890, s 36(2).
46   *Williams v Harris* [1980] ILRM 237 at 241, quoting from Viscount Haldane in *Hugh Stevenson v Aktiengesellschaft* [1918] AC 240 at 246.
47   See *Creagh v Creagh* (1862) 13 Ir Ch R 28, considered at para **[24.25]**, which deals with the right of the personal representative of a deceased partner to have the partnership assets sold, in which Smith MR stated at 47 that the 'executor has a right to have the value ascertained, in the way in which it can be best ascertained, by sale' (quoting Lord Eldon in *Crawshay v Collins* (1808) 15 Ves Jr 218 at 227). See also *Rickard v Rickard* [2016] IECA 158 where former partners in a dissolved partnership 'obstructed' for several years, the sale of partnership property on foot of a court order obtained by their former partner. In her judgment, Irivine J acknowledged that the forced sale of land against the wishes of some of its owners could cause upset, but that the plaintiff had established an entitlement to a court order for the sale and partition of the lands.

On the dissolution of a partnership every partner is entitled, as against the other partners in the firm, and all persons claiming through them in respect of their interests as partners, to have the property of the partnership applied in payment of the debts and liabilities of the firm, and to have the surplus assets after such payment applied in payment of what may be due to the partners respectively after deducting what may be due from them as partners to the firm; and for that purpose any partner or his representatives may on the termination of the partnership apply to the Court to wind up the business and affairs of the firm.

[26.29] It is worth bearing in mind that, as an equitable lien, this right to a forced sale may be defeated by a third party in respect of partnership property, if that third party obtains a legal title to that property, provided that he does so bona fide, for value and without notice of the lien. Since s 39 allows for the forced sale of the property of the partnership only, it is clear that a partner is not entitled to demand the forced sale of assets, which, though used by the partnership, belong to one of the partners.

[26.30] This right to sell the partnership assets entitles a partner to have the assets sold to the best bidder. Kingsmill Moore J observed that:

'[I]n default of agreement, either the surviving partners or the representatives of a deceased partner are entitled to have the value of the partnership assets ascertained by a sale in open market and not by a valuation.'[48]

The right of a partner to force a sale of partnership assets on a general dissolution exists, even if the firm's debts and liabilities could be discharged without such a sale.[49] Thus, every partner has a right to insist that the partnership assets, including goodwill,[50] be sold on the open market and he does not have to accept a valuation therefor. This right, sometimes referred to as a right to a forced sale,[51] applies even where the partnership is being wound up by the court.[52] Only if the assets cannot be sold on the open market will a valuation be made.[53]

Is right of forced sale restricted to partners?

[26.31] The first part of s 39 of the 1890 Act grants the right to a forced sale of the partnership assets to a 'partner' as against all other partners. The right to a forced sale in s 39 is not expressed to be granted to the representatives of a partner, yet the second part of the section goes on to grant 'for that purpose' (ie for the purpose of the forced sale),

---

48 *Meagher v Meagher* [1961] IR 96 at 108, relying on *Hugh Stevenson and Sons v Aktiengesellschaft für Cartonnnagen Industrie* [1918] AC 239; *Burdon v Barkus* (1862) 4 De GF & J 42; *Darby v Darby* (1856) 15 Ves Jr 218; *Featherstonhaugh v Fenwick* (1810) 17 Ves Jr 298 and *Crawshay v Collins* (1808) 15 Ves Jr 218.
49 Partnership Act 1890, s 39; *Hugh Stevenson & Sons Aktiengesellschaft für Cartonnagen-Industrie* [1918] AC 239; *Cook v Collingridge* (1822) Jac 607; *Crawshay v Collins* (1808) 15 Ves Jr 218.
50 Per Kingsmill Moore J: 'Unless the parties otherwise agree there must be a sale of the partnership property including the goodwill', *Meagher v Meagher* [1961] IR 96 at 112. See also *Re David and Matthews* [1899] 1 Ch 378 at 382.
51 See for example *Heslin v Fay (1)* (1884) 15 LR Ir 431 at 446, where Heslin applied for a dissolution of the firm, and Sullivan LC noted that: '[i]f relief were given in the general form, it would confer on Heslin the right to sell the premises by, perhaps, a forced sale.'
52 Per Kingsmill Moore J, *Meagher v Meagher* [1961] IR 96 at 108.
53 Per Kingsmill Moore J, *Meagher v Meagher* [1961] IR 96 at 109.

the right to insist on a winding up and this right is extended to 'any partner or his representatives'. Despite this apparent omission in the early part of this section, it seems clear that the representative of a partner is entitled to force a sale of partnership assets. It would seem that the expression 'representatives' in this section would apply to the personal representative or the Official Assignee of an individual partner as well as a receiver, liquidator or examiner of a corporate partner.

[26.32] Thus in *Creagh v Creagh*,[54] which concerned a deceased partner's estate, Smith MR stated:

'The question then is, whether the surviving partners, instead of settling the account, and agreeing with the executors as to the terms upon which his beneficial interest in the stock is still to be determined, subject still to the probable loss, can take the whole property, do what they please, and compel the executor to take the calculated value? That cannot be, without a contract for it with the testator. The executor has a right to have the value ascertained, in the way in which it can be best ascertained, by sale.'[55]

[26.33] In contrast, the assignee of a partner's share will not be entitled to insist upon the forced sale of partnership assets or the winding up of the partnership, since his rights are expressly restricted by the terms of s 31(2) of the 1890 Act.[56] This provides that the assignee's rights are restricted to receiving a share of the partnership assets and for that purpose to obtain an account from the date of dissolution. In contrast, the other partners are entitled to insist upon a winding up of the partnership as against the assignee, since under the terms of s 39, the assignee is a 'person claiming through' a partner and a partner is entitled to force a sale against such persons.

Subject to contrary agreement

[26.34] Although not expressed to be so, the terms of s 39 of the 1890 Act, like most other rights under the 1890 Act, are subject to contrary agreement between the partners.[57] Thus, in the Supreme Court case of *Meagher v Meagher*,[58] Kingsmill Moore J noted that:

'It is an almost universal rule in winding up a partnership on dissolution that, unless there is a provision to the contrary in the articles, a partner, or the representative of a deceased partner, cannot be forced to accept a valuation of the assets.'[59]

[26.35] Therefore, in determining whether a partnership asset will be subject to such a forced sale, the court will take into account the terms of the partnership agreement regarding the treatment of that asset on the dissolution of the firm. In *Heslin v Fay (1)*,[60] Fay had purchased a premises in North King St in Dublin which he contributed to the partnership as his share of the capital. The partnership business was carried on from

---

54   *Creagh v Creagh* (1862) 13 Ir Ch R 28.
55   *Creagh v Creagh* (1862) 13 Ir Ch R 28 at 47 quoting from Lord Eldon in *Crawshay v Collins* (1808) 15 Ves 218 at 227.
56   See further para **[19.19]** et seq.
57   Partnership Act 1890, s 19. See further para **[5.14]** et seq.
58   *Meagher v Meagher* [1961] IR 96.
59   *Meagher v Meagher* [1961] IR 96 at 108.
60   *Heslin v Fay (1)* (1884) 15 LR Ir 431.

these premises and the partnership agreement provided that in case of 'any dissolution'[61] of the firm, Fay was to have an option to acquire the partnership premises from his co-partners at a value to be agreed pursuant to a valuation mechanism in the agreement. For this reason, the Irish Court of Appeal[62] held that, although Heslin was entitled to a dissolution of the partnership, he was not entitled to force a sale of the partnership premises, but instead it was held that the terms of the partnership agreement governed the rights of the partners regarding the partnership premises.

Where sale will not be forced

[26.36] Despite the apparent absolute terms of s 39, there are a number of instances in which a partner may not be entitled to rely on his right to force a sale of partnership property under s 39. Two of these were considered by the Supreme Court in *Meagher v Meagher*.[63] The first exception is represented by the rule in *Syers v Syers*.[64] In that case, an outgoing partner in a two-man music hall partnership had a one-eighth share in the firm while the continuing partner held the other seven-eighths. Having regard to the nature of the business and the very small interest of the outgoing partner, the House of Lords declined to force the public sale of the partnership assets, but instead ordered the continuing partner to lay proposals before the court for the purchase by him of the outgoing partner's share. In the Supreme Court, Kingsmill Moore J noted that the circumstances of that case were unusual and therefore the case might not be of general application. However, it is thought that an Irish court would exercise its discretion and refuse a public sale of partnership property where an individual partner's share is very small (relative to the other individual shares) and it is not readily saleable to the public.

[26.37] The second situation in which the forced sale of partnership assets will not be allowed is where the assets are incapable of sale. As noted by Kingsmill Moore J: '[w]here an asset is incapable of sale a valuation must be made for there is no other resource [sic] if the parties cannot agree.'[65]

[26.38] In addition to these two exceptional cases, it appears that in certain circumstances, an outgoing partner may be deemed to have relinquished his right to a forced sale. Thus, where a partner, on leaving the partnership, recognises the continuation of the firm's business by the continuing partners, it would be inequitable for him to be granted an order for the sale of the partnership assets.[66]

[26.39] Apart from these limited exceptions, it is apprehended that a court will not refuse to order a forced sale, since to do so would conflict with a partner's fundamental right to have the partnership assets sold and his partnership share liquidated.

---

[61] *Heslin v Fay (1)* (1884) 15 LR Ir 431 at 437.
[62] Sullivan LC, Fitzgibbon and Barry LJJ.
[63] *Meagher v Meagher* [1961] IR 96.
[64] *Syers v Syers* (1876) 1 App Cas 174.
[65] *Meagher v Meagher* [1961] IR 96 at 109, where Kingsmill Moore J relied on *Smith v Mules* (1852) 9 Hare 556 at 572 and *Ambler v Bolton* (1871) LR 14 Eq 427.
[66] See *Sobell v Boston* [1975] 2 All ER 282.

Appointment of Receiver

[26.40] *Haughey v Synnott*[67] concerned the dissolution of a two-partner firm of solicitors. The defendant sought an order under s 28(8) of the Supreme Court of Judicature Act (Ireland) 1877 and Ord 50, r 6 of the Rules of the Superior Courts for the appointment of a receiver or receiver/manager in respect of the partnership's assets, an order conferring certain powers on the receiver or, in the alternative, an order under s 39 of the 1890 Act appointing a receiver to wind up the business or affairs of the partnership. Regarding s 39, Laffoy J observed that insofar as the court would see it as necessary to appoint a receiver to wind up the partnership's business, it would do so following a substantive hearing on the issues and not as part of an application for interlocutory relief, unless it could, for example, be demonstrated that the firm's assets would be in jeopardy pending a substantive hearing. Noting that the defendant's objective appeared to be to have the partnership assets valued, Laffoy J observed that the appointment of a receiver at an interlocutory stage under the equitable jurisdiction of the court was 'definitely not the appropriate mechanism by which the defendant [could] achieve his objective'.[68]

Right and Duty of Partners to Wind up Firm

[26.41] As is clear from the wording of s 39 of the 1890 Act, closely connected with the right of a partner to sell all the partnership assets, is the right of a partner to apply to court to wind up the firm's affairs. While s 39 recognises the right of a partner to apply to court for the firm to be wound up, it is in fact his duty to have the firm's affairs wound up, whether this is done with or without the court's assistance. Thus, in *Meagher v Meagher*[69] Kingsmill Moore J noted that it 'was the duty of the partners and executors to wind up the affairs' of the partnership in that case.[70] Clearly, such a duty only arises where the firm has been dissolved and no agreement to the contrary has been entered into by the partners, eg for the continuation of the business by some of the partners or the sale of the business to third parties. This is because, like most rights conferred on partners by the terms of the 1890 Act, the right to wind up a firm in s 39 may be excluded by an express or implied agreement to the contrary between all the partners.[71]

Winding up is usually best handled by the partners

[26.42] As a general rule, the partners of a dissolved firm are best positioned to oversee its winding up in light of their knowledge of the firm's business. However, where the partners cannot agree on an amicable winding up of the firm, s 39 clearly envisages a winding-up order being granted by the court.

---

67 *Haughey v Synnott* [2011] IEHC 467.
68 *Haughey v Synnott* [2011] IEHC 467 at para 5.2 of the judgment.
69 *Meagher v Meagher* [1961] IR 96.
70 *Meagher v Meagher* [1961] IR 96 at 105. See also *Crean v Quin* (21 June 1976) HC, in which a partnership between the plaintiff and Mr Doyle was dissolved. Kenny J held that the tenancy of the firm's premises between the defendant and the firm was to be taken over by the plaintiff.
71 Partnership Act 1890, s 19.

[26.43] Just because the partnership is being wound up by the court does not deprive the partners of the right to force the sale of the partnership assets. As noted by Kingsmill Moore J:

'Any partner, or the representatives of a deceased partner, has a right to insist that the assets be sold in the open market ... This is so even where the partnership is being wound up by the Court. If one partner is a lunatic or an infant the Court may accept an offer for his share if it appears to be for his benefit, but if the other partners insist on their right to a sale they are entitled to have one.'[72]

[26.44] Where the court grants a winding-up order for a partnership under s 39, it is not clear whether the general authority of all the partners under s 38 to bind the firm for the purposes of the winding up will be subject to the terms of this order. If the winding up is vested by the court in one person only, it would seem to follow that the partners would not have the right to bind the firm under s 38.[73] In order to avoid any confusion in this regard, this matter should ideally be governed by the terms of the court order appointing the person to wind up the firm.[74]

Winding up on application of creditors

[26.45] The right under s 39 of the 1890 Act to apply to court for a winding up is restricted to a partner or his representative. It is to be noted that unlike the position of creditors of companies under the Companies Act 2014,[75] a creditor of a partnership has no standing to seek the winding up of a partnership under the 1890 Act. He may, however, have a right to apply for a court winding up of the partnership under the Companies Act 2014 and this issue is considered elsewhere in this work.[76]

Winding up partner is in a fiduciary position

[26.46] A partner who winds up a firm, whether appointed by a court or not, is treated as being in possession of partnership property as a fiduciary *vis à vis* his co-partners. This is clear from the High Court case of *Williams v Harris*,[77] where McWilliam J adopted the following statement of principle:

'[I]n winding up a partnership the procedure belongs to an equitable jurisdiction which, though theoretically concurrent, is practically exclusive. It depends on the principles which Courts of Equity apply to persons who are in possession of property under circumstances in which they are treated as standing in a fiduciary relationship. It is more

---

[72]   *Meagher v Meagher* [1961] IR 96 at 108.

[73]   Nonetheless the firm may be bound by third parties who deal with such partners on the basis of the ostensible authority of a partner to bind the firm during its winding up. See generally in relation to ostensible authority, para **[10.30]** et seq.

[74]   See for example *Hutcheson v Smith* (1842) 5 Ir Eq R 117.

[75]   Companies Act 2014, ss 585–588. See generally Courtney, *The Law of Companies* (4th edn, 2016) at para [24.026] et seq, Hutchinson, *Keane on Company Law* (5th edn, 2016) at para [38.20] et seq; Forde and Kennedy, *Company Law* (5th edn, 2017) at para 20.27.

[76]   See para **[27.06]** et seq.

[77]   *Williams v Harris* (15 January 1980) HC. Note, however, that the case itself did not involve a winding up, since there was a technical dissolution, rather than a general dissolution of the partnership. The decision was overturned on appeal to the Supreme Court ([1980] ILRM 237), but not in relation to McWilliam J's findings on the fiduciary position of a partner who winds up a firm.

than and different from the procedure which applies when the rights of parties arise merely out of the rules of the common law which apply to contracts.'[78]

[26.47] On this basis, McWilliam J held that the fiduciary relationship, if it is not displaced by parties:

'continues until the partnership has been wound up or, as here, until the terms of the partnership agreement with regard to the retirement of a partner or partners have been completely carried out.'[79]

[26.48] Since the winding up partner is in a fiduciary position *vis à vis* his co-partners, he may not profit from that position.[80] However, the consequences of being a fiduciary may be avoided by the express terms of any agreement between the partners. This principle is illustrated by the facts of *Williams v Harris*.[81] In that case, the partnership agreement for the farming and breeding of bloodstock in Co Tipperary provided for the purchase by the continuing partners of a retiring partner's share in the firm. There was, however, a 19-month delay between the date of the retirement of two partners in that firm and the date they received the purchase price for their share from the continuing partners. Relying on the continuing partners'[82] fiduciary position *vis à vis* the retiring partner, the retiring partner claimed that the continuing partners were liable for interest on the purchase price during this 19-month period. Whilst acknowledging the existence of the fiduciary duty, both the High Court and the Supreme Court[83] stated that the consequences of this fiduciary duty might be excluded by an agreement between the parties. In the High Court, McWilliam J noted that the equitable principles:

'applicable to a partnership continue to apply until the partnership transaction has been completed save only in so far as the application of these principles has been varied by the partnership agreement.'[84]

[26.49] The Supreme Court noted that the partnership agreement provided a complete mechanism for the sale of the retiring partner's share and provided for his share to

---

78 *Williams v Harris* (15 January 1980) HC at pp 7–8 of the transcript, quoting from the judgment of Viscount Haldane in *Hugh Stevenson v Aktiengesellschaft für Cartonnagen-Industrie* [1918] AC 240 at 247.

79 *Williams v Harris* (15 January 1980) HC at p 12.

80 Thus in the Supreme Court case of *Meagher v Meagher* [1961] IR 96, Kingsmill Moore J stated that: 'surviving partners stand in a fiduciary relationship to the representatives of a deceased partner ... a person in a fiduciary position cannot make a profit out of his trusteeship' ([1961] IR 96 at 110). This case also involved a technical rather than a general dissolution and therefore did not involve a winding up.

81 *Williams v Harris* (15 January 1980) HC, [1980] ILRM 237 (SC).

82 They were not winding up partners, since the firm continued in business.

83 In the Supreme Court, Kenny J stated that '[t]he defendants do not dispute the existence of these general equitable principles but say that the terms of the partnership deed prevent them applying to this case. A passage in the speech of Viscount Haldane in *Stevenson's Case* [1918] AC 239 and the terms of s 42 of the 1890 Act ["in the absence of any agreement to the contrary"], show that the terms of the partnership deed may override these general principles' ([1980] ILRM 237 at 241).

84 *Williams v Harris* (15 January 1980) HC at p 12 of the transcript. McWilliam J's judgment was reversed on appeal on the facts, but not as regards the statement of the application of equitable rules to a winding up.

belong to the continuing partners as and from the time of his departure. It held that this operated so as to exclude the equitable principle which otherwise would oblige the continuing partners to pay interest on the purchase price for the 19-month period.

[26.50] In *Meagher v Meagher*,[85] the fiduciary nature of the continuing partners'[86] position was relied upon by the Supreme Court to hold that a former partner was entitled to receive the increase in the value of the partnership assets between the date of his departure from the partnership and the date of realisation of those assets. It is to be noted that in the later case of *Williams v Harris*,[87] the Supreme Court distinguished the earlier *Meagher* case on the basis that there was no partnership agreement of any kind in the *Meagher* case and therefore no exclusion of the fiduciary principles.

III. RETURN OF PREMIUMS

[26.51] Another consequence of the dissolution of a partnership, and one which is dealt with by a separate section of the 1890 Act, is the return of premiums to a partner who has paid them to the existing partners in the firm. The payment of premiums is no longer that widespread in partnerships. A premium was commonly paid by a person to the existing partners in a firm in consideration for the payer being admitted to a fixed term partnership. Indeed in modern professional firms, one is more likely to come across a 'hello payment' to an incoming partner in order to encourage him to join the firm than a payment of a premium from him to the firm.

[26.52] Nonetheless, the payment of premiums has in the past given rise to difficulties where the partnerships were dissolved before the expiry of the agreed term. Since the payment was a personal payment to the existing partners, and not a contribution to the capital of the firm, the payer did not automatically receive it back as part of his repayment of capital on the dissolution of the firm. This gave rise to a separate claim for a return of the premium when the partnership was dissolved prematurely and consequently the development of principles governing such situations. In general terms, where a person pays a premium for admission to a fixed term partnership and that partnership is dissolved prematurely, the court may order the return of such part of the premium as it thinks fit. These principles are contained in s 40 of the 1890 Act which provides that:

> Where one partner has paid a premium to another on entering into a partnership for a fixed term, and the partnership is dissolved before the expiration of that term otherwise than by the death of the partner, the Court[88] may order the repayment of the premium, or of such part thereof as it thinks just, having regard to the terms of the partnership contract and to the length of time during which the partnership has continued; unless
>
> (a) the dissolution is, in the judgment of the Court, wholly or chiefly due to the misconduct of the partner who paid the premium, or

---

85 *Meagher v Meagher* [1961] IR 96.

86 Again, in this case, the partners were not winding up partners, since the firm's business continued.

87 *Williams v Harris* (15 January 1980) HC, [1980] ILRM 237 (SC).

88 By s 45 of the 1890 Act, this refers to every court and judge having jurisdiction in the case. See also, para **[20.13]**.

(b) the partnership has been dissolved by an agreement containing no provision for a return of any part of the premium.

'the court may order the repayment'

[26.53] It is to be noted that by the express terms of s 40, the return of any premium is not mandatory, but discretionary. In exercising its discretion, the court is required to have regard to the conduct of the partner applying for relief and the terms of the partnership agreement. The cases which are considered hereunder give an indication of the way in which the courts will exercise this discretion.

'partnership for a fixed term'

[26.54] Section 40 states that it applies only to fixed term partnerships. This is because in a partnership at will, a partner knows, or certainly ought to know, that the partnership may be dissolved at any time.[89] For this reason, it would be most unwise for a person to pay a premium to join a partnership at will which may be dissolved at any time. If he does, he has no basis for seeking a return of his premium simply because it is dissolved sooner than he had hoped.

'unless ... the partnership has been dissolved by an agreement'

[26.55] Section 40(b) states that the court is not entitled to award the return of a premium where the partnership has been dissolved 'by an agreement containing no provision for a return of any part of the premium'. What is envisaged under this section appears to be a dissolution agreement, probably in writing, which sets out the rights and duties of the partners on the dissolution, but which is silent as to the return of the premium. This silence is taken as indicating an agreement by the partners that the premium will not be returned. Where there is no comprehensive agreement, but simply a consent to the dissolution of the partnership, without any reference to the terms of the dissolution, this consent is not an 'agreement' as envisaged by s 40(b). Thus, it will not deprive the paying partner of his right to a repayment of his premium.

[26.56] This is clear from the pre-1890 Irish case of *Bolton v Carmichael*.[90] This case involved a fixed term partnership between two lawyers, Bolton and Carmichael, for which Bolton had paid a premium of £250. It was held that the partnership had been dissolved, the dissolution originating with Carmichael's misconduct towards Bolton, but was agreed to by an exchange of letters between Carmichael and Bolton's father. These letters constituted a consent to the dissolution of the partnership, without reference to the terms upon which it should be dissolved. Accordingly, Master Henn held that this consent did not deprive Bolton of his right to a return of the premium and thus it did not constitute an 'agreement' to dissolve so as to prevent the return of the premium.[91]

---

89   As to the nature of a partnership at will, see further para **[8.06]** et seq.
90   *Bolton v Carmichael* (1856) 1 Ir Jur (ns) 298.
91   See also *Bury v Allen* (1845) 1 Colly 589; *Astle v Wright* (1856) 25 LJ Ch 864; *Wilson v Johnstone* (1873) 29 LT 93.

'otherwise than by the death of a partner'

[26.57] Section 40 states that the court is not entitled to order a return of a premium where the premature dissolution of the partnership is caused by the death of a partner. The rationale for this exception is that every partner who enters into a partnership, whether paying a premium or not, should envisage the possibility of a partner's death leading to the dissolution of the partnership. For this reason, such a partner cannot subsequently complain when the partnership is so dissolved and he cannot seek the return of his premium on the occurrence of such a death.

Where Dissolution Arises by Virtue of Bankruptcy

[26.58] The rationale for the non-return of premiums on a dissolution caused by the death of a partner is equally applicable to a dissolution caused by the bankruptcy of a partner. Thus, a partner who enters a partnership should equally envisage the bankruptcy of his partner bringing the partnership to a premature end.[92] Therefore, it is apprehended that a court would refuse to order the return of such a premium, unless of course the recipient of the premium accepted it while he was already in financial difficulties which fact he concealed from the partner giving the premium.[93]

'misconduct of partner who paid the premium'

[26.59] Under the terms of s 40(a) of the 1890 Act, the court is not permitted to return the premium, if the dissolution of the partnership is, in the words of the section, 'wholly or chiefly' due to the misconduct of the partner who paid the premium.[94] This does not include a situation where the dissolution is caused by a simple disagreement between the partners or the misconduct of both partners. The partnership in *Bolton v Carmichael*[95] was a fixed term partnership for seven years, but after one year and two months, it was dissolved, primarily by the actions of Carmichael – he did not provide accounts to Bolton as agreed in the partnership agreement and treated him more as a servant than a partner. However, Carmichael alleged that Bolton had made some offensive remarks about him to a third party and disputed Bolton's right to a return of his premium. Nonetheless, Master Henn held that the dissolution was caused by Carmichael and therefore it would be inequitable for him to retain the whole of the premium. On this basis, he ordered the return of a proportion of the premium equal to the unexpired term of the partnership.

---

92 See *Akhurst v Jackson* (1818) 1 Swan 85. It is thought that the same principle might apply to the insolvency of a corporate partner. However, this pre-supposes that the insolvency of a partner will cause the dissolution of the partnership (whether under the terms of the partnership agreement or in the unlikely event that a court held that bankruptcy of an individual partner in s 33(1) of the 1890 Act was equivalent to the insolvency of a corporate partner). As to such a possibility, see generally, para **[23.40]**.

93 *Freeland v Stansfeld* (1854) 23 LJ Ch 923.

94 See for example *Bluck v Capstick* (1879) 41 LT 215; *Wilson v Johnstone* (1873) 29 LT 93; *Atwood v Maude* (1868) LR 3 Ch App 369.

95 *Bolton v Carmichael* (1856) 1 Ir Jur (ns) 298.

Amount of Premium Returned

[26.60] Section 40 grants the court a discretion to order 'the repayment of the premium, or such part thereof as it thinks just, having regard to the term of the partnership contract and to the length of time during which the partnership has continued'. While the court is required to have regard to the term of the partnership agreement, it is apprehended that this does not prevent the court from using its discretion and taking all other circumstances into account. Commonly, in ordering a return of a premium, the court will order the return of that part thereof as is in proportion to the unexpired term of the partnership.[96] However, the court has a complete discretion in this regard and clearly in some instances, the paying partner's conduct or other circumstances may result in a greater or lesser amount being returned.[97]

[26.61] The case of *Cronin v Kehoe*[98] examined what should happen to the unpaid balance of a premium that Dr Cronin had paid to enter into partnership with Dr Kehoe. Dr Kehoe had practised as a general practitioner in New Ross, County Wexford, for many years before Dr Cronin joined his practice in 1991. Drs Kehoe and Cronin entered into a partnership agreement in 1994. As part of that agreement, £27,000 was payable by Dr Cronin to Dr Kehoe in respect of the goodwill brought by Dr Kehoe to the partnership. That £27,000 was payable in two instalments: £12,000 immediately, and £15,000 over the remainder of the partnership at six-monthly intervals. Unfortunately, Dr Cronin died in 1995 (the partnership was dissolved on his death), and Dr Kehoe died in 2008. The proceedings were between their respective personal representatives. Regarding the payment of £27,000, both parties agreed that only £13,500 had been paid by Dr Cronin to Dr Kehoe during his lifetime, and that the £27,000 should be viewed as a premium. Laffoy J agreed that the amount was a premium and that she needed to determine whether the personal representatives of Dr Kehoe were entitled to claim the unpaid balance of the premium from the personal representatives of Dr Cronin. Laffoy J did not view it as correct to resolve the issue by viewing any approach taken on the point as a corollary of s 40, but instead, in finding the balance of the premium remained due to the estate of Dr Kehoe, noted that:

> '... it seems more logical that, if, having paid the whole premium upfront, the estate of the paying partner cannot seek the return of an apportioned part of it on the premature dissolution of the partnership on his death, where part of the premium remains outstanding at the death of the paying partner, the estate of the paying partner should be liable to the other partner for the balance of the premium, subject to any express agreement to the contrary.'

[26.62] However, Laffoy J acknowledged that she had reached this conclusion with 'a certain degree of diffidence'. She indicated that the outcome in a case such as this would be different if the partnership agreement included express provisions regarding how a premium was to be paid and the impact of any premature dissolution of the partnership

---

[96]   As happened in *Bolton v Carmichael* (1856) 1 Ir Jur (ns) 298.
[97]   See for example the New Zealand case of *Janson v McMullen* [1922] NZLR 677, in which Sim ACJ decided to depart from the normal proportion rule in favour of a return of the whole premium, since the main purpose for which the partnership had been entered (the exploitation of certain agencies) had been terminated.
[98]   *Cronin v Kehoe* [2012] IEHC 373.

on any unpaid instalments of premium. She also noted that, in this case, the provision regarding the frequency of instalments did not specify either the number or amount of each instalment. Instead, it provided that the balance would be paid over the remainder of the partnership at six-monthly intervals, which was open to two interpretations: the first that the instalments were only payable while the partnership endured, and the second that if the partnership only continued for one year, the balance was payable in full in two equal instalments, one after six months and one after 12 months. In light of this, it is clear that the court will have regard to the provisions of any partnership agreement in cases regarding unpaid premiums, and the importance of precise drafting should not be underestimated.

IV. POST-DISSOLUTION PROFITS

[26.63] Where a partnership is subject to a technical, rather than a general dissolution, the partnership business is not wound up, but continues after the change in membership of the firm. Where the change in question is the departure (rather than the arrival) of a partner, an issue arises as to the former partner's entitlement to profits earned by his former firm during the period after his departure but before he receives payment for his share in the firm. This issue is addressed by s 42(1) of the 1890 Act.[99] It does this by providing that the former partner is entitled either to a share of the profits of the firm post-dissolution attributable to the use of his share of the partnership assets or to interest at 5% on his share of the partnership assets:

> Where any member of a firm has died or otherwise ceased to be a partner, and the surviving or continuing partners carry on the business of the firm with its capital or assets without any final settlement of accounts as between the firm and the outgoing partner or his estate, then, in the absence of any agreement to the contrary, the outgoing partner or his estate is entitled at the option of himself or his representatives to such share of the profits made since the dissolution as the Court may find to be attributable to the use of his

---

[99] Etherton LJ, in delivering Court of Appeal's judgment in *Hopper v Hopper* [2008] EWCA Civ 1417 (at para 48 of that judgment) summarised s 42 as follows: 'Section 42 governs what happens in relation to post-dissolution profits if (1) the business of the former partnership is continued by one or more of the former partners, not for the purposes of winding up the former partnership, but for the personal benefit of those continuing to run the business, and (2) those persons do not include all the former partners and the personal representatives of the deceased partner, but (3) there are retained within the continuing business all or part of the shares of the assets of the former partnership to which those non-participants in the continuing business were entitled (in their personal capacity or as personal representatives) on dissolution of the former partnership. In summary, this is a familiar situation, well covered by the cases and equitable principles which applied both before and after enactment of the 1890 Act, where one person's property is employed in the business of another, who may or may not be in breach of trust in retaining that property, and the question arises what rights the owner of that property has in respect of profits of the business.' Under s 701(b) of the American Uniform Partnership Act (1997) (Last Amended 2013), in these circumstances a buyout price for the departing partner's share based on the value of the partnership's business at the departure date is calculated and, until such time as that buyout price is paid, the partnership must also pay interest on that buyout price. Under the American Uniform Partnership Act (1914), the departing partner had a right to elect for a share in profits in lieu of interest, but that right was not carried through into the 1997 Act.

share of the partnership assets, or to interest at the rate of five per cent. per annum on the amount of his share of the partnership assets.

[26.64] The rights under s 42(1) to a share of the profits or to interest are optional rather than cumulative and will be considered in turn. While the option may at first sight appear generous to the outgoing partner, it should be viewed as compensation for the fact that the outgoing partner remains liable for partnership obligations which are existing on the date of his departure and for his exposure to additional liabilities as a result of the continuation of the partnership business.[100] In the case of either option, it is necessary first to calculate the outgoing partner's share of the partnership assets.

[26.65] The importance of the former partner, in respect of whom a claim is being made under s 42(1), actually having a share in the partnership assets was highlighted in *Cronin v Kehoe*.[101] Dr Kehoe had practised as a general practitioner in New Ross, County Wexford, for many years before Dr Cronin joined his practice in 1991. Drs Kehoe and Cronin entered into a partnership agreement in 1994. The medical practice was carried out from Dr Kehoe's property, and all surgical instruments, fixtures and fittings were provided by him. Dr Cronin did not introduce any assets to the partnership that he and Dr Kehoe set up in 1994. Dr Cronin died in 1995 (the partnership was dissolved on his death), and Dr Kehoe died in 2008. As part of the proceedings between their respective personal representatives, Dr Cronin's personal representative claimed that she had not exercised her option to claim the amount of the post-dissolution profits as may have been attributable to Dr Kehoe's use of Dr Cronin's share in the partnership's business, and was instead claiming interest at 5% on an amount payable to her in respect of Dr Cronin's share of the partnership's profits between 1994 when it was established, and 1995 when Dr Cronin died. Laffoy J noted that s 42(1) contemplated the payment of interest on the amount of a share in partnership assets, not partnership profits, and on the basis that Dr Cronin had introduced no assets to the partnership, and was only entitled to a share in the profits, Laffoy J found that his personal representative could not maintain a claim under s 42(1).

Calculating a Partner's Share of the Partnership Assets

[26.66] Under s 42(1) of the 1890 Act, the option of the former partner is to have that part of the post-dissolution profits which is attributable to his share of the partnership assets or to interest on his share of the partnership assets. Thus, in either case, it is necessary to determine his share of the partnership assets.

[26.67] In *Sandhu v Gill*,[102] Lord Neuberger held that the reference in s 42 to 'partnership assets' is to the net assets of the partnership, and not the gross assets of the partnership, and that the outgoing partner's share in those assets should be assessed based on the actual portion of the net assets of the partnership to which he would be entitled on conclusion of the winding up process. Where the remaining partners are to carry on the partnership business, again the outgoing partner's share should be

---

[100]   As to these real and potential obligations, see further para **[11.25]** et seq.
[101]   *Cronin v Kehoe* [2012] IEHC 373.
[102]   *Sandhu v Gill* [2005] EWCA Civ 1297.

calculated by reference to the net partnership assets in accordance with s 44(b) of the 1890 Act.

[26.68] The approach to be taken in determining when an outgoing partner's share of partnership assets should be valued was addressed by the Supreme Court in *Meagher v Meagher*.[103] That case involved three brothers who carried on the business of buying houses, renovating them and selling them at a profit. On the death of one brother, the other two brothers continued to carry on the business. The value of the assets of the partnership had increased considerably since the date of death of the first brother, due to a general increase in property prices in Ireland at that time. In considering the deceased partner's estate's claim under s 42(1), the question arose as to whether the value of deceased partner's share in the houses was to be calculated on the date of death or on the date these partnership assets were realised. The deceased's personal representative claimed that the deceased partner's share in the partnership should be valued on the basis of the prices received for the houses when they were sold which was a number of years after the death.

[26.69] In the High Court, Dixon J held that:

'[T]he only such time to ascertain that amount of the deceased's share in the partnership is at the date of his death; otherwise, the amount on which the other partners would have to pay that interest would vary or fluctuate according to the time at which the amount was ascertained. I do not think the [Partnership Act 1890] intended, or indicated any such variable standard and it would be contrary to common sense.'[104]

[26.70] However in the Supreme Court, Kingsmill Moore J (Ó Dálaigh and Maguire JJ concurring) held that a former partner's share in the partnership assets was to be valued at the date of dissolution (ie date of death), but for practical reasons, this valuation was to be achieved by reference to the value achieved for the assets on the date of realisation:

'[T]he valuation of the share at the date of dissolution is not to be based on hypothetical considerations but on the price fetched by an actual sale, whenever held ... Even if only a short period elapses between dissolution and sale, there is likely to be some change in value due to altered circumstances such as alteration in public taste, depreciation, market fluctuation and other matters. The good sense of the parties and the practice of the Court seems to favour the ignoring of such changes and acceptance of the price realised as representing the value at dissolution. To do otherwise is to open the way to endless enquiries and expense and I am of opinion that the ordinary rule should be, as I think it has been, to accept the price realised as the value of the assets on dissolution. But this is a rule of sound practice and not of law, and the procedure of equity is elastic. If the surviving partners or the representatives of a deceased partner make out a plausible case to show that the value at dissolution varied appreciably from that realised by sale, it is within the power of the Court to direct an enquiry as to the amount of the difference and the causes of the difference. The price realised may be due to the personal efforts of a surviving partner from which the representatives of a deceased partner's have no right to benefit.'[105]

---

[103] *Meagher v Meagher* [1961] IR 96.

[104] *Meagher v Meagher* [1961] IR 96 at 99, Dixon J relied on the authority of *Broughton v Broughton* (1854) 5 De GM & G 160.

[105] *Meagher v Meagher* [1961] IR 96 at 109.

[26.71] Thus, the value of a partner's share of the partnership assets is the value of the net assets on dissolution,[106] but as a general rule, this is to be taken as the price realised on the sale of the assets, whenever that may be, unless there is a plausible case that the value at dissolution varied appreciably from that realised by sale.

Option 1: 'profits ... attributable to use of his share'

[26.72] Once the former partner's share of the partnership assets has been determined, the next step is to ascertain the amount of post-dissolution profits which should be relatively straightforward. Then one has to determine what amount of those profits are attributable to the use by the firm of that share. This latter determination may be difficult, since profits will often result from the skill and work of the surviving partners and not from the assets of firm.[107] Indeed, it has been acknowledged by the courts that it involves a certain degree of guesswork since it is 'not an exercise capable of producing a sum by way of a share of the profits which will be capable of being verified as unquestionably right or wrong, for there will be no mathematical or other means of checking its correctness'.[108] In *Meagher v Meagher*,[109] the post-dissolution profits were due primarily to an increase in the value of the partnership assets (ie houses) which appreciated while they remained unsold. For this reason perhaps, the Supreme Court did not make any attempt to ascertain what part of the post-dissolution profits was attributable to the use of the former partner's share of the partnership assets, but rather appears to have assumed that his share of the re-valued partnership assets included his share of the post-dissolution profits.

[26.73] An earlier example of an outgoing partner's entitlement to a share of the post-dissolution profits is to be found in the pre-1890 case of *Pilsworth v Mosse*.[110] In that case, Mosse had shared the profits of a flour-milling partnership with his partner, Pilsworth, so that he received one-third while Pilsworth received two-thirds. After the death of Mosse, his capital remained in the firm and Pilsworth traded on in the partnership business using this capital for a period of three years. Smith MR held that Pilsworth was obliged to pay Mosse's estate a share of the profits of the partnership since his death. However, as is clear from the terms of s 42(1), the outgoing partner is entitled only to that share of the post-dissolution profits as are attributable to his share of the partnership assets. It is important to note that the outgoing partner is not entitled to

---

106 Of course it should be borne in mind that a partner's share of the assets may vary with time, eg if he receives part payment for those assets from the continuing partners during the period in question, see for example the Victoria Court of Appeal case of *Fry v Oddy* [1998] VSCA 26. See also the case of *Sandhu v Gill* [2006] Ch 456.

107 See for example *Featherstonhaugh v Turner* (1858) 25 Beav 382; *Page v Ratcliffe* (1897) 75 LT (ns) 371. In *Pathirana v Pathirana* [1967] 1 AC 233, the Privy Council considered a two-man partnership in a petrol service station in which the partners shared profits equally. A dispute arose between them and the defendant partner gave notice to the plaintiff terminating the partnership. He continued trading from the same premises in his own name using partnership assets (ie petrol supply agreements) and the Privy Council held that the plaintiff partner was entitled to a third of the post-dissolution profits.

108 Per Ormiston J in *Fry v Oddy* [1998] VSCA 26.

109 *Meagher v Meagher* [1961] IR 96 at 110.

110 *Pilsworth v Mosse* (1863) 14 Ir Ch R 163.

share in the post-dissolution profits in the same proportion as his profit share while the partnership was in existence. Thus in this case, Mosse did not receive one-third of the post-dissolution profits but rather a share of the post-dissolution profits 'proportioned to the respective amounts of capital[111] which the said testator and the said Robert Pilsworth had in said concern'.[112] However, this case must not be taken as establishing that in every case it is appropriate for the post-dissolution profits to be shared in proportion to the partners' capital contributions.

[26.74] Since it will often be a difficult matter to prove that the profits in question are 'attributable to the use of his share of the partnership assets', the courts have in the past simplified the former partner's task by proceeding upon the basis that prima facie the profits of a partnership are attributable to the use of its assets.[113] Indeed, the courts have come close to putting an onus on the continuing partners to rebut such a presumption, Romer J holding in *Manley v Sartori*[114] that it 'is for the surviving partners to show, if they can, that the profits have been earned wholly or partly by means other than the utilisation of the partnership assets'.[115] It follows that where the continuing partners fail to produce any evidence to the contrary, then a court is likely to conclude that, subject to a reasonable allowance for the exertions of the continuing partners, all the post-dissolution profits are attributable to the use of the partnership assets.

[26.75] This is highlighted by the decision in *Fry v Oddy*,[116] where the continuing partners in a nine-person law firm claimed that their former partner, Oddy, was not entitled to any of the firm's post-dissolution profits under the Victoria equivalent of s 42(1) of the 1890 Act.[117] They argued that these profits were attributable solely to the skill and exertions of the partners. At first instance, this argument was rejected and after deducting a notional salary for each of the continuing partners' for their exertions in generating these profits, Oddy was held to be entitled to a ninth of the post-dissolution profits. The Victoria Court of Appeal upheld this decision and Brooking J's reasoning highlights that in s 42 litigation, each case depends on its own facts and in the modern world of professional partnerships, care should be taken not to rely blindly on precedent:

> 'If the early cases show one thing, it is that each case depends on its own facts. Sometimes skill, industry, credit and reputation of the continuing partners will be of particular importance in the generation of profits and the assets employed in the business will be of less importance: *Vyse v Foster* (1872) 8 Ch App 309 at 331 where James and Mellish, LJJ instance the case of solicitors. But this was said in 1872 ... But the last half century has seen a transformation in the practice of solicitors. The mega-firm will be courted as the

---

111 The reference is to his share of the partnership capital rather than partnership assets since in this case his share of the partnership assets and his share of the partnership capital were one and the same. This is, of course, not usually the case, see para **[17.05]**.
112 *Pilsworth v Mosse* (1863) 14 Ir Ch R 163 at 187.
113 As in *Meagher v Meagher* [1961] IR 96, *Fry v Oddy* [1998] VSCA 26 and *Manley v Sartori* [1927] 1 Ch 157.
114 *Manley v Sartori* [1927] 1 Ch 157.
115 *Manley v Sartori* [1927] 1 Ch 157 at 166.
116 *Fry v Oddy* [1998] VSCA 26.
117 Victoria Partnership Act 1958, s 46.

prospective tenant of a block of floors in the latest skyscraper. The wasted space of the atrium - a form of conspicuous consumption - emphasises by way of advertisement the firm's standing and success. Sponsorships will be used. Less oblique forms of advertising are commonplace: in newspapers and journals; on television; by public relations exercises; even by the "shopper-docket" offering one free will. Discounts are in terms offered by some firms on a variety of products. Old Gradman wrote everything by hand. Now the pen has been replaced by the word processor, if not by voice recognition software. The new technology is used both for communication and for management of information and activities. With technological change, no large firm could now prosper without its computer on every desk, its giant photocopiers (themselves a source of revenue), its computer notebooks, its fax machines and answering machines, its mobile telephones and pagers, its dictation equipment, its video conferencing facilities. Its library will be to a considerable extent in electronic format. Its drafting will be done with the aid of artificial intelligence. Its requirements in terms of human resources will range from caterers to librarians. Outsourcing may be used. The firm will need a managing partner or general manager or office manager to carry the cares of the practice. It may be so large that some partners hardly know one another ... All this makes the practice of at least the bigger legal firms resemble a manufacturing business, producing and selling at a profit a range of legal and at times related services.'[118]

[26.76] On this basis, Brooking J concluded that all the assets of the partnership contributed to its profits in the sense that they provided the apparatus which enabled the practice to be carried on. Accordingly, in circumstances where the continuing partners had simply denied that any of the post-dissolution profits were attributable to the use of Oddy's share of the assets and in particular since they had not put forward any other basis for determining what share of the profits might be attributable to the use of Oddy's share, it was reasonable for the trial judge to determine that Oddy was entitled to one ninth of these profits, after account had been taken of a notional salary for the continuing partners' exertions in generating those profits.

'as the Court may find'

[26.77] It is worth emphasising that s 42(1) states that the share of post-dissolution profits is the amount that 'the Court may find' to be attributable to the use of the former partner's share of the partnership assets. Thus, the Court has a certain discretion under s 42(1) regarding the amount of profits which it deems are attributable to the outgoing partner's share of the partnership assets. In exercising this discretion, the Court will take account of such factors as the nature of the firm's business, the capital contributed by each partner, the differing skills of the partners, etc.

Credit must be given to continuing partners for their work

[26.78] In calculating what portion of the post-dissolution profits is attributable to the outgoing partner's share of the partnership assets, the court will take account of the time and work of the continuing partners to earn those profits. Any such time and effort will

---

[118] *Fry v Oddy* [1998] VSCA 26 at 34–35.

be valued and deducted from the post-dissolution profits which are payable to the former partner.[119] Thus in *Barr v Barr*,[120] Barron J stated that:

> 'Clearly in considering what profits the assets of the deceased in the Partnership produced it would be necessary to give credit to those working partners for their labours in obtaining those profits.'[121]

[26.79] In *Meagher v Meagher*,[122] the Supreme Court outlined the procedure to be taken in calculating the 'net' value of a partner's share of the post-dissolution profits, in a case in which the profits were derived only from partnership assets:

> 'Unless the parties otherwise agree there must be a sale of the partnership property including the goodwill. When the value of the property has been ascertained by sale, there must be deducted from the total amount realised by the sales of partnership property at any time since dissolution (a) such portion of the sum realised as is attributable to any expenditure on the assets by the surviving partners out of their own assets and not out of partnership property... (b) such amount of the total sum as is properly allowable in respect of the personal superintendence, management and exertions in regard to the partnership business by [the continuing partners].'[123]

Share of profits under s 42(1) includes capital profits

[26.80] The entitlement of a former partner under s 42(1) to the firm's post-dissolution profits includes capital profits as well as income profits. So it was held by the Supreme Court in *Meagher v Meagher*,[124] where the stock of the partnership consisted of renovated houses which the firm sold and Kingsmill Moore J held that a former partner's share will:

---

119 See for example *Fry v Oddy* [1998] VSCA 26, considered at para **[26.75]**. In that case, Ormiston J notes that there is no real consequence whether one deducts this amount from the firm's profits to determine the profits available for distribution to the former partner under s 42 or whether one uses this amount to reduce the outgoing partner's entitlement to the firm's profits. This right has been recognised by statute in Western Australia where s 55(3) of the Partnership Act 1895, as amended, states that: '[i]n determining how far the profits made since the dissolution are attributable to the outgoing partner's capital, the Court shall have regard to the nature of the business, the amount of capital from time to time employed in it, the skill and industry of each partner taking part in it, and the conduct of the parties generally. And the Court may allow to any such continuing partners such remuneration as to the Court seems meet for carrying on the partnership business.'

120 *Barr v Barr* (29 July 1992) HC.

121 *Barr v Barr* (29 July 1992) HC at p 6 of the transcript.

122 *Meagher v Meagher* [1961] IR 96.

123 *Meagher v Meagher* [1961] IR 96 at 112 per Kingsmill Moore J. In the High Court, Dixon J had stated that the order for an account into the profits under s 42 should 'give scope for allowances to the other parties then surviving and the present surviving partner in respect of all proper allowances and remuneration for their efforts in the business' ([1961] IR 96 at 100). He followed the form of order given in the English High Court case of *Manley v Sartori* [1927] 1 Ch 157. His order provided for an account to be made by the Examiner of what would be proper to allow one of the partners in respect of his 'personal superintendence and management of the business'. The Supreme Court overruled this judgment but not in relation to this point.

124 *Meagher v Meagher* [1961] IR 96.

'include any enhanced value which may result from a rise of prices during the period for which the surviving partners retain the assets in their possession and have the use of them.'[125]

[26.81] Although there have been some decisions to the contrary in other jurisdictions,[126] this view is in keeping with the rationale for s 42(1), ie to hasten the settlement of the departing partner's interest[127] and is consistent with the classic common law definition of the term 'profit' by Fletcher Moulton LJ in *Re Spanish*

---

125 *Meagher v Meagher* [1961] IR 96 at 108.
126 Cf the position in England where the High Court held in *Barclays Bank v Bluff* [1982] 1 Ch 172 that s 42(1) does not apply to capital profits and in that case the increase in the value of a farm did not constitute profits under the section. There, the High Court distinguished the Supreme Court's decision on the grounds that in *Meagher v Meagher*, the assets in question were part of the trading stock, while in that case, the assets were the farm upon which the partnership business was carried on. Interestingly, one of the main reasons put forward in *Barclays Bank v Bluff* for the decision in that case was the desire to ensure that the surviving partner would not have the whole benefit of the increase in value of the partnership assets where the departing partner opted for interest at 5% ('On the face of it, this result would be both extraordinary and unjust' at 180). Yet, if the departing partner is aware that his share of the profits includes the capital profits then no injustice will result, since he will probably choose profits over interest. See also the Privy Council decision of *Chandoutrie v Gajadhar* [1987] AC 147 at 154 and the Court of Appeal decision of *Popat v Shonchhatra* [1997] 3 All ER 800, in which *Barclays Bank v Bluff* was approved. The difficulties with the view taken in England are highlighted by *Popat v Shonchhatra*, above. There, the Court of Appeal approved the principle that s 42(1) does not include capital profits. However, in order to grant the applicant partner a share of the capital profits in that case, Nourse LJ introduced the dubious practice of interpreting the term 'profits' in s 24(1) differently from the term 'profits' in s 42(1). He held that in the former section it referred to revenue and capital profits, while in the latter section it referred only to revenue profits. On this basis, he then went on to hold that s 24(1) applied to post as well as pre-dissolution profits and therefore the applicant partner was entitled to a share of the capital profits. The problem with this approach is that the subsections in s 24 are clearly designed to apply during the life of the partnership as is apparent from an analysis of their terms, eg s 24(7) (no person may be introduced as a partner without the consent of the existing partners), s 24(3) (a partner is entitled to interest on any advance made by him above his capital contribution), while s 42(1) is clearly designed for such post-dissolution profits since its margin note describes it as the '[r]ight of outgoing partner in certain cases to share profits made after dissolution'. The decision in *Popat v Shonchhatra* was cited with approval by the Court of Appeal in *Emerson v Estate of Emerson* [2004] EWCA Civ 170. A farming partnership was dissolved on the death of one of the two partners in 1998 but the farm continued to be operated by the surviving partner who had also died by the time the case was heard. During the winding up of the partnership, statutory compensation was received in respect of the 2001 cull of livestock as a result of a foot and mouth outbreak. A portion of the compensation amount included an excess over the value of the livestock that was culled. The question arose as to whether the excess should be treated as a post-dissolution profit under s 42, or whether it represented a post-dissolution capital profit to be divided equally between the continuing partner and the estate of the deceased partner under s 24. The Court of Appeal held that the allocation of the excess was governed by s 24 rather than s 42 (with s 24 presuming an equal division of capital profits). See generally l'Anson Banks, 'Partnership Dissolution' (1995) 1 Commercial Lawyer 16.

Prospecting Co Ltd,[128] which he acknowledged was not realised by the usual accounting practices:

> 'If the total assets of the business at the two dates be compared, the increase which they shew at the later date as compared with the earlier date (due allowance ... being made for any capital introduced into or taken out of the business in the meanwhile) represents in strictness the profits of the business during the period in question.'[129]

[26.82] Thus, Kingsmill Moore J held in *Meagher v Meagher*[130] that a former partner is entitled to this increase in value, whether it is due to the residual value of the asset by reason of keeping it unsold or by expenditure of partnership profits. However, if the increase in value is solely due to the care, supervision and management of the surviving partners, then the increase in value will not be treated as a profit due to the former partner under s 42(1). On the facts of that case, a general increase in property prices had led to an increase in the value of a number of houses which had been renovated and owned by the firm.[131] This was held to be a profit derived by the firm from the use of the deceased partner's share of the assets under s 42(1) and the deceased partner's estate was entitled to this increase.[132]

Option 2: Claim for Interest under s 42(1)

[26.83] The second option for a former partner under s 42(1) is to choose interest of 5% on his share of the partnership assets. Due to the difficulty in establishing with certainty the value of the first option, namely what proportion of the post-dissolution profits are attributable to the use of the outgoing partner's share of the partnership assets, in many cases the easier option will be to choose interest.[133] Unlike the first option, which involves two imponderables, the only imponderable with the second option is the value

---

127 As noted in the American cases of *Casida v Roberts* (1959) 337 P 2d 829; *Emerson v Arnold* (1979) 285 NW 2d 45; *Anderson v Wadeno Silo Co* (1976) 246 NW 2d 45. See also Hurt, Smith, Bromberg and Ribstein, *Bromberg & Ribstein on Limited Liability Partnerships, the Revised Uniform Partnership Act, and the Uniform Limited Partnership Act (2001)* (2018 edn).

128 *Re Spanish Prospecting Co Ltd* [1911] 1 Ch 92.

129 *Re Spanish Prospecting Co Ltd* [1911] 1 Ch 92 at 99.

130 *Meagher v Meagher* [1961] IR 96.

131 Kingsmill Moore J put the matter thus: 'In my opinion, the increase in value of an asset due to a change in prices during the period of its retention can properly be regarded as a profit derived from its use' ([1961] IR 96 at 110). He also gave the example of where the partnership assets are whiskey and the only use made of the whiskey was to keep it locked up, the rise in price would be treated as profit.

132 The post-dissolution profits in that case were attributable solely to an increase in the value of the partnership assets. Accordingly, it was clear that the share of the former partner in these post-dissolution profits which was attributable to his share of the partnership assets was one and the same as his share in the re-valued partnership assets.

133 Of interest is the English decision in *Williams v Williams* [1999] CLY 4095. A partnership between a father and son had dissolved automatically on the death of the father. The administrator of the father's estate brought a claim under s 42 and also sought to recover court interest under the Supreme Court Act 1981. The claim for court interest failed on the basis that interest was already running at the rate of five per cent per annum under s 42 of the 1890 Act.

of the former partner's share of the partnership assets. This option grants the outgoing partner compensation for the retention by the continuing partners of his money in the firm's business by granting him interest, which is simple interest rather than compound interest, at 5% on the value of his share of the partnership assets.

[26.84] *Hutcheson v Smith*[134] did not involve a claim under s 42(1), since the firm's business was not being continued, but was being wound up by one partner. However, the principle underlying s 42(1) is that the continuing partners should not be allowed to have the free use of the former partner's share of the partnership assets and this principle was applied in that case. One partner had charge of the court-ordered winding up of his firm. He had partnership funds in his possession which he had concealed from the court and he appeared to have used them for his own benefit. Accordingly, Brady CB ordered that he pay his co-partner interest of 5% on his co-partner's share of those funds.

Interest is payable on value of former partner's share of partnership assets

[26.85] In calculating the value of the former partner's share of the partnership assets upon which the interest is payable, one takes the value of that share on the date of dissolution and not the date of realisation. As noted by Dixon J in the High Court judgment in *Meagher v Meagher*,[135] where the date of dissolution was the date of death:

> '[I]f the personal representative chooses, as he is so entitled to do, to claim or take five per cent. of that amount, clearly that amount must be an ascertainable amount ascertainable at some specific time, and the only such time to ascertain that amount of the deceased's share in the partnership is at the date of death; otherwise, the amount on which the other partners would have to pay that interest would vary or fluctuate according to the time at which the amount was ascertained. I do not think the Act intended, or indicated, any such variable standard and it would be contrary to common sense.'[136]

[26.86] The same approach was taken by the Supreme Court, where it was held that the interest was calculated on the value of the partnership share on the date of dissolution. Curiously, however, the Supreme Court held that a different approach was to be taken to ascertaining the value of a former partner's share of the partnership assets depending on whether he was opting for interest or post-dissolution profits. It has been noted that the Supreme Court held that in the case of a former partner who opts for post-dissolution profits, his share of the partnership assets is the value of those assets on the date of dissolution, which as a general rule is to be taken as the value on the date of realisation:[137]

> '[I]f the plaintiff elects to take her share of profits instead of interest on the share of the deceased there need be no segregation of [the realisation value] into profits and value of original share. If, however, the plaintiff elects to take 5 per cent per annum on the deceased's share from dissolution there must be an inquiry as to the value of his share on dissolution. In the conduct of this inquiry, regard must be had to the prices fetched on sale, but those must be reduced by any amounts ascertained as a result of [any expenditure on the assets by the surviving partners out of their own assets] and also by such amount as is

---

[134] *Hutcheson v Smith* (1842) 5 Ir Eq R 117.
[135] *Meagher v Meagher* [1961] IR 96.
[136] *Meagher v Meagher* [1961] IR 96 at 99.
[137] See para **[26.70]**.

attributable to the enhancement of value due to the retention of the assets unsold from the date of dissolution to the date of sale of the relevant assets.'[138]

[26.87] According to the Supreme Court, opting for interest deprives the former partner of his share in the increase in the value of the partnership assets between the date of dissolution and the date of realisation of the value of those assets.[139] Yet, if the former partner opts for post-dissolution profits, these are calculated by reference to the value on the date of dissolution, which as a matter of practice is taken to be the value on the date of realisation of the partnership assets (thus taking into account any increase in value of those partnership assets).

[26.88] The decision may be criticised for the inconsistency in the approach to a former partner's share of the firm's assets depending on whether he opts for interest or post-dissolution profits. In the case of a partner seeking post-dissolution profits, it advocates taking the value of a partner's share on the date of dissolution as equivalent to the value on the date of realisation in order to avoid the 'endless enquiries and expense'[140] involved in establishing the value on the date of dissolution. Yet, in the case of a partner seeking interest on his share of the partnership assets, the Supreme Court has no qualms about putting him to the 'endless enquiries and expense' of establishing the value of his share at the date of dissolution. There would seem to be no good reason in principle to distinguish between the value of a former partner's share of the partnership assets, depending on whether the former partner chooses post-dissolution profits or interest under s 42(1). The Supreme Court's decision has justifiably been criticised by legal commentators[141] and this criticism may have been anticipated by Kingsmill Moore J, who emphasised that the rule that the value on the date of realisation should be taken as equivalent to the value on the date of dissolution, was simply a rule of practice and not a rule of law.

[26.89] It is contended that a consistent approach should be taken to establishing the value of a partner's share in the firm whether this value is used to calculate interest at 5% or to calculate the value of post-dissolution profits attributable to that share. For this reason, it is suggested that the Supreme Court decision should instead be read as authority for the following principles:

(a) where there is no appreciable difference in the value of a partner's share of partnership assets between the date of dissolution and realisation, the value on the date of realisation should be taken as equivalent to the value on the date of dissolution;

(b) in a case where the partnership profits are exclusively due to an increase in the value of the partnership stock or assets (as was the case in *Meagher v Meagher*),[142] a partner opting for post-dissolution profits of the firm which are attributable to his share under s 42(1), has the option of taking the increased value of his partnership share between the date of dissolution and realisation as

---

[138] *Meagher v Meagher* [1961] IR 96 at 112.

[139] Cf the position in England: *Barclays Bank Trust Co Ltd v Bluff* [1982] Ch 172.

[140] *Meagher v Meagher* [1961] IR 96 at 109.

[141] *Halsbury's Laws of England/Partnership* (Volume 79 (2014)) at para 200 fn 3; l'Anson Banks, *Lindley & Banks on Partnership* (20th edn, 2017) at para 25-34, fn 133.

[142] *Meagher v Meagher* [1961] IR 96 at 110.

representing those profits, with appropriate deductions for the work or financial contributions of the continuing partners.

[26.90] It is submitted that, insofar as *Meagher v Meagher*[143] states that a different approach should be taken to ascertaining the value of a former partner's share depending on which option is taken under s 42(1), this cannot be supported in principle. Instead it is suggested that whether a former partner is opting for post-dissolution profits attributable to his share of partnership assets or interest on that share, the same test should be applied to determine the value of his share of partnership assets, ie (a) above.

Financial and tax treatment of s 42(1) interest

[26.91] The general rule regarding the payment of the costs of partnership actions is that they are payable out of the assets of the firm.[144] However, where a former partner has to bring an action against the continuing partners to obtain s 42(1) interest, the costs of this action, if paid out of the partnership assets, will have the effect of reducing the partner's share of the partnership assets and consequently the interest payable on this reduced amount. This would clearly discourage any partner taking an action for interest under s 42(1). For this reason, as happened in *O'Connor v Woods*,[145] the court will order that the s 42(1) 'interest is to be calculated on the balance before any deduction is made for costs'.[146] In the same case, it was made clear by Kenny J that interest, which is payable to a former partner on his share of the partnership assets, is subject to income tax.[147]

Opting for Post-dissolution Profits rather than Interest

[26.92] It has been noted that it will usually be easier for a former partner to opt for interest under s 42(1) than post-dissolution profits, since he will not have to prove what amount of the post-dissolution profits were attributable to his share of the partnership assets and he will not have to deduct the amount due to the continuing partners for their efforts in the business. He will simply have to calculate the value of his share of the partnership assets and interest at 5% will be payable thereon. However, where the profits attributable to the former partner's share are easy to establish and exceed 5%, opting for post-dissolution profits will obviously be preferable. The increase in value of the partnership stock of houses in *Meagher v Meagher*[148] is an example of such a case where the profits exceeded 5% per annum. Another example is where the partnership income is derived from the rental of its property, since the rent is likely to be a profit derived from the partnership assets, it may well exceed 5% per annum and with little input from the continuing partners. This may even be the case where the premises are not rented out to a third party but are used by the continuing partner as in *Walmsley v Walmsley*.[149] There, after the death of one partner in a two-man firm, the defendant partner continued

---

143 *Meagher v Meagher* [1961] IR 96.
144 See generally, para **[20.115]**.
145 *O'Connor v Woods* (22 January 1976) HC.
146 *O'Connor v Woods* (22 January 1976) HC at p 22 of the transcript.
147 *O'Connor v Woods* (22 January 1976) HC where at p 22 of the transcript Kenny J noted that '[i]ncome tax may be deducted from it'.
148 *Meagher v Meagher* [1961] IR 96 at 110.
149 *Walmsley v Walmsley* (1846) 3 Jo & La T 556.

in possession of the firm's premises. Sugden LC held that the defendant partner was liable to pay the former partner's estate half of the 'rent' of the firm's premises between the date of dissolution and the date of the appointment of a receiver. This 'rent' was estimated as equivalent to what the receiver subsequently obtained when he leased the premises.

When Option under s 42(1) is to be Exercised

[26.93] It is apparent from the wording of s 42(1) that the former partner does not have to exercise the option to choose between post-dissolution profits or interest until after the court has determined what is the former partner's share of the partnership profits. Thus, the former partner may seek a declaration from the court of the post-dissolution profits attributable to his share of the partnership assets and at that stage decide whether to look for this share or interest at 5%. Thus in *Barr v Barr*,[150] the High Court held that a firm had made a post-dissolution loss, Barron J observing that:

> 'I will declare that no trading profits were made by these assets following the death of the deceased and that accordingly the Plaintiff is entitled to 5% on such sum as was from time to time outstanding.'[151]

Where Payment is made, Profits are Paid off First

[26.94] The general rule of appropriation of payments that when a payment is made into an account, interest is deemed to be paid off first[152] will apply to payments made by a continuing partner to a former partner.[153] Thus where under s 42(1), a continuing partner owes both capital and post-dissolution profits or both capital and interest to a former partner, any payment which is made, without specifying which debt is paid off first, will go to pay off the profits or the interest first.

Where only one Continuing Partner

[26.95] By its express terms, s 42(1) speaks of applying to a situation where there is no final settlement of accounts between the continuing 'partners' and the 'firm' on the one hand and the outgoing partner on the other hand. Prima facie, this would indicate that the section has no application where there is only one continuing 'partner'. However, an examination of the pre-1890 cases indicates that most of them concerned successful claims against a sole continuing 'partner'.[154] Since the 1890 Act was intended to be

---

150   *Barr v Barr* (29 July 1992) HC.
151   *Barr v Barr* (29 July 1992) HC at p 7 of the transcript. Earlier (at p 6) he stated that: 'the Plaintiff is left to her remedy of recovering the capital value of one quarter of the Partnership assets as of the date of the death of her husband together with 5% on any part thereof remaining unpaid.'
152   *Parr's Banking Co Ltd v Yates* [1898] 2 QB 460 and see generally Breslin, *Banking Law* (3rd edn, 2013) at para 8-41 et seq.
153   *Pilsworth v Mosse* (1863) 14 Ir Ch R 163 at 188 per Smith MR.
154   For example *Pilsworth v Mosse* (1863) 14 Ir Ch R 163; *Booth v Parks* (1828) 1 Mol 465; *Walmsley v Walmsley* (1846) 3 Jo & La T 556. See also the Privy Council decision in *Pathirana v Pathirana* [1967] 1 AC 233; *De Renzy* [1924] NZLR 1065 as varied at [1925] BLR 216 (CA).

declaratory of the existing common law,[155] it is contended that s 42(1) must be read as permitting an action against a sole continuing partner. This conclusion can also be supported in principle since there can be no justification for allowing an outgoing partner in a three man firm to receive payment for the use of his share of the partnership assets post-dissolution, while depriving an outgoing partner in a two-man firm of the same payment.

[26.96] However, it must be borne in mind that for s 42(1) to apply there must be a post-dissolution business. If the partners both cease to carry on business, one partner may not claim interest from the other partner under s 42(1). Thus in the New Zealand case of *Draper v Souster*,[156] the High Court refused to order interest under the New Zealand equivalent of s 42(1)[157] on the grounds that when a partnership between two accountants dissolved, there was no continuing business.

Risk on Partner who Continues to Trade

[26.97] While s 42(1) clearly addresses the sharing of post-dissolution profits, it does not address the issue of the liability for post-dissolution trading. In this regard, it is clear that the former partner has the best of both worlds since, although entitled to interest or a share of the post-dissolution profits, he is not liable for any losses made during this trading period.[158] Thus in the pre-Partnership Act case of *Booth v Parks*,[159] Hart LC observed that:

> 'If [the continuing partner] continues it as a trade, it is at his own risque, liable to the option of accounting for profits, or being charged with interest upon the deceased partner's share of the surplus, as taken at his death.'[160]

Exclusion of Right under s 42(1)

[26.98] It is clear from the wording of s 42(1) (ie 'in the absence of any agreement to the contrary') and s 42(2), that the right of an outgoing partner to post-dissolution profits or interest may be excluded by the terms of an agreement between all the partners. Section 42(2) provides that:

> Provided that where by the partnership contract an option is given to surviving or continuing partners to purchase the interest of a deceased or outgoing partner, and that option is duly exercised, the estate of the deceased partner, or the outgoing partner or his estate, as the case may be, is not entitled to any further or other share of the profits; but if any partner assuming to act in exercise of the option does not in all material respects comply with the terms thereof, he is liable to account under the foregoing provisions of this section.

---

155 See generally para **[1.23]** and s 46 of the 1890 Act.
156 *Draper v Souster* [1999] Butterworths Current Law (NZ) 729.
157 New Zealand Partnership Act 1908, s 45.
158 Unless, of course, he is liable under s 36 of the 1890 Act, see generally para **[11.74]** et seq.
159 *Booth v Parks* (1828) 1 Mol 465.
160 *Booth v Parks* (1828) 1 Mol 465 at 466. See also *Creagh v Creagh* (1862) 13 Ir Ch R 28.

[26.99] The effect of an agreement to purchase an outgoing partner's share was considered by the Supreme Court in *Williams v Harris*,[161] where Griffin J held that:

> 'A long line of authorities show that where partnership articles contain a provision requiring the continuing or surviving partners to purchase the share of a retiring or a deceased partner, the articles constitute a contract for the sale of the retiring or deceased partner's share to his partners, and that this is a complete contract, binding all parties, for the purchase of the interest of the retiring or deceased partner on the date provided for in the partnership articles.'[162]

[26.100] In that case, the partnership agreement provided that upon retirement, the share of a retiring partner shall 'as and from the time of his death or ceasing to be a partner ... be purchased and belong to the remaining partners'.[163] The retiring partners received the purchase price for their share 19 months after their retirement, due to a delay in having a valuation of the share fixed by arbitration. The retiring partners claimed interest for this 19-month period at the rate of 5% under s 42(1) of the 1890 Act.[164] Both the High Court and the Supreme Court rejected the claim for interest on the grounds that the terms of the partnership agreement constituted an agreement to the contrary within the terms of s 42(2) and therefore excluded s 42(1) from applying.[165] In the Supreme Court, Griffin J noted that if the parties had wanted to pay interest on the purchase price of the share, this could have been provided in the partnership agreement.[166]

'not entitled to any further or other share of profits'

[26.101] It is curious that s 42(2) provides that the effect of an option to purchase the departing partner's share is that there is no entitlement to any further or other share of the profits, but no reference is made to a right to interest under s 42(1). Nonetheless, it is contended that implicit in this wording is the fact that an agreement to purchase also excludes the right to interest, since it would not make sense to exclude only one of the options under s 42(1) but not the other. Support for this view is to be found in Kenny J's obiter statement in *Williams v Harris*[167] that the plaintiffs would not have been entitled to interest under s 42(1) of the 1890 Act by virtue of the agreement for the purchase of

---

161 *Williams v Harris* [1980] ILRM 237.
162 *Williams v Harris* [1980] ILRM 237 at 238. He relied on *Vyse v Foster* (1874) LR 7 HL 318 and *Hordean v Hordean* [1910] AC 465.
163 *Williams v Harris* [1980] ILRM 237 at 239.
164 See p 5 of the transcript of McWilliam J in the High Court (15 January 1980) HC. Note however that in the Supreme Court, the plaintiffs appeared to rely solely on equitable principles (at 240), though Kenny J commented obiter on their claim under s 42(1).
165 Although in the High Court, McWilliam J held that the retiring partners were entitled to interest on the basis that the continuing partners were in a fiduciary position and could not have the benefit of the purchase money and the retiring partner's share (15 January 1980) HC. In the Supreme Court, the High Court decision was reversed as it was held that the terms of the partnership agreement excluded the application of these equitable principles.
166 See also *Northern Bank v Manning* (December 1976) HC NI in which Murray J held that a clause which provided for a deceased partner's spouse to have a share of the profits and an interest in the property of the firm excluded any statutory or other rights which would have otherwise accrued to his estate (including the right to undrawn profits).
167 *Williams v Harris* [1980] ILRM 237 at 242: 'I may add that, in my opinion, the plaintiffs have not a valid claim under s 42 of the Partnership Act 1890.'

their shares. Thus, it is suggested that the omission of a reference to interest in s 42(2) may be regarded as an oversight. In the High Court judgment in *Williams v Harris*,[168] McWilliam J noted that:

'if there is no right to a share in the profits under the agreement, there can be no possibility of exercising an option under the section [42(1)] to take either a share of the profits or interest at five per cent per annum.'[169]

'that option is duly exercised'

[26.102] Section 42(2) provides that in order to disapply the provisions of s 42(1), the option to purchase the outgoing partner's share must be duly exercised. It is clear from the Supreme Court judgment in *Williams v Harris*,[170] that this will be taken to have occurred even where the completion of the purchase process takes a considerable amount of time. In that case, the valuation of the outgoing partner's share by arbitration took 19 months to complete. However, in the Supreme Court, Griffin J held that as the valuation of the share was 'only an incident in the arrangements for carrying out the contract of purchase',[171] the purchase was regarded as having been duly exercised despite the long delay. Accordingly, it was held that interest was not payable for this 19-month period.

[26.103] The New Zealand case of *De Renzy*[172] involved a surviving partner who wrongly believed that he had an agreement to purchase his former partner's share. There, two brothers were in partnership together and before leaving the country, one brother gave the other an option to buy his share, exercisable within three months of his death. The brother died on his voyage and the surviving brother, believing he had agreed to buy his brother's share, paid a sum to the credit of his estate which he estimated to be the value of the partnership interest. It was held that the survivor was mistaken in his belief that he had a binding agreement to purchase his brother's interest and therefore the option under the New Zealand equivalent of s 42 was not exercised. Instead, the Supreme Court treated this payment as a partial payment under the equivalent of s 42(1)[173] and it held that the proportion of the profits attributable to the retention of the deceased's share had to abate *pro tanto*.

Where purchase price is paid in instalments

[26.104] The agreement for the purchase of an outgoing partner's share may provide for the purchase price to be paid to the outgoing partner in instalments. This is especially relevant in small firms which might have cash-flow problems if the continuing partners were required to pay the purchase price in one lump sum. If interest is to be paid on the instalments, care should be taken to clarify whether the interest payable on each

---

168 *Williams v Harris* (15 January 1980) HC, [1980] ILRM 237 (SC). This aspect of McWilliam J's decision was not overturned by the Supreme Court.

169 *Williams v Harris* (15 January 1980) HC at p 14 of the transcript.

170 *Williams v Harris* [1980] ILRM 237.

171 *Williams v Harris* [1980] ILRM 237 at 238–239.

172 *De Renzy* [1924] NZLR 1065 as varied by the Court of Appeal at [1925] Gazette Law Reports (NZ) 216.

173 New Zealand Partnership Act 1908, s 45(1).

instalment date is to be calculated on the amount of the instalment then payable or on the entire residue of capital unpaid at that time. This precaution was not taken in *Beater v Murray*.[174] There, Charles Murray was a partner in the Dublin firm of Arnott & Co. Under the terms of the partnership deed, on his death his share was to be purchased by the continuing partners. His estate was to receive in four consecutive equal instalments the value of his share in the firm together with interest thereon of 10%. Sullivan MR held that on the date of each instalment, interest was payable on that instalment only, and not on the whole of the capital.[175]

Where delay before decision to purchase former partner's share

[26.105] It is not uncommon for partnership agreements to grant the continuing partners a time period during which they may decide to purchase the former partner's share or not. This raises the question of whether they should have the 'free' use of the former partner's share during this time. The partnership agreement in *Williams v Harris*[176] provided for a period of six months during which the continuing partners were allowed to decide to either purchase the outgoing partner's share or wind up the firm. No claim was made by the retiring partners for interest or a share of the post-dissolution profits during this six-month 'deciding' period. Yet in the High Court, McWilliam J indicated obiter that the retiring partners may have been entitled to a share of the profits for this six-month period. This dicta was not taken up by the Supreme Court on appeal and in view of the Supreme Court's decision that the provisions in the partnership agreement for the sale of the outgoing partner's share were 'a complete contract'[177] between the partners, it is doubted whether this dicta is good law.

V.   DISTRIBUTION OF ASSETS

[26.106] A crucial part of every general dissolution of the firm is its formal winding up, ie the payment of its debts and liabilities and the division of any surplus between the partners. Unless the parties have agreed otherwise, the manner in which the firm's assets and profits and losses (of a revenue or a capital nature) are to be distributed on a winding up of the firm are set out in s 44 of the 1890 Act:

> In settling accounts between the partners after a dissolution of partnership, the following rules shall, subject to any agreement, be observed:
>
> (a) Losses, including losses and deficiencies of capital, shall be paid first out of profits, next out of capital, and lastly, if necessary, by the partners individually in the proportion in which they were entitled to share profits:

---

[174] *Beater v Murray* (1870) 4 ILTR 532.

[175] This runs counter to the principles contained in s 42(1) of the 1890 Act which favour a former partner obtaining the benefit of the totality of his interest in the partnership and for this reason, it is doubted that it would be followed today, see para **[21.144]**.

[176] *Williams v Harris* (15 January 1980) HC.

[177] *Williams v Harris* [1980] ILRM 237 at 238 per Griffin J. Note also Griffin J's comment that if 'the partners had so required, a provision for the payment of interest could have been included in this agreement'.

(b) The assets of the firm including the sums, if any, contributed by the partners to make up losses or deficiencies of capital, shall be applied in the following manner and order:

1. In paying the debts and liabilities of the firm to persons who are not partners therein:

2. In paying to each partner rateably what is due from the firm to him for advances as distinguished from capital:

3. In paying to each partner rateably what is due from the firm to him in respect of capital:

4. The ultimate residue, if any, shall be divided among the partners in the proportion in which profits are divisible.

'subject to any agreement'

[26.107] The rules in s 44 on the distribution of profits and losses amongst the partners are subject to contrary agreement. It is important to bear in mind that, while the partners may replace the rules in s 44, any such agreement will not limit the rights of creditors of the firm to have the partnership assets sold and their debts discharged. Accordingly, the reference to an agreement to the contrary refers to an agreement as to the repayment of capital, advances and the sharing of any surplus or deficit amongst the partners themselves.

Each Stage of s 44(b) Must be Gone Through in Turn

[26.108] In distributing a firm's assets, s 44(b) of the 1890 Act requires that each of its four stages be gone through in turn. If there is a shortfall at any one of the first three stages, that shortfall will be dealt with in accordance with s 44(a), ie the shortfall is first paid out of profits, then capital, then by the partners in proportion to their profit-share, subject to any contrary agreement between the partners.

Advances v Capital

[26.109] Section 44(b) draws a distinction on a distribution of assets between the treatment of an advance by a partner to a firm and capital paid by a partner to a firm.[178] If the contribution made by a partner to a firm is an advance, this amount will be paid out in full, in priority to repayments of capital to the partners. This difference of treatment should be borne in mind by partners when classifying their contributions to the firm, particularly if the payment is being made by them to a firm in financial difficulties.

[26.110] Any loss which arises on the repayment of advances or capital will be shared between the partners in the proportion in which they share profits.[179]

---

[178] See generally regarding this distinction, para **[17.10]**.
[179] Partnership Act 1890, s 44(a).

Interest on advances and on capital

[26.111] Section 24 of the 1890 Act expressly envisages interest being payable on advances[180] made by partners to the firm and implicitly envisages interest being payable on capital contributed by partners to the firm.[181] Nonetheless, when it comes to the distribution of assets on a dissolution, s 44(b) is silent as to the treatment of interest payable on either advances or on capital. It is apprehended that the references in s 44(b) to advances and to capital will be interpreted as including any interest payable thereon and therefore that interest on an advance or capital will be paid off at the same time as the advance or capital, as appropriate.

Residue

[26.112] If there is a residue after the first three stages of s 44(b) have been completed, then under s 44(b)4, this amount is shared by the partners in the same manner in which profits are shared.

'in the proportion in which they are entitled to share profits'

[26.113] Under s 44(a) and 44(b), losses or any residue are distributed in the proportion in which the partners are entitled to share the profits of the firm. In some firms, it is common to have a division of profits based on a system of gradually increasing points for the partners. It is apprehended that in such a case, the proportions to be used for determining the sharing of profits or losses on a final distribution are the proportions of profit share of each partner on the date of dissolution of the firm.

Sharing of Capital Residue or Capital Loss

[26.114] Section 44(a) and 44(b)4 provide that any loss or residue (profits) will be shared between the partners in the proportion in which they share the profits. These sections are traps for the unwary as this sharing of the capital losses or capital profits applies irrespective of the manner in which the partners have contributed to the capital of the firm.[182] Therefore, a partner who contributes all the capital of the firm and shares the profits of the firm evenly with his partner will, in the absence of any agreement to the contrary, share evenly in any capital profit or capital loss on the winding up of the firm. In some cases, this may come as a surprise to the partner who contributes the capital and accordingly the terms for the sharing of capital profits and losses require careful consideration in such partnerships.

[26.115] An example will highlight this issue. A, B and C contributed capital of €2,000 in the following proportions €1,000, €500 and €500 respectively, the partners sharing

---

[180] Partnership Act 1890, s 24(3), which provides that a partner is entitled, subject to contrary agreement between the partners, to interest on an advance beyond the amount of capital agreed to be subscribed by him.

[181] Partnership Act 1890, s 24(4), which provides that, subject to contrary agreement between the partners, a partner is not entitled, before the ascertainment of profits, to interest on the capital subscribed by him.

[182] See also s 24(1) of the 1890 Act and see *Ex p Maude* (1867) 16 LT 577; *Re Weymouth Steam Packet Co* [1891] 1 Ch 66; *Re Wakefield Rolling Stock Co* [1892] 3 Ch 165.

profits and losses equally. On a winding up there is residual capital of only €1,000, thus leaving a capital loss of €1,000. Under the default rules in s 44(a) governing the sharing of capital losses, these are shared in the same proportion as the profit shares, so that A, B and C are required to contribute a third each, ie each notionally contribute €333, giving a notional capital of €2,000. The rationale for this approach is that such a shortfall in the capital is as much a partnership loss as any other shortfall and is made up in the same way, namely by being shared between the partners. The notional capital is then repaid to the partners in accordance with their capital contributions, since s 44(b)3 requires the capital to be repaid to partners 'rateably'. Therefore, A, B and C will notionally receive the €2,000 divided in proportion to their capital contributions ie 2:1:1 so that A will notionally receive his €1,000 back and B and C will receive back €500 each. To get the actual amount received by A, deduct his notional contribution of €333 from the notional amount of capital he should receive (€1,000) to give €666 which he actually receives. Similarly for B and C, deduct their notional contribution of €333 from the notional amount of capital which they were to receive (€500), to give €166 which they will actually receive. So in respect of A's initial capital contribution of €1,000, he gets back €666, and thus he makes a loss of €333. While in respect of B's and C's capital contributions of €500, they get back €166 and thus they also make a loss of €333. The same result could have been achieved by dividing the capital loss of €1,000 equally between A, B and C.

Section 44(b) takes precedence over s 24(1) on a winding up

[26.116] The foregoing example also highlights the fact that although under the default rule partners share capital profits or capital losses in proportion to their profit sharing ratios, any capital (or advances) contributed by partners to the firm are treated as a debt from the firm to the partners. As such, they are postponed by the terms of s 44(b) to third party creditors. As debts they are paid off *rateably* (as required by s 44(b)) so that capital contributions and advances are repaid to the partners in the proportion in which they were contributed (in the above example in the ratio 2:1:1). Therefore, when s 24(1) states that all 'the partners are entitled to *share equally in the capital* and profits of the business', it is important to note that this section does not require the capital contributions by partners to a firm to be paid out equally on a winding up, irrespective of the ratios in which they were contributed. For this reason, s 24(1) must be read as being subject to s 44(b) in relation to capital contributions on a winding up, since these are repaid to the partners *rateably* to the amount of their respective contributions and not shared equally.

[26.117] In this regard, one must bear in mind that the important monetary figure in relation to a partner's capital contribution is the agreed value of his capital contribution, since it is in respect of this figure that a partner is entitled to rank rateably. For example where a partner makes a contribution of capital of €100,000 by contributing the partnership premises to the firm and these premises increase or decrease in value, this fact will not affect his claim for a return of capital of €100,000 and the differential will be regarded as a capital profit or capital loss as appropriate.

Rule in *Garner v Murray*

[26.118] The rule in *Garner v Murray*[183] provides an exception to the general rule that capital losses are shared by the partners in proportion to the ratio in which they share profits.[184] This exception provides that where one partner is insolvent[185] and is therefore unable to contribute to the loss of capital, the solvent partners are not required to make up the shortfall arising from this fact. In such a case, there will be a deficiency in the capital which is to be distributed. Since capital is repaid in the proportions in which it was paid, the end result is that the deficiency will be borne by the partners in proportion to their capital contribution and not their profit share. This is known as the rule in *Garner v Murray*. To take an example, A and B contributed capital of €15,000 in the following proportions €10,000 and €5,000 while C contributed capital in the form of his skill and expertise. The partners agreed to share profits and losses equally. On a winding up, C is insolvent and there is residual capital of only €6,000, thus leaving a capital loss of €9,000. Under the general rules governing the sharing of capital losses, this loss is shared in the same proportion as the profit shares,[186] so that A, B and C are required to contribute a third each (€3,000). However, C is insolvent so he does not have €3,000 to contribute. Under the rule in *Garner v Murray*, A and B do not have to make up C's share and so they only contribute one third each so that they each notionally contribute €3,000 leaving a notional capital of €12,000 (€6,000 plus the residue of €6,000). The notional capital is then repaid to the partners in accordance with their capital contributions.[187] They will notionally receive the €12,000 divided in proportion to their capital contributions ie 2:1, so that A will notionally receive €8,000 and B will notionally receive €4,000. To get the actual amount received by A, deduct his notional contribution of €3,000 from his notional capital repayment of €8,000 to give €5,000 and for B, deduct his notional contribution of €3,000 from his notional capital repayment of €4,000, to give a figure of €1,000. Thus, in respect of A's initial capital contribution of €10,000, he gets back €5,000, and thus he makes a loss of €5,000. While in respect of B's capital contribution of €5,000, he gets back €1,000 and thus he makes a loss of €4,000. Thus A and B suffer varying degrees of losses.[188]

---

[183] *Garner v Murray* [1904] 1 Ch 57.

[184] Cf the position in America, where s 806(c) of the Uniform Partnership Act (1997) (Last Amended 2013) provides that if, in a winding up, a partner does not contribute to the partnership's liabilities (such contributions must be in proportion to the ratios in which profits are shared between the partners), then the other partners who are liable to contribute to those liabilities of the partnership must contribute the additional amount necessary to discharge the partnership's liabilities (again such further contributions should be in proportion to the ratio in which those partners share profits).

[185] It seems that when the insolvent partner's capital account is overdrawn, this deficit is also treated as a capital loss to be shared between all the partners: l'Anson Banks, *Lindley & Banks on Partnership* (20th edn, 2017) at para 25–53.

[186] Partnership Act 1890, s 44(a).

[187] Partnership Act 1890, s 44(b)3.

[188] Note that the same result is achieved by sharing C's deficiency ie €3,000 between A and B in proportion to their capital contributions, so that A is liable for an additional €2,000, (in addition to the €3,000, which he has to contribute), while B is liable for €1,000 (in addition to the €3,000, which he has to contribute). Contrast the earlier example, where C was not insolvent and the capital losses suffered by A, B and C were the same, para **[26.115]**.

Chapter 27

Bankruptcy

INTRODUCTION

[27.01] The effect on a partnership of the bankruptcy of some or all of the partners is only referred to incidentally in the 1890 Act: s 33(1) of the 1890 Act provides that, subject to any agreement between the partners to the contrary, a partnership is dissolved upon the bankruptcy of a partner. Instead, the effect of bankruptcy on a partner and the partners in a firm is dealt with by the general law of bankruptcy. In this chapter, consideration is given to the general law of bankruptcy insofar as it applies to partners and partnerships. An analysis of the law of bankruptcy in general is beyond the scope of this text and reference should be made to the standard works on the area.[1]

[27.02] In 2012, the Personal Insolvency Act 2012 introduced three mechanisms by which an individual debtor, who is unable to pay his debts in full as they fall due, can restructure his debts in conjunction with his creditors (debt relief notices under Chapter 1 of Part 3 of that Act, debt settlement arrangements under Chapter 3 of Part 3 of that Act, and personal insolvency arrangements under Chapter 4 of Part 3 of that Act). The short title of the 2012 Act states one of that Act's objectives as being to enable '... insolvent debtors to resolve their indebtedness (including by determining that debts stand discharged in certain circumstances) in an orderly and rational manner without recourse to bankruptcy ...'. As such, where an individual partner agrees a debt relief notice, a debt settlement arrangement or a personal insolvency arrangement with his creditors under the 2012 Act, that will not equate to a bankruptcy of that partner and, as such, s 33(1) of the 1890 Act will not apply where such an arrangement is entered into. As a result, a detailed consideration of the 2012 Act is outside the scope of this text; however, three points should be noted:

- due to restrictions imposed by the 2012 Act on actions that an insolvent debtor may take where he is subject to such an arrangement, it may be difficult for such a debtor to enter into a partnership;[2]
- partners may wish to include a provision in the partnership agreement regarding what is to happen if an existing partner enters into a debt relief

---

[1] Sanfey and Holohan, *Bankruptcy Law and Practice* (2nd edn, 2010); Forde and Simms, *Bankruptcy Law* (2009). See also the consolidation of the Bankruptcy Act 1988 prepared by the Law Reform Commission and available in the 'Revised Acts' section of its website (www.lawreform.ie). See the Bankruptcy Law Committee Report (1972) prl 2714 and in particular chapter 39 on partnerships. See also 'Unaccomplished reforms in partnership bankruptcy under the Chandler Act' (1940) 49 Yale LJ 908; Ailola, 'Sequestration of a partnership estate in South Africa: some notes on the effect of payment by a partner' (1996) 12 Insolvency Law & Practice 6.

[2] See further para **[4.22]**.

notice, a debt settlement arrangement or a personal insolvency arrangement with his creditors; and

–   if a debtor enters into a debt settlement arrangement or a personal insolvency arrangement under the 2012 Act which is terminated or is deemed to have failed, that termination or deemed failure will trigger an 'act of bankruptcy' under the Bankruptcy Act 1988.[3]

[27.03] While this chapter is primarily concerned with bankruptcy, it also considers the general inability of a partner to pay his debts and it is divided into the following sections:

I.   Winding up of Firms as Unregistered Companies;

II.   Bankruptcy Proceedings;

III. Administration of Firm's and Partner's Estates;

IV.   Arrangements with Creditors.

Overview

[27.04] The law of bankruptcy as it applies to partnerships is a somewhat complex area deriving as it does from a mix of statutory provisions in the 1890 Act, the Bankruptcy Act 1988 and common law decisions, many of which deal with repealed sections of previous bankruptcy legislation. Consequently, the area would benefit from a codification of these various sources of the law of bankruptcy of partners. Surprisingly, this was not one of the recommendations of the Bankruptcy Law Committee in its report on bankruptcy law.[4]

[27.05] The main focus of this chapter is on the effect of the bankruptcy of a partner on his firm. In general terms this is the dissolution of the firm and the vesting of the bankrupt partner's property in the Official Assignee. In practice, the bankrupt partner's interest in the partnership is either sold by the Official Assignee to the other partners or the other partners will wind up the partnership and pay to the Official Assignee the amount which is due to the bankrupt partner. When a partner is declared bankrupt, the main concern is invariably the position of the creditors and in particular the respective rights of the creditors of the partnership and the separate creditors of the bankrupt partner. The common law rules governing the priorities of these respective creditors were known as Lord Loughborough rules, but following the recommendations of the Bankruptcy Law Committee,[5] these important rules have been given a statutory footing and are now contained in s 34 of the Bankruptcy Act 1988. These rules provide for the partnership creditors to have first call on the partnership property and for the separate creditors to have first call on the separate estate of the bankrupt. In doing so, the rules highlight the essential distinction between joint creditors and separate creditors which pervades this area of bankruptcy law, namely that the joint creditors are creditors of the firm while the separate creditors are creditors of the individual partner only. An appreciation of this distinction is required for any consideration of how these rules apply to different bankruptcy situations.

---

[3]   See further para **[27.23]** below.

[4]   See para 39.10.11 of the Bankruptcy Law Committee Report (1972) prl 2714.

[5]   Bankruptcy Law Committee Report (1972), para 39.10.4.

I.   WINDING UP OF FIRMS AS UNREGISTERED COMPANIES

[27.06] Before considering the bankruptcy of a partner and a firm it is proposed to consider the related area of the winding up of a partnership as an unregistered company, since the principal instance in which a partnership may be wound up as an unregistered company is when it is unable to pay its debts. Reference should first be made to the winding up of a partnership under the 1890 Act and then to winding up a partnership under the Companies Act 2014.

Winding up of a Partnership under the 1890 Act

[27.07] Under the combined effect of ss 35 and 39 of the 1890 Act, every partnership may be wound up by means of an application to court. Thus, if a partnership is unable to pay its debts a partner may seek a court dissolution under s 35 on the grounds that the business of the partnership can only be carried on at a loss (s 35(e)) or on the grounds that it is just and equitable (s 35(f)). Once the court has ordered a dissolution, s 39 of the 1890 Act entitles a partner to have the partnership property sold and the debts of the firm paid off and this winding up may be done under the direction of the court. The winding up of a partnership under the 1890 Act is considered in detail elsewhere in this work.[6] Such a winding up will usually be compulsory in the sense that not all the partners will wish to have the firm wound up. Obviously, where winding up is voluntary, there will be no need for court intervention for the winding up to proceed.

[27.08] As will be seen hereunder, certain partnerships may be wound up as unregistered companies under ss 1326 to 1328 of the Companies Act 2014. However in general, only partnerships with eight or more partners may be wound up under that Act. Even then, only the compulsory winding up of those partnerships is permitted under the 2014 Act. Thus, when one refers to the winding up of a partnership, one is generally referring to its winding up under the 1890 Act.

Winding up of Certain Partnerships under Companies Act 2014

[27.09] Under ss 1326 to 1328 of the Companies Act 2014, a partnership of eight or more partners may be wound up as an unregistered company (in the case of an investment limited partnership, there is no limit on the number of partners).[7] A partnership with seven or less members may only be wound up as an unregistered company if it is formed outside the State.[8] This is the effect of s 1326 of the 2014 Act, which provides that:

> For the purposes of this Chapter 'unregistered company' includes ... any partnership, whether limited or not, any association and any company other than—
>
> (a)   a company as defined by *section 2(1)*;
>
> (b)   a partnership, association or company which consists of less than 8 members and is not formed outside the State.

---

6   See para **[26.26]** et seq.

7   Investment Limited Partnerships Act 1994, s 38(3), and see generally para **[29.01]** et seq.

8   This conclusion is based on an interpretation of s 1326(b) in a conjunctive manner, see para **[27.10]**.

For ease of reference, a partnership which satisfies this definition is referred to as a 'qualifying partnership' in the remainder of this chapter.

[27.10] As is clear, s 1326 is very tortuously drafted[9] and it is not immediately obvious what the status is of a partnership with less than eight members but formed outside the State. It seems, however, that the two clauses in s 1326(b) must be interpreted in a conjunctive manner so that such a partnership is not excluded from the definition of an unregistered company and so may be wound up under ss 1326 to 1328.

[27.11] As will be noted, ss 1326 to 1328 allow for the winding up of a partnership by a creditor of the firm. As such, they are the only statutory references to the winding up of a partnership by a creditor, since the 1890 Act does not grant a creditor the right to seek a dissolution or a winding up of a partnership. Thus, a creditor of a non-qualifying partnership may not apply to court for the firm's winding up,[10] but will be restricted to his remedy under the law of bankruptcy.[11]

[27.12] Once a partnership is a qualifying partnership, it may only be compulsorily wound up since a qualifying partnership may not be wound up voluntarily under s 1328.[12] The circumstances in which it may be wound up are set out in s 1328(4) of the Companies Act 2014.[13] These circumstances are:

---

9   In New Zealand there was an implicit recognition of the poor drafting of their equivalent of ss 1326–1328 of the Companies Act 2014 (namely Part XI of the Companies Act 1955) by its replacement in 1993 by ss 240B of the Companies Act 1993 which provides for the liquidation of associations, which term includes a partnership, without any reference to the number of members thereof or the State in which it is formed.

10   Accordingly, the comments of Judge Connolly in the Circuit Court case of *O'Neill v Whelan* (1951) 85 ILTR 111 at 112 must be regarded as referring to a winding up as a result of bankruptcy and not under the companies legislation of the time (the Companies (Consolidation) Act 1908, ss 267–268 the predecessor to both the Companies Act 1963, ss 344–345, and the Companies Act 2014, ss 1326–1328), since the firm in question had only two partners: 'If the partners were not able to discharge the trade debts of the partnership, the creditors would then be entitled to have the partnership wound up under an order of the Court, when all the partnership property would have to be realised.'

11   See para **[27.19]** et seq. Note also the possibility of the appointment of a receiver by way of equitable execution under Ord 45, r 9 of the Rules of the Superior Courts. See further regarding such appointments *Glorney Ltd v O'Byrne* (1951) 85 ILTR 19; *Commissioners of Church Temporalities v Harrington* (1833) 11 LR Ir 127; *Kernohan Estates Ltd v Boyd* [1967] NI 27; *O'Connell v An Bord Pleanála* [2007] IEHC 79. See generally Keane, *Equity and the Law of Trusts* (3rd edn, 2017) at para [21.06] et seq; Wylie, *Irish Land Law* (5th edn, 2013) at para [3.187] et seq; Ó Floinn, *Practice and Procedure in the Superior Courts* (2nd edn, 2008) at p 430.

12   Companies Act 2014, s 1328(3).

13   See for example *Re Royal Victoria Palace Theatre Syndicate* [1873] WN 224, aff'd [1874] WN 8, where a winding up order was made under a predecessor of ss 1326–1328, namely ss 199–200 of the Companies Act 1862 and *Re Bolton Benefit Loan Society Co-op v Booth* (1879) 12 Ch D 679, where a winding up order of the partnership was refused since the number of members was below eight. In that case, the creditor's petition for a winding up was refused and subsequently the court heard an application by one of the partners for the dissolution of the partnership and its winding up.

(a)   the partnership is dissolved;

(b)   the partnership has ceased to carry on business;

(c)   the partnership is carrying on business only for the purposes of its winding up;

(d)   the partnership is unable to pay its debts; or

(e)   the High Court is of the opinion that it is just and equitable that the partnership should be wound up.

[27.13] These grounds are broadly the same as the grounds for winding up a registered company under the Companies Act 2014 though it is to be noted that the five grounds set out above for the winding up of a partnership as an unregistered company are more limited than the eight grounds set out in s 569(1) of the 2014 Act for the winding up of a registered company. Accordingly, reference should be made to the standard company law texts for a detailed consideration of the compulsory winding up of companies.[14] On the winding up of a partnership as an unregistered company, the provisions governing the winding up of companies apply and the High Court or any liquidator appointed may exercise any powers or do any act in the case of a partnership as might be done in relation to the winding up of companies.[15]

[27.14] The first three of the five grounds for the winding up of a partnership as an unregistered company do not require further comment. The fourth ground is that the partnership is unable to pay its debts and it will be considered next.

Unable to pay its debts

[27.15] Section 1329 of the Companies Act 2014 clarifies what is meant by the requirement that an unregistered company be unable to pay its debts. It provides that an unregistered company will be deemed unable to pay its debts:

(a)   if a creditor, by assignment or otherwise, to whom the company is indebted in a sum exceeding €10,000 then due, has served on the company, by leaving it at its principal place of business in the State, or by delivering to the secretary or some director or principal officer of the company, or by serving otherwise in such manner as the court may approve or direct, a demand in writing requiring the company to pay the sum so due, and the company has for 3 weeks after the service of the demand neglected to pay the sum or to secure or compound for it to the satisfaction of the creditor; or

(b)   if any action or other proceeding has been instituted against any member for any debt or demand due or claimed to be due, from the company, or from him in his character of member, and notice in writing of the institution of the action or proceeding having been served on the company by leaving the same at its principal place of business in the State, or by delivering it to the secretary, or some director or principal officer of the company, or by otherwise serving the same in such manner as the court may approve or direct, the company has not within 10 days after service of the notice paid, secured or compounded for the debt or demand, or procured the action or proceeding to be stayed, or indemnified the defendant to his reasonable satisfaction against the action or proceeding, and against all costs, damages and expenses to be incurred by him by reason of the same;

(c)   if in the State or in any country recognised by the Minister for Business, Enterprise and Innovation for the purposes of section s 1417 of the 2014 Act,[16] execution or other process

---

14   Courtney, *The Law of Companies* (4th edn, 2016); Hutchinson, *Keane on Company Law* (5th edn, 2016); Forde and Kennedy, *Company Law* (5th edn, 2017).

15   Companies Act 2014, s 1333.

16   The Companies Act 2014, s 1417 deals with the recognition of winding-up orders of non-European Union states and Denmark.

issued on a judgement, decree or order obtained in any court in favour of a creditor against the company, or any member thereof as such, or any person authorised to be sued as nominal defendant on behalf of the company, is returned unsatisfied;

(d)   if it is otherwise proved to the satisfaction of the court that the company is unable to pay its debts.

In general terms, therefore, a qualifying partnership which satisfies any of these requirements may be wound up on the application of a creditor to court as if it was a company.[17] Accordingly, reference should be made to the standard works on the compulsory winding up of companies.[18]

Position of a limited partner in an investment limited partnership

[27.16] Section 1328 of the Companies Act 2014 provides simply that a qualifying partnership may be wound up as an unregistered company. Accordingly, it is clear that all types of partnerships, whether ordinary, limited or investment limited, may be wound up in this way. However, the provisions of s 1329(3) and (4), in connection with the inability of a partner to pay his debts, are modified in their application to limited partners in investment limited partnerships. Section 38(3) of the Investment Limited Partnerships Act 1994 takes account of the special nature of a limited partner, ie his limited liability for the debts of the firm, by providing that a limited partner in an investment limited partnership is not regarded as being a partner for the purposes of the tests in ss 1329(3) and (4). Thus, the inability of a limited partner in an investment limited partnership to pay a debt due from him as a member of the firm is not a factor in determining whether the firm is unable to pay its debts. The rationale for this exemption is clear, namely that as the liability of a limited partner for the debts of the investment limited partnership is limited to the capital which he has subscribed to the firm, his inability to pay any debt should not be taken into account in determining whether the firm is able to pay its debts.

Position of limited partners in a limited partnership

[27.17] Surprisingly, the same exemption does not apply to limited partners in limited partnerships even though their liability to the firm is limited in almost identical terms to the amount of capital contributed by them. It is apprehended that this is a legislative oversight which should be rectified at the earliest opportunity as there is no reason in principle why a limited partner in an investment limited partnership should be treated differently from a limited partner in an investment limited partnership in this regard.[19]

---

17   For an example of where an unregistered company was wound up, see *Re Welsh Highland Light Railway Co* [1993] BCLC 338.

18   Courtney, *The Law of Companies* (4th edn, 2016); Hutchinson, *Keane on Company Law* (5th edn, 2016); Forde and Kennedy, *Company Law* (5th edn, 2017).

19   Note that the distinction between general partners and limited partners in a limited partnership on the winding up of limited partnerships was initially recognised by the legislature, ie under s 6(4) of the Limited Partnerships Act 1907. This section, which was repealed by s 286 of the Companies (Consolidation) Act 1908, provided for limited partnerships to be wound up under the Companies Acts 1862 to 1900 and that the general partners, but not the limited partners, were to be treated as if they were directors.

Just and Equitable to Wind up the Firm

[27.18] The fifth and final ground for the winding up of a partnership as an unregistered company is on just and equitable grounds. It is indisputable that the winding up by the court of a partnership as an unregistered company on these grounds will be made in the same instances as the winding up by a court of a partnership on just and equitable grounds under s 35(f) of the 1890 Act. Accordingly, reference should be made to the treatment earlier in this work of this ground under s 35(f).[20]

II.   BANKRUPTCY PROCEEDINGS

[27.19] In this section, the mechanics of the bankruptcy procedure against partners and partnerships is examined. A distinction must first be made between the bankruptcy of a firm and the bankruptcy of a partner in a firm. The bankruptcy of a firm necessarily involves the bankruptcy of each of its members,[21] since as has been noted previously, the firm's debts are the debts of each partner.[22] On the other hand, the bankruptcy of a partner does not necessarily bring about the bankruptcy of the firm since, despite the bankruptcy of one partner, the partnership assets may be sufficient to pay all the creditors of the firm. Accordingly, reference will be made throughout this section to two distinct situations: first, where a partner is bankrupt and the firm remains solvent; and second, where the firm is bankrupt, which necessarily involves the bankruptcy of each partner.

The Bankruptcy Act 1988

[27.20] In considering the general law of bankruptcy, reference must be made to both the common law and the Bankruptcy Act 1988,[23] which substantially re-formulated the law of bankruptcy. Sections 30 to 37 of the Bankruptcy Act 1988 are headed 'Partnership Cases' and deal expressly with the bankruptcy of partners and partnerships by reference throughout both to 'partnerships' and 'partners'. On this basis, one can conclude that the 1988 Act prima facie applies to all partnerships (ie ordinary partnerships, limited partnerships and investment limited partnerships) and to ordinary, general and limited partners. This general statement is subject to some qualification. As noted elsewhere in this work, the position of a general partner in a limited partnership and a general partner in an investment limited partnership is akin to that of a partner in an ordinary partnership.[24] There is, therefore, no reason why a general partner should not be subject to the terms of the 1988 Act in the same way as a partner in an ordinary partnership. For this reason, the analysis in this chapter of bankruptcy law as it applies to ordinary partners is equally applicable to general partners in both limited partnerships and investment limited partnerships.

---

[20]   See para **[25.55]** et seq.

[21]   This is also apparent from s 38 of the 1890 Act. The proviso thereto provides that a bankrupt partner cannot bind the firm and thus where all the partners in a firm are bankrupt, the firm is necessarily dissolved since no one person will have authority to act on behalf of the firm.

[22]   See para **[10.01]** et seq.

[23]   As supplemented by the Rules of the Superior Courts, Ord 76.

[24]   See generally in relation to limited partnerships, para **[28.01]** et seq, and in relation to investment limited partnerships, para **[29.01]** et seq.

[27.21] However, the role of the limited partner in a limited partnership and of the limited partner in an investment limited partnership is considerably different from that of a partner in an ordinary partnership. In the case of such a limited partner, his liability for debts of the firm is limited to the amount of his capital contribution.[25] Therefore, bankruptcy laws do not apply to limited partners in limited partnerships and investment limited partnerships in the same way as they apply to ordinary partners and reference should be made to the chapters on limited partnerships and investment limited partnership for a discussion of the modification of bankruptcy law as it applies to limited partners therein.

The Act of Bankruptcy

[27.22] The first substantive area of bankruptcy law for examination is the act of bankruptcy, since before a partner can be adjudicated bankrupt, he must have committed an act of bankruptcy.

There must be an act of bankruptcy

[27.23] The acts of bankruptcy for a partner will in general terms be the same as for an individual and for a detailed consideration of these acts, reference should be made to the standard works on bankruptcy.[26] In brief, these acts are set out in s 7 of the Bankruptcy Act 1988 and unless one of these acts[27] is committed, there can be no bankruptcy.[28] Section 7 reads as follows:

> (1) An individual (in this Act called a 'debtor') commits an act of bankruptcy in each of the following cases—
>
> (a)   if in the State or elsewhere he makes a conveyance or assignment of all or substantially all of his property to a trustee or trustees for the benefit of his creditors generally;
>
> (b)   if in the State or elsewhere he makes a fraudulent conveyance, gift, delivery or transfer of his property or any part thereof;
>
> (c)   if in the State or elsewhere he makes any conveyance or transfer of his property or any part thereof, or creates any charge thereon, which would under this or any other Act be void as a fraudulent preference if he were adjudicated bankrupt;
>
> (ca)   the individual has been subject as a debtor to a Debt Settlement Arrangement which has been terminated under section 83 of the Personal Insolvency Act 2012;
>
> (cb)   the individual has been subject as a debtor to a Debt Settlement Arrangement which under section 84 of the Personal Insolvency Act 2012 is deemed to have failed;
>
> (cc)   the individual has been subject as a debtor to a Personal Insolvency Arrangement which has been terminated under section 122 of the Personal Insolvency Act 2012;
>
> (cd)   the individual has been subject as a debtor to a Personal Insolvency Arrangement which under section 123 of the Personal Insolvency Act 2012 is deemed to have failed;

---

[25]   Save in exceptional circumstances, as to which see para **[28.104]** et seq and para **[29.92]** et seq.

[26]   Sanfey and Holohan, *Bankruptcy Law and Practice* (2nd edn, 2010); Forde and Simms, *Bankruptcy Law* (2009).

[27]   In addition to the acts of bankruptcy mentioned in the text, there is a further act of bankruptcy under s 11(3) of the Auctioneers and House Agents Act 1967. See generally Sanfey and Holohan, *Bankruptcy Law and Practice* (2nd edn, 2010).

[28]   *Ex p Dale* [1893] 1 QB 199.

    (d)   if with intent to defeat or delay his creditors he leaves the State or being out of the State remains out of the State or departs from his dwelling house or otherwise absents himself or evades his creditors;

    (e)   if he files in the Court a declaration of insolvency;

    (f)   if execution against him has been levied by the seizure of his goods under an order of any court or if a return of no goods has been made by the sheriff or county registrar whether by endorsement on the order or otherwise;

    (g)   if the creditor presenting a petition has served upon the debtor in the prescribed manner a bankruptcy summons, and he does not within fourteen days after service of the summons pay the sum referred to in the summons or secure or compound for it to the satisfaction of the creditor.

(2) A debtor also commits an act of bankruptcy if he fails to comply with a debtor's summons served pursuant to section 21(6) of the Bankruptcy (Ireland) Amendment Act, 1872, within the appropriate time thereunder, and section 8(6) of this Act shall apply to such debtor's summons.

Other acts of bankruptcy

[27.24] Section 105 of the Bankruptcy Act 1988 also provides that an act of bankruptcy is committed where a debtor fails to get the approval of both his creditors and the High Court to his proposed arrangement with his creditors under s 105 in Part IV of the 1988 Act. However, while this provision remains in the 1988 Act, it is of no practical use at the time of writing as, since 3 December 2013, a debtor can no longer present a petition for an arrangement under Part IV.[29]

Act of bankruptcy of a partner and partners

[27.25] While acts of bankruptcy by a partner will be the same as those by an individual, there are certain aspects of these acts of bankruptcy which are peculiar to the law of partnership and these are dealt with hereunder.

Act of bankruptcy is personal

[27.26] An act of bankruptcy is personal to the partner who commits it and therefore the bankruptcy of one partner in a firm will not lead to the bankruptcy of his co-partner, since an act of bankruptcy must be proved against each partner. This is the case even though partners are agents for each other.[30] Thus an act of bankruptcy will only bind another partner if the other partner concurs in the act.[31] This point is aptly illustrated by *Re Harris*,[32] which concerned the bankruptcy of one Ms Harris who carried on a garage business in Lower Castlereagh, Co Down. It transpired that a Mr Rand carried on business with Harris and the bankruptcy judge made an order that Rand at the time of

---

[29]   On 3 December 2013, Part 7 of the Courts and Civil Law (Miscellaneous Provisions) Act 2013 (which inserted a new s 86A into the Bankruptcy Act 1988) came into force. The new s 86A provided that from that date, no petition for court protection under Part IV of the 1988 Act could be presented. This resulted from the availability of non-judicial debt settlement mechanisms under the Personal Insolvency Act 2012 as an alternative to bankruptcy under Part IV of the 1988 Act.

[30]   Partnership Act 1890, s 5 and see generally para **[10.01]** et seq.

[31]   *Ex p Blain* (1879) 12 Ch D 522; *Mills v Bennett* (1814) 2 M & s 556; *Ex p Mavor* (1815) 19 Ves 543; *Ex p Addison* (1849) 3 De G & Sm 580.

[32]   *Re Harris* [1939] NI 1.

the adjudication of Harris was her partner and that therefore he also should be adjudged a bankrupt. Rand appealed to the Northern Ireland Court of Appeal which noted that he had not committed any act of bankruptcy and accordingly, the adjudication of bankruptcy was set aside.

[27.27] Since a partner is only bound by the act of bankruptcy if he concurs in it, it has been held that if only one of several partners in a firm execute a deed, which is intended to be executed by all and which conveys for himself and the other partners all their personal property, it is an act of bankruptcy against the executing party only.[33] Similarly, where one partner executes a deed fraudulently in order to convey property to his partner, the execution of the conveyance is an act of bankruptcy only against the first partner.[34]

[27.28] In contrast, a conveyance by one partner of all of his separate property to a trustee, upon trust for sale and the payment of the debts of the firm, is not an act of bankruptcy if made bona fide with the intention of relieving the firm from its difficulties and of enabling it to carry on its business, and if it is not made for the purpose of and does not defraud separate creditors of the partner.[35] Similarly, a bona fide conveyance by one partner to another of all his share in the partnership assets upon trust first to pay the partnership debts and then to retain what is due by the firm to him and thirdly to divide the surplus between the partners is not an act of bankruptcy.[36] This is because such a conveyance does not come within the ambit of s 7(1)(a) of the Bankruptcy Act 1988 as it does no more than allow the assignee to work out the lien which a partner has on the partnership property for what is due by the firm to him.[37]

Joint acts of bankruptcy

[27.29] Partners may commit an act of bankruptcy jointly if they do so with their co-partners. Indeed, a joint adjudication against all the partners in a firm will be made if each has committed an act of bankruptcy during the continuance of the joint debt,[38] although this need not be the same act.[39] Partners will commit a joint act of bankruptcy within the terms of s 7(1)(a) of the Bankruptcy Act 1988, if they assign all their property to a person who undertakes to pay their debts.[40] Similarly, a mortgage of the joint estate by all the partners to secure their separate debts, where the joint creditors are prejudiced, is a joint act of bankruptcy by the partners.[41]

---

[33] *Bowker v Burdekin* (1843) 11 M & W 128.
[34] *Whitwell v Thompson* [1793] 1 Esp 68.
[35] *Abbott v Burbage* (1836) 2 Bing NC 444.
[36] *Payne v Hornby* (1858) 25 Beav 280.
[37] See generally regarding this lien of a partner para **[26.28]** et seq.
[38] *Beasley v Beasley* (1736) 1 Atk 97; *Mills v Bennett* (1814) 2 M & s 556; *Allen v Hartley* (1784) 4 Doug 20; *Dutton v Morrison* (1810) 17 Ves 193; *Hogg v Bridges* (1818) 8 Taunt 200.
[39] *Ex p Bamford* (1809) 15 Ves 449.
[40] See for example *Ex p Zwilchenbart* (1844) 3 MD & D 671.
[41] *Ex p Snowball* (1872) 7 Ch 534.

Bankruptcy Summons

[27.30] The most common way in which bankruptcy proceedings are commenced against a debtor is by a creditor issuing a bankruptcy summons in respect of the debt and if the debt is not thereby satisfied, by the presentation of a bankruptcy petition thereafter.[42]

[27.31] Before petitioning for bankruptcy, the creditor must prove his debt and this is usually done by means of a bankruptcy summons which is issued under s 8 of the Bankruptcy Act 1988. If, after the bankruptcy summons has been served on the debtor, the debtor does not pay the sum therein within 14 days or secure or compound it to the satisfaction of the creditor, the debtor will be deemed to have committed an act of bankruptcy.[43]

Presentation of bankruptcy summons by a partnership or partners

[27.32] Section 8(1) of the Bankruptcy Act 1988 allows a bankruptcy summons to be granted by the High Court to a 'creditor' with a debt of €20,000 (which must be a liquidated sum and in respect of which the creditor must have given at least 14 days' notice in a prescribed form to the debtor of the creditor's intention to apply for that bankruptcy summons, and the debt must remain unpaid). For the purpose of s 8, a creditor is defined as a 'person', which term must be taken to include a partnership.[44] On this basis, it seems clear that where a creditor is a partnership, it may be granted a bankruptcy summons by the High Court against its debtor under s 8(1) of the 1988 Act.

[27.33] Section 8(2) of the Bankruptcy Act 1988 contemplates a situation where two or more persons are creditors of the one debtor and where their individual debt does not exceed €20,000 or more. Section 8(2) states that, provided that these two or more creditors are not partners, they may be granted a bankruptcy summons if their combined indebtedness exceeds €20,000. Curiously, s 8 does not directly address the situation where two or more creditors, who are partners, wish to be granted a bankruptcy summons. This may be because it was apprehended that a firm could be granted a bankruptcy summons as a 'person' under s 8(1) of the 1988 Act.[45]

---

[42] For a consideration of the other means by which a debtor may be adjudicated bankrupt, see generally Sanfey and Holohan, *Bankruptcy Law and Practice* (2nd end, 2010) and Forde and Simms, *Bankruptcy Law* (2009).

[43] Bankruptcy Act 1988, s 7(1)(g).

[44] This is because under s 18(c) of the Interpretation Act 2005, when the term 'person' is used in an Act of the Oireachtas, it is to be construed as importing, inter alia, an 'unincorporated body of persons' and this term clearly includes a partnership. See *Revenue Commissioners v O'Reilly and McGilligan* [1984] ILRM 406 (which considered s 11 of the Interpretation Act 1937, the predecessor to s 18(c) of the 2005 Act), but note that there is some doubt as to whether a partnership of just two is a body of persons, see para **[3.47]**.

[45] Nonetheless, where two or more partners, but not a firm, wish to bring a bankruptcy summons, they cannot benefit from the €20,000 threshold in s 8(2) since partners are expressly excluded. It could be argued that they may rely on the Bankruptcy Act 1988, s 8(1) if they have a joint debt of €20,000 or more. This view rests on the interpretation of the term 'person' in s 8(1) as also including its plural, ie 'persons': Interpretation Act 2005, s 18(a). However, this view is not clear from doubt in view of the express provision in s 8(2) for a situation in which there is more than one creditor. In view of this doubt, the safer course of action is for the partners to bring the action where possible under s 8(1) as a firm.

Bankruptcy Petition

[27.34] Once the debtor has committed an act of bankruptcy, the next step in the process is to petition for the debtor's bankruptcy. The petition by a creditor for the adjudication of a bankrupt must be presented in the High Court.[46]

Petition against debtor partner or debtor firm

[27.35] Where the debtor is either a partner or a partnership, s 11(1)(d) of the Bankruptcy Act 1988 provides that a creditor is entitled to petition for the bankruptcy of that debtor if, inter alia:

> the debtor (whether a citizen or not) is domiciled in the State, or, within 3 years before the date of the presentation of the petition, has ordinarily resided or had a dwelling-house or place of business in the State or has carried on business in the State personally or by means of an agent or manager, or is or within the said period has been a member of a partnership which has carried on business in the State by means of a partner, agent or manager.[47]

Thus, a partner or partners may have a petition in bankruptcy brought against him or them if the partnership carried on business in Ireland within three years of the petition, regardless of whether the partner is an Irish citizen or is resident or domiciled in Ireland.

[27.36] In order to found a joint petition against two or more partners, each of them must have committed an act of bankruptcy, although they need not have committed the same act of bankruptcy.[48] Thus, while a debt owing by a firm will support a bankruptcy petition against all of the partners,[49] a debt owing by one partner only will not support a joint petition against him and his co-partners.[50]

[27.37] Under s 31(1) of the Bankruptcy Act 1988, where the debt is owed by a firm, the creditor may petition against all or any of the partners in the firm:[51]

> Any creditor whose debt is sufficient[52] to entitle him to present a petition for adjudication against all the partners of a firm may present a petition against any one or more partners of the firm without including the others.[53]

[27.38] In *Re McIntire*,[54] one McIntire was in partnership as a general merchant with his brother in Derry city. His brother died and creditors of the firm petitioned for McIntire's

---

46   See definition of 'the court' in s 3 of the Bankruptcy Act 1988.
47   See also Rules of the Superior Courts, Ord 76, r 19 in relation to the format of a creditor's bankruptcy petition.
48   See para **[27.29]**.
49   *Ex p Elton* (1796) 3 Ves 239.
50   *Ex p Clarke* (1832) 1 D & C 544.
51   See for example the successful bankruptcy petition against a partner in respect of a partnership debt under the Insolvent Partnerships (Northern Ireland) 1991 (SR & O 366) in *Re Barry Elliot* [1992] 12 NIJB 44. See also *Ex p Crisp* (1744) 1 Atk 133.
52   As to which, see the Bankruptcy Act 1988, s 11(1)(a).
53   See also *Ex p Battams* [1900] 2 QB 698.
54   *Re McIntire* (1848) Ir Eq R 318.

bankruptcy but their petition did not describe McIntire as the surviving partner of the firm. Nonetheless, Brady LC held that McIntire could be adjudicated bankrupt on foot of liabilities contracted by him and his deceased partner.[55]

Petition against more than one partner

[27.39] Where a petition is presented against more than one partner, s 31(2) of the Bankruptcy Act 1988 gives the High Court a discretion regarding the grant of an order of adjudication:[56]

> Where a petition for adjudication is presented against more than one person the Court may make an order of adjudication against one or more of them and dismiss the petition as to the remainder.

[27.40] Order 76, r 33 of the Rules of the Superior Courts also deals with the situation of petitions against different members of a firm by providing that the petition which was first presented is entitled to be heard first:

> Where two or more petitions are presented against the same debtor, or against debtors being members of the same partnership, the petition which was first presented shall be entitled to be first heard. Where such first petition shall not have been proceeded with to adjudication or where the debtor shows cause against the adjudication thereunder or where delay will be avoided, any other petition may be proceeded with. If the Court shall make adjudication upon such last mentioned petition, all other petitions shall stand dismissed with such costs (if any) as the Court may allow ...

[27.41] Section 123 of the Irish Bankrupt and Insolvent Act 1857 had previously provided for separate petitions against the members of a firm to be consolidated and for all the property of the bankrupts to vest in the Official Assignee and for this purpose for all subsequent petitions to be annexed to and form part of the first petition.[57] However, this section was repealed by the Bankruptcy Act 1988.[58] It is surprising that it was not replaced by an equivalent provision in the 1988 Act, but it may be that this practical difficulty can be overcome by an application by the Official Assignee for a declaratory order from the High Court for the annexation of any subsequent petitions.

More than one petition presented against same partner or firm

[27.42] Order 76, r 33 of the Rules of the Superior Courts addresses the situation where two or more petitions are presented against the same partner or the same firm. In such a situation, the petition which was first presented is entitled to be heard first. Where the first petition is not proceeded with to adjudication, the High Court may proceed with the

---

[55] Note that in *Ex p Haig* (1832) Glas 237, Conyngham LC held that the use of the term 'as surviving partner' in the petition rendered it a joint adjudication. The corollary was held not to apply in *Re McIntire* (1848) Ir Eq R 318, since Brady LC considered *Ex p Haig*, but held that the omission of the term 'as surviving partner' did not render the adjudication a separate commission. *Ex p Haig* must be regarded as overruled insofar as it provided that the omission of this term renders the commission a separate adjudication.

[56] Previously this provision was contained in the Irish Bankrupt and Insolvent Act 1857, s 122.

[57] This section reflected the previous common law: *Re Gowar* (1831) 1 MD & D 1.

[58] Bankruptcy Act 1988, s 6 and 2nd Sch.

other petition and once the partners are adjudicated, all the other petitions are dismissed with such costs as the court allows.[59]

Petition by debtor firm or partner for own bankruptcy

[27.43] In addition to the situation in which a partner or a firm is adjudicated bankrupt on the petition of a creditor, the Bankruptcy Act 1988 also allows a partner or a firm to petition for his or its own bankruptcy where he or it is unable to pay his or its debts.[60]

[27.44] It seems that where the petitioning debtor is a firm, all the partners should join in the bankruptcy petition so as to enable the Official Assignee to administer the partnership property.[61] In *Re Pelan*,[62] one partner in a two-member Belfast based firm petitioned for his own separate bankruptcy. However, he did not have sufficient separate assets to qualify as all the assets in question were partnership assets. Accordingly, Miller J held that he would not adjudicate on the separate petition of the partner, but adjourned the petition in order to allow the other member of the firm to join.

Petition by creditor partner against his co-partner

[27.45] A partner who is a creditor of his co-partner or co-partners may petition against him or them.[63] However, a petitioning partner in such circumstances should be aware that he will not be able to prove against the separate estate of his partner until all the joint creditors have been paid off.[64] In order to be allowed to petition, the debt owed by one partner to another must be recoverable by a direct action. If the debt is only recoverable indirectly by means of an action for account between the partners,[65] a petition will not be allowed until such time as judgment in the action has been obtained. Where the debt is recoverable by a direct action, the petition will also not be allowed where the object of the petitioning partner (or of a creditor at the instigation of the

---

59   The advantage of having one creditor's petition adjudicated in preference to another is that the costs of the petitioner whose petition is adjudicated gain priority in the distribution of the debtor's estate, while the unsuccessful petitioner will normally be liable for his own costs. Order 76, r 167 of the Rules of the Superior Courts.

60   Bankruptcy Act 1988, s 15(1). Before making an order under s 15(1), the High Court is required to consider the type and value of the assets available to the debtor, the extent of his or its liabilities, and whether (in the case of an individual partner) his inability to meet his debts could be more appropriately dealt with by way of a Debt Settlement Arrangement or a Personal Insolvency Arrangement (Bankruptcy Act 1988, s 15(2)). Where the High Court is of the view that a Debt Settlement Arrangement or Personal Insolvency Arrangement under the Personal Insolvency Acts 2012–2015 might be a more appropriate means of dealing with the individual partner's debts, it may adjourn the hearing of his petition to give the debtor an opportunity to enter into one of those arrangements.

61   See *Re Pelan* (1868) 2 ILTR 637. See also Hunter, *Bankruptcy Law and Practice in Northern Ireland* (1984) SLS Publications at para 6.25.

62   *Re Pelan* (1868) 2 ILTR 637.

63   *Ex p Notley* (1833) 1 Mont & Ayr 46; *Ex p Richardson* (1833) 3 D & Ch 244; *Windham v Paterson* (1815) 2 Rose 466; *Ex p Nokes* (1801) 1 Mont Part 108; *Ex p Maberley* (1808) 1 Mont on Part 62.

64   See para [27.151].

65   As regards actions for account generally see para [20.14] et seq.

partner)[66] is not to obtain payment of his debt, but to dissolve the partnership. In such a case, the court will dismiss the petition as an abuse of the process of the court.[67]

Petition by a creditor firm against third party debtor

[27.46] While this chapter is primarily concerned with the bankruptcy of a firm and its partners, a firm may of course be itself a creditor of a third party debtor. As such, a firm may constitute a 'creditor' for the purposes of presenting a petition or the adjudication of its debtor under s 11 of the Bankruptcy Act 1988.[68] This is clear from the express terms of s 36(1) of the 1988 Act which entitle a firm to take proceedings under that Act. The Rules of the Superior Courts also address the situation where a firm is the creditor and Ord 76, r 12(2) provides that: '[a] bankruptcy summons may be granted to a partnership upon the affidavit of one of the partners' while if a firm petitions for the bankruptcy of its debtor, Ord 76, r 20(1) states that:

> A petition by a person other than the debtor shall be signed by the petitioner or, if more than one, by all the petitioners, unless the petitioners are partners, in which case one partner may sign on behalf of himself and the other partners. Any petitioner may sign the petition by his attorney duly authorised by power of attorney in that behalf.[69]

However, if one member of the firm is himself bankrupt, his Official Assignee should be a co-petitioner with the solvent partners.[70]

[27.47] When it comes to proving for the debts on the bankruptcy of the debtor, a firm which is a creditor of the bankrupt may prove through any one of its partners.[71] Where the creditor firm is itself bankrupt, it seems clear that the Official Assignee of the bankrupt firm may prove on the bankruptcy of a debtor of the firm. In *Re Woods*[72]

---

[66] *Ex p Hall* (1838) 3 Deac 405; *Ex p Harcourt* (1815) 2 Rose 214; *Ex p Gallimore* (1816) 2 Rose 424. But cf *Ex p Nash* (1848) 12 Jur 494; *King v Henderson* (1898) AC 720.

[67] *Ex p Christie* (1832) M & B 314; *Ex p Browne* (1810) 1 Rose 151; *Ex p Johnson* (1842) 2 MD & D 678; *Ex p Phipps* (1844) 3 MD & D 505. But cf *Ex p Upfill* (1866) 1 Ch 439.

[68] As noted at para **[27.32]**, in the section which deals with the granting of a bankruptcy summons (s 8 of the Bankruptcy Act 1988) a 'creditor' is referred to as a 'person' which term includes a partnership and that definition is expressed to be only for the purposes of that section. It is curious therefore that when the term petitioning 'creditor' is used in s 11 of the 1988 Act, it is not defined. Nonetheless, it is seems clear that a partnership may be a petitioning creditor: Bankruptcy Act 1988, s 36(1), s 8(1) and Ord 76, r 20(1) of the Rules of the Superior Courts. Of historical interest only, therefore, is *Ex p Sneyds* (1829) 1 Moll 261, in which it was held that a corporation was allowed to be a petitioning creditor in bankruptcy.

[69] As noted at para **[27.50]**, a partner by holding out may take such proceedings. Note also that if the creditor firm is a limited partnership, it is advisable that the creditor's petition should be signed by a general partner rather than a limited partner, in view of the prohibition in the Limited Partnerships Act 1907, s 6(1) on a limited partner taking part in the management of the partnership business. See further para **[28.78]** et seq. Similarly, if a petition is to be signed on behalf of an investment limited partnership it is advisable that it is signed by a general partner, rather than a limited partner, in order to avoid falling foul of the prohibition in the Investment Limited Partnerships Act 1994, s 6 on a limited partner taking part in the conduct of the partnership business. See further para **[29.103]** et seq.

[70] *Ex p Owen* (1884) 13 QBD 113.

[71] *Ex p Mitchell* (1808) 14 Ves 597; *Ex p Hodgkinson* (1815) 19 Ves 291.

[72] *Re Woods* (1875) 9 ILTR 65.

Miller J did not allow such a proof by the Official Assignee for the reason that the firm had already endorsed the bill of exchange for the debt over to a third party for cash.

[27.48] A separate question relates to the granting of a bankruptcy summons to two or more partners, other than on behalf of the firm. In view of the terms of s 8(2) of the Bankruptcy Act 1988, which entitles two or more creditors *who are not partners* to apply for a bankruptcy summons,[73] it is unclear whether partners (other than on behalf of the firm) may bring a bankruptcy petition. It might be argued that under general principles of interpretation, joint creditors may apply for a bankruptcy summons under s 8(1) of the 1988 Act[74] and therefore may bring a bankruptcy petition under s 11(1)(a) of the 1988 Act. However, it is unclear whether this interpretation would be taken by the courts. For this reason, the more prudent approach is for the partners to take the petition separately or on behalf of their firm.

Bankruptcy proceedings, but not adjudication, may issue in firm name

[27.49] Since partners may become bankrupt collectively as well as individually, the express terms of s 36(1) of the Bankruptcy Act 1988 provide that bankruptcy proceedings may be taken against the partners in the name of the firm. This section reads:

> Any two or more persons, being partners, or any person carrying on business under a partnership name, may take proceedings or be proceeded against under this Act in the name of the firm, but in such case the Court may, on application by any person interested, order the names of the persons to be disclosed in such manner, and verified on oath or otherwise, as the Court may direct.

However, if an order of adjudication of bankruptcy is eventually obtained against the firm, it cannot be made against the firm name, but it must be made against the partners individually. Section 36(2) of the 1988 Act goes on to provide that:

> Notwithstanding anything contained in subsection (1) no order of adjudication shall be made against a firm in the firm-name but it shall be made against the partners individually with the addition of the firm name.[75]

Position of Partners by Holding Out

[27.50] The question of whether a partner by holding out may be subject to bankruptcy proceedings as a member of a firm or whether he may take bankruptcy proceedings as a member of a firm against a creditor of the firm is answered by the terms of s 36(1) of the Bankruptcy Act 1988:

> Any two or more persons, being partners, or any person carrying on business under a partnership name, may take proceedings or be proceeded against under this Act in the name of the firm ...

The expression 'or any person carrying on business under a partnership name' clearly is wide enough to include most instances of where a person holds himself out as a member

---

[73]   See further para **[27.33]**.

[74]   See para **[27.32]**, where the interpretation of the term 'person' as including 'persons' is discussed.

[75]   Along the same lines is Ord 76, r 34 of the Rules of the Superior Courts.

of a partnership, eg the position of a salaried partner. Thus, it seems clear that s 36(1) will entitle most partners by holding out to take proceedings as a member of a creditor firm for the bankruptcy of a third party, to have bankruptcy proceedings brought against them as a member of a debtor firm[76] or indeed to petition for the firm's own bankruptcy under s 15 of the 1988 Act.

[27.51] Although not clear from doubt, it is apprehended that an employee would not be regarded as falling within the expression a 'person carrying on business under a partnership name'. This is because the term is used in s 36(1) of the Bankruptcy Act 1988 in the context of a partnership and it is considered that the expression 'carrying on business under a partnership name' in s 36(1) should be interpreted in line with the expression 'carrying on business in common' in s 1(1) of the 1890 Act, in which case, it is clear that it does not include employees.[77] In addition of course, there would be no reason in principle to allow employees to be proceeded against for the bankruptcy of their employers.

Bankruptcy in Specific Situations

Dormant partner

[27.52] As noted elsewhere in this work,[78] a dormant partner is treated for all intents and purposes as an ordinary partner. Accordingly, a dormant partner may be made bankrupt on a petition presented against the firm of which he is a partner[79] or indeed on a petition presented against him personally.[80]

Partner by holding out

[27.53] A person who holds himself out as a partner is 'liable as a partner' under s 14(1) of the 1890 Act. For this reason, a partner by holding out may be adjudicated bankrupt as a member of the firm.[81] This is also clear from the terms of s 36(1) of the Bankruptcy Act 1988, which allows bankruptcy proceedings to be taken against a partner by holding out, since proceedings may be taken in the firm name against any 'person carrying on business under a partnership name'.[82]

Distinct firms

[27.54] Where there are two distinct firms, one of which (X & Y) has partners in common with an other firm (X, Y & Z), a bankruptcy of the larger firm will automatically lead to the bankruptcy of the smaller firm, but not vice versa. This follows because, as has been noted,[83] the bankruptcy of a firm leads to the bankruptcy of each of the partners in that firm (in this example, X, Y and Z). As X and Y will thereby be

---

[76]   See for example *Ex p Hayman* (1878) 8 Ch D 11.
[77]   See generally in relation to the interpretation of this term, para [2.68] et seq.
[78]   See para [6.04] et seq.
[79]   *Ex p Lodge and Fendal* (1790) 1 Ves J 166.
[80]   *Ex p Hamper* (1811) 17 Ves 403; *Ex p Matthews* (1814) 3 V & B 125.
[81]   *Ex p Hayman* (1878) 8 Ch D 11.
[82]   See para [27.50].
[83]   See para [27.19].

bankrupt, the firm of X & Y will of necessity also be bankrupt. Clearly, when the firm X & Y is bankrupt, it will not automatically lead to the bankruptcy of the firm X, Y & Z, since Z may be solvent.

Minor partner

[27.55] Where one partner in a firm is a minor,[84] an adjudication against the firm will be inoperative against the minor partner, but the minor's share of the partnership property will be available for the partnership debts.[85]

Adjudication of Bankruptcy

Adjudication by High Court

[27.56] Under s 14 of the Bankruptcy Act 1988, the High Court may adjudicate a debtor partner or a debtor firm bankrupt on the petition of its creditor and under s 15 of the 1988 Act, the High Court may adjudicate a debtor partner or a debtor firm bankrupt on a petition by the debtor partner or the debtor firm itself. In each case, as regards an individual partner, the Court may adjourn the hearing of the relevant petition if it forms the view that, having regard to the nature and value of the assets available to that partner, the extent of his liabilities, and the contents of any statement of affairs provided by him, his inability to pay his debts could more appropriately be dealt with by a Debt Settlement Arrangement or by a Personal Insolvency Arrangement, in each case under the Personal Insolvency Acts 2012–2015.[86]

Court cannot declare stranger to bankruptcy a partner

[27.57] The Northern Ireland case of *Re Harris*[87] illustrates the principle that a stranger, albeit a partner, to the bankruptcy proceedings of his co-partner cannot be made bankrupt by the court. There, the Northern Ireland Court of Appeal held that in bankruptcy proceedings against Ms Harris, the bankruptcy court had no jurisdiction to make a declaratory order of partnership as against her partner who was a stranger to those proceedings. Accordingly, the Court of Appeal overturned the bankruptcy judge's order that Mr Rand, who was Ms Harris' partner at the time of the adjudication, be adjudged a bankrupt.

Position where bankrupt partner dies before adjudication

[27.58] Section 42 of the Bankruptcy Act 1988 provides that if a bankrupt dies, the High Court may proceed in the bankruptcy as if he were living. Although the section itself does not refer explicitly to the death of a bankrupt after adjudication, the margin note and the heading refer to a 'Bankrupt dying after adjudication' and indeed its predecessor section[88] granted the court the right to proceed in the bankruptcy, where death took place

---

84   Under s 2 of the Age of Majority Act 1985, a minor is a person who has not reached the age of 18 unless he or she is married.

85   *Lovell and Christmas v Beauchamp* [1894] AC 607. See further para **[4.04]** et seq.

86   Bankruptcy Act 1988, ss 14(2) and 15(2).

87   *Re Harris* [1939] NI 1.

88   Irish Bankrupt and Insolvent Act 1857, s 137: 'If any bankrupt shall die after adjudication, the Court may proceed in bankruptcy as if such bankrupt were living.'

'after adjudication'. Therefore, in spite of the apparent breadth of the section, it is suggested that the High Court will only exercise its discretion under s 42 to proceed in the bankruptcy where an adjudication has actually been obtained against the deceased partner. This interpretation is in keeping with the approach taken by the courts in cases where an arranging debtor died before his arrangement was approved by the court[89] and it is in keeping with Part VI of the 1988 Act which provides for a separate procedure where a debtor dies before he can be adjudicated bankrupt, ie a petition for the administration of the estate of a deceased person.

Effect of Adjudication of Bankruptcy

[27.59] The adjudication of a partner as a bankrupt will have an immediate effect on the partnership of which he is a partner. This effect will now be considered.

Dissolution of partnership

[27.60] As noted elsewhere in this work,[90] in the absence of any agreement to the contrary between the partners, the bankruptcy of a partner leads to the automatic dissolution of the firm under s 33(1) of the 1890 Act.[91] The date of dissolution of the partnership is the date upon which the partner is adjudicated bankrupt. Thus in *Provincial Bank of Ireland v Tallon*,[92] Johnston J observed that under s 33(1) of the 1890 Act, the partnership in that case 'became dissolved when the adjudication took place'.[93]

Dissolution is 'subject to any agreement between the partners'

[27.61] The automatic dissolution of a partnership under s 33(1) of the 1890 Act is not, however, absolute, since under the express terms of that section, the dissolution is 'subject to any agreement between the partners'. Where the partners have agreed that the bankruptcy of a partner will not dissolve the partnership but have not agreed to purchase the bankrupt partner's share, the solvent partners will be left with a member of the firm who is bankrupt. This is apt to create considerable practical difficulties in the running of the partnership business. First, and as noted hereafter, the adjudication order will sever any joint tenancy between the bankrupt and his partners and instead the co-owned property will be held by the Official Assignee and the other partners as tenants in common.[94] Second, a bankrupt who trades under a name, other than that under which he was made bankrupt, commits an offence under the Bankruptcy Act 1988 if he fails to disclose the name under which he was adjudicated bankrupt.[95] A bankrupt who trades as a member of a partnership (which is likely to have a name other than his own) may

---

89 See *Re M* (1877) 11 Ir Eq R 46, considered at para **[27.165]**, which considered the predecessor of s 104 of the Bankruptcy Act 1988, ie s 351 of the Irish Bankrupt and Insolvent Act 1857.

90 See para **[23.39]** et seq.

91 For an example of such a dissolution, see *Re Curry* (1848) 12 Ir Eq R 382.

92 *Provincial Bank of Ireland v Tallon* [1938] IR 361.

93 *Provincial Bank of Ireland v Tallon* [1938] IR 361 at 365.

94 See *Provincial Bank of Ireland v Tallon* [1938] IR 361, considered at para **[27.66]** and see also *Morgan v Marquis* (1853) 9 Exch 145 per Parke B at 147–148.

95 Bankruptcy Act 1988, s 129. Another provision likely to create problems for a bankrupt partner in a partnership is the prohibition in s 129 on a bankrupt obtaining credit of €650 or more without disclosing his status as a bankrupt.

easily breach this section. For these reasons, it is usual for the solvent partners in a firm to wish to purchase the bankrupt's share in the partnership. To do so, the solvent partners will have to enter negotiations with the Official Assignee for the purchase of this share. In view of the uncertainty attending such negotiations, it is preferable that the partnership agreement provide:

(1)   That the bankruptcy of one partner will not dissolve the partnership as regards the other partners; and

(2)   That a partner's bankruptcy will lead to his expulsion from the firm, subject to a payment by the continuing partners for his share which payment will be calculated according to an agreed valuation mechanism in the partnership agreement.[96]

Termination of power of bankrupt partner to bind firm

[27.62] Another important effect of the bankruptcy of a partner in a firm is contained in s 38 of the 1890 Act. This section provides primarily for the power of the partners in a dissolved partnership to bind the firm for the purposes of its winding up. However, this section also provides that the power to bind the firm on a winding up does not extend to a bankrupt partner. The proviso to s 38 reads: '[p]rovided that the firm is in no case bound by the acts of a partner who has become bankrupt ...'.

[27.63] It is not immediately clear from the wording of either the 1890 Act or the Bankruptcy Act 1988 whether the expression 'become bankrupt' in s 38 of the 1890 Act relates to the date of the act of bankruptcy or the date of adjudication of bankruptcy. While there is eighteenth century caselaw to the effect that the authority of a partner to bind his firm determines on the date of the act of bankruptcy,[97] these cases were decided when the doctrine of relation back applied, ie where the title of the assignee in bankruptcy related back to the date of the act of bankruptcy. Since this doctrine no longer applies,[98] these authorities are thought to have been rendered inapplicable. Furthermore, it has been held by the High Court in more recent times that a firm dissolves by bankruptcy on the date of adjudication of the bankruptcy.[99] For this reason,[100] it seems clear that the authority of a partner to bind his firm ceases on the date of adjudication and not the date of the act of bankruptcy.[101] Since the proviso to s 38 states that a firm is not bound by the acts of a bankrupt partner, this has practical consequences for persons dealing with a firm which has a bankrupt partner. Thus, a debtor of the firm who knows that one of the partners is bankrupt should ensure that he

---

[96]   See further in relation to such provisions in partnership agreements, para **[21.145]**.

[97]   *Hague v Rolleston* (1768) 4 Burr 2174; *Thomason v Frere* (1809) East 418.

[98]   See para **[27.93]**.

[99]   *Provincial Bank of Ireland v Tallon* [1938] IR 361, see para **[27.60]**.

[100]   But cf *Re Reis* [1904] 1 KB 451 at 455 where it was held that the phrase 'becoming bankrupt' as used in s 47 of the English Bankruptcy Act 1883 meant the date of the act of bankruptcy.

[101]   Of course, the validity of any transactions entered into by a person who has committed an act of bankruptcy may be questioned on other grounds, eg that they constitute a fraudulent preference. See generally Sanfey and Holohan, *Bankruptcy Law and Practice* (2nd edn, 2010) at p 177 et seq.

pays one of the solvent partners the amount owed, since any release by the bankrupt partner of this debt will not bind the firm.

[27.64] By providing that a bankrupt partner cannot bind the firm, s 38 of the 1890 Act also implicitly clarifies that where all the partners in a firm are bankrupt, the firm is necessarily dissolved since in such a case no one person will have authority to act on behalf of the firm.

Automatic vesting of property in Official Assignee

[27.65] Perhaps the major effect of the bankruptcy of a partner under general bankruptcy law is the fact that all of the bankrupt partner's property vests in the Official Assignee for the benefit of his creditors.[102]

[27.66] Where one partner in a firm becomes bankrupt, leaving at least one other solvent partner, the Official Assignee of the bankrupt partner becomes entitled to the separate estate of the bankrupt including his interest in the partnership. In this regard, the Official Assignee becomes a tenant in common with the solvent partner(s) in relation to the partnership property.[103] However, the Official Assignee cannot claim any more than the bankrupt himself would have been entitled to claim, if he had not become bankrupt.[104] The effect of bankruptcy on the assets of a partner was considered in *Provincial Bank of Ireland v Tallon*.[105] The case involved Mr Tallon and Mrs Tallon who were partners, both in the marital and the business sense. Mr Tallon, who was adjudicated bankrupt, owned some property separately and he owned the partnership premises in Drumcondra in Dublin jointly with Mrs Tallon. In these circumstances, Johnston J observed:

> 'When Patrick Tallon became a bankrupt, the position of affairs was this:- The whole of the property owned separately by him vested absolutely and at once in his Assignees, and such interest as he had in the property held jointly by himself and any other person also vested in the Assignees to the extent of that interest ... the Assignees under a commission in bankruptcy against one partner "can only be tenants in common of an undivided moiety subject to all the rights of the other partner".'[106]

---

[102] Bankruptcy Act 1988, s 44(1).

[103] *Provincial Bank of Ireland v Tallon* [1938] IR 361. See also *Fox v Hanbury* (1776) 2 Cowp 445.

[104] Thus in *Re Curry* (1848) Ir Eq R 382 at 387, Macan C stated that: '[n]o doubt where there has been an open avowed partnership between two persons, and a commission issues against one only the other continuing solvent, the assignee can take, and this Court can administer, only the moiety of the partnership stock remaining, after first satisfying in full the just demands of the solvent partner; because this is the utmost extent of the rights of the bankrupt partner and of his creditors under the commission.'

[105] *Provincial Bank of Ireland v Tallon* [1938] IR 361.

[106] *Provincial Bank of Ireland v Tallon* [1938] IR 361 at 365 quoting in part from the judgment of Lord Mansfield in *Fox v Hanbury* (1776) 2 Cowp 445. Despite Johnston J's adoption of the judgment of Lord Mansfield, he held that the partnership property was held by the Assignee as a joint tenant, although it is contended that this is a typographical error since he states: 'On the bankruptcy, therefore, the Assignees and Mrs Tallon became entitled to *equal undivided moieties* as joint tenants in the Drumcondra property', at 365, when it is more correct to refer to *equal undivided moieties as tenants in common*. See generally Wylie, *Irish Land Law* (5th edn, 2013) at para [8.02] et seq.

[27.67] While the Official Assignee is entitled to the bankrupt partner's share in the partnership, it is important to note that he does not become a co-partner with the solvent partners in the firm.[107] As noted hereunder, the interest of the Official Assignee of a bankrupt partner in the partnership property is subject to the joint creditors of the firm being paid in full[108] and the partnership accounts being duly taken and adjusted.[109]

Property held by partner on trust is not vested in Official Assignee

[27.68] Since property which is held by a partner on trust is not beneficially owned by that partner, it follows that such property does not vest in that partner's Official Assignee on his bankruptcy.[110] Thus in *Joy v Campbell*,[111] Redesdale LC held that the property of a partner in a Belfast sugar manufacturing partnership, which he held on trust for a third party, did not vest in that partner's assignees on his bankruptcy.

Where a firm is bankrupt

[27.69] Under s 44(1) of the Bankruptcy Act 1988, where a 'person' is adjudicated bankrupt, all the property of that person vests in the Official Assignee. The term 'person' is interpreted to include a partnership[112] and therefore where a partnership is adjudicated bankrupt (ie where all the partners are adjudicated bankrupt), the assets of the firm vest in the Official Assignee. Thus, when a firm is adjudicated bankrupt, or when a joint adjudication is made against two or more partners, both the joint property of the bankrupts and their separate property vests in the Official Assignee. This is clearly illustrated by the judgment of Miller J in *Re Hind*.[113] That case concerned John Hind & Sons, a Belfast firm of linen manufacturers. The four-partner firm was adjudicated bankrupt and Miller J noted the effect of the bankruptcy of the firm in the following terms:

> '[T]he said firm of John Hind & Sons were adjudicated bankrupts on the 6th of February, 1885, and immediately upon that adjudication all the estates and interests of not only the firm of John Hind & Sons, but also of the several members of that firm, as they respectively stood at that date, became absolutely vested in the assignees under that adjudication, and those assignees were thenceforth bound to assume the entire management and control of these respective estates and interests, and to keep distinct and separate accounts of the joint estates and interest of that firm of John Hind & Sons, as well as of the separate estates and interests of each and every of the several members of that firm, and also to protect to the fullest extent the respective estates and interests in relation

---

107   See s 24(7) of the 1890 Act where it is provided that no person may be introduced as a partner without the consent of all the existing partners.

108   See para **[27.98]**.

109   *Anon* (1700) 3 Salk 61; *Fox v Hanbury* (1776) 2 Cowp 445.

110   Bankruptcy Act 1988, s 44(4)(a).

111   *Joy v Campbell* (1804) 1 Sch & Lef 328.

112   Under s 18 of the Interpretation Act 2005, when the term 'person' is used in an Act of the Oireachtas it is to be construed as importing a body corporate, an unincorporated body of persons as well as an individual. An 'unincorporated body of persons' clearly includes a partnership. As to whether a partnership of two is a 'body of persons', see para **[3.47]** et seq.

113   *Re Hind* (1889) 23 LR Ir 217.

to each other, as between the said firm of John Hind & Sons and the several members of that firm, as well as between the several members of that firm themselves.'[114]

Regulated partnerships

[27.70] The Central Bank Act 1971 used to contain special provisions dealing with the vesting of partnership property in the Official Assignee where the bankrupt firm was the holder of a banking licence; however, those provisions were repealed by the Central Bank Act 1989. The 1971 Act[115] still contains a further act of bankruptcy in addition to those mentioned above.[116] Under that Act, where a creditor obtains a judgment, order or decree against the holder of a banking licence that is a partnership and the judgment relates to the payment of money due by the debtor as a banker, each of the partners is deemed to have committed an act of bankruptcy. However, that provision has been rendered redundant as, at the time of writing, only a body corporate can apply for a banking licence.[117] In addition, the Central Bank of Ireland is entitled to revoke the authorisation of a partnership that operates a regulated business[118] if that partnership is dissolved as a result of the bankruptcy of any partner.[119] The Central Bank may also revoke the authorisation of a money broking business that is a partnership[120] if that partnership is dissolved by the bankruptcy of any partner.

Transfer of bankrupt's property before and after adjudication

[27.71] The assets of a bankrupt partner automatically vest in the Official Assignee under s 44(1) of the Bankruptcy Act 1988. Therefore, any transfer of property belonging to that partner after the date of adjudication, without the authorisation of the Official Assignee, is void. It will commonly occur that the Official Assignee will sell the bankrupt partner's share to the other partners in the firm.[121]

[27.72] In addition, under the Bankruptcy Act 1988, certain transactions made by a bankrupt prior to his bankruptcy may be void as against the Official Assignee as a fraudulent preference of one creditor over the others.[122] However, if the transfer consists only of the transfer of a legal interest, the beneficial interest having being transferred earlier, the transfer will not be void. Such was the case in *Barnett v Jefferson*.[123] There, a partnership owed monies to the defendant and at the same time the Customs Authority

---

114 *Re Hind* (1889) 23 LR Ir 217 at 222–223.
115 Central Bank Act 1971, s 28(1)(e)(iii).
116 At para [27.23].
117 Central Bank Act 1971, s 9.
118 A 'regulated business' is a bureau de change business, a money transmission business, a home reversion firm, a retail credit firm, a debt management firm or a credit servicing firm (Central Bank Act 1997, s 28(1)).
119 Under the Central Bank Act 1989, s 36A.
120 Under the Central Bank Act 1989, s 114(1).
121 See for example *Re Motion, Maule v Davis* (1873) 9 Ch App 192.
122 For a consideration of these transactions see ss 57–59 of the Bankruptcy Act 1988 and s 74 of the Land and Conveyancing Law Reform Act 2009. See generally Sanfey and Holohan, *Bankruptcy Law and Practice* (2nd edn, 2010) and Wylie, *The Land and Conveyancing Law Reform Act 2009: Annotations and Commentary* (2nd edn, 2017) at para [119].
123 *Barnett v Jefferson* (1825) Smi and Bat 159.

owed monies to the partnership. The defendant went with the partners in the firm to the Customs Authority in Newry to arrange for the debt which the Customs Authority owed the firm to be paid to the defendant instead. The clerk of the Customs Authority agreed to do so once he was properly authorised by his superiors. An act of bankruptcy was committed by the partnership between the time they directed the Customs Authority to pay the money and the receipt of authorisation by the clerk from his superiors. The High Court held that the beneficial interest in the money had transferred at the time of the visit to the Customs Authority which was prior to the acts of bankruptcy and, accordingly, the assignee in bankruptcy of the firm failed in his action to recover it from the defendant.

Rights and duties of Official Assignee

[27.73] A further important consequence of the adjudication of a partner or partners as bankrupt is the effect of the rights and duties of the Official Assignee on the partner or partners. Once a partner is adjudicated bankrupt, the Official Assignee is obliged to assume the management and control of the separate estate of the bankrupt. The rights and duties of the assignee in bankruptcy were considered in *Re Hind*[124] in relation to the Belfast firm of John Hind & Sons. There, Miller J noted that the assignees were obliged to comply with the following duties regarding the joint estate of the firm and the separate estate of the partners:

> '[T]o assume the entire management and control of these respective estates and interests, and to keep distinct and separate accounts of the joint estates and interest of that firm of John Hind & Sons, as well as of the separate estates and interests of each and every of the several members of that firm, and also to protect to the fullest extent the respective estates and interests in relation to each other, as between the said firm of John Hind & Sons and the several members of that firm, as well as between the several members of that firm themselves.'[125]

Duty of Official Assignee to ascertain financial position

[27.74] Whether dealing with a partner or an individual, one of the primary duties of the Official Assignee is to ascertain the assets of the bankrupt. Where the bankrupt is a member of a partnership, s 33 of the Bankruptcy Act 1988 requires him to deliver to the Official Assignee a separate statement of affairs in respect of his partnership. In addition, s 32 of the 1988 Act provides that the Official Assignee may obtain information from the partners of the bankrupt. This section states that:

> Where a member of a partnership is adjudicated bankrupt the Official Assignee may require the other partner or partners to deliver to the Official Assignee such accounts and information relating to the partnership estate and the bankrupt's interest therein (duly verified by affidavit if necessary) as the Official Assignee may deem necessary.[126]

---

[124] *Re Hind* (1889) 23 LR Ir 217.

[125] *Re Hind* (1889) 23 LR Ir 217 at 222–223.

[126] A similar provision was previously contained in s 308 of the Irish Bankrupt and Insolvent Act 1857. See also *Re Martindale Ex p Trueman* (1832) 1 Deac and Ch 464.

Inspection of firm's books and accounts

[27.75] As part of his duty to ascertain the financial position of a bankrupt firm, the Official Assignee would be expected to inspect the firm's books and records in order to verify the accounts of the firm. However, where the affairs of the firm are uncomplicated, this may not be necessary. This is apparent from the High Court case of *Rubotham v Young*.[127] There, it was held by McCracken J that in a partnership which had as its sole asset a property and as its sole income the rent therefrom, it was reasonable for the Official Assignee of the bankrupt partner to rely on the unaudited and unverified accounts prepared by the firm's accountants. In view of the straightforward nature of the business, it was not necessary for the Official Assignee to inspect the books or records of the partnership to verify the accounts. It follows that where the business of a partnership is of a more complicated nature, the Official Assignee would be expected to inspect the firm's books and records in order to verify the accounts of the firm.

Right of Official Assignee to get in assets of dissolved partnership

[27.76] It has been noted that when a partner goes bankrupt, the Official Assignee does not become a partner with the solvent partners but becomes a tenant in common with them in respect of the bankrupt partner's share of the partnership property.[128] While not a co-partner with the solvent partners, the Official Assignee has an interest in the assets of the partnership and this is recognised by s 30 of the Bankruptcy Act 1988. This section entitles the Official Assignee to expedite the recovery of the assets of the partnership with a view to the distribution of the bankrupt partner's share in the firm. Section 30 does this by establishing the right of the Official Assignee to get in the assets or debts of the partnership in the name of the partners subject to the consent of the High Court. Section 30 reads:

> Where a member of a partnership is adjudicated bankrupt the Court may authorise the Official Assignee to commence and prosecute any action in the names of the Official Assignee and of the bankrupt's partner to recover any debt due to or any property of the partners, and any release by such partner of any debt or demand to which the action relates shall be void; but notice of the application for authority to commence the action shall be given to the bankrupt's partner and he may show cause against it and on his application the Court may, if it thinks fit, direct that he shall receive his proper share of the proceeds of the action. If the partner does not claim any benefit from the action he shall be indemnified against costs in respect thereof as the Court directs.[129]

Thus, before the High Court will allow the Official Assignee to commence such an action, the other partners may show cause against the application and the Court may provide for an appropriate division of the proceeds of the action. With a view to protecting the interests of the bankrupt's creditors, s 30 provides that any release of the debt by the partners of the bankrupt is void.

---

127 *Rubotham v Young* (23 May 1995) HC.
128 See para **[27.66]**.
129 This section is almost identical to its predecessor, s 278 of the Irish Bankrupt and Insolvent Act 1857 (20 & 21 Vict c 60). Note that it is to s 278 which Johnston J refers in *Provincial Bank v Tallon* [1938] IR 361 at 365-6. See also *Owen ex p* (1884) 13 QBD 113.

[27.77] While s 30 of the Bankruptcy Act 1988 deals with the recovery of debts or property due to the firm, a situation may arise where partnership property is in the hands of the bankrupt partner at the time of the bankruptcy. In such a case, the Official Assignee may take possession of that property and sell it, subject to his having to account for the shares of the other partners therein.[130] As noted by Johnston J in *Provincial Bank of Ireland v Tallon* in considering the partnership property in that case:[131]

> 'The Assignees could of course enter into possession of property of which the bankrupt was in sole possession and of property (if such existed) which was derelict and in the occupation of no one.'[132]

Right of solvent partners to wind up and manage firm

[27.78] As already observed, the Official Assignee of a bankrupt partner does not become a partner with the solvent partners.[133] Rather, the solvent partners are entitled to get in the joint assets of the firm pursuant to the general power of a partner in a dissolved partnership to wind up the affairs of the firm and to complete transactions begun but unfinished at the time of dissolution.[134] As a general rule, the Official Assignee has no right to interfere in this winding up or the management of the partnership business.[135] In contrast, it is the solvent partners who are entitled to use the name of the Official Assignee to get in the assets of the firm on giving the Official Assignee an indemnity therefor, without the necessity for a court order. This is clear from the High Court case of *Provincial Bank of Ireland v Tallon*,[136] where Johnston J observed:

> 'The Court of Bankruptcy, however, cannot interfere with the rights of a solvent partner who has joint assets in his hands or who wishes to get joint assets into his hands in order to administer them in due course. This point was dealt with in the case of *Ex parte Owen*[137] in 1884, where Cotton LJ put the matter this way: "[the bankruptcy] could not prevent the solvent partner from getting in the partnership assets. In my opinion, when one partner in a firm has become a bankrupt, the solvent partner has a right to get in, and to insist on getting in, the assets of the dissolved partnership, and has even a right to use for that purpose the name of the trustee in the bankruptcy on giving him an indemnity." In referring to this right I must, however, emphasise the fact that it exists only in favour of, and to assist a solvent partner. Further it must be observed that the right is one personal to the solvent partner himself and cannot be transferred to another.'[138]

---

130   *Smith v Stokes* (1801) 1 East 363 at 367.
131   *Provincial Bank of Ireland v Tallon* [1938] IR 361.
132   *Provincial Bank of Ireland v Tallon* [1938] IR 361 at 365.
133   See para **[27.67]**.
134   Partnership Act 1890, s 38. See generally in relation to this power, para **[26.26]** et seq.
135   *Ex p Owen* (1884) 13 QBD 113, unless the Official Assignee obtains a court order under s 30 or s 138 of the Bankruptcy Act 1988. Note the right of the Official Assignee to require the solvent partners to furnish him with such accounts and information relating to the partnership as he may deem necessary: Bankruptcy Act 1988, s 32.
136   *Provincial Bank of Ireland v Tallon* [1938] IR 361. In fact Johnston J was considering the predecessor of s 30 (s 278 of the Irish Bankrupt and Insolvent Act 1857). But s 278 is almost identical to s 30 and therefore it is thought that his comments are equally applicable to s 30.
137   *Ex parte Owen* (1884) 13 QBD 113.
138   *Provincial Bank of Ireland v Tallon* [1938] IR 361 at 366.

Since the right to get in and dispose of the partnership assets is personal to the solvent partner, it has been held that a solvent partner could not by suffering a writ of execution to be executed against himself, allow the sheriff to dispose of the partnership assets.[139]

But solvent partner must account to Official Assignee

[27.79] While the Official Assignee may not generally interfere in the winding up or the management of the partnership business, he is entitled to have an account of partnership dealings and a sale and distribution[140] in the same way as the partner he represents would be entitled under s 39 of the 1890 Act to force such a sale on the dissolution of a partnership.[141] That section explicitly states that a partner or his 'representatives' may apply to court for the purposes of enforcing the rights in s 39 and it seems clear that this term includes the Official Assignee.[142] Curiously, s 39 does not grant the right itself to force a sale and distribution to the representatives, but it must be taken that this is implicit, as otherwise, it would be meaningless to grant them the right to go to court to enforce this right.

[27.80] In addition, if any profits are made by the solvent partners during the winding up of the firm, the Official Assignee is entitled to the bankrupt partner's share thereof.[143]

[27.81] It is because of the right of the Official Assignee to a sale and distribution, that it is useful to have a provision in a partnership agreement entitling the continuing partners to buy-out the bankrupt's share.[144] It is clear that any agreement between the bankrupt partner and his co-partners fixing the value at which this share is to be acquired is binding on the Official Assignee.[145]

Exceptional case where Official Assignee may wind up the partnership

[27.82] Although as a general rule, the Official Assignee may not interfere in the winding up of the partnership, *Re Coonan*[146] is authority for the principle that that where the Official Assignee is of the opinion that it would be in the interests of the bankrupt partner or partners, he may make an application to court to wind up the partnership. Support for this view may be found in the wide terms of s 138(1) of the Bankruptcy Act

---

139 See *Fraser v Kershaw* (1856) 25 LJ Ch 445 where at 501, Page Wood VC stated that: '[t]he sheriff can have no such power. It is a power confined to the partner himself, which, when exercised *bona fide*, the Courts have maintained to enable him to proceed in winding up the partnership affairs in due course.' This was quoted with approval by Johnston J, *Provincial Bank of Ireland v Tallon* [1938] IR 361 at 366.

140 *Crawshay v Collins* (1808) 15 Ves Jr 218. See further para **[26.26]** et seq.

141 Assuming that the default position under the 1890 Act applies, ie that the bankruptcy of the partner caused the firm's dissolution under s 33(1) of the 1890 Act.

142 See the New Zealand case of *Re Ward* [1985] 2 NZLR 352.

143 *Crawshay v Collins* (1808) 15 Ves Jr 218. In addition, this principle would appear to underlie the terms of s 42(1) of the 1890 Act.

144 For a comparable clause in a company situation see *Borland's Trustee v Steel Bros & Co* [1901] 1 Ch 279. See further in relation to such clauses, para **[21.129]**.

145 *Whitmore v Mason* (1861) 2 J & H 204.

146 *Re Coonan* (1954), unrep, file no 1276, which is referred to at para 39.6.4 of the Bankruptcy Law Committee Report (1972) prl 2714.

1988, which had no predecessor in the pre-existing bankruptcy legislation. This states that:

> The Court may, upon giving notice to such persons as it may direct, make such orders and give such directions as it thinks proper for winding up and settling the affairs of any partnership or the estate of a deceased person in which the bankrupt has an interest.

Although the section makes no reference to the Official Assignee, it seems likely that any winding up would be conducted by him.

[27.83] Further support for this view is to be found in s 61(3)(g) of the Bankruptcy Act 1988. This section provides that the Official Assignee, for the benefit of the bankrupt partner's estate, may take out letters of administration to any estate without being required to give security. This section is wide enough to enable the Official Assignee to take out letters of administration in respect of a non-bankrupt partner who dies before the partnership has been wound up, with a view to completing the winding up of the partnership.

Set-off in bankruptcy

[27.84] Another important consequence of the adjudication of a partner as bankrupt is the likelihood of a claim for set-off. Typically, when a bankrupt is adjudicated he will have debtors as well as creditors. Where debts are owing to a bankrupt by persons who are also his creditors, the creditors may be entitled to set off their debts against the amounts owed to them by the bankrupt. This raises the whole issue of the right of set-off between firms, partners and third parties on a bankruptcy as distinct from the right of set-off in non-bankruptcy situations, which is considered elsewhere in this work.[147]

[27.85] The right of set-off on bankruptcy is regulated by para 17(1) of the First Schedule to the Bankruptcy Act 1988. It states that:

> Where there are mutual credits or debts as between a bankrupt and any person claiming as a creditor, one debt or demand may be set off against the other and only the balance found owing shall be recoverable on one side or the other.[148]

The rationale for allowing set-off on bankruptcy is to prevent the injustice which would arise if a creditor of a bankrupt, who also owed the bankrupt money, was obliged to pay the bankrupt 100 cent in the euro, yet he would receive less than this from the bankrupt.

[27.86] Under the express terms of para 17(1) of the First Schedule of the Bankruptcy Act 1988, a set-off will only arise where the debts and credits are mutual. Therefore, a debt which is owed to or by a firm (a joint debt) cannot be set off against a debt which is owed to or by a partner (a separate debt) or vice versa as is illustrated by *McCully v Green*.[149] The plaintiff in that case claimed moneys which were due to him by the

---

[147] See para **[12.58]** et seq.

[148] This paragraph replaced s 251 of the Irish Bankrupt and Insolvent Act 1857. Note that para 17(2) of the First Schedule to the Bankruptcy Act 1988 reads: 'Section 36 of the Civil Liability Act 1961 (which provides for the set-off of claims), as amended by section 5 of the Civil Liability (Amendment) Act 1964, shall apply with the substitution in section 36(3) of a reference to subparagraph (1) for the reference to section 251 of the Irish Bankrupt and Insolvent Act 1857.'

[149] *McCully v Green* (1897) 32 ILTR 14.

defendant firm. In response, the defendant firm claimed a set-off in respect of monies owed by the plaintiff to one of the partners in the defendant firm. Although the firm was not in bankruptcy, mutuality of debts is also a requirement of set-off in a non-bankruptcy situation. Accordingly, the set-off was rejected by the County Court where Fitzgibbon J observed:

> 'This set-off cannot be maintained. It is clearly law that where an action is brought against a partnership, one of the partners cannot come in with a debt which is due by the plaintiff to him privately, outside of the partnership, and by setting it off claim thus to defeat the claim against the firm.'[150]

[27.87] A party claiming set-off in a bankruptcy situation is considerably more likely to be prejudiced by the refusal of his set-off, since he may get less than 100 cent in the euro, than where the set-off is claimed against a solvent party, where he is likely to get 100 cent in the euro. For this reason, it is apprehended that in borderline cases, the courts will find the requisite mutuality of debts or credits between the parties on a bankruptcy more easily that in a non-bankruptcy situation.

Waiver of right of set-off against a firm

[27.88] While the position in England is that it is not possible to contract out of the right to set off in a bankruptcy situation,[151] in Ireland there is pre-1890 authority for the principle that a creditor may waive his statutory right of set-off on bankruptcy. In *Deering v Hyndman*,[152] a committee of creditors was appointed to a Belfast partnership of flax spinners, Hind & Sons, which had got into trading difficulties. Hyndman was a member of the committee and the committee decided to recommend the suspension of the firm's business, save for the purposes of winding up the firm. At that time, Hyndman was also a creditor of the firm in the sum of £2,000. A special No 2 account was opened by the firm with its bank so that goods could be sold by the firm for cash out of this account. Evidence was adduced to the effect that it was well-known in Belfast at that time that the effect of this account was to exclude the right of set-off with transactions before its opening, whether bankruptcy ensued or not. After the opening of this account, Hyndman purchased goods worth over £1,000 from the firm for which he didn't pay. Soon afterwards, the firm went into bankruptcy and Hyndman relied on the predecessor of para 17(1) of the First Schedule to the Bankruptcy Act 1988[153] to set off the purchase price of over £1,000 which he owed the firm against the £2,000 which the

---

150 *McCully v Green* (1897) 32 ILTR 14 at 15.

151 *National Westminster Bank Ltd v Halesowen Presswork & Assemblies Ltd* [1972] AC 785, but see, in particular, the dissenting judgment of Lord Cross, in which he favoured the decision of the Irish Court of Appeal in *Deering v Hyndman* (1886) 18 LR Ir 467 over the English Court of Appeal decision in *Rolls Razor Ltd v Cox* [1967] 1 QB 552. Indeed the majority opinion in that case seems to rest as much on the failure of the purported agreement to waive the right of set-off, as much as it does on the supposed principle that it is not possible to waive this right of set-off.

152 *Deering v Hyndman* (1886) 18 LR Ir 323 and affirmed by the Irish Court of Appeal at (1886) 18 LR Ir 467. This decision was considered in detail by the House of Lords in *National Westminster Bank Ltd v Halesowen Presswork & Assemblies Ltd* [1972] AC 785.

153 Ie s 251 of the Irish Bankrupt and Insolvent Act 1857.

firm owed him. The High Court[154] held that the defendant and other creditors had entered into an agreement with the firm for all goods after the suspension to be paid for in cash. By so doing they had waived the statutory right to set off the price of such goods against any debt due to them by the firm on its bankruptcy. In an interesting judgment, O'Brien J held that the legal effect of the opening of the No 2 account:

> 'was the constitution of a new firm, so far as the new dealings were concerned. Hind & Sons, as they existed, were gone. The line was drawn unchangeably between the new and the old. The past was erased, and a new legal entity was brought into existence, constructively by the acts of the parties, with new rights and new engagements. The funds of No 2 account were to bear the demands on No 2 account. It was No 2 account he dealt with, and it is No 2 account that sues him. The contract of sale was made, not with Hind & Sons, but really with Hind & Sons and the other creditors.'[155]

[27.89] On this basis, O'Brien J held that Hyndman could not set-off debts owed to the 'new' firm against debts owed by the 'old' firm. It would be dangerous to accept O'Brien J's conclusion as a statement of the legal effect of opening a suspense account. His reasoning leads to other difficulties beyond simply the right to a set-off, such as the priority of debts owing by the new firm and the old firm. Perhaps what he had in mind was the temporary breathing space allowed to companies under the modern law of examinership.[156] However, even in that situation, there is not the creation of a 'new legal entity', but a different treatment of creditors before and after the examinership. It is for this reason that the judgments of May CJ and Johnson J are to be preferred. May CJ simply held that the right of set-off in bankruptcy may be excluded by the agreement of the creditor while Johnson J similarly held that:

> 'a person who has a benefit given to him by statute may waive it if he thinks fit, but that an individual cannot waive a matter in which the public have an interest ... The right of set-off is a benefit to the individual creditor, and it in no way concerns the public or society whether he relies on it or waives it. And if even an individual creditor agrees for sufficient consideration to waive the right, I fail to see why he should not be at liberty to do so either without bankruptcy or in bankruptcy.'[157]

The decision of the High Court was affirmed by the Irish Court of Appeal (Ashbourne LC, Morris CJ, Fitzgibbon and Barry LJJ).[158]

Allowance to bankrupt partners out of estate

[27.90] It has been observed that all the bankrupt's assets are vested in the Official Assignee on the adjudication of bankruptcy.[159] However, it is clear that the bankrupt will require some money to meet living and other necessary expenses. For this purpose, s 71 of the Bankruptcy Act 1988 provides that the High Court has a discretion to make such allowance to the bankrupt as it thinks proper in the special circumstances of the case,

---

[154] The decision was affirmed by the Irish Court of Appeal at *Deering v Hyndman* (1886) 18 LR Ir 467.

[155] *Deering v Hyndman* (1886) 18 LR Ir 323 at 339.

[156] See generally in relation to examinership, Courtney, *The Law of Companies* (4th edn, 2016) at para [17.001] et seq; Hutchinson, *Keane on Company Law* (5th edn, 2016) at para [37.01] et seq.

[157] *Deering v Hyndman* (1886) 18 LR Ir 323 at 340.

[158] *Deering v Hyndman* (1886) 18 LR Ir 467.

[159] See para **[27.65]**.

although applications for such allowances are rarely encountered in practice.[160] In practice, the court is more likely to have reason to exercise its discretion regarding the financial position of the bankrupt partner in the context of s 65 of the 1988 Act. Under this section, the Official Assignee may apply to the High Court for an order to appropriate all or part of any salary or other income which is payable to the bankrupt. However, in making any such order, the High Court may impose conditions as to the appropriation in light of family responsibilities and the personal situation of the bankrupt.

[27.91] The case of *Re Hunter*[161] illustrates the type of circumstances which the High Court will take into account in making an order under either s 65 or s 71 of the Bankruptcy Act 1988. In that case, James Hunter carried on business as a flour miller for a number of years. However, the day prior to his entering a written agreement with some of his creditors in which he stated that he was unable to pay them, he introduced his two sons into partnership with him. Four months later all three were adjudicated bankrupts. A joint schedule was filed by the three and a separate schedule was filed by James Hunter alone as his two sons had no separate property. An application was then made on behalf of all three bankrupts for an allowance on foot of the joint estate of the bankrupts and the separate estate of James Hunter. Not surprisingly, the claims of the two sons for an allowance were rejected,[162] Miller J observing:

> 'I cannot discover any meritorious claim whatever on the part of either [of the two sons] to any such separate allowance, if there were any room for the exercise of any discretion on the part of this Court, as neither of them brought any capital into the firm, nor rendered any effectual service to that firm and, on the contrary, at the short interval of four months from joining such firm, and before they could have had an opportunity of rendering any such assistance, procured the adjudication of themselves as bankrupts, and the only effect of granting such allowance to each would be, that there would be withdrawn from the estate and creditors of James Hunter £1,000 or thereabouts, which properly belonged to such estate and creditors.'[163]

[27.92] Another factor to be considered by the High Court in determining whether to pay a bankrupt an allowance is likely to be the amount of dividend which has been paid to creditors out of the separate and joint estates. Under previous bankruptcy

---

[160] Previously this right was contained in ss 302 and 303 of the Irish Bankrupt and Insolvent Act 1857.

[161] *Re Hunter* (1872) 7 ILTR 153. Upon appeal the decision was affirmed, see (1872) 7 ILTR 153 at 154.

[162] Miller J expressly overruled *Re Scott* (1863) Ir Jur (ns) 160, a case involving a Cobh shipping partnership, in which the decision in *Ex p Gibbs* (1830) 1 Mont 105 had been reluctantly followed by Lynch J. Instead, Miller J relied expressly on *Ex parte Lomas* (1834) 1 Mon & A 525, which had overruled *Ex p Gibbs* (1830) 1 Mont 105. In two other unreported cases, Lynch J in the Bankruptcy Court had also relied on *Ex p Lomas*, namely in *Re McCarthy and Parsons* (19 January 1860), Bankruptcy Court, and in *Ammerman, Reid and Ryan* (2 January 1863), Bankruptcy Court. In a case heard shortly after *Re Hunter* (1872) 7 ILTR 153, that of *Re W & J Crowe* (4 July 1873), Bankruptcy Court, Miller J rejected an application for a separate allowance for each of the bankrupts on the authority of *Re Hunter*, above.

[163] *Re Hunter* (1872) 7 ILTR 153.

legislation,[164] the court was required to take the amount of dividend into account in determining the allowance to be granted to the bankrupt. While this requirement was repealed by the Bankruptcy Act 1988,[165] it is apprehended that the High Court will take the rate of dividend paid by the bankrupt's estate into account in exercising its discretion under ss 65 and 71 of the 1988 Act. In *Re Lunham*,[166] which was heard under the previous legislation, Lynch J overturned an allowance which was based on the bankrupt's separate estate and *all* the joint estate, since he held that it should have been based on the separate estate and only the bankrupt's share of the joint estate. Thus where the members of a partnership are numerous, the bankrupt partner's share of the joint estate will usually be small and this may impact on the amount of the allowance paid to a partner by the High Court under ss 65 or 71 of the 1988 Act.

Repeal of doctrines of reputed ownership and of relation back

[27.93] It should be noted that some of the previous consequences of an order of adjudication no longer apply. First, the doctrine of reputed ownership allowed the property of a bankrupt which was available for the satisfaction of his debts to include another person's property.[167] This doctrine was abolished by Bankruptcy Act 1988.[168] Second, the doctrine of relation back allowed the Official Assignee's title to a bankrupt's property to relate back to the first act of bankruptcy by the debtor. This doctrine was effectively repealed by s 44(2) of the 1988 Act.

III.   ADMINISTRATION OF FIRM'S AND PARTNERS' ESTATES

[27.94] Once a partner or partners have been adjudicated bankrupt, it is the duty of the Official Assignee to administer their assets for the benefit of the joint creditors, the separate creditors and the joint and separate creditors. In administering the estate of a bankrupt partner, one must reconcile these three different types of debts and in this section, the principles which are applicable thereto are considered.

Joint Estates and Separate Estates

[27.95] In a partnership situation there are three possible ways in which a debt could be owed by a partner(s), ie it could be a joint debt and therefore subject to the joint estate, a separate debt and therefore subject to the separate estate or a joint and separate debt and therefore subject to the joint and separate estates. The joint creditors of the firm are creditors to whom each partner is jointly liable. As is clear from s 9 of the 1890 Act, a contractual debt of the firm will, in the absence of a contrary agreement, be a joint debt

---

164 Irish Bankrupt and Insolvent Act 1857, ss 320 and 303. These sections provided that a bankrupt should not be entitled to an allowance unless a sufficient dividend was paid out of the joint estate and out of the separate estate.

165 Bankruptcy Act 1988, s 6(1) and 2nd Sch.

166 *Re Lunham* (1862) 12 Ir Ch R 471.

167 Irish Bankrupt and Insolvent Act 1857, s 313.

168 Bankruptcy Act 1988, s 6(1) and 2nd Sch. Accordingly, the case of *Re Curry* (1848) 12 Ir Eq R 382 is no longer good law insofar as it deals with this issue.

only and not the separate debt of the partner.[169] The second type of creditor is the separate creditor of a partner and a partner is severally liable to such creditors. Such debts will not usually relate to the firm's business but will be the private debts of the partners. In this regard, these debts are strictly not partnership debts. The third type of debt are those debts which are owed to joint and separate creditors, to whom all the partners are liable both jointly and separately for the same debt. In contrast to s 9 of the 1890 Act, ss 10 to 12 of the 1890 Act provide that the liability of the partners is joint and several where a firm is guilty of a tort, fraud or a breach of trust.[170] The circumstances in which a debt is considered to be either a joint debt, or a joint and several debt are examined in detail earlier in this work.[171]

[27.96] The principles which apply to the distribution of the joint estate and the separate estate are the same, whether the estate to be administered is that of a bankrupt partner or a bankrupt firm. Accordingly, both will be considered simultaneously and any differences which are particular to one situation or the other will be noted.

Right to choose whether joint or separate debt

[27.97] Before considering these rules, it should be noted that there is one situation in which a creditor may be allowed to choose whether to treat his debt as a joint debt or a separate debt. This arises where a firm consists of just two partners, one of whom is an active partner, the other being either a dormant partner or one who is held out as being a partner.[172] In this situation, it seems that a creditor of the firm may choose to treat the debt as a joint debt of the two or as the separate debt of the active partner.[173]

Rules regarding the payment of joint estates and separate estates

[27.98] Perhaps the most important principle of the law of bankruptcy as it applies to partners relates to the respective priority in the administration of the bankruptcy of the firm's debts on the one hand and a partner's separate debts on the other. This principle states that the joint property of the firm is used first to meet the debts of the firm (joint debts) and that the separate property of each partner is used first to meet the separate debts of that partner (separate debts). Only after all the debts of the joint creditors are paid out of the joint estate, are the separate creditors entitled to rely on the joint estate. Only after all the debts of the separate creditors are paid out of the separate estate, are

---

169 See generally in relation to s 9 of the 1890 Act, para **[11.08]** et seq. However, in exceptional circumstances, *Re Gorman Bros* (1949), unrep, file nos 112–1114 (referred to at para 39.7.1 of the Bankruptcy Law Committee Report (1972) prl 2714) is authority for the principle that the joint estates and separate estates of a partner will be consolidated, such as where it is impossible or impractical to separate them. It seems clear that the determining factor in any such decision will be the interests of the creditors. For this reason, it is thought that there is no reason why joint estates and separate estates should not be consolidated if all the joint creditors and separate creditors consent thereto.

170 See generally in relation to ss 10–12 of the 1890 Act, para **[11.14]** et seq.

171 See para **[11.17]** et seq.

172 Technically, of course, this will not be a firm since there will be only one partner in such a case, the other being a partner by holding out.

173 *Ex p Hodgkinson* (1815) 19 Ves Jr 291. See also l'Anson Banks, *Lindley & Banks on Partnership* (20th edn, 2017) at para 27-92.

the joint creditors entitled to rely on the separate estate. This rule is founded on a principle of justice – the firm's creditors are assumed to have given credit to the firm and the partners' creditors are assumed to have given credit to the partners. For this reason, each class of creditors is first confined to the estate to which he was presumed originally to have looked for payment.

[27.99] The resulting rule was stated in the Irish courts more than 200 years ago in *Hayden v Carroll*,[174] where in a case concerning a Waterford banking partnership, Clare LC in the Irish House of Lords observed:

> 'The rule of equity is clear, that in distributing the joint and separate estates of partners in trade who become bankrupts, the joint estate shall be applied first in payment of joint creditors, and the separate estate in discharge of separate debts; and if any surplus remains of either estate after payment of the demands upon it, such surplus shall go in augmentation of the other, that is, the surplus of the joint in augmentation of the separate estate; and the surplus of the separate in augmentation of the joint estate.'[175]

[27.100] This rule is now contained in s 34 of the Bankruptcy Act 1988 which states:

> (1) In the case of partners the joint property shall be applicable in the first instance in payment of their joint debts, and the separate property of each partner shall be applicable in the first instance in payment of his separate debts.

> (2) Where there is a surplus of the joint property, it shall be dealt with as part of the respective separate properties in proportion to the right and interest of each partner in the joint property.

> (3) Where there is a surplus of any separate property, it shall be dealt with as part of the joint property so far as necessary to meet any deficiency in the joint property.

[27.101] Curiously, the only reference in the 1890 Act to the priority of debts is in s 9, which deals with the priority of some several debts and other several debts. This section states that a deceased partner's estate is severally liable for the obligations of the firm which were incurred while the deceased was a partner.[176] In addition, the section provides that this liability is subject in 'England or Ireland to the prior payment of his separate debts'.

Meaning of a surplus

[27.102] The reference in s 34 of the Bankruptcy Act 1988 to the surplus on the joint or the separate estate is to a surplus after all the creditors have been paid one euro in the euro with interest at the rate currently payable on judgment debts.[177]

---

[174] *Hayden v Carroll* (1796) 3 Ridg PC 545. The rule was first stated in 1728 by Lord King in *Ex p Cook* (1728) 2 P Wms 500, though first formulated in *Ex p Crowder* (1715) 2 Vern 706. The rules were incorporated in an order made on 8 March 1794 by Lord Loughborough, which was extended to Ireland by an order of Lord Chancellor Plunkett dated 25 November 1832.

[175] *Hayden v Carroll* (1796) 3 Ridg PC 545 at 605.

[176] See further in relation to this liability, para **[24.40]** et seq.

[177] Bankruptcy Act 1988, s 86(1).

Exceptions to rules in s 34

[27.103] The rules in s 34 of the Bankruptcy Act 1988 are not stated to be subject to any exceptions. However, s 34 is simply a re-formulation of rules of distribution which were first recognised in the eighteenth century and the exceptions to those rules have been recognised since that time. For this reason, it is contended that the exceptions to the rules in s 34 are so well established that they have not been displaced by their omission from s 34, which is not a statement of new rules, but simply the re-formulation of ones that have existed for hundreds of years.[178] This conclusion can be supported in principle, particularly since an examination of these exceptions hereunder shows that they are required in order to ensure that the primary purpose of bankruptcy law is achieved, namely the equal distribution of the bankrupt's estate without any creditor obtaining an unfair advantage over the others.

[27.104] Further support for this view is provided by the case of *Re Budgett*[179] which considered the re-formulation of the rules in England into s 40 of the Bankruptcy Act 1883. Prior to that Act, the rules were contained in the Order of Lord Loughborough from 1794 (which order was adopted in Ireland by an order of Plunkett LC on 25 November 1832). In that case, Chitty J noted that:

> 'when the Legislature passed in the Act of 1883 the 40th section, it seems reasonable and proper to infer, and to adopt the inference as correct, that the Legislature, though now for the first time it put the substance of the Order on the statute-book, intended the law to stand, on the construction of the section, in the same way that it stood previously to the passing of the Act.'[180]

These exceptions to the rules in s 34 are considered in detail hereafter.[181]

Important conceptual difference between joint debts and separate debts

[27.105] The principle underlying s 34 of the Bankruptcy Act 1988 is also to be found in s 74 of the 1988 Act which provides that a joint creditor is not entitled to receive a dividend from the separate estate until all the separate creditors have received the full amount of their debt:

> If one or more of the partners of a firm is a bankrupt, any creditor of the firm shall be entitled to prove his debt or be admitted as a creditor for the purpose of voting in the choice and appointment of a creditors' assignee[182] but such creditor shall not receive any dividend out of the separate estate of the bankrupt until all the separate creditors shall have received the full amount of their respective debts.[183]

---

178 Following the recommendations of the Bankruptcy Law Committee these important rules were quite rightly given a statutory footing in s 34 of the Bankruptcy Act 1988. See the Bankruptcy Law Committee Report (1972) prl 2714 at para 39.10.4.

179 *Re Budgett* [1894] 2 Ch 557.

180 *Re Budgett* [1894] 2 Ch 557 at 561.

181 See para **[27.130]** et seq and **[27.143]** et seq.

182 As to creditors' assignees, see generally Sanfey & Holohan, *Bankruptcy Law and Practice* (2nd edn, 2010) at para 4.34 et seq.

183 The predecessor of this section is s 266 of the Irish Bankrupt and Insolvent Act 1857.

[27.106] It is to be noted that this section allows a joint creditor to prove his debt against the separate estate and vote in relation thereto, yet a separate creditor is not allowed to prove his debt against the joint estate nor vote in relation thereto. This highlights the essential distinction between joint creditors and separate creditors. Joint creditors are creditors of the firm and also creditors of each partner, since each partner is jointly liable for the firm's debts. However, the separate creditor of a partner is not also the creditor of the firm. Therefore, while both the joint creditors and separate creditors are entitled to the surplus on the other's estate, the joint creditors are entitled thereto in a direct fashion (by proving and voting on the separate estate), while the separate creditors are entitled to the surplus in an indirect manner, ie the partner, to which they are the separate creditors, is entitled to the surplus on the joint estate and this surplus then forms part of his separate estate for their benefit.

[27.107] This conceptual difference between joint creditors and separate creditors also explains the differing wording in s 34(2) and 34(3) of the Bankruptcy Act 1988. Section 34(3) provides that any surplus of the separate estate is used to pay off the joint debts, while s 34(2) provides that the surplus of the joint estate shall be used to pay off the separate estates but only 'in proportion to the right and interest of each partner' in the surplus. This ensures that the share of the surplus on the joint estate which belongs to one partner is not used to pay off the separate creditors of his co-partner because the firm is not liable for these debts.

[27.108] This conceptual difference between joint creditors and separate creditors will also explain the sometimes differing treatment of joint creditors and separate creditors in the administration of the respective estates which is discussed in the remainder of this chapter.

Distinct firms

[27.109] The conceptual difference between joint and separate creditors is also relevant in a case where there are two distinct firms, one larger firm (X, Y & Z) and a smaller firm composed of partners who are all members of the larger firm (X & Y). The smaller firm (X & Y) is in a similar position to the separate estate of a partner on the bankruptcy of a single partnership, since the joint creditors of X & Y will not be the creditors of the larger firm, X, Y & Z, in the same way as the separate creditor of a single partner is not the creditor of that firm and thus cannot prove in the bankruptcy of the firm.[184] Applying the same logic, it is thought that the creditors of X & Y cannot prove in the bankruptcy of X, Y & Z. This conclusion runs counter to the authority of the nineteenth century case of *Ex p Worthington*[185] which allowed the creditors of X & Y to prove in the bankruptcy of X, Y & Z. It is contended that this precedent should not be followed by the Irish courts since, to allow the creditors of X & Y to prove in the bankruptcy of X, Y & Z, goes contrary to the well-established principle that separate creditors are not creditors of the partnership. This conclusion can also be supported in principle since the creditors of X & Y relied on the fund of that firm and not that of X, Y & Z. Therefore, allowing them to prove on the latter estate would prejudice the creditors of X, Y & Z who

---

184 See para **[27.141]** et seq.

185 *Ex p Worthington* (1818) 3 Madd 26. This case is noted in Robb, *The Law and Practice of Bankruptcy and Arrangements in Ireland* (1907) at p 216.

relied on that fund.[186] It is curious that this principle was reflected in the superior court rules made under the Supreme Court of Judicature Act (Ireland) 1877[187] but when these rules were repealed in 1905,[188] this particular rule was not replaced.

Substitution of joint debtor for separate debtor and vice versa

[27.110] It has been noted that under s 34 of the Bankruptcy Act 1988, the joint estate will only be applicable to the separate debts of a partner when there is a surplus after all the joint debts have been paid and vice versa. It may therefore be opportune for one class of creditors to claim on the other estate by alleging that the separate debt was in fact adopted by the firm and thus became a joint debt or vice versa. This will not necessarily be an easy matter.

[27.111] The case of *Re Ferrar, ex p Ulster Banking Co*[189] involved a partnership between Ferrar and Simms for the publication of the Belfast Mercury newspaper. The Ulster Banking Company had lent money to Simms which he had used for the purposes of the partnership. Simms became mentally incapacitated and the partnership went bankrupt. The Ulster Banking Company sought to prove for the money lent to Simms against Ferrar as the surviving partner of the firm. Ferrar disputed the bank's claim on the grounds that it was the separate debt of Simms and therefore not provable on the joint estate. Macan J held that in order for a creditor to prove on the joint estate of a firm for a debt incurred by one partner, there must be a positive agreement or sufficient conduct by the other partner from which to infer that the debt was adopted by the firm. It is not sufficient, as happened in this case, that the debt was used by the partner for the purpose of the firm. For there to be a substitution of a joint debtor for a separate debtor, or vice versa, the debtor adopting the debt must consent expressly or implicitly to the adoption of the debt.

[27.112] Not only must the adopting partner or partners agree to the adoption of the debt, but in order to be effective, the creditor must also agree to the change in the nature of his debt, from a separate debt to a joint debt or vice versa. This point is illustrated by *Re Littles*,[190] which involved a River Bann salmon fishing partnership. One partner in

---

186 Note that this view is in line with the current statutory position in England which implicitly overruled *Ex p Worthington*: (currently set out in the Insolvent Partnerships Order 1994, s 175C). This provides that: '[i]f any two or more members of an insolvent partnership constitute a separate partnership, the creditors of such separate partnership shall be deemed to be a separate set of creditors and subject to the same statutory provisions as the separate creditors of any member of the insolvent partnership.'

187 See Part III of the Rules of Court (Ireland) 1899 which set out the Rules of the Supreme Court (Ireland) 1899 (Bankruptcy) and in particular Ord 95 which read: 'If any two or more members of a partnership constitute a separate and independent firm, the creditors of such last-mentioned firm shall be deemed to be a separate set of creditors, and to be on the same footing as the separate creditors of any individual member of the firm. And where any surplus shall arise upon the administration of the assets of such separate or independent firm, the same shall be carried over to the separate estates of the partners in such separate and independent firm according to their respective rights therein.'

188 By Appendix Z of the Rules of the Supreme Court (Ireland) 1905.

189 *Re Ferrar, ex p Ulster Banking Co* (1859) 9 Ir Ch R 11.

190 *Re Littles* (1843) 6 Ir Eq R 197 and on appeal (1847) Ir Eq R 275.

the firm took responsibility for the separate debt of a former partner in the firm. The debt was due by that former partner and another person called Hill to a third party called Knox. On the bankruptcy of the firm, Knox sought to prove on the joint estate for this debt. However, it was held by Brady LC that the debt due to Knox had not been transferred to the firm as there was no evidence to show that Knox accepted the firm as his debtors instead of Hill. Accordingly, Knox was not allowed prove on the joint estate of the firm.

[27.113] It is not a coincidence that the two cases which deal with the substitution of one estate for another deal with the attempted conversion of a separate debt of a partner into the joint debt of the firm, rather than the other way around. This is because on purely practical grounds, it will be easier for a separate creditor to establish a right to prove against the joint estate, than for a joint creditor to establish a right to prove against the separate estate.[191] In the case of a separate creditor proving on the joint estate, the separate creditor need only show that those partners who were not his debtors have become so. In contrast, in the case of a joint creditor proving on the separate estate, he must show that the partner who was his joint debtor with the other partners has taken the debt upon himself alone. The difficulty with proving the latter is that it will not be an easy task to find acts of the partner which are consistent with his taking on of the debt alone. This is because most acts of a partner who is jointly liable with his co-partners for a debt (such as his act in agreeing to pay that debt to the creditor)[192] will be consistent with his remaining jointly liable and will not necessarily indicate that he has become separately liable for the debt.

Converting joint estate into separate estate

[27.114] A related issue to that of the substitution of joint debtors for separate debtors and vice versa is the conversion of what was the joint property of the partnership into the property of one partner. This conversion will also impact upon the joint creditors, since property which would have otherwise been joint property and available first to the joint creditors in priority to the claims of the separate creditors, becomes separate property and thus available first to the separate creditors. Nonetheless, if made bona fide and prior to any act of bankruptcy, the partners are entitled to change the character of partnership property by converting it into the separate property of a partner.[193] *Stuart v Ferguson*[194] establishes that the creditors of a firm cannot prevent the partners from bona fide changing the character of partnership property and converting it into the separate estate of one of them. That case involved a partnership of millers in County Antrim. The defendant claimed that, as a joint creditor of the firm, he had a lien on the joint estate of the firm and therefore disputed the transfer of part of the joint estate into the separate estate of one partner. This was rejected by the Court of Exchequer, where Joy CB noted that creditors of partnerships:

---

191 See l'Anson Banks, *Lindley & Banks on Partnership* (20th edn, 2017) at para 27-99.
192 *Ex p Smith* (1840) 1 MD & D 165; *Ex p Fairlie* (1830) Mont 17; *Ex p Raleigh* (1838) 3 M & A 670.
193 *Ex p Ruffin* (1801) 6 Ves 119, which was approved by Walsh J in *Re Pim* (1881) 7 LR Ir 458.
194 *Stuart v Ferguson* (1832) Hayes 452.

'have no lien; but something approaching to lien, that is, a right to sue, and, by judgement and execution, to obtain possession of the property; but, till then, they cannot prevent the partners from effectually transferring it by *bona fide* alienation.'[195]

[27.115] One of the reasons for allowing such conversions of joint property to separate property is to allow for the orderly dissolution of a partnership. In many cases, this will be in the interests of the creditors, since it may be as part of an arrangement to save the firm's business. This was the case in *Re Pim*[196] where a Cork-based partner, Pim, who was a member of a Scottish firm, entered into an arrangement with the firm's creditors. Pim hoped to return the business to profit on his own account. As part of the arrangement, the partnership was dissolved and the partnership business was transferred to Pim, who gave an indemnity to his former partner in respect of the partnership debts. Walsh J noted the rationale for allowing such conversions of joint property into separate property in the following terms:

'Many cases have occurred upon the distribution between the separate and joint estates, and the principle in all of them, from the great case of Mr Fordyce,[197] has been that if the Court should say that what has been joint or separate property shall always remain so, the consequence would be that no partnership could ever arrange their affairs. Therefore a *bona fide* transmutation of the property is understood to be the act of men acting fairly, winding up the concern, and binds the creditors.'[198]

But agreement to convert property is of no effect if it remains executory

[27.116] While the partners may freely convert joint property into the separate property of the partners, it should be noted that an agreement to transfer partnership property out of the firm will be of no effect if it remains executory, ie if the transfer of the property is dependant on some action which has not been taken. This is illustrated by *Re Fox*,[199] which concerned a partnership agreement between Fox and Doyle for the running of a hotel. The agreement provided that on the death of a partner, the share of the deceased partner should, as from the first of the month following his death, go to and belong to

---

195 *Stuart v Ferguson* (1832) Hayes 452 at 473, quoting from *Campbell v Mallett* (1819) 2 Swan 551 at 575.

196 *Re Pim* (1881) 7 LR Ir 458.

197 Ie *Fordyce's Case* (1871): *Cooke's Bank Law* (8th edn, 1871) at p 531.

198 Walsh J was quoting from the judgment of Lord Eldon in *Ex p Ruffin* (1801) 6 Ves 119 at 127. Walsh J also relied on *Ex p Williams* (1805) 11 Ves Jun 3; *Ex p Peake* (1816) 1 Madd 346; *Ex p Clarkson* (1834) 4 Deac & Chit 56 at 63; *Ex p Walker* (1862) 4 De GF & J 509 (judgment of Knight Bruce LJ). The case of *Duffy v Orr* (1831) 5 Bli (ns) 620 also involved a firm which arranged with its creditors for one partner to be liable for the debts of the firm. In that case, a partnership in Ballsbridge in Dublin which manufactured cotton and muslin got into trading difficulties and entered a deed of composition with its creditors. Under this deed, the creditors agreed to accept less than 100 pence in the pound, that a partner called Duffy should retire from the firm, that he would be released from the debts, and that his partner alone would be liable for them. However, many years later Duffy sought to challenge the amounts owed by one of the creditors and the value of that creditor's security. It was held by Hart LC, and on appeal by the House of Lords, that Duffy could not do so since, having assigned his interest in the partnership to his partner, he had no longer any interest in the arrangement especially as he had acquiesced in the arrangements for many years.

199 *Re Fox* (1915) 49 ILTR 224.

the surviving partner. Under the agreement, the surviving partner was obliged to pay to the personal representatives of the deceased partner such sum as may be due to him on an account being taken. Doyle died, leaving Fox as the sole survivor and two months later Fox died. Nothing was done during the two-month period to effect the provisions of the partnership agreement regarding the transfer of Doyle's share to Fox and thus the agreement to convert the property was held to be executory. O'Connor MR stated:

> 'It occurs to me that the assets of the hotel venture never lost their character of partnership assets. They would have done so if the procedure set forth in article 12 of the partnership deed, to be adopted in the case of the death of a partner, had been carried out. But no such procedure was carried out or any account taken between the deceased and surviving partner. There is nothing in what has occurred to deprive the assets of the hotel of their character of partnership property, and I must therefore hold that the creditors of the partnership are entitled to be paid in full out of the assets of the hotel, and that the surplus of such assets must be divided between the estates of Doyle and Fox.'[200]

Correcting mistakes regarding payments from different estates

[27.117] In dealing with joint and separate estates, it may occur during the administration that a payment is made out of the wrong estate. In such a case, the paying estate is required to be reimbursed by the other estate in respect of the amount which would have had to be paid by the other estate, were it not paid by the paying estate. A good example of this principle is provided by the case of *Re Hind*.[201] That case involved a Belfast firm of flax spinners and linen manufacturers, John Hind & Sons, and one of its creditors, the Rev Charles Hind. After the bankruptcy of the firm, the assignee of the firm paid a joint debt of the firm which was due to Rev Charles Hind out of the separate estates of two of the partners, John and James Hind. Miller J ordered that so much of the payment as would have been paid by the joint estate be repaid to the two separate estates. He noted that:

> '[T]he voluntary payment by the assignees, under such circumstances as stated, of the entire debt due to the Rev Charles Hind out of the separate estates of James Hind and John Hind, at once established the right that the separate estates of James Hind and John Hind should be recouped out of the joint estate to the extent, at all events, of any dividend which would have been properly payable out of the joint estate in respect of the debt which had been due to the Rev. Charles Hind, and had been so altogether discharged out of the respective separate estates of James Hind and John Hind alone.'[202]

[27.118] The converse situation arose in *Re Ferrar, ex p John Davis*[203] since there a creditor had been paid from the joint estate, but it transpired that his debt was the private debt of one partner. Section 79 of the 1988 Act states that:

> The Court may, on the application of the Official Assignee or any creditor or the bankrupt or the arranging debtor, disallow in whole or in part, any debt already proved or admitted.

---

[200] *Re Fox* (1915) 49 ILTR 224 at 225.
[201] *Re Hind* (1889) 23 LR Ir 217.
[202] *Re Hind* (1889) 23 LR Ir 217 at 227.
[203] *Re Ferrar, ex p John Davis* (1859) 9 Ir Ch R 289.

In that case, the application was made by another creditor and by the bankrupt under the predecessor of s 79 of the 1988 Act[204] to disallow the debt so paid and it was granted by Berwick J.[205]

[27.119] Where the mistake in question is not a payment out of the wrong estate, but rather an overpayment to a creditor, the wording of s 79 is wide enough to allow for such an application for the payment to be disallowed.

Secured creditors

[27.120] One of the primary aims of bankruptcy law is to secure equality of distribution of the estate of a bankrupt partner or the estate of a firm and to ensure that no creditor obtains an advantage over the others.[206] This aim is achieved in part by the rule that a creditor whose debt is secured is not allowed to retain his security while also proving in competition with the other creditors for the whole of his debt and thereby reducing the amount available to those other creditors. Otherwise, the creditor would have the best of both worlds. Accordingly, he must either retain his security and prove only for the balance of his debt after taking account of the security, or he may prove for his whole debt if he gives up his security. This principle is contained in para 24(1) of the First Schedule to the Bankruptcy Act 1988:

> If a secured creditor realises his security, he may prove for the balance due to him after deducting the net amount realised and receive dividends thereon but not so as to disturb any dividend then already declared. If he surrenders his security for the general benefit of the creditors, he may prove for his whole debt.

Exception where the security and debt are from different estates

[27.121] One of the underlying principles of the bankruptcy of partners is that joint estates and separate estates are treated distinctly. Thus, a joint creditor who holds separate property of a partner as security for the joint debt is not a secured creditor of the firm. Accordingly, the rule that a secured joint creditor must give all the other joint creditors the benefit of his security does not apply to such security, since the use of this security, coming as it does from the separate estate, does not affect those joint creditors. The same applies to a separate creditor with a security over the firm's property. This is the rationale which underlies the exception that where the security and debt are from separate estates, the secured creditor need not give up his security.

[27.122] This exception is illustrated by *Re Hind*.[207] A Belfast firm, John Hind & Sons, owed one of its creditors, the Rev Charles Hind, certain debts for which two of the partners, John and James Hind, gave security over their own life insurance policies. Miller J held that:

> 'It could not be denied that the Rev Charles Hind could, at any time after the filing of such respective statements of affairs, have proved his debt as thus admitted upon the face of the joint statement of affairs against the joint estate of the bankrupt firm of John Hind &

---

[204] Ie s 263 of the Irish Bankrupt and Insolvent Act 1857.

[205] Although he first required notice of the motion to be served on the assignee and the creditor in question.

[206] See the Bankruptcy Law Committee Report (1972) prl 2714 at para 1.13.1.

[207] *Re Hind* (1889) 23 LR Ir 217.

Sons, and that the Rev Charles Hind, when making such proof, could not have been called upon or required to give credit for or place any value whatever on the separate respective policies so deposited with him by the said James Hind and John Hind, and that the Rev Charles Hind would not, by the making of such proof, have waived, or in any manner prejudiced, his security, as founded upon such respective deposits.'[208]

Proof Against Joint Estate

[27.123] Having considered in general the joint estates and separate estates and the rules for the administration of those estates, it is now proposed to consider in detail the proof of debts against the joint estate and separate estate, beginning with the proof against the joint estate.

Position of a partner

[27.124] One of the underlying principles of bankruptcy law as it applies to partnerships is that a partner cannot compete with his own creditors. For this reason, a partner in a bankrupt firm cannot prove for a debt owed to him by the firm. Otherwise, he would be competing with his own creditors since creditors of the firm are his creditors. This principle was recognised in *McOwen v Hunter*,[209] a case involving the Saint Patrick Insurance Co of Ireland. There Conyngham LC observed:

'[T]he defendant being himself a partner, cannot maintain his claim against the partnership until the demands of the separate creditors are satisfied: and several cases[210] have been cited as decided in bankruptcy, where the claims of the separate creditors were brought into competition with the separate debt of the person, who was a member of the partnership. These cases have been very rightly decided, the principle is unquestionable.'[211]

[27.125] As noted earlier,[212] s 9 of the 1890 Act provides that a deceased partner's estate is liable for the debts of the firm. Accordingly, the rule that a partner cannot prove against the joint estate will also apply to the personal representative of a deceased partner, until such debts are paid or the estate is released from liability.[213]

[27.126] However, once the joint creditors have been paid off, the partners are entitled to receive any sums owing to them by the firm and to do so in priority to separate creditors of the other partners. This is because while a partner is prevented from competing with his own creditors, he is not prevented from competing with the creditors of his co-partners.[214] Indeed, the separate creditors of each partner will not be paid out of the joint estate until all the joint creditors have been paid, including the claims of the other

---

208 *Re Hind* (1889) 23 LR Ir 217 at 223–224.

209 *McOwen v Hunter* (1838) 1 Dr & Wal 347. This statement was obiter as on the facts there was no bankruptcy.

210 *Ex p Reeve* (1804) 9 Ves 588; *Ex p Rawson* (1821) Jac 274; *Ex p Ogle* (1831) 1 Mon 350; *Ex p Carter* (1827) 2 Glynn & J 233.

211 *McOwen v Hunter* (1838) 1 Dr & Wal 347 at 362.

212 See para **[11.10]**.

213 *Ex p Moore* (1826) 2 Gl & J 166; *Nanson v Gordon* (1876) 1 AC 195.

214 Provided that the joint creditors are not thereby prejudiced. Clearly they will not be prejudiced if they have been paid off.

partners.[215] Another way of saying this is that the lien[216] which each partner has upon the partnership assets must be satisfied before the surplus of the joint estate is divided amongst the partners,[217] ie before the surplus can be carried to the account of the separate estate of each partner. A lien in favour of one partner has the effect of increasing that partner's separate estate and in this way operating as effectively as if the separate creditors were given a right to prove against the joint estate in preference to the separate creditors of other partners without such a lien. When the surplus of the joint estate is distributed to the partners, it loses its character as joint estate and becomes the separate estate of the partner to whose account it is carried. Thus, where a partner is owed money by the firm, eg such as an advance made by the partner to the firm, the separate creditors of his co-partners will not be paid out of the partnership assets until the advance has been repaid.[218]

Position of a partner by holding out

[27.127] The rationale for the rule that a partner may not claim on the joint estate until all the joint creditors have been paid off, is to prevent a person from reducing what is available to his own creditors (the joint creditors). As a partner by holding out will have creditors by virtue of s 14(1) of the 1890 Act,[219] which creditors are likely also to be creditors of the firm, a partner by holding out should also be prevented from reducing what is available to them. Therefore, the logic which prevents a 'real' partner from competing with his firm is equally applicable to a partner by holding out and it is submitted that a partner by holding should also be prevented from claiming on the joint estate in competition with the joint creditors.[220]

Ban on proof by partner only applies where there is a bankruptcy

[27.128] It is perhaps self-evident, but nonetheless worth mentioning, that the rule that a partner cannot compete with the joint creditors of the firm only applies when the firm is bankrupt. Thus in *McOwen v Hunter*,[221] McOwen was a member of the firm, Saint Patrick Insurance Co of Ireland, and had paid certain creditors of the firm. He was seeking to be reimbursed out of the funds of the partnership for these payments but was met with the defence that as a partner, he could not maintain a claim against the firm until the demands of the creditors were satisfied. Conyngham LC rejected this defence as the firm was not in bankruptcy. He held that:

---

215 See the Bankruptcy Act 1988, s 34(1) and (2) and para **[27.100]** et seq.

216 A partner's lien is the right of a partner to have the joint estate used to pay off the partnership liabilities and for the surplus to be divided between the partners according to their respective entitlements. See further in relation to such lien, para **[19.50]**.

217 *Ex p Reid* (1814) 2 Rose 84; *Ex p King* (1810) 17 Ves 115.

218 This is because a partner's share in the partnership includes any advances made by him to the firm beyond his capital. See for example *Croft v Pyke* (1733) 3 P Wms 180; *West v Skip* (1749) 1 Ves Sen 239; *Holderness v Shackels* (1828) 8 B & C 612.

219 See generally in relation to partners by holding out, para **[7.01]** et seq.

220 Support for this contention is to be found in *Ex p Sheen* (1877) 6 Ch D 235.

221 *McOwen v Hunter* (1838) 1 Dr & Wal 347.

'I cannot postpone the claims of the creditor, who has been actually proceeded for and proved his debt, merely because there may be other persons, who might be enabled to establish a preferable claim.'[222]

Exceptional cases where partner may prove against joint estate

[27.129] In a number of exceptional situations, a partner may prove on the joint estate in competition with the joint creditors.

Exception where firm dealt with property of a partner fraudulently

[27.130] One exception to the general rule that a partner may not compete with his own (joint) creditors arises where the separate property of one partner has been fraudulently converted by his co-partners to the use of the firm. In such a case, the property is treated as still constituting the property of the defrauded partner and proof is allowed on behalf of that partner against the joint estate in competition with the joint creditors.[223] It is suggested that such a proof should be restricted to the asset which has been fraudulently converted and not allowed in relation to all the joint estate.[224]

Exception where the partner carries on a distinct firm

[27.131] The second exception to the general rule arises where the partner proves against the joint estate as a member of a distinct firm, or where he proves in respect of a distinct trade being carried on by him. To take the example of a distinct firm, if firm A is bankrupt and firm B is one of its creditors, firm B may prove on the joint estate of firm A, even though a partner in firm B is also a partner in firm A. In order for firm B to be allowed prove against the joint estate of firm A, the firms must carry on two distinct trades and the debt must have arisen in the ordinary course of business.[225]

Exception where the partner has obtained an order of discharge

[27.132] The third exception arises where a partner has been discharged from bankruptcy or from the joint debts of the firm. Such a partner is no longer a debtor to the creditors of the firm. In such a situation, if that partner becomes a creditor to the firm, he may prove against the joint estate since he will not be competing with his own creditors by proving against the joint estate.[226]

Position of joint creditors

[27.133] It has already been noted[227] that one of the basic principles underlying the bankruptcy of partners and partnerships is contained in s 34(1) of the Bankruptcy Act 1988, namely that joint creditors have the first claim on the joint estate. Accordingly, the separate creditors of the partners will not receive any of the joint estate until the joint creditors have been paid in full.

---

[222] *McOwen v Hunter* (1838) 1 Dr & Wal 347 at 362.

[223] *Ex p Sillitoe* (1824) 1 Gl & J 382; *Ex p Harris* (1813) 1 Rose 438.

[224] See para **[27.147]**, where this view is further analysed in the context of a claim by a partner against the separate estate of his own partner in the case of property which is fraudulently converted to the separate estate of the co-partner.

[225] *Ex p Cook* (1831) Mont 228; *Ex p Kaye* (1892) 9 Mor 269.

[226] *Ex p Carpenter* (1826) Mont & MacA 1, which was approved by Macan J in *Re McManus* (1858) 7 Ir Ch R 82 at 85–86.

[227] See para **[27.100]**.

Joint creditors who are deferred creditors under s 3 of the 1890 Act

[27.134] However, not all joint creditors will be treated the same and s 3 of the 1890 Act provides that if the debts are due to a creditor under either of the circumstances set out thereunder, they will be postponed until all the claims of the other joint creditors have been satisfied. The two circumstances are:

    (1)   If the debts are in fact a share of the profits of the business or interest varying with the profits, owing to a lender of money to the person engaged or about to engage in the business; or

    (2)   If the debts are in fact a share of the profits of the business owing to a seller of the goodwill of the business who receives that money in consideration for the sale.

[27.135] The nature of the deferment of such a creditor is set out in s 3 itself:

> [T]he lender of the loan and the seller of the goodwill shall not be entitled to recover anything in respect of the share of profits contracted for, until the claims of the other creditors of the borrower or buyer for valuable consideration in money or money's worth have been satisfied.

[27.136] The general priority of payments on a bankruptcy is governed by s 81 of the Bankruptcy Act 1988. This section is stated to be without prejudice to the deferment caused by s 3 of the 1890 Act.[228] Since s 3 of the 1890 Act speaks only of the deferred creditor not being entitled to recover anything in respect of the share of the profits, it is thought that the pre-1890 principle that such deferred creditors are not entitled to prove in the bankruptcy for any purpose, such as voting,[229] is inconsistent with the terms of s 3 and, therefore, no longer good law.[230] The rationale for deferring these joint creditors is that they are receiving the benefits of the successful trading of the firm in the same way as if they were partners and therefore should not be allowed to claim ahead of ordinary creditors, who do not receive such benefits. However, it is contended that this would not justify preventing a deferred creditor from exercising other creditor's rights (such as voting at creditors' meetings) until all the other creditors are paid in full.

[27.137] Sometimes an individual partner will take over the partnership business after the firm's dissolution and as part thereof may take over any loans to the firm. Where that individual subsequently becomes bankrupt, it has been held that the s 3 lender remains a deferred creditor on the bankruptcy of that individual.[231]

Position of separate creditors

[27.138] As already noted,[232] under s 34(1) of the Bankruptcy Act 1988, the separate creditors of a partner cannot prove against the joint estate in competition with the joint creditors of the firm. If a separate creditor is paid out of the joint estate before the joint creditors are paid off, the debt will be disallowed as happened in *Re Ferrar, ex p John Davis*,[233] where the separate creditor's debt was disallowed by Berwick J.

---

228   Bankruptcy Act 1988, s 81(10).

229   *Re Grason* (1879) 12 Ch D 366.

230   On the basis of s 46 of the 1890 Act.

231   *Re Mason* (1899) 1 QB 810.

232   See para **[27.100]**.

233   *Re Ferrar, ex p John Davis* (1859) 9 Ir Ch R 289.

[27.139] Once the joint debts have been paid with interest at the rate currently payable on judgment debts[234] and the liens of the partners are satisfied, s 34(2) of the Bankruptcy Act 1988 requires the surplus of the joint estate to be carried to the separate accounts of each partner in proportion to their shares in the partnership property. In this way, the surplus becomes part of the separate estate of the partners and is used to pay off the separate creditors.

Proof against Separate Estate

[27.140] Consideration will now be given to the issues which arise in relation to the proof by creditors of debts on the separate estate of a partner.

Position of separate creditors

[27.141] Under s 34(1) of the Bankruptcy Act 1988, the separate creditors have the first claim on the separate estate and the joint creditors are only entitled to any surplus which remains after the joint creditors have been paid off.

Deferred creditors under s 3 of the 1890 Act

[27.142] As with joint creditors claiming against the joint estate, not all separate creditors claiming against the separate estate will be treated the same. It had already been noted that s 3 of the 1890 Act provides that if the debts are due to a creditor under either of the circumstances set out in s 3, they will be postponed until all the claims of the other creditors have been satisfied. Reference should be made to the earlier discussion of the application of s 3 to joint creditors as the same principles will apply to a separate creditor claiming against the separate estate.[235]

Position of joint creditors

[27.143] The general rule that the joint creditors are only entitled to any surplus on the separate estate after the separate creditors have been satisfied is subject to a number of exceptions[236] and these appear to apply whether or not all the partners are adjudged bankrupt.[237]

---

[234] Bankruptcy Act 1988, s 86(1).

[235] See further para **[27.134]**.

[236] The existence of such exceptions was recognised by Brady LC in *Re McIntire* (1848) Ir Eq R 318, where at 328–329 he noted that 'there may be some question whether a joint creditor cannot prove against the separate estate. Upon that point I shall not at present give any opinion, as it does not now arise'. One exceptional case, but not a separate category of exceptions, is provided by *Re Williams* (1835) 3 Ir Law Rec (ns) 263. There, Ms Oliver had paid a firm of stockbrokers to purchase shares on her behalf. The shares were never purchased and one of the two partners in the firm, Williams, was declared a bankrupt. There was no suggestion that the bankrupt partner had converted the money to his own use. Ms Oliver claimed against his firm and the separate estate. The assignees in bankruptcy asked Conyngham LC to expunge the claim of Ms Oliver against the separate estate on the grounds that a creditor of the joint estate is not entitled to prove against the separate estate where there is a joint estate and the other partner is not insolvent. Ms Oliver claimed that as the firm was dissolved without notice to her, she was entitled to prove against the joint or separate estate as she thought fit. The court refused to expunge Ms Oliver's proof.

[237] *Re Budgett, Cooper v Adams* [1894] 2 Ch 557; *Re Carpenter* (1890) 7 Mor 270. See also l'Anson Banks, *Lindley & Banks on Partnership* (20th edn, 2017) at para 27-131 et seq.

Exception where no joint estate

[27.144] Where there is no joint estate and no solvent partner,[238] a joint creditor is allowed to be paid out of the separate estates pari passu with the separate creditors.[239] This limit on the general rule that a joint creditor cannot prove in competition with the separate creditors was implicitly recognised by Brady LC in *Re McIntire*[240] when he noted obiter that 'a joint creditor cannot resort to the separate estate of one bankrupt debtor so long as he has the power of so proceeding at law against any solvent partner'.[241]

[27.145] The reason for the general rule against a joint creditor competing with the separate creditors is justified on the grounds that the joint creditor gave credit to the firm and therefore is first confined to the estate to which he was presumed originally to have looked for payment. Accordingly, when there is no joint estate or assets of a solvent partner, the joint creditor is allowed to prove against the separate estate of a bankrupt partner. This is also justifiable on principle, since the individual partners are, after all, jointly liable for the joint debts. However, regardless of how small the joint estate is, once there is a joint estate, the joint creditors will not be permitted to prove against the separate estate in competition with the separate creditors.[242]

[27.146] It is also to be noted that where the joint creditors have paid off the separate creditors fully, the joint creditors may claim against the separate estate.[243] This illustrates the over-riding general principle in relation to a claim by the joint creditors against the separate estate, ie that if the separate creditors are not prejudiced, the joint creditors will be allowed to claim against the separate estate in competition with the separate creditors.

Exception where fraud by partner

[27.147] Where a partner has fraudulently converted partnership property to his own use, this property is regarded as still belonging to the firm and cannot therefore be treated as part of his separate estate. Accordingly, proof on behalf of the joint creditors will be admitted against the separate estate.[244] There is old authority for the view that the proof will be allowed against the separate estate, even where the value of the latter estate may not have been increased by the fraud.[245] However, such a principle is difficult to justify and it is suggested that the claim against the separate estate should be restricted

---

238   There is old authority for the view that the exception still applies where the solvent partner is dead: *Ex p Kendall* (1811) 17 Ves Jr 514. However, it is doubted whether this can be supported in principle since the assets of the solvent partner's estate are available to the joint creditor and therefore it is difficult to see why he should be allowed claim against the bankrupt partner's separate estate and thereby reduce the separate estate.

239   *Re Budgett, Cooper v Adams* [1894] 2 Ch 557.

240   *Re McIntire* (1848) Ir Eq R 318.

241   *Re McIntire* (1848) Ir Eq R 318 at 328, quoting from *Ex p Bauerman* (1838) M & Ch 574.

242   *Ex p Kennedy* (1852) 2 De GM & G 228; *Ex p Peake* (1814) 2 Rose 54; *Ex p Harris* (1816) 1 Madd 583.

243   *Ex p Taitt* (1809) 16 Ves Jr 193.

244   *Ex p Lodge and Fendal* (1790) 1 Ves Jun 166; *Ex p Smith* (1821) 1 Gl & J 74; *Ex p Watkins* (1828) Mont & McA 57.

245   *Lacey v Hill* (1876) 4 Ch D 537, aff'd *sub nom Read v Bailey* (1877) 3 App Cas 94.

to the value of the property which has been fraudulently converted. Otherwise, the separate creditors are prejudiced by having the separate estate disproportionately reduced by the claim of the joint creditors.

[27.148] Similarly, it is contended earlier in this chapter that where the situation is reversed and the separate creditors are allowed prove against the joint estate in the event of a fraudulent conversion of a partner's property by the firm,[246] the claim should also be restricted to the value of the property converted.

Exception where partner carried on a separate trade

[27.149] Another exception to the general rule that the joint creditors cannot prove against the separate estate arises where the separate estate in question is that of a partner who has carried on a separate trade to the firm and thereby become indebted to the firm. In this situation, the firm (or if it is bankrupt, the joint estate) is entitled to prove against the separate estate of the partner in respect of these separate debts in competition with the separate creditors.[247] This exception only applies if the debt has been contracted in the ordinary course of carrying on the distinct business.[248]

Exception where joint creditor petitions for separate bankruptcy?

[27.150] Where the joint creditor is also the petitioning creditor in the bankruptcy of the partner, there is old authority to the effect that the petitioning creditor may claim against the separate estate.[249] However, it is thought that the fairness to the separate creditors of such an exception is questionable. This is because the value of the fund available to the separate creditors is being reduced for no other reason than it was a joint creditor who petitioned for the separate bankruptcy of the partner. In order not to discourage bankruptcy petitions, the Rules of the Superior Courts provide that the costs of a petitioning creditor gain priority in the bankruptcy.[250] It is queried whether it is necessary to give the joint creditor the added bonus of having his claim allowed in competition with the separate creditors.

Position of partner

[27.151] It has been noted that a partner is not allowed prove on the joint estate, since this would involve him in competing with his own creditors (the joint creditors) as he is liable for the joint debts of the firm.[251] This principle is equally applicable to the administration of the separate estate, as it is to the joint estate. This is because if a partner were allowed to claim against the separate estate of his co-partner, this would reduce the size of the surplus to be transferred from the separate estate to the joint estate to pay his joint creditors. For this reason, a partner is not allowed to prove against the

---

[246] This situation is considered para **[27.130]**.

[247] *Ex p Hesham* (1810) 1 Rose 146; *Ex p Castell* (1826) 2 Gl & J 124; *Ex p Johns* (1802) Cooke BL 534.

[248] *Ex p Hargreaves* (1788) 1 Cox 440; *Ex p Sillitoe* (1824) 1 Gl & J 382; *Ex p Williams* (1843) 3 MD & D 433.

[249] *Ex p De Tastet* (1810) 17 Ves 247; *Ex p Hall* (1804) 9 Ves 349; *Ex p Ackerman* (1808) 14 Ves Jr 604.

[250] RSC, Ord 76, r 167.

[251] See para **[27.123]** et seq in relation to the joint estate.

separate estate of his co-partner if by doing so he will reduce the surplus available to the joint estate.[252] It follows that a firm also cannot prove in the bankruptcy of one of its partners, since this is simply a proof by all the partners.[253] However, as with the rule that a partner cannot prove against the joint estate, there are exceptions to this general rule.

Exception where the joint creditors are not prejudiced

[27.152] Where the proof by a partner against the separate estate does not involve that partner competing with the joint creditors, the general rule does not apply since there is no reason in principle why a partner cannot prove in competition with the separate creditors of his co-partners. The fact that a partner can prove on the separate estate of his co-partner provided that his joint creditors are not prejudiced explains the following specific exceptions.

Where no joint debts

[27.153] Where there are no joint debts, a partner will be allowed to prove against the separate estate of his co-partner, since there will obviously be no joint creditor who will be prejudiced thereby. This exception explains the decision in *Re McManus*,[254] which concerned a drapery partnership in Mullingar. One partner, Middleton, had received a bond from his partner, McManus, in relation to money owed to him by McManus. On the bankruptcy of McManus, Middleton tried to prove for the whole amount of his debt against his former partner. One of the separate creditors of the bankrupt partner, Baker & Wardell, objected to this proof by Middleton. However, Macan J held that Baker & Wardell was not a joint creditor of the firm[255] and, therefore, that Middleton could prove on the separate estate since there were no joint debts.

[27.154] It is apprehended that a partner's claim against the separate estate of his co-partner will not be defeated simply by the possibility that there may be joint creditors of the firm. This conclusion rests on the reasoning behind the decision in *McOwen v Hunter*,[256] although that case was not a bankruptcy case and concerned a claim by a partner against his own firm. Nonetheless, the statement of Conyngham LC is thought to be equally applicable to a claim by a partner against the separate estate of his co-partner:

> 'I cannot postpone the claims of the creditor, who has actually proceeded for and proved his debt, merely because there may be other persons, who might be enabled to establish a preferable claim.'[257]

---

[252] See *Ex p Hall* (1804) 9 Ves Jr 349; *Ex p Ackerman* (1808) 14 Ves Jr 604; *Ex p De Tastet* (1810) 17 Ves Jr 247; *Ex p Burnett* (1841) 2 MD & D 357.

[253] *Ex p Turner* (1833) 4 D & C 169.

[254] *Re McManus* (1858) 7 Ir Ch R 82.

[255] Baker & Wardell unsucessfully claimed that they were joint creditors on the grounds that they had known that Middleton was a partner and had extended credit to the firm on the faith of the partnership between the two men. Obiter, Macan J stated that if all the creditors had advanced credit on the faith of the continuing partnership, the court would not have allowed Middleton prove his debt.

[256] *McOwen v Hunter* (1838) 1 Dr & Wal 347.

[257] *McOwen v Hunter* (1838) 1 Dr & Wal 347 at 362.

Where separate estate is insolvent

[27.155] If the separate estate of a partner is insolvent, then there will be no surplus payable to the joint estate. Accordingly, in such a situation, a partner will be allowed to prove against the separate estate since it will not reduce the surplus payable to the joint estate and the joint creditors will not be prejudiced.[258] In fact, the joint creditors are likely to benefit from allowing such a proof since any dividend received by the claiming partner will swell his separate estate for the ultimate benefit of the joint creditors.[259]

Where co-partner paid joint debts

[27.156] Where a partner has paid more than his share of the joint debts, he will be allowed to prove as a separate creditor of his co-partner for the amount which the bankrupt partner ought to have paid. This was the case in *Re Hind*,[260] where one partner, James Hind, had paid £1,700 of the joint debt owed to one of the firm's creditors, while his partner, John Hind, had only paid £800 of that debt. In these circumstances, Miller J allowed James Hind to prove on the bankruptcy of John Hind for £450 so that each would then have contributed equally to the joint debt.[261]

Exception where partner dealt with property of firm fraudulently

[27.157] Where the property of the firm has been fraudulently converted by a partner to his own use, the property is treated as still being the property of the firm and proof is therefore allowed by an innocent partner against the separate estate in competition with the separate creditors.[262] It is contended that such proof should be restricted to the value of the property converted.[263]

Exception where the partner is member of a distinct firm

[27.158] If the debt owed to a partner by the bankrupt partner was incurred by the bankrupt partner carrying on a trade distinct from that of the firm, the partner may prove against the separate estate of his co-partner. The debt must, however, have arisen in the ordinary course of carrying on the distinct business.[264]

Creditors of both Firm and Partners

[27.159] Consideration will now be given to the situation where the firm is jointly liable to a creditor and, at the same time, the partners in the firm are severally liable to the same creditor. In a non-bankruptcy situation, the joint and several creditor has the option

---

258 *Ex p Topping* (1865) 4 De GJ & s 551; *Ex p Head* [1894] 1 QB 638.
259 See *Ex p Head* [1894] 1 QB 638.
260 *Re Hind* (1889) 23 LR Ir 217.
261 See also *Hearn & Cleary* (1947), file number 1081, which is referred to in para 39.8.2 of the Bankruptcy Law Committee Report (1972) prl 2714. See also *Ex p Carpenter* (1826) Mont & McA 1, which was approved by the Macan J in *Re McManus* (1858) 7 Ir Ch R 82. See also *Wood v Dodgson* (1813) 2 M & S 195; *Ex p Watson* (1819) 4 Madd 477.
262 *Ex p Sillitoe* (1824) 1 Gl & J 382; *Ex p Harris* (1813) 1 Rose 438.
263 This is argued at para **[27.147]**.
264 *Ex p Cook* (1831) Mont 228; *Ex p Kaye* (1892) 9 Mor 269.

of suing either all the partners jointly or one or more of them separately.[265] In bankruptcy, a similar rule applies in connection with a creditor's decision to rank against the joint or the separate estates as is noted hereunder.

Rule against double proof and its exception

[27.160] One of the primary aims of bankruptcy law is to achieve an equality of distribution of the estates and to ensure that one creditor does not obtain an unfair advantage over the others.[266] In pursuance of this aim, the rule against double proof provides that a creditor of both the firm and each partner is not allowed to rank as a creditor both against the joint estate and the separate estate, but must elect one or the other.[267] If he were allowed to prove against both the joint and the separate estates, he would be reducing the joint estate for the joint creditors and reducing the separate estate for the separate creditors. In order to make an election, a creditor has a reasonable time to inquire into the comparative solvency of the joint estates and the separate estates.[268]

[27.161] However, para 13 of the First Schedule of the Bankruptcy Act 1988 provides a large class of exceptions to this rule against double proof. Although, by its terms, it implicitly recognises the continued existence of the rule, this paragraph creates so large a class of exceptions as to render the rule of little consequence to creditors. Paragraph 13 states:

> If any bankrupt or arranging debtor, at the date of adjudication or order for protection, is liable in respect of distinct contracts, as a member of two or more distinct firms, or as a sole contractor, and also as member of a firm, the circumstance that such firms are, in whole or in part, composed of the same individuals, or that the sole contractor is also one of the joint contractors, shall not prevent proof in respect of such contracts against the properties respectively liable upon such contracts.[269]

[27.162] This exception covers all liabilities on distinct contracts entered into by a partner as a member in firm A and in firm B or as a partner in a firm and in his individual capacity. Most joint and several liabilities will arise from distinct contracts and therefore fall within the terms of this exception. Thus, if the members of a firm gave a joint and several promissory note, the holder is entitled to prove against the joint estate and the separate estates of the partners.[270] In practice, the only cases in which the rule

---

[265] For a consideration of the manner in which joint and several debts are incurred see para **[11.07]** et seq. Note that if a joint and several creditor sues jointly, he can enforce the judgment against either the partnership property or against the property of each partner or both at once.

[266] See the Bankruptcy Law Committee Report (1972) prl 2714 at para 1.13.1.

[267] *Ex p Bond* (1742) 1 Atk 98; *Ex p Banks* (1740) 1 Atk 106; *Ex p Rowlandson* (1735) 3 PW 405; *Ex p Bevan* (1804) 10 Ves 106; *Ex p Hay* (1808) 15 Ves 4. In *Re Woods* (1875) 9 ILTR 65, the principle against double proof was adopted by Miller J in the context of a bankrupt individual. A bill of exchange had been accepted by him in favour of a firm and the firm had then discounted the bill of exchange to a third party for cash. A claim by the firm against the bankrupt was disallowed since the only person entitled to prove was the holder of the bill of exchange since otherwise there would be double proof against the bankrupt by the firm and the third party.

[268] *Ex p Bond* (1742) 1 Atk 98; *Ex p Bentley* (1790) 2 Cox 218.

[269] The predecessor of this paragraph was Bankruptcy (Ireland) Amendment Act 1872, s 48.

[270] *Simpson v Henning* (1875) LR 10 QB 406.

against double proof will now apply is where the joint and several liability arises from torts, a breach of trust or fraud,[271] and rare cases in which the joint and several liability does not arise by distinct contract.[272]

Where double proof allowed

[27.163] For the exception in para 13 of the First Schedule of the Bankruptcy Act 1988 to apply to a partnership situation, there must be a joint estate and a separate estate. The para 13 exception does not allow double proof against the same estate, even where that estate is carrying on business in two different places. This point is illustrated by *Re Pim*,[273] which concerned the predecessor of para 13.[274] In that case, Pim carried on business as a sole trader in Cork and in partnership in Scotland. As part of the arrangement with the creditors of the Scottish firm, that partnership was dissolved and the business was transferred to Pim who continued to carry on the business there as a sole trader. He also continued to carry on business in Cork as a sole trader until his own bankruptcy in Ireland. A Scottish bank which had granted a loan to the Scottish partnership, sought to prove on Pim's bankruptcy in Ireland and in Scotland on the basis that there were two different estates. Walsh J rejected this claim and held that:

> '[T]his is not a case of two or more firms, it is the case of one individual having business in two places, and having assets in two places connected with the two businesses ... you cannot in such a case say there are two distinct estates to be wound up in bankruptcy ... there was not, at the time of the adjudication in this country, that within [para 13] which it is essential for the bank to establish – an individual, and a firm of which that individual was a member, as Mr Pim was then a sole trader at Cork trading as Deaves, Brothers, and a sole trader at Glasgow trading as A Simpson & Co, the estate to be administered is but one estate.'[275]

As Pim simply had assets in two businesses, there were no separate estates and the rule against double proof applied. Therefore, Walsh J held that the bank could only prove in Pim's estate if it gave credit for so much of the Scottish estate of Pim which it had received or might receive under the bankruptcy[276] in Scotland.

Joint and separate creditor with security

[27.164] It has already been noted that a creditor whose debt is secured is not allowed to prove for his debt without giving up or accounting for his security.[277] However, it has also been seen that this rule does not apply where the debt and the security of a creditor derive from different estates.[278] A creditor who is a joint and separate creditor with security for his debt will not be subject to the rule against double proof since there are two distinct estates. Furthermore, he may split his demand against the two estates. In such a situation the creditor is entitled to do one of two things, namely:

---

271 See para **[11.14]** et seq.
272 See for example the case of *Re Kent County Gas Light and Coke Co Ltd* [1913] 1 Ch 92.
273 *Re Pim* (1881) 7 LR Ir 458.
274 Ie s 48 of the Bankruptcy (Ireland) Amendment Act 1872.
275 *Re Pim* (1881) 7 LR Ir 458 at 466 and at 469.
276 The Scottish equivalent of bankruptcy is sequestration.
277 See para **[27.120]**.
278 See para **[27.121]**.

(a)   prove for the whole of his debt against the non-secured estate and then use his security;[279] or

(b)   give up his security and prove for the whole secured debt against the estate to which the security belongs and prove for the residue against the other estate. [280]

IV. ARRANGEMENTS WITH CREDITORS

[27.165] Under Part IV of the Bankruptcy Act 1988, until 3 December 2013, a debtor who was unable to meet his engagements with his creditors could seek court protection from bankruptcy proceedings with a view to entering into an arrangement with his creditors.[281] With effect from 3 December 2013, a debtor can no longer present a petition for such an arrangement. This change was made in light of the introduction of certain non-judicial debt settlement arrangements (ie personal insolvency arrangements, debt settlement arrangements and debt relief notices) as alternatives to bankruptcy under the Personal Insolvency Act 2012. It was felt that these non-judicial arrangements would be a more appropriate debt solution for individual debtors.

[27.166] The above change was given effect to by the Courts and Civil Law (Miscellaneous Provisions) Act 2013, Pt 7 which inserted a new s 86A into the Bankruptcy Act 1988 precluding a person from presenting a petition for an arrangement under Part IV of the 1988 Act. However, certain decided cases in respect of deeds of arrangement may continue to be relevant when a partnership is in financial difficulties and seeking to negotiate with its creditors. Those cases include:

–   *Re Loré*,[282] where three partners petitioned for an arrangement under the predecessor of Part IV of the 1988 Act and the court held that the requisite number (which was three-fifths) of both the joint estate and of the separate estate were required to approve the arrangement since that was the only way to ensure that the indebtedness of each partner as well as of that of the firm was eliminated by the arrangement.

–   *Re Parrott*,[283] in which Macan J refused to grant the petition for the arrangement of a partner since his co-partners had not agreed to take on the partnership debts themselves.

---

[279] *Ex p Bate* (1838) 3 Deac 358; *Ex p Smyth* (1839) 3 Deac 597; *Ex p Groom* (1837) 2 Deac 265.

[280] *Ex p Ladbroke* (1826) 2 Gl & J 81.

[281] The purpose of arrangements with creditors was considered by Miller J in *Re M* (1877) 11 Ir Eq R 46, a case involving a proposed arrangement between a four partner firm and its creditors. Although he was dealing with the predecessor of Part IV of the Bankruptcy Act 1988 (ss 344–353 of the Irish Bankrupt and Insolvent Act 1857), the following comments of Miller J (at p 49 of his judgment) were equally applicable to arrangements under Part IV: 'The whole purpose of that enactment following the earlier provisions on the same subject was to enable debtors and a substantial majority of their creditors to come to a reasonable arrangement among themselves, such as this Court could approve of, for the settlement of the liabilities of such debtors, and to force such arrangement, when come to, upon an unreasonable minority of the creditors of such debtors, instead of permitting such debtors and their estates to be necessarily subjected to such bankruptcy administration.'

[282] *Re Loré* (1889) 23 LR Ir 365.

[283] *Re Parrott* (1859) 8 Ir Ch R 391.

– *Re Pim*,[284] in which, as part of the arrangement with its creditors, a partnership was dissolved and the business was transferred to one of the partners, Pim, who continued to carry it on. Soon afterwards, Pim himself was forced to attempt to enter an arrangement with his creditors. This was unsuccessful and pursuant to the predecessor of s 105 of the 1988 Act, Pim was adjudicated a bankrupt. On his bankruptcy, the firm's bank sought to rely on a guarantee which Pim had given for loans made to the firm. Pim claimed that this guarantee was discharged by virtue of the agreement of that creditor to the arrangement with the firm. This was rejected by Walsh J who noted that 'nothing short of a clear and express contract to give up the securities' would be sufficient to discharge the securities of a creditor in an arrangement.

– *Duffy v Orr*,[285] which concerned a partnership in Ballsbridge in Dublin that manufactured cotton and muslin. The partnership got into trading difficulties and entered a deed of composition with its creditors whereby they agreed to accept less than 100 pence in the pound. This deed was signed first by Orr, who, after his signature, added the words 'without prejudice to the securities which I hold'. The other creditors added their signatures thereunder and Hart LC held that Orr could not in these circumstances be held to have waived his right to his mortgages over the partnership property and over the separate property of one of the partners. The decision in *Duffy v Orr* is also of interest when considering a partner who retires from his firm under the terms of the arrangement with the creditors. A number of years after the arrangement, Duffy, who appeared to have assigned his interest in the partnership to his co-partner, sought to challenge the amounts owed by one of the creditors as part of the arrangement and the value of that creditor's security. However, it was held by Hart LC, and on appeal, by the House of Lords, that Duffy could not do so, since he had assigned his partnership interest to his co-partner and therefore no longer had any interest in the arrangement. Furthermore, it was held that the delay of nine years in his bringing of the action amounted to acquiescence on his part in those arrangements.

– *Re M*,[286] in which a firm of four partners filed a petition for an arrangement and undertook to sign promissory notes as part of the arrangement. However, the formal confirmation of the proposal was adjourned until the amount of the debts could be ascertained. In the meantime one of the partners died. The surviving partners applied to hold a special sitting under the predecessor of s 104 of the 1988 Act for the purposes of approving the arrangement. Miller J held that the death of one of the partners before the arrangement was confirmed, rendered the arrangement void and it was not possible to carry it into effect by having a special sitting.

– *Re McQuoid*,[287] in which the arranging debtor died after his proposal had been assented to by the requisite majority and confirmed by the High Court with

---

284 *Re Pim* (1881) 7 LR Ir 458.
285 *Duffy v Orr* (1831) 5 Bli (ns) 620.
286 *Re M* (1877) 11 Ir Eq R 46.
287 *Re McQuoid* (1896) 31 ILTR 63.

nothing more remaining to be done by him. The arrangement was allowed to proceed, notwithstanding the debtor's death.

Voluntary Arrangements by Deed

[27.167] It only remains to note the possibility of a voluntary arrangement by deed between a debtor and his creditors.[288] In the latter situation, the arrangement is simply a private contractual arrangement between the debtor and his creditors for the payment of the debts. However, one of the difficulties with a deed of arrangement under the Deeds of Arrangement Act 1887 is that its very execution by a debtor is (where under the terms of the deed of arrangement the debtor transfers some or all of his assets to a third party, with a view to that person distributing those assets for the benefit of his creditors) in fact an act of bankruptcy which may be relied upon by a dissenting creditor, if there is one, to bring a bankruptcy petition.[289]

Registration of a Deed of Arrangement

[27.168] Under s 4(2) of the Deeds of Arrangement Act 1887, a deed of arrangement is defined as any instrument, whether under seal or not, made by, for, or in respect of the affairs of a debtor for the benefit of his creditors generally, otherwise than in pursuance of bankruptcy law. Section 6 of that Act provides that a deed of arrangement must be registered and filed in the Central Office. Under s 5 of the Deeds of Arrangement Act 1887, a deed of arrangement is rendered void if there is a failure to register it within seven clear days of its first execution by the debtor or the creditor, or if it is executed in any place out of Ireland, within seven clear days after the time at which it would, in the ordinary course of post, arrive in Ireland if posted within one week after the execution thereof.

---

[288] See generally, Sanfey and Holohan, *Bankruptcy Law and Practice* (2nd edn, 2010) at para 16.32; Forde and Simms, *Bankruptcy Law* (2009) at para 4-05.

[289] As to acts of bankruptcy, see para **[27.23]**.

PART E
LIMITED PARTNERSHIPS

Chapter 28

Limited Partnerships

INTRODUCTION

[28.01] Up to this, consideration has been given to the ordinary partnership. Three of the basic characteristics of a partner in an ordinary partnership are that:

1. each partner has unlimited liability to the creditors of the firm;[1]
2. each partner is entitled to take part in the management of the firm;[2] and
3. each partner is authorised to bind the firm in relation to the firm's business.[3]

[28.02] In this chapter, consideration will be given to another type of partnership, the limited partnership,[4] and in the succeeding chapter, consideration will be given to the investment limited partnership.

[28.03] A limited partnership is a partnership in which at least one of the partners, known as a limited partner, does not possess the three basic characteristics of a partner in an ordinary partnership. However, at least one of the partners, known as a general partner, will possess these three characteristics[5] and therefore very closely resemble a partner in an ordinary partnership.[6] The primary purpose behind the creation of such

---

1   Partnership Act 1890, ss 9–12 and see generally para **[11.04]**.
2   Subject to contrary agreement between the partners: Partnership Act 1890, s 24(5) and see generally para **[13.03]** et seq.
3   Partnership Act 1890, s 5, which right can be varied under s 19 of the 1890 Act. See generally para **[10.01]** et seq.
4   See generally Ramsay, 'A Comment on Limited Partnerships' (1993) 15 Sydney LR 537; Comment, 'The Limited Partnership' (1936) 45 Yale LJ 895; Queensland Law Reform Commission, *Working Paper on a Bill to Establish Limited Partnerships* (1984) Queensland Law Reform Commission Working Paper 27; Fletcher, 'Limited Partnerships and the Future' (1977) 7 Queensland Law Soc Jo 55; Fletcher, 'Limited Partnerships: Getting it Together ... Eventually' (1989) 19 Queensland Law Soc Jo 285; Lewis, 'The Uniform Limited Partnership Act' (1917) U Penn LR 715.
5   Laffoy J, in *Quigley v Harris* [2008] IEHC 403, commented that unlimited liability is 'the most basic characteristic of a general partner' and observed, at para 61 of her judgment, that the right of a general partner to take part in the management of the partnership's business is subject to any contrary agreement (by reference to l'Anson Banks, *Lindley & Banks on Partnership* (18th edn, 2002)) and that, in other jurisdictions, a limited partner may benefit from limited liability, but still be able to participate in the management of the partnership's business.
6   In *Quigley v Harris* [2008] IEHC 403, Laffoy J did not accept that the term 'general partner' has, as a matter of law, a meaning that exists for all purposes, and rejected a submission that the term 'general partner' could encompass a person who is a partner in a foreign limited partnership with limited liability and no authority to bind the firm, but the ability to participate in its management.

partnerships was to provide a partnership where one or more of the partners limit their liability to creditors of the firm to their capital contribution in much the same way as a shareholder in a limited liability company.[7] In return for this concession, the limited partner is not permitted to take part in the management of the firm or to bind his co-partners.[8] In this way, the limited partnership allows a person to be involved in a firm purely as an investor of his capital and without the risk of him being liable to an unlimited degree to creditors of the firm. Another major difference between limited partnerships and ordinary partnerships is the fact that a limited partnership is required to be registered in a public register. In this way, the public is made aware that, although a partnership, some of the partners have limited liability.

Historical Perspective

[28.04] Limited partnerships have their origins in Italy during the Middle Ages. At that time the nobility were not allowed to engage directly in trade. In order to circumvent this prohibition, they invested through merchants on the basis that they would receive a share of the profits but would not be named as part of the enterprise or be liable for its liabilities.[9] In the eighteenth century, Ireland led the way in the common law world with the creation of this type of partnership. Thus, one of the first common law limited partnerships was created by the passing by the Irish legislature in 1781 of the Anonymous Partnerships Act.[10] This Act granted limited liability to certain partners, called anonymous partners, provided they took no part in the management of the partnership. This Act was adopted subsequently in New South Wales, New Zealand, South Australia and Victoria.[11] However, while limited partnerships continued in these jurisdictions, the Anonymous Partnerships Act of 1781 was repealed in Ireland in 1862[12] and it was not replaced until 1907 with the enactment in Ireland and England of the Limited Partnerships Act of that year (referred to in this chapter as the 1907 Act). By

---

[7]   However, there is the important difference that a company is a separate legal entity so that strictly speaking a shareholder in a company has no liability to the creditors of the company. Rather, he is simply liable towards the company to enable the company meets its obligations.

[8]   The rationale for restricting limited partners from taking part in the management of the partnership is considered at para **[28.105]**.

[9]   Troubat's *Law of Commandatory and Limited Partnership in the United States* (1853) at p 34; l'Anson Banks, *Lindley & Banks on Partnership* (20th edn, 2017) at para 28-02.

[10] 21 & 22 Geo 3, c 46. See, further, Henning, 'The first limited partnership Act' (2015) Comp Law 3(6), 192.

[11] New South Wales: Anonymous Partnerships Act 1853, 17 Vic, c 9; Queensland: Mercantile Act 1867, ss 53–68; South Australia: Anonymous Partnerships Act 1853 17 Vic, c 20; Victoria: Anonymous Partnerships Act 1853, 17 Vic, c 5; New Zealand: Special Partnership Act 1858. Until 2008, the New Zealand legislation was the only one which still traced its history back to the Anonymous Partnerships Act of 1781, since the New Zealand Special Partnership Act of 1858 was consolidated into the Mercantile Law Act 1880 (ss 59–77) and then substantially re-enacted in Part II of the Partnership Act 1908 (ss 48–67). That 1908 Act remained in force until 1 April 2008, when new rules for limited partnerships were introduced by the Limited Partnerships Act 2008.

[12] Companies Act 1862, s 205 and 3rd Sch.

that time, the limited partnership had become popular in continental Europe,[13] where it was known as the partnership *en commandité*.[14]

The Limited Partnerships Act 1907

[28.05] Unlike the 1890 Act, it cannot be said about the 1907 Act that it is a 'model piece of legislation'.[15] As shall be seen, in many respects the 1907 Act raises more questions than it answers regarding the legal treatment of limited partnerships and their members.[16] It is for this reason that it is recommended that the partners in a limited partnership should always have a written partnership agreement which clarifies their respective rights and obligations.[17]

[28.06] However, the 1907 Act does not operate in isolation, since s 7 provides that:

> Subject to the provisions of this Act, the Partnership Act, 1890, and the rules of equity and of common law applicable to partnerships, except so far as inconsistent with the express provisions of the last-mentioned Act, shall apply to limited partnerships.

[28.07] The approach taken by the 1907 Act to creating a body of rules for limited partnerships was to simply presuppose the application of the law of ordinary partnerships to limited partnerships and modify this law in its application to them. For this reason, in considering limited partnerships, it is rarely sufficient to consider the terms of the 1907 Act in isolation and even where a term of the 1907 Act appears to prima facie govern a particular situation, this term must be applied in conjunction with the law of ordinary partnerships,[18] unless the latter is inconsistent with the 1907 Act.[19]

---

[13]   In the United States, the limited partnership has been popular for many years. The key statute is now the Uniform Limited Partnership Act 2001 which, at the time of writing, has been adopted by 21 states and by the District of Columbia. It succeeds the Revised Uniform Limited Partnership Act 1976 (Last Amended 1985). For a comparative analysis of limited partnership law in the UK under the 1907 Act and limited partnership law in the United States, see Berry, 'Limited partnership law in the United States and the United Kingdom: teaching an old dog new tricks?' (2013) Journal of Business Law 2, 160–185.

[14]   For a historical perspective on the introduction of the limited partnership in Ireland, see McKenna, 'On Partnerships with Limited Liability' (1854) 3 Journal of Dublin Statistical Society 1 which was written with a view to supporting its introduction.

[15]   Per Harman LJ in *Keith Spicer Ltd v Mansell* [1970] 1 All ER 462 at 463.

[16]   For example does s 24(8) of the 1890 Act apply to all the partners in a limited partnership (see para **[28.115]**) or just the general partners. Similarly, what is the meaning of the term 'dissolve' in s 6(2) of the 1907 Act (see para **[28.127]**). This sentence was quoted by the Law Commission and the Scottish Law Commission in their 2001 *Limited Partnerships Act 1907: A Joint Consultation Paper* (Consultation Paper No 161; Discussion Paper No 118) at para 1.8.

[17]   The Law Commission and the Scottish Law Commission in their 2001 *Limited Partnerships Act 1907: A Joint Consultation Paper* (Consultation Paper No 161; Discussion Paper No 118) at para 1.9 noted that the author, together with other commentators, had 'strongly emphasised the dangers of using the limited partnership structure without a formal agreement' in the first edition of this work.

[18]   By the law of ordinary partnerships is meant the 1890 Act and the rules of common law and equity which are not inconsistent with that Act.

[19]   Consider for example s 4(4) of the 1907 Act which at first sight appears to be a stand-alone provision governing the capacity of a body corporate to be a limited partner, without reference to general partners. (contd.../)

Since much of the law applicable to ordinary partnerships applies to limited partnerships, reference should always be made to the other chapters of this book on the position under the law of ordinary partnership. In particular, this chapter considers the manner in which the law of limited partnerships is different from that of ordinary partnerships. This will be done under the following headings:

I.   Limited Partnerships in General;

II.   Nature of a Limited Partnership;

III.   Registration of Limited Partnerships;

IV.   Authority of Partners to Bind Firm;

V.   Liability of the Partners in a Limited Partnership;

VI.   Rights of Partners Inter Se;

VII. Financial Rights of Partners in a Limited Partnership;

VIII. Dissolution Otherwise than by Court;

IX.   Dissolution by Court;

X.   Winding Up and Bankruptcy.

Overview

[28.08] The 1907 Act may be criticised for providing a lack of certainty regarding the rights and obligations of general and limited partners. The source of much of this confusion is the fact that the 1907 Act creates a new type of partner, the limited partner, but applies many of the provisions of the 1890 Act to that partner. This is in spite of the fact that the 1890 Act was drafted with only partners with unlimited liability in mind. The application of the 1890 Act results from the fact that the law applicable to limited partnerships was created by super-imposing the 1907 Act on the 1890 Act. As shall be seen, this was done without due effort being made to weave those differing provisions together to produce a coherent body of law suitable for a limited partnership.[20] What results is a workable, but far from perfect, body of law. A perfect example of the difficulties created is provided by the issue of the liability of a limited partner for the obligations of the firm. On the one hand ss 9 and 10 of the 1890 Act apply to a limited partner to make him liable for the debts and obligations of the firm and he is liable to execution or other proceedings for the enforcement of this debt. On the other hand, s 4(2) of the 1907 Act provides that the liability of a limited partner is limited to the capital contributed by him. The attempt to deal with conflicting provisions such as these is contained in s 7 of the 1907 Act which provides that the law of ordinary partnership applies insofar as it is not inconsistent with the 1907 Act. Yet this simple provision does

---

19 (\...contd) However, reference should also be made to s 1(1) of the 1890 Act, which provides that partnership is the relation which exists between 'persons'. That has been interpreted to include bodies corporate and on this basis it may be concluded that bodies corporate can be general partners. See para **[28.34]**.

20 Parts of this paragraph as it appeared in the first edition of this work were quoted by the Law Commission and the Scottish Law Commission in their 2001 *Limited Partnerships Act 1907: A Joint Consultation Paper* (Consultation Paper No 161; Discussion Paper No 118) at para 1.8, and in the Law Commission and the Scottish Law Commission *Partnership Law: Report on a Reference under Section 3(1)(e) of the Law Commissions Act 1965* (Law Com No 283; Scot Law Com No 192) at para 3.44.

not for example clarify whether a limited partner may be the subject of enforcement proceedings for partnership liabilities. It is worth noting that in the Investment Limited Partnerships Act 1994, this mistake is not repeated as there is an express provision that a limited partner in an investment limited partnership is not subject to legal proceedings in respect of a partnership liability.[21]

[28.09] Of course, the partners in a limited partnership may attempt to fill in some of the gaps created by the drafting of the 1907 Act by using a carefully drafted limited partnership agreement. So, for example, the fact that the 1907 Act does not grant a limited partner the right to retire from the firm without first obtaining the consent of all the partners may be circumvented by a contrary provision in the partnership agreement.[22]

[28.10] Finally, the whole approach of the 1907 Act to limited liability is deserving of comment. It treats the limited liability of the limited partners as a privilege which is only obtained by completion of a registration procedure (and it is apprehended, is only maintained by the updating of that registration).[23] This approach in the 1907 Act can be traced back to the fear of limited liability at the time of the enactment of that Act.[24] Since these fears have turned out to be unjustified, it seems clear that limited partnership legislation should take the same approach as that taken by the legislation for limited liability companies and grant the limited partners the security of knowing that their shield of limited liability will not be taken away lightly, instead of the current situation where an administrative error in the registration details will remove the shield.[25]

[28.11] In general therefore, it should perhaps become obvious from the analysis of the 1907 Act hereunder that it would benefit from a substantial overhaul as it applies in Ireland. In 2001, the Law Commission and the Scottish Law Commission published a consultation paper on the reform of limited partnership law.[26] Two years later, in November 2003, they published their Report[27] in which they recommended a number of reforms to the limited partnership framework as it then applied in England, Scotland and Wales, including that the registration of a limited partnership should be conclusive evidence of its existence, only the general partner should be liable for any default in complying with the registration requirements, limited partnerships should disclose their limited liability status, the liability of a limited partner should be capped at the amount of capital actually registered, and guidance should be introduced (in legislation) on the types of activities that a limited partner could carry out without losing his limited liability status. The Commissions also recommended that the registrar of limited

---

21   Investment Limited Partnerships Act 1994, s 22(1).

22   See para **[28.48]**.

23   See para **[28.108]**.

24   See for example McKenna, 'On Partnerships with Limited Liability' (1854) 3 Journal of Dublin Statistical Society 1.

25   See para **[28.72]**.

26   The Law Commission and the Scottish Law Commission (2001) *Limited Partnerships Act 1907: A Joint Consultation Paper* (Consultation Paper No 161; Discussion Paper No 118).

27   The Law Commission and the Scottish Law Commission *Partnership Law: Report on a Reference under Section 3(1)(e) of the Law Commissions Act 1965* (Law Com No 283; Scot Law Com No 192).

partnerships (in the UK, this is the registrar of companies) be given the power to de-register limited partnerships that no longer operate. The UK Government announced, in 2006, that it would proceed with the Commissions' recommendations in respect of limited partnerships, but not those in respect of partnership law generally (which had been the subject of a separate consultation in September 2000[28] and the recommendations in relation to which had been incorporated into the same report as their recommendations on limited partnerships).[29] The Legislative Reform (Limited Partnerships) Order 2009[30] gave effect to some of the Commissions' recommendations ie that the name of a limited partnership disclose its status as such by ending in 'Limited Partnership' or 'LP'[31] and that the certificate of registration be conclusive evidence that a limited partnership came into existence on the date of its registration.[32] The Commissions' remaining recommendations were not, however, introduced into law at that time. On 6 April 2017, the Legislative Reform (Private Fund Limited Partnerships) Order 2017 came into force. It amended the 1907 Act (as it applies in the UK) to introduce a new regime for certain collective investment schemes formed as limited partnerships with a written partnership agreement, with a view to promoting the UK as a location for domiciling funds.[33] Those limited partnerships can elect to be treated as private fund limited partnerships with the result that limited partners will benefit from a white-list of actions they may take which will not be considered as taking part in the management of the limited partnership.[34] Limited partners in a private fund limited partnership will not be obliged to contribute capital.[35] There is no requirement for a court order to wind up a private fund limited partnership[36] and, if it is dissolved at a time when it does not have a general partner, the limited partner(s) can appoint a third party

---

[28]   The Law Commission and the Scottish Law Commission *Partnership Law: A Joint Consultation Paper* (Consultation Paper No 159; Discussion Paper No 111).

[29]   The Law Commission and the Scottish Law Commission *Partnership Law: Report on a Reference under Section 3(1)(e) of the Law Commissions Act 1965* (Law Com No 283; Scot Law Com No 192).

[30]   SI 2009/1940.

[31]   Legislative Reform (Limited Partnerships) Order 2009, art 6.

[32]   Legislative Reform (Limited Partnerships) Order 2009, art 7.

[33]   There was no specific partnership legislation aimed at the asset management and investment funds industry in the UK before the private fund limited partnership was introduced ie there was no equivalent to the Investment Limited Partnerships Act 1994 and limited partnerships were instead used, on a limited basis, by the funds industry, but were governed by the 1907 Act which was perceived by the funds industry as needing significant reform to ensure that it was fit for purpose. As to the limited use made of the 1994 Act in Ireland to date, and the proposals for an imminent reform of that Act, see para **[29.01]** et seq.

[34]   Legislative Reform (Private Fund Limited Partnerships) Order 2017, art 2(5) which introduced a new s 6A into the 1907 Act (as it applies in the UK). Note that art 2(5) of the 2017 Order also introduced a specific provision into the 1907 Act (at s 6A4(b)) which states that the white-list cannot be used as a reference point when establishing when a limited partner in a limited partnership that is not a private fund limited partnership may be taking part in the management of the limited partnership business.

[35]   Legislative Reform (Private Fund Limited Partnerships) Order 2017, art 2(3).

[36]   Legislative Reform (Private Fund Limited Partnerships) Order 2017, art 2(4).

to manage the winding-up.[37] Information on the general nature and term of the private fund limited partnership does not need to be provided on registration,[38] and certain statutory duties which are set out in the 1890 Act and apply to limited partnerships (unless expressly disapplied in the partnership agreement) are expressly disapplied to private fund limited partnerships ie s 28 (the duty of partners to render accounts, etc), s 30 (the duty of a partner not to compete with the firm) and s 36(1) (rights of persons dealing with firm against apparent members of firm).[39] Some more administrative obligations that, in the normal course, apply to limited partnerships are also disapplied including the requirement to publish details of the transfer of a limited partner's interest.[40] Following reports that limited partnerships registered in Scotland were being used as vehicles for criminal activity (such as money laundering, organised crime and tax evasion), and in light of the comparatively significant increase in the number of limited partnerships being registered in Scotland when compared with England, Wales and Northern Ireland,[41] the Department for Business, Energy and Industrial Skills published a '*Review of Limited Partnership Law: call for evidence*' in January 2017, which closed in March 2017. In that call for evidence, views and evidence were sought as to why registrations of limited partnerships in Scotland had increased, the economic uses of limited partnerships, the characteristics of limited partnerships that might enable criminal activity, and other related matters. Following that call for evidence, the Department published a consultation (Limited Partnerships: Reform of Limited Partnership Law) on 30 April 2018,[42] outlining that while evidence provided in response to its January 2017 call for evidence had shown an ongoing need for limited partnerships as business entities, evidence had also been provided of suspected criminal activity involving limited partnerships registered in Scotland. As such, the consultation sought views on how the law in relation to limited partnerships could be reformed to reduce the risk of misuse. In particular, consideration was given to requiring that a UK limited partnership file an annual statement confirming that its principal place of business remains in the UK and providing evidence that the address in question is truly its principal place of business (and not merely an address for service of notices and proceedings). Alternatively, consideration was given to allowing a UK limited partnership to have its principal place of business in another jurisdiction, while requiring it to have an additional service address in its country of registration (ie England and Wales, Scotland, or Northern Ireland). The consultation also sought views on whether UK limited partnerships should be required to prepare accounts and reports similar to those required of a private company, and whether the Registrar of Companies should be

---

37 Legislative Reform (Private Fund Limited Partnerships) Order 2017, art 2(4).

38 Legislative Reform (Private Fund Limited Partnerships) Order 2017, art 2(7).

39 Legislative Reform (Private Fund Limited Partnerships) Order 2017, art 2(4).

40 Legislative Reform (Private Fund Limited Partnerships) Order 2017, art 2(11).

41 The Department of Business, Energy and Industrial Strategy: '*Review of Limited Partnership Law: call for evidence*' (January 2017) noted, at p 18, that between March 2011 and March 2016, there had been a 236% increase in the number of limited partnerships registered in Scotland, whereas the number of limited partnerships registered in England and Wales, and in Northern Ireland, during the same period increased by only 26%.

42 This consultation closed on 23 July 2018. At the time of writing, the Department for Business, Energy and Industrial Skills has not confirmed what reforms may be introduced in light of responses received to the consultation.

given the power to strike-off limited partnerships. In December 2018, the UK government's response to that consultation indicated that it will legislate to require a limited partnership to either keep its principal place of business in the UK or demonstrate that it is continuing some legitimate business activity at a UK address, or demonstrate that it is engaging the services of an agent to provide it with a UK address (that agent must be registered with a UK supervisory body for anti-laundering purposes). The UK government also plans to expand the list of information required from limited partnerships and perhaps require that a confirmation statement be filed annually. It intends to give the Registrar of Companies the power to strike off limited partnerships.

I. LIMITED PARTNERSHIPS IN GENERAL

Popularity of Limited Partnerships

[28.12] While there were only 2,278 limited partnerships registered in Ireland on 31 December 2017,[43] over one-quarter of those limited partnerships were registered in 2017 alone, indicating a resurgence in the popularity of the limited partnership as a vehicle for venture capital and private equity firms, for unregulated investment funds, and for tax-based investments.[44] Like ordinary partnerships, the advantages of limited partnerships over limited liability companies are that they are tax-transparent,[45] are not generally required to file accounts[46] and the partners may withdraw their capital contributions more easily.[47] On the other hand, the great advantage of limited liability companies over ordinary partnerships is the fact that they provide limited liability for their members. The popularity of limited partnerships lies in the fact that they combine the foregoing advantages of ordinary partnerships with the fact that they can also provide limited liability for some of the partners.

Tax-based uses

[28.13] Limited partnerships are commonly used in tax-driven structures because of their tax-transparency. This means that the partnership itself is not taxed but only the individual partners so that a business investment which is carried on though a partnership is subject to a single level of taxation. In a company, both the company and its shareholders are subject to taxation and therefore any such business or investment

---

43 Companies Registration Office Report 2016 at p 32, though it is unlikely that all of these are active, see para **[28.73]**.

44 According to the Companies Registration Office Report 2017, the number of newly registered limited partnerships increased significantly by 676 to 2,278 in 2017. A further 431 limited partnerships had been registered in 2016, representing a significant increase on the 87 registered in 2015, and the 71 registered in 2014.

45 See para **[28.13]**.

46 Save in special circumstances, see the European Communities (Accounts) Regulations 1993 (SI 396/ 1993). These regulations were introduced to implement Council Directive 90/605/ EEC. See generally para **[14.66]** et seq.

47 Cf the position of limited companies under ss 84–87 of the Companies Act 2014. See generally Courtney, *The Law of Companies* (4th edn, 2016) at para [10.097] et seq; Hutchinson, *Keane on Company Law* (5th edn, 2016) at para [16.10] et seq.

may be said to be subject to double taxation. As a vehicle in tax-based transactions, therefore, the limited partnership has the advantage of being able to grant a limited partner protection from liability to third parties for the losses of the firm beyond his capital contribution. Until 1986, a limited partner in a limited partnership could use the losses of the partnership for tax reduction purposes. It was this dual role of the limited partnership in relation to the losses of the firm which led to their popularity as tax avoidance vehicles prior to 1986. Thus, a limited partner whose capital contribution to the limited partnership and consequently his maximum liability was say, £50, could have his share of the trading losses of the firm of say, £1,920 passed on to him and set-off against his other taxable income, even though the limit of his actual loss was £50.[48]

[28.14] In *Reed v Young*,[49] the House of Lords confirmed that the fact that a limited partner was protected against further liability beyond his capital contribution under the 1907 Act was not material to the question of whether he has 'sustained' a trading loss. Accordingly, as between the partners themselves, there was nothing to stop them providing for a limited partner to be liable to share losses over and above the amount of his capital contribution and by so doing ensuring that the limited partner sustained a loss for tax purposes.

[28.15] In 1985, the Revenue Commissioners unsuccessfully challenged this practice in the case of *MacCarthaigh v Daly*[50] and soon after, the government introduced s 46 of the Finance Act 1986.[51] That Act eliminated this practice by restricting the amount which could be set off against a limited partner's[52] taxable income to the amount of capital which he contributes to the firm, rather than to his share of the trading losses of the firm.

---

[48]   These were in fact the amounts which applied in *McCarthaigh v Daly* [1985] IR 73. See para **[28.65]**.

[49]   *Reed v Young* [1986] 1 WLR 649.

[50]   *MacCarthaigh v Daly* [1985] IR 73.

[51]   Now contained in s 1013 of the Taxes Consolidation Act 1997.

[52]   The restriction on a limited partner claiming tax relief on the limited partnership's losses is now contained in the Taxes Consolidation Act 1997. It is to be noted that the definition of 'limited partner' in s 1013 of the Taxes Consolidation Act 1997 is wider than that in the 1907 Act, since it includes, inter alia '(b) a person who is carrying on the trade as a general partner in a partnership, who is not entitled to take part in the management of the trade and who is entitled to have his liabilities, or his liabilities beyond a certain limit, for debts or obligations, incurred for the purposes of the trade, discharged or reimbursed by some other person, (c) a person who carries on the trade jointly with others and who, under the law of any territory outside the State, is not entitled to take part in the management of the trade and is not liable beyond a certain limit for debts or obligations incurred for the purpose of the trade, (d) a person who carries on the trade as a general partner in a partnership otherwise than as an active partner, (e) a person who carries on the trade as a partner in a partnership registered under the law of any territory outside the State, otherwise than as an active partner, or (f) a person who carries on the trade jointly with others under any agreement, arrangement, scheme or understanding which is governed by the law of any territory outside the State, otherwise than as a person who works for the greater part of his or her time on the day-to-day management or conduct of that trade.' (contd.../)

[28.16] Despite this restriction on the amount of losses which can be set-off against tax, limited partnerships continue to be popular as vehicles in tax-based structures, since they still provide the limited partners with the dual advantage of tax transparency and limited liability.

Venture capital vehicles

[28.17] Another important use of limited partnerships is as venture capital vehicles.[53] The limited partnership structure is an attractive structure for venture capitalists because it facilitates a dormant investor (the limited partner) who does not take any part in the management of the firm's funds but who is allowed to limit his liability to the amount of his capital contribution. Such an investor may realise his investment quite easily by withdrawing his capital from the firm and this may be done more easily than if it were capital in a limited liability company.[54] The limited partnership structure also suits the manager of the investment fund (the general partner) since, although he has unlimited liability, he may have an effective cap on his liability by being a limited liability company.[55]

[28.18] It is possible that a requirement to issue a prospectus under the Prospectus (Directive 2003/71/EC) Regulations 2005[56] could arise in respect of an offer of an interest in a limited partnership to the public, as the term 'securities' in the 2005 Regulations[57] is defined by reference to the term 'transferable securities' in the revised Markets in Financial Instruments Directive[58] as transposed into Irish law by the

---

52 (\...contd) In *Quigley v Harris* [2008] IEHC 403, Laffoy J considered whether Mr Harris, a partner in a limited partnership established in the Cook Islands, was a 'general partner' within the meaning of para (d) of the definition of 'limited partner' in s 1013(1). Under the laws of the Cook Islands, he was regarded as a limited partner in the limited partnership. Laffoy J observed that she was first required to determine whether Mr Harris was a limited partner by reference to para (d) by determining the characteristics, rights and obligations attaching to his role as partner under the laws of the Cook Islands in light of s 43 of the Investment Limited Partnerships Act 1994 (as to which, see para **[28.22]**), and, once she had made that determination, she was then required to determine whether, under Irish law, those characteristics, rights and obligations matched those of a general partner within the meaning of para (d). Laffoy J found that, under the laws of the Cook Islands, Mr Harris's liability was not unlimited, meaning that he could not be a 'general partner' within the meaning of para (d).

53 See generally Mitchell, 'Limited Partnerships' (1996) Compliance Monitor 112 regarding the benefits of using a limited partnership as an investment vehicle rather than a unit trust.

54 Although a limited partner will be subject to s 4(3) of the 1907 Act which provides that if he withdraws his capital during the continuance of the partnership, he is liable for the debts and obligations of the firm up to the amount so withdrawn. He may also sell his share in the firm with the consent of the general partners (s 6(5)(b) of the 1907 Act). See also fn **47**.

55 See para **[28.34]**.

56 SI 324/2005, which implements the Prospectus Directive (Directive 2003/71/EC) into Irish law.

57 The term 'securities' was originally defined by reference to the definition of 'transferable securities' in Directive 93/22/EEC (known as the Investment Services Directive) which was replaced by Directive 2004/39/EC (known as MiFID) which was in turn replaced by Directive 2014/65/EU (known as MiFID II).

58 Directive 2014/65/EU.

European Union (Markets in Financial Instruments) Regulations 2017.[59] That definition of 'transferable securities'[60] includes: '... those classes of securities which are negotiable on the capital market ... such as ... shares in companies and other securities equivalent to shares in companies, partnerships or other entities ...' While an analysis of Irish and EU prospectus law is beyond the scope of this work, in practice such an offer to the public and a related requirement to issue a prospectus very rarely happens in respect of a limited partnership.[61]

[28.19] Until the introduction of the European Union (Alternative Investment Fund Managers) Regulations 2013,[62] a limited partnership could have been caught by the terms of the Unit Trusts Act 1990 but that is no longer the case.[63] The 2013 Regulations now provide for the authorisation and operation of managers (AIFMs) of alternative investment funds (AIFs)[64] who manage and/or market AIFs in Ireland, and give effect to the Alternative Investment Fund Managers Directive.[65] An AIFM is a legal person[66] whose regular business is managing one or more AIFs. As such, a limited partnership

---

[59] SI 375/2017.

[60] As set out in the European Union (Markets in Financial Instruments) Regulations 2017, reg 3(1).

[61] Under the previous prospectus regime, set out in the Companies Act 1963 and in the European Communities (Transferable Securities and Stock Exchange) Regulations 1992 (SI 202/1992, which was revoked by the Prospectus (Directive 2003/71/EC) Regulations 2005) the then-applicable definition of 'transferable securities' (as set out in Directive 93/22/EEC) referred only to shares or debentures of a company and equivalent transferable securities (with no reference to partnerships) so that it was unlikely that any requirement to issue a prospectus could arise.

[62] SI 257/2013.

[63] The Unit Trusts Act 1990, as well as applying to unit trust schemes, provided in s 9(1)(a) (which was deleted by the European Union (Alternative Investment Fund Managers) Regulations, reg 64) that it applied to an '... arrangement of a kind ... made for the purpose, or having the effect, solely or mainly, of providing facilities for the participation by the public, as beneficiaries (otherwise than under a trust or through membership of a company, a building society, a friendly society or an industrial and provident society) in profits or income arising from the acquisition, holding, management of securities or any other property whatsoever'. Section 9(1) of the 1990 Act also provided that any such arrangement could not, without the approval of the Central Bank, sell or purchase units of the scheme or make solicitation in respect of such sale or purchase. Thus in general terms, the effect of s 9(1) was to prohibit the sale or purchase of units of a scheme to the public which was designed to facilitate investment in property. Assuming the interest in the partnership was held directly, the question of whether a limited partnership (or indeed an ordinary partnership) which invested in property fell within that section depended on whether it was selling interests in the partnership to the public. In the first edition of this work it was contended that the expression 'public' in s 9(1)(a) should be given its ordinary meaning, so as to mean the public at large and therefore that, in general terms, a private offering of interests in a partnership to a select group of investors would not have fallen foul of the Unit Trusts Act 1990.

[64] An AIF is defined by the Alternative Investment Fund Managers Directive (Directive 2011/61/EU) as a collective investment undertaking which raises capital from a number of investors, with a view to investing it in accordance with a defined investment policy, and which does not require authorisation under UCITS Directive, art 5 (Directive 2009/65/EC).

[65] Directive 2011/61/EU.

[66] European Union (Alternative Investment Fund Managers) Regulations, reg 5(1).

cannot be an AIFM as it is not a legal person. It also cannot be a regulated AIF – this is because the Central Bank of Ireland will only authorise an AIF if it is formed as a unit trust under the Unit Trust Act 1990, as an investment limited partnership under the Investment Limited Partnerships Act 1994, as a common contractual fund under the Investment Funds, Companies and Miscellaneous Provisions Act 2005,[67] as an Irish Collective Asset-management Vehicle (a body corporate) under the Irish Collective Asset-management Vehicles Act 2015, or as an investment company under the Companies Act 2014.[68] As such, a limited partnership under the 1907 Act can neither be an AIFM nor a regulated AIF. As a result, the limited partnership is generally used for unregulated fund structures in Ireland and is only marketed on a private placement basis.

Other uses

[28.20] One interesting use of limited partnerships was as a means of avoiding security of tenure for agricultural tenants in Scotland.[69] The system operated by having the intending tenant form a limited partnership which would take the lease of the land from the landlord. The intending tenant was the general partner in the limited partnership while the landlord was the limited partner. The landlord therefore had his exposure limited to his capital contribution to the firm which was usually nominal. Under the terms of the limited partnership agreement, the landlord (the limited partner) was granted an express power to terminate the partnership on the happening of certain events and in this way to secure the termination of the tenancy.[70] Legislative changes were introduced in Scotland to give greater security of tenure to tenants. Those changes were challenged, with remedial legislation then passed, but related litigation is, at the time of writing, ongoing.[71]

Application of the Limited Partnerships Act 1907 in Ireland

[28.21] Although enacted prior to the establishment of Saorstát Éireann, there can be no doubt that the 1907 Act was carried over into the laws of Ireland in 1922. Any doubts[72] which might have existed about this issue were dispelled in the High Court case of

---

67   The Investment Funds, Companies and Miscellaneous Provisions Act 2005, s 7(2) expressly provides that a common contractual fund is not subject to the 1890 Act, the 1907 Act or the Investment Limited Partnerships Act 1994.

68   See the Central Bank's AIF Rulebook (March 2018) available on its website: www.centralbank.ie.

69   Note that in Scotland, a limited partnership, like an ordinary partnership, is a separate legal entity: Partnership Act 1890, s 4(2). In its *Review of Limited Partnership Law: call for evidence (January 2017)*, the UK government's Department of Business, Enterprise and Industrial Strategy noted that at least 500 Scottish limited partnerships are still active in this area.

70   See Brough, *Miller on Partnership* (2nd edn, 1994) at p 628.

71   See further Shields, 'McMaster v Scottish Ministers – the tenant farmers case' (2017) Jur Rev 2, 113–121; Combe, 'Human rights and limited partnership tenancies, again' (2017) SLT 17, 79–82.

72   Such doubts would have been difficult to justify in view of even the most conservative view of the status of pre-1922 law, ie that of Walsh J (with whom O'Higgins CJ agreed) in *Gaffney v Gaffney* [1975] IR 133, where he felt that statute law only, and not caselaw, was carried forward into Irish law in 1922. (contd.../)

MacCarthaigh v Daly,[73] in which O'Hanlon J accepted the application of the 1907 Act in Ireland.

Foreign Limited Partnerships

[28.22] Section 43 of the Investment Limited Partnerships Act 1994 provides that a limited partnership which is established in or governed by the laws of another state will, in the Irish courts, be subject to the law of that state to determine the liability of the partners and issues regarding the organisation and internal affairs of the firm.[74] By establishing Irish comity for foreign law in this way,[75] the 1994 Act aims to ensure that a foreign court will apply Irish law, if it is faced with similar questions regarding an Irish investment limited partnership and its members. Limited partnerships have, as a result, also benefitted from these comity provisions. In *Quigley v Harris,*[76] Laffoy J observed that s 5 of the 1907 Act was never intended to apply to foreign limited partnerships and that compliance with ss 8, 9 and 10 of the 1907 would present considerable practical difficulties for a foreign limited partnership. She noted in particular that the registration requirement in s 5 of the 1907 Act could not cut across the operation of s 43 of the 1994 Act. In *Quigley v Harris,* Laffoy J had to consider whether Mr Harris, a partner in a limited partnership established in the Cook Islands, was a limited partner for the purposes of the Taxes Consolidation Act 1997. The key issue for consideration was whether he was a 'a person who carries on the trade as a general partner in a partnership otherwise than as an active partner' within the meaning of para (d) of the definition of 'limited partner' in s 1013(1) of the 1997 Act. Under the laws of the Cook Islands, Mr Harris was treated as a limited partner in the limited partnership. Laffoy J observed that, in light of s 43 of the 1994 Act, she first needed to determine the characteristics, rights and obligations attaching to Mr Harris's role as partner under the laws of the Cook Islands and, once she had made that determination, she then needed to determine whether, under Irish law, those characteristics, rights and obligations corresponded to those of a general partner within the meaning of para (d) of the definition of 'limited partner' in s 1013(d) of the 1997 Act. Laffoy J found that, under the laws of the Cook Islands, Mr Harris's liability was not unlimited, meaning that he could not be a 'general partner' within the meaning of para (d).

---

72 (\...contd) The more liberal view is to be found in the judgment of McCarthy J in *Irish Shell Limited v Elm Motors Limited* [1984] ILRM 595, where all pre-1922 law was regarded as having been brought forward into Irish law in 1922. See also *Vone Securities Ltd v Cooke* [1975] IR 59; *McKinley v Minister for Defence* [1992] 2 IR 333.

73 *MacCarthaigh v Daly* [1985] IR 73.

74 Laffoy J, in *Quigley v Harris* [2008] IEHC 403, noted that it was common case between the parties to those proceedings that s 43 of the Investment Limited Partnerships Act 1994 was of general application and was not confined to investment limited partnerships. Laffoy J referenced Murphy, 'Investment Limited Partnerships' (1994) 1 (11) CLP 287 in which the author of that article commented that s 43 had been drafted in that manner as it had been thought that the limitation of liability from which Irish investment limited partnerships were to benefit would be more likely to be recognised in other jurisdictions if, among other matters, Irish law gave recognition to limitation on liability from which foreign limited partnerships benefit.

75 But note that the comity doctrine as the basis for recognising foreign law has been doubted: Binchy, *Irish Conflict of Laws* (1988) at p 13 et seq and at p 585 et seq.

76 *Quigley v Harris* [2008] IEHC 403.

II. NATURE OF A LIMITED PARTNERSHIP

[28.23] In this section, consideration will be given to the nature of a limited partnership and in particular to those aspects of the law of ordinary partnership which are modified or excluded in their application to limited partnerships.

Requirements of a Limited Partnership

[28.24] The requirements for the formation of a limited partnership are contained in s 4(2) of the 1907 Act which states:

> A limited partnership shall not consist, in the case of a partnership carrying on the business of banking, of more than ten persons, and in the case of any other partnership, of more than twenty persons, and must consist of one or more persons called general partners, who shall be liable for all debts and obligations of the firm, and one or more persons to be called limited partners, who shall at the time of entering into such partnership contribute thereto a sum or sums as capital or property valued at a stated amount, and who shall not be liable for the debts or obligations of the firm beyond the amount so contributed.

It can be seen, therefore, that the basic requirement for every limited partnership is that it must consist of at least one general partner and at least one limited partner.

Limited Partnership must have Principal Place of Business in State

[28.25] Before a partnership can be a limited partnership, it must be registered as such under the 1907 Act. Section 8 of the 1907 Act provides that the registration is to be effected by delivering an application for registration:

> to the registrar at the register office in that part of [Ireland][77] in which the principal place of business of the limited partnership is situated or proposed to be situated.

[28.26] Implicitly, therefore, a limited partnership may not be registered unless it has or proposes to have a principal place of business in Ireland. However, a partnership which is initially registered with a principal place of business in Ireland may change its registration details, including its principal place of business, under s 9(1)(c) of the 1907 Act. In view of the rather vague nature of the requirement that a registering firm have a principal place of business in Ireland, it is apprehended that a limited partnership, which registers with a proposed principal place of business in Ireland, may thereafter change it to a place of business outside the State.[78]

---

[77] Note that the term 'United Kingdom' in s 8 of the 1907 Act is here adapted to read Ireland as required by s 3 of the Adaptation of Enactments Act 1922.

[78] Unlike the Investment Limited Partnerships Act 1994, s 12 (which requires an investment limited partnership to have 'at all times' a registered office in the State and a principal place of business in the State (the registered office and the principal place of business can be at the same address)) and the Companies Act 2014, s 50 (which requires a company to have, 'at all times', a registered office in the State), there is no equivalent provision in the 1907 Act that the place of business of the limited partnership be 'at all times' located in the State. As to the position in the UK, see l'Anson Banks, *Lindley & Banks on Partnership* (20th edn, 2017) at para 29-35 [fn 211]. (contd.../)

Number of Partners

[28.27] Like an ordinary partnership, the number of partners in a limited partnership (other than for the business of banking, where the limit is 10)[79] is limited to 20.[80] Under s 1435(5) of the Companies Act 2014, the restriction in s 4(2) of the 1907 Act on the number of partners in a limited partnership[81] does not apply to a limited partnership formed for the purpose of carrying on practice as accountants, where each partner is a statutory auditor, to a limited partnership formed for the purpose of carrying on practice as solicitors, where each partner is a solicitor, to a limited partnership formed for the purpose of carrying on or promoting the business of thoroughbred horse-breeding, or to a limited partnership formed for the purpose of the provision of investment and loan finance and ancillary facilities and services to persons engaged in industrial or commercial activities, being a partnership which consists of not more than 50 partners. In addition, the Minister for Business, Enterprise and Innovation[82] has power under s 1435(2) of the Companies Act 2014 to make an order that the prohibition on more than 20 partners will not apply to the formation of a partnership prescribed by him. If the prohibition on more than 20 partners is contravened, the resulting limited partnership is illegal.[83]

---

[78] (\...contd) See also the comment by the The Law Commission and The Scottish Law Commission in their 2001 *Limited Partnerships Act 1907: A Joint Consultation Paper* (Consultation Paper No 161; Discussion Paper No 118) at para 3.21 that 'the general view appears to be that there is no requirement that the limited partnership must maintain its principal place of business, or indeed conduct any business, in the United Kingdom', and it relied upon this paragraph as it appeared in the first edition of this work. See also para **[28.11]**.

[79] Limited Partnerships Act 1907, s 4(2). Although note that, at the time of writing, only a body corporate can be established as a bank and a limited partnership is not a body corporate. See ss 9 and 9F of the Central Bank Act 1971 which provide that the Central Bank of Ireland shall not propose that the European Central Bank (as the ultimate supervisory authority for banks in the euro area since the introduction of the Single Supervisory Mechanism in November 2014) grant a banking licence to an applicant for authorisation unless that applicant meets various conditions, including that it is a body corporate with its registered office and head office both located in the State.

[80] Limited Partnerships Act 1907, s 4(2). In Great Britain, the Regulatory Reform (Reform of 20 Member Limit in Partnerships etc) Order 2002 (SI 3203/2002), regs 2 and 3 removed any limit on the number of partners in a limited partnership. The limit was later removed in Northern Ireland by The Partnerships etc (Removal of Twenty Member Limit) (Northern Ireland) Order 2003.

[81] Section 1435(5) of the Companies Act 2014 dis-applies the prohibition in s 4(2) of the 1907 Act in the following terms: 'The provisions of section 4 (2) of the 1907 Act shall not apply to a partnership specified in *subsection (1)(c)* nor to a partnership specified in an order made under *subsection (2)*.'

[82] See the Jobs, Enterprise and Innovation (Alteration of Name of Department and Title of Minister) Order 2017 (SI 364/2017).

[83] See generally para **[9.17]** et seq.

Not a Separate Legal Entity

[28.28] A limited partnership is similar to a company in the sense that like a company it is formed and registered under statute.[84] However, unlike a company, an Irish limited partnership does not have a separate legal personality.[85] Like all ordinary Irish partnerships, the law looks to the persons comprising the firm and not the firm itself.[86]

The General and Limited Partners

[28.29] The nature of general partners and limited partners is considered in detail hereunder.[87] In very general terms, a general partner is defined by s 3 of the 1907 Act as simply 'any partner who is not a limited partner' and by s 4(2) which requires every limited partnership to have at least one general partner who is liable for all the debts and obligations of the firm.[88] Similarly, a limited partner is defined by s 4(2) of the 1907 Act which requires every limited partnership to have at least one person (the limited partner) who is obliged to make a capital contribution to the firm and whose liability for the debts and obligations of the firm is limited to the amount of his capital contribution. Provided that there remains at least one general partner and one limited partner, there is nothing to prevent a general partner becoming a limited partner and vice versa.[89]

Form of capital contribution

[28.30] As is noted elsewhere in this text, there is no requirement on a partner in an ordinary partnership to contribute capital to the firm.[90] However, in a limited partnership, a limited partner, but not a general partner, is required to contribute capital to the firm.[91] Capital may be contributed in cash or other property and the details thereof must be stated in the Form LP1,[92] which is the form that is filed with the registrar of limited partnerships on the registration of the limited partnership. The amount contributed by way of capital by each limited partner must also be stated in the Form

---

84   Ie, the Companies Act 2014. See generally Hutchinson, *Keane on Company Law* (5th edn, 2016), Courtney, *The Law of Companies* (4th edn, 2016) and Forde and Kennedy, *Company Law* (5th edn, 2017).
85   See for example *Re Barnard* [1932] 1 Ch 269 and more recently *Mephistopheles Debt Collection Service v Lotay* [1994] 1 WLR 1064.
86   Note that in Scotland, a limited partnership, like an ordinary partnership, is a separate legal entity and this should be borne in mind in considering any Scottish decisions on limited partnerships: Partnership Act 1890, s 4(2). Limited partnerships registered in England, Wales and Northern Ireland do not have separate legal personality.
87   See para **[28.33]** et seq.
88   Note that for certain tax classification purposes, a general partner, who has an asset which is exempt from any enforcement of a debt against the firm or where a limit is placed upon a creditor's entitlement to recover a debt from him, is treated as if he is a limited partner so that he cannot set off his losses beyond the amount of capital which he has contributed: Taxes Consolidation Act 1997, s 1013(4)(b).
89   See generally para **[28.89]** et seq and para **[28.97]**.
90   See para **[17.07]**.
91   Partnership Act 1890, s 4(2).
92   Available in the CRO Forms section of the Companies Registration Office's website: www.cro.ie.

LP3, which must be filed at the same time as LP1. The registrar of limited partnerships is the Registrar of Companies.[93] A bank guarantee by a limited partner of a loan to the firm does not constitute a contribution of cash or property for the purposes of his obligation to make a capital contribution. This is clear from *Rayner & Co v Rhodes*[94] in which a putative limited partner, Rhodes, claimed to have contributed £5,000 to a limited partnership. However, on closer examination, it transpired that this consisted of a running guarantee provided by him to the firm's bank in respect of a loan to the firm. The guarantee was terminable on three months' notice. It was held that, as Rhodes had contributed nothing to the firm, the guarantee amounting only to a future contingent liability, he was not a limited partner and he was held to be a general partner with the consequent unlimited liability to the creditors of the firm.

[28.31] Where capital is contributed in the form of property, s 4(2) of the 1907 Act requires the value of this property to be assessed. It is worth noting that there is no lower limit on the amount of capital to be contributed by a limited partner and, as happens with shareholders in limited liability companies,[95] limited partners will often contribute just €1 and therefore be subject to a maximum exposure of €1, with the balance of their investment in the limited partnership being made by way of loan (often on interest-free terms, and usually subordinated to the loans made to the limited partnership by, for example, banks). Since the commencement of s 110 of the Finance Act 2006,[96] capital contributed to a limited partnership is no longer subject to capital duty. However, the Form LP3 (which used to be filed on registration of a limited partnership to confirm the amount of capital contributed and which had to be stamped at the rate of 1% of the capital contributed)[97] must still be filed on registration of a limited partnership, albeit that while it now states the amount of capital contributed (and the manner in which the contribution is made) capital duty is no longer payable[98] and there is no filing fee. Any increase in the capital of the limited partnership must be notified to the Companies

---

93 The Registrar of Companies, as successor to the Registrar of Joint Stock Companies, is the Registrar of Limited Partnerships: Limited Partnerships Act 1907, s 15. In this context see Hutchinson, *Keane on Company Law* (5th edn, 2016) at para 2.05 in which he notes that 'the name "joint stock company" [is] still sometimes used to describe the limited liability company of today'. See also s 4 of the Constitution (Consequential) Provisions Act 1937.

94 *Rayner & Co v Rhodes* (1926) 24 Ll L Rep 25.

95 Ussher, *Company Law in Ireland* (1986) at p 304.

96 Which amended s 117 of the Stamp Duties Consolidation Act 1999.

97 Note that s 11 of the 1907 Act which provided for the charging of stamp duty on contributions by limited partners was repealed by s 96(1) and the 11th Sch of the Finance Act 1973.

98 Stamp Duties Consolidation Act 1999, s 117 as amended by the Finance Act 2006, s 110. Capital duty under s 117 of the 1999 Act was abolished by the Finance Act 2000, s 110 in respect of transactions taking place on or after 7 December 2005. While it had initially been thought that the provisions for the payment of capital duty in the Stamp Duties Consolidation Act 1999 applied to all partners in a limited partnership, and not just to limited partners, the Revenue Commissioners confirmed in its '*Notes for Guidance on the Stamp Duties Consolidation Act 1999 (as amended by subsequent Acts up to and including the Finance Act 2008)*' (which is updated almost annually) that capital duty had only applied to contributions to a limited partnership by its limited partners, and not by its general partner(s).

Registration Office on Form LP4. Again, capital duty is no longer payable on such an increase and there is no filing fee for this form.[99]

'at the time of entering'

[28.32] Section 4(2) of the 1907 Act provides that the limited partner must make his capital contribution 'at the time of entering' the limited partnership. Significantly, s 5 of the 1907 Act goes on to provide that every limited partnership must be registered in accordance with the Act failing which, each limited partner shall be deemed to be a general partner. The importance of strictly complying with s 4(2) is highlighted by the High Court case of *MacCarthaigh v Daly*.[100] There, the limited partner did not make his capital contribution at the commencement of the partnership, but a number of months later. It was held by O'Hanlon J that this failure resulted in the limited partnership not being registered in accordance with 1907 Act as required by s 5 of the Act and therefore the limited partner was deemed to be a general partner. The importance of strict compliance with the registration requirements should therefore be clear.

Capacity to be a Limited or a General Partner

[28.33] The rules on the capacity of a partner to be a general partner or a limited partner in a limited partnership are, in general terms, the same as those which apply to being a partner in an ordinary partnership and reference should be made to the treatment of that area earlier in this work.[101] In this regard, there is no reason why two different limited partnerships may not be registered where all the partners are the same or indeed where some of the general partners in one partnership are limited partners in the other.[102]

Can a body corporate be a general partner?

[28.34] In one respect however, the 1907 Act makes special provisions regarding the capacity to be a partner in a limited partnership. Section 4(4) states that 'a body corporate may be a limited partner'. No reference is made to whether a body corporate may be a general partner and it might be thought that the inference from s 4(4) is that a body corporate may not be a general partner on the *expressio unius est exclusio alterius* principle.[103] This is, however, not the case. It is clear from s 7 of the 1907 Act that the law applicable to ordinary partnerships also applies to limited partnerships, save insofar as it is inconsistent with the 1907 Act. Under this law of ordinary partnerships, a body corporate may be a partner, subject only to the body corporate having the appropriate objects clause in its memorandum of association.[104] Allowing a body corporate to be a general partner is clearly not inconsistent with the statement in s 4(4) of the 1907 Act

---

[99] Stamp Duties Consolidation Act 1999, s 117 as amended by the Finance Act 2006, s 110.

[100] *MacCarthaigh v Daly* [1985] IR 73.

[101] See para **[4.01]** et seq.

[102] See for example *H Saunders v The Commissioners* (1980) VATTR 53.

[103] Ie, the express mention of one thing is the exclusion of another.

[104] See generally para **[4.16]** and note that a private company limited by shares (as defined in s 2(1) of the Companies Act 2014) has, under s 38 of the 2014 Act, full and unlimited corporate capacity and an objects clause is no longer included in its constitutional documents (s 19 and Sch 1 of the 2014 Act).

that a body corporate may be a limited partner. It follows that a body corporate may also be a general partner. In this way, a general partner can effectively cap his liability to the share capital of the body corporate.[105] This conclusion is in keeping with the High Court decision in *MacCarthaigh v Daly*[106] where the general partner in a limited partnership was a limited liability company. It is also in keeping with the facts of the High Court case of *Bloxham v Companies Act*[107] in which the original limited partnership structure of Bloxham Stockbrokers was outlined. Bloxham Stockbrokers had one limited partner (a limited liability company) and seven individual general partners, and was restructured in 2011, principally for tax reasons. As part of that restructuring, each individual general partner formed an unlimited liability company, and transferred his interest in the limited partnership to that company, which then became a general partner in the partnership.

Limited Partnership must be a Partnership under the 1890 Act

[28.35] By virtue of s 7 of the 1907 Act, the rules on the formation of ordinary partnerships apply to limited partnerships, save insofar as they are inconsistent with the 1907 Act. Accordingly, to be a limited partnership, the members thereof must satisfy the general definition of partnership, ie they must consist of two or more persons carrying on business in common with a view to profit.[108] In the case of limited partnerships, this requirement is supplemented by the condition that at least one of these partners is a general partner and one is a limited partner. Coupled with this is the fact that the requirement that the partners carry on business 'in common' is to a certain degree modified by the restricted role of the limited partner in the management of the firm.[109] However, the other elements of the definition of a partnership are equally applicable to a limited partnership as they are to an ordinary partnership.[110] For example the partners must be carrying on a business with a view to profit and where the partners are not carrying on business or are not doing so with a view to profit,[111] there can be no limited partnership.

Meaning of 'firm', 'firm name' and 'business'

[28.36] Section 3 of the 1907 Act provides that the terms 'firm', 'firm name' and 'business' in the 1907 Act have the same meaning as in the 1890 Act and reference should be made to the earlier treatment of these terms.[112] In addition, s 8 of the 1907 Act

---

105   Subject to the rules of company law on the liability of directors and shareholders for the debts and liabilities of the company in certain exceptional circumstances, see generally Courtney, *The Law of Companies* (4th edn, 2016) at paras [5.001] et seq and [16.149] et seq; Hutchinson, *Keane on Company Law* (5th edn, 2016) at paras [11.16] et seq, [12.18], [15.44], [21.52], [25.87], [27.72], [27.193], [27.253], [30.14] and [33.05].

106   *MacCarthaigh v Daly* [1985] IR 73.

107   *Bloxham and Companies Act* [2017] IEHC 664.

108   Partnership Act 1890, s 1(1).

109   See para **[28.78]**.

110   For a detailed analysis of the definition of partnership, see para **[2.01]** et seq.

111   See for example *MacCarthaigh v Daly* [1985] IR 73.

112   As regards the business, see the Partnership Act 1890, s 45 and see generally, para **[2.49]** et seq. As regards the 'firm' and 'firm-name', see Partnership Act 1890, s 4(1) and see generally para **[3.56]** et seq.

requires that any change in the name of the limited partnership must be notified to the Registrar of Companies.[113]

Limited partnership must comply with Registration of Business Names Act 1963

[28.37] Like any partnership, a limited partnership is obliged to comply with the Registration of Business Names Act 1963 and the terms of this Act which are relevant to ordinary and limited partnerships are considered elsewhere in this work.[114]

[28.38] No distinction is made in the Act between limited partners and general partners. Thus if a limited partnership is using a business name which does not contain the names of all the partners, all the partners therein will be subject to the Registration of Business Names Act 1963. Therefore, they must ensure that the names of both the general and limited partners appear in all business documentation in which the name of the limited partnership appears and also in the registration[115] of the business name with the Registrar of Business Names. However, in neither case is any distinction required to be made between limited and general partners.[116]

[28.39] The failure of the Registration of Business Names Act 1963 to distinguish between limited and general partners is difficult to justify. The rationale for the Act is to provide third parties with the identity of the persons who manage a business and who are liable for its obligations. It is not intended to require details of the dormant investors in an enterprise and it is incongruous that the limited partners are on the one hand prohibited by the 1907 Act from taking any part in the management of the limited partnership, while on the other hand, they are required by the Registration of Business Names Act 1963 to be listed in the firm's letterhead. Accordingly, it is suggested that the application of the Registration of Business Names Act 1963 to limited partnerships is a result of a failure of its drafters to appreciate its application to limited as well as ordinary partnerships and their failure to appreciate the significance of the distinction between general and limited partners in the context of that Act. This oversight should be remedied by excluding limited partners from the 1963 Act or modifying its application to limited partners.[117]

Use of 'limited' in name of a limited partnership

[28.40] One of the primary characteristics of a limited partnership is the fact that the firm must publicise the limited liability of some of the partners by means of the registration of the limited partnership in the Companies Registration Office, with details

---

113 Companies Registration Office Form LP2.
114 See para **[3.70]** et seq.
115 Companies Registration Office Form RBN1A.
116 One commentator has suggested that it would be prudent for the limited partner to indicate after his name that he is a limited partner if it appears in the business letters or in the firm-name: l'Anson Banks, *Lindley & Banks on Partnership* (20th edn, 2017) at para 29-16.
117 This suggestion (as it appeared in the first edition of this work) was noted by The Law Commission and the Scottish Law Commission in their 2001 *Limited Partnerships Act 1907: A Joint Consultation Paper* (Consultation Paper No 161; Discussion Paper No 118) at para 3.38.

of the identity of the general partners and the limited partners. It is therefore surprising that, unlike a limited liability company[118] or indeed an investment limited partnership,[119] there is no requirement on a limited partnership to use the word 'limited' in its name. Indeed, the firm name may simply contain the names of the limited partners. Accordingly, a third party who does not consult the register of limited partnerships may therefore deal with a firm on the basis of its firm name, without knowing that these partners have limited liability. The risk of this occurring is considerably increased by the prohibition in s 27(1) of the Companies Act 2014 on an individual or body which is not a company (which would include a limited partnership) from advertising the fact that it is limited by using the term 'limited' or 'ltd' as the last part of its name.[120] There would appear to be no good reason in principle for this prohibition to apply to limited partnerships and it may result simply from a lack of appreciation by the drafters of the 2014 Act of its application to them. For this reason, it is suggested that it should be repealed in its application to limited partnerships at the earliest opportunity and instead, it is suggested that a limited partnership should be required to use the term 'limited partnership' or 'LP' in its name.[121] In this way, third parties may be put on notice of the limited liability of some of the partners.

Liability of a limited partner as a partner by holding out

[28.41] Under the law of partnership, a person who holds himself out as a partner in an ordinary partnership is liable as a partner (ie with unlimited liability) to third parties who rely on this fact.[122] This raises the question of whether a limited partner who holds himself out as a partner, for example by allowing his name appear in the firm name or in the firm's letterhead, would be liable with unlimited liability on the basis that a third party believed him to have unlimited liability. It seems clear that the answer to this question is in the negative and that his liability will remain limited to his capital contribution, since it is inconceivable that the 1907 Act could grant limited liability to limited partners on the one hand and on the other hand allow the 1890 Act to deprive them of it, insofar as third parties relied on their having unlimited liability. On this basis, it is contended that the application of the doctrine of holding out in s 14(1) of the 1890 Act to limited partners is inconsistent with the very *raison d'être* for limited partnerships. By virtue of s 7 of the 1907 Act, provisions of the 1890 Act which are

---

118 Companies Act 2014, s 26.

119 Investment Limited Partnerships Act 1994, s 12(2) and see further para **[29.47]**.

120 It is worth noting that an examination of the register of limited partnerships will show that the vast majority of limited partnerships have been registered with the term 'limited partnership' or 'LP' as part of their name. The Companies Act 2014, s 26 will, in any event, only be breached if the word 'limited' or 'ltd' (or their Irish equivalents: 'teoranta' or 'teo') is the last word in the limited partnership's name.

121 This is the case in the UK for limited partnerships registered on or after 1 October 2009 (Limited Partnerships Act 1907, s 8B(2), inserted by the Legislative Reform (Limited Partnerships) Order 2009 (SI 2009/1940)); New Zealand (Limited Partnerships Act 2008, s 32(1)), New South Wales (Partnership Act 1892, s 75); Queensland (Partnership (Limited Liability) Act 1988, s 12); Victoria (Partnership Act 1958, s 75). See the American case of *Tilge v Brooks* (1889) 124 Pa 178, in which it was held that a limited partner was not liable as a partner by holding out after his withdrawal from the firm without notice.

122 Partnership Act 1890, s 14(1). See generally in relation to a holding out, para **[7.01]** et seq.

inconsistent with the 1907 Act do not apply to limited partnerships.[123] This conclusion can be supported by the fact that the 1963 Act requires a limited partnership, which does not have the names of all its partners (whether limited or general) in the firm-name, to include them in the letterhead of the firm.[124] It is therefore inconceivable that a limited partner who is complying with the 1963 Act by including his name in the firm's letterhead or in the firm name could be held to be liable as a partner by holding out with unlimited liability.

[28.42] However, where a limited partner represents to third parties that he is a general partner or that he has unlimited liability for the obligations of the limited partnership, it is doubtful that he could rely on the limit on his liability under s 4(2) of the 1907 Act. In such a case, it is thought that under s 14(1) of the 1890 Act or the principles of estoppel by representation underlying that section, the limited partner would be estopped from relying on s 4(2) of the 1907 Act.[125] Similarly, where the limited partner has left the partnership and he allows himself to be held out as a general partner in the firm, there is no reason why s 14(1) of the 1890 Act will not apply to him, since as a former limited partner, he cannot rely on the limit on his liability under s 4(2) of the 1907 Act.

Duration of a Limited Partnership

[28.43] The term of a limited partnership must be stated on the registration of the partnership[126] and any change in the term must be notified to the Registrar of Companies.[127] By virtue of s 7 of the 1907 Act, the rules governing the duration of ordinary partnerships also apply to limited partnerships, subject to the following comments.

Dissolution of partnership by notice

[28.44] Sections 26(1) and 32(c) of the 1890 Act apply to a limited partnership thereby entitling a general partner to dissolve a partnership at will by notice. However, in the absence of a contrary agreement between all the partners, s 6(5)(e) of the 1907 Act provides that a limited partner will not have such a right. A limited partner may, therefore, wish to have a right to dissolve the partnership by notice accorded to him in the limited partnership agreement. Otherwise, he will be bound to remain a partner until the general partners decide to dissolve the partnership, subject to his right to seek a court dissolution on just and equitable grounds.[128]

---

[123] Cf the position of a limited partner in an investment limited partnership, where the use of all or part of a limited partner's name in the firm name results in the limited partner who knowingly permitted it, being liable as a general partner to third parties: Investment Limited Partnerships Act 1994, s 12(4).

[124] Registration of Business Names Act 1963, s 18. See also l'Anson Banks, *Lindley & Banks on Partnership* (20th edn, 2017) at para 29-15 et seq.

[125] In relation to estoppel by conduct generally, see para **[7.32]** et seq.

[126] Limited Partnerships Act 1907, s 8. The form used is Companies Registration Office Form LP1.

[127] Limited Partnerships Act 1907, s 9. The form used is Companies Registration Office Form LP2.

[128] Partnership Act 1890, s 35(f). See generally para **[25.55]**.

No dissolution by death or bankruptcy of a limited partner

[28.45] Unlike the position with ordinary partnerships,[129] under s 6(2) of the 1907 Act, a limited partnership is not automatically dissolved[130] by the death or bankruptcy of a limited partner. This section is not stated to be subject to contrary agreement between the partners.[131] However, it is nonetheless apprehended that all the partners may agree that the limited partnership will dissolve on the death or bankruptcy of a limited partner.[132] This is because by virtue of s 7 of the 1907 Act, the terms of the 1890 Act apply to a limited partnership, save insofar as they are inconsistent with the 1907 Act. One of these terms is s 19 of the 1890 Act, which provides that partners are entitled to vary their rights and duties by agreement. It is thought that the non-dissolution of the limited partnership on the death or bankruptcy of a limited partner may be varied by agreement to the contrary, since there is nothing inconsistent with allowing all the partners in a limited partnership to so agree. Indeed, this approach is in keeping with the general approach of partnership law, which allows all the partners to determine amongst themselves the terms which will govern their arrangement.[133]

[28.46] In the absence of such an agreement, the limited partnership is not dissolved by the death or bankruptcy of a limited partner and accordingly, the estate of a deceased limited partner or his trustee in bankruptcy is not entitled to force a sale of the partnership assets or a winding up of the firm under s 39 of the 1890 Act.[134]

Mental incapacity of a limited partner

[28.47] Unlike the position with an ordinary partnership, s 6(2) of the 1907 Act provides that the lunacy of a limited partner is not a ground for the court to dissolve the partnership (ie under s 35(a) of the 1890 Act) unless dissolution is the only way to realise or ascertain the share of that partner. However, realising a partner's share is not the easiest of matters since it is not an interest in a specific piece of partnership property but is an identical and equal right with the other partners in all the partnership assets.[135] In effect, therefore, if the mentally incapacitated limited partner cannot dispose of his share in the firm to the continuing partners or to a third party, then it will be necessary to dissolve the partnership.

Retirement of a limited partner

[28.48] There seems to be no reason why a limited partner cannot be expressly permitted to retire from a partnership by the other partners in the same way as a partner

---

129 Partnership Act 1890, s 33(1).
130 See para **[28.127]** et seq.
131 Unlike the Partnership Act 1890, s 33(1).
132 For a contrary view see Brough, *Miller on Partnership* (2nd edn, 1994) at p 623.
133 See para **[21.128]** et seq. This analysis (as it appeared in the first edition of this work) was noted by the Law Commission (of England and Wales) and the Scottish Law Commission in their 2001 *Limited Partnerships Act 1907: A Joint Consultation Paper* (Consultation Paper No 161; Discussion Paper No 118) at para 5.32.
134 However, the limited partner or his estate is entitled to the return of his capital contribution, see para **[28.128]**.
135 See generally in relation to the nature of a partnership share, para **[19.03]**.

in an ordinary partnership may retire with the agreement of his co-partners. Where there is no express provision in the limited partnership agreement permitting a limited partner to retire, the consent of all the partners must be obtained to his retirement. In view of the inability of a limited partner to dissolve a partnership by notice,[136] it is useful to have such an express clause in the limited partnership agreement.

[28.49] In this context, s 4(3) of the 1907 Act provides that:

> A limited partner shall not during the continuance of the partnership, either directly or indirectly, draw out or receive back any part of his contribution, and if he does so draw out or receive back any such part[137] shall be liable for the debts and obligations of the firm up to the amount so drawn out or received back.

It might at first appear that this section applies to the situation where a partner is retiring from a limited partnership so as to prevent him from withdrawing his capital. However, the term 'during the continuance of the partnership' must be taken to mean that s 4(3) only applies to a withdrawal of capital while he is a partner in the firm.[138] Thus, where a limited partner retires he will be permitted to withdraw his capital. The contrary interpretation is difficult to support, namely that once a person becomes a limited partner, he would have to leave his capital in the partnership for the life of the partnership, which could be *ad infinitum*.[139] This would operate as an effective bar on any limited partner leaving the partnership, yet the 1907 Act clearly contemplates there being a turnover in the limited partners.[140]

[28.50] Should there be no provision in the limited partnership agreement allowing for retirement and the other partners will not agree to a limited partner retiring, the only other option available to him would seem to be to petition the court for the winding up of the partnership on just and equitable grounds.[141] The importance therefore of a contractual right to retire should be clear.

Retirement of a general partner

[28.51] As with an ordinary partnership, where the partnership agreement does not permit the retirement of a partner, there is no right for a general partner to retire from a limited partnership. Therefore, in such a situation, the consent of all the limited and general partners must be obtained before a general partner may retire. However, unlike a limited partner,[142] the general partner will, in the absence of any agreement to the contrary between the partners, have the right to dissolve a partnership at will by notice.[143]

---

136 Limited Partnerships Act 1907, s 6(5)(e).
137 The word 'he' might have usefully been inserted in this part of the section.
138 See para **[28.111]** and cf the position of limited partners under the Investment Limited Partnerships Act 1994, s 20.
139 This view (as expressed in the first edition of this work) was noted by the Law Commission and the Scottish Law Commission in their 2001 *Limited Partnerships Act 1907: A Joint Consultation Paper* (Consultation Paper No 161; Discussion Paper No 118) at para 4.42.
140 See for example the right of a limited partner to assign his share in the firm: Limited Partnerships Act 1907, s 6(5)(b).
141 Partnership Act 1890, s 35(f).
142 Limited Partnerships Act 1907, s 6(5)(e).
143 Partnership Act 1890, ss 26(1) and 32(c) and see generally, para **[23.13]** et seq.

Limited Partnership as a Collective Investment Scheme?

[28.52] Unlike the situation in England,[144] in Ireland a limited partnership (or an ordinary partnership) cannot be established as a collective investment undertaking subject to the requirements of the Central Bank of Ireland since an undertaking for collective investment in transferable securities (a UCITS) may only be established as a public limited company that is either an investment company with fixed capital, or an investment company with variable capital, a unit trust, a common contractual fund, an Irish collective asset-management vehicle or a special type of partnership, namely, an investment limited partnership formed under the Investment Limited Partnerships Act 1994.[145]

III. REGISTRATION OF LIMITED PARTNERSHIPS

[28.53] Unlike an ordinary partnership, which can be formed without any formality, the very existence of a limited partnership depends on its being registered as such with the Registrar of Companies. Section 5 of the 1907 Act provides that:

> Every limited partnership must be registered as such in accordance with the provisions of this Act, or in default thereof it shall be deemed to be a general partnership, and every limited partner shall be deemed to be a general partner.

[28.54] Under s 15 of the 1907 Act, the Registrar of Companies is also the registrar of limited partnerships.[146] Section 8 of the 1907 Act sets out in detail the particulars of registration to be filed with the Registrar of Companies. It states:

> The registration of a limited partnership shall be effected by sending by post or delivering to the registrar at the register office in that part of [Ireland][147] in which the principal place of business of the limited partnership is situated or proposed to be situated a statement signed by the partners containing the following particulars:
>
> (a) The firm name;[148]
>
> (b) The general nature of the business;
>
> (c) The principal place of business;
>
> (d) The full name of each partner;

---

[144] See s 235 of the Financial Services and Markets Act 2000. Most limited partnerships in the UK, notably partnership schemes, private fund limited partnerships and European Long-term Investment Funds, will constitute collective investment schemes unless a specific exemption applies. See, further, l'Anson Banks, *Lindley & Banks on Partnership* (20th edn, 2017) at paras 29-02 to 29-05, and paras 29-21 to 29-23.

[145] Unit Trusts Act 1990, s 1(1) and European Communities (Undertakings for Collective Investment in Transferable Securities) Regulations 2011 (SI 352/1989), reg 4(6). In relation to investment limited partnerships as collective investment schemes, see para **[29.01]** et seq.

[146] See para **[28.30]**.

[147] Adaptation of the term 'United Kingdom' as required by s 3 of the Adaptation of Enactments Act 1922.

[148] The Registrar of Companies, as registrar of limited partnerships, does not appear to have control over the suitability of the firm name. The Registrar does have control over company names in her capacity as the Registrar of Companies (Companies Act 2014, s 26) and the Minister for Business, Enterprise and Innovation has similar control in respect of the registration of a business name (Registration of Business Names Act 1963, s 14).

    (e)   The term, if any, for which the partnership is entered into, and the date of its commencement;

    (f)   A statement that the partnership is limited, and the description of every limited partner as such;

    (g)   The sum contributed by each limited partner, and whether paid in cash or how otherwise.

A €2.50 fee is payable to the Registrar of Companies on the registration of a limited partnership.[149]

'principal place of business'

[28.55] A firm's principal place of business must be stated on registration. This term is not defined in the 1907 Act, but it may be regarded as being its administrative headquarters from which the central control and management of the firm is carried on.[150]

Time of Filing

[28.56] The form containing the information required by s 8 of the 1907 Act (known as a Form LP1) must be filed in the Companies Registration Office. Under s 5 of the 1907 Act:

> Every limited partnership must be registered as such in accordance with the provisions of this Act, or in default thereof it shall be deemed to be a general partnership, and every limited partner shall be deemed to be a general partner.

[28.57] Thus, a limited partnership will be deemed to be an ordinary partnership and the limited partners are deemed to be general partners if the limited partnership is not registered in accordance with the 1907 Act. For this reason, it is prudent to provide in the limited partnership agreement that the partnership is not to begin to trade until the registration is complete.

'signed by the partners'

[28.58] As required by s 8 of the 1907 Act, the registration form must be signed 'by the partners'. This means that *all* the partners, both general and limited, must sign the Form LP1.[151]

---

149 The Limited Partnership Rules 1907, para 3(a) (SR & O 1907 No 1020), dated 17 December 1907 and made under s 17 of the 1907 Act as amended by the Limited Partnership Regulations 2001 (SI 570/2001), art 3. Under s 17 of the 1907 Act, the Minister for Business, Enterprise and Innovation (adaptation of 'Board of Trade' by s 4 of the Constitution (Consequential) Provisions Act 1937) is entitled to make rules regarding the fees and procedures for the registration of limited partnerships.

150 *Palmer v Caledonian Railway Co* [1892] 1 QB 823; *De Beers Consolidated Mines Ltd v Howe* [1906] AC 455.

151 This is also clear from the terms of the Form LP1 which is prescribed by the Limited Partnerships Rules 1907 (SR & O 1907 No 1020) which states that 'We, the undersigned, being the partners of the firm ...' and requires the signature of each general partner and each limited partner. If the general partner is to be a non-EEA national who intends to come to Ireland to establish a business, the permission of the Minister for Justice and Equality is required. (contd.../)

Term of Partnership to be Stated

[28.59] Under s 8(e) of the 1907 Act, the term of the partnership must be stated in the application for registration. If the partnership does not have a term of years, the Form LP1 which is set out in the Limited Partnerships Rules 1907[152] requires 'the conditions of the existence of the partnership' to be stated.

Statement of Capital Contributed

[28.60] As part of the registration of the limited partnership, a statement of the amount of capital contributed by the limited partners and confirmation as to whether it was contributed by way of cash (or, if not, how it was otherwise contributed) must accompany the particulars of registration using a Form LP3. The Form LP1 must also contain the same information. The requirement for a Form LP3 was introduced as s 117(5) of the Stamp Duties Consolidation Act 1999 (and before that, s 11 of the 1907 Act (which was repealed by Sch II of the Finance Act 1973)) used to prohibit the Registrar of Companies from registering a limited partnership until capital duty was paid. Notwithstanding that companies capital duty was abolished for transactions taking place on or after 7 December 2005,[153] the Form LP3 must still be filed with the Registrar of Companies on the registration of a limited partnership, and signed by a general partner (albeit that, at the time of writing, no filing fee is payable for a Form LP3).

Effect of Registration

[28.61] The effect of the registration of a limited partnership is governed by s 13 of the 1907 Act which states:

> On receiving any statement made in pursuance of this Act the registrar shall cause the same to be filed, and he shall send by post to the firm from whom such statement shall been received a certificate of registration thereof.

It is important to bear in mind that the registration of the limited partnership differs somewhat from the registration of a limited liability company.

[28.62] Registration does not confer the status of 'partnership' on persons who do not satisfy the definition of partnership. In this regard, the registration of a limited partnership is quite different from the registration of a company, since a company comes

---

[151] (\...contd) That evidence must be submitted with the Form LP1, and can include a GNIB card (certificate of registration) or Green Card/Green book (front and back). If the general or a limited partner is an Irish company, its company number must be included on the Form LP1. If the general partner or a limited partner is a non-Irish company, the Form LP1 must be accompanied by a certified copy of its constitutional documents, a copy of its certificate of incorporation, and a copy of any certificate(s) of incorporation on change of name (together with certified translations, if appropriate). If the general partner is a company that is not registered in Ireland, the general partner must also consider Part 21 of the Companies Act 2014, which deals with when a foreign company may need to register a branch in Ireland. See further the Companies Registration Office's Information Leaflet No 6/January 2018 (Limited Partnership Registration).

[152] SR & O 1907, No 1020.

[153] Finance Act 2006, s 110.

into being by virtue of its registration and the issue of a certificate of incorporation.[154] With a limited partnership, the registration is a formality which must be observed to ensure that the limited partners have limited liability, but if the applicants do not satisfy the definition of partnership, registration will not constitute the applicants a partnership whether limited or general. In addition, the certificate of registration of limited partnership issued by the Registrar of Companies[155] is not conclusive evidence of the existence of a limited partnership in Ireland,[156] in contrast to a certificate of incorporation for a company.[157] Under s 16(2) of the 1907 Act, the certificate of registration is simply admissible in evidence in all legal proceedings, both civil and criminal. However, it is not conclusive evidence of registration in accordance with the 1907 Act. In addition, it is to be noted that there is no requirement on a limited partnership to exhibit its certificate of registration at the firm's principal place of business.

Failure to Register in Accordance with the 1907 Act

[28.63] It is an offence under s 12 of the 1907 Act to sign, send or deliver a false statement for registration, knowing it to be false. More significantly, s 5 of the 1907 Act states that if there is a failure to register in accordance with that Act, there is deemed to be a general (ie an ordinary) partnership and every limited partner is deemed to be a general partner (ie an ordinary partner).[158] However, what is not clear from this section is the fact that a finding of ordinary partnership is dependant on the purported partners in

---

154 Companies Act 2014, s 25(2). Contrast also the position in relation to the issue of a certificate of authorisation for an investment limited partnership under s 8(6) of the Investment Limited Partnerships Act 1994, ie the issue of the certificate of authorisation is conclusive evidence of compliance with the requirements of the Act in relation to the formation of an investment limited partnership.

155 Under the terms of para 4 of the Limited Partnership Rules 1907 (SR & O 1907, No 1020) this certificate reads: 'I hereby certify, that the firm X having lodged a Statement of Particulars pursuant to Section 8 of the Limited Partnerships Act 1907, is this day registered as a Limited Partnership.'

156 The position in the UK is now different. The Legislative Reform (Limited Partnerships) Order 2009 inserted a new s 8C into the 1907 Act (as it applies in UK) which provides (with effect from 1 October 2009) that a certificate of registration issued on the registration of a limited partnership is conclusive evidence that a limited partnership came into existence at the date of registration. The implications of the certificate being 'conclusive' were considered in detail by Nugee J in his judgment in *Bank of Beirut SAL and another v HRH Prince Adel El-Hashemite and another; Arab National Bank v HRH Prince Adel El-Hashemite and another* [2015] EWHC 1451 (Ch), in which he noted that once such a certificate issues, the limited partnership must be regarded as having come into operation, irrespective of the circumstances that led to its registration. As such, while the claimant banks had sought orders requiring the registrar of companies (as registrar of limited partnerships) to remove those limited partnerships from the register on the basis that their registration was procured by fraud or forgery, the fact that the registrar had acted bona fide in issuing the certificates of registration meant that it was not open to the Court to make an order directing that those limited partnerships be removed from the register.

157 Companies Act 2014, s 25(4).

158 As regards the nomenclature used, see para **[1.35]**.

the limited partnership being capable of being partners in an ordinary partnership in the first place.[159] Thus if, as happened in *MacCarthaigh v Daly*,[160] the purported partners to the improperly registered limited partnership are not carrying on business with a view to a profit, then they will neither be partners in a limited partnership nor partners in an ordinary partnership since they fail one of the crucial tests for the existence of a partnership.[161] In this regard, s 5 of the 1907 Act must be interpreted as being subject to the definition of partnership in s 1(1) of the 1890 Act.[162]

[28.64] It is important to note that the critical event for the purposes of s 5 of the 1907 Act is the 'registration' of the partnership and not the issue of the certificate of registration, since s 8 states that registration is 'effected' by sending to the Registrar of Companies the details required by that section. Thus, once the correct details regarding the partnership as required by s 8 of the 1907 Act have been filed, registration is complete and the limited partners may safely trade with the benefit of limited liability.[163]

Effect of Incorrect Registration Details

[28.65] *MacCarthaigh v Daly*[164] highlights the importance of ensuring that the initial registration is properly implemented. In that case, a limited partnership for the leasing of assets to the Metropole Hotel in Cork was formed in December of 1977 by an agreement between several professionals who were to be the limited partners in the firm. The limited partners agreed to contribute capital of £50 each and the following February the Form LP1 was filed in the Companies Office (as it then was) containing details of the £50 contributed by each of the limited partners. The certificate of registration was issued by the Registrar of Companies on 16 February 1978. It transpired that the £50 was not actually contributed by each of the limited partners until April 1978. For this reason, the Form LP1 was incorrect when it stated that the limited partners had each contributed £50. In the High Court, O'Hanlon J held that:

> 'Registration of the limited partnership in the present case was achieved by submitting to the registrar, prior to the 16th February, 1978, a statement which omitted, or stated incorrectly, the amount contributed by each limited partner, as, by some oversight, their contributions were not made for some months after registration ... As the registration effected in the present case does not appear to have been effected in accordance with the provisions of the Act, having regard to the irregularity already referred to, it appears to me that the transactions carried out by the parties to the so-called Partnership Agreement during the tax year 1977/78 must, *prima facie*, be regarded as having been carried out by them as general partners.'[165]

---

[159] This issue is briefly discussed in Twomey, 'The Partnership Act 1890 in Ireland' (1996) 8 International Company and Commercial LR 297.

[160] *MacCarthaigh v Daly* [1985] IR 73.

[161] Note that although this was the view expressed by O'Hanlon J in that case, he was constrained for procedural reasons from overturning the decision of the Appeal Commissioner that an ordinary partnership existed in that case.

[162] Limited Partnerships Act 1907, s 7.

[163] Contrast the position of companies, where the issue of the certificate of incorporation is conclusive evidence that an association is a company: Companies Act 2014, s 25(4).

[164] *MacCarthaigh v Daly* [1985] IR 73.

[165] *MacCarthaigh v Daly* [1985] IR 73 at 78–79.

[28.66] It seems that once the mistake is rectified,[166] the limited partnership comes into existence and the limited partners obtain their limited liability, since O'Hanlon J noted that:

> '[I]t was contended on behalf of the appellant that notwithstanding the registration of the limited partnership on the 16th of February, 1978, the requirements of the Act of 1907 had not been complied with and no limited partnership ... came into existence until the requirements of s 4, sub-s 2, of the Act were complied with some months after the relevant tax year had expired (if at all). I am of opinion that this submission is correct.'[167]

[28.67] The lesson to be learnt from this case is that special care should be taken to ensure that any filings which are required to be made under the 1907 Act are accurately and properly made in order to avoid the intended limited partners failing to obtain limited liability.[168] Under s 16(1) of the 1907 Act, any person may inspect the statements filed with the Registrar of Companies in relation to a limited partnership[169] or obtain a certificate of the registration of a limited partnership or a certified copy or extract from the registration statements.[170]

Registration of Changes in a Limited Partnership

[28.68] Section 9(1) of the 1907 Act requires any changes in the particulars of a limited partnership registered under s 8 of the 1907 Act to be notified to the Registrar of Companies within seven days of the change. This section states:

> If during the continuance of a limited partnership any change is made or occurs in—
>
> (a)   the firm name,
>
> (b)   the general nature of the business,
>
> (c)   the principal place of business,
>
> (d)   the partners or the name of any partner,
>
> (e)   the term or character of the partnership,
>
> (f)   the sum contributed by any limited partner,

---

166   However, note that it may not be possible to rectify all mistakes. For example under s 9 of the 1907 Act, changes to the registration details must be notified to the Registrar of Companies within seven days of the change. Clearly, when this period has passed, any subsequent filing will not rectify this omission.

167   *MacCarthaigh v Daly* [1985] IR 73 at 78.

168   Furthermore, once the limited partnership is in existence, the limited partners should take special care to ensure that any changes in the limited partnership are duly registered in accordance with s 9 of the 1907 Act, since a limited partnership which is properly registered initially will fail to be registered in accordance with the 1907 Act, if it fails to keep these details up to date. See para **[28.70]**. See also the Queensland case of *Re Cotton Crops Pty Ltd* [1986] 2 QD R 328, upheld on appeal [1988] 1 QD R 34, where the registration details failed to include the place of residence of the partner and the capital contributions of the limited partners as well as incorrectly stating the principal place of business. It was held that the limited partners were liable as general partners.

169   For a fee of €0.05: Limited Partnership Rules 1907 as amended by the Limited Partnership Regulations 2001 (SI 570/2001), art 3.

170   For a fee of €0.10 for each certificate and, in respect of each certified copy or extract, €0.06 for each folio of 72 words: Limited Partnership Rules 1907 as amended by the Limited Partnership Regulations 2001 (SI 570/2001), art 3.

(g) the liability of any partner by reason of his becoming a limited instead of a general partner or a general instead of a limited partner,

a statement signed by the firm, specifying the nature of the change shall within seven days be sent by post or delivered to the register office in that part of [Ireland][171] in which the partnership is registered.

[28.69] Since the statement must be signed 'by the firm', a general partner, but not a limited partner,[172] may sign this form in the firm name. Under s 9(2) of the 1907 Act, any failure to comply with s 9(1) is an offence by the general partners, but not the limited partners, and as such, is subject to a daily fine.[173] The Companies Registration Office form that is used for the purposes of s 9(1) is a Form LP2 and is subject to a filing fee.[174] Where the change involves an increase in the capital of the firm, a Form LP4 must also be filed. There is no filing fee payable in respect of the Form LP4 and, for increases in the capital of a limited partnership on or after 7 December 2005, capital duty is no longer payable.[175]

Failure to register changes leads to loss of limited liability

[28.70] Of greater significance than the offence of failing to notify changes in the registration details, is the fact that any such failure would, it is apprehended, lead to the firm not being registered in accordance with the 1907 Act and to the partnership consequently being deemed to be an ordinary partnership pursuant to s 5 of that Act. This is because for a limited partnership to be registered in accordance with the 1907 Act, it is clearly not sufficient for the particulars to be correct on the date of registration if they are not also kept up to date by the limited partnership in the light of changing circumstances. Otherwise, the argument goes that s 5 of the 1907 Act would be deprived of any practical significance in providing information to the general public on limited partnerships, since there would be no incentive for the limited partnerships to keep this information up to date. In view of the potential loss of limited liability, extreme care should be taken to notify any change in a limited partnership to the Registrar of Companies within the seven-day time period. In addition, since it is the general partners, and not the limited partners, who are entitled to notify the Registrar of Companies of any change in the registration details, the limited partners might consider insisting on a provision in the limited partnership agreement which provides that no change to the partnership (which requires registration) will take effect until registration is completed.

---

171 Adaptation of the term 'United Kingdom' as required by s 3 of the Adaptation of Enactments Act 1922.

172 See **[28.74]** et seq and the Limited Partnerships Act 1907, s 6(1).

173 Limited Partnerships Act 1907, s 9(2). The original fine of £1 was converted to its euro equivalent by virtue of Council Regulations (EC) No 1103/97, (EC) No 974/98 and (EC) No 2866/98 and the Economic and Monetary Union Act 1998, s 6 and then replaced, by virtue of the Fines Act 2010, with a class E fine (a class E fine is a fine not exceeding €500).

174 The filing fee is €0.30: Limited Partnerships Rules 1907, s 3(b) (SR & O 1907 No 1020) as amended by the Limited Partnership Regulations 2001 (SI 570/2001), art 3.

175 Finance Act 2006, s 110.

In this way, the risk of the limited partners losing their limited liability is considerably reduced.[176]

[28.71] In particular, s 9(1)(e) of the 1907 Act requires the limited partnership to notify the Registrar of Companies of any change in the 'term or character of the partnership'. This requirement is of particular importance for limited partners in formal partnerships (usually fixed term partnerships) which continue after the expiry of the term. This is because this continuation would amount to a change in the term of the partnership, requiring notification to the Registrar under s 9(1)(e) of the 1907 Act. For this reason, the continuation of a limited partnership after the fixed term may be viewed as a trap for unwary limited partners and should be immediately notified to the Registrar in order to prevent them losing their limited liability. It is also important to bear in mind that the arrival or departure of a partner from a limited partnership is a change in the registration particulars and must be registered with the Registrar under s 9(1)(d) of the 1907 Act.

[28.72] It is, however, questioned whether this is the most appropriate way for the legislature to encourage compliance with registration. It is suggested that the present regime is unduly harsh in that it deprives innocent limited partners of their protection of limited liability, where there has been an inadvertent failure to register a change in the registration details. It is inconceivable that the same consequence would apply to a shareholder in a limited liability company, where the company fails to register say the details of a new director. This disproportionate remedy is a relic of the unwarranted fear in the nineteenth century of limited liability and, accordingly, it is contended that it is no longer an appropriate way in which to ensure compliance with the registration requirements of the 1907 Act.

No Power to De-register a Limited Partnership

[28.73] It is somewhat surprising that there is no power in the 1907 Act to strike off from the register of limited partnerships a limited partnership which has ceased to carry on business. However, the Companies Registration Office's Form LP2 (Notice of Change in a Limited Partnership) now includes, as part of the section that must be completed by a limited partnership where there has been a change in its 'term or character',[177] a section for completion if the limited partnership has ceased to carry on business. As a result, the register of limited partnerships now indicates whether a limited partnership has ceased, and the effective date of that cessation. However, as that information (ie whether the limited partnership has ceased to carry on business) is not required by the 1907 Act and is only sought in the Form LP2,[178] it is probable that the penalties for failing to notify the Registrar of Companies of any change, of a type referred to in s 9(1) of the 1907 Act, to the limited partnership does not extend to a

---

[176] See also l'Anson Banks, *Lindley & Banks on Partnership* (20th edn, 2017) at para 29-36 which notes that the failure to register changes where the limited partnership was established on or after 1 October 2009 no longer has the same result in the UK following the amendment of s 5 of the 1907 Act as it applies in UK by the Legislative Reform (Limited Partnerships) Order 2009 (SI 2009/1940).

[177] The Limited Partnerships Act 1907, s 9(1)(e) requires that a notification be made to the Registrar on a change in the term or character of a limited partnership.

[178] It is a relatively recent inclusion in the Form LP2.

failure to notify the Registrar of a cessation of business. As such, it is still possible that the register may provide a misleading picture of the number of true limited partnerships. It is submitted that a requirement to notify the Registrar of the cessation of business by a limited partnership should be added to s 9(1)(e) of the 1907 Act[179] and the Registrar should also be given the power, similar to that which exists for registered companies,[180] to strike off limited partnerships.[181]

IV.   AUTHORITY OF PARTNERS TO BIND FIRM

Authority of General Partner to bind the Firm

[28.74] The authority of a general partner to bind a limited partnership is the same as the authority of a partner in an ordinary partnership.[182] The only additional points to be made are that the position of a general partner is stronger than that of a partner in an ordinary partnership. This is because under s 6(1) of the 1907 Act, the power of a general partner to take part in the management of the business and bind the firm is exclusive to the general partners,[183] since a limited partner is prohibited from doing either, under pain of the loss of his limited liability.[184]

---

179 The Limited Partnerships Act 1907, s 9(1)(e) requires that a notification be made to the Registrar on a change in the term or character of a limited partnership.

180 Ie the Companies Act 2014, ss 725 and 731.

181 Of note is the decision of Nugee J in *Bank of Beirut SAL and another v HRH Prince Adel El-Hashemite and another; Arab National Bank v HRH Prince Adel El-Hashemite and another* [2015] EWHC 1451 (Ch), in which he noted that while the 1907 Act does not contain a provision allowing for deregistration, the entries for the limited partnerships in this particular case (the registrations of which had been procured by fraud) were recorded as having been the subject of fraudulent registration applications, thereby putting anyone checking the register of limited partnership on notice of the issue.

182 See for example *R (on the application of de Silva) v Revenue and Customs Commissioners* [2016] EWCA Civ 40 where Gloster LJ (at para 44) found that a partnership settlement agreement with the Revenue and Customs Commissioners, which had been executed by a general partner, related to the business of the firm, was done in the firm name, demonstrated an intention to bind the firm, and was executed by a person (the general partner) duly authorised to do so. The agreement conferred benefits on the individual partners and Gloster LJ held that it was contractually binding on the appellants as limited partners. This point was not argued on the subsequent appeal. It should also be noted that it is thought that a deed which is executed by all the general partners, and not by the limited partners, is binding on the firm in view of the restricted role of limited partners in the firm. Cf the case of an ordinary partnership, where the deed must be executed by all the partners, para **[10.55]**.

183 As noted by Barrett J in *Camiveo Limited v Dunnes Stores* [2017] IEHC 147 (at para 11 of the judgment), where he observed that Camiveo Limited, as general partner in a limited partnership, had 'complete, sole power and responsibility for managing and administering the business affairs of the partnership'. In the British Columbia Court of Appeal case of *British Columbia Ltd v Tackama Forest Products Ltd* (1992) 91 DLR (4th) 129, it was stated that as regards managing the firm, the managing partner of a limited partnership was in a position more like that of a governing director of a company than a trustee of a will to the beneficiaries.

184 But it is apprehended that the limited partners must consent to any change in the nature of the partnership business, para **[28.80]**.

[28.75] It is usual for any property acquired or investments made by the limited partnership to be in the name of the general partner (albeit for the benefit of all of the partners in the limited partnership)[185] or in the name of a nominee. It is theoretically possible for an asset to be held in the names of all of the partners in a limited partnership (it could not be held in the name of the limited partnership, as a limited partnership does not have separate legal personality and is instead the aggregate of its partners); however, in practice this is very rarely done.

[28.76] As the use of limited partnerships as venture capital and private equity vehicles increased, questions around how security could be taken over the assets of a limited partnership, and against whom that security should be registered, arose more frequently. The assets of a limited partnership are generally held by the general partner(s) (or a nominee) on behalf of the limited partnership, and any security interest in those assets would be granted by the general partner(s) or nominee, as appropriate. As a limited partnership is not a separate legal entity, an asset cannot be held in the name of the limited partnership, but could be held in the names of all of the partners (general and limited) although this would be very unusual. The manner in which assets are to be held should be dealt in the partnership agreement. As to whether, if a general partner or nominee in whose name the asset is held is a company,[186] particulars of the security created should be filed with the Registrar of Companies under Part 7 of the Companies Act 2014, it is submitted that such a filing should be made provided that the security interest that is granted comes within the definition of 'charge' in s 408(1) of the 2014 Act.[187] To the extent that any general partner or nominee is an individual, consideration should also be given to whether any filing under the Bills of Sale Acts is required.[188]

[28.77] On the dissolution of the firm, s 6(3) of the 1907 Act provides that the general partners alone are obliged to wind up the firm, unless the court orders otherwise.

Authority of Limited Partner to bind the Firm

[28.78] The authority of a limited partner, or more accurately the absence of such authority, to bind the limited partnership is dealt with in s 6(1) of the 1907 Act:

> A limited partner shall not take part in the management of the partnership business, and shall not have power to bind the firm:

> Provided that a limited partner may by himself or by his agent at any time inspect the books of the firm and examine into the state and prospects of the partnership business, and may advise with the partners thereon.

> If a limited partner takes part in the management of the partnership business he shall be liable for all debts and obligations of the firm incurred while he so takes part in the management as though he were a general partner.

---

[185] See for example the manner in which property was held by the general partner in a limited partnership in *Camiveo Limited v Dunnes Stores* [2017] IEHC 147.

[186] As defined in the Companies Act 2014, s 2(1).

[187] As to the registration of charges created by companies generally, see Courtney, *The Law of Companies* (4th edn, 2016) at para [20.001] et seq and Hutchinson, *Keane on Company Law* (5th edn, 2016) at para [21.04] et seq.

[188] As to bills of sale, see Breslin, *Banking Law* (3rd edn, 2013) at para 11-60 et seq.

'shall not take part in the management of the partnership business'

[28.79] The expression 'management of the partnership business' is not defined in the 1907 Act[189] and it is unclear where the line is between the 'management of the partnership business' which is prohibited and the right of the limited partner to 'inspect the books of the firm and examine into the state and prospects of the partnership business'[190] and 'advise with the partners thereon.'[191] In view of the possibility of a

---

[189] Cooke J in *Certain Partners in Henderson PFT Secondary Fund II LP v Henderson PFI Secondary Fund II LP* [2013] QB 934 referred to the judgment of Norris J in *Inversiones Frieira SL v Colyzeo Investors I and II LP* [2012] Bus LR 1136 (at pp 1147 and 1150), where Norris J made some general comments around what might and might not constitute participation in the management of the business of a limited partnership. Cooke J commented that: '... the second paragraph of section 6(1) [of the 1907 Act] ... allows for a Limited Partner to inspect the books of the firm, examine the state and prospects of the Partnership business and "advise" with the Partners thereon. Such activity will not constitute participation in the management of the Partnership business. Norris J points out at page 1150 that, having obtained information about the Partnership's affairs, a Limited Partner who examines and analyses the material and confers with other Limited Partners does not thereby become involved in the management of the Partnership. An expression of a view to the General Partner about the performance of the Partnership, or the strategy or future direction of the Partnership, or even a preference about how a particular asset should be dealt with equally does not constitute management. As soon however as there is participation in the decision making process by requiring notice of individual decisions and the ability to make representations about individual decisions, scrutinising and commenting upon the operational business decisions taken by the General Partner, the Limited Partner will be involved in management. There are potentially grey areas no doubt but the conducting of litigation on the part of the Partnership is not one of them.'

[190] In *Inversiones Frieira SL and another v Colyzeo Investors II LP and another* [2012] Bus LR 1136, Norris J's conclusions (at para 23 of his judgment) are a useful summary of the scope of a limited partner's right to inspect the firm's books, and examine its state and prospects. He observed that the right of a partner in an ordinary partnership under s 28 of the 1890 Act to the disclosure of matters regarding the firm's dealings and transactions is as much a right of a limited partner as it is one of an ordinary partner in light of s 7 of the 1907 Act which provides that the provisions of the 1890 Act apply to limited partnerships, subject to the terms of the 1907 Act. He went on to note that the restriction in the first paragraph of s 6(1) of the 1907 Act on a limited partner taking part in the management of the firm's business does not imply that the limited partner's right to information under the second paragraph of s 6(1) is also restricted, in particular as his capital remains at risk, and he has entrusted the conduct of the firm's business to the general partner. See also para **[15.22]**.

[191] Indeed, this distinction is further blurred by s 6(5)(a) of the 1907 Act which provides that, subject to contrary agreement between all the partners (and therefore, including the limited partners): '[a]ny difference arising as to ordinary matters connected with the partnership business may be decided by a majority of the general partners.' Implicit in this provision would appear to be the entitlement of the limited partners to agree that ordinary matters connected with the partnership business may be decided by a decision of the limited as well as the general partners. But it is difficult to reconcile the possibility of limited partners deciding on ordinary matters of partnership business with the prohibition in s 6(1) on their taking part in the management of the partnership. It is contended that this confusion results from poor drafting rather than any desire on the part of the legislature to give the limited partner an expanded role in the management of the firm. (contd.../)

limited partner losing his limited liability, care should be taken to ensure that in his discussions with the general partners regarding the business, the limited partner does not attempt to get involved in managing the firm. It is considered that the concept of advising with the partners entitles the limited partner to establish, by questioning the general partners, the reasons for their management decisions. In putting such questions, it is recommended that the limited partner should not give his own opinion as to what the firm has done or should do in relation to its business. This is because it will be difficult to avoid the conclusion that the proffering of his opinion is an attempt to persuade the general partners of the correctness of his view, which persuasion would clearly constitute his being involved in the management of the firm.[192]

[28.80] However, it is thought that decisions by the limited partners on the basic structure and organisation of the partnership, such as a change in the objectives of the partnership,[193] an increase in the firm's capital, a change to the duration of the firm, a change to the terms of the limited partnership agreement, conversion of a general partner to a limited partner and vice versa,[194] would not be regarded as management decisions.[195] Rather, such decisions relate to the type of limited partnership, in which the limited partners wish to invest their capital and thus these decisions do not fall within the prohibited 'management of the partnership business'. This conclusion can be supported on the basis that, as the limited partner entered into partnership for the original objects, he should not be forced to accept a new object, without having a vote thereon.[196] These decisions go beyond the 'ordinary matters connected with the partnership business' and, therefore, may not be taken by the general partners alone, unless specifically authorised in advance by the limited partners.

---

[191] (\...contd) For this reason, s 6(5)(a) should be read as being subject to s 6(1), so that the involvement of the limited partners in deciding on ordinary matters of partnership business will in general lead to their being deemed to be general partners.

[192] Parts of this analysis (as it appeared in the first edition of this work) were quoted by the Law Commission and the Scottish Law Commission in their 2001 *Limited Partnerships Act 1907: A Joint Consultation Paper* (Consultation Paper No 161; Discussion Paper No 118) at para 4.12.

[193] This would fall within the term 'a change in the nature of the partnership business' as used in s 24(8) of the 1890 Act, so as to require the consent of all the partners.

[194] See, for comparison purposes, the list of permitted activities of a limited partner in an investment limited partnership under s 6(4) of the Investment Limited Partnerships Act 1994. Such a limited partner is in a very similar position to a limited partner in a limited partnership, since he is also prohibited from taking part in the conduct of the partnership business under pain of the loss of his limited liability. These permitted activities include voting as a limited partner on such issues as the dissolution or winding up of the firm, a change in the objectives or policies of the investment limited partnership, the removal of a partner, etc. See para **[29.105]**.

[195] This analysis (as it appeared in the first edition of this work) was quoted by the Law Commission and the Scottish Law Commission in their 2001 *Limited Partnerships Act 1907: A Joint Consultation Paper* (Consultation Paper No 161; Discussion Paper No 118) at para 4.23.

[196] See also para **[28.54]**.

Decisions under the European Communities (Accounts) Regulations 1993

[28.81] In certain exceptional cases a limited partnership is required to file accounts, ie, where all the general partners have themselves limited liability.[197] The involvement of a limited partner in decisions regarding the filing of these accounts might be regarded as involving him in the management of the partnership business. For this reason, reg 8(2) of the European Communities (Accounts) Regulations 1993 creates an express exemption allowing limited partners to deal with such accounting decisions. It provides that a limited partner will not be regarded as taking part in the management of the firm for the purposes of s 6(1) of the 1907 Act, by virtue of his:

(a)   consenting in writing to the exemption of the partnership from the requirement to file accounts under s 357 of the Companies Act 2014; and

(b)   appointing the auditor to the partnership as required by reg 22(1) of the European Communities (Accounts) Regulations 1993.

Inapplicability of ss 15 and 16 of 1890 Act to limited partners

[28.82] In view of the highly restrictive nature of s 6(1) of the 1907 Act, it is contended that ss 15 and 16 of the 1890 Act do not apply to a limited partner.[198] Section 16 of the 1890 Act provides that notice to a 'partner who habitually acts in the partnership business' is deemed to be notice to the firm. However, by virtue of s 6(1) of the 1907 Act, a limited partner is prohibited from taking part in the management of the firm and therefore cannot habitually act in the partnership business. Thus, it is submitted that notice to him will not be deemed to be notice to the firm. Similarly, under s 15 of the 1890 Act, an admission or representation will bind the firm if made by a partner in the ordinary course of the firm's business. As s 6(1) of the 1907 Act prohibits a limited partner from taking part in the management of the firm, he cannot be regarded as being allowed to make admissions or representations in the ordinary course of business of the firm.

Litigation involving the firm

[28.83] In an ordinary partnership, every partner is entitled to bring an action on behalf of a firm.[199] In view of the express wording of s 6(1) of the 1907 Act, it is contended that a limited partner does not have authority to bring an action on behalf of the firm.[200]

---

[197] European Communities (Accounts) Regulations 1993, reg 6 (SI 396/1993).

[198] Ie since they are inconsistent with s 6(1) of the 1907 Act, s 7 of the 1907 Act provides that they do not apply.

[199] See para **[10.53]**.

[200] See the decision of Cooke J in *Certain Limited Partners in Henderson PFI Secondary Fund II LP (a firm) v Henderson PFI Secondary Fund II LP (a firm) and others* [2013] QB 934 where (at para 50) he notes that '[b]y the very terms of section 6(1) of the 1907 Act, a limited partner is not to take part in the management of the partnership business and does not have power to bind the firm, which means that the limited partner cannot act in the name of the partnership in litigation under the first paragraph of that section …'. In *Camiveo Limited v Dunnes Stores* [2017] IEHC 147, there had been a suggestion during the proceedings that Camiveo Limited, the general partner in a limited partnership and the legal owner of the property that was the subject of the dispute, was not the proper plaintiff in the action. (contd.../)

However, an action may be brought against a limited partner in his capacity as an agent of the firm on behalf of the firm. This is because under general partnership law, an action may be brought against a limited partnership in the firm name[201] or in the name of all the partners, including the limited partners.[202]

Where limited partner is a director or shareholder of a general partner

[28.84] In their 2001 Joint Consultation Paper on the 1907 Act,[203] the Law Commission and the Scottish Law Commission noted[204] that a corporate general partner is sometimes established and directed by the limited partners, but that this could lead to a limited partner indirectly participating in the management of the limited partnership. In *PWA Corp v Gemini Group Automated Distribution Systems Inc*,[205] the Ontario Court of Appeal considered various aspects of a dispute between the general partner and limited partners in a limited partnership that operated a computerised reservation system for airline tickets. The limited partners each owned one third of the issued shares in the general partner and had nominated directors to the board of the general partner. This structure seemed to be accepted by the Court of Appeal for Ontario without any consideration as to whether it could equate to the limited partners taking part in the control of the business of the limited partnership itself.[206] However, in *Hutchinson v Bowes*,[207] a limited partner became the chair of an 'advising committee' to the limited partnership. It was held that, in doing so, the limited partner '… did more than advise, they directed and acted, and while they did that they could not escape the consequence of interfering in the transaction of the business by calling themselves an advising committee …'. As such, it is contended that a limited partner who acts as a director or is

---

200 (\...contd) At para 12 of his judgment, Barrett J commented that: '… Camiveo is the general partner in a limited partnership; it has legal ownership of the relevant property and exclusive power to manage and administer the business affairs of the partnership; the rent under the lease is payable to it; it may be that the rent is beneficially payable to another, not unlike the situation where, e.g., a bank has security over a rental stream, but that does not affect the right to sue for the rent where the rent goes unpaid.' The question of whether a limited partner had a right to bring an action did not arise in that case, but it was implicit in Barrett J's judgment that there was no requirement for the limited partners to be involved in the proceedings, even though Camiveo as general partner held the title to the relevant property for the benefit of the limited partnership.

201 Order 14, r 1 of the Rules of the Superior Courts, see generally para **[12.24]**.

202 See para **[12.53]**. Note that in an investment limited partnership, this right is varied by s 22(1) of the Investment Limited Partnerships Act 1994. See further para **[29.112]**.

203 The Law Commission and the Scottish Law Commission (2001) *Limited Partnerships Act 1907: A Joint Consultation Paper* (Consultation Paper No 161; Discussion Paper No 118).

204 The Law Commission and the Scottish Law Commission (2001) *Limited Partnerships Act 1907: A Joint Consultation Paper* (Consultation Paper No 161; Discussion Paper No 118) at para 3.2 of Pt III.

205 *PWA Corp v Gemini Group Automated Distribution Systems Inc* [1993] 103 DLR (4th) 609 (CA, Ontario).

206 The relevant Ontario legislation (the Limited Partnerships Act RSO 1990, c L16) expressly permits a limited partner to advise on the management of the limited partnership's business (s 12(2)), but goes on to provide that if a limited partner 'takes part in the control of the business', the limited partner will be liable as a general partner (s 13(1)).

207 *Hutchinson v Bowes* (1857) 15 UCR 156 (Canada).

a shareholder in the general partner of a limited partnership is at risk of contravening s 6(1) of the 1907 Act on the basis that he is taking part in the management of the business of the limited partnership. The risk is perhaps higher where the limited partner is a director as the statutory default under the Companies Act 2014 is that a company's business is to be managed by its directors,[208] but that statutory default is subject to any regulations contained in the company's constitution, the other provisions of the 2014 Act and any directions given by the shareholders in general meeting by way of special resolution, so the position of a limited partner *qua* shareholder in the general partner remains at risk of contravening s 6(1) of the 1907 Act.[209]

Where limited partner acts on behalf of firm in contravention of s 6(1)

[28.85] If a limited partner attempts to bind the firm, he will of course be liable under the terms of s 6(1) of the 1907 Act for the debts and obligations of the firm incurred during this period.[210] However, the firm will not be bound[211] to third parties who deal with the limited partner in such circumstances,[212] since by the express terms of s 6(1) the

---

[208] Companies Act 2014, s 158(1).

[209] While the 'white list' of actions that may be taken by limited partners in a private fund limited partnership in the UK is broad, that cannot be used as reference point for assessing whether an action taken by a limited partner in a limited partnership is, or is not, equivalent to taking part in the management of the business (s 6A(4)(b) of the 1907 Act as it applies in the UK). That white list includes taking part in decisions about amendments to the partnership agreement, whether the general nature of the partnership business should change, who should run the partnership on day-to-day basis, whether a person should become or cease to be a partner, whether the partnership should end or if its term should be extended, and who should be appointed to wind-up the partnership if it is dissolved at a time when there is no general partner. White-listed activities also include enforcing an entitlement under the partnership agreement or contracting with other partners (as long as that does not involve management of the partnership business), guaranteeing the partnership's obligations, approving the partnership's accounts, reviewing or approving valuations of the partnership's assets, discussing the partnership's business prospects, and consulting or advising with a general partner or anyone appointed to manage or advise the partnership about its affairs or accounts.

[210] As noted by Cooke J in *Certain Limited Partners in Henderson PFI Secondary Fund II LP (a firm) v Henderson PFI Secondary Fund II LP (a firm) and others* [2013] QB 934 at para 60 of his judgment. However, Cooke J's observations at para 69 of the same judgment could be read as implying that during any period for which a limited partner takes part in the management of the firm, he is liable for all of the partnership's debts and liabilities, rather than those incurred during the period for which he takes part in the management of the firm. It is submitted that this is not correct. He also noted (at para 70 of that judgment) that, for the period during which a limited partner takes part in the management of the firm, he 'supplants the general partner and becomes liable as if he were the general partner'. However, it is submitted that this is not correct – such a limited partner would not supplant one or more existing general partners, but would instead become liable as if he were also a general partner.

[211] For a contrary view, see Brough, *Miller on Partnership* (2nd edn, 1994) at p 610 et seq. This argument appears to be that just as the registration of information in the register of business names is not notice thereof to third parties (see para **[3.82]**) so too a third party dealing with a partner in a limited partnership cannot be assumed to be on notice that the partner, with whom he is dealing, is a limited partner.

[212] The firm may be bound if the limited partner had actual authority to bind the firm or the general partners represented to the third party that he had this authority. See generally in relation to the ostensible and actual authority of a partner, para **[10.31]**.

limited partner has no power to bind the firm. The third party will have an action for misrepresentation against the limited partner who wrongfully represented himself to have authority to bind the firm.[213]

V.   LIABILITY OF THE PARTNERS IN A LIMITED PARTNERSHIP

Liability of a General Partner

[28.86] The liability of a general partner for the obligations of a limited partnership is the same as the liability of a partner for the obligations of an ordinary partnership.[214] This is the effect of s 4(2) of the 1907 Act which provides that general partners are 'liable for all debts and obligations of the firm' and reference should be made to the treatment earlier in this work of this area under the law of ordinary partnerships.[215] On occasion, a general partner may delegate the management of the business of the limited partnership to a third party on a contractual basis, but this will not result in the third party becoming a partner in the firm, and the liability of the general partner will remain the same irrespective of whether it has delegated any or all of its management responsibilities.

[28.87] As in ordinary partnerships, the duration of this liability on the departure of a partner is an important issue. In limited partnerships, there is the additional complication that a general partner may become a limited partner.

Departure of general partner from firm

[28.88] In the event of a general partner leaving the limited partnership, notice should be given to persons who dealt with the firm while he was a partner in the same way as a partner in an ordinary partnership is advised to give such notice.[216] This is necessary in order to ensure that the general partner is not liable to persons who dealt with the firm prior to his departure[217] for obligations incurred by the firm thereafter.[218] This raises the question of whether the change in the registration details of the limited partnership is

---

[213]   Unless the third party knew that he was a limited partner and that he was not authorised to act on behalf of the firm. See *Halbot v Lens* [1901] 1 Ch 344.

[214]   See generally para **[10.01]** et seq.

[215]   See l'Anson Banks, *Lindley & Banks on Partnership* (20th edn, 2017) at para 30-08 for criticism of the approach taken by Cooke J in *Certain Limited Partners in Henderson PFI Secondary Fund II LP (a firm) v Henderson PFI Secondary Fund II LP (a firm) and others* [2013] QB 934 where Cooke J observed that a new general partner would automatically assume responsibility for the pre-existing debts of the limited partnership. The view of the current editor of *Lindley & Banks on Partnership* is that Cooke J did not take proper account of s 9 of the 1890 Act which provides that a partner is liable for all debts and obligations of the firm incurred while he is a partner.

[216]   See generally para **[11.74]** et seq.

[217]   However, in relation to persons who did not deal with the firm while he was a partner, it seems that the advertisement of his departure in *Iris Oifigiúil* is sufficient notice to them on the basis that under s 36(2) of the 1890 Act, notice in *Iris Oifigiúil* is notice to such third parties (of the change in the firm) and under s 7 of the 1907 Act, such general principles of partnership law apply to limited partnerships, unless they are inconsistent therewith.

[218]   Partnership Act 1890, s 36(1). See generally, para **[11.85]** et seq.

sufficient notice to such third parties. As has been noted, s 9 of the 1907 Act requires any change in the partners in a firm to be registered with the Registrar of Companies.[219] While the 1907 Act is silent on this point, it is thought that, in the same way as the registration of a change in the register of business names is not notice to persons who had dealings with the firm,[220] so too a change in the register of limited partnerships is not notice to such persons of the departure of a general partner. Although the register of companies is a public register, one cannot expect third parties to check this register in order to determine whether the general partner they have dealt with in the past is still a partner in the limited partnership. Indeed, the 1907 Act itself seems to acknowledge the fact that something more than simply amending the register is generally needed to put third parties on notice by providing that, although the change of a general partner to a limited partner (and of the assignment of a limited partner's interest to another limited partner) is required to be registered in the Registrar of Companies, s 10(1) of the 1907 Act also requires both events to be advertised in *Iris Oifigiúil*.

Change from general partner to limited partner

[28.89] It is possible for a general partner in a limited partnership to become a limited partner, provided, of course, there remains at least one general partner in the firm, as required by s 4(2) of the 1907 Act. To become a limited partner, an existing general partner must contribute capital to the firm, unless he has already done so as a general partner.[221] It seems that the conversion of a general partner to a limited partner would require the consent of the general partners, but not the consent of the limited partners[222] on the grounds that the exposure of the other general partners for the firm's liabilities will be affected by a reduction in the number of general partners, while the limited partners, whose liability remains limited, will not be so affected.

[28.90] As regards obligations incurred by the firm prior to a general partner becoming a limited partner, it is clear that the former general partner will remain liable for those obligations, as if he were still a general partner. In addition, the change of a general partner to a limited partner will not be deemed to be effective until it has been advertised in *Iris Oifigiúil*. Section 10(1) of the 1907 Act states that:

> Notice of any arrangement or transaction under which any person will cease to be a general partner in any firm, and will become a limited partner in that firm, or under which the share of a limited partner in a firm will be assigned to any person, shall be forthwith advertised in [*Iris Oifigiúil*],[223] and until notice of the arrangement or transaction is so

---

[219] See para **[28.68]**.

[220] See para **[3.82]**.

[221] Limited Partnerships Act 1907, s 4(2).

[222] This view is consistent with the other provisions of the 1907 Act, ie the limited partners are prohibited from taking part in the management of the firm (s 6(1)), a limited partner may assign his share to an assignee who becomes a limited partner with the consent of the general partners only (s 6(5)(b)) and a person may be introduced as a partner without the consent of the limited partners (s 6(5)(e)). For a contrary view see l'Anson Banks, *Lindley & Banks on Partnership* (20th edn, 2017) at para 31-17.

[223] Under s 4 of the Adaptation of Enactments Act 1922 the term 'Dublin Gazette' is adapted to read '*Iris Oifigiúil*'.

advertised the arrangement or transaction shall, for the purposes of this Act, be deemed to be of no effect.

[28.91] Thus, the general partner who becomes a limited partner will not benefit from limited liability until that fact is advertised in *Iris Oifigiúil*. The form of this advertisement is set out in the Limited Partnerships Rules 1907.[224] However, advertising in *Iris Oifigiúil* is not sufficient because s 9 of the 1907 Act also requires any change in the 'liability of any partner by reason of his becoming a limited instead of a general partner or a general instead of a limited partner' to be notified to the Registrar of Companies. As already noted,[225] if any failure is made in complying with the notification to the Registrar, s 5 of the 1907 Act provides that 'every limited partner shall be deemed to be a general partner' and therefore the putative limited partner would be deemed to still be a general partner.

[28.92] In relation to pre-existing customers of the firm, it is thought that the requirement in s 10(1) of the 1907 Act that the change be advertised in *Iris Oifigiúil* is not inconsistent with s 36(2) of the 1890 Act and therefore that s 36(2) is not struck down by s 7 of the 1907 Act. Section 36(2) provides that a notice of a change in a firm in *Iris Oifigiúil* operates only 'as notice as to persons who had not dealings with the firm [ie, pre-existing customers] before the date of the dissolution or change so advertised'. For this reason, s 10(1) of the 1907 Act must be read as being subject to s 36(2) of the 1890 Act.[226] Accordingly, the prudent course of action is for pre-existing customers of the firm to be personally notified of any change of a general partner to a limited partner.[227]

Ordinary partnership becoming a limited partnership

[28.93] Another issue which concerns the liability of a general partner arises when partners in an ordinary partnership, without changing the name of the firm, change it to a limited partnership, with the consequence that some of the partners acquire limited liability. It is thought that third parties who deal with the firm before the change are entitled to rely on s 36(1) of the 1890 Act to treat all apparent members of the firm as still being members, until they have notice of any change thereof.[228] Thus, the partner in an ordinary partnership who becomes a limited partner in a limited partnership cannot rely on his limited liability *vis-à-vis* third parties who dealt with him as a partner in the ordinary partnership, unless they are on notice of the change. In this regard, the registration of the limited partnership is insufficient. Similarly, the advertisement of the change in *Iris Oifigiúil* is thought to be insufficient, as under s 36(2) of the 1890 Act,

---

[224] SR & O 1907, No 1020. Paragraph 4 requires the notice to read as follows: 'Pursuant to section 10 of the Limited Partnerships Act, 1907. Notice is hereby given that under an arrangement entered into on the ... day of ... 190 , ... ceases to be a General Partner and becomes a Limited Partner in the firm of ... carrying on business as ... at ... Dated this ... day of ... ,190 . Signature... Witness to the Signature of ... (Name) ... (Address)...'

[225] See para **[28.70]**.

[226] See generally in relation to the application of s 36(2) of the 1890 Act, para **[11.71]** et seq.

[227] For a contrary view see Prime and Scanlan, *The Law of Partnership* (1995), p 352.

[228] See generally para **[11.85]** et seq. See also l'Anson Banks, *Lindley & Banks on Partnership* (20th edn, 2017) at para 29-38.

such an advertisement is only notice to those persons who had no previous dealings with the firm.[229] Accordingly, the prudent course of action is for the limited partner to give notice to each of the third parties who had dealings with him as a partner in the ordinary partnership.

[28.94] Similarly, this change is not required to be advertised in *Iris Oifigiúil* to be effective, since under s 10(1) of the 1907 Act, that section refers only to the change in a limited partnership (of a general partner to a limited partner). It does not apply to a conversion of an ordinary partnership to a limited partnership.[230]

Liability of a Limited Partner

[28.95] Under s 4(2) of the 1907 Act, the liability of a limited partner for the debts and obligations of the firm is limited to his capital contribution.[231] Hereunder, consideration will be given to the extent of this liability, in particular where the limited partner becomes a general partner or where he ceases to be a limited partner.

[28.96] One of the criticisms which can be levelled at the 1907 Act is that, although limiting the liability of a limited partner in this way, it does not expressly exclude the personal liability of every limited partner for the debts and obligations of the firm.[232] Thus, the position is that under ss 9 and 10 of the 1890 Act, a limited partner is liable for the debts and obligations of the firm, albeit that under s 4(2) of the 1907 Act, this liability is limited. The 1907 Act does not contain any provision protecting the limited partner or his separate property from execution or other proceedings for enforcing a partnership debt.[233] However, it is apprehended that any judgment obtained against a limited partner must, of necessity, be limited, so that he enjoys the protection of his

---

229 See l'Anson Banks, *Lindley & Banks on Partnership* (20th edn, 2017) at para 29-38.

230 The reference to 'any firm' on the second line of s 10(1) of the 1907 Act must be construed as a reference to a limited partnership in light of the reference to 'a limited partner in that firm' on the third line thereof.

231 In this regard, the wording of s 4(2) may be criticised for being somewhat vague, since it provides that a limited partnership must consist of at least one limited partner who shall at the time of entering the partnership contribute capital and who shall not be liable for the debts and obligations of the firm beyond the amount so contributed. It could be argued on the basis of this wording that the measure of the limited partner's liability is in fact a sum equal to the capital contributed by him, so that if his capital is exhausted by the partnership, he still has to come up with an equivalent amount to meet the partnership debts. However the use in s 4(2) of the phrase 'shall not be liable for the debts and obligations of the firm beyond the *amounts so contributed*' indicates that this is not the case. In addition, support for this interpretation is provided by s 4(3) which would be meaningless if the limited partner was in fact to be liable for double the amount which he had contributed, since it provides for the limited partner to be liable to the extent of any amount of capital which he has received back from the partnership.

232 Ie, under the Partnership Act 1890, ss 9 and 10.

233 Cf the position of a limited partner in an investment limited partnership under s 22(1) of the Investment Limited Partnerships Act 1994. Parts of this paragraph (as it appeared in the first edition of this work) were quoted by the Law Commission and the Scottish Law Commission in their 2001 *Limited Partnerships Act 1907: A Joint Consultation Paper* (Consultation Paper No 161; Discussion Paper No 118) at para 4.3, albeit that they did not share the same concern. (contd.../)

statutory entitlement to limited liability.[234] One possible way to deal with this issue would be to provide, presumably in the Rules of the Superior Courts, that enforcement of a judgment against a limited partnership sued in its firm name cannot be executed without the consent of the High Court.[235]

Limited partner becoming a general partner

[28.97] Unlike the change of a general partner to a limited partner, the opposite change does not require to be advertised in *Iris Oifigiúil,* although the change in the registration details must be notified to the Registrar of Companies under s 9 of the 1907 Act. As with the change from a general partner to a limited partner, it is thought that such a change would require the consent of the general partners, but not the consent of the limited partners.[236] This is because the general partners are agreeing that the former limited partner will henceforth have authority to bind them by his actions and in this respect their exposure to liability is affected. In contrast, the limited partners, whose liability is limited, will not be affected to the same degree.

[28.98] The notification to the Registrar of Companies of the change of a limited partner to a general partner is a trap for unwary partners. This is because the failure to properly notify the Registrar of this fact results in the firm not being properly registered under s 5 of the 1907 Act and consequently in *all* the limited partners being deemed to be general partners. Accordingly, the limited partners must be vigilant to ensure that all changes to the limited partnership are properly and punctually registered, even those changes, such as the addition of a general partner, which prima facie appear to be in the interests of third parties dealing with the firm by adding another partner with unlimited liability.

[28.99] Once the limited partner becomes a general partner, he does not lose his limited liability in respect of the firm's debts and obligations which were incurred prior to this

---

[233] (...contd) However, in their later *Partnership Law: Report on a Reference under Section 3(1)(e) of the Law Commissions Act 1965* (Law Com No 283; Scot Law Com No 192) at para 17.19 they observed that most of those who had responded to the consultation favoured some clarification being included in the 1907 Act to the effect that s 4(2) excludes any liability, direct or indirect, beyond the amount of the limited partner's capital contribution.

[234] Unless, of course, the limited partner has lost this protection. See further para **[28.104]** et seq. In *Best & Anor v Ghose & Ors* [2018] IEHC 376 (an action against a limited partnership for an account of its management of a particular fund), Baker J refused to grant relief against the fifteenth defendant, a limited partner, on the grounds that it was not involved in the management of the firm and had no documents relating to the fund.

[235] This is the situation in some jurisdictions; see for example the Queensland Partnership (Limited Liability) Act 1988, s 21(2). This reference (as it appeared in the first edition of this work) was noted by the Law Commission and the Scottish Law Commission in their 2001 *Limited Partnerships Act 1907: A Joint Consultation Paper* (Consultation Paper No 161; Discussion Paper No 118) at para 4.5.

[236] This view is consistent with the other provisions of the 1907 Act, ie the limited partners are prohibited from taking part in the management of the firm (s 6(1)), a limited partner may assign his share to an assignee who becomes a limited partner with the consent of the general partners only (s 6(5)(b)) and a person may be introduced as a partner without the consent of the limited partners (s 6(5)(e)). For a contrary view see l'Anson Banks, *Lindley & Banks on Partnership* (20th edn, 2017) at para 31-23.

date. Obviously, his liability will be unlimited for the debts and obligations incurred thereafter.

Termination of liability of limited partner for future debts by assignment

[28.100] Under s 6(5)(b) of the 1907 Act, a limited partner may, with the consent of the general partners, assign his share in the partnership. Under s 10(1) of the 1907 Act, the liability of the limited partner will cease, as regards future debts of the firm, on the date of the advertisement of the assignment in *Iris Oifigiúil*. The form of notice is set out in the Limited Partnerships Rules of 1907.[237] It is worth noting that if the assignment is advertised in *Iris Oifigiúil*, but the change in the details of the partners is not registered with the Registrar of Companies, as required by s 9(1)(d) of the 1907 Act, the new limited partner will be deemed to be a general partner under s 5 of the 1907 Act.[238] Therefore, any person who is taking an assignment of a limited partner's share, should ensure that the registration of this change is duly completed.

Other ways of reducing liability of limited partner for future debts

[28.101] A limited partner who dies, becomes bankrupt or leaves the firm will, pursuant to s 36(3) of the 1890 Act, have no liability for future debts of the firm which are incurred after the date of death or bankruptcy and in the case of his departure, will have no liability for future debts to people who began to deal with the firm after his departure.[239] However, as with partners in ordinary partnerships, in the case of the departure of a limited partner, notice of departure should be given to pre-existing customers of the firm. This is because s 36(1) of the 1890 Act allows persons who had dealt with the firm prior to the departure of a limited partner to treat him as continuing to be a partner until they are on notice of his departure. In addition, notice of departure should be advertised in *Iris Oifigiúil*, since this will be deemed to be notice of the departure to persons who had no dealings with the firm prior to the departure,[240] thereby reducing the likelihood of such persons claiming that the limited partner continued to hold himself out as a partner.[241]

Termination of liability of limited partners for past debts

[28.102] It has been noted elsewhere in this work that where a partner leaves an ordinary partnership, he remains liable for obligations which were incurred while he was a partner.[242] In a limited partnership, when a limited partner leaves the firm, he also remains liable for the obligations incurred while he was a member of the firm, subject of course to the amount of his capital contribution.[243]

---

[237] SR & O 1907, No 1020. Paragraph 4 requires the notice to read as follows: 'Pursuant to section 10 of the Limited Partnerships Act, 1907. Notice is hereby given that under an arrangement entered into on the ... day of ... 190 ... , ... of the firm of ... has assigned his share as a Limited Partner in the above-named firm to ... Dated this...day of ... ,190 ... .Signature ... Witness to the Signature of ... (Name) ... (Address) ...'.

[238] See para **[28.70]**.

[239] See generally para **[11.53]** et seq.

[240] Partnership Act 1890, s 36(2). See generally para **[11.71]**.

[241] See generally in relation to such holding out, paras **[11.75]** and **[7.01]** et seq.

[242] See para **[11.34]** et seq.

[243] Limited Partnerships Act 1907, s 4(2).

When limited partner assigns share

[28.103] The assignment by a limited partner of his share in the firm is permitted by the terms of s 6(5)(b) of the 1907 Act. The 1907 Act is silent as to the effect of such assignment on the obligations of the assignor. It is apprehended that when a limited partner assigns his share to an assignee, he remains liable for any past debts and the new limited partner is liable only for the future debts of the firm.[244] Support for this view is provided by the wording of s 6(5)(b) of the 1907 Act which states simply that 'the assignee shall become a limited partner with all the rights of the assignor'. It is suggested that a more explicit reference would have been required to displace the general position under the 1890 Act, namely that a partner remains liable for debts which were incurred while he was a partner.[245] Furthermore, while a reference is made in s 6(5)(b) to the assignee having all the 'rights of the assignor', no reference is made to the liability of the assignee for the obligations of the assignor. It is to be noted that this contrasts with the express provision in s 18(2) of the Investment Limited Partnerships Act 1994 which provides that the assignee shall 'as of the date of assignment become a limited partner with all the rights *and obligations* of the assignor relating to the investment limited partnership'. Nonetheless, it would be prudent for an assignee to obtain an indemnity from the limited partner in respect of the debts of the firm which were incurred while the assignor was a limited partner.

Loss of Limited Liability by Limited Partner

[28.104] Section 4(2) of the 1907 Act establishes that the limited partner is not liable for the debts or obligations of the firm beyond the amount of capital contributed by him. Unlike a limited partner in an investment limited partnership,[246] a limited partner is only liable for the amounts actually contributed and account is not taken of any amount which is undertaken by him to be contributed.

[28.105] The limited liability which is granted to limited partners can be justified in principle, ie, under the law of ordinary partnerships each partner is personally liable to an unlimited degree for the liabilities of the firm since third parties who deal with a partnership are in fact dealing with the partners individually. This is because a partnership is not a separate legal entity but an aggregate of its members.[247] It follows that there is no entity to be liable and the partners themselves are personally liable for the liabilities of the firm. However this rationale is not present for limited partners, since they are prohibited[248] from taking part in the management of the firm's business and any third parties who deal with the firm cannot be regarded as dealing with them, but rather

---

[244] This analysis (as it appeared in the first edition of this work) was quoted by the Law Commission and the Scottish Law Commission in their 2001 *Limited Partnerships Act 1907: A Joint Consultation Paper* (Consultation Paper No 161; Discussion Paper No 118) at paras 4.43 and 5.25.

[245] See generally para [11.34] et seq. See also l'Anson Banks, *Lindley & Banks on Partnership* (20th edn, 2017) at para 30-25.

[246] Investment Limited Partnerships Act 1994, s 3, see para [29.90].

[247] See generally in relation to the unlimited liability of a partner in an ordinary partnership, para [11.04] et seq and as to the nature of a partnership generally, see para [3.04].

[248] Limited Partnerships Act 1907, s 6(1).

with the general partners. Accordingly, the limited partners are granted limited liability, unless they contravene this prohibition on managing the partnership business.

[28.106] Since the *raison d'être* for limited partnerships is to provide limited liability for the limited partners, it is important to consider the five instances in which this limit on liability may be lost.

1. If a limited partner takes part in the management of the partnership

[28.107] Section 6(1) of the 1907 Act provides that:

> If a limited partner takes part in the management of the partnership business he shall be liable for all debts and obligations of the firm incurred while he so takes part in the management as though he were a general partner.

Since the limited partner will be liable 'as though he were a general partner', if he breaches this prohibition on participating in the management of the firm, it follows that he will lose his limited liability.[249] Even in such a case, his liability may be limited in time, since his unlimited liability will only apply to debts and obligations which were incurred during the period in which the limited partner managed the firm.[250] It is important to note that the guilty limited partner is liable *as though he* were a general partner, but he is not converted into a general partner.[251] The latter conversion would require the consent of all the general partners.[252]

2. Failure of firm to register in accordance with the 1907 Act

[28.108] A limited partner is deemed to be a general partner and thus subject to unlimited liability if there is a failure to register the limited partnership or any change to its registration details in accordance with the 1907 Act. This issue is considered earlier in this chapter.[253]

---

249 See para **[28.105]**.

250 The observations of Cooke J in *Certain Limited Partners in Henderson PFI Secondary Fund II LP (a firm) v Henderson PFI Secondary Fund II LP (a firm) and others* [2013] QB 934 at para 69 of his judgment could be read as implying that during any period for which a limited partner takes part in the management of the firm, he is liable for all of the partnership's debts and liabilities, rather than those incurred during the period for which he takes part in the management of the firm. However, it is submitted that this is not correct.

251 Cooke J in *Certain Limited Partners in Henderson PFI Secondary Fund II LP (a firm) v Henderson PFI Secondary Fund II LP (a firm) and others* [2013] QB 934 at para 70 of his judgment noted that, for the period during which a limited partner takes part in the management of the firm, he 'supplants the general partner and becomes liable as if he were the general partner'. However, it is submitted that this is not correct – such a limited partner would not supplant one or more existing general partners, but would instead become liable as if he were also a general partner.

252 But it is contended that such a conversion does not require the consent of the limited partners. See para **[28.89]**.

253 See para **[28.63]** et seq and para **[28.68]** et seq.

3. Liability between members of the firm may be in excess of capital

[28.109] The limited liability of a limited partner is grounded in the statement in s 4(2) of the 1907 Act that the limited partners are not liable 'for the debts of the firm' beyond the amount of capital contributed by the limited partner. While the liability of the limited partner is limited as regards the debts of the firm *vis-à-vis* creditors, it is not limited as regards his liability to his fellow partners. Therefore, a limited partner who had contributed say capital of £50 to a firm which had trading losses of £13,000 could have agreed with his co-partners to be liable for £1,920 of those trading losses.[254] For this reason, limited partnership agreements usually record the proportion in which the firm's trading losses are to be divided between the partners.

4. General partner becoming a limited partner

[28.110] As already noted,[255] s 10 of the 1907 Act provides that a failure to advertise a change in the status of a general partner to a limited partner in *Iris Oifigiúil* will result in that partner continuing to be a general partner with the consequent unlimited liability. Thus, although technically not a 'loss' of limited liability by a limited partner, since the general partner will never have become a limited partner, it is an example of a situation in which the intended limited partner will not gain limited liability.

5. Withdrawal of capital

[28.111] Section 4(3) of the 1907 Act provides that the limited partner who withdraws his capital or a part of his capital is liable for the debts and obligations of the firm up to the amount so drawn out. Thus, his limited liability is not lost in the true sense of the word, since the limited partner only remains liable up to the amount of capital withdrawn, which obviously can never exceed the amount of capital which he initially contributed. The rationale for this section is clearly that, as limited liability is granted to a limited partner on the basis of the limited partner contributing capital, the amount of this capital which is available to creditors should not be reduced by its withdrawal.[256]

[28.112] The prohibition in s 4(3) of 1907 Act on a limited partner withdrawing his capital only applies 'during the continuance of the partnership' of which he is a member. Thus, when the partnership is dissolved or he is no longer a member of the firm, there is no prohibition on his withdrawing his capital.[257]

---

[254] These were the amounts in *MacCarthaigh v Daly* [1985] IR 73. See also the English case of *Reed v Young* [1986] 1 WLR 649.

[255] See para **[28.90]**.

[256] The Law Commission and the Scottish Law Commission in their 2001 *Limited Partnerships Act 1907: A Joint Consultation Paper* (Consultation Paper No 161; Discussion Paper No 118) at para 2.17 noted that this appeared to be the intention behind s 4(3), quoting from both this paragraph in the first edition of this work and from I'Anson Banks, *Lindley & Banks on Partnership* (17th edn, 1995) at para 30.12 (now at para 30.15 of I'Anson Banks, *Lindley & Banks on Partnership* (20th edn, 2017)).

[257] This view is in keeping with the provision in the second part of s 6(2) of the 1907 Act that the mental incapacity of a limited partner is not a ground for dissolution of the partnership, unless the mentally incapacitated partner's share cannot otherwise be ascertained or realised, ie that section clearly contemplates the withdrawal of capital by a former partner.

VI.   RIGHTS OF PARTNERS INTER SE

Management of the Firm by Limited Partners

[28.113] The restricted role of the limited partners in the management of a limited partnership has been considered earlier in this chapter.[258]

Management of the Firm by General Partners

[28.114] The vesting of the management of the limited partnership in the general partners is achieved indirectly, since it is not referred to in the 1907 Act. Rather, s 5 of the 1890 Act governs this situation. This provides that every partner is the agent of the firm and his other partners for the purpose of the business of the partnership.[259] This provision is supplemented, in relation to general partners, by s 6(5)(a) of the 1907 Act which provides that, subject to any express or implied agreement between the partners, '[a]ny difference arising as to ordinary matters connected with the partnership business may be decided by a majority of the general partners.' Like a partner in an ordinary partnership, the general partner owes his partners, whether limited or general, a fiduciary duty in regard to his management of the firm.[260]

Acts of general partner binding on limited partners

[28.115] It is clear that the limited partners will be bound by the actions of the general partners relating to the ordinary business of the firm, even though they may not have been consulted.[261] However, where the act in question does not relate to the ordinary course of business of the firm, the limited partners will not be bound. Thus, for example, any change in the partnership business will not bind the limited partners. This can be justified in principle since the limited partners contributed their capital to the original partnership business, and not any changed partnership business. Instead, it is contended that s 24(8) of the 1890 Act applies, so as to require the consent of all partners, including the limited partners, to any such change.[262]

---

[258] See para **[28.78]**.

[259] By virtue of s 7 of the 1907 Act, the 1890 Act applies to limited partnerships unless inconsistent with the 1907 Act.

[260] See generally in relation to this duty, para **[15.01]** et seq. See the Ontario Court of Appeal case of *PWA Corp v Gemini Group Automated Distribution System Inc* (1994) 15 OR (3d) 730, regarding the fiduciary obligation of a nominee of a limited partner on the board of directors of a general partner. See also the judgment of Norris J in *BBGP Managing General Partner Ltd v Babcock & Brown Global Partners* [2011] Ch 296, in which he noted that the principle that partners owe one another a 'duty of honesty and good faith' in respect of the business of the partnership applies equally to limited partnerships and ordinary partnerships. See also Buckely, 'Duties of Directors of a General Partner to the Limited Partners' (1993) 67 Australian LJ 934.

[261] Since a limited partner, by virtue of s 5 of the 1890 Act, is bound by the acts of the general partners within the ordinary course business of the firm, see para **[10.82]** et seq.

[262] See also para **[28.80]**.

Admission of New Partners

[28.116] Under s 6(5)(d) of the 1907 Act, unless expressly or impliedly agreed by all the partners to the contrary, the consent of the limited partners is not required for the admission of a new general partner or a new limited partner. Thus, s 24(7) of the 1890 Act will apply (as modified by s 6(5)(d) of the 1907 Act), so that unless agreed otherwise, the consent of all the general partners only will be required for the admission of a partner.[263]

Assignment of a Partner's Share

[28.117] The assignment of a partner's share is dealt with in the 1907 Act and the 1890 Act. A limited partner's share may be assigned under the assignment provisions in the 1907 Act or the more restrictive assignment provisions in the 1890 Act. Since the 1907 Act does not refer to the assignment of a general partner's share, a general partner may only assign his share pursuant to the 1890 Act.

Assignment of a share in a limited partnership under the 1890 Act

[28.118] In the context of ordinary partnerships, it has been noted that, subject to contrary agreement between the partners, a partner may assign his interest in his firm to a third party under s 31 of the 1890 Act.[264] Broadly speaking, the assignee may not interfere in the management of the firm and is entitled to receive the assignor's share of the profits. The assignor remains as the partner in the firm and remains liable as such, despite his assignment of the financial rights attaching to his share. Both a limited partner and a general partner may assign their shares in a limited partnership in this fashion.[265]

Assignment of a limited partner's share under 1907 Act

[28.119] In addition to the rights of a partner to assign his share under s 31 of the 1890 Act, a limited partner in a limited partnership has a more expansive right of assignment granted by the 1907 Act. Under s 6(5)(b) of the 1907 Act, subject to any express or implied agreement to the contrary between all the partners, a limited partner may, with the consent of the general partners, assign his share in the partnership. Unlike an assignment under the 1890 Act, an assignment under this section results in the assignee taking the place of the assignor in the partnership. However, s 10(1) of the 1907 Act provides that the arrangement or transaction under which the share is transferred must be advertised in *Iris Oifigiúil*[266] and until it is so advertised, the assignment is deemed to

---

263 The consent of the general partners is also required for the admission of a limited partner by assignment of an existing limited partner's share: Limited Partnerships Act 1907, s 6(5)(b). See para **[28.119]**.

264 Partnership Act 1890, s 31. See generally para **[19.12]** et seq.

265 This was quoted (by refererence to, among other texts, the first edition of this work) by the Law Commission and the Scottish Law Commission in their 2001 *Limited Partnerships Act 1907: A Joint Consultation Paper* (Consultation Paper No 161; Discussion Paper No 118) at para 5.23.

266 Adaptation of the term 'Dublin Gazette' in s 10(1) of the 1907 Act, as required by s 4 of the Adaptation of Enactments Act 1922.

be of no effect. It has been noted that the assignee should ensure that the change in the firm's membership as a result of the assignment is registered with the Registrar of Companies, as required by s 9 of the 1907 Act, in order to ensure that the partnership is not deemed to be an ordinary partnership.[267]

Incoming Limited Partner is subject to Previously Agreed Variation

[28.120] The assignee of the share of a limited partner in a firm is a derivative partner, in the sense that he takes over the existing share of a partner in the firm *in specie*. As a derivative partner, and in contrast to the position of a newly admitted partner,[268] he will be bound by any variation of the terms of the partnership agreement which was previously consented to by the assignor, even where the variation was not brought to the derivative partner's attention.[269]

VII. FINANCIAL RIGHTS OF PARTNERS IN A LIMITED PARTNERSHIP

Capital of the Firm

[28.121] The capital of a limited partnership is treated differently than that of an ordinary partnership. Limited liability is granted to the limited partners on the basis that the creditors will, instead of having access to the unlimited personal liability of the limited partners, have access to the capital which has been contributed by those partners. Thus under s 4(2) of the 1907 Act, for a limited partnership to exist, it must have a certain amount of capital which may be nominal[270] but which has been contributed by all the limited partners. In contrast to the position of limited partners, the general partners are not required to contribute any capital to the firm,[271] since they are liable to the firm's creditors to an unlimited degree. There is, however, nothing to stop them contributing capital to the firm in the same way as a partner in an ordinary partnership.

[28.122] The importance of a capital contribution by the limited partners is emphasised by the fact that where the limited partners have merely agreed to contribute capital, as distinct from having actually contributed capital to the partnership, a limited partnership will not have come into existence.[272] Thus, as happened in *MacCarthaigh v Daly*,[273] where the capital is not contributed at the formation of the partnership, the putative limited partners will be partners in an ordinary partnership and have unlimited liability. That case also illustrates that care should be taken to ensure that the correct amount of capital contribution (and details of whether it was contributed by way of cash or

---

267 Limited Partnerships Act 1907, s 5. See para **[28.70]**.
268 For the position of a newly admitted partner in the context of variations of the partnership agreement, see para **[5.24]** et seq.
269 *Const v Harris* (1824) T & R 496.
270 *Dickson v MacGregor* (1992) SLT 83.
271 Like partners in ordinary partnerships, see para **[17.07]**.
272 Although there may be an ordinary partnership, if they satisfy the definition of partnership in s 1(1) of the 1890 Act. See generally para **[2.01]** et seq and see *MacCarthaigh v Daly* [1985] IR 73.
273 *MacCarthaigh v Daly* [1985] IR 73.

otherwise) is notified to the Registrar of Companies on the Form LP1 and on the Form LP3.[274] Otherwise, the putative limited partners will be deemed to be general partners.[275]

[28.123] The 1907 Act also contemplates the possibility of a limited partner increasing his capital contribution during the life of the partnership,[276] in which case his liability would be increased correspondingly. On the other hand, the 1907 Act prohibits a limited partner from withdrawing any part of his capital contribution during the partnership, and if he does so, he is liable for the debts and obligations of the firm up to the amount so withdrawn.[277] This is, however, an illusory deterrent since clearly the limited partner would have been liable to the same amount if he had left the capital in the firm. Save for these provisions, the law of ordinary partnerships regarding capital applies to limited partnerships, so that, subject to contrary agreement between the partners:

(a)   a partner, limited or general, is not entitled to interest on capital subscribed by him before the ascertainment of profits,[278] and

(b)   any advance beyond the amount of capital which a partner has agreed to subscribe is subject to interest at 5% per annum.[279]

Sharing of Profit and Loss of the Firm

[28.124] The 1907 Act is silent regarding the sharing of profits and losses between all the partners in a limited partnership. Accordingly, s 24(1) of the 1890 Act determines this issue and therefore, the limited and general partners will share equally in the profits and trading[280] losses of the business, in the absence of any agreement to the contrary.

Filing of Accounts

[28.125] It has been observed that in general, partnerships are not required to file accounts.[281] The rationale for this exemption is that the members of a partnership have unlimited liability and therefore third parties need not be as concerned about their financial affairs as in the case of say limited liability companies. This principle applies equally to limited partnerships, since there will be at least one general partner who has

---

[274]   Neither the Form LP1 nor the Form LP3 provides for the limited partner to confirm the date on which the capital contribution was made, but each limited partner must include a date below both its confirmation of the '[a]mount contributed' by it, and its signature, on the Form LP1 (implying that the contribution must have already been made).

[275]   See para **[28.67]**.

[276]   Limited Partnerships Act 1907, s 9(1)(f).

[277]   Limited Partnerships Act 1907, s 4(3).

[278]   Partnership Act 1890, s 24(4).

[279]   Partnership Act 1890, s 24(3).

[280]   Note the important distinction between on the one hand the fact that the limited partners may be liable inter se for the trading losses of a firm and on the other hand, the fact that they have limited liability *vis-à-vis* third parties for losses of the firm, see para **[28.14]** and para **[28.109]**. This analysis (as it appeared in the first edition of this work) was noted by the Law Commission and the Scottish Law Commission in their 2001 *Limited Partnerships Act 1907: A Joint Consultation Paper* (Consultation Paper No 161; Discussion Paper No 118) at para 5.16.

[281]   See paras **[3.19]** and **[14.64]** et seq.

unlimited liability for the liabilities of the firm. However, the European Communities (Accounts) Regulations 1993[282] require a limited partnership, where all the general partners[283] are companies with limited liability or their equivalent,[284] to file accounts, as if it was a company under the Companies Act 2014.[285] The rationale for this rule is clearly that in such a limited partnership, all the partners will have an effective limit on their liability. For this reason, these partnerships, although *de jure* partnerships, have de facto limited liability for *all* the partners and should be treated as being akin to limited liability companies rather than true partnerships.

VIII. DISSOLUTION OTHERWISE THAN BY COURT

[28.126] Like most aspects of the life of a limited partnership, its dissolution is also dealt with by a combination of the 1907 Act and the 1890 Act. The provisions regarding dissolution which are contained in the 1890 Act will generally apply to a limited partnership. Thus, for example, subject to contrary agreement between the partners, the death or bankruptcy of a *general partner* will dissolve a limited partnership.[286] Any such contrary agreement should be between all the partners (ie general and limited) as required by s 33(1) of 1890 Act. However, in three specific situations the 1907 Act disapplies the 1890 Act in its application to limited partnerships, namely:

1. Section 6(2) of the 1907 Act states that the death[287] or bankruptcy[288] of a limited partner will not dissolve a limited partnership.[289]

2. Section 6(5)(c) of the 1907 Act states that, subject to a contrary agreement between the partners, the partners in a limited partnership are not entitled to dissolve the firm by reason of a limited partner suffering his share to be charged for his separate debt.

3. Section 6(5)(e) of the 1907 Act provides that, subject to a contrary agreement between the partners, a limited partner may not dissolve a partnership by notice.[290]

Death or Bankruptcy of a Limited Partner

[28.127] Section 6(2) of the 1907 Act which provides that the death or bankruptcy of a limited partner will not dissolve a limited partnership is the cause of some uncertainty,

---

[282] SI 396/1993.
[283] Regulation 6 refers to 'partnerships where all the members thereof who do not have a limit on their liability'.
[284] Ie, entities which are equivalent to companies with limited liability, see further para **[14.66]** et seq.
[285] References to the Companies (Amendment) Act 1986 in the European Communities (Accounts) Regulations 1993 are to be construed as references to the Companies Act 2014 (Companies Act 2014, s 5 and Sch 6).
[286] Application of s 33(1) of the 1890 Act pursuant to the terms of s 7 of the 1907 Act.
[287] As to the position of a corporate partner which is wound up or put into examinership, see generally para **[23.36]**.
[288] As to the position of a corporate partner which becomes insolvent, see generally para **[23.40]**.
[289] It is contended that this is subject to contrary agreement between the parties, see para **[28.45]**.
[290] See further para **[28.44]**.

since it is not clear what is meant by the statement that the partnership will not dissolve. As is noted earlier in this work, the term dissolution may mean a general or a technical dissolution.[291] A general dissolution is a change in the membership of the firm leading to its winding up. A technical dissolution is a change in the membership of a firm where the firm continues to operate as before the change.

[28.128] If the term 'dissolution' as used in s 6(2) is taken to mean a technical dissolution, it creates numerous practical difficulties. Thus, it would prohibit the return of capital to the deceased partner's estate or the bankrupt partner, on the basis that they are still members of the firm and it would mean that the personal representative and the trustee in bankruptcy would become partners in his place. Such a consequence of the death or bankruptcy of a limited partner is difficult to justify since it purports to treat the firm as a separate legal entity which is contrary to the accepted meaning of a partnership as constituting the partners for the time being in the firm.[292] These problems do not arise if the term 'dissolved' is interpreted as referring to a general dissolution of the limited partnership. On this basis, s 6(2) provides that while the death or bankruptcy of a limited partner does not give rise to a general dissolution, it does not prohibit a technical dissolution. Thus, there is a technical dissolution of a partnership every time there is a death or bankruptcy of a limited partner.[293] In this way, the representative of the deceased partner or the trustee in bankruptcy is not entitled to force a sale of the partnership assets or a winding up of its affairs.[294] However, they are entitled to a return of the limited partner's capital, since the partnership has been technically dissolved by the departure of the limited partner.[295]

---

[291] See para **[23.07]**.

[292] See generally in relation to the nature of a partnership, para **[3.04]**.

[293] Unless, of course, there is an agreement to the contrary amongst the partners providing, eg, for the personal representative of the deceased partner or the trustee in bankruptcy to take the limited partner's place. As to the possibility of the partners agreeing that the death or bankruptcy of a partner will not dissolve the partnership, see para **[28.45]**. Interpreting s 6(2) of the 1907 Act as referring to a general dissolution, but not a technical dissolution, also assists in reconciling the conflict between s 6(2) and s 4(2) of the 1907 Act which would otherwise arise on the death or bankruptcy of a sole limited partner. Thus, under s 6(2), the death or bankruptcy of a limited partner will lead to the technical (rather than the general) dissolution of the partnership but where he is the sole limited partner, s 4(2) will take precedence so that it will be generally dissolved, para **[28.129]**.

[294] Which would be the case under the Partnership Act 1890, s 39. See generally, para **[26.28]**.

[295] Thus the original partnership is not 'continuing' which, if it were, would prevent the return of capital under the terms of s 4(3) of the 1907 Act, see para **[28.112]**. The personal representative or trustee in bankruptcy may also rely on s 42(1) of the 1890 Act to claim any profits arising after the technical dissolution of the firm, where those profits are attributable to the use by the firm of the former limited partner's share of the partnership assets or interest on that share, as to which see para **[26.60]** et seq. This analysis (as it appeared in the first edition of this work) was noted by the Law Commission and the Scottish Law Commission in their 2001 *Limited Partnerships Act 1907: A Joint Consultation Paper* (Consultation Paper No 161; Discussion Paper No 118) at para 5.33.

Where the sole limited partner dies or goes bankrupt

[28.129] It has been concluded that s 6(2) of the 1907 Act must be interpreted as preventing the general dissolution of a partnership where a limited partner dies or becomes bankrupt. A valid criticism that may be made of this section is that it does not contemplate a situation where the bankruptcy or death occurs to the sole limited partner. In this regard, one must bear in mind that s 4(2) of the 1907 Act defines a limited partnership as a partnership with at least one general partner and one limited partner. Therefore, if the sole limited partner dies or becomes bankrupt, the partnership will no longer comply with s 4(2) of the 1907 Act and therefore must in fact no longer be a limited partnership. It may, of course, be an ordinary partnership if there are two or more general partners.[296] If, however, there is only one general partner and the sole limited partner dies or becomes bankrupt then it is contended that the terms of s 4(2) of the 1907 Act will take precedence over s 6(2) of the 1907 Act, so as to allow for the general dissolution of this former partnership.

General Partner's Share being Charged for Separate Debt

[28.130] Section 6(5)(c) of the 1907 Act provides that the other partners shall not be entitled to dissolve the partnership by reason of any limited partner suffering his share to be charged for his separate debt. Since this section applies only to a situation where a limited partner's share is being charged, s 33(2) of the 1890 Act will continue to apply to a general partner who suffers his share to be charged for his separate debt. Section 33(2) of the 1890 Act provides that, in such a case, the partnership may be dissolved at the option of the other partners. It has been noted that an agreement that a limited partnership will dissolve on the bankruptcy of a limited partner must be between all the general and limited partners;[297] so too it is thought that *all* the other partners (including the limited partners) must consent to the dissolution of the partnership under s 33(2) of the 1890 Act on the general partner's share being charged.[298] It is apprehended that the giving of such consent would not be regarded as involving the limited partner in the management of the firm contrary to s 6(1) of the 1907 Act.

Death or Bankruptcy of a Sole General Partner

[28.131] Section 4(2) of the 1907 Act requires there to be one general partner for a limited partnership to exist. Accordingly, on the death of a sole general partner, the limited partnership is automatically dissolved. Section 33(1) of the 1890 Act does not apply to such a situation, insofar as it would otherwise permit partners to agree that their

---

296 The remaining general partners will constitute an ordinary partnership from the date of death on the basis that they satisfy s 1(1) of the 1890 Act.

297 See para **[28.45]**.

298 This analysis (as it appeared in the first edition of this work) was noted by The Law Commission and the Scottish Law Commission in their 2001 *Limited Partnerships Act 1907: A Joint Consultation Paper* (Consultation Paper No 161; Discussion Paper No 118) at para 5.34 where they shared the same view. For a contrary view, see l'Anson Banks, *Lindley & Banks on Partnership* (20th edn, 2017) at para 32-05 where the current editor indicates that a limited partner can exercise the option to dissolve the partnership under s 33(2) *or* join with the other partners in exercising that option.

partnership will not dissolve on the death of the *sole* general partner,[299] since that is plainly inconsistent with s 4(2) of the 1907 Act.[300]

[28.132] The position of a sole general partner who becomes bankrupt is somewhat different, since, although bankrupt, he will continue to exist for the purposes of s 4(2) of the 1907 Act. Thus, where all the partners agree that the bankruptcy of a general partner will not dissolve the partnership, the bankruptcy of the sole general partner will not dissolve the partnership.[301] However, while technically possible, in practical terms, having a sole general partner who is bankrupt will lead to considerable restrictions on the general partner, and accordingly on the limited partnership.[302] For this reason, it will usually be appropriate for the limited partnership agreement to provide for the bankruptcy of a sole general partner to lead to the firm's dissolution.

IX. DISSOLUTION BY COURT

Section 35 of 1890 Act applies

[28.133] The power of a court to dissolve an ordinary partnership under s 35 of the 1890 Act is equally applicable to a limited partnership.[303] Section 35(a) of the 1890 Act, which provides for the dissolution of a partnership where a partner is of unsound mind, is, however, subject to s 6(2) of the 1907 Act. This provides that:

> [T]he lunacy of a limited partner shall not be a ground for dissolution of the partnership by the court unless the lunatic's share cannot be otherwise ascertained or realised.

Thus, the dissolution of a limited partnership in the case of the mental incapacity of a limited partner can be avoided, for example, where that partner's share is realised by the other partners arranging to buy it. It is apprehended that a derisory offer by the continuing partners for that partner's share would not satisfy this requirement.

Court likely to take account of limited partner's restricted role

[28.134] The 1907 Act makes no other modification to the application of s 35 of the 1890 Act to limited partnerships. Thus, a limited or a general partner may apply to court for a dissolution of the partnership in any of the cases set out in that section. However, under s 35 of the 1890 Act, the court has an absolute discretion whether to grant a dissolution and it is likely to exercise this discretion in such a way as to take account of the fact that a limited partner is in essence a dormant investor in a limited partnership. For example where it is the limited partner's conduct which forms the basis for the application, it is likely that to justify a court-ordered dissolution, this should be more severe than the conduct of a general partner, in view of the very limited role of the

---

[299] This situation was contemplated in the case of an investment limited partnership, since under s 37 of the Investment Limited Partnerships Act 1994 the death or bankruptcy of a sole general partner causes the immediate dissolution of the partnership, *notwithstanding any agreement to the contrary between the partners.*

[300] And therefore not applicable to limited partnerships pursuant to s 7 of the 1907 Act.

[301] Cf the position under the Investment Limited Partnerships Act 1994, fn **299**.

[302] See generally para **[27.59]** et seq.

[303] As to the dissolution of a partnership by court order, see generally para **[25.01]** et seq.

limited partner in the management of the firm.[304] On the other hand, where the limited partner is the applicant, his restricted role means that a court is likely to be more tolerant of a general partner's behaviour *vis-à-vis* the limited partners than between partners in an ordinary partnership.

X. WINDING UP AND BANKRUPTCY

Winding Up

[28.135] Once the limited partnership is dissolved, whether by court order or by the actions of the partners, it is the general partners who are charged with the winding up of the firm. Section 6(3) of the 1907 Act provides that '[i]n the event of the dissolution of a limited partnership its affairs shall be wound up by the general partners unless the court otherwise orders'.

[28.136] If the general partners were guilty of misconduct, bankrupt or dead, it is conceived that the limited partners could apply to court under s 39 of the 1890 Act for the court to appoint a third party to wind up the partnership. In view of the prohibition on limited partners managing the firm,[305] it would appear to be inadvisable for limited partners to be involved in the firm's winding up, particularly as s 38 of the 1890 Act states that after the dissolution of a partnership the authority of each partner to bind the firm continues and the rights and obligations of the partners continue insofar as necessary to wind up the affairs of the partnership.

Winding up as an unregistered company

[28.137] An application for the winding up of a limited partnership may be made under Chapter 3 of Part 22 of the Companies Act 2014 in the same way as for an ordinary partnership. Accordingly, reference should be made to the analysis of this area earlier in this text.[306]

---

[304] Indeed, were it not for the 1907 Act stating that a limited partner is a partner, it seems that a limited partner might not constitute a 'partner' under the 1890 Act. This is because the limited partner has no control over the partnership business and arguably might not be carrying on business in common (as required by the definition of partnership in s 1(1) of the 1890 Act) with the general partners.

[305] Limited Partnerships Act 1907, s 6(1).

[306] See para **[27.06]** et seq. It was held in the Irish case of *Re Rodger & Limited Partnership Act 1907* (unreported, 1911 cited in *Halsbury's Laws of England* (1912) Vol 22 at p 113) that as no rules had been framed under the 1907 Act in Ireland for the winding up of a limited partnership, a limited partnership could be wound up under the predecessor of Part X of the Companies Act 1963 (ie Part VIII of the Companies (Consolidation) Act 1908 (8 Edw 7, c 69) (the predecessor of both Chapter 3 of Part 22 of the Companies Act 2014, and its predecessor, Part X of the Companies Act 1963) and the rules made thereunder). Note that in England (but not in Ireland), the Bankruptcy Act 1914 provided that limited partnerships could not be wound up as an unregistered companies and this was continued in England by s 398 of the Companies Act 1948 (11 & 12 Geo 6, c 38). However, a limited partnership in Great Britain can now be wound up as an unregistered company under the Insolvency Act 1986 and the Insolvent Partnerships Order 1994 (SI 2421/1994), subject to some limitations on the ability of partners to petition for such a winding-up. See further l'Anson Banks, *Lindley & Banks on Partnership* (20th edn, 2017) at para 27-14.

Bankruptcy

[28.138] As is clear from s 37 of the Bankruptcy Act 1988, a limited partnership is treated as an ordinary partnership for the purposes of bankruptcy and the law of bankruptcy is considered in detail elsewhere in this work.[307] Accordingly, reference will be made hereunder only to those instances where special rules apply to limited partnerships. Since the position of a general partner in a limited partnership is akin to that of a partner in an ordinary partnership,[308] there is no reason why a general partner should not be fully subject to bankruptcy law. However, in view of the limited liability of the limited partner,[309] differing rules will apply to him on bankruptcy.

Vesting of partnership property in Official Assignee

[28.139] It has been noted previously that on the bankruptcy of *all* the partners in an ordinary partnership, the partnership property vests in the Official Assignee for the benefit of the firm's creditors.[310] But in a limited partnership, the liability of the limited partners is limited, so s 37 of the Bankruptcy Act 1988 provides that the entire assets of the limited partnership vest in the Official Assignee when *all the general partners* are adjudicated bankrupt, regardless of whether the limited partners are bankrupt or not.[311]

[28.140] It has been observed that a general partner in a limited partnership may be a company,[312] yet s 37 of the Bankruptcy Act 1988 is drafted with only individuals in mind, since it refers solely to the bankruptcy of a general partner and not to the liquidation or winding up of an insolvent general partner. The failure of s 37 to recognise the possibility that a general partner in a limited partnership may be a company is regrettable. Therefore, it remains to be seen whether a court will interpret s 37 as applicable to a case where one of the general partners is a company which is being wound up or liquidated as a result of its insolvency.[313]

Non-dissolution of firm on bankruptcy of limited partner

[28.141] In view of the restricted role of the limited partner in the management of the firm and his limited liability, the bankruptcy of a limited partner does not have the same impact upon a limited partnership as the bankruptcy of an ordinary partner. Accordingly, unlike the situation in an ordinary partnership,[314] s 6(2) of the 1907 Act provides that a limited partnership shall not be dissolved by the bankruptcy of a limited partner.

---

[307] See para **[27.01]** et seq.

[308] See para **[28.03]**.

[309] Save in exceptional circumstances where he loses this limited liability, as to which see para **[28.104]** et seq.

[310] *Re Hind* (1889) 23 LR Ir 17 and the Bankruptcy Act 1988, s 44(1). See generally para **[27.69]** et seq.

[311] Previously, s 345(8) of the Companies Act 1963 which was repealed by s 6 of the Bankruptcy Act 1988, (2nd Sch), provided that the assets of the limited partnership vest in the Official Assignee only where *all* the partners, both limited and general, were adjudicated bankrupt.

[312] See para **[28.34]**.

[313] See further para **[23.40]** et seq where the question of whether the bankruptcy of a partner is akin to the winding up of an insolvent company, is discussed.

[314] See the Partnership Act 1890, s 33(1) and para **[27.60]**.

Position of a limited partner on bankruptcy

[28.142] A limited partner's liability is restricted to the amount of his capital contribution to the firm and in this regard his position in a limited partnership where all of the general partners are bankrupt is like that of a postponed creditor. In general,[315] he is not liable to contribute to the assets of the firm beyond his capital contribution and if there is a surplus after all the firm's liabilities are discharged, he will be entitled to his share of that surplus. Save for this,[316] a limited partnership is treated as if it were an ordinary partnership.[317] Significantly, there is no prohibition on a creditor of the firm presenting a petition for bankruptcy against a limited partner under s 31 of the Bankruptcy Act 1988,[318] although such a petition is only likely to be brought where the limited partner has lost the protection of limited liability.

[28.143] Similarly:

(a) the Official Assignee can take an action to recover a firm debt in the name of a limited partner (s 30 of the Bankruptcy Act 1988);

(b) a limited partner in a limited partnership is required to provide the Official Assignee with accounts and other information on the firm on the bankruptcy of his partner (s 32 of the Bankruptcy Act 1988);

(c) limited partners may be named in bankruptcy proceedings against a limited partnership (s 36 of the Bankruptcy Act 1988);

(d) a limited partner who is adjudicated bankrupt (for example in a situation where he has lost the protection of limited liability) is obliged to deliver a statement of affairs of the partnership to the Official Assignee (s 33 of the Bankruptcy Act 1988);

(e) a person who is jointly party to a contract with a bankrupt limited partner may sue or be sued on that contract without joining the bankrupt partner (s 35 of the Bankruptcy Act 1988).

Where only one general partner

[28.144] A situation which may arise is where there is only one general partner in a limited partnership and he is adjudged bankrupt. This occurred in the English High Court case of *Re Barnard*.[319] In that case, Farwell J held that there was no joint estate and all the debts of the limited partnership were provable in the bankruptcy of the general partner, regardless of whether the firm was bankrupt or not. However, it is questioned whether this reasoning should be followed here. The conclusion that there is no joint estate is difficult to justify in theory, as there will always be a limited partner who is jointly liable for the partnership obligations, albeit that his liability is limited.

---

[315] But subject to the instances in which he may lose his limited liability, see para **[28.104]** et seq.

[316] And also subject to the earlier comments on the non-dissolution of the partnership on the bankruptcy of a limited partner (para **[28.141]**) and the vesting of partnership property in the Official Assignee (para **[29.139]**).

[317] Bankruptcy Act 1988, s 37.

[318] Contrast the position of a limited partner in an investment limited partnership under s 23 of the Investment Limited Partnerships Act 1994, para **[29.213]**.

[319] *Re Barnard* [1932] 1 Ch 269.

This is because the 1907 Act does not exclude the limited partner from liability for the partnership obligations, but simply provides that his liability is limited to his capital contribution. Indeed, a further difficulty with this theory arises if the limited partner has lost his protection of limited liability. In such a case there would be a joint estate since the creditors would have unlimited recourse to the assets of the single general partner and also unlimited recourse to the assets of the limited partner as if he was also a general partner.

Petitioning for bankruptcy

[28.145] If a petition is to be signed on behalf of a limited partnership for its own bankruptcy or for the bankruptcy of a debtor of the firm, it is advisable that it be signed by a general partner, rather than a limited partner. Otherwise, the limited partner may be contravening the prohibition on his taking part in the management of the partnership business.[320]

---

[320] Limited Partnerships Act 1907, s 6(1). See further para **[28.78]** et seq.

Chapter 29

Investment Limited Partnerships

INTRODUCTION

[29.01] Up to this, consideration has been given to the two oldest forms of partnership in Ireland, namely the ordinary partnership, which is governed by the 1890 Act, and the limited partnership, which was created by the 1907 Act. The next type of partnership to be considered is the investment limited partnership (ILP), which was introduced into Irish law by the Investment Limited Partnerships Act 1994 (the 1994 Act). This partnership is a very different creature from either the ordinary partnership or the limited partnership, since it is a collective investment scheme whose legal structure is a partnership. An ILP comes into existence when it receives a certificate of authorisation from the Central Bank of Ireland,[1] and is subject to a specific Central Bank authorisation and supervision regime as an alternative investment fund (AIF) within the Irish legal framework for AIFs and alternative investment fund managers which derives from European Union law.

[29.02] The legal framework applicable to ILPs comprises the 1994 Act, together with:

- the Alternative Investment Fund Managers' Directive,[2] which was transposed into Irish law by the European Union (Alternative Investment Fund Managers) Regulations 2013 (the Irish AIFMD Regulations);[3]

- the AIFMD Level 2 Regulation;[4] and

- the Central Bank AIF Rulebook,[5] published in July 2013 and which is updated from time to time. It sets out conditions[6] for both ILPs and for other entities

---

[1]   The Investment Limited Partnerships Act 1994, s 3 which defines an ILP as 'a partnership which holds a certificate of authorisation issued in accordance with this Act', and s 8(6) of the 1994 Act which provides for the issue of that certificate of authorisation by the Central Bank.

[2]   Directive 2011/65/EU of the European Parliament and of the Council of 8 June 2011 on alternative investment fund managers.

[3]   SI 257/2013, as amended.

[4]   Commission Delegated Regulation (EU) No 231/2013 of the European Parliament and of the Council with regard to exemptions, general operating conditions, depositaries, leverage, transparency and supervision.

[5]   At the time of writing, the current edition of the Central Bank AIF Rulebook is the March 2018 edition.

[6]   Under the Investment Limited Partnerships Act 1994, s 7(2)(b), the Central Bank may impose such conditions on ILPs 'as it considers appropriate and prudent for the purposes of the orderly and proper regulation' of ILPs.

which can be authorised as AIFs.[7] The Central Bank lists further conditions relating to the authorisation and supervision of AIFs separately on its website.[8]

If there is a conflict between the terms of the Central Bank AIF Rulebook, and the terms of the 1994 Act, the Irish AIFMD Regulations or the AIFMD Level 2 Regulation, the relevant provisions of the 1994 Act, the Irish AIFMD Regulations, or the AIFMD Level 2 Regulation, as appropriate, will prevail over the relevant provisions of the Central Bank AIF Rulebook.[9]

[29.03] The Irish AIFMD Regulations[10] define an AIF as follows:

'alternative investment fund' or 'AIF' means a collective investment undertaking, including investment compartments thereof, which—

(a)   raises capital from a number of investors, with a view to investing it in accordance with a defined investment policy for the benefit of those investors, and

(b)   does not require authorisation under Directive 2009/65/EC of the European Parliament and of the Council of 13 July 2009 on the coordination of laws, regulations and administrative provisions relating to undertakings for collective investment in transferable securities (UCITS).[11]

[29.04] The investment limited partnership framework has proven considerably less popular than originally expected in Ireland. At the time of writing, there are only seven investment limited partnerships with authorisations from the Central Bank of Ireland.[12] As mentioned above,[13] an investment limited partnership is subject to a specific authorisation and supervision regime by the Central Bank as an AIF, but the Irish funds industry has long viewed the current investment limited partnership framework as having considerable limitations which lessen its attractiveness both domestically, and to international private equity firms.

[29.05] In July 2017, the Minister for Finance and Public Expenditure and Reform announced that approval had been given for a Bill to be drafted to amend the Investment Limited Partnerships Act 1994. The purpose of the Bill is to align the investment limited partnership framework with the framework introduced by the Alternative Investment Fund Managers Directive, and to further enhance Ireland's status as a fund domicile. At

---

[7]   Such as unit trusts under the Unit Trust Act 1990, investment companies under the Companies Act 2014, common contractual funds under the Investment Funds, Companies and Miscellaneous Provisions Act 2005, and Irish Collective Asset-management Vehicles under the Irish Collective Asset-management Vehicles Act 2015.

[8]   These can be found in the 'AIF' section of the Central Bank's website. The Central Bank has also published an AIFMD Q&A which provides additional, non-binding, guidance. At the time of writing, that AIFMD Q&A is in its 30th edition and can also be found in the 'AIF' section of the Central Bank's website.

[9]   Central Bank AIF Rulebook: Introduction.

[10]   European Union (Alternative Investment Fund Managers) Regulations 2013, reg 5.

[11]   Known as the UCITS Directive.

[12]   Central Bank of Ireland Register of Authorised Investment Limited Partnerships (31 October 2018).

[13]   See, further, para **[29.01]** above.

the time of writing, that Bill is known as the Investment Limited Partnership and Irish Collective Asset-management Vehicle (Amendment) Bill 2017, but only draft Heads of Bill have been prepared.[14]

[29.06] While the proposed modernisation of the Irish ILP framework will be a welcome development for the funds industry, the further alignment of the ILP framework with the Alternative Investment Fund Managers Directive framework will also be of considerable benefit when assessing the duties to which the various parties involved with an ILP (most notably, the general partner, any alternative investment fund manager, and the custodian) are subject. Under the current framework, for example, to establish the duties to which the custodian of the ILP is subject, one must examine the 1994 Act, the Irish AIFMD Regulations, the AIFMD Level 2 Regulation and the Central Bank AIF Rulebook, and check for any additional conditions on the Central Bank's website. The terminology is also not aligned: the term 'custodian' is used in the 1994 Act,[15] while the Irish AIFMD Regulations, the AIFMD Level 2 Regulation and the Central Bank AIF Rulebook use the term 'depositary' throughout. An alternative investment fund manager appointed to an AIF that is an ILP is subject to requirements imposed by both the Irish AIFMD Regulations and the AIFMD Level 2 Regulations, and to the conditions set out by the Central Bank in the Central Bank AIF Rulebook and on its website. However, if a general partner of an ILP is appointed as its alternative investment fund manager, that general partner will not only be subject to the provisions of the 1994 Act in its capacity as general partner, but to three other sets of laws or conditions referable to its status as alternative investment fund manager.

[29.07] The ILP will be examined under the following headings:

    I.   General;

    II.   Nature of an ILP;

---

[14] In its Government Legislation Programme for Autumn 2018, the Government confirmed that the Heads of Bill had been prepared and that the Bill itself was a priority for publication. In the UK, steps have also been taken to promote the UK as a location for domiciling funds. On 6 April 2017, the Legislative Reform (Private Fund Limited Partnerships) Order 2017 came into force. Rather than introducing a stand-alone regime similar to that introduced by the 1994 Act in Ireland, the 2017 Order instead amended the Limited Partnerships Act 1907 (as it applies in the UK) to introduce a new regime for certain collective investment schemes formed as limited partnerships with written partnership agreements. Those limited partnerships can now elect to be treated as 'private fund limited partnerships' with the result that their limited partners benefit from a white-list of actions they may take which will not be considered as taking part in the management of the limited partnership. Limited partners in a private fund limited partnership are also not obliged to contribute capital. There is no requirement for a court order to wind up a private fund limited partnership and, if it is dissolved at a time when it does not have a general partner, the limited partners can appoint a third party to manage the winding-up. Information on the general nature and term of the private fund limited partnership does not need to be provided on registration, and certain statutory duties which are set out in the 1890 Act and apply to limited partnerships generally (unless expressly disapplied in the partnership agreement) are expressly disapplied to private fund limited partnerships ie s 28 (the duty of partners to render accounts, etc), s 30 (the duty of a partner not to compete with the firm) and s 36(1) (rights of persons dealing with firm against apparent members of firm).

[15] Which, at s 8(1)(c), provides that the custodian must be a 'depositary' within the meaning of reg 22(3) of the Irish AIFMD Regulations.

    III.   Authorisation of an ILP;

    IV.   Liability of the Limited Partners;

    V.   Authority of the Partners;

    VI.   Rights and Duties of the Partners;

    VII.   Regulation of ILPs;

    VIII.   Termination of ILPs.

Overview

[29.08] The passing of the 1994 Act represented the first major change in partnership law in nearly a century. For this reason alone it is interesting to briefly refer to some of those terms of the 1994 Act which modify the application of the law of partnership to ILPs, particularly where those modifications are not required by the special nature of an ILP.

[29.09] For example one of the main problems associated with the 1890 Act is that the default partnership agreement provided by the terms of that Act is inappropriate for many modern partnerships. In particular, it has been seen that the default position under the 1890 Act is that the departure of a partner from a firm or his bankruptcy or death automatically causes that firm's dissolution. This may then lead to the unnecessary winding up of successful partnerships.[16] This problem is avoided in ILPs by virtue of s 37 of the 1994 Act which provides that any change in the partners or the bankruptcy or death of a partner[17] does not dissolve the ILP. In this way, the 1994 Act takes a more realistic approach to modern partnerships, by assuming that on the occurrence of one of these events, the continuing partners will invariably wish to avoid winding up the firm. The 1994 Act contains a number of other much needed reforms of the law of partnership, albeit in relation to ILPs only, such as the dis-application of the prohibition on firms of more than 20 partners[18] (a prohibition which has outgrown its usefulness);[19] its provision of a power to appoint inspectors to ILPs in much the same way as applies to companies;[20] its recognition of the potential value to partners of their partnership interest as security by providing that the mortgage of a partnership interest will not lead to the dissolution of the partnership;[21] and the exemption of limited partners from being subject to a petition for bankruptcy in relation to the debts of the partnership.[22]

[29.10] If changes such as these to the partnership landscape have been suitable for ILPs since 1994 (and as further enhancements to the ILP regime are expected), it is submitted that there is no reason why those changes and enhancements should not also be applied to both ordinary and limited partnerships.

---

[16]   See generally para **[23.32]** et seq.

[17]   Provided there is more than one general partner.

[18]   Now set out in s 1435(1) of the Companies Act 2014. See further para **[29.41]** et seq.

[19]   Investment Limited Partnerships Act 1994, s 4(4). As regards the position in ordinary partnerships, see para **[4.29]** et seq.

[20]   Investment Limited Partnerships Act 1994, s 26.

[21]   Investment Limited Partnerships Act 1994, s 37, cf the Partnership Act 1890, s 33(2).

[22]   Investment Limited Partnerships Act 1994, s 23. Contrast the position of a limited partner in a limited partnership under the 1907 Act, para **[28.142]**.

I.   GENERAL

Background

[29.11] The ILP was created in 1994 in order to fill a perceived gap in the range of investment vehicles suitable for investors who were interested in collective investment opportunities in Ireland. After considering the limited partnership structures used in jurisdictions such as the Cayman Islands, Bermuda, America and particularly the American Revised Uniform Limited Partnership Act (1985)[23] and the Delaware Limited Partnership Act,[24] the Investment Limited Partnerships Bill was drafted. The Bill was passed into law on 12 July 1994, coming into effect on 25 July 1994.[25]

Characteristics of an ILP

[29.12] In general terms, an ILP is a partnership between one or more general partners and one or more limited partners, the principal business of which, as expressed in the partnership agreement, is the investment of its funds in property.[26] Like the position in limited partnerships formed under the 1907 Act, a general partner in an ILP has unlimited liability for the debts and obligations of the firm, while a limited partner is not liable for the debts and obligations of the firm beyond the amount of his capital contribution.[27]

[29.13] However, these basic requirements are not sufficient for a partnership to constitute an ILP. Since an ILP is defined as 'a partnership which holds a certificate of authorisation' from the Central Bank,[28] an ILP only comes into existence on the receipt of this certificate of authorisation.[29] The Central Bank, as the authority responsible for

---

23   This has now been replaced in many US states by the Uniform Limited Partnership Act (2001) (Last Amended 2013). For a general discussion of this Act, see Geu and Nekritz, 'Expectations for the Twenty-First Century: An Overview of the New Limited Partnership Act' (American Bar Association, Probate & Property, January/February 2002, 47–55).

24   See generally, the annotation of the 1994 Act by Declan Murphy, available at www.westlaw.ie. For a general discussion of the Delaware Act, see Smith, 'Limited Partnerships – Expanded opportunities under Delaware's 1988 Revised Uniform Limited Partnership Act' (1990) 15 Delaware Journal of Corporate Law 43. The applicable limited partnership legislation in Delaware is now the Delaware Revised Uniform Limited Partnership Act, set out in Chapter 17 of Title 6 to the Delaware Code.

25   Investment Limited Partnerships Act 1994 (Commencement) Order 1994, s 2 (SI 213/1994). See generally, the annotation of the 1994 Act by Declan Murphy, available at www.westlaw.ie. For further information on the background to the Act and in particular some of the tax considerations see Murphy, 'Investment Limited Partnerships' (1994) CLP 287 and the papers from the Irish Centre for Commercial Law Studies conference on the 1994 Act, dated 6 October 1994.

26   Investment Limited Partnerships Act 1994, s 5(1)(a) and (b). The Investment Limited Partnerships Act 1994, s 3 defines 'property' as real or personal property of any kind (including securities), wherever located.

27   Investment Limited Partnerships Act 1994, s 3. The instances in which a limited partner loses his limited liability are dealt with at para **[29.92]** et seq.

28   Investment Limited Partnerships Act 1994, s 3.

29   Investment Limited Partnerships Act 1994, s 5(1)(f).

the authorisation and supervision of ILPs, will only authorise an ILP as an AIF. The conditions which must be satisfied before the Central Bank will issue such a certificate are considered in detail later in this chapter.[30] Where a partnership fails to obtain the certificate of authorisation, it will not be an ILP,[31] but will be an ordinary partnership, assuming it otherwise satisfies the definition of partnership in s 1(1) of the 1890 Act.[32] In such a case, the proposed limited partners will have unlimited liability for the debts of the firm.[33]

[29.14] An ILP can be established as either a qualifying investor AIF, or as a retail investor AIF. A qualifying investor AIF can be marketed to investors who meet the criteria set out in Chapter 2 of the Central Bank AIF Rulebook, ie the investor must:

- be a '*professional client*' within the meaning of Annex II of the Markets in Financial Instruments Directive;[34]

- receive an appraisal from an EU bank, MiFID investment firm or UCITS management company confirming that he has the appropriate expertise, experience and knowledge to adequately understand the investment in the qualifying investor AIF; or

- certify that he is an informed investor by providing the following:

  - written confirmation that he has such knowledge of, and experience in, financial and business matters as would enable him to properly evaluate the merits and risks of the prospective investment; or

  - written confirmation that his business involves, whether for his own account or the account of others, the management, acquisition or disposal of property of the same kind as the property of the qualifying investor AIF.[35]

A retail investor AIF is one which may be marketed to retail investors. Retail investors are investors who are not eligible to invest in qualifying investor AIFs (ie investors with less experience, knowledge and expertise).[36]

---

[30]   See para **[29.65]** et seq.

[31]   The Investment Limited Partnerships Act 1994, s 3 defines an ILP as 'a partnership which holds a certificate of authorisation issued in accordance with this Act'.

[32]   See generally in relation to this definition, para **[2.01]** et seq.

[33]   Investment Limited Partnerships Act 1994, s 8(7).

[34]   The original Markets in Financial Instruments Directive (Directive 2004/39/EC) was repealed by the revised Markets in Financial Instruments Directive (Directive 2014/65/EU, art 94 with effect from 3 January 2018. The Central Bank AIF Rulebook still referes to the original Directive 'as amended' however the meaning of 'professional client' in both Directives is the same. A professional client for the purposes of each Directive is one who possesses the experience, knowledge and expertise to make his own investment decisions and properly assess the risks that he incurs, and he must comply with further criteria set out in Annex II to the Directive.

[35]   Central Bank AIF Rulebook, p 101.

[36]   Central Bank AIF Rulebook: Definitions, p 13.

As a Partnership, an ILP is subject to Partnership law

[29.15] As is clear from the strict regulation of ILPs, they are primarily collective investment undertakings. However, they are nonetheless partnerships and, as such, they are not only subject to the terms of the 1994 Act, but are also subject to the general principles of partnership law and in particular the terms of the 1890 Act. This is clear from s 4(1) of the 1994 Act which states:

> Subject to the provisions of this Act, the Act of 1890, and the rules of equity and of common law applicable to partnerships, except so far as they are inconsistent with the express provisions of the last-mentioned Act, shall apply to investment limited partnerships.[37]

Accordingly, when considering the legal position of an ILP, it is not sufficient to consider only the terms of the 1994 Act and the Irish Alternative Investment Fund Managers Directive framework.[38] Reference must also be made to the law of ordinary partnerships and, in each case, an assessment must be made as to whether these principles are consistent with the terms of the 1994 Act.

ILP is first a Collective Investment Undertaking

[29.16] It is important to bear in mind that, although an ILP is structurally a partnership, the *raison d'être* for the 1994 Act was to create a new form of collective investment undertaking and an ILP is first a collective investment undertaking and second a partnership. In broad terms, a collective investment undertaking is a scheme whereby investors pool their funds and those funds are managed by a third party. By pooling their resources in this way, the investors are more easily able to diversify the assets in which they invest. The ILP was intended to be a useful method for such collective investment since it provides, inter alia, limited liability to the investors[39] and an easy structure in which to invest and withdraw capital.

[29.17] It is interesting to note that the term collective investment undertaking does not figure prominently in the 1994 Act, and on a first reading thereof, one might be forgiven for failing to appreciate that an ILP is a collective investment undertaking. This only becomes apparent from the fact that the Central Bank, which issues the authorisation for an ILP,[40] will only authorise an ILP as an AIF (and not as any other type of regulated vehicle), and an AIF is defined in the Irish AIFMD Regulations as a collective investment undertaking.[41] As a collective investment undertaking, an ILP is subject to the strict regulation of such schemes imposed by the Central Bank for the benefit of investors in those undertakings. Thus, an ILP only comes into existence if the Central

---

[37] The reference to the inconsistency of the rules of common law and equity with the 1890 Act is superfluous, since the 1890 Act itself provides that these rules will not apply if they are inconsistent with that Act.

[38] See para **[29.02]**.

[39] Except in certain rare cases where the protection of limited liability is lost by the limited partners, see para **[29.92]** et seq.

[40] Investment Limited Partnerships Act 1994, s 3.

[41] European Union (Alternative Investment Fund Managers) Regulations 2013, reg 5(1).

Bank says so and the Central Bank has the power to terminate this existence.[42] On a practical level, such issues as minor amendments to the partnership agreement cannot be effected by the partners without the consent of the Central Bank.[43]

[29.18] The wide-ranging powers of the Central Bank in relation to the regulation of ILPs are clear from s 7(1) and 7(2)(a) of the 1994 Act:

(1) Notwithstanding any other powers which may be available to the Bank under any other enactment, order or regulation, the Bank may impose such conditions for the authorisation of an investment limited partnership as it considers appropriate and prudent for the purposes of the orderly and proper regulation of investment limited partnerships.

(2)(a) Conditions imposed under *subsection (1)* may be imposed generally, or by reference to particular investment limited partnerships, or by reference to any other matter the Bank considers appropriate and prudent for the purposes of the orderly and proper regulation of the business of investment limited partnerships.

[29.19] This power to impose conditions for the authorisation of an ILP includes a power to impose such further conditions from time to time as the Central Bank considers appropriate. The Central Bank imposes those conditions on ILPs through the Central Bank AIF Rulebook,[44] which replaced the previous conditions which the Central Bank had imposed on ILPs by way of its Non-UCITS Notices.[45] The Central Bank also lists certain conditions relating to the authorisation and supervision of AIFs separately on its website.[46] The letter of authorisation issued by the Central Bank to an ILP when it is authorised as an AIF will list the definitive set of conditions that apply to that ILP.[47] The Central Bank may grant derogations from the Central Bank AIF Rulebook, but those are considered on a case-by-case basis[48] and applications for a derogation must be accompanied by a 'detailed and comprehensive rationale supporting the request'.[49] Any such derogations must be published in the AIF's prospectus.[50]

Contravention of Central Bank's conditions

[29.20] Under s 39(c) of the 1994 Act, where an ILP contravenes any conditions in relation to its authorisation or business imposed by the Central Bank, it will be guilty of

42 See further para **[29.65]** et seq.
43 Investment Limited Partnerships Act 1994, s 11(2). Central Bank AIF Rulebook at p 52 (in respect of an ILP authorised as a retail investor AIF) and p 113 (in respect of an ILP authorised as a qualifying investor AIF).
44 The Central Bank AIF Rulebook must be read in conjunction with the 1994 Act, the Irish AIFMD Regulations and the AIFMD Level 2 Regulation.
45 The Non-UCITS Notices (known as the NU Series of Notices) were first introduced by the Central Bank in January 1996, and were a comprehensive set of conditions governing ILPs which themselves superseded ILP1, a set of conditions imposed by the Central Bank in July 1994 in conjunction with the introduction of the 1994 Act into Irish law.
46 At the time of writing, these can be found in the 'AIF' section of the Central Bank's website.
47 Central Bank: AIFMD Questions and Answers (30th edn, 4 May 2018) at ID 1014.
48 Central Bank: AIFMD Questions and Answers (30th edn, 4 May 2018) at ID 1071.
49 Central Bank: AIFMD Questions and Answers (30th edn, 4 May 2018) at ID 1071.
50 Central Bank AIF Rulebook at p 57 (in respect of an ILP authorised as a retail investor AIF) and p 119 (in respect of an ILP authorised as a qualifying investor AIF).

an offence and any partner in the firm who is in default[51] is liable to a maximum fine of €1,093,750 or to imprisonment of up to 15 years.[52] Of perhaps greater concern to certain ILPs is the power of the Central Bank to revoke an ILP's authorisation for a breach of these conditions.[53] In addition, s 34 of the 1994 Act allows for preventative action to be taken, by authorising the Central Bank to apply to court for an order prohibiting the ILP, the general partner or the custodian from contravening the condition in question, and for this purpose, the court may grant interim or interlocutory relief.

[29.21] Under reg 49 of the Irish AIFMD Regulations, if the Central Bank is satisfied that an AIF (such as an ILP) has failed to comply, or is likely to fail to comply, with any condition or requirement imposed on it by the Irish AIFMD Regulations or otherwise, the Central Bank may give written directions to the ILP to take one or more of various actions set out in reg 39(3) of those Regulations. Such actions may include the suspension of business, a requirement to raise capital, or a requirement to comply with the condition or requirement that it has breached.

ILP is not subject to the 1907 Act

[29.22] It is important to bear in mind that although an ILP is a form of limited partnership, in the sense that it has one or more limited partners, it is not governed by the 1907 Act. Section 4(2) of the 1994 Act expressly provides that the 'provisions of the Limited Partnerships Act, 1907, shall not apply to investment limited partnerships'.

ILPs and Capital Contributions under Investment Intermediaries Act 1995 and the Markets in Financial Instruments Regulations 2017

[29.23] By virtue of s 2(1) of the Investment Intermediaries Act 1995, the capital contribution of a partner in an ILP is an 'investment instrument' for the purposes of that Act. In general terms, therefore, any advice regarding the purchase, sale, subscription or underwriting of such capital contributions is caught by the terms of the 1995 Act and must be given by an investment business firm which has been authorised by the Central Bank.[54] Similarly, an interest in an investment limited partnership is a 'financial instrument' under the European Union (Markets in Financial Instruments) Regulations

---

[51] Although the Investment Limited Partnerships Act 1994, s 39(c) refers to a 'partner in default' being guilty of an offence, this term is not defined in the section. However, s 270 of the Companies Act 2014 provides that the term 'in default' in respect of any officer of a company means any officer 'who authorises or who, in breach of his or her duty as such officer, permits the default mentioned in the provision'. It has been suggested that a similar meaning will be given to the expression 'partner in default': (see the annotated consolidation of the 1994 Act prepared by Declan Murphy and available at www.westlaw.ie (where he refers to the predecessor of s 270 of the 2014 Act: s 383 of the Companies Act 1963)).

[52] Investment Limited Partnerships Act 1994, s 40. The original fine of £500,000 was converted to its euro equivalent by virtue of Council Regulations (EC) No 1103/97, (EC) No 974/98 and (EC) No 2866/98 and the Economic and Monetary Union Act 1998, s 6 and then, by virtue of s 9 of the Fines Act 2010, multiplied by 1.75 to give the current amount.

[53] Investment Limited Partnerships Act 1994, s 29.

[54] See generally Clarke and Murphy's annotation of the Investment Intermediaries Act 1995, available at www.westlaw.ie. (contd.../)

2017,[55] meaning that the provision of investment advice or other investment services in respect of an interest in an ILP may only be provided by an appropriately authorised investment firm.

[29.24] However, an ILP itself is not an investment business firm so as to require authorisation by the Central Bank under the Investment Intermediaries Act 1995.[56] This is logical since an ILP is subject to its own regulatory regime under the terms of the 1994 Act and therefore does not require to be governed by the terms of the Investment Intermediaries Act 1995. An ILP also does not require authorisation by the Central Bank under the European Union (Markets in Financial Instruments) Regulations 2017, as reg 4(1)(p) of those Regulations specifically exempts collective investment undertakings from their scope.

Popularity of ILPs

[29.25] Because of the specialised nature of ILPs as collective investment undertakings, until the introduction of the Alternative Investment Fund Managers Directive framework, they were only of relevance to a small number of sophisticated investors. Despite the ability to structure an AIF as an ILP following the introduction of the Alternative Investment Fund Managers Directive framework in 2013, the ILP remains unpopular, with only seven ILPs authorised at the time of writing.[57] The impending reform of the ILP regime is designed to address this issue, and make the ILP a more attractive structure both domestically and internationally.

[29.26] The ILP also benefits from a favourable tax regime, enhanced further by the Finance Act 2013, which inserted a new section, s 739J, into the Taxes Consolidation Act 1997 in relation to the tax treatment of ILPs. An ILP is not chargeable to tax on its income or gains.[58] Instead, its income and gains are treated as if they had accrued directly to the limited partners in proportion to their interests in the ILP.[59] The ILP must file a return in respect of each year of assessment, setting out details of the profits that have arisen to the ILP in respect of the capital contributions made by the limited partners, and setting out the name and address of each limited partner, together with details of the amount of that profit to which that limited partner is entitled.[60]

---

[54]   (\...contd) Note that most of the 1995 Act no longer applies to investment firms, the majority of which are now authorised or deemed authorised under the Markets in Financial Instruments Directive (Directive 2014/65/EU), transposed into Irish law by the European Union (Markets in Financial Instruments) Regulations 2017.

[55]   By virtue of coming within the definition of 'transferable securities' in the European Union (Markets in Financial Instruments) Regulations 2017, reg 3(1).

[56]   The Investment Intermediaries Act 1995, s 2(6) which expressly excludes from the definition of investment business firm those collective investment undertakings which are already regulated by the Central Bank (which, by definition, will be the case with ILPs).

[57]   Central Bank, Register of Authorised Investment Limited Partnerships (31 October 2018).

[58]   Taxes Consolidation Act 1997, s 739J(2)(a).

[59]   Taxes Consolidation Act 1997, s 739J(2)(b).

[60]   Taxes Consolidation Act 1997, s 739J(3). The ILP must also include such other information as the Revenue Commissioners may require.

[29.27] Interest which arises on a deposit to which an ILP is entitled is not subject to deposit interest retention tax.[61] An ILP has always been exempt from companies' capital duty under Part 8 of the Stamp Duties Consolidation Act 1999.[62]

Recognition of Foreign Limited Partnerships

[29.28] Section 43 of the 1994 Act provides that a limited partnership which is established in or governed by the laws of another state will, in the Irish courts, be subject to the law of that state to determine the liability of the partners and issues regarding the organisation and internal affairs of the firm.[63] By establishing Irish comity for foreign law in this way,[64] the 1994 Act aims to ensure that a foreign court will apply Irish law, if it is faced with similar questions regarding an Irish ILP and its members.

II.   NATURE OF AN ILP

[29.29] The key to understanding the nature of an ILP is recognising that it only comes into existence when the Central Bank grants it a certificate of authorisation.[65] For this reason, the authorisation process plays a significant role in the law of ILPs and this is considered in detail hereunder.[66] However, before an application for the authorisation of an ILP will even be considered by the Central Bank, certain basic structural requirements must be satisfied and these requirements will now be considered.

Principal Business of ILP must be Investment in Property

[29.30] Before a partnership will be considered an ILP, s 5(1)(a) of the 1994 Act requires its principal business to be the investment of its funds in real or personal property[67] (including securities).[68]

---

61   Taxes Consolidation Act 1997, s 739J(4).

62   The exemption for ILPs is set out at s 115 of the Stamp Duties Consolidation Act 1999. In contrast, a limited partnership formed under the 1907 Act was subject to companies capital duty until 7 December 2005, when companies capital duty was abolished by the Finance Act 2006, s 110.

63   Laffoy J, in *Quigley v Harris* [2008] IEHC 403, noted that it was common case between the parties to those proceedings that s 43 of the 1994 Act was of general application and was not confined to ILPs. Laffoy J referenced Murphy, 'Investment Limited Partnerships' (1994) 1 (11) CLP 287 in which the author of that article commented that s 43 of the 1994 Act had been drafted in that manner as it had been thought that the limitation of liability from which Irish ILPs were to benefit would be more likely to be recognised in other jurisdictions if, among other matters, Irish law gave recognition to limitations on liability from which foreign limited partnerships benefit. See, further, para **[28.22]** regarding the decision in *Quigley v Harris*.

64   But note that the comity doctrine as the basis for recognising foreign law has been doubted: Binchy, *Irish Conflict of Laws* (1988) at p 13 et seq and at p 585 et seq.

65   Investment Limited Partnerships Act 1994, s 5(1)(f).

66   See para **[29.65]** et seq.

67   Investment Limited Partnerships Act 1994, s 5(1)(a).

68   Investment Limited Partnerships Act 1994 (see definition of 'property' at s 2).

At least one General Partner and one Limited Partner

[29.31] Like an ordinary partnership, s 5(1)(b) of the 1994 Act requires an ILP to have at least two members. However, as with a limited partnership under the 1907 Act, one of the partners must be a limited partner and one of them must be a general partner.[69]

It must have an Alternative Investment Fund Manager

[29.32] If the ILP is to be established as a retail investor AIF, it must appoint an alternative investment fund manager authorised within the EU, and the general partner may be appointed to that role. If the ILP is to be established as a qualifying investor AIF, it may appoint an alternative investment fund manager that is authorised in Ireland, one that is authorised in another EU Member State and allowed to passport its activities into Ireland, or one that is authorised outside the EU. Again, the general partner may be appointed to this role.[70] Unless it is required by the Irish AIFMD Regulations to appoint an alternative investment fund manager at an earlier date, an ILP authorised as a qualifying investor AIF on or after 22 July 2013 by the Central Bank must appoint an alternative investment fund manager within two years from its date of launch.[71]

A body corporate may be a limited or a general partner

[29.33] Although it is the position under partnership law generally,[72] s 5(2) of the 1994 Act specifically acknowledges the fact that a body corporate may be a partner in an ILP since it states that '[a] body corporate with or without limited liability may be a general partner or a limited partner and a partnership may be a limited partner'. This is an important practical issue, since by having a limited liability company as a general partner, it is possible to effectively limit the liability of the general partner to the amount of capital of that company.[73]

But one general partner must be a body corporate

[29.34] Although there is no requirement under the 1994 Act that a general partner be a body corporate, it is an implicit requirement of the Central Bank since the Central Bank AIF Rulebook provides that the AIF must, in its prospectus, disclose the registered office of the general partner.[74] The Central Bank's Guidance on AIF Applications for

---

[69] Compare the similar requirement for limited partnerships under Limited Partnerships Act 1907, s 4(2), considered at para **[28.24]**.

[70] An analysis of the authorisation and supervision regime for alternative investment fund managers is outside the scope of this work, but is set out in the Irish AIFMD Regulations, the AIFMD Level 2 Regulations and in the Central Bank AIF Rulebook.

[71] Central Bank AIF Rulebook at p 113.

[72] See para **[2.35]**.

[73] Subject to the rules of company law on the liability of directors and shareholders for the debts and liabilities of the company in certain exceptional circumstances, see generally Courtney, *The Law of Companies* (4th edn, 2016) at paras [5.001] et seq and [16.149] et seq; Hutchinson, *Keane on Company Law* (5th edn, 2016) at paras [11.16] et seq, [25.87] and [27.75]; Forde and Kennedy, *Company Law* (5th edn, 2017) at paras 4-51 et seq, 4-74 et seq and 7-131 et seq.

[74] Central Bank AIF Rulebook, p 61 (in respect of an ILP authorised as a retail investor AIF) and p 121 (in respect of an ILP authorised as a qualifying investor AIF). The Central Bank is permitted to impose such a condition by the Investment Limited Partnerships Act 1994, s 7.

Authorisation[75] also sets out the Central Bank's expectations regarding the board of directors of a general partner (ie that it will include directors who have experience in relation to the organisation of the relevant form of AIF).

Is the general partner subject to minimum capital requirements?

[29.35] While before the Alternative Investment Fund Managers Directive framework was introduced in Ireland in 2013 there was a requirement that at least one general partner have a minimum capital of €125,000,[76] that requirement no longer applies to the general partner of an ILP acting *qua* general partner.[77] Since 2013, an ILP can only be authorised by the Central Bank as an AIF, and must have an alternative investment fund manager. That alternative investment fund manager is itself subject to an authorisation and supervision regime, whether by the Central Bank or by its equivalent in another jurisdiction, and it is subject to specific capital requirements as set out in both the Irish AIFMD Regulations and in the AIFMD Level 2 Regulation. As a result, there is no need to impose minimum capital requirements on the general partner *qua* general partner. However, if a general partner is itself appointed as the alternative investment fund manager of the ILP, it will also need to comply with those requirements, and will itself be regulated by the Central Bank or its equivalent in another jurisdiction.

Can a partnership be a general partner?

[29.36] The express terms of s 5(2) of the 1994 Act provide that 'a partnership may be a limited partner', but the section is silent as regards the ability of a partnership to be general partner. It might be thought that on the basis of the *expressio unius est exclusio alterius* principle,[78] this implies that a partnership may not be a general partner. However, it is suggested that this is not the case and once one general partner is a body corporate (as required by the Central Bank), the other general partners may be partnerships.[79] Under s 3 of the 1994 Act, a general partner is defined as a 'person' which term is broad enough to include a partnership.[80] The disapplication of the *expressio unius* principle may also be supported by the fact that the 1994 Act provides that the law of ordinary partnership applies to ILPs, subject to it not being inconsistent

---

[75]   Set out in the 'AIF' section of the Central Bank's website.

[76]   Non-UCITS Notice 5.13, see para **[29.19]**.

[77]   It used to be the case that such a general partner or (it seemed) all of them where there was more than one general partner, had to supply the Central Bank with its half-yearly financial and annual audited accounts and attend bi-annual meetings with the Central Bank. Where the ILP had a non-resident general partner, it had (between 1994 and 1996) also been under an obligation to supply the Central Bank with its annual audited accounts. The foregoing obligations no longer apply since the introduction of the Alternative Investment Fund Managers Directive framework into Irish law.

[78]   Ie the express mention of one thing is the exclusion of another.

[79]   A similar issue arises in relation to bodies corporate being general partners under the Limited Partnerships Act 1907, s 4(4) which simply states that a 'body corporate may be a limited partner'. See para **[28.34]**, where it is concluded that bodies corporate may be general partners relying upon, inter alia, *MacCarthaigh v Daly* [1985] IR 73.

[80]   See para **[2.36]**.

with the provisions of that Act,[81] and under this law a firm may be a partner.[82] In addition, the checklist required by the Central Bank in respect of an ILP's partnership agreement[83] recognises that not all general partners will be bodies corporate where it refers to 'a general partner which is a body corporate'.[84] The express reference in s 5(2) to a limited partner only may perhaps be explained by the fact that the Central Bank requires one general partner to be a body corporate and in most cases there will be just one general partner, while there will be many limited partners.

The Limited Partner

[29.37] Every ILP must have at least one limited partner[85] who is defined by s 3 of the 1994 Act as a:

> [P]erson who has been admitted to an investment limited partnership as a limited partner in accordance with the partnership agreement and who shall, at the time of entering into such partnership, contribute or undertake to contribute a stated amount to the capital of the partnership and, except as provided by *sections 6, 12, 20* and *38* of this Act, shall not be liable for the debts or obligations of the firm beyond the amount so contributed or undertaken.

'in accordance with the partnership agreement'

[29.38] The proposed limited partner in an ILP must ensure that he is admitted in accordance with the procedure set down in the partnership agreement. This is because under the strict wording of s 3 of the 1994 Act, a failure to do so will result in him not being a limited partner. In the event of such a failure,[86] it is conceived that the other general partners and limited partners (assuming that there are at least one of each)[87] could constitute an ILP amongst themselves of which he is not a member.[88]

---

81 See para **[29.15]**.

82 See para **[2.36]**.

83 In the 'AIF' section of its website, the Central Bank provides a detailed checklist of the terms that it requires to be included in an ILP's partnership agreement if it is to be authorised as a retail investor AIF, and an equivalent checklist for an ILP's partnership agreement if it is to be authorised as a qualifying investor AIF.

84 Note also that a firm may be a general partner under the American Uniform Limited Partnership Act (1985) and under the Uniform Limited Partnership Act 2001 (Last Amended 2013). Hurt, Smith, Bromberg and Ribstein, *Bromberg & Ribstein on Limited Liability Partnerships, the Revised Uniform Partnership Act, and the Uniform Limited Partnership Act (2001)* (2018 edn). See *Frigidaire Sales Corp v Union Properties Inc* (1977) 562 P 2d 244.

85 Investment Limited Partnerships Act 1994, s 5(1)(b).

86 It is unlikely that he would be held to be a general partner, since he is not likely to satisfy the requirement that general partners be admitted to the partnership as a general partner in accordance with the partnership agreement: the Investment Limited Partnerships Act 1994, s 3.

87 To satisfy the requirement in the Investment Limited Partnerships Act 1994, s 5(1)(b) that the firm have at least one limited partner and one general partner.

88 However, if the failed limited partner carries on business in common with the partners in the ILP, there may exist a concurrent partnership between him and the ILP. (contd.../)

Capital contribution of limited partner

[29.39] The contribution made by a limited partner to the capital of an ILP may be satisfied either in cash or other property.[89] It must however be made or undertaken to be made 'at the time of entering into'[90] the partnership. Where the contribution is in the form of non-cash, the value of the property must be the fair market value of the property at the time of the transfer of the property to the firm.[91] The contribution of capital in the form of the provision of services by the limited partner to the firm is expressly prohibited.[92] Section 5(4) of the 1994 Act re-states the self-evident proposition of partnership law that the provision of a loan by a limited partner to the ILP does not constitute a capital contribution.

The General Partner

[29.40] A general partner is defined in s 3 of the 1994 Act as:

> [A] person who has been admitted to an investment limited partnership as a general partner in accordance with the partnership agreement, and who shall be personally liable for the debts and obligations of the investment limited partnership.

The general partner, like a partner in an ordinary partnership, has unlimited liability for the debts and obligations of the firm. It is to be noted that, unlike the limited partner, the general partner is not required to contribute any capital to the ILP. However, like the limited partner,[93] the general partner must be admitted in accordance with the terms of the partnership agreement, failing which, he will not be a general partner.[94] The Central Bank AIF Rulebook includes a further condition relating to the appointment of a general partner in an ILP, namely that, subject to certain exceptions, an ILP cannot appoint a general partner who would acquire any shares carrying voting rights which would then

---

88 (\...contd) In this way, he may be a partner with, as distinct from *in* the ILP, assuming he could be regarded as carrying on business in common with that ILP with a view to profit, as required by the terms of the Partnership Act 1890, s 1(1) (see generally para **[2.01]** et seq). Of course, he will be an ordinary partner in such a partnership with the consequent unlimited liability. (See *MacCarthaigh v Daly* [1985] IR 73, where the proposed limited partner was held to be a general partner under the Limited Partnerships Act 1907, s 5, due to a failure to register as a limited partner in accordance with the provisions of the 1907 Act. Note however, s 5 of the 1907 Act expressly provides for this eventuality in the event of a failure to register in accordance with that Act). While this outcome is technically possible, in practice it may be unlikely to occur, since the putative limited partner, if he acts as a limited partner, is unlikely to satisfy the requirement that he be carrying on business 'in common' with the other partners. This is because of the restrictions on a limited partner from taking part in the conduct of the business of the ILP.

89 Investment Limited Partnerships Act 1994, s 5(3).

90 See the definition of a limited partner in the Investment Limited Partnerships Act 1994, s 3.

91 Investment Limited Partnerships Act 1994, s 3.

92 Investment Limited Partnerships Act 1994, s 5(4).

93 See para **[29.38]**.

94 If he does not comply with those requirements, he may be an ordinary partner with, as distinct from in, the ILP so formed. See fn **88** where the same point is made regarding limited partners.

enable the general partner to exercise significant influence over the management of the entity (the 'issuing body') in which the shares are issued.[95]

No Maximum Number of Partners

[29.41] Unlike an ordinary or limited partnership,[96] an ILP is not limited in the number of partners it can have. This is because the prohibition in s 1435(1) of the Companies Act 2014 on more than 20 partners in a partnership does not by its express terms apply to 'an investment limited partnership within the meaning of the Investment Limited Partnerships Act 1994'[97] or to partnerships formed under 'some other statute'[98] (which would also of itself exclude an ILP from the prohibition in s 1435(1) on the basis that an ILP is formed under the 1994 Act). There is further language in s 4(4) of the 1994 Act confirming that s 376 of the Companies Act 1963[99] does not apply to ILPs.

Not a Separate Legal Entity

[29.42] An ILP, like an ordinary partnership, is not a separate legal entity. So, for example, proceedings are taken against the general partners and not against the firm itself.[100] In much the same way as an ordinary partnership has some of the traits of a separate legal entity,[101] the 1994 Act does provide the ILP with some of these characteristics. Indeed, the ILP has even more of the characteristics of a separate legal entity than either the ordinary or limited partnership. For example unlike either of those partnerships, an ILP is not dissolved by a change in identity of the limited or general partners, in the absence of any agreement to the contrary between the partners.[102] Similarly, the death or bankruptcy of a limited or general partner will not dissolve the partnership, in the absence of any agreement to the contrary between the partners.[103]

The ILP Agreement

[29.43] Unlike an ordinary or limited partnership,[104] an ILP must be governed by a written partnership agreement. This is implicit in the requirement that the application for authorisation to the Central Bank must be accompanied by the partnership

---

[95] Central Bank AIF Rulebook at p 19 (in respect of an ILP authorised as a retail investor AIF) and p 103 (in respect of an ILP authorised as a qualifying investor AIF). This requirement is not applicable to investments in other investment funds, or to a venture capital, development capital or private equity AIF, provided that its prospectus states its intention to exercise legal and management control over underlying investments.

[96] See para **[4.29]** and para **[28.27]**.

[97] Companies Act 2014, s 1435(4).

[98] Companies Act 2014, s 1435(1)(b).

[99] The reference to s 376 of the Companies Act 1963 is deemed by s 5 and para 11(1) of Schedule 6 to the Companies Act 2014 to be a reference to its successor, s 1435(1) of the Companies Act 2014.

[100] Investment Limited Partnerships Act 1994, s 22(1).

[101] See para **[3.07]** et seq.

[102] Investment Limited Partnerships Act 1994, s 37(1)(i).

[103] Investment Limited Partnerships Act 1994, s 37(1)(iii).

[104] See para **[2.11]**.

agreement (with original signatures). The term 'partnership agreement' is defined by s 3 of the 1994 Act as:

> any valid written agreement of the partners governed by the law of the State and subject to the exclusive jurisdiction of the courts of the State, as to the affairs of an investment limited partnership and the conduct of its business as may be amended, supplemented or restated from time to time.

Furthermore, the terms of the investment limited partnership agreement must comply with certain basic requirements set out in the 1994 Act. Failure to comply with these requirements will result in the ILP not being authorised by the Central Bank. The Central Bank AIF Rulebook also sets out a number of items in respect of which provision should be made in the partnership agreement of an ILP.[105] As part of the application process for ILP authorisation, in addition to providing the partnership agreement itself, a lengthy checklist must also be submitted to the Central Bank[106] confirming that various matters are addressed in the partnership agreement, and indicating which clause of the partnership agreement deals with each of those matters. There is a separate checklist for a retail investor AIF and for a qualifying investor AIF.

Required terms of the investment limited partnership agreement

[29.44] It is clear from the definition of the investment limited partnership agreement that it may be amended, supplemented or restated from time to time.[107] The 1994 Act requires that the agreement comply with the following:

1. It must govern the affairs and the conduct of the business of the ILP.[108]
2. It must be in writing and signed by all the limited and general partners, be governed by the laws of Ireland and subject to the exclusive jurisdiction of the Irish courts.[109]
3. The principal business of the partnership must be stated.[110]
4. It must appoint a custodian.[111]
5. It must provide that its terms are subject to the exclusive jurisdiction of the courts of Ireland.[112]
6. It must contain the conditions and procedures for the replacement or admission of a general partner and custodian (including the replacement of a general partner or custodian by the Central Bank under s 30 of the 1994 Act). These provisions must also ensure that the limited partners are protected in the event of the replacement of a general partner or a custodian, although not in the event of additional general partners or custodians being admitted.[113] The Central

---

105 See para **[29.44]**.
106 The checklists for each of a retail investor AIF and for a qualifying investor AIF are available in the 'Forms' part of the 'AIF' section of the Central Bank's website
107 Investment Limited Partnerships Act 1994, s 3.
108 Investment Limited Partnerships Act 1994, s 3.
109 Investment Limited Partnerships Act 1994, s 3.
110 Investment Limited Partnerships Act 1994, s 5(1)(a).
111 Investment Limited Partnerships Act 1994, s 3.
112 Investment Limited Partnerships Act 1994, s 3.
113 Investment Limited Partnerships Act 1994, s 5(1)(d).

Bank AIF Rulebook also contains a similar requirement in respect of the replacement of the general partner or alternative investment fund manager (or management company, if one is appointed) whether at the initiative of the Central Bank or the ILP,[114] and in respect of the replacement of the depositary.[115]

In addition to the foregoing, the Central Bank AIF Rulebook also requires that the investment limited partnership agreement provide for a number of other matters, including the following matters:

1. The maximum annual fee charged by, as relevant, the general partner, the alternative investment fund manager, and any management company.[116]

2. In respect of a qualifying investor AIF only, the remuneration and expenditure which the general partner, depositary and any management company are entitled to charge the ILP, how that is to be calculated, and related costs to be borne by the ILP.[117]

3. In respect of a retail investor AIF only, if it is to be allowed to borrow and to secure any such borrowings on the assets of the retail investor AIF, express permission to do so.[118]

4. That the ILP's assets will be entrusted to a depositary for safe keeping.[119]

5. The maximum charge relating to the redemption or repurchase of units in the ILP.[120]

6. The conditions for contributions or withdrawals of contributions of partners' capital.[121]

7. The conditions and manner of the application of income.[122]

8. The rules for the valuation of assets.[123]

---

[114] Central Bank AIF Rulebook, p 35 (in respect of an ILP authorised as a retail investor AIF) and p 104 (in respect of an ILP authorised as a qualifying investor AIF).

[115] Central Bank AIF Rulebook, p 35 (in respect of an ILP authorised as a retail investor AIF) and p 105 (in respect of an ILP authorised as a qualifying investor AIF).

[116] Central Bank AIF Rulebook, p 20 (for a retail investor AIF) and p 103 (for a qualifying investor AIF).

[117] Central Bank AIF Rulebook, p 104.

[118] Central Bank AIF Rulebook, p 23.

[119] Central Bank AIF Rulebook, p 35 (in respect of a retail investor AIF) and p 104 (in respect of an ILP authorised as a qualifying investor AIF). See para [29.58] for further details of the requirement that an ILP's custodian be a 'depositary' within the meaning of the Irish AIFMD Regulations, reg 22(3).

[120] Central Bank AIF Rulebook, p 35 (in respect of an ILP authorised as a retail investor AIF) and p 103 (in respect of an ILP authorised as a qualifying investor AIF).

[121] Central Bank AIF Rulebook, p 35 (in respect of an ILP authorised as a retail investor AIF) and p 107 (in respect of an ILP authorised as a qualifying investor AIF).

[122] Central Bank AIF Rulebook, p 35 (in respect of an ILP authorised as a retail investor AIF) and p 104 (in respect of an ILP authorised as a qualifying investor AIF).

[123] Central Bank AIF Rulebook, p 38 et seq (in respect of an ILP authorised as a retail investor AIF) and p 106 et seq (in respect of an ILP authorised as a qualifying investor AIF).

[29.45] In addition to the foregoing requirements, the partnership agreement may contain the cases in which the calculation of the net asset value and the redemption of units in the firm may be suspended and the procedure therefor. However, suspension may be provided for only in exceptional cases where the circumstances so require and where it is justified, having regard to the interests of the partners.[124]

Amendment of the partnership agreement

[29.46] The all pervasive power of the Central Bank in relation to ILPs is apparent from the fact that, notwithstanding any term to the contrary, the investment limited partnership agreement may only be varied by an instrument in writing signed by or on behalf of all of the partners if that amendment has been approved by the Central Bank.[125]

The Name of an ILP

[29.47] As part of the application for authorisation as an ILP, the applicant firm must supply its proposed name.[126] The Central Bank may refuse to authorise an ILP by a name which is, in its opinion, undesirable, although an appeal against such a refusal may be taken in the High Court.[127] In addition, any amendment to the name of an ILP must be approved by the Central Bank before it will take effect.[128] As part of its name, an ILP must use any one of the following:[129]

    (a)   'investment limited partnership';

    (b)   'ILP';

    (c)   'comhpháirtíocht theoranta infheistíochta'; or

    (d)   'cti'.

If an ILP fails to comply with this obligation, any partner in the firm[130] who is in default, is guilty of an offence and liable to a maximum fine of €1,093,750, or to imprisonment for up to 15 years.[131]

---

124 Central Bank AIF Rulebook, p 37 (for a retail investor AIF) and p 106 (for a qualifying investor AIF).

125 Investment Limited Partnerships Act 1994, s 11(2) and Central Bank AIF Rulebook, p 52 (in respect of an ILP authorised as a retail investor AIF) and p 113 (in respect of an ILP authorised as a qualifying investor AIF).

126 Investment Limited Partnerships Act 1994, s 8(4)(a), see further para **[29.68]**.

127 Investment Limited Partnerships Act 1994, s 8(8).

128 Investment Limited Partnerships Act 1994, s 11(2).

129 Investment Limited Partnerships Act 1994, s 12(2).

130 In view of the restricted role of the limited partner in the conduct of the business of the firm (see the Investment Limited Partnerships Act 1994, s 6(1) and para **[29.103]**), this is most likely to be a general partner.

131 Investment Limited Partnerships Act 1994, s 40. The original fine of £500,000 was converted to its euro equivalent by virtue of Council Regulations (EC) No 1103/97, (EC) No 974/98 and (EC) No 2866/98 and the Economic and Monetary Union Act 1998, s 6 and then, by virtue of s 9 of the Fines Act 2010, multiplied by 1.75 to give the current amount.

Name cannot be changed without Central Bank consent

[29.48] An ILP may not change its name without the prior consent of the Central Bank.[132]

Name must not contain name of limited partner

[29.49] The role of a limited partner in an ILP is that of a dormant investor who takes no part in the management of the business of the firm and accordingly is not liable to third parties for the debts of the firm, beyond the amount he contributes in capital to the firm. For this reason, the 1994 Act prohibits the impression being given that the limited partner manages the firm's business. It does this by prohibiting the name of a limited partner, or a distinctive part thereof, from being part of the name of an ILP.[133]

[29.50] Under s 12(4) of the 1994 Act, where a limited partner knowingly allows his name or part thereof to be used in the name of the firm, he is liable, as if he were a general partner, to any person who does not actually know he was not a general partner and who extends credit to the firm. If the limited partner assigns his partnership share, his liability under this section does not pass to the assignee,[134] and if he ceases to be a limited partner, he is not relieved of this liability.[135] It is worth noting that unlike a holding out under s 14(1) of the 1890 Act,[136] there is no requirement for the third party to prove that he gave credit to the firm 'on the faith of' the representation that the limited partner was a general partner. He must simply show that he extended credit to the firm.

[29.51] The term 'extends credit' to the firm is not defined in the 1994 Act. However, it is similar to the requirement for a holding out under s 14(1) of the 1890 Act, ie that a third party has 'given credit' to the firm in which the person is being held out to be a partner. It has been noted elsewhere in this work[137] that this term, as used in s 14(1) of the 1890 Act, is not to be given a technical meaning, but should be taken to mean any transaction entered into by a third party with the firm. It is suggested that the term 'extends credit' in s 12(4) of the 1994 Act should be given a similar generic meaning.

Must comply with Registration of Business Names Act 1963

[29.52] While s 12(3) of the 1994 Act prohibits a limited partner from allowing his name to be used in the firm name, an ILP, like any partnership, is subject to the terms of the Registration of Business Names Act 1963. Indeed, because of the requirement in s 12(3) of the 1994 Act that a limited partner's name may not be used as part of the firm name, all ILPs will *ipso facto* be subject to the 1963 Act, since that Act applies to partnerships which carry on business under a name, other than that of all the partners.

---

[132] Central Bank AIF Rulebook, p 52 (in respect of a retail investor AIF) and p 113 (in respect of an ILP authorised as a qualifying investor AIF).

[133] Investment Limited Partnerships Act 1994, 12(3).

[134] Investment Limited Partnerships Act 1994, s 18(2).

[135] Investment Limited Partnerships Act 1994, s 21.

[136] See generally para [7.01] et seq.

[137] See para [7.32] et seq above. See the Australian case of *Lynch v Stiff* [1943] 68 CLR 428.

The application of the 1963 Act to partnerships is considered elsewhere in this work.[138] For present purposes, it remains to be noted that no distinction is made in the 1963 Act between limited partners and general partners. Accordingly, the names of the general and limited partners must appear in all business letters, circulars and catalogues in which the business name appears and in the registration form[139] for filing the business name with the Registrar of Business Names. However, in neither case is any distinction required to be made between limited and general partners. Nonetheless, it might be prudent for the limited partners to indicate that they are limited partners after their name.

The Registered Office of an ILP

[29.53] Unlike an ordinary partnership or a limited partnership, but like a company,[140] an ILP is obliged to maintain a registered office in Ireland.[141] The ILP is also obliged to maintain a principal place of business in Ireland which may be the same address as its registered office.[142] Under the express terms of s 12(1) of the 1994 Act, all communications and notices 'may' be addressed to the principal place of business, although this is *ipso facto* not obligatory. If an ILP fails to comply with the obligation to maintain a registered office and principal place of business, any partner[143] in the firm who is in default is guilty of an offence and liable to a maximum fine of €1,093,750 or to imprisonment of up to 15 years.[144]

ILP Must Maintain a Register of Interests

[29.54] Further increasing the practical similarities between an ILP and a company[145] is the fact that an ILP is obliged to maintain a register of the interests in the partnership.[146] This register must contain the following information:

(a)   the name and address of each partner;

(b)   the amount and date of contribution of each partner;

(c)   the amount undertaken to be contributed by each partner; and

(d)   the amount and date of any return of contribution to a partner.

The register is prima facie evidence of each of these matters. The register must be updated within five days of any change in particulars and is open to inspection by any

---

138   See para **[3.70]** et seq.

139   Companies Office Form RBN1A.

140   Companies Act 2014, s 50.

141   Investment Limited Partnerships Act 1994, s 12(1).

142   Investment Limited Partnerships Act 1994, s 12(1).

143   In view of the restricted role of the limited partner in the conduct of the business of the firm (see the Investment Limited Partnerships Act 1994, s 6(1) and see para **[29.103]**) this is most likely to be a general partner.

144   Investment Limited Partnerships Act 1994, s 12(5) and s 40. The original fine of £500,000 was converted to its euro equivalent by virtue of Council Regulations (EC) No 1103/97, (EC) No 974/98 and (EC) No 2866/98 and the Economic and Monetary Union Act 1998, s 6 and then, by virtue of s 9 of the Fines Act 2010, multiplied by 1.75 to give the current amount.

145   See the equivalent requirement on companies under s 169 of the Companies Act 2014.

146   Investment Limited Partnerships Act 1994, s 13.

partner or custodian of the ILP during business hours.[147] If default is made in maintaining the register, each general partner shall, upon summary conviction, incur a penalty of a class C fine for each day the default continues and must indemnify any person who thereby suffers a loss.[148]

ILP Must Appoint an Alternative Investment Fund Manager

[29.55] An ILP authorised as a retail investor AIF must appoint an alternative investment fund manager.[149] That alternative investment fund manager must itself be authorised within the EU, and the general partner of the ILP may be appointed to that role. If the ILP is to be established as a qualifying investor AIF, it must appoint an alternative investment fund manager that is authorised in Ireland, one that is authorised in another EU Member State and allowed to passport its activities into Ireland, or one that is authorised outside the EU. Unless it is required by the Irish AIFMD Regulations to appoint an alternative investment fund manager at an earlier date, an ILP authorised as a qualifying investor AIF on or after 22 July 2013 by the Central Bank must appoint an alternative investment fund manager within two years from its date of launch.[150] Again, the general partner may be appointed to this role.[151]

An ILP Cannot Act as Alternative Investment Fund Manager

[29.56] While certain types of qualifying investor AIF's may be internally managed (ie the AIF itself may be appointed as the alternative investment fund manager), this is not the case with an ILP authorised as a qualifying investor AIF as an alternative investment fund manager must be a 'legal person'.[152]

Duties of the Alternative Investment Fund Manager

[29.57] The AIFMD Level 2 Regulation provides the framework for the duties of an alternative investment fund manager. For example the senior management of an alternative investment fund manager is responsible for the implementation of the ILP's general investment policy, and the approval of the ILP's investment strategy.[153] It is also responsible for the establishment, maintenance, implementation and review of written

---

[147] Investment Limited Partnerships Act 1994, ss 13(1) and (2).

[148] Investment Limited Partnerships Act 1994, s 13(4). The original fine of £1,000 was converted to its euro equivalent by virtue of Council Regulations (EC) No 1103/97, (EC) No 974/98 and (EC) No 2866/98 and the Economic and Monetary Union Act 1998, s 6 and then, by virtue of s 6 of the Fines Act 2010, became a class C fine (a fine not exceeding €2,500). Compare s 173 of the Companies Act 2014. Unlike that section, s 13 of the 1994 Act does not provide for the register to be rectified, although the Central Bank arguably has this power under its general powers in s 33(1) of the 1994 Act to order such a rectification.

[149] Central Bank AIF Rulebook at p 52.

[150] Central Bank AIF Rulebook at p 113.

[151] An analysis of the authorisation and supervision regime for alternative investment fund managers is outside the scope of this work, but is set out in the Irish AIFMD Regulations, the AIFMD Level 2 Regulations and in the Central Bank AIF Rulebook.

[152] European Union (Alternative Investment Fund Managers) Regulations, reg 5(1).

[153] AIFMD Level 2 Regulation, reg 60(2).

policies and procedures in respect of the ILP's valuation processes and procedures,[154] and must (without prejudice to the requirements of Irish law and the ILP's partnership agreement) ensure that valuation methodologies of a certain standard are used.[155] The alternative investment fund manager must also ensure that the ILP's assets are valued fairly and appropriately.[156] An alternative investment fund manager will require authorisation from the Central Bank or from an equivalent regulatory authority in another jurisdiction, and the Irish AIFMD Regulations provide for the authorisation of, and operating conditions for, Irish-authorised alternative investment fund managers. Chapter 3 of the Central Bank AIF Rulebook also sets out conditions regarding the operating conditions, remuneration, organisational requirements, directors, record-keeping obligations, and permitted activities of alternative investment fund managers authorised by it, together with requirements regarding the relationship between the alternative investment fund manager and the Central Bank, and duties in respect of its financial control and management information. The letter of authorisation that is issued by the Central Bank to an alternative investment fund manager will set out the definitive list of conditions to which that alternative investment fund manager's authorisation is subject.

ILP Must Have Appointed a Custodian

[29.58] Under s 5(1)(c) of the 1994 Act, before an ILP will be granted an authorisation by the Central Bank, it must have appointed a custodian which has a place of business in Ireland and which is eligible to act as custodian in accordance with s 8 of the 1994 Act (ie the proposed custodian must be a 'depositary' within the meaning of reg 22(3) of the Irish AIFMD Regulations).[157] That custodian must have an appropriate level of expertise and experience to enable it to carry out its duties as set out in the Central Bank AIF Rulebook,[158] the Irish AIFMD Regulations, and the AIFMD Level 2 Regulation. It must also have sufficient resources to effectively conduct its business and it must organise and control its internal affairs in a reasonable manner with proper records and adequate arrangements for ensuring that employees are suitable, adequately trained and properly

---

[154] AIFMD Level 2 Regulation, reg 67(1).

[155] AIFMD Level 2 Regulation, reg 67(1).

[156] AIFMD Level 2 Regulation, reg 71(1).

[157] The definition of 'custodian' in the Investment Limited Partnerships Act 1994, s 3 was amended by the Irish AIFMD Regulations, reg 67 to require that any custodian be eligible to act as such in accordance with s 8 of the 1994 Act. To be eligible to act as custodian for an ILP in accordance with s 8 of the 1994 Act, the custodian must, under s 8(1)(c) of the 1994 Act, be a 'depositary' within the meaning of reg 22(3) of the Irish AIFMD Regulations. In general terms, this means that (in respect of an ILP under the 1994 Act) only banks, investment firms authorised as such under the framework of the Markets in Financial Instruments Directive (Directive 2014/59/EU (which replaced Directive 2004/39/EC) and which was transposed into Irish law by the European Union (Markets in Financial Instruments) Regulations 2017 (SI 375/2017), as amended) and investment firms authorised as such under the Investment Intermediaries Act 1995 may act as custodians. The Central Bank AIF Rulebook sets out (at Chapter 5) certain conditions regarding capital and governance in respect of a depositary that is an investment firm authorised under the Investment Intermediaries Act 1995.

[158] Central Bank AIF Rulebook, Chapter 5.

supervised.[159] The custodian will be subject to the duties set out in s 24 of the 1994 Act and any additional duties as are specified by the Central Bank.[160] There must be a written agreement in place with the custodian[161] and the assets of the ILP must be entrusted for safekeeping to the custodian.[162] Section 24(1)(c) of the 1994 Act states that the custodian:

> must ensure that an investment limited partnership's income is applied in accordance with this Act or regulations made hereunder, directions of the Bank *or* the partnership agreement.

[29.59] It is unclear why this section is framed in a disjunctive rather than a conjunctive manner. It is thought that this must be a typographical error, as it must have been intended that the custodian ensure compliance with all these matters. Nonetheless, a custodian who is alleged to have committed an offence by his failure to comply with this section[163] would appear to have a possible defence, namely that this section must be interpreted strictly (since it creates an offence).[164]

[29.60] In addition to any contractual obligation which a custodian may have to the general partners under the terms of the custodian agreement, he is also under a statutory obligation to carry out the instructions of the general partner, unless they conflict with the terms of the 1994 Act, any regulations made thereunder, any direction of the Central Bank or the partnership agreement.[165]

General partner and custodian must be independent

[29.61] Section 8(2) of the 1994 Act states that one person cannot be both a general partner and a custodian of an ILP. This is because the custodian is intended to be a third party who ensures the independent nature of the ILP for the benefit of the limited partners (the investors). This point is explicitly made in the Central Bank AIF Rulebook, which provides[166] that an AIF may only enter into a transaction with inter alia a general partner, depositary or alternative investment fund manager, or with their delegates or group companies, where they are negotiated at arms' length, and that transactions must be in the best interests of the limited partners.[167]

---

[159] Central Bank AIF Rulebook at p 187.

[160] The Investment Limited Partnerships Act 1994, s 7(2)(b) gives the Central Bank the power to impose such further conditions as it considers 'appropriate and prudent' for the purposes of regulating, inter alia, custodians. These are set out in the Central Bank AIF Rulebook and the Central Bank will set out the definitive list of conditions in the letter that it sends to the custodian when the related AIF is authorised (Central Bank AIF Rulebook at p 186).

[161] European Union (Alternative Investment Fund Managers) Regulations, reg 22(1).

[162] European Union (Alternative Investment Fund Managers) Regulations, reg 22(8).

[163] Investment Limited Partnerships Act 1994, s 24(3).

[164] *Frescati Estates v Walker* [1975] IR 177; *CW Shipping Co Ltd v Limerick Harbour Commissioners* [1989] ILRM 416 at 424.

[165] Investment Limited Partnerships Act 1994, s 24(1)(a).

[166] Central Bank AIF Rulebook at p 46 (in respect of retail investor AIFs) and p 112 (in respect of qualifying investor AIFs).

[167] Limited partners are included in the scope of the term 'unit holders' in the Central Bank AIF Rulebook. The previous iteration of this requirement (in Non-UCITS Notice 7, para 11) referred to 'partners' rather than to 'unit holders' but that had been interpreted as a reference to limited partners only (see para **[29.48]** of the first edition of this work).

No Obligation upon ILP to file Accounts in Companies Registration Office

[29.62] It has been noted elsewhere in this work that as a general rule, partnerships are not required to file accounts.[168] Despite the treatment of an ILP in some cases as being akin to a company,[169] it is does not as a general rule have to file accounts in the Companies Registration Office. It does, of course, have extensive reporting obligations to the Central Bank which are considered hereunder.[170]

Unless all the general partners have limited liability

[29.63] Like ordinary and limited partnerships, an ILP is subject to the terms of the European Communities (Accounts) Regulations 1993.[171] These provide that a partnership, in which all the partners with unlimited liability (ie the general partners in an ILP) are companies with limited liability or their equivalent,[172] is required to file accounts as if it were a company under the Companies Act 2014. The rationale for this rule is that in such a partnership all the partners will effectively have limited liability and should therefore be treated in the same way as limited liability companies in relation to the filing of their accounts.

But Central Bank has granted an exemption

[29.64] As noted elsewhere in this chapter, the ILP is required to provide the Central Bank with an annual report and audited accounts.[173] The Central Bank has exercised its power under s 15 of 1994 Act to exempt an ILP which falls within the European Communities (Accounts) Regulations 1993[174] from its terms.[175] To be entitled to that exemption,[176] the ILP must have as its 'sole' business the investment of funds in property with the aim of spreading investment risk and giving its partners the benefit of the management of its assets. As previously noted,[177] under s 5(1)(a) of the 1994 Act, an ILP may be formed where its 'principal', as distinct from its sole, business is the

---

168 See para **[14.64]**.
169 See for example the appointment of inspectors to ILPs under the Investment Limited Partnerships Act 1994, s 26, considered at para **[29.174]** and the power of a partner to contract with the ILP as if he was a third party under s 19(2) of the 1994 Act, considered at para **[29.116]**.
170 See para **[29.176]** et seq.
171 SI 396/1993.
172 For those partnerships which are caught by this expression see the terms of reg 6 of the European Communities (Accounts) Regulations 1993 which are considered para **[14.66]** et seq.
173 See further in relation to this requirement, para **[29.176]** et seq.
174 SI 396/1993.
175 This exemption is set out in the 'AIF' section of the Central Bank's website.
176 This power is based on the right in Article 5 of Council Directive 78/660/EEC for Member States to derogate from Council Directives 90/604/EEC and 90/605/EEC in the case of investment companies. Article 5(2)(a) defines investment companies as undertakings whose sole object is the investment of funds in property with the sole aim of spreading risk and giving members the benefit of the results of the management of assets.
177 See para **[29.30]**.

investment of its funds in property, so that not every ILP will benefit from this exemption.

III. AUTHORISATION OF AN ILP

[29.65] Having considered the nature of an ILP, it is now proposed to look in detail at the authorisation process and the additional requirements to be satisfied by an ILP before it will be authorised by the Central Bank. The importance of this process cannot be underestimated, since the very existence of an ILP is dependant on the Central Bank issuing such an authorisation.[178]

Central Bank must be Satisfied as to Competence and Probity

[29.66] Before the Central Bank will authorise an ILP, it must be satisfied with various matters in respect of the proposed general partner(s) and the proposed custodian. The proposed custodian must be a depositary within the meaning of reg 22(3) of the AIFMD Regulations,[179] and either:

(a) the proposed general partners, or any one of them, must be authorised by the Central Bank as an alternative investment fund manager[180] or must be authorised as such by the competent authority in its home Member State or in its Member State of reference;[181] or

(b) the proposed general partners or any one of them must satisfy the Central Bank as to their competence and probity.[182]

If the proposed general partner or any one of them is not already authorised as an alternative investment fund manager (ie as set out in (a) above) the Central Bank will not authorise the ILP if, in the Central Bank's opinion, the general partners are not of sufficiently good repute or lack the experience required for the performance of their duties.[183] Since the limited partner is in essence, a dormant investor in the partnership, the Central Bank is not concerned about his repute or experience.

But authorisation does not constitute a warranty by the Central Bank

[29.67] Section 36 of the 1994 Act expressly provides that the grant of an authorisation by the Central Bank does not constitute a warranty by it as to the creditworthiness or financial standing of an ILP, its partners or its custodians. Curiously, this section does

---

[178] Investment Limited Partnerships Act 1994, s 5(1)(f).

[179] As to which, see para **[29.58]**.

[180] Under Part 2 of the Irish AIFMD Regulations.

[181] Such authorisation would be under Chapter II of the Alternative Investment Fund Managers Directive as transposed into the laws of that Member State. A 'member state of reference' is relevant where the alternative investment fund manager is from a non-EU jurisdiction and wants to inter alia manage an EU AIF (such as an ILP under the 1994 Act). In that case, the Alternative Investment Fund Managers Directive sets out rules for determining which EU Member State will be treated as the 'home member state' of that non-EU alternative investment fund manager and which regulatory authority will have oversight of its activities in the EU.

[182] Investment Limited Partnerships Act 1994, s 8(1)(a).

[183] Investment Limited Partnerships Act 1994, s 8(1)(b).

not go on to provide that the Central Bank is not liable for any loss caused to third parties by the actions of an authorised ILP. This is in contrast to legislation governing the regulation by the Central Bank of banks,[184] unit trusts,[185] investment companies[186] and investment intermediaries.[187] Whether this fact could be used to successfully argue that the Central Bank is liable to limited partners or third parties who suffer losses at the hands of an authorised ILP is doubtful,[188] especially as every ILP authorised as a retail investor AIF must issue a prospectus which states that:

> 'The Central Bank shall not, by virtue of its authorisation of this Retail Investor AIF or by reason of its exercise of functions conferred on it by legislation in relation to this Retail Investor AIF, be liable for any default of the Retail Investor AIF. Authorisation of this Retail Investor AIF does not constitute a warranty by the Central Bank as to the creditworthiness or financial standing of the various parties to the Retail Investor AIF.'[189]

And every ILP authorised as a qualifying investor AIF must issue a prospectus which states that:

> 'The Central Bank shall not be liable by virtue of its authorisation of this Qualifying Investor AIF or by reason of its exercise of the functions conferred on it by legislation in relation to this Qualifying Investor AIF for any default of the Qualifying Investor AIF. Authorisation of this Qualifying Investor AIF does not constitute a warranty by the Central Bank as to the creditworthiness or financial standing of the various parties to the Qualifying Investor AIF.'[190]

Application for Authorisation

[29.68] Once the foregoing basic requirements for an ILP are satisfied by the partnership, it may make an application for authorisation in writing to the Central Bank.[191] In the case of an application for authorisation as a retail investor AIF, the application must be made by the proposed alternative investment fund manager and the general partner(s). In the case of a qualifying investor AIF, the application must be made by the proposed alternative investment fund manager, the general partner(s) and the depositary. The application must be accompanied by a fee of €1,250,[192] and detailed

---

184 Central Bank Act 1971, s 9(5). See also s 25A of the Central Bank Act 1989 (as inserted by s 69 of the Central Bank Act 1997).

185 Unit Trusts Act 1990, s 4(6).

186 Companies Act 2014, s 1397.

187 Investment Intermediaries Act 1995, s 53.

188 See the annotation of the 1994 Act by Declan Murphy, available at www.westlaw.ie. It would seem to be a difficult matter to impose such liability in view of the High Court decision in *McMahon v Ireland* [1988] ILRM 610. For a discussion of this case, see McGrath, 'Tort – Negligence – The Duty of Care and the World at Large' (1987) DULJ 163. See also the Privy Council case of *Yeun Kun Yeu v AG of Hong Kong* [1987] 3 WLR 776 which was followed by the High Court in *McMahon v Ireland*, above and the Privy Council case of *Davis v Radcliffe* [1990] 1 WLR 821.

189 Central Bank AIF Rulebook at p 62.

190 Central Bank AIF Rulebook at p 123.

191 Investment Limited Partnerships Act 1994, s 8(3).

192 Investment Limited Partnerships Act 1994 (Authorisation Fee) Regulations, 1994 (SI 402/ 1994) made pursuant to s 8(4) of the 1994 Act. (contd.../)

application forms and appendices to those application forms, together with related authorisation guidance, are set out in the 'AIF' section of the Central Bank's website. The Central Bank requires the directors of any general partner to have relevant experience and those directors must be approved by the Central Bank in advance of the authorisation application being made.[193] As part of the application process, a statement signed by the proposed general partner containing the following information must be provided:[194]

1. The name of the ILP;[195]
2. The general nature of its investment objectives;
3. Its registered office and its principal place of business in Ireland;
4. Its commencement date and its term or a statement that it is of unlimited duration;
5. The full name and address of the proposed general partner(s);
6. Where the proposed general partner is a body corporate which is not incorporated in Ireland, a statement that it has complied with the requirements of s 1302 of the Companies Act 2014[196] and its registration number;
7. The full name and address of the proposed custodian.

The Central Bank's application forms also seek, inter alia, the following information:

1. Details in respect of the alternative investment fund manager and other service providers to the ILP, including legal advisors and auditors.
2. Details of how the fund will be marketed, together with various other letters and confirmations specific to the type of business that the ILP will carry on.

[29.69] In addition to the signed application form and the statement of the general partner under s 8(4) of the 1994 Act, the ILP must also submit originals of both its partnership agreement and the agreement with its custodian to the Central Bank, together with copies of material contracts entered into by it, its prospectus, and details of any derogations from the Central Bank AIF Rulebook which have been granted to it.

[29.70] The Central Bank provides, in the section of its website dealing with AIFs, checklists in respect of the terms that must be included in the partnership agreement, the agreement with the alternative investment fund manager, and the agreement with the

---

192 (\...contd) The original fee of £1,000 was converted to its euro equivalent by virtue of Council Regulations (EC) No 1103/97, (EC) No 974/98 and (EC) No 2866/98 and the Economic and Monetary Union Act 1998, s 6.

193 An online individual questionnaire must be completed in respect of each such director, even if they have been previously approved by the Central Bank in relation to a qualifying investor AIF.

194 Investment Limited Partnerships Act 1994, s 8(4); Central Bank Regulatory Requirements and Guidance for AIFs: AIF Applications for Authorisation (revision dated 3 July 2013).

195 The Central Bank may refuse to authorise an ILP by a name which is in its opinion undesirable, although an appeal against such a refusal shall lie to the High Court: Investment Limited Partnerships Act 1994, s 8(8).

196 The Investment Limited Partnerships Act 1994, s 8(4A) refers to s 352 of the Companies Act 1963 which is deemed, by virtue of s 5 and para 11(1) of Sch 6 to the Companies Act 2014 to be a reference to s 1302 of the Companies Act 2014.

custodian, confirming which clause of each of those agreements meets specific requirements imposed by the AIFMD framework.

Failure by general partner to sign statement

[29.71] If the proposed general partner fails to sign the application for authorisation as an ILP, any other limited or general partner (or an assignee of a partner's interest) who is affected may petition the High Court to direct the signing of the application for authorisation.[197] This right does not extend to a failure by the alternative investment fund manager or (in the case of a qualifying investor AIF) the depositary to sign the application form – neither a limited partner nor a general partner may seek to direct the signing of the form by either of those parties.

Changes to some particulars are ineffective without Central Bank's consent

[29.72] If, after the authorisation for an ILP has issued, any change occurs in certain of the particulars submitted to the Central Bank as part of the application process by the general partner under s 8(4) of the Act, s 28(2) of the 1994 Act provides that this change will not come into effect until the Central Bank has approved it. A general partner is required to submit a statement of the change to the Central Bank within five days thereof and the change will only take effect on the issue of a letter by the Central Bank consenting to the change.[198] Where the change in question is a change in the name of the ILP, this change will not take effect until the Central Bank has issued an amended certificate of authorisation.[199]

Even a change in name or address of custodian?

[29.73] One of the particulars which must be submitted to the Central Bank as part of the application process is the name and address of the ILP's custodian. Prima facie, one of the effects of s 28(2) of the 1994 Act is that a custodian, who has as one of its clients an ILP, will not be able to change its name or address without the Central Bank issuing a letter of consent to the change. This possibility arises from the loose drafting of s 8(4)(f) and s 28(2) of the 1994 Act. Clearly what concerns the Central Bank is that the custodian of the ILP's funds meets the definition of 'depositary' in the Irish AIFMD Regulations[200] and for this reason, its identity must be notified to the Central Bank as part of the application process. However, the Central Bank cannot have any interest in

---

197 Investment Limited Partnerships Act 1994, s 8(5).
198 Investment Limited Partnerships Act 1994, s 28(1).
199 Investment Limited Partnerships Act 1994, s 28(2).
200 European Union (Alternative Investment Fund Managers) Regulation 2013, reg 22(3). The combined effect of reg 22(3) and s 8(1) of the 1994 Act is that, in general terms, only banks, investment firms authorised as such under the framework of the Markets in Financial Instruments Directive (Directive 2014/59/EU (which replaced Directive 2004/39/EC) and which was transposed into Irish law by the European Union (Markets in Financial Instruments) Regulations 2017 (SI 375/2017), as amended) and investment firms authorised as such under the Investment Intermediaries Act 1995 may act as custodians for an ILP. The Central Bank AIF Rulebook sets out (at Chapter 5) certain conditions regarding capital and governance where the depositary is an investment firm authorised under the Investment Intermediaries Act 1995.

the corporate housekeeping of the custodian. Accordingly, it is suggested that when s 28(2) refers to any change in the 'particulars specified in s 8(4)(a) to (f) with respect to the investment limited partnership', this should, it is submitted, be interpreted as any change in the identity of the ILP's custodian and not, as any change in the name or address of the custodian. In this way, the custodian, who happens to have an ILP as a client, may change its name or address without requiring the consent of the Central Bank. Since this interpretation is by no means certain, this matter should be clarified by an appropriate amendment to the 1994 Act.

Where Failure of Central Bank to take a Decision on Authorisation

[29.74] If the Central Bank refuses or fails to take a decision on an application for authorisation of an ILP within three months of a complete application, one of the proposed general partners may apply to the High Court which may direct the Central Bank to take a decision within such time as the court may direct.[201]

Criteria for Refusal of Authorisation

[29.75] In addition to the Central Bank being obliged to refuse the authorisation where it is not satisfied as to the competence and probity of the general partner or it has not been demonstrated to it that the proposed custodian is a depositary within the meaning of reg 22(3) of the Irish AIFMD Regulations,[202] the Central Bank may refuse authorisation where:

(a)   the applicant fails to fulfil the requirements set down in the 1994 Act or by the Central Bank under that Act; or

(b)   the applicant fails to satisfy the Central Bank that it will be able to satisfy the conditions imposed by the Central Bank; or

(c)   the Central Bank is not satisfied that authorisation would be in the best interests of the proper and orderly regulation of ILPs.[203]

Notification of refusal

[29.76] The Central Bank is required by s 9(1) of the 1994 Act to notify an applicant of a refusal of authorisation and the reasons therefor. There is no time period directly imposed on the Central Bank within which the notification of refusal is to be made, but it seems that it should be done within three months of the date upon which a proper application was submitted. This is because under s 9(2) of the 1994 Act, where the Central Bank fails to take a decision within three months of submission, a general partner may apply to the High Court for a direction for the Central Bank to make the decision.

---

201   Investment Limited Partnerships Act 1994, s 32.
202   Investment Limited Partnerships Act 1994, s 8(1), see further para **[29.66]**.
203   Investment Limited Partnerships Act 1994, s 8(9).

Criteria for Revocation of Authorisation

[29.77] Where the Central Bank has previously authorised an ILP, it is entitled to revoke that authorisation where it appears to the Central Bank that:

(a)   the requirements for the authorisation of the ILP are no longer satisfied;

(b)   it is desirable in the interests of the limited partners;

(c)   the general partner or custodian has contravened any provision of the 1994 Act or any condition imposed thereunder or has furnished the Central Bank with false, inaccurate or misleading information.[204]

[29.78] The Central Bank may also revoke the authorisation of an ILP at the request of the general partner or custodian, unless the revocation would not be in the interests of the limited partners or if any matter concerning the ILP should first be investigated.[205] The Central Bank must publish a notice of a revocation of authorisation in *Iris Oifigiúil* and in one national daily newspaper within five days of the revocation.[206]

[29.79] The Central Bank is also entitled to replace a general partner (or custodian) in similar circumstances[207] to those in which it may revoke an ILP's authorisation. In some cases, this option may be preferred by the Central Bank, since it is more likely to be in the interests of the limited partners.

Effect of revocation

[29.80] Section 37(2)(b) of the 1994 Act provides that the revocation of a firm's authorisation leads to its automatic dissolution.[208] This modifies the application of the law of partnership which would otherwise apply to ILPs. Thus, notwithstanding the fact that under the law of partnership, the ILP would otherwise be regarded as an existing partnership, the effect of this section is that the ILP (which of course depends for its existence on the authorisation of the Central Bank)[209] is immediately dissolved by the revocation of its authorisation. The reference in s 37(2)(b) to dissolution is clearly to the general dissolution of the firm since the firm will not be allowed to carry on its business.[210] Under the general law of partnership on such a dissolution, the partners in the ILP are entitled to have the partnership property sold and applied in the payment of the firm's debts and liabilities and to apply to court for the firm to be wound up.[211]

---

204   Investment Limited Partnerships Act 1994, s 29(1).

205   Investment Limited Partnerships Act 1994, s 29(2).

206   Investment Limited Partnerships Act 1994, s 29(3).

207   This issue is considered in more detail para **[29.148]** et seq.

208   Investment Limited Partnerships Act 1994, s 37(2)(b).

209   Investment Limited Partnerships Act 1994, s 5(1)(f).

210   As to the distinction between a general dissolution and a technical dissolution, see para **[23.07]**.

211   Partnership Act 1890, s 39. See also the situations in which the winding up of an ILP (that has had its authorisation withdrawn) may be avoided: Investment Limited Partnerships Act 1994, s 37(3).

Appeal of Refusal or Revocation of Authorisation

[29.81] In addition to the judicial review remedies[212] which may be available where an authorisation has been refused or revoked by the Central Bank, the 1994 Act sets out a restricted form of appeal procedure to the High Court. Under s 32, where the Central Bank refuses an application for authorisation or revokes an existing authorisation, any aggrieved party, including a limited partner, may apply to the High Court for a review. Any application must be made on notice to the Central Bank, the general partner and the custodian and where a general partner brings the application or receives notice of it, he must advise the limited partners who are entitled to be heard at the application. As is clear from the following analysis, the process is somewhat restricted in nature and for that reason the term 'review' as used in s 32 to describe this process is more apt than the term 'appeal'.

Onus of proof on applicant

[29.82] Although not expressly stated, it appears from the wording of s 32(2) of the 1994 Act that the onus is on the applicant to prove his case, since it states that the court shall confirm the decision, unless it is satisfied that the procedures laid down by that Act have not been satisfied. This onus on the applicant is heavy, since under s 32(2), he must prove that the requirements of the 1994 Act, or the criteria for the refusal of an authorisation or the revocation of an authorisation, have not been satisfied in any 'material respect'. In addition, the application will be unsuccessful if the Central Bank proves that it had some 'material' upon which it could reasonably conclude that these criteria had been satisfied.

[29.83] The applicant's position is even more difficult in the case of a revocation of authorisation, since while the Central Bank is required to give reasons for its refusal to grant an authorisation,[213] it is not required to give any reasons for its decision to revoke an authorisation.[214] It is contended that there is no good reason for this distinction.

Court may not order authorisation to be granted

[29.84] In a case taken against the refusal or revocation of the authorisation of an ILP under s 32(2), the High Court is not entitled to order the Central Bank to grant an authorisation, but its power extends merely to setting aside the decision of the Central Bank.[215] Obviously, in the case of the setting aside of a decision to revoke an authorisation, this will be as good as an order for the authorisation to be re-granted. However, where the decision being set aside is the Central Bank's refusal to grant the original authorisation, the High Court is simply empowered to direct the Central Bank to reconsider the decision.[216]

---

[212] As to judicial review actions generally see Chapters 10 and 11 of Hogan and Morgan, *Administrative Law in Ireland* (4th edn, 2010); Bradley, *Judicial Review* (2000).

[213] Investment Limited Partnerships Act 1994, s 9(1).

[214] Investment Limited Partnerships Act 1994, s 29.

[215] Investment Limited Partnerships Act 1994, s 32(3).

[216] Investment Limited Partnerships Act 1994, s 32(3).

Certificate of Authorisation is Conclusive

[29.85] Once the Central Bank issues a certificate of authorisation for an ILP, the certificate is conclusive evidence[217] of compliance with all the requirements of the 1994 Act in relation to the formation and authorisation of an ILP.[218]

[29.86] While the certificate of authorisation is conclusive evidence of the formation of an ILP, it should be noted that the Central Bank has power to amend at any time the conditions upon which it authorised an ILP, if it regards this as being necessary for the orderly and proper regulation of the business of ILPs.[219]

ILP Must Comply with Central Bank's Conditions

[29.87] An ILP is required to comply with all requirements set down from time to time by the Central Bank.[220] In this respect, the Central Bank is granted quite far-reaching powers to impose conditions for the authorisation of ILPs generally or to impose conditions on specific ILPs, general partners or custodians. The only requirement for the imposition of such conditions is that the Central Bank considers that they are appropriate or prudent for the orderly and proper regulation of the general partners, custodians or ILPs. The 1994 Act contains a non-inclusive list of matters to which these conditions may relate.[221]

[29.88] The Central Bank is also entitled to amend the conditions contained in the grant of authorisation at any time after the authorisation is granted.[222] Any failure by an ILP, custodian or general partner to comply with the Central Bank's conditions will constitute

---

[217] Note, however, that in *Maher v Attorney General* [1973] IR 140, it was held that a similar provision in s 44(2)(a) of the Road Traffic Act 1968 was declared unconstitutional since it made a certificate of the level of alcohol in the blood conclusive evidence of the matter certified. This was held to pre-empt the judicial function. Note however that this case was concerned with a criminal offence unlike s 8(6) of the 1994 Act.

[218] Investment Limited Partnerships Act 1994, s 8(6). Similar wording is to be found in s 25(4) of the Companies Act 2014 but cf the position in relation to the issue of the certificate of registration of a limited partnership under the Limited Partnerships Act 1907, s 13, para **[28.62]**.

[219] Investment Limited Partnerships Act 1994, s 7(3). As there is no provision under the 1994 Act for an appeal regarding the conditions imposed by the Central Bank, the only possible recourse would be to administrative law remedies, see generally Hogan and Morgan, *Administrative Law in Ireland* (4th edn, 2010).

[220] Investment Limited Partnerships Act 1994, s 5(1)(e). Note that the Central Bank is entitled to impose additional conditions on ILPs under s 7 of the 1994 Act.

[221] This list is set out in the Investment Limited Partnerships Act 1994, s 7(4), ie the (a) investment policies of the ILP, (b) contents of prospectus and other information disseminated by the firm, (c) criteria for the appointment of a custodian, (d) vesting of assets in the custodian, (e) issue of reports by the ILP, and (f) any other supervisory or reporting requirements.

[222] Investment Limited Partnerships Act 1994, s 7(3).

an offence punishable by a maximum fine of €1,093,750 and imprisonment of up to 15 years.[223]

Conditions issued by the Central Bank

[29.89] The Central Bank first issued conditions for the authorisation of ILPs in July 1994 by means of Central Bank Notice ILP 1. This notice was replaced by the NU Series of Notices which was issued in January 1996. The NU Series of Notices was then replaced by the Central Bank AIF Rulebook in July 2013. The terms of the Central Bank AIF Rulebook are considered hereunder in relation to the regulation of ILPs.[224] In addition to imposing specific conditions for the initial authorisation of ILPs, the Central Bank AIF Rulebook sets out the ongoing supervisory requirements for ILPs, and the Central Bank also lists further conditions in the 'AIF' section of its website. It is important to note that the Central Bank has indicated that the letter of authorisation issued by the Central Bank to an ILP when it is authorised as an AIF will list the definitive set of conditions that apply to that ILP.[225] The Central Bank may grant derogations from the Central Bank AIF Rulebook, and these will generally be listed in the prospectus.[226]

IV. LIABILITY OF THE LIMITED PARTNERS

[29.90] The definition of a limited partner in s 3 of the 1994 Act establishes that he is not liable for the obligations of the firm beyond the amount of capital contributed or undertaken to be contributed by him to the firm. It is important to bear in mind that the liability of a limited partner depends on him being a member of a valid ILP which in turn depends on the issue of the authorisation of the Central Bank.[227] Accordingly, a limited partner will not benefit from limited liability until this authorisation has issued.

[29.91] Under the law applicable to ordinary partnerships, each partner is personally liable to an unlimited degree for the obligations of the firm. As noted elsewhere in this work,[228] the unlimited liability of a partner in an ordinary partnership is based on the fact that a partnership is not a separate legal entity and therefore third parties who deal with a partnership are in fact dealing with the partners individually. For this reason, the partners in an ordinary partnership are personally liable for the obligations of the firm in the same way as if the third parties were dealing with them individually. However, this

---

[223] Investment Limited Partnerships Act 1994, s 40. Under s 41(1) of the 1994 Act, where the offence is committed by a body corporate with the consent or approval, or was facilitated by any wilful neglect on the part, of any person being a director, manager, secretary, member of any committee or management or other controlling authority of such body, that person shall also be guilty of an offence. The original fine of £500,000 was converted to its euro equivalent by virtue of Council Regulations (EC) No 1103/97, (EC) No 974/98 and (EC) No 2866/98 and the Economic and Monetary Union Act 1998, s 6 and then, by virtue of s 9 of the Fines Act 2010, multiplied by 1.75 to give the current amount.

[224] See para **[29.146]** et seq.

[225] Central Bank: AIFMD Questions and Answers (30th edn, 4 May 2018) at ID 1014.

[226] See para **[29.19]**.

[227] See para **[29.65]** et seq.

[228] See para **[28.105]**.

rationale is not present for limited partners in ILPs, since they are prohibited[229] from taking part in the conduct of the firm's business. Therefore, any third parties who deal with the firm cannot be regarded as dealing with them but with the general partners. This reasoning is behind the grant to limited partners of limited liability and also the loss of this protection when they contravene this prohibition. In view of the importance to investors of limited liability, consideration will now be given to the loss of this liability where the limited partner takes part in the management of the firm and also to the other situations in which it may be lost.

Loss of Limited Liability

[29.92] The actual (and in some cases the perceived) loss by the limited partners of their limited liability will arise in each of the following five instances.

1. Limited partner taking part in the conduct of the business

[29.93] The first situation in which a limited partner will lose his protection of limited liability is where he takes part in the conduct of the business of the ILP.[230] As noted, the rationale for granting the limited partner limited liability is the fact that he does not take part in the conduct of the firm's business. The corollary of this is that he is liable as if he were a general partner if he takes part in the conduct of the business. Section 6 of the 1994 Act[231] states that the limited partner is liable as a general partner if each of the following conditions is met:

(a)   The limited partner must have taken part in the conduct of the business of the firm in its dealings with third parties. Thus, if the ILP was doing business with the partners of the firm, the limited partner would not be liable.

(b)   The firm must be insolvent before the limited partner will be liable.

(c)   The debts or obligations for which the limited partner is liable must have been incurred by a third party who, at the time the debt or obligation was incurred, reasonably believed, based upon the conduct of the limited partner, that he was a general partner. This requirement implies that there must be some degree of culpability on the part of the limited partner, since his conduct should be sufficient to convince a reasonable man that he was a general partner. To this extent, it is comparable to the doctrine of holding out in an ordinary partnership which requires the alleged partner by holding out to represent himself, or knowingly suffer himself to be represented, as a partner.[232]

---

229   Investment Limited Partnerships Act 1994, s 6(2). Compare the limited liability of limited partners in limited partnerships, para **[28.95]** et seq.

230   Investment Limited Partnerships Act 1994, s 6(2).

231   This section is clearly based on s 303 of the American legislation on limited partnerships, ie the Revised Uniform Limited Partnership Act of 1985. While that Act remains applicable in a number of US states, it has been replaced in many US states by the Uniform Limited Partnership Act 2001 (Last Amended 2013) which provides a full shield against liability to limited partners in s 303 of that Act, which provides that: '[a] limited partner is not personally liable, directly or indirectly, by way of contribution or otherwise, for a debt, obligation, or other liability of the partnership solely by reason of being or acting as a limited partner, even if the limited partner participates in the management and control of the limited partnership ...'

232   See generally in relation to the degree of culpability required of a person for him to be held liable as a partner by holding out under the Partnership Act 1890, s 14(1), para **[7.12]** et seq.

(d)   The obligation must have been incurred during the period when the limited partner participated in the conduct of the firm's business.

Certain activities are permitted by the express terms of s 6 of the 1994 Act which will not deprive a limited partner of his protection of limited liability. These activities are considered elsewhere in this chapter.[233]

2. Use of limited partner's name in firm name

[29.94] Where a limited partner knowingly allows his name or part thereof to be used in the name of the ILP, he is liable as if he were a general partner (with unlimited liability) to any person who does not actually know he was not a general partner and who extends credit to the firm.[234] It is worth noting that the standard of proof for both the third party and the limited partner is high under this section – first, to establish liability the third party must show that the limited partner knowingly allowed his name to be used as part of the firm name, while to avoid liability the limited partner has to show that the third party actually knew that he was a limited partner.

3. Expiry of fixed term partnership

[29.95] Section 38(4) of the 1994 Act provides that where a fixed term partnership reaches the end of its term, the limited partners are liable for the debts and obligations 'purportedly incurred on behalf of the investment limited partnership thereafter'. This provision is remarkably wide-ranging and is deserving of consideration as technically it may provide for the loss of limited liability by the limited partners.

[29.96] First, s 38(4) is concerned with investment limited partnership agreements which provide for the partnership to last for a fixed duration. This is clear since it provides that if liabilities are incurred after the end of that term, the limited partners are liable therefor. Curiously, the question of the extent of the partner's liability is not explicitly addressed by s 38(4). It simply states that the 'limited partners shall be liable for the debts and obligations purportedly incurred'. It is apprehended that the grant of limited liability under s 3 of the 1994 Act takes precedence over this section so that the liability of the limited partners is still limited to their capital contribution. If it was intended that s 38(4) would provide unlimited liability for the limited partners, it is contended that more explicit language would be required to override the terms of s 3. It is submitted therefore that s 38(4) must be taken to confer liability on the limited partners up to the amount of their capital contribution after the final day of the partnership term.

[29.97] However, there is no certainty that a court will take this view and in view of the possibility, albeit remote, that a court would interpret s 38(4) as providing a limited partner with unlimited liability for the debts incurred after the expiry of the fixed term, the drafters of investment limited partnership agreements might be well advised to draft open-ended partnership agreements rather than fixed term agreements. Another precaution would be for a limited partner in a fixed term partnership which has come to

---

233   See para **[29.105]**.

234   Investment Limited Partnerships Act 1994, s 12(4). Cf the position of a limited partner in a limited partnership who allows his name to be used in the firm name, para **[28.41]**.

an end to advise all those persons who had dealings with the firm of the fact that the partnership is dissolved, so as to prevent such persons entering arrangements with the ILP on the misapprehension that it still exists.[235] In doing so, the limited partner will be relying on the terms of s 36(1) of the 1890 Act, ie that a person who had dealings with a firm is only entitled to treat all apparent members of the firm as still being members until he has notice of the change.

Position of general partner under s 38(4)

[29.98] At this juncture, it is proposed to briefly consider the position of the general partner under s 38(4) of the 1994 Act. It is strange that s 38(4) refers only to the liability of the limited partners for the debts and obligations incurred after the expiry of the term of a fixed term ILP. Nonetheless, it is apprehended that the general partners will also remain liable for these obligations under general principles of partnership law[236] on the grounds that these principles apply to ILPs since they are not inconsistent with the terms of s 38(4) or the rest of the 1994 Act.[237] In this regard, s 38(4) of the 1994 Act requires any one general partner[238] to advertise in *Iris Oifigiúil* the dissolution of the fixed term partnership by the expiry of its term. Curiously, however, there is no reference in the 1994 Act to the effect of such a notice and for this reason, it is apprehended that the provisions of the 1890 Act will apply to such a notice, on the grounds that those provisions are not inconsistent with the 1994 Act. Thus, only those persons who had no previous dealings with the firm will be deemed to be on notice of the advertised dissolution.[239]

4. Repayment of capital to a limited partner

[29.99] A limited partner is not entitled to a return[240] of all or part of his capital, unless at the time and immediately following the return, the general partner certifies that the ILP will be able to pay its debts as they fall due. However, where there is a return of capital without such a certificate and the firm becomes insolvent within four months, the amount so paid shall be repaid by the limited partner with interest of 5% per annum[241] to the extent that such sum is required to discharge an obligation of the firm which was incurred while that partner's capital represented an asset of the firm. Although not strictly a loss of limited liability, since the liability of the limited partner remains limited to the amount of his withdrawn capital plus interest, this is a situation where the limited partner loses his limit on liability in the sense that he may have an unanticipated liability.

---

235   In doing so, the third parties would be relying on the Partnership Act 1890, s 36(1).
236   Partnership Act 1890, s 36(1). See further para **[11.49]** et seq.
237   Since under the Investment Limited Partnerships Act 1994, s 4(1), the rules of common law and the provisions of the 1890 Act apply to ILPs, except in so far as they are inconsistent with the 1994 Act.
238   Investment Limited Partnerships Act 1994, s 4(3).
239   Partnership Act 1890, s 36(2). See further para **[11.71]**.
240   A release of any undertaking forming part of a capital contribution is regarded as constituting such a return of capital: Investment Limited Partnerships Act 1994, s 20(3).
241   Or such further sum as may be fixed by the Minister for Business, Enterprise and Innovation: Investment Limited Partnerships Act 1994, s 20(2).

5. Overvaluing of non-cash capital contribution

[29.100] The final situation in which a limited partner may lose his limited liability is in fact a perceived, rather than a real, loss of the limit on his liability. Under the terms of s 5 of the 1994 Act, a limited partner may satisfy his requirement to contribute capital to the firm by means of a non-cash contribution. The value of the property so contributed is deemed to be its fair market value. This leaves room for a situation where, for example, a limited partner contributes property to his firm which is accepted by the partners in satisfaction of his obligation to contribute capital of say €100,000. If it subsequently transpires that the fair market value of the property at the time of the transfer was only €30,000, this will leave the limited partner with a further €70,000 to contribute to the firm.

V.   AUTHORITY OF THE PARTNERS

[29.101] This part of the chapter considers the authority of the general partners to bind the ILP and the authority, or more accurately the absence of the authority, of the limited partners to bind the firm.

General Partner is Authorised to Bind the Firm

[29.102] A general partner in an ILP is in a similar position to a partner in an ordinary partnership. Section 5 of the 1890 Act applies to the general partner and accordingly each general partner is the agent of the firm and his other partners for the purpose of the business of the firm.[242] This point is reiterated by s 6(1) of the 1994 Act which states that 'all letters, contracts, deeds, instruments and documents whatsoever' shall be entered into by the general partner on behalf of the firm and by s 17 of the 1994 Act which states:

> Any debt or obligation incurred by a general partner in the conduct of the business of an investment limited partnership shall be a debt or obligation of the investment limited partnership.

Reference should be made to the analysis of the authority of a partner to bind a firm earlier in this work, as this is equally applicable to a general partner in an ILP.[243]

Limited Partner is Prohibited from Binding Firm

[29.103] In return for being granted limited liability, the limited partner is not allowed take part in the conduct of the firm's business and is therefore prohibited from binding the firm.[244] Section 6(1) of the 1994 Act states:

> A limited partner shall not take part in the conduct of the business of the investment limited partnership and in particular shall not have power to contract on behalf of the investment limited partnership and all letters, contracts, deeds, instruments and

---

[242]   The Investment Limited Partnerships Act 1994, s 4(1) and the Partnership Act 1890, s 5. See generally in relation to s 5 of the 1890 Act, para **[10.82]** et seq.

[243]   See para **[10.01]** et seq.

[244]   Compare the restriction on a limited partner in a limited partnership from taking part in the management of the partnership business: Limited Partnerships Act 1907, s 6(1). See para **[28.79]**.

documents whatsoever shall be entered into by the general partner on behalf of the investment limited partnership.

[29.104] In view of the highly restrictive nature of s 6(1) of the 1994 Act, it seems that the provisions of ss 15 and 16 of the 1890 Act will not apply to a limited partner, since both are inconsistent with s 6(1) of the 1994 Act.[245] Section 16 of the 1890 Act provides that notice to a 'partner who habitually acts in the partnership business' is deemed to be notice to the firm. However, by virtue of s 6(1) of the 1994 Act, a limited partner is prohibited from taking part in the conduct of the business of the firm and therefore cannot be said to habitually act in the partnership business. Thus, notice to a limited partner will not be deemed to be notice to the firm. As regard s 15, this provides that an admission or representation will bind a firm if made by a partner in the ordinary course of the firm's business. As s 6(1) of the 1994 Act prohibits a limited partner from taking part in the conduct of the business of the firm, it is apprehended that an admission or representation made by him will not bind the ILP.

Permitted activity for a limited partner

[29.105] Section 6(4) of the 1994 Act outlines a number of activities which may be undertaken by a limited partner, without fear of him being in breach of the prohibition in s 6(1) and regardless of the frequency with which he undertakes these activities. The list of permitted activities is as follows:

> A limited partner does not take part in the conduct of the business of an investment limited partnership within the meaning of this Act solely by doing any one or more of the following, irrespective of the frequency of such acts:
>
> (a) being a contractor for, or being an agent or employee of, the investment limited partnership or a general partner or acting as a director, officer or shareholder of a general partner which is a body corporate;
>
> (b) consulting with and advising a general partner with respect to the business of the investment limited partnership;
>
> (c) investigating, reviewing, or being advised as to the accounts or business affairs of the investment limited partnership or exercising any right conferred by this Act;
>
> (d) acting as surety or guarantor or providing any other form of security for the investment limited partnership either generally or in respect of specific obligations;
>
> (e) voting as a limited partner on one or more of the following matters:
>
>> (i) the dissolution and winding up of the investment limited partnership;
>>
>> (ii) the purchase, sale, exchange, lease, mortgage, pledge, or other acquisition or transfer of any asset or assets by or on behalf of the investment limited partnership;
>>
>> (iii) the incurring or renewal of any indebtedness of the investment limited partnership;
>>
>> (iv) a change in the objectives or policies of the investment limited partnership;

---

[245] And provisions of the 1890 Act which are inconsistent with the 1994 Act do not apply to ILPs: Investment Limited Partnerships Act 1994, s 4(1).

> (v) the admission, removal or withdrawal of a general or limited partner or custodian and the continuation of the business of the investment limited partnership thereafter;
>
> (vi) transactions in which one or more of the general partners have an actual or potential conflict of interest with one or more of the limited partners.

[29.106] In general terms, these permitted activities arise in two distinct situations. First, where the limited partner is acting in another capacity such as a director of a general partner which happens to involve him in the conduct of the business of the firm. This is on the assumption that such activities are being done by him in that capacity and not in his capacity as a limited partner. Thus, as is clear from s 6(4), a limited partner may also be an agent or employee of the ILP, an agent or employee of a general partner or indeed a director, officer or shareholder of a general partner.

[29.107] Second, the permitted activities arise where the limited partner has an expansive role in his own right in the internal affairs of the firm. Thus, the limited partner may, inter alia, act as a guarantor of the firm's obligations or have a right to vote on the transfer of the firm's assets, the incurring of indebtedness by the firm or a change in the general partners, limited partners or custodian.[246] In general terms, however, and in contrast to a limited partner in a limited partnership, an ILP limited partner has a greater scope to influence certain business decisions of the firm. In particular, it seems clear that a vote by a limited partner on the transfer of any asset by the ILP or the incurring or renewal of indebtedness by it would, if it were not for s 6(4), be viewed as taking part in the conduct of the firm's business.

Activities not mentioned in s 6(4)

[29.108] Section 6(5) of the 1994 Act provides that if the limited partner does an activity, which is not a permitted activity listed in s 6(4), this does not *ipso facto* mean that he is taking part in the conduct of the firm's business. By expressly excluding the principle *expressio unius est exclusio alterius*,[247] s 6(5) requires each activity to be judged on its merits to see if it constitutes the taking part in the conduct of the firm's business.[248]

---

[246] See para **[29.138]** et seq in relation to the right of a limited partner to vote on the admission of a new limited partner.

[247] Ie the express mention of one thing is the exclusion of another.

[248] In the UK, the new form private fund limited partnership introduced by the Legislative Reform (Private Fund Limited Partnerships) Order 2017 contains a non-exhaustive 'white list' of actions that a limited partner in a private fund limited partnership may undertake without losing its limited liability. While the 'white list' of actions that may be taken by limited partners in a private fund limited partnership in the UK is broad, that list cannot be used as a reference point for assessing whether an action taken by a limited partner in a UK limited partnership which is not a private fund limited partnership is, or is not, equivalent to taking part in the management of the business (Limited Partnerships Act 1907, s 6A(4)(b) as it applies in the UK).

Where limited partner is involved in decision to file accounts

[29.109] One activity not expressly permitted by s 6(4) is the involvement of a limited partner in the decisions regarding the filing of accounts on behalf of the firm. An ILP, where all the general partners have themselves limited liability (ie if they are limited liability companies or their equivalent),[249] is required to file accounts under the European Communities (Accounts) Regulations 1993[250] as if it were a company under the Companies Act 2014, unless it has been exempted by the Central Bank under s 15 of the 1994 Act. The Central Bank has, in the 'AIF' section of its website, confirmed that it has exercised its power under s 15 of 1994 Act to exempt an ILP which falls within the scope of the 1993 Regulations from its terms.[251] To be entitled to that exemption,[252] the ILP must have as its 'sole' business the investment of funds in property with the aim of spreading investment risk and giving its partners the benefit of the management of its assets. As previously noted,[253] under s 5(1)(a) of the 1994 Act, an ILP may be formed where its 'principal', as distinct from its sole, business is the investment of its funds in property, so that not every ILP will benefit from this exemption. If an ILP does not benefit from that exemption, the limited partner may be required to do the following:

(a) consent in writing to the exemption of the ILP from the requirement to file accounts under s 357 of the Companies Act 2014, and

(b) appoint the auditor to the ILP as required by reg 22 of the 1993 Regulations.

[29.110] However, reg 8(2) of the European Communities (Accounts) Regulations 1993[254] specifically envisages limited partners in limited partnerships being required to make either of these decisions. Accordingly, it states that in such a case, a limited partner in a limited partnership will not be regarded as taking part in the management of the firm for the purposes of s 6(1) of the 1907 Act. However, no reference is made to an ILP. This can, of course, be explained in part by the fact that the 1994 Act had not been enacted prior to the 1993 Regulations. It would of course be preferable if this anomaly was rectified by legislation. Nonetheless, it is apprehended that where a limited partner in an ILP takes part in either of these activities, he will not, for that reason alone, be regarded as taking part in the conduct of the firm's business.

Inspecting and advising on partnership books

[29.111] Although not expressly listed as a permitted activity in s 6(4) of the 1994 Act, s 19(1)(b) entitles a limited partner by himself or by an agent to inspect the books[255] of his firm, with such assistance of the general partner as may be reasonably required.

---

249 See para **[29.63]**.

250 SI 396/1993.

251 This power is based on the right in Article 5 of Council Directive 78/660/EEC entitling Member States to derogate from Council Directives 90/604/EEC and 90/605/EEC in the case of investment companies. Article 5(2)(a) defines investment companies as undertakings whose sole object is the investment of funds in property with the sole aim of spreading risk and giving members the benefit of the results of the management of assets.

252 The exemption is set out in the 'AIF' section of the Central Bank's website.

253 See para **[29.30]**.

254 SI 396/1993.

255 As to distinction between partnership 'books' and partnership 'accounts' see para **[21.91]**.

When he has the results of his inspection, the limited partner is entitled to advise all the partners on these results.[256] This activity of advising the partners on these results is undoubtedly a permitted activity which will not result in the loss by a limited partner of his limited liability. Any other conclusion would lead to a conflict between the terms of s 6(1) and s 19(1)(b) which could not be justified in principle.

Legal proceedings

[29.112] Another possible activity of a limited partner which is not mentioned in s 6(4) of the 1994 Act is litigation on behalf of his firm. This issue is, however, dealt with in s 22(1) of the 1994 Act.[257] This section provides an express restriction on a limited partner instituting any legal proceedings in respect of any liability owed by or to his ILP (including proceedings to enforce a foreign judgment). Such proceedings may be instituted only by (or indeed, against) one or more of the general partners. This provision emphasises the role of the limited partner as a dormant investor with no involvement in the day-to-day running of the firm. It seems clear that a breach by the limited partner of this restriction would be a breach of the prohibition on his taking part in the conduct of the business of the ILP, thereby leading to his loss of limited liability. However, in exceptional cases, a limited partner may be entitled to take a derivative action on behalf of the firm. Section 22(3) of the 1994 Act provides that a limited partner may, in certain circumstances, bring a derivative action on behalf of the ILP. The availability of a derivative action further emphasises the similarity between a limited partner and a shareholder in a limited company. This section allows a derivative action where the general partners, with the authority to bring such proceedings, refuse to do so, provided that the High Court determines that the refusal is oppressive to the limited partner or in disregard of his interests as a limited partner.[258] In light of the express permission of such an action by s 22(3), it is clear that it would not constitute the taking part in the conduct of the business of the ILP by the limited partner so as to lead to his loss of limited liability.

---

[256] As to the meaning of advising on these results, see para **[28.79]** in the context of a similar expression for limited partners for limited partnerships.

[257] The margin note for s 22 is clearly incorrect as it states 'Cessation of limited partner on assignment'. This is obviously intended as the margin note for s 21. An appropriate margin note for s 22 would be 'Legal proceedings by or against ILPs'.

[258] Compare the right to bring a derivative action under company law, see Courtney, *The Law of Companies* (4th edn, 2016) at para [11.111] et seq; Hutchinson, *Keane on Company Law* (5th edn, 2016) at para [26.23]; Forde and Kennedy, *Company Law* (5th edn, 2017) at para 11-45 et seq. In addition, the Investment Limited Partnerships Act 1994, s 26(2) allows the High Court to appoint an inspector on the application of the Central Bank to investigate the affairs of an ILP, where there are circumstances suggesting that the limited partners are being oppressed or their interests as limited partners are disregarded. Compare the right of shareholders under s 212 of the Companies Act 2014 to seek a remedy from the High Court for oppressive conduct.

Is ILP Bound by Limited Partner who Conducts Business?

[29.113] As already noted,[259] where a limited partner takes part in the conduct of the business of an ILP with non-partners[260] in breach of s 6(1) and the firm becomes insolvent, he will be liable as if he were a general partner during the period he took part in the conduct of the business. A separate issue is whether the firm itself will be bound by the act of the limited partner. It seems clear that the firm will not be bound[261] to third parties who deal with the limited partner in such circumstances,[262] since by the express terms of s 6(1), the limited partner has no power to bind the firm and therefore the third party cannot claim that the limited partner had ostensible authority to bind the firm.[263] The third party will of course have an action for misrepresentation against the limited partner who wrongfully represented himself to have authority to bind the firm.[264]

VI. RIGHTS AND DUTIES OF THE PARTNERS

Rights and Duties of the Limited and General Partners

[29.114] In Part C of this work, consideration is given to the rights and duties of partners inter se and when considering the rights and duties of partners in an ILP, reference should be made thereto. In this section, consideration will given to those rights and duties which are peculiar to limited partners and general partners in ILPs. First, however, consideration will be given to those areas which are relevant to both types of partners in an ILP.

Resolving differences as to business of firm

[29.115] Subject to an express or an implied term of the partnership agreement, any difference arising as to matters connected with the business of an ILP is decided by the

---

259 See para **[29.93]**.
260 Under the Investment Limited Partnerships Act 1994, s 6(2), it would appear that a limited partner will not lose the protection of limited liability where he takes part in the conduct of the business of the firm in its dealings with partners in the firm. He would however be guilty of a breach of s 6(1) but curiously this is not an offence under the 1994 Act, since s 39 only makes it an offence for the ILP, rather than the limited partner, to contravene the provisions of the Act. On this basis the limited partner would not be subject to the penalties set out in s 40 of the 1994 Act.
261 Support for a contrary view is to be found regarding the position of limited partners under the Limited Partnerships Act 1907, s 6, see Brough, *Miller on Partnership* (2nd edn, 1994) at p 610 et seq. His argument appears to be that just as the registration of information in the register of business names is not notice thereof to third parties, (para **[3.82]**) so too a third party dealing with a partner in a limited partnership cannot be assumed to be on notice that the partner he is dealing with is a limited partner.
262 Unless of course the general partners have expressly authorised the limited partner to act on behalf of the firm.
263 The firm may be bound if the limited partner had actual authority to bind the firm or the general partners represented to the third party that he had this authority. See generally in relation to the ostensible and actual authority of a partner, para **[10.31]** et seq.
264 The third party would not have any action, if he knew that he was a limited partner and was not authorised to act on behalf of the firm.

general partner or a majority of the general partners.[265] If the partnership agreement alters this provision to include the limited partners in the decision-making process, care should be taken to ensure that the matters, upon which the limited partners are entitled to decide, do not involve the limited partners in the conduct of the business of the firm. If they do, the limited partner runs the risk of being liable as a general partner for obligations incurred during that period in the event of the subsequent insolvency of the ILP.[266]

Right of any partner to transact business with firm

[29.116] Under the law applicable to ordinary partnerships, the firm is not a separate legal entity but is an aggregate of the partners for the time being in the firm.[267] However, it has been noted that in the case of ILPs, the application of this view of partnerships, known as the aggregate theory, is substantially diluted[268] and it is further diluted by the terms of s 19(2) of the 1994 Act. This section increases the perception of an ILP as a quasi-separate legal entity, by providing that a limited or general partner may transact business with the ILP of which he is a member as if he was a third party, subject to any conditions imposed by the Central Bank. Section 19(2) states that:

> Notwithstanding any rules of equity or common law applicable to partnerships, but subject to conditions imposed by the Bank, a partner may enter into any contract, including for the lending of money, or transact any business with an investment limited partnership, and such partner shall have the same rights and obligations with respect thereto as a person who is not a partner.

[29.117] Clearly any contract between a partner, especially a general partner, and the ILP will involve a potential conflict of interest for the partner. The law applicable to ordinary partnerships implies a fiduciary duty upon a partner in his partnership dealings and thus he must act in the firm's interest rather than his own.[269] The Central Bank AIF Rulebook clarifies the application of this duty to transactions between an ILP and its general partner.

Must be on arms' length basis

[29.118] The Central Bank AIF Rulebook[270] provides that any transactions carried out between the ILP and a general partner[271] must be carried out at arms' length and in the best interests of the limited partners. The Central Bank AIF Rulebook goes on to clarify that such a transaction will be permitted if:

---

265 Investment Limited Partnerships Act 1994, s 19(1)(a).
266 See generally in relation to such liability, para **[29.93]**.
267 See generally para **[3.04]**.
268 See para **[29.42]**.
269 See generally in relation to this duty, para **[15.01]** et seq.
270 Central Bank AIF Rulebook at p 46 (in respect of an ILP authorised as a retail investor AIF) and p 112 (in respect of an ILP authorised as a qualifying investor AIF).
271 Or a delegate or group company of a general partner ('group company' is defined in the Central Bank AIF Rulebook, p 10 as a member company of a group of associated or related companies). (contd.../)

(a)   there is a certified valuation of the transaction by a person approved by the custodian[272] as independent and competent; or

(b)   it is executed on best terms on organised investment exchanges under their rules; or

(c)   if (a) and (b) are impractical, the custodian is satisfied that it is carried out as if effected on arms' length terms and in the best interests of the unitholders.[273]

Yet partner will not be deferred creditor

[29.119] Under s 44(b) of the 1890 Act, a partner who is owed money by the firm is not entitled to be repaid this amount on the distribution of the firm's assets, until all the creditors of the firm have been paid off. However, this rule is modified in its application to ILPs. This is because under s 19(2) of the 1994 Act, a partner who transacts business with the ILP is stated to have 'the same rights and obligations' as a non-partner, so that such general or limited partners rank equally with the other creditors of the firm.

Right of any partner to assign his partnership share as security

[29.120] The right of any partner in an ILP to assign his partnership share arises under general partnership law, ie under s 31 of the 1890 Act. By virtue of this section, a limited or general partner is entitled to assign his interest in an ILP as security to a third party.[274] In addition to the right to assign a partnership share under s 31 of the 1890 Act, a limited partner, but not a general partner, in an ILP has a right to assign his partnership interest as security pursuant to s 18(3) of the 1994 Act. The limited partner also has a right to make an outright assignment of his partnership share,[275] but for present purposes, reference is made only to the right to assign his share as security.

[29.121] There are some minor differences between s 31 of the 1890 Act and s 18(3) of the 1994 Act which are worth noting, since the general partner will only be entitled to assign his share pursuant to the former provision. First, unlike s 31, the right in s 18(3) is expressly stated to apply, not just to the partnership interest but also to 'any part' of the partnership interest. Nonetheless, it is thought that there is no reason in principle why a general partner should not be entitled to assign only part of his partnership share under s 31.[276] Second, s 18(3) expressly states that the assignor is not relieved of any of his

---

[271]   (\...contd) The provisions regarding transactions being at arms' length and in the best interests of the limited partners also apply to transactions between the ILP and a management company, depositary, alternative investment fund manager or investment manager (or any delegate or group company of any of them). If the transaction is between the ILP and the depositary, it is the ILP itself which makes the assessments referred to at (a) and (c) in para **[29.118]** rather than the depositary.

[272]   Referred to in the Central Bank AIF Rulebook as the 'depositary'.

[273]   The Central Bank AIF Rulebook definition of 'unit holder' (at p 14) includes a limited partner in an ILP.

[274]   See generally in relation to this right, para **[19.12]** et seq.

[275]   Investment Limited Partnerships Act 1994, s 18(2), see further para **[29.126]**.

[276]   See further para **[19.25]**.

obligations to the firm. Although, not expressly stated in s 31, the same is obviously true of an assignment by a general partner under that section.[277]

Rights and Duties of the Limited Partners

Right of limited partner to inspect books and advise on results

[29.122] Although a limited partner is prohibited from taking part in the conduct of the partnership business,[278] he is entitled to ascertain the state of the partnership business. Thus, a limited partner is entitled by himself or by an agent to inspect the books[279] of his firm, with such assistance of the general partner as may be reasonably required.[280] When he has the results of his inspection, the limited partner is entitled to advise all the partners on these results.[281] This activity, ie advising the partners on these results, is not expressly listed as a permitted activity within s 6(4)(c) of the 1994 Act but it seems clear that it will not result in the loss by a limited partner of his limited liability.[282]

Restricted right of limited partner to a return of capital

[29.123] In an ordinary partnership, there is no restriction on a partner obtaining a return of his capital contribution in the absence of any contrary agreement between the partners. However, in an ILP, s 20 of the 1994 Act provides that a limited partner is only entitled to a return of his capital contribution,[283] if the firm is certified by the sole general partner, or a majority of the general partners, to be able to pay its debts in full as they fall due at the time of and immediately after the return.[284] It is important to note that s 20 does not grant a right to a return of capital, but only dictates the terms upon which such a return is to be made. Therefore, there is nothing to prevent the partnership agreement from prohibiting the limited partners from obtaining a return of any part of their capital during the life of the partnership.

Return of capital without certificate of solvency

[29.124] Where there is a return of capital without the required certificate of solvency and the firm becomes insolvent in the four month period following the return of capital,

---

[277] Although in that case there is an indemnity implied from the purchaser or assignee for value of the share in favour of the assignor in respect of the partnership obligations, see para **[19.24]**. It is thought that the same would not apply to the assignee of a partnership share as security.

[278] Investment Limited Partnerships Act 1994, s 6(1).

[279] As to the distinction between partnership 'books' and 'accounts' see para **[21.91]**.

[280] Investment Limited Partnerships Act 1994, s 19(1)(b).

[281] Investment Limited Partnerships Act 1994, s 19(1)(b).

[282] See para **[29.111]**.

[283] A return of capital is deemed to occur anytime a limited partner receives the assets of the firm (or is released from his undertaking to contribute to the capital) which reduces the value of his share in the firm (calculated on the value of the firm's net assets) below the amount contributed or undertaken to be contributed by him in the register of interests: Investment Limited Partnerships Act 1994, s 20(4). As to the register of interests see para **[29.54]**.

[284] Investment Limited Partnerships Act 1994, s 20(1). Cf the position of a limited partner in a limited partnership who wishes to obtain a return of his capital, para **[28.17]**.

the capital is repayable by the limited partner to the firm with interest at 5% per annum calculated on a daily basis,[285] if such contribution is necessary to discharge the obligations of the ILP which were incurred during the period that such contribution was an asset of the firm.

Limited partner may have a right to retire

[29.125] The retirement of a limited partner from the ILP is envisaged by s 21 of the 1994 Act.[286] This section provides that a limited partner will cease to be a limited partner on the return of the whole of his contribution, including the release of any undertaking to contribute to the firm. Like the terms of s 20, this section does not grant the limited partner a right to retire, but simply provides for him to cease to be a partner where he is entitled to a return of his capital. It is up to the partners themselves to determine if and how a limited partner may be entitled to a return of his capital or to retire from the firm. Section 21 of the 1994 Act provides that, notwithstanding any term of the partnership agreement, such retirement will not relieve the limited partner of any obligation which he has incurred as a result of his breach of s 6 (participation in the conduct of the partnership business), s 12 (allowing his name to be used in firm name) or s 20 (the return of capital to him in the absence of a certificate of solvency).

Outright assignment by limited partner of his share

[29.126] Reference has been made already to the assignment of a limited partner's share as security.[287] Consideration will now be given to the outright assignment of a limited partner's share. This is governed by ss 18 and 21 of the 1994 Act. These sections are, however, not without difficulty. Section 18(2) provides:

> Subject to subsection (1) a limited partner may assign absolutely the whole or any part of his partnership interest and an assignee shall as of the date of such assignment become a limited partner with all of the rights and obligations of the assignor relating to the investment limited partnership, including the obligation of the assignor to make contributions in respect of the partnership interest or the part thereof assigned but excluding any liability of the assignor arising pursuant to *section 6, 12* or *20.*

[29.127] Thus, on the assignment of his interest, the outgoing limited partner ceases to be liable for the debts and obligations of the firm, save insofar as they relate to his participation in the conduct of the firm's business in contravention of s 6, s 12 or s 20.[288] The legal effect of an assignment by a limited partner of his partnership share is completed by the terms of s 21 of the 1994 Act which provides that '[a] limited partner shall cease to be a limited partner of an investment limited partnership on the absolute assignment of all of his partnership interest ...'.

---

[285] Or such further sum as may be fixed by regulation made by the Minister for Business, Enterprise and Innovation: Investment Limited Partnerships Act 1994, s 20(2).

[286] In view of the incorrect margin note for s 22, see fn **257** above, it is thought that the margin note for s 22 is in fact the correct margin note for s 21, ie 'Cessation of limited partner upon assignment'.

[287] See para **[29.120]**.

[288] Cf the position under the Limited Partnerships Act 1907, where the assignor does not cease to be liable for the debts of the firm which were incurred by the firm while he was a partner, see para **[28.103]**.

[29.128] It is worth noting that s 21 only applies where there is an assignment of all of a limited partner's share. However, s 18(2) envisages a situation where only part of the partnership share is assigned. It is thought that where there is an assignment of part only of a partnership share, the liabilities of the limited partner will be shared between the assignee and assignor, in proportion to their respective share of the pre-assignment interest. On this basis, it is apprehended that after the assignment, the assignor and the assignee would both be limited partners in the ILP.

Interaction of s 18(1) with s 18(2)

[29.129] The interaction of s 18(1) and 18(2) is worthy of consideration as they are curiously drafted:

(1) Notwithstanding anything provided in the partnership agreement, a person may be admitted to an investment limited partnership as a limited partner with the consent of the general partner, or if more than one general partner, of all of them, and if by assignment, subject to *subsection (2)* without any requirement to obtain the consent of the existing limited partners.

(2) Subject to *subsection (1)* a limited partner may assign absolutely the whole or any part of his partnership interest and an assignee shall as of the date of such assignment become a limited partner with all of the rights and obligations of the assignor relating to the investment limited partnership, including the obligation of the assignor to make contributions in respect of the partnership interest or the part thereof assigned but excluding any liability of the assignor arising pursuant to *section 6, 12 or 20*.

Admission of a limited partner by creation of new partnership interest

[29.130] Both subsections deal with the admission of limited partners to an ILP. As has been seen, s 18(2) deals with the admission of a limited partner by way of assignment of an existing limited partner's share. Thus, when s 18(1) deals with the general admission of a limited partner, this must be taken as referring to the admission of a limited partner by the creation of a new partnership interest. The reference in s 18(1) that '[n]otwithstanding anything provided in the partnership agreement, a person may be admitted' as a limited partner with the consent of the general partner(s), would seem to indicate that the consent of the general partner(s) is a *sufficient* requirement for entry into the partnership. Thus, once this requirement is satisfied, the new limited partner must be admitted regardless of the terms of the partnership agreement. However, while the consent of all the general partners is sufficient, a lesser requirement may be imposed, so that it is possible, for example, to require the consent of a majority of the general partners and a majority of the limited partners to the admission of a new limited partner. This is the same as the approach under ordinary partnership law where the partners themselves may agree to be bound by a majority vote regarding the admission of a new partner.[289]

Admission of a limited partner by assignment

[29.131] While s 18(1) deals with the admission of a limited partner by the creation of a new partnership interest, the admission of a new limited partner by the assignment of a limited partner's share is expressly dealt with by s 18(2). This section is stated to be

---

[289] See para **[21.102]**.

'subject to *subsection (1)*'. Although not clear from doubt, it is thought that as both sections deal with the admission of a limited partner to the firm, this phrase must be interpreted as applying the same preconditions to the admission of a limited partner by assignment of a limited partner's interest under s 18(2), as apply to the admission of a limited partner by the creation of a new partnership interest under s 18(1).[290] This would also seem to be the effect of the reference in s 18(1) to 'and if by assignment, subject to *subsection (2)*'. On this basis it may be concluded that notwithstanding the terms of the partnership agreement, the consent of all the general partners is a *sufficient* requirement for the admission of a limited partner by the assignment of a limited partner's share. Equally, a lesser requirement may be imposed, so that it is possible, for example, to require the consent of a majority of the general partners and a majority of the limited partners to the admission of a new limited partner by way of assignment as is the case with the admission of partners in an ordinary partnership.[291]

[29.132] Thus, a limited partner must be admitted to an ILP where all the general partners consent, regardless of whether the admission is by way of assignment or by the creation of a new partnership interest. The rationale for the crucial role of the general partners in the admission of new limited partners is that they have unlimited liability for conduct of the partnership business and therefore should be able to decide on the identity of their partners.

Admission of a limited partner by assignment: Interaction of ss 18(2) and 21

[29.133] Another curious aspect to the drafting of those provisions of the 1994 Act which deal with the assignment of a partnership share is the interaction of s 18(2) with s 21. Section 18(2) deals with the admission of a limited partner to the ILP by way of assignment of a limited partner's share while s 21 deals with the assignment of a limited partner's share without reference to the admission of the assignee as a partner in the ILP. As previously noted,[292] it is implicit from the terms of s 18(1) and 18(2) that the partnership agreement may require the consent of all of the general partners for the admission of a new limited partner by assignment of a limited partner's share.[293] Section 21 then goes on to provide that on the absolute assignment of a limited partner's share, the assignor ceases to be a limited partner. This section does not contemplate the position where the assignor has made the assignment and thus ceased to be a limited partner under the terms of s 21, but the assignee has not been admitted to the partnership due to the refusal of the general partners to consent to such an admission. This gives rise

---

[290] Compare the situation for limited partnerships, ie the assignment of limited partner's share in a limited partnership requires the consent of all the general partners, unless the partners agree to the contrary: Limited Partnerships Act 1907, s 6(5)(b), see generally para **[28.119]**.

[291] See further para **[21.102]**.

[292] See para **[29.131]**.

[293] However, as s 18(2) is itself not clearly drafted, it might be argued that it should be interpreted as not being subject to the requirement in s 18(1) that the admission of a partner may be subject to the general partner's consent. If one takes this interpretation of s 18(2) then there is no impediment to the assignment of a limited partner's share and to the admission of the assignee and thus no conflict between s 18(2) and s 21. However, while s 18(1) and 18(2) are poorly drafted, this interpretation is difficult to justify in view of the wording of s 18(1) that it is subject to s 18(2), see para **[29.131]**.

to the situation where the assignor is no longer a limited partner but the assignee is not allowed to become the limited partner in his place.[294]

[29.134] It is regrettable that this interaction between s 18(2) and s 21 has not been addressed by the 1994 Act. However, from a drafting perspective, this issue should be addressed in the ILP agreement by providing that the admission of a new limited partner, by the assignment of limited partner's share, does not require the consent of the general partners. Alternatively the partnership agreement could prohibit the assignment of a limited partner's interest without the consent of all the general partners.

Admission of a new limited partner: role of Central Bank

[29.135] In contrast to the position of a general partner,[295] a limited partner may be admitted to an ILP without the need for any involvement on the part of the Central Bank. Such consent is not required, whether the new limited partner is admitted by acquiring another limited partner's interest pursuant to s 18(2) or by the creation of a new partnership interest pursuant to s 18(1).

[29.136] As previously noted,[296] in both instances of the admission of a new limited partner, the consent of the general partners is a sufficient requirement for admission to the ILP. When it comes to the question of whether the existing limited partners should have a say in the admission of a new limited partner, the 1994 Act distinguishes between the two ways in which a new limited partner may be admitted.

Admission of a limited partner by creating a new partnership interest: consent of partners

[29.137] As previously noted,[297] s 18(1) of the 1994 Act deals with the admission of limited partners by the creation of new partnership interests by providing that a limited partner 'may' be admitted into the partnership with the consent of all the general partner(s). Since this is simply sufficient for the admission of new limited partners, there is nothing to stop the partners agreeing that a new limited partner may be admitted subject to other conditions, such as the consent of a majority of the partners, general and limited. Indeed, s 6(4)(e)(v) of the 1994 Act envisages the limited partners voting on the admission of a limited partner and expressly provides that such voting will not result in the limited partner being regarded as taking part in the conduct of the business of the firm.

Admission of limited partner by assignment: consent of partners

[29.138] Section 18(2) governs the admission of a new partner by means of the assignment of an existing limited partner's interest. It has been noted that s 18(2) is to be interpreted as subject to s 18(1) and so requiring the consent of all the general partners to the assignment to be sufficient for the admission of the new partner.[298] In view of the permissive nature of this section it seems clear that a limited partner may be admitted

---

294 See also the annotation of the 1994 Act by Declan Murphy, available at www.westlaw.ie.
295 Investment Limited Partnerships Act 1994, s 11(3), see para **[29.143]**.
296 See para **[29.132]** et seq.
297 See para **[29.130]**.
298 See para **[29.131]**.

subject to other conditions, such as the consent of a majority of the general partners. However, s 18(1) expressly provides that in the case of an admission by assignment pursuant to s 18(2), the consent of the limited partners is not required irrespective of the terms of the partnership agreement.

[29.139] Thus, the 1994 Act allows the limited partners to have a say in the admission of a limited partner by way of the creation of another partnership interest, but not where the admission is by way of assignment of a limited partner's share. The only possible justification for this approach is that in the case of an assignment of a limited partner's share, it is regarded as inadvisable to allow the other limited partners have a possible veto over the transfer, since this would have the effect of fettering a limited partner's right to realise his investment in the fund. In contrast, where a limited partner is being admitted by the creation of a new partnership interest, allowing the limited partners have a say does not involve a limited partner in realising his investment.[299]

Incoming limited partners are subject to previously agreed variation

[29.140] The assignee of the share of a limited partner in a firm is a derivative partner, in the sense that he takes over the existing share of a partner in the firm *in specie*. As a derivative partner, and in contrast to the position of a partner by the creation of a new partnership share, he is bound by any variation of the terms of the partnership agreement which was consented to by the outgoing partner, even where the variation was not brought to the derivative partner's attention.[300]

Limited partner exempted from having to register place of business

[29.141] A limited partner which is incorporated outside of Ireland is not by virtue of its investment in an Irish ILP required to register under Part 21 of the Companies Act 2014 as having a place of business in Ireland.[301] Clearly, this exemption will not apply if the limited partner establishes a place of business separate from its investment in the ILP.

Rights and Duties of the General Partners

Right of a general partner to retire

[29.142] As is the case with ordinary partnerships, a general partner is entitled to retire from an ILP provided that there is such a right contained in the partnership agreement. Where the retiring partner is the sole general partner, the firm which remains will no longer constitute an ILP, since it will not satisfy the requirement in s 3 of the 1994 Act that it have at least one general partner. This fact is recognised by s 37(2)(a) of the 1994

---

299 By way of contrast, under the Delaware Revised Uniform Limited Partnership Act, set out in Chapter 17 of Title 6 to the Delaware Code, the limited partners have a say in the admission of new limited partners by way of the assignment of a limited partner's share unless otherwise provided in the partnership agreement.

300 *Const v Harris* (1824) T & R 496.

301 Investment Limited Partnerships Act 1994, s 7(6). Section 7(6) refers to Part XI of the Companies Act 1963. Under s 5 and para 11(1) of Sch 6 to the Companies Act 2014, this is deemed to be a reference to Chapter 21 of the Companies Act 2014. Note that, instead of referring to a 'place of business', Chapter 21 refers to a 'branch'.

Act which states that the retirement of the sole general partner will cause the immediate dissolution of the firm. However, if within 35 days of the retirement of the sole general partner, the limited partners unanimously elect one or more general partners who are approved by the Central Bank, the business of the ILP need not be wound up.[302]

Addition or replacement of a general partner

[29.143] The crucial role of the Central Bank in the life of an ILP is highlighted by the fact that a general partner may not be replaced, nor may any additional general partners be appointed, without the prior approval of the Central Bank.[303]

Exclusion of liability for the general partner or indemnification is void

[29.144] The fact that ILPs are collective investment undertakings and the consequent desire to ensure that (in circumstances where the general partners, or any one of them, are not authorised by the Central Bank as an alternative investment fund manager[304] or are not authorised as such by the competent authority in its home Member State or in its Member State of reference)[305] the assets thereof are protected explains s 24(4) of the 1994 Act. This section provides that any provision in the investment limited partnership agreement or in any contract with the ILP is void, insofar as it provides for a general partner's liability in relation to the ILP to be excluded for negligence, default, breach of duty or breach of trust or for the general partner to be indemnified by the firm for such liability.[306] An ILP is however entitled to indemnify a general partner for liability incurred by him in defending proceedings in which judgment is given in his favour or in which he is acquitted.[307]

Duty of general partner

[29.145] The general partner is under a fiduciary duty to all his fellow general and limited partners, in the same way as a partner in an ordinary partnership.[308]

---

302 Investment Limited Partnerships Act 1994, s 37(3).
303 Investment Limited Partnerships Act 1994, s 11(3).
304 European Union (Alternative Investment Fund Managers) Regulations 2013, Pt 2.
305 Such authorisation would be under Chapter II of the Alternative Investment Fund Managers Directive as transposed into the laws of that Member State. A 'member state of reference' is relevant where the alternative investment fund manager is from a non-EU jurisdiction and wants to inter alia manage an EU AIF (such as an ILP under the 1994 Act). In that case, the Alternative Investment Fund Managers Directive sets out rules for determining which EU Member State will be treated as the 'home member state' of that non-EU alternative investment fund manager and which regulatory authority will have oversight of its activities in the EU. Where the general partner(s) is/are so authorised, they are subject to a detailed authorisation and supervision regime; see further para **[29.32]**.
306 Investment Limited Partnerships Act 1994, s 24(2).
307 Investment Limited Partnerships Act 1994, s 24(2).
308 See generally in relation to such fiduciary duties, para **[15.01]** et seq. While one aspect of this fiduciary duty was re-iterated by NU 7 of the NU Series of Notices which provided that the general partner must act independently and solely in the interests of all the partners, that was not expressly replicated in the Central Bank AIF Rulebook.

VII. REGULATION OF ILPs

[29.146] This part of the chapter deals with the regulation of ILPs. The vast majority of the regulations concerning ILPs arises from the fact that they are collective investment undertakings. Accordingly, a detailed consideration of these regulations is beyond the scope of a work such as this on partnership law. Reference should be made to the Central Bank AIF Rulebook for a detailed list of the restrictions on the business activities of an ILP.[309]

Investment, Borrowing and Related Restrictions

[29.147] Where an ILP is to be authorised as a qualifying investor AIF, it must have a minimum subscription of €100,000 or its equivalent in other currencies,[310] and each investor to whom it is marketed must:

- be a '*professional client*' within the meaning of Annex II of the Markets in Financial Instruments Directive;[311]

---

[309] See in particular Chapter 1 which, inter alia, prohibits an ILP authorised as a retail investor AIF from granting loans or acting as a guarantor on behalf of third parties. This prohibition will not prevent that ILP from acquiring debt securities or securities which are not fully paid. Chapter 1, in respect of retail investor AIFs, also contains restrictions on investments (including investments in securities, cash, investment funds and financial derivatives), restrictions on its borrowing powers, restrictions on its dealings in financial derivative instruments, and restrictions on the entry into by it of repurchase (repo) contracts and securities lending transactions, together with detailed provisions regarding the valuation of, and dealings in, partnership assets and the interests of the limited partners. There are less onerous restrictions set out in Chapter 2 which apply to an ILP authorised as a qualifying investor AIF. These include (subject to exceptions) restrictions on raising capital through the issue of debt securities, making loans and giving guarantees. Chapter 2 also sets out very limited investment restrictions for qualifying investor AIFs, and provisions regarding the valuation of, and dealings in, partnership assets and the interests of the limited partners. The Central Bank AIF Rulebook also provides for specific variations of both the retail investor AIF (including venture or development capital or private equity retail investor AIFs, real estate retail investor AIFs, and guaranteed retail investor AIFs) and the qualifying investor AIF (including loan originating qualifying investor AIFs). In each of those cases, some of the more general restrictions are disapplied (for eg, a loan originating qualifying investor AIF can lend) and some additional, bespoke, conditions are imposed.

[310] Central Bank AIF Rulebook, p 101. There are some exceptions to the minimum subscription requirement in respect of a qualifying investor AIF set out in that section, including in respect of an investment by the general partner, the management company or the alternative investment fund manager.

[311] The original Markets in Financial Instruments Directive (Directive 2004/39/EC) was repealed by the revised Markets in Financial Instruments Directive (Directive 2014/65/EU, art 94) with effect from 3 January 2018. The Central Bank AIF Rulebook still referes to the original Directive 'as amended' however the meaning of 'professional client' in both Directives is the same. A professional client for the purposes of each Directive is one who possesses the experience, knowledge and expertise to make his own investment decisions and properly assess the risks that he incurs, and he must comply with further criteria set out in Annex II to the Directive.

- have received an appraisal from an EU bank, MiFID investment firm or UCITS management company confirming that he has the appropriate expertise, experience and knowledge to adequately understand the investment in the qualifying investor AIF; or
- have certified that he is an informed investor by providing the following:
  - written confirmation that he has such knowledge of, and experience in, financial and business matters as would enable him to properly evaluate the merits and risks of the prospective investment; or
  - written confirmation that his business involves, whether for his own account or the account of others, the management, acquisition or disposal of property of the same kind as the property of the qualifying investor AIF.

Replacement for Cause of a General Partner or Custodian

[29.148] Just as it is a requirement for the authorisation of an ILP that the general partner(s) demonstrate competence, probity, good repute and experience to perform their duties,[312] so too s 30 of the 1994 Act entitles the Central Bank to replace such persons who fail to reach these requisite standards. Under this section, the Central Bank may replace a general partner or custodian with another general partner or custodian if the Central Bank is satisfied as to any one of the following:

(a) the general partner or custodian has failed to demonstrate the competence, probity or experience in the discharge of their functions reasonably required by them;

(b) the general partner or custodian is not of sufficiently good repute;

(c) it is undesirable in the interests of the limited partners that the person should remain as a general partner or custodian;

(d) the general partner or custodian has contravened any provision of the 1994 Act or regulations imposed thereunder or in purported compliance with any such provision supplied the Central Bank with false,[313] inaccurate or misleading information.

Notice of proposed replacement

[29.149] Section 31 of the 1994 Act imports one of the principles of natural justice, ie *audi alteram partem*, to the procedure for the replacement of a custodian or a general partner. Section 31(1) provides that the Central Bank is required to give the general partner or custodian notice of its intention to replace him. Curiously, this section requires the Central Bank to notify the general partner of the identity of the proposed new general partner, but it does not require the Central Bank to give the custodian notice of the identity of the new custodian. The partner or custodian has 15 days within which to make written representations to the Central Bank and this time period may be extended by the Central Bank for the purposes of receiving representations from the

---

[312] Investment Limited Partnerships Act 1994, s 8(1).

[313] Note that there is no requirement that this be done knowingly, cf the requirement for an offence under the Investment Limited Partnerships Act 1994, s 16(11) that the false information in the annual report to the Central Bank be given knowingly.

limited partners.[314] In order to ensure that principles of natural justice are observed, the Central Bank is required to have regard to these representations in determining whether to replace the general partner or the custodian.[315] For this purpose, any one general partner[316] is required to notify the limited partners of the receipt of a notice of his proposed replacement from the Central Bank,[317] and if he is in default, he is guilty of an offence and liable to a maximum fine of €1,093,750 or to imprisonment of up to 15 years and is required to indemnify any person who thereby suffers loss.[318] The Central Bank AIF Rulebook also requires that the ILP have approved and documented procedures in place to be followed to replace the general partner or custodian (whether at the instigation of the Central Bank or otherwise).[319]

[29.150] Upon the replacement of a general partner or custodian, he ceases to be a partner or custodian of the firm and his powers and duties devolve upon his replacement. Any decision by the Central Bank to replace a general partner or custodian is subject to review by the High Court on the application of any aggrieved party (including a limited partner).[320] As previously noted,[321] the onus of proof is on the applicant to prove, in the case of the replacement of a general partner or custodian, that the 1994 Act was not complied with in a material respect or that there was no material before the Central Bank, on which it could reasonably have concluded that any one of the four conditions for the replacement of a general partner or custodian was satisfied. If this is the case, the High Court is empowered to set aside the decision of the Central Bank.[322]

However the general partner's liability remains

[29.151] Once a general partner is replaced in an ILP, the question arises as to his liability for the debts and obligations of the firm. This issue is addressed by s 30(2) of the 1994 Act, which provides that the liability of a general partner in respect of the debts and obligations of the firm is not affected by his replacement. Accordingly, the general rules regarding the liability of a partner for the debts of his firm after his departure will apply.[323] Therefore, a general partner who is removed from the firm remains liable for the obligations incurred while he was a partner and he may, in certain cases, be liable for debts incurred by the firm even after his departure to persons who had dealings with the

---

314 Investment Limited Partnerships Act 1994, s 31(3).
315 Investment Limited Partnerships Act 1994, s 31(4).
316 Investment Limited Partnerships Act 1994, ss 31(2) and 4(3).
317 Investment Limited Partnerships Act 1994, s 31(2).
318 Investment Limited Partnerships Act 1994, ss 31(5) and 40. The original fine of £500,000 was converted to its euro equivalent by virtue of Council Regulations (EC) No 1103/97, (EC) No 974/98 and (EC) No 2866/98 and the Economic and Monetary Union Act 1998, s 6 and then, by virtue of s 9 of the Fines Act 2010, multiplied by 1.75 to give the current amount.
319 Central Bank AIF Rulebook at p 54 (in respect of an ILP authorised as a retail investor AIF) and pp 115–116 (in respect of an ILP authorised as a qualifying investor AIF).
320 Investment Limited Partnerships Act 1994, s 32(1).
321 See para **[29.82]**.
322 Investment Limited Partnerships Act 1994, s 32(3).
323 Partnership Act 1890, s 17(2) and s 36(1), see generally in relation the liability of a former partner for the obligations of the firm, para **[11.25]** et seq.

firm while he was a partner, but who were unaware of his departure. Accordingly, a replaced general partner in an ILP should take steps to ensure that any pre-existing clients of the firm are notified of his departure, in the same way as if he was a partner in an ordinary partnership.[324]

Replacement not removal of a general partner or custodian

[29.152] It is worth noting that the Central Bank is not entitled to simply remove a general partner or custodian from an ILP, rather s 30(1) simply entitles it to replace him and so the Central Bank is obliged to find another general partner or custodian, as appropriate. If this search is unsuccessful, the Central Bank may be forced to exercise its powers under s 29 of the 1994 Act to revoke the authorisation of the ILP. In most cases, it is anticipated that the replacement option will be in the interests of the investors (the limited partners).

Replacement or Addition of General Partner or Custodian

[29.153] Quite apart from the replacement of a general partner or custodian for misconduct under s 31 of the 1994 Act, there may be times when it is proposed that a general partner be replaced for administrative or personal reasons or indeed there may be a desire to admit more general partners to the firm. The strong regulatory role of the Central Bank is evidenced by the fact that a general partner or a custodian may not be replaced by another general partner or custodian, nor may any additional general partners be appointed to an ILP, without the prior approval of the Central Bank.[325]

[29.154] The Central Bank AIF Rulebook also requires that the investment limited partnership agreement[326] include details of the procedure to be followed to replace the general partner or custodian (whether at the instigation of the Central Bank or otherwise) and provisions to ensure the protection of the limited partners[327] if such a replacement occurs.[328] Where the custodian is to be replaced, the procedures that are to be followed by the ILP must have been approved by the general partner, and both the retiring custodian and the incoming custodian must confirm, to the Central Bank, that they are satisfied with the transfer of assets from the retiring custodian to the incoming custodian.[329] An ILP may only terminate the custodian's appointment when a new

---

[324] See generally para **[11.76]**.

[325] Investment Limited Partnerships Act 1994, s 11(3). Non-compliance with this section is an offence under s 11(4).

[326] The Central Bank AIF Rulebook refers to 'constitutional document', which is defined (at p 10) as including an ILP's partnership agreement.

[327] The Central Bank AIF Rulebook refers to 'unit holders', which is defined (at p 14) as including the limited partners in an ILP.

[328] Central Bank AIF Rulebook, pp 35, 36 and 54 (in respect of an ILP authorised as a retail investor AIF) and pp 104, 105, 115 and 116 (in respect of an ILP authorised as a qualifying investor AIF).

[329] Central Bank AIF Rulebook, pp 35, 36 and 54 (in respect of an ILP authorised as a retail investor AIF) and pp 104, 105, 115 and 116 (in respect of an ILP authorised as a qualifying investor AIF).

custodian has been appointed, or if the ILP's authorisation as an AIF is revoked by the Central Bank.[330]

The Custodian

[29.155] Because an ILP is primarily a collective investment undertaking which happens to be structured as a partnership, the custodian plays a very significant role in its operations. This is reflected in the fact that an ILP must have a custodian before it will be issued with its authorisation, and that the custodian must have a place of business in Ireland.[331]

The Custodian must be a Depositary

[29.156] The custodian must be a 'depositary' as specified in reg 22(3) of the Irish AIFMD Regulations.[332] In general terms, in respect of an ILP under the 1994 Act, only banks, investment firms authorised as such under the framework of the Markets in Financial Instruments Directive,[333] and investment firms authorised as such under the Investment Intermediaries Act 1995, may act as custodians.[334] While before the Alternative Investment Fund Managers Directive framework was introduced there was a requirement under the NU Series of Notices[335] that the accounts of the custodian (both annual and half-yearly) be provided to the Central Bank (unless the custodian was a credit institution or a branch of a credit institution), that requirement no longer applies as the entities which may fill the role of custodian in respect of an ILP are themselves subject to authorisation and supervision regimes, whether by the Central Bank or by an equivalent regulatory authority in another jurisdiction. Information on the agreement between the ILP and the custodian must be supplied to the Central Bank as part of the ILP's application for authorisation.[336] The ILP's alternative investment fund manager can enter into the contract with the custodian instead of the ILP, if the alternative investment

---

330 Central Bank AIF Rulebook, pp 35, 36 and 54 (in respect of an ILP authorised as a retail investor AIF) and pp 104, 105, 115 and 116 (in respect of an ILP authorised as a qualifying investor AIF).

331 Investment Limited Partnerships Act 1994, s 5(1)(c).

332 Investment Limited Partnerships Act 1994, ss 5(1)(c) and 8(1)(c).

333 Directive 2014/59/EU (which replaced Directive 2004/39/EC) and which was transposed into Irish law by the European Union (Markets in Financial Instruments) Regulations 2017 (SI 375/2017), as amended.

334 Irish AIFMD Regulations, reg 22(3)(a)(i)–(iii) inclusive. The Central Bank AIF Rulebook sets out (at Chapter 5) certain conditions regarding capital and governance in respect of a depositary that is an investment firm authorised under the Investment Intermediaries Act 1995.

335 Non-UCITS Notice 7.12.

336 The Central Bank requires a checklist to be completed as part of the application process, specifying the clause in the agreement with the custodian that deals with specific points, including its tasks, delegation of functions, liability, the services to be provided, and the circumstances in which the appointment of the custodian can be terminated. The requirement for clauses of that nature in the agreement with the custodian, and the requirement that the agreement be in writing, each originate from the AIFMD Level 2 Regulation, reg 83. The Central Bank's checklists can be found in the 'AIF' section of the Central Bank's website.

fund manager is managing a number of AIFs and the custodian is fulfilling the role of custodian for each of those AIFs.[337]

The role of the custodian

[29.157] As the name suggests, the custodian's role is to hold the assets of the firm in safekeeping and to generally ensure that the ILP is complying with the partnership agreement,[338] and in particular to ensure that the financial transactions executed by the firm are done so in accordance with the partnership agreement, the 1994 Act, the regulations issued thereunder and any directions of the Central Bank.[339] The *raison d'être* for the custodian is to ensure that the assets of the firm are not dissipated by the general partners to the detriment of the limited partners. Section 24 of the 1994 Act lists certain obligations of the custodian,[340] including an obligation to report on the conduct of the general partners in the management of the firm to the limited partners. This report is included in the annual report of the firm which is required to be filed with the Central Bank.[341] The custodian is also required to deal with the Central Bank in an 'open and cooperative manner'.[342]

Custodian must carry out instructions of general partner

[29.158] In addition to any contractual obligation which a custodian may have to the general partners under the terms of the custodian agreement, unless the general partners,

---

[337] Commission Delegated Regulation (EU) No 231/2013, reg 83.

[338] Under the Investment Limited Partnerships Act 1994, s 5(1)(c), the custodian is described as the person in whom the assets of the ILP are entrusted for safekeeping and who is charged with verifying that the business of the ILP is conducted in accordance with the partnership agreement and with such powers and duties as are specified in s 24 and by the Central Bank.

[339] A list of the duties of a custodian are set out in s 24 of the 1994 Act. The AIFMD Level 2 Regulation also sets out, in Chapter IV, Section 3, a number of obligations on the depositary appointed in respect of an AIF, including in relation to cash monitoring, the safe-keeping of assets, the verification of ownership interests in assets, record-keeping, risk assessments, checking procedures in relation to subscriptions and redemptions, verifying valuation procedures, monitoring compliance by an AIF with investment restrictions and borrowing limits to which it is subject, and oversight in respect of the distribution of the AIF's income. It may, subject to certain conditions, delegate its safe-keeping functions, but it must monitor the delegate's compliance with its obligations, and retain overall liability for compliance with the applicable requirements of the Alternative Investment Fund Managers Directive framework.

[340] Under the Investment Limited Partnerships Act 1994, s 24(2), the custodian is required to carry out such additional duties as the Central Bank may specify by means of conditions imposed under s 7(2)(b) of the 1994 Act. The Central Bank imposes these conditions by way of the Central Bank AIF Rulebook which, at Chapter 5, sets out requirements in respect of the depositary (an ILP's custodian must be a 'depositary'.

[341] Investment Limited Partnerships Act 1994, s 16(1). The Central Bank AIF Rulebook, Chapter 5, also requires the depositary to enquire into the conduct of inter alia the general partner(s) in each accounting period and report on that conduct to the limited partners (limited partners are within the scope of the Central Bank AIF Rulebook's definition of 'unit holders') (at p 14 of the Central Bank AIF Rulebook).

[342] Central Bank's Regulatory Requirements and Guidance for AIFs (AIF Depositaries): issued 3 July 2013, available on its website.

or any one of them, is authorised by the Central Bank as an alternative investment fund manager[343] or is authorised as such by the competent authority in its home Member State or in its Member State of reference,[344] the custodian is under a statutory obligation to carry out the instructions of the general partner, unless they conflict with the terms of the 1994 Act, the regulations made thereunder, any direction of the Central Bank or the investment limited partnership agreement.[345]

Custodian is obliged to act independently and solely in interests of partners

[29.159] Under the Central Bank AIF Rulebook,[346] the custodian cannot have directors in common with inter alia the general partner. As well as any duty which a custodian may have to the firm under the terms of the custodian agreement, the Irish AIFMD Regulations[347] provide that the custodian must act honestly, fairly, professionally, independently and in the interest of the AIF (ie the ILP) and the investors in the AIF (ie the partners). The requirement that the custodian act in the interests of the ILP and its partners must be treated with caution. This is because both s 24(2) and s 7(2)(b) of the 1994 Act require the custodian to carry out such additional duties as may be specified by the Central Bank. The Central Bank has a role as the guardian of the ILP industry as a whole,[348] and for this reason, it seems that these additional duties imposed upon the custodian may be in the interests of this industry and not solely in the interests of the partners.

[29.160] Any breach by the custodian of his duties under s 24 of the 1994 Act will result in him being guilty of an offence and liable to a maximum fine of €1,093,750 or to imprisonment for up to 15 years.[349] In addition, he is required to indemnify any person who thereby suffers loss.[350]

---

[343] European Union (Alternative Investment Fund Managers) Regulations 2013, Pt 2.

[344] Such authorisation would be under Chapter II of the Alternative Investment Fund Managers Directive as transposed into the laws of that Member State. A 'member state of reference' is relevant where the alternative investment fund manager is from a non-EU jurisdiction and wants to inter alia manage an EU AIF (such as an ILP under the 1994 Act). In that case, the Alternative Investment Fund Managers Directive sets out rules for determining which EU Member State will be treated as the 'home member state' of that non-EU alternative investment fund manager and which regulatory authority will have oversight of its activities in the EU.

[345] Investment Limited Partnerships Act 1994, s 24(1)(a).

[346] Central Bank AIF Rulebook, Chapter 5.

[347] European Union (Alternative Investment Fund Managers) Regulations 2013, reg 22(10).

[348] See for example the Central Bank's power to impose conditions generally or by reference to a particular ILP for the purposes of the orderly and proper regulation of ILPs: Investment Limited Partnerships Act 1994, s 7(2)(a).

[349] Investment Limited Partnerships Act 1994, s 40.

[350] From the third party's perspective, this statutory right has the benefit over an action in negligence that the third party will not have to satisfy the 'proximity test' to be entitled to damages, see the annotation of the 1994 Act by Declan Murphy, available at www.westlaw.ie. The original fine of £500,000 was converted to its euro equivalent by virtue of Council Regulations (EC) No 1103/97, (EC) No 974/98 and (EC) No 2866/98 and the Economic and Monetary Union Act 1998, s 6 and then, by virtue of s 9 of the Fines Act 2010, multiplied by 1.75 to give the current amount.

Any exclusion of liability or indemnification is void

[29.161] The paternalistic approach of the 1994 Act to investors in ILPs is emphasised by s 24(2). This states that where the custodian provides in his contract with the ILP for his liability in relation to the firm to be excluded for negligence, default, breach of duty or breach of trust or to be indemnified for such liability, that provision shall be void.[351] An ILP is, however, entitled to indemnify a custodian for liability incurred by him in defending proceedings in which judgment is given in his favour or he is acquitted.[352]

Terms which must be included in custodian agreement

[29.162] The highly regulated nature of collective investment undertakings is further evidenced by the fact that the custodian agreement must be submitted to the Central Bank as part of the application for authorisation of the ILP.[353] In addition, the Central Bank's checklists for custodian agreements require them to contain the terms which follow.

Custodian liable for loss for negligence and wilful default

[29.163] The custodian agreement must provide that the custodian will exercise due care and diligence in the discharge of his duties and will be liable to the limited and general partners for any loss arising from negligence, fraud, bad faith, wilful default or recklessness in the performance of those duties.[354] This requirement is consistent with the terms of s 24(2) of the 1994 Act[355] which provides that any provision exempting a custodian for liability or indemnifying him for any negligence, default, breach of duty or breach of trust is void.

Liability of custodian is not affected by delegation to third party

[29.164] The custodian agreement is required to provide that the liability of a custodian will not be affected by the fact that he has entrusted some or all of the assets in his safe keeping to a third party.[356]

---

351   Investment Limited Partnerships Act 1994, s 24(2).

352   Investment Limited Partnerships Act 1994, s 24(2).

353   The Central Bank's application forms for authorisation as either a retail investor AIF or a qualifying investor AIF each require that the agreement with the depositary (ie the custodian) (with original signatures) accompany the application for authorisation.

354   The Central Bank's checklists for agreements with the custodian/depositary set out these requirements. Those checklists are available on the 'AIF' section of the Central Bank's website.

355   See para **[29.168]**.

356   The Central Bank's checklists for agreements with the custodian/depositary set out these requirements. Those checklists are available on the 'AIF' section of the Central Bank's website.

The Auditor

[29.165] The auditor of an ILP is unlike the auditor of a company,[357] since he has obligations to the ILP and its members on the one hand and to the Central Bank on the other hand. Indeed, pursuant to the Central Bank's role as regulator[358] of the ILP sector, s 16(7) of the 1994 Act authorises the Central Bank to require the auditor of an ILP to provide it 'with such information as it may specify' in relation to the audit of the ILP. In providing this information, the Central Bank may require the auditor to ignore his duty to the ILP.[359] Since these interests may sometimes conflict, s 16(8) of the 1994 Act specifically provides that the auditor shall not incur liability to the ILP, its partners, creditors or other interested parties by reason of his compliance with his obligations to the Central Bank.

[29.166] As part of his duty to the Central Bank, the auditor is required to report to the Central Bank, without delay, in the event of his discovering any financial irregularities in the ILP[360] or where requested by the Central Bank to report on any specific obligation of a financial nature under the Act or the conditions imposed thereunder.[361] In either case, the auditor must send a copy of the report to the ILP[362] and any failure by the auditor to send the report to the Central Bank and a copy to the ILP shall result in his being guilty of an offence and liable to a maximum fine of €1,093,750 or to imprisonment of up to 15 years.[363]

[29.167] For its part, the Central Bank is required to supply to the auditor financial returns made by the ILP to the Central Bank where the auditor requires them to fulfil his duty under the Act.[364]

---

357   See generally in relation to the status of a statutory auditor to a company, Courtney, *The Law of Companies* (4th edn, 2016) at para 18.237; Hutchinson, *Keane on Company Law* (5th edn, 2016) at para [30.148] et seq; Forde and Kennedy, *Company Law* (5th edn, 2017) at para 19-23 et seq.

358   Although this term is nowhere used in the 1994 Act or in the Central Bank AIF Rulebook, there can be no doubt that this accurately describes the role of the Central Bank *vis-à-vis* ILPs. See para **[29.18]**.

359   Investment Limited Partnerships Act 1994, s 16(7)(b), which provides that the Central Bank may require the auditor to 'act independently of the ILP'.

360   Investment Limited Partnerships Act 1994, s 16(3), which sets out six situations in which the auditor is required to report to the Central Bank.

361   Investment Limited Partnerships Act 1994, s 16(4).

362   Investment Limited Partnerships Act 1994, s 16(6).

363   Investment Limited Partnerships Act 1994, s 16(10) (as amended by s 40 of the Companies (Amendment) (No2) Act 1999). Section 40 of the Companies (Amendment) (No 2) Act 1999 removed the requirement in s 16(10) that the auditor indemnify any person who suffered a loss as a result of the auditor's breach of s 16(3), (4) or (6). The original fine of £500,000 was converted to its euro equivalent by virtue of Council Regulations (EC) No 1103/97, (EC) No 974/98 and (EC) No 2866/98 and the Economic and Monetary Union Act 1998, s 6 and then, by virtue of s 9 of the Fines Act 2010, multiplied by 1.75 to give the current amount.

364   Investment Limited Partnerships Act 1994, s 16(5).

Any exclusion of liability or indemnification is void

[29.168] Where in its contract with the ILP, the auditor provides for its liability in relation to the ILP to be excluded for negligence, default, breach of duty or breach of trust or to be indemnified by the firm for such liability, that provision shall be void.[365] An ILP is, however, entitled to indemnify an auditor for liability incurred by him in defending proceedings in which judgment is given in his favour or he is acquitted.[366]

The Terms of the Prospectus Issued by an ILP

[29.169] Every ILP must publish a prospectus containing sufficient information for prospective partners in the firm to make an informed judgment of the investment.[367] The provisions of the Companies Act 2014 on the content and form of prospectuses do not apply to a prospectus issued by an ILP.[368] Instead, the prospectus must comply with the terms of the Central Bank AIF Rulebook.

[29.170] Where an ILP is a qualifying investor AIF and is, as such, not subject to the same Central Bank restrictions as those imposed by the Central Bank on the investment and borrowing powers of an ILP authorised as a retail investor AIF (because a qualifying investor AIF is marketed to qualifying investors only),[369] this fact must be stated in the prospectus in a form of words approved by the Central Bank.[370] There must be a description in the prospectus of the potential conflicts of interest which could arise between the general partners and the ILP[371] with details, where applicable, of how these are going to be resolved.[372]

[29.171] Where an ILP fails to comply with the conditions imposed by the Central Bank for the issue of the prospectus, the general partner is guilty of an offence[373] and subject to a maximum fine of €1,093,750 or to imprisonment for up to 15 years. He is also liable to any person who suffers a loss in reliance upon such a prospectus which is in any

---

[365] Investment Limited Partnerships Act 1994, s 24(2).
[366] Investment Limited Partnerships Act 1994, s 24(2).
[367] Investment Limited Partnerships Act 1994, ss 7(4)(b) and 14(1); Central Bank AIF Rulebook, p 56 et seq (in respect of an ILP authorised as a retail investor AIF) and pp 118 et seq (in respect of an ILP authorised as a qualifying investor AIF).
[368] Investment Limited Partnerships Act 1994, s 14(2) which refers to the Companies Acts 1963 to 1990 which reference is deemed, by virtue of s 5(3) and Sch 6 of the Companies Act 2014 to be a reference to the Companies Act 2014.
[369] As to who constitutes a 'qualifying investor', see para **[29.14]**.
[370] The Central Bank AIF Rulebook at p 122 provides that the prospectus must, when specifying its minimum subscription requirements, include the following statement in a prominent position: 'While this Qualifying Investor AIF is authorised by the Central Bank, the Central Bank has not set any limits or other restrictions on the investment objectives, the investment policies or on the degree of leverage which may be employed by the Qualifying Investor AIF.'
[371] In addition to listing other potential conflicts of interest that could arise, including as between the alternative investment fund manager (if not a general partner) and the AIF.
[372] Central Bank AIF Rulebook at p 63 (in respect of an ILP authorised as a retail investor AIF) and p 123 (in respect of an ILP authorised as a qualifying investor AIF).
[373] Investment Limited Partnerships Act 1994, s 7(7).

material respect inaccurate or which omits material information required by the Central Bank.[374]

Powers and Duties of the Central Bank

[29.172] One of the distinguishing features of an ILP from either an ordinary partnership or a limited partnership is the fact that it is a collective investment undertaking. As such, the Central Bank will have an important role in ensuring that it is properly managed for the protection of investors in the scheme. Accordingly, the 1994 Act gives the Central Bank wide-ranging powers not only as regards the initial authorisation of the ILP, but also during the life of the firm.

Power of entry

[29.173] Section 25 of the 1994 Act grants the Central Bank wide powers of entry,[375] enquiry and inspection at all reasonable times in relation to the records of:

(a)   ILPs, general partners and custodians;

(b)   any associated undertakings[376] of the general partner and custodian; and

(c)   any other person associated with the ILP.[377]

Power to appoint an inspector

[29.174] Section 26 of the 1994 Act entitles the Central Bank to apply to the High Court to appoint one or more inspectors to investigate the affairs of an ILP or any associated undertaking, where there are circumstances suggesting that the limited partners are not being given all the information on the firm which they might reasonably expect, they are being oppressed or there has been some wrongdoing in the running of the firm. This section was clearly based on Part II of the Companies Act 1990 (now Part 13 of the Companies Act 2014) which provided for the appointment of inspectors to companies. The court appointed inspector to an ILP has considerable powers to enable him prepare a detailed report on the ILP, including the power to examine persons on oath and extend the powers of inspection with the approval of the High Court to any other ILP, any body corporate or present or former associated undertakings of the ILP. Having considered the inspector's report, the High Court may wind up the ILP or make an order for the remedying of any disability[378] suffered by any person whose interests were affected by the conduct of the affairs of the ILP.[379]

---

[374]   Investment Limited Partnerships Act 1994, s 14(3). The original fine of £500,000 was converted to its euro equivalent by virtue of Council Regulations (EC) No 1103/97, (EC) No 974/98 and (EC) No 2866/98 and the Economic and Monetary Union Act 1998, s 6 and then, by virtue of s 9 of the Fines Act 2010, multiplied by 1.75 to give the current amount.

[375]   See generally, the annotation of the 1994 Act by Declan Murphy, available at www.westlaw.ie, where the author notes that the word 'and' has been omitted from s 25(2)(a) before the phrase 'for those purposes'.

[376]   This is defined in the Investment Limited Partnerships Act 1994, s 25(4)(a) and includes partnerships.

[377]   This expression is not defined by the 1994 Act.

[378]   This term should, it seems, be interpreted as synonymous with the term 'loss': see generally, the annotation of the 1994 Act by Declan Murphy, available at www.westlaw.ie.

[379]   Investment Limited Partnerships Act 1994, s 26(10).

Power to require information

[29.175] The general partner and custodian are required to provide the Central Bank with such information and returns as the Central Bank may specify from time to time. In addition, the Central Bank may require information regarding any associated undertakings[380] of the ILP, if it is materially relevant to the proper appraisal of the business of the ILP or, curiously, of the associated undertaking. One would have thought that the power to seek information in relation to an associated undertaking should be allowed only insofar as it is materially relevant to the ILP. Yet s 27(3) allows the Central Bank to seek such information even if it is only relevant to the associated undertaking itself. Whether this was intended by the draftsman is open to doubt since it is difficult to justify in principle. A person who knowingly provides false information to the Central Bank is guilty of an offence and liable to a maximum fine of €1,093,750 or to imprisonment of up to 15 years.[381] In addition to the foregoing right to require specific information, the Central Bank requires the following information on an ongoing basis.

Annual, half-yearly reports and monthly returns of the ILP

[29.176] An ILP authorised as a qualifying investor AIF is required to publish and file an annual (audited) report with the Central Bank.[382] An ILP authorised as a retail investor AIF is required to publish and file both an annual (audited) report and a half-yearly report with the Central Bank.[383] Each must also file monthly and quarterly statistical returns with the Central Bank.[384]

Annual report and accounts of ILP

[29.177] An ILP is required by s 16(2) of the 1994 Act to maintain audited accounts. The Central Bank may impose conditions on the form, content and periodicity of the accounts of an ILP, as it deems appropriate.[385] The annual report of an ILP, including the accounts of the firm, which are submitted to the Central Bank must be audited by a person empowered to audit accounts under the Companies Act 2014.[386] The annual report must comply with the requirements of the Irish AIFMD Regulations[387] and the

---

380 As defined in the Investment Limited Partnerships Act 1994, s 25(4)(a).

381 Investment Limited Partnerships Act 1994, ss 27(4) and 40. The original fine of £500,000 was converted to its euro equivalent by virtue of Council Regulations (EC) No 1103/97, (EC) No 974/98 and (EC) No 2866/98 and the Economic and Monetary Union Act 1998, s 6 and then, by virtue of s 9 of the Fines Act 2010, multiplied by 1.75 to give the current amount.

382 Investment Limited Partnerships Act 1994, s 16(1); Central Bank AIF Rulebook at p 126, which also sets out detailed information as to what should be included in those reports.

383 Investment Limited Partnerships Act 1994, s 16(1); Central Bank AIF Rulebook at p 70, which also sets out detailed information as to what should be included in those reports.

384 Central Bank AIF Rulebook at p 55 (in respect of an ILP authorised as a retail investor AIF) and pp 116–117 (in respect of an ILP authorised as a qualifying investor AIF).

385 Investment Limited Partnerships Act 1994, s 15(2).

386 Investment Limited Partnerships Act 1994, s 16(2) refers to the 'Companies Acts'; by virtue of Schedule 1 Part 2 of the Interpretation Act 2005 and s 5(3) of the Companies Act 2014, this is deemed to be a reference to the Companies Act 2014.

387 European Union (Alternative Investment Fund Managers) Regulations 2013, reg 23.

Central Bank AIF Rulebook,[388] and it must contain an auditor's report.[389] The auditor's report to the limited partners, including any qualifications to that report, must be reproduced in full in the annual report that is submitted to the Central Bank.[390] Where a general partner or a custodian knowingly supplies false information to an auditor, he is guilty of an offence and liable to a maximum fine of €1,093,750 or to imprisonment of up to 15 years.[391] In addition, he is obliged to indemnify any person who suffers loss as a result of the supply of this information.[392]

[29.178] Under s 25(1) of the 1994 Act, every[393] general partner and custodian of an ILP must keep, at an office within Ireland, such books and records (including accounts) as may be specified from time to time by the Central Bank. The custodian and general partner are required to notify the Central Bank of the address of every office at which such books or records are kept.

Failure of ILP to file annual report

[29.179] Where an ILP fails to publish and file an annual report with the Central Bank in accordance with its requirements, each general partner shall be guilty of an offence and shall indemnify any person who thereby suffers loss.[394]

[29.180] In addition, an ILP which fails to take all reasonable steps to ensure compliance with the requirement to file an annual report with the Central Bank under s 16(1) or to keep accounts and records under s 25(1), is guilty of an offence, unless it had reasonable grounds for believing and did believe that a competent and reliable person was charged with compliance and was in a position to ensure it.[395]

Personal liability of officers of general partner regarding accounts of ILP

[29.181] It has been noted elsewhere[396] that a general partner which is a limited liability company may thereby effectively limit its liability for the obligations of the ILP to the amount of capital in the company. However in certain situations, the officers or former officers of a general partner (which terms include a director of a general partner)[397] will

388 Central Bank AIF Rulebook at p 70 et seq (in respect of an ILP authorised as a retail investor AIF) and p 126 et seq (in respect of an ILP authorised as a qualifying investor AIF).
389 Investment Limited Partnerships Act 1994, s 16(2).
390 Central Bank AIF Rulebook at p 70 (in respect of an ILP authorised as a retail investor AIF) and p 126 (in respect of an ILP authorised as a qualifying investor AIF).
391 Investment Limited Partnerships Act 1994, ss 16(11) and 40.
392 Investment Limited Partnerships Act 1994, s 16(11).
393 The use of the word 'every' in s 25(1) negatives the assumption in s 4(3) that a reference to a general partner means any one general partner, where there is more than one.
394 Investment Limited Partnerships Act 1994, s 16(9). Unlike an action in negligence, an action under this statutory right to damages does not require the third party to satisfy the 'proximity test' before being entitled to damages, see generally, the annotation of the 1994 Act by Declan Murphy, available at www.westlaw.ie.
395 Investment Limited Partnerships Act 1994, s 35(8).
396 See para **[29.33]**.
397 The Investment Limited Partnerships Act 1994, s 35(6) which states: 'In this section "officer" in relation to a general partner includes a director, a person in accordance with whose directions the directors are accustomed to act, or the secretary.'

have personal liability, without any limitation, for the debts and liabilities of the ILP. Before personal liability will arise, s 35 of the 1994 Act requires there to have been a failure by the ILP to publish and file with the Central Bank an annual report under s 16(1) or a failure by the ILP to keep books and records of the firm in Ireland and notify the Central Bank of the location thereof under s 25(1). If the High Court considers that, on the winding up of an ILP which is unable to pay its debts, this failure to comply with s 16(1) or s 25(1) contributed to its inability to pay its debts or resulted in substantial uncertainty as to the assets, liabilities, client money or investment instruments of the ILP or substantially impeded its orderly winding up,[398] then the High Court has a discretion to impose personal liability, without limitation, on the officer of the general partner responsible for the contravention, for all or part of the ILP's debts and liabilities.[399] A High Court order imposing personal liability on the officers of the general partner may only be made on the application of the liquidator of the ILP, the Central Bank, a creditor or a limited partner in the firm.[400] There will be no liability if the officer took all reasonable steps to secure compliance with the ILP's obligations under s 16(1) or s 25(1), or if he had reasonable grounds for believing and did believe that a competent and reliable person was charged with compliance and was in a position to ensure it.

[29.182] Under s 35(6), an 'officer' of a general partner includes a director, secretary or 'person in accordance with whose directions or instructions the directors are accustomed to act', ie a shadow director. Unlike the case of shadow directors in companies,[401] there is no exemption for professional advisers who advise directors on the firm's affairs. This may have been an accidental oversight by the drafters of the 1994 Act and as the High Court has a discretion whether to declare an officer of a general partner liable for the debts of the ILP, it is apprehended that the High Court is unlikely to make such professional advisers personally liable where the directors are simply acting in accordance with their professional advice.

The officers and directors of the ILP

[29.183] In addition to providing personal liability upon an officer of a general partner, s 35 also provides that where a person, who is a member or director of an ILP, fails to take all reasonable steps to secure compliance with the requirements in s 16(1) or s 25(1), he shall be guilty of an offence.[402] This section is curious for two reasons, first there cannot be any person who is a director of an ILP, since it is a partnership. Second, a limited partner is a 'member' of a firm, yet it cannot be expected that a limited partner should be required to take reasonable steps to ensure the firm complies with s 16(1) or s 25(1), since limited partners are prohibited from taking part in the conduct of the firm's business. The most plausible explanation for this rather curious provision would appear to be that it was intended to refer to the members or directors of a general

---

[398] Compare the Companies Act 1990, ss 203 and 204, upon which s 35 appears to be based (now s 609 of the Companies Act 2014).

[399] Investment Limited Partnerships Act 1994, s 35(1).

[400] Investment Limited Partnerships Act 1994, s 35(1).

[401] Cf the Companies Act 2014, s 221(1) and see generally the annotation of the 1994 Act by Declan Murphy, available from www.westlaw.ie.

[402] Investment Limited Partnerships Act 1994, s 35(8).

partner. In its present form, it makes little sense and does not achieve what was its presumed intention, to make directors and officers of the general partner guilty of an offence where they fail to take all reasonable steps to ensure that the firm's annual report is filed with the Central Bank and that the firm keeps at its offices, books and records of the firm. As this section purports to create a criminal offence, there can be little doubt that the courts will interpret the wording strictly and thereby render it meaningless.[403]

Central Bank as registrar of ILPs

[29.184] The Central Bank, as well as being the body appointed to authorise and supervise the operation of ILPs, is also the place for the maintenance of the central register of such partnerships. This aspect of the supervisory role of the Central Bank is akin to that of the Registrar of Companies in the Companies Registration Office.[404] The Central Bank is obliged to maintain a record of each ILP authorised by it and all statements filed in relation to ILPs. A copy or extract from these records, certified by a director or secretary[405] of the Central Bank, shall be admissible in evidence as of equal validity as the original document.

Right of inspection of register

[29.185] Under s 10(1) of the 1994 Act, members of the public are entitled to inspect and obtain copies on the payment of any relevant fees of:

(a)   the partnership agreement of an ILP;[406]

(b)   the prospectus of an ILP;

(c)   particulars filed with the Central Bank by the ILP under s 8(4)(e);[407]

(d)   particulars filed with the Central Bank as a result of the supervisory requirements of the Central Bank under s 8(4)(f);[408] and

(e)   the annual report of an ILP filed with the Central Bank and any statement by the auditor of the ILP filed with the Central Bank under s 16(3), 16(4) or 16(7)(a).

---

[403]   *Frescati Estates v Walker* [1975] IR 177; *CW Shipping Co Ltd v Limerick Harbour Commissioners* [1989] ILRM 416 at 424.

[404]   This is achieved by the Investment Limited Partnerships Act 1994, s 10 which applies s 370 of the Companies Act 1963 (now deemed to be a reference to ss 891–893 of the Companies Act 2014 by virtue of s 5(3) and sch 6 of the Companies Act 2014) relating to the inspection, production and evidence of documents kept by the Registrar of Companies to ILPs, save that the reference therein to registrar is to be construed as a reference to the Central Bank.

[405]   The Companies Act 2014, s 892 refers inter alia to an 'officer authorised by the Minister' and s 2(1) of the Companies Act 2014 defines 'officer' (in respect of a body corporate) as including a director or secretary.

[406]   The drafting of s 10(1) is somewhat confusing as a comma appears to have been omitted on the fifth line thereof, before the phrase 'the particulars'.

[407]   Ie, the name and address of the general partner(s) and if a company not incorporated in the State, a statement that it has complied with s 1302 of the Companies Act 2014 and its registration number.

[408]   Ie, the name and address of the custodian.

Central Bank has discretion to publish names of ILPs

[29.186] There is no obligation upon the Central Bank to publish in *Iris Oifigiúil* a list of ILPs authorised by it, since s 10(2) provides simply that the Central Bank 'may' publish such a list, with such details of the other matters filed with the Central Bank in relation thereto and available for inspection as it considers appropriate. In contrast, the Central Bank is obliged to publish a notice of the revocation of the authorisation of an ILP in *Iris Oifigiúil*.[409]

Power of summary intervention by Central Bank

[29.187] In addition to its wide-ranging powers to impose and amend conditions for the authorisation of ILPs[410] and for the general supervision of ILPs,[411] s 33 of the 1994 Act authorises the Central Bank to summarily intervene in the business of an ILP to give directions to an ILP in certain circumstances, including but not limited to its winding up or the suspension of the assignment of any partnership interest. These circumstances arise when the Central Bank is of the opinion that:

(a) it is in the public interest or the interests of the proper and orderly regulation of ILPs; or

(b) any of the requirements for authorising an ILP are no longer satisfied; or

(c) the ILP, custodian or general partner—

  (i) is unlikely to meet its obligations to creditors; or

  (ii) has contravened the Act or the conditions imposed thereunder or furnished[412] false or misleading information to the Central Bank; or

  (iii) has inadequate capital resources, in light of its volume and nature of business; or

  (iv) is in breach of the capital or other financial requirements of the Central Bank.

[29.188] Section 33(6) provides for a review of the Central Bank's directions by the High Court, although like the review procedure in s 32,[413] there would appear to be a heavy onus of proof upon the applicant, since it must be established that the requirements of the 1994 Act have not been complied with in any material respect or that there was no evidence upon which the Central Bank could reasonably conclude that the criteria for making such directions had existed or that the directions made by the Central Bank were disproportionate.

---

[409] Investment Limited Partnerships Act 1994, s 29(3).

[410] Investment Limited Partnerships Act 1994, s 7(2) and 7(3).

[411] Investment Limited Partnerships Act 1994, s 7(4)(f).

[412] Note that there is no requirement that this be done 'knowingly'; cf the requirement for an offence under the Investment Limited Partnerships Act 1994, s 16(11) that the false information in the annual report to the Central Bank be given knowingly.

[413] See further para **[29.82]**.

Scheme for termination of custodian's or general partner's business

[29.189] Under s 33(10) of the 1994 Act, the Central Bank is also entitled to apply to the High Court for an order directing the custodian or general partner[414] to prepare, in consultation with the Central Bank, a scheme for the orderly termination of its own business and the discharge of its liabilities and to submit the final scheme to court for approval. To make such an application, the Central Bank must be of the opinion that, even if directions were imposed upon the custodian or general partner under s 33, the circumstances giving rise to the directions are unlikely to be rectified.

VIII. TERMINATION OF ILPs

[29.190] In this section, consideration will be given to the end of the life of the ILP, namely its dissolution, its bankruptcy and its winding up.

Dissolution of ILPs otherwise than by Court

[29.191] The dissolution of an ILP, otherwise than by the court, is dealt with by a combination of the 1994 Act and the 1890 Act. The provisions regarding dissolution contained in the 1890 Act are, however, substantially modified in their application to an ILP and it is proposed to examine the manner in which the 1994 Act achieves these modifications. Before doing so, it is important to bear in mind that, to the extent that the dissolution provisions of the 1890 Act are not inconsistent with the 1994 Act, these provisions will apply to an ILP.[415] Accordingly, in considering the dissolution of an ILP, regard should always be had to treatment of the dissolution of ordinary partnerships earlier in this work.[416]

Acts of dissolution

[29.192] It has been noted elsewhere in this chapter[417] that the Central Bank has the power to revoke the authorisation of an ILP under s 29 of the 1994 Act, in cases of default or where it is in the interests of the limited partners. Section 37(2)(b) of the 1994 Act provides that on the revocation of an authorisation, an ILP automatically dissolves.

[29.193] Dissolution will also occur where an ILP has just one general partner and he is subject to any of the following events:[418] death, incapacity, retirement, bankruptcy, removal, resignation, insolvency, dissolution, or winding up.

[29.194] However, if within 35 days of any of these events, the limited partners unanimously elect a replacement general partner(s), who is approved by the Central

---

[414] The Investment Limited Partnerships Act 1994, s 33(10) which refers to the custodian and 'partner'. However, as s 33(10) depends on s 33(1) (which refers to directions being given to a custodian or 'general partner'), the reference in s 33(10) to 'partner' must be taken as meaning the 'general partner'.

[415] Investment Limited Partnerships Act 1994, s 4(1).

[416] See Part D of this work.

[417] See para **[29.77]** et seq.

[418] Investment Limited Partnerships Act 1994, s 37(2)(a).

Bank, the business of the ILP need not be wound up but may be resumed and continued.[419]

Dissolution by act of partners

[29.195] Where the firm is purported to be dissolved by an act of the partners themselves, such as a vote by the partners or dissolution under the terms of the investment limited partnership agreement or by notice of one partner,[420] the dissolution will only take effect after the notice of dissolution has been signed by any one general partner, delivered to the Central Bank[421] and published in *Iris Oifigiúil*.[422]

[29.196] Section 19(1)(a) of the 1994 Act provides that, subject to any express or implied term of the partnership agreement, any differences arising as to matters connected with the partnership business, and this would include a vote on the dissolution of the firm, requires a majority vote of the general partners.[423] Thus, the investment limited partnership agreement legitimately may provide for the limited partners to have a vote on the dissolution and winding up of the firm. In such a case, s 6(4)(e)(i) of the 1994 Act expressly provides that such activity would not be regarded as constituting the taking part in the conduct of the business of the firm, so as to deprive the limited partners of their protection of limited liability.

Expiry of fixed term partnership

[29.197] As with ordinary partnerships,[424] a fixed term ILP will dissolve on the expiry of the term. However, in contrast to an ordinary partnership, the general partner is required to put a notice in *Iris Oifigiúil* of the dissolution of an ILP by the expiry of its term.[425] However, there is no provision in the 1994 Act regarding the effect of such a notice. For this reason, it is apprehended that the provisions of the 1890 Act regarding the effect of a notice in *Iris Oifigiúil* on the dissolution of a partnership will apply to such a notice. Since the 1994 Act does not deem it necessary to make it an offence for the general partner to fail to so advertise, it is thought that it is solely in his own interest to advertise the dissolution, ie in order to reduce his liability to persons who had no dealings with the ILP. Thus, it is apprehended that in accordance with the law of ordinary partnerships, only those persons who had no previous dealings with the ILP will be deemed to be on notice of the advertised dissolution of the ILP and not those persons who had dealings with the ILP.[426]

---

[419] Investment Limited Partnerships Act 1994, s 37(3).
[420] Were it not for the terms of the Investment Limited Partnerships Act 1994, s 38(1), notice by any one partner to his co-partners of his desire to dissolve the partnership would be sufficient per se to dissolve a partnership at will: Partnership Act 1890, ss 26(1) and 32(c).
[421] It seems clear that this right may not be varied by agreement between the partners under the Partnership Act 1890, s 19, since that section applies only to 'the mutual rights and duties of partners' and not where, as in this case, the rights of the Central Bank are involved.
[422] Investment Limited Partnerships Act 1994, s 38(1).
[423] Investment Limited Partnerships Act 1994, s 19(1)(a).
[424] Partnership Act 1890, s 32(a), see generally para **[23.47]** et seq.
[425] Investment Limited Partnerships Act 1994, s 38(4).
[426] Partnership Act 1890, s 36(1) and 36(2) and see further para **[11.70]** et seq.

[29.198] Section 38(4) of the 1994 Act provides that, on the dissolution of a fixed term partnership by the expiry of its term, the limited partners are liable for the debts and obligations 'purportedly incurred on behalf of the ILP thereafter'. This remarkably wide-ranging provision is considered elsewhere in this chapter.[427]

Non-dissolution events

[29.199] Section 37 of the 1994 Act sets out a number of situations which do not cause the dissolution of an ILP, many of which cause the dissolution of a partnership under the 1890 Act. These will be considered next.

General or limited partner's share being charged for separate debt

[29.200] A partner in an ILP may grant any form of security interest over his share in the firm and, in contrast to an ordinary partnership,[428] this will not entitle the other partners to dissolve the firm.

Change in constitution of firm

[29.201] In an ordinary partnership, any change in the constitution of the firm leads to the firm's dissolution.[429] In contrast, s 37(1) of the 1994 Act provides that an ILP is not dissolved by any change in the limited or general partners, and in particular is not dissolved by the admission, replacement, departure, bankruptcy, death, dissolution or winding up of a limited or a general partner, unless the partner in question is the sole general partner.[430] In broad terms the section treats the ILP as approaching the status of a separate legal personality, since it prima facie provides for the identity or status of the partners to be irrelevant to the existence of the firm, save in the case of the sole general partner. However, this section is not without its difficulties.

[29.202] First, there is an apparent conflict between s 37(1)(iii) and s 5(1)(b) of the 1994 Act. On the one hand, s 5(1)(b) states that an ILP 'shall ... consist of one or more general partners and one or more limited partners'. Yet s 37(1)(iii) states that:

> [N]otwithstanding anything contained in the Act of 1890, an investment limited partnership shall not be terminated or dissolved by ... the death, incapacity, bankruptcy, removal, resignation, dissolution or winding-up of a limited partner or a general partner, where there is more than one general partner.

[29.203] Section 37(2)(a) then goes on to provide that if these events happen to a sole general partner, the ILP will dissolve. Therefore, it would seem to be implicit in s 37(1)(iii) that an ILP is not dissolved where the sole limited partner is removed or dies or otherwise ceases to exist. Yet it is difficult to reconcile this with the requirement in s 5(1)(b) that every ILP must have at least one limited partner. It is suggested that this conflict should be resolved by resorting to general principles and that since every ordinary partnership must have two partners and every limited partnership must have one general partner and one limited partner, s 37(1)(iii) should be read as being subject to s 5, so that an ILP will not exist where there is no limited partner. On this basis, it is

---

427 See para **[29.95]** et seq.
428 Partnership Act 1890, s 33(2).
429 See para **[23.09]**.
430 Investment Limited Partnerships Act 1994, s 37(1)(i) and (iii).

contended such an ILP will not exist and it should, in the words of s 37(1), be terminated or dissolved.[431]

[29.204] A second issue concerning s 37(1)(iii) relates to the wording used in that section. In essence, the purpose of s 37(1)(iii) is to prevent a partner in an ILP exercising his right to wind up the firm under s 39 of the 1890 Act in the event of one of the partners dying, becoming incapacitated, bankrupt, being removed, resigning, being dissolved[432] or wound up. Unfortunately, this purpose is achieved by providing that these events will not lead to the partnership being 'dissolved'. In partnership law, this term is somewhat ambiguous since it can mean general dissolution, in the sense of the winding up of a partnership, but it can also mean a technical dissolution, in the sense of any change in the membership of a continuing firm.[433] Interpreting s 37(1)(iii) to mean that these seven events cause a technical dissolution of an ILP would lead to the absurd result that where a partner is removed from an ILP, the firm is not technically dissolved, but that he remains a member of the firm. For this reason, it is apprehended that the intention of s 37(1)(iii) is that these events do not cause a general dissolution of the firm.

[29.205] This still leaves open the possibility that these seven events may or may not cause a technical dissolution of the partnership. Because of the physical nature of four of these events, namely, death, removal, resignation and dissolution, the firm must undergo a technical dissolution, since it will not be possible for the partners affected to continue as members of the partnership. However in the other three events, namely, incapacity, bankruptcy and winding-up, the affected partner has the capacity to remain a partner in the ILP and thus it is thought that s 37(1)(iii) must be interpreted as meaning that there will not even be a technical dissolution in such cases. Thus a partner, who is incapacitated, bankrupt or being wound up, will remain a member of the ILP, unlike a partner who is deceased, removed, dissolved or has resigned.[434]

Dissolution of an ILP by Court Order

[29.206] The power of a court to dissolve an ordinary partnership under s 35 of the 1890 Act is equally applicable to the dissolution of an ILP.[435]

---

[431] It is possible that an ILP with two or more general partners, but no limited partners, will be an ordinary partnership. On the other hand, if there is simply one general partner and no limited partners, there can be no partnership of any nature and the firm must be dissolved since a partnership must have at least two members: Partnership Act 1890, s 1(1).

[432] This term clearly refers to the dissolution of a company or firm. It is apprehended that the dissolution of a corporate partner is equivalent to the death of an individual partner, see para **[23.36]**. A similar argument can be made in the case of the dissolution of a firm, which is itself a member of an ILP, although the dissolution of a firm is not as final an event as the dissolution of a company.

[433] See generally para **[23.07]**.

[434] These former partners who are dead, removed, dissolved or resigned will not therefore be able to rely on the Partnership Act 1890, s 39 but will be able to rely on s 42 of the 1890 Act, see generally paras **[26.26]** et seq and **[26.63]**.

[435] See generally in relation to the Partnership Act 1890, s 35 and para **[25.01]** et seq.

[29.207] The 1994 Act does not modify the application of s 35 of the 1890 Act to ILPs. Thus, a limited or a general partner may apply to court for a dissolution of the ILP in any of the cases set out in that section. However, under s 35 of the 1890 Act, the court is not obliged to grant a dissolution in the cases arising under that section. Rather, the section provides that the court 'may decree a dissolution' and a court is likely to exercise this discretion in such a way as to take account of the restricted role of a limited partner in the ILP. Thus, where it is the limited partner's conduct which forms the ground for the application, it is likely that to justify a court order, this conduct should be more severe than the conduct of a general partner, in view of the limited role of the limited partner in the management of the ILP. Conversely, where the limited partner is the applicant, his restricted role means that the court is more likely to be tolerant of a general partner's behaviour towards a limited partner in an ILP than that of a partner in an ordinary partnership

Winding up of an ILP

[29.208] Once an ILP is dissolved, whether by court order or by a non-judicial event, s 39 of the 1890 Act entitles the partners to have the partnership property sold and the debts and liabilities of the firm paid off and for that purpose, any partner may apply to court to wind up the firm. In view of the restriction on the limited partners taking part in the conduct of the partnership business,[436] it is apprehended that the limited partners should not take part in the winding up of the firm for fear of losing their limited liability.[437] Indeed it is surprising that the 1994 Act does not expressly entrust the winding up of the firm to the general partners, as is done in the case of limited partnerships.[438]

Winding up of an ILP as an unregistered company

[29.209] An ILP may be wound up as an unregistered company under Part 22 of the 2014 Act in the same way as an ordinary partnership, save that the restriction on the application of Part 22 to partnerships of eight partners or more[439] is expressly disapplied by s 38(3) of the 1994 Act in the case of ILPs. Thus, all ILPs which are formed in Ireland may be wound up as unregistered companies. In addition, s 1326 of the 2014 Act, which outlines the instances in which a partnership is deemed to be unable to pay its debts, does not apply to limited partners.[440] In this way, the financial position of the limited partner does not have any effect on the question of whether the ILP should be wound up. Reference should be made to the analysis of Part 22 of the 2014 Act earlier in this text.[441]

---

[436] Investment Limited Partnerships Act 1994, s 6(1).

[437] See generally para **[29.103]** et seq.

[438] Limited Partnerships Act 1907, s 6(3).

[439] This restriction is imposed by the Companies Act 2014, s 1326.

[440] The Investment Limited Partnerships Act 1994, s 38(3) which modifies the terms of the Companies Act 1963, s 345(5)(b) and (c) (now the Companies Act 2014, s 1328) in their application to limited partners.

[441] See para **[27.06]** et seq.

Bankruptcy

[29.210] The law of bankruptcy is considered in detail elsewhere in this work.[442] As has been noted previously, the Bankruptcy Act 1988, by its simple reference to 'partners' and 'partnerships' prima facie applies to ILPs and to general and limited partners.[443] Accordingly, reference will be made hereunder only to those instances where special rules apply to ILPs. Since the position of a general partner in an ILP is akin to that of a partner in an ordinary partnership,[444] there is no reason why a general partner should not be subject to bankruptcy law in the same way as a partner in an ordinary partnership. However, the role of the limited partner in an ILP is somewhat different from that of a partner in an ordinary partnership and for this reason, different rules will apply to him.

Petitioning for bankruptcy

[29.211] If a petition is to be signed on behalf of the ILP for its own bankruptcy or for the bankruptcy of a debtor of the firm, it is advisable that it be signed by a general partner, rather than a limited partner, in order to avoid contravening the prohibition on a limited partner taking part in the management of the partnership business.[445]

Non-dissolution of ILP on bankruptcy of limited partner

[29.212] In an ordinary partnership, the bankruptcy of a partner leads to the automatic dissolution of the partnership, unless there is a contrary agreement between the partners.[446] In view of the restricted role of the limited partner in the management of the ILP and the limit on his liability to his capital contributed to the firm, the bankruptcy of a limited partner does not have the same impact on the ILP. This explains the provision in s 37(1)(iii) of the 1994 Act that an ILP shall not be terminated or dissolved by the bankruptcy of a limited partner.

Position of limited partners on bankruptcy of ILP

[29.213] In contrast to the partial manner in which limited partners in limited partnerships are excluded from a firm's bankruptcy,[447] limited partners in ILPs are expressly excluded from ss 30–32 and 36 of the Bankruptcy Act 1988. Section 23 of the 1994 Act provides that:

> For the purposes of the application of sections 30, 31, 32 and 36 of the Bankruptcy Act, 1988, a limited partner shall not be regarded as a partner of an investment limited partnership.

The exclusion of limited partners in ILPs from these bankruptcy provisions reinforces their status as passive investors who will lose their capital contribution on the bankruptcy of the partnership, but will not be subject to bankruptcy proceedings.

---

442 See para **[27.01]** et seq.
443 See para **[27.20]** et seq.
444 See para **[29.40]**.
445 Investment Limited Partnerships Act 1994, s 6(1). See further para **[29.93]**.
446 Partnership Act 1890, s 33(1). See generally para **[27.60]**.
447 See para **[28.142]** et seq.

Exclusion of s 31 of the Bankruptcy Act 1988

[29.214] The most significant provision of the Bankruptcy Act 1988 from which limited partners are excluded is s 31. As a result of its disapplication, a creditor of an ILP cannot present a petition for bankruptcy against a limited partner in that firm. However, it seems that this is not absolute. This is because s 22 of the 1994 Act provides that in legal proceedings against the firm for a debt, a limited partner may be made a party thereto, or named therein, if he is liable for the debt, as a result of the loss of his limited liability under s 6 or s 20 of the 1994 Act. Therefore, if the bankruptcy proceedings relate to a debt arising under s 6 or s 20 of the 1994 Act, then it seems that they may be taken against the limited partner. Although s 23 of the 1994 Act does not admit such an exception on its face, clearly allowing bankruptcy proceedings to be taken against a limited partner who has acted as a general partner (in breach of s 6) or received back his capital when the firm is unable to pay its debts (in breach of s 20), can be supported in principle.

Exclusion of ss 30, 32 and 36 of the Bankruptcy Act 1988

[29.215] The other sections of the Bankruptcy Act 1988 from which the limited partner is excluded are ss 30, 32 and 36. Thus, the Official Assignee cannot take an action to recover a debt from the ILP in the name of a limited partner (s 30), a limited partner is not required to provide the Official Assignee with accounts and other information on the ILP on the bankruptcy of his general partner (s 32) and a limited partner may not be named in bankruptcy proceedings against an ILP (s 36).[448]

[29.216] A limited partner in an ILP is not excluded from bankruptcy law in general, but only from ss 30–32 and 36 of the Bankruptcy Act 1988. Thus, a limited partner is subject to all other principles of bankruptcy. For example a limited partner remains subject to s 33 of the 1988 Act which deals with the duty of a partner, who is himself adjudicated bankrupt, to deliver a statement of affairs to the Official Assignee in relation to the partnership.

Vesting of partnership property in Official Assignee

[29.217] It has been noted earlier in this work that on the bankruptcy of *all* the partners in a firm, the partnership property vests in the Official Assignee for the benefit of his creditors.[449] In a limited partnership, s 37 of the Bankruptcy Act 1988 provides for the modification of this rule, so that the partnership property is vested in the Official Assignee where the general partners alone are adjudicated bankrupt.[450] Although the role of a limited partner in an ILP is very similar to that of a limited partner in a limited partnership, s 37 of the 1988 Act does not apply to ILPs. This can, in part, be explained by the fact that ILPs were only created in 1994, after the passing of the 1988 Act.

---

448 Clearly the exclusion of s 32 would not apply, where the bankruptcy relates to a debt for which the limited partner is liable under the Investment Limited Partnerships Act 1994, ss 6 or 20. See para **[29.214]**, where the same point is made in relation to the Bankruptcy Act 1988, s 31.

449 See *Re Hind* (1889) 23 LR Ir 17 and the Bankruptcy Act 1988, s 44(1). See generally para **[27.69]**.

450 See para **[28.139]**.

[29.218] Nonetheless, it is curious that the rule that the assets of a partnership only vest in the Official Assignee on the bankruptcy of each of the partners was not modified in its application to ILPs. This is especially so, when one considers that a limited partner in an ILP is even further protected from the bankruptcy of his firm than a limited partner in a limited partnership. For this reason, it is thought that the failure of the 1994 Act to provide that the property of an ILP vests in the Official Assignee on the bankruptcy of the general partners alone is simply a drafting oversight. Indeed, in light of the other terms of the 1994 Act, it can be argued that the Act, and in particular, s 23, implicitly achieves this purpose. This argument goes that s 23 provides that a limited partner is not a partner for the purposes of, inter alia, s 31 of the Bankruptcy Act 1988 and therefore may not be adjudicated bankrupt on the basis of the debts of the firm. For this reason, and bearing in mind the limited liability of a limited partner for the debts of the firm, it would be illogical to prevent the partnership property from vesting in the Official Assignee, where all the general partners are bankrupt, simply because the limited partners are not also bankrupt. While this argument can be supported in principle, it would of course have been preferable if this modification to the vesting of the property of an ILP in the Official Assignee had been expressly enacted by the legislature, rather than leaving it to a court to find that it is implicit in the terms of s 23 of the 1994 Act.

Chapter 30

LLPs, Legal Partnerships and Multi-disciplinary Practices

INTRODUCTION

[30.01] As mentioned earlier in this work,[1] one of the statutory provisions which expressly prohibits the formation of certain types of partnership is contained in the Solicitors Act 1954. Under s 59 of that Act, a solicitor is prohibited from carrying on business as a solicitor in partnership with a person who has not been admitted as a solicitor.[2] Further, at the time of writing, practising barristers are not permitted to enter into any professional partnership, whether with one another, or with others.[3] The Legal Services Regulation Act 2015 (referred to in this chapter as the 2015 Act) will, when commenced in full, change the position considerably. It will allow practising barristers to enter into partnerships with other practising barristers, and with practising solicitors, and these new forms of partnership will be known as 'legal partnerships'. Under the 2015 Act, it will also be possible for practising lawyers (both solicitors and barristers) to enter into partnerships with non-lawyers, known as 'multi-disciplinary practices'. In a significant development for the Irish legal profession, both partnerships of solicitors, and legal partnerships, will be able to apply for authorisation as a 'limited liability partnership' (sometimes referred to as an 'LLP'), with the partners in that partnership then benefitting from limited liability.[4] Unlike the UK however, Ireland's new LLP framework will, for the time being, only be available to the legal profession.

[30.02] This Chapter will consider the new partnership structures under the 2015 Act under the following headings:

  I.   Background to the 2015 Act.

  II.   The Role of the Legal Services Regulatory Authority.

  III.   Legal Partnerships.

  IV.   Limited Liability Partnerships.

  V.   Multi-Disciplinary Practices.

---

[1]   See para [9.10].

[2]   The Solicitors Act 1954, s 59(1) states that: 'A solicitor shall not wilfully – (a) act, in business carried on by him as a solicitor, as agent for an unqualified person so as to enable that person to act as a solicitor ...' Since every partner is an agent for his co-partners (see para [10.07]), a solicitor, who is in partnership with an unqualified person, is (at the time of writing) in breach of this section.

[3]   *Code of Conduct for the Bar of Ireland* (version as adopted on 23 July 2014) at para 7.14.

[4]   This will be a substantial change for partnerships of solicitors who, to date, have had unlimited liability for the obligations of the partnership. See, further, Ryan, 'Limited Liability for Solicitors – the story now' (Winter 2015) The Parchment 42–43.

I.   BACKGROUND TO THE 2015 ACT

Recommendations of Fair Trade Commission

[30.03] Since 1990, a considerable amount of work has been carried out to examine how the Irish legal profession could be reformed.[5] In March 1990, the Fair Trade Commission[6] recommended that there:

> 'should be the greatest possible freedom allowed to individual solicitors and barristers to decide themselves upon the most suitable form of business organisation through which to offer their services to clients, with adequate safeguards to ensure the preservation of standards.'

Possibility of 'incorporated practices' of solicitors

[30.04] While the Solicitors (Amendment) Act 1994[7] provided that the Law Society of Ireland could make regulations allowing for 'incorporated practices' of solicitors, at the time of writing, the relevant section of that Act has not yet been commenced, and as a result, no such regulations have yet been made.

Competition Authority 2006 Report

[30.05] In December 2006, the Irish Competition Authority published a report on *Competition in Professional Services: Solicitors and Barristers*,[8] as part of a wider study that it had undertaken in relation to eight professions; solicitors, barristers, engineers, architects, dentists, optometrists, veterinary surgeons and medical practitioners. It observed[9] that, notwithstanding the recommendations of the Fair Trade Commission,[10] lawyers operating in Ireland continued to be subject to, among other restrictions, a number of partnership-related restrictions such as:

-   barristers not being permitted to enter into partnership with one another;
-   barristers not being permitted to enter into partnership with solicitors, or with any other person;

---

[5]   See the Fair Trade Commission, *Report of Study into Restrictive Practices in the Legal Profession* (March 1990), the Organisation for Economic Co-Operation & Development, *Regulatory Reform in Ireland* (2001), the Report of the Legal Costs Working Group (November 2005), and the Report of the Legal Costs Implementation Advisory Group (November 2006). For a detailed review of the work that has taken place to review, and suggest reforms for, the legal profession in Ireland, see Byrne, McCutcheon, Bruton and Coffey, *Byrne and McCutcheon on the Irish Legal System* (6th edn, 2014).

[6]   Fair Trade Commission, *Report of Study into Restrictive Practices in the Legal Profession* (March 1990) at para 11.35.

[7]   Solicitors (Amendment) Act 1994, s 70.

[8]   The Competition Authority's 2006 *Report on Competition in Professional Services: Solicitors & Barristers*, available at https://www.ccpc.ie/business/wp-content/uploads/sites/3/2017/03/Solicitors-and-barristers-full-report.pdf with an executive summary available at https://www.ccpc.ie/business/wp-content/uploads/sites/3/2017/03/Exec-Summary.pdf.

[9]   At p 89 of the Competition Authority's 2006 Report.

[10] See para **[30.03]**.

- solicitors not being permitted to enter into partnership with any person other than another solicitor;
- firms of solicitors not being permitted to incorporate, limit their liability, or have owners that are not solicitors.

[30.06] In its 2006 Report, the Competition Authority observed that the legal profession in Ireland was in need of 'substantial reform' and made 29 recommendations[11] with the aim of aligning the structure of the Irish legal profession with that of other jurisdictions, including England and Wales, Northern Ireland, Australia and New Zealand. Some of the Competition Authority's key findings were as follows:

- The prohibition on barristers forming partnerships was severely hampering competition in the provision of legal services. The Competition Authority commented that if barristers were permitted to form partnerships, the sharing of costs, work, risk and professional reputation that would result from this would lead to economies of scale and greater efficiencies.[12]
- The restriction in the Solicitors Act 1954[13] that prevents practising solicitors from entering into partnership with persons who have not been admitted as solicitors has been a contributing factor to the business model for the provision of legal services in Ireland being overly rigid.[14]
- The potential for alternative practice structures for the Irish legal profession should be examined.[15]

[30.07] Notably, in its 2006 Report, the Competition Authority did not make any recommendations regarding limited liability partnerships as it did not see any clear competition benefits and noted that they could pose additional risks for consumers of the services of solicitors.[16] Instead, the Competition Authority commented that, while there could be other reasons why limited liability partnerships should be permitted, that analysis was outside the scope of the Competition Authority's remit and was instead to be considered by the Law Reform Commission.[17]

---

[11] Recommendation 11 (at p xiv of the Competition Authority's 2006 Report) was that barristers should be allowed to form partnerships, subject to appropriate regulation, and Recommendation 12 (also at page xiv of the Competition Authority's 2006 Report) was that the Legal Services Commission should undertake research into alternative business structures for the Irish legal market. That Legal Services Commission, which was proposed by the Competition Authority's 2006 Report, was never established.

[12] At p vi of the Competition Authority's 2006 Report.

[13] Solicitors Act 1954, s 59.

[14] At p 81 of the Competition Authority's 2006 Report.

[15] At page xiv of the Competition Authority's 2006 Report.

[16] At p 104 of the Competition Authority's 2006 Report. The Competition Authority noted a risk that the limit on liability that would be available to partners in limited liability partnerships could disincentivise partnerships of solicitors from adopting 'effective risk management systems to control negligence and malfeasance'.

[17] At p 104 of the Competition Authority's 2006 Report.

Programme for Government 2011–2016

[30.08] In its Programme for Government (Government for National Recovery 2011–2016), the Irish Government undertook[18] to put in place independent regulation of the legal profession to improve access and competition.

EU/IMF Programme of Financial Support

[30.09] The EU/IMF Programme of Financial Support for Ireland (entered into on 16 December 2010 between the Irish Government, the European Commission, the European Central Bank and the International Monetary Fund) also required the Government to introduce laws to '… remove restrictions to trade and competition in sheltered sectors including … the legal profession' and to implement, among other recommendations, those of the Competition Authority.[19]

Legal Services Regulation Bill 2011

[30.10] Arising out of the commitments made by the then Government as part of its Programme for Government 2011–2016, and commitments already made by the previous Government as part of the EU/IMF Programme of Financial Support for Ireland, the Legal Services Regulation Bill was first published in October 2011. It was not, however, signed into law until 30 December 2015 (as the 2015 Act). That delay was largely attributable to the priority given to other commitments made as part of the EU/IMF Programme of Financial Support for Ireland, and to the lengthy debates that took place on the Bill as it progressed through the Houses of the Oireachtas.

The 2015 Act

[30.11] In its final form, the 2015 Act represents a significant overhaul of the legal profession in Ireland, in particular regarding both business models, and regulation. In addition to establishing the Legal Services Regulatory Authority (referred to in this chapter as the Authority), which will oversee both solicitors and barristers in Ireland, the 2015 Act introduces, at Part 8 of that Act, three new partnership-based business models for the legal profession:

- legal partnerships;
- limited liability partnerships; and
- multi-disciplinary practices;

each of which will be considered in this chapter.[20] The definition of 'legal partnership', and the definition of 'multi-disciplinary practice', each refers to that structure as being a 'partnership formed under the law of the State'. As such, while not expressly stated in the 2015 Act, it is clear that the law in relation to ordinary partnerships will apply to

---

[18] At p 51 of the Programme for Government (Government for National Recovery 2011-2016).

[19] At p 24 of the EU/IMF Programme of Financial Support for Ireland (16 December 2010).

[20] Aside from the provisions of the 2015 Act which are of most relevance to partnership law and which are considered in detail in this chapter, the 2015 Act also provides for a Legal Practitioners Disciplinary Tribunal to be established, and reforms the law in relation to legal costs. For further information on the 2015 Act generally, see the *Annual Review of Irish Law 2015*, 1(1), 519–534.

both legal partnerships and multi-disciplinary practices (ie the 1890 Act, together with relevant caselaw). Nothing in the 2015 Act would appear to restrict a legal partnership or a multi-disciplinary practice from being established as a limited partnership under the Limited Partnerships Act 1907. However, as partnerships of solicitors are traditionally established as ordinary partnerships rather than as limited partnerships, a similar approach could reasonably be expected of legal partnerships. The 2015 Act does, however, expressly provided that, in respect of a limited liability partnership, the provisions of the 1890 Act will apply to an Irish limited liability partnership, save to the extent that those provisions are inconsistent with ss 122 to 132 of the 2015 Act (which deal with the liability and authorisation of limited liability partnerships).[21] This express reference to the relevance of the 1890 Act to Irish limited liability partnerships emphasises the distinction between that type of partnership, and a limited liability partnership in the UK, which is a body corporate, and not a partnership at all.[22]

'Relevant business'

[30.12] Before considering the new partnership-based business models under the 2015 Act in more detail, it is worth noting that only a partnership of solicitors, or a legal partnership, will be able to seek authorisation as a limited liability partnership under Part 8 of the 2015 Act. This is because the 2015 Act only allows a 'relevant business' to apply for such authorisation,[23] and defines a 'relevant business' as a partnership of solicitors or a legal partnership.[24] The possibility of limited liability is expected to prove attractive to the majority of partnerships of solicitors, in particular due to the limitations it will place on liability for the risks to which partners are exposed, and the potential reduction in the cost of professional indemnity insurance.[25]

A Multi-disciplinary Practice cannot be an LLP

[30.13] A multi-disciplinary practice, which will be a 'partnership' under s 2 of the 2015 Act, is not a 'relevant business' under s 99 of the 2015 Act. It will, therefore, not be entitled to be authorised as a limited liability partnership.

Most of the 2015 Act has not yet been Commenced

[30.14] At the time of writing, only a small number of sections of the 2015 Act have been commenced, including:

---

21 Legal Services Regulation Act 2015, s 123(6). In contrast, s 1(5) of the UK's Limited Liability Partnerships Act 2000 provides that partnership law does not apply to limited liability partnerships formed under that Act. While s 15(c) of that Act allows for regulations to be made which apply 'any law relating to partnerships' to UK limited liability partnerships, at the time of writing no such regulations have yet been made.

22 See further paras **[30.39]** and **[30.40]**.

23 Legal Services Regulation Act 2015, s 125(1) and (2).

24 Legal Services Regulation Act 2015, s 99.

25 In a speech delivered on 16 November 2017, the Minister for Justice and Equality confirmed that he would be 'pressing on for the early roll-out of Limited Liability Partnerships' in light of the 'incentive to legal business that can be offered' by their introduction.

– section 118, which requires the Authority to carry out a public consultation on the regulation, monitoring and operation of legal partnerships, and to provide both initial and final reports to the Minister for Justice and Equality;[26] and

– section 119, which requires the Authority to make an initial report to the Minister on the establishment, regulation, monitoring, operation and impact of multi-disciplinary practices, to carry out a subsequent public consultation, and to then provide a final report (with the Authority's recommendations) to the Minister.[27]

[30.15] None of the other sections of Part 8 of the 2015 Act, which deals with legal partnerships, limited liability partnerships and multi-disciplinary practices, have been commenced at the time of writing. In particular, the sections of that Act which require the Authority to make regulations for the operation of legal partnerships, limited liability partnerships, and multi-disciplinary practices are not yet in force.[28] In light of this, at the time of writing, much remains unknown regarding how legal partnerships and multi-disciplinary practices will operate in practice. In respect of limited liability partnerships, the matters that remain to be dealt with by regulation are less wide-ranging,[29] so, for a partnership of solicitors that may wish to seek authorisation as a limited liability partnership, it will be more straightforward to assess at this stage what the additional requirements will be. However, parties wishing to form a legal partnership will first need to see what regulations are published by the Authority under s 116 of the 2015 Act in respect of legal partnerships themselves, and then examine any regulations published by the Authority under s 130 of the 2015 Act in respect of limited liability partnerships.

II.   THE ROLE OF THE LEGAL SERVICES REGULATORY AUTHORITY

[30.16] The Authority was established with effect from 1 October 2016.[30] Since its establishment, it has carried out a public consultation on the regulation, monitoring and operation of legal partnerships, and provided two reports to the Minister for Justice and Equality.[31] It has also provided an initial report to the Minister on multi-disciplinary practices, carried out a subsequent public consultation, and provided a further report to the Minister on the establishment, regulation, monitoring and operation of multi-

---

26 Commenced by the Legal Services Regulation Act 2015 (Sections 118 to 120) (Commencement) Order 2016 (SI 630/2016).

27 Commenced by the Legal Services Regulation Act 2015 (Sections 118 to 120) (Commencement) Order 2016 (SI 630/2016).

28 The relevant sections of the 2015 Act are s 116 (in respect of legal partnerships and multi-disciplinary practices) and s 130 (in respect of limited liability partnerships).

29 See paras **[30.51]**, **[30.52]**, **[30.56]** and **[30.59]** below.

30 Legal Services Regulation Act 2015 (Establishment Day) Order 2016 (SI 507/2016). Certain provisions of Part 2 of the 2015 Act, dealing with the governance of the Authority, were also commenced with effect from 19 July 2016 by the Legal Services Regulation Act 2015 (Commencement of Certain Provisions) Order 2016 (SI 383/2016).

31 Legal Services Regulation Act 2015, s 118. See further para **[30.21]** et seq below.

disciplinary practices in Ireland.[32] What seems clear from these reports[33] is that the Authority's priority is the establishment of regulatory frameworks for both legal partnerships and limited liability partnerships.[34] A framework for multi-disciplinary practices is unlikely to be introduced in Ireland in the near future.[35]

[30.17] On 1 February 2018, in response to a question in Dáil Éireann, the Minister for Justice and Equality gave an update on the activities of the Authority since its establishment on 1 October 2016, noting the number of public consultations the Authority had carried out, and the number of reports that it had provided to the Minister. The Minister confirmed that the Government was continuing to 'give policy priority' to the introduction of legal partnerships, but that the Authority was also focused on its staffing and resourcing needs, and the roll-out of its other functions, including its public complaints role. The Authority indicated, in the minutes of its April 2018 meeting, that it is working towards implementing the framework for legal partnerships in the third quarter of 2018. In its April 2018 First Strategic Plan, it also signalled its intention to introduce the enabling framework for LLPs in the fourth quarter of 2018. At the time of writing, the regulations have not been made, but the Authority has confirmed that they have been drafted and that it is informally consulting with the relevant professional bodies in relation to those drafts.

III. LEGAL PARTNERSHIPS

[30.18] A 'legal partnership' is a partnership formed under the laws of Ireland by written agreement between at least two legal practitioners, one of whom must be a practising barrister. The other partners may be both practising solicitors and practising barristers, or practising barristers only. The legal partnership must be formed for the purpose of providing legal services.[36]

[30.19] The provisions in relation to legal partnerships are set out in ss 100 to 121 of the 2015 Act. At the time of writing, the only section of the 2015 Act relating directly to legal partnerships that has been commenced is s 118, which requires that the Authority

---

32   Legal Services Regulation Act 2015, s 119. See further para **[30.63]** et seq below.

33   The Authority has also published a report under s 120 of the 2015 Act (Legal Services Regulatory Authority, *Certain Issues Relating to Barristers, Report to the Minister for Justice and Equality, Mr Charles Flanagan TD*, 29 September 2017), on issues relating to barristers but, as this did not address issues specific to partnership law, it is not covered in detail in this chapter. That report did, however, note that the prohibition on barristers holding client moneys needs to be addressed, as it is likely to be an impediment to the formation of a legal partnership between a practising solicitor (who can hold client moneys) and a practising barrister (who cannot).

34   See further para **[30.23]**.

35   See further para **[30.71]**.

36   The 2015 Act does not contain a comprehensive definition of 'legal services'. Instead, at s 2(1) of the 2015 Act, 'legal services' are simply defined as legal services provided by a person, whether as a solicitor or as a barrister. Although not directly relevant, it is to be noted that in the Solicitors (Amendment) Act 1994, s 2, the term 'legal services' is defined as 'services of a legal or financial nature provided by a solicitor arising from that solicitor's practice as a solicitor, and includes any part of such services'.

carry out a public consultation in relation to legal partnerships, and provide both initial and final reports to the Minister for Justice and Equality.

Consultations and Reports in relation to Legal Partnerships

Consultation on legal partnerships

[30.20] Under s 118(1) of the 2015 Act, the Authority was tasked with carrying out a public consultation on the regulation, monitoring and operation of legal partnerships within six months of its establishment on 1 October 2016,[37] and submitting a report[38] on that consultation, with any recommendations that the Authority wished to make, to the Minister for Justice and Equality. The Authority began that public consultation on 24 February 2017, seeking feedback on a number of topics, including the registration requirements for legal partnerships, and the form that the register of legal partnerships that the Authority must establish and maintain[39] should take. As practising solicitors are already able to enter into partnership with one another, the public consultation was principally focused on issues that might arise as a result of two different types of legal practitioner (ie a practising solicitor and a practising barrister), each of which is subject to different professional obligations, entering into partnership with one another. A key issue for the consultation was how the different roles that both solicitors and barristers would play in a legal partnership could be reconciled with the joint and several liability of partners in an ordinary partnership under the 1890 Act. Most notably, the requirements imposed on solicitors and barristers in relation to client money are very different: solicitors are allowed to hold client money while, under s 45 of the 2015 Act, barristers are not.

Initial report on legal partnerships

[30.21] The Authority submitted its initial report on legal partnerships to the Minister for Justice and Equality on 31 March 2017, following the public consultation.[40] Key points made by the Authority in that initial report were that:

- the regulations to be developed by the Authority in respect of legal partnerships will need to balance the need for flexibility and competition in the legal profession, with protecting consumers of legal services;[41]
- a flexible regulatory approach will be needed, in particular as there will be two different types of legal partnership: barrister–barrister, and barrister–solicitor;[42] and
- it is, in theory, possible that different regulatory obligations will be imposed on solicitors who are partners in legal partnerships, to those imposed on barristers who are partners in legal partnerships.[43]

---

37 Legal Services Regulation Act 2015, s 118(2).
38 Legal Services Regulation Act 2015, s 118(3).
39 Under the Legal Services Regulation Act 2015, s 117(1)(a).
40 The initial report on legal partnerships dated 31 March 2017 is available on the website of the Authority (www.lsra.ie).
41 At p 11 of its initial report on legal partnerships dated 31 March 2017.
42 At p 11 of its initial report on legal partnerships dated 31 March 2017.
43 At p 11 of its initial report on legal partnerships dated 31 March 2017.

[30.22] While supportive of the proposed introduction of legal partnerships as business models for the provision of legal services in Ireland, the Authority recommended[44] that the remaining provisions of the 2015 Act, as they relate to legal partnerships, should not be commenced until the Authority has had an opportunity to carry out further consultations on various matters relating to the regulation, operation and monitoring of legal partnerships. Such matters include professional indemnity insurance requirements, accounting reporting requirements, the approach to be taken to dissolving legal partnerships in financial difficulties, and the timeframe for the commencement of the provisions of the 2015 Act regarding the authorisation of limited liability partnerships. The Authority also commented that it would need time to arrange the staff, office-space and IT necessary to enable it to establish and maintain a register of legal partnerships, and committed to providing a further report to the Minister for Justice and Equality by 31 July 2017.

Further report on legal partnerships

[30.23] The Authority provided a further (short) report on legal partnerships to the Minister for Justice and Equality on 31 July 2017. In that report, it confirmed that it was separately consulting on matters relating to legal partnerships, barristers, and multi-disciplinary practices, and that the matters arising out of these consultations needed to be considered together. For example the issue of whether barristers can hold client moneys was relevant to both the consultation on barristers, and the consultation on legal partnerships. The Authority again observed that further steps should be taken before the provisions of the 2015 Act in respect of legal partnerships (which would include the requirement for the Authority to make regulations in respect of their regulation, monitoring and operation) are commenced. The Authority noted its intention to carry out further, targeted, consultations,[45] and expressed the view that work in relation to Parts 3 and 6 of the 2015 Act[46] should be completed first, before new business models, such as the framework for legal partnerships, are introduced.[47]

[30.24] However, the Authority later indicated, in the minutes of its April 2018 meeting, that it is working towards implementing the framework for legal partnerships in the third quarter of 2018. At the time of writing, the regulations have not been made, but the Authority has confirmed that they have been drafted and that it is informally consulting with the relevant professional bodies in relation to those drafts.

Regulations on operation of legal partnerships

[30.25] When the issues in respect of legal partnerships that will be the subject of further, more targeted, consultations by the Authority are resolved, the Authority will then be expected to make a number of regulations under s 116 of the 2015 Act regarding

---

[44] At pp 26–27 of its initial report on legal partnerships dated 31 March 2017.

[45] Under the Legal Services Regulation Act 2015, s 118(1)(b), the Authority is allowed to carry out periodic public consultations on the regulation, monitoring and operation of legal partnerships.

[46] Dealing, respectively, with the conduct of inspections of solicitors and barristers, and complaints and disciplinary procedures in respect of solicitors and barristers.

[47] In its further report on legal partnerships of 31 July 2017, the Authority also noted that office space and staffing remained an issue for it.

the operation and management of legal partnerships. An indicative, but not exhaustive, list of the items that may be covered by those regulations is set out in s 116(3) and (4) of the 2015 Act and includes the following:

- the standards to be observed in the provision of legal services to clients, including in respect of professional and ethical conduct, client confidentiality, and the provision of information to clients;
- the rights, duties and responsibilities of a legal partnership in respect of client moneys;
- appropriate systems of control, including systems for risk management and financial control;
- the management of conflicts of interest;
- record-keeping;
- compliance with the 2015 Act and regulations made by the Authority under the 2015 Act;
- names that may be used by the legal partnership; and
- advertising by the legal partnership of its services.

Requirements of the 2015 Act relating to Legal Partnerships

[30.26] While most of the requirements regarding the regulation, monitoring and operation of legal partnerships will be contained in the regulations which the Authority will make under s 118 of the Act, the 2015 Act does contain certain requirements in relation to legal partnerships, and these are set out in more detail below.

The partnership agreement must be in writing

[30.27] For a legal partnership to exist, the partnership agreement must be in writing, at least one partner must be a practising barrister, and each party to the written partnership agreement must be either a practising solicitor or a practising barrister.[48]

Types of partners

[30.28] A practising solicitor or a practising barrister may provide legal services as a partner in a legal partnership, or as an employee of a legal partnership.[49] This will be a seminal change for practising barristers who have historically not been permitted to enter into partnership with one another, or with one or more practising solicitors. If an existing partnership of solicitors wishes to admit practising barristers to its partnership, while the mechanism for doing so is not expressly provided for in the 2015 Act, it appears relatively clear that such a partnership will need to meet the requirements of the 2015 Act (and any regulations made by the Authority under s 118 of that Act) as they apply to legal partnerships, and then notify the Authority, before commencing business, that it intends to provide legal services as a legal partnership.

---

[48] See the definition of 'legal partnership' in Legal Services Regulation Act 2015, s 2(1).
[49] Legal Services Regulation Act 2015, s 100(1).

Commencement and cessation of business by a legal partnership

[30.29] A legal partnership that plans to provide legal services must notify the Authority before commencing business,[50] and must also notify the Authority when it ceases to provide legal services.[51] Before providing those services, it must have an appropriate professional indemnity insurance policy in place.[52]

Register of Legal Partnerships

[30.30] The Authority will be required to maintain a register of legal partnerships who notify the Authority of their intention to provide legal services.[53] That register must be available for inspection by the public, free of charge.[54] At the time of writing, the Authority has not yet confirmed the form that the register will take,[55] but signalled in both its initial report of 31 March 2017 and in its further report of 31 July 2017 that adequate office accommodation, staffing, and IT resources needed to be put in place before any register could be established or operated.

[30.31] Where a registered legal partnership later notifies the Authority that it has ceased to provide legal services, the Authority must remove the name of that legal partnership from the register of legal partnerships.[56]

[30.32] In its initial report to the Minister for Justice and Equality on 31 March 2017,[57] the Authority commented that the register of legal partnerships should contain information similar to that which is contained on the file of a company maintained by the Irish Companies Registration Office ie:

- the type of partnership;
- the date of its registration;
- the address of the partnership;
- the names of the partners in the partnership;
- whether the partnership is active or dissolved; and
- whether the annual returns of the partnership are up-to-date.

The Authority is also considering whether information on disciplinary action taken in respect of the legal partnership or its partners should also be included on the register. It does not appear that a legal partnership will be required to file a copy of its partnership agreement with the Authority.

---

50 Legal Services Regulation Act 2015, s 104(1).
51 Legal Services Regulation Act 2015, s 104(2).
52 Legal Services Regulation Act 2015, s 105.
53 Legal Services Regulation Act 2015, s 117(1)(a).
54 Legal Services Regulation Act 2015, s 117(3).
55 The Legal Services Regulation Act 2015, s 117(3), provides that the register must be in 'an appropriate format'.
56 Legal Services Regulation Act 2015, s 117(2).
57 See para 63 on page 19 of that initial report on legal partnerships dated 31 March 2017.

Will a legal partnership be automatically registered on notification?

[30.33] In its initial report on legal partnerships to the Minister for Justice and Equality, the Authority acknowledged that s 104 of the 2015 Act (which requires the legal partnership to notify the Authority of its intention to provide legal services) may imply that registration is somewhat automatic, whereas s 105 of that Act implies that a further step is necessary, ie a confirmation that appropriate professional indemnity insurance is in place, between notification and entry on the register of legal partnerships. The Authority stated in that initial report that it will continue to carefully consider what its powers are in this regard when formulating the regulations in relation to the register of legal partnerships.

Can registration of a legal partnership be revoked by the Authority?

[30.34] The 2015 Act does not provide for what happens if a partner in a legal partnership breaches a provision of the 2015 Act, or of any regulation made under that Act, regarding the registration of the legal partnership. In its initial report to the Minister for Justice and Equality, the Authority indicated[58] that it might need to take advice on how a breach by a partner in (or by an employee of) a legal partnership could lead to the Authority taking 'material action' against the legal partnership, and what type of action the Authority might be able to take. As to what happens when a registered legal partnership no longer meets the conditions to be registered as such (perhaps because the only partner that is a practising barrister leaves the partnership), the Authority is also taking advice as to whether it will have the power to then remove that legal partnership from the register, without necessarily affecting the right of the remaining partners to continue to practice law on an ongoing basis.[59]

Will a legal partnership need to make ongoing filings with the Authority?

[30.35] In its initial report to the Minister, the Authority confirmed[60] that it would need to take further advice on its ability to require ongoing updates to a legal partnership's record on the register of legal partnerships, but clearly indicated that the information on the register should be up-to-date and relevant, and that perhaps the benchmark for the information to be provided to the Authority should be the information that a company incorporated under the Companies Act 2014 is obliged to provide to the registrar of companies. That would be likely to include:

- changes in the composition of the partners (in particular, a change leading to the partners no longer constituting a 'legal partnership' by virtue of the departure of the only remaining practising barrister from the partnership);
- changes to the partnership's address; and
- perhaps a requirement to file some form of annual declaration or return.

If the register is to include information regarding complaints or disciplinary proceedings in respect of the partnership or its partners, this is also likely to result in notification obligations where a complaint is made or disciplinary action is taken. Again, the

---

58 At p 21 of the Authority's initial report on legal partnerships dated 31 March 2017.
59 At p 23 of the Authority's initial report on legal partnerships, dated 31 March 2017.
60 At pp 22–23 of the Authority's initial report on legal partnerships, dated 31 March 2017.

Authority's final approach to ongoing filings will only become clear once regulations are made by it under the 2015 Act.

[30.36] Once the framework for legal partnerships comes into operation, the Authority will be required[61] to review the operation of Part 8 of the 2015 Act as it relates to legal partnerships within four years, and report to the Minister for Justice and Equality within one year of that review beginning. Further, periodic reviews must then be carried out by the Authority every five years.

IV. LIMITED LIABILITY PARTNERSHIPS

Background

[30.37] Limited liability partnerships have existed in the United States since 1991, having been introduced in response to litigation against partnerships of lawyers and partnerships of accountants regarding their roles in advising on the establishment of loan and savings associations which failed in large numbers. To protect the innocent partners in those partnerships against future claims for vicarious liability, it was proposed that partners in a registered limited liability partnership would not be liable for liabilities arising from negligence committed by another partner. This proposal went on to form the basis of the first LLP statute.[62]

[30.38] As a result of high profile negligence cases against professional partnerships in the United Kingdom,[63] pressure was brought to bear by large accountancy partnerships on the British parliament to introduce limited liability for partners in ordinary partnerships. The result was the Limited Liability Partnerships Act 2000, which introduced limited liability partnerships to England and Wales, and to Scotland.[64] Limited liability partnerships were later introduced in Northern Ireland with effect from November 2004 under the Limited Liability Partnerships Act (Northern Ireland) 2002.[65] That 2002 Act was repealed by the Companies Act 2006, which extended the Limited Liability Partnerships Act 2000 to Northern Ireland.[66]

---

61   Under the Legal Services Regulation Act 2015, s 121.

62   At the time of writing, in all but nine US states, there is a full corporate-type liability shield, while in the remaining states, the partners remain vicariously liable for ordinary contractual debts. In all other respects, these partnerships are subject to the law of ordinary partnerships. See generally Hurt, Smith, Bromberg and Ribstein, *Bromberg & Ribstein on Limited Liability Partnerships, the Revised Uniform Partnership Act, and the Uniform Limited Partnership Act* (2018 edn).

63   Such as *ADT Ltd v BDO Binder Hamlyn* [1996] BCC 808, in which an award of £65m was made on foot of a finding of negligent misrepresentation.

64   See l'Anson Banks, *Lindley & Banks on Partnership* (20th edn, 2017) at para 2-39 et seq.

65   C 12 (NI).

66   The Companies Act 2006, s 1286(2), repealed the Limited Liability Partnerships Act (Northern Ireland) 2002 with effect from 1 October 2009, with s 1286(1)(a) of the 2006 Act then extending the laws in effect in Great Britain at that time in relation to limited liability partnerships (including the Limited Liability Partnerships Act 2000) to Northern Ireland.

[30.39] In contrast to the framework envisaged for limited liability partnerships in Ireland, which is explained further below, limited liability partnerships formed under the Limited Liability Partnerships Act 2000 in the United Kingdom:

- are bodies corporate with separate legal personality;[67] and
- are not partnerships for the purposes of the 1890 Act.[68]

In Ireland, a limited liability partnership authorised under the 2015 Act will be an ordinary partnership (rather than a body corporate with separate legal personality), and will have started life as either a partnership of solicitors, or a legal partnership.[69] The provisions of the 1890 Act will apply to an Irish limited liability partnership, save to the extent that those provisions are inconsistent with ss 122 to 132 of the 2015 Act (which deal with the authorisation of limited liability partnerships).[70]

[30.40] In light of the differences between limited liability partnerships in the UK (which are not actually partnerships at all and are, instead, bodies corporate with separate legal personality) and limited liability partnerships as they will exist within the framework of the 2015 Act (as ordinary partnerships to which the 1890 Act will largely apply), the growing body of English caselaw on limited liability partnerships will be of considerably less persuasive authority in Ireland than caselaw relating to the 1890 Act or to the Limited Partnership Act 1907.[71]

Key features of an Irish limited liability partnership

Must be a partnership of solicitors, or a legal partnership

[30.41] The 2015 Act provides that[72] a limited liability partnership is a 'relevant business in respect of which an authorisation, granted under section 125, is for the time being in force'. A 'relevant business' is defined by the 2015 Act as being either a partnership of solicitors or a legal partnership.[73] As a partnership, by its nature, involves more than one person, it is clear that a solicitor who practices as a sole practitioner will

---

67 Limited Liability Partnerships Act 2000, s 1(2).

68 Limited Liability Partnerships Act 2000, s 1(5).

69 Another fundamental differences between a UK limited liability partnership, and an Irish limited liability partnership, is that the members of the UK limited liability partnership are the agents of the partnership (and not of one another).

70 Legal Services Regulation Act 2015, s 123(6). In contrast, s 1(5) of the UK's Limited Liability Partnerships Act 2000 provides that partnership law does not apply to limited liability partnerships formed under that Act. While s 15(c) of that Act allows for regulations to be made which apply 'any law relating to partnerships' to UK limited liability partnerships, at the time of writing no such regulations have yet been made. Certain regulations made under the 2000 Act apply certain default rules to UK limited liability partnerships which are broadly similar to some of the rules set out in the 1890 Act, but a UK limited liability partnership remains a body corporate, even if those default provisions apply. See, further, l'Anson Banks, *Lindley & Banks on Partnership* (20th edn, 2017) at para 2-40, and Blackett-Ord and Haren, *Partnership Law* (5th edn, 2015) at para 25.29 et seq.

71 See further Keane, 'LLP service' (November 2017) Law Society Gazette at p 44.

72 Legal Services Regulation Act 2015, s 99.

73 Legal Services Regulation Act 2015, s 99.

not be able to benefit from the limitation on liability which will be available to practising solicitors and practising barristers who are in partnership with one another.[74] It is also clear that a multi-disciplinary practice will not be able to seek authorisation as a limited liability partnership.[75]

Limitation on liability

[30.42] The limited liability partnership itself will not have limited liability. Rather, each partner in an Irish limited liability partnership will not (as a result of being a partner in that limited liability partnership) be personally liable for the debts, obligations or liabilities of:

- the limited liability partnership itself;[76]
- himself or herself, *qua* partner in the limited liability partnership;[77]
- another partner in the limited liability partnership;[78] or
- any employee, agent or representative of the limited liability partnership.[79]

This limitation on liability, from which each partner in a limited liability partnership will benefit, will apply whether the debt, obligation or liability arises in contract, tort or otherwise.[80]

[30.43] In this respect, limited liability partnerships will not only differ from ordinary partnerships under the 1890 Act insofar as the partners will not have unlimited liability for the debts of the limited liability partnership, but they will also differ from limited partnerships under the Limited Partnerships Act 1907, since all the partners in a limited liability partnership will benefit from a limit on their personal liability for the partnership's obligations, yet will still be entitled to participate in the management of the partnership (in contrast to the position of a limited partner in a limited partnership under the 1907 Act).[81] The possibility of limited liability is expected to prove attractive to the majority of partnerships of solicitors, in particular as it will enable the risks to which

---

74　The Solicitors (Amendment) Act 1994, s 70 allows the Law Society of Ireland to make regulations allowing for 'incorporated practices' of solicitors however, at the time of writing, no such regulations have been made. If such regulations are made at a later date, and provide for a sole practitioner to set up an 'incorporated practice', it is possible that the benefit of limited liability could then be available to a solicitor operating as a sole practitioner through an incorporated practice. It is, of course, conceivable that in the future the limited liability partnership structure for lawyers, and thus the benefit of limited liability, could be extended to sole practitioners (whether solicitors or barristers) by providing for a single member limited liability partnership, in much the same way as it is possible to incorporate a company with just one member (Companies Act 2014, s 17(4)).

75　See further Ryan, 'Limited Liability for Solicitors – the story now' (Winter 2015) The Parchment, 42–43, which briefly considers the limitations of the multi-disciplinary practice model in other jurisdictions.

76　Legal Services Regulation Act 2015, s 123(1)(a).

77　Legal Services Regulation Act 2015, s 123(1)(b).

78　Legal Services Regulation Act 2015, s 123(1)(c).

79　Legal Services Regulation Act 2015, s 123(1)(d).

80　Legal Services Regulation Act 2015, s 123(1).

81　See, further, para **[28.78]** et seq.

partners are exposed to be managed, and as it could lead to a reduction in the cost of professional indemnity insurance. [82]

[30.44] There are, however, certain circumstances in which a partner in a limited liability partnership will not have the benefit of the limitation on liability set out in s 123 of the 2015 Act, and these circumstances are set out in more detail below.

Exception to limitation on liability – pre-authorisation of limited liability partnership

[30.45] If the relevant debt, obligation or liability arises from an act or omission of the relevant partner which took place before the date on which the limited liability partnership was authorised under the 2015 Act, the limitation on liability will not be available to that partner. [83]

Exception to limitation on liability – fraud or dishonesty

[30.46] If the relevant debt, obligation or liability arises from an act or omission of a partner which involves fraud or dishonesty, and which was either the subject of a finding of misconduct[84] under Part 6 of the 2015 Act, or constituted an offence for which that partner was convicted, the limitation on liability will not apply to that partner. [85]

---

[82] According to the Smith & Williamson, *Survey of Irish law firms 2012/2013*, 94% of firms that were surveyed favoured the introduction of limited liability partnerships. In the Smith & Williamson *5th Annual Law Firm Survey* (2016/2017), 69% of the top 20 firms of solicitors in Ireland signalled their intention to convert to limited liability partnerships, with 44% of those top 20 firms planning to do so within two years of that survey being conducted (subject to the relevant provisions of the 2015 Act being commenced).

[83] Legal Services Regulation Act 2015, s 123(5).

[84] The Legal Services Regulation Act 2015, s 50(1) provides that an act or omission of a practising solicitor or practising barrister may constitute misconduct (a) where it involves fraud or dishonesty, (b) where it relates to the provision, by that lawyer, of legal services which were substantially inadequate, (c) where it does not occur in relation to the provision of legal services, but would justify a finding that the lawyer is 'not a fit and proper person to engage in the provision of legal services', (d) where it constitutes an offence under the 2015 Act, (e) where it constitutes a breach by a solicitor of the Solicitors Acts 1954 to 2015 or any regulations made thereunder, (f) where it constitutes an offence committed by a solicitor under the Solicitors Acts 1954 to 2015, (g) where (in the case of a barrister) it is likely to bring the profession of barristers into disrepute or, in the case of a solicitor, is likely to bring the profession of solicitors into disrepute, (h) in the case of a managing legal practitioner of a multi-disciplinary practice, where it constitutes a failure by him or her to comply with his or her obligations under the 2015 Act as managing legal practitioner, (i) where an arrestable offence has been committed or, where a crime or offence is committed outside Ireland, it would be an arrestable offence if committed in Ireland, (j) where a 'grossly excessive' amount of costs is sought by the solicitor or barrister in respect of the provision of legal services, (k) where it constitutes a breach of the 2015 Act or any regulations made thereunder, or (l) where s 215(1) of the 2015 Act is breached (which requires a practising solicitor or practising barrister, who has accepted instructions to appear in court on behalf of a client in custody, not to withdraw from the case without the permission of the court before which the client is scheduled to appear next).

[85] Legal Services Regulation Act 2015, s 123(2).

Exception to limitation on liability – unrelated purposes

[30.47] If the relevant debt, obligation or liability was incurred by a partner for a purpose that is not related to the business of the limited liability partnership, that partner will not benefit from the limitation on liability.[86]

Exception to limitation on liability – tax

[30.48] If the relevant debt or obligation[87] relates to any 'tax' within the meaning of s 960A of the Taxes Consolidation Act 1997, the limitation on liability will not apply to the relevant partner.[88]

The impact of the limitation on liability on partnership property

[30.49] The 2015 Act provides that the limitation on liability from which a partner in a limited liability partnership will benefit will not prevent enforcement action being taken against the property of the limited liability partnership in respect of any debt, obligation or liability. By way of example, a bank which has lent to the limited liability partnership, and taken a security interest in the assets of the limited liability partnership, may enforce its security over those assets, but may not pursue the partners personally for the purpose of recovering any outstanding debt which remains after it has enforced its security and applied the proceeds towards discharge of the debt.[89]

[30.50] Further, if the partners in a limited liability partnership transfer the property of that partnership for the benefit of one or more of the partners, this will be a 'conveyance' within the meaning of s 7 of the Bankruptcy Act 1988, meaning that such a conveyance will be subject to the provisions of the 1988 Act regarding fraudulent conveyances and fraudulent preference of creditors. If that transfer constitutes a fraudulent conveyance or fraudulent preference, it is liable to be avoided under ss 57 or 58 of the 1988 Act, and the transfer itself will constitute an 'act of bankruptcy'.[90] Further, such a transfer will also be a 'conveyance' for the purposes of s 74 of the Land and Conveyancing Law Reform Act 2009, meaning that if it is made with the intention of defrauding a creditor or other person, the transfer will be voidable by any person who is prejudiced by it.[91]

---

[86] Legal Services Regulation Act 2015, s 123(3).

[87] The tax-related carve-out from the protection of limited liability at the Legal Services Regulation Act 2015, s 123(4) refers to a 'debt or obligation' of the partner, rather than to a 'debt, obligation or liability' of that partner (as is the case with the other carve-outs from the limitation on liability in s 123); however, it is submitted that nothing turns on that variation in wording.

[88] Legal Services Regulation Act 2015, s 123(4). This reference to 'tax' includes any debt or obligation in respect of, among others, income tax, corporation tax, capital gains tax, value-added tax, excise duty, stamp duty, gift tax, inheritance tax, local property tax, the income levy, the parking levy in urban areas, the domicile levy or the universal social charge.

[89] Legal Services Regulation Act 2015, s 124(1).

[90] As to the effect of an 'act of bankruptcy', see para **[27.23]** et seq.

[91] Land and Conveyancing Law Reform Act 2009, s 74(3), save where the property is transferred for valuable consideration and the partner or partners to whom it is transferred do not, in good faith, have notice of the fraudulent intention at the time of the transfer.

Authorisation of Limited Liability Partnerships

Application for authorisation

[30.51] The 2015 Act does not contain any detailed information regarding the proposed authorisation regime for limited liability partnerships, but instead provides for the Authority to make regulations[92] regarding:

- the application form for authorisation as a limited liability partnership;
- the information that must be provided to the Authority by the partnership of solicitors or legal partnership when submitting an application form for authorisation;[93] and
- the fee that must accompany the application for authorisation.

At the time of writing, no such regulations have yet been made.

Conditions of authorisation

[30.52] While the regulations to be made by the Authority under ss 125(3) and 130 of the 2015 Act may include further conditions that must be met if the Authority is to grant an authorisation to a partnership of solicitors or a legal partnership to operate as a limited liability partnership, the 2015 Act also provides that the Authority must be satisfied with the following before granting an authorisation:

- where the applicant is a legal partnership, that it has professional indemnity insurance in place, in respect of those partners in the legal partnership that are practising barristers, which meets the requirements of the regulations that the Authority is required to make[94] under s 47 of the 2015 Act regarding, inter alia, limited liability partnerships; and
- where the applicant is a partnership of solicitors, or in respect of any partners in a legal partnership that are practising solicitors, that there is professional indemnity insurance in place which meets the requirements of s 26 of the Solicitors Act 1994.[95]

Effective date of authorisation

[30.53] The Authority must make its decision as to whether to authorise a partnership of solicitors or a legal partnership as a limited liability partnership within 60 days of receiving a properly-completed application for authorisation.[96] The authorisation granted by the Authority must be by way of written notice to the applicant partnership of solicitors or legal partnership, and will be effective from the date specified in that notice.[97]

---

[92] Legal Services Regulation Act 2015, ss 125(3) and 130.
[93] Under the Legal Services Regulation Act 2015, s 130(2)(b), that information is expected to include, at a minimum, the name and address of each of the partners in the firm of solicitors or legal partnership, the full name of the firm of solicitors or legal partnership, and the address from which the firm of solicitors or legal partnership ordinarily carries on its business.
[94] At the time of writing, those regulations have not yet been made.
[95] Legal Services Regulation Act 2015, s 125(4) and (5).
[96] Legal Services Regulation Act 2015, s 125(9).
[97] Legal Services Regulation Act 2015, s 125(6).

Cessation of authorisation

[30.54] If a limited liability partnership no longer wishes to operate as such, it must notify the Authority of the date on which it plans to cease operating as a limited liability partnership,[98] and its authorisation shall be deemed to have been revoked as of the date specified in that notice.[99] The form that such a notice is to take, and any fee payable to the Authority for filing such a notice, will be set out in the regulations that are yet to be made by the Authority.[100]

[30.55] If a limited liability partnership fails to maintain professional indemnity insurance to the standard required by the 2015 Act,[101] its authorisation will be deemed to have been revoked as of the date on which the partnership ceased to meet that requirement.[102]

Information to clients and creditors

[30.56] Once the authorisation to operate as a limited liability partnership is received by the partnership of solicitors or legal partnership, the partnership will then be required to inform both its clients and its creditors that it will be operating as a limited liability partnership. The Authority may also prescribe (by way of regulations) further information that must be provided by the limited liability partnership to its clients and creditors[103] but, at the time of writing, such regulations have not yet been made.

Name of limited liability partnership

[30.57] A limited liability partnership must carry on business using a name that ends with 'limited liability partnership' or 'LLP'.[104] Unlike an ordinary or limited partnership, a limited liability partnership is not within the category of 'persons to be registered' under s 3 of the Registration of Business Names Act 1963.[105] As such, it will not need to register its business name with the registrar of companies (as registrar of business names) under s 4 of the 1963 Act. Instead, the Authority will establish and maintain a register of limited liability partnerships,[106] which will be available for public inspection, free of charge. While a limited liability partnership, by virtue of not coming within the category of 'persons to be registered' under s 3 of the 1963 Act, is not required by s 18 of that Act to publish the names and nationalities of its partners on its

---

98   Legal Services Regulation Act 2015, s 129(1).
99   Legal Services Regulation Act 2015, s 129(2).
100 Legal Services Regulation Act 2015, s 129(4).
101 Legal Services Regulation Act 2015, s 125(5).
102 Legal Services Regulation Act 2015, s 129(3).
103 Legal Services Regulation Act 2015, ss 125(7) and 130(2)(c).
104 Legal Services Regulation Act 2015, s 125(8)(a). The 2015 Act, at s 132, amends s 27 of the Companies Act 2014 to confirm that the use of the term 'limited' by a limited liability partnership will not be subject to the restriction in s 27(1) of the 2014 Act on a company or an individual using inter alia the word 'limited' or any abbreviation thereof in the last part of its name.
105 Legal Services Regulation Act 2015, s 131, which provides that s 3 of the Registration of Business Names Act 1963 does not apply to limited liability partnerships.
106 See further para **[30.58]**.

stationery, it will instead be required to include its name (ie the name ending in 'limited liability partnership' or 'LLP') on its stationery, and on other documents.[107] Prior to being authorised as a limited liability partnership, however, the relevant partnership of solicitors, or legal partnership, will have been subject to the requirements of the 1963 Act.[108]

Register of limited liability partnerships

[30.58] Once the provisions of the 2015 Act relating to limited liability partnerships are commenced, the Authority must set up and maintain a register of limited liability partnerships.[109] The register will contain the following details about each limited liability partnership that is authorised by the Authority:

- the names of each of the partners in the partnership, and their respective addresses;[110]
- the full name of the partnership[111] (which must end in 'limited liability partnership' or 'LLP');[112]
- the address from which the partnership ordinarily carries on business;[113]
- the date from which the partnership's authorisation as a limited liability partnership takes effect;[114]
- if applicable, details of any order of the High Court which suspends the partnership's authorisation as a limited liability partnership,[115] together with details of the suspension period and any conditions imposed by the High Court;
- if applicable, details of any order of the High Court which revokes the partnership's authorisation as a limited liability partnership;[116]
- the date from which the partnership's authorisation as a limited liability partnership is deemed to have been revoked[117] following the receipt, by the Authority, of a notice from the limited liability partnership under s 129(1) of the 2015 Act of its intention to cease operating as such[118] (the date will be the date that is specified in that notice);

---

[107] Legal Services Regulation Act 2015, s 125(8)(b).
[108] See para **[3.70]** et seq in respect of ordinary partnerships (a partnership of solicitors, and a legal partnership, will each be an ordinary partnership prior to being authorised as a limited liability partnership under the 2015 Act).
[109] Legal Services Regulation Act 2015, s 126(1).
[110] Legal Services Regulation Act 2015, s 126(2)(a).
[111] Legal Services Regulation Act 2015, s 126(2)(b).
[112] Legal Services Regulation Act 2015, s 125(8)(a).
[113] Legal Services Regulation Act 2015, s 126(2)(b).
[114] Legal Services Regulation Act 2015, s 126(2)(c).
[115] Legal Services Regulation Act 2015, s 126(1)(d). Such an order would be made under Legal Services Regulation Act 2015, s 128, on the application of the Authority and on notice to the limited liability partnership.
[116] Legal Services Regulation Act 2015, s 126(1)(e). Such an order would be made under the Legal Services Regulation Act 2015, s 128 on the application of the Authority and on notice to the limited liability partnership.
[117] Under the Legal Services Regulation Act 2015, s 129(2).
[118] Legal Services Regulation Act 2015, s 126(5).

– the date from which the partnership's authorisation as a limited liability partnership is deemed to have been revoked[119] as a result of it not having suitable professional indemnity insurance in place.[120]

[30.59] The register of limited liability partnerships must be publicly available, and capable of being inspected free of charge.[121] It remains to be seen whether the Authority will (as the Companies Registration Office does in respect of companies) only make general information publicly available, and charge a fee for copies of particular filings made by a limited liability partnership. The form of the register must be one which the Authority views as appropriate,[122] but, at the time of writing, further details as to the format of the register are not yet available. The Authority is also empowered[123] to make further regulations setting out information that a limited liability partnership must provide to the Authority to enable it to assess the partnership's compliance with the requirements imposed on it by the 2015 Act.

Powers of the Authority

[30.60] The Authority will be entitled to issue directions to a limited liability partnership to take or to refrain from taking specific steps if it believes that the limited liability partnership is not complying with the 2015 Act.[124] If the Authority plans to issue such a direction to a limited liability partnership, it must notify the partnership in writing, setting out the nature of the breach, the directions that it plans to make, and asking the partnership to make observations on those matters within a particular time-frame.[125] If the Authority gives a written direction to the partnership, the partnership will have a right of appeal to the High Court.[126] If the partnership fails to comply with the direction, the Authority may apply to the High Court for an order requiring the partnership to comply with the direction, or alternatively suspending or revoking the partnership's authorisation as a limited liability partnership.[127]

Consultations and reports by the Authority

[30.61] Unlike in relation to legal partnerships and multi-disciplinary practices, the 2015 Act does not require the Authority to carry out public consultations or to publish reports in relation to limited liability partnerships. However, in both its initial and further reports to the Minister for Justice and Equality on legal partnerships,[128] the

---

[119] Under the Legal Services Regulation Act 2015, s 129(3).

[120] Legal Services Regulation Act 2015, s 126(5). The requirements as to professional indemnity insurance for limited liability partnerships are set out in Legal Services Regulation Act 2015, s125(5). Revocation of a limited liability partnership's authorisation as a result of a failure to have suitable professional indemnity insurance in place would appear to be automatic (Legal Services Regulation Act 2015, s 129(3)).

[121] Legal Services Regulation Act 2015, s 126(6).

[122] Legal Services Regulation Act 2015, s 126(6).

[123] By the Legal Services Regulation Act 2015, s 130(1)(d).

[124] Legal Services Regulation Act 2015, s 127(1).

[125] Legal Services Regulation Act 2015, s 127(2).

[126] Legal Services Regulation Act 2015, s 127(4).

[127] Legal Services Regulation Act 2015, s 128.

[128] See para **[30.21]** et seq.

Authority signalled that it wanted to be given further time to carry out targeted consultations on a variety of further matters, including access by legal partnerships to limited liability. Theoretically, it would be possible for the provisions of the 2015 Act dealing with limited liability partnerships to be commenced, with a view to enabling partnerships of solicitors to apply for authorisation as limited liability partnerships, while issues around the regulation, monitoring and operation of legal partnerships are resolved. However, it is not yet clear whether, from a policy perspective, a staggered implementation of the provisions of the 2015 Act regarding legal partnerships and limited liability partnerships is desirable. Much will depend on the issues raised as part of any further consultations carried out by the Authority, and whether those issues can be successfully addressed by the regulations that the Authority may make under the 2015 Act. At the time of writing, the most recent update from the Authority was as part of its April 2018 First Strategic Plan, when it signalled its intention to introduce the enabling framework for LLPs in the fourth quarter of 2018. At the time of writing, the regulations have not been made, but the Authority has confirmed that they have been drafted and that it is informally consulting with the relevant professional bodies in relation to those drafts.

V.   MULTI-DISCIPLINARY PRACTICES

[30.62] The 2015 Act contains a framework for the creation of multi-disciplinary practices, which will be partnerships between two or more individuals, at least one of whom is a 'legal practitioner' (ie a practising solicitor or a practising barrister) with a view to providing both legal and non-legal services. This business model would, by way of example, enable a partnership to be formed between a practising solicitor and a tax advisor, or between a practising barrister and an accountant.[129] However, as previously noted,[130] a multi-disciplinary practice is not entitled to be authorised as a limited liability partnership.

---

[129]   The case of *Gulliver v Brady & ors p/a Matheson Ormsby Prentice* [2003] IESC 68 is worth noting. A memorandum of understanding had been entered into between the parties to the effect that, subject to the fulfilment of certain conditions, Mr Gulliver (a tax advisor, and not a practising solicitor) would be admitted as a full equity partner in the defendant solicitors' partnership. One of those conditions was that at least 75% of the equity partners would not vote against his admission as a partner. However, a resolution was passed that precluded his admission as a partner, with Mr Gulliver then claiming that he had been made a partner, and had acted as a full equity partner, before that resolution had been passed. The dispute was referred to arbitration, and then settled, with Mr Gulliver leaving the firm. Of note is the wording of the memorandum of understanding, which appeared to contemplate an arrangement similar to a multi-disciplinary practice, with the firm agreeing to use '... best endeavours to facilitate the establishment of a dedicated tax advisory group [within the firm] to complement and assist in the development of the existing taxation advisor service ... It is further agreed ... that subject to regulatory constraints an integral element of this agreement is the commitment of the parties hereto to put in place a mechanism by which [Gulliver] will ... be admitted as a full profit sharing partner of [the firm] with effect from the 1st day of January 2003.'

[130]   See para **[30.13]**.

Consultations and Reports

Initial report on multi-disciplinary practices

[30.63] The Authority was required, under s 119(1) of the 2015 Act, to submit an initial report on the establishment, regulation, monitoring, operation and impact of multi-disciplinary practices in Ireland to the Minister for Justice and Equality within six months of its establishment (ie by 31 March 2017). In preparing that report, the Authority was asked to examine, among other matters, multi-disciplinary practices in other jurisdictions[131] and the expected consequences of setting up multi-disciplinary practices in Ireland.[132]

---

[131] The jurisdictions considered in detail as part of the initial report on multi-disciplinary practices dated 31 March 2017 were:

- Australia: multi-disciplinary practices can be established in each of New South Wales, Victoria, the Australian Capital Territory, Tasmania, Queensland and Western Australia;
- Canada: multi-disciplinary practices have been introduced on a very limited basis in Canada. In Ontario, lawyers can practise with paralegals and some other regulated professions, and share profits with them, while in both Québec and British Columbia, lawyers may practise and share profits with certain other regulated professionals;
- England and Wales: 'legal disciplinary practices' were allowed from 31 March 2009 onwards, whereby non-lawyers could own up to 25% of a law firm, and persons authorised to carry out certain activities could enter into partnership with one another (solicitors, barristers, licensed conveyancers, notaries, patent attorneys, trade mark attorneys, legal executives and costs lawyers). The 'legal disciplinary practices' regime was then replaced by the 'alternative business structures' model. 'Alternative business structures' are bodies that can provide legal services in England and Wales, with up to 100% of their owners being non-lawyers and no restriction on their legal form (ie an 'alternative business structure' could be a body corporate, a partnership etc);
- Scotland: the Legal Services (Scotland) Act 2010 allows solicitors to provide legal services using various different business models, including partnerships or incorporated practices (up to 49% of which can be owned by 'non-qualifying investors' from certain other regulated professions);
- the US: while the report from the American Bar Association's Commission on the Future of Legal Services (2014-16) stated that the '... Model Rules of Professional Conduct prohibit nonlawyer ownership of law firms, nonlawyer management of law firms, and sharing fees with nonlawyers (except under very limited circumstances). Almost every US jurisdiction follows this restriction', multi-disciplinary practices are allowed in Washington DC, and in Washington State;
- Singapore: law practices can have non-lawyer employee ownership of up to 25%;
- Hong Kong, New Zealand and South Africa: in each of these jurisdictions, the potential for different business models for lawyers has been examined, but multi-disciplinary practices have not been introduced;
- Denmark: multi-disciplinary practices are not permitted;
- Germany, Italy, the Netherlands and Spain: in each of these jurisdictions, lawyers can enter into multi-disciplinary practices with members of certain other professions.

[132] Legal Services Regulation Act 2015, s 119(2).

[30.64] The Authority presented its initial report to the Minister on 31 March 2017. The initial report was less than encouraging about the introduction of multi-disciplinary practices as a partnership model for the legal profession, noting that while the 2015 Act suggests a framework for multi-disciplinary practices in Ireland, 'it does not pre-empt the decision of whether this new form of business structure should be introduced at all'.[133] The Authority's initial report noted that the market share of multi-disciplinary practices in jurisdictions where multi-disciplinary practices can be established is extremely small.

Public consultation on multi-disciplinary practices

[30.65] The Authority was then required[134] to carry out a public consultation in respect of matters identified in its initial report, and key issues which it wished to examine were:

- whether the multi-disciplinary practice model should be introduced in Ireland at all (as contemplated by the 2015 Act or in an adapted form);

- what features of the multi-disciplinary practice model might prove attractive, or might alternatively pose barriers to entry;

- what the legal profession would like to achieve through the introduction of the multi-disciplinary practice model; and

- in light of the evidence obtained on behalf of the Authority from other jurisdictions that the market share for multi-disciplinary practices in those jurisdictions is comparatively small, whether the multi-disciplinary practice model would, in fact, be transformative for the Irish legal market.[135]

Further report on multi-disciplinary practices

[30.66] The Authority was required to submit a final report on multi-disciplinary practices to the Minister for Justice and Equality within six months of its initial report,[136] and that report was submitted on 29 September 2017.[137]

Experience of other jurisdictions

[30.67] The Authority, in this further report, again noted[138] the experience gathered from other jurisdictions regarding the introduction of multi-disciplinary practices, ie that uptake is slow, that market share is small, and that limited liability is a feature (unlike in

---

133 At p 5 of the report.
134 Legal Services Regulation Act 2015, s 119(3).
135 See further Savage 'The cost of the one stop shop' (2017) 22(4) The Bar Review 14.
136 Legal Services Regulation Act 2015, s 119(3).
137 Legal Services Regulatory Authority, *Multi-Disciplinary Practices, Further Report to the Minister for Justice and Equality, Mr Charles Flanagan TD*, 29 September 2017. The Authority (at para 1.9 of that further report) was concerned that it had not received responses from many of the potential stakeholders that it had identified (only five responses were received).
138 At p 25 of the further report on multi-disciplinary practices dated 29 September 2017.

Ireland, where it is not proposed that multi-disciplinary practices be able to avail of the limited liability partnership model).[139]

[30.68] The Authority raised a number of other issues in its further report. It observed that the inability of multi-disciplinary practices to avail of the limited liability partnership model will make them less attractive as a business model.[140] Further, as multi-disciplinary practices would facilitate partnership between lawyers and non-lawyers, issues of client confidentiality and legal privilege caused the Authority some concern.[141] The potential for 'passive' investment in multi-disciplinary practices was also raised as an issue, in particular in light of the potential for conflict where the business plan of the multi-disciplinary practice does not focus to the same extent on maximising profit as would be the case with a non-legal partnership.[142] The Authority also noted its fundamental objective as being the regulation of the provision of legal services in Ireland and observed that there is a strong argument that it should not be regulating members of multi-disciplinary practices that are not members of the legal profession.[143]

[30.69] The Authority observed that it could take a restrictive approach to the regulation of multi-disciplinary practices, by restricting who could be a partner in such a practice, and the services that those partners could provide. However, as that could restrict the ability of a multi-disciplinary practice to deliver legal services in an innovative manner, the Authority also signalled the possibility of regulating the operations of a multi-disciplinary practice, rather than its structure.[144]

Recommendations of the Authority

[30.70] The Authority's recommendations, set out in Part 4 of its further Report, were as follows:

-   the Authority's resources should be directed, in the first instance, towards the introduction of legal partnerships and limited liability partnerships;
-   the other functions of the Authority, in particular the complaints process, should also be a key focus area; and
-   the issue of multi-disciplinary practices could be considered further.

[30.71] In light of the concerns expressed by the Authority in both its initial and further reports on multi-disciplinary practices, at the time of writing it is not clear whether the multi-disciplinary practice model will be available to the Irish legal market in the near

---

139 Separately, the Authority noted that other jurisdictions in which multi-disciplinary practices had been introduced had not reported difficulties regarding ethical behaviour or standards being maintained.
140 Paragraphs 3.44–3.45 of the further report on multi-disciplinary practices dated 29 September 2017.
141 Paragraphs 3.46–3.63 of the further report on multi-disciplinary practices dated 29 September 2017.
142 Paragraphs 3.64–3.67 of the further report on multi-disciplinary practices dated 29 September 2017.
143 Paragraph 3.71 of the further report on multi-disciplinary practices dated 29 September 2017.
144 Paragraphs 3.93–3.94 of the further report on multi-disciplinary practices dated 29 September 2017.

future, whether in the form contemplated by the 2015 Act or at all.[145] The minutes of the eighth meeting of the Authority held on 14 September 2017 confirm[146] the Authority's approach as being that the focus should be placed on progressing legal partnerships and limited liability partnerships, and that the Authority 'would not move on the issue of [multi-disciplinary practices] at this time'.[147]

Authorisation and Operation of Multi-disciplinary Practices

[30.72] While multi-disciplinary practices are not expected to be introduced as a business model for the legal profession in Ireland in the near future (if, indeed, at all), it is worth briefly considering the framework for multi-disciplinary practices that is set out in the 2015 Act. At the outset, it is worth bearing in mind that the Authority may make regulations regarding a number of aspects of the operation and management of multi-disciplinary practices, but has not yet done so and is not expected to do so in the near future.[148] Also, in both its initial and further reports on multi-disciplinary practices, the Authority commented that it does not consider the framework contained in the 2015 Act for multi-disciplinary practices to be binding on the Authority, and indicated the Authority's view as being that it has the freedom to propose an alternative structure for multi-disciplinary practices (perhaps if it developed an alternative structure that could be more manageable from regulatory perspective, and more likely to be attractive to the Irish legal profession).[149]

A multi-disciplinary practice can provide legal and non-legal services

[30.73] A multi-disciplinary practice is a partnership between two or more individuals which provides both legal and non-legal services.[150] A written partnership agreement

---

[145] The Legal Services Regulatory Authority, Annual Report 2016, at p 8 emphasised legal partnerships and limited liability partnerships as the key new business models introduced by the 2015 Act, and in respect of multi-disciplinary practices, referred to the 2015 Act as providing a 'pathway ... for the introduction, on foot of formal research and public consultations, of [multi-disciplinary practices]'.

[146] At Item 4.2 of those minutes.

[147] In its September 2017 report under s 120 of the 2015 Act (Legal Services Regulatory Authority, *Certain Issues Relating to Barristers, Report to the Minister for Justice and Equality, Mr Charles Flanagan TD*, 29 September 2017), the Authority stated that issues concerning legal partnerships, multi-disciplinary practices and barristers cannot be dealt with separately and should be viewed as a whole, and that further consideration should be given to matters such as the holding of client moneys by barristers in a legal partnership or multi-disciplinary practice structure as part of the consultations on those business models.

[148] Those regulations would be made by the Authority under the Legal Services Regulation Act 2015, s 116, which applies to both legal partnerships and multi-disciplinary practices, and has not, at the time of writing, been commenced.

[149] The Authority's view in this respect is predicated on the Legal Services Regulation Act 2015, s 119, which obliges the Authority to make recommendations in relation to the establishment, regulation, operation and monitoring of multi-disciplinary practices. In light of this, the Authority views it as '... permissible and within its statutory remit to propose a different structure ...'.

[150] Legal Services Regulation Act 2015, s 2(1).

must exist between the partners,[151] and at least one of the partners must be a legal practitioner (ie a practising solicitor or a practising barrister). Practising solicitors and practising barristers can each be partners in, or employees of, a multi-disciplinary practice,[152] but a partner in such a practice need not provide legal services or, indeed, any other services.[153]

A multi-disciplinary practice is a partnership

[30.74] The definition of 'multi-disciplinary practice' in s 2(1) of the 2015 Act makes clear that a multi-disciplinary practice will be a partnership as a matter of Irish law. As previously noted,[154] a multi-disciplinary practice is not entitled to limited liability.

Partners are jointly and severally liable

[30.75] It follows that each partner in a multi-disciplinary practice will be jointly and severally liable for his own acts and omissions, those of his fellow partners in the partnership, and those of the partnership's employees.[155] The provisions of Part 8 of the 2015 Act are in addition to all rights and obligations that a legal practitioner might otherwise have, and such legal practitioners are also subject to the misconduct provisions of the 2015 Act.[156]

Commencement and cessation of business

[30.76] A multi-disciplinary practice that intends to provide legal services must notify the Authority before doing so, and must also notify the Authority when ceasing to provide those services.[157] The Authority must maintain a register of multi-disciplinary practices notified to it, and that register must be available to the public for inspection, free of charge.[158] At the time of writing, the Authority has not yet confirmed the form that the register will take.[159] Where a registered multi-disciplinary practice later notifies the Authority that it has ceased to provide legal services, the Authority must remove the name of that multi-disciplinary practice from the register.[160]

---

[151] The definition of 'multi-disciplinary practice' at the Legal Services Regulation Act 2015, s 2(1) provides that a multi-disciplinary practice is one which is formed under the laws of Ireland 'by written agreement'.

[152] Legal Services Regulation Act 2015, s 102(1).

[153] Legal Services Regulation Act 2015, s 107(3).

[154] See para **[30.13]**.

[155] Legal Services Regulation Act 2015, s 107(1).

[156] Legal Services Regulation Act 2015, s 109. The acts and omissions on the part of a legal practitioner which could constitute misconduct are set out in the Legal Services Regulation Act 2015, s 50.

[157] Legal Services Regulation Act 2015, s 106. Forms and fees in respect of such notifications may be prescribed.

[158] Legal Services Regulation Act 2015, s 117.

[159] The Legal Services Regulation Act 2015, s 117(3), provides that the register must be in 'an appropriate format'.

[160] Legal Services Regulation Act 2015, s 117(2).

Sharing of fees and other income

[30.77] A partner in a multi-disciplinary practice will, under the 2015 Act, be allowed to share fees or other income arising from the provision of services (legal or non-legal) by the multi-disciplinary practice with another partner in that practice, irrespective of whether either or both partners are practising solicitors or practising barristers.[161]

Restrictions on being a partner

[30.78] Unlike legal partnerships and limited liability partnerships, a multi-disciplinary practice may comprise partners who are not practising solicitors or practising barristers. While practising solicitors and practising barristers must separately confirm to the Law Society of Ireland and to the Bar of Ireland, respectively, that they are not in breach of various laws, s 107(4) of the 2015 Act sets out the types of person who may not be a partner in a multi-disciplinary practice in an attempt to apply a similar standard to those partners in a multi-disciplinary practice who are legal practitioners, and those who are not. Unless a person listed below (other than a person who comes within any of the first three categories) has successfully obtained a High Court order allowing him to become a partner in a multi-disciplinary practice on the basis that it is 'reasonable and proportionate' for such an order to be made, the following persons may not become partners in a multi-disciplinary practice:

– a person in respect of whom the High Court has made an order[162] that prohibits him from providing legal services otherwise than as an employee;

– a person in respect of whom the High Court has made an order[163] suspending him from practice as a legal practitioner unless the order is made at a time that he is a partner in a multi-disciplinary practice, and expressly allows him to continue as a partner in that multi-disciplinary practice;[164]

– a person who has been struck off the roll of practising barristers or the roll of solicitors on foot of a High Court order;[165]

– a solicitor who is not a solicitor qualified to practise, within the meaning of the Solicitors Act 1954, as a result of his name having been struck off the roll of solicitors, his suspension from practice, a refusal to issue him with a practising certificate under s 49 of the 1954 Act, a suspension of his practising certificate under s 58 of the 1954 Act, or him having given an undertaking to the High Court not to practise as a solicitor (or an equivalent event occurs in respect of a person who is a solicitor in another jurisdiction);[166]

---

161 Legal Services Regulation Act 2015, s 107(2).
162 Under the Legal Services Regulation Act 2015, s 85(7)(c).
163 Under the Legal Services Regulation Act 2015, s 85 (7)(d).
164 The restriction on such a person being a partner in a multi-disciplinary practice will remain in effect only for so long as the suspension order is in place.
165 Under the Legal Services Regulation Act 2015, s 85(7)(c) or s 85(7)(f).
166 Referred to in the Legal Services Regulation Act 2015, s 107 as an 'unqualified person'.

- a person who, having been a qualified barrister in Ireland, has been disbarred (or, where he is a barrister in another jurisdiction, has been disbarred under the laws of that jurisdiction);[167]
- a person who has been restricted as a director[168] or is deemed[169] to have been so restricted;
- a person who has been disqualified as a director, or is deemed to have been so disqualified;[170]
- a person convicted on indictment of an offence;
- a person convicted of an offence involving fraud, dishonesty or breach of trust;
- a person convicted of an offence involving money laundering or terrorist financing;[171]
- a person who is an undischarged bankrupt (whether in Ireland or in another jurisdiction);
- a person convicted outside Ireland for an offence consisting of acts or omissions that, if done or made in Ireland, would constitute an offence triable on indictment;
- a person disqualified under the law of another state (whether pursuant to an order of a judge or a tribunal or otherwise) from being appointed or acting as a director or secretary of a body corporate or an undertaking.

A partner in a multi-disciplinary practice must be a natural person

[30.79] A partner in a multi-disciplinary practice must be an individual.[172]

Day-to-Day Operation of a Multi-disciplinary Practice

Managing legal practitioner

[30.80] Each multi-disciplinary practice must appoint at least one partner in the practice (who must be a practising solicitor or practising barrister) to the position of 'managing legal practitioner' with responsibility for managing and supervising the provision of legal services by the practice, and compliance with the requirements of the 2015 Act.[173] If the multi-disciplinary practice does not have a managing legal practitioner for a period of at least seven days, it must notify the Authority and cease providing legal services until one is appointed.[174] If the managing legal practitioner believes that the practice is providing, or is likely to provide, legal services in a manner that is not compliant with the 2015 Act, he must take all reasonable steps to remedy that position

---

167 Unless he sought to be disbarred himself with a view to instead being admitted to the roll of solicitors.
168 Under the Companies Act 2014, s 819.
169 By virtue of Part 14, Ch 5 of the Companies Act 2014.
170 Within the meaning of Part 14, Ch 4 of the Companies Act 2014 and whether by virtue of that Chapter or any other provisions of the 2014 Act.
171 Each within the meaning of the Criminal Justice (Money Laundering and Terrorist Financing) Act 2010 (as amended).
172 Legal Services Regulation Act 2015, ss 1(2) and 107(8).
173 Legal Services Regulation Act 2015, s 108(1) and 108(3).
174 Legal Services Regulation Act 2015, s 108(2).

within 14 days. The 2015 Act also imposes obligations on the managing legal practitioner to ensure that the practice maintains separate accounting records in respect of the legal services and the other services provided by it, to ensure that money connected with the provision of legal services is held in a separate bank account, and to ensure that fees and other income arising from the provision of legal services are held in a separate bank account.[175]

Written procedures

[30.81] A multi-disciplinary practice must have written procedures in place to ensure that it provides legal services in accordance with the 2015 Act, any relevant regulations and the professional principles set out in s 13(5) of the 2015 Act,[176] and to enable the managing legal practitioner to comply with his obligations under the 2015 Act.[177] Those procedures may be supplemented by any procedures required by regulation to be put in place.[178] All partners and employees of the practice must be subject to those procedures and must be obliged to comply with the directions of the managing legal practitioner. The procedures must not induce any legal practitioner to provide legal services in a manner which would not comply with the 2015 Act and any relevant regulations.

More substantive conditions on operation and management will be set out in regulations

[30.82] While the 2015 Act sets out a small number of obligations on multi-disciplinary practices regarding, for example, letters of engagement[179] and the requirement that the practice have in place a professional indemnity insurance policy in respect of the provision of legal services,[180] substantial powers are reserved to the Authority under s 116 of the 2015 Act to make regulations regarding the operation and management of multi-disciplinary practices. Those regulations may deal with matters such as professional and ethical standards, confidentiality, the provision of information to clients, obligations regarding money received from clients, the management and control of the practice, control systems (in particular, covering risk management and financial control), managing conflicts of interest, compliance with the obligations imposed by the 2015 Act and related regulations, record-keeping, the practice name(s), advertising of services, the opening and keeping of bank accounts, and the practice's accounting records. No such regulations have yet been made and, in light of the priority being given by the Authority to the frameworks for both legal partnerships and limited liability partnerships, and the Authority's reservations in respect of multi-disciplinary practices

---

175 Legal Services Regulation Act 2015, s 110(4).
176 Those professional principles are that legal practitioners shall act with independence and integrity, act in the best interests of their clients, maintain proper standards of work, comply with such duties as are rightfully owed to the court when exercising a right of audience or conducing litigation, and keep clients' affairs confidential (subject to any professional obligation, including any obligation as an officer of the court).
177 Legal Services Regulation Act 2015, s 110.
178 Under the Legal Services Regulation Act 2015, s 116(4)(a), the Authority may make regulations specifying additional procedures that are to form part of the written procedures required by the 2015 Act.
179 Legal Services Regulation Act 2015, s 111.
180 Legal Services Regulation Act 2015, s 112.

generally,[181] it seems unlikely that any such regulations in relation to multi-disciplinary practices will be introduced in the near future.

Powers of the Authority

[30.83] If the multi-disciplinary practice has breached its obligation to have a managing legal practitioner, the Authority can direct it to appoint one.[182] If the Authority reasonably believes that there is a breach of Part 8 of the 2015 Act (or regulations made under that Part), it must notify the multi-disciplinary practice or the managing legal practitioner, in writing, of that belief, the reasons for it and the measures that the practice or the managing legal practitioner must take and invite observations. Depending on the outcome, the Authority may then issue a direction to the practice or the managing legal practitioner to take particular steps.[183]

[30.84] The Authority may also apply to the High Court[184] for an order suspending or ceasing the provision of legal services by the practice if the practice or the managing legal practitioner, as appropriate, fails to comply with a notice from the Authority under s 114 of the 2015 Act.[185] The High Court may also make an order requiring the practice or, as appropriate, the managing legal practitioner, to comply with a direction issued by the Authority. Both the Authority and the managing legal practitioner have a right of appeal to the Court of Appeal against the High Court order.[186] Once the High Court makes an order, a notice setting out the effect of that order must be published in *Iris Oifigiúil* and in such other manner as the Authority may consider appropriate.[187]

[30.85] As and when the framework for multi-disciplinary practices comes into operation, the Authority will be required[188] to review the operation of Part 8 of the 2015 Act as it relates to multi-disciplinary practices within two years, and report to the Minister for Justice and Equality within one year of that review beginning. Further, periodic, reviews must then be carried out every five years.

---

[181]   See paras **[30.70]** and **[30.71]** above.
[182]   Legal Services Regulation Act 2015, s 114(3).
[183]   Legal Services Regulation Act 2015, s 114(1) and 114(4). The practice or the managing legal practitioner has a right to appeal the issue of a direction to the High Court under Legal Services Regulation Act 2015, s 114(5). The High Court can then confirm, revoke or vary the Authority's direction (Legal Services Regulation Act 2015, s 114(7)).
[184]   Under the Legal Services Regulation Act 2015, s 115.
[185]   See para **[30.83]**.
[186]   Legal Services Regulation Act 2015, s 115(6).
[187]   Legal Services Regulation Act 2015, s 115(7).
[188]   Under the Legal Services Regulation Act 2015, s 121.

Index